POLITICS IN AMERICA

POLITICS IN

AMERICA

SIXTH EDITION

Thomas R. Dye

Emeritus McKenzie
Professor of Government
Florida State University

PEARSON

Prentice
Hall

Upper Saddle River, New Jersey 07458

Library of Congress Cataloging in Publication Data

Dye, Thomas R.
    Politics in America / Thomas R. Dye—6th ed., National ed.
        p. cm.
    Includes bibliographical references and index.
    ISBN 0–13–153450–5
    1. United States—Politics and government.   I. Title.

JK276.D926 2005
320.473—dc22   2004025193

Editorial Director: Charlyce Jones Owen
Acquisitions Editor: Glenn Johnston
Editorial Assistant: Suzanne Remore
Marketing Manager: Kara Kindstrom
Marketing Assistant: Jennifer Lang
Managing Editor: Lisa Iarkowski
Production Liaison: Fran Russello
Permissions Supervisor: Lisa Black
Manufacturing Buyer: Sherry Lewis
Design Manager: Anne Nieglos
Interior Design: Susan Walrath

Cover Design: Susan Walrath
Cover Illustration/Photo: Lester Lefkowitz/ImageBank/
Getty Images, Inc. and Siede Preis/Photodisc Green/Getty
Images, Inc.
Illustrator (Interior): Mirella Signoretto
Photo Researcher: David Tietz
Image Permission Coordinator: Debbie Hewitson
Composition/Full-Service Project Management:
Bruce Hobart/Pine Tree Composition
Printer/Binder: Courier Companies, Inc.

Credits and acknowledgments borrowed from other sources and reproduced, with permission, in this textbook appear on page PC-1.

Pearson Education LTD. London
Pearson Education Singapore, Pte. Ltd
Pearson Education, Canada, Ltd
Pearson Education–Japan
Pearson Education Australia PTY, Limited

Pearson Education North Asia Ltd
Pearson Educación de Mexico, S.A. de C.V.
Pearson Education Malaysia, Pte. Ltd
Pearson Education, Upper Saddle River, New Jersey
PEARSON Prentice Hall

10 9 8 7 6 5 4 3 2 1

ISBN 0-13-153450-5

To my students over the years,
who taught me more than I taught them.

Brief Contents

Contents

PART III   Participants

People strive for power—to get the most of what there is to get.

Harold Lasswell

PART IV   Institutions

Authority is the expected and legitimate possession of power.
Harold Lasswell

PART V   Outcomes

*That political science concentrates upon the influential does not imply
the neglect of the total distribution of values throughout the community.
. . . The emphasis upon the probability that the few (elite) will get the
most does not imply that the many (mass) do not profit from some political changes.*

Harold Lasswell

Preface

Politics is an activity by which people try to get more of whatever there is to get. It is not about the pursuit of liberty as much as it is about the struggle over the allocation of values in society. Simply put, it is about "who gets what, when, and how."

By using Lasswell's classic definition of politics as the unifying framework, *Politics in America, Sixth Edition*, strives to present a clear, concise, and stimulating introduction to the American political system. Politics consists of all of the activities—reasonable discussion, impassioned oratory, campaigning, balloting, fund raising, advertising, lobbying, demonstrating, rioting, street fighting, and waging war—by which conflict is carried on. Managing conflict is the principal function of the political system and power is the ultimate goal.

By examining the struggle for power—the participants, the stakes, the processes, and the institutional arenas—*Politics in America, Sixth Edition*, introduces students to the politics that is the basis for our democracy.

Why Politics in America?

Instructors teaching the Introductory American Government course find engaging their students to be the most difficult task facing them. *Politics in America, Sixth Edition*, is written to be lively and absorbing, reflecting the teaching philosophy that *stimulating students' interest in politics and public affairs is the most important goal of an introductory course*. Interesting examples and controversial debates spark students' interest and keep them connected to the material. The struggle for power in society is not a dull topic, and textbooks should not make it so.

Politics in America, Sixth Edition, strives for a balanced presentation, but "balanced" does not mean boring. It does not mean the avoidance of controversy. Liberal and conservative arguments are set forth clearly and forcefully. Race and gender are given particular attention, not because it is currently fashionable to do so, but because American politics has long been driven by these factors. As in previous editions, the trademark of this book continues to be its desire to pull students into the debate that is our political system.

Organization

Part I, "Politics," begins with Lasswell's classic definition of politics and proceeds to describe the nature and functions of government and the meaning of democracy. It poses the question. How democratic is the American political system? It describes the American political culture: its contradictions between liberty and conformity, political equality and economic inequality, equality of opportunity and inequality of results, the role of ideology—liberalism and conservatism, thus laying the groundwork for understanding the struggle over who gets what.

Part II, "Constitution," describes the politics of constitution making—deciding how to decide. It describes how the struggle over the U.S. Constitution reflected the distribution of power in the new nation. It focuses on the classic arguments of the Founders for limiting and dividing governmental power and the structural arrangements designed to accomplish this end.

Part III, "Participants," begins by examining individual participation in politics—the way people acquire and hold political opinions and act on them through voting and protest activity. It examines the influences of family, school, gender, race, and the role of media in shaping political opinion. It describes how organization concentrates power—to win public office in the case of party organizations, and to influence policy in the case of interest groups. It assesses the role of personal ambition in politics and the role of money.

Part IV, "Institutions," describes the various governmental arenas in which the struggle for power takes place—the Congress, the presidency, the bureaucracy, the courts. More important, it evaluates the power that comes with control of each of these institutions.

Part V, "Outcomes," deals with public policies—the result of the struggle over the allocation of values. It is especially concerned with the two fundamental values of American society—liberty and equality. Each is examined in separate chapters, as are economic policies, welfare policies, and national security policies.

New to the Sixth Edition

Americans went to the polls in 2004 in numbers never seen before and percentages not seen in forty years. Perhaps it was a lesson learned in 2000 that a few hundred votes can change the Electoral College vote and determine the presidency. Perhaps it was the projected closeness of the race between Bush and Kerry, or concern over the continuing war in Iraq, or an increased turnout of religious people concerned with growing secularism in society. Perhaps all of these conditions combined to inspire Americans to renew their commitment to the political system.

The Sixth Edition of *Politics in America* describes the recent changes in the political landscape of the nation. It updates students on the war on terrorism and the restrictions on freedom that it has inspired. It describes and analyzes the presidential and congressional election of 2004: the campaign strategies of George W. Bush and John F. Kerry; the impact of the war in Iraq; campaign finance "reform" and how it was evaded during the campaign; popular images of Bush and Kerry and the issues considered most important by the voters; the Republican victory in the congressional elections and the growing polarization on Capitol Hill.

The Sixth Edition also assesses bias in the media and how it has been modified by newer cable network broadcasting and the Internet; it describes new leadership in Congress, including Senate Republican Leader Bill Frist, Sen. Hillary Clinton, and House Democratic Leader Nancy Pelosi; it describes charges of partisanship in the Supreme Court (especially in *Bush vs. Gore*) and controversial court decisions on cross burning, gay marriage, and the rights of enemy combatants captured on the battlefield.

As in previous editions, the Sixth Edition invites controversy and spirited discussion in the classroom. It raises "politically incorrect" issues—affirmative action and "diversity" in education; rising income inequality in America; how much campaign contributions affect congressional voting; amending the Constitution to ban gay marriages; when is the right to disobey the law; what is the appropriate justification for the use of military force; is the American government really "Of, by, and for the people."

New Features

- *What Do You Think?* "What Government Programs Do You Support?"
- *What Do You Think?* "Beliefs about Fairness"
- *People in Politics:* Bill O'Reilly, "The No Spin Zone?"
- *Up Close:* Why the Founders Created an Electoral College
- *People in Politics:* Arnold, from Bodybuilder to Superstar to Governor.
- *What Do You Think?* "Do Gender Stereotypes Affect Voting?"
- *Up Close:* "The Generation Gap in News"
- *A Conflicting View:* "Fox News, 'Fair and Balanced'?"
- *Up Close:* "The Brief History of Money in Politics"
- *Up Close:* "New Ways to Evade Campaign Reform Laws"
- *A Conflicting View:* "Payback, Money and Medicare"
- *Up Close:* "Polarization on Capitol Hill"
- *People in Politics* "Bill First M.D., Leading the Senate"
- *Up Close:* "Tips on Lobbying Congress"
- *Up Close:* "Contrasting Presidential Styles"
- *What Do You Think?* "How Would You Rate Federal Agencies?"
- *People in Politics:* "George Bush and 'Operator Iraqi Freedom'"
- *Up Close:* "How to Use the Freedom of Information Act"
- *Up Close:* "Women and the Courts"
- *What Do You Think?* "Do You Have Confidence in the Supreme Court?"
- *A Conflicting View.* "Terrorism Requires Restrictions on Civil Liberties"
- *Up Close.* "Why We Can Burn the Flag but Not a Cross"

The Sixth Edition provides a variety of new instructional aids, including running marginal Web site addresses on the topics under discussion.

Instructional Features

Interactive Chapter Opening Survey Each chapter opens with a brief poll called "Think about Politics" that alerts students to the crucial issues the chapter covers and the impact of those issues on their lives. This tool can be used to get students thinking about how and why politics is important to them as individuals and as members of a community.

Text and Features The body of each chapter is divided into text and features. The text provides the framework of understanding American politics. Each chapter begins with a brief discussion of power in relation to the subject matter of the chapter: for example, limiting governmental power (Chapter 3, "The Constitution"), dividing governmental power (Chapter 4, "Federalism"), and the power of the media (Chapter 6, "Mass Media"). By focusing the beginning of each chapter on questions of power, students can more easily set the chapter content in the context of Lasswell's definition of politics.

The features in each chapter provide timeliness, relevance, stimulation, and perspective. Each boxed feature in the Sixth Edition of *Politics in America* is designed to encourage students to voice their opinions and explore those of others. If the key to learning is active involvement, students should be encouraged to read and respond whenever possible.

- **"What Do You Think?"**: These features pose controversial questions to students and provide national opinion survey data. They cover a wide range of interests designed to stimulate classroom discussion. Examples include: "Can You Trust the Government?" "Is American Government 'Of, By and For the People'?" "Are You a Liberal or a Conservative?" "Does Money Buy Influence in Washington?" "How Would You Rate the Presidents?" "Should We Judge Presidents on Private Character or Performance in Office?" "How Much Money Does the Government Waste?" "What Constitutes Sexual Harassment?"

- **"A Conflicting View"**: These features challenge students to rethink conventional notions about American politics. They are designed to be controversial and to start students thinking about the push and pull that is politics. "Conflicting View" features include: "An Economic Interpretation of the Constitution," "Objections to the Constitution by an Anti-Federalist," "The War on Drugs Threatens Individual Liberty," "The Constitution Should Be Color-Blind."

- **"Compared to What?"**: These features provide students with global context by comparing the United States with other nations. Discussions include "Freedom and Democracy around the World," as well as such topics as the size of government, tax burdens, voter turnout, political parties, television culture, health care, and the earnings gap between men and women.

- **"People in Politics"**: These features are designed to personalize politics for students, to illustrate to them that the participants in the struggle for power are real people. They discuss where prominent people in politics went to school, how they got started in politics, how their careers developed, and how much power they came to possess. Both historical—John Locke and James Madison—and current figures, such as Arnold Schwarzeneggar, Ralph Nader, Colin Powell, and Ted Kennedy are discussed.

- **"Up Close"**: These features illustrate the struggle over who gets what. They range over a wide variety of current political conflicts, such as "Sex, Lies, and Impeachment," "Abortion, the 'Hot Button' Issue," "Dirty Politics," "AARP: The Nation's Most Powerful Interest Group," "The Christian Coalition: Organizing the Faithful," "Is Welfare Reform Working?" A special feature, "How to Run for Office," provides practical advice on how to get into electoral politics.

- **"Across the USA"**: These features provide maps that summarize important statistical and demographic information relevant to American politics.

Learning Aids Each chapter contains a running glossary in the margin to help students master important concepts, Web sites where students can obtain additional information direct from political sources, a chapter outline, a summary, and a list of annotated suggested readings, as well as marginal questions that relate to the chapter opening survey.

Technology Initiatives

With the development of new technologies, we have discovered more and more ways of helping students and instructors to further understand and analyze information. In this edition, we have made every effort to give both instructors and students a large array of multimedia tools to help with both the presentation and the learning of the material.

- **New! Make It Real** is a comprehensive Web site that contains dynamic simulations developed by Prentice Hall exclusively for American Government. In addition to simulations, Make It Real also contains activities on civic participation, interactive timelines and maps, quizzes, primary source documents, Census 2000 data, and exercises in visual literacy. Students will use information such as real election results, real demographics, maps and voting score cards. Self-study quizzes are available for the student to take to make sure they understand the concepts used in completing the simulations and other activities.

- **New and Improved Evaluating Online Resources for Political Science with Research Navigator™:** Our newest addition to the reliable Internet guide for political science, Prentice Hall's new Research Navigator™ keeps instructors and students abreast of the latest news and information and helps students create top quality research papers. From finding the right articles and journals, to citing sources, drafting and writing effective papers, and completing research assignments, Research Navigator simplifies and streamlines the entire process. It offers extensive help on the research process and three exclusive databases full of relevant and reliable source material including EBSCO's Content-Select Academic Journal Database, *The New York Times* Search-by-Subject Archive, and "Best of the Web" Link Library.

  A unique access code for Research Navigator™ is provided on the inside front cover of the booklet. The booklet contains an introduction to the Internet. Evaluating Online Resources for Political Science with Research Navigator is FREE when packaged with *Politics in America* and available for stand-alone sale. Take a tour on the web at http://www.researchnavigator.com
- **Improved Companion Website™** (www.prenhall.com/dye): Students can now take full advantage of the World Wide Web to enrich the study of American government through the *Politics in America* Website. Interactive Web exercises guide students to do research with a series of questions and links.
- **Evaluating Online Resources for Political Science with Research Navigator (ISBN 0-13-192288-2):** This timely supplement provides an introduction to the Internet and the numerous political sites on the World Wide Web. It describes e-mail, list servers, browsers, and how to document sources. It also includes Web addresses for the most current and useful political Web sites.

OneKey Instructors and students will find all of their resources—all in one place—all organized around the chapters of this text for maximum convenience and flexibility in OneKey, Prentice Hall's new and exclusive one-stop shop. Among the resources available for each chapter include all of the Make It Real simulations, chapter assessment with e-book PDF in feedback, flashcards, crossword puzzles, chapter opening questions, chapter outline/summary. For the instructor, OneKey also contains: Instructors Manual and Test Item File, powerpoints, image bank, audio of great speeches and video clips from campaigns and advertisements.

Supplements Available for the Instructor

- **New Instructor's Resource CD-ROM:** New from Prentice Hall, the Instructor's Resource CD-ROM allows you maximum flexibility as you prepare your lectures and manage your class. For presentation use, this CD contains a database featuring most of the art from the text, more than 30 video and audio segments of classical and contemporary political science footage, and several simulations from Make It Real. An easy to use interface (organized logically by chapter) allows you to customize your lectures with your own original material and the assets we've provided.
- **Instructor's Manual with Test Item File:** For each chapter, a summary, review of concepts, lecture suggestions and topic outlines, and additional resource materials—including a guide to media resources—are provided. An electronic version is also available on the Instructor's Resource CD-ROM.

  Thoroughly reviewed and revised to ensure test highest level of quality and accuracy, the test item file offers over 1,800 questions in multiple choice, true/false, and essay format with page references to the text.
- **Prentice Hall Test Manager:** A computerized test bank contains the items from the Test Item File. The program allows full editing of questions and the addition of instructor-generated items. Suitable for Windows and Macintosh versions.
- **American Government Transparencies, Series VI:** This set of over 100 four-color transparency acetates reproduces illustrations, charts, and maps from the text as well as from additional sources. An instructor's guide is also available.
- **Prentice Hall Custom Video: How a Bill Becomes a Law:** This 25-minute video chronicles an environmental law in Massachusetts—from its start as one citizen's concern to its passage in Washington, D.C. Students see step-by-step the process of how a bill becomes a law complete through narrative and graphics. Call your local Prentice Hall representative for details.
- **PowerPoint Gallery:** For each chapter, the PowerPoint Gallery provides electronic files for each figure and table in the text, along with pre-created PowerPoint slides ready for customization. With the use of this tool you may create a dynamic PowerPoint presentation or print your own customized 4-

color transparencies. (Available in the Faculty Resources section of the Companion Web Site™.)

- **Films for the Humanities and Social Sciences:** With a qualifying order of textbooks from Prentice Hall, you may select from a high quality library of political science videos from Films for the Humanities and Sciences. Please contact your local representative for a complete listing.

Supplements Available for the Student

- **Practice Tests:** Includes chapter outlines, study notes, a glossary, and practice tests designed to reinforce information in the text and help students develop a greater understanding of American government and politics.

Supplementary Books and Readings for American Government

Each of the following books features specialized topical coverage allowing you to tailor your American Government course to suit the needs of your region or your particular teaching style. Featuring contemporary issues or timely readings, any of the following books are available for a discount when bundled with *Politics in America.* Please visit our Online Catalog at www.prenhall.com/dye for additional details.

Government's Greatest Achievements: From Civil Rights to Homeland Security, 20th ed.
Paul C. Light, Brookings Institute
ISBN: 0-13-110192-7 © 2004

Issues in American Political Life: Money, Violence, and Biology, 4th ed.
Robert Thobaben, Wright State University
Donna Schlagheck, Wright State University
Charles Funderburk, Wright State University
ISBN: 0-13-0336726 © 2002

Choices: An American Government Reader—Custom Publishing
Gregory Scott, University of Central Oklahoma
Katherine Tate, University of California–Irvine
Ronald Weber, University of Wisconsin–Milwaukee
ISBN: 0-13-0219916 © 2002

Civil Rights and Liberties: Provocative Questions and Evolving Answers, 2nd ed.
Harold Sullivan, The City University of New York
ISBN: 0-13-1174355 © 2001

21 Debated: Issues in American Politics, 2nd ed.
Gregory Scott, University of Central Oklahoma
Loren Gatch, University of Central Oklahoma
ISBN: 0-13-1841785 © 2005

Government and Politics in the Lone Star State: Theory and Practice, 4th ed.
L. Tucker Gibson, Trinity University
Clay Robison, The Houston Chronicle
ISBN: 0-13-0340502 © 2002

Rethinking California: Politics and Policy in the Golden State
Matthew Cahn, California State University–Northridge
H. Eric Schockman, University of Southern California
David Shafie, Ohio University
ISBN: 0-13-0282677 © 2001

Strategies for Active Citizenship
Kateri M. Drexler
Gwen Garcelon
ISBN: 0-13-1172956 © 2005

Political Science: Evaluating Online Resources with Research Navigator, 2005
Melissa Payton
ISBN: 0-13-192288-2

The Political Science Student Writer's Manual, 4th ed.
Gregory M. Scott, University of Central Oklahoma
Stephen M. Garrison, University of Central Oklahoma
ISBN: 0-13-0404470 © 2002

Smoking and Politics: Policy Making and the Federal Bureaucracy, 5th ed.
A. Lee Fritschler, Dickinson College
James M. Hoefler, Dickinson College
ISBN: 0-13-4358015 © 1996

Real Politics in America series is another resource for contemporary instructional material. To bridge the gap between research and relevancy, we have launched a new series of supplemental books with the help of series editor Paul Herrnson of the University of Maryland. More descriptive than quantitative, more case study than data study, these books cut across all topics to bring students relevant details in current political science research. From exploring the growing phenomenon of direct democracy to who runs for the state legislature, these books show students that real political science is meaningful and exciting. Available for a discount when bundled with *Politics in America*. Please see your Prentice Hall representative or access www.prenhall.com for a complete listing of titles in the series.

Acknowledgments

Politics in America, Sixth Edition, reflects the influence of many splendid teachers, students, and colleagues who have helped me over the years. I am grateful for the early guidance of Frank Sorauf, my undergraduate student adviser at Pennsylvania State University, and James G. Coke, my Ph.D. dissertation director at the University of Pennsylvania. Georgia Parthemos at the University of Georgia and Malcolm Parsons at Florida State University gave me my first teaching posts. But my students over the years contributed most to my education—notably Susan MacManus, Kent Portney, Ed Benton, James Ammons, Aubrey Jewitt, and especially John Robey.

Several of my colleagues gave advice on various parts of this book. Glen Parker (on Congress), Suzanne Parker (on public opinion), James Gwartney (on economics), Robert Lichter (on the mass media), Charles Barrioux (on Bureaucracy), and especially Harmon Zeigler, whose knowledge of politics is unbounded.

I would like to thank James Corey of High Point University for preparing the annotated Constitution and Chris Cardone for editorial management in the early stages of this Fifth Edition.

Finally, I would like to thank the many reviewers who evaluated the text and contributed invaluable advice:

Charles W. Chapman, University of Texas at Brownsville
John Pratt, Cedar Valley College
James Corey, High Point University
Christopher C. Lovett, Emporia State University
Kevin R. den Dulk, Grand Valley State University
Wayne Pryor, Brazosport College
James W. Lamare, Florida Atlantic University
Roger Marietta, Darton College
Paul Davis, Truckee Meadows Community College
Earl T. Sheridan, University of North Carolina

Thomas R. Dye

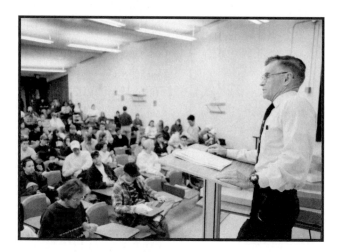

THOMAS R. DYE, Emeritus McKenzie Professor of Government at Florida State University regularly taught large introductory classes in American politics and was University Teacher of the Year in 1987. He received his B.A. and M.A. degrees from Pennsylvania State University and his Ph.D. degree from the University of Pennsylvania. He is the author of numerous books and articles on American government and public policy, including. *The Irony of Democracy, Politics in States and Communities, Understanding Public Policy, Who's Running America, American Politics in the Media Age, Power in Society, Politics, Economics, and the Public, and American Federalism: Competition Among Governments.* His books have been translated into many languages, including Russian and Chinese, and published abroad. He has served as president of the Southern Political Science Association, president of the Policy Studies Organization, and secretary of the American Political Science Association. He has taught at the University of Pennsylvania, the University of Wisconsin, and the University of Georgia, and served as a visiting scholar at Bar-Ilan University, Israel, the Brookings Institution in Washington, D.C., and elsewhere. He is a member of Phi Beta Kappa, Omicron Delta Kappa, and Phi Kappa Phi, and is listed in most major biographical directories. Additional information is available at www.thomasrdye.com.

POLITICS IN AMERICA

POLITICS:
WHO GETS WHAT, WHEN, AND HOW

Politics and Political Science

Politics is deciding "who gets what, when, and how." It is an activity by which people try to get more of whatever there is to get—money, prestige, jobs, respect, sex, even power itself. Politics occurs in many different settings. We talk about office politics, student politics, union politics, church politics, and so forth. But political science usually limits its attention to *politics in government.*

Political science is the study of politics, or the study of who gets what, when, and how. The *who* are the participants in politics—voters, special-interest groups, political parties, television and the press, corporations and labor unions, lawyers and lobbyists, foundations and think tanks, and both elected and appointed government officials, including members of Congress, the president and vice president, judges, prosecutors, and bureaucrats. The *what* of politics are public policies—the decisions that governments make concerning social welfare, health care, education, national defense, law enforcement, the environment, taxation, and thousands of other issues that come before governments. The *when* and *how* are the political process—campaigns and elections, political reporting in the news media, television debates, fund raising, lobbying, decision making in the White House and executive agencies, and decision making in the courts.

Political science is generally concerned with three questions. *Who governs? For what ends? By what means?* Throughout this book, we are concerned with who participates in politics, how government decisions are made, who benefits most from those decisions, and who bears their greatest costs (see Figure 1.1).

Politics would be simple if everyone agreed on who should govern, who should get what, who should pay for it, and how and when it should be done. But conflict arises from disagreements over these questions, and sometimes the question of confidence in the government itself underlies the conflict (see *What Do You Think?* "Can You Trust the Government?"). Politics arises out of conflict, and it consists of all the activities—reasonable discussion, impassioned oratory, balloting, campaigning, lobbying, parading, rioting, street fighting, terrorism, and waging war—by which conflict is carried on.

FIGURE 1.1   Who Gets What, When, and How

Political science is the study of politics. The distinguished political scientist Harold Lassvell entitled his most popular book *Politics: Who Gets What, When and How.* The first topic of politics is "Who?" (that is, who are the participants in politics, both within and outside of government?), "When and how are political decisions made?" (that is, how do the institutions and processes of politics function?), and "What outcomes are produced?" (that is, what public policies are adopted?). Shown here are some of the topics of concern to political science.

Who Governs: Participants

Governmental	*Nongovernmental*
President and White House staff	Voters
Executive Office of the President, including Office of Management and Budget	Campaign contributors
	Interest-group leaders and members
Cabinet officers and executive agency heads	Party leaders and party identifiers in the electorate
Bureaucrats	Corporate and union leaders
Congress members	Media leaders, including press and television anchors and reporters
Congressional staff	
Supreme Court justices	Lawyers and lobbyists
Federal appellate and district judges	Think tanks and foundation personnel

When and How: Institutions and Processes

Institutions	*Processes*
Constitution	Socialization and learning
Separation of powers	Opinion formation
Checks and balances	Party identification
Federalism	Voting
Judicial review	Contributing
Amendment procedures	Joining organizations
Electoral system	Talking politics
Presidency	Running for office
Congress	Campaigning
Senate	Polling
House of Representatives	Fund raising
	Parading and demonstrating
Courts	Nonviolent direct action
Supreme Court	Violence
Appellate courts	
District courts	Agenda setting
	Lobbying
Parties	Logrolling
National committees	Deciding
Conventions	Budgeting
State and local organizations	Implementing and evaluating
	Adjudicating
Press and television	

What Outcomes: Public Policies

Civil liberties	Energy
Civil rights	Environmental protection
Equality	Economic development
Criminal justice	Economic stability
Welfare	Taxation
Social Security	Government spending and deficits
Health	National defense
Education	Foreign affairs

politics   Deciding who gets what, when, and how.

political science   The study of politics: who governs, for what ends, and by what means.

THINK AGAIN

Should any group other than the government have the right to use force?

government   Organization extending to the whole society that can legitimately use force to carry out its decisions.

Politics and Government

What distinguishes governmental politics from politics in other institutions in society? After all, parents, teachers, unions, banks, corporations, and many other organizations make decisions about who gets what in society. The answer is that only **government** decisions can *extend to the whole society*, and only government can *legitimately use force.* Other institutions encompass only a part of society: for exam-

Conflict exists in all political activities as participants struggle over who gets what, when, and how. From the streets to the Congress to the White House, participants in the political process compete to further their goals and ambitions.

ple, students and faculty in a college, members of a church or union, employees or customers of a corporation. And individuals have a legal right to voluntarily withdraw from nongovernmental organizations. But governments make decisions affecting everyone, and no one can voluntarily withdraw from government's authority (without leaving the country, and thus becoming subject to some other government's authority). Some individuals and organizations—muggers, gangs, crime families—occasionally use physical force to get what they want. But only governments can use force legitimately—that is, people generally believe it is acceptable for the government to use force if necessary to uphold its laws, but they do not extend this right to other institutions or individuals.

Most people would say that they obey the law in order to avoid fines and stay out of prison. But if large numbers of people all decided to disobey the law at the same time, the government would not have enough police or jails to hold them all.

The government can rely on force only against relatively small numbers of offenders. Most of us, most of the time, obey laws out of habit—the habit of compliance. We have been taught to believe that law and order are necessary and that government is right to punish those who disobey its laws.

Government thus enjoys **legitimacy**, or rightfulness, in its use of force.[1] A democratic government has a special claim to legitimacy because it is based on the consent of its people, who participate in the selection of its leaders and the making of its laws. Those who disagree with a law have the option of working for its

American Political Science Association
Association of college and university teachers advises students how to study political science.
www.apsanet.org

THINK AGAIN

Is violence ever justified as a means of bringing about political change?

legitimacy Widespread acceptance of something as necessary, rightful, and legally binding.

Can You Trust the Government?

Americans are suspicious of big government. Many do not trust the government in Washington to "do what is right." Trust in government has varied over the years, as measured by polls asking, "How much of the time do you think you can trust the government in Washington to do what is right? Just about always? Most of the time? Some of the time? None of the time?" During the early years of the Johnson Administration (and even earlier, during the Kennedy and Eisenhower presidencies), public confidence in government was high. But in the late '60s and early '70s defeat and humiliation in Vietnam appeared to diminish public confidence. On the heels of the Vietnam experience came the Watergate scandal and President Richard Nixon's forced resignation in 1974—the first resignation of a president in U.S. history—causing public confidence in government to fall further.

Throughout the long years of decline in public confidence in government, television broadcast many negative images of government and public policy. Television producers seldom consider good news as "news" but instead focus on violence, scandal, corruption, and incompetence (see Chapter 6, "Mass Media: Setting the Political Agenda").

But public confidence in government can be restored, as it was in part during the Reagan presidency. Perhaps President Reagan's personal popularity was part of the reason that popular confidence in government rose.

Economic recessions erode public confidence in government. People expect the president and Congress to lead them out of "hard times." George Bush's Gulf War success raised public confidence only temporarily; the perceived failure of his administration to act decisively to restore the nation's economic health helped to send public confidence in government back down. Sustained growth in the economy during the 1990s under President Clinton improved public trust in government.

The terrorist attack of September 11, 2001, rallied Americans behind their government as no other event since the Japanese attack on Pearl Harbor in 1941. American flags sprouted from homes, businesses, and automobiles. Trust in government "to do the right thing" leaped to levels not seen since the 1960s. This dramatic rise in trust after "9/11" leveled off in 2002, but still remained higher than at any time in recent years.

Public Confidence, That the Federal Government Can Be Trusted to "Do What is Right Most of the Time"

Source: 1992–2004 data from Gallup Opinion Polls (http://www.gallup.com/poll/topics/trust_gov.asd), Copyright © 1992–2004, The Gallup Organization, see also Arthur H. Miller, "Confidence in Government during the 1980's," *American Politics Quarterly* 19 (April 1991): 147–73. See also Marc J. Hetherington and Suzanne Globetti, "Political Trust and Racial Policy Preferences," *American Journal of Political Science* 46 (April, 2002): 253–275.

change by speaking out, petitioning, demonstrating, forming interest groups or parties, voting against unpopular leaders, or running for office themselves. Since people living in a democracy can effect change by "working within the system," they have a greater moral obligation to obey the law than people living under regimes in which they have no voice. However, there may be some occasions when "civil disobedience" even in a democracy may be morally justified (see *A Conflicting View:* "Sometimes It's Right to Disobey the Law").

THINK AGAIN

Is it ever right to disobey the law?

The Purposes of Government

All governments tax, penalize, punish, restrict, and regulate their people. Governments in the United States—the federal government in Washington, the 50 state governments, and the more than 86,000 local governments—take nearly 40 cents out of every dollar Americans earn. Each year, the Congress enacts about 500 laws; federal bureaucracies publish about 19,000 rules and regulations, the state legislatures enact about 25,000 laws; and cities, counties, school districts, and other local governments enact countless local ordinances. Each of these laws restricts our freedom in some way. Each dollar taken out of our wages or profits reduces our freedom to choose what to do with our money.

Why do people put up with governments? An answer to this question can be found in the words of the Preamble to the Constitution of the United States:

> We the people of the United States, in Order to form a more perfect Union, establish Justice, insure domestic Tranquility, provide for the common defense, promote the general Welfare, and secure the Blessings of Liberty to ourselves and our Posterity, do ordain and establish this Constitution for the United States of America.

To Establish Justice and Insure Domestic Tranquility Government manages conflict and maintains order. We might think of government as a **social contract** among people who agree to allow themselves to be regulated and taxed in exchange for protection of their lives and property. No society can allow individuals or groups to settle their conflicts by street fighting, murder, kidnapping, rioting, bombing, or terrorism. Whenever government fails to control such violence, we describe it as "a breakdown in law and order." Without the protection of government, human lives and property are endangered, and only those skilled with fists and weapons have much of a chance of survival. The seventeenth-century English political philosopher Thomas Hobbes described life without government as "a war where every man is enemy to every man," where people live in "continual fear and danger of violent death."[2]

To Provide for the Common Defense Many anthropologists link the origins of government to warfare—to the need of early communities to protect themselves from raids by outsiders and to organize raids against others. Since the Revolutionary War, the U.S. government has been responsible for the country's defense. During the long Cold War, when America confronted a nuclear-armed, expansionist-minded, communist-governed Soviet Union, the United States spent nearly half of the federal budget on national defense. With the end of the Cold War, defense spending fell to about 15 percent of the federal budget, but defense spending has begun to creep upward again as the nation confronts the new war on terrorism. National defense will always remain a primary responsibility of United States government.

The King Center Atlanta-based center commemorates the life and teachings of Martin Luther King, Jr. *www.theKingCenter.com*

Internet Encyclopedia of Philosophy

At this site, you can find a concise description of social contract theory along with a discussion of John Locke's writing. *www.utm.edu/research/iep/*

DefenseLink Official site of the U.S. Department of Defense, with current news as well as links to Army, Navy, Air Force, Marine, and other defense agencies. *www.defenselink.gov*

social contract Idea that government originates as an implied contract among individuals who agree to obey laws in exchange for protection of their rights.

Sometimes It's Right to Disobey the Law

Civil disobedience is the nonviolent violation of laws that people believe to be unjust. Civil disobedience denies the *legitimacy,* or rightfulness, of a law and implies that a higher moral authority takes precedence over unjust laws. It is frequently a political tactic of minorities. (Majorities can more easily change laws through conventional political activity.)

Why resort to civil disobedience in a democracy? Why not work within the democratic system to change unjust laws? In 1963 a group of Alabama clergy posed these questions to Martin Luther King, Jr., and asked him to call off mass demonstrations in Birmingham, Alabama. King, who had been arrested in the demonstrations, replied in his now famous "Letter from Birmingham City Jail":

> One may well ask, "How can you advocate breaking some laws and obeying others?" The answer is found in the fact that there are unjust laws. I would be the first to advocate obeying just laws. One has not only a legal but a moral responsibility to obey just laws. Conversely, one has a moral responsibility to disobey unjust laws.

King argued that *nonviolent direct action* was a vital aspect of democratic politics. The political purpose of civil disobedience is to call attention or "to bear witness" to the existence of injustices. Only laws regarded as unjust are broken, and they are broken openly, without hatred or violence. Punishment is actively sought rather than avoided, since punishment will further emphasize the injustice of the laws.

The objective of nonviolent civil disobedience is to stir the conscience of an apathetic majority and to win support for measures that will eliminate the injustices. By accepting punishment for the violation of an unjust law, persons practicing civil disobedience demonstrate their sincerity. They hope to shame the majority and to make it ask itself how far it is willing to go to protect the status quo. Thus, ac-

Dr. Martin Luther King, Jr., shown here marching in Mississippi with his wife, Coretta Scott King, and others, used civil disobedience to advance the rights of African Americans during the 1950s and 1960s. (Copyright Flip Schulke)

cording to King's teachings, civil disobedience is clearly differentiated from hatred and violence:

> One who breaks an unjust law must do it openly, lovingly (not hatefully as the white mothers did in New Orleans when they were seen on television screaming "nigger, nigger, nigger") and with a willingness to accept the penalty. I submit that an individual who breaks a law that conscience tells him is unjust, and willingly accepts the penalty by staying in jail to arouse the conscience of the community over its injustice, is in reality expressing the very highest respect for law.

In 1964 Martin Luther King, Jr., received the Nobel Peace Prize in recognition of his extraordinary contributions to the development of nonviolent methods of social change.

Source: Martin Luther King, Jr., "Letter from Birmingham City Jail," April 16, 1963.

---

public goods Goods and services that cannot readily be provided by markets, either because they are too expensive for a single individual to buy or because if one person bought them, everyone else would use them without paying.

To Promote the General Welfare Government promotes the general welfare in a number of ways. It provides **public goods**—goods and services that private markets cannot readily furnish either because they are too expensive for individuals to buy for themselves (for example, a national park, a highway, or a sewage disposal plant) or because if one person bought them, everyone else would "free-ride," or use them without paying (for example, clean air, police protection, or national defense).

Nevertheless, Americans acquire most of their goods and services on the **free market,** through voluntary exchange among individuals, firms, and corporations. The **gross domestic product** (GDP)—the dollar sum of all the goods and services produced in the United States in a year—amounts to more than $10 trillion. Government spending in the United States—federal, state, and local governments combined—amounts to about $3 trillion, or an amount equivalent to 30 percent of the gross domestic product.

Governments also regulate society. Free markets cannot function effectively if individuals and firms engage in fraud, deception, or unfair competition, or if contracts cannot be enforced. Moreover, many economic activities impose costs on persons who are not direct participants in these activities. Economists refer to such costs as **externalities.** A factory that produces air pollution or wastewater imposes external costs on community residents who would otherwise enjoy cleaner air or water. A junkyard that creates an eyesore makes life less pleasant for neighbors and passersby. Many government regulations are designed to reduce these external costs.

To promote general welfare, governments also use **income transfers** from taxpayers to people who are regarded as deserving. Government agencies and programs provide support and care for individuals who cannot supply these things for themselves through the private job market, for example, ill, elderly, and disabled people, and dependent children who cannot usually be expected to find productive employment. The largest income transfer programs are Social Security and Medicare, which are paid to the elderly regardless of their personal wealth. Other large transfer payments go to farmers, veterans, and the unemployed, as well as to a wide variety of businesses. As we shall see, the struggle of individuals and groups to obtain direct government payments is a major motivator of political activity (see What Do You Think? "What Government Programs Do You Support?").

To Secure the Blessings of Liberty All governments must maintain order, protect national security, provide public goods, regulate society, and care for those unable to fend for themselves. But *democratic* governments have a special added responsibility—to protect individual liberty by ensuring that all people are treated equally before the law. No one is above the law. The president must obey the Constitution and laws of the United States, and so must members of Congress, governors, judges, and the police. A democratic government must protect people's freedom to speak and write what they please, to practice their religion, to petition, to form groups and parties, to enjoy personal privacy, and to exercise their rights if accused of a crime.

The concentration of government power can be a threat to freedom. If a democratic government acquires great power in order to maintain order, protect national security, or provide many collective goods and services, it runs the risk of becoming too powerful for the preservation of freedom. The question is how to keep government from becoming so pervasive it threatens the individual liberty it was established to protect.

The Meaning of Democracy

Throughout the centuries, thinkers in many different cultures contributed to the development of democratic government. Early Greek philosophers contributed the word **democracy,** which means "rule by the many." But there is no single definition of *democracy,* nor is there a tightly organized system of democratic thought.

free market Free competition for voluntary exchange among individuals, firms, and corporations.

gross domestic product (GDP) The dollar sum of all the goods and services produced in a nation in a year.

externalities Costs imposed on people who are not direct participants in an activity.

income transfers Government transfers of income from taxpayers to persons regarded as deserving.

democracy Governing system in which the people govern themselves, from the Greek term meaning "rule by the many."

What Government Programs Do You Support?

Although many Americans lack confidence in their government in general, they support many specific programs of the government. In somewhat of a paradox, Americans often express distrust in the federal government, yet at the same time approve of many of the programs and activities of that government.

The Council on Excellence in Government, which conducted this poll, believes that the most highly regarded programs are those that serve (or potentially serve) all Americans, rather than target groups.

Support for Government Programs

Support a Great Deal	Percent
Social Security	69
The Armed Forces	64
Medicare	64
Enforcing workplace safety	63
Enforcing laws against discrimination	61
Programs for public schools	61
Enforcing food and drug safety	60
College student loans	56
Enforcing minimum wage laws	56
Enforcing environmental protection laws	55
Federal law enforcement, such as the FBI	45
Enforcing family and medical leave laws	40
NASA and the space program	34
Affirmative action programs	29
Welfare programs	24

Source: Council Excellence in Government nationwide survey, February, 1997. www.excelgov.org. Reprinted by permission of Council on Excellence in Government.

 U.S. Information Agency

Official government site defining democracy, individual rights, and the culture of democracy
www.usinfo.state.gov/products/ pubs/whatsdem

democratic ideals
Individual dignity, equality before the law, widespread participation in public decisions, and public decisions by majority rule, with one person having one vote.

It is better, perhaps, to speak of democratic traditions than of a single democratic ideology.

Unfortunately, the looseness of the term *democracy* allows it to be perverted by *anti*democratic governments. Hardly a nation in the world exists that does not *claim* to be "democratic." Governments that outlaw political opposition, suppress dissent, discourage religion, and deny fundamental freedoms of speech and press still claim to be "democracies," "democratic republics," or "people's republics" (for example, the Democratic People's Republic of Korea is the official name of Communist North Korea). These governments defend their use of the term *democracy* by claiming that their policies reflect the true interests of their people. But they are unwilling to allow political freedoms or to hold free elections in order to find out whether their people really agree with their policies. In effect, they use the term as a political slogan rather than a true description of their government.[3]

The actual existence of **democratic ideals** varies considerably from country to country, regardless of their names (see *Compared to What?* "Freedom and Democracy around the World"). A meaningful definition of democracy must include the following ideals: recognition of the dignity of every individual; equal protection under the law for every individual; opportunity for everyone to participate in pub-

Freedom and Democracy around the World

Worldwide progress toward freedom over the past half-century has been impressive. In 1950 there were 22 democracies accounting for 31 percent of the world population that were said to be "free." Another 21 nations with restricted democratic practices were labeled "partly free"; they accounted for an additional 11.9 percent of the world population. By 2000, democracy had spread to 120 "free" countries that constituted 58 percent of the world population; an additional 5 percent lived in nations labeled "partly free." In all, about 63 percent of the world population were living in democracies. Nonetheless, "not-free" authoritarian and totalitarian regimes governed more than one-third of the world's population.[*]

Worldwide progress toward freedom and democracy has been evident since 1989 notably as a result of the collapse of communism in Eastern Europe and the demise of the Soviet Union.

One way to assess the degree of democracy in a governmental system is to consider its record in en-suring political freedoms—enabling citizens to participate meaningfully in government—and individual liberties. A checklist for political freedoms might include whether the chief executive and national legislature are elected; whether elections are generally fair, with open campaigning and honest tabulation of votes; and whether multiple candidates and parties participate. A checklist for individual liberties might include whether the press and broadcasting are free and independent of the government; whether people are free to assemble, protest, and form opposition parties; whether religious institutions, labor unions, business organizations, and other groups are free and independent of the government; and whether individuals are free to own property, travel, and move their residence.

The Freedom House is a NewYork-based think tank that regularly surveys political conditions around the world (see map).

---

[*]Freedom House, *Democracy's Century* (New York: Freedom House, 2001).

Source: Reprinted by permission of Freedom House, 2002.

lic decisions; and decision making by majority rule, with one person having one vote.

Individual Dignity The underlying value of democracy is the dignity of the individual. Human beings are entitled to life and liberty, personal property, and equal protection under the law. These liberties are *not* granted by governments; they belong to every person born into the world. The English political philosopher John Locke (1632–1704) argued that a higher "natural law" guaranteed liberty to every person and that this natural law was morally superior to all human laws and governments. Each individual possesses "certain inalienable Rights, among these are Life, Liberty, and Property."[4] When Thomas Jefferson wrote his eloquent defense of the American Revolution in the Declaration of Independence for the Continental Congress in Philadelphia in 1776, he borrowed heavily from Locke (perhaps even to the point of plagiarism):

> We hold these truths to be self-evident, that all Men are created equal, that they are endowed by their Creator with certain unalienable Rights, that among these are Life, Liberty and the Pursuit of Happiness—That to secure these Rights, Governments are instituted among Men, deriving their just powers from the Consent of the Governed, that whenever any Form of Government becomes destructive of these Ends, it is the Right of the People to alter or to abolish it.

Individual dignity requires personal freedom. People who are directed by governments in every aspect of their lives, people who are "collectivized" and made into workers for the state, people who are enslaved—all are denied the personal dignity to which all human beings are entitled. Democratic governments try to minimize the role of government in the lives of citizens.

Equality True democracy requires equal protection of the law for every individual. Democratic governments cannot discriminate between blacks and whites, or men and women, or rich and poor, or any groups of people in applying the law. Not only must a democratic government refrain from discrimination itself, but it must also work to prevent discrimination in society generally. Today our notion of equality extends to equality of opportunity—the obligation of government to ensure that all Americans have an opportunity to develop their full potential.

Participation in Decision Making Democracy means individual participation in the decisions that affect individuals' lives. People should be free to choose for themselves how they want to live. Individual participation in government is necessary for individual dignity. People in a democracy should not have decisions made *for* them but *by* them. Even if they make mistakes, it is better that they be permitted to do so than to take away their rights to make their own decisions. The true democrat would reject even a wise and benevolent dictatorship because it would threaten the individual's character, self-reliance, and dignity. The argument for democracy is not that the people will always choose wise policies for themselves, but that people who cannot choose for themselves are not really free.

Majority Rule: One Person, One Vote Collective decision making in democracies must be by majority rule, with each person having one vote. That is, each person's vote must be equal to every other person's, regardless of status, money, or fame. Whenever any individual is denied political equality because of race, sex, or wealth, then the government is not truly democratic. Majorities are

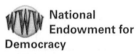

Freedom House
A think tank monitoring the ongoing evolution of global human rights and liberty; provides an annual world survey covering freedom's progress throughout the state system. *www.freedomhouse.org/*

THINK AGAIN

Should important decisions in a democracy be submitted to voters rather than decided by Congress?

National Endowment for Democracy

Private advocacy group for worldwide democracy and human rights. *www.ned.org*

not always right. But majority *rule* means that all persons have an equal say in decisions affecting them. If people are truly equal, their votes must count equally, and a majority vote must decide the issue, even if the majority decides foolishly.

The Paradox of Democracy

What if a *majority* of the people decide to attack the rights of some unpopular individuals or minority groups? What if hate, prejudice, or racism infects a majority of people and they vote for leaders who promise to "get rid of the Jews" or "put blacks in their place" or "bash a few gays"? What if a majority of people vote to take away the property of wealthy people and distribute it among themselves.[5] Do we abide by the principle of majority rule and allow the majority to do what it wants? Or do we defend the principle of individual liberty and limit the majority's power? If we enshrine the principle of majority rule, we are placing all our confidence in the wisdom and righteousness of the majority of the people. Yet we know that democracy means more than majority rule, that it also means freedom and dignity for the individual. How do we resolve this **paradox of democracy**—the potential for conflict between majority rule and individual freedom?

Limiting the Power of Majorities The Founders of the American nation were not sure that freedom would be safe in the hands of the majority. In *The Federalist Papers* in 1787, James Madison warned against a direct democracy: "Pure democracy . . . can admit of no cure for the mischiefs of faction. . . . There is nothing to check the inducements to sacrifice the weaker party, or an obnoxious individual."[6] So the Founders wrote a Constitution and adopted a Bill of Rights that limited the power of government over the individual, that placed some personal

THINK AGAIN

In a democracy should "majority rule" be able to limit the rights of members of an unpopular or dangerous minority?

THINK AGAIN

Is government trying to do too many things that should be left to individuals?

paradox of democracy
Potential for conflict between individual freedom and majority rule.

The paradox of democracy balances the principle of majority rule against the principle of individual liberty. When the German people voted Adolf Hitler and the Nazi Party into power, did majority rule give the Nazis free rein to restrict the individual liberties of the people? Or did those who abhorred the trespasses of their government have the right to fight against its power?

Political sociologists have observed that the military in totalitarian societies has a distinct body language. Soldiers in Nazi Germany and, as seen here, communist North Korea used a "goose step" when on parade—a march in which the knee is unbent and the foot, encased in a heavy boot, is stamped on the ground, providing a powerful image of authority and force. In democratic societies, the goose step is not employed, indeed, it is regarded as somewhat ridiculous.

liberties beyond the reach of majorities. They established the principle of **limited government**—a government that is itself restrained by law. Under a limited government, even if a majority of voters wanted to, they could not prohibit communists or atheists or racists from speaking or writing. Nor could they ban certain religions, set aside the rights of criminal defendants to a fair trial, or prohibit people from moving or quitting their jobs. These rights belong to individuals, not to majorities or governments.

Totalitarianism: Unlimited Government Power No government can be truly democratic if it directs every aspect of its citizens' lives. Individuals must be free to shape their own lives, free from the dictates of governments or even majorities of their fellow citizens. Indeed, we call a government with *un*limited power over its citizens totalitarian. Under **totalitarianism**, the individual possesses no personal liberty. Totalitarian governments decide what people can say or write; what unions, churches, or parties they can join, if any; where people must live; what work they must do; what goods they can find in stores and what they will be allowed to buy and sell; whether citizens will be allowed to travel outside of their country; and so on. Under a totalitarian government, the total life of the individual is subject to government control.

Constitutional Government Constitutions, written or unwritten, are the principal means by which governmental powers are limited. Constitutions set forth the liberties of individuals and restrain governments from interfering with these liberties. Consider, for example, the opening words of the First Amendment to the U.S. Constitution: "Congress shall make no law respecting an establishment of religion, or prohibiting the free exercise thereof." This amendment places religious belief beyond the reach of the government. The government itself is restrained by law. It cannot, even by majority vote, interfere with the personal liberty to worship as one chooses. In addition, armed with the power of judicial review, the courts can declare unconstitutional laws passed by majority vote of Congress or state legislatures (see "Judicial Power" in Chapter 13).

Throughout this book we examine how well limited constitutional government succeeds in preserving individual liberty in the United States. We examine free

limited government
Principle that government power over the individual is limited, that there are some personal liberties that even a majority cannot regulate, and that government itself is restrained by law.

totalitarianism Rule by an elite that exercises unlimited power over individuals in all aspects of life.

speech and press, the mass media, religious freedom, the freedom to protest and demonstrate, and the freedom to support political candidates and interest groups of all kinds. We examine how well the U.S. Constitution protects individuals from discrimination and inequality. And we examine how far government should go in protecting society without destroying individual liberty (see *Up Close:* "Terrorism's Threat to Democracy" on page 18).

Direct Versus Representative Democracy

In the Gettysburg Address, Abraham Lincoln spoke about "a government of the people, by the people, for the people," and his ringing phrase remains an American ideal. But can we take this phrase literally? More than 281 million Americans are spread over 4 million square miles. If we brought everyone together, standing shoulder to shoulder, they would occupy 66 square miles. One round of five-minute speeches by everyone would take over 2,500 years. "People could be born, grow old, and die while they waited for the assembly to make one decision."[7]

Direct democracy (also called pure or participatory democracy), where everyone actively participates in every decision, is rare. The closest approximation to direct democracy in American government may be the traditional New England town meeting, where all of the citizens come together face to face to decide about town affairs. But today most New England towns vest authority in a board of officials elected by the townspeople to make policy decisions between town meetings, and professional administrators are appointed to supervise the day-to-day town services. The town meeting is rapidly vanishing because citizens cannot spend so much of their time and energy in community decision making.

Representative democracy recognizes that it is impossible to expect millions of people to come together and decide every issue. Instead, representatives of the people are elected by the people to decide issues on behalf of the people. Elections must be open to competition so that the people can choose representatives who reflect their own views. And elections must take place in an environment of free speech and press, so that both candidates and voters can freely express their views. Finally, elections must be held periodically so that representatives can be thrown out of office if they no longer reflect the views of the majority of the people.

New Rules Project
An organization advocating local government solutions and "direct democracy," including the New England town meeting. *www.newrules.org*

direct democracy
Governing system in which every person participates actively in every public decision, rather than delegating decision making to representatives.

representative democracy
Governing system in which public decision making is delegated to representatives of the people chosen by popular vote in free, open, and periodic elections.

Direct democracy still lives in many New England towns, where citizens come together periodically to pass laws, elect officials, and make decisions about such matters as taxation and land use.

No government can claim to be a representative democracy, then, unless

1. Representatives are selected by vote of all the people.
2. Elections are open to competition.
3. Candidates and voters can freely express themselves.
4. Representatives are selected periodically.

So when we hear of "elections" in which only one party is permitted to run candidates, candidates are not free to express their views, or leaders are elected "for life," then we know that these governments are not really democracies, regardless of what they may call themselves.

Throughout this book, as we examine how well representative democracy works in the United States, we consider such issues as participation in elections—why some people vote and others do not—whether parties and candidates offer the voters real alternatives, whether modern political campaigning informs voters or only confuses them, and whether elected representatives are responsive to the wishes of voters. These are the kinds of issues that concern political science.

THINK AGAIN

Is the government run by a few big interests looking out for themselves?

Who Really Governs?

Democracy is an inspiring ideal. But is democratic government really possible? Is it possible for millions of people to govern themselves, with every voice having equal influence? Or will a small number of people inevitably acquire more power than others? To what extent is democracy attainable in *any* society, and how democratic is the American political system? That is, who really governs?

The Elitist Perspective "Government is always government by the few, whether in the name of the few, the one, or the many."[8] This quotation from political scientists Harold Lasswell and Daniel Lerner expresses the basic idea of **elitism**. All societies, including democracies, divide themselves into the few who have power and the many who do not. In every society, there is a division of labor. Only a few people are directly involved in governing a nation; most people are content to let others undertake the tasks of government. The *elite* are the few who have power; the *masses* are the many who do not. This theory holds that an elite is inevitable in any social organization. We cannot form a club, a church, a business, or a government without selecting some people to provide leadership. And leaders will always have a perspective on the organization different from that of its members.

In any large, complex society, then, whether or not it is a democracy, decisions are made by tiny minorities. Out of more than 281 million Americans, only a few thousand individuals at most participate directly in decisions about war and peace, wages and prices, employment and production, law and justice, taxes and benefits, health and welfare. Even the people themselves have doubts about the accuracy of Lincoln's words, "a government of, by and for the people." (See *What Do You Think? "Is the American Government 'Of, By and For the People'?"*)

Elitism does *not* mean that leaders always exploit or oppress members. On the contrary, elites may be very concerned for the welfare of the masses. Elite status may be open to ambitious, talented, or educated individuals from the masses or may be closed to all except the wealthy. Elites may be very responsive to public opinion, or they may ignore the usually apathetic and ill-informed masses. But whether

elitism Theory that all societies, even democracies, are divided into the few who govern and the many who do not.

elites are self-seeking or public spirited, open or closed, responsive or unresponsive, it is they and not the masses who actually make the decisions.

Contemporary elite theory argues that power in America is concentrated in a small *institutional* elite. Sociologist C. Wright Mills popularized the term *power elite* in arguing that leaders of corporations, the military establishment, and the national government come together at the top of a giant pyramid of power.[9] Other social scientists have found that more than half of the nation's total assets are concentrated in the 100 largest corporations and 50 largest banks; that the officers and directors of these corporations and banks interact frequently with leaders of government, the mass media, foundations, and universities, and that these leaders are drawn disproportionately from wealthy, educated, upper-class, white, male, Anglo-Saxon Protestant groups in American society.[10]

Most people do not regularly concern themselves with decision making in Washington. They are more concerned with their jobs, family, sports, and recreation than they are with politics. They are not well informed about tax laws, foreign policy, or even who represents them in Congress. Since the "masses" are largely apathetic and ill informed about policy questions, their views are likely to be influenced more by what they see and hear on television than by their own experience. Most communication flows downward from elites to masses. Elitism argues that the masses have at best only an indirect influence on the decisions of elites.

Opinion polls indicate that many Americans agree with the elitist contention that government is run by "a few big interests" (see Figure 1.2).

The Pluralist Perspective No one seriously argues that all Americans participate in *all* of the decisions that shape their lives; that majority preferences *always* prevail; that the values of life, liberty, and property are *never* sacrificed; or that every American enjoys equality of opportunity. Nevertheless, most American political scientists argue that the American system of government, which they describe as "pluralist," is the best possible approximation of the democratic ideal in a large, complex society. Pluralism is designed to make the theory of democracy "more realistic."[11]

Pluralism is the belief that democracy can be achieved in a large, complex society by competition, bargaining, and compromise among organized groups and

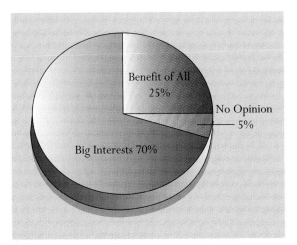

C. Wright Mills
Web site devoted to Mills, with photos, books, and writings.
www.cwrightmills.org

pluralism Theory that democracy can be achieved through competition among multiple organized groups and that individuals can participate in politics through group memberships and elections.

FIGURE 1.2 Public Opinion about Who Runs the Country

Would you say the government is pretty much run by a few big interests looking out for themselves or that it is run for the benefit of all the people?

Source: The Gallup Poll, July 6–9, 2000. Copyright © 1996–2004 by The Gallup Organization.

Benefit of All 25%

No Opinion 5%

Big Interests 70%

Terrorism's Threat to Democracy

The horrifying images of "9/11" will not be easily forgotten—America's tallest skyscrapers exploding in flames and crumbling to earth—images projected over and over again on the nation's television screens. Commercial airliners, loaded with fuel and passengers, flown at high speeds directly into the symbols of America's financial and military power—the World Trade Center in New York and the Pentagon in Washington. Within minutes, thousands of lives are lost on American soil—more than at any time since the Civil War. After September 11 America found itself in a new war, a war against worldwide networks of terrorists.

The Goal of Terrorism   Terrorism is violence directed against innocent civilians to advance political goals. As barbaric as terrorism appears to civilized peoples, it is not without a rationale. Terrorists are not "crazies." Their first goal is to announce in the most dramatic fashion their own grievances, their commitment to violence, and their disregard for human life, often including their own. In its initial phase the success of a terrorist act is directly related to the publicity it receives. Terrorist groups jubilantly claim responsibility for their acts. The more horrendous, the more media coverage, the more damage, the more dead—all add to the success of the terrorists in attracting attention to themselves.

A prolonged campaign of terrorism is designed to inspire pervasive fear among people, to convince them that their government cannot protect them, and to undermine their confidence in their political system. If the government fails to suppress terrorism, people become ever more fearful, more willing to accept restrictions on liberties, and more open to the appeals of demagogues who promise to restore order to protect people at any cost. Or a weakened government may resort to "negotiations" with the leaders of terrorist groups, implicitly granting them legitimacy and providing them the opportunity to advance their goals.

America's Response   But America's response to the terrorist attacks of September 11, 2001, was precisely the *opposite* of the intention of the terrorists. National pride, confidence in national leadership, and faith in human nature, all soared among the American people in the aftermath of the attack. Patriotism flourished. Flags flew from businesses, homes, and automobiles. The attack united the country in a way that no other event since the 1941 Japanese attack on Pearl Harbor had done. Trust in government rose to highs not seen since the 1960s. Popular support for military action was overwhelming.

Security vs. Liberty   However, threats to national security have historically resulted in challenges to individual liberty. Abraham Lincoln suspended the *writ of habeas corpus* (the requirement that authorities bring defendants before a judge and show cause for their detention) during the Civil War. (Only after the war did the U.S. Supreme Court hold that he had no authority to suspend the writ.[*])

---

[*]Ex parte Milligan (1866).

See Robert A. Pape, "The Strategic Logic of Suicide Terrorism," *American Political Science Review* 97 (August 2003): 343–361.

Democracy Net
Democracy site of the League of Women Voters linking ZIP codes to your federal, state, and local representatives. ***www.dnet.org***

that individuals can participate in decision making through membership in these groups and by choosing among parties and candidates in elections.

Pluralists recognize that the individual acting alone is no match for giant government bureaucracies, big corporations and banks, the television networks, labor unions, or other powerful interest groups. Instead, pluralists rely on *competition* among these organizations to protect the interests of individuals. They hope that countervailing centers of power—big business, big labor, big government—will check one another and prevent any single group from abusing its power and oppressing individual Americans.

Individuals in a pluralist democracy may not participate directly in decision making, but they can join and support *interest groups* whose leaders bargain on their behalf in the political arena. People are more effective in organized groups—for

The horrifying images of "9/11" will not be easily forgotten—America's tallest skyscrapers exploding and crumbling to earth—images projected over and over again on the nation's television screens.

In February 1942, shortly after the Japanese attack on Pearl Harbor, President Franklin D. Roosevelt authorized the removal and internment of Japanese Americans living on the West Coast. The U.S. Supreme Court upheld this flagrant violation of the Constitution,[†] not until 1988 did the U.S. Congress vote reparations and make public apologies to the surviving victims.

New Restrictions on Americans The "9/11" terrorist attack on America inspired Congress and the president to enact and enforce greater restrictions on individual liberty than the nation had experienced

[†]Korematsu p. U.S., 323 U.S. 214 (1944).

since World War II. Congress passed the Patriot Act that, among other things, allows searches without notice to the suspect; grants "roving" wiretap warrants that allow government eavesdropping on any telephones used by suspects; allows the interception of e-mail; allows investigators to obtain information from creditcard companies, banks, libraries, and other businesses; authorizes the seizure of properties used to commit or facilitate terrorism; and allows the detention of noncitizens charged with terrorism. President George W. Bush created a new Department of Homeland Security reorganizing more than forty federal agencies that have a role in combating terrorism. All of these measures enjoyed widespread popular support.

Terrorism and Democracy Terrorism has brought mixed blessings to American democracy. It has succeeded in uniting Americans, inspiring patriotism, and increasing their trust in government. But it has also inspired a greater willingness to accept new restrictions on individual liberty. In the past, restrictions on individual liberty have been relaxed when the perceived crisis has subsided. How long will the "war on terrorism" last? Will Americans be asked to sacrifice additional liberties in this war? How far are Americans willing to go in sacrificing individual liberty to achieve national security?

example, the Sierra Club for environmentalists, the American Civil Liberties Union (ACLU) for civil rights advocates, the National Association for the Advancement of Colored People (NAACP) and the Urban League for African Americans, the American Legion and Veterans of Foreign Wars for veterans, and the National Rifle Association (NRA) for opponents of gun control.

According to the pluralist view, the Democratic and Republican parties are really coalitions of groups: the national Democratic Party is a coalition of union members, big-city residents, blacks, Catholics, Jews, and, until recently, southerners; the national Republican Party is a coalition of business and professional people, suburbanites, farmers, and white Protestants. When voters choose candidates and parties, they are helping to determine which interest groups will enjoy a better reception in government.

 The Terrorism Research Center

News and information on terrorist attacks around the world and list of terrorist organizations.
www.terrorism.com

Is the American Government "Of, By and For the People"?

Do you think of the government in Washington as OUR government or as THE government? If a democratic government is truly "of, by and for the people," we would expect that the people would think of it as their own. But national opinion polls indicate the majority of Americans do *not* believe that the government belongs to them:

Q. When you think and talk about government, do you tend to think of it more as THE government or as OUR government?

THE government	55%
OUR government	42
Not sure	3

Indeed, a majority do *not* believe that we have a government today that is "of, by and for the people."

Q. One goal that Americans have traditionally considered important is to have a government that is "of, by and for the people"—meaning that it involves people and represents them. In your opinion, do we have a government today that is "of, by and for the people"?

Yes	39%
No	54
Not sure	7

Source: Council on Excellence in Government, as reported in *The Polling Report,* June, 1999.

Pluralists contend that there are multiple leadership groups in society (hence the term *pluralism*). They contend that power is widely dispersed among these groups; that no one group, not even the wealthy upper class, dominates decision making; and that groups that are influential in one area of decision making are not necessarily the same groups that are influential in other areas of decision making. Different groups of leaders make decisions in different issue areas.

Pluralism recognizes that public policy does not always coincide with majority preferences. Instead, public policy is the "equilibrium" reached in the conflict among group interests. It is the balance of competing interest groups, and therefore, say the pluralists, it is a reasonable approximation of society's preferences.

Democracy in America

Is democracy alive and well in America today? Elitism raises serious questions about the possibility of achieving true democracy in any large, complex society. Pluralism is more comforting; it offers a way of reaffirming democratic values and providing some practical solutions to the problem of individual participation in a modern society.

There is no doubt about the strength of democratic ideals in American society. These ideals—individual dignity, equality, popular participation in government, and majority rule—are the standards by which we judge the performance of the American political system. But we are still faced with the task of describing the reality of American politics.

This book explores who gets what, when, and how in the American political system; who participates in politics; what policies are decided upon; and when and how these decisions are made. In so doing, it raises many controversial questions about the realities of democracy, elitism, and pluralism in American life. But this book does not supply the answers; as a responsible citizen, you have to provide your own answers. At the completion of your studies, you will have to decide for yourself whether the American political system is truly democratic. Your studies will help inform your judgment, but, in the end, you yourself must make that judgment. That is the burden of freedom.

SUMMARY NOTES

- Politics is deciding who gets what, when, and how. It occurs in many different settings, but political science focuses on politics in government.

- Political science focuses on three central questions:
  Who governs?
  For what ends?
  By what means?

- Government is distinguished from other social organizations in that it
  Extends to the whole society
  Can legitimately use force

- The purposes of government are to
  Maintain order in society
  Provide for national defense
  Provide "public goods"
  Regulate society
  Transfer income
  Protect individual liberty

- The ideals of democracy include
  Recognition of individual dignity and personal freedom
  Equality before the law
  Widespread participation in decision making
  Majority rule, with one person equaling one vote

- The principles of democracy pose a paradox: How can we resolve conflicts between our belief in majority rule and our belief in individual freedom?

- Limited government places individual liberty beyond the reach of majorities. Constitutions are the principal means of limiting government power.

- Direct democracy, in which everyone participates in every public decision, is very rare. Representative democracy means that public decisions are made by representatives elected by the people, in elections held periodically and open to competition, in which candidates and voters freely express themselves.

- Threats to national security have historically reduced the scope of individual liberty in our nation. The terrorist attack on America of September 11, 2001, inspired greater unity, patriotism, and trust in government among the people. But it also brought greater restrictions on individual liberty.

- Who really governs? The elitist perspective on American democracy focuses on the small number of leaders who actually decide national issues, compared to the mass of citizens who are apathetic and ill informed about politics. A pluralist perspective focuses on competition among organized groups in society, with individuals participating through group membership and voting for parties and candidates in elections.

- How democratic is American government today? Democratic ideals are widely shared in our society. But you must make your own informed judgment about the realities of American politics.

KEY TERMS

politics 4
political science 4
government 4
legitimacy 5
social contract 7
public goods 8
free market 9
gross domestic product (GDP) 9
externalities 9
income transfers 9
democracy 9

SUGGESTED READINGS

Barker, Lucius J., Mack H. Jones, and Katherine Tate. *African-Americans and the American Political System.* Upper Saddle River, NJ.: Prentice Hall, 1999. A dynamic analysis of how African Americans fare within the prevailing theoretical, structural, and functioning patterns of the American political system.

Cronin, Thomas J. *Direct Democracy.* Cambridge, Mass.: Harvard University Press, 1989. A thoughtful discussion of direct versus representative democracy, as well as a review of initiative, referendum, and recall devices.

Dahl, Robert A. *Democracy and Its Critics.* New Haven, Conn.: Yale University Press, 1989. A defense of modern democracy from the pluralist perspective.

Dye, Thomas R., and Harmon Zeigler. *The Irony of Democracy.* 12th ed. New York: Wadsworth, 2003. An interpretation of American politics from the elitist perspective.

Fukuyama, Francis. *Trust.* New York: Free Press, 1995. Argues that the breakdown of trust in America—not only in the government but at a person-to-person level—is burdening the nation with formal rules and regulations, lengthy contracts, bureaucracy, lawyers, and lawsuits.

Lasswell, Harold. Politics: *Who Gets What, When, and How.* New York: McGraw-Hill, 1936. Classic description of the nature of politics and the study of political science by America's foremost political scientist of the twentieth century.

Mills, C. Wright. *The Power Elite.* New York: Oxford University Press, 1956. Classic Marxist critique of elitism in American society, setting forth the argument that "corporate chieftains," "military warlords," and a "political directorate" come together to form the nation's power elite.

Neiman, Max. *Defending Government: Why Big Government Works.* Upper Saddle River, N.J.: Prentice Hall, 2000. A spirited defense of how big government can improve lives of people.

Page, Benjamin I., and Robert Y. Shapiro. *The Rational Public.* Chicago: University of Chicago Press, 1992. An examination of fifty years of public opinion polls convinces these authors that American government is generally responsive to the views of the majority.

Putnam, Robert D. *Bowling Alone: The Collapse and Revival of the American Community.* New York: Simon & Schuster, 2001. An argument that Americans are increasingly disconnected from one another, harming the health of democracy.

THE MAP OF FREEDOM

Freedom and democracy are not absolutes, they can develop in stages. No country allows its citizens complete freedom and no country can completely eliminate it. The map in this simulation describes countries as free, partly free, or not free, based on the criteria of political rights (right to vote, free and fair elections, participation of minorities, etc.). You will be asked to finish the map by describing the countries as "free," "partly free," or "not free."

POLITICAL CULTURE:
IDEAS IN CONFLICT

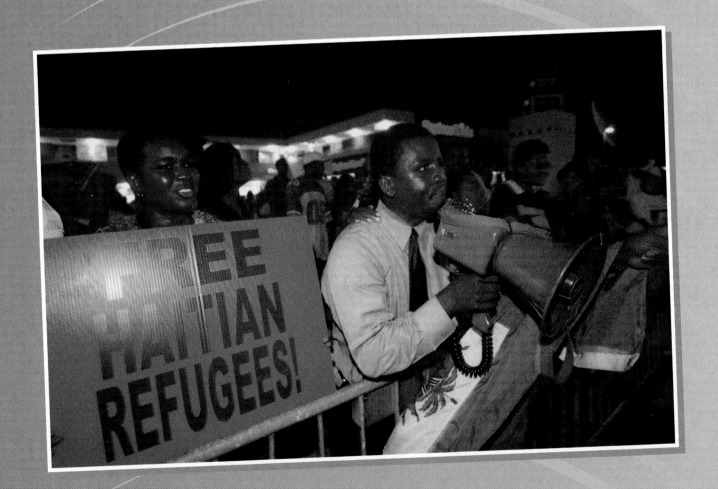

Political Culture

Ideas have power. We are all influenced by ideas—beliefs, values, symbols—more than we realize. Ideas provide us with rationalizations for ways of life, with guides for determining right and wrong, and with emotional impulses to action. Political institutions are shaped by ideas, and political leaders are constrained by them.

The term **political culture** refers to widely shared ideas about who should govern, for what ends, and by what means. **Values** are shared ideas about what is good and desirable. Values provide standards for judging what is right or wrong. **Beliefs** are shared ideas about what is true. Values and beliefs are often related. For example, if we believe that human beings are endowed by God with rights to life, liberty, and property, then we will value the protection of these rights. Thus beliefs can justify values.

Cultural descriptions are generalizations about the values and beliefs of many people in society, but these generalizations do not apply to everyone. Important variations in values and beliefs may exist within a society, these variations are frequently referred to as **subcultures** and may arise from such diverse bases as religion, racial or ethnic identity, or political group membership.

Contradictions between Values and Conditions Agreement over values in a political culture is no guarantee that there will not be contradictions between these values and actual conditions. People both in and out of politics frequently act contrary to their professed values. No doubt the most grievous contradiction between professed national beliefs and actual conditions in America is found in the long history of slavery, segregation, and racial discrimination. The contradiction between the words of the Declaration of Independence that "all men are created equal" and the practices of slavery and segregation became the "American dilemma."[1] But this contradiction does not mean that professed values are worthless; the very existence of the gap between values and behavior becomes a motivation for change. The history of the civil rights movement might be viewed as an effort to "bear witness" to the contradiction between the belief in equality and the existence of segregation and discrimination.[2] Whatever the obstacles to racial equality in America, these obstacles would be even greater if the nation's political culture did *not* include a professed belief in equality.

THINK ABOUT POLITICS

1 Do you consider yourself politically conservative, moderate, or liberal?
Conservative ●
Moderate ●
Liberal ●

2 Are income differences in America widening?
Yes ● No ●

3 Is it the government's responsibility to reduce income differences between people?
Yes ● No ●

4 If incomes were made more equal, would people still be motivated to work hard?
Yes ● No ●

5 Do Americans today still have the opportunity to significantly improve their condition in life?
Yes ● No ●

6 Should the U.S. government curtail immigration to America?
Yes ● No ●

7 Should illegal immigrants be denied welfare benefits?
Yes ● No ●

8 Is American culture racist and sexist?
Yes ● No ●

Ask yourself if your answers to these questions are widely shared by most citizens of the United States. Your answers probably reflect not only your own beliefs and values but also those of the political culture to which you belong.

Inconsistent Applications A political culture does not mean that shared principles are always applied in every circumstance. For example, people may truly believe in the principle of "free speech for all, no matter what their views might be," and yet when asked whether racists should be allowed to speak on a college campus, many people will say no. Thus general agreement with abstract principles of freedom of speech, freedom of the press, and academic freedom does not always ensure their application to specific individuals or groups.[3] Americans are frequently willing to restrict the freedoms of particularly obnoxious groups. A generation ago it was alleged communists and atheists whose freedoms were questioned. Over time these groups have become less threatening, but today people are still willing to restrict the liberties of racists, pro-abortion or anti-abortion groups, "skinheads," and neo-Nazis, and people who resemble terrorists.

Conflict The idea of political culture does not mean an absence of conflict over values and beliefs. Indeed, much of politics involves conflict over very fundamental values. The American nation has experienced a bloody civil war, political assassinations, rioting and burning of cities, the forced resignation of a president, and other direct challenges to its political foundations. Indeed, much of this book deals with serious political conflict. Yet Americans do share many common ways of thinking about politics.

Individual Liberty

No political value has been more widely held in the United States than individual liberty. The very beginnings of our history as a nation were shaped by **classical liberalism**, which asserts the worth and dignity of the individual. This political philosophy emphasizes the rational ability of human beings to determine their own destinies, and it rejects ideas, practices, and institutions that submerge individuals into a larger whole and thus deprive them of their dignity. The only restriction on the individual is not to interfere with the liberties of others.

Political Liberty Classical liberalism grew out of the eighteenth-century Enlightenment, the Age of Reason in which great philosophers such as Voltaire, John Locke, Jean Jacques Rousseau, Adam Smith, and Thomas Jefferson affirmed their faith in reason, virtue, and common sense. Classical liberalism originated as an attack on the hereditary prerogatives and distinctions of a feudal society, the monarchy, the privileged aristocracy, and the state-established church.

Classical liberalism motivated America's Founders to declare their independence from England, to write the U.S. Constitution, and to establish the Republic. It rationalized their actions and provided ideological legitimacy for the new nation. The founders adopted the language of John Locke, who argued that a natural law, or moral principle, guaranteed every person "certain inalienable Rights," among them "Life, Liberty, and Property," and that human beings form a social contract with one another to establish a government to help protect their rights. Implicit in the social contract and the liberal notion of freedom is the belief that governmental activity and restrictions on the individual should be kept to a minimum.

Economic Freedom Classical liberalism as a political idea is closely related to capitalism as an *economic* idea. **Capitalism** asserts the individual's right to own private property and to buy, sell, rent, and trade that property in a free market. The

---

political culture Widely shared views about who should govern, for what ends, and by what means.

values Shared ideas about what is good and desirable.

beliefs Shared ideas about what is true.

subcultures Variations on the prevailing values and beliefs in a society.

Philosophy Pages
History of Western philosophy and discussion of major democratic philosophers, including John Locke, Jean Jacques Rousseau, and Thomas Hobbes, among others.
www.philosophypages.com

classical liberalism Political philosophy asserting the worth and dignity of the individual and emphasizing the rational ability of human beings to determine their own destinies.

capitalism Economic system asserting the individual's right to own private property and to buy, sell, rent, and trade that property in a free market.

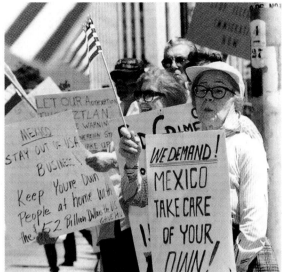

Proposition 187, a ballot initiative in California in 1994 denying state services to illegal immigrants, exposed a clash of cultures in Los Angeles.

economic version of freedom is the freedom to make contracts, to bargain for one's services, to move from job to job, to join labor unions, to start one's own business. Capitalism stresses individual rationality in economic matters—freedom of choice in working, producing, buying, and selling—and limited governmental intervention in economic affairs. Classical liberalism emphasizes individual rationality in voter choice—freedom of speech, press, and political activity—and limitations on governmental power over individual liberty. In classical liberal politics, individuals are free to speak out, to form political parties, and to vote as they please—to pursue their political interests as they think best. In classical liberal economics, individuals are free to find work, to start businesses, and to spend their money as they please—to pursue their economic interests as they think best. The role of government is restricted to protecting private property, enforcing contracts, and performing only those functions and services that cannot be performed by the private market.

The value of liberty in these political and economic spheres has been paramount throughout our history. Only equality competes with liberty as the most honored value in the American political culture.

Heritage Foundation

This think tank site includes a ranking of over 150 nations on an "Index of Economic Freedom." The U.S. ranks sixth; Hong Kong ranks first. *www.heritage.org*

Dilemmas of Equality

Since the bold assertion of the Declaration of Independence that "all men are created equal," Americans have generally believed that no person has greater worth than any other person. The principle of equal worth and dignity was a radical idea in 1776, when much of the world was dominated by hereditary monarchies, titled nobilities, and rigid caste and class systems. Belief in equality drove the expansion of voting rights in the early 1800s and ultimately destroyed the institution of slavery. Abraham Lincoln understood that equality was not so much a description of reality as an ideal to be aspired to: "a standard maxim for a free society which should be familiar to all, and revered by all; constantly looked to, constantly labored for, and even though never perfectly attained, constantly approximated and thereby augmenting the happiness and value of life to all people of all colors everywhere."[4] The millions who immigrated to the United States viewed this country as a land not only of opportunity but of *equal* opportunity, where everyone, regardless of birth, could rise in wealth and status based on hard work, natural talents, and perhaps good luck.

Today, most Americans agree that no one is intrinsically "better" than anyone else. This belief in equality, then, is fundamental to Americans, but a closer examination shows that throughout our history it has been tested, as beliefs and values so often are, by political realities.

Political Equality The nation's Founders shared the belief that the law should apply equally to all—that birth, status, or wealth do not justify differential application of the laws. But *legal equality* did not necessarily mean **political equality,** at least not in 1787, when the U.S. Constitution was written. The Constitution left the issue of voter qualifications to the states to decide for themselves. At that time, all states imposed either property or taxpayer qualifications for voting. Neither women nor slaves could vote anywhere. The expansion of voting rights to universal suffrage required many bitter battles over the course of two centuries. The long history of the struggle over voting rights illustrates the contradictions between values and practices (see the section "Securing the Right to Vote" in Chapter 5). Yet in the absence of the *value* of equality, voting rights might have remained restricted.

Center for Equal Opportunity

Think tank advocating equality of opportunity over equality of results.
www.ceousa.org

Equality of Opportunity The American ideal of equality extends to **equality of opportunity**—the elimination of artificial barriers to success in life. The term *equality of opportunity* refers to the ability to make of oneself what one can, to develop one's talents and abilities, and to be rewarded for one's work, initiative, and achievement. Equality of opportunity means that everyone comes to the same starting line in life, with the same chance of success, and that whatever differences develop over time do so as a result of abilities, talents, initiative, hard work, and perhaps good luck.

Americans do not generally resent the fact that physicians, engineers, airline pilots, and others who have spent time and energy acquiring particular skills make more money than those whose jobs require fewer skills and less training. Neither do most Americans resent the fact that people who risk their own time and money to build a business, bring new or better products to market, and create jobs for others make more money than their employees. Nor do many Americans begrudge multimillion-dollar incomes to sports figures, rock stars, and movie stars whose talents entertain the public. And few Americans object when someone wins a million-dollar lottery, as long as everyone who entered the lottery had an equal chance at winning. Americans are generally willing to have government act to ensure equality of opportunity—to ensure that everyone has an equal chance at getting an education, landing a job, and buying a home, and that no barriers of race, sex, religion, or ethnicity bar individual advancement. Differences arise over whether special efforts such as *affirmative action* should be undertaken to overcome the effects of past discriminatory barriers (see the section "Affirmative Action in the Courts" in Chapter 15). But the ideal of equality of opportunity is widely shared.

political equality Belief that the law should apply equally to all and that every person's vote counts equally.

equality of opportunity Elimination of artificial barriers to success in life and the opportunity for everyone to strive for success.

equality of results Equal sharing of income and material goods regardless of one's efforts in life.

Equality of Results **Equality of results** refers to the equal sharing of income and material rewards. Equality of results means that everyone starts *and finishes* the race together, regardless of ability, talent, initiative, or work. Those who argue on behalf of this notion of equality say that if individuals are truly equal, then everyone should enjoy generally equal conditions in life. According to this belief, we should appreciate an individual's skills, work, knowledge, and contributions to society without creating inequalities of wealth and income. Government should act to *transfer* wealth and income from the rich to the poor to increase the total happiness of all members of society.

But equality of results, or absolute equality, is *not* a widely shared value in the United States. This notion of equality was referred to as "leveling" by Thomas Jefferson and generally has been denounced by the nation's political leadership—and by most Americans—then and now:

> To take from one, because it is thought his own industry and that of his fathers has acquired too much, in order to spare to others who have not exercised equal industry and skill, is to violate arbitrarily . . . the guarantee to everyone the free exercise of his industry and the fruits acquired by it.[5]

The taking of private property from those who acquired it legitimately, for no other reason than to equalize wealth or income, is widely viewed as morally wrong. Moreover, many people believe that society generally would suffer if incomes were equalized. Absolute equality, in this view, would remove incentives for people to work, save, or produce. Everyone would slack off, production would decline, goods would be in short supply, and everyone would end up poorer than ever. So some inequality may be essential for the well-being of society.

Thus Americans believe strongly in equality of opportunity but not necessarily equality of results (see *What Do You Think?* "Beliefs About Fairness"). Americans seek fairness rather than equality of wealth and income.

Fairness Americans value "fairness" even though they do not always agree on what is fair. Most Americans support a "floor" on income and material well-being—a level that no one, regardless of his or her condition, should be permitted to fall below—even though they differ over how high that floor should be. Indeed, the belief in a floor is consistent with the belief in equality of opportunity; extreme poverty would deny people, especially children, the opportunity to compete in life.[6] But very few Americans want to place a "ceiling" on income or wealth. This unwillingness to limit top income extends to nearly all groups in the United States, the poor as well as the rich. Generally, Americans want people who cannot provide for themselves to be well cared for, especially children, the elderly, the ill, and the disabled. They are often willing to "soak the rich" when searching for new tax sources, believing that the rich can easily afford to bear the burdens of government. But, unlike citizens in other Western democracies, Americans generally do *not* believe that government should equalize incomes.

Equality in Politics *versus* Economics Americans make a clear distinction between the *private economic* sphere of life and the *public political* sphere.[7] In the private economic sphere, they value the principle of "earned deserts," meaning that individuals are entitled to what they achieve through hard work, skill, talent, risk, and even good luck. They are willing to tolerate inequalities of result in economics. Self-interested behavior in the marketplace is seen as appropriate and even beneficial, if properly constrained by rules that apply equally to everyone. But in the public political sphere, Americans value absolute equality—one person, one vote. They condemn disparities of power and influence among individuals. Self-interested behavior in politics is seen as corrupt.

Monticello
Biography, letters, and a "Day in the Life" of Thomas Jefferson.
www.monticello.org

Beliefs about Fairness

Americans believe that there is "plenty of opportunity" to get ahead and that the economic system of the United States is "basically fair." They do NOT believe that everyone's income should be made more equal. And they believe that "hard-working initiative" and "getting the right education or training" is the key to success in life. However, a substantial percentage of Americans acknowledge that "parents and family" and "connections" also play an important role in success.

Q. Some people say there's not much opportunity in America today—that the average person doesn't have much chance to really get ahead. Others say there's plenty of opportunity and anyone who work hard can go as far as they want. How you feel about this?

Plenty of opportunity	81%
Not much opportunity	17
Don't know	2

Q. Do you think the economic system in United States is basically fair, since all Americans have an equal opportunity to succeed, or basically unfair, since all Americans do not have an opportunity to succeed?

Basically fair	68%
Basically unfair	29
No opinion	3

Q. Do you believe that incomes should be more equal because everybody's contribution to society is equally important?

Yes	37%
No	61
No opinion	2

Q. I am going to read several reasons why some people get ahead and succeed in life and others do not. Please tell me how important it is as a reason for a person's success.

	Most or very important
Hard work and initiative	92%
Getting the right education or training	92
Parents and family	87
Willingness to take risks	69
Connections, knowing the right people	68
Ability or talent one is born with	60
Physical appearance, good looks	50
Good luck, in right place at right time	43
Money inherited from family	41
Gender (whether male or female)	33
Member of particular race/ethnic group	30

Source: James R. Kluegel and Eliot R. Smith, *Beliefs About Inequality* (New York: Aldine de Gruyter, 1986); Gallup Poll Special Report, "Have and Have-Nots: Perceptions of Fairness and Opportunity—1998," www.gallup.com

As long as the economic and political spheres of life are perceived as separate, then economic inequalities and political equalities can exist side by side in a society.

Inequality of Income and Wealth

THINK AGAIN

Are income differences in America widening?

Conflict in society is generated more often by inequalities among people than by hardship or deprivation. Material well-being and standards of living are usually expressed in aggregate measures for a whole society—for example, gross domestic product per capita, income per capita, average life expectancy, infant mortal-

Income and Inequality

Capitalism has proven successful in creating wealth. The free market system has provided Americans with more purchasing power than any other people. ("Purchasing power parity" is a statistic used by international economists to adjust for the cost of living differences in measuring how much it costs to purchase a standard "basket" of goods and services.) However, relatively high incomes of average Americans exists side by side with relatively high inequality among Americans. The United States ranks well below many European countries in measures of income inequality. (The "Gini index" is a statistic used by economists to measure income equality/inequality.) But poverty and inequality exists side by side in most of the world's less-developed countries (not ranked below).

Rank by purchasing power	Rank by equality (Gini index)
1. **United States**	1. Denmark
2. Switzerland	2. Czech Republic
3. Norway	3. Japan
4. Belgium	4. Sweden
5. Denmark	5. Finland
6. Canada	6. Norway
7. Japan	7. Italy
8. Netherlands	8. Belgium
9. Ireland	9. Germany
10. Australia	10. Canada
11. Germany	11. South Korea
12. Finland	12. Poland
13. France	13. Spain
14. Sweden	14. Netherlands
15. United Kingdom	15. Taiwan
16. Italy	16. France
17. Taiwan	17. Greece
18. Israel	18. Switzerland
19. Spain	19. Portugal
20. South Korea	20. Israel
21. Portugal	21. Ireland
22. Greece	22. United Kingdom
23. Czech Republic	23. **United States**
24. Poland	24. Costa Rica
25. Mexico	25. Mexico

Source: Rank by purchasing power, *The Economist Pocket World in Figures,* 2003; rank by Gini index, Central Intelligence Agency, *The World Factbook,* 2003. Both sources rank many more nations.

ity rate. These measures of societal well-being are vitally important to a nation and its people, but *political* conflict is more likely to occur over the *distribution* of well-being *within* a society. Unequal distributions can generate conflict even in a very affluent society with high levels of income and a high standard of living (see *Compared to What?* "Income and Inequality").

Inequality of Income Let us examine inequality of income in the United States systematically. Figure 2.1 divides all American households into two groups—the lowest one-fifth in income and the highest one-fifth—and shows the shares (percentage) of total household income received by each of these groups over the

Global Policy Forum
Information on many global issues. Click to "social and economic policy" and then to "inequality of wealth and income" for cross-national data.
www.globalpolicy.org

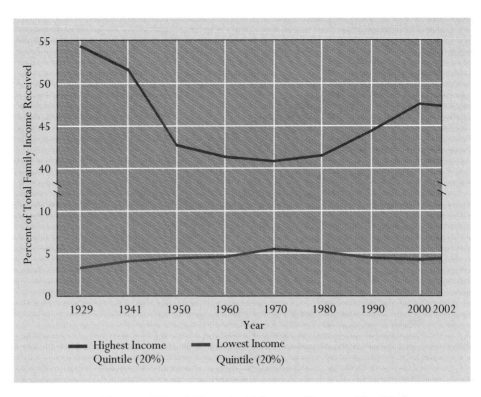

FIGURE 2.1   Shares of Total Household Income Received by Highest and Lowest Income Groups

years. (If perfect income equality existed, each fifth of American households would receive 20 percent of all personal income.) The poorest one-fifth received only 3.5 percent of all household income in 1929; today, this group does a little better, at 4.2 percent of household income. The highest one-fifth received 54.4 percent of all household income in 1929; today, its percentage stands at 46.2.

However, while income differences in the United States have declined over the long run, inequality has actually *increased* in recent years. The income of the poorest households declined from 5.4 to 4.3 percent of total income between 1970 and 2000; the income of the highest quintile rose from 40.9 to 47.4 percent of total income. This reversal of historical trends has generated both political rhetoric and serious scholarly inquiry about its causes.

Explaining Recent Increases in Income Inequality Recent increases in income inequality in the United States are a product of several social and economic trends: (1) the decline of the manufacturing sector of the economy (and the loss of many relatively high-paying blue-collar jobs) and the ascendancy of the communications, information, and service sectors of the economy (with a combination of high-paying and low-paying jobs); (2) the rise in the number of two-wage families, making single-wage, female-headed households relatively less affluent; (3) demographic trends, which include larger proportions of aged and larger proportions of female-headed families; and (4) global competition, which restrains wages in unskilled and semiskilled jobs while rewarding people in high-technology, high-productivity occupations.

Inequality of Wealth Inequalities of wealth in the United States are even greater than inequalities of income. *Wealth* is the total value of a family's assets—

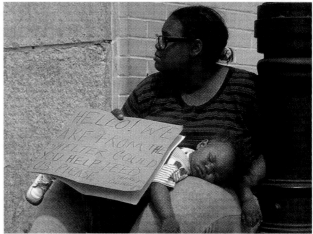

Income and wealth differences between the "haves" and the "have-nots" increased in America during the 1980s and the early 1990s.

bank accounts, stocks, bonds, mutual funds, business equity, houses, cars, and major appliances—minus outstanding debts, such as credit card balances, mortgages, and other loans. The top 1 percent of families in the United States owns over 40 percent of all family wealth. Inequality of wealth appeared to be diminishing until the mid-1970s, but in recent years it has surged sharply. Not surprisingly, age is the key determinant of family wealth; persons age fifty to sixty-five are by far the wealthiest, with persons over sixty-five close behind; young families generally have less than one-third of the assets of retirees.

Social Mobility

Political conflict over inequality might be greater in the United States if it were not for the prospect of **social mobility**. All societies are stratified, or layered, but societies differ greatly in the extent to which people move upward or downward in income and status over a lifetime or over generations. When there is social mobility, people have a good opportunity to get ahead if they study or work long and hard, save and invest wisely, or display initiative and enterprise in business affairs (however, see *A Conflicting View: "Success Is Determined by the Bell Curve"*). Fairly steep inequalities may be tolerated politically if people have a reasonable expectation of moving up over time, or at least of seeing their children do so.

How Much Mobility? The United States describes itself as the land of opportunity. The really important political question may be how much real opportunity exists for individual Americans to improve their conditions in life relative to others. The impression given by Figure 2.1 is one of a static distribution system, with families permanently placed in upper or lower fifths of income earners. But there is considerable evidence of both upward and downward movement by people among income groupings.[8] About a third of the families in the poorest one-fifth will move upward within a decade, and about a third of families in the richest one-fifth will fall out of this top category. However, there appears to have been some slowing of this mobility in recent years; one's chances of escaping the bottom have diminished somewhat. Thus the nation is currently experiencing not only an increase in inequality but also a slowing of social mobility.

social mobility Extent to which people move upward or downward in income and status over a lifetime or generations.

Success Is Determined by the Bell Curve

Most Americans believe in social mobility—the idea that anyone who studies or works hard, saves and invests wisely, and makes good use of his or her talents, initiative, and enterprise can get ahead. But a controversial book, *The Bell Curve* by Richard J. Herrnstein and Charles Murray, sets forth the argument that general intelligence largely determines success in life. General intelligence, the authors contend, is distributed among the population in a bell-shaped curve, with most people clustered around the median, smaller numbers with higher intelligence (a "cognitive elite") at one end, and an unfortunate few trailing behind at the other end (see graph). Over time, say Herrnstein and Murray, intelligence is becoming ever more necessary for the performance of key jobs in the "information society." The result will be the continuing enhancement of the power and wealth of the cognitive elite and the further erosion of the lifestyle of the less intelligent.

Even more controversial than the authors' claim that general intelligence determines success is their contention that general intelligence is mostly (60 percent) genetic. Because intelligence is mostly inherited, programs to assist the underprivileged are useless or even counterproductive.

The cognitive elite, the authors predict, will continue to distance themselves from the masses in knowledge, skills, technical competence, income, and power while social problems will be concentrated among the "dullest." Indeed, they amass statistics showing that educational deficiencies, emotional problems, welfare reliance, early childbirth, and even criminal behavior are disproportionately concentrated in low-intelligence groups (see table).

But critics of *The Bell Curve* point out the lack of consensus on the role of genetics in intelligence. In-

Population Distribution of IQ Scores

deed, recent research on infant development indicates that brain activity and the interconnections among brain cells are greatly affected by early human interaction. Infants in a stimulating environment—who are frequently coddled, spoken to, and sung to, for example—exhibit more brain activity than those with little environmental stimuli. Moreover, the implication of the bell curve thesis is that social classes and elitism are both natural and inevitable—and therefore that most efforts to ensure equality of opportunity are useless. Finally, a racial dimension Herrnstein and Murray add to their argument is unnecessary to their thesis. Although they claim that the differences between African Americans, whites, and Asians on IQ tests should not matter if every individual were judged separately on IQ, clearly their argument reinforces racial stereotypes.

	Cognitive Class	High School Dropout	Women on Welfare Assistance	Mean Age at First Childbearing	Convictions (young white males)
I	Very Bright	0%	0%	27.2 years	3%
II	Bright	0	2	25.6	7
III	Normal	6	8	23.4	15
IV	Dull	35	17	21.0	21
V	Very Dull	55	31	19.8	14

Source: Table adapted from various chapters in Herrnstein and Murray, *The Bell Curve* (1994).

Mobility, Class Conflict, and Class Consciousness Social mobility and the expectation of mobility, over a lifetime or over generations, may be the key to understanding why **class conflict**—conflict over wealth and power among social classes—is not as widespread or as intense in America as it is in many other nations. The *belief* in social mobility reduces the potential for class conflict because it diminishes **class consciousness**, the awareness of one's class position and the feeling of political solidarity with others in the same class in opposition to other classes. If class lines were impermeable and no one had any reasonable expectation of moving up or seeing his or her children move up, then class consciousness would rise and political conflict among classes would intensify.

Most Americans describe themselves as "middle class" rather than "rich" or "poor" or "lower class" or "upper class." There are no widely accepted income definitions of "middle class." The federal government officially defines a "poverty level" each year based on the annual cash income required to maintain a decent standard of living ($18,244 in 2002 for a family of four). Roughly 12 percent of the U.S. population lives with annual cash incomes below this poverty line. (For more discussion, see the section on "Poverty in the United States" in Chapter 17.) This is the only income group in which a majority of people describe themselves as poor.[9] Large majorities in every other income group identify themselves as middle class. So it is no surprise that presidents, politicians, and political parties regularly claim to be defenders of America's "middle class"!

Race, Ethnicity, and Immigration

America has always been an ethnically and racially pluralist society. All groups were expected to adopt the American political culture—including individual liberty, economic freedom, political equality, and equality of opportunity—and to learn American history and the English language. The nation's motto "E Pluribus Unum" (from many, one) is inscribed on its coins. Yet each of America's racial and ethnic groups brings its own traditions and values to the American political culture.

African Americans Historically African Americans constituted the nation's largest minority. Blacks composed about 20 percent of the population at the time the U.S. Constitution was written in 1787 (although as we shall see in Chapter 3 an enslaved African American was to be counted as only 3/5ths of a person in the original Constitution). Heavy European immigration in the late nineteenth century diluted the black population to roughly 12 percent of the nation's total. As late as 1900, most African Americans (90 percent) were still concentrated in the Southern states. But World Wars I and II provided job opportunities in large cities of the Northeast and Midwest. Blacks could not cast ballots in most Southern counties, but they could "vote with their feet." The migration of African Americans from the rural South to the urban North was one of the largest internal migrations in our history. Today only about half of the nation's African Americans live in the South—still more than in any other region but less of a concentration than earlier in American history. Today the nation's 36 million African Americans comprise 12.3 percent of the total population of the United States (see Figure 2.2). "African-American Politics in Historical Perspective" is discussed in Chapter 15, as well as the long struggle against slavery, segregation, and discrimination. This struggle has given African Americans a somewhat different perspective on American politics (see "Race and Opinion" in Chapter 5).

THINK AGAIN

Is American culture racist and sexist?

class conflict Conflict between upper and lower social classes over wealth and power.

class consciousness Awareness of one's class position and a feeling of political solidarity with others within the same class in opposition to other classes.

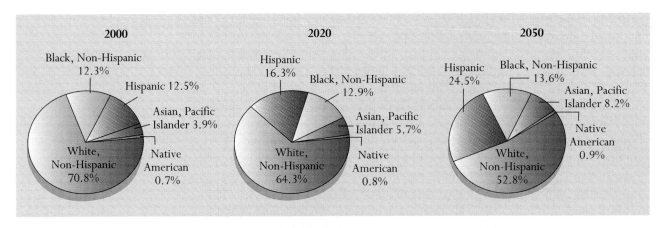

FIGURE 2.2   Racial and Ethnic Composition of the United States 2000, 2020, 2050

Source: U.S. Bureau of the Census (Middle Series).

Hispanic Americans Hispanics are now the nation's largest minority. The term *Hispanic* generally refers to persons of Spanish-speaking ancestry and culture; it includes Mexican Americans, Cuban Americans, and Puerto Ricans. Today there are an estimated 37 million Hispanics in the United States, or 12.5 percent of the total population. The largest subgroup is Mexican Americans, some of whom are descendants of citizens living in Mexican territory that was annexed to the United States in 1848, but most of whom have come to the United States in accelerating numbers in recent years. The largest Mexican American populations are found in Texas, Arizona, New Mexico, and California. The second-largest subgroup is Puerto Ricans, many of whom move back and forth from the island to the mainland, especially New York City. The third-largest subgroup is Cubans, most of whom have fled from Castro's Cuba. They live mainly in the Miami metropolitan area. The politics of each of these Hispanic groups differs somewhat (see "Hispanic Politics" in Chapter 15).

A Nation of Immigrants The United States is a nation of immigrants, from the first "boat people" (Pilgrims) to the latest Haitian refugees and Cuban *balseros* ("rafters"). Historically, most of the people who came to settle in this country did so because they believed their lives would be better here, and American political culture today has been greatly affected by the beliefs and values they brought with them. Americans are proud of their immigrant heritage and the freedom and opportunity the nation has extended to generations of "huddled masses yearning to be free"—words emblazoned on the Statue of Liberty in New York's harbor. Today about 8 percent of the U.S. population is foreign-born.

Immigration policy is a responsibility of the national government. It was not until 1882 that Congress passed the first legislation restricting entry into the United States of persons alleged to be "undesirable" and virtually all Asians. After World War I, Congress passed the comprehensive Immigration Act of 1921, which established maximum numbers of new immigrants each year and set a quota for immigrants for each foreign country at 3 percent of the number of that nation's foreign-born who were living in the United States in 1910, later reduced to 2 percent of the number living here in 1890. These restrictions reflected anti-immigration feelings that were generally directed at the large wave of Southern and

Immigration places responsibility on public schools to provide for the needs of children from different cultures. Here, Latino pupils assemble in Santa Ana, California.

Eastern European Catholic and Jewish immigrants (from Poland, Russia, Hungary, Italy, and Greece) entering the United States prior to World War I (see Figure 2.3). It was not until the Immigration and Naturalization Act of 1965 that national origin quotas were abolished, replaced by preference categories for close relatives of U.S. citizens, professionals, and skilled workers.

Immigration "reform" was the announced goal of Congress in the Immigration Reform and Control Act of 1986, also known as the Simpson-Mazzoli Act. It sought to control immigration by placing principal responsibility on employers; it set fines for knowingly hiring an illegal alien. However, it allowed employers to

The U.S. Coast Guard may intercept boats at sea and return their occupants to their country of origin. But once immigrants reach the U.S. shore, they are entitled to a hearing in any deportation proceedings.

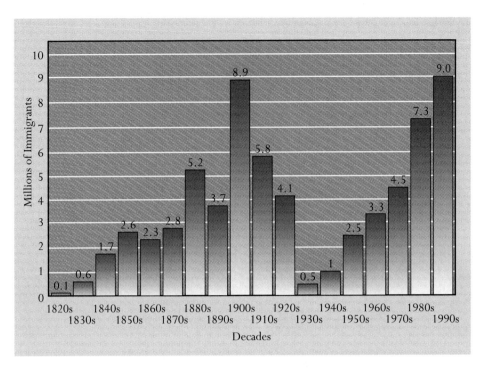

FIGURE 2.3   **Legal Immigration to the United States by Decades**

Source: Statistical Abstract of the United States, 2002, p. 10.

 Center for Immigration Studies

Advocacy organization for strengthening enforcement of immigration law.
www.cis.org

accept many different forms of easily forged documentation and at the same time subjected them to penalties for discriminating against legal foreign-born residents. To win political support, the act granted amnesty to illegal aliens who had lived in the United States since 1982. But the act failed to reduce the flow of either legal or illegal immigrants.

Today, roughly a million people per year are admitted *legally* to the United States as "lawful permanent residents" (persons who have needed job skills or who have relatives who are U.S. citizens) or as "political refugees" (persons with "a well-founded fear of persecution" in their country of origin). In addition, each year more than 25 million people are awarded temporary visas to enter the United States for study, business, or pleasure.

Source: Steve Kelley.

Illegal Immigration   The United States is a free and prosperous society with more than 5,000 miles of borders (2,000 with Mexico) and hundreds of international air- and seaports. In theory, a sovereign nation should be able to maintain secure borders, but in practice the United States has been unwilling and unable to do so. Estimates of illegal immigration vary widely, from the official U.S. Bureau of Immigration and Citizenship Services (formerly the Immigration and Naturalization Service, INS) estimate of 400,000 per year (about 45 percent of the legal immigration) to unofficial estimates ranging up to 3 million per year. The government estimates that about 4 million illegal immigrants currently reside in the United States; unofficial estimates range up to 10 million or more. Many illegal immigrants slip across U.S. borders or enter ports with false documentation; many more overstay tourist, worker, or student visas.[10]

As a free society, the United States is not prepared to undertake massive roundups and summary deportations of millions of illegal residents. The Fifth and Fourteenth Amendments to the U.S. Constitution require that every *person* (not just citizen) be afforded "due process of law." The government may turn back persons at the border or even hold them in detention camps. The Coast Guard may intercept boats at sea and return persons to their country of origin.[11] Aliens have no constitutional right to come to the United States. However, once in the United States, whether legally or illegally, every person is entitled to due process of law and equal protection of the laws. People are thus entitled to a fair hearing prior to any government attempt to deport them. Aliens are entitled to apply for asylum and present evidence at a hearing of their "well-founded fear of prosecution" if

WHAT DO YOU THINK?

Could You Pass the Citizenship Test?

To ensure that new citizens "understand" the history, principles, and form of government of the United States, the INS administers a citizenship test. Could you pass it today?

Answer correctly at least 18 of 30 questions to pass:

1. How many stars are there on our flag?
2. What do the stars on the flag mean?
3. What color are the stripes?
4. What do the stripes on the flag mean?
5. What is the date of Independence Day?
6. Independence from whom?
7. What do we call a change to the Constitution?
8. How many branches are there in our government?
9. How many full terms can a president serve?
10. Who nominates judges of the Supreme Court?
11. How many Supreme Court justices are there?
12. Who was the main writer of the Declaration of Independence?
13. What holiday was celebrated for the first time by American colonists?
14. Who wrote the Star-Spangled Banner?
15. What is the minimum voting age in the U.S.?
16. Who was president during the Civil War?
17. Which president is called the "Father of our Country"?
18. What is the 50th state of the Union?
19. What is the name of the ship that brought the Pilgrims to America?
20. Who has the power to declare war?
21. What were the 13 original states of the U.S. called?
22. In what year was the Constitution written?
23. What is the introduction to the Constitution called?
24. Which president was the first Commander-in-Chief of the U.S. Army and Navy?
25. In what month do we vote for the president?
26. How many times may a senator be re-elected?
27. Who signs bills into law?
28. Who elects the president of the U.S.?
29. How many states are there in the U.S.?
30. Who becomes president if both the president and V.P. die?

Answers: 1. 50; 2. One for each state in the Union, 3. Red and white, 4. They represent the 13 original states, 5. July 4, 6. England, 7. Amendments, 8. 3, 9. 2, 10. The president, 11. 9, 12. Thomas Jefferson, 13. Thanksgiving, 14. Francis Scott Key, 15. 18, 16. Abraham Lincoln, 17. George Washington, 18. Hawaii, 19. *The Mayflower*, 20. The Congress, 21. Colonies, 22. 1787, 23. The Preamble, 24. George Washington, 25. November, 26. There is no limit at the present time, 27. The president, 28. The Electoral College, 29. 50, 30. Speaker of the House of Representatives.

Source: Bureau of Citizenship and Immigration Services.

returned to their country. Experience has shown that the only way to reduce the flow of illegal immigration is to control it at the border, an expensive and difficult but not impossible task. Localized experiments in border enforcement have indicated that, with significant increases in personnel and technology, illegal immigration can be reduced by half or more.

Bureau of Citizenship and Immigration Services

Official site with information on immigration laws, citizenship requirements, etc. (previously INS).
www.immigration.gov

Citizenship Persons born in the United States are U.S. citizens. People who have been lawfully admitted into the United States and granted permanent residence, and who have resided in the United States for at least five years and in their home state for the last six months, are eligible for naturalization as U.S. citizens. Federal district courts as well as offices of the INS may grant applications for citizenship. By law, the applicant must be over age eighteen, be able to read, write, and speak English, possess good moral character, and understand and demonstrate an attachment to the history, principles, and form of government of the United States (see *What Do You Think?* "Could You Pass the Citizenship Test?").

Ideologies: Liberalism and Conservatism

An **ideology** is a consistent and integrated system of ideas, values, and beliefs. A political ideology tells us who *should* get what, when, and how; that is, it tells us who *ought* to govern and what goals they *ought* to pursue. When we use ideological terms such as *liberalism* and *conservatism*, we imply reasonably integrated sets of values and beliefs. And when we pin ideological labels on people, we imply that those people are fairly consistent in the application of these values and beliefs in public affairs. In reality, neither political leaders nor citizens always display integrated or consistent opinions; many hold conservative views on some issues and liberal views on others.[12] Many Americans avoid ideological labeling, either by describing themselves as "moderate" or "middle-of-the-road" or by simply declining to place themselves on an ideological scale. But as Figure 2.4 shows, among those who choose an ideological label to describe their politics, conservatives consistently outnumber liberals. (See also *Across the USA:* "Liberalism and Conservatism" on page 42.)

THINK AGAIN

Do you consider yourself politically conservative, moderate, or liberal?

American Conservative Union

Conservative news and views and rankings of Congress members on conservative index. *www.conservative.org*

ideology Consistent and integrated system of ideas, values, and beliefs.

conservatism Belief in the value of free markets, limited government, and individual self-reliance in economic affairs, combined with a belief in the value of tradition, law, and morality in social affairs.

Despite inconsistencies in opinion and avoidance of labeling, ideology plays an important role in American politics. Political *elites*—elected and appointed officeholders; journalists, editors, and commentators; party officials and interest-group leaders; and others active in politics—are generally more consistent in their political views than nonelites and are more likely to use ideological terms in describing politics.[13]

Modern Conservatism: Individualism plus Traditional Values Modern **conservatism** combines a belief in free markets, limited government, and individual self-reliance in economic affairs with a belief in the value of tradition, law, and morality in social affairs. Conservatives wish to retain our historical commitments to individual freedom from governmental controls; reliance on individual initiative and effort for self-development; a free-enterprise economy with a minimum of governmental intervention; and rewards for initiative, skill, risk, and hard work. These views are consistent with the early classical liberalism of Locke, Jefferson, and the nation's Founders, discussed at the beginning of this chapter. The result is a confusion of ideological labels: modern conservatives claim to be the true inheritors of the (classical) liberal tradition.

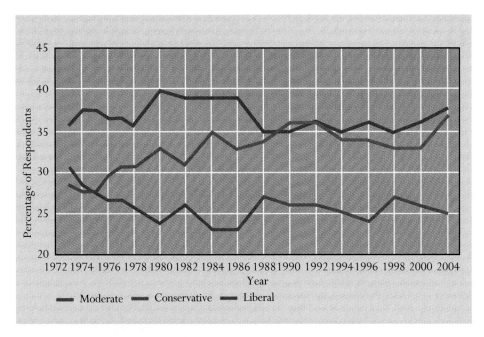

FIGURE 2.4   Americans: Liberal, Moderate, Conservative

Source: General Social Surveys, National Opinion Research Center, University of Chicago; Updated from *The American Enterprise*, January/February 2000, and Gallup, 2004.

Modern conservatism does indeed incorporate many classical liberal ideals, but it also has a distinct ideological tradition of its own. Conservatism is less optimistic about human nature. Traditionally, conservatives have recognized that human nature includes elements of irrationality, ignorance, hatred, and violence. Thus they have been more likely to place their faith in *law* and *traditional values* than in popular fads, trends, or emotions. To conservatives, the absence of law does not mean freedom but, rather, exposure to the tyranny of terrorism and violence. They believe that without the guidance of traditional values, people would soon come to grief through the unruliness of their passions, destroying both themselves and others. Conservatives argue that strong institutions—family, church, and community—are needed to control individuals' selfish and immoral impulses and to foster civilized ways of life.

It is important to note that conservatism in America incorporates different views of the role of government in economic versus social affairs. Conservatives generally prefer *limited noninterventionist government in economic affairs*—a government that relies on free markets to provide and distribute goods and services; minimizes its regulatory activity; limits social welfare programs to the "truly needy"; keeps taxes low; and rejects schemes to equalize income or wealth. On the other hand, conservatives would *strengthen government's power to regulate social conduct.* They support restrictions on abortion; endorse school prayer; favor a war on drugs and pornography; oppose the legitimizing of homosexuality; support the death penalty; and advocate tougher criminal penalties.

Modern Liberalism: Governmental Power to "Do Good"   Modern **liberalism** combines a belief in a strong government to provide economic security and protection for civil rights with a belief in freedom from government

Young Americans for Freedom

The "YAF" archives site contains background on the conservative organization and conservative views on key issues of the day.
www.yaf.com

Americans for Democratic Action

The ADA is the nation's oldest liberal political action organization.
www.adaction.org

liberalism Belief in the value of strong government to provide economic security and protection for civil rights, combined with a belief in personal freedom from government intervention in social conduct.

Liberalism and Conservatism

States might be classified in terms of their voters' self-identification in opinion surveys as liberal, moderate, or conservative. The most conservative state is Utah (45 percent conservative, 37 percent moderate, 13 percent liberal), followed by Indiana (42 percent conservative, 39 percent moderate, 13 percent liberal). The most liberal states are Massachusetts (26 percent conservative, 42 percent moderate, 26 percent liberal), New York (29 percent conservative, 39 percent moderate, 26 percent liberal), and New Jersey (28 percent conservative, 40 percent moderate, 26 percent liberal).

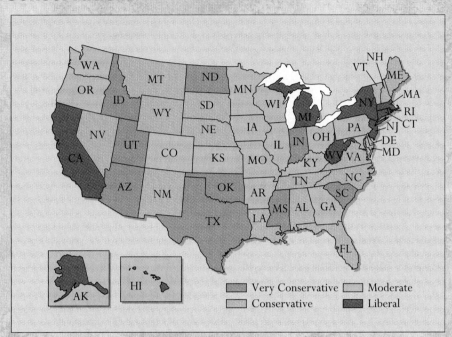

Source: Gerald C. Wright, Robert S. Erikson, and John P. McIver, "Public Opinion and Policy Liberalism in the American States," *American Journal of Political Science* 31 (November 1987): 980–1001. Reprinted by permission of the University of Wisconsin Press.

intervention in social conduct. Modern liberalism retains the classical liberalism commitment to individual dignity, but it emphasizes the importance of social and economic security for the whole population. In contrast to classical liberalism which looked at governmental power as a potential threat to personal freedom, modern liberalism looks on the power of government as a positive force for eliminating social and economic conditions that adversely affect people's lives and impede their self-development. The modern liberal approves of the use of governmental power to correct the perceived ills of society (see *People in Politics:* "Barbara Boxer, Defending Liberalism in Congress" on page 44).

Today's liberals believe that government can change people's lives by working to end racial and sexual discrimination, abolish poverty, eliminate slums, create jobs, uplift the poor, provide medical care for all, educate the masses, protect the environment, and instill humanitarian values in everyone. The prevailing impulse is to "do good," to perform public services, and to assist the least fortunate in society, particularly the poor and minorities. Modern liberalism is impatient with what it sees as the slow progress of individual initiative and private enterprise toward solving socioeconomic problems, so it seeks to use the power of the national government to find solutions to society's troubles.

Bill O'Reilly
Popular Web site for conservative views as well as promotion of O'Reilly programs, books, editorials, etc. *www.billoreilly.com*

Bill O'Reilly, "The No Spin Zone?"

Bill O'Reilly assures "fair and balanced" broadcast journalism to Fox News viewers. He describes his popular TV show as a "no spin zone" and refers to himself as an "independent." Yet O'Reilly has emerged as the nation's most popular voice of conservatism on television.

O'Reilly boasts of an Irish Catholic working-class upbringing in Long Island. He graduated from Catholic Marist College, briefly taught in a Miami high school, and earned a master's degree from Boston University in journalism. He bounced around the country as a reporter for various TV stations, and by 1986 he had become a top correspondent for ABC News. He eventually replaced David Frost as anchor of the TV tabloid *Inside Edition,* but left that job in 1995 to earn a master's degree from the John F. Kennedy School of Government at Harvard University.

The Fox News network recruited O'Reilly to create a new evening talk show, *The O'Reilly Factor.* The show quickly grew into the most watched program on cable news, out-distancing even *Larry King Live.*

O'Reilly mixes humor with bombast. He ferociously attacks liberals bold enough to come on his show as guests. He constantly interrupts guests, both liberal and conservative, to broadcast his own views. He is convinced that liberal "secularists" are waging war against religion and traditional moral values. His favorite targets include Hollywood liberals, Hillary Clinton, Jesse Jackson, and the American Civil Liberties Union. The occasional twinkle in his Irish eyes tempers his often venomous commentary.

Modern liberalism defines equality somewhat differently from the way classical liberalism does. Classical liberalism stresses the value of equality of opportunity. Individuals should be free to make the most of their talents and skills, but differences in wealth or power that are a product of differences in talent, initiative, risk taking, and skill are accepted as natural. In contrast, modern liberalism contends that individual dignity and equality of opportunity depend in some measure on *reduction of absolute inequality* in society. Modern liberals believe that true equality of opportunity cannot be achieved where significant numbers of people are suffering from hopelessness, hunger, treatable illness, or poverty. Thus modern liberalism supports government efforts to reduce inequalities in society.

Liberals also have different views of the role of government in economic versus social affairs. Liberals generally prefer an active, powerful government in economic affairs—a government that provides a broad range of public services; regulates business; protects civil rights; protects consumers and the environment; provides generous unemployment, welfare, and Social Security benefits; and reduces economic inequality. But many of these same liberals would limit the government's power to regulate social conduct. They oppose restrictions on abortion; oppose school prayer; favor "decriminalizing" marijuana use and "victimless" offenses like public intoxication and vagrancy; support gay rights and tolerance toward alternative lifestyles; oppose government restrictions on speech, press, and protest; oppose the death penalty; and strive to protect the rights of criminal defendants. Liberalism is the prevailing ideology among college professors (see Figure 2.5).

Barbara Boxer, Defending Liberalism in Congress

Perhaps no one has been more successful in defending liberal causes in Congress than California's outspoken U.S. senator, Barbara Boxer. Her political résumé boasts awards and honors from such organizations as Planned Parenthood (family planning, reproductive health, and abortion rights), the Sierra Club (environmental causes), Mobilization against AIDS, Anti-Defamation League (civil rights), and Public Citizen (consumer affairs).

A graduate of Brooklyn College with a B.A. in economics, Boxer worked briefly as a stockbroker before moving to San Francisco, where she became a journalist and later a campaign aide to a local congressional representative. Her political career is based in Marin County, a trendy, upper-class, liberal community north of San Francisco, where she first won elected office as a member of the County Board of Supervisors. She was elected to the U.S. House of Representatives from her Marin County district in 1982 and quickly won a reputation as one of the most liberal members of the House. Appointed to the House Armed Services Committee, she became a leading critic of defense spending and virtually every weapon requested by the military.

When her state's liberal Democratic senator, Alan Cranston, announced he would not seek reelection to the Senate in the wake of his censure in the Keating Five affair, Boxer sought the open seat. Her opponent, conservative Republican radio and TV commentator Bruce Herschensohn, hammered at Boxer's 143 overdrafts at the House bank, her frequent absenteeism, and her extensive use of congressional perks. But with the help of Clinton's 1992 landslide (47 to 32 percent) victory over George Bush in California, Boxer eked out a 48 to 46 percent victory over Herschensohn. Her victory, together with that of Dianne Feinstein, gave California a historical first—two women U.S. senators.

Boxer quickly emerged as a powerful force in the U.S. Senate on behalf of abortion rights. She led the Senate fight for a federal law protecting abortion clinics from obstruction by demonstrators. On the Environmental and Public Works Committee she helped block efforts to relax federal environmental regulations. She led the movement to oust Republican senator Bob Packwood from the Senate on charges of sexually harassing staff members. She helped lead the fight for the Family Medical Leave Act, passed in the early days of the Clinton administration, as well as the Freedom of Access to [Abortion] Clinics Act. She was reelected by a wide margin in 1998.

Youth and Ideology Young people are more likely to hold liberal views than their elders. Especially on social issues, young people, 18–24, are more likely to describe themselves as liberals (see Table 2.1). Older adults are more likely to describe themselves as conservatives on social as well as economic issues.

U.S. Senator Barbara Boxer

The official Web site of U.S. Senator Barbara Boxer of California contains biographical material, information about Boxer's committee assignments, and her stands on various political issues.
www.senate.gov/~boxer/

FIGURE 2.5 Ideology Among Professors

Source: American Enterprise, vol. 2, July/August 1991, http://www.TAEmag.com. Published by the American Enterprise Institute for Public Policy Research, Washington,DC..

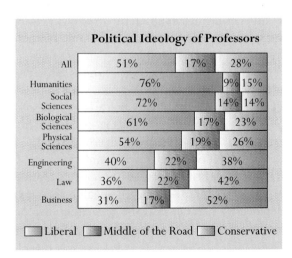

TABLE 2.1 Ideology and Age

Thinking about social issues, would you say your views on social issues are conservative, moderate, or liberal?

Age	Conservative	Moderate	Liberal
18–24	27%	36%	36%
25–38	33	34	31
39 plus	40	38	19

Thinking about economic issues, would you say your views on economic issues are conservative, moderate, or liberal?

Age	Conservative	Moderate	Liberal
18–24	33%	40%	26%
25–38	39	39	20
39 plus	47	38	12

Source: Gallup Poll reported May 20, 2003. Copyright © 2003 by The Gallup Organization.

Dissent in the United States

Dissent from the principal elements of American political culture—individualism, free enterprise, democracy, and equality of opportunity—has arisen over the years from both the *left* and the *right*. The **left** generally refers to socialists and communists, but it is sometimes used to brand liberals. The **right** generally refers to fascists and extreme nationalists, although it is sometimes used to stamp conservatives. Despite their professed hostility toward each other, **radicals** on the left and right share many characteristics. Both are **extremist**. They reject democratic politics, compromise, and coalition building as immoral, and they assert the supremacy of the "people" over laws, institutions, and individual rights. Extremists view politics with hostility, although they may make cynical use of democratic politics as a short-term tactical means to their goals.

Conspiracy theories are popular among extremists. For example, the left sees a conspiracy among high government, corporate, and military chieftains to profit from war; the right sees a conspiracy among communists, intellectuals, the United Nations, and Wall Street bankers to subordinate the United States to a world government. The historian Richard Hofstadter has referred to this tendency as "the paranoid style of politics."[14] Both the left and right are intolerant of the opinions of others and are willing to disrupt and intimidate those with whom they disagree. Whether shouting down speakers or disrupting meetings or burning crosses and parading in hoods, the impulse to violence is often present in those who subscribe to radical politics.

Antidemocratic Ideologies Dissent in the United States has historical roots in antidemocratic movements that originated primarily outside its borders. These movements have spanned the political spectrum from the far right to the far left.

left A reference to the liberal, progressive, and/or socialist side of the political spectrum.

right A reference to the conservative, traditional, anticommunist side of the political spectrum.

radicalism Advocacy of immediate and drastic changes in society, including the complete restructuring of institutions, values, and beliefs. Radicals may exist on either the extreme left or extreme right.

extremism Rejection of democratic politics and the assertion of the supremacy of the "people" over laws, institutions, and individual rights.

At the far-right end of this spectrum lies **fascism**, an ideology that asserts the supremacy of the state or race over individuals. The goal of fascism is unity of people, nation, and leadership—in the words of Adolf Hitler: *"Ein Volk, Ein Reich, Ein Führer"* (One People, One Nation, One Leader). Every individual, every interest, and every class are to be submerged for the good of the nation. Against the rights of liberty or equality, fascism asserts the duties of service, devotion, and discipline. Its goal is to develop a superior type of human being, with qualities of bravery, courage, genius, and strength. The World War II defeat of the two leading fascist regimes in history—Adolf Hitler's Nazi Germany and Benito Mussolini's fascist Italy—did not extinguish fascist ideas. Elements of fascist thought are found today in extremist movements in both the United States and Europe.

Marxism arose out of the turmoil of the Industrial Revolution as a protest against social evils and economic inequalities. Karl Marx (1818–83), its founder, was not an impoverished worker but rather an upper-middle-class intellectual unable to find an academic position. Benefiting from the financial support of his wealthy colleague Friedrich Engels (1820–95), Marx spent years writing *Das Kapital* (1867), a lengthy work describing the evils of capitalism, especially the oppression of factory workers (the proletariat) and the inevitability of revolution. The two men collaborated on a popular pamphlet entitled *The Communist Manifesto* (1848), which called for a workers' revolution: "Workers of the world, unite. You have nothing to lose but your chains."

It fell to Vladimir Lenin (1870–1924) to implement Marx and Engels's revolutionary ideology in the Russian Revolution in 1917. According to **Leninism**, the key to a successful revolution is the organization of small, disciplined, hard-core groups of professional revolutionaries into a centralized totalitarian party. To explain why Marx's predictions about the ever-worsening conditions of the masses under capitalism proved untrue (workers' standards of living in Western democracies rose rapidly in the twentieth century), Lenin devised the theory of imperialism: advanced capitalist countries turned to war and colonialism, exploiting the Third World, in order to make their own workers relatively prosperous.

Communism is the outgrowth of Marxist-Leninist ideas about the necessity of class warfare, the inevitability of a worldwide proletarian revolution, and the con-

fascism Political ideology in which the state and/or race is assumed to be supreme over individuals.

Marxism The theories of Karl Marx, among them that capitalists oppress workers and that worldwide revolution and the emergence of a classless society are inevitable.

Leninism The theories of Vladimir Lenin, among them that advanced capitalist countries turned toward war and colonialism to make their own workers relatively prosperous.

communism System of government in which a single totalitarian party controls all means of production and distribution of goods and services.

 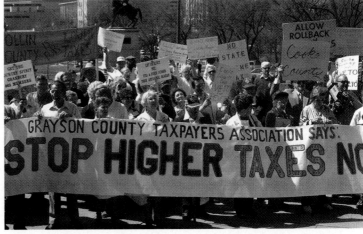

Liberals' concern about efforts to curtail social welfare programs reflects their support of strong government, whereas conservatives' demands for tax cuts reflect their preference for government that encourages self-reliance and individual initiative.

Are You a Liberal or a Conservative?

Not everyone consistently takes a liberal or a conservative position on every issue. But if you find that you agree with more positions under one of the following "liberal" or "conservative" lists, you are probably ready to label yourself ideologically.

	You are Liberal If You Agree That	**You Are Conservative If You Agree That**
Economic policy	Government should regulate business to protect the public interest. The rich should pay higher taxes to support public services for all. Government spending for social welfare is a good investment in people.	Free-market competition is better at protecting the public than government regulation. Taxes should be kept as low as possible. Government welfare programs destroy incentives to work.
Crime	Government should place primary emphasis on alleviating the social conditions (such as poverty and joblessness) that cause crime.	Government should place primary emphasis on providing more police and prisons and stop courts from coddling criminals.
Social policy	Government should protect the right of women to choose abortion and fund abortions for poor women. Government should pursue affirmative action programs on behalf of minorities and women in employment, education, and so on. Government should keep religious prayers and ceremonies out of schools and public places.	Government should restrict abortion and not use taxpayer money for abortions. Government should not grant preferences to anyone based on race or sex. Government should allow prayers and religious observances in schools and public places.
National security policy	Government should support "human rights" throughout the world. Military spending should be reduced now that the Cold War is over.	Government should pursue the "national interest" of the United States. Military spending must reflect a variety of new dangers in this post Cold-War period.
You generally describe yourself as	"caring" "compassionate" "progressive"	"responsible" "moderate" "sensible"
and you describe your political opponents as	"extremists" "right-wing radicals" "reactionaries"	"knee jerks" "bleeding hearts" "left-wing radicals"

centration of all power in the "vanguard of the proletariat"—the Communist Party. Communism justifies violence as a means to attain power by arguing that the bourgeoisie (the capitalistic middle class) will never voluntarily give up its control over "the means of production" (the economy). Democracy is only "window dressing" to disguise capitalist exploitation. The Communist Party justifies authoritarian single-party rule as the "dictatorship of the proletariat." In theory, after a period of rule by the Communist Party, all property will be owned by the government, and a "classless" society of true communism will emerge.

Socialist Party USA News and views from America's Socialist party. *http://sp-usa.org*

Socialism Socialism shares with communism a condemnation of capitalist profit making as exploitative of the working classes. Communists and socialists agree on the "evils" of industrial capitalism: the concentration of wealth, the insensitivity of the profit motive to human needs, the insecurities and suffering brought on by the business cycle, the conflict of class interests, and the tendency of capitalist nations to involve themselves in imperialist wars. However, socialists are committed to the democratic process as a means of replacing capitalism with collective ownership of economic enterprise. Socialists generally reject the notion of violent revolution as a way to replace capitalism and instead advocate peaceful, constitutional roads to bring about change. Moreover, many socialists are prepared to govern in a free society under democratic principles, including freedom of speech and press and the right to organize political parties and oppose government policy. Socialism is egalitarian, seeking to reduce or eliminate inequalities in the distribution of wealth. It attempts to achieve equality of results, rather than mere equality of opportunity.

The End of History? Much of the history of the twentieth century has been the struggle between democratic capitalism and totalitarian communism. Thus the collapse of communism in Eastern Europe and the Soviet Union, symbolized by the tearing down of the Berlin Wall in 1989, as well as the worldwide movement toward free markets and democracy at the end of the twentieth century, has been labeled the **end of history**.[15] Democratic revolutions were largely inspired by the realization that free-market capitalism provided much higher standards of living than communism. The economies of Eastern Europe were falling further and further behind the economies of the capitalist nations of the West. Similar comparative observations of the successful economies of the Asian capitalist "Four Tigers"—South Korea, Taiwan, Singapore, and Hong Kong—even inspired China's communist leadership to experiment with market reforms. Communism destroyed the individual's incentive to work, produce, innovate, save, and invest in the future. Under communism, production for government goals (principally a strong military) came first; production for individual needs came last. The result was long lines at stores, shoddy products, and frequent bribery of bureaucrats to obtain necessary consumer items. More important, perhaps, the concentration of both economic and political power in the hands of a central bureaucracy proved to be incompatible with democracy. Communism relies on central direction, force, and repression. Communist systems curtail individual freedom and prohibit the development of separate parties and interest groups outside of government.

Capitalism does not *ensure* democracy; some capitalist nations are authoritarian. But economic freedom inspires demands for political freedom. Thus market reforms, initiated by communist leaders to increase productivity, led to democracy movements, and those movements eventually dismantled the communist system in Eastern Europe and the old Soviet Union.

socialism System of government involving collective or government ownership of economic enterprise, with the goal being equality of results, not merely equality of opportunity.

end of history The collapse of communism and the worldwide movement toward free markets and political democracy.

Political extremists of the left and right often have more in common than they would like to admit. Although decidedly different in their political philosophies, both members of right-wing American neo-Nazi groups and members of left-wing communist groups reject democratic politics and assert the supremacy of the "people" over laws, institutions, and individual rights. Gregory Johnson (left) was the catalyst for the flag burning controversy that is still raging in Congress today. Buford O'Neal Furrow, Jr. (right), was arrested for opening fire on children in a Jewish day care center in California. Several children died in this attack.

Academic Radicalism Marxism survives on campuses today largely as an academic critique of the functioning of capitalism.[16] It provides some disaffected academics with ideas and language to attack everything that disturbs them about the United States—from poverty, racism, and environmental hazards to junk food, athletic scholarships, and obnoxious television advertising—conveniently blaming the "profit motive" for many of the ills of American society.

Contemporary radicals argue that the institutions of capitalism have conditioned people to be materialistic, competitive, and even violent. The individual has been transformed into a one-dimensional person in whom genuine humanistic values are repressed.[17] Profitability, rather than humanistic values, remains the primary criterion for decision making in the capitalist economy, and thus profitability is the reason for poverty and misery despite material abundance. Without capitalist institutions, life would be giving, cooperative, and compassionate. Only a *radical restructuring* of social and economic institutions will succeed in liberating people from these institutions to lead humanistic, cooperative lives.

To American radicals, the problem of social change is truly monumental, because capitalist values and institutions are deeply rooted in this country. Since most people are not aware that they are oppressed and victimized, the first step toward social change is consciousness raising—that is, making people aware of their misery.

The agenda of academic radicalism has been labeled **politically correct** (PC) thinking. Politically correct thinking views American society as racist, sexist, and homophobic. Overt bigotry is not the real issue, but rather Western institutions,

 National Association of Scholars

Association of college and university professors opposed to PC restrictions on campus.
www.nas.org

politically correct (PC)
Repression of attitudes, speech, and writings that are deemed racist, sexist, homophohic (anti-homosexual), or otherwise "insensitive."

language, and culture, which systematically oppress and victimize women, people of color, gays, and others.

Academic radicalism "includes the assumption that Western values are inherently oppressive, that the chief purpose of education is political transformation, and that all standards are arbitrary.[18] In PC thinking, "everything is political." Therefore curriculum, courses, and lectures—even language and demeanor—are judged according to whether they are politically correct or not. Universities have always been centers for the critical examination of institutions, values, and culture, but PC thinking does not really tolerate open discussion or debate. Opposition is denounced as "insensitive," racist, sexist, or worse, and intimidation is not infrequent (see *Up Close:* "Political Correctness versus Free Speech on Campus" in Chapter 14).

SUMMARY NOTES

- Ideas are sources of power. They provide people with guides for determining right and wrong and with rationales for political action. Political institutions are shaped by the values and beliefs of the political culture, and political leaders are restrained in their exercise of power by these ideas.

- The American political culture is a set of widely shared values and beliefs about who should govern, for what ends, and by what means.

- Americans share many common ways of thinking about politics. Nevertheless, there are often contradictions between professed values and actual conditions, problems in applying abstract beliefs to concrete situations, and even occasional conflict over fundamental values.

- Individual liberty is a fundamental value in American life. The classical liberal tradition that inspired the nation's Founders included both political liberties and economic freedoms.

- Equality is another fundamental American value. The nation's Founders believed in equality before the law; yet political equality, in the form of universal voting rights, required nearly two centuries to bring about.

- Equality of opportunity is a widely shared value; most Americans are opposed to artificial barriers of race, sex, religion, or ethnicity barring individual advancement. But equality of results is not a widely shared value; most Americans support a "floor" on income and well-being for their fellow citizens but oppose placing a "ceiling" on income or wealth.

- Income inequality has increased in recent years primarily as a result of economic and demographic changes. Most Americans believe that opportunities for individual advancement are still available, and this belief diminishes the potential for class conflict.

- Liberal and conservative ideologies in American politics present somewhat different sets of values and beliefs, even though they share a common commitment to individual dignity and private property. Generally, liberals favor an active, powerful government to provide economic security and protection for civil rights but oppose government restrictions on social conduct. Generally, conservatives favor minimal government intervention in economic affairs and civil rights but support many government restrictions on social conduct.

- Many Americans who identify themselves as liberals or conservatives are not always consistent in applying their professed views. Populists are liberal on economic issues but conservative in their views on social issues. Libertarians are conservative on economic issues but liberal in their social views.

- Liberal and conservative ideas evolve over time in response to new challenges and changing conditions. Neo-conservatives share the historical classical liberal concerns about the nation's social problems but no longer believe that solutions can be found in large-scale, costly bureaucratic government programs. Neo-liberals retain their faith in the power of government but focus their attention on efforts to promote economic growth as a prerequisite to solving social problems.

- The collapse of communism in Eastern Europe and the former Soviet Union and the worldwide movement toward free markets and democracy have undermined support for socialism throughout the world. Yet Marxism survives in academic circles as a critique of the functioning of capitalism.

SUGGESTED READINGS

Ebenstein, Alan, William Ebenstein, and Edwin Fogelman. *Today's Isms: Communism, Fascism, Capitalism, Socialism.* 11th ed. Upper Saddle River, N.J.: Prentice Hall, 2000. A concise description and history of the major isms.

Herrnstein, Richard J., and Charles Murray. *The Bell Curve: Intelligence and Class Structure in American Life.* New York: Free Press, 1994. A controversial argument that success in life is mainly a result of inherited intelligence and that a very bright "cognitive elite" will continue to distance themselves from the duller masses.

Huntington, Samuel P. *American Politics: The Promise of Disharmony.* Cambridge, Mass.: Harvard University Press, 1981. An examination of the gaps between the promise of the American ideals of liberty and equality and the performance of the American political system.

Ingersoll, David E., Richard K. Matthews, and Andrew Davidson. *The Philosophical Roots of Modern Ideology: Liberalism, Communism, Fascism, Islamism.* 3rd ed. Upper Saddle River, N.J.: Prentice Hall, 2001. Overview of political ideologies, including extensive quotes from original sources, from Locke, Jefferson, Madison, Marx, and Lenin to Gorbachev, Hitler, and Khomeini.

Ryscavage, Paul. *Income Inequality in America.* Armonk, N.Y.: M.E. Sharpe, 1999. A careful analysis of current trends toward income inequality in the United States.

Tocqueville, Alexis de. *Democracy in America* (1835). Chicago: University of Chicago Press. 2000. Classic early assessment of American political culture by French traveler.

Wolff, Edward N. *Top Heavy.* 2nd Ed. New York: News Press, 2002. A fact-filled report on the increasing inequality of wealth in America, together with a proposal to tax wealth as well as income.

Wray, J. Harry. *Sense and Non-Sense: American Culture and Politics.* Upper Saddle River, N.J.: Prentice Hall, 2001. Introduction to American political culture and the values that influence political life in the United States today.

MAKE IT REAL

POLITICAL SURVEY: WHAT DO YOU BELIEVE?

Political culture consists of widely shared beliefs, values, and norms concerning the relationship of citizens to government and to one another. However, just because they are widely shared does not mean they are universally shared. To what degree do you share beliefs with the general population? With your generation? With your classmates? In this simulation you will complete a questionnaire to see how your political beliefs compare with those of people around you.

3

THE CONSTITUTION:
LIMITING GOVERNMENTAL POWER

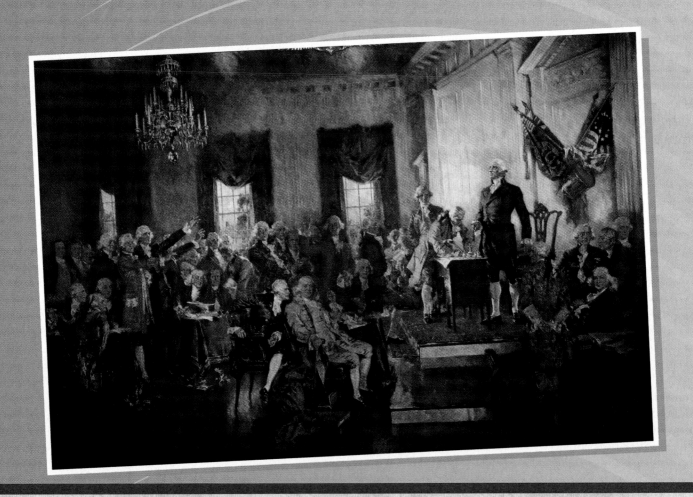

Constitutional Government

Constitutions govern government. **Constitutionalism**—a government of laws, not of people—means that those who exercise governmental power are restricted in their use of it by a higher law. If individual freedoms are to be placed beyond the reach of government and beyond the reach of majorities, then a constitution must truly limit the exercise of authority by government. It does so by setting forth individual liberties that the government—even with majority support—cannot violate.

A **constitution** legally establishes government authority. It sets up governmental bodies (such as the House of Representatives, the Senate, the presidency, and the Supreme Court in the United States). It grants them powers. It determines how their members are to be chosen. And it prescribes the rules by which they make decisions.

Constitutional decision making is deciding how to decide; that is, it is deciding on the rules for policy making. It is not policy making itself. Policies will be decided later, according to the rules set forth in the constitution.

A constitution cannot be changed by the ordinary acts of governmental bodies; change can come only through a process of general popular consent.[1] The U.S. Constitution, then, is superior to ordinary laws of Congress, orders of the president, decisions of the courts, acts of the state legislatures, and regulations of the bureaucracies. Indeed, the Constitution is "the supreme law of the land."

The Constitutional Tradition

Americans are strongly committed to the idea of a written constitution to establish government and limit its powers. In fact, the Constitutional Convention of 1787 had many important antecedents.

The Magna Carta, 1215 English lords, traditionally required to finance the king's wars, forced King John to sign the Magna Carta, a document guaranteeing their feudal rights and setting the precedent of a limited government and monarchy.

The Mayflower Compact, 1620 Puritan colonists, while still aboard the Mayflower, signed a compact establishing a "civil body politic . . . to enact just and equal laws . . . for the general good of the colony, unto which we promise all due submission and obedience." After the Puritans landed at Plymouth, in what is today Massachusetts, they formed a colony based on the Mayflower Compact, thus setting a precedent of a government established by contract with the governed.

WWW **National Constitution Center**
Located in Philadelphia Independence Mall, this museum is devoted to explaining the U.S. Constitution.
www.constitutioncenter.org

The Colonial Charters, 1624–1732 The charters that authorized settlement of the colonies in America were granted by royal action. For some of the colonies, the British king granted official proprietary rights to an individual, as in Maryland (granted to Lord Baltimore), Pennsylvania (to William Penn), and Delaware (also to Penn). For other colonies, the king granted royal commissions to companies to establish governments, as in Virginia, Massachusetts, New Hampshire, New York, New Jersey, Georgia, and North and South Carolina. Royal charters were granted directly to the colonists themselves only in Connecticut and Rhode Island. These colonists drew up their charters and presented them to the king, setting a precedent in America for written contracts defining governmental power.

The "Charter Oak Affair" of 1685–88 began when King James II became displeased with his Connecticut subjects and issued an order for the repeal of the Connecticut Charter. In 1687 Sir Edmund Andros went to Hartford, dissolved the colonial government, and demanded that the charter be returned. But Captain John Wadsworth hid it in an oak tree. After the so-called Glorious Revolution in England in 1688, the charter was taken out and used again as the fundamental law of the colony. Subsequent British monarchs silently acquiesced in this restoration of rights, and the affair strengthened the notion of loyalty to the constitution rather than to the king.

The Declaration of Independence, 1776 The First Continental Congress, a convention of delegates from twelve of the thirteen original colonies, came together in 1774 to protest British interference in American affairs. But the Revolutionary War did not begin until April 19, 1775. The evening before, British regular troops marched out from Boston to seize arms stored by citizens in Lexington and Concord, Massachusetts. At dawn the next morning, the Minutemen—armed citizens organized for the protection of their towns—engaged the British regulars in brief battles, then harassed them all the way back to Boston. In June of that year, the Second Continental Congress appointed George Washington Commander-in-Chief of American forces and sent him to Boston to take command of the American militia surrounding the city. Still, popular support for the Revolution remained limited, and even many members of the Continental Congress hoped only to force changes—not to split off from Britain.

As this hope died, however, members of the Continental Congress came to view a formal Declaration of Independence as necessary to give legitimacy to their cause and establish the basis for a new nation. Accordingly, on July 2, 1776, the Continental Congress "Resolved, that these United Colonies are, and, of right, ought to be free and independent States." Thomas Jefferson had been commissioned to write a justification for the action, which he presented to the congress on July 4, 1776. In writing the Declaration of Independence, Jefferson lifted several phrases directly from the English political philosopher John Locke asserting the rights of individuals, the contract theory of government, and the right of revolution. The declaration was signed first by the president of the Continental Congress, John Hancock.

constitutionalism A government of laws, not people, operating on the principle that governmental power must be limited and government officials should be restrained in their exercise of power over individuals.

constitution The legal structure of a political system, establishing governmental bodies, granting their powers, determining how their members are selected, and prescribing the rules by which they make their decisions. Considered basic or fundamental, a constitution cannot be changed by ordinary acts of governmental bodies.

After numerous drafts by Thomas Jefferson, including such changes as the deletion of a clause condemning the slave trade that offended North Carolina and Georgia, the Declaration of Independence was accepted by the majority of the Continental Congress on July 4, 1776. The document then became "the unanimous declaration of the thirteen United States of America" on July 19, and was signed by all members of the Continental Congress on August 2. Shown in this painting are (left to right) Benjamin Franklin, Thomas Jefferson, Robert Livingston, John Adams, and Roger Sherman.

U.S. History
The Independence Hall Association Web site with "Documents of Freedom" including Mayflower Compact, Declaration of Independence, Articles of Confederation, etc. *www.ushistory.org*

The Revolutionary War ended when British General Charles Cornwallis surrendered at Yorktown, Virginia, in October 1781. But even as the war was being waged, the new nation was creating the framework of its government.

The Articles of Confederation, 1781–1789 Although Richard Henry Lee, a Virginia delegate to the Continental Congress, first proposed that the newly independent states form a confederation on July 6, 1776, the Continental Congress did not approve the Articles of Confederation until November 15, 1777, and the last state to sign them, Maryland, did not do so until March 1, 1781. Under the Articles, Congress was a single house in which each state had two to seven members but only one vote. Congress itself created and appointed executives, judges, and military officers. It also had the power to make war and peace, conduct foreign affairs, and borrow and print money. But Congress could *not* collect taxes or enforce laws directly; it had to rely on the states to provide money and enforce its laws. The United States under the Articles was really a confederation of nations. Within this "firm league of friendship" (Article III of the Articles of Confederation), the national government was thought of as an alliance of independent states, not as a government "of the people."

Troubles Confronting a New Nation

Two centuries ago the United States was struggling to achieve nationhood. The new U.S. government achieved enormous successes under the Articles of Confederation: It won independence from Great Britain, the world's most powerful colonial nation at the time; it defeated vastly superior forces in a prolonged war for independence; it established a viable peace and won powerful allies (notably, France) in the international community; it created an effective army and navy, established a postal system, and laid the foundations for national unity. But despite these successes in war and diplomacy, the political arrangements under the Articles were unsatisfactory to many influential groups—notably, bankers and investors who held U.S. government bonds, plantation owners, real estate developers, and merchants and shippers.

Constitution Society

Web site includes comprehensive list of founding documents, essays, and commentaries on the Constitution.
www.constitution.org

Financial Difficulties Under the Articles of Confederation, Congress had no power to tax the people directly. Instead, Congress had to ask the states for money to pay its expenses, particularly the expenses of fighting the long and costly War of Independence with Great Britain. There was no way to force the states to make their payments to the national government. In fact, about 90 percent of the funds requisitioned by Congress from the states was never paid, so Congress had to borrow money from wealthy patriot investors to fight the war. Without the power to tax, however, Congress could not pay off these debts. Indeed, the value of U.S. governmental bonds fell to about 10 cents for every dollar's worth because few people believed the bonds would ever be paid off. Congress even stopped making interest payments on these bonds.

Commercial Obstacles Under the Articles of Confederation, states were free to tax the goods of other states. Without the power to regulate interstate commerce, the national government was unable to protect merchants from heavy tariffs imposed on shipments from state to state. Southern planters could not ship their agricultural products to northern cities without paying state-imposed tariffs, and northern merchants could not ship manufactured products from state to state without interference. Merchants, manufacturers, shippers, and planters all wanted to develop national markets and prevent the states from imposing tariffs or restrictions on interstate trade. States competed with one another by passing low tariffs on foreign goods (to encourage the shipment of goods through their own ports) and high tariffs against one another's goods (to protect their own markets). The result was a great deal of confusion and bad feeling—as well as a great deal of smuggling.

Currency Problems Under the Articles, the states themselves had the power to issue their own currency, regulate its value, and require that it be accepted in payment of debts. States had their own "legal tender" laws, which required creditors to accept state money if "tendered" in payment of debt. As a result, many forms of money were circulating: Virginia dollars, Rhode Island dollars, Pennsylvania dollars, and so on. Some states (Rhode Island, for example) printed a great deal of money, creating inflation in their currency and alienating banks and investors whose loans were being paid off in this cheap currency. If creditors refused payment in a particular state's currency, the debt could be abolished in that state. So finances throughout the states were very unstable, and banks and creditors were threatened by cheap paper money.

Civil Disorder In several states, debtors openly revolted against tax collectors and sheriffs attempting to repossess farms on behalf of creditors who held unpaid mortgages. The most serious rebellion broke out in the summer of 1786 in western Massachusetts, where a band of 2,000 insurgent farmers captured the courthouses in several counties and briefly held the city of Springfield. Led by Daniel Shays, a veteran of the Revolutionary War battle at Bunker Hill, the insurgent army posed a direct threat to investors, bankers, creditors, and tax collectors by burning deeds, mortgages, and tax records to wipe out proof of the farmers' debts.

Shays's Rebellion, as it was called, was finally put down by a small mercenary army, paid for by well-to-do citizens of Boston.

Reports of Shays's Rebellion filled the newspapers of the large eastern cities. George Washington, Alexander Hamilton, James Madison, and many other prominent Americans wrote their friends about it. The event galvanized property owners to support the creation of a strong central government capable of dealing with "radicalism." Only a strong central government, they wrote one another, could "insure domestic tranquility," guarantee "a republican form of government," and protect property "against domestic violence." It is no accident that all of these phrases appear in the Constitution of 1787.

The Road to the Constitutional Convention In the spring of 1785, some wealthy merchants from Virginia and Maryland met at Alexandria, Virginia, to try to resolve a conflict between the two states over commerce and navigation on the Potomac River and Chesapeake Bay. George Washington, the new nation's most prominent citizen, took a personal interest in the meeting. As a wealthy plantation owner and a land speculator who owned more than 30,000 acres of land upstream on the Potomac, Washington was keenly interested in commercial problems under the Articles of Confederation. He lent his great prestige to the Alexandria meeting by inviting the participants to his house at Mount Vernon. Out of this conference came the idea for a general economic conference for all of the states, to be held in Annapolis, Maryland, in September 1786.

The Annapolis Convention turned out to be a key stepping-stone to the Constitutional Convention of 1787. Instead of concentrating on commerce and navigation between the states, the delegates at Annapolis, including Alexander Hamilton and James Madison, called for a general constitutional convention to suggest remedies to what they saw as defects in the Articles of Confederation.

In an attempt to prevent the foreclosure of farms by creditors, Revolutionary War veteran Daniel Shays led an armed mass of citizens in a march on a western Massachusetts court-house. This uprising, which came to be known as Shays's Rebellion, exposed the Confederation's military weakness and increased support for a strong central government.

On February 21, 1787, the Congress called for a convention to meet in Philadelphia for the "sole and express purpose" of *revising* the Articles of Confederation and reporting to the Congress and the state legislatures "such alterations and provisions therein as shall, when agreed to in Congress and confirmed by the states, to render the federal Constitution adequate to the exigencies of government and the preservation of the union." Notice that Congress did not authorize the convention to write a new constitution or to call constitutional conventions in the states to ratify a new constitution. State legislatures sent delegates to Philadelphia expecting that their task would be limited to revising the Articles and that revisions would be sent back to Congress and state legislatures for their approval. But that is not what happened.

WWW **George Washington Papers**

The life of George Washington with images, maps, documents, and papers.
http://gwpapers.virgina.edu

The Nation's Founders The fifty-five delegates to the Constitutional Convention, which met in Philadelphia in the summer of 1787, quickly discarded the congressional mandate to merely "revise" the Articles of Confederation. The Virginia delegation, led by James Madison, arrived before a quorum of seven states had assembled and used the time to draw up an entirely new constitutional document. After the first formal session opened on May 25 and George Washington was elected president of the convention, the Virginia Plan became the basis of discussion. Thus, at the very beginning of the convention, the decision was made to scrap the Articles of Confederation altogether, write a new constitution, and form a new national government.[2]

The Founders were very confident of their powers and abilities. They had been selected by their state legislatures (only Rhode Island, dominated by small farmers, refused to send a delegation). When Thomas Jefferson, then serving in the critical post of ambassador to France (the nation's military ally in the Revolutionary War), first saw the list of delegates, he exclaimed, "It is really an assembly of demigods." Indeed, among the nation's notables, only Jefferson and John Adams (then serving as ambassador to England) were absent. The eventual success of the convention, and the ratification of the new Constitution, resulted in part from the enormous prestige, experience, and achievements of the delegates themselves.

WWW **Our Documents**

National Archives Web site with access to 100 "milestone documents" in American history.
www.ourdocuments.gov

Above all, the delegates at Philadelphia were cosmopolitan. They approached political, economic, and military issues from a "continental" point of view. Unlike most Americans in 1787, their loyalties extended beyond their states. They were truly nationalists.[3]

Consensus in Philadelphia

THINK AGAIN

Was the original constitution of 1787 a truly democratic document?

The Founders shared many ideas about government. We often focus our attention on *conflict* in the Convention of 1787 and the compromises reached by the participants, but the really important story of the Constitution is the *consensus* that was shared by these men of influence.

Liberty and Property The Founders had read John Locke and absorbed his idea that the purpose of government is to protect individual liberty and property. They believed in a natural law, superior to any human-made laws, that endowed each person with certain inalienable rights—the rights to life, liberty, and property. They believed that all people were equally entitled to these rights. Most of them, including slave owners George Washington and Thomas Jefferson, un-

George Washington, Founder of a Nation

From the time he took command of the American Revolutionary forces in 1775 until he gave his Farewell Address to the nation in 1796 and returned to his Mount Vernon plantation, George Washington (1732–99) was, indeed, "First in war, first in peace, first in the hearts of his countrymen." His military success, combined with his diplomacy and practical political acumen, gave him overwhelming moral authority, which he used to inspire the Constitutional Convention, to secure the ratification of the Constitution, and then to guide the new nation through its first years.

Washington was raised on a Virginia plantation and inherited substantial landholdings, including his Mount Vernon plantation on the Potomac River. He began his career as a surveyor. His work took him deep into the wilderness of America's frontier. This experience later served him well when at age twenty-one, he was appointed an officer in the Virginia militia. In 1754 he led a small force toward the French Fort Duquesne, but after a brief battle at makeshift "Fort Necessity," he was obliged to retreat. In 1755 British Major General Edward Braddock asked the young militia officer to accompany his heavy regiments on a campaign to dislodge the French from Fort Duquesne. Braddock disregarded Washington's warnings about concealed ways of fighting in the New World; Braddock's parading redcoat forces were ambushed by the French and Indians near Pittsburgh, and the general was killed. Washington rallied what remained of the British forces and led them in a successful retreat back to Virginia.

Washington was viewed by Virginians as a hero, and at age twenty-two he was appointed by the Virginia Assembly "Colonel of the Virginia Regiment and Commander in Chief of all Virginia Forces." But regular British officers ridiculed the militia forces and asserted their authority over Washington. British General John Forbes occupied Fort Duquesne, renamed it Fort Pitt, and gave Washington's men the task of garrisoning it.

In 1759, having completed his service in the French and Indian Wars, Washington left his military post and returned to plantation life. He married a wealthy widow, Martha Custis, expanded his plantation holdings, and prospered in western land speculation.

The Virginia legislature elected Washington to attend the First Continental Congress in September 1774. Washington was the most celebrated veteran of the French and Indian Wars who was still young enough (forty-two) to lead military forces in a new struggle. John Adams of Massachusetts was anxious to unite the continent in the coming contest, and he persuaded the Second Continental Congress to give the Virginian command of the American revolutionary forces surrounding the British army in Boston in 1775.

Throughout the Revolutionary War Washington persevered by employing many of the tactics later defined as the principles of guerrilla warfare. By retreating deep into Pennsylvania's Valley Forge, Washington avoided defeat and saved his army. His bold Christmas night attack against Hessian troops at Trenton, New Jersey, encouraged French intervention on America's behalf. Slowly Washington was able to wear down the British resolve to fight. In the end, he succeeded in trapping a British army at Yorktown, Virginia. Assisted by a French naval blockade, he accepted the surrender of Lord Cornwallis and 8,000 of his men on October 19, 1781.

Perhaps Washington's greatest contribution to democratic government occurred in 1783 in Newburgh, New York, near West Point, where the veterans of his Continental Army were encamped. Despite their hardships and ultimate victory in the Revolutionary War, these soldiers remained unpaid by Congress. Indeed, Congress ignored a series of letters, known as the Newburgh Addresses, that threatened military force if Congress continued to deny benefits to the veterans. Washington was invited to Newburgh by officers who hoped he would agree to lead a military coup against the Congress. But when Washington mounted the platform he denounced the use of force and the "infamous propositions" contained in their earlier addresses to Congress. There is little doubt that he could have chosen to march on the Congress with his veteran army and install himself as military dictator. World history is filled with revolutionary army leaders who did so. But Washington chose to preserve representative government.

One of the few noncontroversial decisions of the Constitutional Convention in 1787 was the selection of George Washington to preside over the meetings. He took little part in the debates; however, his enormous prestige helped to hold the convention together and later to win support for the new Constitution.

derstood that the belief in personal liberty conflicted with the practice of slavery and found the inconsistency troubling.

Social Contract The Founders believed that government originated in an implied contract among people. People agreed to establish government, obey laws, and pay taxes in exchange for protection of their natural rights. This social contract gave government its legitimacy—a legitimacy that rested on the consent of the governed, not with gods or kings or force. If a government violated individual liberty, it broke the social contract and thus lost its legitimacy.

Representative Government Although most of the world's governments in 1787 were hereditary monarchies, the Founders believed the people should have a voice in choosing their own representatives in government. They opposed hereditary aristocracy and titled nobility. Instead, they sought to forge a republic. **Republicanism** meant government by representatives of the people. The Founders expected the masses to consent to be governed by their leaders—men of principle and property with ability, education, and a stake in the preservation of liberty. The Founders believed the people should have only a limited role in directly selecting their representatives: they should vote for members of the House of Representatives, but senators, the president, and members of the Supreme Court should be selected by others more qualified to judge their ability.

Limited Government The Founders believed unlimited power was corrupting and a concentration of power was dangerous. They believed in a written constitution that limited the scope of governmental power. They also believed in dividing power within government by creating separate bodies able to check and balance one another's powers.

Nationalism Most important, the Founders shared a belief in **nationalism**—a strong and independent national (federal) government with power to govern directly, rather than through state governments. They sought to establish a government that would be recognized around the world as representing "We the people of the United States." Not everyone in America shared this enthusiasm for a strong federal government; indeed, opposition forces, calling themselves Anti-Federalists, almost succeeded in defeating the new Constitution. But the leaders meeting in Philadelphia in the summer of 1787 were convinced of the need for a strong central government that would share power with the states.

Conflict in Philadelphia

Consensus on basic principles of government was essential to the success of the Philadelphia convention. But conflict over the implementation of these principles not only tied up the convention for an entire summer but later threatened to prevent the states from ratifying, or voting to approve, the document the convention produced.

Representation Representation was the most controversial issue in Philadelphia. Following the election of George Washington as president of the convention, Governor Edmund Randolph of Virginia rose to present a draft of a new constitution. This Virginia Plan called for a legislature with two houses: a lower house chosen by the people of the states, with representation according to population;

republicanism Government by representatives of the people rather than directly by the people themselves.

nationalism Belief that shared cultural, historical, linguistic, and social characteristics of a people justify the creation of a government encompassing all of them; the resulting nation-state should be independent and legally equal to all other nation-states.

TABLE 3.1 Constitutional Compromise

The Virginia Plan	The New Jersey Plan	The Connecticut Compromise The Constitution of 1787
Two-house legislature, with the lower house directly elected based on state population and the upper house elected by the lower.	One-house legislature, with equal state representation, regardless of population.	Two-house legislature, with the House directly elected based on state population and the Senate selected by the state legislatures; two senators per state, regardless of population.
Legislature with broad power, including veto power over laws passed by the state legislatures.	Legislature with the same power as under the Articles of Confederation, plus the power to levy some taxes and to regulate commerce.	Legislature with broad power, including the power to tax and to regulate commerce.
President and cabinet elected by the legislature.	Separate multiperson executive, elected by the legislature, removable by petition from a majority of the state governors.	President chosen by an Electoral College.
National judiciary elected by the legislature.	National judiciary appointed by the executive.	National judiciary appointed by the president and confirmed by the Senate.
"Council of Revision" with the power to veto laws of the legislature.	National Supremacy Clause similar to that found in Article VI of the 1787 Constitution.	National Supremacy Clause: the Constitution is "the supreme Law of the Land."

and an upper house to be chosen by the lower house (see Table 3.1). Congress was to have the broad power to "legislate in all cases to which the separate States are incompetent, or in which the harmony of the United States may be interrupted." Congress was to have the power to nullify state laws that it believed violated the Constitution, thus ensuring the national government's supremacy over the states. The Virginia Plan also proposed a *parliamentary* form of government, in which the legislature (Congress) chose the principal executive officers of the government as well as federal judges. Finally, the Virginia Plan included a curious "council of revision," with the power to veto acts of Congress.

Delegates from New Jersey and Delaware objected strongly to the great power given to the national government in the Virginia Plan, the larger representation it proposed for the more populous states, and the plan's failure to recognize the role of the states in the composition of the new government. After several weeks of debate, William Paterson of New Jersey submitted a counterproposal. The New Jersey Plan called for a single-chamber Congress in which each state, regardless of its population, had one vote, just as under the Articles of Confederation. But unlike the Articles, the New Jersey Plan proposed separate executive and judicial branches of government and the expansion of the powers of Congress to include levying taxes and regulating commerce. Moreover, the New Jersey Plan included a National Supremacy Clause, declaring that the Constitution and federal laws would supersede state constitutions and laws.

Debate over representation in Congress raged into July 1787. At one point, the convention actually voted for the Virginia Plan, 7 votes to 3, but without New York, New Jersey, and Delaware, the new nation would not have been viable.

The Great Compromise

James Madison University Web site on Madison with information on constitutional compromises, including the slavery compromise.
www.jmu.edu/madison

Eventually, Roger Sherman of Connecticut came forward with a compromise. This Connecticut Compromise—sometimes called the Great Compromise—established two houses of Congress: in the upper house, the Senate, each state would have two members regardless of its size; in the lower body, the House of Representatives, each state would be represented according to population. Members of the House would be directly elected by the people; members of the Senate would be selected by their state legislatures. Legislation would have to pass both houses to be enacted. This compromise was approved by the convention on July 16.

Slavery Another conflict absorbing the attention of the delegates was slavery. In 1787 slavery was legal everywhere except in Massachusetts. Nevertheless, the delegates were too embarrassed to use the word *slave* or *slavery* in their debates or in the Constitution itself. Instead, they referred to "other persons" and "persons held to service or labour."

Delegates from the southern states, where slaves were a large proportion of the population, believed slaves should be counted in representation afforded the states, but not counted if taxes were to be levied on a population basis. Delegates from the northern states, with small slave populations, believed that "the people" counted for representation purposes should include only free persons. The Connecticut Plan included the now-infamous Three-fifths Compromise: three-fifths of the slaves of each state would be counted for purposes both of representation in the House of Representatives and for apportionment for direct taxes.

Slave owners also sought protection for their human "property" in the Constitution itself. They were particularly concerned about slaves running away to other states and claiming their freedom. So they succeeded in writing into the Constitution (Article IV, Section 2) a specific guarantee: "No person held to Service or Labour in one State . . . escaping into another, shall . . . be discharged from such Service or Labour, but shall be delivered up on Claim of the Party to whom such Service or Labour may be due."

Yet another compromise dealt with the slave trade. The capture, transportation, and "breaking in" of African slaves was considered a nasty business, even by southern planters. Many wealthy Maryland and Virginia plantations were already well supplied with slaves and thus could afford the luxury of conscience to call for an end to slave importation. But other planters from the less-developed southern states, particularly South Carolina and Georgia, wanted additional slave labor. The final compromise prohibited the slave trade—but not before the year 1808, thereby giving the planters twenty years to import all the slaves they needed before the slave trade ended.

Voter Qualifications Another important conflict centered on qualifications for voting and holding office in the new government. Most of the delegates believed that voters as well as officeholders should be men of property. (Only Benjamin Franklin went so far as to propose universal *male* suffrage.) But delegates argued over the specific wording of property qualifications, their views on the subject reflecting the source of their own wealth. Merchants, bankers, and manufacturers objected to making the ownership of a certain amount of land a qualification for officeholding. James Madison, a plantation owner himself, was forced to admit that "landed possessions were no certain evidence of real wealth. Many enjoyed them who were more in debt than they were worth."

After much debate, the convention approved a constitution without any expressed property qualifications for voting or holding office, except those that the states might impose themselves: "The Electors in each State shall have the

Although hotly debated, the issue of slaveholding was not resolved by the Founders in either the Declaration of Independence or the Constitution. As a result, the practice of buying and selling slaves—and the debate over this practice—continued for years to come, until political conflict exploded in the Civil War.

Qualifications requisite for Electors of the most numerous Branch of the State Legislature." At the time, every state had property qualifications for voting, and women were not permitted to vote or hold office. (The New Jersey Constitution of 1776 enfranchised women as well as men who owned property, but in 1787, a new state law limited the vote to "free white male citizens.")

Resolving the Economic Issues

The Founders were just as concerned with "who gets what, when, and how" as today's politicians are. Important economic interests were at stake in the Constitution. Historian Charles A. Beard pointed out that the delegates to the Constitutional Convention were men of wealth: planters, slaveholders, merchants, manufacturers, shippers, bankers and investors, and land speculators. Moreover, most of the delegates owned Revolutionary War bonds that were now worthless and would remain so unless the national government could obtain the tax revenues to pay them off[4] (see *A Conflicting View:* "An Economic Interpretation of the Constitution"). But it is certainly not true that the Founders acted only out of personal interest. Wealthy delegates were found on both sides of constitutional debates, arguing principles as well as economic interests.[5]

Levying Taxes A central purpose of the Constitution was to enable the national government to levy its own **taxes**, so that it could end its dependence on state contributions and achieve financial credibility. The very first power given to Congress in Article 1, Section 8, is the power to tax: "The Congress shall have Power to lay and collect Taxes, Duties, Imposts and Excises, to pay the Debts and provide for the common Defence and general Welfare."

The financial credit of the United States and the interests of Revolutionary War bondholders were guaranteed by Article VI in the Constitution, which specifically declared that the new government would be obligated to pay the debts of the old government. Indeed, the nation's first secretary of the treasury, Alexander

Constitutional Law
Cornell University Law School overview of the Constitution.
www.law.cornell.edu/topics/ constitutional

taxes Compulsory payments to the government.

An Economic Interpretation of the Constitution

Charles Beard, historian and political scientist, provided the most controversial historical interpretation of the origin of American national government in his landmark book. *An Economic Interpretation of the Constitution of the United States* (1913). Not all historians agree with Beard's economic interpretation, but all concede that it is a milestone in understanding the U.S. Constitution. Beard closely studied unpublished financial records of the U.S. Treasury Department and the personal letters and financial accounts of the fifty-five delegates to the Philadelphia convention. He concluded that they represented the following five economic interest groups, each of which benefited from specific provisions of the Constitution:

- *Public security interests* (persons holding U.S. bonds from the Revolutionary War: 37 of the 55 delegates). The taxing power was of great benefit to the holders of public securities, particularly when it was combined with the provision in Article VI that "all Debts contracted and Engagements entered into, before the Adoption of this Constitution, shall be as valid against the United States under this Constitution, as under the Confederation." That is, the national government would be obliged to pay off all those investors who held U.S. bonds, and the taxing power would give the national government the ability to do so on its own.
- *Merchants and manufactures* (persons engaged in shipping and trade: 11 of the 55 delegates). The Interstate Commerce Clause, which eliminated state control over commerce, and the provision in Article I, Section 9, which prohibited the states from taxing exports, created a free-trade area, or "common market," among the thirteen states.
- *Bankers and investors* (24 of 55 delegates). Congress was given the power to make bankruptcy laws, to coin money and regulate its value, to fix standards of weights and measures, to punish counterfeiting, to establish post offices and post roads, to pass copyright and patent laws to protect authors and inventors, and to punish piracies and felonies committed on the high seas. Each of these powers is a specific asset to bankers and investors as well as merchants, authors inventors, and shippers.
- *Western land speculators* (persons who purchased large tracts of land west of the Appalachian Mountains: 14 of the 55 delegates). If western settlers were to be protected from the Indians, and if the British were to be persuaded to give up their forts in Ohio and open the way to American westward expansion, the national government could not rely on state militias but must have an army of its own. Western land speculators welcomed the creation of a national army that would be employed primarily as an Indian-fighting force over the next century.
- *Slave owners* (15 of the 55 delegates). Protection against domestic insurrection also appealed to the southern slaveholders' deep-seated fear of a slave revolt. The Constitution permitted Congress to outlaw the *import of slaves* after the year 1808. But most southern planters were more interested in protecting their existing property and slaves than they were in extending the slave trade, and the Constitution provided an explicit advantage to slaveholders in Article IV, Section 2 (later revoked by the Thirteenth Amendment, which abolished slavery), by specifically requiring the forced return of slaves who might escape to free states.

Beard argued that the members of the Philadelphia convention who drafted the Constitution were, with a few exceptions, immediately, directly, and personally interested in, and derived economic advantages from, the establishment of the new system. But many historians disagree with Beard's emphasis on the economic motives of the Founders. The Constitution, they point out, was adopted in a society that was fundamentally democratic, and it was adopted by people who were primarily middle-class property owners, especially farmers, rather than owners of businesses. The Constitution was not just an economic document, although economic factors were certainly important. Since most of the people were middle class and owned private property, practically all Americans were interested in the protection of property.

Under the Articles of Confederation, each state issued its own currency. Differences in currency regulation from state to state led to financial uncertainty and inflation. By creating a national currency and putting the national government in charge of the money supply, the Founders hoped to restore stability and control inflation.

Hamilton, made repayment of the national debt the first priority of the Washington Administration.

The original Constitution placed most of the tax burden on consumers in the form of **tariffs** on goods imported into the United States. For more than a century, these tariffs provided the national government with its principal source of revenue. Tariffs were generally favored by American manufacturers, who wished to raise the price paid for foreign goods to make their home-produced goods more competitive. No taxes were permitted on *exports*, a protection for southern planters, who exported most of their tobacco and, later, cotton. Direct taxes on individuals were prohibited (Article 1, Section 2) except in proportion to *population*. This provision prevented the national government from levying direct taxes in proportion to income until the Sixteenth Amendment (income tax) was ratified in 1913.

The power to tax and spend was given to Congress, not to the president or executive agencies. Instead, the Constitution was very specific: "No Money shall be drawn from the Treasury, but in Consequence of Appropriations made by Law." This is the constitutional basis of Congress's "power of the purse."

Regulating Commerce The new Constitution gave Congress the power to "regulate Commerce with foreign Nations, and among the several States" (Article 1, Section 8), and it prohibited the states from imposing tariffs on goods shipped across state lines (Article 1, Section 10). This power created what we call today a **common market**; it protected merchants against state-imposed tariffs and stimulated trade among the states. States were also prohibited from "impairing the Obligation of Contracts"—that is, passing any laws that would allow debtors to avoid their obligations to banks and other lenders.

Protecting Money The Constitution also ensured that the new national government would control the money supply. Congress was given the power to coin money and regulate its value. More important, the states were prohibited from issuing their own paper money, thus protecting bankers and creditors from the repayment of debts in cheap state currencies. (No one wanted to be paid for goods or labor in Rhode Island's inflated dollars.) If only the national government could issue money, the Founders hoped, inflation could be minimized.

tariff Tax imposed on imported products (also called a customs duty).

common market Unified trade area in which all goods and services can be sold or exchanged free from customs or tariffs.

Protecting National Security

At the start of the Revolutionary War, the Continental Congress had given George Washington command of a small regular army—"Continentals"—paid for by Congress and also had authorized him to take command of state militia units. During the entire war, most of Washington's troops had been state militia. (The "militia" in those days was composed of every free adult male, each was expected to bring his own gun.) Washington himself had frequently decried the militia units as undisciplined, untrained, and unwilling to follow his orders. He wanted the new United States to have a *regular* army and navy, paid for by the Congress with its new taxing power, to back up the state militia units.

War and the Military Forces Congress was authorized to "declare War," to raise and support a regular army and navy, and to make rules regulating these forces. It was also authorized to call up the militia, as it had done in the Revolution, in order to "execute the Laws of the Union, suppress Insurrections and repel Invasions." When the militia are called into national service, they come under the rule of Congress and the command of the president.

The United States relied primarily on militia—citizen-soldiers organized in state units—until World War I. The regular U.S. Army, stationed in coastal and frontier forts, directed most of its actions against Native Americans. The major actions in America's nineteenth-century wars—the War of 1812 against the British, the Mexican War of 1846–48, the Civil War in 1861–65, and the Spanish-American War in 1898—were fought largely by citizen-soldiers from these state units.

Commander-in-Chief Following the precedent set in the Revolutionary War, the new president, who everyone expected to be George Washington, was made "Commander-in-Chief of the Army and Navy of the United States, and of the Militia of the several States, when called into the actual Service of the United States." Clearly, there is some overlap in responsibility for national defense: Congress has the power to declare war, but the president is Commander-in-Chief. During the next two centuries, the president would order U.S. forces into 200 or more military actions, but Congress would pass an official Declaration of War only five times. Conflict between the president and Congress over war-making powers continues to this day (see the section "Commander-in-Chief" in Chapter 11).

Foreign Affairs The national government also assumed full power over foreign affairs and prohibited the states from entering into any "Treaty, Alliance, or Con-

On May 1, 2003, President Bush landed on an aircraft carrier and declared "Mission Accomplished"— the end of major combat operations in Iraq. But guerrilla attacks on U.S. troops continued. By August more soldiers had died in the aftermath of the war than during the capture of Baghdad.

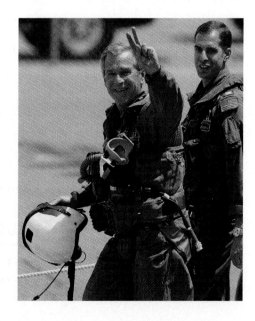

federation." The Constitution gave the president, not Congress, the power to "make Treaties" and "appoint Ambassadors." However, the Constitution stipulated that the president could do these things only "by and with the Advice and Consent of the Senate," indicating an unwillingness to allow the president to act autonomously in these matters. The Senate's power to "advise and consent" to treaties and appointments, together with the congressional power over appropriations, gives the Congress important influence in foreign affairs. Nevertheless, the president remains the dominant figure in this arena.

The Structure of the Government

The Constitution that emerged from the Philadelphia convention on September 17, 1787, founded a new government with a unique structure. That structure was designed to implement the Founders' beliefs in nationalism, limited government, republicanism, the social contract, and the protection of liberty and property. The Founders were realists; they did not have any romantic notions about the wisdom and virtue of "the people." James Madison wrote, "A dependence on the people is, no doubt, the primary control on the government, but experience has taught mankind the necessity of auxiliary precautions." The key structural arrangements in the Constitution—national supremacy, federalism, republicanism, separation of powers, checks and balances, and judicial review—all reflect the Founders' desire to create a strong national government while at the same time ensuring that it would not become a threat to liberty or property.

THINK AGAIN

Should a large state like California, with 32 million people, elect more U.S. senators than a small state like Wyoming, with only half a million people?

National Supremacy The heart of the Constitution is the National Supremacy Clause of Article VI:

> This Constitution, and the Laws of the United States which shall be made in Pursuance thereof, and all Treaties made, or which shall be made, under the Authority of the United States, shall be the supreme Law of the Land; and the Judges in every State shall be bound thereby, any Thing in the Constitution or Laws of any State to the Contrary notwithstanding.

This sentence ensures that the Constitution itself is the supreme law of the land and that laws passed by Congress supersede state laws. This National Supremacy Clause establishes the authority of the Constitution and the U.S. government.

Federalism The Constitution *divides power* between the nation and the states (see Chapter 4). It recognizes that both the national government and the state governments have independent legal authority over their own citizens: both can pass their own laws, levy their own taxes, and maintain their own courts. The states have an important role in the selection of national officeholders—in the apportionment of congressional seats and in the allocation of electoral votes for president. Most important, perhaps, both the Congress and three-quarters of the states must consent to changes in the Constitution itself.

Republicanism To the Founders, a *republican* government meant the delegation of powers by the people to a small number of gifted individuals "whose wisdom may best discern the true interest of their country, and whose patriotism and love of justice will be least likely to sacrifice it to temporary or partial considerations."[6] The Founders believed that enlightened leaders of principle and property with ability, education, and a stake in the preservation of liberty could govern the people better than the people could govern themselves. So they gave the voters only a limited voice in the selection of government leaders.

TABLE 3.2   Decision-Making Bodies in the Constitution of 1787

House of Representatives	Senate	President	Supreme Court
Members alloted to each state "according to their respective numbers," but each state guaranteed at least one member.	"Two senators from each state" (regardless of the size of the state).	Single executive.	No size specified in the Constitution, but by tradition, nine.
Two-year term. No limits on number of terms that can be served.	Six-year term. No limits on number of terms that can be served.	Four-year term (later limited to two terms by the Twenty-second Amendment in 1951).	Life term.
Directly elected by "the People of the several States."	Selected by the state legislatures (later changed to direct election by the Seventeenth Amendment in 1913).	Selected by "Electors," appointed in each state "In such Manner as the Legislature thereof may direct" and equal to the total number of U.S. senators and House members to which the state is entitled in Congress.	Appointed by the president, "by and with the Advice and Consent of the Senate."

The Electoral College Official FEC site

Provides brief history of the electoral college and a description of how it works. **www.fec.gov/pages/ecmenu**

referenda Proposed laws or constitutional amendments submitted to the voters for their direct approval or rejection, found in state constitutions but not in the U.S. Constitution.

The Constitution of 1787 created *four* decision-making bodies, each with separate numbers, terms of office, and selection processes (see Table 3.2). Note that in the *original* Constitution only one of these four bodies—the House of Representatives—was to be directly elected by the people. The other three were removed from direct popular control: state legislatures selected U.S. senators; "electors" (chosen at the discretion of the state legislatures) selected the president; the president appointed Supreme Court and other federal judges (see *Up Close:* "Why the Founders created an Electoral college to choose the president").

Democracy? The Founders believed that government rests ultimately on "the consent of the governed." But their notion of republicanism envisioned decision making by *representatives* of the people, not the people themselves (see *A Conflicting View:* "Let the People Vote on National Issues"). The U.S. Constitution does not provide for *direct* voting by the people on national questions, that is, unlike many state constitutions today, it does *not* provide for national **referenda**. Moreover, as noted earlier, only the House of Representatives (sometimes referred to even today as "the people's house") was to be elected directly by voters in the states.

These republican arrangements may appear "undemocratic" from our perspective today, but in 1787 the U.S. Constitution was more democratic than any other governing system in the world. Although other nations were governed by monarchs, emperors, chieftains, and hereditary aristocracies, the Founders recognized that government depended on the *consent of the governed.* Later democratic impulses in America greatly altered the original Constitution (see "Constitutional Change" later in this chapter) and reshaped it into a much more democratic document.

Why the Founders Created an Electoral College to Choose the President

In the 2000 presidential election, Democrat Al Gore received about 500,000 more votes nationwide than Republican George W. Bush. But Bush won the presidency with 271 "electoral votes" to Gore's 267. Why did the Founders decide to have "Electors" choose the president? Why not allow the people themselves to directly elect their president?

The Founders believed in "republicanism," not "democracy." They believed that the people should entrust governmental power to a small number of gifted individuals "whose wisdom may best discern the true interest of their country, and whose patriotism and love of justice will be least likely to sacrifice it to temporary or partial consideration."

At the Constitutional Convention of 1787 the Founders considered several systems for electing the president: direct election by the people, election by the Congress, election by the state legislatures, or election by citizens especially chosen to be "Electors."

Election by a direct popular vote had the least support in the Convention. Not only did the Founders distrust direct democracy, but they also worried that the 4 million people spread over 1,000 miles of Atlantic seaboard would have little knowledge or information about candidates from outside their own state, and that they would most likely vote for a "favorite son" from their own state. The result might be that no candidate would win a popular majority, or that the choice of the president would be decided by the largest most populous state, with little opportunity for candidates from smaller states to win the office.

The Founders also considered giving the Congress the power to choose the president. But the debates suggested that the Founders worried that this procedure would encourage unseemly political bargaining and corruption in the Congress itself. Moreover, it would upset the notion of separation of powers and checks and balances, the basic framework of the government that the Founders were creating.

Recognizing the pitfalls of both direct election of the president and election by Congress, the Founders turned to election of the president by the states. The first idea was to allow the state legislatures to select the president. But in the Constitution of 1787 the state legislatures were already charged with responsibility of electing U.S. Senators. So the Founders argued about whether to give additional power to state legislatures or to set up a separate system of presidential "Electors" in the states. Following much argument, the Founders finally decided on a compromise: Electors in each state, equal to the total number of House and Senate members from that state, would choose the president. However, *state legislatures* would decide how to choose Electors.

The Founders designed the Electoral College to ensure that the winning presidential candidate had support distributed across the nation—support in small states as well as large. (Small states are actually overrepresented in the Electoral College, owing to the fact that each state has two Electors based on their representation in the U.S. Senate regardless of their population.) Opponents of the Electoral College worry about the possibility of electing a president who receives fewer popular votes than his opponent, as occurred in the Bush-Gore election in 2000 (and the Harrison-Cleveland election of 1888). Indeed, if one candidate's popular support is heavily concentrated in a few states while the other candidate maintains a slim popular lead in enough states to win the needed majority of the Electoral College, this will be the outcome. But the Founders deliberately structured the Electoral College so that voters in a few populous states could not themselves determine the outcome. (See "Should We Scrap the Electoral College?" in Chapter 8.)

Separation of Powers and Checks and Balances

The Founders believed that unlimited power was corrupting and that the concentration of power was dangerous. James Madison wrote, "Ambition must be made to counteract ambition." The **separation of powers** within the national government—the creation of separate legislative, executive, and judicial branches in Articles I, II, and III of the Constitution—was designed to place internal controls on governmental power. Power is not only apportioned among three branches of government,

separation of powers
Constitutional division of powers among the three branches of the national government—legislative, executive, and judicial.

A CONFLICTING VIEW

Let the People Vote on National Issues

"Direct democracy" means that the people themselves can initiate and decide policy questions by popular vote. The Founders were profoundly skeptical of this form of democracy. They had read about direct democracy in the ancient Greek citystate of Athens, and they believed the "follies" of direct democracy far outweighed any virtues it might possess. It was not until more than 100 years after the U.S. Constitution was written that widespread support developed in the American states for direct voter participation in policy making. Direct democracy developed in states and communities, and it is to be found today *only* in state and local government.

Why not extend our notion of democracy to include nationwide referenda voting on key public issues? Perhaps Congress should be authorized to place particularly controversial issues on a national ballot, Perhaps a petition signed by at least 1 million voters should also result in a question being placed on a national ballot.

Proponents of direct voting on national issues argue that national referenda would

- Enhance government responsiveness and accountability to the people.
- Stimulate national debate over policy questions.
- Increase voter interest and turnout on election day.
- Increase trust in government and diminish feelings of alienation from Washington.
- Give voters a direct role in policy making.

Opponents of direct democracy, from our nation's Founders to the present, argue that national referenda voting would

- Encourage majorities to sacrifice the rights of individuals and minorities.
- Lead to the adoption of unwise and unsound policies because voters are not sufficiently informed to cast intelligent ballots on many complex issues.
- Prevent consideration of alternative policies or modifications or amendments to the proposition set forth on the ballot. (In contrast, legislators devote a great deal of attention to writing, rewriting, and amending bills, as well as seeking out compromises among interests.)
- Enable special interests to mount expensive referendum campaigns; the outcomes of referenda would be heavily influenced by paid television advertising.

How would voters' decisions in national referenda differ from current government policies? A national poll on key policy issues produced the results shown here.

THINK AGAIN

In which do you have the most trust and confidence? President, Congress, Supreme Court

checks and balances
Constitutional provisions giving each branch of the national government certain checks over the actions of other branches.

but, perhaps more important, each branch is given important **checks and balances** over the actions of the others (see Figure 3.1 on page 72). According to Madison, "The constant aim is to divide and arrange the several offices in such a manner as that each may be a check on the other." No bill can become a law without the approval of both the House and the Senate. The president shares legislative power through the power to sign or to veto laws of Congress, although Congress may override a presidential veto with a two-thirds vote in each house. The president may also suggest legislation, "give to the Congress Information of the State of the Union, and recommend to their Consideration such Measures as he shall judge necessary and expedient." The president may also convene special sessions of Congress.

However, the president's power of appointment is shared by the Senate, which confirms cabinet and ambassadorial appointments. The president must also secure

Question: *Suppose that on election day this year you could vote on key issues as well as candidates. Please tell me whether you would vote for or against each one of the following propositions. (27 items read in random order)*

	Vote for	Vote against	No opinion
1. *Balanced budget amendment	83%	14%	3
2. Raising the minimum wage	83%	15%	2
3. *English as the official language	82%	16%	2
4. Life sentences for drug dealers	80%	17%	3
5. Death penalty for murder	79%	18%	3
6. *Congressional term limits amendment	74%	23%	3
7. *Prayer in public school amendment	73%	25%	2
8. *Reducing all government agencies	71%	23%	6
9. Two-year cutoff for welfare without work	71%	24%	5
10. Mandatory job retraining	69%	25%	6
11. *Doctor-assisted suicide	68%	29%	3
12. *School choice	59%	37%	4
13. *Teaching creationism in public schools	58%	36%	6
14. *Ban on partial-birth abortions	57%	39%	4
15. Ban on assault rifles	57%	42%	1
16. *Five-year freeze on legal immigration	50%	46%	4
17. *Federal flat tax system	49%	39%	12
18. Reducing social spending	44%	53%	3
19. Reducing defense spending	42%	54%	4
20. Abortion ban except to save mother's life	42%	56%	2
21. Reestablishing relations with Cuba	40%	49%	11
22. *School busing for racial balance	34%	62%	4
23. Legalization of gay marriages	28%	67%	5
24. Selling off public lands	24%	70%	6
25. Legalization of marijuana	24%	73%	3
26. Withdrawal of U.S. from United Nations	17%	77%	6
27. *Racial preferences in jobs and school	14%	83%	3

Issues on which current public policy differs from popular preference.

Source: *The Gallup Poll Monthly,* May 1996. Copyright © 1996 by The Gallup Organization.

the advice and consent of the Senate for any treaty. The president must execute the laws, but it is Congress that provides the money to do so. The president and the rest of the executive branch may not spend money that has not been appropriated by Congress. Congress must also authorize the creation of executive departments and agencies. Finally, Congress may impeach and remove the president from office for "Treason, Bribery, or other High Crimes and Misdemeanors."

Members of the Supreme Court are appointed by the president and confirmed by the Senate. Traditionally, this court has nine members, but Congress may determine the number of justices. More important, Congress must create lower federal district courts as well as courts of appeal. Congress must also determine the number of these judgeships and determine the jurisdiction of federal courts. But the most important check of all is the Supreme Court's power of judicial review.

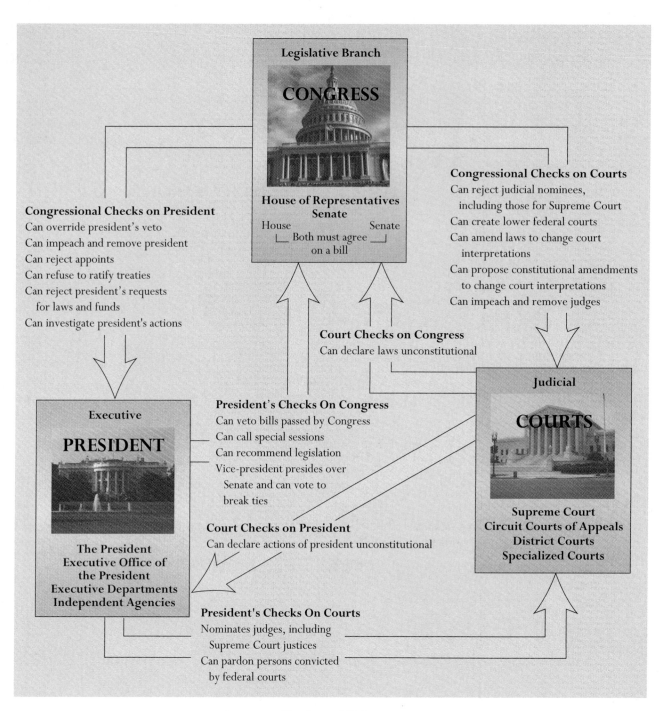

Congressional Checks on President

Can override president's veto

Can impeach and remove president

Can reject appoints

Can refuse to ratify treaties

Can reject president's requests
  for laws and funds

Can investigate president's actions

Legislative Branch

CONGRESS

**House of Representatives
Senate**

House   Senate

└─ Both must agree ─┘
      on a bill

Congressional Checks on Courts

Can reject judicial nominees,
  including those for Supreme Court

Can create lower federal courts

Can amend laws to change court
  interpretations

Can propose constitutional amendments
  to change court interpretations

Can impeach and remove judges

Court Checks on Congress

Can declare laws unconstitutional

President's Checks On Congress

Can veto bills passed by Congress

Can call special sessions

Can recommend legislation

Vice-president presides over
  Senate and can vote to
  break ties

Executive

PRESIDENT

**The President
Executive Office of
the President
Executive Departments
Independent Agencies**

Judicial

COURTS

**Supreme Court
Circuit Courts of Appeals
District Courts
Specialized Courts**

Court Checks on President

Can declare actions of president unconstitutional

President's Checks On Courts

Nominates judges, including
  Supreme Court justices

Can pardon persons convicted
  by federal courts

FIGURE 3.1   Checks and Balances

Judicial review, which is not specifically mentioned in the Constitution itself, is the power of the judiciary to overturn laws of Congress and the states and actions of the president that the courts believe violate the Constitution (see "Judicial Power" in Chapter 13). Judicial review, in short, ensures compliance with the Constitution.

Many Federalists, including Alexander Hamilton, believed the Constitution of 1787 clearly implied that the Supreme Court could invalidate any laws of Congress or presidential actions it believed to be unconstitutional. Hamilton wrote in 1787, "[Limited government] . . . can be preserved in no other way than through the

judicial review Power of the U.S. Supreme Court and federal judiciary to declare laws of Congress and the states and actions of the president unconstitutional and therefore legally invalid.

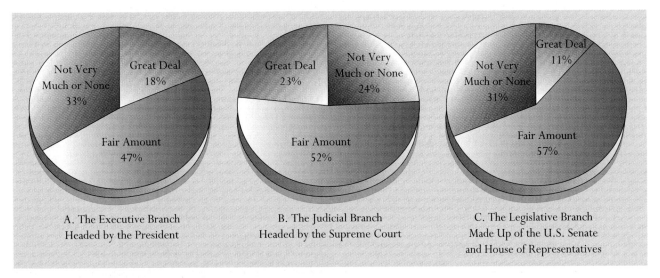

A. The Executive Branch
Headed by the President

B. The Judicial Branch
Headed by the Supreme Court

C. The Legislative Branch
Made Up of the U.S. Senate
and House of Representatives

FIGURE 3.2 Trust and Confidence in the Three Branches of Government

As you know, the federal government is made up of three branches: an Executive branch, headed by the President, a Judicial branch, headed by the U.S. Supreme Court, and a Legislative branch, made up of the U.S. Senate and House of Representatives. How much trust and confidence do you have at this time in [A,B,C]— a great deal, a fair amount, not very much, or none at all? (Mechanism not shown.)

Source: Gallup Poll, July, 2000, as reported in *The Polling Report*, www.pollingreport.com. Copyright © 2000 by The Gallup Organization.

medium of courts of justice, whose duty it is to declare all acts contrary to the manifest tenor of the Constitution void."[7] But it was not until *Marbury v. Madison* in 1803 that Chief Justice John Marshall asserted a Supreme Court ruling that the Supreme Court possessed the power of judicial review over laws of Congress. (See *People in Politics:* "John Marshall and Early Supreme Court Politics" in Chapter 13.) Today the American people express more trust and confidence in the Supreme Court than in either the president or the Congress (see Figure 3.2).

Conflict over Ratification

Today the U.S. Constitution is a revered document, but in the winter of 1787–88, the Founders had real doubts about whether they could get it accepted as "the supreme Law of the Land." Indeed, the Constitution was ratified by only the narrowest of margins in the key states of Massachusetts, Virginia, and New York.

The Founders adopted a **ratification** procedure that was designed to enhance chances for acceptance of the Constitution. The ratification procedure written into the new Constitution was a complete departure from what was then supposed to be the law of the land, the Articles of Confederation, in two major ways. First, the Articles of Confederation required that amendments be approved by *all* of the states. But since Rhode Island was firmly in the hands of small farmers, the Founders knew that unanimous approval was unlikely. So they simply wrote into their new Constitution that approval required only nine of the states. Second, the Founders called for special ratifying conventions in the states rather than risk submitting the Constitution to the state legislatures. Because the Constitution placed many prohibitions on the powers of states, the Founders believed that special constitutional ratifying conventions would be more likely to approve the document than would state legislatures.

ratification Power of a legislature to approve or reject decisions made by other bodies. State legislators or state conventions must ratify constitutional amendments submitted by Congress. The U.S. Senate must ratify treaties made by the president.

FIGURE 3.3 The Fight over Ratification

Source: Map from p. 118, retitled "The Fight Over Ratification," from Encyclopedia of American History by Richard B. Morris, editor and Jeffrey B. Morris, assistant editor. Copyright 1953, © 1961, 1965, 1970, 1976 by Harper & Row Publishers, Inc. Reprinted by permission of HarperCollins Publishers, Inc.

The Founders enjoyed some important tactical advantages over the opposition. First, the Constitutional Convention was held in secret; potential opponents did not know what was coming out of it. Second, the Founders called for ratifying conventions to be held as quickly as possible so that the opposition could not get itself organized. Many state conventions met during the winter months, so it was difficult for some rural opponents of the Constitution to get to their county seats in order to vote (see Figure 3.3 above).

The Founders also waged a very professional (for 1787–88) media campaign in support of the Constitution. James Madison, Alexander Hamilton, and John Jay issued a series of eighty-five press releases, signed simply "Publius," on behalf of the Constitution. Major newspapers ran these essays, which were later collected and published as *The Federalist Papers.* The essays provide an excellent description and explanation of the Constitution by three of its writers and even today serve as a principal reference for political scientists and judges faced with constitutional ambiguities (see *People in Politics:* "James Madison and the Control of 'Faction'"). Two of the most important *Federalist Papers* are reprinted in the Appendix to this textbook.

Nevertheless, opponents of the Constitution—the Anti-Federalists—almost succeeded in defeating the document in New York and Virginia. They charged that the new Constitution would create an "aristocratic tyranny" and pose a threat to the "spirit of republicanism." They argued that the new Senate would be an aristocratic upper house and the new president a ruling monarch. They complained that neither the Senate nor the president were directly elected by the people. They also argued that the new national government would trample state governments and deny the people of the states the opportunity to handle their own political and economic affairs. Virginia patriot Patrick Henry urged the defeat of the

James Madison and the Control of "Faction"

The most important contributions to American democracy by James Madison (1751–1836) were his work in helping to write the Constitution and his insightful and scholarly defense of it during the ratification struggle. Indeed, Madison is more highly regarded by political scientists and historians as a *political theorist* then as the fourth president of the United States.

Madison's family owned a large plantation in Virginia. He graduated from the College of New Jersey (now Princeton University) at eighteen and assumed a number of elected and appointed positions in Virginia's colonial government. In 1776 Madison drafted a new Virginia Constitution. While serving in Virginia's Revolutionary assembly, he met Thomas Jefferson; the two became lifetime political allies and friends. In 1787 Madison represented Virginia at the Constitutional Convention and took a leading role in its debates over the form of a new federal government.

Madison's political insights are revealed in *The Federalist Papers,* a series of eighty-five essays published in major newspapers in 1787–88, all signed simply "Publius." Alexander Hamilton and John Jay contributed some of them, but Madison wrote the two most important essays. Number 10, which explains the nature of political conflict (faction) and how it can be "controlled", and Number 51, which explains the system of separation of powers and checks and balances (both reprinted in the Appendix of this textbook). According to Madison, "controlling faction" was the principal task of government.

What creates faction? Madison believed that conflict is part of human nature. In all societies, we find "a zeal for different opinions concerning religion, concerning government, and many other points," as well as "an attachment to different leaders ambitiously contending for preeminence and power." Even when there are no serious differences among people, these "frivolous and fanciful distinctions" will inspire "unfriendly passions" and "violent conflicts."

Clearly, Madison believed conflict could arise over just about any matter. Yet "the most common and durable source of factions, has been the various and unequal distribution of property." That is, economic conflicts between rich and poor and between people with different kinds of wealth and sources of income are the most serious conflicts confronting society.

Madison argued that factions could best be controlled in a republican government extending over a large society with a "variety of parties and interests." He defended republicanism (representative democracy) over "pure democracy," which he believed "incompatible with personal security, or the rights of property." And he argued that protection against "factious combinations" can be achieved by including a great variety of competing interests in the political system so that no one interest will be able to "outnumber and oppress the rest." Modern pluralist political theory (see Chapter 1) claims Madison as a forerunner.

Constitution "to preserve the poor Commonwealth of Virginia." Finally, their most effective argument was that the new Constitution lacked a bill of rights to protect individual liberty from government abuse (see *A Conflicting View:* "Objections to the Constitution by an Anti-Federalist" on page 83).

A Bill of Rights

It may be hard to imagine today, but the original Constitution had no **Bill of Rights**. This was a particularly glaring deficiency because many of the new state constitutions proudly displayed these written guarantees of individual liberty.

The Founders certainly believed in limited government and individual liberty, and they did write a few liberties into the body of the Constitution, including protection against ex post facto laws, a limited definition of treason, a guarantee of the writ of habeas corpus, and a guarantee of trial by jury (see Chapter 14).

Bill of Rights Written guarantees of basic individual liberties; the first ten amendments to the U.S. Constitution.

Canada's Parliamentary System

The United States and Canada are both democracies, but there are very important differences in the way Americans and Canadians govern themselves.

Canada is recognized as a constitutional monarchy rather than a republic. Officially the head of state for Canada is the Queen of England, who is represented in Canada by a Governor-General. The Governor-General, and occasionally the queen, undertake ceremonial roles in Canada. The Canadian government was initially established by the British North American Act of 1867, passed by the British Parliament.

Rather than a separation of powers between the legislative, executive, and judicial branches of government as in the United States, governmental powers in Canada are concentrated in the hands of the Prime Minister and his Cabinet. The Prime Minister is the leader of the majority party in the Canadian House of Commons. The PM names the Cabinet. The PM and the Cabinet are themselves members of the House of Commons. All legislation is initiated by the PM and the Cabinet for submission to the House of Commons. Passage is almost always assured because the PM's party controls the House of Commons. In the event of a defeat of a PM and the

Cabinet, usually on a motion of censure or went of confidence, the PM and the Cabinet resign, and the Governor-General calls for new elections to the House of Commons. There is no specific "term" of office for the PM and Cabinet; they stay in office as long as they have the support of the House of Commons. However, by tradition, new elections are always held sometime within a five-year period. Occasionally, "by-elections" are held to replace Members of Parliament who have died or resigned.

The House of Commons currently includes 301 Members of Parliament (MPs). The Canadian Senate usually rubber-stamps legislation passed by the House of Commons, although occasionally it adds amendments or clarifications that are accepted by the House of Commons. The Senate is appointed by the Prime Minister, membership is generally considered an honor rather than a responsibility. Currently, five parties are represented in the House of Commons (see *Compared to What?* "Canada's Multiparty System" in Chapter 7). The Liberal Party currently holds a majority; its leader, Paul Martin, is the Prime Minister. The second-largest party in the House of Commons is officially known as the Opposition, and its leader the Leader of the Opposition.

Canadians view their parliamentary system as more responsible and responsive than the separate presidential and congressional branches of the U.S. government.

Parenthetical numbers indicate how many seats each province has in the House of Commons.

Objections to the Constitution by an Anti-Federalist

Virginia's George Mason was a delegate to the Constitutional Convention of 1787, but he refused to sign the final document and became a leading opponent of the new Constitution. Mason was a wealthy plantation owner and a heavy speculator in western (Ohio) lands. He was a friend of George Washington's, but he considered most other political figures of his day to be "babblers" and he generally avoided public office. However, in 1776 he authored Virginia's Declaration of Rights, which was widely copied in other state constitutions and later became the basis for the Bill of Rights. Although an ardent supporter of states' rights, he attended the Constitutional Convention of 1787 and, according to James Madison's notes on the proceedings, was an influential force in shaping the new national government. His refusal to sign the Constitution and his subsequent leadership of the opposition to its ratification made him the recognized early leader of the Anti-Federalists.

Mason's first objection to the Constitution was that it included no Bill of Rights. But he also objected to the powers given to the Senate, which was not directly elected by the people in the original document; to the federal courts; and to the president. He was wary of the Necessary and Proper Clause, which granted Congress the power to "make all laws which shall be necessary and proper" for carrying out the enumerated powers—those specifically mentioned in the Constitution. Mason correctly predicted that this clause would be used to preempt the powers of the states.

In his "objections to the Constitution" Mason wrote,

> There is no declaration of rights; and the laws of the general government being paramount to the laws and constitutions of the several States, the declaration of rights in the separate States are no security.

> Senators are not the representatives of the people, or amenable to them.

> The judiciary of the United States is so constructed and extended as to absorb and destroy the judiciaries of the several States; thereby rendering law as tedious, intricate and expensive. . .

> Under their own construction of the general clause at the end of the enumerated powers, the Congress may . . . extend their power as far as they shall think proper; so that the State Legislatures have no security for the powers now presumed to remain to them; or the people for their rights.

Note that virtually all of Mason's objections to the original Constitution had to be remedied at a later date. The Bill of Rights was added as the first ten amendments. Eventually (1913) the Seventeenth Amendment provided for the direct election of U.S. senators. And Mason correctly predicted that the federal judiciary would eventually render the law "tedious, intricate, and expensive" and that the Necessary and Proper Clause, which he refers to as "the general clause at the end of the enumerated powers," would be used to expand congressional powers at the expense of the states.

The Federalists argued that there was really no need for a bill of rights because (1) the national government was one of **enumerated powers** only, meaning it could not exercise any power not expressly enumerated, or granted, in the Constitution; (2) the power to limit free speech or press, establish a religion, or otherwise restrain individual liberty was not among the enumerated powers; (3) therefore it was not necessary to specifically deny these powers to the new government. But the Anti-Federalists were unwilling to rest fundamental freedoms on a thin thread of logical inference from the notion of enumerated powers. They wanted specific written guarantees that the new national government would not interfere with the rights of individuals or the powers of the states. So Federalists at the New York, Massachusetts, and Virginia ratifying conventions promised to support the addition of a bill of rights to the Constitution in the very first Congress.

enumerated powers
Powers specifically mentioned in the Constitution as belonging to the national government.

TABLE 3.3 The Bill of Rights

Guaranteeing Freedom of Expression

First Amendment prohibits the government from abridging freedom of speech, press, assembly, and petition.

Guaranteeing Religious Freedom

First Amendment prohibits the government from establishing a religion or interfering with the free exercise of religion.

Affirming the Right to Bear Arms and Protecting Citizens from Quartering Troops

Second Amendment guarantees the right to bear arms.
Third Amendment prohibits troops from occupying citizens' homes in peacetime.

Protecting the Rights of Accused Persons

Fourth Amendment protects against unreasonable searches and seizures.
Fifth Amendment requires an indictment by a grand jury for serious crimes; prohibits the government from trying a person twice for the same crime; prohibits the government from taking life, liberty, or property without due process of law; and prohibits the government from taking private property for public use without fair compensation to the owner.
Sixth Amendment guarantees a speedy and public jury trial, the right to confront witnesses in court, and the right to legal counsel for defense.
Seventh Amendment guarantees the right to a jury trial in civil cases.
Eighth Amendment prohibits the government from setting excessive bail or fines or inflicting cruel and unusual punishment.

Protecting the Rights of People and States

Ninth Amendment protects all other unspecified rights of the people.
Tenth Amendment reserves to the states or to the people those powers neither granted to the federal government nor prohibited to the states in the Constitution.

WWW James Madison
The legacy of Madison organized by topic.
www.jmu.edu/madison

A young member of the new House of Representatives, James Madison, rose in 1789 and presented a bill of rights that he had drawn up after reviewing more than 200 recommendations sent from the states. Interestingly, the new Congress was so busy debating new tax laws that Madison had a difficult time attracting attention to his bill. Eventually, in September 1789, Congress approved a Bill of Rights as ten **amendments,** or formal changes, to the Constitution and sent them to the states. (Congress actually passed twelve amendments. One was never ratified; another, dealing with pay raises for Congress, was not ratified by the necessary three-quarters of the states until 1992.) The states promptly ratified the first ten amendments to the Constitution (see Table 3.3 above), and these changes took effect in 1791.

The Bill of Rights was originally designed to limit the powers of the new *national* government. The Bill of Rights begins with the command "Congress shall make no law. . . ." It was not until after the Civil War that the Constitution was amended to also prohibit states from violating individual liberties. The Fourteenth Amendment, ratified in 1868, includes the command "No State shall. . . ." It prohibits the states from depriving any person of "life, liberty or property, without due process of law," or abridging "the privileges or immunities of citizens of the United States," or denying any person "equal protection of the laws." Today virtually all of the liberties guaranteed in the Constitution protect individuals not only from the national government but also from state governments.

amendment Formal change in a bill, law, or constitution.

Constitutional Change

The purpose of a constitution is to govern government—to place limits on governmental power. Thus government itself must not be able to alter or amend a constitution easily. Yet the U.S. Constitution has changed over time, sometimes by formal amendment and other times by judicial interpretation, presidential and congressional action, and general custom and practice.

Amendments A constitutional amendment must first be proposed, and then it must be ratified. The Constitution allows two methods of *proposing* a constitutional amendment: (1) by passage in the House and the Senate with a two-thirds vote, or (2) by passage in a national convention called by Congress in response to petitions by two-thirds of the state legislatures. Congress then chooses the method of *ratification,* which can be either (1) by vote in the legislatures of three-fourths of the states, or (2) by vote in conventions called for that purpose in three-fourths of the states (see Figure 3.4 below).

Of the four possible combinations of proposal and ratification, the method involving proposal by a two-thirds vote of Congress and ratification by three-quarters of the legislatures has been used for all the amendments except one. Only for the Twenty-first Amendment's repeal of Prohibition did Congress call for state ratifying conventions (principally because Congress feared that southern Bible Belt state legislatures would vote against repeal). The method of proposal by national convention has never been used.

In addition to the Bill of Rights, most of the constitutional amendments ratified over the nation's 200 years have expanded our notion of democracy. Today the Constitution includes 27 amendments, which means that only 17 (out of more

THINK AGAIN

Should the Constitution be amended to guarantee that equal rights shall not be denied based on sex?

 The Anti-Federalist Papers

Essays by Anti-Federalists opposed to the ratification of the Constitution. *www.thisnation.com/library/ antifederalist*

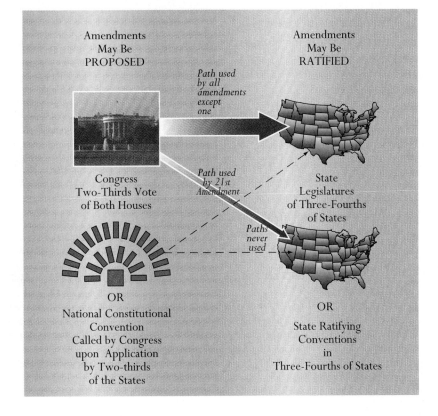

**FIGURE 3.4
Constitutional Amendment Process**

The Constitution set up two alternative routes for proposing amendments and two for ratifying them. One of the four possible combinations has actually been used for all except one (the Twenty-first) amendment. However, in our time there have been persistent calls for a constitutional convention to propose new amendments permitting school prayer, making abortion illegal, and requiring a balanced national budget.

Figure labels:
Amendments May Be PROPOSED
Amendments May Be RATIFIED
Path used by all amendments except one
Path used by 21st Amendment
Paths never used
Congress Two-Thirds Vote of Both Houses
OR
National Constitutional Convention Called by Congress upon Application by Two-thirds of the States
State Legislatures of Three-Fourths of States
OR
State Ratifying Conventions in Three-Fourths of States

Equal Rights Amendment (ERA) Proposed amendment to the Constitution guaranteeing that equal rights under the law shall not be denied or abridged on account of sex. Passed by Congress in 1972, the amendment failed to win ratification by three of the necessary three-fourths of the states.

than 10,000) proposed amendments have been ratified since the passage of the Bill of Rights. It is possible to classify the amendments that have been ratified into the broad categories of constitutional processes, Prohibition, income tax, individual liberty, and voting rights (see Table 3.4 below).

Amending the U.S. Constitution requires not only a two-thirds vote in both houses of Congress, reflecting *national* support, but also ratification by three-fourths of the states, reflecting widespread support within the states. The fate of the **Equal Rights Amendment**, popularly known as the ERA, illustrates the need for nationwide consensus in order to amend the Constitution. The Equal Rights Amendment is a simple statement to which the vast majority of Americans agree, according to public opinion polls: "Equality of rights under the law shall not be denied or abridged by the United States or any state on account of sex." Congress passed the ERA in 1972 with far more than the necessary two-thirds vote; both Republicans

TABLE 3.4 Amendments to the Constitution Since the Bill of Rights

Perfecting Constitutional Processes

Eleventh Amendment (1798) forbids federal lawsuits against a state by citizens of another state or nation

Twelfth Amendment (1804) provides separate ballots for president and vice president in the Electoral College to prevent confusion.

Twentieth Amendment (1933) determines the dates for the beginning of the terms of Congress (January 3) and the president (January 20).

Twenty-second Amendment (1951) limits the president to two terms.

Twenty-fifth Amendment (1967) provides for presidential disability.

Twenty-seventh Amendment (1992) prevents Congress from raising its own pay in a single session.

The Experiment with Prohibition

Eighteenth Amendment (1919) prohibits the manufacture, sale, or transportation of intoxicating liquors.

Twenty-first Amendment (1933) repeals the Eighteenth Amendment.

The Income Tax

Sixteenth Amendment (1913) allows Congress to tax incomes.

Expanding Liberty

Thirteenth Amendment (1865) abolishes slavery.

Fourteenth Amendment (1868) protects life, liberty, and property and the privileges and immunities of citizenship and provides equal protection of the law.

Expanding Voting Rights

Fifteenth Amendment (1870) guarantees that the right to vote shall not be denied because of race.

Seventeenth Amendment (1913) provides for the election of senators by the people of each state.

Nineteenth Amendment (1920) guarantees that the right to vote shall not be denied because of sex.

Twenty-third Amendment (1961) gives the District of Columbia electoral votes for presidential elections.

Twenty-fourth Amendment (1964) guarantees that the right to vote shall not be denied because of failure to pay a poll tax or other tax.

Twenty-sixth Amendment (1971) guarantees that the right to vote shall not be denied to persons eighteen years of age or older.

and Democrats supported the ERA, and it was endorsed by Presidents Nixon, Ford, and Carter as well as most other national political leaders and organizations. By 1978, thirty-five state legislatures had ratified the amendment—three states short of the necessary thirty-eight (three-quarters). (Five states subsequently voted to rescind, or cancel, their earlier ratification. However, because there is no language in the Constitution regarding rescission, there is some disagreement about the constitutionality of this action.) Promising that the "ERA won't go away," proponents of the amendment have continued to press their case. But to date Congress has not acted to resubmit the ERA to the states.

Judicial Interpretations Some of the greatest changes in the Constitution have come about not by formal amendment but by interpretations of the document by federal courts, notably to U.S. Supreme Court.

Indeed, through **judicial review,** the U.S. Supreme Court has come to play the central role in giving meaning to the Constitution. Judicial review is the power of federal courts, and ultimately the Supreme Court, to declare laws of Congress and actions of the president unconstitutional and therefore invalid. This power was first asserted by Chief Justice John Marshall in the case of *Marbury vs. Madison* in 1803 (see *People in Politics:* "John Marshall and Early Supreme Court Politics" in Chapter 13). It is now an important part of the system of checks and balances (see Figure 3.1). This power is itself an interpretation of the Constitution, because it is not specifically mentioned in the document.

Supreme Court interpretations of the Constitution have given specific meaning to many of our most important constitutional phrases. Among the most important examples of constitutional change through judicial interpretation are the important meanings given to the Fourteenth Amendment, particularly its provisions that "No State shall . . . deprive any person of life, liberty, or property, without due process of law; nor deny to any person within its jurisdiction the equal protection of the laws":

- Deciding that "equal protection of the laws" requires an end to segregation of the races (*Brown v. Board of Education of Topeka,* 1954, and subsequent decisions).

- Deciding that "liberty" includes a woman's right to choose an abortion, and that the term *person* does not include the unborn fetus (*Roe v. Wade,* 1973, and subsequent decisions).

- Deciding that "equal protection of the laws" requires that every person's vote should be weighed equally in apportionment and districting plans for the House of Representatives, state legislatures, city councils, and so on (*Baker v. Carr,* 1964, and subsequent decisions).

Presidential and Congressional Action Congress and the president have also undertaken to interpret the Constitution. Nearly every president, for example, has argued that the phrase "executive Power" in Article II includes more than the specific powers mentioned afterward. Thomas Jefferson purchased the Louisiana Territory from France in 1803 even though there is no constitutional authorization for the president, or even the national government, to acquire new territory. Presidents from George Washington to Richard Nixon have argued that Congress cannot force the executive branch to turn over documents it does not wish to disclose (see Chapter 11).

Congress by law has tried to restrict the president's power as Commander-in-Chief of the Armed Forces by requiring the president to notify Congress when U.S.

judicial review The power of federal courts to declare laws of Congress and actions of the president unconstitutional.

troops are sent to "situations where imminent involvement in hostilities is clearly indicated" and limiting their stay to sixty days unless Congress authorizes an extension. This War Powers Act (1973), passed by Congress over President Richard Nixon's veto in the immediate aftermath of the Vietnam War, has been ignored by every president to date (see Chapter 11). Yet it indicates that Congress has its own ideas about interpreting the Constitution.

Custom and Practice Finally, the Constitution changes over time as a result of generally accepted customs and practice. It is interesting to note, for example, that the Constitution never mentions political parties. (Many of the Founders disapproved of parties because they caused "faction" among the people.) But soon after Thomas Jefferson resigned as President Washington's first secretary of state (in part because he resented the influence of Secretary of the Treasury Alexander Hamilton), the Virginian attracted the support of Anti-Federalists, who believed the national government was too strong. When Washington retired from office, most Federalists supported John Adams as his successor. But many Anti-Federalists ran for posts as presidential electors, promising to be "Jefferson's men." Adams won the presidential election of 1796, but the Anti-Federalists organized themselves into a political party, the Democratic-Republicans, to oppose Adams in the election of 1800. The party secured pledges from candidates for presidential elector to cast their electoral vote for Jefferson if they won their post, then the party helped win support for its slate of electors. In this way the Electoral College was transformed from a deliberative body where leading citizens from each state came together to decide for themselves who should be president into a ceremonial body where pledged electors simply cast their presidential vote for the candidate who had carried their state in the presidential election. (For a full discussion of the current operation of the Electoral College, see *Up Close:* "Understanding the Electoral College" in Chapter 8.)

SUMMARY NOTES

■ The true meaning of constitutionalism is the limitation of governmental power. Constitutions govern governments; they are designed to restrict those who exercise governmental power. Constitutions not only establish governmental bodies and prescribe the rules by which they make their decisions, but, more important, they also limit the powers of government.

■ The American tradition of written constitutions extends back through the Articles of Confederation, the colonial charters, and the Mayflower Compact to the thirteenth-century English Magna Carta. The Second Continental Congress in 1776 adopted a written Declaration of Independence to justify the colonies' separation from Great Britain. All of these documents strengthened the idea of a written contract defining governmental power.

■ The movement for a Constitutional Convention in 1787 was inspired by the new government's inability to levy taxes under the Articles of Confederation, its inability to fund the Revolutionary War debt, obstacles to interstate commerce, monetary problems, and civil disorders, including Shays's Rebellion.

■ The nation's Founders—fifty-five delegates to the Constitutional Convention in Philadelphia in 1787—shared a broad consensus on liberty and property, the social contract, republicanism, limited government, and the need for a national government.

■ The Founders compromised their differences over representation by creating two co-equal houses in the Congress: the House of Representatives, with members apportioned to the states on the basis of population and directly elected by the people for two-year terms, and the Senate, with two members allotted to each state regardless of its population and originally selected by state legislatures for six-year terms.

■ The infamous slavery provisions in the Constitution—counting each slave as three-fifths of a person for purposes of taxation and representation, guaranteeing the return of escaped slaves, and postponing the end of the slave trade for twenty years—were also compromises. Voter qualifications in national elections were left to the states to determine.

■ The structure of the national government reflects the Founders' beliefs in national supremacy, federalism, republicanism, separation of powers, checks and balances, and judicial review.

■ The original Constitution gave the people very little influence on their government: only members of the House of Representatives were directly elected; senators were elected by state legislatures; the president was elected indirectly by "electors" chosen in each state; and members of the Supreme Court and federal judiciary were appointed for life by the president and confirmed by the Senate. Over time, the national government became more democratic through the expansion of voting rights, the direct election of senators, the emergence of political parties, and the practice of voting for presidential electors pledged to cast their vote for the candidates of one party.

■ The separation of powers and checks and balances written into the Constitution was designed, in Madison's words, "to divide and arrange the several offices in such a manner as that each may be a check on the other." Judicial review was not specifically described in the original Constitution, but the Supreme Court soon asserted its power to overturn laws of Congress and the states, as well as presidential actions, that the Court determined to be in conflict with the Constitution.

■ Opposition to the new Constitution was strong. Anti-Federalists argued that it created a national government that was aristocratic, undemocratic, and a threat to the rights of the states and the people. Their concerns resulted in the Bill of Rights: ten amendments added to the original Constitution, all designed to limit the power of the national government and protect the rights of individuals and states.

■ Over time, constitutional changes have come about as a result of formal amendments, judicial interpretations, presidential and congressional actions, and changes in custom and practice. The most common method of constitutional amendment has been proposal by two-thirds vote of both houses of Congress followed by ratification by three-fourths of the state legislatures.

KEY TERMS

constitutionalism   54
constitution   54
republicanism   60
nationalism   60
taxes   63

tariff   65
common market   65
referenda   68
separation of powers   69
checks and balances   70

judicial review   72
ratification   73
Bill of Rights   75
enumerated powers   77
amendment   78

Equal Rights Amendment
   (ERA)   80
judicial review   81

SUGGESTED READINGS

Beard, Charles. *An Economic Interpretation of the Constitution.* New York: Macmillan, 1913. A classic work setting forth the argument that economic self-interest inspired the Founders in writing the Constitution.

Finkelman, Paul. *Slavery and the Founders.* 2nd ed. Armark NY: M.E. Sharpe, 2000. A critical account of the Founders' attitudes toward slavery and the resulting 3/5th's compromise.

Frohren, Bruce. Ed. *The American Republic: Primary Sources.* Indianapolis: Liberty Fund Inc., 2002. Excellent collection of earliest American documents, from the Mayflower Compact to the Declaration of Independence.

Madison, James, Alexander Hamilton, and John Jay. *The Federalist Papers.* New York: Modern Library, 1937. These eighty-five collected essays, written in 1787–88 in support of ratification of the Constitution, remain the most important commentary on that document. Numbers 10 and 51 (reprinted in the Appendix) ought to be required reading for all students of American government.

McDonald, Forrest B. *Novus Ordo Seculorum.* Lawrence: University Press of Kansas, 1986. A description of the intellectual origins of the Constitution and the "new secular order" that it represented.

Peltason, J.W. and Sue Davis. *Understanding the Constitution.* 16th ed. New York: Harcourt Brace, 2004. Of the many books that explain the Constitution, this is one of the best. It contains explanations of the Declaration of Independence, the Articles of Confederation, and the Constitution. The book is written clearly and well suited for undergraduates.

Rossiter, Clinton L. 1787, *The Grand Convention.* New York: Macmillan, 1960. A very readable account of the people and events surrounding the Constitutional Convention in 1787, with many insights into the conflicts and compromises that took place there.

Storing, Herbert J. *What the Anti-Federalists Were For.* Chicago: University of Chicago Press, 1981. An examination of the arguments of the Anti-Federalists in opposition to the ratification of the Constitution.

MAKE IT REAL

THE CONSTITUTION: WHAT IF YOU WERE A FOUNDING FATHER?

The democratic principles that guide this nation are embodied in the Constitution, or are they? In this simulation, it is 1789 and you have been asked to make final revisions on the Constitution. You will be challenged to apply some of the principles, both modern and traditional, to the original Constitution. Decide whether or not to include these principles and see how your choices might affect the Constitution and American history.

The Constitution of the United States

THE PREAMBLE

We the People of the United States, in Order to form a more perfect Union, establish Justice, insure domestic Tranquility, provide for the common defense, promote the general Welfare, and secure the Blessings of Liberty to ourselves and our Posterity, do ordain and establish this Constitution for the United States of America.

"We, the people." Three simple words, yet of profound importance and contentious origin. Every government in the world at the time of the Constitutional Convention was some type of monarchy wherein sovereign power flowed from the top. The Founders of our new country rejected monarchy as a form of government and proposed instead a republic, which would draw its sovereignty from the people.

The Articles of Confederation that governed the U.S. from 1776 until 1789 started with: "We the under signed Delegates of the States." Early drafts of the new constitution started with: "We, the states . . ." But again, the Founders were not interested in another union of states but rather the creation of a new national government. Therefore, "We, the states" was changed to "We, the people." The remainder of the preamble describes the generic functions of government. These would apply to almost any type of government. Some have proven more critical than others. For example, "promote the general welfare" has been cited as the authority for social welfare programs of the federal government.

ARTICLE I—THE LEGISLATIVE ARTICLE

Legislative Power

The very first article in the Constitution established the legislative branch of the new national government. Why did the framers start with the legislative power instead of the executive branch? Under the Articles of Confederation, the legislature was the only functional instrument of government. Therefore, the framers truly believed it was the most important component of the new government.

Section 1 All legislative Powers herein granted shall be vested in a Congress of the United States, which shall consist of a Senate and House of Representatives.

Section 1 established a bicameral (two-chamber) legislature or an upper (Senate) and lower (House of Representatives) organization of the legislative branch.

House of Representatives: Composition; Qualifications; Apportionment; Impeachment Power

Section 2 Clause 1. The House of Representatives shall be composed of Members chosen every second Year by the People of the several States, and the Electors in each State shall have the Qualifications requisite for Electors of the most numerous Branch of the State Legislature.

This section sets the term of office for House members (2 years) and indicates that those voting for Congress will have the same qualifications as those voting for the state legislatures. Originally, states limited voters to white property owners. Some states even had religious disqualifications, such as Catholic or Jewish. Most property and religious qualifications for voting were removed by the 1840s, but race and gender restrictions remained.

Clause 2. No Person shall be a Representative who shall not have attained to the Age of twenty five Years, and been seven Years a Citizen of the United States, and who shall not, when elected, be an inhabitant of that State in which he shall be chosen.

This section sets forth the basic qualifications of a representative: at least 25 years of age, a U.S. citizen for at least 7 years, and a resident of a state. Note that the Constitution does not require a person to be a resident of the district he or she represents. At the time the Constitution was written, life expectancy was about 43 years of age. So a person 25 years old was middle aged. Considering today's life expectancy of about 78 years, the equivalent age of 25 would be about 45. The average age of a current representative is 53. Because of the specificity of the Constitution as to the qualifications for office, the U.S. Supreme Court ruled that term limits could not be imposed.

Clause 2 does not specify how many terms a Representative can serve in Congress. One provision of the Republican House *Contract with America* "The Citizens Legislature Act" called for term limits for legislators. This provision was not enacted. Subsequently some states passed legislation to limit the terms of their U.S. Representatives. Because of the specificity of the qualifications for office, the USSC ruled in *U.S. Term Limits, Inc. v. Thornton*, 514 U.S. 779 (1995) that term limits for U.S. legislators could not be imposed by any state but would require a constitution amendment.

Clause 3. Representatives and direct Taxes[1] shall be appointed among the several States which may be included within this Union, according to their respective Numbers, which shall be determined by adding to the whole Number of free Persons, including those bound to Service for a Term of Years, and excluding Indians not taxed, three fifths of all other Persons.[2] The actual Enumeration shall be made within three Years after the first Meeting of the Congress of the United States, and within every subsequent Term of ten Years in such Manner as they shall by Law direct. The Number of Representatives shall not exceed one for every thirty Thousand, but each State shall have at Least one Representative, and until such enumeration shall be made, the State of New Hampshire shall be entitled to chuse three, Massachusetts eight Rhode Island and Providence Plantations one, Connecticut five, New York six, New Jersey four, Pennsylvania eight, Delaware one, Maryland six, Virginia ten, North Carolina five, South Carolina five, and Georgia three.

This clause contains the Three-Fifths Compromise wherein American Indians and Blacks were only counted as 3/5 of a person for congressional representation purposes. This clause also addresses the question of congressional reapportionment every 10 years, which requires a census. Since the 1911 Reapportionment Act, the size of the House of Representatives has been set at 435. This is the designated size that is reapportioned every 10 years. Based on changes of population, some states gain and some states lose representatives. This clause also provides that every state, regardless of population, will have at least one (1) representative. Currently, seven states have only one representative.

Clause 4. When vacancies happen in the Representation from any State, the Executive Authority thereof shall issue Writs of Election to fill such Vacancies.

This clause provides a procedure for replacing a U.S. representative in the case of death, resignation, or expulsion from the House. Essentially, the governor of the representative's state will assign a successor. Generally, if less than half a term is left, the governor will appoint a successor. If more than half a term is remaining, most states require a special election to fill the vacancy.

Clause 5. The House of Representatives shall chuse their Speaker and other Officers, and shall have the sole Power of Impeachment.

Only one officer of the House is specified—the Speaker. All other officers are decided by the House.

This clause also gives the House authority for impeachments (accusations) against officials of the executive and judicial branches.

Senate Composition: Qualifications, Impeachment Trials

Section 3 Clause 1. The Senate of the United States shall be composed of two Senators from each State, *chosen by the Legislature thereof*,[3] for six Years and each Senator shall have one Vote.

This clause treats each state equally—all have two senators each. Originally, senators were chosen by state legislators, but since passage and ratification of the 17th Amendment, they are now elected by popular vote. This clause also establishes the term of a senator—6 years—three times that of a House member.

Clause 2. Immediately after they shall be assembled in Consequence of the first Election, they shall be divided as equally as may be into three Classes. The Seats of the Senators of the first Class shall be vacated at the Expiration of the second Year, of the second Class at the Expiration of the fourth Year, and of the third Class at the Expiration of the sixth Year, so that one third may be chosen every second Year *and if Vacancies happen by Resignation, or otherwise, during the Recess of the Legislature of any State, the Executive thereof may make temporary Appointments until the next Meeting of the Legislature which shall then fill such Vacancies.*[4]

To prevent a wholesale election of senators every six years, this clause provides that one-third of the Senate will be elected every two years. Senate vacancies are filled similar as the House—either appointment by the governor or a special election.

Clause 3. No person shall be a Senator who shall not have attained to the Age of thirty Years, and been nine Years a Citizen of the United States, and who shall not, when elected be an Inhabitant of that State for which he shall be chosen.

This clause sets forth the qualifications for U.S. senator: at least 30 years old, a U.S. citizen for at least nine years, and a citizen of a state. The equivalent age of 30 today would be 54 years old. The average age of a U.S. senator at present is 58.3 years.

Clause 4. The Vice President of the United States shall be President of the Senate but shall have no Vote, unless they be equally divided.

The only constitutional duty of the vice president is specified in this clause—president of the Senate. This official only has a vote if there is a tie vote in the Senate; then the vice president's vote breaks the tie.

Clause 5. The Senate shall chuse their other Officers, and also a President pro tempore, in the Absence of the Vice President, or when he shall exercise the Office of President of the United States

One official office in the U.S. Senate is specified—temporary president, who fills in during the vice president's absence (which is normally the case). All other Senate officers are designated and selected by the Senate.

---

[1]Modified by the 16th Amendment
[2]Replaced by Section 2, 14th Amendment

[3]Repealed by the 17th Amendment
[4]Modified by the 17th Amendment

Clause 6. The Senate shall have the sole Power to try all Impeachments. When sitting for that Purpose, they shall be on Oath or Affirmation. When the President of the United States is tried, the Chief Justice shall preside. And no Person shall be convicted without the Concurrence of two thirds of the Members present.

Judgment in Cases of impeachment shall not extend further than to removal from Office, and disqualification to hold and enjoy any Office of honor. Trust or Profit under the United States, but the Party convicted shall nevertheless be liable and subject to Indictment, Trial, Judgment and Punishment according to Law.

The Senate acts as a trial court for impeached federal officials. If the accused is the president, the Chief Justice of the U.S. Supreme Court presides. Otherwise, the vice president normally presides. Conviction of the charges requires a 2/3 majority vote of those senators present at the time of the vote. Conviction results in the federal official's removal from office and disqualification to hold any other federal appointed office. Removal from office does not bar further prosecution under applicable criminal or civil laws, nor does it apparently bar one from elected office. A current representative, Alcee L. Hastings, was removed as a federal district judge. He subsequently ran for Congress and now represents Florida's 23rd Congressional District.

Congressional Elections: Times, Places, Manner

Section 4   The Times, Places and Manner of holding Elections for Senators and Representatives, shall be prescribed in each State by the Legislature thereof, but the Congress may at any time by Law make or alter such Regulations, except as to the Places of chusting Senators.

The Congress shall assemble at least once in every Year, *and such Meeting shall be on the first Monday in December, unless they shall by Law appoint a different Day.*[5]

The states determine the place and manner of electing representatives and senators, but Congress has the right to make or change these laws or regulations, except for the election sites. Congress is required to meet annually, and now, by law, annual meetings begin in January.

Powers and Duties of the Houses

Section 5   Clause 1. Each House shall be the Judge of the Elections, Returns and Qualifications of its own Members, and a Majority of each shall constitute a Quorum to do Business, but a smaller Number may adjourn from day to day, and may be authorized to compel the Attendance of absent Members, in such Manner, and under the Penalties as each House may provide.

This clause enables each legislative branch to essentially make its own rules. Normally, to take a vote, a quorum is necessary. But if no votes are scheduled, fewer than a quorum can convene a session.

Clause 2. Each House may determine the Rules of its Proceedings, punish its Members for disorderly Behaviour, and with the Concurrence of two thirds, expel a Member.

Essentially, each branch promulgates its own rules and punishes its own members. The ultimate punishment is expulsion of the member, which requires

---

[5]Changed by the 20th Amendment

a 2/3 vote. Expulsion does not prevent the member from running again.

Clause 3. Each House shall keep a Journal of its Proceedings, and from time to time publish the same, excepting such Parrs as may in their Judgment require Secrecy, and the Yeas and Nays of the Members of either House on any question shall, at the Desire of one fifth of those Present, be entered on the Journal

An official record called the Congressional Record, House Journal, etc., is kept for all sessions. It is a daily account of House and Senate floor debates, votes, and members' remarks. However, a record is not printed if a proceeding is closed to the public for security reasons. Many votes are by voice vote, and if at least 1/5 of the members request, a recorded vote of Yeas and Nays will be conducted and recorded. This procedure permits analysis of congressional role-call votes.

Clause 4. Neither House, during the Session of Congress shall, without the Consent of the other, adjourn for more than three days, nor to any other Place than that in which the two Houses shall be sitting.

This clause prevents one branch from adjourning for a long period of time or to some other location without the consent of the other branch.

Rights of Members

Section 6   Clause I. The Senators and Representatives shall receive a Compensation for their Services, to be ascertained by Law, and paid out of the Treasury of the United States. They shall in all Cases, except Treason Felony and Breach of the Peace, be privileged from Arrest during then Attendance at the Session of their respective Houses, and in going to and returning from the same, and for any Speech or Debate in either House, they shall not be questioned in any other Place.

This section ensures that senators and congressional representatives will be paid a salary from the U.S. Treasury. This salary is determined by no other than the legislature. According to the Library of Congress legislative Web site THOMAS "The current salary for members of Congress is $145,100. A small number of leadership positions, like Speaker of the House, receive a somewhat higher salary." In addition, members of Congress receive many other benefits; free health care, fully funded retirement system, free gyms, 26 free round trips to their home state or district, etc. This section also provides immunity from arrest or prosecution for congressional actions on the floor or in travel to and from the Congress. For example, few members of Congress have ever been charged with drunk driving.

Clause 2. No Senator or Representative, shall, during the Time for which he was elected, be appointed to any civil Office under the Authority of the United States, which shall have been created, or the Emoluments whereof shall have been encreased during such time; and no Person holding any Office under the United States, shall be a Member of either House during his Continuance in Office.

This section prevents the U.S. from adopting a parliamentary democracy, since congressional members cannot hold executive offices and members of the executive branch cannot be members of Congress.

Legislative Powers: Bills and Resolutions

Section 7 Clause 1. All Bills for raising Revenue shall originate in the House of Representatives; but the Senate may propose or concur with Amendments as on other Bills.

This clause specifies one of the few powers specific to the U.S. House—revenue bills.

Clause 2. Every Bill which shall have passed the House of Representatives and the Senate, shall, before it becomes a Law, be presented to the President of the United States; If he approve be shall sign it, but if nor he shall return it, with his Objections to that House in which it shall have originated, who shall enter the Objections at large on their Journal, and proceed to reconsider it. If after such Reconsideration two thirds of that House shall agree to pass the Bill, it shall be sent, together with the Objections, to the other House, by which it shall likewise be reconsidered, and if approved by two thirds of that House, it shall become a Law. But in all such Cases the Votes of both Houses shall be determined by yeas and Nays, and the Names of the Persons voting for and against the Bill shall be entered on the Journal of each House respectively. If any Bill shall not be returned by the President within ten Days (Sundays excepted) after it shall have been presented to him, the Same shall be a Law, in like Manner as if he had signed it, unless the Congress by their Adjournment prevent its Return, in which Case it shall not be a Law.

The heart of the checks and balances system is contained in this clause. Both the House and Senate must pass a bill and present it to the president. If the president falls to act on the bill within 10 days (not including Sundays), the bill will automatically become law. If the president signs the bill, it becomes law. If the president vetoes the bill and sends it back to Congress, this body may override the veto by a 2/3 vote in each branch. This vote must be a recorded vote.

Clause 3. Every Order, Resolution, or Vote to which the Concurrence of the Senate and House of Representatives may be necessary (except on a question of Adjournment) shall be presented to the President of the United States; and before the Same shall take Effect, shall be approved by him, or being disapproved by him, shall be repassed by two thirds of the Senate and House of Representatives, according to the Rules and Limitations prescribed in the Case of a Bill.

This clause covers every other type of legislative action other than a bill. Essentially, the same procedures apply in most cases. There are a few exceptions. For example, a joint resolution proposing a new congressional amendment is not subject to presidential veto.

Powers of Congress

Section 8 Clause 1. The Congress shall have Power To lay and collect Taxes, Duties, Imposts and Excises, to pay the Debts and provide for the common Defence and general Welfare of the United States, but all Duties, Imposts and Excises shall be uniform throughout the United States.

To borrow Money on the credit of the United States;

To regulate Commerce with foreign Nations, and among the several States, and with the Indian Tribes;

To establish an uniform Rule of Naturalization, and uniform Laws on the subject of Bankruptcies throughout the United States;

To coin Money, regulate the Value thereof, and of foreign Coin, and fix the Standard of Weights and Measures;

To provide for the Punishment of counterfeiting the Securities and current Coin of the United States;

To establish Post Offices and post Roads;

To promote the Progress of Science and useful Arts, by securing for limited Times to Authors and Inventors the exclusive Right to their respective Writings and Discoveries;

To constitute Tribunals inferior to the supreme Court;

To define and punish Piracies and Felonies committed on the high Seas, and Offences against the Law of Nations;

To declare War, grant Letters of Marque and Reprisal, and make Rules concerning Captures on Land and Water;

To raise and support Armies, but no Appropriation of Money to that Use shall be for a longer Term than two Years;

To provide and maintain a Navy;

To make Rules for the Government and Regulation of the land and naval Forces;

To provide for calling for the Militia to execute the Laws of the Union, suppress Insurrections and repel Invasions;

To provide for organizing, arming, and disciplining, the Militia, and for governing such Part of them as may be employed in the Service of the United States, reserving to the States respectively, the Appointment of the Officers, and the Authority of training the Militia according to the discipline prescribed by Congress;

This *extensive* clause establishes what are known as the "expressed" or "specified" powers of Congress. In theory, this serves as a limit or brake on congressional power.

Clause 2. To exercise exclusive Legislation in all Cases whatsoever, over such District (not exceeding ten Miles square) as may, by Cession of particular States, and the Acceptance of Congress, become the Seat of the Government of the United States, and to exercise like Authority over all Places purchased by the Consent of the Legislature of the State in which the Same shall be, for the Erection of Forts, Magazines, Arsenals, dock Yards, and other needful Buildings—And

This clause establishes the seat of the federal government, which was first started in New York but eventually was moved to Washington, D.C., when both Maryland and Virginia ceded land to the new national government, which then established the District of Columbia.

Clause 3. To make all Laws which shall be necessary and proper for carrying into Execution the foregoing Powers, and all other Powers vested by this Constitution in the Government of the United States, or in any Department or Officer thereof.

This clause, known as the "Elastic Clause," provides the basis for the doctrine of "implied" congressional powers, which was first introduced in the U.S. Supreme Court case of *McCulloch v. Maryland,* 1819. This doctrine tremendously expanded the power of Congress to pass legislation and make regulations.

Powers Denied to Congress

Section 9. Clause 1. The Migration or Importation of such Persons as any of the States now existing shall think proper to admit, shall not be prohibited by the Congress prior to the Year one thousand eight hundred and eight, but a Tax or duty may be imposed on such Importation, not exceeding ten dollars for each Person.

This clause was part of the Three-Fifths Compromise. Essentially, the new Congress was prohibited from stopping the importation of slaves until 1808,

but it could impose a head tax, not to exceed ten dollars for each slave.

Clause 2. The Privilege of the Writ of Habeas Corpus shall not be suspended, unless when in Cases of Rebellion or Invasion the public Safety may require it.

Congress cannot suspend the writ of habeas corpus except in cases of rebellion or invasion. The writ of habeas corpus permits a judge to inquire about the legality of detention or deprivation of liberty of any citizen.

Clause 3. No Bill of Attainder or ex post facto Law shall be passed.

This provision prohibits Congress from passing either a bill of attainder (forfeiture of property in capital cases) or ex post facto laws (retroactive crimes after passage of legislation). Similar restrictions were enshrined in many state constitutions.

Clause 4. No Capitation, or other direct. Tax shall be laid, unless in Proportion to the Census or Enumeration herein before directed to be taken.[6]

This clause prevents Congress from passing an Income tax. Only with passage of the 16th Amendment in 1913 did Congress gain this power.

Clause 5. No Tax or Duty shall be laid on Articles exported from any State.

This section establishes free trade within the U.S. The federal government cannot tax state exports.

Clause 6. No Preference shall be given by any Regulation of Commerce or Revenue to the Ports of one State over those of another; nor shall Vessels bound to, or from one State, be obliged to enter, clear, or pay Duties in another.

This clause also applies to free trade within the U.S. The national government cannot show any preference to any state or maritime movements among the states.

Clause 7. No Money shall be drawn from the Treasury, but in Consequence of Appropriations made by Law, and a regular Statement and Account of the Receipts and Expenditures of all public Money shall be published from time to time.

This provision of the Constitution prevents any expenditure unless it has been specifically provided for in an appropriations bill. At the beginning of most fiscal years, Congress has not completed its work on the budget. Technically, the government cannot spend any money according to this provision and would have to shut down. So Congress normally passes a Continuing Resolution Authority providing temporary authority to continue to spend money until the final budget is approved and signed into law.

Clause 8. No Title of Nobility shall be granted by the United States. And no Person holding any Office of Profit or Trust under them, shall, without the Consent of Congress, accept of any present,

[6]Modified by the 16th Amendment.

Emolument, Office, or Title, of any kind whatever, from any King, Prince, or foreign State.

Feudalism would not be established in the new country. We would have no nobles. No federal official can even accept a title of nobility (even honorary) without permission of Congress.

Powers Denied to the States

This section sets out the prohibitions on state actions.

Section 10 Clause 1. No State shall enter into any Treaty. Alliance, or Confederation; grant Letters of Marque and Reprisal, coin Money, emit Bills of Credit, make any Thing but gold and silver Coin a Tender in Payment of Debts, pass any Bill of Attainder, ex post facto Law, or Law impairing the Obligation of Contracts of grant any Title of Nobility.

This particular clause is a laundry list of denied powers. Note that these restrictions cannot even be walved by Congress. States are not to engage in foreign relations, nor acts of war. A letter of Marque and Reprisal was used during these times to provide legal cover for privateers. The federal government's currency monopoly is established. The sanctity of contracts is specified. And similar state prohibitions are specified for bills of attainder, ex post facto, etc.

Clause 2. No State shall, without the Consent of the Congress, lay any Imposts or Duties on Imports or Exports, except what may be absolutely necessary for executing its inspection Laws: and the net Produce of all Duties and Imposts, laid by any State on Imports or Exports, shall be for the Use of the Treasury of the United States, and all such Laws shall be subject to the Revision and Controul of the Congress.

This section establishes the monopoly control of the national government in matters of both national and international trade. The only concession to states is health and safety inspections.

Clause 3. No State shall, without the Consent of Congress, lay any Duty of Tonnage, keep Troops, or Ships of War in time of Peace, enter into any Agreement or Compact with another State, or with a foreign Power, or engage in War, unless actually invaded, or in such imminent Danger as will not admit of delay.

This final section of the Legislative article establishes the war monopoly power of the national government. The only exception to state action is actual invasion or threat of imminent danger.

ARTICLE II—THE EXECUTIVE ARTICLE

This article establishes an entirely new concept in government—an elected executive power.

Nature and Scope of Presidential Power

Section 1 Clause 1. The executive Power shall be vested in a President of the United States of America. He shall hold his Office during the Term of four Years and, together with the Vice President, chosen for the same Term, be elected as follows

This clause establishes the executive power in the office of the president of the United States of America. It also establishes a second office—vice president. A four-year term was established, but no limit on the number of terms. A limit was later established by the 22nd Amendment.

Clause 2. Each State shall appoint, in such Manner as the Legislature thereof may direct, a Number of Electors, equal to the whole Number of Senators and Representatives to which the State may be entitled in the Congress: but no Senator or Representative, or Person holding an Office of Trust or Profit under the United States, shall be appointed an Elector.

This paragraph essentially establishes the Electoral College to choose the president and vice president.

Clause 3. The Electors shall meet in their respective States, and vote by Ballot for two Persons, of whom one at least shall not be an Inhabitant of the same State with themselves. And they shall make a List of all the Persons voted for, and of the Number of Votes for each; which List they shall sign and certify, and transmit sealed to the Seat of the Government of the United States, directed to the President of the Senate. The President of the Senate shall, in the Presence of the Senate and House of Representatives, open all the Certificates, and the Votes shall then be counted. The Person having the greatest Number of Votes shall be the President, if such Number be a Majority of the whole Number of Electors appointed; and if there be more than one who have such Majority, and have an equal Number of Votes, then the House of Representatives shall immediately chuse by Ballot one of them for President; and if no Person have a Majority, then from the five highest on the List the said House shall in like Manner chuse the President. But in chusing the President, the Votes shall be taken by States, the Representation from each State having one Vote; A quorum for this Purpose shall consist of a Member or Members from two thirds of the States, and a Majority of all the States shall be necessary to a Choice. In every Case, after the Choice of the President, the Person having the greatest Number of Votes of the Electors shall be the Vice President. But if there should remain two or more who have equal Votes, the Senate shall chuse from them by Ballot the Vice President.[7]

This paragraph has been superseded by the 12th Amendment. The original language did not require a separate vote for president and vice president. This resulted in a tied vote in the Electoral College in 1800 when both Thomas Jefferson and Aaron Burr received 73 electoral votes. The 12th Amendment requires a separate vote for each. Only one of the two can be from the state of the elector. This means that it is highly unlikely that the presidential and vice presidential candidates would be from the same state. This question arose in the 2000 election when Dick Cheney, who lived and worked in Texas, had to reestablish his residence in Montana.

The original language provided for a House election in the case of no majority vote or a tie vote among the top five candidates. The amendment lowered the number of candidates to the top three. The Senate is to select the vice president if a candidate does not have an electoral majority or in the case of a tie vote. The Senate considers only the top two candi-

dates. The amendment also clarifies that the qualifications of the vice president are the same as those for president.

Clause 4. The Congress may determine the Time of chusing the Electors, and the Day on which they shall give their Votes; which Day shall be the same throughout the United States.

Congress is given the power to establish a uniform day and time for the state selection of electors.

Clause 5. No Person except a natural born Citizen, or a Citizen of the United States, at the time of the Adoption of this Constitution, shall be eligible to the Office of President; neither shall any Person be eligible to that Office who shall not have attained to the Age of thirty five Years, and been fourteen Years a Resident within the United States.

The qualifications for the offices of president and vice president are specified here—at least 35 years old, 14 years' resident in the U.S., and a natural-born citizen or citizen of the U.S. The 14th Amendment clarified who is a citizen of the U.S., a person born or naturalized in the U.S. and subject to its jurisdiction. But the term "natural-born citizen" is unclear and has never been further defined by the judicial branch. Does it mean born in the U.S. or born of U.S. citizens in the U.S. or somewhere else in the world? Unfortunately, there is no definitive answer.

Clause 6 In Case of the Removal of the President from Office, or of his Death, Resignation, or Inability to discharge the Powers and Duties of the said Office, the Same shall devolve on the Vice President, and the Congress may by Law provide for the Case of Removal, Death, Resignation, or Inability, both of the President and Vice President, declaring what Officer shall then act as president, and such Officer shall act accordingly, until the Disability be removed, or a President shall be elected.[8]

This clause has been modified by the 25th Amendment. Upon the death, resignation, or impeachment conviction of the president, the vice president becomes president. The new president nominates a new vice president, who assumes the office, if approved by a majority vote in both congressional branches. The president is also now able to notify the Congress of his inability to perform his office.

Clause 7. The President shall, at stated Times, receive for his Services, a Compensation which shall neither be increased nor diminished during the Period of which he shall have been elected, and he shall not receive within that Period any other Emolument from the United States, or any of them.

This section covers the compensation of the president, which cannot be increased or decreased during his office. The current salary is $400,000/year.

Clause 8. Before he enter on the Execution of his Office, he shall take the following Oath or Affirmation—"I do solemnly swear (or affirm) that I will faithfully execute the Office of President of the United States, and will to the best of my Ability, preserve, protect and defend the Constitution of the United States."

---

[7]Changed by the 12th and 20th Amendments

[8]Modified by the 25th Amendment

This final clause in Section 1 is the oath of office administered to the new president.

Powers and Duties of the President

Section 2   Clause 1. The President shall be the Commander in Chief of the Army and Navy of the United States, and of the Militia of the several States, when called into the actual Service of the United States, he may require the Opinion, in writing, of the principal Officer in each of the executive Departments, upon any Subject relating to the Duties of their respective Offices, and he shall have the Power to grant Reprieves and Pardons for Offences against the United States, except in Cases of Impeachment.

This clause establishes the president as Commander-in-Chief of the U.S. armed forces. George Washington was the only U.S. president to actually lead U.S. armed forces during the Whiskey Rebellion. The second provision provides the basis for cabinet meetings that are used to acquire the opinions of executive department heads. The last provision provides an absolute pardon or reprieve power from the president. The provision was controversial, but legal, when former President Clinton pardoned fugitive Marc Rich.

Clause 2. He shall have Power, by and with the Advice and Consent of the Senate to make Treaties, provided two thirds of the Senators present concur, and he shall nominate, and by and with the Advice and Consent of the Senate, shall appoint Ambassadors, other public Ministers and Consuls, Judges of the supreme Court, and all other Officers of the United States, whose Appointments are not herein otherwise provided for, and which shall be established by Law but the Congress may by Law vest the Appointment of such inferior Officers, as they think proper in the President alone, in the Courts of Law, or in the Heads of Departments.

This clause covers two important presidential powers; treaty making and appointments. The president (via the State Department) can negotiate treaties with other nations, but these do not become official until ratified by a 2/3 vote of the U.S. Senate. The president is empowered to appoint judges, ambassadors, and other U.S. officials (cabinet officers, military officers, agency heads, etc.) subject to Senate approval. The Congress can and does delegate this approval to the president in the case of inferior officers. For example, junior military officer promotions are not submitted to the Senate, but senior officer promotions are.

Clause 3. The President shall have Power to fill up all Vacancies that may happen during the Recess of the Senate, by granting Commissions which shall expire at the End of their next Session.

This provision allows recess appointments of the officials listed in Clause 2 above. These commissions automatically expire unless approved by the Senate by the end of the next session. Presidents have used this provision to fill jobs when the nomination process is stalled. Some of these appointments have been very controversial. The regular nomination was stalled because the Senate did not want to confirm the nominee.

Section 3   He shall from time to time give to the Congress Information of the State of the Union, and recommend to their Considera-

tion such Measures as he shall judge necessary and expedient, he may, on extraordinary Occasions convene both Houses, or either of them and in Case of Disagreement between them, with Respect to the Time of Adjournment, he may adjourn them to such Time as he shall think proper, he shall receive Ambassadors and other public Ministers, he shall take Care that the Laws be faithfully executed, and shall Commission all the Officers of the United States.

This section provides for the annual State of the Union address to a joint session of Congress and the American people. The president is also authorized to call special meetings of either the House or Senate. If there is disagreement between the House and Senate regarding adjournment, the president is empowered to adjourn them. This would be extremely rare. The president formally receives other nations' ambassadors. The next to last provision to faithfully execute laws provides the basis for the whole administrative apparatus of the presidency. All officers of the U.S. receive a formal commission from the president (most of these are signed with a signature machine).

Section 4   The President, Vice President and all civil Officers of the United States, shall be removed from Office on Impeachment for, and Conviction of, Treason, Bribery, or other high Crimes and Misdemeanors.

This section provides the constitutional authority for the impeachment and trial of the president, vice president, and all civil officers of the U.S. for treason, bribery, or other high crimes and misdemeanors (the exact meaning of this phrase is unclear and is often more political than judicial).

ARTICLE III—THE JUDICIAL ARTICLE

Judicial Power, Courts, Judges

Section 1   The judicial Power of the United States, shall be vested in one supreme Court, and in such inferior Courts as the Congress may from time to time ordain and establish. The Judges, both the supreme and inferior Courts, shall hold their Offices during good Behaviour, and shall, at stated Times, receive for their Services, a Compensation, which shall not be diminished during their Continuance in Office.

This section establishes the judicial branch in very general terms. It specifically provides only for the Supreme Court. Congress is given the responsibility to flesh out the court system. It initially did so in the Judiciary Act of 1789, when it established 13 district courts (one for each state), and 3 appellate courts. All federal judges hold their offices for life and can only be removed for breaches of good behavior—a very nebulous term. Federal judges have been removed for drunkenness, accepting bribes, and other misdemeanors. To date, no justice of the U.S. Supreme Court has ever been removed.

The salary of federal judges is set by congressional act, but can never be reduced. Although the American Bar Association and the Federal Bar Association consider federal judges' salaries inadequate, most Americans would probably disagree. Federal district judges earn $145,100/year, appellate judges

$153,900, and Supreme Court justices $178,300. The Chief Justice is paid $186,300. These are lifetime salaries, even upon retirement.

Jurisdiction

Section 2 The judicial Power shall extend to all Cases, in Law and Equity, arising under this Constitution, the Laws of the United States, and Treaties made, or which shall be made, under their Authority,—to all Cases affecting Ambassadors, other public Ministers and Consuls,—to all Cases of admiralty and maritime Jurisdiction,—to Controversies to which the United States shall be a Party,—to Controversies between two or more States; between a State and Citizens of another State;[9]—between Citizens of different States,—between Citizens of the same State claiming Lands under Grants of different States, and between a State, or the Citizens thereof, and foreign States, Citizens, or Subjects.

In all Cases affecting Ambassadors, other public Ministers and Consuls, and those in which a State shall be Party, the supreme Court shall have original Jurisdiction. In all the other Cases before mentioned, the supreme Court shall have appellate Jurisdiction, both as to Law and Fact, with such Exceptions, and under such Regulations as Congress shall make.

The Trial of all Crimes, except in Cases of Impeachment, shall be by Jury; and such Trial shall be held in the State where the said Crimes shall have been committed; but when not committed within any State, the Trial shall be at such Place or Places as the Congress may by Law have directed.

This section establishes the original and appellate jurisdiction of the U.S. Supreme Court. With the Congress of Vienna's 1815 establishment of "diplomatic immunity," the U.S. Supreme Court no longer hears cases involving ambassadors. Since 1925, the Supreme Court no longer hears every case on appeal but can select which cases it will accept, which is now only about 150 cases per year. This section also establishes the right of trial by jury for federal crimes.

Treason

Section 3 Treason against the United States, shall consist only in levying War against them, or in adhering to their Enemies, giving them Aid and Comfort. No Person shall be convicted of Treason unless on the Testimony of two Witnesses to the same overt Act, or on Confession in open Court.

The Congress shall have Power to declare the Punishment of Treason, but no Attainder of Treason shall work Corruption of Blood, or Forfeiture except during the Life of the Person attainted.

Treason is the only crime defined in the U.S. Constitution. Congress established the penalty of death for treason convictions. Note that two witnesses are required to convict anyone of treason. Even in cases of treasonable conduct, seizure of estates is prohibited.

ARTICLE IV—INTERSTATE RELATIONS

Full Faith and Credit Clause

Section 1 Full Faith and Credit shall be given in each State to the public Acts, Records, and judicial Proceedings of every other State. And the Congress may by general Laws prescribe the Manner in which such Acts, Records and Proceedings shall be proved, and the Effect thereof.

This section provides that the official acts, records of one state will be recognized and given credence by other states, e.g., marriages and divorces.

Privileges and Immunities, Interstate Extradition

Section 2 Clause 1. The Citizens of each State shall be entitled to all Privileges and Immunities of Citizens in the several States.

This clause requires states to treat citizens of other states equally. For example, when driving in another state, my driver's license is recognized. One area not so clear is that of charging higher state tuitions at educational institutions for out-of-state students.

Clause 2. A person charged in any State with Treason, Felony or other Crime, who shall flee from Justice, and be found in another State, shall on Demand of the executive Authority of the State from which he fled, be delivered up, to be removed to the State having Jurisdiction of the Crime.

Extradition is the name of this clause. A criminal fleeing to another state, if captured, can be returned to the state where the crime was committed. But this is not an absolute. A state's governor can refuse, for good reason, to extradite someone to another state.

Clause 3. No person held to Service or Labour in one State, under the Laws thereof, escaping into another, shall, in Consequence of any Law or Regulation therein, be discharged from such Service or Labour, but shall be delivered up on Claim of the Party to whom such Service or Labour may be due.[10]

This clause was included to cover runaway slaves. It has been made inoperable by the 13th Amendment, which abolished slavery.

Admission of States

Section 3 New States may be admitted by the Congress into this Union but no new State shall be formed or erected within the Jurisdiction of any other State, nor any State to be formed by the Junction of two or more States, or Parts of States, without the Consent of the Legislatures of the States concerned as well as of the Congress.

The Congress shall have Power to dispose of and make all needful Rules and Regulations respecting the Territory or other Property belonging to the United States, and nothing in this Constitution shall be so construed as to Prejudice any Claims of the United States, or of any particular State.

This section concerns the admission of new states to the Union. In theory, no state can be created from part of another state without permission of the state legislature. But West Virginia was formed from Virginia during the Civil War without the permission of Virginia, which was part of the Confederacy. With fifty states now part of the Union, this section has not been used for many decades. The only future use may be in the case of Puerto Rico or perhaps Washington, D.C.

Republican Form of Government

Section 4 The United States shall guarantee to every State in this Union a Republican Form of Government, and shall protect each

---

[9]Modified by the 11th Amendment

[10]Repealed by the 13th Amendment

of them against Invasion, and on Application of the Legislature, or of the Executive (when the Legislature cannot be convened) against domestic Violence.

This section commits the federal government to guarantee a republican form of government to each state and protect the state against foreign invasion or domestic insurrection.

ARTICLE V—THE AMENDING POWER

The Congress, whenever two thirds of both Houses shall deem it necessary, shall propose Amendments to this Constitution, or, on the Application of the Legislatures of two thirds of several States, shall call a Convention for proposing Amendments, which, in either Case, shall be valid to all Intents and Purposes, as Part of this Constitution, when ratified by the Legislatures of three fourths of the several States, or by Conventions in three fourths thereof, as the one or the other Mode of Ratification may be proposed by the Congress, Provided that no Amendment which may be made prior to the Year One thousand eight hundred and eight shall in any Manner affect the first and fourth Clauses in the Ninth Section of the first Article, and that no State, without its Consent, shall be deprived of its equal Suffrage in the Senate.

Amendment to the U.S. Constitution can be originated by a 2/3 vote in both the U.S. House and Senate or by 2/3 of the state legislatures asking for a convention to propose amendments. Proposed amendments, by either route, must be approved by 3/4 of state legislatures or by 3/4 of conventions convened in the states for purposes of ratification. Only one amendment has been ratified by the convention method—Amendment 21 to repeal the 18th Amendment establishing Prohibition.

Thousands of amendments have been proposed; few have been passed by 2/3 vote in each branch of Congress. The Equal Rights Amendment was one such case, but it was not ratified by 3/4 of state legislatures. There have only been 27 successful amendments to the U.S. Constitution.

ARTICLE VI—THE SUPREMACY ACT

Clause 1. All Debts contracted and Engagements entered into, before the Adoption of this Constitution, shall be as valid against the United States under the Constitution, as under the Confederation.

This clause made the new national government responsible for all debts incurred during the Revolutionary War. This was very important to banking and commercial interests.

Clause 2. This Constitution, and the Laws of the United States which shall be made in Pursuance thereof, and all Treaties made, or which shall be made, under the Authority of the United States, shall be the supreme Law of the Land, and the Judges in every State shall be bound thereby, any Thing in the Constitution or Laws of any State to the Contrary notwithstanding.

This is the National Supremacy Clause, which provides the basis for the supremacy of the national government.

Clause 3. The Senators and Representatives before mentioned, and the Members of the several State Legislatures, and all executive and judicial Officers, both of the United States and of the several States, shall be bound by Oath or Affirmation, to support this Constitution, but no religious Test shall ever be required as a Qualification to any Office or public Trust under the United States.

This clause requires essentially all federal and state officials to swear or affirm their allegiance to and support of the U.S. Constitution. Note that a religious test was prohibited for federal office. However, some states used religious tests for voting and office qualification until the 1830s.

ARTICLE VII—RATIFICATION

The Ratification of the Conventions of nine States, shall be sufficient for the Establishment of this Constitution between the States so ratifying the Same.

Done in Convention by the Unanimous Consent of the States present the Seventeenth Day of September in the Year of our Lord one thousand seven hundred and Eighty seven and of the Independence of the United States of America the Twelfth. *In Witness whereof We have hereunto subscribed our Names.*

AMENDMENTS

Realizing the unanimous ratification of the 13 states of the new Constitution might never have occurred, the framers wisely specified that only 9 states would be needed for ratification. Even this proved to be a test of wills between Federalists and Anti-Federalists, leading to publication of the great political work *The Federalist Papers*.

THE BILL OF RIGHTS

[The first ten amendments were ratified on December 15, 1791, and form what is known as the "Bill of Rights."]

The Bill of Rights applied initially only to the federal government and not to state or local governments. Beginning in 1925 in the case of *Gitlow v. New York*, the U.S. Supreme Court began to selectively incorporate the Bill of Rights, making its provisions applicable to state and local governments. There are only three exceptions, which will be discussed at the appropriate amendment.

AMENDMENT 1— RELIGION, SPEECH, ASSEMBLY, AND POLITICS

Congress shall make no law respecting an establishment of religion, or prohibiting the free exercise thereof; or abridging the freedom of speech, or of the press; or the right of the people peaceably to assemble, and to petition the Government for a redress of grievances.

This is the godfather of all amendments in that it protects five fundamental freedoms: religion, speech, press, assembly, and petition. Note that the press is the only business that is specifically protected by the U.S. Constitution. Freedom of religion and speech are two of the most contentious issues and generate a multitude of Supreme Court cases.

AMENDMENT 2—MILITIA AND THE RIGHT TO BEAR ARMS

A well-regulated Militia, being necessary to the security of a free State, the right of the people to keep and bear Arms, shall not be infringed.

This amendment is the favorite of the National Rifle Association. This amendment also has not been incorporated for state/local governments; that is, state and local governments are free to regulate arms within their respective jurisdictions. There is also controversy as to the meaning of this amendment. Some believe that it specifically refers to citizen militias, which were common at the time of the Constitution but now have been replaced by permanent armed forces. Therefore, is the amendment still applicable? Do private citizens need weapons for the security of a free state?

AMENDMENT 3—QUARTERING OF SOLDIERS

No Soldier shall, in time of peace be quartered in any house, without the consent of the Owner, nor in time of war, but in manner to be prescribed by law.

It was the practice of the British government to insist that colonists provide room or board to British troops. This amendment was designed to prohibit this practice. Today, military and naval bases provide the necessary quarters.

AMENDMENT 4—SEARCHES AND SEIZURES

The right of the people to be secure in their persons, houses, papers, and effects, against unreasonable searches and seizures, shall not be violated, and no Warrants shall issue, but upon probable cause, supported by Oath or affirmation, and particularly describing the place to be searched, and the persons or things to be seized.

This is an extremely important amendment to prevent the abuse of state police powers. Essentially, unreasonable searches or seizures of homes, persons, or property cannot be undertaken without probable cause or a warrant that specifically describes the place to be searched, the person involved, and suspicious things to be seized.

AMENDMENT 5—GRAND JURIES, SELF-INCRIMINATION, DOUBLE JEOPARDY, DUE PROCESS, AND EMINENT DOMAIN

No person shall be held to answer for a capital, or otherwise infamous crime, unless on a presentment or indictment of a Grand jury, except in cases arising in the land or naval forces, or in the Militia, when in actual service in time of War or public danger; nor shall any person be subject for the same offence to be twice put in jeopardy of life or limb, nor shall be compelled in any criminal case to be a witness against himself, nor be deprived of life, liberty, or property, without due process of law, nor shall private property be taken for public use, without just compensation.

Only a grand jury can indict a person for a federal crime. This provision does not apply to state/local governments. This amendment also covers double jeopardy, or being tried twice for the same crime in the same jurisdiction. Note that since the federal government and state governments are different jurisdictions, one could be tried in each jurisdiction for essentially the same crime. For example, it is a federal crime to kill a congressperson. It is also a state crime to murder anyone. Further, this amendment also covers the prohibition of self-incrimination. Pleading the 5th Amendment used to be common in Mafia cases, but recently was used by Enron witnesses. The deprivation of life, liberty, or property by any level of government is prohibited unless due process of law is applied. Finally, private property may not be taken under the doctrine of "eminent domain" unless the government provides just compensation.

AMENDMENT 6—CRIMINAL COURT PROCEDURES

In all criminal prosecutions, the accused shall enjoy the right to a speedy and public trial, by an impartial jury of the State and district wherein the crime shall have been committed, which district shall have been previously ascertained by law, and to be informed of the nature and cause of the accusation, to be confronted with the witnesses against him, to have compulsory process for obtaining witnesses in his favor, and to have the Assistance of Counsel for his defence.

This amendment requires public trials by jury for criminal prosecutions. Anyone accused of a crime is guaranteed the right to be informed of the charges; confront witnesses; to subpoena witnesses for their defense; and to have a lawyer for their defense. Currently, the government must provide a lawyer for a defendant unable to afford one.

AMENDMENT 7—TRIAL BY JURY IN COMMON LAW CASES

In Suits at common law, where the value in controversy shall exceed twenty dollars, the right of trial by jury shall be preserved, and no fact tried by a jury shall be otherwise re-examined in any Court of the United States, than according to the rules of the common law.

This amendment is practically without meaning in modern times. Statutory law has largely superseded common law. Federal civil law suits with a guaranteed jury are now restricted to cases that exceed $50,000. The Bill of Rights, which includes the right to trial by jury, applied orginally only to the national government. Beginning in 1925, the USSC began a selective process of incorporating provisions in the Bill of Rights and making them applicable to state/local governments as well. There are just a few provisions that have not been thus incorporated. Trial by jury is one. Some state/local governments have trials by judges, not by juries.

AMENDMENT 8—BAIL, CRUEL AND UNUSUAL PUNISHMENT

Excessive bail shall not be required, nor excessive fines imposed, nor cruel and unusual punishments inflicted.

Capital punishment is covered by this amendment, which also prohibits excessive bail. But this is rela-

tive. Million-dollar bails are not uncommon in some cases. One federal judge offered voluntary castration for sex offenders in lieu of jail time. Higher courts held this to be a cruel or unusual punishment. But it is the death penalty that generates the most heated controversy. Court cases challenging the constitutionality of capital punishment cite this amendment's language prohibiting cruel and unusual punishment. For a period of 4 years, the USSC banned capital punishment. When states modified their statutes to provide a two part judicial process of guilt determination and punishment, the USSC allowed the reinstitution of capital punishment by the states.

AMENDMENT 9—RIGHTS RETAINED BY THE PEOPLE

The enumeration in the Constitution of certain rights, shall not be construed to deny or disparage others retained by the people.

This amendment implies that there may be other rights of the people not specified by the previous amendments. Indeed, the Warren Court established the right to privacy even though it is not specifically mentioned in any previous amendment. Some would claim the persons have a right to adequate medical care and education.

AMENDMENT 10—RESERVED POWERS OF THE STATES

The powers not delegated to the United States by the Constitution, nor prohibited by it to the States, are reserved to the States respectively, or to the people.

The 10th Amendment was seen as the reservoir of reserved powers for state governments. If the national government had been limited only to expressed powers in Article 1, Section 8, of the Constitution, this would have been the case. But the doctrine of implied national government powers, which was established by the U.S. Supreme Court in *McCulloch v. Maryland* in 1819, made the intent of this amendment almost meaningless. What reserved powers that were retained by the states were virtually removed by the U.S. Supreme Court's decision in the *Garcia v. San Antonio Metropolitan Transit Authority* case in 1985, which basically told state/local governments not to look to the courts to protect their residual rights but rather to their political representatives. In subsequent cases, the USSC has retreated somewhat from this position when the court found the federal government encroaching in state jurisdictional areas.

AMENDMENT 11—SUITS AGAINST THE STATES

[Ratified February 7, 1795]

The Judicial power of the United States shall not be construed to extend to any suit in law or equity, commented or prosecuted against one of the United States by Citizens of another State, or by Citizens or Subjects of any Foreign State.

Article 3 of the U.S. Constitution originally allowed federal jurisdiction in cases of one state citizen against another state citizen or state. This amendment removes federal jurisdiction in this area. In essence, states may not be sued in federal court by citizens of another state or country.

AMENDMENT 12—ELECTION OF THE PRESIDENT

[Ratified June 15, 1804]

The Electors shall meet in their respective states, and vote by ballot for President and Vice-President, one of whom, at least, shall not be an inhabitant of the same state with themselves; they shall name in their ballots the person voted for as President, and in distinct ballots the person voted for as Vice-President, and they shall make distinct lists of all persons voted for as President, and of all persons voted for as Vice-President, and of the number of votes for each, which lists they shall sign and certify, and transmit sealed to the seat of the government of the United States, directed to the President of the Senate;—The President of the Senate shall, in presence of the Senate and House of Representatives, open all the certificates and the votes shall then be counted;—The person having the greatest number of votes for President, shall be the President, if such number be a majority of the whole number of Electors appointed; and if no person have such majority, then from the persons having the highest numbers not exceeding three on the list of those voted for as President, the House of Representatives shall choose immediately, by ballot, the President. But in choosing the President, the votes shall be taken by states, the representation from each state having one vote; a quorum for this purpose shall consist of a member or members from two-thirds of the states, and a majority of all states shall be necessary to a choice. And if the House of Representatives shall not choose a President whenever the right of choice shall devolve upon them, *before the fourth day of March next following*, then the Vice-President shall act as President, as in the case of the death or other constitutional disability of the President.[11] The person having the greatest number of votes as Vice-President, shall be the Vice-President, if such a number be a majority of the whole numbers of Electors appointed, and if no person have a majority, then from the two highest numbers on the list, the Senate shall choose the Vice-President, a quorum for the purpose shall consist of two-thirds of the whole number of Senators, and a majority of the whole number shall be necessary to a choice. But no person constitutionally ineligible to the office of President shall be eligible to that of Vice-President of the United States.

This was a necessary amendment to correct a flaw in the Constitution covering operations of the Electoral College. In the election of 1800, both Thomas Jefferson and Aaron Burr, of the same Democratic-Republican Party, received the same number of electoral votes, 73, for president. Article II of the original Constitution specified that each elector would cast two ballots. It did not specify for whom. This amendment clarifies that the electoral vote must be specific for president and vice president. The original Constitution provided that if no candidate received a majority of electoral votes, the House would decide from the candidates with the top five vote totals. This amendment reduces the candidate field to the top three vote totals. If the House delays in this selection past the fourth day of March, the elected vice president will act as president until the House selects the president. The original Constitution provided that the candidate with the second highest number of electoral votes would become vice president.

---

[11]Changed by the 20th Amendment

This amendment, which requires a separate vote tally for vice president, provides for selection by the U.S. Senate if no vice presidential candidate receives an electoral vote majority.

AMENDMENT 13—PROHIBITION OF SLAVERY

[Ratified December 6, 1865]

Section 1 Neither slavery nor involuntary servitude, except as a punishment for crime whereof the party shall have been duly convicted, shall exist within the United States, or any place subject to their jurisdiction.

Section 2 Congress shall have power to enforce this article by appropriate legislation.

This is the first of the three Civil War amendments. Slavery is prohibited under all circumstances. Involuntary servitude is also prohibited unless it is a punishment for a convicted crime.

AMENDMENT 14—CITIZENSHIP, DUE PROCESS, AND EQUAL PROTECTION OF THE LAWS

[Ratified July 9, 1868]

Section 1 All persons born or naturalized in the United States, and subject to the jurisdiction thereof, are citizens of the United States and of the State wherein they reside. No State shall make or enforce any law which shall abridge the privileges or immunities of citizens of the United States; nor shall any State deprive any person of life, liberty, or property, without due process of law; nor deny to any person within its jurisdiction the equal protection of the laws.

This section defines the meaning of U.S. citizenship and protection of these citizenship rights. It also establishes the Equal Protection Clause that each state must guarantee to its citizens. It extended the provisions of the 5th Amendment of due process and protection of life, liberty, and property and made these applicable to the states.

Section 2 Representatives shall be apportioned among the several States according to their respective numbers, counting the whole number of persons in each State, excluding Indians not taxed. But when the right to vote at any election for the choice of electors for President and Vice President of the United States, Representatives in Congress, the Executive and Judicial officers of a State, or the members of the Legislature thereof, is denied to any of the male inhabitants of such State, being twenty-one[12] years of age, and citizens of the United States, or in any way abridged, except for participation in rebellion, or other crime, the basis of representation therein shall be reduced in the proportion which the number of such male citizens shall bear to the whole number of male citizens twenty-one years of age in such State.

This section changes the Three-Fifths Clause of the original Constitution. Now all male citizens, 21 or older, will be used to calculate representation in the House of Representatives. If a state denies the right to vote to any male 21 or older, the number of denied citizens will be deducted from the overall state total to determine representation.

Section 3 No person shall be a Senator or Representative in Congress, or elector of President and Vice President, or bold any of-

[12]Changed by the 26th Amendment

fice, civil or military under the United States, or under any State, who, having previously taken an oath, as a member of Congress, or as an officer of the United States, or as a member of any State legislature, or as an executive or judicial officer of any State, to support the Constitution of the United States, shall have engaged in insurrection or rebellion against the same, or given aid or comfort to the enemies thereof. But Congress may by a vote of two-thirds of each House, remove such disability.

This section disqualifies from federal office or elector for president or vice president anyone who rebelled or participated in an insurrection against the Constitution. This was specifically directed against citizens of southern states. Congress by a 2/3 vote could override this provision.

Section 4 The validity of the public debt of the United States, authorized by law, including debts incurred for payment of pensions and bounties for services in suppressing insurrection or rebellion, shall nor be questioned. But neither the United States nor any State shall assume or pay any debt or obligation incurred in aid of insurrection or rebellion against the United States or any claim for the loss or emancipation of any slave, but all such debts, obligations and claims shall be held illegal and void.

Section 5 The Congress shall have power to enforce, by appropriate legislation, the provisions of this article.

Sections 4 and 5 cover the Civil War debts.

AMENDMENT 15—THE RIGHT TO VOTE

[Ratified February 3, 1870]

Section 1 The right of citizens of the United States to vote shall not be demed or abridged by the United States or by any State on account of race, color, or previous condition of servitude.

Section 2 The Congress shall have power to enforce this article by appropriate legislation.

This final Civil War amendment state that voting rights could not be denied by any states on account of race, color, or previous servitude. Unfortunately, it did not mention gender. Accordingly, all male citizens 21 or over were guaranteed the right to vote by this amendment.

AMENDMENT 16—INCOME TAXES

[Ratified February 3, 1913]

The Congress shall have power to lay and collect taxes on incomes, from whatever source derived, without apportionment among the several States, and without regard to any census or enumeration.

Article 1, Section 9, of the original Constitution prohibited Congress from enacting a direct tax (head tax) unless in proportion to a census. Congress in 1894 passed an income tax law, levying a 2 percent tax on incomes over $4,000. In 1895, the U.S. Supreme Court in a split decision (5–4) found that the income tax was a direct tax not apportioned among the states and was thus unconstitutional. Thus, Congress proposed an amendment allowing it to enact an income tax. Once this amendment was ratified, the flow of tax money to Washington increased tremendously.

AMENDMENT 17—DIRECT ELECTION OF SENATORS

[Ratified April 8, 1913]

The Senate of the United States shall be composed of two Senators from each State, elected by the people thereof, for six years and each Senator shall have one vote. The electors in each State shall have the qualifications requisite for electors of the most numerous branch of the State legislatures.

When vacancies happen in the representation of any State in the Senate, the executive authority of such State shall issue writs of election to fill such vacancies: Provided, That the legislature of any State may empower the executive thereof to make temporary appointment until the people fill the vacancies by election as the legislature may direct.

This amendment shall not be so construed as to affect the election or term of any Senator chosen before it becomes valid as part of the Constitution.

Prior to this amendment, U.S. senators were selected by state legislatures. Now U.S. senators would be selected by popular vote in each state. Further, the governor of each state may fill vacancies, subject to state laws.

AMENDMENT 18—PROHIBITION

[Ratified January 16, 1919, Repealed December 5, 1933 by Amendment 21]

Section 1   After one year from the ratification of this article the manufacture, sale, or transportation of intoxicating liquors within, the importation thereof into, or the exportation thereof from the United States and all territory subject to the jurisdiction thereof for beverage purposes is hereby prohibited.

Section 2   The Congress and the several States shall have concurrent power to enforce this article by appropriate legislation.

Section 3   This article shall be inoperative unless it shall have been ratified as an amendment to the Constitution by the legislatures of the several States, as provided in the Constitution, within seven years from the date of the submission hereof to the States by the Congress.[13]

This amendment was largely the work of the Women's Christian Temperance Union and essentially banned the manufacture, sale, or transportation of alcoholic beverages. Unintended consequences of this attempt to legislate morality were the brewing of "bathtub gin" and moonshine liquor, the involvement of the mob in importing liquor from Canada, and the "Untouchables" of Elliott Ness. Fortunately, this ill-fated social experiment was corrected by the 21st Amendment. This is also the first amendment where Congress fixed a period for ratification—7 years.

AMENDMENT 19—FOR WOMEN'S SUFFRAGE

[Ratified August 18, 1920]

The right of the citizens of the United States to vote shall not be denied or abridged by the United States or by any State on account of sex.

Congress shall have power, by appropriate legislation, to enforce the provision of this article.

---

[13]Repealed by the 21st Amendment

At long last, women achieved voting parity with men.

AMENDMENT 20—THE LAME DUCK AMENDMENT

[Ratified January 23, 1933]

Section 1   The terms of the President and Vice President shall end at noon on the 20th day of January, and the terms of the Senators and Representatives at noon on the 3d day of January, of the years in which such terms would have ended if this article had not been ratified, and the terms of their successors shall then begin.

Section 2   The Congress shall assemble at least once in every year, and such meeting shall begin at noon on the 3d day of January, unless they shall by law appoint a different day.

Section 3   If, at the time fixed for the beginning of the term of the President, the President elect shall have died, the Vice President elect shall become President. If a President shall not have been chosen before the time fixed for the beginning of his term, or if the President elect shall have failed to qualify, then the Vice President elect shall act as President until a President shall have qualified, and the Congress may by law provide for the case wherein neither a President elect nor a Vice President elect shall have qualified, declaring who shall then act as President, or the manner in which one who is to act shall be selected, and such person shall act accordingly until a President or Vice President shall have qualified.

Section 4   The Congress may by law provide for the case of the death of any of the persons from whom the House of Representatives may choose a President whenever the right of choice shall have developed upon them, and for the case of the death of any of the persons from whom the Senate may choose a Vice President whenever the right of choice shall have devolved upon them.

Section 5   Sections 1 and 2 shall take effect on the 15th day of October following the ratification of this article.

Section 6   This article shall be inoperative unless it shall have been ratified as an amendment to the Constitution by the legislatures of three-fourths of the several States within seven years from the date of its submission.

Called the Lame Duck amendment, this amendment fixes the dates for the end of presidential and legislative terms. A new president is elected in November, but the current president remains in office until January 20 of the following year. Thus, the term "lame duck." Legislative terms begin earlier, on January 3.

AMENDMENT 21—REPEAL OF PROHIBITION

[Ratified December 5, 1933]

Section 1   The eighteenth article of amendment to the Constitution of the United States is hereby repealed.

Section 2   The transportation or importation into any State, Territory, or possession of the United States for delivery or use therein of intoxicating liquors, in violation of the laws thereof, is hereby prohibited.

Section 3   This article shall be inoperative unless it shall have been ratified as an amendment to the Constitution by conventions in the several States, as provided in the Constitution, within seven years from the date of the submission hereof to the States by the Congress.

This unusual amendment nullified the 18th Amendment. The end of Prohibition unless prohibited by state laws.

AMENDMENT 22—NUMBER OF PRESIDENTIAL TERMS

[Ratified February 27, 1951]

Section 1 No person shall be elected to the office of the President more than twice, and no person who has held the office of President, or acted as President, for more than two years of a term to which some other person was elected President shall be elected to the office of the President more than once. But this article shall not apply to any person holding the office of President when this article was proposed by the Congress, and shall not prevent any person who may be holding the office of President, or acting as President, during the term within which this article becomes operative from holding the office of President or acting as President during the remainder of such term.

Section 2 This article shall be inoperative unless it shall have been ratified as an amendment to the Constitution by the legislatures of three-fourths of the several states within seven years from the date of its submission to the states by the Congress.

This amendment could be called the Franklin D. Roosevelt amendment. It was FDR who broke the previous unwritten pattern of no more than two-term presidents. Democrat Roosevelt won an unprecedented four terms as president. When the Republicans took control of the Congress in 1948, they pushed through the 22nd Amendment, limiting the U.S. president to a lifetime of two full four-year terms of office.

AMENDMENT 23—PRESIDENTIAL ELECTORS FOR THE DISTRICT OF COLUMBIA

[Ratified March 29, 1961]

Section 1 The District constituting the seat of government of the United States shall appoint in such manner as the Congress may direct:

A number of electors of President and Vice President equal to the whole number of Senators and Representatives in Congress to which the District would be entitled if it were a state, but in no event more than the least populous state, they shall be in addition to those appointed by the states, but they shall be considered for the purposes of the election of President and Vice President, to be electors appointed by a state, and they shall meet in the District and perform such duties as provided by the twelfth article of amendment.

Section 2 The Congress shall have power to enforce this article by appropriate legislation

This amendment gave electoral votes to the citizens of Washington, D.C., which is not a state and thus not included in the original scheme of state electoral votes. Currently, Washington, D.C., has 3 electoral votes, bringing the total of presidential electoral votes to 538. Puerto Ricans are citizens of the U.S. but have no electoral votes.

AMENDMENT 24—THE ANTI-POLL TAX AMENDMENT

[Ratified January 23, 1964]

Section 1 The right of citizens of the United States to vote in any primary or other election for President or Vice President, for electors for President or Vice President or for Senator or Representative in Congress, shall not be denied or abridged by the United States or any state by reason of failure to pay any poll tax or other tax.

Section 2 The Congress shall have power to enforce this article by appropriate legislation.

The poll tax was a procedure used mostly in southern states to discourage poor white and black voters from registering to vote. Essentially, one would have to pay a tax to register to vote. The tax was not much—around $34/year. But for a poor white or black voter, this might not be disposable income. As part of the assault against disenfranchisement of voters, the poll tax was abolished. Literacy tests, another device to disqualify voters, were abolished by the Voting Rights Act of 1965.

AMENDMENT 25—PRESIDENTIAL DISABILITY, VICE PRESIDENTIAL VACANCIES

[Ratified February 10, 1967]

Section 1 In case of the removal of the President from office or his death or resignation, the Vice President shall become President.

Section 2 Whenever there is a vacancy in the office of the Vice President, the President shall nominate a Vice President who shall take the office upon confirmation by a majority vote of both Houses of Congress.

Section 3 Whenever the President transmits to the President pro tempore of the Senate and the Speaker of the House of Representatives his written declaration that he is unable to discharge the powers and duties of his office, and until he transmits to them a written declaration to the contrary, such powers and duties shall be discharged by the Vice President as Acting President.

Section 4 Whenever the Vice President and a majority of either the principal officers of the executive departments or of such other body as Congress may by law provide, transmit to the President pro tempore of the Senate and the Speaker of the House of Representatives their written declaration that the President is unable to discharge the powers and duties of his office, the Vice President shall immediately assume the powers and duties of the office as Acting President.

Thereafter, when the President transmits to the President pro tempore of the Senate and the Speaker of the House of Representatives his written declaration that no inability exists, he shall resume the powers and duties of his office unless the Vice President and a majority of either the principal officers of the executive departments, or of such other body as Congress may by law provide, transmit within four days to the President pro tempore of the Senate and the Speaker of the House of Representatives their written declaration that the President is unable to discharge the powers and duties of his office. Thereupon Congress shall decide the issue, assembling within forty-eight hours for that purpose if not in session. If the Congress, within twenty-one days after receipt of the latter written declaration, or, if Congress is not in session, within twenty-one days after Congress is required to assemble, determines by two-thirds vote of both Houses that the President is unable to discharge the powers and duties of his office, the Vice President shall continue to discharge the same as Acting President otherwise the President shall resume the powers and duties of his office.

During the administration of President Woodrow Wilson, his final year in office, in 1919, was marked by serious illness. It is rumored that his wife acted as president. There was no constitutional provision to cover an incapacitating illness of a president. So this amendment provides a procedure for this eventuality. The president can inform congressional lead-

ers of his incapacitation and the vice president takes over. When he recovers, the president can so inform congressional leaders and he resumes office.

But the amendment also recognizes that the president may not be able or wish to indicate this debilitation; so the vice president and a majority of cabinet members can inform congressional leaders and the vice president takes over. When the president informs congressional leadership that he is back in form, he resumes the presidency unless the vice president and majority of the cabinet disagree. Then Congress must decide. The likelihood that this procedure will ever be used is relatively very small.

The most immediate importance of this amendment concerns the office of vice president. The original Constitution did not address the issue of a vacancy in this office. So the 25th Amendment established the procedure, just in time! This amendment was ratified in 1967. In 1973, the sitting vice president, Spiro Agnew, resigned his office. Under the provisions of this amendment, President Nixon nominated Gerald Ford as vice president. As a former member of the House, the Congress quickly approved him. But a year later, President Nixon also resigned. Now Vice President Ford became President Ford, and he in turn appointed Nelson Rockefeller as the new vice president. So, now for the first time in our history, we had both a president and vice president, neither of whom was elected by the Electoral College.

AMENDMENT 26—EIGHTEEN-YEAR-OLD VOTE

[Ratified July 1, 1971]

Section 1 The right of citizens of the United States, who are 18 years of age or older, to vote, shall not be denied or abridged by the United States or by any state on account of age.

Section 2 The Congress shall have power to enforce this article by appropriate legislation.

During the Vietnam War, 18 year olds were being drafted and sent out to possibly die in the service of their country. Yet they did not even have the right to vote. This incongruity led to the 22nd Amendment, which lowered the legal voting age from 21 to 18.

AMENDMENT 27—CONGRESSIONAL SALARIES

[Ratified May 7, 1992]

No law varying the compensation for the services of the Senators and Representatives shall take effect until an election of Representatives shall be intervened.

This is a "sleeper" amendment that was part of 12 amendments originally submitted by the first Congress to the states for ratification. The states only ratified 10 of the 12, which collectively became known as the Bill of Rights. But since Congress did not set a time limit for ratification, the other two amendments remained on the table. Much to the shock of the body politic, in 1992, 3/4 of the states ratified original amendment 12 of 12. This reflected the disgust of seeing Congress continuing to increase its salary and benefits. The amendment delays any increase of compensation for at least one election cycle.

Annotations by James Corey, High Point University.

4

FEDERALISM:
DIVIDING GOVERNMENTAL POWER

Indestructible Union, Indestructible States

In December 1860 South Carolina seceded from the Union and in April 1861 authorized its state militia to expel U.S. troops from Fort Sumter in Charleston harbor. Although there is no provision in the Constitution for states leaving the Union, eleven southern states—South Carolina, Mississippi, Florida, Alabama, Georgia, Louisiana, Texas, Virginia, Arkansas, Tennessee, and North Carolina, in that order—argued that the Union was a voluntary association and they were entitled to withdraw.[1] President Abraham Lincoln declared these states to be in armed rebellion and sent federal troops to crush the "rebels." The result was the nation's bloodiest war: more than 250,000 battle deaths and another 250,000 deaths from disease and privation, out of a total population of less than 30 million.

Following the Civil War, Chief Justice Salmon P. Chase confirmed what had been decided on the battlefield. "The Constitution in all its provisions looks to an indestructible union, composed of indestructible states."[2]

Federalism divides power between two separate authorities—the nation and the states—each of which enforces its own laws directly on its citizens. Both the nation and the states pass laws, impose taxes, spend money, and maintain their own courts. Neither the nation nor the states can dissolve the Union or amend the Constitution without the consent of the other. The Constitution itself is the only legal source of authority for both the states and the nation, the states do not get their power from the national government, and the national government does not get its power from the states. Both national and state governments derive their power directly from the people.

American federalism differs from a **unitary system** of government, in which formal authority rests with the national government, and whatever powers are exercised by states, provinces, or subdivisions are given to those governments by the national government. Most of the world's governments—including France and Britain—are unitary. Federalism also differs from a **confederation** of states, in which the national government relies on the states for its authority, not the people (see Figure 4.1). Under the Articles of Confederation of 1781, the United States was a confederation. The national government could not even levy taxes, it had to ask the states for revenue. Like the United States, a number of other countries were confederations before establishing federal systems, and today new types of

FIGURE 4.1 The Federal, Confederation, and Unitary Systems of Government

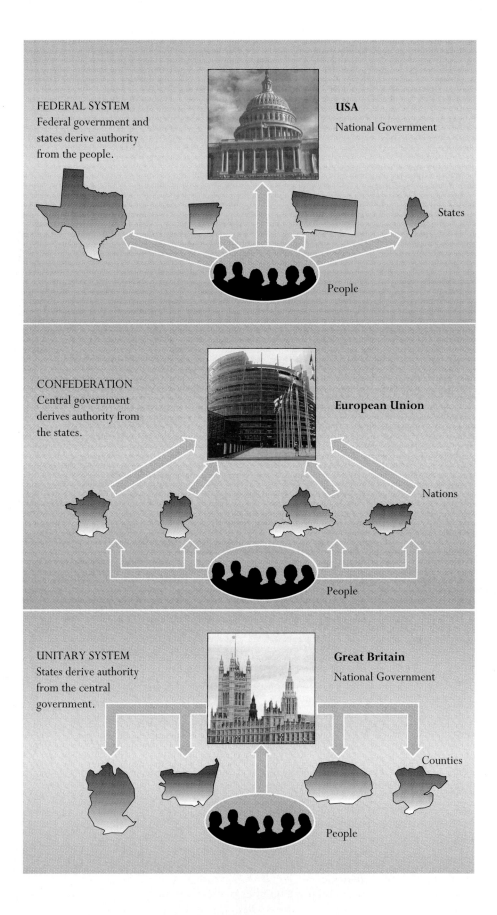

FEDERAL SYSTEM
Federal government and states derive authority from the people.

USA
National Government

States

People

CONFEDERATION
Central government derives authority from the states.

European Union

Nations

People

UNITARY SYSTEM
States derive authority from the central government.

Great Britain
National Government

Counties

People

confederations with limited functions are being formed (see *Compared to What?* "The European Union").

People in the United States often think of the *federal government* when the word *government* comes up. In fact, today there are more than 87,000 American governments. These state and local governments are important in American life, for they provide such essential day-to-day services as schools, water, and police and fire departments (see Table 4.1). However, the U.S. Constitution, the supreme law of the land, recognizes the existence of only the national government and the states. Local governments have no guarantees of power—or even existence—under the U.S. Constitution. Whatever powers they have are given to them by their state governments. States can create or abolish local governments, grant or withhold their powers, or change their boundaries without their consent. Some local governments have powers guaranteed in *state* constitutions, and some are even given **home rule**—the power to pass laws affecting local affairs, so long as those laws do not conflict with state or federal laws. About 60,000 of these 87,000 governments have the power to levy taxes to support activities authorized by state law.

In short, the American federal system is large and complex, with three levels of government—national, state, and local—sharing power. Indeed, the numbers and complexity of governments in the United States make **intergovernmental relations**—all of the interactions among these governments and their officials—a major concern of political scientists and policy makers.

Why Federalism? The Argument for a "Compound Republic"

The nation's Founders believed that "republican principles" would help make government responsible to the people, but they also argued that "auxiliary precautions" were necessary to protect the liberties of minorities and individuals. They believed that majority rule in a democratic government made it particularly important to devise ways to protect minorities and individuals from "unjust" and "interested" *majorities*. They believed that federalism would better protect liberty, disperse power, and manage "faction" (conflict).

federalism A constitutional arrangement whereby power is divided between national and subnational governments, each of which enforces its own laws directly on its citizens and neither of which can alter the arrangement without the consent of the other.

unitary system Constitutional arrangement whereby authority rests with the national government, subnational governments have only those powers given to them by the national government.

confederation Constitutional arrangement whereby the national government is created by and relies on subnational governments for its authority.

home rule Power of local government to pass laws affecting local affairs, so long as those laws do not conflict with state or federal laws.

THINK AGAIN

Which level of government deals best with the problems it faces?

intergovernmental relations Network of political, financial, and administrative relationships between units of the federal government and those of state and local governments.

TABLE 4.1 How Many American Governments?	
U.S. government	1
States	50
Counties	3,034
Municipalities	19,431
Townships	16,506
Special districts	35,356
School districts	13,522
All governments	87,900

Source: Statistical Abstract of the United States, 2002, p. 260.

The European Union

The European Union incorporates features of both federalism and confederation. The EU includes fifteen member nations—Austria, Belgium, Denmark, Finland, France, Germany, Greece, Ireland, Italy, Luxembourg, the Netherlands, Portugal, Spain, Sweden, and the United Kingdom—and embraces 374 million people. It grew slowly from a European Economic Community established in 1957 (designed to reduce and eventually abolish all tariffs among member nations), through a European Community established in 1965 (designed to create a single market free of all barriers to the movement of goods, services, capital, and labor), to its much more unified European Union established in 1991. The objectives of the European Union are to

- Promote economic progress through a single market and a single currency.
- Assert the identity of the European Union in international affairs, through common foreign and security policies and actions in international crises.
- Promote the free movement of persons and products throughout member nations.
- Promote European citizenship, not to replace national citizenship but to complement it and confer civil and political rights on European citizens.

Council of the European Union

The Council is the EU's principal decision-making body. It is composed of the foreign ministers of the member nations. Each country takes the presidency for six months; the Council votes by majority, although each country's vote is weighted differently. Germany, France, Italy, and the United Kingdom each have ten votes; Spain has eight; Belgium, Greece, the Netherlands, and Portugal have five; Austria and Sweden have four; Ireland, Denmark, and Finland have three; and Luxembourg has two. The Council meets in Brussels.

European Parliament

Deputies of the European Parliament (626) are directly elected every five years by the European Union's 374 million citizens. The major political parties operating in each of the member nations nominate candidates. The Parliament oversees the EU budget and passes on proposals to the Council of Ministers and the Commission. The Parliament also passes on new applicants to the EU.

The Commission

The Commission of the EU supervises the implementation of EU treaties, implements EU policies, and manages EU funds. It is composed of 20 commissioners appointed by member governments. The five largest countries—France, Germany, Italy, Spain, and the United Kingdom—appoint two commissioners each; the remaining countries appoint one commissioner each.

The Court of Justice

A Court of Justice hears complaints about member governments' treaty violations and interprets EU treaties and legislation. Its fifteen justices are appointed by the member governments and serve six-year terms.

The "Euro"

Perhaps the most far-reaching accomplishment of the EU was the introduction of the "euro"—a single European currency for use in all member states. The euro was first introduced January 1, 1999, and officially replaced old national currencies—such as francs, marks, pesetas, and lira—on January 1, 2002. However, the United Kingdom, Sweden, and Denmark have refused to substitute the euro for their own currency.

European Union Online Official EU site

Describes the structure of the organization, its membership current issues, etc.
www.europa.eu.int

Protecting Liberty Constitutional guarantees of individual liberty do not enforce themselves. The Founders argued that to guarantee liberty, government should be structured to encourage "opposite and rival" centers of power *within* and *among* governments. So they settled on both *federalism*—dividing powers between the national and state governments—and *separation of powers*—the dispersal of power among branches within the national government.

In the compound republic of America, the power surrendered by the people is first divided between two distinct governments, and then the portion allotted to each is sub-

The future of the European Union remains under discussion. Will there be a common Bill of Rights guaranteeing Europeans individual liberties and protections against government? Will European governments create a common military? Will the European Union admit additional nations—Poland, the Czech Republic, or Hungary, for example? How will the voting strength of large nations and small nations be balanced? How much power will be allocated to the central European Union government relative to the powers of member nations? Note that these questions were the same as many of those discussed in the American Constitutional Convention of 1787 (see Chapter 3).

divided among distinct and separate departments. Hence a double security arises to the rights of the people. The different governments will control each other, at the same time that each will be controlled by itself.[3]

Thus the Founders deliberately tried to create competition within and among governmental units as a means of protecting liberty. Rather than rely on the "better motives" of leaders, the Founders sought to construct a system in which governments and government officials would be constrained by competition with other governments and other government officials: "Ambition must be made to counteract ambition."[4]

Council of State Governments

Official Organization of U.S. states, providing information on their governmental structures, officials, and current issues. **www.csg.org**

Dispersing Power Federalism distributes power widely among different sets of leaders, national as well as state and local officeholders. The Founders believed that multiple leadership groups offered more protection against tyranny than a single set of all-powerful leaders. State and local government offices also provide a political base for the opposition party when it has lost a national election. In this way, state and local governments contribute to party competition in the United States by helping to tide over the losing party after electoral defeat at the national level so that it can remain strong enough to challenge incumbents at the next election. And finally, state and local governments often provide a training ground for national political leaders. National leaders can be drawn from a pool of leaders experienced in state and local government.

Increasing Participation Federalism allows more people to participate in the political system. With more than 87,000 governments in the United States—state, county, municipality, township, special district, and school district—nearly a million people hold some kind of public office (See *What Do You Think?* "Which Government Seems Closer to You?").

Improving Efficiency Federalism also makes government more manageable and efficient. Imagine the bureaucracy, red tape, and confusion if every governmental activity—police, schools, roads, fire fighting, garbage collection, sewage disposal, and so forth—in every local community in the nation were controlled by a centralized administration in Washington. Government can become arbitrary when a bureaucracy far from the scene directs local officials. Thus decentralization often softens the rigidity of law.

Ensuring Policy Responsiveness Federalism encourages policy responsiveness. The existence of multiple governments offering different packages of benefits and costs allows a better match between citizen preferences and public policy. Americans are very mobile. People and businesses can "vote with their feet" by relocating to those states and communities that most closely conform to their own policy preferences. This mobility not only facilitates a better match between citizen preferences and public policy but also encourages competition between states and communities to offer improved services at lower costs.[5]

Encouraging Policy Innovation The Founders hoped that federalism would encourage policy experimentation and innovation. Today federalism may seem like a "conservative" idea, but it was once the instrument of liberal reformers. Federal programs as diverse as the income tax, unemployment compensation, Social Security, wage and hour legislation, bank deposit insurance, and food stamps were all state programs before becoming national undertakings. Today much of the current "liberal" policy agenda—mandatory health insurance for workers, child-care programs, notification of plant closings, government support of industrial research and development—has been embraced by various states. The phrase **laboratories of democracies** is generally attributed to the great progressive jurist Supreme Court Justice Louis D. Brandeis, who used it in defense of state experimentation with new solutions to social and economic problems.[6]

laboratories of democracy
A reference to the ability of states to experiment and innovate in public policy.

Managing Conflict Federalism allows different peoples to come together in a nation without engendering irresolvable conflict. Conflicts between geographically separate groups in America are resolved by allowing each to pursue its own poli-

Which Government Seems Closer to You?

Americans seem to favor governments closer to home. Most surveys show that Americans have greater confidence in their local governments than in their state or federal government. Americans feel most "connected" to their local government and least "connected" to the federal government.

Sources: Responses on confidence from Gallup, September, 2003; responses on connectedness from Council for Excellence in Government, July, 1999.

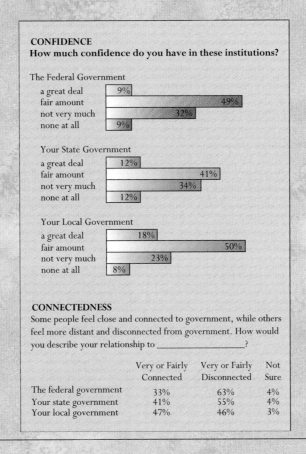

CONFIDENCE
How much confidence do you have in these institutions?

The Federal Government
- a great deal — 9%
- fair amount — 49%
- not very much — 32%
- none at all — 9%

Your State Government
- a great deal — 12%
- fair amount — 41%
- not very much — 34%
- none at all — 12%

Your Local Government
- a great deal — 18%
- fair amount — 50%
- not very much — 23%
- none at all — 8%

CONNECTEDNESS
Some people feel close and connected to government, while others feel more distant and disconnected from government. How would you describe your relationship to _____?

	Very or Fairly Connected	Very or Fairly Disconnected	Not Sure
The federal government	33%	63%	4%
Your state government	41%	55%	4%
Your local government	47%	46%	3%

cies within its separate state or community instead of battling over a single national policy to be applied uniformly throughout the land.

Some Important Reservations Despite the strengths of federalism, it has its problems. First of all, federalism can obstruct action on national issues. Although decentralization may reduce conflict at the national level, it may do so at the price of "sweeping under the rug" very serious national injustices (see *A Conflicting View:* "The Dark Side of Federalism" on page 114). Federalism also permits local leaders and citizens to frustrate national policy, to sacrifice national interest to local interests. Decentralized government provides an opportunity for local NIMBYs (people who subscribe to the motto *"Not In My Back Yard"*) to obstruct airports, highways, waste disposal plants, public housing, drug rehabilitation centers, and many other projects that would be in the national interest.

The Dark Side of Federalism

Segregationists once regularly used the argument of "states rights" to deny equal protection of the law to African Americans. Indeed, *states' rights* became a code word for opposition to federal civil rights laws. In 1963 Governor George Wallace invoked the states' rights argument when he stood in the doorway at the University of Alabama to prevent the execution of a federal court order that the university admit two African American students and integrate. Federal marshals were on hand to enforce the order, and Wallace only temporarily delayed them. Shortly after his dramatic stand in front of the television cameras, he retreated to his office. Later in his career, Wallace sought African American votes, declaring, "I was wrong. Those days are over."

Federalism in America remains tainted by its historical association with slavery, segregation, and discrimination. In the Virginia and Kentucky Resolutions of 1798, Thomas Jefferson and James Madison asserted the doctrine of "nullification," claiming that states could nullify unconstitutional laws of Congress. Although the original intent of this doctrine was to counter congressional attacks on a free press under the Alien and Sedition Acts of 1798, it was later revived to defend slavery. John C. Calhoun of South Carolina argued forcefully in the years before the Civil War that slavery was an issue for the states to decide and the Constitution gave Congress no power to interfere with slavery in the southern states or in the new western territories.

In the years immediately following the Civil War, the issues of slavery, racial inequality, and African American voting rights were *nationalized*. Nationalizing these issues meant removing them from the jurisdiction of the states and placing them in the hands of the national government. The Thirteenth, Fourteenth, and Fifteenth Amendments to the Constitution were enforced by federal troops in the southern states during the post–Civil War Reconstruction era. But after the Compromise of 1876 led to the withdrawal of federal troops from the southern states, legal and social segregation of African Americans became a "way of life" in the region. Segregation was *denationalized*, which reduced national conflict over race but exacted a high price from the nation's African American population. Segregationists asserted the states' rights argument so often in defense of racial discrimination that it became a code phrase for racism. Not until the 1950s and 1960s were questions of segregation and equality again made into national issues. The civil rights movement asserted the supremacy of national law and in 1954 won a landmark decision in the case of *Brown v. Board of Education of Topeka,* when the U.S. Supreme Court ruled that segregation enforced by state (or local) officials violated the Fourteenth Amendment's guarantee that no state could deny any person the equal protection of the law. Later the *national* Civil Rights Act of 1964 outlawed discrimination in private employment and businesses serving the public.

Only now that national constitutional and legal guarantees of equal protection of the law are in place is it possible to reassess the true worth of federalism. Having established that federalism will not mean racial inequality, Americans are now free to explore the values of decentralized government.

In an attempt to block the admission of two African American students to the University of Alabama in 1963, Governor George Wallace barred the door with his body in the face of U.S. federal marshals. The tactic did not succeed, and the two students were admitted.

Finally, federalism permits the benefits and costs of government to be spread unevenly across the nation. For example, some states spend more than twice as much on the education of each child in the public schools as other states do. Taxes in some states are more than twice as high per capita as they are in other states. Welfare benefits in some states are more than twice as high as in other states. Competition among states may keep welfare benefits low in states that want to discourage poor people from moving there. Thus federalism obstructs uniformity in policy.

The Original Design of Federalism

The U.S. Constitution *originally* defined American federalism in terms of (1) the powers expressly delegated to the national government plus the powers implied by those that are specifically granted, (2) the concurrent powers exercised by both states and the national government, (3) the powers reserved to the states, (4) the powers denied by the Constitution to both the national government and the states, and (5) the constitutional provisions giving the states a role in the composition of the national government (see Figure 4.2).

Delegated Powers The U.S. Constitution lists seventeen specific grants of power of Congress, in Article I, Section 8. These are usually referred to as the **delegated, or enumerated, powers.** They include authority over war and foreign affairs, authority over the economy ("interstate commerce"), control over the money supply, and the power to tax and spend "to pay the debts and provide for the common defence and general welfare." After these specific grants of power comes the power "to make all laws which shall be necessary and proper for carrying into execution the foregoing powers, and all other powers vested by this Constitution in the government of the United States or in any department or officer thereof." This statement is generally known as the **Necessary and Proper Clause,** and it is the principal source of the national government's **implied powers**—powers not specifically listed in the Constitution but inferred from those that are.

National Supremacy The delegated and implied powers, when coupled with the assertion of "national supremacy" (in Article VI), ensure a powerful national government. The **National Supremacy Clause** is very specific in asserting the supremacy of federal laws over state and local laws:

> This Constitution, and the laws of the United States which shall be made in pursuance thereof, and all treaties made, or which shall be made, under the authority of the United States, shall be the supreme law of the land, and the Judges in every state shall be bound thereby, any thing in the constitution or laws of any state to the contrary notwithstanding.

Concurrent and Reserved Powers Despite broad grants of power to the national government, the states retain considerable governing power. **Concurrent powers** are those recognized in the Constitution as belonging to *both* the national and state governments, including the power to tax and spend, make and enforce laws, and establish courts of justice. The Tenth Amendment reassured the states that "the powers not delegated to the United States . . . are reserved to the States respectively, or to the people." Through these **reserved powers,** the states

delegated, or enumerated, powers Powers specifically mentioned in the Constitution as belonging to the national government.

THINK AGAIN

In which level of government do you have the most confidence?

Necessary and Proper Clause Clause in Article I, Section 8, of the U.S. Constitution granting Congress the power to enact all laws that are "necessary and proper" for carrying out those responsibilities specifically delegated to it. Also referred to as the Implied Powers Clause.

implied powers Powers not mentioned specifically in the Constitution as belonging to Congress but inferred as necessary and proper for carrying out the enumerated powers.

National Supremacy Clause Clause in Article VI of the U.S. Constitution declaring the constitution and laws of the national government "the supreme law of the land" superior to the constitutions and laws of the states.

concurrent powers Powers exercised by both the national government and state governments in the American federal system.

reserved powers Powers not granted to the national government or specifically denied to the states in the Constitution that are recognized by the Tenth Amendment as belonging to the state governments. This guarantee, known as the Reserved Powers Clause, embodies the principle of American federalism.

POWERS GRANTED BY THE CONSTITUTION

NATIONAL GOVERNMENT
Delegated Powers

Military Affairs and Defense
- Provide for the common defense (I-8).
- Declare war (I-8).
- Raise and support armies(I-8).
- Provide and maintain a navy (I-8).
- Define and punish piracies (I-8).
- Define and punish offenses against the law of nations (I-8).
- Provide for calling forth the militia to execute laws, suppress insurrections, and repel invasions (I-8).
- Provide for organizing, arming, and disciplining the militia (I-8).
- Declare the punishment of treason (III-3).

Economic Affairs
- Regulate commerce with foreign nations, among the several states, and with Indian tribes (I-8).
- Establish uniform laws on bankruptcy (I-8).
- Coin money and regulate its value (I-8).
- Fix standards of weights and measures (I-8).
- Provide for patents and copyrights (I-8).
- Establish post offices and post roads (I-8).

Governmental Organization
- Constitute tribunals inferior to the Supreme Court (I-8, III-1).
- Exercise exclusive legislative power over the seat of government and over certain military installations (I-8).
- Admit new states (IV-3).
- Dispose of and regulate territory or property of the United States (IV-3).

"Implied" Powers
- Make laws necessary and proper for carrying the expressed powers into execution (I-8).

NATIONAL AND STATE GOVERNMENTS
Concurrent Powers

- Levy taxes (I-8).
- Borrow money (I-8).
- Contract and pay debts (I-8).
- Charter banks and corporations (I-8).
- Make and enforce laws (I-8).
- Establish courts (I-8).
- Provide for the general welfare (I-8).

STATE GOVERNMENTS
Reserved to the States

- Regulate intrastate commerce.
- Conduct elections.
- Provide for public health, safety, and morals.
- Establish local government.
- Maintain the militia (National Guard).
- Ratify amendments to the federal Constitution (V).
- Determine voter qualifications (I-2).

"Reserved" Powers

- Powers not delegated to national government nor denied to the States by the Constitution (X).

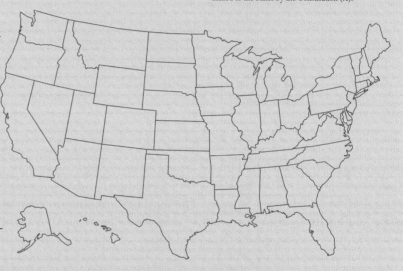

POWERS DENIED BY THE CONSTITUTION

NATIONAL GOVERNMENT

- Give preference to the ports of any state (I-9).
- Impose a tax or duty on articles exported from any state (I-9).
- Directly tax except by apportionment among the states on a population basis (I-9), now superseded as to income tax (Amendment XVI).
- Draw money from the Treasury except by appropriation (I-9).

NATIONAL AND STATE GOVERNMENTS

- Grant titles of nobility (I-9).
- Limit the suspension of habeas corpus (I-9).
- Issue bills of attainder (I-10).
- Make ex post facto laws (I-10).
- Establish a religion or prohibit the free exercise of religion (Amendment I).
- Abridge freedom of speech, press, assembly, or right of petition (Amendment I).
- Deny the right to bear arms protected (Amendment II).
- Restrict quartering of soldiers in private homes (Amendment III).
- Conduct unreasonable searches or seizures. (Amendment IV).
- Deny guarantees of fair trials (Amendment V, Amendment VI, and Amendment VII).
- Impose excessive bail or unusual punishments (Amendment VII).
- Take life, liberty, or property without due process (Amendment V).
- Permit slavery (Amendment XIII).
- Deny life, liberty, or property without due process of law (Amendment XIV).
- Deny voting because of race, color, previous servitude (Amendment XV), sex (Amendment XIX), or age if 18 or over (Amendment XXVI).
- Deny voting because of nonpayment of any tax (Amendment XXIV).

STATE GOVERNMENTS

Economic Affairs
- Use legal tender other than gold or silver coin (I-10).
- Issue separate state coinage (I-10).
- Impair the obligation of contracts (I-10).
- Emit bills of credit (I-10).
- Levy import or export duties, except reasonable inspection fees, without the consent of Congress (I-10).
- Abridge the privileges and immunities of national citizenship (Amendment XIV)
- Make any law that violates federal law (Amendment VI).
- Pay for rebellion against the United States or for emancipated slaves (Amendment XIV)

Foreign Affairs
- Enter into treaties, alliances, or confederations (I-10).
- Make compact with a foreign state, except by congressional consent (I-10).

Military Affairs
- Issue letters of marque and reprisal (I-10).
- Maintain standing military forces in peace without congressional consent (I-10).
- Engage in war, without congressional consent, except in imminent danger or when invaded (I-10).

FIGURE 4.2 Original Constitutional Distribution of Powers

Under the Constitution of 1787, certain powers were delegated to the national government, other powers were shared by the national and state governments, and still other powers were reserved for state governments alone. Similarly, certain powers were denied by the Constitution to the national government, other powers were denied to both the national and state governments, and still other powers were denied only to state governments. Later amendments especially protected individual liberties.

generally retain control over property and contract law, criminal law, marriage and divorce, and the provision of education, highways, and social welfare activities. (But for a discussion of increasing federal involvement in crime fighting, traditionally a "reserved" power of the states, see *A Conflicting View:* "Don't Make Everything a Federal Crime!") The states control the organization and powers of their own local governments. Finally, the states, like the federal government, retain the power to tax and spend for the general welfare.

"Look, the American people don't want to be bossed around by federal bureaucrats. They want to be bossed around by state bureaucrats."

Source: © 2002 Robert Mankoff from cartoonbank.com. All Rights Reserved.

Powers Denied to the States The Constitution denies the states some powers in order to safeguard national unity. States are specifically denied the power to coin money, enter into treaties with foreign nations, interfere with the "obligation of contracts," levy taxes on imports or exports, or engage in war.

Powers Denied to the Nation and the States The Constitution denies some powers to both national and state government—namely, the powers to abridge individual rights. The Bill of Rights originally applied only to the national government, but the Fourteenth Amendment, passed by Congress in 1866 and ratified by 1868, provided that the states must also adhere to fundamental guarantees of individual liberty.

State Role in National Government The states are basic units in the organizational scheme of the national government. The House of Representatives apportions members to the states by population, and state legislatures draw up the districts that elect representatives. Every state has at least one member in the House of Representatives, regardless of its population. Each state elects two U.S. senators, regardless of its population. The president is chosen by the electoral votes of the states, with each state having as many electoral votes as it has senators and representatives combined. Finally, three-fourths of the states must ratify amendments to the U.S. Constitution.

State Obligations to Each Other To promote national unity, the Constitution requires the states to recognize actions and decisions taken by other states. Article IV requires the states to give "Full Faith and Credit . . . to the public Acts, Records, and judiciary Proceedings of every other State." This provision ensures that contracts, property ownership, insurance, civil judgments, marriages and divorces, among other things, made in one state are recognized in all states.

Recently, controversy has arisen over recognition of gay and lesbian marriages or "civil unions." A strict reading of Article IV would suggest that if any state legalized same-sex marriages, all states would be obliged to recognize them. (In 1999 the Vermont Supreme Court prohibited discrimination against gay marriages.) Anticipating this issue, the Congress passed a Defense of Marriage Act in 1996 stating that "No State . . . shall be required to give effect to any public act, record, or judicial proceeding of any other State respecting a relationship between persons of the same sex that is treated as a marriage. . ." The Congress relied on language in the next sentence of Article IV: "the Congress may by general law prescribe the Manner in which such Acts, Records and Proceedings shall be proved, *and the Effect thereof*" (italics added). It is not altogether clear whether this constitutional language in the second sentence allows Congress to nullify the "Full Faith and Credit" clause in the first sentence. If Vermont or any other state persists in recognizing gay marriages, the issue may end up in the Supreme Court (see also "Privacy and the Constitution" in Chapter 14).

Don't Make Everything a Federal Crime!

Political officeholders in Washington are continually pressured to make "a federal crime" out of virtually every offense in society. Neither Democrats nor Republicans, liberals nor conservatives, are willing to risk their political futures by telling their constituents that crime fighting is a state and local responsibility. So Washington lawmakers continue to add common offenses to the ever lengthening list of federal crimes.

Traditionally, federal crimes were limited to a relatively narrow range of offenses, including counterfeiting and currency violations; tax evasion, including alcohol, tobacco, and firearm taxes; fraud and embezzlement; robbery of federally insured banks; murder or assault of a federal official; and violations of customs and immigrations laws. While some federal criminal laws overlapped state laws, most criminal activity—murder, rape, robbery, assault, burglary, theft, auto theft, gambling, sex offenses, and so on—fell under state jurisdiction. Indeed, the *police power* was believed to be one of the "reserved" powers states referred to in the Tenth Amendment.

But over time Congress has made more and more offenses *federal* crimes. Today federal crimes range from drive-by shootings to obstructing sidewalks in front of abortion clinics. Any violent offense motivated by racial, religious, or ethnic animosity is a "hate crime" subject to federal investigation and prosecution. "Racketeering" and "conspiracy" (organizing and communicating with others about the intent to commit a crime) is a federal crime. The greatest impact of federal involvement in law enforcement is found in drug-related crime. Drug offenders may be tried in either federal or state courts, or both. Federal drug laws, including those pro-hibiting possession, carry heavier penalties than those of most states.

The effect of federalizing crime is to subject citizens to the possibility of being tried twice for the same crime—in federal court and in state court for an offense that violates both federal and state criminal codes. The U.S. Supreme Court has held that such multiple prosecution does *not* violate the Double Jeopardy Clause of the Fifth Amendment—"nor shall any person be subject for the same offense to be twice put in jeopardy of life or limb" (*Heath vs. Alabama,* 474 U.S. 82 (1985)). In the well-publicized Rodney King case, a California state jury acquitted police officers of beating King, but a federal court jury later convicted them of violating King's civil rights.

Another effect of federalizing crime is to further fragment an already fragmented law enforcement structure in the United States. The federal government's principal investigative agencies are the Federal Bureau of Investigation (FBI) and the Drug Enforcement Administration (DEA), both units of the Department of Justice; the Bureau of Alcohol, Tobacco, and Firearms (ATF) and the Internal Revenue Service (IRS) in the Treasury Department; and the Customs Bureau and Immigration and Naturalization Service (INS) in the Department of Homeland Security. Efforts to combine these law enforcement agencies have consistently foundered in bureaucratic battles. It is not uncommon at a major crime scene to see FBI, DEA, and ATF agents mingling with officers from state-level agencies, county sheriff's departments, and local police forces.

Yet, despite growing federalization of crime, state and local governments in America continue to bear the major burden of law enforcement. Over 10 million people are arrested and charged with offenses from misdemeanors to felonies in the United States today. But only about 50,000 people are prosecuted for crime by federal authorities in federal courts.

The Evolution of American Federalism

American federalism has evolved over 200 years from a state-centered division of power to a national-centered system of government. Although the original constitutional wordings have remained in place, power has flowed toward the national government since the earliest days of the Republic. American federalism has been forged in the fires of political conflicts between states and nation, conflicts that have usually been resolved in favor of the national government. (See *Up Close:* "Historical Markers in the Development of American Federalism."). Generalizing

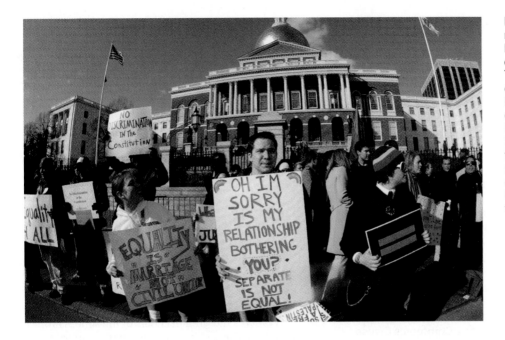

about the evolution of American federalism is no easy task. But let us try to describe broadly some major periods in the evolution of federalism, then look at five specific historical developments that had far-reaching impact on that evolution.

State-Centered Federalism, 1787–1868 From the adoption of the Constitution of 1787 to the end of the Civil War, the states were the most important units in the American federal system. It is true that during this period the legal foundation for the expansion of national power was being laid, but people looked to the states for resolving most policy questions and providing most public services. Even the issue of slavery was decided by state governments. The supremacy of the national government was frequently questioned, first by the Anti-Federalists (including Thomas Jefferson) and later by John C. Calhoun and other defenders of slavery.

Dual Federalism, 1868–1913 The supremacy of the national government was decided on the battlefields of the Civil War. Yet for nearly a half-century after that conflict, the national government narrowly interpreted its delegated powers, and the states continued to decide most domestic policy issues. The resulting pattern has been described as **dual federalism.** Under this pattern, the states and the nation divided most governmental functions. The national government concentrated its attention on the "delegated" powers—national defense, foreign affairs, tariffs, interstate commerce, the coinage of money, standard weights and measures, post office and post roads, and the admission of new states. State governments decided the important domestic policy issues—education, welfare, health, and criminal justice. The separation of policy responsibilities was once compared to a layer cake, with local governments at the base, state governments in the middle, and the national government at the top.[7]

Cooperative Federalism, 1913–1964 The distinction between national and state responsibilities gradually eroded in the first half of the twentieth century. American federalism was transformed by the Industrial Revolution and the development of a national economy, by the federal income tax in 1913, which shifted financial resources to the national government, and by the challenges of two world

dual federalism Early concept of federalism in which national and state powers were clearly distinguished and functionally separate.

Historical Markers in the Development of American Federalism

Among the most important events in the development of American federalism: (1) the Supreme Court's decision in *McCulloch v. Maryland* in 1819 giving a broad interpretation of the Necessary and Proper Clause; (2) the victory of the national government in the Civil War 1861–65; (3) the establishment of a national system of civil rights based on the Fourteenth Amendment culminating in the Supreme Court's desegregation decision in *Brown v. Board of Education;* (4) the expansion of the national government's power under the Interstate Commerce Clause during the Great Depression of the 1930s; and (5) the growth of federal revenues after the passage of the Sixteenth (income tax) Amendment in 1913.

McCulloch v. Maryland and the Necessary and Proper Clause

Political conflict over the scope of national power is as old as the nation itself. In 1790 Secretary of the Treasury Alexander Hamilton proposed the establishment of a national bank. Congress acted on Hamilton's suggestion in 1791, establishing a national bank to serve as a depository for federal money and to aid the federal government in borrowing funds. Jeffersonians believed the national bank was a dangerous centralization of government. They objected that the power to establish the bank was nowhere to be found in the enumerated powers of Congress.

Hamilton replied that Congress could derive the power to establish a bank from grants of authority in the Constitution relating to money, in combination with the clause authorizing Congress "to make all laws which shall be necessary and proper for carrying into execution the foregoing powers."

The question finally reached the Supreme Court in 1819, when the State of Maryland levied a tax on the national bank and the bank refused to pay it. In the case of *McCulloch v. Maryland,* Chief Justice Marshall accepted the broader Hamiltonian version of the Necessary and Proper Clause: "Let the end be legitimate, let it be within the scope of the Constitution, and all means which are appropriate, which are plainly adopted to that end, which are not pro-

hibited but consistent with the letter and the spirit of the Constitution, are constitutional."[*]

The *McCulloch* case firmly established the principle that the Necessary and Proper Clause gives Congress the right to choose its means in carrying out the enumerated powers of the national government. Because of this broad interpretation of the Necessary and Proper Clause, today Congress can devise programs, create agencies, and establish national laws on the basis of long chains of reasoning from the most meager phrases of the constitutional text.

Secession and Civil War

The Civil War was the greatest crisis of the American federal system. Did a state have the right to oppose national law to the point of secession, that is, withdrawing from the federal Union? The question of secession was decided on Civil War battlefields between 1861 and 1865. Yet the states' rights doctrine and political disputes over the character of American federalism did not disappear with General Robert E. Lee's surrender at Appomattox. In addition to establishing that states cannot secede from the federal union, the Civil War led to three constitutional amendments clearly aimed at limiting state power in the interests of individual freedom. The Thirteenth Amendment eliminated slavery in the states; the Fifteenth Amendment prevented states from denying the vote on the basis of race, color, or previous enslavement; and the Fourteenth Amendment declared,

> No State shall make or enforce any law which shall abridge the privileges or immunities of citizens of the United States; nor shall any state deprive any person of life, liberty, or property, without due process of law; nor deny to any person within its jurisdiction the equal protection of the laws.

During the post–Civil War Reconstruction era (1866–77), Congress passed several laws designed to enforce these amendments—laws guaranteeing the right to vote, providing remedies for the denial of rights by any person acting under "the color of law" (any public official), and prohibiting discrimination in public accommodation.[†] But after 1877, Congress gave up its efforts to reconstruct southern society, and the Supreme Court also failed to uphold these Reconstruction laws.

National Guarantees of Civil Rights

However, in the twentieth century, the Supreme Court began to build a national system of civil rights based on the Fourteenth Amendment. First, the Court held that the Fourteenth Amendment prevented states from interfering with free speech, free press, or religious practices. But it was not until 1954, in the desegregation decision in *Brown v. Board of Education of Topeka,* that the Court began to call for the full assertion of national authority on behalf of civil rights.[‡] When it decided that the Fourteenth Amendment prohibited the states from segregating the races in public schools, the Court was asserting national authority over longstanding practices in many of the states.

But in the years following *Brown,* some state officials tried to prevent the enforcement of a national law. Governor Orval Faubus called out the Arkansas National Guard to prevent a federal court from desegregating Little Rock Central High School in 1957. President Dwight D. Eisenhower responded by ordering the Arkansas National Guard removed and sent units of the U.S. Army to enforce national authority. This presidential action reinforced the principle of national supremacy in the American political system.

The Expansion of Interstate Commerce

The growth of national power under the Interstate Commerce Clause of the Constitution is another important development in the evolution of American federalism. For many years, the U.S. Supreme Court

In a long bloody war to establish national supremacy, the North's ultimate victory served to prove once and for all that the federal union cannot be dissolved.

narrowly defined *interstate commerce* to mean only the movement of goods and services across state lines. Until the late 1930s, it insisted that agriculture, mining, manufacturing, and labor relations were outside the reach of the delegated powers of the national government. However, when confronted with the Great Depression of the 1930s and Franklin Roosevelt's threat to add enough members to the Supreme Court to win favorable rulings, the Court yielded. It redefined *interstate commerce* to include any activity that "substantially affects" the national economy.[§] Indeed, the Court frequently approved of congressional restrictions on economic activities that had only very indirect effects on interstate commerce.[‖]

The Income Tax and Federal Grants

In the famous Northwest Ordinance of 1787, which provided for the governing of the territories west of the Appalachian Mountains, Congress made grants of land for the establishment of public schools. Then in the Morrill Land Grant Act of 1862, Congress provided grants of land to the states to promote higher education, especially agricultural and mechanical studies. Federal support for "A and M" or "land grant" universities continues today.

With the money provided to Washington by the passage of the Sixteenth (income tax) Amendment in 1913, Congress embarked on cash grants to the states. Among the earliest cash grant programs were the Federal Highway Act of 1916 and the Smith-Hughes Act of 1917 (vocational education). With federal money came federal direction. For example, states that wanted federal money for highways after 1916 had to accept uniform standards of construction and even a uniform road-numbering system (U.S. 1, U.S. 30, and so on). Shortly after these programs began, the U.S. Supreme Court considered the claim that these federal grants were unconstitutional intrusions into areas "reserved" for the states. But the Court upheld grants as a legitimate exercise of Congress's power to tax and spend for the general welfare.[¶]

---

[*]*McCulloch v. Maryland,* 4 Wheaten 316 (1819).

[†]*Civil Rights Acts of 1866, 1872, and 1875.*

[‡]*Brown v. Board of Education of Topeka, Kansas,* 347 U.S. 483 (1954).

[§]*National Labor Relations Board v. Jones & Laughlin Steel Corporation,* 301 U.S. 1 (1937).

[‖]*Wickard v. Filburn,* 317 U.S. 128 (1938).

[¶]*Massachusetts v. Mellon, Framingham v. Mellon,* 262 U.S. 447 (1923).

cooperative federalism
Model of federalism in which national, state, and local governments work together exercising common policy responsibilities.

 The Close Up Foundation

A nonprofit, nonpartisan citizenship education organization with excellent historical materials about federalism's evolution and information about federalism issues. A related link on the Close Up site contains the complete text of the pro-states' rights 1798 Kentucky and Virginia Resolutions (authored by Jefferson). ***www.closeup.org***

centralized federalism
Model of federalism in which the national government assumes primary responsibility for determining national goals in all major policy areas and directs state and local government activity through conditions attached to money grants.

During the Great Depression of the 1930s, the massive public works projects sponsored by the federal government under President Franklin Roosevelt's New Deal reflected the emergence of cooperative federalism. Programs of the Work Progress Administration, like the one shown here, were responsible for the construction of buildings, bridges, highways, and airports throughout the country.

wars and the Great Depression. In response to the Great Depression of the 1930s, state governors welcomed massive federal public works projects under President Franklin D. Roosevelt's New Deal program. In addition, the federal government intervened directly in economic affairs, labor relations, business practices, and agriculture. Through its grants of money, the national government cooperated with the states in public assistance, employment services, child welfare, public housing, urban renewal, highway building, and vocational education.

This new pattern of federal-state relations was labeled **cooperative federalism**. Both the nation and the states exercised responsibilities for welfare, health, highways, education, and criminal justice. This merging of policy responsibilities was compared to a marble cake: "As the colors are mixed in a marble cake, so functions are mixed in the American federal system."[8] Yet even in this period of shared national-state responsibility, the national government emphasized cooperation in achieving common national and state goals. Congress generally acknowledged that it had no direct constitutional authority to regulate public health, safety, or welfare. Instead, it relied primarily on its powers to tax and spend for the general welfare, providing financial assistance to state and local governments to achieve shared goals. Congress did not usually legislate directly on local matters.

Centralized Federalism, 1964–1980 Over the years, it became increasingly difficult to maintain the fiction that the national government was merely assisting the states to perform their domestic responsibilities. By the time President Lyndon B. Johnson launched the Great Society program in 1964, the federal government clearly had its own *national* goals. Virtually all problems confronting American society—from solid-waste disposal and water and air pollution to consumer safety, home insulation, noise abatement, and even "highway beautification"—were declared to be national problems. Congress legislated directly on any matter it chose, without regard to its *enumerated powers* and without pretending to render only financial assistance. The Supreme Court no longer concerned itself with the reserved powers of the states, and the Tenth Amendment lost most of its meaning. The pattern of national-state relations became **centralized federalism**. As for the cake analogies, one commentator observed, "The frosting had moved to the top, something like a pineapple upside-down cake."[9]

New Federalism, 1980–1985 New **federalism** was a phrase frequently applied to efforts to reverse the flow of power to Washington and to return responsibilities to states and communities. (The phrase originated in the administration of Richard M. Nixon, 1969–74, who used it to describe general revenue sharing—making federal grants to state and local governments with few strings attached.) New Federalism was popular early in the administration of President Ronald Reagan, who tried to reduce federal involvement in domestic programs and encourage states and cities to undertake greater policy responsibilities themselves. The result was that state and local governments were forced to rely more on their own sources of revenue and less on federal money. Still, centralizing tendencies in the American federal system continued. While the general public usually gave better marks to state and local governments than to the federal government, paradoxically that same public also favored greater federal involvement in policy areas traditionally thought to be state or local responsibilities (see Figure 4.3).

Representational Federalism, 1985–1995 Despite centralizing tendencies, it was still widely assumed prior to 1985 that the Congress could not directly legislate how state and local governments should go about performing their traditional functions. However, in its 1985 *Garcia v. San Antonio Metropolitan Transit Authority* decision, the U.S. Supreme Court appeared to remove all barriers to direct

new federalism Attempts to return power and responsibility to the states and reduce the role of the national government in domestic affairs.

Which level of government should run the following programs?

Service to immigrants
Federal 60%
State 15%
Local 6%

Welfare
Federal 40%
State 38%
Local 17%

Health care for the disabled, poor, and elderly
Federal 36%
State 28%
Local 18%

Opportunity for minorities
Federal 35%
State 30%
Local 28%

Air/water quality
Federal 35%
State 40%
Local 22%

Public education
Federal 21%
State 47%
Local 30%

Child care
Federal 16%
State 34%
Local 29%

Employment and job training
Federal 15%
State 59%
Local 24%

Law enforcement
Federal 15%
State 36%
Local 45%

FIGURE 4.3 Public Views about Which Level of Government Should Run Various Programs

Source: Gallup/CNN/USA Today Poll, reported in *The Polling Report,* February 10, 1997. Copyright © 1996–2004 by The Gallup Organization.

Medicare for the elderly was added to Social Security in 1965 as part of President Lyndon B. Johnson's Great Society program. Increasingly, health care has come to be viewed as a federal government responsibility. A Republic-controlled congress added prescription drug coverage in 2003, albeit with "gaps" that Democrats vowed to eliminate.

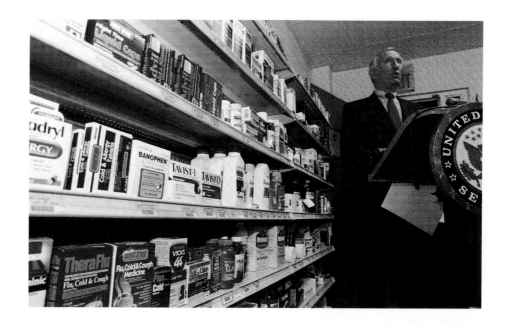

THINK
AGAIN

Should the national government be able to prosecute a high school student for bringing a gun to school?

representational federalism
Assertion that no constitutional division of powers exists between the nation and the states but the states retain their constitutional role merely by selecting the president and members of Congress.

congressional legislation in matters traditionally reserved to the states. The case arose after Congress directly ordered state and local governments to pay minimum wages to their employees. The Court dismissed arguments that the nature of American federalism and the Reserved Powers Clause of the Tenth Amendment prevented Congress from directly legislating in state affairs. It said that the only protection for state powers was to be found in the states' role in electing U.S. senators, members of the U.S. House of Representatives, and the president. The Court's ruling asserts a concept known as **representational federalism**: Federalism is defined by the role of the states in electing members of Congress and the president, not by any constitutional division of powers. The United States is said to retain a federal system because its national officials are selected from subunits of government—the president through the allocation of Electoral College votes to the states and the Congress through the allocation of two Senate seats per state and the apportionment of representatives based on state population. Whatever protection exists for state power and independence must be found in the national political process, in the influence of state and district voters on their senators and representatives. In a strongly worded dissenting opinion in *Garcia*, Justice Lewis Powell argued that if federalism is to be retained, the Constitution—not Congress—should divide powers. "The states' role in our system of government is a matter of constitutional law, not legislative grace. . . . [This decision] today rejects almost 200 years of the understanding of the constitutional status of federalism."[10]

Federalism Revived?

In recent years federalism has experienced a modest revival. The U.S. Supreme Court today appears to be somewhat more respectful of the powers of states and somewhat less willing to see these powers trampled upon by the national government.[11]

In 1995 the U.S. Supreme Court issued its first opinion in more than sixty years that recognized a limit on Congress's power over interstate commerce and reaffirmed the Founders' notion of a national government with only the powers enumerated in the Constitution.[12] The Court found that the federal Gun-Free School

Zones Act was unconstitutional because it exceeded Congress's powers under the Interstate Commerce Clause. When a student, Alfonso Lopez, was apprehended at his Texas high school carrying a .38 caliber hand-gun, federal agents charged him with violating the *federal* Gun-Free School Zones Act of 1990.

The U.S. government argued that the act was a constitutional exercise of its interstate commerce power, because "violent crime reduces the willingness of individuals to travel to areas within the country that are perceived to be unsafe." But after reviewing virtually all of the key commerce clause cases in its history, the Court determined that an activity must *substantially affect* interstate commerce in order to be regulated by Congress. Chief Justice William H. Rehnquist, writing for the majority in a 5 to 4 decision in *U.S. vs. Lopez*, even cited James Madison with approval: "The powers delegated by the proposed Constitution to the federal government are few and defined. Those which are to remain in the state governments are numerous and indefinite" (*Federalist*, No. 45).

In another victory for federalism, the U.S. Supreme Court ruled in 1996 in *Seminole Tribe v. Florida* that the Eleventh Amendment shields states from lawsuits by private parties that seek to force states to comply with federal laws enacted under the commerce power.[13] And in 1999 in *Alden v. Maine,* the Supreme Court held that states were also shielded in their own courts from lawsuits in which private parties seek to enforce federal mandates. In an opinion that surveyed the history of American federalism, Justice Kennedy wrote: "Congress has vast power but not all power. . . . When Congress legislates in matters affecting the states it may not treat these sovereign entities as mere prefectures or corporations."[14]

In defense of federalism, the Supreme Court invalidated a provision of a very popular law of Congress—the Brady Handgun Violence Protection Act. The Court decided in 1997 that the law's command to local law enforcement officers to conduct background checks on gun purchasers violated "the very principle of separate

National Conference of State Legislatures

This conference site provides information on 50 state legislatures and the issues they confront. **www.ncsl.org**

Former presidential Press Secretary James Brady was permanently disabled in the assassination attempt on President Reagan in 1981. Brady and his wife led the effort to pass the Brady Act, which, among other things, ordered state and local officials to conduct background checks on gun purchasers. The Supreme Court held that portion of the act to be an unconstitutional violation of the principle of federalism.

Should Violence Against Women Be a Federal Crime?

When a student at VPI (Virginia Polytechnic Institute) was raped, she argued that the attack violated the federal Violence against Women Act of 1994, a popular bill that passed overwhelmingly in Congress and was signed by President Bill Clinton. The act allowed victims of "gender motivated violence," including rape, to sue their attackers for monetary damages in *federal* court. The U.S. government defended its constitutional authority to involve itself in crimes against women by citing the Interstate Commerce Clause, arguing that crimes against women interfered with interstate commerce, the power over which is given to the national government in Article I of the Constitution.

But in 2000 the U.S. Supreme Court said, "If accepted, this reasoning would allow Congress to reg-ulate any crime whose nationwide, aggregated impact has substantial effects on employment, production, transit, or consumption. Moreover, such reasoning will not limit Congress to regulating violence, but may be applied equally as well to family law and other areas of state regulation since the aggregate effect of marriage, divorce, and childrearing on the national economy is undoubtedly significant." The Court reasoned that "the Constitution requires a distinction between what is truly national and what is truly local, and there is no better example of the police power, which the Founders undeniably left reposed in the States and denied the central government." In Justice Scalia's opinion, allowing Congress to claim that violence against women interfered with interstate commerce would open the door to federalizing all crime because all crime affects interstate commerce.

Source: U.S. v. Morrison, May 15, 2000.

state sovereignty." The Court affirmed that the federal government "may neither issue directives requiring the states to address particular problems, nor command the states' officers, or those of their political subdivisions, to administer or enforce the federal regulatory program" (*Printz v. U.S.*, 521 U.S. 890 (1997).[15] And the Court held that in the Violence against Women Act, Congress also invaded the reserved police power of the states[16] (see *What Do You Think?* "Should Violence Against Women Be a Federal Crime?").

The Supreme Court's apparent revival of federalism has been greeted with cautious optimism. However, all of the recent Supreme Court rulings reaffirming federalism have come in narrow 5 to 4 decisions. The closeness of these votes, together with these decisions' contrast to more than a half-century of case law in support of national power, provide no guarantee that in the future the Supreme Court will continue to move in the direction of strengthening federalism.

Money and Power Flow to Washington

THINK AGAIN

When the federal government requires states to provide safe drinking water, clean air, or access for the handicapped, should it provide funds to carry out these mandates?

Over the years, power in the federal system has flowed to Washington because tax money has flowed to Washington. With its financial resources, the federal government has been able to offer assistance to state and local governments and thereby involve itself in just about every governmental function performed by these governments. Today the federal government is no longer one of *enumerated* or *delegated* powers. No activities are really *reserved* to the states. Through its power to tax and spend for the *general welfare*, the national government is now deeply involved in welfare, education, transportation, police protection, housing, hospitals, urban development, and other activities that were once the exclusive domain of state and local government (see *Up Close:* "How Congress Set a National Drinking Age").

How Congress Set a National Drinking Age

Traditionally the *reserved* powers of the states included protection of the health, safety, and well-being of their citizens. The *enumerated* powers of Congress in the Constitution did not include regulating the sale and consumption of alcoholic beverages. Every state determined its own minimum age for drinking.

When the Twenty-sixth Amendment to the Constitution was passed in 1971, guaranteeing eighteen-year-olds the right to vote, most states lowered their minimum drinking age to eighteen. But by the early 1980s, some states had raised their minimums back to twenty-one in response to reports of teenage drinking and driving. Indeed, the National Transportation Safety Board reported that teenagers were statistically more likely to be involved in alcohol-related deaths than nonteenagers. The National Student Association, restaurant owners, and the beverage industry claimed that the selection of *all* teenagers for restriction was age discrimination. Whatever the merits of the argument, the issue was widely considered to be a *state* concern.

But the minimum drinking age became a national issue as a result of emotional appeals by groups such as Mothers Against Drunk Driving (MADD). Tragic stories told at televised committee hearings by grieving relatives of dead teenagers swept away federalism arguments. A few Congress members tried to argue that a national drinking age infringed on the powers of the state in a matter traditionally under state control. However, the new law did not directly mandate a national drinking age. Instead, it ordered the withholding of 10 percent of all federal highway funds from any state that failed to raise its minimum drinking age to twenty-one. States retained the rights to ignore the national minimum and give up a portion of their highway funds. (Congress used this same approach in 1974 in establishing a national 55-mile-per-hour speed limit.) Opponents of this device labeled it federal blackmail and a federal intrusion into state responsibilities. For some state officials, then, the issue was not teen drinking but rather the preemption of state authority.

Proponents of the legislation cited the *national* interest in setting a uniform minimum drinking age. They argued that protecting the lives of young people outweighed the states' interest in preserving their authority. Moreover, teens were crossing state lines to drink in states with lower drinking ages. New York, for example, with a minimum drinking age of nineteen, was attracting teenagers from Pennsylvania and New Jersey, where the drinking age was twenty-one. Reports of "bloody borders" were used to justify national action to establish a uniform drinking age. Although the Reagan White House had pledged to return responsibility to the states, it did not wish to offend the nation's mothers on such an emotional issue. Despite initial reservations, President Ronald Reagan supported the bill and signed it into law in 1984.

From a purely constitutional perspective, Congress simply exercised its power to spend money for the general welfare; it did not *directly* legislate in an area *reserved* to the states. Technically, states remain free to set their own minimum drinking age. Despite heated arguments in many state legislatures, all of the states adopted the twenty-one-year-old minimum national drinking age by 1990.

Appeals by groups such as Mothers Against Drunk Driving (MADD) helped overcome concerns that legislation effectively setting a national drinking age would infringe on state authority.

Grants-in-aid Today grant-in-aid programs are the single most important source of federal influence over state and local activity. A **grant-in-aid** is defined as "payment of funds by one level of government (national or state) to be expended by another level (state or local) for a specified purpose, usually on a matching-funds basis (the federal government puts up only as much as the state or locality) and in accordance with prescribed standards of requirements."[17] No state or local government is *required* to accept grants-in-aid. Participation in grant-in-aid programs is voluntary. So in theory, if conditions attached to the grant money are too oppressive, state and local governments can simply decline to participate and pass up these funds.

About one-quarter of all state and local government revenues currently come from federal grants. Federal grants are available in nearly every major category of state and local government activity. Over 500 separate grant programs are administered by various federal agencies. So numerous and diverse are these grants that state and local officials often lack information about their availability, purpose, and requirements. "Grantmanship"—knowing where and how to obtain federal grants—is highly valued in state and local governments. Federal grants can be obtained to preserve historic buildings, develop minority-owned businesses, aid foreign refugees, drain abandoned mines, control riots, and subsidize school milk programs, and so on. However, welfare (including cash benefits and food stamps) and health (including Medicaid for the poor) account for two-thirds of federal aid money (see Figure 4.4).

Thus many of the special projects and ongoing programs carried out today by state and local governments are funded by grants from the federal government. These funds have generally been dispersed as either categorical grants or block grants.

■ *Categorical Grant:* A grant for a specific, narrow project. The project must be approved by a federal administrative agency. About 90 percent of federal aid money is distributed in the form of categorical grants. Categorical grants can be distributed on a project basis or a formula basis. Grants made on a project basis are distributed by federal administrative agencies to state or local governments that compete for project funds in their applications. Federal agencies have a great deal of discretion in selecting specific projects for support, and

grants-in-aid Payments of funds from the national government to state or local governments or from a state government to local governments for specific purposes.

FIGURE 4.4 Purposes of Federal Grants to State and Local Governments

Over one-fifth of all state and local government revenues are derived from federal grants. Federal grants-in-aid to state and local governments are especially vital in the areas of health and welfare.

Source: Budget of United States Government, 2004.

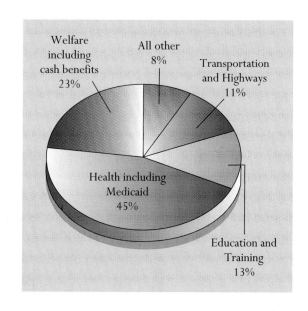

Welfare including cash benefits 23%

All other 8%

Transportation and Highways 11%

Health including Medicaid 45%

Education and Training 13%

Liberals, Conservatives, and Federalism

From the earliest days of the Republic, American leaders and scholars have argued over federalism. Political interests that constitute a majority at the national level and control the national government generally praise the virtue of national supremacy. Political interests that do not control the national government but exercise controlling influence in one or more states generally see great merit in preserving the powers of the states.

In recent years, political conflict over federalism—over the division between national versus state and local responsibilities and finances—has tended to follow traditional "liberal" and "conservative" political cleavages. Generally, liberals seek to enhance the power of the *national* government because they believe people's lives can be changed—and bettered—by the exercise of national governmental power. The government in Washington has more power and resources than do state and local governments, which many liberals regard as too slow, cumbersome, weak, and unresponsive. Thus liberalism and centralization are closely related in American politics. The liberal argument for national authority can be summarized as follows:

- There is insufficient concern about social problems by state and local governments. The federal government must take the lead in civil rights, equal employment opportunities, care for the poor and aged, the provision of adequate medical care for all Americans, and the elimination of urban poverty and blight.
- It is difficult to achieve change when reform-minded citizens must deal with 50 state governments and more than 85,000 local governments. Change is more likely to be accomplished by a strong central government.
- State and local governments contribute to inequality in society by setting different levels of services in education, welfare, health, and other public functions. A strong national government can ensure uniformity of standards throughout the nation.
- A strong national government can unify the nation behind principles and ideals of social justice and economic progress. Extreme decentralization may favor local or regional "special" interests at the expense of the general "public" interest.

In contrast, conservatives generally seek to return power to *state and local* governments. Conservatives are skeptical about the "good" that government can do and believe that adding to the power of the national government is not an effective way of resolving society's problems. On the contrary, they argue that "government is the problem, not the solution." Excessive government regulation, burdensome taxation, and inflationary government spending combine to restrict individual freedom, penalize work and savings, and destroy incentives for economic growth. Government should be kept small, controllable, and close to the people. The conservative argument for state and local autonomy can be summarized as follows:

- Grass-roots government promotes a sense of self-responsibility and self-reliance.
- State and local governments can better adapt public programs to local needs and conditions.
- State and local governments promote participation in politics and civic responsibility by allowing more people to become involved in public questions.
- Competition between states and cities can result in improved public programs and services.
- The existence of multiple state and local governments encourages experimentation and innovation in public policy, from which the whole nation may gain.

There is no way to settle the argument over federalism once and for all. Debates about federalism are part of the fabric of American politics.

---

they can exercise direct control over the projects. Most categorical grants are distributed to state or local governments according to a fixed formula set by Congress. Medicaid and Food Stamps (see Chapter 17) are the largest categorical grant programs.

- *Block Grant:* A grant for a general governmental function, such as health, social services, law enforcement, education, or community development. State and local governments have fairly wide discretion in deciding how to spend federal block grant money within a functional area. For example, cities receiving "community development" block grants can decide for themselves about specific neighborhood development projects, housing projects, community facilities, and so on. All block grants are distributed on a formula basis set by Congress. Federal administrative agencies may require reports and adherence to rules and guidelines, but they do not choose which specific projects to fund. Only about 10 percent of federal grant-in-aid money is distributed in the form of block grants.

"Devolution" Controversy over federalism—what level of government should do what and who should pay for it—is as old as the nation itself (see *A Conflicting View:* "Liberals, Conservatives, and Federalism"). Beginning in 1995, with a new Republican majority in both houses of Congress and Republicans holding a majority of state governorships, debates over federalism were renewed. The new phrase was **devolution**—the passing down of responsibilities from the national government to the states.

Welfare reform turned out to be the key to devolution. Bill Clinton once promised "to end welfare as we know it," but it was a Republican Congress in 1996 that did so. After President Clinton had twice vetoed welfare reform bills, he and Congress finally agreed to merge welfare reform with devolution. A new Temporary Assistance to Needy Families program (see Chapter 17) replaced direct federal cash aid welfare "entitlements." The new program:

- Establishes block grants with lump-sum allocations to the states for cash welfare payments.

- Grants the states broad flexibility in determining eligibility and benefit levels for persons receiving such aid.

- Limits the use of federally aided cash grants for most recipients to two continuing years and five years over their lifetime.

- Allows states to deny additional cash payments for children born to women already receiving welfare assistance and allowing states to deny cash payments to parents under eighteen who do not live with an adult and attend school.

Since Franklin D. Roosevelt's New Deal, with its federal guarantee of cash Aid to Families with Dependent Children (AFDC), low-income mothers and children had enjoyed a federal "entitlement" to welfare payments. But welfare reform, with its devolution of responsibility to the states, ended this 60-year-old federal entitlement. Note, however, that Congress continues to place "strings" on the use of federal welfare funds, including a two-year limit on continuing payments to beneficiaries in a five-year lifetime limit.

Political Obstacles to Devolution and Federalism Politicians in Washington are fond of the rhetoric of federalism. They know that Americans generally prefer governments closer to home. Yet at the same time they confront strong political pressures to "DO SOMETHING!" about virtually every problem that confronts individuals, families, or communities, whether or not doing so may overstep the enumerated powers of the national government. Politicians gain very little by telling their constituents that a particular problem—violence in the schools, domestic abuse, physician-assisted suicide, and so on—is not a federal responsibility and should be dealt with at the state or local level of government.

WWW Urban Institute
Washington think tank offers viewpoints on federalism and issues confronting state/local government. ***www.urban.org***

devolution Passing down of responsibilities from the national government to the states.

Moreover, neither presidents nor members of Congress are inclined to restrain their own power. Both liberals and conservatives in Washington are motivated to tie their own strings to federal grant-in-aid money, issue their own federal mandates, and otherwise "correct" what they perceive to be errors or inadequacies of state policies.

Coercive Federalism: Preemptions and Mandates

Traditionally, Congress avoided issuing direct orders to state and local governments. Instead, it sought to influence them by offering grants of money with federal rules, regulations, or "guidelines" attached. In theory at least, states and communities were free to forgo the money and ignore the strings attached to it. But increasingly Congress has undertaken direct regulation of areas traditionally reserved to the states and restricted state authority to regulate these areas. And it has issued direct orders to state and local governments to perform various services and comply with federal law in the performance of these services.

Federal Preemptions The supremacy of federal laws over those of the states, spelled out in the National Supremacy Clause of the Constitution, permits Congress to decide whether or not there is **preemption** of state laws in a particular field by federal law. In **total preemption**, the federal government assumes all regulatory powers in a particular field—for example, copyrights, bankruptcy, railroads, and airlines. No state regulations in a totally preempted field are permitted. **Partial preemption** stipulates that a state law on the same subject is valid as long as it does not conflict with the federal law in the same area. For example, the Occupational Safety and Health Act of 1970 specifically permits state regulation of any occupational safety or health issue on which the federal Occupational Safety and Health Administration (OSHA) has *not* developed a standard; but once OSHA enacts a standard, all state standards are nullified. A specific form of partial preemption called **standard partial preemption** permits states to regulate activities in a field already regulated by the federal government, as long as state regulatory standards are at least as stringent as those of the federal government. Usually states must submit their regulations to the responsible federal agency for approval, the federal agency may revoke a state's regulating power if that state fails to enforce the approved standards. For example, the federal Environmental Protection Agency (EPA) permits state environmental regulations that meet or exceed EPA standards.

Federal Mandates Federal **mandates** are direct orders to state and local governments to perform a particular activity or service or to comply with federal laws in the performance of their functions. Federal mandates occur in a wide variety of areas, from civil rights to minimum-wage regulations. Their range is reflected in some recent examples of federal mandates to state and local governments:

- *Age Discrimination Act, 1986:* Outlaws mandatory retirement ages for public as well as private employees, including police, fire fighters, and state college and university faculty.

- *Asbestos Hazard Emergency Act, 1986:* Orders school districts to inspect for asbestos hazards and remove asbestos from school buildings when necessary.

- *Safe Drinking Water Act, 1986:* Establishes national requirements for municipal water supplies; regulates municipal waste treatment plants.

preemption Total or partial federal assumption of power in a particular field, restricting the authority of the states.

total preemption Federal government's assumption of all regulatory powers in a particular field.

partial preemption Federal government's assumption of some regulatory powers in a particular field, with the stipulation that a state law on the same subject as a federal law is valid if it does not conflict with the federal law in the same area.

standard partial preemption Form of partial preemption in which the states are permitted to regulate activities already regulated by the federal government if the state regulatory standards are at least as stringent as the federal government's.

mandates Direct federal orders to state and local governments requiring them to perform a service or to obey federal laws in the performance of their functions.

Arnold: From Bodybuilder, to Superstar, to Governor

Arnold's message to California Governor Grey Davis was "Hasta la vista, baby!" In 2003 Davis became only the second governor in history to be recalled by the voters. Arnold himself had never held political office. He had risen from an impoverished immigrant who barely spoke English, to champion bodybuilder, to world-famous movie star, to Kennedy family in-law, to governor of America's largest state.

Eighteen states include recall provisions in their constitutions: petitions signed by a specified number of voters (12 percent in California) force an incumbent official to face the voters and risk being ousted before the end of their terms. Petition drives for a California governor's recall had failed on thirty-one previous occasions; even Governor Ronald Reagan faced three recall attempts. The recall grew out of the Progressive Movement of the early twentieth century, which advanced elements of direct democracy, including the initiative and referendum, in American politics. But the initiative, referendum, and recall exist only at the state level; America's Founders were extremely skeptical of direct democracy (see Chapter 1, "Direct versus Representative Democracy" and Chapter 3, "The Structure of the Government").

So what did Grey Davis do to deserve ouster only one year after his reelection to a second term? Unlike impeachment, a successful recall does not require specific charges of malfeasance or criminal conduct in office. Voters can recall an officeholder for any reason, or for no reason. But Davis was particularly inept: he failed to act decisively during California's electricity blackouts of 2000 and 2001, which resulted in higher utility bills; he engaged in reckless spending despite an economic downturn and consequently drowned the state in red ink; and perhaps most enraging to voters, he tripled the car tax, raising license fees from about $70 to $210 for the average passenger car.

Arnold's father had been a local police chief in Austria and a Nazi Party member prior to World War II. Arnold donated hundreds of thousands of dollars to the Simon Wiesenthal Center, a Jewish human rights organization, and asked the Center to investigate his father's activities.

The Center found no evidence that his father had committed any war crimes. Arnold spent his teenage years developing his body in the hope of one day becoming Mr. Universe. At age 20 he fulfilled his dream, and then came to America to pursue his second goal, to become a movie actor. His 1982 *Conan the Barbarian* became a cult classic; in 1984 he starred in *The Terminator* and later made two sequels.

Arnold revealed an interest in politics by becoming involved with the Special Olympics and serving on President George H. W. Bush's Council on Physical Fitness. In 2002 he sponsored a California ini-

■ *Clean Air Act, 1990:* Bans municipal incinerators and requires auto emission inspections in certain urban areas.

■ *Americans with Disabilities Act, 1990:* Requires all state and local government buildings to promote handicapped access.

■ *National Voter Registration Act, 1993:* Requires states to register voters at driver's license, welfare, and unemployment compensation offices.

■ *No Child Left Behind Act, 2001:* Requires states and their school districts to test public school pupils.

State and local governments frequently complain that the costs imposed on them by complying with such federal mandates are seldom reimbursed by Washington.

unfunded mandates
Mandates that impose costs on state and local governments (and private industry) without reimbursement from the federal government.

"Unfunded" Mandates Federal mandates often impose heavy costs on states and communities. When no federal monies are provided to cover these costs, the mandates are said to be **unfunded mandates**. Governors, mayors, and other state and local officials have often urged Congress to stop imposing unfunded mandates on states and communities. Private industries have long voiced the tiative to spend more money for before- and after-school programs. He offered very few specifics in his campaign for governor: "I am a man of the people"; "We have tough choices ahead"; "For the people to win, politics as usual must lose." When the liberal *Los Angeles Times* charged Arnold with "groping" women on movie sets, Arnold's wife, television personality Maria Shriver, daughter of Robert Kennedy, came to his defense. His poll numbers ac-

tually went up following the charges. Davis lost the recall vote 54 to 46 percent. Arnold won 48 percent of the vote in the 135-candidate race. As a moderate Rebublican, he won easily over the Democratic Lieutenant Governor and a conservative Republican state senator, among many others. But in a Democratic state, with a Democratic-controlled legislature, can *The Terminator* end California's financial problems?

same complaint. Regulations and mandates allow Congress to address problems while pushing the costs of doing so onto others.

Homeland Security The Constitution gives the federal government the responsibility for national defense. The terrorist attack on the World Trade Center in New York and the Pentagon in Washington, September 11, 2001, began what President George W. Bush described as a long and difficult to "war on terrorism." Washington reorganized itself, creating a new Department of Homeland Security (see Chapter 12), and allocated billions of dollars for homeland defenses. But the "first responders" to any terrorist attack are state and local police, fire, medical, and other emergency agencies. States, counties, and cities now face unprecedented and permanent responsibilities in homeland security, even including dealing with the results of nuclear, biological, and chemical attacks. Governors, mayors, city and county officials, and especially police, fire, and emergency officers, have urged the Congress to provide more federal funding and resources to state and local agencies for homeland security. Congress has responded with billions of dollars in additional aid, but states and communities claim that assistance for their "first responders" is inadequate.

- The struggle for power between the national government and the states over two centuries has shaped American federalism today.

- Federalism is the division of power between two separate authorities, the nation and the state, each of which enforces its own laws directly on its citizens and neither of which can change the division of power without the consent of the other.

- American federalism was designed by the Founders as an additional protection for individual liberty by providing for the division and dispersal of power among multiple units of government.

- Federalism has also been defended as a means of increasing opportunities to hold public office, improving governmental efficiency, ensuring policy responsiveness, encouraging policy innovation, and managing conflict.

- However, federalism can also obstruct and frustrate national action. Narrow state interests can sometimes prevail over national interests or the interests of minorities within states. Segregation was long protected by theories of states' rights. Federalism also results in uneven levels of public services through the nation.

- Power has flowed to the national government over time, as the original state-centered division of power has evolved into a national-centered system of government. Among the most important historical influences on this shift in power toward Washington have been the Supreme Court's broad interpretation of national power, the national government's victory over the secessionist states in the Civil War, the establishment of a national system of civil rights based on the Fourteenth Amendment, the growth of a national economy governed by Congress under its interstate commerce power, and the national government's accumulation of power through its greater financial resources.

- Federal grants to state and local governments have greatly expanded the national government's powers in areas previously regarded as *reserved* to the states.

- Federal grants are available for most state and local government activities, but health and welfare account for about two-thirds of these grants.

- Although Congress has generally refrained from directly legislating in areas traditionally *reserved* to the states, federal power in local affairs has grown as a result of federal rules, regulations, and guidelines established as conditions for the receipt of federal funds.

- The Supreme Court in its *Garcia* decision in 1985 removed all constitutional barriers to direct congressional legislation in matters traditionally reserved to the states. Establishing the principle of representational federalism, the Court said that states could defend their own interests through their representation in the national government.

- Representational federalism focuses on the role of the states in electing national officials—the president through the allocation of Electoral College votes to the states, the Senate through the allocation of two seats for each state, and the House through the appointment of representatives based on the state's population.

- Recent efforts at the "devolution" of federal responsibilities for welfare resulted in an end to federal individual "entitlements" to cash welfare payments and their replacement with block grants for cash aid to the states. But Congress continues to place "strings" on the use of federal welfare grants to the states.

federalism   103
unitary system   103
confederation   103
home rule   103
intergovernmental relations   103
laboratories of democracy   106
delegated, or enumerated, powers   109

Necessary and Proper Clause   109
implied powers   109
National Supremacy Clause   109
concurrent powers   109
reserved powers   109
dual federalism   113
cooperative federalism   116

centralized federalism   116
new federalism   117
representational federalism   118
grant-in-aid   122
devolution   124
preemption   125
total preemption   125
partial preemption   125

standard partial preemption   125
mandates   125
unfunded mandates   126

SUGGESTED READINGS

Beer, Samuel H. *To Make a Nation: The Rediscovery of American Federalism.* Cambridge, Mass.: Harvard University Press, 1993. A historical account of the development of both federalism and nationalism in American political philosophy.

Dye, Thomas R. *American Federalism: Competition among Governments.* Lexington, Mass.: Lexington Books, 1990. A theory of "competitive federalism" arguing that rivalries among governments improve public services while lowering taxes, restrain the growth of government, promote innovation and experimentation in public policies, inspire greater responsiveness to the preferences of citizen-taxpayers, and encourage economic growth.

Elazar, Daniel J. *The American Partnership.* Chicago: University of Chicago Press, 1962. Classic study of the historical evolution of federalism, stressing the nation-state sharing of policy concerns and financing, from the early days of the Republic, and the politics behind the gradual growth of national power.

Greve, Michael S. *Real Federalism.* Washington, D.C.: AEI Press, 1999. Why real "competitive" federalism matters and how it can be achieved in the current political environments.

Nagel, Robert F. *The Implosion of Federalism.* New York: Oxford University Press, 2001. America's political institutions are collapsing into the center, reducing the opportunity for competition and participation.

Ostrum, Vincent. *The Meaning of American Federalism.* San Francisco: ICS Press, 1991. A theoretical examination of federalism, setting forth the conditions for a self-governing society and arguing that multiple, overlapping units of government, with various checks on one another's power, provide a viable democratic system of conflict resolution.

O'Toole, Laurence J., ed. *American Intergovernmental Relations.* 3rd ed. Washington, D.C.: CQ Press, 1999. A collection of readings, both classic and contemporary, describing the theory, history, and current problems of intergovernmental relations in America.

Peterson, Paul E. *The Price of Federalism.* Washington, D.C.: Brookings Institution, 1995. Historical, theoretical, and empirical perspectives merged into a new, timely model of federalism that would allocate social welfare functions to the national government and education and economic development to states and communities.

Van Horn, Carl E. *The State of the States.* 3rd ed. Washington, D.C.: CQ Press, 1996. An assessment of the challenges facing state governments as a result of the devolution revolution.

5

OPINION AND PARTICIPATION:
THINKING AND ACTING IN POLITICS

THINK
ABOUT POLITICS

1 Should political leaders pay attention to public opinion polls when making decisions for the country?
Yes ● No ●

2 Do you believe that your representative in Congress cares about your personal opinion on important issues?
Yes ● No ●

3 Can you name the two U.S. senators from your state?
Yes ● No ●

4 Is our government really legitimate when only about half the people vote in presidential elections?
Yes ● No ●

5 Do you identify yourself with the same political party as your family?
Yes ● No ●

6 Is it appropriate for religious leaders to try to influence how people vote?
Yes ● No ●

7 Have you ever personally called or written to your representative in Congress?
Yes ● No ●

8 Do you think you will ever run for public office yourself?
Yes ● No ●

By thinking about politics and acting on your political opinions—voting, talking to friends, writing letters, joining organizations, attending meetings and rallies, contributing money, marching in demonstrations, or running for office yourself—you are participating in politics.

Politics and Public Opinion

For most Americans, politics is not as interesting as football or basketball, or the sex lives of celebrities, or prime-time television entertainment. Although politicians, pollsters, and commentators frequently assume that Americans have formed opinions on major public issues, in fact, most have not given them very much thought. Nevertheless, **public opinion** commands the attention of politicians, the news media, and political scientists.

Public opinion is given a lot of attention in democracies because democratic government rests on the consent of the governed. The question of whether public opinion *should* direct government policy has confounded political philosophers for centuries. Edmund Burke, writing in 1790, argued that democratic representatives should serve the *interests* of the people, but not necessarily conform to their *will*, in deciding questions of public policy. In contrast, other political philosophers have evaluated the success of democratic institutions by whether or not they produce policies that conform to popular opinion.

Major shifts in public opinion in the United States generally translate into policy change. Both the president and Congress appear to respond over time to *general* public preferences for "more" or "less" government regulation, "more" or "less" government spending, "getting tough on crime," "reforming welfare," and so on.[1] But public opinion is often weak, unstable, ill informed, or nonexistent on *specific* policy issues. Consequently, elected officials have greater flexibility in dealing with these issues—and, at the same time, there is an increase in the influence of lobbyists, interest groups, reporters, commentators, and others who have direct access to policy makers. Moreover, the absence of well-formed public opinion on an issue provides interest groups and the media with the opportunity to influence policy indirectly by shaping popular opinion.

Politicians read the opinion polls. And even though many elected representatives claim that they exercise independent judgment about what is best for the nation in their decision making, we can be reasonably sure their "independent judgment" is influenced at least in part by what they think their constituents want. Public opinion commands the attention of politicians because even if only a small number of voters cast their ballots on the basis of the candidates' policy positions, those votes are still important. The

Can We Believe the Polls?

Survey research is a flourishing political enterprise. The national news media—notably CBS, NBC, ABC, and CNN television networks, the *New York Times* and the *Washington Post,* and *Time* and *Newsweek* magazines—regularly sponsor independent national surveys, especially during election campaigns. Major survey organizations—the American Institute of Public Opinion (Gallup), Louis Harris and Associates, National Opinion Research Center (NORC), the Roper Organization, National Election Studies (University of Michigan)—have been in business for a long time and have files of survey results going back many years. Political candidates also contract with private marketing and opinion research firms to conduct surveys in conjunction with their campaigns.

Public opinion surveys depend on the selection of a *random sample* of persons chosen in a way which ensures that every person in the *universe* of people about whom information is desired has an equal chance of being selected for interviewing. National samples, representative of all adults or all voters, usually include only about 1,000 persons. First, geographical areas (for example, counties or telephone area codes) that are representative of all such areas in the nation are chosen. Then residential telephone numbers are randomly selected within these areas. Once the numbers have been selected at random, the poll taker does not make substitutions but calls back several times if necessary to make contact so as not to bias the sample toward people who stay at home.

Even when random-selection procedures are closely followed, the sample may not be truly representative of the universe. But survey researchers can estimate the *sampling error* through the mathematics of probability. The sampling error is usually expressed as a percentage range—for example, plus or minus 3 percent—above and below the sample response within which there is a 95 percent likelihood that the universe response would be found if the entire universe were questioned. For example, if 65 percent of the survey respondents favor the death penalty and the sampling error is calculated at plus or minus 3 percent, then we can say there is a 95 percent probability that a survey of the whole population (the universe) would produce a response of between 62 and 68 percent in favor of the death penalty.

"Loaded" or "leading" questions are often used by unprofessional pollsters simply to produce results favorable to their side of an argument. An even worse abuse in telephone polling is the "push poll"—questions asked by political campaign workers posing as independent pollsters, deliberately worded to create an opinion—for example, "If you knew that Congressman Smith would soon be indicted for child molestation, would you vote for him?"

Professional pollsters strive for questions that are clear and precise, easily understood by the respondents, and as neutral and unbiased as possible. Nevertheless, because all questions have a potential bias, it is often better to examine *changes over time* in response to identically worded questions. Perhaps the best-known continuing question in public opinion polling is the presidential approval rating: "Do you approve or disapprove of the way _____ is handling his job as president?" Changes over time in public response to this question alert scholars, commentators, and presidents themselves to their public standing (see Chapter 11).

A survey can only measure opinions *at the time* it is taken. A few days later public opinion may change, especially if major events that receive heavy television coverage intervene. Some political pollsters conduct continuous "tracking" surveys until election night in order to catch last-minute opinion changes.

---

public opinion Aggregate of preferences and opinions of individuals on significant issues.

survey research Gathering of information about public opinion by questioning a representative sample of the population.

cynical stereotype of the politician who reads the opinion polls before taking stands on the issues is often embarrassingly accurate.

All this attention to public opinion has created a thriving industry in public opinion polling and **survey research**. Polls have become a fixture of American political life (see *Up Close:* "Can We Believe the Polls?"). But how much do Americans really think about politics? How informed, stable, and consistent is public opinion?

Knowledge Levels Most Americans do *not* follow politics closely enough to develop well-informed opinions on many public issues (see Figure 5.1). Low levels of knowledge about government and public affairs make it difficult for people

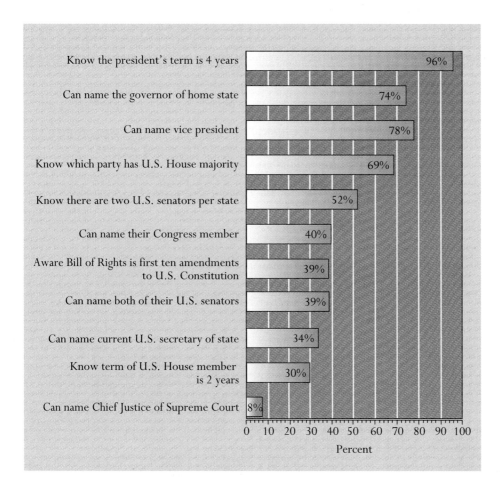

FIGURE 5.1 What Do Americans Know about Politics?

Politics is not the major interest of most Americans, and as a result, knowledge about the political system is limited. Less than one-third of the general public knows the names of their representatives in Congress or their U.S. senators, and knowledge of specific foreign and domestic matters is even more limited.

Source: Data from Robert S. Erikson and Kent L. Tedin, *American Public Opinion,* 6th ed. (New York: Macmillan, 2002). p. 55 citing various polls by Gallup. Harris, National Opinion Research Center (NORC), and CBS/*New York Times.* Similar "shocking" results are regularly reported in national polls; see, for example, Richard Morin, "Who's in Control? Many Don't Know or Care," *Washington Post,* January 29, 1996.

to form opinions on specific issues or policy proposals. Many opinion surveys ask questions about topics that people had not considered before being interviewed. Few respondents are willing to admit that they know nothing about the topic or have "no opinion." Respondents believe they should provide some sort of answer, even if their opinion was nonexistent before the question was asked. The result is that the polls themselves "create" opinions.[2]

The "Halo Effect" Many respondents give "good citizen" or socially respectable answers, whether they are truthful or not, even to an anonymous interviewer. This **halo effect** leads to an *underestimation* of the true extent of prejudice, hatred, and bigotry. Another common example of the halo effect is the fact that people do not like to admit that they do not vote. Surveys regularly report higher percentages of people saying they voted in an election than the actual number of ballots cast. Moreover, postelection surveys almost always produce higher percentages of people who say they voted for the winner than the actual vote tally for the winner. Apparently poll respondents do not like to admit that they backed the loser.

Inconsistencies Because so many people hold no real opinion on political issues, the wording of a question frequently determines their response. People respond positively to positive phrases (for example, "helping poor people," "improving education," "cleaning up the environment") and negatively to negative phrases (for example, "raising taxes," "expanding governmental power," "restricting choice").

Gallup
Oldest public opinion organization, with latest polls and large archive.
www.gallup.com

THINK AGAIN

Should political leaders pay attention to public opinion polls when making decisions for the country?

halo effect Tendency of survey respondents to provide socially acceptable answers to questions.

Abortion:
The "Hot-Button" Issue

Although public opinion may be weak or nonexistent on many policy questions, there are a few "hot-button" issues in politics—issues on which virtually everyone has an opinion and many people feel very intensely about.

Abortion is one such highly sensitive issue. Both *pro-choice* proponents of legalized abortion and *pro-life* opponents claim to have public opinion on their side. *Interpretation* of the poll results becomes a political activity itself. Consider, for example, re-

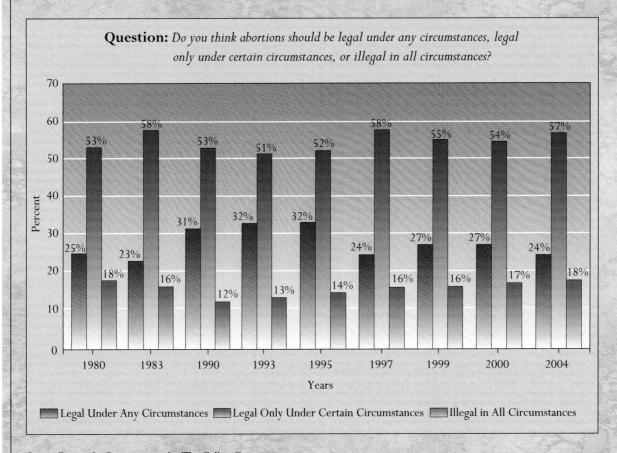

Question: *Do you think abortions should be legal under any circumstances, legal only under certain circumstances, or illegal in all circumstances?*

Legal Under Any Circumstances ■ Legal Only Under Certain Circumstances ■ Illegal in All Circumstances

Source: Copyright © 1980–2004 by The Gallup Organization.

The wording of questions, combined with weak or nonexistent opinion, often produces inconsistent responses. For example, when asked whether they agreed or disagreed with the statement that "people should have the right to purchase a sexually explicit book, magazine, or movie, if that's what they want to do," an overwhelming 80 percent endorsed the statement. However, when the same respondents were also asked whether they agreed with the opposite statement that "community authorities should be able to prohibit the selling of magazines or movies they consider to be pornographic," 65 percent approved of this view as well.[3]

The Polling Report
Recent public opinion polls on policy issues, political actors, government institutions, etc.
www.pollingreport.com

sponses to the general question posed in the graph pictured here.

Pro-choice forces interpret these results as overwhelming support for legalized abortion; pro-life commentators interpret these results as majority support for restricting abortion. Indeed, public opinion appears to support *specific restrictions* on abortion (see below).

In short, most Americans appear to want to keep some abortions legal but they believe that government should place certain restrictions on the practice.

Question: *Do you favor or oppose each of the following proposals?*

Percentage saying:

A law requiring doctors to inform patients about alternatives to abortion before performing the procedure — 88% / 11%

A law requiring women seeking abortions to wait 24 hours before having the procedure done — 78% / 19%

A law requiring women under 18 to get parental consent for any abortion — 73% / 24%

A law requiring that the husband of a married woman be notified if she decides to have an abortion — 72% / 26%

A law making it illegal to perform an abortion procedure conducted in the last six months of pregnancy, known as "partial-birth abortion," except when necessary to save the mother's life — 70% / 25%

☐ Favor ☐ Oppose

Source: Gallup, CNN, *USA Today,* as reported on Public Opinion Online, www.publicagenda.org, October, 2003. Copyright © 2003 by The Gallup Organization.

Instability Many people answer survey questions impulsively without very serious consideration. This lack of thought often results in an apparent instability of opinions—people giving contradictory responses to the same question when asked it at different times. Indeed, when identical questions are asked just a few months apart, 20 percent or more of respondents may switch sides! Instability is somewhat less on issues that are intensely debated (for example, abortion), it is somewhat greater on issues that receive less media attention (for example, oil drilling in Alaska).[4]

Public Agenda Online

Recent opinion polls on a variety of policy issues.
www.publicagenda.org

FIGURE 5.2 What's to Worry About?

Public concerns shift over time, as indicated by changing responses to the question, "What is the most important problem facing America?" In recent years, Americans have been alternately concerned about the economy, unemployment, drugs, and crime. Terrorism appeared as a top concern after the September 11, 2001, attack on America. But by 2004 the economy reemerged as the public's "most important problem."

Source: Gallup opinion polls. 2002 figures are averages of polls conducted in Jan., Feb., Mar., Apr., May, June, July, Aug., and Sept. 2002. 2000 figures are averages of polls conducted in Mar., June, and Oct. 2000. 1995 figures are averages of polls conducted in Jan. and July 1995. 1992 figures are averages of polls conducted in Mar., May, Aug./Sept. 1992. 1987 figures are averages of polls conducted in Jan. and April 1987. 1984 figures are averages of polls conducted in Feb., June, Aug., and Sept. 1984. 1980 figures are averages of polls conducted in Mar., June, Sept., Oct., and Nov. 1980. Copyright © 1980, 1984, 1988, 1992, 1996, 1997, 2000, 2002, 2004 The Gallup Organization.

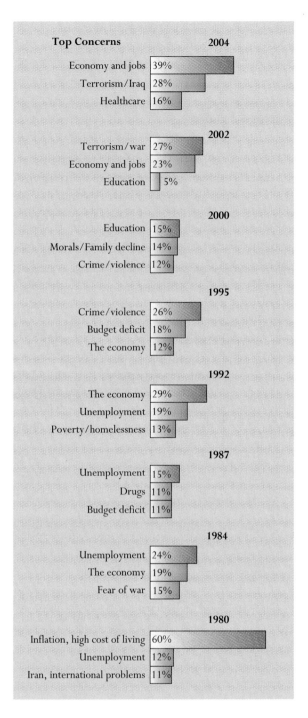

Salience People are likely to think about issues that receive a great deal of attention in the mass media—television, newspapers, magazines. **Salient issues** are those that people think about most—issues on which they hold stronger and more stable opinions. These are issues that people feel relate directly to their own lives, such as abortion (see *Up Close:* "Abortion: The 'Hot-Button' Issue" on pages 140–141). Salient issues are, therefore, more important in politics.

Salient issues change over time. In general, during recessions the most salient issue is "Jobs, Jobs, Jobs!"—that is, unemployment and the economy. During inflationary periods, the issue is "the high cost of living." During wartime, the war itself becomes the public's principal concern. A gasoline shortage can turn public

salient issues Issues about which most people have an opinion.

concern toward energy issues. The Gallup Opinion Organization regularly asks Americans what they think is "the most important problem facing America." The results are shown in Figure 5.2. These salient issues drive the political debate of the times.[5]

Socialization: The Origins of Political Opinions

Where do people acquire their political opinions? Political **socialization** is the learning of political values, beliefs, and opinions (see *Compared to What?* "How 'Exceptional' Is Opinion in America?" on page 144 for a look at the results of different socialization patterns in other lands). It begins early in life when a child acquires images and attitudes toward public authority. Preschool children see "police officer" and "president" as powerful yet benevolent "helpers." These figures—police officer and president—are usually the first recognized sources of authority above the parents who must be obeyed. They are usually positive images of authority at these early ages:

Q: What does the policeman do?
A: He catches bad people.[6]

Even the American flag is recognized by most U.S. preschoolers, who pick it out when asked, "Which flag is your favorite?" These early positive perceptions about political figures and symbols may later provide *diffuse support* for the political system—a reservoir of goodwill toward governmental authority that lends legitimacy to the political order.

Family The family is the first agent of socialization, and some family influences appear to stay with people over a lifetime.[7] Children in the early school grades (3 to 5) begin to identify themselves as Republicans or Democrats. These childhood party identifications are almost always the same as those of the parents. Indeed, parent-child correspondence in party identification may last a lifetime.[8] The children who abandon the party of their parents tend to become independents rather than identify with the opposition party. However, party identification appears to be more easily passed on from parent to child than specific opinions on policy questions. Perhaps the reason is that parental party identifications are known to children, but few families conduct specific discussions of policy questions.

School Political revolutionaries once believed that the school was the key to molding political values and beliefs. After the communist revolutions in Russia in 1917 and China in 1949, the schools became the focus of political indoctrination of the population. Today political battles rage in America over textbooks, teaching methods, prayer in schools, and other manifestations of politics in the classroom. But no strong evidence indicates a causal relationship between what is taught in the schools and the political attitudes of students.

Certainly the schools provide the factual basis for understanding government—how the president is chosen, the three branches of government, how a law is passed. But even this elemental knowledge is likely to fade if not reinforced by additional education or exposure to the news media or discussion with family or peers.

The schools *try* to inculcate "good citizenship" values, including support for democratic rules, tolerance toward others, the importance of voting, and the legitimacy (rightfulness) of government authority. Patriotic symbols and rituals abound in the classroom—the flag, the Pledge of Allegiance—and students are taught to

socialization Learning of values, beliefs, and opinions.

How "Exceptional" Is Opinion in America?

Do Americans differ much from Europeans in their social and political values? The American political culture places great value on individual liberty, limited government intervention in people's personal lives, equality of opportunity, and individual responsibility for one's own fate in life (see Chapter 2). The strong American commitment to these values has been labeled American "exceptionalism," suggesting that people in other nations, including the Western European democracies, are not as strongly committed to these values as are people in the United States.

The values of the political culture influence opinion on many specific issues. If the American political culture is truly "exceptional," Americans should differ significantly from Europeans on questions dealing with individual liberty, social mobility, and the role of government in society. And, indeed, cross-national survey research results do show significant differences between Americans and Europeans on these issues (see table).

Americans believe strongly in an "opportunity" society where people get ahead by their own efforts. Other peoples are more committed to a "security" society where the government assumes principal responsibility for their well-being. For example, Americans are much less likely to agree that the role of government is to reduce income differences between people or to "provide everyone with a guaranteed basic income." Americans are less likely than others (with the possible exception of the independent-minded Australians) to believe that government "should provide a job for everyone who wants one." Finally, Americans, more than other free peoples, believe in the possibility of upward social mobility—"improving our standard of living."

	"Government should reduce differences between high and low incomes"	"Government should provide everyone with a guaranteed basic income"	"Government should provide a job for everyone who wants one"	"In my country, people like me have a good chance of improving our standard of living"
United States	29%	21%	45%	72%
Australia	44	38	40	61
Switzerland	43	43	50	59
Great Britain	64	61	59	37
Netherlands	65	50	75	26
Germany	61	56	77	40
Austria	81	57	80	47
Italy	82	67	82	45
Hungary	80	79	92	33

Source: Surveys for the International Social Survey Program by National Opinion Research Center (United States), by Social and Community Planning Research, London (Great Britain), by Zentrum for Umfragen, Methoden, und Analysen, Mannheim (West Germany), by Ricerca Sociale e di Marketing, Milan (Italy), by Institute für Soziologie, Graz University (Austria), by Australian National Research School of Social Sciences. Reported in *American Enterprise* 1 (March/April 1990) 115–17.

respect the institutions of government. Generally the younger the student, the more positive the attitudes expressed toward political authority.[9] Yet despite the efforts of the schools to inspire support for the political system, distrust and cynicism creep in during the high school years. Although American youth retain a generally positive view of the political system, they share with adults increasing skepticism toward specific institutions and practices. During high school, students acquire some ability to think along liberal-conservative dimensions. The college experience appears to produce a "liberalizing" effect: College seniors tend to be more liberal than entering freshmen. But over the years following graduation, liberal views tend to moderate.

Although no direct evidence indicates that the schools can inculcate democratic values, people with more education tend to be more tolerant than those with less education and to be generally more supportive of the political system (see Table 5.1). This pattern suggests that the effects of schooling are gradual and subtle (see also *What Do You Think?* college students opinions).

Church Religious beliefs and values may also shape political opinion. *Which* religion an individual identifies with (for example, Protestant, Catholic, Jewish) affects public opinion. So does *how important* religion is in the individual's life. It is difficult to explain exactly how religion affects political values, but we can observe differences in the opinions expressed by Protestants, Catholics, and Jews; by people who say their religious beliefs are strong versus those who say they are not; and between fundamentalists (those who believe in a literal interpretation of the Bible) and nonfundamentalists. Religion shapes political attitudes on a variety of issues, including abortion, drugs, the death penalty, homosexuality, and prayer in public schools[10] (see Table 5.2 on page 147). Religion also plays a measurable role in political ideology. Fundamentalists are more likely to describe themselves as conservatives than as moderates, and very few accept the liberal label.[11]

The United States is one of the most religious societies in the world, in terms of the proportion of the people who say they believe in God (96 percent), who say God has guided them in making decisions in their life (77 percent), who say they belong to an organized religion (70 percent), who say that religion is "very important" in their own life (60 percent), and who say they attend church at least once a month (58 percent). Most Americans believe religion should play an important role in addressing "all or most of today's problems" (64 percent), and they lament that religion is "losing its influence" in American life (69 percent).

At the same time, however, most Americans are concerned about religious leaders exercising influence in political life. Most respondents say it is "not appropriate for religious leaders to talk about their political beliefs as part of their religious

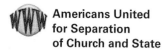

THINK AGAIN

Is it appropriate for religious leaders to try to influence how people vote?

Christian Coalition Organization advocating greater Christian involvement in politics and government. *www.cc.org*

Americans United for Separation of Church and State Advocacy organization opposed to religious influence in government. *www.au.org*

TABLE 5.1 Education and Tolerance

	Percentage Responding "Yes" (by highest degree completed)				
	No High School	High School	Junior College	College Degree	Total
If such a person wanted to make a speech in your community, should he be allowed to speak?					
Atheist (anti-religion)	47%	72%	83%	88%	69%
Racist	47	61	69	77	61
Homosexual	51	76	85	90	73
Should such a person be allowed to teach in a college or university?					
Atheist (anti-religion)	29%	49%	65%	72%	49%
Racist	35	42	52	58	45
Homosexual	40	66	80	83	64

Source: General Social Survey, Cumulative Index, 2000 (Chicago: National Opinion Research Center), Cross tabulations by Nikita Desai, Department of Political Science, Purdue University.

College Students' Opinions

College students' opinions today appear to be somewhat more conservative then they were a generation ago, in the 1970s. While most students identify themselves politically as "middle-of-the-road," there are somewhat more "conservative" self-identifiers, and fewer "liberal" self identifiers than 35 years ago. On policy issues, students today are more likely to support the death penalty, believe the courts are too lenient with criminals, and oppose legalization of marijuana. (However, students are somewhat more liberal on these issues today than in the 1980s and 1990s.) Students in the 1970s confronted an unpopular war in Vietnam, faced a military draft, and were more likely to experiment with drugs and alternative lifestyles. Today's students confront greater economic competition and increased educational requirements for employment. They are more concerned with their financial future than students were a generation ago.

However, college students remain somewhat more liberal than the general population. Moreover, college seniors and graduate students are more liberal than first-year students; students at prestigious Ivy League universities are more liberal than students at state universities and community colleges; and students in humanities and social sciences are more liberal than students in engineering, physical sciences, and business. Over the years following graduation, many of these liberal predispositions tend to moderate.

Political Opinions of College Students

	1972	1995	2003
Political ideology			
Far left	2%	3%	3%
Liberal	33	21	25
Middle-of-the road	48	50	51
Conservative	16	20	20
Far right	1	2	1
Policy issues			
Abolish the death penalty	33	21	32
Courts are too concerned with rights of criminals	50	73	64
Marijuana should be legal	47	34	40

Source: Data taken from various issues of *The Chronicle of Higher Education,* reporting annual polls by the American Council of Education.

activities (61 percent), "religious leaders should not try to influence how people vote in elections" (64 percent), and "religious groups should *not* advance their beliefs by being involved in politics and working to affect policy" (54 percent).[12]

Age and Opinion Age group differences in politics and public opinion are sometimes referred to as the **generation gap.** On most of the issues shown in Table 5.3, older people appear to be more conservative than younger people. Older people are less likely than younger people to favor the legalization of marijuana, to allow abortion for any reason, or to allow homosexuals to teach in college; older people are more likely to identify themselves as "conservative." Younger Americans in general appear to be less interested and involved in politics than older Americans, they are less likely to keep up with political news, and, perhaps most importantly, are less likely to vote (see Table 5.3 and the discussion later in this chapter).

generation gap Differences in politics and public opinion among age groups.

TABLE 5.2 Religion and Public Opinion

Opinion	Affiliation			Faith		Belief That the Bible Is		
	Protestant	**Catholic**	**Jew**	**Strong**	**Not Very Strong**	**Literal Word of God**	**Inspired by God**	**Book of Fables**
Abortion for any reason should be legal	36%	35%	79%	26%	47%	23%	44%	67%
Legalize marijuana	19	23	43	14	28	13	23	45
Support death penalty	60	65	69	68	79	69	78	71
Remove book that favored homosexuality from library	42	31	15	46	31	54	24	17
Support prayer in public school	67	60	17	70	57	78	55	33

Source: General Social Survey, Cumulative Index, 2000 (Chicago: National Opinion Research Center). Cross-tabulations by Nikita Desai, Department of Political Science, Purdue University.

How can we explain the generation gap in politics and public opinion? The generation gap may be a product of **generational effects**—historical events that affect the views of those who lived through them. For example, the "Depression generation"—those persons who grew up during the Great Depression of the 1930s—may give greater support to government income-security programs because of this experience. The "baby boomers"—those persons who were born in the high-birthrate years following World War II (1946–64)—experienced the civil rights movement, the war in Vietnam, and changes in sexual morality, all of which may affect their views on many social issues.

The large size of the baby-boom generation makes their views especially important in politics. On some issues it is possible to identify a distinctive baby-boom generational viewpoint. For example, with regard to abortion, baby boomers are generally more supportive of legal abortion under various circumstances than either younger or older persons. However, over time much of the distinctiveness of the baby-boom generation has faded. As baby boomers have matured, their views have fitted more into common patterns of opinion.

generational effects
Historical events that affect the views of those who lived through them.

Source: PEANUTS reprinted by permission of United Feature Syndicate, Inc.

TABLE 5.3   Age and Public Opinion

	Under 30	55 and Over
Marijuana should be made legal	35%	17%
Allow homosexuals to teach in college	88	61
Allow abortion for any reason	44	32
Describe oneself as:		
Liberal	35	19
Moderate	33	43
Conservative	33	49
Read news about presidential campaign	42	71
Pay attention to national news	33	57
Vote in presidential election	24	65

Source: Questions from various *National Election Studies* and *General Social Surveys*, 1996–2000.

A generation gap in opinion may also be a product of **life-cycle effects**—changes in life circumstances associated with age that affect one's views. Young people are expected to be idealistic. As they age and take on the responsibilities of raising children, holding a job, and paying a mortgage, they become more practical in outlook. The elderly are less amenable to social change, especially changes in morals. There is some limited evidence of life-cycle effects, but they are difficult to sort out from generational effects.[13]

life-cycle effects   Changes in life circumstances associated with age that affect one's views.

Media Influence   Television is the major source of political information for Americans. More than two-thirds report that they receive "all or most" of their news from television, making newspapers, magazines, books, and radio secondary

Religion helps to shape politics and public opinion. Here Catholics protest a tax-supported New York museum's showing of an exhibit that included a feces-smeared painting of the Virgin Mary.

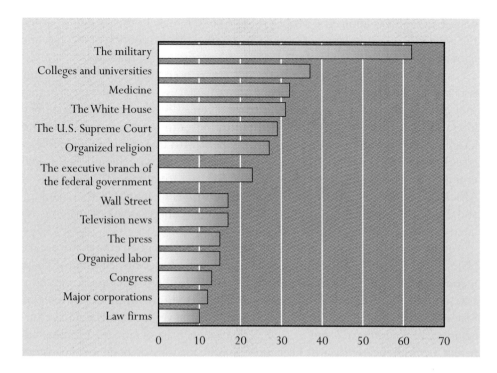

FIGURE 5.3 Public Confidence in Institutions (Percent Saying They Have a Great Deal of Confidence)

Source: The Harris Poll® #18, March 10, 2004. © 2004, Harris Interactive Inc. Reproduced by permission of Harris Interactive®. All rights reserved.

to television as a source of political information (see Chapter 6). Moreover, Americans rate television the "most believable" channel of communication.

But the effect of television on opinion is not really in persuading people to take one side of an issue or another. Instead, the principal effect is in *setting the agenda* for thinking and talking about politics. Television does not tell people *what* to think, but it does tell them what to think *about* (see Chapter 6, "Mass Media: Setting the Political Agenda"). Television coverage determines matters of general public concern. Without coverage, the general public would not know about, think about, or discuss most events, personalities, and issues. Media attention creates issues, and the amount of attention given an issue determines its importance. (We return to the discussion of media power in Chapter 6.)

Institutional Confidence. Americans express varying degrees of confidence in the major institutions of society. It seems reasonable to believe that public opinion would be more responsive to messages from institutions in which the American public has a great deal of confidence, as opposed to those institutions that failed to generate much confidence.

Interestingly, the only institution in society in which a majority of Americans regularly express "a great deal of confidence" is the *military*. Fewer than half of Americans express a great deal of confidence in the *president* and the *Supreme Court*, although these institutions rank higher than universities, medicine, television news, religion, or the press. Relatively few Americans express great confidence in the *Congress*. Lawyers and law firms regularly show up in national polls as the least trusted institutions in America (see Figure 5.3)

Ideology and Opinion

Ideology helps to shape opinion. Many people, especially politically interested and active people, approach policy questions with a fairly consistent and integrated set of principles—that is, an *ideology* (see Chapter 2). Liberal and conservative ideas about the proper role of government in the economy, about the regulation of social conduct, about equality and the distribution of income, and about civil rights influence people's views on specific policy questions.

To what extent do self-described liberals and conservatives differ over specific issues? Can we predict people's stances on particular issues by knowing whether they call themselves liberal or conservative? Generally speaking, self-described liberals and conservatives do differ in their responses to specific policy questions, although some take policy positions inconsistent with their proclaimed ideology (see Table 5.4). People who describe themselves as liberal generally favor governmental efforts to reduce income inequalities and to improve the positions of African Americans, other minorities, and women. Overall, it appears that ideology and opinion are fairly well linked—that the liberal-conservative dimension is related to opinions on specific policy questions.[14]

Yet it is also true that substantial percentages of self-described conservatives take liberal policy positions, and self-described liberals take conservative positions. These inconsistencies may show that significant portions of the population do not consistently apply ideological principles when determining their position on specific issues. The consistent application of ideology to policy issues may be more characteristic of the interested and active few than of the mass of citizens. Or these apparent inconsistencies may arise because people are focusing on different dimensions of liberalism and conservatism when they label themselves. That is, some people who label themselves conservatives may hold traditional social views about abortion, homosexuality, prayer in the schools, crime, and pornography, but they want government to guarantee economic security. Or these same people may label them-

TABLE 5.4 Ideology and Opinion

| | Percentage Agreeing | | | |
	Liberals	Moderates	Conservatives	Total
Equality				
"Government should reduce income differences"	33%	24%	20%	25%
"Government should not concern itself with income differences"	27	23	50	32
Courts' treatment of criminals				
"Too harsh"	5	2	0	2
"Not harsh enough"	83	91	92	89
"About right"	12	8	8	9
Social issues				
Favor legalizing marijuana	52	32	20	35
Favor school prayer	43	61	69	58
Oppose busing for racial balance in public schools	70	79	88	77

Source: *General Social Survey, Cumulative Index,* 2000 (Chicago: National Opinion Research Center). Cross-tabulations by Nikita Desai, Department of Political Science, Purdue University.

selves liberal based on their view of the role of government in the economy, even though they hold traditional views about social conduct. In short, a single liberal-conservative dimension may be inadequate for describing the ideology of Americans, and this inadequacy explains the apparent inconsistencies.

Gender and Opinion

A **gender gap** in public opinion—a difference of opinion between men and women—occurs on only a few issues. Interestingly, a gender gap does *not* appear on women's issues: abortion, the role of women in business and politics, whether one would vote for a qualified woman for president, or whether men are better suited for political office. On these issues, men and women do not differ significantly (see Figure 5.4).

However, gender gap differences are apparent on a variety of contemporary issues (see Figure 5.4). Many polls report that women are:

- More likely to favor an activist role for government

- More often opposed to U.S. military intervention

- More supportive of restrictions on firearms

- More supportive of spending on social programs

- More supportive of affirmative action

And there is some evidence that these gender gap differences are recognized by many voters and affect their choices at the polls (see *What Do You Think?* Do Gender Stereotypes Affect Voting?).

Politically, the most important gender gap is in party identification. Women are more likely to identify themselves as Democrats, and men more likely to identify themselves as Republicans. This difference emerged in the 1980s, when men were more likely than women to support Republican president Ronald Reagan. (Group differences in party identification are discussed at length in Chapter 7.)

Race and Opinion

Opinion over the extent of discrimination in the United States and over the causes of and remedies for racial inequality differs sharply across racial lines. Most whites believe there is very little discrimination toward African Americans in jobs, housing, or education and that differences between whites and blacks in society occur as a result of a lack of motivation among black people. Most African Americans strongly disagree with these views and believe that discrimination continues in employment, housing, and education and that differences between whites and blacks in standards of living are "mainly due to discrimination" (see Figure 5.5).

African Americans generally support a more positive role for government in reducing inequality in society. Approximately two out of every three believe that government should do more to reduce income differences between rich and poor. Blacks favor busing to achieve racial balance in public schools, a view not shared by many whites. Given these preferences for a strong role for government, it is not surprising that more blacks than whites identify themselves as liberals. Note, however, that about one-quarter of black people identify themselves as conservative.

Center for Women in Politics

Extensive information on women officeholders, as well as gender gap data on voting and attitudes on public policy.
www.rci.rutgers.edu/~cawp

National Urban League

Organization devoted to advancing the economic well-being of African-Americans, often reflecting opinions of the growing black middle class. Publishes annual *State of Black America*.
www.nul.org

gender gap Aggregate differences in political opinions of men and women.

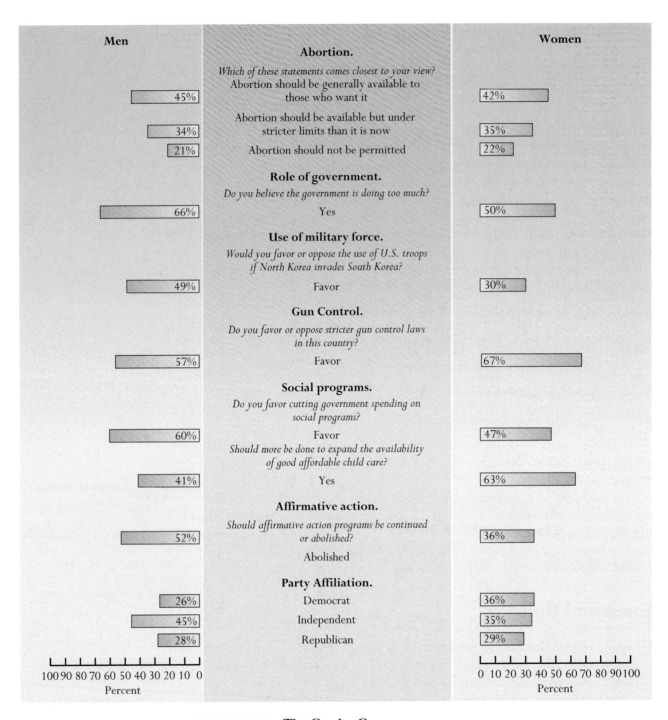

FIGURE 5.4 The Gender Gap

Source: Reprinted by permission of Center for American Women and Politics, Eagleton Institute of Politics, Rutgers, The State University of New Jersey.

And indeed, on certain social issues—crime, drugs, school prayers—majorities of black people take conservative positions. However, black support for the death penalty is significantly less than white support.

African Americans are much more likely than whites to support governmental actions and programs to improve the position of black people and other minorities. Levels of support for affirmative action depend on the wording of the question, but regardless of wording, blacks are more likely to support racial and minority

Do Gender Stereotypes Affect Voting?

Overall, women are just as successful as men as candidates for Congress, state legislatures and statewide offices. Fewer women run for these offices than men, but when they do they are just as likely to win. However, this does not mean that the gender of a candidate makes no difference to voters. On the contrary, voters use gender to make inferences about a candidate's traits, beliefs, and issue positions.

Male voters tend to prefer men over women candidates, and women voters tend to prefer women at the ballot box. This predisposition to male or female candidates is largely explained by gender stereotypes about candidate beliefs, issue competency, and presumed policy position. Voters tend to believe that women will do a better job at protecting Social Security, while men will be better at handling foreign affairs and dealing with crime. And women voters trust women candidates on the abortion issue.

	Man	Neutral	Woman
Q. If two equally qualified candidates were running for office, one a man and the other a woman, do you think you would be more inclined to vote for the man or the woman?			
Men	35%	49%	16%
Women	24%	38%	39%

	Man	Neutral	Woman
Q. Please tell me who do you think would probably do a better job of handling these issues in Congress: a man or a woman?			
Protecting Social Security	23%	36%	42%
Handling foreign affairs	56	29	15
Dealing with crime	51	28	21
Q. Now please tell me who would be more likely to take these positions in Congress: the man or woman?			
Change politics as usual	33%	21%	46%
Take your position on abortion	21%	15%	64%

Source: Data from Kira Sanbonmatsu, "Gender Stereotypes and Vote Choice," *American Journal of Political Science*, 46 (January 2002): 23. Copyright © 2002 by Blackwell Publishing. Reprinted by permission of the publisher.

---

preferences than whites. For example, both blacks and whites say they "favor affirmative action programs in business," with blacks more likely to do so than whites. However, if the question specifies "preferential treatment" for blacks and minorities, whites oppose affirmative action and blacks support it.

Policy and Opinion

Does public opinion determine government policy? It is widely assumed that in a democracy, government policy will be heavily influenced by public opinion. Yet, as noted earlier, public opinion is weak or nonexistent on many policy questions; it is frequently inconsistent and unstable; and it is poorly informed about many policy issues. Under these circumstances, political leaders—presidents and members of Congress, bureaucrats, judges, and other public officials—are relatively unconstrained by mass opinion in policy decisions (see *What Do You Think?* "Should Government Leaders Pay More Attention to Public Opinion in Policy Making?"). Moreover, in the absence of well-formed public opinion on an issue, other political actors—lobbyists and lawyers, interest-group spokespersons, journalists and

THINK AGAIN

Do you believe that your representative in Congress cares about your personal opinion on important issues?

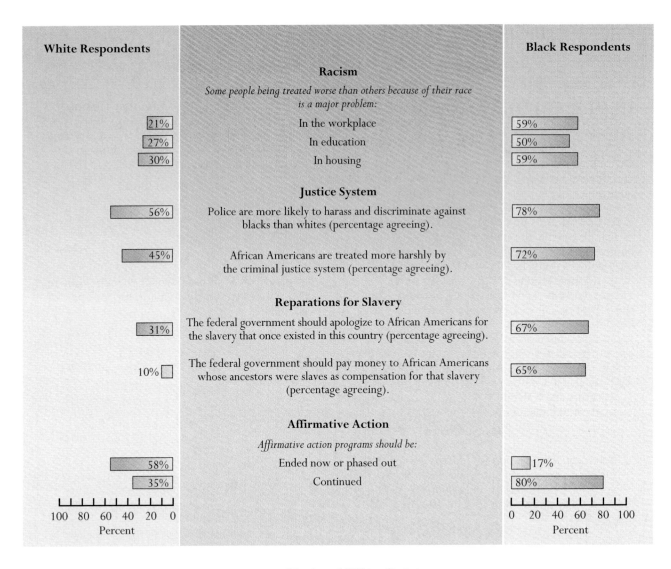

White Respondents

Black Respondents

Racism

Some people being treated worse than others because of their race is a major problem:

	In the workplace	
21%		59%
27%	In education	50%
30%	In housing	59%

Justice System

Police are more likely to harass and discriminate against blacks than whites (percentage agreeing).

56% — 78%

African Americans are treated more harshly by the criminal justice system (percentage agreeing).

45% — 72%

Reparations for Slavery

The federal government should apologize to African Americans for the slavery that once existed in this country (percentage agreeing).

31% — 67%

The federal government should pay money to African Americans whose ancestors were slaves as compensation for that slavery (percentage agreeing).

10% — 65%

Affirmative Action

Affirmative action programs should be:

| 58% | Ended now or phased out | 17% |
| 35% | Continued | 80% |

100 80 60 40 20 0
Percent

0 20 40 60 80 100
Percent

FIGURE 5.5 Black and White Opinions

Blacks and whites differ over the extent of racism in the United States as well as over what, if anything, should be done about it.

Source: Various national opinion surveys, reported in Public Agenda Online, 2004.

commentators, television reporters and executives—can influence public policy by communicating directly with government officials, claiming to represent the public. They can also influence public policy indirectly by molding and shaping public opinion.

The weakness of public opinion on many policy issues increases the influence of elites, that small group of people who are interested and active in public affairs, who call or write their elected representatives; who join organizations and contribute money to causes and candidates; who attend meetings, rallies, and demonstrations; and who hold strong opinions on a wide variety of public issues. According to political scientist V. O. Key, Jr., the linkage between ordinary citizens and democratic government depends heavily on "that thin stratum of persons referred to variously as the political elite, the political activists, the leadership echelons, or the influentials."[15] Thus political *participation* appears to be the essential link between opinion and policy.

Students at Augustana College react to the verdict in the nationally televised trial of O.J. Simpson for murder. Simpson was found not guilty by the jury. The verdict focused national attention on the great differences between the beliefs of whites and African Americans about the role of racism in the criminal justice system.

Individual Participation in Politics

Democracies provide a variety of ways for individuals to participate in politics. People may run for, and win, public office; take part in marches, demonstrations, and protests; make financial contributions to political candidates or causes; attend political meetings, speeches, and rallies; write letters to public officials or to newspapers; wear a political button or place a bumper sticker on their car; belong to organizations that support or oppose particular candidates or take stands on public issues; attempt to influence friends while discussing candidates or issues; and vote in elections. Individuals may also participate in politics passively, by simply following political issues and campaigns in the media, acquiring knowledge, forming opinions about public affairs, and expressing their views to others. These forms of political participation can be ranked according to their order of frequency (see Figure 5.6). Only a little more than half of the voting-age population vote in presidential elections, and far fewer vote in congressional and state and local elections.

THINK AGAIN

Do you think you will ever run for public office yourself?

Securing the Right to Vote

Popular participation in government is part of the very definition of democracy. The long history of struggle to secure the right to vote—**suffrage**—reflects the democratizing of the American political system.

The Elimination of Property Qualifications, 1800–1840 The Constitution of 1787 left it to the states to determine voter qualifications. The Founders generally believed that only men of property had a sufficient "stake in society" to exercise their vote in a "responsible" fashion. However, the Founders could not agree on the wording of property qualifications for insertion into the Constitution, so they left the issue to the states, feeling safe in the knowledge that at the time every state had property qualifications for voting. Yet over time, Jeffersonian and

suffrage Legal right to vote.

Should Government Leaders Pay More Attention to Public Opinion in Policy Making?

Over 200 years ago, the British parliamentarian Edmund Burke told his constituents: "Your representative owes you, not his industry only, but his judgment, and he betrays you instead of serving you, if he sacrifices it to your opinion." Since then "Burkian representation" has come to mean using one's own judgment in governmental decision making and paying little or no attention to public opinion polls. Indeed, many politicians boast of their own courage and independence and their willingness to ignore opinion polls on major issues.

But the American people believe that the country would be much better off if politicians paid *more* attention to public opinion.

Q. If the leaders of the nation followed the views of the public more closely, do you think that the nation would be better off, or worse off than it is today?

Better	81%
Worse	10%

Indeed, most Americans believe that members of Congress should "read up on the polls" in order to "get a sense of the public's views."

Q. Please tell me which statement you agree with most. (A) When members of Congress are thinking about how to vote on an issue, they should read up on the polls, because this can help them get a sense of the public's views on the issue. (B) When members of Congress are thinking about how to vote on an issue, they should not read the polls, because this will distract them from thinking about what is right.

Should read polls	67%
Should not read polls	26%

But fewer than one-third of the members of Congress believe that the American people know enough to form wise opinions on public issues. When Congress members themselves were questioned—"*Do you think the American public knows enough about the issues you face to form wise opinions about what should be done about these issues, or not?*"—the results (Yes—31 percent, No—47 percent, Maybe—17 percent) indicated that Congress members do not have a very high regard for the "wisdom of the people," no matter what they say in their political speeches.

Source: Center on Policy Alternatives, as reported in *The Polling Report,* February 15, 1999.

Jacksonian principles of democracy, including confidence in the judgment of ordinary citizens, spread rapidly in the new Republic. The states themselves eliminated most property qualifications by 1840. Thus before the Civil War (1861–65), the vote had been extended to virtually all *white males* over twenty-one years of age.

The Fifteenth Amendment, 1870 The first important limitation on state powers over voting came with the ratification of the Fifteenth Amendment: "The right of citizens of the United States to vote shall not be denied or abridged by the United States or by any state on account of race, color, or previous condition of servitude." The object of this amendment, passed by the Reconstruction Congress after the Civil War and ratified in 1870, was to extend the vote to former black slaves and prohibit voter discrimination on the basis of race. The Fifteenth Amendment also gave Congress the power to enforce black voting rights "by appropriate legislation." The states retain their right to determine voter qualifications, *as long as they do not practice racial discrimination,* and Congress has the power to pass legislation ensuring black voting rights.

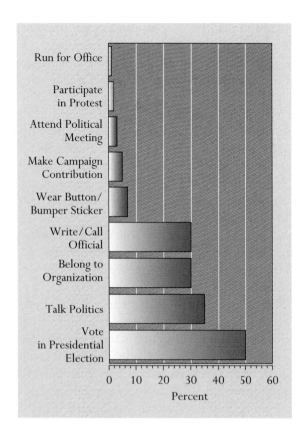

FIGURE 5.6 Political Participation

Only a small percentage of the American people are actively engaged in the political process, yet they receive most of the media attention. Less than 1 percent of the population runs for office at any level of government, and only about half of all voting-age Americans bother to go to the polls even in a presidential election.

Source: National Election Studies Cumulative File. See also M. Margaret Conway, *Political Participation in the United States,* 3rd ed. (Washington, D.C.: CQ Press, 2000).

Continued Denial of Voting Rights, 1870–1964 For almost 100 years after the adoption of the Fifteenth Amendment, white politicians in the southern states were able to defeat its purposes. Social and economic pressures and threats of violence were used to intimidate many thousands of would-be black voters.

There were also many "legal" methods of disenfranchisement, including a technique known as the **white primary**. So strong was the Democratic Party throughout the South that the Democratic nomination for public office was tantamount to election. Thus *primary elections* to choose the Democratic nominee were the only elections in which real choices were made. If black people were prevented from voting in Democratic primaries, they could be effectively disenfranchised. Therefore, southern state legislatures resorted to the simple device of declaring the Democratic Party in southern states a private club and ruling that only white people could participate in its elections—that is, in primary elections. Blacks were free to vote in "official" general elections, but all whites tacitly agreed to support the Democratic, or "white man's," Party in general elections, regardless of their differences in the primary. Not until 1944, in *Smith v. Allwright,* did the Supreme Court declare the white primary unconstitutional and bring primary elections under the purview of the Fifteenth Amendment.[16]

From an estimated 5 percent of voting-age black people registered in southern states in the 1940s, black registration rose to an estimated 20 percent in 1952, 25 percent in 1956, 28 percent in 1960, and 39 percent in 1964. But this last figure was still only about half of the comparable figure for white registration in the South. Despite the Fifteenth Amendment, many local registrars in the South succeeded in barring black registration by an endless variety of obstacles, delays, and frustrations. Application forms for registration were lengthy and complicated, even a minor error, like underlining rather than circling in the "Mr.—Mrs.—Miss" set

white primary Democratic Party primary elections in many southern counties in the early part of the twentieth century that excluded black people from voting.

of choices, as instructed, would lead to rejection. **Literacy tests** were the most common form of disenfranchisement. Many a black college graduate failed to interpret "properly" the complex legal documents that were part of the test. White applicants for voter registration were seldom asked to go through these lengthy procedures.

The Civil Rights Act, the Twenty-fourth Amendment, and the Voting Rights Act, 1964–65

The Civil Rights Act of 1964 made it unlawful for registrars to apply unequal standards in registration procedures or to reject applications because of immaterial errors. It required that literacy tests be in writing and made a sixth-grade education a presumption of literacy. In 1970 Congress outlawed literacy tests altogether.

The Twenty-fourth Amendment to the Constitution, ratified in 1964, made **poll taxes**—taxes required of all voters—unconstitutional as a requirement for voting in national elections. In 1966 the Supreme Court declared poll taxes unconstitutional in state and local elections as well.[17]

In early 1965 civil rights organizations led by Martin Luther King, Jr., effectively demonstrated against local registrars in Selma, Alabama, who were still keeping large numbers of black people off the voting rolls. Registrars there closed their offices for all but a few hours every month, placed limits on the number of applications processed, went out to lunch when black applicants appeared, delayed months before processing black applications, and used a variety of other methods to keep blacks disenfranchised. In response to the Selma march, Congress enacted the strong Voting Rights Act in 1965. The U.S. attorney general, upon evidence of voter discrimination, was empowered to replace local registrars with federal registrars, abolish literacy tests, and register voters under simplified federal procedures. Southern counties that had previously discriminated in voting registration hurried to sign up black voters just to avoid the imposition of federal registrars. The Voting Rights Act of 1965 proved to be very effective, and Congress has voted to extend it over the years.

literacy test Examination of a person's ability to read and write as a prerequisite to voter registration, outlawed by Voting Rights Act (1965) as discriminatory.

poll taxes Taxes imposed as a prerequisite to voting; prohibited by the Twenty-fourth Amendment.

Passage of the Voting Rights Act of 1965 opened the voting booth to millions of black voters formerly kept from the polls by a variety of discriminatory regulations in the South. Here African Americans in rural Alabama in 1966 line up at a local store to cast their votes in a primary that focused on an issue central to their existence—segregation.

The turn of the century saw the acceleration of the women's suffrage movement. Although Woodrow Wilson expressed support for granting the vote to women even before he took office in 1912, it took the activities of women "manning the homefront" during World War I to persuade the male electrorate to pass the Nineteenth Amendment and give women access to the ballot box throughout the nation.

The Nineteenth Amendment, 1920 Following the Civil War, many of the women who had been active in the abolitionist movement to end slavery turned their attention to the condition of women in the United States. As abolitionists, they had learned to organize, conduct petition campaigns, and parade and demonstrate. Now they sought to improve the legal and political rights of women. In 1869 the Wyoming territory adopted women's suffrage, later, several other western states followed suit. But it was not until the Nineteenth Amendment was added to the U.S. Constitution in 1920 that women's right to vote in all elections was constitutionally guaranteed.

The Twenty-sixth Amendment, 1971 The movement for eighteen-year-old voting received its original impetus during World War II. It was argued successfully in Georgia in 1944 that because eighteen-year-olds were being called upon to fight and die for their country, they deserved to have a voice in the conduct of government. However, this argument failed to convince adult voters in other states; qualifications for military service were not regarded as the same as qualifications for rational decision making in elections. In state after state, voters rejected state constitutional amendments designed to extend the vote to eighteen-year-olds.

Congress intervened on behalf of eighteen-year-old voting with the passage of the Twenty-sixth Amendment to the Constitution.[18] The states quickly ratified this amendment in 1971 during a period of national turbulence over the Vietnam War. Many supporters of the amendment believed that protests on the campuses and streets would be reduced if youthful protesters were given the vote.

The National Voter Registration Act, 1993 The National Voter Registration Act of 1993, popularly known as the "Motor Voter Act," mandates that the states offer people the opportunity to register to vote when they apply for driver's licenses or apply for welfare services. States must also offer registration by mail, and they must accept a simplified registration form prepared by the Federal Election Commission. Finally, it bars states from removing the names of people from registration lists for failure to vote. Did the "**Motor Voter Act**" work? Careful

"Motor Voter Act" Federal mandate that states offer voter registration at driver's licensing and welfare offices.

research indicates that it succeeded in increasing voter registration, but its effects on actual turnout at the polls were very limited.[19] Apparently, easy registration does not automatically increase voter turnout.

Why Vote?

Deciding whether to cast a vote in an election is just as important as deciding which candidate to vote for. *About half of the voting-age population in the United States typically fails to vote, even in presidential elections.* Voter **turnout**—the number of actual voters in relation to the number of people eligible to register and vote—is even lower in off-year congressional and state elections, when presidential elections are not held. Turnout in local elections (for example, city, county, school board) is even lower when these elections are held separately from national elections. Voter turnout in presidential elections steadily declined for several decades (see Figure 5.7). The three-way presidential race in 1992 temporarily reversed the downward trend. But in 2004 voter turnout surged to levels not seen since the 1960s. Various explanations have been offered: the expected closeness of the election, the

turnout Number of voters who actually cast ballots in an election, as a percentage of people eligible to register and vote.

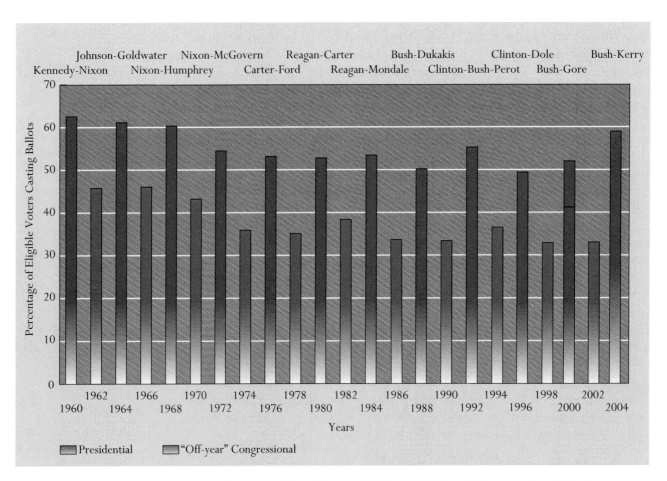

FIGURE 5.7   Voter Turnout in Presidential and Congressional Elections

Voter turnout is always higher in years with a presidential election. However, voter turnout has generally declined since 1960, even in presidential election years. The exception came in 1992, when intense interest in the contest between George Bush and Bill Clinton—spiced by the entry of independent Ross Perot—led to a higher-than-normal turnout. In 1996 fewer than half of voting-age Americans bothered to cast ballots. However, in 2004 voter turnout rose to levels not seen since the 1960's.

experience of 2000 when only a few votes in Florida decided the outcome, the war in Iraq, and an increasing concern with "moral values" that seemed to motivate devout churchgoers to go to the polls.

Why vote? Usually, this question is asked in the negative: Why do so many people fail to register and vote? But greater insight into the question of voter participation can be obtained if we try to understand what motivates the people who do go to the polls.

The Rational Voter From a purely "rational" perspective, an individual should vote only if the costs of voting (time spent in registering, informing oneself about the candidates, and going to the polls) are *less* than the expected value of having the preferred candidate win (the personal benefits gained from having one's candidate win), multiplied by the probability that one's own vote will be the deciding vote. Why vote when registering, following the political news, and getting to the polls take away time from work, family, or leisure activity? Why vote when the winner will not really change one's life for the better, or even do things much differently from what the loser would have done? Most important, why vote when the chance that one individual vote will determine who wins is very small? Thought of in this fashion, the wonder is that millions of Americans continue to vote.

The "rational" model can explain voter turnout only by adding "the intrinsic rewards of voting" to the equation. These rewards include the ethic of voting, patriotism, a sense of duty, and allegiance to democracy. People exercise their right to vote out of respect for that right rather than for any personal tangible benefit they expect to receive. They can look at the voting returns on television later in the evening, knowing they were part of an important national event. These psychological rewards do not depend on whether a single vote determines the outcome. Millions of people vote out of a sense of duty and commitment to democracy.

The Burden of Registration Voter **registration** is a major obstacle to voting. Not only must citizens care enough to go to the polls on election day; they must also expend time and energy, weeks before the election, to register. Registration usually occurs at a time when interest in the campaign is far from its peak. It may involve a trip to the county courthouse and a procedure more complicated than voting itself. The registration requirement reduces voter turnout significantly. Approximately 85 percent of *registered voters* turn out for a presidential election, but this figure represents only about 50 percent of the *voting-age population*. This discrepancy suggests that registration is a significant barrier to participation.

Registration is supposed to prevent fraud. Voters must identify themselves on Election Day and show they have previously registered in their districts as voters; once they have voted, their names are checked off and they cannot vote again. Registration was adopted by most states in the early twentieth century as a reform designed to reduce the fraudulent voting that was often encouraged and organized by political machines. "Vote early and vote often" was the rallying cry of many party bosses, who sent their legions to the polls for repeated voting. (Registration did not end all voting fraud; some enterprising old party bosses continued to cast votes for registered persons who had died—"the tombstone vote"—or moved away.) But the trade-off for reducing fraud was to create an additional burden on the voter: registration.

Burdensome Ballots Deciding upon voting times, places, equipment, and ballots is the responsibility of state governments, most of which pass on this responsibility to their county governments. County elected or appointed "super-

State of the Vote
Official Web site of the National Association of Secretaries of State (state voting officials) urging young people to register and vote.
www.stateofthevote.org

registration Requirement that prospective voters establish their identity and place of residence prior to an election in order to be eligible to vote.

Voter registration is designed to prevent fraud, but it also tends to discourage people from exercising their right to vote. Spanish language registration forms, where they are used, may ease the burden of registration for some.

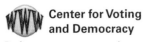

Center for Voting and Democracy

Reform organization devoted to expanding voter participation; Web site includes data on voter turn out nationally and by state.
www.fairvote.org

visors of elections" function throughout the nation preparing ballots and handling the streams of voters on election day. Nationwide, over 1 million "poll workers," usually volunteers from the local Democratic and Republican party organizations, assist in the voting process and later the counting of votes.

The contested 2000 presidential election spotlighted many of the flaws of ballots and vote counting throughout the nation. That election revealed the variety of voting methods used among the states and even within the same state.[20] Some states and counties use traditional paper or mark-sense ballots, others older lever machines and punch-card ballots, while still others are progressing toward electronic voting equipment. Paper and punch-card ballots regularly produce "overvotes" (where voters mark or punch votes for more than one candidate for the same office) or "undervotes" (where voters fail to make a selection for a particular office), or otherwise spoil their ballot. These ballots are "uncounted"; nationwide, they usually amount to about 2 percent of all ballots cast. Many state laws are fuzzy regarding when and how to conduct "recounts"—requiring election officials to undertake a second or third counting of the ballots. Reformers generally recommend touch screen voting machines, carefully designed ballot layouts, better training of poll workers, uniform rules for recounts, and better voter education programs, including sample ballots distributed well before election day.

The Politics of Voter Turnout

Politics drives the debate over easing voter registration requirements. Democrats generally favor minimal requirements—for example, same-day registration, registration by mail, and registration at welfare and motor vehicle licensing offices. They know that nonvoters are heavily drawn from groups that typically support the Democratic Party, including the less-educated, lower-income, and minority groups. Republicans are often less enthusiastic about easing voting requirements, but it is politically embarrassing to appear to oppose increased participation. It is not surprising that the Motor Voter Act of 1993 was a product of a Democratic Congress and a Democratic president, Bill Clinton.

The Stimulus of Competition The more lively the competition between parties or between candidates, the greater the interest of citizens and the larger the voter turnout. When parties and candidates compete vigorously, they make news and are given large play by the mass media. Consequently, a setting of competitive politics generates more political stimuli than does a setting with weak competition. People are also more likely to perceive that their votes count in a close contest, and thus they are more likely to cast them. Moreover, when parties or candidates are fighting in a close contest, their supporters tend to spend more time and energy campaigning and getting out the vote.

Political Alienation People who feel politics is irrelevant to their life—or who feel they cannot personally affect public affairs—are less likely to vote than people who feel they themselves can affect political outcomes and that these outcomes affect their life. Given the level of **political alienation** (two-thirds of respondents agree with the statement, "Most public officials are not really interested in the problems of people like me"),[21] it is surprising that so many people vote. Alienation is high among voters, and it is even higher among nonvoters.

Intensity Finally, as we might expect, people who feel strongly about politics and who hold strong opinions about political issues are more likely to vote than people who do not. For example, people who describe themselves as *extreme* liberals or *extreme* conservatives are more likely to vote than people who describe themselves as moderates.

Explaining Turnouts The general decline in U.S. voter turnout over the last several decades has generated a variety of explanations. This decline has occurred despite an easing of registration requirements and procedures over time. It may be a product of increasing distrust of government (see *What Do You Think?* "Can You Trust the Government?" in Chapter 1), which is related to political alienation. People who distrust the government are likely to feel they have little influence in politics. They are therefore less likely to go to the trouble of registering and voting. The focus of the media, particularly television, on corruption in government, sex scandals involving politicians, conflicts of interest, waste and inefficiency, and negative campaign advertising may add to popular feelings of alienation.

Another explanation focuses on the expansion of the electorate to include young people eighteen to twenty-one years of age. Young people do not vote in the same proportions as older people (see Figure 5.8). After the electorate was expanded by the Twenty-sixth Amendment to include persons eighteen years of age and over, voter turnout actually dropped, from 60.9 percent in the 1968 presidential election to 55.2 percent in the 1972 presidential election, the largest turnout decline in successive presidential elections.

Still another explanation focuses on the declining role of party organizations in the political system. Strong party organizations, or machines, that canvassed neighborhoods, took citizens to the courthouse to register them, contacted them personally during campaigns, and saw to it that they got to the polls on election day have largely disappeared (see Chapter 7).

political alienation Belief that politics is irrelevant to one's life and that one cannot personally affect public affairs.

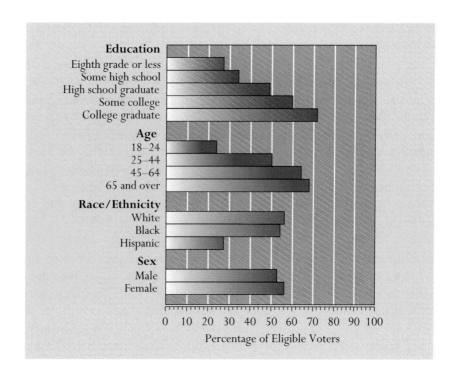

FIGURE 5.8 Voter Turnout by Social Groups

Although there is virtually no gender gap in who goes to the polls, voter turnout increases with education, age, and income. Major efforts to "get out the vote" in the African American community have raised voter turnout to nearly that of whites, but turnout among Hispanics continues to lag.

Source: U.S. Bureau of the Census, *Statistical Abstract of the United States,* 2004. Data for 2000 presidential election.

Regardless of the explanations offered, it is interesting to note that most European democracies report higher voter turnout rates than the United States (see *Compared to What?* "Voter Turnout in Western Democracies").

Voters and Nonvoters

Who votes and who doesn't? The perceived benefits and costs of voting apparently do not fall evenly across all social groups. Nonvoting would generate less concern if voters were a representative cross section of nonvoters. But voters differ from nonvoters in politically important ways.

Voters are better educated than nonvoters. Education appears to be the most important determinant of voter turnout (see Figure 5.7). It may be that schooling promotes an interest in politics, instills the ethic of citizen participation, or gives people a better awareness of public affairs and an understanding of the role of elections in a democracy. Education is associated with a sense of confidence and political *efficacy,* the feeling that one can indeed have a personal impact on public affairs.

Age is another factor affecting voter participation. Perhaps because young people have more distractions, more demands on their time in school, work, or new family responsibilities, nonvoting is greatest among eighteen- to twenty-four-year-olds. In contrast, older Americans are politically influential in part because candidates know they turn out at the polls.

High-income people are more likely to vote than are low-income people. Most of this difference stems from the fact that high-income people are more likely to be well educated and older. But poor people may also feel alienated from the political system—they may lack a sense of political efficacy; they may feel they have little control over their own lives, let alone over public affairs. Or poor people may simply be so absorbed in the problems of life that they have little time or energy to spend on registering and voting.[22]

Voter Turnout in Western Democracies

Other Western democracies regularly report higher voter turnout rates than the United States (see figure). Yet in an apparent paradox, Americans seem to be more supportive of their political institutions, less alienated from their political system, and even more patriotic than citizens of Western European nations. Why, then, are voter turnouts in the United States so much lower than in these other democracies?

The answer to this question lies primarily in the legal and institutional differences between the United States and the other democracies. First of all, in Austria, Australia, Belgium, and Italy, voting is *mandatory*. Penalties and the level of enforcement vary within and across these countries. Moreover, registration laws in the United States make voting more difficult than in other countries. In Western Europe, all citizens are required to register with the government and obtain identification cards. These cards are then used for admission to the polls. In contrast, voter registration is entirely voluntary in the United States, and voters must reregister if they change residences. Nearly 50 percent of the U.S. population changes residence at least once in a five-year period, thus necessitating reregistration.

Parties in the United States are more loosely organized, less disciplined, and less able to mobilize voters than are European parties. Moreover, many elections in the United States, notably elections for Congress, are not very competitive. The United States organizes congressional elections by district with winner-take-all rules, whereas many European parliaments are selected by proportional representation, with seats allocated to parties based on national vote totals. Proportional representation means every vote counts toward seats in the legislative body. Thus greater competition and proportional representation may encourage higher voter turnout in European democracies.

But cultural differences may also contribute to differences in turnout. The American political culture, with its tradition of individualism and self-reliance and its reluctance to empower government (see Chapter 2), encourages Americans to resolve their problems through their own efforts rather than looking to government for solutions. Government is not as central to Americans as it is to Europeans, and therefore getting to the polls on election day is not seen as so important.

Average Turnout, 1991–2000

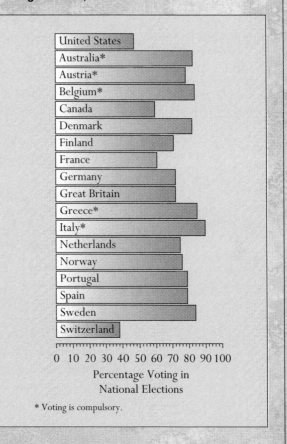

Source: Center for Voting and Democracy, 2002, www.fairvote.org. Reprinted by permission.

Income and education differences between participants and nonparticipants are even greater when other forms of political participation are considered. Higher-income, better-educated people are much more likely to be among those who make campaign contributions, who write or call their elected representatives, and who join and work in active political organizations.[23]

Historically, race was a major determinant of nonvoting. Black voter turnout, especially in the South, was markedly lower than white voter turnout. African Americans continue today to have a slightly lower overall voter turnout than whites, but most of the remaining difference is attributable to differences between blacks and whites in educational and income levels. Blacks and whites at the same educational and income levels register and vote with the same frequency. Indeed, in cities where African Americans are well organized politically, black voter turnout may exceed white voter turnout.[24]

The greatest disparity in voter turnout is between Hispanics and others. Low voter participation by Hispanics may be a product of language differences, lack of cultural assimilation, or noncitizenship status.

Nonvoting: What Difference Does It Make?

THINK AGAIN

Is our government really legitimate when only about half the people vote in presidential elections?

How concerned should we be about low levels of participation in American politics? Certainly the democratic ideal envisions an active, participating citizenry. Democratic government, asserts the Declaration of Independence, derives its "just powers from the consent of the governed." The legitimacy of democratic government can be more easily questioned when half of the people fail to vote. That is, it is easier to question whether the government truly represents "the people" when only half of the people vote even in a presidential election. Voting is an expression of good citizenship, and it reinforces attachment to the nation and to democratic government. Nonvoting suggests alienation from the political system.

However, the *right* to vote is more important to democratic government than voter turnout. The nineteenth-century English political philosopher John Stuart Mill wrote, "Men, as well as women, do not need political rights in order that they may govern, but in order that they may not be misgoverned."[25] As long as all adult Americans possess the right to vote, politicians must consider their interests. "Rulers and ruling classes are under a necessity of considering the interests of those who have the suffrage."[26] Democratic governments cannot really ignore the interests of anyone who can vote. People who have the right to vote, but who have voluntarily chosen not to exercise it in the past, can always change their minds, go to the polls, and "throw the rascals out."

Indeed, a huge army of nonvoters "hangs over the democratic process like a bomb ready to explode and change the course of history.[27] Some commentators view this latent "bomb" with alarm, but others view it as a potential resource in hard times. The last major surge in voting turnout occurred in 1932 in the midst of the Depression, when voters went to the polls in droves to oust incumbent Herbert Hoover and elect Franklin D. Roosevelt, who changed the role of government in the economy.

Voluntary nonvoting is not the same as being denied the suffrage. Politicians can indeed ignore the interests of people denied the vote by restrictive laws or practices or by intimidation or force. But when people choose not to exercise their right to vote, they may be saying that they do not believe their interests are really affected by government. The late Senator Sam Ervin is widely quoted on the topic of nonvoters:

> I'm not going to shed any crocodile tears if people don't care enough to vote. I don't believe in making it easy for apathetic lazy people. I'd be extremely happy if nobody in the United States voted except for the people who thought about the issues and made up their own minds and wanted to vote.[28]

But the class bias in voting presents another concern. It is frequently argued that greater overall turnout by better-educated, higher-income, older whites tilts the political system toward the interests of upper socioeconomic classes at the expense of poorer, less-educated, younger, black, and Hispanic people.[29] Thus the people we would expect to be most in need of government help are least represented among voters. This underrepresentation not only harms their policy interests but also contributes even further to their feelings of political alienation.

However, it is difficult to predict that major changes would occur in specific public policies if all socioeconomic groups voted with the same frequency. As we have already observed, rich and poor, black and white, often share the same opinions on policy issues or differ only in degree. The likely policy consequences of increased voter participation may be overestimated by scholars and commentators.[30]

Protest as Political Participation

Protests, marches, and demonstrations are important forms of political participation. Indeed, the First Amendment guarantees the right "peaceably to assemble, and to petition the government for a redress of grievances." A march to the steps of Congress, a mass assembly of people on the Washington Mall with speakers, sign waving, and songs, and the presentation of petitions to government officials are all forms of participation protected by the First Amendment.

Protests Protests are generally designed to call attention to an issue and to motivate others to apply pressure on public officials. In fact, protests are usually directed at the news media rather than at public officials themselves. If protesters could persuade public officials directly in the fashion of lobbyists and interest groups, they would not need to protest. Protests are intended to generate attention and support among previously uncommitted people—enough so the ultimate targets of the protest, public officials, will be pressured to act to redress grievances.

Coverage by the news media, especially television, is vital to the success of protest activity. The media not only carry the protesters' message to the mass public but also inform public officials about what is taking place. Protests provide the media with "good visuals"—pictorial dramatizations of political issues. The media welcome opportunities to present political issues in a confrontational fashion because confrontation helps capture larger audiences. Thus protesters and the media use each other to advance their separate goals.

Protests are most commonly employed by groups that have little influence in electoral politics. They were a key device of the civil rights movement at a time when many African Americans were barred from voting. In the absence of protest, the majority white population—and the public officials they elected—were at best unconcerned with the plight of black people in a segregated society. Protests, including a dramatic march on Washington in 1963 at which Martin Luther King, Jr., delivered his inspirational "I Have a Dream" speech, called attention to the injustices of segregation and placed civil rights on the agenda of decision makers.

Protests can be effectively employed by groups that are relatively small in number but whose members feel very intensely about the issue. Often the protest is a means by which these groups can obtain bargaining power with decision makers. Protests may threaten to tarnish the reputations of government officials or private corporations, or may threaten to disrupt their daily activities or reduce their business through boycotts or pressure on customers. If the protest is successful, protest

Protest Net
Radical organization provides calendar of protests against military actions, world trade, animal experiments, etc.
www.protest.net

protests Public marches or demonstrations designed to call attention to an issue and motivate others to apply pressure on public officials.

How to Run for Office

Many rewards come with elected office—the opportunity to help shape public policy, public attention and name recognition, and many business, professional, and social contacts. But there are many drawbacks as well—the absence of privacy, a microscopic review of one's past, constant calls, meetings, interviews and handshaking, and perhaps most onerous of all, the continual need to solicit campaign funds.

Before You Run—Getting Involved

Get involved in various organizations in your community:

- Neighborhood associations.
- Chambers of commerce, business associations.
- Churches and synagogues (become an usher, if possible, for visibility).
- Political groups (Democratic or Republican clubs, League of Women Voters, and so on).
- Parent-Teacher Associations (PTAs).
- Service clubs (Rotary, Kiwanis, Civitan, Toastmasters).
- Recreation organizations (Little League, flag football, soccer leagues, running and walking clubs, for example, as participant, coach, or umpire).

Deciding to Run—Know What You're Doing

In deciding to run, and choosing the office for which you wish to run, you should become thoroughly familiar with the issues, duties, and responsibilities.

- Attend council or commission meetings, state legislative sessions, and/or committee hearings.
- Become familiar with current issues and officeholders, and obtain a copy of and read the budget.
- Learn the demographics of your district (racial, ethnic, and age composition; occupational mix; average income; neighborhood differences). If you do not fit the prevailing racial, ethnic, or age composition, think about moving to another district.
- Memorize a brief (preferably less than seven seconds) answer to the question, "Why are you running?"

Getting in the Race

Contact your county elections department to obtain the following:

- Qualifying forms and information.
- Campaign financing forms and regulations.
- District and street maps for your district.
- Recent election results in your district.
- Election-law book or pamphlet.
- Voter registration lists (usually sold as lists, or labels, or tapes).
- Contact your party's county chairperson for advice; convince the party's leaders that you can win. Ask for a list of their regular campaign contributors.

Raising Money

The easiest way to finance a campaign is to be rich enough to provide your own funds. Failing that, you must:

- Establish a campaign fund, according to the laws of your state.
- Find a treasurer/campaign-finance chairperson who knows many wealthy, politically involved people.
- Invite wealthy, politically involved people to small coffees, cocktail parties, dinners; give a brief campaign speech and then have your finance chairperson solicit contributions.
- Follow up fund-raising events and meetings with personal phone calls.
- Be prepared to continue fund-raising activities throughout your campaign; file accurate financial disclosure statements as required by state law.

Getting Organized

Professional campaign managers and management firms almost always outperform volunteers. If you cannot afford professional management, you must rely on yourself or trusted friends to perform the following:

- Draw up a budget based on reasonable expectations of campaign funding.
- Interview and select a professional campaign-management firm, or appoint a trusted campaign manager.
- Ask trusted friends from various clubs, activities, neighborhoods, churches, and so on, to meet and serve as a campaign committee. If your district is racially or ethnically diverse, make sure all groups are represented on your committee.
- Decide on a campaign theme; research issues important to your community; develop brief, well-articulated positions on these issues.
- Open a campaign headquarters with desks and telephones. Buy a cell phone; use call forwarding; stay in contact. Use your garage if you can't afford an office.

- Arrange to meet with newspaper editors, editorial boards, TV station executives, and political reporters. Be prepared for tough questions.
- Hire a media consultant or advertising agency, or appoint a volunteer media director who knows television, radio, and newspaper advertising.
- Arrange a press conference to announce your candidacy. Notify all media well in advance. Arrange for overflow crowd of supporters to cheer and applaud.
- Produce eyecatching, inspirational 15- or 30-second television and radio ads that present a favorable image of you and stress your campaign theme.
- Prepare and print attractive campaign brochures, signs, and bumper stickers.
- Hire a local survey-research firm to conduct telephone surveys of voters in your district, asking what they think are the most important issues, how they stand on them, whether they recognize your name and your theme, and how they plan to vote. Be prepared to change your theme and your position on issues if surveys show strong opposition to your views.

On the Campaign Trail

Campaigns themselves may be primarily media centered or primarily *door-to-door* ("retail") or some combination of both.

- Buy media time as early as possible from television and radio stations; insist on prime-time slots before, during, and after popular shows.
- Buy newspaper ads; insist on their placement in popular, well-read sections of the paper.
- Attend every community gathering possible, just to be seen, even if you do not give a speech. Keep all speeches short. Focus on one or two issues that your polls show are important to voters.
- Recruit paid or unpaid volunteers to hand out literature door-to-door. Record names and addresses of voters who say they support you.
- Canvass door-to-door with a brief (seven-second) self-introduction and statement of your reasons for running. Use registration lists to identify members of your own party, and try to address them by name. Also canvass offices, factories, coffee shops, shopping malls—anywhere you find a crowd.
- Organize a phone bank, either professional or volunteer. Prepare *brief* introduction and phone statements. Record names of people who say they support you.

- Know your opponent: Research his or her past affiliations, indiscretions if any, previous voting record, and public positions on issues.
- Be prepared to "define" your opponent in negative terms. Negative advertising works. But be fair: Base your comments on your opponent's public record. Emphasize his or her positions that clearly deviate from your district voters' known preferences.

Primary versus General Elections

Remember that you will usually have to campaign in two elections—your party's primary and the general election.

- Before the primary, identify potential opposition in your own party, try to dissuade them from running.
- Allocate your budget first to win the primary election. If you lose the primary, you won't need any funds for the general election.
- In general elections, you must broaden your appeal without distancing your own party supporters. Deemphasize your party affiliation unless your district regularly elects members of your party, in a close district or a district that regularly votes for the opposition party, stress your independence and your commitment to the *district's* interests.

On Election Day

Turning out your voters is the key to success. Election day is the busiest day of the campaign for you and your staff.

- Use your phone bank to place as many calls as possible to party members in your district (especially those who have indicated in previous calls and visits that they support you). Remind them to vote; make sure your phone workers can tell each voter where to go to cast his or her vote.
- Solicit volunteers to drive people to the polls.
- Assign workers to as many polling places as possible. Most state laws require that they stay a specified distance from the voting booths. But they should be in evidence with your signs and literature to buttonhole voters before they go into the booths.
- Show up at city or county election office on election night with prepared victory statement thanking supporters and pledging your service to the district. (Also draft a courteous concession statement pledging your support to the winner, in case you lose.)
- Attend victory party with your supporters; meet many "new" friends.

leaders can then offer to end the protest in exchange for concessions from their targets.

Civil Disobedience Civil disobedience is a form of protest that involves breaking what are perceived as "unjust" laws. The purpose is to call attention to the existence of injustice. In the words of Martin Luther King, Jr., civil disobedience "seeks so to dramatize the issue that it can no longer be ignored"[31] (see *A Conflicting View:* "Sometimes It's Right to Disobey the Law" in Chapter 1). Those truly engaging in civil disobedience do not attempt to evade punishment for breaking the law but instead willingly accept the penalty. By doing so, they demonstrate not only their sincerity and commitment but also the injustice of the law. Cruelty or violence directed at the protesters by police or others contributes further to the drama of injustice. Like other protest activity, the success of civil disobedience depends on the willingness of the mass media to carry the message to both the general public and the political leadership.

Violence Violence can also be a form of political participation. Indeed, political violence—for example, assassinations, rioting, burning, looting—has been uncomfortably frequent in American politics over the years (see *A Conflicting View:* "American Politics as Violence" in Chapter 1). It is important to distinguish violence from protest. Peaceful protest is constitutionally protected. Often, organized protest activity harnesses frustrations and hostilities, directs them into constitutionally acceptable activities, and thus avoids violence. Likewise, civil disobedience should be distinguished from violence. Civil disobedience breaks only "unjust" laws, without violence, and willingly accepts punishment without trying to escape.

civil disobedience Form of public protest involving the breaking of laws believed to be unjust.

Effectiveness How effective are protests? Protests can be effective in achieving some goals under some conditions. But protests are useless or even counter-

Cruelty or violence directed at peaceful protesters further dramatizes their cause. In Jackson, Mississippi in 1963, segregationists poured mustard, ketchup, and sugar over lunch counter sit-in protesters. But far more serious violence, including murder, was perpetrated against civil rights protesters in the 1960s.

productive in pursuit of other goals under other conditions. Here are some generalizations about the effectiveness of protests:

- Protests are more likely to be effective when directed at specific problems or laws rather than at general conditions that cannot readily be remedied by governmental action.

- Protests are more likely to be effective when targeted toward public officials who are capable of granting the desired concession or resolving the specific problem. Protests with no specific targets and protests directed at officials who have no power to change things are generally unproductive.

- Protests are more likely to succeed when the goal is limited to gaining access or representation in decision making or to placing an issue on the agenda of decision makers.

- Protests are not always effective in actually getting laws changed and are even less effective in ensuring that the impact of the changes will really improve the conditions that led to the protest.

Public officials can defuse protest activity in a variety of ways. They may greet protesters with smiles and reassurances that they agree with their goals. They may disperse symbolic satisfaction without any tangible results. They may grant token concessions with great publicity, perhaps remedying a specific case of injustice while doing little to affect general conditions. Or public officials may claim to be constrained either legally or financially from doing anything—the "I-would-like-to-help-you-but-I-can't" strategy. Or public officials can directly confront the protesters by charging that they are unrepresentative of the groups they are trying to help.

Perhaps the most challenging and sometimes the most effective kind of protest is to run for public office (see *Up Close:* "How to Run for Office" on pages 168–169). Whether at the local level, such as the school board, or at the state or national level, the participation of one individual as a candidate—even when not elected—can make a difference in public affairs.

SUMMARY NOTES

- Public opinion commands the attention of elected public officials in a democracy, yet many Americans are poorly informed and unconcerned about politics; their opinions on public issues are often changeable and inconsistent. Only a few highly salient issues generate strong and stable opinions.

- Political socialization—the learning of political values, beliefs, and opinions—starts at an early age. It is influenced by family, school, church, age group, and the media.

- Ideology also shapes opinion, especially among politically interested and active people who employ fairly consistent liberal or conservative ideas in forming their opinions on specific issues.

- Race and gender also influence public opinion. Blacks and whites differ over the extent of discrimination in the United States, as well as over its causes and remedies. Men and women tend to differ over issues involving the use of force. In recent years, women have tended to give greater support to the Democratic Party than men have.

- Individuals can exercise power in a democratic political system in a variety of ways. They can run for public office, take part in demonstrations and protests, make financial contributions to candidates, attend political events, write letters to newspapers or public officials, belong to political organizations, vote in elections, or simply hold and express opinions on public issues.

- Securing the right to vote for all Americans required nearly 200 years of political struggle. Key victories included the elimination of property qualifications by 1840, the Fifteenth Amendment in 1870 (eliminating restrictions based on race), the Nineteenth Amendment in 1920 (eliminating restrictions based on gender), the Civil Rights Act of 1964 and Voting Rights Act of 1965 (eliminating racial obstacles), the Twenty-fourth Amendment in 1964 (eliminating poll taxes), and the Twenty-sixth Amendment in 1971 (extending the right to vote to eighteen-year-olds).

- About half of the voting-age population fails to vote even in presidential elections. Voter turnout has steadily declined in recent decades. Voter registration is a major obstacle to voting. Turnout is affected by competition as well as by feelings of political alienation and distrust of government. Young people have the poorest record of voter turnout of any age group.

- Voluntary nonvoting is not as serious a threat to democracy as denial of the right to vote. Nevertheless, the class bias in voting may tilt the political system toward the interests of higher-income, better-educated, older whites at the expense of lower-income, less-educated, younger minorities.

- Protest is an important form of participation in politics. Protests are more commonly employed by groups with little direct influence over public officials. The object is to generate attention and support from previously uncommitted people in order to bring new pressure on public officials to redress grievances. Media coverage is vital to the success of protests.

KEY TERMS

public opinion   132
survey research   132
halo effect   133
salient issues   136
socialization   137

generation gap   140
generational effects   141
life-cycle effects   142
gender gap   145
suffrage   149

white primary   151
literacy test   152
poll taxes   152
"Motor Voter Act"   153
turnout   154

registration   155
political alienation   157
protests   161
civil disobedience   164

SUGGESTED READINGS

Asher, Herbert. *Polling and the Public: What Every Citizen Should Know.* 4th ed. Washington, D.C.: CQ Press, 1998. Explains methods of polling and how results can be influenced by wording, sampling, and interviewing techniques; also covers how polls are used by the media and in campaigns.

Conway, M. Margaret. *Political Participation in the United States.* 3rd ed. Washington, D.C.: CQ Press, 2000. A comprehensive summary of who participates in politics and why.

Conway, M. Margaret, Gertrude A. Stevernagel, and David Ahern. *Women and Political Participation.* Washington, D.C.: CQ Press, 1998. An examination of cultural change and women's participation in politics, including treatment of the gender gap in political attitudes and the impact of women's membership in the political elite.

Erikson, Robert S., and Kent L. Tedin. *American Public Opinion,* 6th ed. Longman, 2002. A comprehensive review of the forces influencing public opinion and an assessment of the influence of public opinion in American politics.

Greenstein, Fred I. *Children and Politics.* New Haven, Conn.: Yale University Press, 1985. Early research on what children know about politics and how they learned it.

Page, Benjamin I., and Robert Y. Shapiro. *The Rational Public: Fifty Years of Trends in Americans' Policy Preferences.* Chicago: University of Chicago Press, 1992. An argument that government policies generally reflect public opinion.

Stimson, James A. *Public Opinion in America: Moods, Cycles, and Swings.* 2nd ed. Boulder, Colo.: Westview Press, 1998. A systematic analysis of swings and cycles in "policy moods" that roughly correspond to liberal and conservative views concerning the effectiveness of government in dealing with perceived problems.

Wald, Kenneth D. *Religion and Politics in the United States.* 4th ed. Rowman & Littlefield, 2003. An explanation of the impact of religion on American political culture, the policy process, and voting behavior.

Walton, Hanes, and Robert C. Smith. *African American Politics and the African American Quest for Universal Freedom.* New York: Pearson Longman, 2002. A comprehensive American government textbook emphasizing the diversity of African American opinions and behavior.

Zaller, John R. *The Nature and Origins of Mass Opinion.* New York: Cambridge University Press, 1992. An effort to develop and test a conceptual model of how people form political preferences, how political views and arguments diffuse through the population, and how people evaluate this information and convert their reactions into public opinion.

MAKE IT REAL

PUBLIC OPINION: SPIN DETECTION

The Opinion Outreach and Public Survey has been declining in recent years due to a lack of leadership and expertise. As the new Director of Research, your job is to correct the problems in questions, methods, and interpretation. Each survey question tries to make a generalization about a population (all the people being described) by interviewing a sample (all of the people actually surveyed). You will have a toolbox that contains all of the resources you need to fix the survey so that the report is reliable and valid. Your ability to produce a quality report will determine the fate of your organization.

6

MASS MEDIA:
SETTING THE POLITICAL AGENDA

THINK
ABOUT POLITICS

The Power of the Media

Politics—the struggle over who gets what, when, and how—is largely carried out in the **mass media**. The arenas of political conflict are the various media of mass communication—television, newspapers, magazines, radio, books, recordings, motion pictures, and the Internet. What we know about politics comes to us largely through these media. Unless we ourselves are admitted to the White House Oval Office or the committee rooms of Congress or dinner parties at foreign embassies, or unless we ourselves attend political rallies and demonstrations or travel to distant battlefields, we must rely on the mass media to tell us about politics. Furthermore, few of us ever have the opportunity to personally evaluate the character of presidential candidates or cabinet members or members of Congress, or to learn their views on public issues by talking with them face to face. Instead, we must learn about people as well as events from the mass media.

Great power derives from the control of information. *Who knows what* helps to determine *who gets what.* The media not only provide an arena for politics; they are themselves players in that arena. The media not only report on the struggles for power in society; they are themselves participants in those struggles. The media have long been referred to as America's "fourth branch" of government—and for good reason.[1]

The Power of Television Television is the most powerful medium of communication. It is the first true *mass* communication medium. Virtually every home in the United States has a television set, and the average home has the set turned on for about seven hours a day. Television is regularly chosen over other news media by Americans as the most common news source.

Americans turn to *local* TV news broadcasts as their most regular source of news. Daily newspapers are read by less than half of the adult public (see Figure 6.1). The national network evening news shows (*NBC Nightly News, ABC World News Tonight, CBS Evening News*) have lost viewership in recent years. But viewership of cable CNN, Fox News Cable, CNBC, and MSNBC is rising. Television weekly news magazines, notably CBS's *60 Minutes* and ABC's 20/20 have also become major sources of news for many Americans.

A growing number of Americans, especially young people, are turning to online news sources (see *Up Close* "The Generation Gap in News").

During a national crisis—for example, the terrorist attack of 9/11—Americans become even more dependent on television for their news. When asked "Where would you go first," for information during a crisis, 66 percent of Americans said they would turn on their TV sets. CNN was mentioned most often.[2]

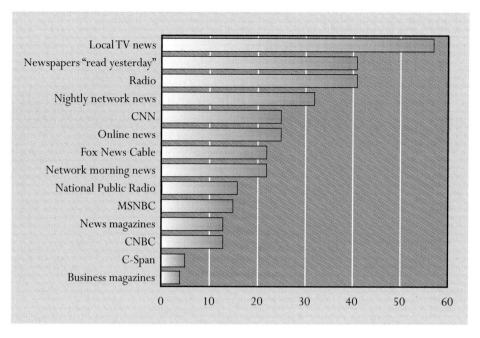

FIGURE 6.1 **Where Americans Get Their News**

Source: Adapted from the Pew Research Center for the People and the Press, "Public News Habits," www.people-press.org/ (June 9, 2002).

Note: More than one answer accepted in survey, so the sum adds up to well over 100%.

Believability Television is also rated by Americans as the most *believable* medium of communication. Compared to television news, print sources are generally seen as less believable, with one exception, the *Wall Street Journal.* CNN is rated highest among all news sources (see Table 6.1). Not many people rate the tabloids as very believable.

Newspapers and Magazines Less than one-half of the adult population reads one or another of the nation's 1,500 daily newspapers. But the nation's prestige newspapers—the *New York Times, Washington Post,* and *Wall Street Journal*—are regularly read by government officials, corporate chiefs, interest-group leaders, and

mass media All means of communication with the general public, including television, newspapers, magazines, radio, books, recordings, motion pictures, and the Internet.

TABLE 6.1 **Believing in the Media**

Believe all or most of what you see and hear (percent)

Wall Street Journal	41%	*Time*	29%
CNN	39%	Your daily paper	25%
60 Minutes	34%	*New York Times*	24%
C-Span	33%	*Newsweek*	24%
Local TV news	33%	*USA Today*	23%
ABC News	30%	*AOL News*	13%
CBS News	29%	*People*	10%
NBC News	29%	*National Enquirer*	4%

Source: Pew Research Center for the People and the Press. http://www.people-press.org. Reprinted by permission of Pew Research Center for the People & The Press.

The Generation Gap in News

Young people are far less likely to spend time watching the news than than older people. Indeed, people 65 and older or nearly twice as likely as those under 30 to watch television news. And older people are more than twice as likely to read a newspaper.

However, young people are more likely than older people to hear radio news, perhaps because radio news periodically interrupts music programming. And young people are the principal consumers of online news. Yet overall, young people are exposed to far less news than seniors.

The News Generation Gap

	18–29	30–49	50–64	65+
Watch TV news	40	52	62	73
Local TV	28	41	49	52
Network evening news	17	25	38	46
Cable TV news	16	23	30	35
Morning TV news	11	16	21	27
Read newspaper	26	37	52	59
Listen to radio news	34	49	42	29
News magazines	12	13	15	13
Online news	31	30	24	7
No news (yesterday)	33	19	15	12

Source: Pew Research Center for People and the Press. http://www.people-press.org. Reprinted by permission of Pew Research Center for the People & The Press.

other media people. Stories appearing in these newspapers are generally picked up by daily papers around the country, and these stories almost always appear on national network television.

The leading weekly newsmagazines—*Time, Newsweek,* and *U.S. News & World Report*—reach a smaller but more politically attentive audience than do newspapers. Magazines of political commentary—for example, the *Nation* (liberal), *New Republic* (liberal), *National Review* (conservative), *American Spectator* (conservative), *Weekly Standard* (conservative), *Public Interest* (neo-conservative), and *Washington Monthly* (neo-liberal)—reach very small but politically active audiences.

Television's Emotional Communication The power of television derives not only from its large audiences but also from its ability to communicate emotions as well as information. Television's power is found in its visuals—angry faces in a rioting mob, police beating an African American motorist, wounded soldiers being unloaded from a helicopter—scenes that convey an emotional message. Gripping pictures can inflame public opinion, inspire a clamor for action, and even pressure the government into hasty action. (This "CNN effect" has been cited as a cause of the disastrous American intervention in Somalia in 1992; visuals of starving children forced the Bush administration to airlift relief supplies and later to send troops to monitor distribution. The effort failed, and American lives were lost.)

Moreover, television focuses on the faces of individuals as well as on their words, portraying honesty or deception, humility or arrogance, compassion or

Network Television
All major networks now maintain news sites on the Web.
www.cbsnews.com
www.abcnews.com
www.cnn.com
www.msnbc.com
www.foxnews.com

indifference, humor or meanness, and a host of other personal characteristics. Skillful politicians understand that *what* one says may not be as importants as *how* one says it. Image triumphs over substance on television.[3]

Influence on Decision Makers The media's impact on political decision makers is vastly more significant than their impact on ordinary viewers. Media stories often relate more directly to the immediate concerns of politicians and government officials. They are more attentive to these stories; they are often asked to respond or comment upon news stories. They correctly perceive that media coverage of particular events and issues sets the agenda for public discussion. Even media stories that have relatively little widespread public interest can create a buzz "inside the Beltway," that is, within Washington circles.

The Myth of the Mirror Media people themselves often deny that they exercise great power. They sometimes claim that they only "mirror" reality. They like to think of themselves as unbiased reporters who simply narrate happenings and transmit videotaped portrayals of people and events as they really are. But whether or not the editors, reporters, producers, or anchors acknowledge their own power, it is clear that they do more than passively mirror reality.

Sources of Media Power

Government and the media are natural adversaries. (Thomas Jefferson once wrote that he would prefer newspapers without government to a government without newspapers. But after serving as president, he wrote that people who never read newspapers are better informed than those who do, because ignorance is closer to the truth than the falsehoods spread by newspapers.) Public officials have long been frustrated by the media. But the U.S. Constitution's First Amendment guar-

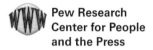

Pew Research Center for People and the Press

Information, including opinion polls, on the media.
http://www.people-press.org

THINK AGAIN

Do the media mirror what is really news, rather than deciding themselves what's important and then making it news?

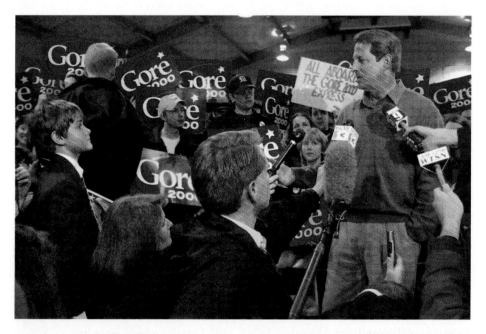

Politicians have a love-hate relationship with the media. They crave the recognition and celebrity that the media can confer on them, but they also fear attack from the media.

antee of a free press anticipates this conflict between government and the media. It prohibits government from resolving this conflict by silencing its critics.

Media professionals—television and newspaper reporters, editors, anchors, and producers—are not neutral observers of American politics but rather are active participants. They not only report events but also discover events to report, assign them political meaning, and predict their consequences (see *People in Politics:* "Stars of the Network News: Rather, Jennings, and Brokaw"). They seek to challenge government officials, debate political candidates, and define the problems of society. They see their profession as a "sacred trust" and themselves as the true voice of the people in public affairs.

Newsmaking Deciding what is "news" and who is "newsworthy"— newsmaking—is the most important source of media power. It is only through the media that the general public comes to know about events, personalities, and issues. Media attention makes topics public, creates issues, and elevates personalities from obscurity to celebrity. Each day, editors, producers, and reporters must select from millions of events, topics, and people those that will be videotaped, written about, and talked about. The media can never be a "picture of the world" because the whole world cannot be squeezed into the picture. The media must decide what is and is not "news."

Decisions about what will be news both influence popular discussion and cue public officials about topics they must turn their attention to. Politicians cannot respond to reporters' questions by saying, "I don't know," or "That's not important," or "No comment." Media attention to a topic *requires* public officials to respond to it. Moreover, the media decide how important an issue or person or event is by their allocation of time and space. Topics given early placement on the newscast and several minutes of airtime or that receive front-page newspaper coverage with headlines and pictures are believed to be important by viewers and readers.

Politicians have a love-hate relationship with the media. They need media attention to promote themselves, their message, and their programs. They crave the exposure, the name recognition, and the celebrity status that the media can confer. At the same time, they fear attack by the media. They know the media are active players in the political game, not just passive spectators. The media seek sensational stories of sin, sexuality, corruption, and scandal in government to attract viewers and readers, and thus the media pose a constant danger to politicians. Politicians understand the power of the media to make or break their careers.

Agenda Setting Agenda setting is the power to decide what will be decided. It is the power to define society's "problems," to create political issues, and to set forth alternative solutions. Deciding which issues will be addressed by government may be even more important than deciding how the issues will be resolved. The distinguished political scientist E. E. Schattschneider once wrote, "He who determines what politics is about runs the country."[4]

The real power of the media lies in their ability to set the political agenda for the nation. This power grows out of their ability to decide what is news. Media coverage determines what both citizens and public officials regard as "crises" or "problems" or "issues" to be resolved. Conditions ignored by the media seldom get on the agenda of political leaders. Media attention forces public officials to speak on the topic, take positions, and respond to questions. Media inattention allows problems to be ignored by government. "TV is the Great Legitimator. TV confers reality. Nothing happens in America, practically everyone seems to agree, until it happens on television."[5]

 Newspaper Web Sites
Virtually all major daily newspapers have Web sites that summarize each day's stories. For national news the most frequently consulted sites are *USA Today, Wall Street Journal, New York Times, Washington Post.*
www.usatoday.com
www.nytimes.com
www.washingtonpost.com
www.wallstreetjournal.com

newsmaking Deciding what events, topics, presentations, and issues will be given coverage in the news.

agenda setting Deciding what will be decided, defining the problems and issues to be addressed by decision makers.

Stars of the Network News

From left to right: Network news anchors Tom Brokaw, Dan Rather, and Peter Jennings.

Television news strives for credibility. Anchors are chosen not only for their personal appearance but also for the credibility they can lend to the news. The recognized all-time champion of credibility was CBS's Walter Cronkite, who for many years was "the most trusted man in America," according to all of the national polls.

Each night about 28 million Americans watch one of three men: Dan Rather, Peter Jennings, or Brian Williams (who replaced 20-year veteran anchor Tom Brokaw in 2004). No other individuals—not presidents, movie stars, or popes—have had such extensive contact with so many people. These network celebrities are recognized and heard by more people than anyone else on the planet. The networks demand that an anchor be the network's premier journalist, principal showman, top editor, star, symbol of news excellence, and single most important living logo.

Anchors, then, are both celebrities and newspeople. They are chosen for their mass appeal, but they must also bring journalistic expertise to their jobs. The anchors help select from thousands of hours of videotapes and hundreds of separate stories that will be squeezed into the twenty-two minutes of nightly network news (eight minutes are reserved for commercials). Each minute represents approximately 160 spoken words; the total number of words on the entire newscast is less than found on a single newspaper page. These inherent restrictions of the medium give great power to the anchors and their executive producers through their selection of what Americans will see and hear about the world each night.

All three network anchors are middle-aged, Anglo-Saxon, male Protestants. All share liberal and reformist social values and political beliefs.

Dan Rather, who deliberately projects an image of emotional intensity, has created both strong attachments and heated animosities among his audiences. He is most despised by conservatives because of his undisguised and passionate liberal views. Rather worked his way up through the ranks of CBS News following graduation from Sam Houston State College. He was a reporter and news director for the CBS affiliate station in Houston, then chief of the CBS London Bureau, and later Vietnam correspondent. He came to national prominence in 1966 as a CBS White House correspondent and took over the anchor position from Walter Cronkite in 1981.

The Canadian born Peter Jennings projects an image of thoughtful, urbane sophistication. He is widely traveled (his father was a journalist), but his formal education ended in the tenth grade. ABC's *World News Tonight with Peter Jennings* devotes slightly more time to international news than do its rival news shows.

The first change in anchors in two decades occurred when Brian Williams replaced the retiring Tom Brokaw at *NBC Nightly News* in 2004. Williams attended George Washington University and Catholic University, both in Washington, before becoming a White House intern under President Jimmy Carter. He served as a lobbyist for the American Association of Broadcasters before becoming a news reporter at stations in Philadelphia and Washington. He won the coveted NBC job as Chief White House News Correspondent in 1994 and became a regular face on NBC broadcasts.

The ratings race among the anchors is very close. Indeed, the closeness of those ratings may be driving the shows toward even more sensational themes, violent confrontations, and dramatic hype.

Political issues do not just "happen." The media are crucial to their development. Organized interest groups, professional public relations firms, government bureaucracies, political candidates, and elected officials all try to solicit the assistance of the media in shaping the political agenda. Creating an issue, publicizing it, dramatizing it, turning it into a "crisis," getting people to talk about it, and ultimately forcing government to do something about it are the tactics of agenda setting. The participation of the mass media is vital to their success.[6]

Interpreting The media not only decide what will be news; they also interpret the news for us. Editors, reporters, and anchors provide each story with an *angle*, an interpretation that places the story in a context and speculates about its meaning and consequences. The interpretation tells us what to think about the news.

News is presented in "stories." Reporters do not report facts; they tell stories. The story structure gives meaning to various pieces of information. Some common angles or themes of news stories are these:

- *Good guys versus bad guys:* for example, corrupt officials, foreign dictators, corporate polluters, and other assorted villains versus honest citizens, exploited workers, endangered children, or other innocents.

- *Little guys versus big guys:* for example, big corporations, the military, or insensitive bureaucracies versus consumers, taxpayers, poor people, or the elderly.

- *Appearance versus reality:* for example, the public statements of government officials or corporate executives versus whatever contradicting facts hardworking investigative reporters can find.

News is also "pictures." A story without visuals is not likely to be selected as television news in the first place. The use of visuals reinforces the angle. A close-up shot can reveal hostility, insincerity, or anxiety on the face of villains or can show fear, concern, sincerity, or compassion on the face of innocents. To emphasize elements of a story, an editor can stop the action, use slow motion, zoom the lens, add graphics, cut back and forth between antagonists, cut away for audience reaction, and so on. Videotaped interviews can be spliced to make the interviewees appear knowledgeable, informed, and sincere or, alternatively, ignorant, insensitive, and mean-spirited. The media jealously guard the right to edit interviews themselves, rejecting virtually all attempts by interviewees to review and edit their own interviews.

Socializing The media have power to socialize audiences to the political culture. News, entertainment, and advertising all contribute to **socialization**—to the learning of political values. Socialization through television and motion pictures begins in early childhood and continues throughout life. Most of the political information people learn comes to them through television—specific facts as well as general values. Election coverage, for example, shows "how democracy works," encourages political participation, and legitimizes the winner's control of government. Advertising shows Americans desirable middle-class standards of living even while it encourages people to buy automobiles, detergent, and beer, and entertainment programming socializes them to "acceptable" ways of life. Political values such as racial tolerance, sexual equality, and support for law enforcement are reinforced in movies, situation comedies, and police shows. Realistic "docudramas" seize on specific political themes, from abortion, to homosexuality, to drug use, to child abuse, to AIDS. Entertainment news programming such as the highly popular *60 Minutes* is now regular prime-time fare.

Groups hoping for free media coverage of their cause can improve their chances by framing their protests in dramatic form. Here, members of an animal-rights group attract the press by getting arrested during a protest against the fur industry, in which they painted themselves with red paint and wore leghold traps.

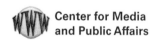

Center for Media and Public Affairs
Studies of news and entertainment media, including election coverage.
www.cmpa.com

socialization The learning of a culture and its values.

Persuading The media, in both paid advertising and news and entertainment programming, engage in direct efforts to change our attitudes, opinions, and behavior. Newspaper editorials have traditionally been employed for direct persuasion. A great deal of the political commentary on television news and interview programs is aimed at persuading people to adopt the views of the commentators. Even many entertainment programs and movies are intended to promote specific political viewpoints. But most direct persuasion efforts come to us through paid advertising.

Corporations may use their advertising dollars not only to promote sales of their product but also to convey the message that they are good citizens—sensitive to the environment, concerned with worker and consumer safety, devoted to providing more and better jobs, goods, and services to America.

Political campaigning is now largely a media battle, with paid political advertisements as the weapons. Candidates rely on professional campaign-management firms, with their pollsters, public relations specialists, advertising-production people, and media consultants, to carry on the fight (see Chapter 8).

Governments and political leaders must rely on persuasion through the mass media to carry out their programs. Presidents can take their message directly to people in televised speeches, news conferences, and the yearly State of the Union message. Presidents by custom are accorded television time whenever they request it. In this way, they can go over the heads of Congress and even the media executives and reporters themselves to communicate directly with the people.

In short, persuasion is central to politics, and the media are the key to persuasion.

The Business of the Media

National Association of Broadcasters

News and views of the media industry from their trade association.

www.nab.org

The business of the media is to gather mass audiences to sell to advertisers. Economic interest drives all media to try to attract and hold the largest numbers of readers and viewers in order to sell time and space to advertisers. Over one-quarter of all prime-time television (8–11 P.M.) is devoted to commercial advertising. Americans get more than one minute of commercials for every three minutes of news and entertainment. Television networks and commercial stations charge advertisers on the basis of audience estimates made by rating services. One rating service, A. C. Nielsen, places electronic boxes in a national sample of television homes and calculates the proportion of these homes that watch a program (the rating), as well as the proportion of homes with their television sets turned on that watch a particular program (the share). Newspapers' and magazines' advertising revenue is based primarily on circulation figures (see Table 6.2).

Soft Fluff versus Hard Programming Lightweight entertainment—"soft fluff"—prevails over serious programming in virtually all media, but particularly on television. Critics of the "boob tube" abound in intellectual circles, but the mass public clearly prefers fluffy entertainment programming. Political scientist Doris Graber writes:

> Although "lightweight" programming draws the wrath of many people, particularly intellectual elites, one can argue that their disdain constitutes intellectual snobbery. Who is to say that the mass public's tastes are inferior to those of elites? . . .Proof is plentiful that the mass public does indeed prefer light entertainment to more serious programs.[7]

And it is the mass public that advertisers want to reach. Channels devoted to highbrow culture, including public television stations, languish with low ratings.

TABLE 6.2 The Largest Circulation U.S. Newspapers and Magazines

Daily Newspapers		Magazines	
Rank Newspaper	**Circulation**	**Rank Magazine**	**Circulation**
1. *USA Today* (Arlington, Va.)	2,136,068	1. *AARP Modern Maturity*	17,360,979
2. *Wall Street Journal* (New York, N.Y.)	1,800,607	2. *Reader's Digest*	12,078,469
3. *Times* (New York, N.Y.)	1,113,000	3. *TV Guide*	9,067,124
4. *Times* (Los Angeles)	925,135	4. *Better Homes and Gardens*	7,605,204
5. *Post* (Washington, DC)	746,724	5. *National Geographic*	6,774,138
6. *Daily News* (New York, N.Y.)	715,070	6. *Good Housekeeping*	4,699,736
7. *Tribune* (Chicago)	679,327	7. *Family Circle*	4,634,069
8. *Post* (New York, N.Y.)	590,061	8. *Woman's Day*	4,205,049
9. *Newsday* (Long Island, N.Y.)	578,809	9. *TIME*	4,111,927
10. *Chronicle* (Houston)	552,052	10. *Ladies' Home Journal*	4,101,347

Source: Editor and Publisher International Yearbook 2003. Copyright © 2003 VNU Business Media, Inc. Used with permission.

News as TV Entertainment Increasingly news is being presented as television entertainment. In recent years there has been a dramatic increase in the number of entertainment-oriented, quasi-news programming, sometimes referred to as the "soft news media."[8] Soft news comes mainly in two formats: talk shows, both daytime and nighttime; and tabloid news programs (see Table 6.3). Even late-night entertainment programs—Jay Leno, David Letterman, Conan O'Brien—include comedy monologues that occasionally refer to political events or issues.

Soft news is no major source of information for people who are not interested in politics or public affairs. It is true, of course, that most soft news programming favors celebrity gossip, murder trials, sex scandals, disasters, and other human interest stories. But on some high-profile news issues these programs provide an otherwise inattentive public with what little information it absorbs.

TABLE 6.3 TV Soft News Programming

Network news magazines

Dateline NBC
20/20
Primetime Live
48 Hours
60 Minutes

Late-night TV talk shows

Jay Leno
David Letterman
Conan O'Brien
Politically Incorrect

Daytime TV talk shows

Oprah Winfrey
Rosie O'Donnell
Regis and Kelly
Geraldo Rivera
Phil Donahue

Network TV soft news

Extra
Entertainment Tonight
Inside Edition
A Current Affair
Access Hollywood

Cable TV soft news

E! Network
Black Entertainment Television
Comedy Central's *Daily Show*
MTV News

"Bad news" is far more likely to be seen on television than "good news." The 1999 shooting at Columbine High School in Colorado was one of the most widely covered news stories of the year.

60 Minutes attracts more viewers than any other soft news program. *Dateline* and *20/20* are not far behind. (Arguably these programs are oriented toward a somewhat more sophisticated audience than talk shows or tabloid news programs.) These programs, as well as *Entertainment Tonight* and Oprah Winfrey attract more viewers than any of the nightly network newscasts.

Politicians themselves have come to understand the importance of soft news programming in reaching segments of the public that seldom watch news programs, speeches or debates, or campaign advertising. Presidential candidates welcome invitations to appear with Oprah, or Leno, or Letterman, and try to reformulate their messages in a light, comedic style that fits the program.

The Media Conglomerates Mega-mergers in recent years have created corporate empires that spread across multiple media—television, film, newspapers, music, and the Internet. Conglomerate media corporations combined television broadcasting and cable programming, movie production and distribution, magazine and book publication, music recording, Internet access, and even sports and recreation. The seven multinational corporations listed in Table 6.4 currently dominate world media and cultural interests.

The Politics of the News

The politics of the news media are shaped by (1) their *economic interest,* (2) their *professional environment,* and (3) their *ideological leanings.*

Sensationalism The economic interest of the media—the need to capture and hold audience attention—creates a bias toward "hype" in the selection of news, its presentation, and its interpretation. To attract viewers and readers, the media bias the news toward violence, conflict, scandal, corruption, sex, scares of various sorts, and the personal lives of politicians and celebrities. News is selected primarily for its emotional impact on audiences, its social, economic, or political significance is secondary to the need to capture attention.

News must "touch" audiences personally, arouse emotions, and hold the interest of people with short attention spans. Scare stories—street crime, drug use, AIDS, nuclear power plant accidents, global warming, and a host of health alarms—make "good" news, for they cause viewers to fear for their personal safety. The sex lives of politicians, once by custom off limits to the press, are now public "affairs." Scandal and corruption among politicians, as well as selfishness and greed among business executives, are regular media themes.[9]

Negativism The media are biased toward bad news. Bad news attracts larger audiences than good news. Television news displays a pervasive bias toward the negative in American life—in government, business, the military, politics, education, and everywhere else. Bad-news stories on television vastly outnumber good-news stories.

Good news gets little attention. For example, television news watchers are not likely to know that illegal drug use is declining in the United States, that both the air and water are measurably cleaner today than in past decades, that the nuclear power industry has the best safety record of any major industry in the United States, and that the aged in America are wealthier and enjoy higher incomes than the nonaged. Television has generally failed to report these stories or, even worse, has implied that the opposite is true. Good news—stories about improved health

TABLE 6.4 The Media Empires

AOL-Time Warner

Television: HBO, TNT, TBS, CNN, CNNSI, CNNFN, Cinemax, Time Warner Cable
Motion Pictures: Warner Brothers, New Line Cinema, Castle Rock, Looney Tunes
Magazines: Time, People, Sports Illustrated, Fortune, plus twenty-eight other specialty magazines
Books: Warner Books, Little, Brown Publishing, Book-of-the-Month Club
Music: Warner Brothers Records, Atlantic Records, Elektra
Sports and Entertainment: Atlanta Braves, Atlanta Hawks, World Championship Wrestling
Internet: AOL, Netscape, CompuServe

Walt Disney

Television: ABC-TV, plus ten stations; ESPN, ESPN-2, Disney Channel, A&E, EI, Life-time
Motion Pictures: Walt Disney Pictures, Miramax, Touchstone
Music: Walt Disney Records, Mammoth
Sports and Recreation: Disney theme parks in Florida, California, France, Japan; cruise line; Anaheim, Mighty Ducks

Viacom

Television: CBS, plus thirty-four TV stations: MTV, TNN, Nickelodeon, Showtime, VH1, Nick-At-Nite
Motion Pictures: Paramount Pictures, Spelling, Viacom
Books: Simon & Schuster, Scribner, Free Press
Music: Famous Music Publishing
Sports and Recreation: Blockbuster Video, SportsLine, plus five Paramount parks

NewsCorp (Fox)

Television: Fox Network plus fifteen TV stations; Fox News, Fox Sports, Fox Family Channel, National Geographic Channel
Motion Pictures: 20th Century Fox, Searchlight
Books: HarperCollins
Magazines: TV Guide
Music: Mushroom Records
Sports and Recreation: Los Angeles Dodgers

Seagram

Television: USA Network
Motion Pictures: Universal Pictures
Music: MCA, Geffen, Def Jam, Motown
Sports and Recreation: Universal Studios theme parks in California and Florida

Sony

Television: Game Show Network
Motion Pictures: Columbia Pictures, Sony Pictures, Tri Star
Music: Columbia Records, Epic Records, Nashville Records
Sports and Recreation: Sony Theaters

General Electric

Television: NBC Network plus thirteen TV stations; CNBC, MSNBC

Source: Thomas R. Dye, *Who's Running America? The Bush Restoration,* 6th ed. (Upper Saddle River, N.J.: Prentice Hall, 2002).

statistics, longer life spans, better safety records, higher educational levels, for example—seldom provides the dramatic element needed to capture audience attention. The result is an overwhelming bad-news bias, especially on television.[10]

Muckraking The professional environment of reporters and editors predisposes them toward an activist style of journalism once dubbed **muckraking**. Reporters today view themselves as "watchdogs" of the public trust. They see themselves in

muckraking Journalistic exposés of corruption, wrongdoing, or mismanagement in government, business, and other institutions of society.

noble terms—enemies of corruption, crusaders for justice, defenders of the disadvantaged. "The watchdog function, once considered remedial and subsidiary. . .[is now] paramount: the primary duty of the journalists is to focus attention on problems and deficits, failures and threats."[11] Their professional models are the crusading "investigative reporters" who expose wrongdoing in government, business, the military, and every other institution in society—except the media.

Many reporters go beyond the watchdog role and view themselves as adversaries of government. They see it as their job to expose politicians by unmasking their disguises, debunking their claims, and piercing their rhetoric. In short, until proven otherwise, political figures of any party or persuasion are presumed to be opponents. Even on entertainment shows, politicians are usually depicted as corrupt, hypocritical, and self-seeking, and business executives as crooked, greedy, and insensitive. Reporters are particularly proud of their work when it results in official investigations.

The "Feeding Frenzy" Occasionally, muckraking episodes grow into "**feeding frenzies**"—intense coverage of a scandal or event that blocks out most other news. Political scientist Larry Sabato describes the feeding frenzy: "In such situations a development is almost inevitably magnified and overscrutinized, the crush of cameras, microphones, and people, combined with the pressure of instant deadlines and live broadcasts, hype events and make it difficult to keep them in perspective. When a frenzy begins to gather, the intensity grows exponentially. . .. Television news time is virtually turned over to the subject of the frenzy."[12] Increasingly stiff competition among the media for attention and the need for round-the-clock cable news to fill long hours contribute to feeding frenzies.

Liberalism in the Newsroom The activist role that the media have taken upon themselves means that the personal values of reporters, editors, producers, and anchors are a very important element of American politics. The political values of the media are decidedly liberal and reformist. Political scientist Doris A. Graber writes about the politics of the media: "Economic and social liberalism prevails, especially in the most prominent media organizations. So does a preference for an internationalist foreign policy, caution about military intervention, and some suspicion about the ethics of established large institutions, particularly big business and big government."[13] Most Americans agree that media news coverage is biased and the bias is in a liberal direction (see *What Do You Think?* "Are the Media Biased?").

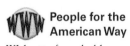

People for the American Way

Web site founded by Hollywood "liberals" to combat "right-wing" influence.
www.pfaw.org

"feeding frenzy" Intense media coverage of a scandal or event that blocks out most other news.

Liberalism in Hollywood With a few exceptions, Hollywood producers, directors, writers, studio executives, and actors are decidedly liberal in their political views, especially when compared with the general public. Of the Hollywood elite, more than 60 percent describe themselves as liberal and only 14 percent as conservative,[14] whereas in the general public, self-described conservatives outnumber liberals by a significant margin. Hollywood leaders are five times more likely to be Democrats than Republicans, and Hollywood is a major source of Democratic Party campaign funds. On both economic and social issues, the Hollywood elite is significantly more liberal than the nation's general public or college-educated public.[15] (However, see *A Conflicting View,* "Fox News 'Fair and Balanced'?").

The question remains, however, how much political influence Hollywood exercises over its audiences. Many television shows and motion pictures have little political content, they are designed almost exclusively to entertain, to gather the

Are the Media Biased?

Are the media biased, and if so in what direction—liberal or conservative? Arguments over media bias have grown in intensity as the media have come to play a central role in American politics.

Nearly three out of four Americans (74 percent) see "a fair amount" or "a great deal" of media bias in news coverage (see table below). And of those who see a bias, over twice as many see a liberal bias rather than a conservative bias. Indeed, even liberals see a liberal bias in the news; it is not a perception limited to conservatives, although they are more likely to see it. The liberal bias is much more likely to be seen by college graduates than by people who did not finish high school. It is also more likely to be seen by political activists than by those who engage in little or no political activity. However, African Americans are likely to see a conservative bias in the news, in contrast to the liberal bias perceived more often by whites.

Political bias is not Americans' only complaint about the national news media. Indeed, the most common complaint is that the media "ignore people's privacy" (80 percent). And majorities also complain about "one-sided coverage" (63 percent), "too negative" (61 percent), and "too much influence" (58 percent)—and they believe the media "abuse freedom of the press" (52 percent).

At the same time, Americans have high expectations of the role of the media in society: they expect the media to protect them from "abuse of power" by government, to hold public officials accountable, and to point out and help solve the problems of society.

Perceptions of Media Bias

	How Much Bias? "A Great Deal" or "Fair Amount" (%)	Direction of Bias	
		Liberal (%)	Conservative (%)
All	74	43	19
Race			
White	75	46	15
Black	64	24	40
Education			
Less than high school	56	29	33
High school graduate	75	42	19
College graduate	81	57	19
Ideology			
Liberal	70	41	22
Moderate	70	30	16
Conservative	81	57	19
Political Activism			
High	82	54	14
Low	76	42	22
None	65	34	22

Source: Data from *Media Monitor,* May/June 1997, Center for Media and Public Affairs, Washington, D.C. Reprinted by permission.

largest audiences for advertisers, and to sell theater tickets. Even shows or movies with political themes or pronounced political biases may not influence audiences as much as Hollywood would wish.

Conservatism on Talk Radio Talk radio is the one medium where conservatism prevails. The single most listened-to talk radio show is the *Rush Limbaugh*

Fox News: "Fair and Balanced"?

For many years conservatives complained about the liberal tilt of television news. But despite their ample financial resources, conservative investors failed to create their own network or purchase an existing one. It was an Australian billionaire, Rupert Murdoch, who eventually came to the rescue of American conservatives.

Murdoch's global media empire, News Corp, includes Fox Network, Fox News Cable, 20th Century Fox, the *New York Post, The Times* and *The Sun* of London, HarperCollins Publishing, thirty-five local TV stations, and the Los Angeles Dodgers. He began his career by injecting glitz and vulgarity into previously dull Australian newspapers he inherited. The formula worked worldwide: the *New York Post* became a noisy tabloid after Murdoch took over (most memorable headline: "HEADLESS BODY FOUND IN TOPLESS BAR"), and Fox TV entertainment airs even more vulgar shows than the mainstream networks.

Murdoch himself is not particularly conservative in his politics, but he recognized an unfilled market for conservative views on American television. In 1996 he founded Fox News and hired Roger Ailes (former TV ad producer for Richard Nixon, Ronald Reagan, and George Bush) to head up the new net-

work. Ailes quickly signed Bill O'Reilly (see *People in Politics* in Chapter 2) for an hourlong nightly conservative talk show. Brit Hume, one of the few prominent TV reporters considered to be a conservative, was made managing editor.

Fox proclaims "fair and balanced" news—"We report, you decide." The implication is that mainstream media has a liberal bias and that Fox is rectifying it with its own fair and balanced reporting. According to Fox, if its reporting appears conservative, it is only because the country has become so accustomed to left-leaning media that a truly balanced network just seems conservative.

Regular news reporting on Fox is not much different than other networks, except that Fox may cover some stories ignored by the mainstream media, e.g. political correctness to run amok on college campuses, ridiculous environmental regulations, hypocrisy among Hollywood liberals, etc. But it is the talk and commentary shows that outrage liberals and warm the hearts of conservatives. Liberals bold enough to appear on Fox are badgered mercilessly, while conservative guests are tossed softball questions.

The bottom line, financially as well as politically, is that Fox News is now the most watched cable news network, even surpassing CNN. Whatever its flaws, Fox News had added diversity of views to American television.

Accuracy in Media
A self-described watchdog organization critical of liberal bias in the media.
www.aim.org

Show, whose host regularly bashes "limousine liberals," "femi-Nazis," "environmental wackos," and "croissant people."[16] Talk radio might be portrayed as "call-in democracy." Callers respond almost immediately to reported news events. Call-in shows are the first to sense the public mood. Callers are not necessarily representative of the general public. Rather they are usually the most intense and outraged of citizens. But their complaints are early warning signs for wary politicians.

Mediated Elections

Political campaigning is largely a media activity, and the media, especially television, shape the nation's electoral politics.

The Media and Candidate-Voter Linkage The media are the principal link between candidates and the voters. At one time, political party organizations performed this function, with city, ward, and precinct workers knocking on doors, distributing campaign literature, organizing rallies and candidate appearances, and getting out the vote on election day. But television has largely replaced party organizations and personal contact as the means by which candidates communicate with voters. Candidates come directly into the living room via television—on the nightly news, in broadcast debates and interviews, and in paid advertising (see Table 6.5).

Media campaigning requires candidates to possess great skill in communications. Candidates must be able to project a favorable media *image*. The image is a composite of the candidate's words, mannerisms, appearance, personality, warmth, friendliness, humor, and ease in front of a camera. Policy positions have less to do with image than the candidate's ability to project personal qualities—leadership, compassion, strength, and character.

Television places an especially important emphasis on personal communication skills. Print media—newspapers and magazines—communicate only what is said. But *television communicates not only what is said but also how it is said*. For example, newspaper reports of Ronald Reagan's commonplace speeches and time-worn slogans failed to capture his true audience appeal, the folksy, warm, comfortable, reassuring manner, the humor and humility, and the likable personality that made Reagan "the Great Communicator." Reagan prevailed over hostile reporters, editors, and commentators because he was able to effectively communicate directly to mass audiences.

The Media and Candidate Selection The media strongly influence the early selection of candidates. Media coverage creates **name recognition**, an essential quality for any candidate. Early media "mentions" of senators, governors, and other political figures as possible presidential contenders help to sort out the field even before the election year begins. Conversely, media inattention can condemn aspiring politicians to obscurity.

Conservative talk-show host Rush Limbaugh became the symbol for the talk-radio phenomenon of the 1990s. In addition to his daily three-hour radio broadcast, Limbaugh also had a nightly syndicated television show.

TABLE 6.5	Sources of Political Campaign News in Presidential Election Years		

Over time network news (ABC, CBS, NBC) has been declining as a major source of campaign news, while cable news (CNN, MSNBC, Fox) has been gaining. The Internet has also gained ground as a source of campaign news, yet it was cited by only 11 percent of Americans as their source of "most news."

News Sources	1992	1996	2000
Television	82%	72%	70%
Cable	29	21	36
Network	55	36	22
Local	29	23	21
Newspapers	57	60	39
Radio	12	19	15
Internet	—	3	11
Magazines	9	11	4

Note: Respondents were asked, "How did you get most of your news about the presidential election campaign? From television, from newspapers, from radio, from magazines or from the Internet?" Television users were then asked, "Did you get most of your news about the presidential campaign from network TV news, from local TV news, or from cable news networks such as CNN or MSNBC?" Respondents could name two sources.

Source: Pew Research Center for the People and the Press data from a telephone survey of 1,113 voters, November 10–12, 2000, http://www.people-press.org/post00que.htm.

Name recognition Public awareness of a candidate—whether they even know his or her name.

Serious presidential campaigns now begin at least six months before the New Hampshire primary (or almost a year and a half before the November presidential election). This early time period, "the invisible primary," is increasingly critical for campaigns.[17] Candidates must position themselves relative to competitors in their own party—build their name recognition, raise poll numbers, and build a campaign war chest. Inasmuch as campaign contributions are just beginning to come in, candidates have relatively little money to spend on paid advertising. They are forced to focus their efforts on attracting media attention by staging media events and issuing press releases. But from the media's perspective, campaign news is neither timely nor immediately relevant. Candidates must try to win media coverage by catering to the conflict and horse race stories preferred by the media. Press releases and speeches focused on issues are most likely to be ignored.

The media sort out the serious candidates early in a race. They even assign front-runner status, which may be either a blessing or a curse, depending on subsequent media coverage. In presidential primaries, the media play the *expectations game*, setting vote margins that the front-runner must meet in order to maintain *momentum*. If the front-runner does not win by a large enough margin, the media may declare the runner-up the "real" winner. This sorting out of candidates by the media influences not only voters, but—more important—financial contributors. The media-designated favorite is more likely to receive campaign contributions; financial backers do not like to waste money on losers. And as contributions roll in, the favorite can buy more television advertising, adding momentum to the campaign.

In presidential elections, the media sorting process places great emphasis on the early primary states, particularly New Hampshire, whose primary in early February is customarily the first contest in a presidential election year. Less than 1 percent of convention delegates are chosen by this small state, but media coverage is intense, and the winner quickly becomes the media-designated front-runner.[18]

The Media as Kingmakers In the early months of campaign, media coverage of candidates and their standing in public opinion polls tend to move together. Candidates who receive heavy media coverage usually do well in the polls. Good poll ratings create more media coverage. Good poll ratings and increased media coverage inspire campaign contributions, which then allow candidates to buy television advertising to further increase their poll numbers. Media-sponsored public opinion polls play an important role in kingmaking. The CBS/*New York Times* poll, the NBC/Associated Press poll, the ABC/*Washington Post* poll, and the CNN/*USA Today* poll are widely reported; they become the benchmarks for voters, telling them who the winners and losers are.

The name of the game for candidates early in the race is *exposure*. Even appearances on entertainment shows, once considered "unpresidential," are now highly valued by political candidates. They vie to appear on *Larry King Live* and on late-night talk shows hosted by Jay Leno, David Letterman, and Conan O'Brien.

Media Effects on the Campaign Political candidates are aware of the importance of the media to their success. Their campaign managers must be "media-savvy" and they must hire media consultants early in the campaign. Candidates are advised to arrange daily newsworthy events to keep their name and image in the news. Television producers, reporters, and editors do not like to receive position papers on substantive issues or to present "talking heads"—shots only of the faces

Drudge Report
Controversial site that links to stories not always carried by mainstream media. Links to all major media outlets.
www.drudgereport.com

In spite of the growing importance of the Internet, most people continue to get campaign and election news from television.

of speakers. Rather they prefer attention-getting, action-oriented, emotion-laden videotape. Candidates and their managers know this and so they attract media attention and resort to *media events*—staged activities designed to polish the image of the candidate. Candidates arrange to appear at police conventions, at schools, at hazardous waste sites, on aircraft carriers, at flag factories, and so on in order to project an image on television of their concern for crime, education, the environment, national defense, patriotism, and the like. (See also "Campaign Strategies" in Chapter 8.)

The Media and the Horse Race The media give election campaigns **horse-race coverage**: reporting on who is ahead or behind, what the candidates' strategies are, how much money they are spending, and, above all, what their current standing in the polls is. Such stories account for more than half of all television news coverage of an election. Additional stories are centered on *campaign* issues—controversies that arise on the campaign trail itself, including verbal blunders by the candidate—and *character* issues, such as the sex life of the candidate. In contrast, *policy* issues typically account for only about one-third of the television news stories in a presidential election campaign.[19]

The Bad News Bias The media's bad-news bias is evident in election campaigns as well as in general news reporting. Negative stories about all presidential candidates usually outnumber positive stories. The media generally see their function in political campaigns as reporting on the weaknesses, blunders, and vulnerabilities of the candidates. It might be argued that exposing the flaws of the candidates is an important function in a democracy. But the media's negative reporting about candidates and generally skeptical attitude toward their campaign speeches, promises, and advertisements may contribute to political alienation and cynicism among voters.

The media focus intense scrutiny on the personal lives of candidates—their marriages, sex lives, drug or alcohol use, personal finances, past friendships, military service, club memberships, and other potential sources of embarrassment. Virtually any past error in judgment or behavior by a candidate is given heavy coverage. But the media defend their attention to personal scandal on the ground that they are reporting on the "character issue." They argue that voters must have information on candidates' character as well as on their policy positions.

The Shrinking Sound Bite Reporters and newsroom anchors dominate television broadcasting. They report roughly three-quarters of all campaign news themselves. The candidates are allocated less than 15 percent of the time devoted to campaign news stories. (Other sources—pundits, commentators, voters, etc.—account for the remaining airtime.) The candidates themselves have very little direct contact with audiences in network news. The average **sound bite**—time allowed the candidates to speak on their own behalf—has shrunk to less than eight seconds!

The Media and Political Bias The media are very sensitive to charges of bias toward candidates or parties. Media people are overwhelmingly liberal and Democratic but generally try to deflect charges of political bias during an election campaign by giving almost equal coverage to both Democratic and Republican candidates. Moreover, the media report negatively on both Republicans and Democrats, although some scholars count more negative stories about Republican candidates.

horse-race coverage Media coverage of electoral campaigns that concentrates on who is ahead and who is behind, and neglects the issues at stake.

sound bite Words actually spoken by candidates themselves on news broadcasts.

The media are generally more critical of front-runners than of underdogs during a campaign. A horse race loses audience interest if one horse gets too far ahead, so the media tend to favor the underdog. "Frontrunners and incumbents consistently experienced the least balanced, least favorable news coverage."[20] During the presidential primary season, media attacks on an early favorite may result in gains for the underdog, who then becomes the new object of attack.

Freedom versus Fairness

THINK AGAIN

Should the media be legally required to be fair and accurate in reporting political news?

Complaints about the fairness of media are as old as the printing press. Most early newspapers in the United States were allied with political parties, they were not expected to be fair in their coverage. It was only in the early 1900s that many large newspapers broke their ties with parties and proclaimed themselves independent. And it was not until the 1920s and 1930s that the norms of journalistic professionalism and accuracy gained widespread acceptance.

The Constitution protects the *freedom* of the press; it was not intended to guarantee *fairness*. The First Amendment's guarantee of freedom of the press was originally designed to protect the press from government attempts to silence criticism. Over the years, the U.S. Supreme Court has greatly expanded the meaning of the free-press guarantee.

No Prior Restraint The Supreme Court has interpreted freedom of the press to mean that government may place no **prior restraint** on speech or publication (that is, before it is said or published). Originally, this doctrine was designed to prevent the government from closing down or seizing newspapers. Today, the doctrine prevents the government from censoring any news items. In the famous case of the Pentagon Papers, the *New York Times* and *Washington Post* undertook to publish secret information stolen from the files of the State Department and Defense Department regarding U.S. policy in Vietnam while the war was still going on. No one disputed the fact that stealing the secret material was illegal. What was at issue was the ability of the government to prevent the publication of stolen documents in order to protect national security. The Supreme Court rejected the national security argument and reaffirmed that the government may place no prior restraint on publication.[21] If the government wishes to keep military secrets, it must not let them fall into the hands of the American press.

Press versus Electronic Media In the early days of radio, broadcast channels were limited, and anyone with a radio transmitter could broadcast on any frequency. As a result, interference was a common frustration of early broadcasters. The industry petitioned the federal government to regulate and license the assignment and use of broadcast frequencies.

The Federal Communications Commission (FCC) was established in 1934 to allocate broadcast frequencies and to license stations for "the public interest, convenience and necessity." The act clearly instructed the FCC: "Nothing in this Act shall be understood or construed to give the Commission the power of censorship." However, the FCC views a broadcast license and exclusive right to use a particular frequency as a *public trust*. Thus broadcasters, unlike newspapers and magazines, are licensed by a government agency and supposed to operate in the *public interest*.

The Ownership Controversy Until recently the FCC did not permit a single firm or individual to own both a leading TV station and a leading newspaper in the

Federal Communication Commission

The FCC's official Web site with announcements and consumer information. *www.fcc.gov.*

prior restraint Power of government to prevent publication or to require approval before publication, generally prohibited by the First Amendment.

same city. This FCC rule was defended as necessary to ensure diversity and competition in the news. But early in 2003 the FCC proposed to drop this rule as "no longer in the public interest." The FCC's new argument was that the old rule failed to recognize the explosion of media channels—hundreds of cable TV channels, satellite television, and the Internet. The major media corporations (see Table 6.2), not surprisingly, strongly supported dropping the ownership rule, as did the Bush administration. (The Chairman of the FCC, Michael Powell, is the son of Secretary of State Colin Powell.) But liberal interest groups, including Ralph Nader who founded Common Cause, rallied against the change, arguing that big corporations would eventually squeeze out independent stations and monopolize the news. But the FCC, by a 3–2 vote of the commissioners, dropped the ownership rule. It is likely that this action will encourage the continuing concentration of media ownership.

The Equal-Time Requirement The FCC requires radio and television stations that provide airtime to a political candidate to offer competing candidates the same amount of airtime at the same price. Stations are not required to give free time to candidates, but if stations choose to give free time to one candidate, they must do so for the candidate's opponents. But this **equal-time rule** does *not* apply to newscasts, news specials, or even long documentaries, nor does it apply to talk shows like *Larry King Live* (see *People in Politics:* "Larry King Live"). Nor does it apply to presidential press conferences or presidential addresses to the nation, although the networks now generally offer free time for a "Democratic response" to a Republican president, and vice versa. A biased news presentation does not require the network or station to grant equal time to opponents of its views. And it is important to note that newspapers, unlike radio and television, have never been required to provide equal time to opposing views (see *Compared to What?* "America's TV Culture in Perspective").

Libel and Slander

Communications that wrongly damage an individual are known in law as **libel** (when written) and **slander** (when spoken). The injured party must prove in court that the communication caused actual damage and was either false or defamatory. A damaging falsehood or words or phrases that are defamatory (such as "Joe Jones is a rotten son of a bitch") are libelous and are not protected by the First Amendment from lawsuits seeking compensation.

Public Officials Over the years, the media have sought to narrow the protection afforded public officials against libel and slander. In 1964 the U.S. Supreme Court ruled in the case of *New York Times v. Sullivan* that public officials did not have a right to recover damages for false statements unless they are made with "malicious intent."[22] The **Sullivan rule** requires public officials not only to show that the media published or broadcast false and damaging statements but also to prove they did so knowing that their statements were false and damaging or that they did so with "reckless disregard" for the truth or falsehood of their statements. The effect of the Sullivan rule is to free the media to say virtually anything about public officials. Indeed, the media have sought to expand the definition of "public officials" to "public figures"—that is, to include anyone they choose as the subject of a story.

"Absence of Malice" The First Amendment protects the right of the media to be biased, unfair, negative, sensational, and even offensive. Indeed, even *damaging*

equal-time rule Federal Communications Commission (FCC) requirement that broadcasters who sell time to any political candidate must make equal time available to opposing candidates at the same price.

THINK AGAIN

Should the media report on all aspects of the private lives of public officials?

libel Writings that are false and malicious and are intended to damage an individual.

slander Oral statements that are false and malicious and are intended to damage an individual.

Sullivan rule Court guideline that false and malicious statements regarding public officials are protected by the First Amendment unless it can be proven they were known to be false at the time they were made or were made with "reckless disregard" for their truth or falsehood.

Larry King Live

Who turned presidential politics into talk-show entertainment? A strong argument can be made that Larry King was personally responsible for changing the nature of presidential campaigning. It was Larry King who nudged frequent talk-show guest Ross Perot into the presidential arena. And it was Larry King who demonstrated to the candidates that the talk-show format was a good way to reach out to the American people.

Larry King's supremacy in talk-show politics came late in life, after a half-century of hustling and hard knocks, no college education, bouts of gambling followed by bankruptcy, and multiple marriages. King has written five books about himself, describing his rise from Brooklyn neighborhoods; his friendships with Jackie Gleason, Frank Sinatra, and other celebrities; and his hardscrabble life. As he tells it, he hung around a New York radio station for five years before taking a bus to Miami to try his luck first as a disk jockey and later as a sports announcer. After a decade in Miami, he had his own TV interview show, a talk show on radio, and a newspaper column, and he was color commentator for the Miami Dolphins. He lived the fast life, running up huge debts and dealing in shady financial transactions. He was arrested in 1971 on grand larceny charges; they were dropped only because the statute of limitations had expired. He lost his TV and radio shows and his newspaper column. He ended up in Shreveport, Louisiana, doing play by play for the World Football League. In 1975 he was bankrupt but back in Miami doing radio. In 1978 he moved to Washington to launch his Mutual Network radio talk show. As radio talk shows gained popularity, so did King. When CNN started twenty-four-hour broadcasting in 1982, the network turned to King to do an evening interview show, *Larry King Live*. At first, the show merely filled the space between the evening and the late news. A decade later, the show was making news itself.

King's success is directly attributable to his accommodating style. He actually listens to his guests; he lets them speak for themselves; he unashamedly plugs their books, records, and movies. He does *not* attack his guests; he does not assume the adversarial, abrasive style preferred by reporters like Sam Donaldson, Dan Rather, and Mike Wallace, or interviewers like Bill O'Reilly. An old-fashioned liberal himself, King appears comfortable interviewing politicians of every stripe. He lets guests talk about themselves. He tosses "softball" questions: "If I were to interview the president about an alleged sexual affair, I wouldn't ask if he'd had one, I'd ask him, 'How does it feel to read these things about yourself?'"

With his emphasis on feelings, emotions, and motives rather than on facts, it is little wonder that King's style attracts politicians . . . or that *Larry King Live* is the highest rated show on CNN.

Source: Adapted from "A King Who Can Listen." *Time*, 10/5/92; © 1992 Time, Inc., reprinted by permission.

---

falsehoods may be printed or broadcast as long as the media can show that the story was not deliberately fabricated by them with malicious intent, that is, if the media can show an "absence of malice."

Shielding Sources The media argue that the First Amendment allows them to refuse to reveal the names of their sources, even when this information is required in criminal investigations and trials. Thus far, the U.S. Supreme Court has not given blanket protection to reporters to withhold information from court proceedings. However, a number of states have passed *shield laws* protecting reporters from being forced to reveal their sources.

Politics and the Internet

The development of any new media of communications invariably affects political life. Just as, first, radio and, later, television reshaped politics in America, today the Internet is having its own unique impact on public affairs. The Internet pro-

America's TV Culture in Perspective

America is a TV culture. Americans rely more on television for news and entertainment than people in other advanced industrial nations do. Perhaps more important, Americans have greater confidence in the media than other peoples do. Consider, for example, the question "Would you say you have a great deal of confidence, only some confidence, hardly any confidence, or no confidence at all in the media—press, radio, and television?" When this question was asked of a national sample of Americans, 69 percent responded that they had a great deal or at least some confidence in the media. But majorities in four other countries—France, Great Britain, Germany, and Spain—said they had little or no confidence in the media (see "confidence in the media" figure).

How much do the media influence key decisions in society? A majority of people in both the United States and these same European nations believe the media exert a large influence on public opinion. Americans appear to be closer to unanimity on this point (88 percent) than are Europeans. When people are asked how much influence the media exerts on particular governing institutions—the executive, the legislature, and the judiciary—Americans are much more likely to perceive strong media influence than are Europeans (see "media influence" figure).

Source: Adapted from Lawrence Parisot, "Attitudes about the Media: A Five Country Study," Public Opinion 43 (January/February 1988): 18, 60.

Have confidence in the media

France	48%
Germany	42%
Great Britain	38%
Spain	46%
USA	69%

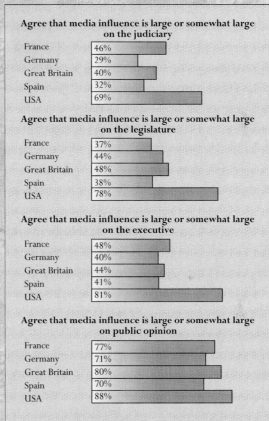

Agree that media influence is large or somewhat large on the judiciary

France	46%
Germany	29%
Great Britain	40%
Spain	32%
USA	69%

Agree that media influence is large or somewhat large on the legislature

France	37%
Germany	44%
Great Britain	48%
Spain	38%
USA	78%

Agree that media influence is large or somewhat large on the executive

France	48%
Germany	40%
Great Britain	44%
Spain	41%
USA	81%

Agree that media influence is large or somewhat large on public opinion

France	77%
Germany	71%
Great Britain	80%
Spain	70%
USA	88%

vides a channel for *interactive mass participation* in politics. It is unruly and chaotic by design. It offers the promise of abundant and diverse information in the opportunity for increased political participation. It empowers anyone who can design a Web site to spread their views, whether their views are profound and public-spirited or hateful and obscene.

Chaotic by Design During the Cold War, the RAND Corporation, a technological research think tank, proposed the Internet as a communications network that might survive a nuclear attack. It was deliberately designed to operate without any central authority or organization. Should any part of the system be destroyed, messages would still find their way to their destinations. The later development of the World Wide Web language allowed any connected computer

" INTERESTING.....IT'S LIKE A PORTABLE 500K FILE and YOU DON'T HAVE TO WAIT FOR IT
TO DOWNLOAD.... AND YOU SAY IT'S CALLED A NEWSPAPER ? "

(© 1997 Jim Borgman, Cincinnati Enquirer. Reprinted with permission of King Feature Syndicate.)

in the world to communicate with any other connected computer. And introduction of the World Wide Web in 1992 also meant that users no longer needed computer expertise to communicate. By 1995 Americans were buying more computers than television sets and sending more e-mail than "snail mail." Since then, Internet usage has continued to mushroom (see Figure 6.2).

Political Web Sites Abound The Internet is awash in political Web sites. The simple query "politics" on a standard search program can return well over a million matches. Almost all federal agencies, including the White House, Congress, the federal judiciary, and executive departments and agencies, maintain Web sites. Individual elected officeholders, including all members of Congress, maintain sites that include personal biographies, committee assignments, legislative accom-

FIGURE 6.2
Growth of Internet Users

Source: Statistical Abstract of the United States, 2004.

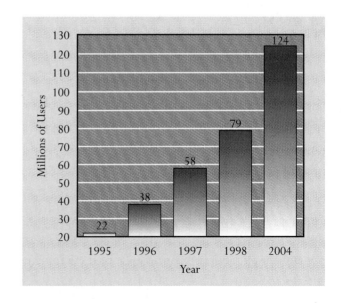

plishments, issue statements, and press releases. The home pages of the Democratic and Republican parties offer political news, issue positions, opportunities to become active in party affairs, and invitations to send them money. No serious candidate for major public office lacks a Web site; these campaign sites usually include flattering biographies, press releases, and, of course, invitations to contribute financially to the candidates' campaigns. All major interest groups maintain Web sites—business, trade, and professional groups; labor unions; ideological and issue groups; women's, religious, environmental, and civil rights groups. Indeed, this virtual tidal wave of politics on the Internet may turn out to offer too much information in too fragmented a fashion, thereby simply adding to apathy and indifference.

Internet Uncensored The Internet allows unrestricted freedom of expression, from scientific discourses on particle physics and information on the latest developments in medical science, to invitations to join in paramilitary "militia" and offers to exchange pornographic photos and messages. Commercial sex sites outnumber any other category on the Web.

 Annenberg Public Policy Center
The Annenberg Center of the University of Pennsylvania conducts research on political use of the media, including the Internet.
www.appcpenn.org

Congress unsuccessfully attempted to outlaw "indecent" and "patently offensive" material on the Internet and its Communications Decency Act of 1996. But the U.S. Supreme Court gave the Internet First Amendment protection in 1997 in *Reno v. American Civil Liberties Union.*[23] The Court recognized the Internet as an important form of popular expression protected by the Constitution. Congress had sought to make it a federal crime to send or display "indecent" material to persons under 18 years of age (material describing or displaying sexual activities or organs in "patently offensive" fashion). But the Supreme Court reiterated its view that government may not limit the adult population to "only what is fit for children." The Court decision places the burden of filtering Internet messages on parents. Filtering software can be installed on home computers, but a First Amendment issue arises when it is installed on computers in public libraries.

The Privacy Problem While the Internet facilitates the exercise of the right of free expression, it poses a problem for the right of privacy. Government and private industry have been collecting information on individuals for many years, from driving records to credit reports. But the Internet offers a vastly expanded and easily accessible source of data on individuals, including their earnings, purchases, hobbies, medical condition, reading habits, and more. Surfing the Internet may seem anonymous but it is not. Web sites can easily track visitors and may even send out "cookies"—files quietly stored in visitors' computers that continue to provide identification and information. Encryption (coding) programs are available, but the Federal Bureau of Investigation demands "recovery keys" from manufacturers in order to maintain surveillance.

Media Effects: Shaping Political Life

What effects do the media have on public opinion and political behavior? Let us consider media effects on (1) information and agenda setting, (2) values and opinions, and (3) behavior. These categories of effects are ranked by the degree of influence the media are likely to have over us. The strongest effects of the media are on our information levels and societal concerns. The media also influence values and opinions, but the strength of media effects in these areas is diluted by many

 THINK AGAIN

Is your choice of candidates in elections affected by their advertising?

The Media Age

The print media—newspapers, magazines, and books—have played a major role in American politics since colonial times. But today the electronic media—radio, television, and cable television—dominate in political communication.

Radio was widely introduced into American homes in the 1920s and 1930s, allowing President Franklin D. Roosevelt to become the first "media president," directly communicating with the American people through radio "fireside chats." After World War II, the popularity of television spread quickly; between 1950 and 1960, the percentage of homes with TV sets grew from 9 to 87.

Some notable political media innovations over the years:

- **1952:** The first paid commercial TV ad in a presidential campaign appeared, on behalf of Dwight D. Eisenhower. The black-and-white ad began with a voice-over—"Eisenhower answers the nation!"—followed by citizens asking favorable questions and Eisenhower responding, and ending with a musical jingle: "I like Ike." Although crude by current standards, it nevertheless set a precedent in media campaigning.

- **1952:** The "Checkers speech" by Eisenhower's running mate, Richard M. Nixon, represented the first direct television appeal to the people over the heads of party leaders. Nixon was about to be dumped from the Republican ticket for hiding secret slush-fund money from campaign contributors. He went on national television with an emotional appeal, claiming that the only personal item he ever took from a campaign contributor was his daughters' little dog, Checkers. Thousands of viewers called and wired in sympathy. Ike kept Nixon on the ticket.

- **1960:** The first televised debate between presidential candidates featured a youthful, handsome John F. Kennedy against a shifty-eyed Richard M. Nixon with a pronounced "five o'-clock shadow." Nixon doggedly scored debater points, but JFK presented a cool and confident image and spoke directly to the viewers. The debate swung the popular tide toward Kennedy, who won in a very tight contest. Nixon attributed his defeat to his failure to shave before the broadcast.

- **1964:** The first "negative" TV ad was the "Daisy Girl" commercial sponsored by the Lyndon Johnson campaign against Republican conservative Barry Goldwater. It implied that Goldwater would start a nuclear war. It showed a little girl picking petals off a daisy while an ominous voice counted down "10-9-8-7 . . ." to a nuclear explosion, followed by a statement that Lyndon Johnson could be trusted to keep the peace.

- **1976:** President Gerald Ford was the first incumbent president to agree to a televised debate. (No televised presidential debates were held in the Nixon-Humphrey race in 1968 or in the Nixon-McGovern race in 1972. Apparently Nixon had learned his lesson.) Ford stumbled badly, and Jimmy Carter went on to victory.

- **1982:** CNN (Cable News Network), introduced by the maverick media mogul Ted Turner, began twenty-four-hour broadcasting.

- **1991:** The Persian Gulf War was the first war to be fought live on television. (Although film and videotape reports of the Vietnam War had been important molders of public opinion in America, the technology of that era did not allow live reporting.) In the Gulf War, the Iraqi government permitted CNN to continue live broadcasts from Baghdad, including spectacular coverage of the first night's air raids on the city.

- **1992:** In the presidential election, television talk shows became a major focus of the campaign. Wealthy independent candidate Ross Perot actually conducted an all-media campaign, rejecting

other influences. Finally, it is most difficult to establish the independent effect of the media on behavior.

Information and Agenda-Setting Effects The media strongly influence what we know about our world and how we think and talk about it. Years ago, foreign-policy expert Bernard Cohen, in the first book to assess the effects of the media on foreign policy, put it this way: "The mass media may not be successful

The first televised presidential election debates were in 1960 between Senator John F. Kennedy and Vice President Richard Nixon. Nixon came armed with statistics, but his dour demeanor, "five o'clock shadow," and stiff presentation fared poorly in contrast to Kennedy's open, relaxed, confident air.

in-person appearances in favor of such media techniques as half-hour "infomercials."

- **1994–95:** The arrest and trial of celebrity O.J. Simpson on murder charges so dominated the national news that more television time was devoted to the O.J. story than to the actions of the president and Congress.
- **1996:** The presidential election was given less television time and newspaper space than previous elections. Clinton's large lead throughout the campaign, public boredom with Whitewater and other scandals, and Dole's lackluster performance frustrated reporters in search of drama. Network TV news gave Clinton twice as much positive coverage as Dole.
- **1997–98:** Sex scandals involving Bill Clinton dominated the news and talk shows, but public opinion polls gave the president the highest approval ratings of his two terms in office.

- **2000:** On election night, the networks prematurely called the presidential election, first for Gore and then for Bush, causing confusion among the public and embarrassment for the networks. A "Florida feeding frenzy" ensued over the next month as television blanketed every phase of that state's recount, from local election officials staring at punch-card ballots to state and U.S. Supreme Court arguments.
- **2001:** Dramatic television coverage of commercial aircraft crashing into the World Trade Center and videotape of the collapse of the twin giant buildings shocked Americans and inspired the "War on Terrorism."
- **2003:** Reporters were "embedded" with American troops in the Iraqi War, providing ground-level narratives and video of combat.

in telling people what to think, but the media are stunningly successful in telling their audience what to think about."[24] (see *Up Close:* "The Media Age").

However, **information overload** diminishes the influence of the media in determining what we think about. So many communications are directed at us that we cannot possibly process them all. A person's ability to recall a media report depends on repeated exposure to it and reinforcement through personal experience. For example, an individual who has a brother in a trouble spot in the Middle East

information overload
Situation in which individuals are subjected to so many communications that they cannot make sense of them.

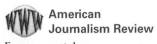

American Journalism Review

Features articles on current topics in print and television reporting, together with links to newspapers, television networks and stations, radio stations, media companies, etc. *www.ajr.org*

is more likely to be aware of reports from that area of the world. But too many voices with too many messages cause most viewers to block out a great deal of information.

Information overload may be especially heavy in political news. Television tells most viewers more about politics than they really want to know. Political scientist Austin Ranney writes, "The fact is that for most Americans politics is still far from being the most interesting and important thing in life. To them, politics is usually confusing, boring, repetitious, and above all irrelevant to the things that really matter in their lives."[25]

Effects on Values and Opinions The media often tell us how we *should* feel about news events or issues, especially those about which we have no prior feelings or experiences. The media can reinforce values and attitudes we already hold. However, the media seldom *change* our preexisting values or opinions. Media influence over values and opinions is reduced by **selective perception**, mentally screening out information or opinions we disagree with. People tend to see and hear only what they want to see and hear. For example, television news concentration on scandal, abuse, and corruption in government has not always produced the liberal, reformist values among viewers that media people expected. On the contrary, the focus of network executives on governmental scandals—Watergate, the Iran-Contra scandal, the sexual antics of politicians, congressional check kiting, and so on—has produced feelings of general political distrust and cynicism toward government and the political system. These feelings have been labeled **television malaise**, a combination of social distrust, political cynicism, feelings of powerlessness, and disaffection from parties and politics that seems to stem from television's emphasis on the negative aspects of American life.

The media do not *intend* to create television malaise; they are performing their self-declared watchdog role. They expect their stories to encourage liberal reform of our political institutions. But the result is often alienation rather than reform.

Direct Effects on Public Opinion Can the media change public opinion, and if so, how? For many years, political scientists claimed that the media had

selective perception
Mentally screening out information or opinions with which one disagrees.

television malaise
Generalized feelings of distrust, cynicism, and powerlessness stemming from television's emphasis on the negative aspects of American life.

Late night television is now a popular campaign forum. Young people rely heavily on the Jay Leno, David Letterman, and Conan O'Brien shows for their political news.

only minimal effects on public opinions and behavior. This early view was based largely on the fact that newspaper editorial endorsements seldom affected people's votes. But serious research on the effects of television tells a different story.

THINK
AGAIN

Are media professionals—news reporters, editors, anchors—the true voice of the people in public affairs?

In an extensive study of eighty policy issues over fifteen years, political scientists examined public opinion polls on various policy issues at a first point in time, then media content over a following interval of time, and finally public opinion on these same issues at the end of the interval. The purpose was to learn if media content—messages scored by their relevance to the issue, their salience in the broadcast, their pro/con direction, the credibility of the news source, and quality of the reporting—changed public opinion. Most people's opinions remained constant over time (opinion at the first time period is the best predictor of opinion at the second time period). However, when opinion did change, it changed in the direction supported by the media. "News variables alone account for nearly half the variance in opinion change." Other findings include the following:

- Anchors, reporters, and commentators have the greatest impact on opinion change. Television newscasters have high credibility and trust with the general public. Their opinions are crucial in shaping mass opinion.

- Independent experts interviewed by the media have a substantial impact on opinion, but not as great as newscasters themselves.

- A popular president can also shift public opinion somewhat. Unpopular presidents do not have much success as opinion movers, however.

- Interest groups on the whole have a slightly negative effect on public opinion. "In many instances they seem actually to have antagonized the public and created a genuine adverse effect"; such cases include Vietnam War protesters, nuclear freeze advocates, and other demonstrators and protesters, even peaceful ones.[26]

Effects on Behavior Many studies have focused on the effects of the media on behavior: studies of the effects of TV violence, studies of the effects of television on children, and studies of the effects of obscenity and pornography.[27] Although it is difficult to generalize from these studies, television appears more likely to reinforce behavioral tendencies than to change them. For example, televised violence may trigger violent behavior in children who are already predisposed to such behavior, but televised violence has little behavioral effect on average children.[28] Nevertheless, we know that television advertising sells products. And we know that political candidates spend millions to persuade audiences to go out and vote for them on election day. Both manufacturers and politicians create name recognition, employ product differentiation, try to associate with audiences, and use repetition to communicate their messages. These tactics are designed to affect our behavior both in the marketplace and in the election booth.

Political ads are more successful in motivating a candidate's supporters to go to the polls than they are in changing opponents into supporters. It is unlikely that voters who dislike a candidate will be persuaded by political advertising to change their votes. But many potential voters are undecided, and the support of many others is dubbed "soft." Going to the polls on election day requires effort—people have errands to do, it may be raining, they may be tired. Television advertising is more effective with the marginal voters.

- The mass media in America not only report on the struggle for power, they are participants themselves in that struggle.

- It is only through the media that the general public comes to know about political events, personalities, and issues. Newsmaking—deciding what is or is not "news"—is a major source of media power. Media coverage not only influences popular discussion but also forces public officials to respond.

- Media power also derives from the media's ability to set the agenda for public decision making—to determine what citizens and public officials will regard as "crises," "problems," or "issues" to be resolved by government.

- The media also exercise power in their interpretation of the news. News is presented in story form, pictures, words, sources, and story selection all contribute to interpretation.

- The media play a major role in socializing people to the political culture. Socialization occurs in news, entertainment, and advertising.

- The politics of the media are shaped by their economic interest in attracting readers and viewers. This interest largely accounts for the sensational and negative aspects of news reporting.

- The professional environment of newspeople encourages an activist, watchdog role in politics. The politics of most newspeople are liberal and Democratic.

- Political campaigning is largely a media activity. The media have replaced the parties as the principal linkage between candidates and voters. But the media tend to report the campaign as a horse race, at the expense of issue coverage, and to focus more on candidates' character than on their voting records or issue positions.

- The First Amendment guarantee of freedom of press protects the media from government efforts to silence or censor them and allows the media to be "unfair" when they choose to be. The Federal Communications Commission exercises some modest controls over the electronic media, since the rights to exclusive use of broadcast frequencies is a *public trust*.

- Public officials are afforded very little protection by libel and slander laws. The Supreme Court's Sullivan rule allows even damaging falsehoods to be written and broadcast as long as newspeople themselves do not deliberately fabricate lies with "malicious intent" or "reckless disregard."

- Media effects on political life can be observed in (1) information and agenda setting, (2) values and opinions, and (3) behavior—in that order of influence. The media strongly influence what we know about politics and what we talk about. The media are less effective in changing existing opinions, values, and beliefs than they are in creating new ones. Nevertheless, the media can change many people's opinions, based on the credibility of news anchors and reporters. Direct media effects on behavior are limited. Political ads are more important in motivating supporters to go to the polls, and in swinging undecided or "soft" voters, than in changing the minds of committed voters.

mass media   170
newsmaking   173
agenda setting   173
socialization   175
muckraking   179

"feeding frenzy"   180
name recognition   183
horse-race coverage   185
sound bite   185
prior restraint   186

equal-time rule   187
libel   187
slander   187
Sullivan rule   187

information overload   193
selective perception   194
television malaise   194

Alterman, Eric. *What Liberal Media?* New York: Simon & Schuster, 2003. A contrarian argument that the media does *not* have a liberal bias but rather bends over backward to include conservative views.

Ansolabehere, Stephen, Roy Behr, and Shanto Iyengar. *The Media Game: American Politics in the Television Age.* New York: Macmillan, 1993. A comprehensive text assessing the changes in the political system brought about by the rise of television since the 1950s.

Fallows, James. *Breaking the News: How the Media Undermine American Democracy.* New York: Pantheon, 1996. An argument that today's arrogant, cynical, and scandal-minded news reporting is turning readers and viewers away and undermining support for democracy.

Goldberg, Bernard *Bias: A CBS Insider Exposes How the Media Distort the News.* New York: Perennial, 2003. The title says it all.

Graber, Doris A. *Mass Media and American Politics.* 6th ed. Washington, D.C.: CQ Press, 2002. A wide-ranging description of media effects on campaigns, parties, and elections, as well as on social values and public policies.

Lichter, Robert S., Stanley Rothman, and Linda S. Lichter. *The Media Elite.* Bethesda, Md.: Adler and Adler, 1986. A thorough study of the social and political values of top leaders in the mass media, based on extensive interviews of key people in the most influential media outlets.

Patterson, Thomas E. *Out of Order.* New York: Random House, 1994. The antipolitical bias of the media poisons national election campaigns; policy questions are ignored in favor of the personal characteristics of candidates, their campaign strategies, and their standing in the horse race.

Prindle, David F. *Risky Business.* Boulder, Colo.: Westview Press, 1993. An examination of the politics of Hollywood, its liberalism, activism, self-indulgence, and celebrity egotism.

Sabato, Larry J. *Feeding Frenzy: How Attack Journalism Has Transformed American Politics.* New York: Free Press, 1992. A strong argument that the media prefer "to employ titillation rather than scrutiny" and as a result produce "trivialization rather than enlightenment."

POLITICAL PARTIES:
ORGANIZING POLITICS

1 Generally speaking, how would you identify yourself: as a Republican. Democrat, independent, or something else?
   Republican ● Democrat ●
   Independent ● Other ●

2 Which major political party better represents the interests of people like yourself?
   Republican ● Democrat ●

3 Does the Republican Party favor the rich more than the middle class or poor?
   Yes ● No ●

4 Does the Democratic Party favor the poor more than the middle class or rich?
   Yes ● No ●

5 Which major party does a better job of protecting the Social Security system?
   Republican ● Democrat ●

6 Which major party does a better job of handling foreign affairs?
   Republican ● Democrat ●

7 Should elected officials be bound by their party's platform?
   Yes ● No ●

8 Do we need a third party to challenge the Republican and Democratic parties?
   Yes ● No ●

How much power do political parties really have to determine who gets what in America? We hear the terms *Republican* and *Democratic* linked to people and to policies, but do these parties have real power beyond that of organizing for elections?

The Power of Organization

In the struggle for power, organization grants advantage. Italian political scientist Gaetano Mosca once put it succinctly: "A hundred men acting uniformly in concert, with a common understanding, will triumph over a thousand men who are not in accord and can therefore be dealt with one by one."[1] Thus politics centers on organization—on organizing people to win office and to influence public policy.

Political organizations—parties and interest groups—function as intermediaries between individuals and government. They organize individuals to give them power in selecting government officials—who governs—and in determining public policy—for what ends. Generally, **political parties** are more concerned with winning public office in elections than with influencing policy, whereas *interest groups* are more directly concerned with public policy and involve themselves with elections only to advance their policy interests (see Figure 7.1). In other words, parties and interest groups have an informal division of functions, with parties focusing on personnel and interest groups focusing on policy. Yet both organize individuals for more effective political action.

American Parties: A Historical Perspective

Parties are *not* mentioned in the Constitution. Indeed, the nation's Founders regarded both parties and interest groups as "actions," citizens united by "some common impulse of passion, or of interest, adverse to the rights of other citizens, or to the permanent and aggregate interests of the community." The Founders viewed factions as "mischievous" and "dangerous."[2] Yet the emergence of parties was inevitable as people sought to organize themselves to exercise power over who governs (see Figure 7.2 on page 207).

The Emergence of Parties: Federalists and Democratic-Republicans
In his Farewell Address, George Washington warned the nation about political parties: "Let me . . . warn you in the most solemn manner against the baneful effects of the spirit of party generally."[3] As president, Washington stood above the factions that were coalescing around his secretary of treasury, Alexander Hamilton, and around his former secretary of

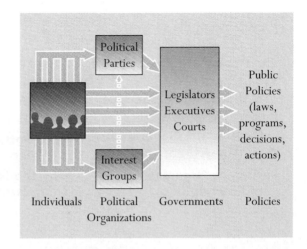

FIGURE 7.1 Political Organizations as Intermediaries

All political organizations function as intermediaries between individuals and government. Parties are concerned primarily with winning elected office, interest groups are concerned with influencing policy.

political organizations
Parties and interest groups that function as intermediaries between individuals and government.

political parties
Organizations that seek to achieve power by winning public office.

Federalists Those who supported the U.S. Constitution during the ratification process and who later formed a political party in support of John Adams's presidential candidacy.

Anti-Federalists Those who opposed the ratification of the U.S. Constitution and the creation of a strong national government.

majority Election by more than 50 percent of all votes cast in the contest.

state, Thomas Jefferson. Jefferson had resigned from Washington's cabinet in 1793 to protest the fiscal policies of Hamilton, notably his creation of a national bank and repayment of the state's Revolutionary War debts with federal funds. Washington had endorsed Hamilton's policies, but so great was the first president's prestige that Jefferson and his followers directed their fire not against Washington but against Hamilton, John Adams, and their supporters, who called themselves **Federalists** after their leaders' outspoken defense of the Constitution during the ratification process. By the 1790s, Jefferson and Madison, as well as many **Anti-Federalists** who had initially opposed the ratification of the Constitution, began calling themselves *Republicans* or *Democratic-Republicans,* terms that had become popular after the French Revolution in 1789.

Adams narrowly defeated Jefferson in the presidential election of 1796. This election was an important milestone in the development of the parties and the presidential election system. For the first time, two candidates campaigned as members of opposing parties, and candidates for presidential elector in each state pledged themselves as "Adams's men" or "Jefferson's men." By committing themselves in advance of the actual presidential vote, these pledged electors enabled voters in each state to determine the outcome of the presidential election.

Party activity intensified in anticipation of the election of 1800. Jefferson's Democratic-Republican Party first saw the importance of organizing voters, circulating literature, and rallying the masses to their causes. Many Federalists viewed this early party activity with disdain. Indeed, the Federalists even tried to outlaw public criticism of the federal government by means of the Alien and Sedition Acts of 1798, which among other things made it a crime to publish false or malicious writings against the (Federalist) Congress or president or to "stir up hatred" against them. These acts directly challenged the newly adopted First Amendment guarantees of freedom of speech and press. But in the election of 1800, the Federalists went down to defeat. Democratic-Republican electors won a **majority** (more than half the votes cast) in the Electoral College.

However, the original Constitution provided that each presidential elector could cast two votes, the person getting the most votes won the presidency and the runner-up won the vice presidency. If no one won a majority, the president would be elected by the House of Representatives. In 1800 each Democratic-Republican elector cast one of his votes for Jefferson and the other for Aaron Burr, Jefferson's vice presidential running mate. But the result was an unintended tie between Jefferson and Burr, throwing the election into the House of Representatives. (The

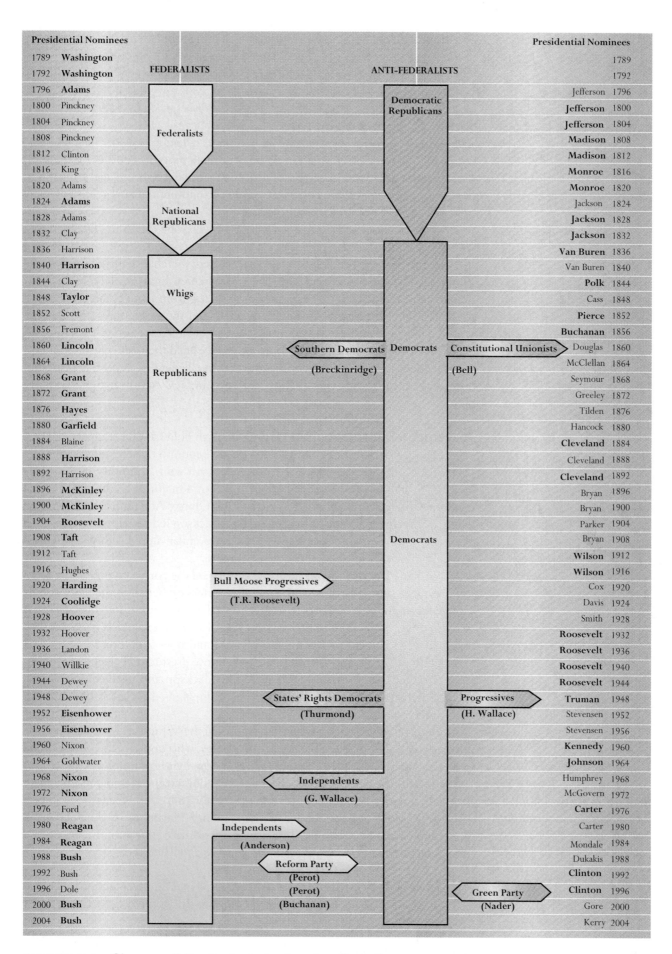

FIGURE 7.2 Change and Continuity in the American Party System

Twelfth Amendment, ratified in 1804, remedied the problem by requiring electors to cast separate votes for president and vice president.) A few disgruntled Federalists in the House considered giving Burr their votes just to embarrass Jefferson, and the ambitious Burr encouraged this chicanery. But in the end, the House selected Jefferson. President Adams and the Federalists turned over the reins of government to Jefferson and the Democratic-Republicans.

The election of 1800 was a landmark in American democracy—the first time that control of government passed peacefully from one party to another on the basis of an election outcome. As commonplace as that may seem to Americans today, the peaceful transfer of power from one group to another remains a rarity in many political systems around the world.

Jefferson's Democratic-Republican Party—later to be called the Democrats—was so successful that the Federalist Party never regained the presidency or control of Congress. The Federalists tended to represent merchants, manufacturers, and shippers, who were concentrated in New York and New England. The Democratic-Republicans tended to represent agrarian interests, from large plantation owners to small farmers. In the mostly agrarian America of the early 1800s, the Democratic-Republican Party prevailed. Jefferson easily won reelection in 1804, and his allies, James Madison and James Monroe, overwhelmed their Federalist opponents in subsequent presidential elections. By 1820, the Federalist Party had ceased to exist. Indeed, for a few years, it seemed as if the new nation had ended party politics.

Jacksonian Democrats and Whigs

Partisan politics soon reappeared, however. The Democratic-Republicans had already begun to fight among themselves by the 1824 presidential election. Andrew Jackson won a **plurality** (at least one more vote than anyone else in the race) but not a majority of the popular and Electoral College vote, but he then lost to John Quincy Adams in a close decision by the factionalized House of Representatives. Jackson led his supporters to found a new party, the **Democratic Party**, to organize popular support for his 1828 presidential bid, which succeeded in ousting Adams.

Jacksonian ideas both *democratized* and *nationalized* the party system. Under Jackson, the Democratic Party began to mobilize voters on behalf of the party and its candidates. It pressed the states to lower property qualifications for voting in order to recruit new Democratic Party voters. The electorate expanded from 365,000 voters in 1824 to well over a million in 1828 and over 2 million in 1840. The Democratic Party also pressed the states to choose presidential electors by popular vote rather than by state legislatures. Thus Jackson and his Democratic successor, Martin Van Buren, ran truly national campaigns directed at the voters in every state.

At the same time, Jackson's opponents formed the Whig Party, named after the British party of that name. Like the British Whigs, who opposed the power of the king, the American Whigs charged "King Andrew" with usurping the powers of Congress and the people. The Whigs quickly adopted the Democrats' tactics of national campaigning and popular organizing. By 1840, the Whigs were able to gain the White House, running William Henry Harrison—nicknamed "Old Tippecanoe" from his victory at Tippecanoe over Native Americans in 1811—and John Tyler and featuring the slogan "Tippecanoe and Tyler too."

Post-Civil War Republican Dominance

Whigs and Democrats continued to share national power until the slavery conflict that ignited the Civil War de-

plurality Election by at least one vote more than any other candidate in the race.

Democratic Party One of the main parties in American politics; it traces its origins to Thomas Jefferson's Democratic-Republican Party, acquiring its current name under Andrew Jackson in 1828.

stroyed the old party system. The Republican Party had formed in 1854 to oppose the spread of slavery to the western territories. By the election of 1860, the slavery issue so divided the nation that four parties offered presidential candidates: Lincoln the Republican, Stephen A. Douglas the northern Democrat, John C. Breckinridge the southern Democrat, and John Bell the Constitutional Union Party candidate. No party came close to winning a majority of the popular vote, but Lincoln won in the Electoral College.

The new party system that emerged from the Civil War featured a victorious **Republican Party** that generally represented the northern industrial economy and a struggling Democratic Party that generally represented a southern agricultural economy. The Republican Party won every presidential election from 1860 to 1912 except for two victories by Democratic reformer and New York governor Grover Cleveland (see *Up Close:* "The Donkey and the Elephant").

Yet the Democratic Party offered a serious challenge in the election of 1896 and realigned the party affiliations of the nation's voters. The Democratic Party nominated William Jennings Bryan, a talented orator and a religious fundamentalist. Bryan sought to rally the nation's white "have-nots" to the Democratic Party banner, particularly the debt-ridden farmers of the South and West. His plan was to stimulate inflation (and thus enable debtors to pay their debts with "cheaper," less valuable dollars) through using plentiful, western-mined "free silver," rather than gold, as the monetary standard. He defeated Cleveland's faction and the "Gold Democrats" in the 1896 Democratic Party convention with his famous Cross of Gold speech: "You shall not crucify mankind upon a cross of gold."

But the Republican Party rallied its forces in perhaps the most bitter presidential battle in history. It sought to convince the nation that high tariffs, protection for manufactures, and a solid monetary standard would lead to prosperity for industrial workers as well as the new tycoons. The campaign, directed by Marcus Alonzo Hanna, attorney for John D. Rockefeller's Standard Oil Company, spent an unprecedented $16 million (an amount in inflation-adjusted dollars that has never been equaled) to elect Republican William McKinley, advertised as the candidate who would bring a "full dinner pail" to all. The battle also produced one of the largest voter turnouts in history. McKinley won in a landslide. Bryan ran twice again but lost by even larger margins. The Republican Party solidified the loyalty of industrial workers, small-business owners, bankers, and large manufactures, as well as black voters, who respected "the party of Lincoln" and despised the segregationist practices of the southern Democratic Party.

So great was the Republican Party's dominance in national elections that only a split among Republicans enabled the Democrat Woodrow Wilson to capture the presidency in 1912. Republican Theodore Roosevelt (who became president following McKinley's assassination and had won reelection in 1904) sought to recapture the presidency from his former protégé, Republican William Howard Taft. In the **GOP** convention ("Grand Old Party," as the Republicans began labeling themselves), party regulars rejected the unpredictable Roosevelt in favor of Taft, even though Roosevelt had won the few primary elections that had recently been initiated. An irate Teddy Roosevelt launched a third, progressive party, the "Bull Moose," which actually outpolled the Republican Party in the 1912 election—the only time a third party has surpassed one of the two major parties in U.S. history. But the result was a victory for the Democratic candidate, former Princeton political science professor Woodrow Wilson. Following Wilson's two terms, Republicans again reasserted their political dominance with victories by Warren G. Harding, Calvin Coolidge, and Herbert Hoover.

Republican Party One of the two main parties in American politics, it traces its origins to the antislavery and nationalist forces that united in the 1850s and nominated Abraham Lincoln for president in 1860.

GOP "Grand Old Party"— popular label for the Republican Party.

The Donkey and the Elephant

The popular nineteenth-century cartoonist Thomas Nast is generally credited with giving the Democratic and Republican parties their current symbols: the donkey and the elephant. In *Harper's Weekly* cartoons in the 1870s, Nast critically portrayed the Democratic Party as a stubborn mule "without pride of ancestry nor hope of posterity." During this period of Republican Party dominance, Nast portrayed the Republican Party as an elephant, the biggest beast in the political jungle. Now both party symbols are used with pride.

"A LIVE JACKASS KICKING A DEAD LION."
And such a Lion! and such a Jackass!

In the 1870 cartoon on the left, published following the death of Lincoln's Secretary of War E. M. Stanton. Nast shows a donkey (labeled "Copperheads," a disparaging term for the mostly Democratic northerners who were sympathetic to the South during the Civil War) kicking the dead Stanton, who is portrayed as a lion. The 1874 cartoon on the right features the elephant as the Republican Vote and the donkey masquerading as a lion.

THINK AGAIN

Does the Democratic Party favor the poor more than the middle class or rich?

New Deal Policies of President Franklin D. Roosevelt during the depression of the 1930s that helped form a Democratic Party coalition of urban working-class, ethnic, Catholic, Jewish, poor, and southern voters.

The New Deal Democratic Party The promise of prosperity that empowered the Republican Party and held its membership together faded in the light of the Great Depression. The U.S. stock market crashed in 1929, and by the early 1930s, one-quarter of the labor force was unemployed. Having lost confidence in the nation's business and political leadership, in 1932 American voters turned out incumbent Republican President Herbert Hoover in favor of Democrat Franklin D. Roosevelt, who promised the country a **New Deal**.

More than just bringing the Democrats to the White House, the Great Depression marked another party realignment. This time, traditionally Republican voting groups changed their affiliation and enabled the Democratic Party to dominate national politics for a generation. This realignment actually began in 1928, when Democratic presidential candidate Al Smith, a Catholic, won many northern, urban, ethnic voters away from the Republican Party. By 1932, a majority New Deal Democratic coalition had been formed in American politics. It consisted of the following groups:

Franklin Roosevelt campaigning among coal miners in West Virginia during the presidential election campaign of 1932. Roosevelt's optimism and "can-do" attitude in the face of the Great Depression helped cement the New Deal Democratic coalition that won him the presidency.

- Working classes and union members, especially in large cities.

- White ethnic groups who had previously aligned themselves with Republican machines.

- Catholics and Jews.

- African Americans, who ended their historic affiliation with the party of Lincoln to pursue new economic and social goals.

- Poor people, who associated the New Deal with expanded welfare and Social Security programs.

- Southern whites, who had provided the most loyal block of Democratic voters since the Civil War.

To be sure, this majority coalition had many internal factions: southern "Dixiecrats" walked out of the Democratic Party convention in 1948 to protest a party platform that called for an end to racial discrimination in employment. But the promise of a New Deal—with its vast array of government supports for workers, elderly and disabled people, widows and children, and farmers—held this coalition together reasonably well. President Harry Truman's **Fair Deal** proved that the coalition could survive its founder, Franklin D. Roosevelt. Republican Dwight D. Eisenhower made inroads into this coalition by virtue of his personal popularity and the Republican Party's acceptance of most New Deal programs. But John F. Kennedy's "New Frontier" demonstrated the continuing appeal of the Democratic Party tradition. Lyndon Johnson's **Great Society** went further than the programs of any of his predecessors in government intervention in the economic and social life of the nation. Indeed, it might be argued that the Great Society laid the foundation for a political reaction that eventually destroyed the old Democratic coalition and led to yet another new party alignment (see Figure 7.3).

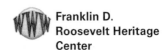 **Franklin D. Roosevelt Heritage Center**
Biography on F.D.R. and information on the New Deal. *www.fdrheritage.org*

Fair Deal Policies of President Harry Truman extending Roosevelt's New Deal and maintaining the Democratic Party's voter coalition.

Great Society Policies of President Lyndon Johnson that promised to solve the nation's social and economic problems through government intervention.

FIGURE 7.3 The Parties in Presidential Voting

Despite the dominance of the Democratic Party in terms of numbers of registered voters, Republicans have won more presidential elections since 1952, indicating that, at the presidential level, voters are not always loyal to their party. Democrat Al Gore won the popular vote in 2000 but lost the Electoral College vote.

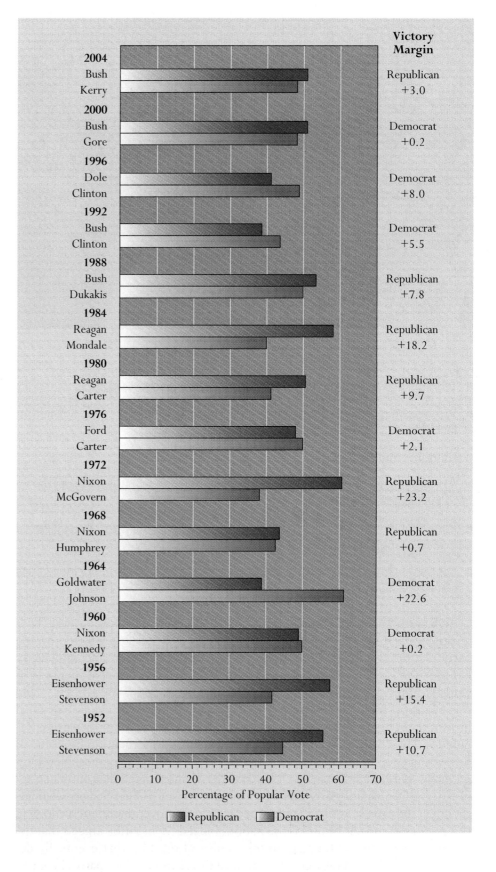

A New Republican Majority The American political system underwent massive convulsions in the late 1960s as a result of both the civil rights revolution at home and an unpopular war in Vietnam. Strains were felt in all of the nation's political institutions, from the courts to the Congress to the presidency. And when Lyndon Johnson announced his decision not to run for reelection in 1968, the Democratic Party erupted in a battle that ultimately destroyed its majority support among presidential voters.

At the 1968 Democratic Party convention in Chicago, Vice President Hubert Humphrey controlled a majority of the delegates inside the convention hall, but antiwar protesters dominated media coverage outside the hall. When Chicago police attacked unruly demonstrators with batons, the media broadcast to the world an image of the nation's turmoil. In the presidential campaign that followed, both candidates—Democrat Hubert Humphrey and Republican Richard Nixon—presented nearly identical positions supporting the U.S. military commitment in Vietnam while endorsing a negotiated, "honorable" settlement of the war. But the image of the Democratic Party became associated with the street protesters. Inside the convention hall, pressure from women and minorities led party leaders to adopt changes in the party's delegate-selection process for future conventions to assure better representation of these groups—at the expense of Democratic officeholders (see "Making Party Rules" later in this chapter for more details).

In 1972 the Democratic Party convention strongly reflected the views of antiwar protesters, civil rights advocates, feminist organizations, and liberal activists generally. The visibility of these activists, who appeared to be well to the left of both Democratic Party voters and the electorate in general, allowed the Republican Party to portray the Democratic presidential nominee, George McGovern, as an unpatriotic liberal, willing to "crawl to Hanoi" and to sacrifice the nation's honor for peace. It also allowed the Republicans to characterize the new Democratic Party as soft on crime, tolerant of disorder, and committed to racial and sexual quotas in American life. Richard Nixon, never very popular personally, was able to win in a landslide in 1972. The Watergate scandal and Nixon's forced resignation only temporarily stemmed the tide of "the new Republican majority." Democrat Jimmy Carter's narrow victory over Republican Gerald R. Ford in 1976 owed much to the latter's pardon of Nixon.

The Reagan Coalition Under the leadership of Ronald Reagan, the Republican Party was able to assemble a majority coalition that dominated presidential elections in the 1980s, giving Reagan landslide victories in 1980 and 1984 and George Bush a convincing win in 1988. The **Reagan Coalition** consisted of the following groups:

- Economic conservatives concerned about high taxes and excessive government regulation, including business and professional voters who had traditionally supported the Republican Party.

- Social conservatives concerned about crime, drugs, and racial conflict, including many white ethnic voters and union members who had traditionally voted Democratic.

- Religious fundamentalists concerned about such issues as abortion and prayer in schools.

- Southern whites concerned about racial issues, including affirmative action programs.

Democratic Party
Web site of the Democratic National Committee (DNC)

With news, press releases, policy positions, etc.
www.democrat.org

Does the Republican Party favor the rich more than the middle class or poor?

Republican Party
Web site of the Republican National Committee (RNC)

With GOP news, press releases, policy positions, etc.
www.rnc.org

Reagan Coalition
Combination of economic and social conservatives, religious fundamentalists, and defense-minded anticommunists who rallied behind Republican President Ronald Reagan.

President Ronald Reagan created a Republican majority coalition in the 1980s by uniting Republican factions—economic conservatives, social conservatives, religious fundamentalists, and anti-Communists—and adding many Southern white Democrats.

 Reagan Information Page

Web site celebrating Reagan's presidential achievements. **www.presidentreagan.info**

 Democratic Leadership Council/New Democrats Online

Moderate Democrats in the House and Senate set forth their views. **www.ndol.org**

Democratic Leadership Council Organization of party leaders who sought to create a "new" Democratic Party to appeal to middle-class, moderate voters.

■ Internationalists and anticommunists who wanted the United States to maintain a strong military force and to confront Soviet-backed Marxist regimes around the world.

Reagan held this coalition together in large part through his personal popularity and his infectious optimism about the United States and its future. Although sometimes at odds with one another, economic conservatives, religious fundamentalists, and internationalists could unite behind the "Great Communicator." Reagan's presidential victory in 1980 helped to elect a Republican majority to the U.S. Senate and encouraged Democratic conservatives in the Democrat-controlled House of Representatives to frequently vote with Republicans. As a result, Reagan got most of what he asked of Congress in his first term: cuts in personal income taxes, increased spending for national defense, and slower growth of federal regulatory activity. With the assistance of the Federal Reserve Board, inflation was brought under control. But Reagan largely failed to cut government spending as he had promised, and the result was a series of huge federal deficits. Reagan appointed conservatives to the Supreme Court and the federal judiciary (see Chapter 13), but no major decisions were reversed (including the *Roe v. Wade* decision, protecting abortion); social conservatives had to be content with the president's symbolic support.

During these years, the national Democratic Party was saddled with an unpopular image as the party of special-interest groups. As more middle-class and working-class voters deserted to the GOP, the key remaining loyal Democratic constituencies were African Americans and other minorities, government employees, union leaders, liberal intellectuals in the media and universities, feminist organizations, and environmentalists. Democratic presidential candidates Walter Mondale in 1984 and Michael Dukakis in 1988 were obliged to take liberal positions to win the support of these groups in the primary elections. Later, both candidates sought to move toward the center of the ideological battleground in the general election. But Republican Party strategists were able to "define" Mondale and Dukakis through negative campaign advertising (see Chapter 8) as liberal defenders of special-interest groups. The general conservative tilt of public opinion in the 1980s added to the effectiveness of the GOP strategy of branding Democratic presidential candidates with the "*L* word" (*liberal*).

Clinton and the "New" Democrats Yet even while Democratic candidates fared poorly in presidential elections, Democrats continued to maintain control of the House of Representatives, to win back control of the U.S. Senate in 1986, and to hold more state governorships and state legislative seats than the Republicans. Thus the Democratic Party retained a strong leadership base on which to rebuild itself.

During the 1980s, Democratic leaders among governors and senators came together in the **Democratic Leadership Council** to create a "new" Democratic Party closer to the center of the political spectrum. The chair of the Democratic Leadership Council was the young, energetic, and successful governor of Arkansas, Bill Clinton. The concern of the council was that the Democratic Party's traditional support for social justice and social welfare programs was overshadowing its commitment to economic prosperity. Many council members argued that a healthy economy was a prerequisite to progress in social welfare. Not all Democrats agreed with the council agenda. African American leaders (including the Reverend Jesse Jackson), as well as liberal and environmental groups, feared that the priorities of the council would result in the sacrifice of traditional Democratic Party commitments to minorities, poor people, and the environment.

In the 1992 presidential election, Bill Clinton was in a strong position to take advantage of the faltering economy under George Bush, to stress the "new" Democratic Party's commitment to the middle class, and to avoid being labeled as a liberal defender of special interests. At the same time, he managed to rally the party's core activist groups—liberals, intellectuals, African Americans, feminists, and environmentalists. Many liberals in the party deliberately soft-pedaled their views during the 1992 election in order not to offend voters, hoping to win with Clinton and then fight for liberal programs later. Clinton won with 43 percent of the vote, to George Bush's 38 percent. Independent Ross Perot captured a surprising 19 percent of the popular vote, including many voters who were alienated from both the Democratic and the Republican parties. Once in office, Clinton appeared to revert to liberal policy directions rather than to pursue the more moderate line he had espoused as a "new" Democrat. As Clinton's ratings sagged, the opportunity arose for a Republican resurgence.

Republican Resurgence A political earthquake shook Washington in the 1994 congressional elections, when the Republicans for the first time in forty years captured the House of Representatives, regained control of the Senate, and captured a majority of the nation's governorships. For the first time in history Republicans won more seats in the South than the Democrats. This southern swing to the Republicans in congressional elections seemed to confirm the realignment of southern voters that had begun earlier in presidential elections. Just two years after a Democratic president had been elected, the GOP won its biggest nationwide victory since the Great Depression.

Clinton Holds On Following the Republican victory, the Democratic Party appeared to be in temporary disarray. The new Republican House Speaker, Newt Gingrich, tried to seize national policy leadership; Clinton was widely viewed as a failed president. But the Republicans quickly squandered their political opportunity. They had made many promises in a well-publicized "Contract with America"—a balanced federal budget, congressional term limits, tax cuts, welfare reform, and more—but they delivered little. Majority Leader Bob Dole failed by one vote to pass the Balanced Budget Amendment in the Senate. President Clinton took an unexpectedly hard line toward GOP spending cuts and vetoed several budget bills. When the federal government officially "closed down" for lack of appropriated funds, the public appeared to blame Republicans. Polls showed a dramatic recovery in the president's approval ratings. Clinton skillfully portrayed GOP leaders, especially Newt Gingrich, as "extremists" and himself as a responsible moderate prepared to trim the budget, reduce the deficit, and reform welfare, "while still protecting Medicare, Medicaid, education, and the environment." By early 1996, Clinton had set the stage for his reelection campaign.

Bill Clinton is the first Democratic president to be reelected since Franklin D. Roosevelt. Clinton rode to victory on a robust economy. Voters put aside doubts about Clinton's character, and they ignored Republican Bob Dole's call for tax reductions. Clinton won with 49 percent of the popular vote to Dole's 41 percent and Perot's 8 percent. But Clinton's victory failed to rejuvenate the Democratic Party's fortunes across the country. The GOP retained its majorities in both houses of Congress.

2000—A Nation Divided The nation was more evenly divided in 2000 between the Democratic and Republican parties than perhaps at any other time in history. Democrat Al Gore won a narrow victory in the popular vote for presi-

MoveOn
Website of the liberal wing of the Democratic Party.
www.moveon.org

dent, but after a month-long battle for Florida's electoral vote, Republican George W. Bush emerged as a winner of the Electoral College vote, 271 to 267 (see Chapter 8). Not only was the presidential vote almost tied but both houses of Congress were split almost evenly between Democrats and Republicans. The Republican Party lost seats in the House of Representatives in 1998 and again in 2000. Yet the GOP still retained a razor-thin margin of control of that body. In the Senate, the 2000 election created a historic 50–50 tie between Democrats and Republicans. The vote of the Senate's presiding officer, Republican Vice President Dick Cheney, would have given the GOP the narrowest of control of that body. But in 2001, Vermont's Republican Senator Jim Jeffords decided to switch his support to the Democratic Party, swinging control of the Senate to the Democrats (see Chapter 10).

The Republican Party defied tradition in 2002 by regaining control of the Senate and expanding their majority in the House. Historically, the party in control of the White House *lost* seats in midterm elections. But in an era in which presidents are not supposed to have coattails, especially in midterm congressional elections, President George W. Bush campaigned energetically across the country for GOP candidates, focusing attention on the war on terrorism. Democratic complaints about the weak economy were muted. Bush's intense efforts appeared to motivate Republican voters; a higher-than-usual midterm voter turnout resulted in Republican victories in hotly contested Senate and House races across the country. Bush's White House Press Secretary proclaimed "President Bush and the Republican Party have made history."

Republicans Take Control In 2004, the GOP consolidated its control over the White House, Senate, and House of Representatives. Throughout the 2004 election campaign, polls showed the nation evenly split, with Republican President Bush and Democratic Senator Kerry running nezck and neck. There was considerable fear of another contested presidential election and concern that the popular vote winner might again lose in the Electoral College. But Republicans showed unexpected strength, with Bush winning both the popular vote and the Electoral College vote. Turnout was high—about 59 percent of persons eligible to vote. (Republican turnout may have been helped by referenda banning same-sex marriage that appeared on the ballot in eleven states; polls consistently show regular churchgoers tending to vote Republican.) Republicans added to their controlling margins in both the House and the Senate. Even the Democratic Senate leader, Tom Daschle of South Dakota, lost his bid for reelection. President Bush claimed a mandate for Republican efforts to simplify the tax code and to allow younger workers to invest part of their Social Security taxes in the stock market, and continued to aggressively pursue the war on terrorism throughout the world.

Political Parties and Democratic Government

THINK
AGAIN

Should elected officials be bound by their party's platform?

"Political parties created democracy, and modern democracy is unthinkable save in terms of the parties."[4] Traditionally, political scientists have praised parties as indispensable to democratic government. They have argued that parties are essential for organizing popular majorities to exercise control over government. The development of political parties in all the democracies of the world testifies to the underlying importance of parties to democratic government. But political parties in the United States have lost their preeminent position as instruments of democracy. Other structures and organizations in society—interest groups, the mass media, independent campaign organizations, primary elections, social welfare agencies—now perform many of the functions traditionally regarded as prerogatives of political parties. Nevertheless, the Democratic and Republican parties remain important organizing structures for politics in the United States.

"Responsible" Parties in Theory In theory, political parties function in a democracy to organize majorities around broad principles of government in order to win public office and enact these principles into law. A "responsible" party should:

- Adopt a platform setting forth its principles and policy positions.

- Recruit candidates for public office who agree with the party's platform.

- Inform and educate the public about the platform.

- Organize and direct campaigns based on platform principles.

- Organize the legislature to ensure party control in policy making.

- Hold its elected officials responsible for enacting the party's platform.

If responsible, disciplined, policy-oriented parties competed for majority support, *if* they offered clear policy alternatives to the voters, and *if* the voters cast their ballots on the basis of these policy options, *then* the winning party would have a "policy mandate" from the people to guide the course of government. In that way, the democratic ideal of government by majority rule would be implemented.

Winning Wins over Principle However, the **responsible party model** never accurately described the American party system. The major American parties have been loose coalitions of individuals and groups seeking to attract sufficient votes to gain control of government. *Winning has generally been more important than any principles or policies.* America's major parties must appeal to tens of millions of voters in every section of the nation and from all walks of life. If a major party is to acquire a majority capable of controlling the U.S. government, it cannot limit its appeal by relying on a single unifying principle. Instead, it must form coalitions of voters from as many sectors of the population as it can. Major American parties therefore usually do not emphasize particular principles or ideologies so much as try to find a common ground of agreement among many different people. This emphasis does not mean no policy differences exist between the American parties. On the contrary, each party tends to appeal to a distinctive coalition of interests, and therefore each party expresses somewhat distinctive policy views (see *What Do You Think?* "Which Party Does a Better Job?").

In their efforts to win, major American political parties strive to attract the support of the large numbers of people near the center of public opinion. Generally more votes are at the center of the ideological spectrum—the middle-of-the-road—than on the extreme liberal or conservative ends. Thus *no real incentive exists for vote-maximizing parties to take strong policy positions in opposition to each other.* As the Democratic and Republican policy positions approach the center, the parties seem to echo each other, and critics attack them as Tweedledee and Tweedledum (see Figure 7.4).

Party and Ideology Despite incentives for the parties to move to the center of the political spectrum, the Republican and Democratic parties are perceived by the public as ideologically separate. The electorate tends to perceive the Republican Party as conservative and the Democratic Party as liberal.

responsible party model
System in which competitive parties adopt a platform of principles, recruiting candidates and directing campaigns based on the platform, and holding their elected officials responsible for enacting it.

Which Party Does a Better Job?

What do Americans think of the Democratic and Republican parties? Generally speaking, the Democratic Party has been able to maintain an image of "the party of the common people," and the Republican Party has long been saddled with an image of "favoring the rich."

But when it comes to popular perceptions of each party's ability to deal with problems confronting the nation, the Democratic and Republican parties appear evenly matched. The Republican Party is trusted to "do a better job" in handling foreign affairs and maintaining a strong national defense. It also enjoys a reputation of being better at "holding down taxes."

The Democratic Party enjoys its greatest advantage on "compassion issues" like helping poor, elderly, and homeless people. And the Democrats have long enjoyed the support of the high-voter-turnout over-sixty-five age group because it is trusted to do a better job "protecting the Social Security system."

Source: Various polls reported in *The Polling Report,* November 22, 1999, September 10, 2001, January 28, 2002, August 11, 2003.

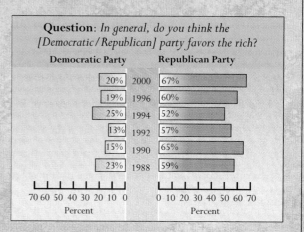

Question: *In general, do you think the [Democratic / Republican] party favors the rich?*

	Democratic Party	Year	Republican Party
	20%	2000	67%
	19%	1996	60%
	25%	1994	52%
	13%	1992	57%
	15%	1990	65%
	23%	1988	59%

Percent (70 60 50 40 30 20 10 0) Percent (0 10 20 30 40 50 60 70)

Question: *I am going to read a list of issues and I want you to tell me whether, overall, you think the Democrats or the Republicans would do a better job with this issue. ("Don't Know" responses not shown.)*

Democratic Party		Republican Party
	Republican Advantages	
16%	Dealing with Terrorists	51%
32%	Keeping U.S. Strong	46%
29%	Crime	40%
	Fairly Evenly Divided	
38%	Taxes	41%
42%	Economy	40%
45%	Federal Budget	44%
	Democratic Advantages	
52%	Social Security	37%
55%	Health Care	38%
54%	Environment	21%

Percentage (80 60 40 20 0) Percentage (0 20 40 60 80)

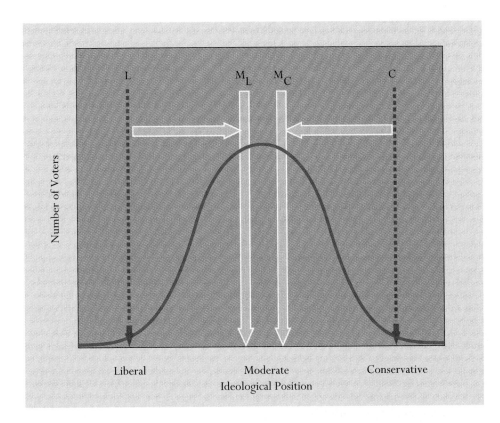

FIGURE 7.4 Winning versus Principle

Why don't we have a party system based on principles, with a liberal party and a conservative party, each offering the voters a real ideological choice? Let's assume that voters generally choose the party closest to their own ideological position. If the liberal party (L) took a strong ideological position to the left of most voters, the conservative party (C) would move toward the center, winning more moderate votes, even while retaining its conservative supporters, who would still prefer it to the more liberal opposition party. Likewise, if the conservative party took a strong ideological position to the right of most voters, the liberal party would move to the center and win. So both parties must abandon strong ideological positions and move to the center, becoming moderate in the fight for support of moderate voters.

Indeed, polls suggest that Republican voters described themselves as conservatives for more often than as liberals. And Democratic voters are more likely to identify themselves as liberals than as conservatives, although many like to think of themselves as moderates (see Table 7.1).

This relationship between ideological self-identification and party self-identification is relatively stable over time. It suggests that the parties are not altogether empty jars. Later we will observe that Democratic and Republican party activists (notably, delegates to the party conventions) are even more ideologically separate than Democratic and Republican Party voters.

Democratic and Republican party activists have become a more ideologically separate in recent years. And voters have become increasingly aware of this **party polarization**. Indeed many voters are now prepared to say that the Democratic Party is more liberal and the Republican Party is more conservative on a variety

party polarization The tendency of the Democratic Party to take more liberal positions and the Republican Party to take more conservative positions on key issues.

TABLE 7.1 Party and Ideology Among Voters		
	Democratic Voters	**Republican Voters**
Liberal	34%	11%
Moderate	46	38
Conservative	16	49

Source: As reported in the *New York Times*, August 14, 2000.

of high-profile issues, including government services and spending, government provision of health insurance, and government help to African-Americans.[5]

The Erosion of Traditional Party Functions Parties play only a limited role in campaign organization and finance. Campaigns are generally directed by professional campaign management firms or by the candidates' personal organizations, not by parties. Party organizations have largely been displaced in campaign activity by advertising firms, media consultants, pollsters, and others hired by the candidates themselves (see Chapter 8).

Most political candidates today are self-recruited. American political parties also play only a limited role in recruiting candidates for elected office. People initiate their own candidacies, first contacting friends and financial supporters. Often in state and local races, candidates contact party officials only as a courtesy, if at all.

The major American political parties cannot really control who their **nominee**—the party's entry in a general election race—will be. Rather, party **nominations** for most elected offices are won in *primary elections.* In a **primary election**, registered voters select who will be their party's nominee in the general election. Party leaders may endorse a candidate in a primary election and may even work to try to ensure the victory of their favorite, but the voters in that party's primary select the nominee.

Candidates usually communicate directly with voters through the mass media. Television has replaced the party organization as the principal medium of communication between candidates and voters. Candidates no longer rely much on party workers to carry their message from door to door. Instead, candidates can come directly into the voters' living rooms via television.

Even if the American parties wanted to take stronger policy positions and to enact them into law, they would not have the means to do so. *American political parties have no way to bind their elected officials to the party platform or even to their campaign promises.* Parties have no strong disciplinary sanctions to use against members of Congress who vote against the party's policy position. The parties cannot deny them renomination. At most, the party's leadership in Congress can threaten the status, privileges, and pet bills of disloyal members (see Chapter 10). Party cohesion, where it exists, is more a product of like-mindedness than of party discipline.

American political parties no longer perform social welfare functions—trading off social services, patronage jobs, or petty favors in exchange for votes. Traditional party organizations, or **machines**, especially in large cities, once helped immigrants get settled in, found **patronage** jobs in government for party workers, and occasionally provided aid to impoverished but loyal party voters. But *government bureaucracies have replaced the political parties as providers of social services.* Government employment agencies, welfare agencies, civil service systems, and other bureaucracies now provide the social services once undertaken by political machines in search of votes.

Divided Party Government Finally, to further confound the responsible party model, Americans seem to prefer **divided party government**—where one party controls the executive branch while the other party controls one or both houses of the legislative branch. Over the last forty years, American presidents have been more likely to face a Congress in which the opposition party controls one or both houses than to enjoy their own party's full control of Congress.[6] (Divided party government in the states—where one party controls the governorship and the opposition party controls one or both houses of the state legislature—is also in-

nominee Political party's entry in a general election race.

nomination Political party's selection of its candidate for a public office.

primary elections Elections to choose party nominees for public office; may be open or closed.

machine Tightly disciplined party organization, headed by a boss, that relies on material rewards—including patronage jobs—to control politics.

patronage Appointment to public office based on party loyalty.

divided party government One party controls the executive branch while the other party controls one or both houses of the legislative branch.

creasing over time).[7] Divided party control of government makes it difficult for either party to fully enact its platform.

It is noteworthy that American public opinion seems to prefer divided party government over unified party control: *"Do you think it is better when one party controls both the presidency and the Congress, better when control is split between the Democrats and Republicans, or doesn't it matter?"*: Better one party—23.8%; Better control split—52.4%; Doesn't matter—23.8%.[8]

Party Finances

Parties as well as candidates raise hundreds of millions of dollars in every election year. (Later, in Chapter 8, we will examine campaign financing by candidates themselves.) At the national level, contributions to the parties go to the Democratic and Republican National Committees, and to the Democratic and Republican House and Senatorial Committees (see Table 7.2).

The Partisan Tilt of Campaign Contributions The Republican Party has generally been able to raise and spend more money in each election cycle than the Democratic Party. But the dollar differences have narrowed over the years. Perhaps more interesting are the differences in sources of support for each party. Broken down by sector (as in Table 7.3), the Democratic Party relies more heavily on lawyers and law firms, on the TV, movie and music industry (Hollywood), teachers and public sector employee unions, and industrial and building trade unions. Business interests divide their contributions, but they tilt toward the Republican Party, notably the health-care industry, insurance, manufacturing, oil and gas, automotive, and general and special contractors.

Center for Responsive Politics
Source of information on campaign finances—contributor, recipients, PACs, lobbyists, etc.
www.opensecrets.org

Closing the Soft Money Loophole Prior to 2002, political contributions given directly to the Democratic and Republican parties were unlimited as to their

TABLE 7.2 Party Finances (million $)

	2004	2002	2000
Totals			
Democratic Party	$618	$463	$520
Republican Party	744	691	715
National Committees			
Dem. National Com.	299	162	260
Rep. National Com.	330	284	379
House Party Committees			
Dem. Cong. Camp. Com.	76	103	105
Nat'l Rep. Cong. Com.	156	211	145
Senate Party Committees			
Dem. Senatorial Camp. Com.	76	143	104
Nat'l Rep. Senatorial Camp.com.	69	125	96

Source: Federal Elections Commission

TABLE 7.3 Contributors to the Republican and Democratic Parties by Sector

Democratic Party	Republican Party
1. Lawyers/law firms	1. Real estate
2. Securities/investment	2. Health professionals
3. Real estate	3. Securities/investment
4. TV/movies/music	4. Lawyers/law firms
5. Business services	5. Insurance
6. Health professionals	6. Manufacturing/distributing
7. Education	7. Oil and gas
8. Lobbyists	8. Business services
9. Computers/Internet	9. General contractors
10. Insurance	10. Automotive
11. Public sector unions	11. Computers/Internet
12. Commercial banks	12. Commercial banks
13. Industrial unions	13. Special trade contractors
14. Building trade unions	14. Retail sales
15. Liberal/ideological	15. Food and beverage

Source: Center for Responsive Politics. Candidate committees, miscellaneous, and "retired" excluded from this table.

amounts. Nearly all **soft money** was raised in large contributions—indeed, the reason soft money was so popular with parties was that it allowed big donors to give without having to abide by the limits imposed on direct campaign contributions. Direct contributions to the candidates were referred to as "hard money" and limited as to the amount any individual could contribute. Technically, soft money was supposed to be used for party building, get-out-the-vote drives, or general party advertising ("Vote Democratic" or "Vote Republican"). But, in reality, both parties used their soft money in direct support of their candidates, rather than building the party.

But the Bipartisan Campaign Finance Reform Act of 2002 banned national party committees from accepting or spending unregulated soft money. Contributions to national party committees were limited to $2,000, the same limitation that applies to direct contributions to candidates (see "Rising Campaign Cash" in Chapter 8).

Parties as Organizers of Elections

Despite the erosion of many of their functions, America's political parties survive as the principal institutions for organizing elections. Party nominations organize electoral choice by narrowing the field of aspiring office seekers to the Democratic and Republican candidates in most cases. Very few independents or third-party candidates are elected to high political office in the United States. **Nonpartisan elections**—elections in which there are no party nominations and all candidates run without an official party label—are common only in local elections, for city council, country commission, school board, judgeships, and so on. Only Nebraska has nonpartisan elections for its unicameral (one-house) state legislature. Party conventions are still held in many states in every presidential year,

soft money Campaign contributions, not subject to regulated limits, given to a party for activities such as party building or voter registration, but not directly for campaigns. Soft-money contributions to national parties were banned in 2002.

nonpartisan elections Elections in which candidates do not officially indicate their party affiliation; often used for city, country, school board, and judicial elections.

Political parties as organizers of elections. (a) The Executive Committee of the Republican National Convention in Chicago in 1880. Conventions emerged as the main way for parties to select candidates in the nineteenth century. (b) Al Gore celebrates after winning the nation's first Republican primary in New Hampshire. Today, party candidates are determined by primary elections rather than by convention. (c) Parties also seek to attract voters through registration drives. (d) George W. Bush campaigning on his way to the Republican National Convention in Philadelphia. Parties provide the organizational structure for political campaigns.

but these conventions seldom have the power to determine the parties' nominees for public office.

Party Conventions Historically, party nominations were made by caucus or convention. The **caucus** was the earliest nominating process, party leaders (party chairs, elected officials, and "bosses") would simply meet several months before the election and decide on the party's nominee themselves. The early presidents— Thomas Jefferson, James Madison, James Monroe, and John Quincy Adams— were nominated by caucuses of Congress members. Complaints about the exclusion of people from this process led to nominations by convention—large meetings of delegates sent by local party organizations—starting in 1832. Andrew Jackson was the first president to be nominated by convention. The convention was considered more democratic than the caucus.

For nearly a century, party conventions were held at all levels of government— local, state, and national. City or country conventions included delegates from local **wards** and **precincts**, who nominated candidates for city or county office, for

caucus Nominating process in which party leaders select the party's nominee.

ward Division of a city for electoral or administrative purposes or as a unit for organizing political parties.

precinct Subdivision of a city, county, or ward for election purposes.

the state legislature, or even for the House of Representatives when a congressional district fell within the city or country. State conventions included delegates from counties, and they nominated governors, U.S. senators, and other statewide officers. State parties chose delegates to the Republican and Democratic national conventions every four years to nominate a president.

Party Primaries Today, primary elections have largely replaced conventions as the means of selecting the Democratic and Republican nominees for public office.[9] Primary elections, introduced as part of the progressive reform movement of the early twentieth century, allow the party's *voters* to choose the party's nominee directly. The primary election was designed to bypass the power of party organizations and party leaders and to further democratize the nomination process. It generally succeeded in doing so, but it also had the effect of seriously weakening political parties, since candidates seeking a party nomination need only appeal to party *voters*—not *leaders*—for support in the primary election.[10]

Types of Primaries There are some differences among the American states in how they conduct their primary elections.[11] **Closed primaries** allow only voters who have previously registered as Democrats or Republicans (or in some states voters who choose to register as Democrats or Republicans on primary election day) can cast a ballot in their chosen party's primary. Closed primaries tend to discourage people from officially registering as independents, even if they think of themselves as independent, because persons registered as independents cannot cast a ballot in either party's primary.

Open primaries allow voters to choose on election day which party primary they wish to participate in. Anyone, regardless of prior party affiliation, may choose to vote in either party's primary election. Voters simply request the ballot of one party or the other.[12] Open primaries provide opportunities for voters to cross over party lines and vote in the primary of the party they usually do not support. Opponents of open primaries have argued that these types of primary elections allow for **raiding**—organized efforts by one party to get its members to cross over to the opposition party's primary and defeat an attractive candidate and thereby improve the raiding party's chances of winning the general election. But there is little evidence to show that large numbers of voters connive in such a fashion.

Louisiana is unique in its nonpartisan primary elections. All candidates, regardless of their party affiliation, run in the same primary election. If a candidate gets over 50 percent of the vote, he or she wins the office, without appearing on the general election ballot. If no one receives over 50 percent of the primary election votes, then the top two vote-getters, regardless of party, face each other in the general election.

Some states hold a **runoff primary** when no candidate receives a majority or a designated percentage of the vote in the party's first primary election. A runoff primary is limited to the two highest vote-getters in the first primary. Runoff elections are more common in the southern United States. In most states, only a plurality of votes is needed to win a primary election.

General Elections Several months after the primaries and conventions, the **general election** (usually held in November, on the first Tuesday after the first Monday for presidential and most state elections) determines who will occupy elective office. Winners of the Democratic and Republican primary elections must face each other—and any independent or third-party candidates—in the general

closed primaries Primary elections in which voters must declare (or have previously declared) their party affiliation and can cast a ballot only in their own party's primary election.

open primaries Primary elections in which a voter may cast a ballot in either party's primary election.

raiding Organized efforts by one party to get its members to cross over in a primary and defeat an attractive candidate in the opposition party's primary.

runoff primary Additional primary held between the top two vote-getters in a primary where no candidate has received a majority of the vote.

general election Election to choose among candidates nominated by parties and/or independent candidates who gained access to the ballot by petition.

Primaries 2004: Democrats Seek "Electability"

The Democrats lost their two most popular presidential candidates even before the "pre-primary" when former Vice President Al Gore and New York Senator Hillary Clinton both announced that they would not seek their party's nomination. Both had led in Democratic opinion polls before their announcements. Their decisions to forego the race brought a small army of Democratic candidates into the race.

The "pre-primary" season began in earnest in August, 2003. Connecticut Senator Joe Lieberman initially led in name recognition but soon fell to fourth or fifth place as a battle progressed. Massachusetts Senator John Kerry and Missouri Congressman Dick Gephardt were getting double-digit numbers in the polls. Former NATO Commander General Wesley Clark also appeared to be a serious contender; he was rumored to be the choice of Bill and Hillary Clinton.

The Dean Bubble By early November the media began to focus on a little-known Vermont governor, Howard Dean. Dean separated himself from the other candidates with his heated opposition to the war in Iraq and his vitriolic attacks on President Bush. The media was entranced with his lurid anti-Bush rhetoric and his passionate "Hate Bush" followers. Dean was also successful in exploiting the Internet to tap into his most zealous followers to amass $50 million in campaign funds, the largest war chest of any Democratic candidate. But could money and passion win votes in the early primaries?

Iowa and New Hampshire Grass-roots Democrats in the Iowa caucuses and New Hampshire primary appeared unfazed by Dean's intensity or the media attention given him. Many admired his "raw meat" attacks on Bush, but more seemed committed to finding an "electable" Democrat. John Kerry's relatively low-key yet well-organized work in Iowa and New Hampshire paid off. He surprised the pundits, commentators, and pollsters with come-from-behind victories in both states. Dean was stunned. He reacted with a high-volume shouting speech which appeared to confirm the voters' notion that he was too emotional and perhaps too unstable for the presidency.

Front-loaded Victories Kerry's Iowa and New Hampshire victories gave him much-needed momentum for a series of Democratic primaries that had been moved up into February. By March 2nd, Kerry had effectively won the Democratic nomination. (He lost only to Clark in Oklahoma and Edwards in South Carolina.) His Democratic poll numbers skyrocketed. One by one his competitors dropped out. North Carolina Senator John Edwards ended up a distant second in the primary voting. Although Kerry's liberal voting record matched that of his mentor, Ted Kennedy, he appeared moderate in contrast to Dean. And perhaps the youthful-looking Edwards did not appear to have the necessary experience to win what Democrats expected to be a hard fought election. Kerry's Vietnam War heroism set him apart from the other candidates and reassured voters that he would be a capable Commander-in-Chief. (He had voted for the war in Iraq, but later criticized its execution.)

A Long Campaign The front loading of the primary season in 2004 produced a Democratic challenger to President Bush a full eight months before the general election in November. Kerry's victories reported in the media catapulted the Massachusetts Senator to near-even standing with Bush. Indeed, the Bush camp decided to begin running television campaign advertisements in early March. The stage was set for a long and brutal general election campaign.

election. Voters in the general election may choose any candidate, regardless of how they voted earlier in their party's primary or whether they voted in the primary at all.

Independent and minor-party candidates can get on the general election ballot, although the process is usually very difficult. Most states require independent candidates to file a petition with the signatures of several thousand registered voters. The number of signatures varies from state to state and office to office, but it may range up to 5 or 10 percent of *all* registered voters, a very large number that, in a big state especially, presents a difficult obstacle. The same petition requirements

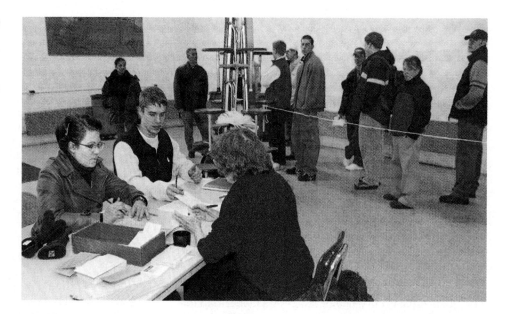

Voter turn-out among 18 to 21 year olds is lower than any other age group. Here, University of New Hampshire students register to vote in the 2000 election.

usually apply to minor parties, although some states automatically carry a minor party's nominee on the general election ballot if that party's candidate or candidates received a certain percentage (for example, 10 percent) of the vote in the previous general election.

Where's the Party?

The Democratic and Republican parties are found in different political arenas (see Figure 7.5). There is, first of all, the **party-in-the-electorate**—the voters who identify themselves as Democrats or Republicans and who tend to vote for the candidates of their party. The party-in-the-electorate appears to be in decline today. Party loyalties among voters are weakening. More people identify themselves as independents, and more **ticket splitters** divide their votes between candidates of different parties for different offices in the same general election, and more voters cast their ballots without regard to the party affiliation of the candidates than ever before.

The second locus of party activity is the **party-in-the-government**—officials who received their party's nomination and won the general election. The party-in-the-government includes members of Congress, state legislators and local government officials, and elected members of the executive branch, including the president and governors.

Party identification and loyalty among elected officeholders (the party-in-the-government) are generally stronger than party identification and loyalty among the party-in-the-electorate. Nevertheless, party loyalties among elected officials have also weakened over time. (We examine the role of parties in Congress in Chapter 9 and the president's party role in Chapter 10.)

Finally, there is the **party organization**—national and state party officials and workers, committee members, convention delegates, and others active in the party. The Democratic and Republican party organizations formally resemble the American federal system, with national committees, officers and staffs, and national conventions, 50 state committees, and more than 3,000 country committees with city, ward, and precinct levels under their supervision. State committees are not very

party-in-the-electorate
Voters who identify themselves with a party.

ticket splitter Person who votes for candidates of different parties for different offices in a general election.

party-in-the-government
Public officials who were nominated by their party and who identify themselves in office with their party.

party organization
National and state party officials and workers, committee members, convention delegates, and others active in the party.

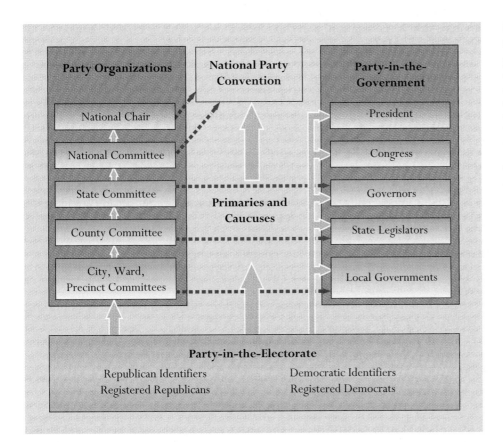

FIGURE 7.5 Where's the Party?

Even among Americans who strongly identify with a major party, there are differences among those who are strictly members of the party-in-the-electorate (voters), those who are members of the party-in-the-government (elected officials), and those who are members of the party organization (national and state party committee members).

responsive to the direction of the national committee; and in most states, city and country party organizations operate quite independently of the state committees. In other words, no real hierarchy of authority exists in American parties.

National Party Structure The Democratic and Republican national party conventions possess *formal* authority over the parties. They meet every four years not only to nominate candidates for president and vice president but also to adopt a party platform, choose party officers, and adopt rules for the party's operation. Because the convention is a large body that meets for only three or four days, however, its real function is to ratify decisions made by national party leaders, as well as to formally nominate presidential and vice presidential candidates.

The Democratic and Republican national committees, made up of delegates from each state and territory, are supposed to govern party affairs *between* conventions. But the *real* work of the national party organizations is undertaken by the national party chairs and staff. The national chair is officially chosen by the national committee but is actually chosen by the party's presidential candidate. If the party wins the presidency, the national chair usually serves as a liaison with the president for party affairs. If the party loses, the chair may be replaced before the next national convention. The national chair is supposed to be neutral in the party's primary battles, but when an incumbent president is seeking reelection, the national chair and staff lean very heavily in the president's favor.

State Party Organizations State party organizations consist of a state committee, a state chair who heads the committee, and a staff working at the state capital. Democratic and Republican state committees vary from state to state in

Election World
Links to party Web sites in many nations of the world, with latest election results.
www.electionsworld.org

composition, organization, and function. The state party chair is generally selected by the state committee, but this selection is often dictated by the party's candidate for governor. Membership on the state committee may range from about a dozen up to several hundred. The members may be chosen through party primaries or by state party conventions. Generally, representation on state committees is allocated by counties, but occasionally other units of government are recognized in state party organizations.

Most state party organizations maintain full-time staffs, including an executive director and public relations, fund-raising, and research people. These organizations help to raise campaign funds for their candidates, conduct registration drives, provide advice and services to their nominees, and even recruit candidates to run in election districts and for offices where the party would otherwise have no names on the ballot. Services to candidates may include advertising and media consulting, advice on election-law compliance, polling, research (including research on opponents), registration and voter identification, mailing lists, and even seminars on campaign techniques.

State committees are also supposed to direct the campaigns for important statewide elections—governors and U.S. senators. They are supposed to serve as central coordinating agencies for these election campaigns and as the party's principal fund-raising organization in the state. Today the role of the state committee is very often limited, however, because most candidates have their own campaign organizations.

Legislative Party Structures The parties organize the U.S. Senate and House of Representatives, and they organize most state legislatures as well. The majority party in the House meets in caucus to select the speaker of the house as well as the House majority leader and whip (see "Organizing Congress: Party and Leadership" in Chapter 10). The minority party elects its own minority leader and whip. The majority party in the Senate elects the president pro tempore, who presides during the (frequent) absences of the vice president, as well as the Senate majority leader and whip. The minority party in the Senate elects its own minority leader and whip. Committee assignments in both the House and the Senate are allocated on a party basis; committee chairs are always majority-party members.

County Committees The nation's 3,000 Republican and 3,000 Democratic county chairs probably constitute the most important building blocks in party organization in the nation. City and county party officers and committees are chosen in local primary elections; they cannot be removed by state or national party authorities.

National Party Conventions

The Democratic and Republican parties are showcased every four years at the national party **convention**. The official purpose of these four-day fun-filled events is the nomination of the presidential candidates and their vice presidential running mates. Yet the presidential choices have usually already been made in the parties' **presidential primaries** and caucuses earlier in the year. By midsummer convention time, delegates pledged to cast their convention vote for one or another of the presidential candidates have already been selected. Not since 1952, when the Democrats took three convention ballots to select Adlai Stevenson as their pres-

convention Nominating process in which delegates from local party organizations select the party's nominees.

presidential primaries Primary elections in the states in which voters in each party can choose a presidential candidate for its party's nomination. Outcomes help determine the distribution of pledged delegates to each party's national nominating convention.

idential candidate, has convention voting gone beyond the first ballot.[13] The possibility exists that in some future presidential race no candidate will win a majority of delegates in the primaries and caucuses, and the result will be a *brokered* convention in which delegates will exercise independent power to select the party nominee. But this event is unlikely.

The Democratic and Republican national conventions are really televised party rallies, designed to showcase the presidential nominee, confirm the nominee's choice for a running mate, and inspire television viewers to support the party and its candidates in the forthcoming general election. Indeed, the national party conventions are largely media events, carefully staged to present an attractive image of the party and its nominees. Party luminaries jockey for key time slots at the podium, and the party prepares slick videotaped commercials touting its nominee for prime-time presentation.

Convention Delegates Over time, the spread of presidential primary elections has taken the suspense out of the national party conventions. As late as 1968, fewer than half of the delegates were selected in primary elections. But today, the selection of more than 80 percent of pledged delegates by the party's primary voters has greatly diminished the role of party officials in presidential selection.

Both parties award **delegates** to each state in rough proportion to the number of party voters in the state. Democratic Party rules currently require that all popularly elected delegates from each state be awarded to the presidential candidates according to their proportion of that state's primary or caucus vote, after the candidates reach a 15 percent vote threshold. Republican Party rules allow states either to apportion their delegates according to the primary or caucus vote or to adopt a winner-take-all system of awarding all state delegates to the state's primary election victor.

Convention delegates are generally party activists, ideologically motivated and strongly committed to their presidential candidates. Democratic delegates are much more *liberal* than Democratic voters, and Republican delegates are more *conservative* than Republican voters (see Figure 7.6). There is a slight tendency for Democratic and Republican delegates to differ in social backgrounds, usually more African Americans, women, public employees, and union members are found among Democratic delegates than among Republican delegates.

delegates Accredited voting members of a party's national presidential nominating convention.

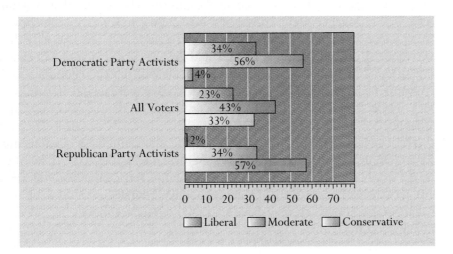

FIGURE 7.6 Ideologies of Voters versus Party Activists

Democratic and Republican party activists (convention delegates in 2000) are far more likely to hold divergent liberal and conservative views than voters generally.

Source: As reported in the *New York Times*, August 14, 2000.

Making Party Rules National party conventions make rules for the party, including rules governing the selection of delegates at the next party convention. Democrats are especially likely to focus on delegate selection rules. In 1972 the Democratic Party responded to charges that African Americans, women, and other minorities were underrepresented among the delegates by appointing a special commission chaired by Senator George McGovern to "reform" the party. The McGovern Commission took "affirmative steps" to ensure that the next convention would include "goals" for the representation of African Americans, women, and other minorities among the delegates in proportion to their presence in the Democratic electorate. The effect of these reforms was to reduce the influence of Democratic officeholders (members of Congress, governors, state legislators, and mayors) at the convention and to increase the influence of ideologically motivated activists. Later rule changes eliminated the *unit vote,* in which all delegates from a state were required to vote with the majority of the state's delegation and which required that all delegates who were pledged to a candidate vote for that candidate unless *released* by the candidate.

Then, in the 1980s, the Democratic Leadership Council pressed the party to reserve some convention delegate seats for **superdelegates**—elected officials and party leaders not bound to one candidate—with the expectation that these delegates would be more moderate than the liberal party activists. The notion was that the superdelegates would inject more balanced, less ideological political judgments into convention deliberations, thus improving the party's chances of victory in the general elections. As a result, many Democratic senators, governors, and members of Congress now attend the convention as superdelegates. If presidential candidates ever fail to win a majority of delegates in the primaries, these superdelegates may some day control a nomination.

Party Platforms National conventions also write party **platforms**, setting out the party's goals and policy positions. Because a party's platform is not binding on its nominees, platform *planks* are largely symbolic, although they often provide heated arguments and provide distinct differences between the parties to present to voters (see *Up Close:* "Democratic and Republican Platforms: Can You Tell the Difference?").

Selecting a Running Mate Perhaps the only suspense remaining in national party conventions centers on the presidential nominee's choice of a vice presidential running mate. Even a presidential candidate who has decided on a running mate well in advance of the convention may choose to wait until the convention to announce the choice, otherwise there would be little real "news value" to the convention, and the television networks would give less coverage to it. By encouraging speculation about who the running mate will be, the candidate and the convention manager can sustain media interest. (For a discussion of various strategies in selecting a running mate, see "The Vice Presidential Waiting Game" in Chapter 11.)

The convention *always* accepts the presidential candidate's recommendation for a running mate. No formal rules require the convention to do so, but it would be politically unacceptable for the convention to override the first important decision of the party's presidential nominee. Convention delegates set aside any personal reservations they may have and unanimously endorse the presidential nominee's choice.

superdelegates Delegates to the Democratic Party national convention selected because of their position in the government or the party and not pledged to any candidate.

platform Statement of principles adopted by a political party at its national convention (specific portions of the platform are known as planks); a platform is not binding on the party's candidates.

Democratic and Republican Platforms: Can You Tell the Difference?

Iraq

A "We cannot allow a failed state in Iraq that inevitably would become a haven for terrorists and a destabilizing force in the Middle East."

B ". . . today there are more than 50 million newly freed people in the nation of Afghanistan and Iraq—America is safer."

Taxes

A "We will roll back the tax cuts for those making more than $200,000."

B "Tax reform is necessary to achieve tax simplicity, efficiency, fairness, and predictability. . . . In particular we must: Make the tax relief of 2001 and 2003 permanent."

Foreign Policy

A "They rush to force before exhausting diplomacy. They bully rather than persuade. They act alone when they could assemble a team."

B "We are defending the peace by taking the fight to the enemy. We are confronting terrorists overseas so that we do not have to confront them here at home."

Health-care

A "We will offer individuals and businesses tax credits to make quality, reliable health coverage more affordable."

B "Enact Health Savings Accounts which allow individuals to save and pay for their health-care tax free."

Social Security

A "We are absolutely committed to preserving Social Security."

B "Social Security needs to be strengthened and enhanced for our children and grandchildren . . . Each of today's workers should be free to direct a portion of their payroll taxes to personal investments for their retirement."

Other

A "Their energy policy is simple: government by big oil, of big oil, and for big oil."

B "We will curb the burden of frivolous lawsuits . . . One of their nominees made his fortune as a trial lawyer . . . They offer no hope for reform of this badly broken system."

A "We will raise the minimum wage to $7.00."

B "We strongly support the policy that prevents taxpayers dollars from being used to encourage the future destruction of human embryos."

A "We will create new jobs and protect existing ones by ending tax breaks for companies that ship jobs overseas."

B "We support legislation requiring a supermajority vote in both houses of Congress to raise taxes."

Source: Excerpts from Democratic [A] and Republican [B] party platforms, 2004.

party identification Self-described identification with a political party, usually in response to the question, "Generally speaking, how would you identify yourself: as a Republican, Democrat, independent, or something else?"

dealignment Declining attractiveness of the parties to the voters, a reluctance to identify strongly with a party, and a decrease in reliance on party affiliation in voter choice.

Campaign Kickoff The final evening of the national conventions is really the kickoff for the general election campaign. The presidential nominee's acceptance speech tries to set the tone for the fall campaign. Party celebrities, including defeated presidential candidates, join hands at the podium as a symbol of party unity. Presidential and vice presidential candidates, spouses, and families assemble under balloons and streamers, amid the happy noise and hoopla, to signal the start of the general election campaign. . . . TV coverage helps provide the parties with small postconvention "bumps" in the polls.[14]

Party Voters

Traditionally, the Democratic Party has been able to claim to be the majority party in the United States (see Figure 7.7). In opinion polls, those who "identify" with the Democratic Party generally outnumber those who "identify" with the Republican Party. (**Party identification** is determined by response to the question, "Generally speaking, how would you identify yourself: as a Republican, Democrat, independent, or something else?") But the Democratic Party advantage among the voters eroded over time, partly as a result of a gradual increase in the number of people who call themselves independents.

Dealignment **Dealignment** describes the decline in attractiveness of the political parties to the voters, the growing reluctance of people to identify themselves with either party, and a decrease in reliance on a candidate's party affiliation

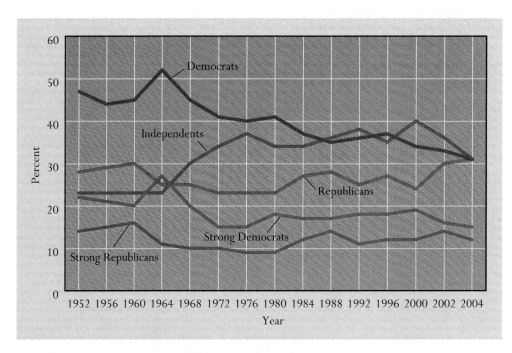

FIGURE 7.7 Party Identification in the Electorate

For many years, the Democratic Party enjoyed a substantial lead in party identification among voters. This Democratic lead eroded in the late 1960s as more people began to identify themselves as independents. Independent identification suggests that many voters have become disillusioned with both parties. Relatively few people consider themselves "strong" Democrats or Republicans.

Source: Data from *National Election Studies,* University of Michigan.

in voter choice. Dealignment is evident not only in the growing numbers of self-described independents but also in the declining numbers of those who identify themselves as "strong" Democrats or Republicans. In short, the electorate is less partisan than it once was.

Party Loyalty in Voting Despite the decline in partisan identification in the electorate, it is important to note that *party identification is a strong influence in voter choice in elections.* Most voters cast their ballot for the candidate of their party. This is true in presidential elections (see Figure 7.8) and even more true in congressional and state elections. Those who identify themselves as Democrats are somewhat more likely to vote for a Republican presidential candidate than those who

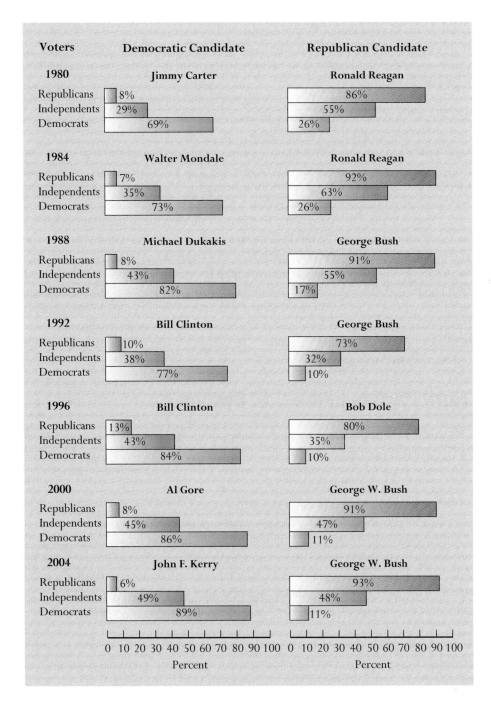

Voters	Democratic Candidate	Republican Candidate
1980	**Jimmy Carter**	**Ronald Reagan**
Republicans	8%	86%
Independents	29%	55%
Democrats	69%	26%
1984	**Walter Mondale**	**Ronald Reagan**
Republicans	7%	92%
Independents	35%	63%
Democrats	73%	26%
1988	**Michael Dukakis**	**George Bush**
Republicans	8%	91%
Independents	43%	55%
Democrats	82%	17%
1992	**Bill Clinton**	**George Bush**
Republicans	10%	73%
Independents	38%	32%
Democrats	77%	10%
1996	**Bill Clinton**	**Bob Dole**
Republicans	13%	80%
Independents	43%	35%
Democrats	84%	10%
2000	**Al Gore**	**George W. Bush**
Republicans	8%	91%
Independents	45%	47%
Democrats	86%	11%
2004	**John F. Kerry**	**George W. Bush**
Republicans	6%	93%
Independents	49%	48%
Democrats	89%	11%

0 10 20 30 40 50 60 70 80 90 100   0 10 20 30 40 50 60 70 80 90 100
Percent   Percent

FIGURE 7.8

Republican, Democratic, and Independent Voters in Presidential Elections

As the percentages here indicate, in recent years registered Democrats have been more likely to "cross over" and vote for a Republican candidate for president than registered Republicans have been to vote for the Democratic presidential candidate.

Source: New York Times.

identify themselves as Republicans are to vote for a Democratic presidential candidate. Republican Ronald Reagan was able to win more than one-quarter of self-identified Democrats in 1980 and 1984, earning these crossover voters the label "Reagan Democrats."[15]

Realignment? Although Democratic Party loyalty has eroded over the last thirty years, it is not clear whether or not this erosion is a classic party **realignment**.[16] Most scholars agree that party realignments occurred in the presidential elections of 1824 (Jackson, Democrats), 1860 (Lincoln, Republicans), 1896 (Bryan, Democrats), and 1932 (Roosevelt, Democrats). This historical sequence gave rise to a theory that realigning elections occur every thirty-six years. According to this theory, the election of 1968 should have been a realigning one. It is true that Richard Nixon's 1968 victory marked the beginning of a 24-year Republican era in presidential election victories that was broken only by Jimmy Carter in 1976. But there was relatively little shifting of the party loyalties of major social groups, and the Democratic Party remained the dominant party in the electorate and in Congress.

The Democratic Party still receives *disproportionate* support from Catholics, Jews, African Americans, less educated and lower income groups, blue-collar workers, union members, and big-city residents. The Republican Party still receives *disproportionate* support from Protestants, whites, more educated and higher income groups, white-collar workers, nonunion workers, and suburban and small-town dwellers (see *Up Close:* "The Donkeys and the Elephant"). Disproportionate support does not mean these groups *always* give a majority of their votes to the indicated party, but only that they give that party a larger percentage of their votes than the party receives from the general electorate. This pattern of social-group voting and party identification has remained relatively stable over the years, even though the GOP has made some gains among many of the traditionally Democratic groups (see Figure 7.9). The only major *shift* in social-group support has occurred among southern whites. This group has shifted from heavily Democratic in party identification to a substantial Republican preference. Thus it is questionable whether a true party realignment has occurred[17] (see *Across the USA:* "Democratic and Republican Party Strength in the States").

Third Parties in the U.S. System

Despite the cultural and electoral barriers to victory, **third parties**, more accurately called minor parties, are a common feature of American politics. These parties can be roughly classified by the role they play in the political system.

Ideological Parties Ideological parties exist to promote an ideology rather than to win elections. They use the electoral process to express their views and to rally activists to their cause, and they measure success not by victory at the polls but by their ability to bring their name and their views to the attention of the American public. The socialist parties, which have run candidates in virtually every presidential election in this century, are prime examples of ideological parties in the United States (see also *Up Close:* "The Libertarian Party: A Dissenting Voice").

Protest Parties Protest parties arise around popular issues or concerns that the major parties have failed to address. An important historical example of a protest party is the Populist Party of the late 1800s. It arose as a protest by mid-

---

realignment Long-term shift in social-group support for various political parties that creates new coalitions in each party.

third party Political party that challenges the two major parties in an election.

ideological party Third party that exists to promote an ideology rather than to win elections.

THINK AGAIN

Do we need a third party to challenge the Republican and Democratic parties?

Libertarian Party
This Web site reflects the Libertarian Party's strong ideological commitments to individual liberty, free markets, and nonintervention in world affairs. *www.lp.org*

protest party Third party that arises in response to issues of popular concern which have not been addressed by the major parties.

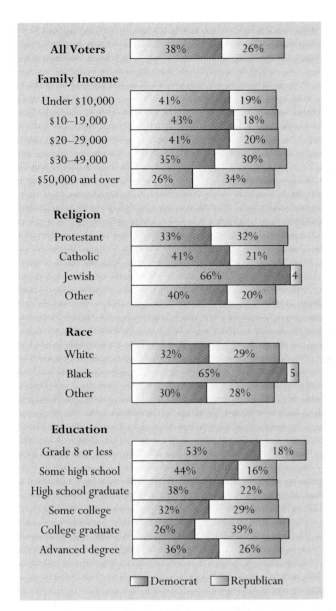

All Voters

	Democrat	Republican
All Voters	38%	26%

Family Income

	Democrat	Republican
Under $10,000	41%	19%
$10–19,000	43%	18%
$20–29,000	41%	20%
$30–49,000	35%	30%
$50,000 and over	26%	34%

Religion

	Democrat	Republican
Protestant	33%	32%
Catholic	41%	21%
Jewish	66%	4
Other	40%	20%

Race

	Democrat	Republican
White	32%	29%
Black	65%	5
Other	30%	28%

Education

	Democrat	Republican
Grade 8 or less	53%	18%
Some high school	44%	16%
High school graduate	38%	22%
Some college	32%	29%
College graduate	26%	39%
Advanced degree	36%	26%

☐ Democrat   ☐ Republican

FIGURE 7.9 Social-Group Support for the Democratic and Republican Parties

The Democratic Party draws disproportionate support from low-income, less educated, Catholic, Jewish, and African American voters. The Republican Party relies more heavily on support from high-income, college-educated, white Protestant voters.

Source: Data from *National Election Studies,* University of Michigan.

western farmers against eastern railroads, "trusts" and monopolies, and the gold standard. The Populists threatened to capture the wave of popular support for railroad regulation, cheap money, and anti-monopoly legislation, and thus they endangered the established Democratic and Republican parties. But when the Democratic Party nominated William Jennings Bryan in 1896, the Populist Party officially endorsed Bryan and temporarily disappeared as a significant independent political organization. Populist ideas were set forth again in a new Progressive Party, which nominated Robert M. La Follette for president in 1924; the Democratic and Republican parties both nominated conservative candidates that year, helping La Follette to win almost 17 percent of the popular vote.

Not all major protest movements have been accompanied by the formation of third parties. Indeed, protest leaders have often argued that a third-party effort distracts the movement from a more effective strategy of capturing control of one or both of the major parties. The labor-union-organizing movement of the 1930s and the civil rights and antiwar movements of the 1960s did not spark a separate

Democratic and Republican Party Strength in the States

The Democratic and Republican parties compete in every state. But sectionalism is evident in the "Republican L"—the strength of the Republican party in the Mountain and Southern states. The Democratic Party is becoming bicoastal—strong in the Northeast and the Pacific Coast. Of the four largest states, California and New York lean Democratic, while Texas and Florida lean Republican.

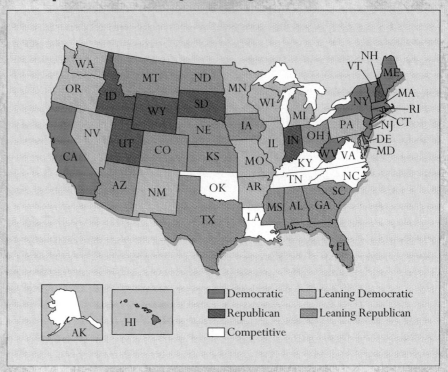

Democratic
Republican
Competitive
Leaning Democratic
Leaning Republican

third party but instead worked largely *within* the dominant Democratic Party to advance their goals.

Single-Issue Parties **Single-issue parties** have frequently formed around a particular cause. Single-issue parties are much like protest parties, although somewhat narrower in their policy focus. The Greenback Party of the late 1800s shared with the Populists a desire for cheap inflated currency in order to ease the burden of debt and mortgage payments by farmers. But the Greenback Party focused on a single remedy: an end to the gold standard and the issuance of cheap currency—"greenbacks."

Perhaps the most persistent of minor parties over the years has been the Prohibition Party. It achieved temporary success with the passage of the Eighteenth Amendment to the U.S. Constitution in 1919, which prohibited the manufacture, sale, or transportation of "intoxicating liquors," only to see its "noble experiment" fail and be repealed by the Twenty-first Amendment.

Today the Green Party provides an example of a single-issue party, with its primary emphasis on environmental protection. However, the Green Party itself contends that it is "part of the worldwide movement that promotes ecological wisdom, social justice, grassroots democracy and non-violence."

Splinter Parties Finally, many third parties in American politics are really **splinter parties**, parties formed by a dissatisfied faction of a major party. Splinter

WWW Green Party
Although centered on the issue of "ecological wisdom," the Green web site also promotes "grassroots democracy," "social justice," "peace," "feminism," and "diversity." *www.greens.org*

single-issue party Third party formed around one particular cause.

splinter party Third party formed by a dissatisfied faction of a major party.

The Libertarian Party: A Dissenting Voice

Would you like to see the federal income tax repealed; the Internal Revenue Service abolished; foreign aid ended; all U.S. troops brought home from overseas; and individual choice "in all matters," from abortion to gun control to drug use? Would you like to eliminate government farm subsidies; end federal support for public broadcasting, science, and the arts; and "privatize" education and "charitize" welfare? These are the campaign promises of the Libertarian Party, whose presidential candidates' names appeared on the ballot in all fifty states in 1992, 1996, and 2000.

The Libertarian Party is unique in its uncompromising commitment to the classical liberal, eighteenth-century ideals of John Locke and Adam Smith. Libertarians oppose all interference by government in the private lives of citizens. They support unregulated free markets and the protection of private property rights. Thus they oppose environmental regulations, consumer protection laws, and laws that infringe on private property or "take" property for government use without just compensation to owners. They also oppose government efforts to regulate private morals—including laws outlawing drug use, prostitution, gambling, and pornography—believing these activities should be the exclusive choice of consenting individuals. Libertarians are strict noninterventionists in International affairs; they are opposed to the North Atlantic Treaty Organization (NATO) alliance, to foreign aid, to military involvements outside of U.S. territory, and to virtually all spending for national defense.

Although the Libertarian Party candidate for president regularly receives less than 1 percent of the popular vote, Libertarian ideas have entered the nation's policy debates and influenced both major parties. Republican candidates have frequently adopted Libertarian arguments on behalf of deregulation of market activities; Democratic candidates frequently use Libertarian arguments about individual "choice" in the areas of abortion, school prayer, and homosexual activity. And both the Democratic and the Republican parties have vocal "isolationist" wings that borrow Libertarian, noninterventionist arguments against foreign aid, international alliances, and military expenditures. Thus the Libertarian Party, like other ideological parties, functions to promote ideas rather than win elections.

---

parties may form around a particular individual, as did the Progressive (Bull Moose) Party of Theodore Roosevelt in 1912. As a popular former president, Teddy Roosevelt won more than 27 percent of the popular vote, outpolling Republican candidate William Howard Taft but allowing Democrat Woodrow Wilson to win the presidency.

Splinter parties also may emerge from an intense intraparty policy dispute. For example, in 1948 the States' Rights (Dixiecrat) Party formed in protest to the civil rights (fair employment practices) plan in the Democratic Party platform of that year and nominated Strom Thurmond for president. In 1968 George Wallace's American Independent Party won nearly 14 percent of the popular vote. Wallace attacked school desegregation and busing to achieve racial balance in schools, as well as crime in the streets, welfare "cheats," and meddling federal judges and bureaucrats. He abandoned his third-party organization in 1972 to run in the Democratic presidential primary elections. Following some Democratic primary victories, he was shot and disabled for life.

Third Party Prospects In recent years, polls have reported that a majority of Americans favor the idea of a third party. But support for the *general* idea of a third party has never been matched by voter support for *specific* third-party or independent presidential candidates (see Table 7.4). Moreover, it is very difficult for a third party or independent candidate to win electoral votes (see *Up Close:*

Ralph Nader, the nation's most visible interest-group entrepreneur, continues his fight against auto companies, speaking here to Toledo residents unhappy with tax breaks given to Daimler-Chrysler to keep its plant in the city. In the 2000 presidential election, Nader was the Green Party's nominee. But he lost the Green nomination in 2004 and ran as an independent.

"Understanding the Electoral College" in Chapter 8). Only Theodore Roosevelt, Robert M. La Follette, and George C. Wallace managed to win any electoral votes in the past century. The Reform Party, founded by billionaire Ross Perot in 1992, was the latest serious attempt to create a nationwide third-party (see *Up Close* "The Rise and Fall of the Reform Party").

Why the Two-Party System Persists

The two-party system is deeply ingrained in American politics. Although third parties have often made appearances in presidential elections, no third-party candidate has ever won the Oval Office. (Lincoln's new Republican Party in 1860

TABLE 7.4 Twentieth-Century Third-Party Presidential Votes

Third-Party Presidential Candidates	Popular Vote (percentage)	Electoral Votes (number)
Theodore Roosevelt (1912), Progressive (Bull Moose) Party	27.4%	88
Robert M. La Follette (1924), Progressive Party	16.6	13
George C. Wallace (1968), American Independent Party	13.5	46
John Anderson (1980), Independent	6.6	0
Ross Perot (1992), Independent	18.9	0
Ross Perot (1996), Reform Party	8.5	0
Ralph Nader (2000), Green Party	2.7	0
Ralph Nader (2004) Independent	0.4	0

The Rise and Fall of the Reform Party

While anyone with a Web site can create a virtual political party, establishing a new *national* party with a place on the general election ballot in all fifty states is a monumental task. It requires $100 million or more and tens of thousands of working supporters throughout the nation. It is a task fit only for an eccentric, energetic, media-wise billionaire.

When the pint-sized Texas billionaire Ross Perot first announced on *Larry King Live* in 1992 that he intended to run for president, he was not taken very seriously in Washington. But he quickly motivated tens of thousands of supporters in a grass-roots effort, "United We Stand," that succeeded in placing his name on ballot in all fifty states. He used his own money, nearly $100 million, to build a nationwide organization. Early in the campaign his poll numbers mushroomed to 35 percent, higher than any independent candidate's support in the history of modern polling. His twangy Texas quotes activated audiences. His political support came mostly from the center of the political spectrum—people who identified themselves as independent rather than as Democrats or Republicans Perot participated in the first three-way presidential television debates, and won 19 percent of popular vote in the general election, the highest percentage won by a third-party candidate since Teddy Roosevelt in 1912. But Perot's voters were spread across the nation and therefore he failed to win a single electoral vote.

But the temperamental tycoon proceeded to turn his independent "United We Stand" organization into a political party—the Reform Party. The party not only enjoyed ballot access in all of the states, but because of Perot's 1992 vote showing, the Reform Party qualified for federal campaign matching funds in 1996 and again in 2000. Perot's popular support in early polls in 1996 languished and he was given little chance of winning any state's electoral votes. He was excluded from the presidential debates. On Election Day he won fewer than half of the votes (9 percent) that he had garnered four years earlier, and again failed to win any state's electoral votes.

The Reform Party imploded at a raucus midsummer 2000 convention with rival factions almost coming to blows over control of the microphone. Firebrand conservative commentator Pat Buchanan appeared to control a majority of the delegates. But Perot followers, as well as Minnesota Governor Jesse Ventura, viewed Buchanan's candidacy as a hostile takeover of the Reform Party. The Federal Election Commission recognized Buchanan as the official nominee and awarded him the $12.6 million due to the Reform Party based on Perot's vote total in 1996. But Buchanan's right-wing rhetoric attracted less than 1 percent of the voters. Running on the Green Party, Ralph Nader outpolled the Reform Party and its future was left in doubt.

By 2004 some states dropped the Reform Party from their ballots. Ralph Nader laid claim to their ballot status in other states. But the Reform Party no longer functioned as a national party.

---

might be counted as an exception, but it quickly became a major party.) Very few third-party candidates have won seats in Congress. Many other democracies have multiple-party systems, so the question arises as to why the United States has had a two-party system throughout its history.[18] (See *Compared to What?* "Canada's Multiparty Systems.")

Cultural Consensus One explanation of the nation's two-party system focuses on the broad consensus supporting the American political culture (see Chapter 2). The values of democracy, capitalism, free enterprise, individual liberty, religious freedom, and equality of opportunity are so widely shared that no party challenging these values has ever won much of a following. There is little support in the American political culture for avowedly fascist, communist, authoritarian, or other antidemocratic parties. Moreover, the American political culture includes a strong belief in the separation of church and state. Political parties with religious affiliations, common in European democracies, are absent from American politics. Socialist parties have frequently appeared on the scene under various labels—the

Reform Party
The Reform Party site provides information about founder Ross Perot and the principles of and news about the party.
www.reformparty.org

Canada's Multiparty System

Canada's governing House of Commons is currently composed of 301 constituencies, or "ridings," in that nation's ten provinces and two territories. They are allocated to the provinces and territories roughly in accordance with population. The winner (by plurality, not necessarily majority) of a parliamentary election is seated in the House of Commons as Member of Parliament or "MP." The party that wins the largest number of seats in the general election forms the "Government," that is, it names the Prime Minister and the Cabinet.

Currently there are five parties represented in the House of Commons. The majority party is the Liberal Party, whose leader, Paul Martin, is the Prime Minister. The Liberal Party pledges itself to "human dignity, responsibility, and individual freedom, within the framework of a just society . . . the enhancement of our unique and diverse cultural community, recognition of Canada's two official languages, and preservation of the Canadian identity in a global society." The Liberal Party came to power in 1997.

Traditionally, the opposition to the Liberal Party was provided by the Progressive Conservative Party. The Progressive Conservatives regularly call for cuts in taxes, a balanced budget, and less red tape in government. But both the Liberal and Progressive Conservative parties are more liberal in their programs and policies than either the Democratic or Republican party in the United States.

Recently, Canadian conservatives, particularly those from the western provinces, created a new political party to replace their Reform Party. This new party, the Canadian Alliance, presents itself as a truly conservative party, and a party that opposes the "disintegration" of Canada—that is, the increasingly separatist views of French-speaking Canadians particularly in the province of Quebec.

The Bloc Québécois is devoted to the achievement of sovereignty for Quebec. It advocates "the promotion of a national identity based on a common language, French, a specific culture and history and the territory of Quebec." Once Quebec sovereignty has been achieved, then the Bloc Québécois is prepared to enter into a partnership agreement with the other provinces of Canada. The Bloc pledges to respect the rights of the English-speaking minority in Quebec.

The New Democratic Party advocates an even stronger role for government in the economy than the Liberal Party and an even more comprehensive social welfare system. It also supports "an agenda for women's equality," "gay and lesbian rights," "equity and access for persons with disabilities," and respect for "aboriginal treaty rights." Perhaps even more controversial is its opposition to American influence in Canadian affairs, including its opposition to the North American Free Trade Agreement (NAFTA).

Canada's multiparty system allows voters to align themselves more closely with their preferred political views. But a multiparty system may also someday prevent a majority party from controlling the government. The result may be either new elections or the creation of a coalition of minority parties, each sharing some Cabinet positions. Moreover, Canada's multiparty system has accentuated regional and language differences—the more conservative western provinces versus the more liberal eastern provinces, the separatist movement in Quebec, and the continuing battles over language, French versus English.

Socialist Party, the Socialist Labor Party, and the Socialist Workers Party. But the largest popular vote ever garnered by a socialist candidate in a presidential election was the 6 percent won by Eugene V. Debs in 1912. In contrast, socialist parties have frequently won control of European governments.

On broad policy issues, most Americans cluster near the center. This general consensus tends to discourage multiple parties. There does not appear to be sufficient room for them to stake out a position on the ideological spectrum that would detach voters from the two major parties.

This cultural explanation blends with the influence of historical precedents. The American two-party system has gained acceptance through custom. The nation's first party system developed from two coalitions, Federalists and Anti-Federalists, and this dual pattern has been reinforced over two centuries.

Winner-Take-All Electoral System Yet another explanation of the American two-party system focuses on the electoral system itself. Winners in presidential and congressional elections, as well as in state gubernatorial and legislative elections, are usually determined by a plurality, winner-take-all vote. Even in elections that require a majority of more than 50 percent to win—which may involve a runoff election—only one party's candidate wins in the end. Because of the winner-take-all nature of U.S. elections, parties and candidates have an overriding incentive to broaden their appeal to a plurality or majority of voters. Losers come away empty-handed. There is not much incentive in such a system for a party to form to represent the views of 5 or 10 percent of the electorate.

Americans are so accustomed to winner-take-all elections that they seldom consider alternatives. In some countries, legislative bodies are elected by **proportional representation,** whereby all voters cast a single ballot for the party of their choice and legislative seats are then apportioned to the parties in proportion to their total vote in the electorate. Minority parties are assured of legislative seats, perhaps with as little as 10 or 15 percent of the vote. If no party wins 50 percent of the votes and seats, the parties try to form a coalition of parties to establish control of the government. In these nations, party coalition building to form a governing majority occurs *after* the election rather than *before* the election, as it does in winner-take-all elections systems.

Legal Access to the Ballot Another factor in the American two-party system may be electoral system barriers to third parties. The Democratic and Republican nominees are automatically included on all general election ballots, but third-party and independent candidates face difficult obstacles in getting their names listed. In presidential elections, a third-party candidate must meet the varied requirements of fifty separate states to appear on their ballots along with the Democratic and Republican nominees. These requirements often include filing petitions signed by up to 5 or 10 percent of registered voters. In addition, states require third parties to win 5 or 10 percent of the vote in the last election in order to retain their position on the ballot in subsequent elections. In 1980 independent John Anderson gained access to the ballot in all fifty states, as did independent Ross Perot in 1992. But just doing so required a considerable expenditure of effort and money that the major parties were able to avoid.

proportional representation
Electoral system that allocates seats in a legislature based on the proportion of votes each party receives in a national election.

SUMMARY NOTES

- Organization grants advantage in the struggle for power. Political parties organize individuals and groups to exercise power in democracies by winning elected office.

- Political parties are not mentioned in the U.S. Constitution, yet they have played a central role in American political history. Major party realignments have occurred at critical points in American history, as major social groups shifted their political loyalties.

- In theory, political parties are "responsible" organizations that adopt a principled platform, recruit candidates who support the platform, educate the public about it, direct

an issue-oriented campaign, and then organize the legislature and ensure that their candidates enact the party's platform.

- But in the American two-party system, winning office by appealing to the large numbers of people at the center of the political spectrum becomes more important than promoting strong policy positions. American parties cannot bind elected officials to campaign promises anyway.

- American parties have lost many of their traditional functions over time. Party nominations are won by individual candidates in primary elections rather than through selection by party leaders. Most political candidates are self-selected, they organize their own campaigns. Television has replaced the party as the principal means of educating the public. And government bureaucracies, not party machines, provide social services.

■ Party nominations are won in primary elections as earlier caucus and convention methods of nomination have largely disappeared. Party primary elections in the various states may be open or closed and may or may not require runoff primaries. The nominees selected in each party's primary election then battle each other in the general election.

■ The parties battle in three major arenas. The *party-in-the-electorate* refers to party identification among voters. The *party-in-the-government* refers to party identification and organization among elected officials. The *party organization* refers to party offices at the local, state, and national levels.

■ The Democratic and Republican parties are structured to include national party conventions, national committees with chairs and staff, congressional party organizations, state committees, and county and local committees.

■ Since presidential nominations are now generally decided in primary elections—with pledged delegates selected

before the opening of the national conventions and with party platforms largely symbolic and wholly unenforceable on the candidates—the conventions have become largely media events designed to kick off the general election campaign.

■ *Dealignment* refers to a decline in the attractiveness of the parties to the voters, a growing reluctance of people to identify strongly with either party, and greater voter willingness to cross party lines. Despite dealignment, party identification remains a strong influence in voter choice.

■ Opinion polls indicate that most Americans support the general idea of a third party, but throughout the twentieth century no third-party presidential candidate won very many votes.

■ In the United States, many aspects of the political system—including cultural consensus, the winner-take-all electoral system, and legal restrictions to ballot access—place major obstacles in the way of success for third parties and independent candidates. Although never successful at gaining federal office in significant numbers, ideological, protest, single-issue, and splinter third parties have often been effective at getting popular issues on the federal agenda.

KEY TERMS

SUGGESTED READINGS

Beck, Paul, and Marjorie Hershey. *Party Politics in America.* 10th ed. New York: Longman, 2003. An authoritative text on the American party system—party organizations, the parties-in-government, and the parties-in-the-electorate.

Downs, Anthony. *An Economic Theory of Democracy.* New York: Harper & Row, 1957. The classic work describing rational choice winning strategies for political parties and explaining why there is no incentive for vote-maximizing parties in a two-party system to adopt widely separate policy positions.

Keefe, William J. *Parties, Politics, and Public Policy in America.* 9th ed. Washington, D.C.: CQ Press, 2003. A comprehensive survey of American political parties, from the nominating process to campaign finance and the changing affiliations of voters.

Lowi, Theodore E., and Joseph Romange. *Debating the Two Party System.* Boulder, Colo.: Rowman & Littlefield, 1997. Lowi argues that the two-party system is no longer adequate to represent the people of a diverse nation; Romange counters that two parties help unify the country and instruct Americans about the value of compromise.

Rosenstone, Steven J., Roy L. Behr, and Edward H. Lazarus. *Third Parties in America.* 2nd ed. Princeton, N.J.: Princeton University Press, 1996. A review of the history of third parties in American politics with an analysis of the various causes of third-party movements.

Wattenberg, Martin P. *The Decline of American Political Parties, 1952–1992.* Cambridge, Mass.: Harvard University Press, 1994. An authoritative discussion of increasing negative attitudes toward the parties and the growing dealignment in the electorate.

White, John Kenneth and Daniel M. Shen. *New Party Politics.* 2nd ed. Belmont, Calif.:, Wordsworth, 2004. Historical approach to evolution of the American party system.

MAKE IT REAL

THE GREAT AMERICAN DIVIDE

Following the 1932 election, the New Deal Democrats—a new coalition of union households, immigrant workers, and people hurt by the Great Depression—established a voting base which dominated the Congress until Newt Gingrich led the Republican Revolution in 1994. Now, as memories of the New Deal fade and the agenda of American politics shifts, the alignments of the 1930s and 1940s hold less and less relevance. The Democrats will need to create a new voting base if it hopes to return to power. In this simulation, you will study the factors that led to the 1932 election and then try to decide where the Democrats had their support in the 2000 election.

THE POLITICAL HORIZON

Every four years, during the presidential election season, the parties write their platforms, which delineate their principles and policy position and proposals. While these platforms are not binding on individual candidates, they are a good indicator of what that party considers important. This simulation contains two parts, in the first part you can explore which party holds views closest to your own. In the second part you can test your knowledge of the issue positions espoused by the various parties.

8

CAMPAIGNS AND ELECTIONS:
DECIDING WHO GOVERNS

THINK
ABOUT POLITICS

1 Should elected officials be bound by their campaign promises?
Yes ● No ●

2 Do you think that personal ambition, rather than civic duty, motivates most politicians?
Yes ● No ●

3 Do career politicians serve their constituents better than those who go into politics for just a short time?
Yes ● No ●

4 Should people vote on the basis of a candidate's personal character rather than his or her policy positions?
Yes ● No ●

5 Would you vote for a candidate who used negative ads to discredit an opponent?
Yes ● No ●

6 Do political campaign contributions have too much influence on elections and government policy?
Yes ● No ●

7 Are high campaign costs discouraging good people from becoming candidates?
Yes ● No ●

8 Should presidents be elected by direct popular vote?
Yes ● No ●

What real power do you have in a democracy? By casting ballots, citizens in a democracy have the power to determine who will represent them, who will make up the government under which they live. You, then, are an integral part of the democratic process every time you vote in an election.

Elections in a Democracy

Democratic government is government by "the consent of the governed." Elections give practical meaning to this notion of "consent." Elections allow people to choose among competing candidates and parties and to decide who will occupy public office. Elections give people the opportunity to pass judgment on current officeholders, either by reelecting them (granting continued consent) or by throwing them out of office (withdrawing consent).

In a representative democracy, elections function primarily to choose personnel to occupy public office—to decide "who governs." But elections also have an indirect influence on public policy, allowing voters to influence policy directions by choosing between candidates or parties with different policy priorities. Thus elections indirectly influence "who gets what"—that is, the outcomes of the political process.

Elections as Mandates? However, it is difficult to argue that elections serve as "policy mandates"—that is, that elections allow voters to direct the course of public policy. Frequently, election winners claim a **mandate**—overwhelming support from the people—for their policies and programs. But for elections to serve as policy mandates, four conditions have to be met:

1. Competing candidates have to offer clear policy alternatives.
2. The voters have to cast their ballots on the basis of these policy alternatives alone.
3. The election results have to clearly indicate the voters policy preferences.
4. Elected officials have to be bound by their campaign promises.[1]

As we shall see, *none* of these conditions is fully met in American elections. Often candidates do not differ much on policy questions, or they deliberately obscure their policy positions to avoid offending groups of voters. Voters themselves frequently pay little attention to policy issues in elections but rather vote along traditional party lines or group affiliations, or on the basis of the candidate's character, personality, or media image.

Elections are more about choosing personnel ("Who Governs") than they are about directing the course of future policy. The focus is on the candidates more than the issues.

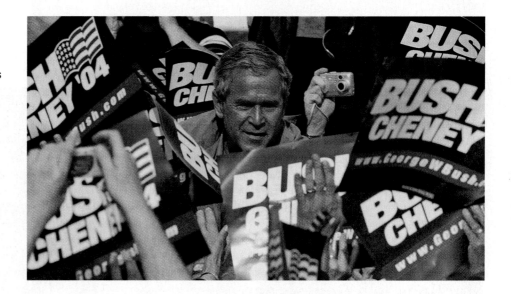

Moreover, even in elections in which issues seem to dominate the campaign, the outcome may not clearly reflect policy preferences. Candidates take stands on a variety of issues. It is never certain on which issues the voters agreed with the winner and on which issues they disagreed yet voted for the candidate anyway.

Finally, candidates often fail to abide by their campaign promises once they are elected. Some simply ignore their promises, assuming voters have forgotten about the campaign. Others point to changes in circumstances or conditions as a justification for abandoning a campaign pledge.

Retrospective Voting Voters can influence future policy directions through **retrospective voting**—votes cast on the basis of the performance of incumbents, by either reelecting them or throwing them out of office.[2] Voters may not know what politicians will do in the future, but they can evaluate how well politicians performed in the past. When incumbent officeholders are defeated, it is reasonable to assume that voters did not like their performance and that newly elected officials should change policy course if they do not want to meet a similar fate in the next election. But it is not always clear what the defeated incumbents did in office that led to their ouster by the voters. Nor, indeed, can incumbents who won reelection assume that all of their policies are approved of by a majority of voters. Nevertheless, retrospective voting provides an overall judgment of how voters evaluate performance in office.

Protection of Rights Elections also provide protection against official abuse. The long struggle for African American voting rights in the United States was premised on the belief that once black people acquired the right to vote, government would become more responsive to their concerns. In signing the Voting Rights Act of 1965, President Lyndon Johnson expressed this view: "The vote is the most powerful instrument ever devised by man for breaking down injustice and destroying the terrible walls which imprison men because they are different from other men."[3] The subsequent history of racial politics in America (see Chapter 15) suggests that the vote is more effective in eliminating discriminatory laws than it is in resolving social or economic inequities. Nevertheless, *without* the vote, we can be certain that government would have very little incentive to respond to popular needs.

THINK AGAIN

Should elected officials be bound by their campaign promises?

mandate Perception of popular support for a program or policy based on the margin of electoral victory won by a candidate who proposed it during a campaign.

retrospective voting Voting for or against a candidate or party on the basis of past performance in office.

Power and Ambition

Personal ambition is a driving force in politics. Politics attracts people for whom *power*—the drive to shape the world according to one's own beliefs and values—and *celebrity*—the public attention, deference, name recognition, and social status that accompany public office—are more rewarding than money, leisure, or privacy. "Political office today flows to those who want it enough to spend the time and energy mastering its pursuit. It flows in the direction of ambition—and talent."[4]

Communication Skills Another important personal qualification is the ability to communicate with others. Politicians must know how to talk, and talk, and talk—to large audiences, in press conferences and interviews, on television, to reporters, to small groups of financial contributors, on the phone, at airports and commencements, to their staffs, on the floor of Congress or the state legislature. It matters less what politicians say than how they look and sound saying it. They must communicate sincerity, compassion, confidence, and good humor, as well as ideas.

Professionalism Politics is increasingly characterized by **professionalism**. "Citizen officeholders"—people with business or professional careers who get into politics part time or for short periods of time—are being driven out of political life by career politicians—people who enter politics early in life as a full-time occupation and expect to make it their career. Politics increasingly demands all of a politician's time and energy. At all levels of government, from city council to state legislatures to the U.S. Congress, political work is becoming full-time and year-round.

Careerism Professional political careers begin at a relatively early age. **Careerism** in politics begins when ambitious young people seek out internships and staff positions with members of Congress, with congressional committees, in state legislators' or governors' offices, in mayors' offices, or in council chambers. Others volunteer to work in political campaigns. Many find political mentors from whom they learn how to organize campaigns, contact financial contributors, and deal with the media. Soon they are ready to run for local office or the state legislature. Rather than challenge a strong incumbent, they may wait for an open seat to be

THINK AGAIN

Do you think that personal ambition, rather than civic duty, motivates most politicians?

professionalism In politics, a reference to the increasing number of officeholders for whom politics is a full-time occupation.

careerism In politics, a reference to people who started young working in politics, running for and holding public office, and made politics their career.

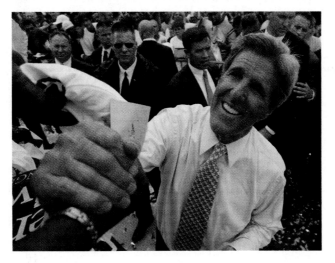

Success in politics requires not only talent, but also personal ambition and the willingness to sacrifice time, energy, privacy, and often family life as well.

Former President Clinton prepares for an interview with reporters from the television news show *60 Minutes.* Successful politicians are skilled communicators; most truly enjoy the hard work and constant interaction with other people their careers entail.

created by retirement, by reapportionment, or by its holder seeking another office. Over time, running for and holding elective office become their career.

Lawyers in Politics The prevalence of lawyers in politics is an American tradition. Among the fifty-five delegates to the Constitutional Convention in 1787, some twenty-five were lawyers. The political dominance of lawyers continues today, with lawyers filling more than half of U.S. Senate seats and nearly half of the seats in the U.S. House of Representatives.

It is sometimes argued that lawyers dominate in politics because of the parallel skills required in law and politics. Lawyers represent clients, so they can apply their professional experience to represent constituents in Congress. Lawyers are trained to deal with statutory law, so they are assumed to be reasonably familiar with the United States Code (the codified laws of the U.S. government) when they arrive in Congress to make or amend these statutes.

But it is more likely that people attracted to politics decide to go to law school fully aware of the tradition of lawyers in American politics. Moreover, political officeholding at the state and local level as well as in the national government can help a struggling lawyer's private practice through free public advertising and opportunities to make contacts with potential clients. Finally, there are many special opportunities for lawyers to acquire public office in "lawyers only" posts as judges and prosecuting attorneys in federal, state, and local governments. Law school graduates who accept modest salaries as U.S. attorneys in the Justice Department or in state or county prosecuting offices can gain valuable experience for later use in either private law practice or politics.

Most of the lawyers in the Congress, however, have become professional politicians over time. They have left their legal practices behind.

The Advantages of Incumbency

In theory, elections offer voters the opportunity to "throw the rascals out." But in practice, voters seldom do so. **Incumbents,** people already holding public office, have a strong advantage when they seek reelection. The reelection rates of incumbents for *all* elective offices—city council, mayor, state legislature, governor,

incumbent Candidate currently in office seeking reelection.

and especially Congress—are very high. Since 1950, more than 90 percent of all members of the House of Representatives who have sought reelection have been successful. The success rate of U.S. Senate incumbents is not as great, but it is still impressive; since 1950, more than 70 percent of senators seeking reelection have been successful.

Why do incumbents win so often? This is a particularly vexing question, inasmuch as so many people are distrustful of government and hold politicians in low esteem. Congress itself is the focal point of public disapproval and even ridicule. Yet people seem to distinguish between Congress as an institution—which they distrust—and their own members of Congress—whom they reelect. The result is something of a contradiction: popular members of Congress serving in an unpopular Congress (see *What Do You Think?* "Why Do Voters Reelect Members of an Unpopular Congress?" in Chapter 10). Three major advantages tend to enhance incumbents' chances of winning: name recognition, campaign contributions, and the resources of office.

Name Recognition One reason for incumbents' success is that they begin the campaign with greater **name recognition** than their challengers, simply because they are the incumbent and their name has become familiar to their constituents over the previous years. Much of the daily work of all elected officials, especially members of Congress, is really public relations. Name recognition is a strategic advantage at the ballot box, especially if voters have little knowledge of policy positions or voting records. Voters tend to cast ballots for recognizable names over unknowns. Cynics have concluded that there is no such thing as bad publicity, only publicity. Even in cases of well-publicized scandals, incumbent members of Congress have won reelection; presumably voters preferred "the devil they knew" to the one they did not.

The somewhat lower rate of reelection of Senate versus House members may be a result of the fact that Senate challengers are more likely to have held high-visibility offices—for example, governor or member of Congress—before running for the Senate. Thus Senate challengers often enjoy some name recognition even before the campaign begins. Greater media attention to a statewide Senate race also helps to move the challenger closer to the incumbent in public recognition. In contrast, House challengers are likely to have held less visible local or state legislative offices or to be political novices, and House races attract considerably less media attention than Senate races do.

Campaign Contributions Incumbents have a strong advantage in raising campaign funds, simply because individuals and groups seeking access to those already in office are inspired to make contributions (see Table 8.1). **Challengers** have no immediate favors to offer; they must convince a potential contributor that they will win office and also that they are devoted to the interests of their financial backers.[5]

Contributing individuals and interest groups show a strong preference for incumbents over challengers. They do not wish to offend incumbent officeholders by contributing to their challengers; doing so risks both immediate retribution and future "freezing out" in the likely event of the challengers' defeat. Thus only when an incumbent has been especially hostile to an organization's interest or in rare cases where an incumbent seems especially vulnerable will an interest group support a challenger. Yet challengers need even larger campaign war chests than incumbents to be successful. Challengers must overcome the greater name

name recognition Public awareness of a political candidate—whether they know his or her name.

challengers In politics, a reference to people running against incumbent officeholders.

TABLE 8.1 Incumbent Advantage in Fund Raising

Senate	2002	2004
Average Incumbent Raised	$5,803,639	$7,212,068
Average Challenger Raised	1,013,314	869,688
House		
Average Incumbent Raised	898,382	982,941
Average Challenger Raised	197,608	171,551

Source: Center for Responsive Politics; figures for 2002 and 2004 congressional elections.

recognition of incumbents, their many office resources, and their records of constituency service. Thus even if incumbents and challengers had equal campaign treasuries, incumbents would enjoy the advantage.

Resources of Office Successful politicians use their offices to keep their names and faces before the public in various ways—public appearances, interviews, speeches, and press releases. Congressional incumbents make full use of the **franking privilege** (free use of the U.S. mails) to send self-promotional newsletters to tens of thousands of households in their district at taxpayers' expense. They travel on weekends to their district virtually year-round, using tax-funded travel allowances, to make local appearances, speeches, and contacts.

Members of Congress have large staffs working every day over many years with the principal objective of ensuring the reelection of their members. Indeed, Congress is structured as an "incumbent-protection society" organized and staffed to help guarantee the reelection of its members (see "Home Style" in Chapter 10). Service to constituents occupies the energies of congressional office staffs both in Washington and in local district offices established for this purpose. Casework wins voters one at a time: tracing lost Social Security checks, ferreting out which federal loans voters qualify for and helping them with their applications, and performing countless other personal favors. These individual "retail-level" favors are supplemented by larger scale projects that experienced members of Congress can bring to their district or state (roads, dams, post offices, buildings, schools, grants, contracts), as well as undesirable projects (landfills, waste disposal sites, halfway houses) that they can keep out of their district. The longer incumbents have occupied the office, the more favors they have performed and the larger their networks of grateful voters.

Campaign Strategies

Campaigning is largely a media activity, especially in presidential and congressional campaigns. Media campaigns are highly professionalized, relying on public relations and advertising specialists, professional fund raisers, media consultants, and pollsters. Campaign management involves techniques that strongly resemble those employed in marketing commercial products. Professional media campaign management includes developing a **campaign strategy**: compiling computerized mailing lists and invitations for fund-raising events; selecting a campaign theme and

franking privilege Free use of the U.S. mails granted to members of Congress to promote communication with constituents.

campaign strategy Plan for a political campaign, usually including a theme, an attempt to define the opponent or the issues, and an effort to coordinate images and messages in news broadcasts and paid advertising.

coming up with a desirable candidate image; monitoring the progress of the campaign with continual polling of the voters; producing television tapes for commercials, newspaper advertisements, signs, bumper stickers, and radio spots; selecting clothing and hairstyles for the candidate; writing speeches and scheduling appearances; and even planning the victory party.

 Campaigns and Elections

The Web site for "Campaigns and Elections," a magazine directed toward candidates, campaign managers, political TV advertisers, political consultants, and lobbyists.
www.campaignline.com

Selecting a Theme Finding the right theme or "message" for a campaign is essential; this effort is not greatly different from that of launching an advertising campaign for a new detergent. A successful theme or "message" is one that characterizes the candidate or the electoral choice confronting the voters. A campaign theme need not be controversial; indeed, it need not even focus on a specific issue. It might be as simple as "a leader you can trust"—an attempt to "package" the candidate as competent and trustworthy.

Most media campaigns focus on candidates' personal qualities rather than on their stands on policy issues. Professional campaigns are based on the assumption that a candidate's "image" is the most important factor affecting voter choice. This image is largely devoid of issues, except in very general terms: for example, "tough on crime," "stands up to the special interests," "fights for the taxpayer," or "cares about you."

Negative Campaigning: "Defining" the Opponent A media campaign also seeks to "define" the opponent in negative terms. The original negative TV ad is generally identified as the 1964 "Daisy Girl" commercial, aired by the Lyndon B. Johnson presidential campaign (see *Up Close:* "Dirty Politics"). Negative ads can serve a purpose in exposing the record of an opponent. But **negative campaigning** risks an opponent's counterattack charges of "mudslinging," "dirty tricks," and "sleaze."

negative campaigning
Speeches, commercials, or advertising attacking a political opponent during a campaign.

Research into the opponent's public and personal background ("oppo research") provides the data for negative campaigning. Previous speeches and writings can be mined for embarrassing or mean-spirited statements. The voting record of the opponent can be scrutinized for unpopular policy positions. Any evils that occurred during an opponent's term of office can be attributed to him or her, either directly ("She knew and conspired in it") or indirectly ("He should have known and done something about it"). Personal scandals or embarrassments can be developed as evidence of "character." If campaign managers fear that highly personal attacks on an opponent will backfire, they may choose to leak the information to reporters and try to avoid attribution of the story to themselves or their candidate.

Negative advertising is often blamed on television's dominant role in political campaigns. "The high cost of television means now that you have to go for the jugular."[6] A political consultant summarized the current rules of political engagement as follows:

1. Advertise early if you have the money. . . .
2. Go negative early, often, and right through election day, if necessary.
3. Appeal to the heart and gut, rather than to the head.
4. Define your opponent to the voters before he or she can define him/herself or you.
5. If attacked, hit back even harder.
6. It's easier to give voters a negative impression of your opponent than it is to improve their image of you.[7]

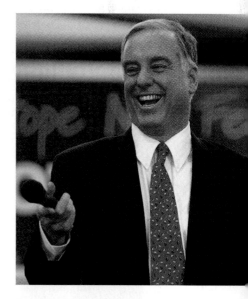

An early leader in the Democratic polls. Vermont Government Howard Dean appeared too excitable after the Iowa caucus.

Dirty Politics

Political campaigning frequently turns ugly with negative advertising that is vicious and personal. It is widely believed that television's focus on personal character and private lives—rather than on policy positions and governmental experience—encourages negative campaigning. But vicious personal attacks in political campaigns began long before television. They are nearly as old as the nation itself.

"If Jefferson is elected," proclaimed Yale's president in 1800, "the Bible will be burned and we will see our wives and daughters the victims of legal prostitution." In 1864 *Harper's Weekly* decried the "mudslinging" of the day, lamenting that President Abraham Lincoln was regularly referred to by his opponent as a "filthy storyteller, despot, liar, thief, braggart, buffoon, monster, Ignoramus Abe, robber, swindler, tyrant, fiend, butcher, and pirate."

Television's first memorable attack advertisement was the "Daisy Girl" commercial broadcast by Lyndon Johnson's presidential campaign in 1964 against his Republican opponent, Barry Goldwater. Although never mentioning Goldwater by name, the purpose of the ad was to "define" him as a warmonger who would plunge the world into a nuclear holocaust. The ad opens with a small, innocent girl standing in an open field plucking petals from a daisy and counting, "1, 2, 3 . . ." When she reaches 9, an ominous adult male voice begins a countdown: "10, 9, 8 . . ." as the camera closes in on the child's face. At "zero," a mushroom cloud appears, reflected in her eyes, and envelops the screen. Lyndon Johnson's voice is heard: "These are the stakes."

The infamous Willie Horton ad, broadcast by an independent organization supporting Republican George Bush in 1988, portrayed Democrat Michael Dukakis as weak on crime prevention. It featured a close-up mug shot of a very threatening convicted murderer, Willie Horton, with a voice proclaiming, "Dukakis not only opposes the death penalty, he allowed first-degree murderers to have weekend passes from prison. One was Willie Horton who murdered a boy in a robbery, stabbing him nineteen times. Despite a life sentence, Horton received ten weekend passes from prison." A final photo shows Dukakis, with a voice-over announcing, "Weekend prison passes, Dukakis weak on crime."

"Attack ads" have multiplied in recent elections at all levels of government. John Kerry had volunteered for Vietnam following his graduation from Yale. In four months as commander of a small "swift boat" he won a Silver Star, a Bronze Star, and three Purple Hearts. But an independent group, Swift Boat Veterans for the Truth, challenged the legitimacy of Kerry's medals in a series of TV ads. Later, the Swift Boat group redirected their attacks toward Kerry's post Vietnam behavior as a leader in the Vietnam Veterans against the War. These ads showed a young Kerry at a congressional hearing accusing his fellow veterans of terrible atrocities, "murdering civilians, cutting off heads, and burning villages." These ads corresponded to a slight drop in Kerry's poll numbers.

But Bush's service in the Texas National Guard during the Vietnam War was also a target of attack. Bush joined the Guard with the possible help of family friends, but he won his wings as a fighter pilot and was honorably discharged after five years. The Texas Guard was never called active-duty and Bush never saw combat. But a CBS News report by Dan Rather, based on forged documents, asserted that Bush failed to meet all of his Guard responsibilities. Later CBS News recanted the charge. The affair may have helped Bush somewhat, by convincing viewers that Dan Rather and others at CBS were biased against him.

What are the effects of negative advertising? First of all, it works more often than not. Controlled experiments indicate that targets of attack ads are rated less positively by people who have watched these ads. But another effect of negative advertising is to make voters more cynical about politics and government in general. There is conflicting evidence about whether or not negative campaigning by opposing candidates reduces voter turnout.

What, if anything, can be done? Government regulation of political speech directly contravenes the First Amendment. American democracy has survived negative campaigning for a long time.

Source: Kathleen Hall Jamieson, *Dirty Politics, Deception, Distraction, and Democracy* (New York: Oxford University Press, 1992); also Stephen Ansolabehere et al., "Does Attack Advertising Demobilize the Electorate?" *American Political Science Review* 88 (December 1994): 829–38; Kim Fridkin Kahn and Patrick J. Kenney, "Do Negative Campaigns Mobilize or Suppress Turnout?" *American Political Science Review* 93 (December, 1999): 877–89.

Frames from Lyndon Johnson's 1964 "Daisy Girl" commercial.

Does negative campaigning really work? Professional campaign managers and consultants are convinced that negative ads are effective—more effective than positive ads. Regarding ads praising one's own qualities, they say "save them for your tombstone." But political science research suggests that the success of negative campaigning depends on the situations in which candidates find themselves. Overall negative campaigning does not appear to be more effective than positive political ads for every candidate.[8] However, candidates who are running far behind, as well as challengers who are campaigning against incumbents, are more likely to turn to negative campaigning and more likely to have success going on the attack.[9]

Using Focus Groups and Polling Focus group techniques can help in selecting campaign themes and identifying negative characteristics in opponents. A **focus group** is a small group of people brought together to view videotapes, listen to specific campaign appeals, and respond to particular topics and issues. Media professionals then develop a campaign strategy around "hot-button" issues—issues that generate strong responses by focus groups—and avoid themes or issues that fail to elicit much interest.

The results of focus group work can then be tested in wider polling. Polling is a central feature of professional campaigning. Serious candidates for national and statewide offices almost always employ their own private polling firms, distinct from the national survey organizations that supply the media with survey data. Initial polling is generally designed to determine candidates' name recognition—the extent to which the voters recognize the candidates—and whatever positive and negative images are already associated with their names.

Campaign polling is highly professionalized, with telephone banks, trained interviewers, and computer-assisted-telephone-interviewing (CATI) software that records and tabulates responses instantly and sends the results to campaign managers. In well-financed campaigns, polling is continual throughout the campaign, so that managers can assess progress on a daily basis. Polls chart the candidate's progress and, perhaps more important, help assess the effectiveness of specific campaign themes. If the candidate appears to be gaining support, the campaign stays on course. But if the candidate appears to be falling in the polls, the campaign manager comes under intense pressure to change themes and strategies. As election day nears, the pressure increases on the trailing candidate to "go negative"—to launch even more scathing attacks on the opponent.

Incumbent versus Challenger Strategies Campaign strategies vary by the offices being sought, the nature of the times, and the imagination and inventiveness of the candidates' managers. But incumbency is perhaps the most important factor affecting the choice of a strategy. The challenger must attack the record of the incumbent, deplore current conditions in the city, state, or nation; and stress the need for change. Challengers are usually freer to take the offensive; incumbents must defend their record in office and either boast of accomplishments during their term or blame the opposition for blocking them. Challengers frequently opt for the "outsider" strategy, capitalizing on distrust and cynicism toward government.

News Management News management is the key to the media campaign. News coverage of the candidates is more credible in the eyes of viewers than paid advertisements. The campaign is planned to get the maximum favorable "free" ex-

THINK AGAIN

Would you vote for a candidate who used negative ads to discredit an opponent?

focus group In a political context, a small number of people brought together in a comfortable setting to discuss and respond to themes and issues, allowing campaign managers to develop and analyze strategies.

posure on the evening news. Each day a candidate must do something interesting and "newsworthy," that is, likely to be reported as news. Pictures are as important as words. Candidates must provide good **photo ops** for the media—opportunities where they can be photographed in settings or backgrounds that emphasize their themes. For example, if the theme is patriotism, then the candidate appears with war veterans, at a military base, or at a flag factory. If the theme is education, the candidate appears at a school; if crime control, then with police officers; if environmentalism, then in a wilderness area; if the economy, then at a closed factory or unemployment line or soup kitchen for the homeless.

Themes must be stated in concise and catchy **sound bites** that will register in the viewers' minds. Candidates now understand that the news media will select only a few seconds of an entire day of speech making for broadcast. The average length of a network news sound bite has shrunk from forty-five to seven seconds over the last thirty years. Thus extended or serious discussion of issues during a campaign is sacrificed to the need for one-liners on the nightly news. Indeed, if a campaign theme cannot fit on a bumper sticker, it is too complex.

Consequently, each day's campaigning is a series of photo ops and sound bites, all prepared with the evening news in mind. Between events, candidates must scramble to various fund-raising events—dinners, parties, personal meetings with large contributors. Thus candidates balance their time between "getting out the message" and finding ways to pay for getting it out.

Paid Advertising Television "spot" ads must be prepared prior to and during the campaign. They involve employing expensive television advertising and production firms well in advance of the campaign and keeping them busy revising and producing new ads throughout the campaign to respond to changing issues or opponents' attacks. Commercial advertising is the most expensive aspect of the campaign. Heavy costs are incurred in the production of the ads and in the purchase of broadcast time. The Federal Communications Commission (FCC) does not permit television networks or stations to charge more than standard commercial rates for political ads, but these rates are already high. Networks and stations are required to offer the same rates and times to all candidates, but if one candidate's campaign treasury is weak or exhausted, an opponent can saturate broadcast airtime.

Free Airtime All candidates seek free airtime on news and talk shows, but the need to gain free exposure is much greater for underfunded candidates. They must go to extremes in devising media events, and they must encourage and participate in free televised debates. The debate format is particularly well suited for candidates who cannot match their opponents in paid commercial advertising. Thus well-funded and poorly funded candidates may jockey over the number and times of public debates.

photo ops Staged opportunities for the media to photograph the candidate in a favorable setting.

sound bites Concise and catchy phrases that attract media coverage.

How Much Does It Cost to Get Elected?

Getting elected to public office has never been more expensive (see *Up Close:* "A Brief History of Money in Politics"). The professionalization of campaigning and the heavy costs of television advertising drive up the costs of running for office. Campaign costs are rising with each election cycle (see Figure 8.1). In the presidential election year 2004, campaign spending by *all* presidential and congres-

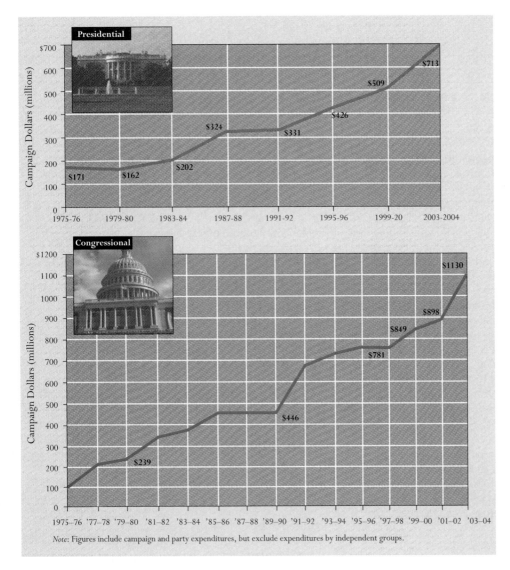

FIGURE 8.1 **The Growing Costs of Campaigns**

Source: Reprinted by permission of Center for Responsive Politics.

Note: Figures include campaign and party expenditures, but exclude expenditures by independent groups.

sional candidates, the Democratic and Republican parties, and independent political organizations is estimated to have topped *$4 billion.*

Congressional Costs The typical winning campaign for a seat in the House of Representatives costs nearly $900,000. House members seeking to retain their seats must raise this amount *every two years.* The typical winning campaign for a U.S. Senate seat costs $5 to $7 million. But Senate campaign costs vary a great deal from state to state; Senate seats in the larger states may cost $20 million or $40 million or more.

The upward spiral in congressional campaign spending continued through 2004 with over $1 *billion* spent by all House and Senate candidates (see Table 8.2). New York's high-profile Senate race in 2002 between Democrat Hillary Clinton and Republican Rick Lazio attracted a combined $85 million in contributions from across the nation. A new individual spending record was set by multimillionaire Democrat Jon Corzine in his successful bid for a U.S. Senate seat from New Jersey in 2002; Corzine spent about $60 million of his *own* money.

Spending for House seats also varies a great deal from one race to another. (The spending record for a House seat is held by former Speaker Republican Newt Gingrich of Georgia, who spent more than $7.5 million awaiting reelection in 1998.)

THINK AGAIN

Are high campaign costs discouraging good people from becoming candidates?

A Brief History of Money in Politics

In 1757, in his race for a seat in the Virginia House of Burgesses, George Washington was reprimanded for purchasing and distributing more than a quart of whiskey per voter in his district. But for the first fifty years or so of American independence, campaign costs were relatively low. The population was small, and only white males who owned property—about one of every five adults—were allowed to vote. But as the population grew, and property requirements were abolished, campaign costs rose. By 1840 the practice of buying votes was well established in the nation's cities.

Rising campaign costs in the early nineteenth century required candidates to begin soliciting funds from businesses, industries, and wealthy individuals. These contributors, in turn, increasingly sought favors from a government that was becoming more and more involved in economic matters. During the Civil War, Abraham Lincoln wrote:

> As a result of the war, corporations have become enthroned, and an era of corruption in high places will follow. The money power of the country will endeavor to prolong its rule by preying on the prejudices of the people until all wealth is concentrated in a few hands.

During the industrial revolution following the Civil War, historian Richard Hofstadter describes what may have been the high-water mark of corruption in American politics: "Capitalists seeking land grants, tariffs, bounties, favorable currency policies, freedom from regulatory legislation and economic reform, supplied campaign funds, fees, and bribes, and plied politicians with investment opportunities." Banks, railroads, and oil and mining companies became the major sources of campaign cash in national politics; in local politics, campaigns were funded by utilities, saloons, gambling halls, houses of prostitution, and racetracks. According to historian George Thayer. "Standard Oil did everything to the Pennsylvania Legislature except refine it." The presidential election of 1896 set a record for campaign spending that would not be surpassed in equivalent dollars until the 1970s. U.S. Senator Marcus Alonzo Hanna, general counsel for John D. Rockefeller's Standard Oil Company, raised between $6 and $7 million for the winner, Republican William McKinley, while his Democratic opponent William Jennings Bryan spent only about a half million dollars.

Political campaign costs rose again following the Seventeenth Amendment (1913), which instituted the direct election of U.S. senators; the nineteenth Amendment, which won women the right to vote; and the expanding use of primary elections to choose party candidates. Fortunately for politicians who began to need more campaign money to reach more voters, the New Deal vastly increased government involvement in the economy and thereby raised the incentives for business interests to fork over more money to ensure that their interests would be protected in policymaking. Labor unions became a major source of campaign funds in 1936 when the newly formed Congress of Industrial Organizations (CIO) contributed a half million dollars to Franklin D. Roosevelt's presidential campaign.

During the 1950s and 1960s, each of the major parties enjoyed the support of wealthy "superdonors"—the Mellons and Rockefellers on the Republican side and the Kennedys and Harrimans on the Democratic side. But a turning point in campaign finance history occurred after the Watergate revelations of secret donations to the 1972 Nixon reelection campaign, especially the $2 million individual contribution by insurance magnate Clement Stone. The result was the passage of the Federal Election Campaign Act, creating the Federal Elections Commission (FEC) and placing limits on direct campaign contributions to candidates by individuals and organizations.

But the reforms envisioned by the act were quickly undermined by an explosion in the number of political action committees, vast increases in unlimited "soft money" contributions to the parties, and the U.S. Supreme Court decision in *Buckley v. Valeo* declaring that individuals (and by implication independent organizations) may spend as much as they wish to express their own views and advance their own candidacies. The result was a skyrocketing of political campaign spending and an even greater dependence on big money sources of campaign funds than before the passage of the act.

The Bipartisan Campaign Finance Reform Act of 2002 was designed to close "loopholes" in the earlier reform act. It banned unlimited soft money contributions to the parties, limited individual contributions to candidates to $2,000 per election. But contributions to independent organizations ("527s") remained unregulated. These groups were prohibited from coordinating their ads with candidates or parties, but they played a major role in the 2004 election (see *Up Close:* "New Ways to Evade Campaign Finance Reform").

Source: Excerpted from *A Brief History of Money in Politics,* Center for Responsive Politics, Washington, D.C., 1999.

TABLE 8.2　The Cost of Getting Elected to Congress

Senate

Average Democratic Incumbent	$8,582,559
Average Democratic Challenger	$772,381
Average Republican Incumbent	$5,750,211
Average Republican Challenger	$1,126,857
Most Expensive Campaign	Tom Daschle (D, SD) $17.4 million (lost)

House of Representatives

Average Democratic Incumbent	$918,481
Average Democratic Challenger	$174,694
Average Republican Incumbent	$1,041,327
Average Republican Challenger	$192,960
Most Expensive Campaign	Martin Frost (D, TX), $3.9 million (lost)

Source: Center for Responsive Politics.

In nearly two-thirds of all House districts, one candidate (almost always the incumbent) outspends his or her opponent by a factor of ten to one or more. Only about 16 percent of House campaigns are financially competitive; that is, neither candidate spends more than twice as much as his or her opponent. In the remaining 84 percent of House campaigns, one candidate spends more than twice as much as his or her opponent.[10]

Presidential Costs　More cash is spent in every presidential election than in the previous election (see Table 8.3). Over $500 million was spent by all presidential candidates in the 2000 election, and spending for the 2004 election ran in excess of $700 million.

Raising Campaign Cash

Fund raising to meet the high costs of campaigning is the most important hurdle for any candidate for public office. Campaign funds come from a wide range of sources—small donors, big donors, interest group PAC's of every stripe, labor

TABLE 8.3　Presidential Campaign Funding

	Contributions	Public Funding	Public Convention Funding	Total
2004	529.2	149.2	35.0	713.5
2000	351.7	147.7	29.5	528.9
1996	248.3	152.7	24.7	425.7
1992	198.5	110.5	22.1	331.1
1988	213.8	92.2	18.4	324.4
1984	105.0	80.8	16.2	202.0

Source: Reprinted by permission of Center for Responsive Politics. Figures for 2004 are preliminary.

Center for Responsive Politics

The site of an organization devoted to the study of campaign finance laws, the role of money in elections, PACs, "soft money," and special-interest groups.

www.opensecrets.org

unions, even taxpayers. In some cases, candidates pay their own way (or most of it). More typically, however, candidates for high public office—particularly incumbents—have become adept at running their campaigns using other people's money, not their own.

Public Money Presidential campaigns can be partly funded with taxpayer money through an income tax checkoff system. Each year taxpayers are urged to check the box on their tax forms which authorizes $3 of their tax payment to go to the Federal Elections Commission for distribution to presidential candidates' campaigns as well as to political party conventions. However, taxpayers are becoming less and less willing to allow their tax monies to go into political campaigning (even though the $3 checkoff does not add to the taxpayers' total taxes). Only about 11 percent of taxpayers currently check the box. The Presidential Election Campaign Fund has been in jeopardy of not having enough money to make its promised payments to the candidates and parties.

Presidential candidates may opt out of taxpayer-financed funding if they choose to do so. This allows them to spend as much money as they wish, but they receive no public money. Nonetheless, all presidential candidates, and all candidates for Congress, must abide by federal campaign finance laws (see below).

Small Donations Millions of Americans participate in campaign financing, either by giving directly to candidates or the parties or by giving to political action committees, which then distribute their funds to candidates. For members of Congress, small donors typically make up less than 20 percent of their campaign funds. The proportion is higher for presidential candidates. Under federal law, donations under $200 need not be itemized, so contributors' names and addresses are recorded only by the candidates and parties, not passed along to the Federal Election Commission as part of the public record.

Large Individual Donors "Fat cats" are the preferred donors. These are the donors whose names are on the candidates' Rolodexes. They are the ones in attendance when the president, the Speaker of the House, or other top political dignitaries travel around the country doing fund raisers. They are also the ones who are wined, dined, prodded, and cajoled in a seemingly ceaseless effort by the parties and the candidates to raise funds for the next election.

In its 2002 campaign finance reform legislation, Congress raised the maximum individual contribution to federal candidates to $2,000 (up from $1,000 in the 2000 election). Fat cats are expected to give the maximum, and indeed even more. They can do so by giving their maximum $2,000 once in the primary election and a second time in the general election. And their spouses can do the same. And, of course, they can also give to the parties and to independent political organizations committed to helping their preferred candidates.

Candidate Self-Financing Candidates for federal office also pump millions into their own campaigns. There are no federal restrictions on the amount of money individuals can spend on their own campaign.[11] Leading the field in the last two presidential races was publishing magnate Steve Forbes, whose unsuccessful bids for the Republican nomination for president were largely funded with millions from his personal fortune. Senate and House candidates frequently put $50,000 to $100,000 or more of their own money into their campaigns, through outright gifts or personal loans. (Candidates who loan themselves the money to run are able to pay themselves back later from outside contributions.)

Candidates seek to appear "in touch" with ordinary voters. John Kerry made many efforts to overcome his image as too serious, too aloof, too senatorial, during the campaign.

Issue Ads Issue ads are produced independently by interest groups. Issue ads advocate policy positions rather than explicitly advising voters cast their ballots for or against particular candidates. But most of these ads leave little doubt about which candidate is being supported or targeted. Beginning in 2002, money spent for issue ads must be reported to the Federal Elections Commission. The Bipartisan Campaign Reform Act of 2002 does not permit issue ads mentioning the name of a candidate. It also bans issue ads 60 days before a general election and 30 days before a primary election. However, there are no dollar limits on the size of contributions to these groups (often referred to as 527s from the section of the Internal Revenue code under which they operate.

What Do Contributors "Buy"?

What does money buy in politics? A cynic might say that money can buy anything—for example, special appropriations for public works directly benefiting the contributor, special tax breaks, special federal regulations. Public opinion views big-money contributions as a major problem in the American political system (see *What Do You Think? "Does Money Buy Influence in Washington?"* on page 255). Scandals involving the direct (quid pro quo) purchase of special favors, privileges, exemptions, and treatments have been common enough in the past, and they are likely to continue in the future. But campaign contributions are rarely made in the form of a direct trade-off for a favorable vote. Such an arrangement risks exposure as bribery and may be prosecuted under the law. Campaign contributions are more likely to be made without any *explicit* quid pro quo but rather with a general understanding that the contributor has confidence in the candidate's good judgment on issues directly affecting the contributor. The contributor expects the candidate to be smart enough to figure out how to vote in order to keep the contributions coming in the future.

THINK AGAIN

Do political campaign contributions have too much influence on elections and government policy?

issue ads Ads that advocate policy positions rather than explicitly supporting or opposing particular candidates.

BOTTOM LINERS

© 1999 Tribune Media Services, Inc.
All Rights Reserved.   11/23

"Ultimately, I want to get into political fund raising
. . . I'm just here to make some contacts."

Source: © Tribune Media Services, Inc. All Rights Reserved.
Reprinted with permission.

The Big-Money Contributors Big-money contributors—businesses, unions, professional associations—pump millions into presidential and congressional elections. Figure 8.2 lists the top fifty contributors to candidates and parties since 1989. Note that union contributions are heavily weighted toward Democrats, as are the contributions of the Association of Trial Lawyers. Businesses and business associations tend to split their contributions between the parties, but Republicans usually get the largest share.

Buying Access to Policy Makers Large contributors expect to be able to call or visit and present their views directly to "their" officeholders. At the presidential level, major contributors who cannot get a meeting with the president expect to meet at least with high-level White House staff or cabinet officials. At the congressional level, major contributors usually expect to meet or speak directly with their representative or senator. Members of Congress boast of responding to letters, calls, or visits by any constituent, but contributors can expect a more immediate and direct response than noncontributors can. Lobbyists for contributing organizations routinely expect and receive a hearing from members of Congress.

political action committee (PAC) Organization created by a corporation, union, or other interest group to collect and distribute campaign funds to candidates.

Political Action Committees Political action committees (PACs) are the most reliable source of money for reelection campaigns in Congress. Corporations and unions are not allowed to contribute directly to campaigns from corporate or union funds, but they may form PACs to seek contributions from managers and stockholders and their families, or union workers and their families. PACs are organized not only by corporations and unions but also by trade and professional associations, environmental groups, and liberal and conservative ideological groups.

Does Money Buy Influence in Washington?

Americans are clearly troubled by the role money plays in politics. About two-thirds believe excessive influence of political contributions on elections and government policy is a major problem with the system. A similar proportion feel this way about the conflicts of interest created when elected officials solicit or accept political contributions while they are making policy decisions. An even greater percentage believe the high cost of campaigns discourages good people from running for office.

Money is believed to obstruct good government in a variety of ways. At the very least, it is seen as distracting people's representatives from the jobs they were elected to do. A solid majority think elected officials in Washington spend too much time on political fund raising. But many see money's effects as much more pernicious than simply reducing the efficiency of the federal government. More than half of Americans believe political contributions often buy influence in Washington for one group by denying another group its fair say; as many as half think money often determines who gets elected and appointed to federal office. Nearly half see the influence of money in politics seriously undermining democratic ideals by often leading elected officials to support policies they don't personally believe are best for the country.

Major Problems with Political System	Percentage Responding "Yes"
"Political contributions have too much influence on elections and government policy"	66%
"Elected officials seek or receive political contributions while making decisions about issues of concern to those giving money"	65
"Elected officials spend too much of their time raising money for election campaigns"	63
"Good people are being discouraged from becoming candidates because of the high costs of campaigns"	71

How Frequently Does the Use of Money Buy Political Influence in Washington?	Percentage Responding "Often"
"Gives one group more influence by keeping another from having its fair say"	55%
"Determines election outcomes"	52
"Gets someone appointed to office who would not otherwise be considered"	50
"Keeps important legislation from being passed"	48
"Leads elected officials to support policies they don't think are best for the country"	45

Source: Princeton Survey Research Associates for the Center for Responsive Politics, *Money and Politics Survey, 1997.*

The wealthiest PACs are based in Washington, D.C. (see "PAC Power" in Chapter 9). PACs are very cautious; their job is to get a maximum return on their contributions, winning influence and goodwill with as many lawmakers as possible in Washington. There's no return on their investment if their recipients lose at the polls, therefore most PACs—particularly business PACs—give most of their dollars to incumbents seeking reelection.

Buying Government Assistance Many individual large contributors do business with government agencies. They expect any representative or senator

Rank	Contributor	Total Contributions	% Dem.	% Rep.	Rank	Contributor	Total Contributions	% Dem.	% Rep.
1.	American Federation of State/County/Municipal Employees	$34,944,356	98%	1%	25.	National Rifle Assn	$14,345,042	13%	86%
2.	National Assn of Realtors	$24,159,780	50%	49%	26.	AFL-CIO	$14,143,542	88%	11%
3.	National Education Assn	$23,382,034	86%	13%	27.	American Bankers Assn	$13,753,323	39%	60%
4.	Assn of Trial Lawyers of America	$23,310,366	89%	10%	28.	Time Warner	$13,408,561	70%	28%
5.	Communications Workers of America	$21,968,716	98%	1%	29.	SBC Communications	$13,032,502	34%	65%
6.	Service Employees International Union	$21,865,215	88%	11%	30.	Verizon Communications	$12,617,393	38%	61%
7.	Intl Brotherhood of Electrical Workers	$21,522,812	96%	3%	31.	BellSouth Corp	$12,427,578	43%	56%
8.	Carpenters & Joiners Union	$20,995,637	68%	31%	32.	Microsoft Corp	$12,327,062	58%	41%
9.	Teamsters Union	$20,838,115	85%	13%	33.	National Beer Wholesalers Assn	$12,207,798	30%	69%
10.	American Medical Assn	$20,632,636	28%	71%	34.	EMILY's List	$11,777,389	100%	0%
11.	Altria Group (Philip Morris)	$20,567,067	41%	57%	35.	Sheet Metal Workers Union	$11,687,901	97%	2%
12.	FedEx Corp	$20,500,993	33%	66%	36.	Ernst & Young	$11,672,581	31%	67%
13.	Laborers Union	$20,497,632	86%	13%	37.	Lockheed Martin	$11,486,880	39%	60%
14.	United Auto Workers	$19,832,550	98%	0%	38.	JP Morgan Chase & Co	$11,455,069	49%	50%
15.	AT&T	$19,484,567	47%	52%	39.	RJR Nabisco/ RJ Reynolds Tobacco	$10,959,872	11%	88%
16.	American Federation of Teachers	$19,291,514	99%	0%	40.	American Dental Assn	$10,898,735	43%	56%
17.	Goldman Sachs	$18,607,643	50%	49%	41.	Morgan Stanley	$10,850,938	34%	65%
18.	Machinists & Aerospace Workers Union	$18,429,464	98%	0%	42.	Blue Cross/Blue Shield	$10,757,914	42%	57%
19.	United Food & Commercial Workers Union	$18,318,526	98%	1%	43.	American Hospital Assn	$10,748,440	44%	55%
20.	Citigroup Inc	$17,080,206	48%	50%	44.	National Assn of Insurance & Financial Advisors	$10,629,255	37%	62%
21.	United Parcel Service	$16,859,844	29%	70%	45.	General Electric	$10,596,818	46%	53%
22.	National Auto Dealers Assn	$16,474,442	29%	70%	46.	American Institute of CPAs	$10,381,169	37%	62%
23.	National Assn of Home Builders	$14,930,228	38%	61%	47.	Union Pacific Corp	$10,131,658	22%	77%
24.	National Assn of Letter Carriers	$14,608,734	71%	27%	48.	Credit Union National Assn	$10,110,853	43%	56%
					49.	Deloitte Touche Tohmatsu	$10,108,211	28%	71%
					50.	United Steelworkers of America	$10,089,196	97%	2%

FIGURE 8.2   All Time Big-Money Contributors

Source: Center for Responsive Politics "Top All Time Donor Profiles" www.opensecrets.org

they have supported to intervene on their behalf with these agencies, sometimes acting to cut red tape, ensure fairness, and expedite their cases, and other times pressuring the agencies for a favorable decision. Officials in the White House or the cabinet may also be expected to intervene on behalf of major contributors. There is little question raised when the intervention merely expedites consideration of a contributor's case, but pressure to bend rules or regulations to get favorable decisions raises ethical problems for officeholders (see "Congressional Ethics" in Chapter 10).

Individual Contributors Those who contribute to presidential and/or congressional campaign funds do so for a variety of reasons. Some contributors are ideologically motivated. They make their contributions based on their perception of the ideological position of the candidate (or perhaps their perception of the candidate's opponent). They may make contributions to congressional candidates across the country who share their policy views. Liberal and conservative networks of contributors can be contacted through specialized mailing lists—for example, liberals through television producer Norman Lear's People for the American Way. Feminists have been effective in soliciting individual contributions across the country and funneling them very early in a campaign to women candidates through EMILY's List. Ideological contributors may only get the satisfaction of knowing that they are financially backing their cause in the political process. Some contributors simply enjoy the opportunity to be near and to be seen with high-ranking politicians. Politicians pose for photos with contributors, who later frame the photos and hang them in their office to impress their friends, associates, and customers. About 7 to 10 percent of the population claims in national surveys to have contributed to candidates running for public office. Contributors are disproportionately high-income, older people with strong partisan views (see Figure 8.3).

Fund-Raising Chores Fund raising occupies more of a candidate's time than any other campaign activity. Candidates must personally contact as many individual contributors as possible. They work late into the evening on the telephone with potential contributors. Fund-raising dinners, cocktail parties, barbecues, fish frys, and so on, are scheduled nearly every day of a campaign. The candidate is expected to appear personally to "press the flesh" of big contributors. Movie and rock stars and other assorted celebrities may also be asked to appear at fund-

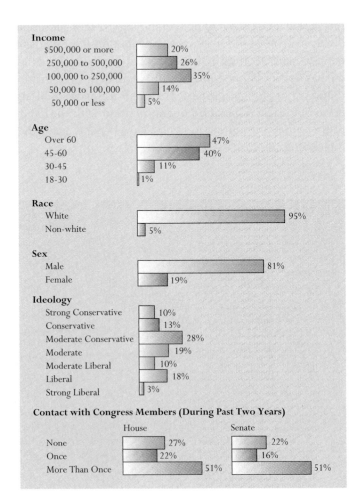

FIGURE 8.3
Characteristics of Individual Political Contributors

Contributors to political campaigns generally have been older, and have higher incomes than most Americans. Whites and males contribute more than blacks and females, and conservatives contribute more than liberals.

Source: John Green, Paul Herrnson, Lynda Powell, Clyde Wilcox, "Individual Congressional Campaign Contributions," press release, June 9, 1998, Center for Responsive Politics.

raising affairs to generate attendance. Dinners may run to $2,000 a plate in presidential affairs, although often less in Senate or House campaigns. Tickets may be "bundled" to well-heeled individual contributors or sold in blocks to organizations. Fund-raising techniques are limited only by the imagination of the campaign manager.

Regulating Campaign Finance

The **Federal Election Commission (FEC)** is responsible for enforcing limits on individual and organizational contributions to all federal elections, administering the public funding of presidential campaigns, and requiring full disclosure of all campaign financial activity in presidential and congressional elections. Enforcement of these federal election and campaign finance laws lies in the hands of the six-member FEC. Appointed by the president to serve staggered six-year terms, commission members are traditionally split 3 to 3 between Republicans and Democrats.

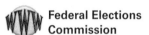
Federal Elections Commission
The FEC Web site contains ample information on the important regulations and statutes relating to campaign finance. *http://www.fec.gov*

Federal Election Commission (FEC) Agency charged with enforcing federal election laws and disbursing public presidential campaign funds.

Limits on Contributions The FEC now limits direct individual contributions to a candidate's campaign to $2,000 per election and organizational contributions to $5,000 per election. But there are many ways in which individuals and organizations can legally surmount these limits. Contributors may give a candidate $2,000 for each member of their family in a primary election and then another $2,000 per member in the general election. Organizations may generate much more than the $5,000 limit by bundling (combining) $2,000 additional contributions from individual members. (Soft-money contributions—unregulated amounts given to the national parties officially for "party building" but actually used in support of candidates—were banned in 2002.) Independent organizations can spend whatever they wish in order to promote their political views, so long as these organizations do so "without cooperation or consultation with the candidate of his or her campaign." Finally, as noted, individuals may spend as much of their own money on their own campaigns as they wish.[11]

Celebrity entertainers are a major source of campaign funding for Democratic candidates. They attract crowds to hear the candidates and open their wallets.

Reporting By law, every candidate for federal office must file periodic reports with the FEC detailing both the income and the expenditures of their campaign. Individual contributors who give an aggregate of $200 or more must be identified by name, address, occupation, and employer. All PAC and party contributions, no matter how large or small, must also be itemized. In addition, PACs themselves must file reports with the FEC at least four times a year, detailing both the contributions received by the PAC and the names of candidates and other groups that received the PAC's donations.

Federal Funding of Presidential Elections Federal funding, financed by the $3 checkoff box on individual income tax returns, is available to presidential candidates in primary and general elections, as well as to major-party nominating conventions. Candidates seeking the nomination in presidential primary elections can qualify for federal funds by raising $5,000 from private contributions no greater than $250 each in each of twenty states. In the general election, Democratic and Republican nominees are funded equally at levels determined by the FEC. In order to receive federal funding, presidential candidates must agree to FEC limits on their campaign spending in both primary and general elections.

Federal funding pays about one-third of the primary campaign costs of presidential candidates and all the *official* presidential campaign organization costs in the general election. The parties also receive federal funds for their nominating conventions.

Campaign Finance Reform Unregulated soft money contributions to the parties grew rapidly during the 1990s. These contributions represented a giant black hole in the original Federal Election Campaign Act of 1974. Contributions made directly to a candidate's campaign—hard money contribution—were limited (originally to $1,000). But individuals, organizations, corporations, and unions could contribute as much as they wanted to the Democratic and Republican national parties. These contributions were supposed to be for party building, voter registration, getting out the vote, etc., but in fact went into candidate campaigning.

In the 2000 Republican presidential primaries, U.S. Senator John McCain made campaign finance reform his principal issue. He surprised the Republican Party leaders by defeating George W. Bush in the New Hampshire primary that year. Bush and both Democratic and Republican leaders decided to jump on the campaign finance reform bandwagon, although with little real enthusiasm. In 2002 a somewhat reluctant Congress finally passed the Bipartisan Campaign Finance Reform Act (see Table 8.4).

Among other things, this act eliminates soft money contributions to the parties; increases the individual contribution limit to candidates' campaigns from $1,000 to $2,000; prohibits independent groups from coordinating their campaign spending with candidates or parties; does not allow independent groups to mention the name of a candidate in their issue ads; and bans independent groups from broadcasting their views in the final days of a campaign.

But contributions to nonprofit independent groups remain unregulated. Big money contributors who can no longer provide large amounts of cash to candidates or to parties *can* establish nonprofit independent groups (known as "527s", referring to their Internal Revenue Service code) to accept big contributions to enable them to produce and broadcast campaign advertisements (see *Up Close* "New Ways to Evade Campaign Finance Reform").

TABLE 8.4 **Campaign Finance Rules, 2004**

General

All federal election contributions and expenditures must be reported to the Federal Election Commission, which may investigate and prosecute violators.

All contributions over $200 must be reported, with name, address, and occupation of contributor.

No foreign contributions can be made.

There are no restrictions on how much individuals may spend on their own campaigns (*Buckley vs. Valeo*).

No large contributions (soft money) may be made to the national parties; party contributions by individuals and committees are limited.

Presidential Primaries

Federal matching funds are available for money raised by candidates from individual donors giving $250 dollars or less. To be eligible, the primary candidate must raise $5,000 in each of twenty states in contributions of $250 or less.

Presidential Elections

The federal government pays all campaign costs of major party candidates and contributes to the costs of party conventions. The federal government will also pay part of the costs of minor party candidates who win between 5 and 25 percent of the vote.

Limits on Contributions

Donor	Candidate	PAC	National Party	State/Local	Special
Individual	$2,000	$5,000	$25,000	$10,000	Biennial total: $95,000
National party	5,000	5,000	—	—	—
State/local party	5,000	5,000	—	—	—
PAC (multi-candidate)	5,000	5,000	1,500	5,000	—
PAC (single-candidate)	2,000	5,000	25,000	10,000	—

Millionaire Amendment

If a candidate spends more of his own money beyond specified thresholds (e.g., $350,000 for House candidates), contribution limits for his or her opponent are tripled.

Independent Group Expenditures

Independent individuals or groups airing TV or radio ads must not coordinate with candidates or parties in order to avoid contribution limits.

Election Communications

Independent individuals or groups may not broadcast TV or radio ads referring to a candidate 60 days prior to a general election or 30 days prior to the primary election.

Note: This table summarizes the Bipartisan Campaign Finance Reform Act of 2002.

The act was challenged as a violation of First Amendment free speech rights, but upheld by the U.S. Supreme Court in *McConnell vs. Federal Elections Commission*, December 10, 2003. (See also Chapter 14.)

The Presidential Campaign: The Primary Race

The phrase *presidential fever* refers to the burning political ambition required to seek the presidency. The grueling presidential campaign is a test of strength, character, endurance, and determination. It is physically exhausting and mentally and emotionally draining. Every aspect of the candidates' lives—and the lives of their families—is subject to microscopic inspection by the news media. Most of this coverage is critical, and much of it is unfair. Yet candidates are expected to han-

New Ways to Evade Campaign Finance Reform

The Bipartisan Campaign Finance Reform Act was supposed to eliminate big money contributions from national elections. After years of struggle, reformers thought they had eliminated loopholes that allow individuals, corporations, and labor unions to pump millions of dollars into presidential and congressional campaigns.

But campaign cash is like the Pillsbury doughboy: push it in one place and it pops out in another. The act banned big soft money contributions to the parties. But Congress did not block individuals or nonprofit independent groups from spending as much as they want to broadcast their own views. So early in the 2004 election campaign, big money contributors and political savvy consultants, especially in the Democratic Party, began to build a network of nonprofit organizations—organizations into which they could funnel millions of dollars and expect to see them broadcast issue ads in favor of their candidates during the campaign. (These organizations became popularly known as "527s," in reference to the section in the U.S. Tax Code authorizing them.)

George Soros, one of the world's richest men, has given away billions to promote democracy in former Soviet bloc nations, including his birthplace, Hungary. In addition, Soros funds a wide variety of liberal causes through his Open Society Institute. In 2003, he declared financial war on George Bush. He gave millions to a series of often newly created liberal organizations. Among the recipients of his political generosity:

MoveOn, an organization originally formed by Silicon Valley entrepreneurs to defend President Bill Clinton against impeachment.

Americans Coming Together (ACT), an organization formed by officers of the AFL-CIO, the Sierra Club, and the Service Employees International Union "to mobilize voters to defeat George W. Bush and elect progressive candidates across all America."

America Votes, created by former Texas Gov. Ann Richards and her daughter to coordinate get-out-the-vote of anti-George Bush groups.

Partnership for America's Families, another group formed by the Service Employees International Union to get "progressive" voters to the polls in big cities.

Voices for Working Families, created by the AFL-CIO to "mobilize the votes primarily of minorities and women."

The Media Fund, organized by President Clinton's Deputy White House Chief of Staff to raise big money to buy TV and radio ads.

Moving America Forward, created to increase Hispanic Democratic voting in the southwestern states.

Grassroots Democrats, organized by the Communications Workers of America union and the Association of Trial Lawyers to raise contributions under the new campaign finance law.

Billionaires for Bush, a tongue-in-cheek organization opposed to Bush's reelection.

These organizations and others like them can accept millions of dollars.

dle it all with grace and humor, from the earliest testing of the waters through a full-fledged campaign.

Media Mentions Politicians with presidential ambitions may begin by promoting presidential *mentions* by media columnists and commentators. The media help to identify "presidential timber" years in advance of a presidential race simply by drawing up lists of potential candidates, commenting on their qualifications, and speculating about their intentions. Mentions are likely to come to prominent governors or senators who start making speeches outside of their state, who grab the media spotlight on a national issue, or who simply let it be known to the media "off the record" that they are considering a presidential race. Visiting New Hampshire and giving speeches there is viewed as "testing the waters" and a signal of presidential ambitions.

Presidential Credentials Political experience as vice president, governor, U.S. senator, or member of Congress not only inspires presidential ambition but also provides vital experience in political campaigning. However, virtually all presidential candidates testify that the presidential arena is far more challenging than politics at any other level. The experience of running for and holding high public office appears to be a political requirement for the presidency. Some presidential aspirants (for example, General Wesley Clark in 2004) have tried to make a virtue of their lack of previous political office holding, no doubt hoping to attract support from the many Americans who disdain "politics as usual." But for over a century no major party nominee for president has not previously held office as vice president, governor, U.S. senator, or member of Congress except World War II hero General Dwight D. Eisenhower.

The Decision to Run The decision to run for president involves complex personal and political calculations. Ambition to occupy the world's most powerful office must be weighed against the staggering costs—emotional as well as financial—of a presidential campaign.

Serious planning, organizing, and fund raising must begin at least two years before the general election. A staff must be assembled—campaign managers and strategists, fund raisers, media experts, pollsters, issues advisers and speech writers, lawyers and accountants—and supporters must be identified in key states throughout the nation. Paid and volunteer workers must be assembled (see Figure 8.4). Leaders among important interest groups must be contacted. A general cam-

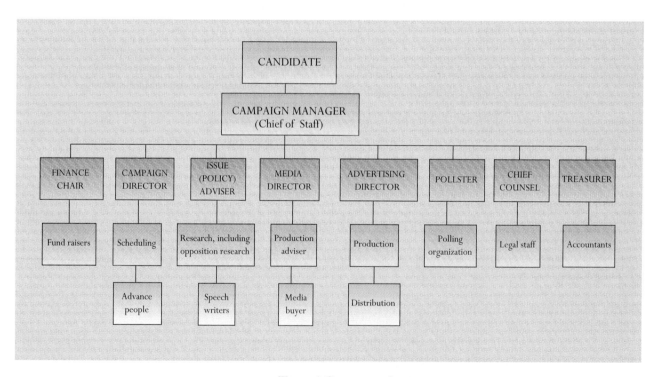

FIGURE 8.4 Typical Campaign Organization

Campaign organizations vary, but most assign someone to perform these tasks: funding, scheduling appearances, speech writing, media production and buying, polling, advertising, legal compliance, and check writing, even if, in local campaigns, all these tasks must be performed by the candidate or his or her family members.

paign strategy must be developed, an organization put in place, and several millions of dollars in campaign contributions pledged in advance of the race. Often the decision to run hinges on whether initial pledges of campaign contributions appear adequate. The serious candidate must be able to anticipate contributions of $25 million or more for primary elections. Most of this work must be accomplished in the pre-primary season—the months after Labor Day of the year preceding the election, and before the first primary election.

A Strategy for the Primaries The road to the White House consists of two separate races: the primary elections and caucuses leading to the Democratic and Republican party nominations, and the general election. Each of these races requires a separate strategy. The primary race requires an appeal to party activists and the more ideologically motivated primary voters in key states. The general election requires an appeal to the less partisan, less attentive, more ideologically moderate general election voters. Thus the campaign strategy developed to win the nomination must give way after the national conventions to a strategy to win the November general election.

Primary Campaigns Primary campaigns come in different varieties. An incumbent president with no serious competition from within his own party can safely glide through his party's primaries, saving campaign money for the general election. In contrast, the party out of the White House typically goes through a rough-and-tumble primary (and pre-primary) season, with multiple presidential aspirants. And when no incumbent president is running for reelection, both parties experience heavy party infighting among multiple presidential hopefuls.

Candidates strive during the pre-primary season to win media attention, to climb the poll ratings, and raise campaign funds. Early front runners must beware of stumbles and gaffs; they must be prepared for close scrutiny by the media; and they must expect to be the targets of their competitors. Not infrequently, early front runners lose their momentum even before the first primary elections.[12]

Primary voters are heavily weighted toward party activists, who are more ideologically motivated than the more moderate voters in general elections. Democratic primary voters are more liberal, and Republican primary voters are more conservative, than the voters in the November general election. Democratic primary voters include large numbers of the party's core constituents—union members, public employees, minorities, environmentalists, and feminists.

Presidential candidates must try to appeal not only to the ideological predispositions of their party's primary voters, but also convince them of their "electability"—the likelihood that they can win the party's nomination and more importantly go on to win the presidential election. Often primary voters are torn between voting for their favorite candidate based on his or her ideological and issue positions, or voting for the most electable candidate.

The New Hampshire Primary The primary season begins in the winter snows of New Hampshire, traditionally the first state to hold a presidential primary election. New Hampshire is far more important *strategically* to a presidential campaign than it is in delegate strength. As a small state, New Hampshire supplies fewer than 1 percent of the delegates at the Democratic and Republican conventions. But the New Hampshire primary looms very large in media coverage and hence in overall campaign strategy. Although the popular Democratic Iowa party caucuses are held even earlier, New Hampshire is the nation's first primary, and the media begin speculating about its outcome and reporting early state-poll results months in advance.

The New Hampshire primary inspires **retail politics**—direct candidate contact with the voters. Presidential aspirants begin visiting New Hampshire in the year preceding the primary elections, speaking at town hall meetings, visiting with small groups, standing outside of supermarkets, walking through restaurants, greeting workers at factories and offices, and so on. These personal contacts bypass the media's filtering and interpreting of the candidate's personality and message. Retail politics is largely confined to New Hampshire, a small state and a year of pre-primary time to reach voters personally. And there is some evidence that voters who actually meet candidates come away with a more favorable view of them.[13]

The "expectations" game is played with a vengeance in the early primaries. Media polls and commentators set the candidates' expected vote percentages, and the candidates and their spokespersons try to deflate these expectations. On election night, the candidates' **spin doctors** sally forth among the crowds of television and newspaper reporters to give a favorable interpretation of the outcome. The candidates themselves appear at campaign headquarters (and, they hope, on national television) to give the same favorable spin to the election results. But the media itself—particularly the television network anchors and reporters and commentators—interpret the results for the American people, determining the early favorites in the presidential horse race.

New Hampshire provides the initial *momentum* for the presidential candidates. "Momentum" is more than just a media catchword. The Democratic and Republican winners in New Hampshire have demonstrated their voter appeal, their "electability." Favorable New Hampshire results inspire more financial contributions and thus the resources needed to carry the fight into the next group of primary elections. Unfavorable New Hampshire results tend to dry up contributions; weaker candidates may be forced into an early withdrawal.

The Front-End Strategy A **front-end strategy** places heavy emphasis on the results from New Hampshire and other early primary states. This strategy involves spending all or most of the candidate's available resources—time, energy, and money—on the early primary states, in the hopes that early victories will provide

retail politics Direct candidate contact with individual voters.

spin doctor Practitioner of the art of spin control, or manipulation of media reporting to favor one's own candidate.

front-end strategy Presidential political campaign strategy in which a candidate focuses on winning early primaries to build momentum.

Democratic presidential hopefuls line up for a debate prior to the New Hampshire primary, won by Massachusetts Senator John Kerry (third from right). Others are Missouri's Dick Gephardt, New York's Al Sharpton, Ohio's Dennis Kucinich, Connecticut's Joe Lieberman, North Carolina's John Edwards, Illinois' Carol Moseley-Braun, and Vermont's Howard Dean.

the momentum, in media attention and financial contributions, to continue the race.

Big-State Strategy Presidential aspirants who begin the race with widespread support among party activists, heavy financial backing, and strong endorsements from the major interest groups can focus their attention on the big-state primaries. A **big-state strategy** generally requires more money, more workers, and better organization than a front-end strategy. But the big states—California, New York, Texas, Florida, Pennsylvania, Ohio, and Michigan—have the most delegates. The results of these primaries may determine the Democratic and Republican nominees, assuming that most or all of them are won by the same candidates. It is rare that more than two candidates in each party survive as credible candidates after the big states have made their selections. By this stage of the race, many uncommitted delegates begin to commit themselves and their convention votes to the leader.

Front Loading Presidential nominees are now selected by early March. State legislators in a number of states expressed their frustration over the media attention given to tiny New Hampshire by moving up the dates of their presidential primary elections. (The New Hampshire Legislature responded by officially setting its primary date one week earlier than any other state's primary.) In 2004 many big states, including California, Connecticut, Georgia, Massachusetts, Minnesota, New York, and Ohio, held their primary on March 2; Florida and Texas held theirs on March 7; and Michigan held its primary on February 7.

This **front loading** of presidential primaries appears to favor the candidate who peaks in the polls in the first six weeks of the primary season.[14]

Convention Showplace Once a presidential candidate has enough votes to assure nomination, this uncrowned winner must prepare for the party's convention.

big-state strategy
Presidential political campaign strategy in which a candidate focuses on winning primaries in large states because of their high delegate counts.

front loading The scheduling of presidential primary elections early in the year.

Presidential candidates usually submit their choice for vice president in the run-up to the party's national convention. George W. Bush's 2000 running mate, Dick Cheney, was viewed by some as having been chosen to lend an air of maturity to the Republican ticket. Cheney was Secretary of Defense in Bush's father's administration.

Bush v. Gore, 2000

The 2000 presidential election turned out to be one of the most bitterly contested races in the nation's history, an election that was "too close to call" for over a month after balloting!

Early Campaign Strategies

By traditional expectations, Democrat Al Gore's election should have been a "slam dunk." The nation was enjoying economic prosperity, low unemployment, low inflation, budget surpluses, and a relative peace. Traditionally under such conditions, Americans have kept the incumbent party in the White House.

But the campaign started off very badly for Al Gore. The vice president was perceived as a stiff, wooden prop for his boss, the flawed yet charismatic Bill Clinton. Gore trailed George W. Bush badly in opinion polls for the first eight months of the election year.

George W. Bush's campaign rested largely on his personal appeal to voters—his warmth, good humor and general likability. Early on, he settled on the theme of "compassionate conservatism," trying to appeal to independents, minorities, and especially women.

The Race Narrows

Al Gore's fortunes changed dramatically at the Democratic convention in August. In a deliberate effort to overcome his image of formality, he planted a passionate kiss on his wife as he strode to the podium. He reinvented himself, this time as a populist fighting for "working people" against the powerful special interests—the oil companies, the insurance companies, the hated HMOs. His voice was stronger, his rhetoric more powerful, and even if his new persona seemed somewhat artificial, he struck a chord with the American people. Perhaps more importantly, Gore distanced himself from the scandals of the Clinton administration, even while simultaneously claiming credit for eight years of prosperity. His running mate selection, U.S. Senator Joseph Lieberman of Connecticut, the first Jew to appear on a major party ticket and an outspoken critic of Bill Clinton's scandalous behavior, was widely applauded. The selection seemed to affirm Al Gore's claim "I am my own man." Gore won a huge convention "bounce" in the polls.

Electoral Vote Strategies

The Bush campaign conceded New York, California, and most of the north-eastern states to Gore. The Gore campaign conceded Texas and most of the southern and mountain states to Bush. The battleground states were Pennsylvania, Ohio, Michigan, Illinois, Wisconsin, and especially Florida. Bush's younger brother, Jeb Bush, had been elected governor of Florida in 1998 and Republicans controlled both houses of the legislature.

The Battle after the Bell

The morning after election day, it was clear that Al Gore had won the nationwide popular vote. But the Electoral College outcome depended on Florida's 25 electoral votes. Bush's lead in Florida, after several machine recounts and the count of absentee ballots, was 930 votes out of 6 million cast in that state.

Armies of lawyers descended on Florida. The Gore campaign demanded hand recounts of the votes. Bush's lawyers argued that the hand counts in these counties were late, unreliable, subjective, and open to partisan bias. Gore's lawyers argued that the Palm Beach "butterfly" ballot was confusing (the Gore/Lieberman punch hole was positioned third instead of second under Bush/Cheney; Buchanan's punch hole was positioned second). They also argued that partially detached "chads" (small perforated squares in the punch cards that should fall out when the voter punches the ballot) should be inspected to ascertain the "intent" of the voter.

The Florida Supreme Court ordered that hand counts continue, setting back the Florida legislature's enacted deadline for the receipt of county votes by more than a week to November 26, 2000.

Florida's secretary of state (separately elected Republican Katherine Harris) certified the state's vote immediately after the Court's new deadline. Bush was declared the winner by 537 votes.

A President Chosen by the Supreme Courts

In *Bush v. Gore,* finally decided on December 12, the U.S. Supreme Court held that "the use of standardless manual recounts violates the Equal Protection and Due Process clauses of the Constitution" and that "Florida statutory law cannot reasonably be thought to require the counting of improperly marked ballots." The effect of the decision was to let stand the Florida secretary of state's certification of Bush as the winner of that state's 25 electoral votes and the winner of the Electoral College vote for president, 271 to 267.

But the Supreme Court's 5–4 decision followed ideological lines. The five justices in the majority included acknowledged conservatives Rehnquist, Scalia, and Thomas, together with moderates O'Connor and Kennedy. The minority included the acknowledged ideological liberals, Stevens, Bryer, and Ginsburg, together with Souter. Yet, despite the prolonged contest, the bitter feelings of many of the participants, and the apparent ideological split, George W. Bush was recognized as the elected president of the United States immediately after the Supreme Court's historic decision.

Organizing and orchestrating convention forces, dominating the platform and rules writing, enjoying the nominating speeches and the traditional roll call of the state delegations, mugging for the television camera when the nominating vote goes over the top, submitting the vice presidential nominee's name for convention approval, and preparing and delivering a rousing acceptance speech to begin the fall campaign are just a few of the many tasks awaiting the winner—and the winner's campaign team.

The Presidential Campaign: The General Election Battle

Buoyed by the conventions—and often by postconvention bounces in the polls— the new nominees must now face the general electorate.

General Election Strategies Strategies in the general election are as varied as the imaginations of campaign advisers, media consultants, pollsters, and the candidates themselves. As noted earlier, campaign strategies are affected by the nature of the times and the state of the economy; by the incumbent or challenger status of the candidate; by the issues, conditions, scandals, or events currently being spotlighted by the media; and by the dynamics of the campaign itself as the candidates attack and defend themselves. (see *Up Close*. "Bush v. Kerry, 2004").

Presidential election campaigns must focus on the **Electoral College**. The president is not elected by the national popular vote total but rather by a majority of the *electoral* votes of the states. Electoral votes are won by plurality, winner-take-all popular voting in each of the states. Thus a narrow plurality win in a state delivers *all* of that state's electoral votes. Big-state victories, even by very narrow margins, can deliver big electoral prizes. The biggest prizes are California with 54 electoral votes, New York with 33, and Texas with 32. With a total of 538 electoral votes at stake, *the winner must garner victories in states that total a minimum of 270 electoral votes*. (See *What Do You Think?* "Should We Scrap the Electoral College?" on page 270.)

Targeting the Swing States In focusing on the most populous states, with their large electoral votes, candidates must decide which of these states are "winnable," then direct their time, energy, and money to these **swing states**. Candidates cannot afford to spend too much effort in states that already seem to be solidly in their column, although they must avoid the perception that they are ignoring these strong bases of support. Neither can candidates waste much effort on states that already appear to be solidly in their opponent's column. So the swing states receive most of the candidates' time, attention, and television advertising money.

The Presidential Debates The nationally televised presidential debates are the central feature of the general election campaign. These debates attract more viewers than any other campaign event. Moreover, they enable a candidate to reach undecided voters and the opponent's supporters, as well as the candidate's own partisans. Even people who usually pay little attention to politics may be drawn in by the drama of the confrontation (see *Up Close*: "The Presidential Debates" on page 274).

Electoral College The 538 presidential electors apportioned among the states according to their congressional representation (plus 3 for the District of Columbia) whose votes officially elect the president and vice president of the United States.

swing states States that are not considered to be firmly in the Democratic or Republican column.

Bush v. Kerry

John F. Kerry wrapped up the Democratic nomination in the early spring, and his poll numbers quickly matched those of President Bush. Despite one of the most liberal voting records in Congress, Kerry appeared to be a "moderate" in contrast to his boisterous primary opponent, Vermont Governor Howard Dean (See *Up Close:* "Primaries 2004" in Chapter 7). At the Democratic National Convention Kerry took the stage with a snappy military salute, "I'm John Kerry and I'm reporting for duty!" The early intent was to use his war hero's status to demonstrate his ability to be Commander-in-Chief in time of war. It was a risky strategic decision because President Bush was perceived in all of the polls as a "strong leader" in the war on terrorism. But events thirty-five years ago seemed irrelevant in 2004. Kerry got very little "bounce" from the Democratic Convention.

George Bush had little choice but to make the war on terrorism his major theme. Bush's advisors believed it was to their candidate's advantage to make terrorism the "chief concern" of Americans, rather than the economy. They believed that in wartime most voters wanted a "strong leader," "decisive," and a "man of his word"—qualities in whom the polls indicated Bush was strongest. Kerry was to be cast as a "waffler"—first voting to authorize military force against Iraq and then later voting against a bill to finance operations there. Kerry supported continuing U.S. military efforts in Iraq, but he attacked Bush's decision to invade Iraq without the support of other United Nations members. He referred to Iraq as "the wrong war, the wrong place, the wrong time," and accused Bush of a "colossal error of judgment" in shifting anti-terrorist efforts to catch Osama bin Laden in Afghanistan to the attack on Iraq.

Bush maintained a slim lead in the polls throughout the spring and summer, a lead that he was to lose briefly after the first presidential debate in October. Kerry's carefully-crafted image in the debate seemed to reassure many Americans that he too would make a strong Commander-in-Chief. He claimed that Bush had "misled" the American people about the existence of weapons of mass destruction in Iraq, that he failed to "exhaust the remedies of the United Nations," and that he, Kerry, would not commit American troops to battle without satisfying "the global test." Bush jumped on the phrase "the global test" to claim that Kerry would place America's security in the hands of the United Nations: "I'll never turn over America's national security needs to leaders of other countries." Kerry was judged by the polls as the winner of the debates. But Bush had found a theme—that Kerry was indecisive, that he flip-flopped, and that he would hesitate to act when confronted with threats to national security. Within a week, Bush regained his slim lead in the polls.

As election day neared, the rhetoric became more bitter. Bush had "lied" about the reasons for the war in Iraq, rather than simply being misinformed by the intelligence community about the existence of weapons of mass destruction in Saddam's hands. It was charged that Bush secretly intended to bring back the draft and that he would cut social security benefits for the elderly. Kerry was "unfit for command": early in his career he had accused his fellow veterans of committing atrocities in Vietnam. The terrorists were hoping for a Kerry victory. The nation would not be "safe" if Kerry won.

Bush succeeded in making Iraq part of the war on terrorism: "We will fight the terrorists abroad, rather than fight them at home." Kerry could never fully take advantage of the controversial war: he had voted for it in the first place. He said he would call upon our allies in the United Nations to help in Iraq, but it seemed unlikely to many Americans that UN members who opposed the war would want to assist the U.S.

Contrary to expectations, Americans went to the polls in record numbers. And while Iraq and terrorism ranked high among their concerns, they cited "moral values" as the most important issue in the election. Bush's folksy image and his moral values seemed to match their own. He was "honest and trustworthy," he "took a clear stand," he was "decisive" and "better at handling the war on terrorism." He not only won a majority of the popular vote (51 to 48%), but also helped to increase the Republican majorities in the House and Senate.

The debates allow viewers an opportunity to see and hear candidates together and to compare their responses to questions as they stand side by side. The debates give audiences a better view of the candidates than they can get from thirty-second commercial ads or seven-second news sound bites. Viewers can at least judge how the candidates react under pressure.

However, the debates emphasize candidate image over substantive policy issues. Candidates must appear presidential. They must appear confident, compassionate, concerned, and good humored. They must not appear uncertain or unsure of themselves, or aloof or out of touch with viewers, or easily upset by hostile questions. They must avoid verbal slips or gaffes or even unpolished or awkward gestures. They must remember that the debates are not really debates so much as joint press conferences in which the candidates respond to questions with rehearsed mini-speeches and practiced sound bites.

The Electoral College Vote In recent presidential elections, the Democratic candidates (Clinton in 1992 and 1996 and Gore in 2000) have won the north-eastern states, including New York; the upper midwestern states, including Michigan and Illinois; and, perhaps most importantly, the West Coast, including California (see *Across the USA*: "How the States Voted" on page 272). Republican presidential candidates (Bush in 1992, Dole in 1996, and Bush in 2000 and 2004) have shown greater strength in the Great Plains and Rocky Mountain states and in the south-eastern states (forming a Republican "L" on the Electoral College map). If these patterns continue in presidential elections, Democrats can depend on two of the four largest Electoral College vote states in 2004, California (55) and New York (31), while Republicans can feel comfortable in the other two, Texas (34) and Florida (27). The Electoral College battleground may be states such as Ohio, Pennsylvania, and Missouri—"swing states" that have cast their votes alternatively for Democratic and Republican candidates in recent presidential elections.

The Voter Decides

The Center for Voting and Democracy
A site with material on possible changes in the Electoral College.
www.fairvote.org

Understanding the reasons behind the voters' choice at the ballot box is a central concern of candidates, campaign strategists, commentators, and political scientists. Perhaps no other area of politics has been investigated so thoroughly as voting behavior. Survey data on voter choice have been collected for presidential elections for the past half century.[15] We know that voters cast ballots for and against candidates for a variety of reasons—party affiliation, group interests, characteristics and images of the candidates themselves, the economy, and policy issues. But forecasting election outcomes remains a risky business.

Party Affiliation Although many people claim to vote for "the person, not the party," party identification remains a powerful influence in voter choice. Party ties among voters have weakened over time, with increasing proportions of voters labeling themselves as independents or only weak Democrats or Republicans, and more voters opting to split their tickets or cross party lines than did so a generation ago (see Chapter 7). Nevertheless, party identification remains one of the most important influences on voter choice. Party affiliation is more important in congressional than in presidential elections, but even in presidential elections the tendency to see the candidate of one's own party as "the best person" is very strong.

Should We Scrap the Electoral College?

Americans were given a dramatic reminder in 2000 that the president of the United States is not elected by nationwide popular vote but rather by a majority of the electoral votes of the states.

How the Electoral College Works

The Constitution grants each state a number of electors equal to the number of its congressional representatives and senators combined (see map). Because representatives are apportioned to the states on the basis of population, the electoral vote of the states is subject to change after each ten-year census. No state has fewer than three electoral votes, because the Constitution guarantees every state two U.S. senators and at least one representative. The Twenty-third Amendment granted three electoral votes to the District of Columbia even though it has no voting members of Congress. So winning the presidency requires winning in states with at least 270 of the 538 total electoral votes.

Voters in presidential elections are actually choosing a slate of presidential electors pledged to vote for their party's presidential and vice presidential candidates. The names of electors seldom appear on the ballot, only the names of the candidates and their parties. The slate that wins a plurality of the popular vote in a state (more than any other slate, not necessarily a majority) casts all of the state's vote in the Electoral College. (This "winner-take-all" system in the states is not mandated by the Constitution; a state legislature could allocate a state's electoral votes in proportion to the split in the popular vote. The winner-take-all system in the states helps ensure that the Electoral College produces a majority for one candidate.

The Electoral College never meets at a single location; rather, electors meet at their respective state capitols to cast their ballots around December 15, following the general election on the first Tuesday after the first Monday of November. The results are sent to the presiding officer of the Senate, the vice president who in January presides over their count in the presence of both houses of Congress and formally announces the results. These procedures are usually considered a formality, but the U.S. Constitution does not require that electors cast their vote for the winning presidential candidate in their state, and occasionally "faithless electors" disrupt the process, although none has ever changed the outcome.

If no candidate wins a majority of electoral votes, the House of Representatives chooses the president from among the three candidates with the largest number of electoral votes, with each state casting one vote. The Constitution does not specify how House delegations should determine their vote, but by House rules, the state's vote goes to the candidate receiving a majority vote in the delegation.

The Historical Record

Only two presidential elections have ever been decided formally by the House of Representatives. In 1800 Thomas Jefferson and Aaron Burr tied in the Electoral College because the Twelfth Amendment had not yet been adopted to separate presidential from vice presidential voting; all the Democratic-Republican electors voted for both Jefferson and Burr, creating a tie. In 1824 Andrew Jackson won the popular vote and more electoral votes than anyone else but failed to get a majority. The House chose John Quincy Adams over Jackson, causing a popular uproar and ensuring Jackson's election in 1828.

In addition, in 1876, the Congress was called on to decide which electoral results from the southern states to validate; a Republican Congress chose to validate enough Republican electoral votes to allow Republican Rutherford B. Hayes to win, even though Democrat Samuel Tilden had won more popular votes. Hayes promised the Democratic southern states that in return for their acknowledgment of his presidential claim, he would end the military occupation of the South.

In 1888, the Electoral College vote failed to reflect the popular vote. Benjamin Harrison received 233 electoral votes to incumbent president Grover Cleveland's 168, even though Cleveland won about 90,000 more popular votes than Harrison. Harrison served a single lackluster term; Cleveland was elected for a second time in 1892, the only president to serve two nonconsecutive terms.

2000—Gore Wins but Loses

Al Gore won the nationwide popular vote, receiving about 500,000 more votes (out of the more than 100 million ballots cast) than George W. Bush. But the vote in several states was extremely close. On election night, Gore was reported to have won 262 electoral votes to Bush's 246—that is, neither candidate had the necessary 270. The key turned out to be Florida's 25 electoral votes. (New Mexico's 5 votes eventually went to Gore.) The Florida secretary of state declared Bush the winner by a few hundred votes out of 6 million cast in that state. The Gore campaign demanded hand recounts, especially in heavily Democratic counties in south Florida (including Palm Beach County, where the ballot was said to be confusing to voters). The Bush campaign responded that hand counts are subjective, unreliable, and open to partisan bias. For over a month neither Bush nor Gore would concede the election. Suits were initiated by both candidates in both federal and Florida states courts. Finally the U.S. Supreme Court rejected Gore's appeal; Florida's 25 votes went to Bush and he was declared the winner.

What Would Replace the Electoral College?

Constitutional proposals to reform the Electoral College have circulated for nearly two hundred years, but none has won widespread support. These reform proposals have included (1) election of the president by direct national popular vote; (2) allocation of each state's electoral vote in proportion to the popular vote each candidate received in the state; (3) allocation of electoral votes to winners of each congressional district and two to the statewide winners.

But most reform proposals create as many problems as they resolve. If the president is to be elected by direct nationwide popular vote, should a plurality vote be sufficient to win? Or should a national runoff be held in the event that no one receives a majority in the first election? Would proportional allocation of electoral votes encourage third-party candidates to enter the race in order to deny the leading candidate a majority?

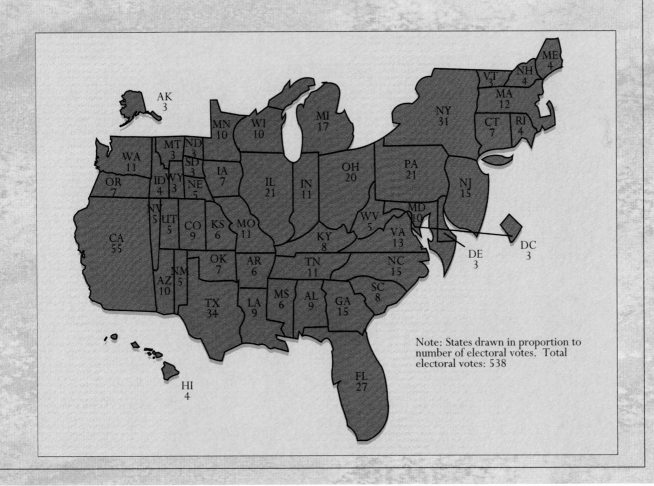

Note: States drawn in proportion to number of electoral votes. Total electoral votes: 538

How the States Voted

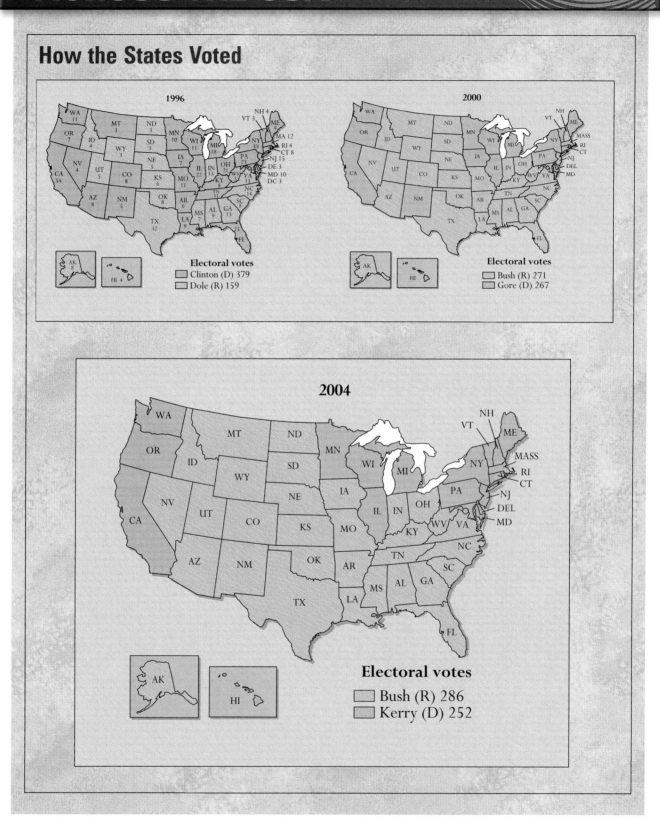

1996

Electoral votes
- Clinton (D) 379
- Dole (R) 159

2000

Electoral votes
- Bush (R) 271
- Gore (D) 267

2004

Electoral votes
- Bush (R) 286
- Kerry (D) 252

2004	Kerry(Democrat)	Bush (Republican)
Party		
Democrat	90%	9%
Republican	7%	92%
Independent	45%	48%
Ideology		
Liberal	84%	12%
Moderate	45%	53%
Conservative	18%	80%
Economy		
Excellent	10%	88%
Good	14%	82%
Not Good	80%	16%

2000	Gore (Democrat)	Bush (Republican)
Party		
Democrat	86%	11%
Republican	8%	91%
Independent	45%	47%
Ideology		
Liberal	80%	13%
Moderate	52%	44%
Conservative	17%	81%
Economy		
Excellent	53%	46%
Good	37%	53%
Not Good	47%	49%

1996	Clinton (Democrat)	Dole (Republican)
Party		
Democrat	84%	10%
Republican	13%	80%
Independent	43%	35%
Ideology		
Liberal	78%	11%
Moderate	57%	33%
Conservative	20%	71%
Economy		
Better	66%	26%
Same	46%	45%
Worse	27%	57%

FIGURE 8.5 Party, Ideology, and Nature of the Times in Presidential Voting

Those who identify themselves as members of a major political party are highly likely to vote for the presidential candidates of their party. Likewise, those who identify themselves as liberals are more likely than average to vote for Democrats, and those who identify themselves as conservatives are more likely to vote for Republicans in presidential elections. In addition, voters who see the economic picture as better are more likely to vote for the incumbent, those who are concerned about the nation's economy are more likely to vote against the incumbent.

Source: Election exit polls, Voter News Service, National Election Pool.

Consider the three presidential elections (see Figure 8.5). Self-identified Republicans voted overwhelmingly for Bush in 1992, for Dole in 1996, and for George W. Bush in 2000. Self-identified Democrats voted overwhelmingly for Clinton in 1992 and 1996, for Gore in 2000, and for Kerry in 2004.

Because Republican identifiers are outnumbered in the electorate by Democratic identifiers, Republican presidential candidates, and many Republican

The Presidential Debates

Presidential debates attract more viewers than any other campaign activity. Most campaign activities—speeches, rallies, motorcades—reach only supporters. Such activities may inspire supporters to go to the polls, contribute money, and even work to get others to vote their way. But televised debates reach undecided voters as well as supporters, and they allow candidates to be seen by supporters of their opponent. Even if issues are not really discussed in depth, people see how presidential candidates react as human beings under pressure.

Kennedy-Nixon

Televised presidential debates began in 1960 when John F. Kennedy and Richard M. Nixon confronted each other on a bare stage before an America watching on black-and-white TV sets. Nixon was the vice president in the popular presidential administration of Dwight Eisenhower; he was also an accomplished college debate-team member. He prepared for the debates as if they were college debates, memorizing facts and arguments. But he failed to realize that image triumphs over substance on television. By contrast, Kennedy was handsome, cool, confident; whatever doubts the American people may have had regarding his youth and inexperience were dispelled by his polished manner. Radio listeners tended to think that Nixon won, and debate coaches scored him the winner. But television viewers preferred the glamorous young Kennedy. The polls shifted in Kennedy's direction after the debate, and he won in a very close general election.

Carter-Ford

President Lyndon Johnson avoided debating in 1964, and Nixon, having learned his lesson, declined to debate in 1968 and 1972. Thus televised presidential debates did not resume until 1976, when incumbent president Gerald Ford, perceiving he was behind in the polls, agreed to debate challenger Jimmy Carter. Ford made a series of verbal slips. Carter was widely perceived as having won the debate, and he went on to victory in the general election.

Reagan-Carter and Reagan-Mondale

It was Ronald Reagan who demonstrated the true power of television. Reagan had lived his life in front of a camera. It was the principal tool of both of his trades—actor and politician. In 1980 incumbent president Jimmy Carter talked rapidly and seriously about programs, figures, and budgets. But Reagan was master of the stage; he was relaxed, confident, joking. He appeared to treat the president of the United States as an overly aggressive, impulsive younger man, regrettably given to exaggeration. When it was all over, it was clear to most viewers that Carter had been bested by a true professional in media skills.

However, in the first of two televised debates with Walter Mondale in 1984, Reagan's skills of a lifetime seemed to desert him. He stumbled over statistics and groped for words. Reagan's poor performance raised the only issue that might conceivably defeat him—his age. The president had looked and sounded old. But in the second debate, Reagan laid the perfect trap for his questioners. When asked about his age and capacity to lead the nation, he responded with a serious dead-pan expression to a hushed audience and waiting America: "I want you to know that I will not make age an issue in this campaign. I am not going to exploit for political purposes [pause] my opponent's youth and inexperience." The studio audience broke into uncontrolled laughter. Even Mondale had to laugh. With a classic one-liner, Reagan buried the age issue and won not only the debate but also the election.

Bush-Dukakis

In 1988 Michael Dukakis ensured his defeat with a cold, detached performance in the presidential debates, beginning with the very first question. When CNN anchor Bernard Shaw asked, "Governor, if Kitty Dukakis were raped and murdered, would you favor an irrevocable death penalty for the killer?" The question demanded an emotional reply. Instead, Dukakis responded with an impersonal recitation of his stock position on law enforcement. Bush seized the opportunity to establish a more personal relationship with the viewers: Voters responded to Bush, electing him.

Clinton-Bush-Perot

The three-way presidential debates of 1992 drew the largest television audiences in the history of presidential debates. In the first debate, Ross Perot's Texas twang and down-home folksy style stole the show. Chided by his opponents for having no governmental experience, he shot back, "Well, they have a point. I don't have any experience in running up a $4 trillion dollar debt." But it was Bill Clinton's smooth performance in the second debate, with its talk-show format, that seemed to wrap up the election. Ahead in the polls, Clinton appeared at ease walking about the stage and responding to audience questions with sympathy and sincerity. By contrast, George Bush appeared stiff and formal, and somewhat ill at case with the "unpresidential" format.

Clinton-Dole

A desperate Bob Dole, running 20 points behind, faced a newly "presidential" Bill Clinton in their two 1996 debates. (Perot's poor standing in the polls led to his exclusion.) Dole tried to counter his image as a grumpy old man in the first encounter; his humor actually won more laughs from the audience than Clinton. Dole injected more barbs in the second debate, complaining of "ethical problems in the White House." But Clinton remained cool and comfortable, ignoring the challenger and focusing on the nation's economic health. Viewers, most of whom were already in Clinton's court, judged him the winner of both debates.

Bush-Gore

Separate formats were agreed upon for three debates—the traditional podium, a conference, table, and a town hall setting. Gore was assertive, almost to the point of rudeness, but both candidates focused on policy differences rather than on personal attacks. Viewers gave Gore the edge in these debates but they found Bush more likable. Bush appeared to benefit more in the post-debate polls.

Bush-Kerry

Kerry prepared well for the three debates. He appeared tall, earnest, confident, well-informed, and "presidential." He spoke forcefully, avoiding the qualifying clauses and lengthy sentences that had plagued his speeches in the past. Bush appeared uncomfortable, scowling at Kerry's answers, often repeating himself, and failing to "connect" with his audiences. Polls showed Kerry winning each debate.

congressional candidates as well, *must* appeal to independent and Democratic crossover voters.

Group Voting We already know that various social and economic groups give disproportionate support to the Democratic and Republican parties (see Chapter 7). So it comes as no surprise that recent Democratic presidential candidates have received disproportionate support from African Americans, Catholics, Jews, less-educated, and union workers; Republican presidential candidates have fared better among whites, Protestants, and better-educated voters (see Figure 8.6 on page 277). That is, these groups have given a larger percentage of their vote to the Democratic or Republican candidates than the candidate received from the total electorate.

Race and Gender Gaps Among the more interesting group voting patterns is the serious *gender gap* affecting recent Republican candidates. Although Reagan won the women's vote in both 1980 and 1984, his vote percentages among men were considerably higher than among women. George H. W. Bush lost the women's vote in both 1988 and 1992. In 1996 the gender gap widened, with a 54 percent of women voting for Clinton as opposed to only 38 percent for Dole, and continued in 2000 with women giving Gore 54 percent of the vote as opposed to Bush's 43 percent. Again in 2004 women gave Democrat John F. Kerry 54 pecent of their vote. African Americans have long constituted the most loyal group of Democratic voters, regularly giving the Democratic presidential nominee up to 90 percent or more of their vote. The overall Hispanic vote is Democratic, although a significant portion of Hispanics, notably Cuban Americans in Florida, vote Republican.

Candidate Image In an age of direct communication between candidates and voters via television, the image of candidates and their ability to relate to audiences have emerged as important determinants of voter choice. As party and group identifications have moderated and independent and middle-of-the-road identifications among voters have grown, the personal characteristics of candidates have become central to many voters. Indeed, the personal qualities of candidates are most important in the decision of less partisan, less ideological voters. Candidate image is most important in presidential contests, inasmuch as presidential candidates are personally more visible to the voter than candidates for lesser offices.[16]

It is difficult to identify exactly what personal qualities appeal most to voters. Warmth, compassion, strength, confidence, honesty, sincerity, good humor, appearance, and "character" all seem important. "Character" has become a central feature of media coverage of candidates (see Chapter 6). Reports of extramarital affairs, experimentation with drugs, draft dodging, cheating in college, shady financial dealings, conflicts of interest, or lying or misrepresenting facts receive heavy media coverage because they attract large audiences. But it is difficult to estimate how many voters are swayed by so-called character issues.

Attractive personal qualities can win support from opposition-party identifiers and people who disagree on the issues. John F. Kennedy's handsome and youthful appearance, charm, self-confidence, and disarming good humor defeated the heavy-jowled, shifty-eyed, defensive, and ill-humored Richard Nixon. Ronald Reagan's folksy mannerisms, warm humor, and comfortable rapport with television audiences justly earned him the title "The Great Communicator." Reagan disarmed his critics by laughing at his own personal flubs—falling asleep at meetings, forgetting names—and by telling his own age jokes. His personal appeal

THINK
AGAIN

Should people vote on the basis of a candidate's personal character rather than his or her policy positions?

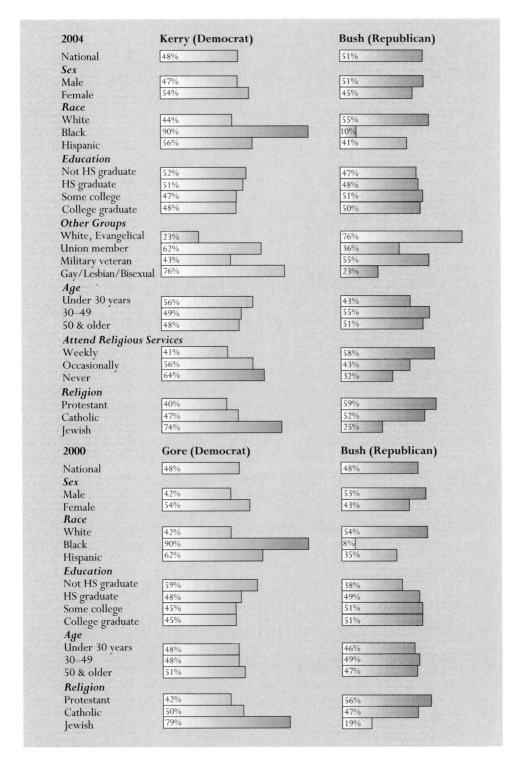

FIGURE 8.6 Group Voting in Presidential Elections

Democratic presidential candidates regularly do better among African American, Hispanic, lower-income, less-educated voters. The gender gap—men tending to vote Republican and women Democratic—first emerged in the Reagan years. Increasingly, white religious voters are casting their ballots for Republican candidates.

Source: Election exit polls, Voter News Service, National Election Pool.

won more Democratic voters than any other Republican candidate has won in modern history, and he won the votes of many people who disagreed with him on the issues.

Bush's resolute position on Iraq and the war on terrorism created a popular image of him as "a strong leader," someone who "has clear stands on issues," and is "honest and trustworthy." He is also seen as having a "strong religious faith." Kerry was seen as someone who "will bring needed change," "cares about people like me," and is "intelligent" (see Table 8.5). Bush was also seen as friendly and likeable, while Kerry was seen as somewhat aloof and austere.

An important reservation regarding image voting: although many voters cite favorable or unfavorable personal characteristics of the candidates as the reason for their vote, it turns out that Democratic voters usually perceive favorable attributes in Democratic candidates and unfavorable attributes in Republican candidates, and Republican voters see just the opposite. In other words, the voters' perceptions of the candidates' personal qualities are influenced by the voters' party identifications and perhaps by their group affiliations as well. Thus evaluations of the candidates' personal characteristics may not be a significant independent determinant of voter choice, especially for people who identify themselves as strong Democrats or Republicans.

The Economy Fairly accurate predictions of voting outcomes in presidential elections can be made from models of the American economy. Economic conditions at election time—recent growth or decline in personal income, the unemployment rate, consumer confidence, and so on—are related to the vote given the incumbent versus the challenger. Ever since the once-popular Republican incumbent Herbert Hoover was trounced by Franklin Roosevelt as the Great Depression of the 1930s deepened, politicians have understood that voters hold the incumbent party responsible for hard economic times.

Perhaps no other lesson has been as well learned by politicians: hard economic times hurt incumbents and favor challengers. The economy may not be the only important factor in presidential voting, but it is certainly a factor of great impor-

TABLE 8.5 Images of Bush and Kerry 2004

Considering the following qualities and characteristics, please state whether you think each one better describes John F. Kerry or George W. Bush.

Percentage who said:		Kerry	Bush
25%	Will bring needed change	95%	4%
17%	Has clear stand on issues	23%	75%
16%	Strong leader	14%	85%
11%	Honest, trustworthy	28%	70%
10%	Cares about people like me	76%	23%
8%	Intelligent	91%	7%
7%	Strong religious faith	9%	90%

tance.[17] Some evidence indicates that it is not voters' *own* personal economic well-being that affects their vote but rather voter perception of *general* economic conditions. People who perceive the economy as getting worse are likely to vote against the incumbent party, whereas people who think the economy is getting better support the incumbent.[18] Thus voters who thought the economy was getting *worse* in 1992 supported challenger Bill Clinton over incumbent president George Bush. But the reverse was true in 1996; more people thought the economy was better, and the people who thought so voted heavily for incumbent Bill Clinton. In 2000, Gore won the votes of those who thought the economy was "excellent," but economic voting did not seem to be as influential as in previous presidential races. The economy was cited as "most important" by about one-fifth of the voters in 2004 and Kerry won the vast majority of these voters.

Issue Voting Casting one's vote exclusively on the basis of the policy positions of the candidates is rare. Most voters are unaware of the specific positions taken by candidates on the issues. Indeed, voters often believe that their preferred candidate agrees with them on the issues, even when this is not the case. In other words, voters project their own policy views onto their favorite candidate more often than they decide to vote for a candidate because of his or her position on the issues.

However, when asked specifically about issues, voters are willing to name those they care most about (see Table 8.6). Voters do not always make their choices based on a candidate's stated policy positions, but voters *do* strongly favor candidates whose policy views they assume match their own. Only when a key issue takes center stage do voters really become aware of what the candidates actually propose to do. In the 1992, 1996, and 2000 elections, the economy was the issue that voters cared about most. In all three elections, Clinton and Gore won the votes of the people most concerned about the economy (see Table 8.6).

To the surprise of many commentators, "moral values" was cited as the most important issue by voters leaving the polls in 2004. Bush won over three-quarters of these voters. Faith and family appeared to underlie concern with moral values. Bush had never disguised his religious faith. Bans on same-sex

TABLE 8.6 Issues the Voters Cared about in 2004

Presidential Vote of Those Who Listed Issue as "Most Important"

Rank	Percentage who said:		Who they voted for: Kerry	Bush
1	21%	Moral values	19%	78%
2	20%	Economy/jobs	82%	16%
3	18%	Terrorism	15%	85%
4	15%	Iraq	76%	23%
5	8%	Health care	79%	20%
6	5%	Taxes	47%	53%
7	4%	Education	75%	24%

marriage were on referenda ballots in eleven states and may have helped inspire a heavy turnout for Bush.

Bush had tried to portray the war in Iraq as part of a broader war on terrorism. But while Bush won the votes of people concerned with terrorism, Kerry won the votes of those concerned with the war in Iraq. Voters opposed to the war in Iraq went heavily for Kerry, while supporters of the war voted heavily for Bush.

SUMMARY NOTES

- In a democracy, elections decide "who governs." But they also indirectly affect public policy, influencing "who gets what."

- Although winning candidates often claim a mandate for their policy proposals, in reality few campaigns present clear policy alternatives to the voters, few voters cast their ballots on the basis of policy considerations, and the policy preferences of the electorate can seldom be determined from election outcomes.

- Nevertheless, voters can influence future policy directions through retrospective judgments about the performance of incumbents, returning them to office or turning them out. Most retrospective voting appears to center on the economy.

- Personal ambition for power and celebrity drives the decision to seek public office. Political entrepreneurship, professionalism, and careerism have come to dominate political recruitment; lawyers have traditionally dominated American politics.

- Incumbents begin campaigns with many advantages: name recognition, financial support, goodwill from services they perform for constituents, large-scale public projects they bring to their districts, and the other resources of office.

- Campaigning for office is largely a media activity, dominated by professional advertising specialists, fund raisers, media consultants, and pollsters.

- The professionalization of campaigning and the heavy costs of a media campaign drive up the costs of running for office. These huge costs make candidates heavily dependent on financial support from individuals and organizations. Fund raising occupies more of a candidate's time than any other campaign activity.

- Campaign contributions are made by politically active individuals and organizations, including political action committees. Many contributions are made in order to gain access to policy makers and assistance with government business. Some contributors are ideologically motivated; others merely seek to rub shoulders with powerful people.

- Presidential primary election strategies emphasize appeals to party activists and core supporters, including the more ideologically motivated primary voters.

- In the general election campaign, presidential candidates usually seek to broaden their appeal to moderate, centrist voters while holding on to their core supporters. Campaigns must focus on states where the candidate has the best chance of gaining the 270 electoral votes needed to win.

- Voter choice is influenced by party identification, group membership, perceived image of the candidates, economic conditions, and, to a lesser extent, ideology and issue preferences.

KEY TERMS

SUGGESTED READINGS

Abramson, Paul R., John H. Aldrich, and David W. Rohde. *Change and Continuity in the 2000 Elections.* Washington, D.C.: CQ Press, 2002. An in-depth analysis of the 2000 presidential and congressional elections assessing the impact of party loyalties, presidential performance, group memberships, and policy preferences on voter choice.

DiClerico, Robert, ed. *Campaigns and Elections in America.* Upper Saddle River, N.J.: Prentice Hall, 2000. Essays by leading scholars on the nominating process, campaign finance, media campaigning, turnout, voter choice, and the party system.

Fiorina, Morris P. *Retrospective Voting in American National Elections.* Princeton, N.J.: Princeton University Press, 1988. Argues that retrospective judgments guide voter choice in presidential elections.

Flanigan, William H., and Nancy H. Zingale. *Political Behavior of the American Electorate.* 11th ed. Washington, D.C.: CQ Press, 2002. A brief but comprehensive summary of the extensive research literature on the effects of party identification, opinion, ideology, the media, and candidate image on voter choice and election outcomes.

Iyengar, Shanto, and Stephen Ansolabehere. *Going Negative: How Political Advertisements Shrink and Polarize the Electorate.* New York: Free Press, 1996. The real problem with negative political ads is not that they sway voters to support one candidate over another, but that they reinforce the belief that all are dishonest and cynical.

Matalin, Mary, and James Carville. *All's Fair: Love, War and Running for President.* New York: Random House and Simon & Schuster, 1994. Inside the presidential campaign of George Bush and Bill Clinton in 1992 by their respective campaign directors, who were romantically involved and were married after the campaign.

Polsby, Nelson W., and Aaron Wildavsky. *Presidential Elections: Strategies and Structures.* 10th ed. New York: Chatham House, 2000. Updated classic on presidential campaign strategies.

Rosenstone, Steven. *Forecasting Presidential Elections.* New Haven, Conn.: Yale University Press, 1985. A discussion of the models employed to forecast presidential election outcomes based on unemployment, inflation, and personal income statistics.

Sabato, Larry J., and Glenn R. Simpson. *Dirty Little Secrets: The Persistence of Corruption in American Politics.* New York: Random House Times Books, 1996. A political scientist and a journalist combine to produce a lurid report on unethical and corrupt practices in campaigns and elections.

Sorauf, Frank J. *Inside Campaign Finance.* New Haven, Conn.: Yale University Press, 1992. A comprehensive description of campaign financing in America, individual contributions, PACs, party funds, independent organizations, soft money, intermediaries and brokers, and so on, together with a balanced appraisal of the prospects and potential consequences of reform.

MAKE IT REAL

ELECTION IN ACTION: 2004 PRESIDENTIAL ELECTION

No presidential election in recent history illustrated not only the importance of every vote but the importance of a candidate's campaign tactics in accumulating votes, and more importantly how those votes translate into Electoral College votes. And although the Electoral College's continued existence has been hotly disputed, it still forms the backbone strategy of anyone who is seriously considering a run at the presidency. Also playing a huge role in determining the outcome of the 2000 presidential campaign were the continued importance of raising money (lots of it) and the influence of third party candidates on the race. In this simulation you will become the presidential campaign manager of either the Republicans or the Democrats for the 2004 race. But watch out—you need to raise enough money and skillfully position your candidate on the issues to fend off potential third party candidates to win the White House.

9

INTEREST GROUPS:
GETTING THEIR SHARE
AND MORE

THINK
ABOUT POLITICS

1 Do special-interest groups in America obstruct the majority of citizens' wishes on public policy?
Yes ● No ●

2 Should people join an interest group such as the American Association of Retired Persons for its discounts, magazines, and travel guides even if they disagree with its policy goals?
Yes ● No ●

3 Should state and local governments use taxpayers' money to lobby Congress to get federal funds?
Yes ● No ●

4 Should former government officials be allowed to lobby their former colleagues?
Yes ● No ●

5 Should interest groups be prohibited from making large campaign contributions in their effort to influence public policy?
Yes ● No ●

6 If a lobbyist makes a campaign contribution to a Congress member, hoping to gain support for a bill, is this a form of bribery?
Yes ● No ●

7 Is organized interest-group activity a cause of government gridlock?
Yes ● No ●

What role do interest groups play in politics? Their organization, their money, and their influence in Washington raise the possibility that interest groups, rather than individuals, may in fact hold the real power in politics. They may be the "who" that determines the "what" that the rest of us get.

Interest-Group Power

Organization is a means to power—to determining who gets what in society. Interest groups are organizations that seek to influence government policy. Organization concentrates power and concentrated power prevails over unorganized interests. The First Amendment to the Constitution recognizes "the right of the people peaceably to assemble and to petition the government for a redress of grievances." Americans thus enjoy a fundamental right to organize themselves to influence government.

Electoral versus Interest-Group Systems The *electoral system* is organized to represent geographically defined constituencies—states and congressional districts in Congress. The *interest-group system* is organized to represent economic, professional, ideological, religious, racial, gender, and issue constituencies. In other words, the interest-group system supplements the electoral system by providing people with another avenue of participation. Individuals may participate in politics by supporting candidates and parties in elections, and also by joining **interest groups**, organizations that pressure government to advance their interests.[1]

Interest group activity provides more direct representation of policy preferences than electoral politics. At best, individual voters can influence government policy only indirectly through elections (see Chapter 8). Elected politicians try to represent many different—and even occasionally conflicting—interests. But interest groups provide concentrated and direct representation of policy views in government.

Checking Majoritarianism The interest-group system gives voice to special interests, whereas parties and the electoral system cater to the majority interest. Indeed, interest groups are often defended as a check on **majoritarianism**, the tendency of democratic governments to allow the faint preferences of a majority to prevail over the intense feelings of minorities. However, the interest-group system is frequently attacked because it obstructs the majority from implementing its preferences in public policy.

Concentrating Benefits While Dispersing Costs Interest groups seek special benefits, subsidies, privileges, and protections from the government. The costs of these *concentrated* benefits are usually *dispersed* to all taxpayers, none of whom individually bears enough added cost to merit spending time, energy, or money to organize a group to oppose the benefit. Thus the interest-group system concentrates benefits to the few and

THINK
AGAIN

Do special-interest groups in America obstruct the majority of citizens' wishes on public policy?

disperses costs to the many. The system favors small, well-organized, homogeneous interests that seek the expansion of government activity at the expense of larger but less well-organized citizen-taxpayers. Over long periods of time, the cumulative activities of many special-interest groups, each seeking concentrated benefits to themselves and dispersed costs to others, result in what has been termed **organizational sclerosis**, a society so encrusted with subsidies, benefits, regulations, protections, and special treatments for organized groups that work, productivity, and investment are discouraged and everyone's standard of living is lowered.

Origins of Interest Groups

James Madison viewed interest groups—which he called "factions"—as a necessary evil in politics. He defined a faction as "a number of citizens, whether amounting to a majority or a minority of the whole, who are united and actuated by some common impulse of passion, or of interest, adverse to the rights of other citizens, or to the permanent and aggregate interests of the community." He believed that interest groups not only conflict with each other but, more important, also conflict with the common good. Nevertheless, Madison believed that the origin of interest groups was to be found in human nature—"a zeal for different opinions concerning religion, concerning government, and many other points"—and therefore impossible to eliminate from politics.[2]

Protecting Economic Interests Madison believed that "the most common and durable source of factions, has been the various and unequal distribution of property." With genuine insight, he identified *economic interests* as the most prevalent in politics: "a landed interest, a manufacturing interest, a mercantile interest, a moneyed interest, with many lesser interests." From Madison's era to the present, businesspeople and professionals, bankers and insurers, farmers and factory workers, merchants and shippers have organized themselves to press their demands on government (see *Up Close:* "Superlobby: The Business Roundtable").

Advancing Social Movements Major social movements in American history have spawned many interest groups. Abolitionist groups were formed before the Civil War to fight slavery. The National Association for the Advancement of Colored People (NAACP) emerged in 1909 to fight segregation laws and to rally public support against lynching and other violence against African Americans. Farm organizations emerged from the populist movement of the late nineteenth century to press demands for railroad rate regulation and easier credit terms. The small trade unions that workers formed in the nineteenth century to improve their pay and working conditions gave way to large national unions in the 1930s as workers sought protection for the rights to organize, bargain collectively, and strike. The success of the women's suffrage movement led to the formation of the League of Women Voters in the early twentieth century, and a generation later the feminist movement inspired the National Organization for Women (NOW).

Seeking Government Benefits As government expands its activities, it creates more interest groups. Wars create veterans' organizations. The first large veterans' group—the Grand Army of the Republic—formed after the Civil War and

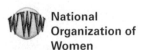
NAACP
Oldest civil rights organization, working on behalf of African Americans.
www.naacp.org

National Organization of Women
An organization of "feminist activists" concerned with abortion rights, lesbian rights, sexual harassment, affirmative action, and electing feminists.
www.now.org

interest groups
Organizations that seek to influence government policy.

majoritarianism Tendency of democratic governments to allow the faint preferences of the majority to prevail over the intense feelings of minorities.

organizational sclerosis
Society encrusted with so many special benefits to interest groups that everyone's standard of living is lowered.

Superlobby: The Business Roundtable

The Business Roundtable was established in 1972 "in the belief that business executives should take an increased role in the continuing debates about public policy."* The organization is composed of the chief executives of the 200 largest corporations in America and is financed through corporate membership fees.

The power of the Business Roundtable stems in part from its "firm rule" that a corporate chief executive officer (CEO) cannot send a substitute to its meetings. Moreover, corporate CEOs lobby the Congress in person rather than sending paid lobbyists. Members of Congress are impressed when the chair of IBM appears at a congressional hearing on business regulation or when the chair of GTE speaks to a congressional committee about taxation, or when the chair of Prudential talks to Congress about Social Security, or when the head of B. F. Goodrich testifies before the Senate Judiciary Committee about antitrust policy. One congressional staff member explained, "If a corporation sends its Washington representative to our office, he's probably going to be shunted over to a legislative assistant. But the chairman of the board is going to get in to see the senator." Another aide echoed those sentiments: "Very few members of Congress would not meet with the president of a Business Roundtable corporation."†

---

*Quotations about the reasons for the establishment of the Business Roundtable from "The History of the Business Roundtable," 1998.

†*Time*, April 13, 1981, pp. 76–77.

---

successfully lobbied for bonus payments to veterans over the years. Today the American Legion, the Veterans of Foreign Wars, and the Vietnam Veterans of America engage in lobbying the Congress and monitor the activities of the Department of Veterans Affairs. As the welfare state grew, so did organizations seeking to obtain benefits for their members, including the nation's largest interest group, the American Association of Retired Persons (AARP). Over time, organizations seeking to protect and expand welfare benefits for the poor also emerged (see *People in Politics:* "Marian Wright Edelman, Lobbying for the Poor"). Federal grant-in-aid programs to state and local governments inspired the development of governmental interest groups—the Council of State Governments, the National League of Cities, the National Governors Association, the U.S. Conference of Mayors, and so on—so that it is not uncommon today to see governments lobby other governments. Expanded government support for education led to political activity by the National Education Association, the American Federation of Teachers, the American Association of Land Grant Colleges and Universities, and other educational groups.

Responding to Government Regulation As more businesses and professions came under government regulation in the twentieth century, more organizations formed to protect their interests, including such large and powerful groups as the American Medical Association (doctors), the American Bar Association (lawyers), and the National Association of Broadcasters (broadcasters). Indeed, the issue of regulation—whether of public utilities, interstate transportation, mine safety, medicines, or children's pajamas—always causes the formation of interest groups. Some form to demand regulation; others form to protect their members from regulatory burdens.

 Business Roundtable

Organization representing largest U.S. corporations.
www.broundtable.org

 Children's Defense Fund

Advocacy organization for welfare programs.
www.childrendefense.org

(a)

(b)

(c)

(d)

(e)

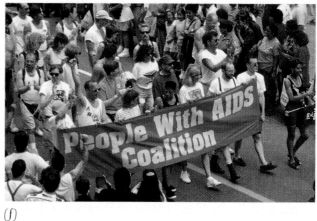
(f)

From (a) the Whiskey Rebellion of 1794 to (b) violent early union protests like the Haymarket Riot of 1886 to (c) Carrie Nation's battle to ban liquor and (d) the women's suffrage movement of the late nineteenth and early twentieth centuries to (e) the civil rights marches of the 1960s and (f) the gay rights marches of the 1990s, protest has bad a long and strong history for interest groups in the United States. Some protests have been violent and others peaceful, but by addressing key issues of the time, all have prompted public debate, and many have resulted in changes in public policy.

Marian Wright Edelman, Lobbying for the Poor

As founder and president of the Children's Defense Fund, Marian Wright Edelman has become legendary in Washington as a persuasive and persistent lobbyist on behalf of civil rights and social welfare legislation. A close friend of the Kennedy family, Edelman regularly testifies at Senate committee hearings, providing rapid-fire statistics on the effects of poverty on African American children. Each year the Children's Defense Fund, with a staff of more than a hundred in its Washington headquarters, produces numerous reports on infant mortality, homelessness, prenatal care, child nutrition, drug use, child abuse, teenage pregnancy, and single-parent households.

Marian Wright grew up in segregated rural South Carolina, the academically gifted daughter of a Baptist minister with a strong commitment to social justice. At an early age, she worked at the Wright House for the Aged, which her father had established. She entered all-black Spelman College in Atlanta and studied abroad at the Sorbonne in Paris and the University of Geneva, intending to take up a career in the foreign service. But Wright changed her career plans when she became involved in the early civil rights struggles in Atlanta. After graduating from Spelman, she entered Yale Law School to prepare herself in civil rights law. Upon her graduation in 1963, she immediately went to work for the National Association for the Advancement of Colored People Legal Defense Fund and traveled to Mississippi, where for four years she undertook the dangerous work of defending civil rights workers. In 1967 she met Peter Edelman, a Harvard Law School graduate and legislative aide to Senator Robert Kennedy; together they persuaded Kennedy to personally tour the most poverty-stricken areas of the Mississippi Delta, where the senator directly confronted hungry children living in miserable conditions.

The following year Wright and Edelman were married and settled in Washington, where she established the Washington Research Project, a public-interest research and lobbying organization on behalf of President Lyndon Johnson's War on Poverty. She maintained her Washington base even while directing the Harvard University Center for Law and Education during the several years that her husband served as vice president of the University of Massachusetts. In 1973 she organized the Children's Defense Fund (CDF) in Washington, "a strong national voice for children and family." The Children's Defense Fund describes its mission: "to leave no child behind." It was the principal lobbying group behind the Head Start program as well as federal child care and the Family Leave Act of 1993.

Marian Wright Edelman has been especially effective as an advocate of social welfare programs with her lively style, sense of urgency, and wealth of information about children in poverty. In 2000 Edelman received the Presidential Medal of Freedom, the nation's highest civilian award.[*]

[*]*New York Times.* February 27, 1986, p. A10.

The Organized Interests in Washington

There are more than 1 million nonprofit organizations in the United States, several thousand of which are officially registered in Washington as lobbyists.[3] Trade and professional associations and corporations are the most common lobbies in Washington, but unions, public-interest groups, farm groups, environmental groups, ideological groups, religious and civil rights organizations, women's groups, veterans and defense-related groups, groups organized around a single issue (for example, Mothers Against Drunk Driving), and even organizations representing state and local governments also recognize that they need to be "where the action is." Among this huge assortment of organizations, many of which are very influential in their highly specialized field, there are a number of well-known organized interests. Even a partial list of organized interest groups (see Table 9.1) demonstrates the breadth and complexities of interest-group life in American politics.

TABLE 9.1 • Major Organized Interest Groups, by Type

Business

Business Roundtable
National Association of Manufacturers
National Federation of Independent Businesses
National Small Business Association
U.S. Chamber of Commerce

Trade

American Bankers Association
American Gas Association
American Iron and Steel Institute
American Petroleum Institute
American Truckers Association
Automobile Dealers Association
Home Builders Association
Motion Picture Association of America
National Association of Broadcasters
National Association of Real Estate Boards

Professional

American Bar Association
American Medical Association
Association of Trial Lawyers
National Education Association

Union

AFL-CIO
American Federation of State, County, and Municipal Employees
American Federation of Teachers
International Brotherhood of Teamsters
International Ladies' Garment Workers Union
National Association of Letter Carriers
United Auto Workers
United Postal Workers
United Steel Workers

Agricultural

American Farm Bureau Federation
National Cattlemen's Association
National Farmers Union
National Grange
National Milk Producers Federation
Tobacco Institute

Women

League of Women Voters
National Organization for Women

Public Interest

Common Cause
Consumer Federation of America
Public Citizen
Public Interest Research Groups

Ideological

American Conservative Union
Americans for Constitutional Action (conservative)
Americans for Democratic Action (liberal)
People for the American Way (liberal)

Single Issue

Mothers Against Drunk Driving
National Abortion Rights Action League
National Rifle Association
National Right to Life Committee
Planned Parenthood Federation of America
National Taxpayers Union

Environmental

Environmental Defense Fund
Greenpeace
National Wildlife Federation
National Resources Defense Council
Nature Conservancy
Sierra Club
Wilderness Society

Religious

American Israel Public Affairs Committee
Anti-Defamation League of B'nai B'rith
Christian Coalition
National Council of Churches
U.S. Catholic Conference

Civil Rights

American Civil Liberties Union
American Indian Movement
Mexican-American Legal Defense and Education Fund
National Association for the Advancement of Colored People
National Urban League
Rainbow Coalition
Southern Christian Leadership Conference

Age Related

American Association of Retired Persons
Children's Defense Fund

Veterans

American Legion
Veterans of Foreign Wars
Vietnam Veterans of America

Defense

Air Force Association
American Security Council
Army Association
Navy Association

Government

National Association of Counties
National Conference of State Legislators
National Governors Association
National League of Cities
U.S. Conference of Mayors

U.S. Chamber of Commerce

Representing business, "3 million companies of all sizes." ***www.uschamber.com***

Business and Trade Organizations Traditionally, economic organizations have dominated interest-group politics in Washington. There is ample evidence that economic interests continue to play a major role in national policy making, despite the rapid growth over the last several decades of consumer and environmental organizations. Certainly in terms of the sheer number of organizations with offices and representatives in Washington, business and professional groups and occupational and trade associations predominate. More than half of the organizations with offices in Washington are business or trade associations, and all together these organizations account for about 75 percent of all of the reported lobbying expenditures.[4]

Business interests are represented, first of all, by large inclusive organizations, such as the U.S. Chamber of Commerce, representing thousands of local chambers of commerce across the nation; the National Association of Manufacturers; the Business Roundtable, representing the nation's largest corporations; and the National Federation of Independent Businesses, representing small business. Specific business interests are also represented by thousands of **trade associations**. These associations can closely monitor the interests of their specialized memberships. Among the most powerful of these associations are the American Bankers Association, the American Gas Association, the American Iron and Steel Institute, the National Association of Real Estate Boards, the American Petroleum Institute, and the National Association of Broadcasters. In addition, many individual corporations and firms achieve representation in Washington by opening their own lobbying *offices or by hiring* experienced professional lobbying and law firms.

Professional Associations Professional associations rival business and trade organizations in lobbying influence. The American Bar Association (ABA), the American Medical Association (AMA), and the National Education Association (NEA) are three of the most influential groups in Washington. For example, the American Bar Association, which includes virtually all of the nation's practicing attorneys, and its more specialized offspring, the American Association of Trial Lawyers, have successfully resisted efforts to reform the nation's tort laws (see *A Conflicting View:* "America Drowning in a Sea of Lawsuits," Chapter 13).

Many years ago, the AMA fought against national health insurance plans, arguing that socialized medicine would erode quality medical care. But when Medicare for the aged and Medicaid for the poor were pushed forward by President Lyndon Johnson in 1965, the AMA switched tactics, supporting the legislation as a means of bringing vast sums of tax money into the nation's health care system. Initially the strategy proved immensely profitable: Medicare and Medicaid spending grew rapidly in the federal budget. Government payments also now account for nearly one-third of the average doctor's income. However, the AMA eventually learned that government money is almost always accompanied by government efforts to regulate costs and practices. The AMA has been forced to accept government payment schedules for various procedures. The Medicare and Medicaid programs encourage beneficiaries to enroll in health maintenance organizations (HMOs) which in turn often check physicians' practices and procedures. The AMA remains vigorously opposed to any limits on physicians' decisions about care for their patients. But only about 32 percent of the nation's physicians are now members of the AMA, down from nearly 65 percent thirty years ago. Today many physicians believe they are better represented by more specialized medical groups (for example, the American College of Surgeons, the American Academy of Family Physicians, the American Society of Internal Medicine), especially in negotiations over government fee schedules for particular procedures.

Organized Labor Labor organizations have declined in membership over the last several decades. The percentage of the nonagricultural work force belonging to unions has declined from about 37 percent in the 1950s to about 13 percent today. This decline has occurred primarily as a result of changes in the economy: rapid growth of professional, managerial, finance, technical, sales, and service em-

 American Medical Association

Professional organization of doctors that both lobbies and publishes medical research in the prestigious *Journal of the American Medical Association* (JAMA) *www.ama-assn.org*

trade associations Interest groups composed of businesses in specific industries.

ployment, where unions are weakest; and slower growth or stagnation of manufacture, mining, and construction employment, where unions are strongest. Yet even in manufacturing, union membership today is only about 20 percent of the work force.

Nevertheless, labor unions remain a major political influence in Congress and the Democratic Party. The AFL-CIO is a federation of sixty-eight separate unions with more than 13 million members. The AFL-CIO has long maintained a large and capable lobbying staff in Washington, and it provides both financial contributions and campaign services (registration, get-out-the-vote, information, endorsements) for members of Congress it favors. Many of the larger individual unions also maintain offices in Washington and offer campaign contributions and services.

Today union influence is greatest among government employees, including teachers. About 38 percent of all public sector employees are unionized. The American Federation of State, County, and Municipal Employees (AFSCME), the National Education Association (NEA), the American Federation of Teachers (AFT), and the Teamsters Union (which recruits public employees in sanitation and transportation) are among the few unions growing in membership.

Labor union political campaign contributions (see "PAC Power" below) remain a major source of union influence in Washington. The AFSCME, NEA, Teamsters, United Auto Workers, United Steel Workers, Electrical Workers, Machinists, and Letter Carriers, as well as the AFL-CIO itself, are regularly ranked among the top contributors in congressional elections. Almost all union campaign contributions go to Democratic candidates.

Farm Organizations Even though the farm population of the United States has declined from about 25 percent of the total population in the 1930s to less than 3 percent today, farmers—especially large agricultural producers—remain a very potent political force in Washington. Agricultural interests are organized both into large inclusive groups, such as the American Farm Bureau Federation and the National Grange, and into very effective specialized groups, such as the National Milk Producers and the National Cattlemen's Association. Small and low-income farmers are represented by the National Farmers Union.

Women's Organizations Women's organizations date back to the antislavery societies in pre-Civil War America. The first generation of feminists—Lucretia Mott, Elizabeth Cady Stanton, Lucy Stone, and Susan B. Anthony—learned to organize, hold public meetings, and conduct petition campaigns as abolitionists. After the Civil War, women are successful in changing many state laws that abridged the rights of married women and otherwise treated them as "chattel" (property) of their husbands. Women were also prominent in the Anti-Saloon League, which succeeded in outlawing prostitution and gambling in every state except Nevada and provided a major source of support for the Eighteenth Amendment (Prohibition). In the early twentieth century, the feminist movement concentrated on obtaining the vote (suffrage) for women. Today the League of Women Voters—a broad-based organization that provides information to voters—backs registration and get-out-the-vote drives and generally supports measures seeking to ensure honesty and integrity in government.

Interest in feminist politics revived in the wake of the civil rights movement of the 1960s. New organizations sprang up to compete with the conventional activities of the League of Women Voters by taking a more activist stance toward women's issues. The largest of these organizations is the National Organization for Women (NOW), founded in 1966.

Religious Groups Churches and religious groups have a long history of involvement in American politics—from the pre-Civil War antislavery crusades, to the prohibition effort in the early twentieth century, to the civil rights movement of the 1960s. The leadership for the historic Civil Rights Act of 1964 came from the Reverend Martin Luther King, Jr., and his Southern Christian Leadership Conference. Today religious groups span the political spectrum, from liberal organizations such as the National Council of Churches and Anti-Defamation League of B'nai B'rith, to conservative and fundamentalist organizations, such as the Christian Coalition, often referred to as the "religious right" (see *Up Close:* "The Christian Coalition: Organizing the Faithful").

The American Israel Public Affairs Committee is regularly ranked as one of Washington's most powerful lobbies (see *Up Close:* "Washington's Most Powerful Lobbies" later in this chapter). It is actually a foreign policy lobby rather than a religious lobby, although its support is concentrated in the American Jewish community. It lobbies on behalf of Israel's interests, including continuing substantial foreign aid.

Public-Interest Groups **Public-interest groups** claim to represent broad classes of people—consumers, voters, reformers, or the public as a whole. Groups with lofty-sounding names, such as Common Cause, Public Citizen, and the Consumer Federation of America, perceive themselves as balancing the narrow, "selfish" interests of business organizations, trade associations, unions, and other "special" interests. Public-interest groups generally lobby for greater government regulation of consumer products, public safety, campaign finance, and so on. Their reform agenda, as well as their call for a larger regulatory role for government, makes them frequent allies of liberal ideological groups, civil rights organizations, and environmental groups.[5]

Many public-interest groups were initially formed in the 1970s by "entrepreneurs" who saw an untapped "market" for the representation of these interests. Among the most influential public-interest groups are Common Cause, a self-styled "citizens' lobby," and the sprawling network of organizations created by consumer advocate Ralph Nader (see *People in Politics:* "Ralph Nader, People's Lobbyist"). Common Cause tends to focus on election-law reform, public financing of elections, and limitations on political contributions. The Nader organization began as a consumer protection group focusing on auto safety but soon spread to encompass a wide variety of causes.

Single-Issue Groups Like public-interest groups, **single-issue groups** appeal to principle and belief. But as their name implies, single-issue groups concentrate their attention on a single cause. They attract the support of individuals with a strong commitment to that cause. Single-issue groups have little incentive to compromise their position. They exist for a single cause; no other issues really matter to them. They are by nature passionate and often shrill. Their attraction to members is the intensity of their beliefs.

Among the most vocal single-issue groups in recent years have been the organizations on both sides of the abortion issue. The National Abortion Rights Action League (NARAL) describes itself as "pro-choice" and opposes any restrictions on a woman's right to obtain an abortion. The National Right-to-Life Committee

WWW Christian Coalition Organization "defending our godly heritage" by giving "people of faith a voice in government". *www.cc.org*

WWW Public Citizen Organization founded by Ralph Nader, devotes its site to "protecting health, safety and democracy" as well as lobbying for "strong citizen and consumer protection laws." *www.publiccitizen.com*

public-interest groups Interest groups that claim to represent broad classes of people or the public as a whole.

single-issue groups Organizations formed to support or oppose government action on a specific issue.

The Christian Coalition: Organizing the Faithful

Christian fundamentalists, whose religious beliefs are based on a literal reading of the Bible, have become a significant political force in the United States through effective organization. Perhaps the most influential Christian fundamentalist organization today is the Christian Coalition, with nearly 2 million active members throughout the country.

Fundamentalist Christians are opposed to abortion, pornography, and homosexuality; they favor the recognition of religion in public life, including prayer in schools; and they despair at the decline of traditional family values in American culture, including motion pictures and television broadcasting. Historically, fundamentalist Protestant churches avoided politics as profane and concentrated evangelical efforts on saving individual souls. Their few ventures into worldly politics—notably the prohibition movement in the early twentieth century—ended in defeat. Their strength tended to be in the southern, rural, and poorer regions of the country. They were widely ridiculed in the national media.

In the 1960s, television evangelism emerged as a religious force in the United States. The Reverend Pat Robertson founded the Christian Broadcasting Network (CBN) and later purchased the Family Channel. But efforts by social conservatives to build a "moral majority" for political action largely failed, as did Robertson's presidential candidacy in 1988. Televangelists, including Jerry Falwell and Tammy Fay Baker, suffered popular disdain following some well-publicized scandals.

Although officially nonpartisan, the Coalition became an important force in Republican politics; religious fundamentalists may constitute as much as one-third of the party's voter support. The Christian Coalition does not officially endorse candidates, but its voter guides clearly indicate which candidates reflect the coalition's position on major issues. The distribution of millions of these guides, mostly in churches on the weekend before the Tuesday election, was credited with helping Republicans capture control of Congress in 1994. The political influence of the Christian Coalition in Republican politics, and the "religious right" generally, ensures that most GOP candidates for public office publicly express support for a "profamily" agenda. This agenda includes a constitutional amendment allowing prayer in public schools; vouchers for parents to send their children to private, religious schools; banning late-term abortions as well as banning the use of taxpayer funds to pay for abortions; restrictions on pornography on cable television and the Internet; and opposition to human embryo research and human cloning.

---

describes itself as "pro-life" and opposes abortion for any reason other than to preserve the life of the mother. Other prominent single-issue groups include the National Rifle Association (opposed to gun control) and Mothers Against Drunk Driving (MADD).

Ideological Groups **Ideological organizations** pursue liberal or conservative agendas, often with great passion and considerable financial resources derived from true-believing contributors. The ideological groups rely heavily on computerized mailings to solicit funds from persons identified as holding liberal or conservative views. The oldest of the established ideological groups is the liberal Americans for Democratic Action (ADA), well known for its annual liberalism ratings of members of the Congress according to their support for or rejection of programs of concern. The American Conservative Union (ACU) also rates members of Congress each year. Overall, Democrats do better on the liberal list and Republicans on the conservative list, although both parties include some Congress members who occasionally vote on the opposite side of the fence from the majority of their fellow party members (see Table 9.2). Other interest groups, such as the AFL-CIO, the National Taxpayers Union, and the National Abortion Rights

National Rifle Association

The National Rifle Association site is devoted to opposing gun control legislation as well as employing the Second Amendment in it anti–gun control argument.
www.nra.org

ideological organizations
Interest groups that pursue ideologically based (liberal or conservative) agendas.

Ralph Nader, People's Lobbyist

Much of the credit for the growth of public-interest groups in recent decades goes to Ralph Nader, the self-appointed "people's lobbyist" who achieved national celebrity as an advocate of consumer protection laws. From seat belts and nonsmoking sections to nuclear power regulation, insurance rates, food and drug legislation, and worker safety. Nader's influence has been widely felt in American society.

The child of Lebanese immigrants who operated a small bakery in Winsted, Connecticut, Nader graduated from the Woodrow Wilson School of Public and International Affairs at Princeton University magna cum laude, then went on to Harvard Law School, where he earned an LL.B. with distinction in 1958. After a short stint in the army, Nader opened a private law practice in Hartford, Connecticut, but soon left to travel throughout the world, working as a free-lance journalist for the *Christian Science Monitor.*

An article that Nader wrote for the *Harvard Law Review* on auto design and safety brought him to the attention of then-Acting Secretary of Labor (later U.S. Senator from New York) Daniel Patrick Moynihan. Moynihan hired the young attorney as a staff consultant on highway safety. While employed at the Department of Labor, Nader wrote and published his book *Unsafe at Any Speed* (1965), which charged that General Motors Corporation preferred styling to safety. Nader was thrust further into the national spotlight when he sued General Motors for invading his privacy by hiring private detectives to investigate him.

With his $16 million in settlement money (plus substantial royalty and speaking income), Nader began to construct an organizational colossus.

In 1971 Nader started Public Citizen, Inc., to enlist members of the general public in a broad array of causes. Among these causes: *Congress Watch,* which directly lobbies Congress on health, safety, and environmental issues, as well as campaign finance reform; *The Health Research Group,* which lobbies the Food and Drug Administration for greater regulation, including tobacco restrictions; *The Litigation Group,* which generates class-action suits against corporations and governments; *The Critical Mass Energy Project,* which opposes nuclear energy and the oil and gas industry; *Global Trade Watch,* which opposes free trade as a threat to the environment; and *Buyers Up,* a home heating-oil cooperative that also monitors quality of gasoline sold to consumers.

Capitalizing on his campus popularity, Nader formed hundreds of Public Interest Research Groups (PIRGs) and overcame the "free-rider" problem by pressuring university administrators on many campuses to add PIRG dues to student activities fees.

Nader has resigned from direct participation in most of the organizations he founded, leaving them to be managed by a new generation of consumer advocates. Nader ran for president in 1996 as a Green Party (environmental protection) candidate. But he campaigned very little and refused to solicit contributions. In public appearances he often seemed argumentative and self-righteous. He ended up with less than 1 percent of the popular vote nationwide.

Nader's decision to actively campaign for the presidency in 2000 angered many of his liberal Democratic friends. They believed that most of his nearly 3 million votes nationwide (about 3 percent of the popular vote) would otherwise have gone to Democrat Al Gore. Nader ran again in 2004 but not all of the states granted him ballot position. He won less than one percent of the vote.

Action League, also rate members of Congress, but these groups have a narrower focus than the ADA and ACU. Yet another prominent ideological group, People for the American Way, was formed by television producer Norman Lear to coordinate the efforts of liberals in the entertainment industry as well as the general public, but it issues no ratings.

Government Lobbies The federal government's grant-in-aid programs to state and local governments (see Chapter 4) have spawned a host of lobbying efforts by these governments in Washington, D.C. Thus state- and local-government tax-

TABLE 9.2 Ideological Interest-Group Ratings for U.S. Senators

ADA Americans for Democratic Action (liberal)			ACU American Conservative Union (conservative)		
"100s"			**"100s"**		
Mikulski	(D-MD)	100	Murkowski	(R-AK)	100
Sarbanes	(D-MD)	100	Kyl	(R-AZ)	100
Kennedy	(D-MA)	100	Allard	(R-CO)	100
Corzine	(D-NJ)	100	Craig	(R-ID)	100
Reed	(D-RI)	100	Brownback	(R-KS)	100
"95s"			Roberts	(R-KS)	100
			Bunning	(R-KY)	100
Durbin	(D-IL)	95	McConnell	(R-KY)	100
Levin	(D-MI)	95	Lott	(R-MS)	100
Stabenow	(D-MI)	95	Burns	(R-MT)	100
Dayton	(D-MN)	95	Frist	(R-TN)	100
Clinton	(D-NY)	95	Hutchinson	(R-TX)	100
Conrad	(D-ND)	95	Bennett	(R-UT)	100
Jeffords	(I-VT)	95	Enzi	(R-WY)	100
Leahy	(D-VT)	95	Thomas	(R-WY)	100
"Zeros'			**"Zeros"**		
Murkowski	(R-AK)	0	Akaka	(D-HI)	0
Kyl	(R-AZ)	0	Inouye	(D-HI)	0
Roberts	(R-KS)	0	Durbin	(D-IL)	0
Buning	(R-KY)	0	Mikulski	(D-MD)	0
McConnell	(R-KY)	0	Stabenow	(D-MI)	0
Lott	(R-MS)	0	Sarbanes	(D-MD)	0
Frist	(R-TN)	0	Kennedy	(D-MA)	0
Most Liberal Republicans			Levin	(D-MI)	0
			Reed	(D-RI)	0
Collins	(R-ME)	35	Leahy	(D-VT)	0
Spector	(R-PA)	35	**Most Liberal Republicans**		
Smith	(R-OR)	35	Snowe	R-ME	65
Campbell	(R-CO)	30	Collins	R-ME	55
Snowe	(R-ME)	30	Spector	R-PA	50
Most Consecutive Democrats			Chaffee	R-RI	50
Miller	(D-GA)	30	**Most Consecutive Democrats**		
Breaux	(D-LA)	65	Nelson	(D-NE)	55
			Miller	(D-GA)	50
			Breaux	(D-LA)	45

Source: Americans for Democratic Action, www.adaction.org; American Conservative Union, www.conservative.org

payers foot the bill to lobby Washington to transfer federal taxpayers' revenues to states and communities. The National Governors Association occupies a beautiful marble building, the Hall of the States, in Washington, along with representatives of the separate states and many major cities. The National League of Cities and the National Association of Counties also maintain large Washington offices, as does the U.S. Conference of Mayors. The National Conference of State Legislators sends its lobbyists to Washington from its Denver headquarters. These groups pursue a wide policy agenda and often confront internal disputes. But they are united in their support for increased federal transfers of tax revenues to states and cities.

Leaders and Followers

Organizations require leadership. And over time leaders develop a perspective somewhat different from that of their organizations' membership. A key question in interest-group politics is how well organization leaders represent the views of their members.

Interest-Group Entrepreneurs People who create organizations and build membership in those organizations—**interest-group entrepreneurs**—have played a major role in strengthening the interest-group system in recent decades. These entrepreneurs help overcome a major obstacle to the formation of strong interest groups—the *free-rider* problem.

Free-riders are people who benefit from the efforts of others but do not contribute to the costs of those efforts. Not everyone feels an obligation to support organizations that represent their interests or views. Some people feel that their own small contribution will not make a difference in the success or failure of the organization's goals and, moreover, that they will benefit from any successes even if they are not members. Indeed, most organizations enroll only a tiny fraction of the people they claim to represent. The task of the interest-group entrepreneur is to convince people to join the organization, either by appealing to their sense of obligation or by attracting them through tangible benefits.

Marketing Membership Interest-group entrepreneurs make different appeals for membership depending on the nature of the organization. Some appeal to passion or purpose, as, for example, those who seek to create ideological (liberal or conservative) organizations, public-interest organizations committed to environmental or consumer protection or governmental reform, and single-issue organizations devoted to the support or opposition of a single policy issue (gun control, abortion, and so on). Entrepreneurs of these organizations appeal to people's sense of duty and commitment to the cause rather than to material rewards of membership. By using sophisticated computerized mailing lists, they can solicit support from sympathetic people.[6]

Business, trade, and professional organizations usually offer their members many tangible benefits in addition to lobbying on behalf of their economic interests. These benefits may include magazines, journals, and newsletters that provide access to business, trade, and professional information as well as national conventions and meetings that serve as social settings for the development of contacts, friendships, and business and professional relationships. Some organizations also offer discount travel and insurance, credit cards, and the like, that go only to dues-paying members.

It is generally easier to organize smaller, specialized economic interests than larger, general, noneconomic interests. People more easily recognize that their own membership is important to the success of a small organization, and economic interests are more readily calculated in dollar terms.

Large organizations with broad goals—such as advancing the interests of all veterans or all retired people or all automobile drivers—must rely even more heavily on tangible benefits to solicit members. Indeed, some organizations have succeeded in recruiting millions of members (for example, the AARP with 36 million

interest-group entrepreneurs Leaders who create organizations and market memberships.

free-riders People who do not belong to an organization or pay dues, yet nevertheless benefit from its activities.

members, the American Automobile Association with 28 million members), most of whom have very little knowledge about the policy positions or lobbying activities of the organization. These members joined to receive specific benefits—magazines, insurance, travel tips, discounts. Leaders of these organizations may claim to speak for millions of members, but it is unlikely that these millions all share the policy views expressed by the leaders.

Organizational Democracy and Leader/Member Agreement Most organized interest groups are run by a small group of leaders and activists. Few interest groups are governed democratically; members may drop out if they do not like the direction their organization is taking but rarely do they have the opportunity to directly challenge or replace the organization's leadership. Relatively few members attend national meetings, vote in organizational elections, or try to exercise influence within their organization. Thus the leadership may not always reflect the views of the membership, especially in large organizations that rely heavily on tangible benefits to recruit members. Leaders of these organizations enjoy considerable freedom in adopting policy positions and negotiating, bargaining, and compromising in the political arena.

The exception to this rule is the single-issue group. Because the strength of these groups is in the intensity of their members' beliefs, the leaders of such groups are closely tied to their members' views. They cannot bargain or compromise these views or adopt policy positions at variance with those of their members.

Class Bias in Membership Americans are joiners. A majority of the population belong to at least one organization, most often a church. Yet membership in organized interest groups is clearly linked to socioeconomic status. Membership is greatest among professional and managerial, college-educated, and high-income persons.[7]

The Washington Lobbyists

Washington is a labyrinth of interest representatives—lawyers and law firms; independent consultants; public and governmental relations firms; business, professional, and trade associations; and advocates of special causes. It is estimated that more than 15,000 people in Washington fit the definition of **lobbyist,** a person working to influence government policies and actions. This figure suggests at least twenty-eight lobbyists for every member of Congress. Roughly $1.5 *billion* are spent on direct lobbying activities *each year;*[8] this figure does *not* include political campaign contributions. The top spenders for direct lobbying are listed in Table 9.3.

Who Are the Lobbyists? Lobbyists in Washington share a common goal—to influence the making and enforcing of laws—and common tactics to achieve this goal. Many lobbyists are the employees of interest-group organizations who devote all of their efforts to their sponsors.

Other lobbyists are located in independent law, consulting, or public relations firms that take on clients for fees (see Table 9.4). Independent lobbyists, especially law firms, are often secretive about whom they represent, especially when they represent foreign governments. Lobbyists frequently prefer to label their activities as "government relations," "public affairs," "regulatory liaison," "legislative counseling," or merely "representation."

lobbyist Person working to influence government policies and actions.

TABLE 9.3 Top Lobbying Spenders

Rank	Organization	Annual Spending
1	Chamber of Commerce of the U.S.	$26,160,160
2	Business Roundtable	$21,480,000
3	American Medical Assn.	$16,640,000
4	General Electric	$16,020,000
5	Edison Electric Institute	$12,000,000
6	American Hospital Assn.	$11,950,000
7	Philip Morris	$11,220,000
8	Lockheed Martin	$11,170,000
9	Verizon Communications	$10,480,000
10	Schering-Plough Corp.	$9,180,000
11	Seniors Coalition	$9,022,096
12	National Assn. of Realtors	$8,920,000
13	General Motors	$8,805,620
14	Assn of American Railroads	$8,760,160
15	Ford Motor Co.	$8,008,000
16	Boeing Co.	$7,820,000
17	American Council of Life Insurance	$7,712,090
18	Blue Cross/Blue Shield	$7,655,822
19	AT&T	$7,480,000
19	Pharmaceutical Research & Mfrs of America	$7,480,000

Source: Reprinted by permission of the Center for Responsive Politics, *Influence, Inc.* 2000. There is considerable change from year to year in the list, depending on the nature of the legislation before Congress.

In reality, many independent lawyers and lobbyists in Washington are "fixers" who offer to influence government policies for a price. Many are former government officials—former Congress members, cabinet secretaries, White House aides, and the like—who "know their way around." Their personal connections help to "open doors" to allow their paying clients to "just get a chance to talk" with top officials.

TABLE 9.4 Washington's Top Independent Lobbying Firms

Rank/Organization

1	Cassidy & Associates	11	Podesta/Mattoon
2	Verner, Liipfert et al.	12	Quinn Gillespie & Assoc.
3	Patton Boggs LLP	13	Dutko Group
4	Akin, Gump et al.	14	Timmons & Co.
5	Preston, Gates et al.	15	Clark & Weinstock
6	Van Scoyoc Associates	16	Hooper, Owen et al.
7	PricewaterhouseCoopers	17	Paul Magliocchetti Assoc.
8	Washington Counsel Ernst & Young	18	Hogan & Hartson
9	Barbour, Griffith & Rogers	19	Carmen Group
10	Williams & Jensen	20	Griffin, Johnson et al.

Source: Reprinted by permission of the Center for Responsive Politics, 2000.

Washington's Most Powerful Lobbies

Fortune magazine sponsored a survey of more than 2,000 Washington "insiders," including members of Congress, their staffs, and White House officials, asking them to rank the most powerful lobbyists in the capital. The results were as follows:

The "Power 25"

1. American Association of Retired Persons
2. American Israel Public Affairs Committee
3. National Federation of Independent Business
4. National Rifle Association of America
5. AFL-CIO
6. Association of Trial Lawyers of America
7. Christian Coalition
8. Credit Union National Association
9. National Right to Life Committee
10. American Medical Association
11. Chamber of Commerce of the U.S.A.
12. Independent Insurance Agencies of America
13. National Association of Manufacturers
14. American Farm Bureau Federation
15. National Restaurant Association
16. National Association of Home Builders of the U.S.
17. National Association of Realtors
18. National Association of Broadcasters
19. Motion Picture Association of America
20. American Bankers Association
21. National Education Association
22. Health Insurance Association of America
23. American Council of Life Insurance
24. National Beer Wholesalers Association
25. Veterans of Foreign Wars of the United States

Source: Reprinted from *Fortune,* December 8, 1997. Copyright © 1997 Time, Inc. Reprinted by permission of *Fortune.*

Some lobbying organizations rely heavily on their campaign contributions to achieve lobbying power; others rely on large memberships, and still others on politically active members who concentrate their attention on a narrow range of issues (see *Up Close:* "Washington's Most Powerful Lobbies").

Washington's army of lobbyists includes many former members of Congress. Lobbying is a favorite occupation of former members; they can command much higher salaries as lobbyists than they did as Congress members. Lobbying firms are pleased to have people who know the lawmaking process from the inside and who can easily "schmooze" with their former colleagues.

Regulation of Lobbies The Constitution's First Amendment guarantee of the right "to petition the government for a redress of grievances" protects lobbying. But the government can and does regulate lobbying activities, primarily through disclosure laws. The Regulation of Lobbying Act requires lobbyists to register and to report how much they spend, but definitions of *lobbying* are unclear and enforcement is weak. Many large lobbying groups—for example, the National Association of Manufacturers, the American Bankers Association, and Americans for Constitutional Action—have never registered as lobbyists. These organizations claim that because lobbying is not their principal activity, they need not register under the law. In addition, financial reports of lobbyists grossly underestimate the extent of lobbying in Congress because the law requires reports of only money spent for *direct* lobbying before Congress, not money spent for public relations or grass-roots mobilization of members to pressure Congress. Another weakness in the law is that it applies only to attempts to influence Congress, it does not regulate lobbying activities in administrative agencies or litigation in the courts.

Tax laws require nonprofit organizations to refrain from direct lobbying in order to retain their tax-free status. Under current tax law, individual contributions to

TABLE 9.5 The Most Heavily Lobbied Issues*

1. Budget/appropriations	12. Energy
2. Taxation/Internal Revenue Code	13. Education
3. Health issues	14. Banking
4. Trade (Domestic and Foreign)	15. Agriculture
5. Environmental/Super Fund	16. Financial Institutions/Investments/ Securities
6. Labor/Antitrust/Workplace	
7. Medicare/Medicaid	17. Natural Resources
8. Transportation	18. Aviation/Airlines
9. Defense	19. Clean Air/Water
10. Copyright/Patent/Trademark	20. Utilities
11. Government Issues/Nuclear	

Source: Reprinted by permission of Center for Responsive Politics, 2000.

*Ranked by number of Lobbyists

nonprofit charitable and educational organizations are tax deductible, and the income of these organizations is tax free. But these organizations risk losing these tax preferences if a "substantial part" of their activities is "attempting to influence legislation." Thus, for example, Washington think tanks such as the Brookings Institution, the American Enterprise Institute, and the Heritage Foundation refrain from direct lobbying even though they make policy recommendations. But the line between public affairs "education" and "lobbying" is very fuzzy.

What Issues Are Lobbied Most Not surprisingly, tax and spending bills are the most heavily lobbied types of legislation in Washington. Virtually all groups have an interest in the thousands of pages of the U.S. Internal Revenue Code and the thousands of exemptions, exclusions, and special treatments in it. And, of course, virtually all groups have an interest in maximizing government spending that benefits their interests. Top lobbying issues, as determined by reports of registered lobbyists, are shown in Table 9.5.

The Fine Art of Lobbying

Any activity directed at a government decision maker with the hope of influencing decisions is a form of **lobbying**. (The term arose from the practice of waiting in the lobbies of legislative chambers to meet and persuade legislators.) For organized interests, lobbying is continuous—in congressional committees, in congressional staff offices, at the White House, at executive agencies, at Washington cocktail parties. If a group loses a round in Congress, it continues the fight in the agency in charge of executing the policy, or it challenges the policy in the courts. The following year it resumes the struggle in Congress: it fights to repeal the offending legislation, to weaken amendments, or to reduce the agency's budget enough to cripple enforcement efforts.

Lobbying techniques are as varied as the imagination of interest-group leaders, but such activities generally fall into seven categories: (1) public relations; (2) access; (3) information; (4) grass-roots mobilization; (5) protests and demonstrations; (6) coalition building; and (7) campaign support. In the real world

American League of Lobbyists

Lobbyists have their own Web site, one devoted to "ethical conduct" in the lobbying process and the "advancement of the lobbying profession."
www.alldc.org

lobbying Activities directed at government officials with the hope of influencing their decisions.

of Washington power struggles, all these techniques may be applied simultaneously or innovative techniques may be discovered and applied at any time (see Figure 9.1).

Public Relations Many interest groups actually spend more of their time, energy, and resources on **public relations**—developing and maintaining a favorable climate of opinion in the nation—than on direct lobbying of Congress. The mass media—television, magazines, newspapers—are saturated with expensive ads by oil companies, auto companies, chemical manufacturers, trade associations, teachers' unions, and many other groups, all seeking to create a favorable image for themselves with the general public. These ads are designed to go well beyond promoting the sale of particular products; they portray these organizations as patriotic citizens, protectors of the environment, providers of jobs, defenders of family values, and supporters of the American way of life. Generally, business interests have an advantage in the area of public relations because public relations and sales and marketing activities are synonymous. But paid advertising is less credible than news stories and media commentary. Hence interest groups generate a daily flood of press releases, media events, interviews, reports, and studies for the media. Media news stories appear to favor liberal public interest groups (see Table 9.6).

Access "Opening doors" is a major business in Washington. To influence decision makers, organized interests must first acquire **access** to them. Individuals who have personal contacts in Congress, the White House, or the bureaucracy (or who

public relations Building and maintaining goodwill with the general public.

access Meeting and talking with decision makers, a prerequisite to direct persuasion.

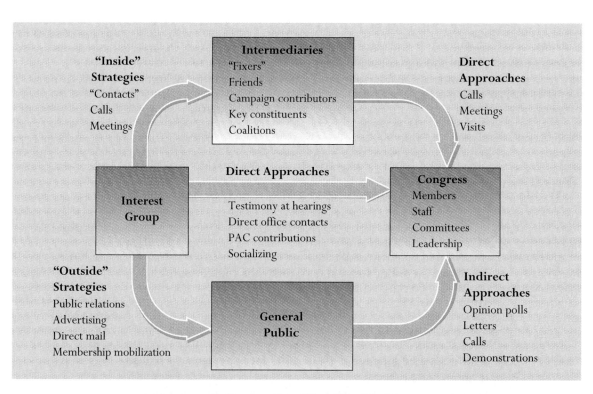

FIGURE 9.1   A Guide to the Fine Art of Lobbying
Interest groups seek to influence public policy both directly through lobbying and campaign contributions (inside strategy) and indirectly through public relations efforts to mold public opinion (outside strategy).

say they do) sell their services at high prices. Washington law firms, public relations agencies, and consultants—often former insiders—all offer their connections, along with their advice, to their clients. The personal prestige of the lobbyist, together with the group's perceived political influence, helps open doors in Washington.

Washington socializing is often an exercise in access—rubbing elbows with powerful people. Well-heeled lobbyists regularly pay hundreds, even thousands, of dollars per plate at fund-raising dinners for members of Congress. Lobbyists regularly provide dinners, drinks, travel, vacations, and other amenities to members of Congress, their families, and congressional staff, as well as to White House and other executive officials. These favors are rarely provided on a direct quid pro quo basis in exchange for votes. Rather, they are designed to gain access—"just a chance to talk."

"Schmoozing," building personal relationships, consumes much of a lobbyist's time and the client's money. It is difficult to know how much this contributes to actual success in passing, defeating, or amending legislation. But, to quote one client: "I figured that half of the money I spend on lobbying is wasted. Trouble is, I don't know which half."[9]

Information Once lobbyists gain access, their knowledge and information become valuable resources to those they lobby. Members of Congress and their staff look to lobbyists for *technical expertise* on the issue under debate as well as *political information* about the group's position on the issue. Members of Congress must vote on hundreds of questions each year, and it is impossible for them to be fully informed about the wide variety of bills and issues they face. Consequently many of them (and administrators in the executive branch as well) come to depend on trusted lobbyists.

Lobbyists also spend considerable time and effort keeping informed about bills affecting their interests. They must be thoroughly familiar with the "ins and outs" of the legislative process—the relevant committees and subcommittees, their schedules of meetings and hearings, their key staff members, the best moments to act, the precise language for proposed bills and amendments, the witnesses for

TABLE 9.6 Television News Coverage of Interest Groups

Type of Interest Group	Percent of All Interest Group References
Citizen groups	45.6
Think tanks	4.3
Corporations	24.3
Trade associations	13.0
Professional associations	3.8
Labor unions	4.0
Other[a]	5.1
Total	100.1

Data from 295 newscasts during 1995, alternating among broadcasts by ABC, CBS, CNN *Headline News*, and NBC. There were 847 references to groups. These references were contained in 548 distinct stories.

[a]Veterans, nonprofits, churches, and other groups.

Source: Jeffrey M. Berry, *The New Liberalism*, Copyright © 1999 by the Brookings Institution. Reprinted by permission.

hearings, and the political strengths and weaknesses of the legislators themselves. In their campaign to win congressional and bureaucratic support for their programs, lobbyists engage in many different types of activities. Nearly all testify at congressional hearings and make direct contact with government officials on issues that affect them. In addition, lobbyists provide the technical reports and analyses used by congressional staffs in their legislative research. Engaging in protest demonstrations is a less common activity, in part because it involves a high risk of alienating some members of Congress.

Experienced lobbyists develop a reputation for accurate information. Most successful lobbyists do not supply faulty information; their success depends on maintaining the trust and confidence of decision makers. A reputation for honesty is as important as a reputation for influence.

Grass-Roots Mobilization

Many organized interests lobby Congress from both the *outside* and the *inside*. From the outside, organizations seek to mobilize **grass-roots lobbying** of members of Congress by their constituents. Lobbyists frequently encourage letters and calls from "the folks back home." Larger organized interests often have local chapters throughout the nation and can mobilize these local affiliates to apply pressure when necessary. Lobbyists encourage influential local people to visit the office of a member of Congress personally or to make a personal phone call on behalf of the group's position. And, naturally, members are urged to vote for or against certain candidates, based on their policy stances (see *Up Close:* "AARP: The Nation's Most Powerful Interest Group").

Experienced lawmakers recognize attempts by lobby groups to orchestrate "spontaneous" grass-roots outpourings of cards and letters. Pressure mail is often identical in wording and content. Nevertheless, members of Congress dare not ignore a flood of letters and telegrams from home, for the mail shows that constituents are aware of the issue and care enough to sign their names.

Another grass-roots tactic is to mobilize the press in the home district of a member of Congress. Lobbyists may provide news, analyses, and editorials to local newspapers and then clip favorable articles to send to lawmakers. Lobby groups may also buy advertisements in hometown newspapers.

Protests and Demonstrations

Interest groups occasionally employ protests and demonstrations to attract media attention to their concerns and thereby apply pressure on officials to take action. For these actions to succeed in getting issues on the agenda of decision makers in Congress, in the White House, and in executive agencies, participation by the media, especially television, is essential. The media carry the message of the protest or demonstration both to the general public and directly to government officials (see "Protest as Political Participation" in Chapter 5).

Organized interest groups most often resort to protests and demonstrations when (1) they are frustrated in more traditional "inside" lobbying efforts; and/or (2) they wish to intensify pressure on officials at a specific point in time. Demonstrations typically attract media attention for a short time only. But media coverage of specific events can carry a clear message—for example, farmers driving tractors through Washington to protest farm conditions; motorcyclists conducting a giant "bike-in" to protest laws requiring helmets; cattle raisers driving steers down the Washington Mall to protest beef prices. The potential drawbacks to such activities are that the attention is short-lived and the group's reputation may be tarnished if the protest turns nasty or violent.

AARP
The AARP site covers issues and provides information relevant to the concerns of citizens who are 50 years of age or older.
www.aarp.org

grass-roots lobbying
Attempts to influence government decision making by inspiring constituents to contact their representatives.

AARP: The Nation's Most Powerful Interest Group

The American Association of Retired Persons (AARP) is the nation's largest and most powerful interest group, with more than 36 million members. The AARP's principal interests are the Social Security and Medicare system programs, the nation's largest and most expensive entitlements.

Like many other interest groups, the AARP has grown in membership not only by appealing to the political interests of retired people but also by offering a wide array of material benefits. For a $12.50 annual fee, members are offered a variety of services, including discounted rates on home, auto, life and health insurance; discounted mail-order drugs, tax advisory services; discounted rates on hotels, rental cars, and so on; a newsletter, *The AARP Bulletin*; a semi-monthly magazine, *Modern Maturity*, and for babyboomers now reaching their 50s, a new magazine, *My Generation*.

The political power of senior citizens is so great that prospects for limiting current or even future increases in government benefits for the elderly are slim. Social Security is said to be the "third rail of American politics—touch it and you're dead."

Critics of the AARP argue that its lobbyists in Washington do not fairly represent the views of the nation's senior citizens, that few of its members know what its lobbying arm does at the nation's capital. Indeed, in the struggle over prescription drug coverage under Medicare in 2003, the AARP leadership was accused of favoring its own interest in selling private insurance over the interests of its members in receiving government-paid insurance. AARP keeps its dues low, and consequently its membership high, through its business ties with insurance companies, its magazine advertising revenue, and commercial royalties revenues for endorsing products and services.

Source: Reprinted, with permission, from the April 1997 issue of *Reason* Magazine, Copyright 2000 by the Reason Foundation, 3415 S. Sepulveda Blvd. Suite 400, Los Angeles, CA, 90034, www.reason.com.

The Christian Coalition remains a major political force, especially within the Republican Party. Here, George W. Bush addresses the Coalition during the Republican presidential primaries in 2000.

Coalition Building Interest groups frequently seek to build **coalitions** with other groups in order to increase their power. Coalitions tend to form among groups with parallel interests: for example, the National Organization for Women, the League of Women Voters, and the National Abortion Rights Action League on women's issues. Coalitions usually form temporarily around a single piece of legislation in a major effort to secure or prevent its passage.

Campaign Support Perhaps the real key to success in lobbying is the campaign contribution. Interest-group contributions not only help lobbyists gain access and a favorable hearing but also help elect people friendly to the group's goals. As the costs of campaigning increase, legislators must depend more heavily on the contributions of organized interests.

Most experienced lobbyists avoid making electoral threats. Amateur lobbyists sometimes threaten legislators by vowing to defeat them at the next election, but this tactic usually produces a hostile reaction among members of Congress. Legislators are likely to respond to crude pressures by demonstrating their independence and voting against the threatening lobbyist. Moreover, experienced members of Congress know that such threats are empty; lobbyists can seldom deliver enough votes to influence the outcome of an election.

Experienced lobbyists also avoid offering a campaign contribution in exchange for a specific vote.[10] Crude "vote buying" (bribery) is illegal and risks repulsing politicians who refuse bribes. **Bribery,** when it occurs, is probably limited to very narrow and specific actions—payments to intervene in a particular case before an administrative agency; payments to insert a very specific break in a tax bill or a specific exemption in a trade bill; payments to obtain a specific contract with the government. Bribery on major issues is very unlikely; there is too much publicity and too many participants for bribery to be effective (but see *Up Close:* "The Cash Constituents of Congress" in Chapter 10).

THINK AGAIN

If a lobbyist makes a campaign contribution to a Congress member, hoping to gain support for a bill, is this a form of bribery?

coalition A joining together of interest groups (or individuals) to achieve a common goal.

bribery Giving or offering anything of value in an effort to influence government officials in the performance of their duties.

PAC Power

Organized interest groups channel their campaign contributions through **political action committees (PACs)**. PACs are organized by corporations, labor unions, trade associations, ideological and issue-oriented groups, and cooperatives and nonprofit corporations to solicit campaign contributions and distribute them to political candidates.

Distributing PAC Money Because PAC contributions are in larger lumps than individual contributions, PAC contributions often attract more attention from members of Congress. The PACs listed in Table 9.7 gave millions of dollars to finance the campaigns of their potential allies in 2000.

Most PACs use their campaign contributions to acquire access and influence with decision makers. Corporate, trade, and professional PAC contributions go overwhelmingly to incumbents, regardless of party. Leaders of these PACs know that incumbents are rarely defeated, and they do not wish to antagonize even unsympathetic members of Congress by backing challengers. However, ideological and issue-oriented PACs are more likely to allocate funds according to the candi-

political action committees (PACs) Organizations that solicit and receive campaign contributions from corporations, unions, trade associations, and ideological and issue-oriented groups, and their members, then distribute these funds to political candidates.

TABLE 9.7 The Big Money PACs in 2000

Nearly 4,000 PACs made contributions to presidential and congressional candidates in 1999–2000. The 25 largest contributors are listed.

Rank/Organization	Total	Democrats	Republicans
1 National Assn. of Realtors	$3,423,441	41%	69%
2 Assn. of Trial Lawyers of America	$2,661,000	86%	13%
3 American Fedn. of St./Cnty/Munic. Employees	$2,590,074	95%	5%
4 Teamsters Union	$2,565,495	93%	7%
5 National Auto Dealers Assn.	$2,498,700	32%	68%
6 Intl. Brotherhood of Electrical Workers	$2,470,125	96%	4%
7 Laborers Union	$2,255,900	90%	9%
8 Machinists/Aerospace Workers Union	$2,188,138	99%	1%
9 United Auto Workers	$2,155,050	99%	1%
10 American Medical Assn.	$2,028,354	48%	52%
11 Service Employees International Union	$1,871,774	89%	11%
12 National Beer Wholesalers Assn.	$1,871,500	21%	79%
13 Carpenters & Joiners Union	$1,869,920	84%	15%
14 National Assn. of Home Builders	$1,824,599	36%	64%
15 United Parcel Service	$1,755,065	35%	65%
16 United Food & Commercial Workers Union	$1,743,652	97%	2%
17 National Education Assn.	$1,717,125	95%	5%
18 Verizon Communications	$1,677,617	33%	67%
19 American Bankers Assn.	$1,657,615	35%	64%
20 American Federation of Teachers	$1,599,555	98%	2%
21 National Rifle Assn.	$1,583,574	15%	84%
22 Marine Engineers Union	$1,578,432	58%	42%
23 SBC Communications	$1,561,738	42%	58%
24 National Assn. of Letter Carriers	$1,552,350	84%	16%
25 Credit Union National Assn.	$1,526,584	49%	51%

Source: Reprinted by permission of the Center for Responsive Politics.

Emily's List

Fund raising is the greatest obstacle to mounting a successful campaign against an incumbent. And the most difficult problem facing challengers is raising money *early* in the campaign, when they have little name recognition and little or no standing in the polls.

EMILY's List is a politically adroit and effective effort to support liberal Democratic women candidates by infusing *early money* into their campaigns. EMILY stands for Early Money is Like Yeast, because "it makes the dough rise." Early contributions provide the initial credibility that a candidate, especially a challenger, needs in order to solicit additional funds from individuals and organizations. EMILY is a fund-raising network of thousands of contributors, each of whom pays $100 to join and pledges to give at least $100 to two women from a list of candidates prepared by EMILY's leaders. Most of the contributors are professional women who appreciate EMILY's screening of pro-choice, liberal women candidates around the country.

EMILY's List was begun in 1985, by a wealthy heir to a founder of IBM, Ellen Malcolm. Women challengers for congressional races traditionally faced frustration in fund raising. Incumbent male office-holders enjoyed a huge fund-raising advantage be-

cause contributors expected them to win and therefore opened their wallets to gain access and good-will. EMILY's List has helped to overcome defeatism among both women candidates and contributors.

Senator Barbara Milkulski, Democrat of Maryland and an early beneficiary of EMILY's List, at a news conference.

WWW EMILY's List
Political network for pro-choice Democratic women that raises early money for women candidates.
www.emilyslist.org

dates' policy positions and voting records. Labor PACs give almost all of their contributions to Democrats. Ideological and issue-oriented PACs give money to challengers as well as incumbents; in recent years, these groups collectively favored Democrats as women's, environmental, abortion rights, and elderly groups proliferated. (See *Up Close:* "EMILY's List.")

The pattern of contributing to congressional incumbents resulted in a shift of contributions from Democrats to Republicans when the GOP took control of both houses of Congress after the 1994 election. PAC money is less important in the Senate than in the House. PAC contributions account for about 35 percent of House campaign contributions; they only account for about 20 percent of Senate campaign contributions. Actually, PACs contribute more *dollars* to the average senator than to the average House member. But because Senate campaigns cost so much more than House campaigns, PAC contributions are *proportionally* less. Senators must rely more on individual contributions than House members do.

Instead of bribery, organized interests contribute to an incumbent member of Congress over a long period of time and leave it to the lawmaker to figure out how to retain their support. Only when a legislator consistently works against an organized interest will it consider contributing to that lawmaker's opponent in an election.

Payback: Money and Medicare

After years of struggle, Congress finally passed a prescription drug benefit for Medicare recipients in 2003. The bill was one of the most heavily lobbied pieces of legislation in the Congress in many years. The House and Senate passed very different measures, and the conference committee required months of behind-the-scenes negotiations before sending the bill to both chambers for final passage.

The principal beneficiaries of the bill were supposed to be the nation's senior citizens. And indeed the AARP was heavily involved in every stage of the bill's progress. But the biggest campaign contributors, and arguably the biggest beneficiaries of the final bill, were the drug manufacturers, the health maintenance organizations (HMOs), and the insurance industry.

The House passed the final bill by a close vote of 220–215. An analysis of congressional voting on the bill shows that lawmakers who voted to approve the legislation received an average of roughly twice as much in campaign contributions from the drug companies, HMOs, and insurance companies, as those who voted against the bill.

Republicans controlled the House as well as the Senate, and Republicans were generally more favorable toward the positions taken by these industries. So is no surprise that Republican Congress members on average received much larger contributions from these industries than Democrats, even Democrats who supported the industries' positions.

PAC Contributions and the Prescription Drug Vote in the House

	Average Contributions 1990–2003	
	Supporters	Opponents
Drug manufacturers	27,618	11,308
HMOs	11,582	6,630
Health insurers	19,510	10,128

Payback Representatives of organized interest groups say that their PAC contributions are designed to buy access—"a chance to talk"—with members of Congress, their staffs, and executives in the administration (see "What Do Contributors Buy?" in Chapter 8). Both interest groups and government officials usually deny that campaign contributions can "buy" support.

Nevertheless, the pattern of campaign contributions by major industries corresponds closely with the pattern of congressional voting on many key issues. Congress members who receive the largest PAC contributions from an industry group tend to vote in favor of that group's position. Congress members who oppose the industry's position generally receive far less (see *Up Close*: "Payback: Money and Medicare").

Lobbying the Bureaucracy

Lobbying does not cease after a law is passed. Rather, interest groups try to influence the implementation of the law. Interest groups know that bureaucrats exercise considerable discretion in policy implementation (see "Bureaucratic Power" in Chapter 12). Thus many interests spend as much or more time and energy trying to influence executive agencies than Congress.

Lobbying the bureaucracy involves various types of activities, including monitoring regulatory agencies for notices of new rules and regulatory changes; providing reports, testimony, and evidence in administrative hearings; submitting contract and grant applications and lobbying for their acceptance; and monitoring the performance of executive agencies on behalf of group members.

Groups may try to influence the creation of a new agency to carry out the law or influence the assignment of implementation to an existing "friendly" agency. They may try to influence the selection of personnel to head the implementing agency. They may lobby the agency to devote more money and personnel to enforcement of the law (or less, depending on a group's preference). They may argue for strict rules and regulations—or loose interpretations of the law—by the implementing agencies. Lobbyists frequently appear at administrative hearings to offer information. They often undertake to sponsor test cases of administrative regulations on behalf of affected members. In short, lobbying extends throughout the government.[11]

Iron Triangles In general, interest groups strive to maintain close working relationships with the departments and agencies that serve their members or regulate their industries. Conversely, bureaucracies seek to nourish relationships with powerful "client" groups that are capable of pressuring Congress to expand their authority and increase their budgets. Both bureaucracies and interest groups seek close working relationships with the congressional committees that exercise jurisdictions over their policy function. Finally, members of Congress seek the political and financial support of powerful interest groups, and members also seek to influence bureaucrats to favor supportive interest groups.

The mutual interests of congressional committee members, organized groups, and bureaucratic agencies come together to form what has been labeled the "iron triangles" of American government. **Iron triangles** refer to stable relationships among interest groups, congressional committees, and administrative agencies functioning in the same policy area. Each of the three sides of these triangles depends on the support of the other two; their cooperation serves their own interests (see Figure 9.2).

In an iron triangle, bureaucracies, interest groups, and congressional committees "scratch each other's backs." Bureaucrats get political support from interest groups in their requests for expanded power and authority and increased budgetary allocations. Interest groups get favorable treatment of their members by the bureaucracy. Congressional committee members get political and financial

iron triangles Mutually supportive relationships among interest groups, government agencies, and legislative committees with jurisdiction over a specific policy area.

FIGURE 9.2 Iron Triangles

The iron triangle approach provides a convenient way to look at the interrelationship among interest groups, executive agencies, and congressional committees. As this example shows, veterans' interest groups work closely with both the Department of Veterans Affairs (executive agency) and the House Veterans Affairs Committee.

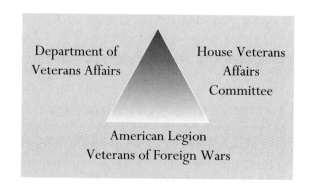

Department of Veterans Affairs

House Veterans Affairs Committee

American Legion Veterans of Foreign Wars

support from interest groups, as well as favorable treatment for their constituents and contributors who are served or regulated by the bureaucracy.

Iron triangles are more likely to develop in specialized policy areas over which there is relatively little internal conflict. However, conflict, rather than cooperation, is more likely to characterize bureaucratic—congressional—interest-group relationships when powerful, diverse interests are at stake. For example, the Occupational Safety and Health Administration is caught between the demands of labor unions and industry groups. The U.S. Forest Service is caught between the demands of environmental groups and the lumber industry. The Environmental Protection Agency is pressured by environmental groups as well as by industry and agriculture. These kinds of conflicts break open the iron triangles or prevent them from forming in the first place.

Policy Networks Generally, we think of American government in terms of the separate branches—Congress, the president and the bureaucracy, and the courts—with interest groups portrayed as external to government itself. But it is also possible to envision government as a series of **policy networks**—interactions in a common policy area among interest-group leaders and lobbyists, members of Congress and their staff personnel, executive agency officials, lawyers and consultants, foundation and think tank people, and even reporters and journalists assigned to the field. Policy networks develop among people who share some knowledge and interest in a policy field—for example, weapons procurement, housing, environment, transportation, or energy—and who regularly interact with each other in the policy arena. Policy networks may include people who differ strongly with each other as well as people who share similar views. What they have in common is their policy expertise and regular interaction. They can participate in negotiations and reach compromises as well as try to outwit and outmaneuver each other.

Revolving Doors It is not uncommon in Washington for people in a policy network to switch jobs, moving from a post in the government to a job in the private sector, or vice versa, or moving to different posts within the government. In one example, an individual might move from a job in a corporation (Pillsbury or General Mills) to the staff of an interest group (American Farm Bureau Federation), and then to the executive agency charged with implementing policy in the field (U.S. Department of Agriculture) or to the staff of a House or Senate committee with jurisdiction over the field (House Agricultural Committee or Senate Agriculture, Nutrition, and Forestry Committee). The common currency of moves within a network is both policy expertise and contacts within the field.

The term **revolving doors** is often used to criticize people who move from a government post (where they acquired experience, knowledge, and personal contacts) to a job in the private sector as a consultant, lobbyist, or salesperson. Defense contractors may recruit high-ranking military officers or Defense Department officials to help sell weapons to their former employers. Trade associations may recruit congressional staffers, White House staffers, or high-ranking agency heads as lobbyists, or these people may leave government service to start their own lobbying firms. Attorneys from the Justice Department, the Internal Revenue Service, and federal regulatory agencies may be recruited by Washington law firms to represent clients in dealings with their former employers.

Former members of Congress are considered the most viable commodity a lobby firm can offer their clients. The Center for Responsive Politics reports that 125 to 150 former Congress members are lobbyists, many of them among the highest

policy networks Interaction in a common policy area among lobbyists, elected officials, staff personnel, bureaucrats, journalists, and private-sector experts.

revolving doors The movement of individuals from government positions to jobs in the private sector, using the experience, knowledge, and contacts they acquired in government employment.

paid in the profession. When asked, lobbyists themselves, especially former members of Congress, acknowledge that their success depends mostly on "schmoozing" with their former colleagues.[12]

Concern about revolving doors centers not only on individuals cashing in on their knowledge, experience, and contacts obtained through government employment, but also on the possibility that some government officials will be tempted to tilt their decisions in favor of corporations, law firms, or interest groups that promise these officials well-paid jobs after they leave government employment.

The Ethics in Government Act limits postgovernment employment in an effort to reduce the potential for corruption. Former members of Congress are not permitted to lobby Congress for one year after leaving that body. Former employees of executive agencies are not permitted to lobby their agency for one year after leaving government service, and they are not permitted to lobby their agency for two years on any matter over which they had any responsibility while employed by the government.

Lobbying the Courts

Interest groups play an important role in influencing federal courts. Many of the key cases brought to the federal courts are initiated by interest groups. Indeed, **litigation** is becoming a favored instrument of interest-group politics. Groups that oppose a new law or an agency's action often challenge it in court as unconstitutional or as violating the law. Interest groups bring issues to the courts by (1) supplying the attorneys for individuals who are parties to a case; (2) bringing suits to the courts on behalf of classes of citizens; or (3) filing companion **amicus curiae** (literally "friend of the court") arguments in cases in which they are interested.

The nation's most powerful interest groups all have legal divisions specializing in these techniques. The American Civil Liberties Union is one of the most active federal court litigants on behalf of criminal defendants (see *Up Close:* "Politics and the ACLU" in Chapter 14). The early civil rights strategy of the National Association for the Advancement of Colored People (NAACP) was directed by its Legal Defense and Education Fund under the leadership of Thurgood Marshall (see *People in Politics:* "Thurgood Marshall" in Chapter 15). The NAACP chose to sponsor a suit by Linda Brown against the Board of Education in her hometown—Topeka, Kansas—in order to win the historic 1954 desegregation decision.[13] The National Abortion Rights Action League (NARAL) is active in sponsoring legal challenges to abortion restrictions. The Environmental Defense Fund and the Natural Resources Defense Council specialize in environmental litigation.

The special rules of judicial decision making preclude direct lobbying of judges by interest groups (see "The Special Rules of Judicial Decision Making" in Chapter 13). Directly contacting federal judges about a case, letter writing, telephoning, and demonstrating outside of federal courtrooms are all considered inappropriate conduct. They inspire more resentment than support among federal judges. However, interest groups have been very active in direct lobbying of Congress over judicial appointments. Key interest groups supporting abortion rights—the National Abortion Rights Action League, People for the American Way, the National Organization for Women, and so on—have played a central role in confirmation battles (see *Up Close:* "The Confirmation of Clarence Thomas" in Chapter 13).

litigation Legal dispute brought before a court.

amicus curiae Person or group other than the defendant or the plaintiff or the prosecution that submits an argument in a case for the court's consideration.

Politics as Interest-Group Conflict

Politics can be viewed as a struggle among interest groups over government policy. Interest groups, rather than individual citizens, can be viewed as the principal participants in American politics.

Pluralism as Democratic Politics Pluralism (see Chapter 2) is the idea that democracy can be preserved in a large, complex society through individual membership in interest groups that compete, bargain, and compromise over government policy. Individuals are influential in politics only when they act as part of, or on behalf of, groups. (Only leaders of organizations participate directly in policy making.) The group becomes the essential bridge between the individual and the government. Pluralists argue that interest-group politics is a natural extension of the democratic ideals of popular participation in government, freedom of association, and competition over public policy.

Pluralism portrays public policy at any given time as the equilibrium reached in the struggle among interest groups to influence policy (see Figure 9.3). This equilibrium is determined by the relative influence of interest groups. Changes in the relative influence of any interest group can be expected to result in changes in public policy; policy will move in the direction desired by the groups gaining in influence and away from the desires of groups losing influence.

According to this view of political life, government plays a passive role, merely "refereeing" group struggles. Public policy at any given moment represents the "equilibrium" point of the group pressures—the balance of competing interests. The job of politicians is to function as brokers of group interests, arranging compromises and balancing interests.

Balancing Group Power Pluralism assumes that compromises *can* be arranged and that interests *can* be balanced in relatively stable fashion. It assumes that no single interest will ever become so dominant that it can reject compromise and proceed to impose its will on the nation without regard for the interests of other people. This assumption is based on several beliefs. The first is that interest groups act as a check on each other and that a system of *countervailing power* will protect the interests of all. For example, the power of big business will be checked by the countervailing power of big labor and big government.

A second belief is that *overlapping group membership* will tend to moderate the demands of particular groups and lead to compromise. Because no group can command the undivided loyalty of all its members, its demands will be less drastic and

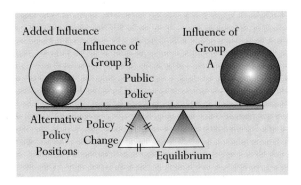

FIGURE 9.3 The Interest-Group Model

According to pluralist theorists, policy in a democracy is the result of various special-interest groups "reaching equilibrium"—arriving at a compromise position that requires all parties to give up something but gives all parties something they wanted.

its leaders more amenable to compromise. If the leaders of any group go too far with their demands, those of its members who also belong to other groups endangered by these immoderate demands will balk.

A third belief is that radical programs and doctrinaire demands will be checked by the large, unorganized, but potentially significant *latent interest group* that is composed of all Americans who believe in toleration, compromise, and democratic processes.

Interest-Group Politics: How Democratic? There are several problems with accepting pluralism as the legitimate heir to classic democratic theory. Democratic theory envisions public policy as the rational choice of individuals with equal influence who evaluate their needs and reach a majority decision with due regard for the rights of others. This traditional theory does not view public policy as a product of interest-group pressures. In fact, classic democratic theorists viewed interest groups and even political parties as intruders into an individualistic brand of citizenship and politics. Today critics of pluralism charge that interest groups dominate the political arena, monopolize access to governmental power, and thereby restrict individual participation rather than enhance it.

Pluralism contends that different groups of leaders make decisions about different issues, but critics charge that these leaders do not necessarily compete with each other. Rather, groups of leaders often allow other groups of leaders to govern their own spheres of influence without interference. Accommodation, rather than competition, may be the prevailing style of leadership interaction: "You scratch my back, and I'll scratch yours."

Another assumption of pluralism is that group membership enhances the individual's influence on policy. But only rarely are interest groups democratically governed. Individuals may provide the numerical strength for organizations, but interest groups are usually run by a small elite of officers and activists. Leaders of corporations, banks, labor unions, medical associations, and bar associations—whose views and agendas often differ from those of their membership—remain in control year after year. Very few people attend meetings, vote in organizational elections, or make their influence felt within their organization. Indeed, people believe that "special interest groups" are "what is wrong with government today" (see Table 9.8).

TABLE 9.8 Public Views of Interest Groups

Among the following, which one or two would you say are most responsible for what is wrong with government today?

Special interest groups	38%
The media	29
Elected officials	24
Political parties	24
The public	14
Government employees	6
Other	8
Not sure	2

Source: As reported in *The Polling Report*, November 11, 2003.

Finally, pluralists hope that the power of diverse institutions and organizations in society will roughly balance out and prevent the emergence of a power monopoly. Yet inequality of power among organizations is commonplace. Examples abound of narrow, organized interests achieving their goals at the expense of the broader, unorganized public. Furthermore, producer interests, bound together by economic ties, usually dominate less well-organized consumer groups and groups based on noneconomic interests. Special interests seeking governmental subsidies, payments, and "entitlements" regularly prevail over the broader yet unorganized interests of taxpayers.

Interest-Group Politics: Gridlock and Paralysis Even if the pluralists are correct that the public interest is only the equilibrium of special-interest claims, some consensus among major interest groups is required if government is to function at all. Democracies require a sense of community and common purpose among the people. If the demands of special interests displace the public interest, government cannot function effectively. Uncompromising claims by conflicting special interests create policy *gridlock.* Yet if politicians try to placate every special interest, the result is confusing, contradictory, and muddled policy—or worse, no policy at all.

Interest-group paralysis and the resulting inability of government to act decisively to resolve national problems weaken popular confidence in government. "The function of government is to govern. A weak government, a government which lacks authority, fails to perform its function, is immoral in the same sense in which a corrupt judge, a cowardly soldier, or an ignorant teacher, is immoral."[14]

Over time, the continued buildup of special protections, privileges, and treatments in society results in "institutional sclerosis." Economist Mancur Olson argues that the accumulation of special interest subsidies, quotas, and protections leads to economic stagnation. Interest groups focus on gaining distributive advantages— a larger share of the pie for themselves—rather than on growth of the whole economy—a larger pie.[15] Major interest groups are more interested in winning income transfers to themselves through government action than in promoting the growth of national income. The more entrenched the interest-group system becomes, the slower the growth of the national economy.

THINK AGAIN

Is organized interest-group activity a cause of government gridlock?

SUMMARY NOTES

- Organizations concentrate power, and concentrated power prevails over diffused power. Interest groups are organizations that seek to influence government policy.

- The interest-group system supplements the electoral system as a form of representation. The electoral system is designed to respond to broad, majority preferences in geographically defined constituencies. The interest-group system represents narrower, minority interests in economic, professional, ideological, religious, racial, gender, and issue constituencies.

- Interest groups originated to protect economic interests, to advance social movements, to seek government benefits, and to respond to government activity. As government has expanded into more sectors of American life, more interest groups have formed to influence government policy.

- Washington lobbying groups represent a wide array of organized interests. But business, trade, and professional associations outnumber labor union, women's, public-interest, single-issue, and ideological groups.

- Interest-group formation has been aided in recent decades by entrepreneurs who create and build group memberships. They urge people to join organizations either by appealing to their sense of obligation or by providing an array of direct tangible benefits.

- Most organized groups are dominated by small groups of leaders and activists. Few groups are governed democratically, members who oppose the direction of the organization usually drop out rather than challenge the leadership. Group membership and especially group leadership overrepresent educated, upper-middle-class segments of the population.

- Lobbying activities include advertising and public relations, obtaining access to government officials, providing them with technical and political information, mobilizing constituents, building coalitions, organizing demonstrations, and providing campaign support. Bribery is illegal, and most lobbyists avoid exacting specific vote promises in exchange for campaign contributions.

- Organized political action committees (PACs) proliferated following the 1974 "reform" of campaign finance laws. Most PAC money goes to incumbents; interest-group leaders know that incumbents are rarely defeated.

- The mutual interests of organized groups, congressional committees, and bureaucratic agencies sometimes come together to form "iron triangles" of mutual support and cooperation in specific policy areas. In many policy areas, loose "policy networks" emerge among people who share an interest and expertise—although not necessarily opinions—about a policy and are in regular contact with each other.

- The "revolving door" problem emerges when individuals use the knowledge, experience, and contacts obtained through government employment to secure high-paying jobs with corporations, law firms, lobbying and consulting firms, and interest groups doing business with their old agencies.

- Interest groups influence the nation's courts not only by providing financial and legal support for issues of concern to them but also by lobbying Congress over judicial appointments.

- Pluralism views interest-group activities as a form of democratic representation. According to the pluralists, public policy reflects the equilibrium of group influence and a reasonable approximation of society's preferences. Competition among groups, overlapping group memberships, and latent interest groups all combine to ensure that no single group dominates the system.

- Critics of pluralism warn that interest groups may monopolize power and restrict individual participation in politics rather than enhance it. They note that interest groups are not usually democratically governed, nor are their leaders or members representative of the general population. They warn that accommodation rather than competition may characterize group interaction and that narrow producer interests tend to achieve their goals at the expense of broader consumer (taxpayer) interests.

- The growing power of special interests, when combined with the declining power of parties and the fragmentation of government, may lead to grid-lock and paralysis in policy making. The general public interest may be lost in the conflicting claims of special interests.

KEY TERMS

interest groups 284
majoritarianism 284
organizational sclerosis 284
trade associations 289
public-interest groups 291
single-issue groups 291

ideological organizations 292
interest-group entrepreneurs 295
free-riders 295
lobbyist 296
lobbying 299

public relations 300
access 300
grass-roots lobbying 302
coalition 304
bribery 304
political action committees (PACs) 305

iron triangles 308
policy networks 309
revolving doors 309
litigation 310
amicus curiae 310

SUGGESTED READINGS

Berry, Jeffrey M. *The Interest Group Society*. White Plains, N.Y.: Longman, 1997. An overview of lobbying in all three branches of government as well as grass-roots lobbying, within the context of democratic (Madisonian) theory.

Berry, Jeffrey M. *The New Liberalism: The Rising Power of Citizen Groups*. Washington, D.C.: Brookings Institution Press, 1999. A description of the increasing number and activities of liberal interest groups in Washington and their success in defeating both business and conservative groups.

Cigler, Allan J., and Burdett A. Loomis, eds. *Interest Group Politics*. 6th ed. Washington, D.C.: CQ Press, 2002. A collection of essays examining interest-group politics.

Goldstein, Kenneth M. *Interest Groups, Lobbying and Participation in America*. New York: Cambridge University Press, 2003. When and why people join interest groups, how they are recruited, and how groups try to influence legislation.

Hernson, Paul S., Ronald G. Shaiko, and Clyde Wilcox. The *Interest Group Connection: Electioneering, Lobbying and Policymaking*. Boston: Chatham House, 2003. Interest group activities in the electoral, legislative, judicial, and policymaking processes.

Lowi, Theodore J. *The End of Liberalism*. New York: Norton, 1969. The classic critique of "interest-group liberalism," describing how special interests contribute to the growth of government and the development of "clientism."

Olson, Mancur. *The Logic of Collective Action*. Cambridge, Mass.: Harvard University Press, 1965. A highly theoretical inquiry into the benefits and costs to individuals of joining groups and the obstacles (including the free-rider problem) to forming organized interest groups.

Olson, Mancur. *The Rise and Decline of Nations*. New Haven, Conn.: Yale University Press, 1982. Argues that, over time, the development of powerful special-interest lobbies has led to institutional sclerosis, inefficiency, and slowed economic growth.

Schlozman, Kay Lehman, and John T. Tierney. *Organized Interests and American Democracy*. New York: Harper & Row, 1986. Comprehensive examination of interest groups in American politics, with original survey data from Washington lobbyists.

Wolpe, Bruce E., and Bertram J. Levine. *Lobbying Congress*. 2nd ed. Washington, D.C.: CQ Press, 1996. A practical guide to lobbying on Capitol Hill written by experienced lobbyists.

MAKE IT REAL

LOBBYING AMERICA

This activity allows you to try your hand at the "art" of lobbying. You will take on the role of being the newest lobbyist in Washington and you need to earn a reputation for success. As a representative of an influential interest group, you will be given a specific amount of time and money. Your job is to get your own legislation passed. How well you allocate your resources will determine whether or not you are successful!

10

CONGRESS:
POLITICS ON
CAPITOL HILL

THINK
ABOUT POLITICS

1 Should members of Congress be limited in the number of terms they can serve?
Yes ● No ●

2 Should congressional districts be drawn to ensure that minorities win seats in Congress in rough proportion to their populations in the states?
Yes ● No ●

3 Do Congress members spend too much time in their home districts seeking re-election?
Yes ● No ●

4 Is the nation better served when president and the majority in Congress are from the same party?
Yes ● No ●

5 Is it ethical for Congress members to pay special attention to requests for assistance by people who make large campaign contributions?
Yes ● No ●

6 Are there too many lawyers in Congress?
Yes ● No ●

7 Are members of Congress obliged to vote the way their constituents wish, even if they personally disagree?
Yes ● No ●

Who are the members of Congress? How did they get there, and how do they manage to stay there? How did Congress—the official institution for deciding who gets what in America—get its powers, and how does it use them?

The Powers of Congress

James Madison argued that the control of "faction" was "the principal task of modern legislation."[1] He meant that in enacting laws, legislators were really balancing interests, finding compromises, and resolving conflicts. Public policies—laws, regulations, and budgets—represent temporary balances of power among conflicting interests. As the relative power of these interests changes over time, new laws, amendments, and increases or decreases in funding will be enacted, reflecting new balances of power.

Constitutional Powers The Constitution gives very broad powers to Congress. "All legislative Powers herein granted shall be vested in a Congress of the United States, which shall consist of a Senate and House of Representatives." The nation's Founders envisioned Congress as the first and most powerful branch of government. They equated national powers with the powers of Congress and gave Congress the most clearly specified role in national government.

Article I empowers Congress to levy taxes, borrow and spend money, regulate interstate commerce, establish a national money supply, establish a post office, declare war, raise and support an army and navy, establish a court system, and pass all laws "necessary and proper" to implement these powers. Congress may also propose amendments to the Constitution or (with a two-thirds vote of both the House and the Senate) admit new states. In the event that no presidential candidate receives a majority of votes in the Electoral College, the House of Representatives selects the president. The Senate has two additional powers, it is called on for advice and consent to treaties, and it confirms presidential nominations to executive and judicial posts. The House has the power to impeach, and the Senate to try any officer of the U.S. government, including the president. Each congressional session convenes on January 3 following congressional elections in November of even-numbered years.

Institutional Conflict Over two centuries, the separate branches of the national government—the Congress, the presidency and the executive branch, and the Supreme Court and federal Judiciary—have struggled for power and preeminence in governing. This struggle for power among the separate institutions is precisely what the Founders envisioned. In writing the Constitution, they sought to create "opposite and rival interests" among the separate branches of the national government. "The constant aim," explained Madison, "is to divide and arrange the several offices in such a manner as that each may be a check on the other."[2] (see Appendix, *Federalist Papers*, No. 51). From time to time, first the Congress, then the presidency, and occasionally the Supreme Court have appeared to become the most powerful branch of government.

"The President Initiates, Congress Deliberates" Throughout much of the twentieth century, Congress ceded leadership in national policy making to the president and the executive branch. Congress largely responded to the policy initiatives and spending requests originating from the president, executive agencies, and interest groups. Congress did not merely ratify or "rubber-stamp" these initiatives and requests; it played an independent role in the policy-making process. But this role was essentially a deliberative one, in which Congress accepted, modified, amended, or rejected the policies and budget requests initiated by others.

It is easier for the Congress to obstruct the policy initiatives of the president than it is to assume policy leadership itself. Congress can defeat presidential policy proposals, deny presidential budget requests, delay or reject presidential appointments, investigate executive agencies, hold committee hearings to spotlight improprieties, and generally immobilize the executive branch. It can investigate and question nominees for the Supreme Court and the federal judiciary; it can legislate changes in the jurisdiction of the federal courts; and it can try to reverse court decisions by amending laws or the Constitution itself. The Congress can even threaten to impeach the president or federal judges. But these are largely reactive, obstructionist actions, usually accompanied by a great deal of oratory.

Dividing Congressional Power: House and Senate Congress must not only share national power with the executive and judicial branches of government; it must share power within itself. The framers of the Constitution took the advice of the nation's eldest diplomat, Benjamin Franklin: "It is not enough that your legislature should be numerous; it should also be divided. . . . One division should watch over and control the other, supply its wants, correct its blunders, and cross its designs, should they be criminal or erroneous."[3] Accordingly, the U.S. Congress is **bicameral**—composed of two houses (see Figure 10.1).

No law can be passed and no money can be spent unless both the House of Representatives and the Senate pass identical laws. Yet the House and the Senate have very different constituencies and terms. The House consists of 435 voting members, elected from districts within each state apportioned on the basis of equal population. (The average congressional district since the 1990 census has a population of 571,700; the House also includes nonvoting delegates from Puerto Rico, the District of Columbia, Guam, the Virgin Islands, and American Samoa.) All House members face election every two years. The Senate consists of 100 members serving six-year terms, elected by statewide constituencies. Senate terms are staggered so that one-third of senators are elected every two years (see Table 10.1).

The House of Representatives, with its two-year terms, was designed to be more responsive to the popular mood. Representatives are fond of referring to their chamber as "the people's House," and the Constitution requires that all revenue-raising bills originate in the House. The Senate was designed to be a smaller, more deliberative body, with its members serving six-year terms. Indeed, the Senate is the more prestigious body. House members frequently give up their seats to run for the Senate; the reverse has seldom occurred. Moreover, the Senate exercises

U.S. House of Representatives
Official Web site of the House, with schedule of floor and committee actions, legislative information, and links to every Representative's Web site and every committee Web site.
www.house.gov

congressional session
Each Congress elected in November of even-numbered years meets the following January 3 and remains in session for two years. Since the first Congress to meet under the Constitution in 1789, Congresses have been numbered by session (for example, 107th Congress 2001–2003, 108th Congress 2003–2005, 109th Congress 2005–2007).

bicameral Any legislative body that consists of two separate chambers or houses; in the United States, the Senate represents 50 statewide voter constituencies, and the House of Representatives represents voters in 435 separate districts.

HOUSE OF REPRESENTATIVES · SENATE

House Chamber — Old House Chamber — Rotunda — Old Senate Chamber — President's Room — Vice President's Room — Senate Chamber

FIGURE 10.1 **Corridors of Power in Congress**

The architecture and floor plan of the Capitol Building in Washington reflect the bicameral division of Congress, with one wing for the House of Representatives and one for the Senate.

certain powers not given to the House: the power to ratify treaties and the power to confirm federal judges, ambassadors, cabinet members, and other high executive officials.

Domestic versus Foreign and Defense Policy

Congress is more powerful in domestic than in foreign and military affairs. It is freer to reject presidential initiatives in domestic policy areas such as welfare, health, education, the environment, and taxation. But Congress usually follows presidential leadership in foreign and defense policy even though constitutionally the president and Congress share power in these arenas. The president is "Commander-in-Chief" of the armed forces, but only Congress can "declare war." The president appoints and receives ambassadors and "makes treaties," but the Senate must confirm appointments and provide "advice and consent" to treaties. Historically presidents have led the nation in matters of war and peace. Presidents have sent U.S. troops beyond the borders of the United States in military actions on more than two hundred occasions. In contrast, Congress has formally declared war only five times: the War of 1812, the Mexican War in 1846, the Spanish-American War in 1898, World War I in 1917, and World War II in 1941. Congress did not declare war in the Korean War (1950–53), the Vietnam War (1965–73), the Persian Gulf War (1991), or the wars in Afghanistan (2002) or Iraq (2003).

The Vietnam experience inspired Congress to try to reassert its powers over war and peace. Military embarrassment, prolonged and indecisive fighting, and accumulating casualties—all vividly displayed on national television—encouraged Congress to challenge presidential war-making power. The War Powers Act of 1973, passed over the veto of President Richard Nixon, who was weakened by the Watergate scandal, sought to curtail the president's power to commit U.S. military forces to combat (see "Commander-in-Chief" in Chapter 11). But this act has not proven effective, and both Republican and Democratic presidents have continued to exercise war-making powers.

WWW U.S. Senate Official Senate Web site, with floor and committee schedules, Senate news, and links to each Senator's Web site. *www.senate.gov*

TABLE 10.1 Comparing the House and Senate

	House of Representatives	Senate
Terms	Two years	Six years
Members	435	100
Elections	All every two years	One-third every two years
Constituencies	Congressional districts	States
Unique powers	Originate tax bills	Advise and consent to (ratify) treaties by two-thirds vote
	Bring impeachment charges	Confirm appointments
		Try impeachment charges
Debate on bills	Limited by Rules Committee	Unlimited, except by unanimous consent or vote of cloture (three-fifths)
Member prestige	Modest; smaller personal staffs, fewer committee assignments	High: larger personal staffs, more committee assignments, always addressed as "Senator"
Leadership	Hierarchical, with speaker, majority and minority leaders and whips and committees, especially Rules, concentrating power	Less hierarchical, with each senator exercising more influence on leadership, committees, and floor votes
Committees	Twenty standing and select committees	Twenty standing and select committees
	Each member on about five committees	Each member on about seven committees
	Difficult to bypass	Easier to bypass

The Power of the Purse Congress's real power in both domestic and foreign (defense) policy centers on its **power of the purse**—its power over federal taxing and spending. Only Congress can "lay and collect Taxes, Duties, Imposts and Excises" (Article I, Section 8), and only Congress can authorize spending: "No Money shall be drawn from the Treasury, but in Consequence of Appropriations made by Law" (Article I, Section 9).

Congress jealously guards these powers. Presidents initiate taxing and spending policies by sending their budgets to the Congress each year (see "The Bureaucracy and the Budgetary Process" in Chapter 12 for details). But Congress has the last word on taxing and spending. The most important bills that Congress considers each year are usually the budget resolutions setting ceilings on various categories of expenditures and the later appropriations bills authorizing specific expenditures. It is often in these appropriations bills that Congress exercises its greatest influence over national policy. Thus, for example, the Congress's involvement in foreign affairs centers on its annual consideration of appropriations for foreign aid, its involvement in military affairs centers on its annual deliberations over the defense appropriations bill, and so on.

power of the purse
Congress's exclusive, constitutional power to authorize expenditures by all agencies of the federal government.

oversight Congressional monitoring of the activities of executive branch agencies to determine if the laws are being faithfully executed.

Oversight of the Bureaucracy Congressional **oversight** of the federal bureaucracy is a continuing process by which Congress reviews the activities of the executive branch. The *formal* rationale of oversight is to determine whether the purposes of laws passed by Congress are being achieved by executive agencies and whether appropriations established by Congress are being spent as intended. Often the *real* purpose is to influence executive branch decisions, secure favorable treatment for friends and constituents, embarrass presidential appointees, undercut political support for particular programs or agencies, lay the political groundwork for budgetary increases or decreases for an agency, or simply enhance the power of congressional committees and subcommittees and those who chair them.

Oversight is carried out primarily through congressional committees and subcommittees. Individual senators and representatives can engage in a form of oversight simply by writing or calling executive agencies, but committees and their staffs carry on the bulk of oversight activity. Because committees and subcommittees specialize in particular areas of policy making, each tends to focus its oversight activities on particular executive departments and agencies. Oversight is particularly intense during budget hearings. Subcommittees of both the House and the Senate Appropriations Committees are especially interested in how money is being spent by the agencies they oversee.

Senate Advice and Consent and Confirmation of Presidential Appointments
The Constitution provides that the President must obtain the **advice and consent** of the Senate for treaties "provided that two-thirds of the Senators present concur." In fact, the Senate has seldom provided "advice" to the president regarding treaties prior to their submission to the Senate for "consent." The president enjoys a high degree of autonomy over U.S. foreign policy (see "Global Leader" in Chapter 11). The process of treaty ratification begins when a president submits an already negotiated treaty to the Senate. Once submitted, treaties are automatically referred to the Senate Foreign Relations Committee. That Committee cannot make changes in the treaty itself; it can either reject the treaty or forward it to the full Senate. The Senate itself cannot make changes in the formal treaty but must accept or reject it. Ratification requires a two-thirds vote. The Senate can, however, express its reservations to a treaty and/or instruct the president how the treaty is to be interpreted.[4]

The Senate also exercises a special power over the president and the executive branch of government through its constitutional responsibility for approving presidential appointments of key executive officers, including Cabinet members, ambassadors, and other high officials (see "Congressional Constraints on the Bureaucracy" in Chapter 12). And the Senate exercises a special power over the judicial branch through its constitutional responsibility to ratify presidential appointments to the federal judiciary including the Supreme Court (see "The Politics of Selecting Judges" in Chapter 13). Confirmation of appointments requires only a simple majority vote of the Senate.

Agenda Setting and Media Attention
Congressional **hearings** and investigations often involve agenda setting—bringing issues to the public's attention and placing them on the national agenda. For agenda-setting purposes, congressional committees or subcommittees need the assistance of the media. Televised hearings and investigations are perhaps the most effective means by which Congress can attract attention to issues as well as to itself and its members.

Hearings and investigations are similar in some ways, but hearings are usually held on a specific bill in order to build a record of both technical information (what is the problem and how legislation might be crafted to resolve it) and political information (who favors and who opposes various legislative options). In contrast, investigations are held on alleged misdeeds or scandals. Although the U.S. Supreme Court has held that there must be some "legislative purpose" behind a **congressional investigation**, that phrase has been interpreted very broadly indeed.[5]

The *formal* rationale for congressional investigations is that Congress is seeking information to assist in its lawmaking function. But from the earliest Congress to the present, the investigating powers of Congress have often been used for

John Ashcroft, former U.S. Senator from Missouri, during his confirmation hearings to become Bush's Attorney General. Ashcroft would later lead the fight for the controversial Patriot Act as part of the war on terror.

confirmation The constitutionally required consent of the Senate to appointments of high-level executive officials by the president and appointments of federal judges.

advice and consent The constitutional power of the U.S. Senate to reject or ratify (by a two-thirds vote) treaties made by the president.

congressional hearings Congressional committee sessions in which members listen to witnesses who provide information and opinions on matters of interest to the committee, including pending legislation.

congressional investigation Congressional committee hearings on alleged misdeeds or scandals.

political purposes: to rally popular support for policies or programs favored by Congress; to attack the president, other high officials in the administration, or presidential policies or programs; to focus media attention and public debate on particular issues; or simply to win media coverage and popular recognition for members of Congress. Congressional investigators have the legal power to subpoena witnesses (force them to appear), administer oaths, compel testimony, and initiate criminal charges for contempt (refusing to cooperate) and perjury (lying). These powers can be exercised by Congress's regular committees and subcommittees and by committees appointed especially to conduct a particular investigation.

Congress cannot impose criminal punishments as a result of its investigations. But the information uncovered in a congressional investigation can be turned over to the U.S. Department of Justice, which may proceed with its own criminal investigation and perhaps indictment and trial of alleged wrongdoers in federal courts.

Congressional investigations have long been used as an opportunity for Congress to expose wrongdoing on the part of executive branch officials. The first congressional investigation (1792) examined why General Arthur St. Clair had been defeated by the Indians in Ohio; the Crédit Mobilier investigations (1872–73) revealed scandals in the Grant Administration; the Select Committee on Campaign Practices, known universally as the "Watergate Committee," exposed the activities of President Richard Nixon's inner circle that led to impeachment charges and Nixon's forced resignation; a House and Senate Joint Select Committee conducted the Iran-Contra investigation in the Reagan Administration; the Senate Special Whitewater Committee investigated matters related to Bill and Hillary Clinton's real estate investments in Arkansas.

Impeachment and Removal Potentially Congress's most formidable power is that of impeaching and removing from office the president, other officers of the United States, and federal judges, including Supreme Court justices. Congress can do so only for "Treason, Bribery or other High Crimes and Misdemeanors." The House of Representatives has the sole authority to bring charges of impeachment by a simple majority vote. Impeachment is analogous to a criminal indictment; it does not remove an officer but merely subjects him or her to trial by the Senate. Only the Senate, following a trial, can remove the federal official from office, and then only by a two-thirds vote.

Bill Clinton is the second president in the nation's history to be impeached by the U.S. House of Representatives. (Andrew Johnson was the first in 1867; after a one-month trial in the Senate, the "guilty" vote fell one short of two-thirds needed for removal. President Richard Nixon resigned just prior to an impending impeachment vote in 1974.) The 1998 House impeachment vote split along partisan lines, with Republicans voting "yes" and Democrats voting "no." Two Articles of Impeachment were passed, one for perjury before a grand jury and one for obstruction of justice. In the subsequent Senate trial, only 45 senators (less than a majority and far less than the needed two-thirds) voted to convict President Clinton on the first charge, and only 50 voted to convict on the second (see *Up Close:* "Sex, Lies, and Impeachment" in Chapter 11).

Congressional Apportionment and Redistricting

The Constitution states that "Representatives . . . shall be apportioned among the several states . . . according to their respective Numbers." It orders an "actual enumeration" (census) every ten years. And it provides that every state shall have at

THINK AGAIN

Should congressional districts be drawn to ensure that minorities win seats in Congress in rough proportion to their populations in the states?

least one representative, in addition to two senators, regardless of population. But the Constitution is silent on the size of the House of Representatives. Congress itself determines its own size; for more than a century, it allowed itself to grow to accommodate new states and population growth. In 1910 it fixed the membership of the House at 435.

The effect of doing so has been to expand the population of House districts over the years. Following the 2000 census, House districts have populations of about 650,000. It is sometimes argued that such large House constituencies prevent meaningful communication between citizens and their representatives. (The Framers originally envisioned House districts of no more than 30,000 people.) But expanding the size of the House would complicate its work, reduce the influence of individual members, require more procedural controls, and probably strengthen the power of party leaders.

Apportionment Apportionment refers to the allocation of House seats to the states after each ten-year census. The Constitution does not specify a mathematical method of apportionment; Congress adopted a complex "method of equal proportion" in 1929, which so far has withstood court challenges (see *Across the USA:* "Reapportionment, 2000," which shows the current apportionment, together with the states that gained and lost seats after the 2000 census).

Malapportionment Historically, State legislatures were notorious for their **malapportionment**—congressional (and state legislative) districts with grossly unequal numbers of people. Some congressional districts had twice the average number of people per district, and others had only half as many. In a district twice the size of the average district, the value of an individual's vote was heavily diluted. In a district half the size of the average, the value of an individual's vote was greatly magnified.

Enter the Supreme Court Prior to 1962, the Supreme Court refused to intervene in apportionment, holding that this question belonged to the state legislatures and that the federal courts should avoid this "political thicket." So the Supreme Court's decision in the landmark case *Baker v. Carr* (1962) came as a surprise. The Court ruled that inequalities in voters' influence resulting from different-size districts violated the Equal Protection Clause of the Fourteenth Amendment. The case dealt with a complaint about Tennessee's state legislative districts, but the Court soon extended its holding to congressional districts as well.[6] The conception of political equality from the Declaration of Independence to Lincoln's Gettysburg Address, to the Fourteenth, Fifteenth, Seventeenth, and Nineteenth Amendments, can mean only one thing—one person, one vote."[7]

The shift in the Supreme Court's policy raised a new question: How equal must districts be in order to guarantee voters "equal protection of the law"? The courts have ruled that only official U.S. Bureau of the Census figures may be used: estimated changes since the last census may *not* be used. In recent years, the courts have insisted on nearly exact mathematical equality in congressional districts in a state.

"Enumeration" The U.S. Constitution is very specific in its wording: It calls for an "actual Enumeration" (Article I, Section 2) of the population in each ten-year census. However, the U.S. Bureau of the Census has considered the use of samples and estimates to correct what it perceives to be "undercounts." Undercounting is said to occur when certain populations are difficult to identify and count on an individual basis, populations such as recent non-English-speaking immigrants or

apportionment The allocation of legislative seats to jurisdictions based on population. Seats in the U.S. House of Representatives are apportioned to the states on the basis of their population after every ten-year census.

malapportionment Unequal numbers of people in legislative districts resulting in inequality of voter representation.

Reapportionment, 2000

Since 1910, the number of seats in the House of Representatives has remained constant at 435. Each ten-year census requires a reapportionment of seats among states based on their populations. States with rapid population growth such as Arizona. Texas, Georgia, and Florida gain seats (each of the states gained two seats following the 2000 census). States with slow population growth lose seats (New York and Pennsylvania both lost two seats). The newly apportioned House convened in January 2003.

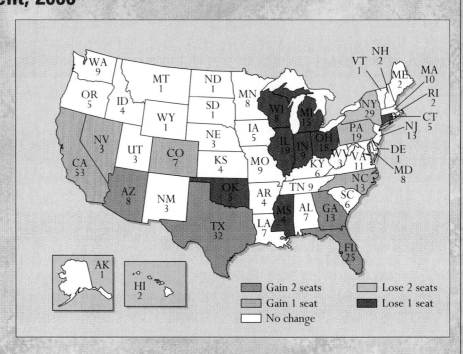

residents of neighborhoods likely to mistake government census takers for law enforcement officers or other unwelcome government officials. Political leaders (usually Democrats) of states and cities with large immigrant and minority populations have favored the substitution of samples and estimates for actual head counts. However, the U.S. Supreme Court held in 1999 that the Census Act of 1976 prohibits sampling for purposes of apportioning House members among the states.[8] Congress may use sampling for determining the allocation of grant-in-aid funds if it wishes.

Redistricting Redistricting refers to the drawing of boundary lines of congressional districts following the census. After each census, some states gain and others lose seats, depending on whether their populations have grown faster or slower than the nation's population. In addition, population shifts within a state may force districting changes. Congressional district boundaries are drawn by state legislatures in each state, a state's redistricting act must pass both houses of the state legislature and win the governor's signature (or be passed over a gubernatorial veto). The U.S. Justice Department and the federal judiciary are also deeply involved in redistricting issues, particularly questions of whether or not redistricting disadvantages African Americans or other minorities.

Gerrymandering Gerrymandering is the drawing of district lines for political advantage (see Figure 10.2). The population of districts may be equal, yet the dis-

redistricting Drawing of legislative district boundary lines following each ten-year census.

gerrymandering Drawing district boundary lines for political advantage.

FIGURE 10.2 The Original Gerrymander

The term *gerrymander* immortalizes Governor Elbridge Gerry (1744–1814) of Massachusetts, who in 1811 redistricted the state legislature to favor Democrats over Federalists. A district north of Boston was designed to concentrate, and thus "waste," Federalist votes. This political cartoon from the *Boston Gazette,* March 26, 1812, depicted the new district lines as a salamander, dubbing the process the "gerrymander."

trict boundaries are drawn in such a fashion as to grant advantage or disadvantage to specific groups of voters. Gerrymandering has long been used by parties in control of the state legislatures to maximize their seats in Congress and state legislatures.

Gerrymandering, with the aid of sophisticated computer-mapping programs and data on past voting records of precincts, is a highly technical task. But consider a simple example where a city is entitled to three representatives and the eastern third of the city is Republican but the western two-thirds is Democratic (see Figure 10.3). If the Republicans could draw the district lines, they might draw them along a north-south direction to allow their party to win in one of the three districts. In contrast, if Democrats could draw the district lines, they might draw them along an east-west direction to allow their party to win all three districts by diluting the Republican vote. Such dividing up and diluting of a strong minority to deny it the power to elect a representative is called **splintering**. Often gerrymandering is not as neat as our example; district lines may twist and turn, creating grotesque patterns in order to achieve the desired effects. Another gerrymandering strategy—**packing**—is the heavy concentration of one party's voters in a single district in order to "waste" their votes and allow modest majorities of the party doing the redistricting to win in other districts.

Partisan Gerrymandering

Generally, partisan gerrymandering does not violate federal court standards for "equal protection" under the Fourteenth Amendment. There is no constitutional obligation to allocate seats "to the contending parties in proportion to what their anticipated statewide vote will be."[9] However, the federal courts may intervene in political gerrymandering if it "consistently degrades a voter's or a group of voters' influence on the political process as a whole."[10]

splintering Redistricting in which a strong minority is divided up and diluted to prevent it from electing a representative.

packing Redistricting in which partisan voters are concentrated in a single district, "wasting" their majority vote and allowing the opposition to win by modest majorities in other districts.

FIGURE 10.3

Gerrymandering in Action

Depending on how an area is divided into districts, the result may benefit one party or the other. In this example, dividing the area so one district has virtually all the Republicans gives that party a victory in that district while ceding the other two districts to the Democrats. In contrast, Democrats benefit when Republican voters are divided among the three districts so that their votes are splintered.

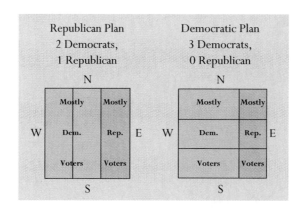

These vague standards set forth by the U.S. Supreme Court open the door to judicial intervention in particularly grievous cases of partisan gerrymandering.

Re-redistricting The redrawing of congressional districts usually occurs after each ten-year census. However, several states have been embroiled in a second round of redistricting, notably Texas. (If one party dominated a state legislature during the first redistricting after the census, and drew district lines in a partisan fashion, there is then a strong temptation for the opposition party to undertake a second round of partisan redistricting if it subsequently wins control of the state legislature.) It is theoretically possible that redistricting could be undertaken every time a state legislature changes party control. If this becomes a common practice in the states, partisan wrangling over redistricting may tie up state legislatures for years.

Incumbent Gerrymandering Yet another problem confronting state legislatures in redistricting is the preservation of incumbent Congress members, that is, **incumbent gerrymandering**. Incumbents generally have sufficient political clout with their state parties to inspire efforts in the legislature to protect their districts.

Incumbent gerrymandering means drawing district lines in such a way so as to ensure that districts of incumbents include enough supporters of their party to provide a high probability of their reelection. But often ensuring incumbents' security and maximizing the party's total number of seats are conflicting goals. It is not always possible to redraw district lines in such a way as to protect incumbents and at the same time ensure the largest number of party seats in a state. Incumbents themselves want the largest number of their party's voters packed in their district. But this tactic may result in losses for their party in other districts that have been robbed of party voters. Redistricting almost always confronts incumbents with new voters—voters that were previously in a different incumbent's district. As a result, incumbents usually have a somewhat more difficult reelection campaign following redistricting than in other elections.[11]

Racial Gerrymandering Racial gerrymandering to disadvantage African Americans and other minorities violates both the Equal Protection Clause of the Fourteenth Amendment and the Voting Rights Act of 1965. The Voting Rights Act specifies that redistricting in states with a history of voter discrimination or low voter participation must be "cleared" in advance with the U.S. Justice Department. The act extends special protection not only to African American voters but also to Hispanic, Native American, Alaska Native, and Asian voters.

incumbent gerrymandering
Drawing legislative district boundaries to advantage incumbent legislators.

In 1982 Congress strengthened the Voting Rights Act by outlawing any electoral arrangement that has the effect of weakening minority voting power. This *effects test* replaced the earlier *intent test,* under which redistricting was outlawed only if boundaries were intentionally drawn to dilute minority political influence. In *Thornburg v. Gingles* (1986), the Supreme Court interpreted the effects test to require state legislatures to redistrict their states in a way that maximizes minority representation in Congress and the state legislatures.[12] The effect of this ruling was to require **affirmative racial gerrymandering**—the creation of predominately African American and minority districts (labeled "majority-minority" districts) whenever possible. Following the 1990 census, redistricting in legislatures in states with large minority populations was closely scrutinized by the U.S. Justice Department and the federal courts. The result was a dramatic increase in African American and Hispanic representation in Congress (see Figure 10.7 later in this chapter).

However, the Supreme Court later expressed constitutional doubts about bizarre-shaped districts based *solely* on racial composition. In a controversial 5 to 4 decision in *Shaw v. Reno* (1993), Justice Sandra Day O'Connor wrote, "Racial gerrymandering, even for remedial purposes, may balkanize us into competing racial factions. . . . A reapportionment plan that includes in one district individuals who have little in common with one another but the color of their skin bears an uncomfortable resemblance to political apartheid"[13] (see Figure 10.4). Later the Court held that the use of race as the "predominant factor" in dividing district lines in unconstitutional: "When the state assigns voters on the basis of race, it engages in the offensive and demeaning assumption that voters of a particular race, because of their race, think alike, share the same political interests and will prefer the same candidates at the polls."[14] But the Court has stopped short of saying that *all* race-conscious districting is unconstitutional.

Partisanship Interacts with Race Racial gerrymandering appears to help Republican congressional candidates. If African American voters are concentrated in heavily black districts, the effect is to "bleach" surrounding districts of Democratic-leaning black voters and thus improve the chances for Republican victories.

affirmative racial gerrymandering Drawing district boundary lines to maximize minority representation.

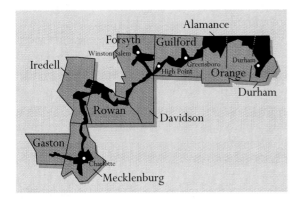

FIGURE 10.4 Affirmative Racial Gerrymandering

North Carolina's Twelfth Congressional District was drawn up to be a "majority-minority" district by combining African American communities over a wide region of the state. The U.S. Supreme Court in *Shaw v. Reno* (1993) ordered a court review of this district to determine whether it incorporated any common interest other than race. The North Carolina legislature redrew the district in 1997, lowering its black population from 57 to 46 percent, yet keeping its lengthy connection of black voters from Charlotte to Greensboro.

Republican Party congressional gains in the South during the 1990s may be partly attributed to racial gerrymandering.[15] In what has been described as a "paradox of representation," the creation of majority-minority districts brought more minority members to Congress, but it also led to a more conservative House of Representatives, as Republicans gained seats previously held by white liberal Democrats.[16]

Republican led efforts to "pack" black (Democratic) voters into relatively few districts suffered a setback in 2003 when the U.S. Supreme Court recognized that doing so might diminish the power of African-American voters overall. The Court approved of a plan that "unpacked" some heavily concentrated majority-minority districts in Georgia. The Court reasoned that the result would be to create additional black "influence" districts where African-American voters would not be in a majority but would be a large influential voting bloc.[17]

Getting to Capitol Hill

Members of Congress are independent political entrepreneurs—selling themselves, their services, and their personal policy views to the voters in 435 House districts and 50 states across the country. They initiate their own candidacies, raise most of their campaign funds from individual contributors, put together personal campaign organizations, and get themselves elected with relatively little help from their party. Their reelection campaigns depend on their ability to raise funds from individuals and interest groups and on the services and other benefits they provide to their constituents.

Are there too many lawyers in Congress?

Roll Call
This online magazine covers a variety of current topics about Congress but is especially strong on stories dealing with running for Congress and/or campaign financing.
www.rollcall.com

Who Runs for Congress? Members of Congress come from a wide variety of backgrounds, ranging from acting and professional sports to medicine and the ministry. However, exceptionally high percentages of senators and representatives have prior experience in at least one of three fields—law, business, or public service (see Table 10.2). Members of Congress are increasingly career politicians, people who decided early in life to devote themselves to running for and occupying public office.[18] The many lawyers, by and large, are *not* practicing attorneys. Rather, the typical lawyer-legislator is a political activist with a law degree. These are people who graduated from law school and immediately sought public jobs—as federal or state prosecuting attorneys, as attorneys for federal or state agencies, or as staff assistants in congressional, state, or city offices. They used their early job experiences to make political contacts and learn how to organize a political campaign, find financial contributors, and deal with the media. Another group of Congress members are former businesspeople—not employees of large corporations, but people whose personal or family businesses brought them into close contact with government and their local community, in real estate, insurance, franchise dealerships, community banks, and so forth.

Competition for Seats Careerism in Congress is aided by the electoral advantages enjoyed by incumbents over challengers. Greater name recognition, advantages in raising campaign funds, and the resources of congressional offices all combine to limit competition for seats in Congress and to reelect the vast majority of incumbents (see "The Advantages of Incumbency" in Chapter 8). The result is an incumbent reelection percentage for House members that usually exceeds 90 percent. The average reelection rate for U.S. senators is more than 80 percent (see Figure 10.5).

TABLE 10.2 Backgrounds of Congress Members

	House			Senate			Congress
	D	R	Total	D	R	Total	Total
Occupation							
Actor/entertainer		2	2				2
Aeronautics		2	2	1		1	3
Agriculture	8	18	26		5	5	31
Artistic/Creative		1	2*				2*
Business/Banking	56	109	165	9	16	25	190
Clergy	1	1	2				2
Education	50	37	88*	7	5	12	100*
Engineering	1	7	8		1	1	9
Health Care	4	1	5				5
Homemaker/Domestic	2	2	4				4
Journalism	3	7	11*	1	5	6	17*
Labor	5	2	7		2	2	9
Law	86	75	161	29	30	60	221†
Law Enforcement	6	3	9				9
Medicine	5	11	16		3	3	19
Military		3	3		1	1	4
Professional Sports		1	1		1	1	2
Public Service/Politics	77	68	145	17	13	30	175
Real Estate	3	27	30	2	1	3	33
Secretarial/Clerical		2	2				2
Technical/Trade	1	3	4				4
Miscellaneous	1	3	4				4
Religion							
African Methodist Episcopal	3		3				3
Baptist	33	33	66	1	5	6	72
Christian Church	4		4				4
Christian Reformed Church		2	2				2
Christian Scientist		5	5				5
Eastern Orthodox		2	2	1	1	2	4
Episcopalian	10	24	34	3	7	10	44
Jewish	24	1	26*	9	2	11	37*
Lutheran	9	10	19	3	1	4	23
Methodist	16	34	50	7	5	12	62
Mormon	3	9	12	1	4	5	17
Pentecostal		4	4				4
Presbyterian	11	26	37	3	10	13	50
Roman Catholic	71	53	124	14	11	25	149
Seventh-Day Adventist	1	1	2				2
Unitarian	1	1	2	1		1	3
United Church of Christ/ Congregationalist		2	2	3	2	6†	8†
Unspecified, Protestant	12	22	34	2	2	4	38
Unspecified, other	7		7		1	1	8

*Includes Independent Bernard Sanders of Vermont.

†Includes Independent James M. Jeffords of Vermont.

Source: Congressional Quarterly Weekly Report, January 25, 2003, for 108th Congress, 2003–2005.

FIGURE 10.5
Incumbent Advantage

Despite periodic movements to "throw the bums out," voters in most districts and states routinely reelect their members of Congress. In recent decades, more than 90 percent of representatives and 80 percent of senators who have sought reelection have been returned to Congress by votes in their districts or states.

House	Year	Senate
99%	2002	88%
97%	2000	83%
98%	1998	91%
94%	1996	95%
92%	1994	83%
93%	1992	86%
96%	1990	96%
98%	1988	85%
98%	1986	75%
96%	1984	90%
92%	1982	93%
91%	1980	55%
95%	1978	68%
97%	1976	64%
90%	1974	92%
96%	1972	80%
97%	1970	79%
99%	1968	83%
90%	1966	97%
88%	1964	87%
94%	1962	85%
95%	1960	97%

House Percent: 100 80 60 40 20 0
Senate Percent: 0 20 40 60 80 100

Aspirants for congressional careers are well advised to wait for open seats. **Open seats** in the House of Representatives are created when incumbents retire or vacate the seat to run for higher office. These opportunities occur on average in about 10 percent of House seats in each election. But every ten years reapportionment creates many new opportunities to win election to Congress. Reapportionment creates new seats in states gaining population, just as it forces out some incumbents in states losing population. Redistricting also threatens incumbents with new constituencies, where they have less name recognition, no history of casework, and perhaps no common racial or ethnic identification. Thus forced retirements and electoral defeats are more common in the first election following each ten-year reapportionment and redistricting of Congress.

Winning Big Not only do incumbent Congress members usually win, they usually win big. Over 70 percent of House members win by margins of 60 percent or more or run unopposed. (In recent years, 10 to 18 percent of House members have had no opposition in the general election.) Senate races are somewhat more competitive. Senate challengers are usually people who have political experience and name recognition as members of the House, governors, or other high state officials. Even so, most Senate incumbents seeking reelection are victorious over their challengers.

Most members of Congress, then, sit comfortably in **safe seats**—that is, they regularly win reelection by a large margin of the vote (see Table 10.3).

open seat Seat in a legislature for which no incumbent is running for reelection.

safe seat Legislative district in which the incumbent regularly wins by a large margin of the vote.

TABLE 10.3 Winning Big: House and Senate Elections Won by 60 Percent or More of the Vote

	House	Senate
1984	78.9%	65.5%
1986	84.5	50.0
1988	87.3	37.5
1990	79.5	66.7
1992	65.0	46.4
1994	63.0	48.0
1996	68.0	30.0
1998	77.2	65.5
2000	81.1	69.0
2002	84.7	57.1
2004	79.7	52.9

Source: Harold Stanley and Richard G. Niemi, *Vital Statistics on American Politics* 2002–2004. Washington, D.C.: CQ Press, 2004; plus calculations by author.

Turnover Despite a high rate of reelection of incumbents in Congress, about 15 percent of members arrive new to their jobs each session. **Turnover** occurs more frequently as a result of retirement, resignation (sometimes to run for higher office), or reapportionment (and the loss of an incumbent's seat) that it does as a result of an incumbent's defeat in a bid for reelection. Roughly 10 percent of Congress members voluntarily leave office when their term expires.[19]

Congressional Term Limits? Public distrust of government helped to fuel a movement in the states to limit congressional terms. Several states attempted to limit their state's House members to four two-year terms and their senators to two six-year terms. Proponents of congressional term limits argued that career politicians become isolated from the lives and concerns of average citizens, that they acquire an "inside the Beltway" (the circle of highways that surrounds Washington) mentality. They also argued that term limits would increase competition, creating "open-seat" races on a regular basis and encouraging more people to seek public office.

Opponents of congressional term limits argued that they infringe on the voters' freedom of choice. If voters are upset with the performance of their Congress members, they can limit their terms by not reelecting them. But if voters wish to keep popular and experienced legislators in office, they should be permitted to do so. Opponents also argued that inexperienced Congress members would be forced to rely more on the policy information supplied them by bureaucrats, lobbyists, and staff people—thus weakening the institution of Congress.

But the U.S. Supreme Court ruled in 1995 that the states themselves cannot limit the terms of their members of Congress. "If the qualifications set forth in the text of the Constitution are to be changed, that text must be amended."[20] In a controversial 5 to 4 decision, the Court held that the Founders intended age, citizenship, and residency to be the *only* qualifications for members of Congress.

It is not likely that the necessary two-thirds of both houses of Congress will ever vote for a constitutional amendment to limit their own stay in office. Thus, the Supreme Court's decision effectively killed the movement for congressional term limits.

THINK AGAIN

Should members of Congress be limited in the number of terms they can serve?

turnover Replacement of members of Congress by retirement or resignation, by reapportionment, or (more rarely) by electoral defeat, usually expressed as a percentage of members newly elected.

Why Do Voters Reelect Members of an Unpopular Congress?

Congress is the least popular branch of government. Public approval of Congress is well below that of the presidency and the Supreme Court. What accounts for this lack of popularity? The belief that members of Congress "spend more time thinking about their own political futures than they do in passing legislation" may contribute to this sentiment.

But public distrust of Congress may also arise from a misunderstanding of democratic government. "People do not wish to see uncertainty, conflicting options, long debate, competing interests, confusion and compromised imperfect solutions. . . . They often see a patently unrealistic form of democracy."[*]

But in an apparent paradox, most voters *approve of their own* representative (see figure below), even while Congress itself is the object of popular distrust and ridicule. A majority of voters believe that their own representatives "deserve reelection."

This apparent contradiction is explained in part by differing expectations: Americans expect Congress to deal with national issues, but they expect their own representatives to deal with local concerns and even personal problems. Members of Congress understand this concern and consequently devote a great deal of their time to constituent service. Indeed, many members of Congress try to dissociate themselves from Congress, attacking Congress in their own campaigns and contributing to negative images of the institution. Finally, the national news media are highly critical of Congress, but local news media frequently portray local members of Congress in a more favorable light.

Q. "Do you approve of the way the U.S. Congress is handling its job?"

Q. "Do you approve or disapprove of the way the representative from your own congressional district is handling his or her job?"

---

[*]John R. Hibbing and Elizabeth Theiss-Morse, *Congress as Public Enemy* (Cambridge: Cambridge University Press, 1995), p. 147. Also cited by Roger H. Davidson and Walter J. Oleszak, *Congress and Its Members* 9th ed. (Washington, D.C.: CQ Press, 2004), p. 487.

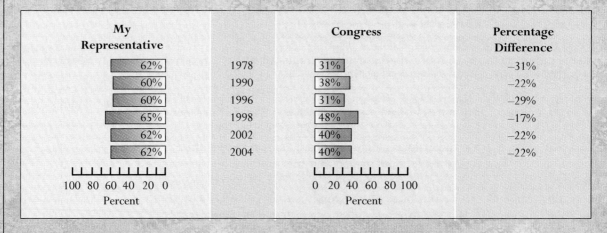

My Representative		Congress	Percentage Difference
62%	1978	31%	−31%
60%	1990	38%	−22%
60%	1996	31%	−29%
65%	1998	48%	−17%
62%	2002	40%	−22%
62%	2004	40%	−22%

Percentage of Those Expressing Approval of Their Representatives and Congress

Source: Data from surveys by the Gallup Organization, as reported in www.thepollingreport.com

The Congressional Electorate Congressional elections generally fail to arouse much interest among voters. Indeed, only about 60 percent of the general public can name one U.S. senator from their state, and only about 40 percent can name both of their U.S. senators. Members of the House of Representatives fare no better: less than half of the general public can name their representative. But even constituents who know the names of their congressional delegation seldom know anything about the policy positions of these elected officials or about their votes on specific issues. Turnout in congressional *general elections* averages only about 35 percent in off-year (nonpresidential) elections. Turnout in congressional *primary elections* seldom exceeds 15 to 20 percent of persons eligible to vote. This lack of public attentiveness to congressional elections gives a great advantage to candidates with high name recognition, generally the incumbents (see *What Do You Think?* Why Do Voters Reelect Members of an Unpopular Congress).

Independence of Congressional Voting Congressional voting is largely independent of presidential voting. The same voters who elected Republican presidents in 1968, 1972, 1980, 1984, and 1988 simultaneously elected Democratic majorities to the House of Representatives. And while reelecting Democratic President Bill Clinton in 1996, voters simultaneously reelected Republican majorities in the House and Senate. In 2000, Republicans maintained a razor-thin margin in the House, despite Gore's popular vote victory. Only in 2004 did voters elect a Republican president and add to Republican majorities in the House and Senate. It is unlikely that voters deliberately seek to impose *divided party government* on the nation. Rather, they cast their presidential and congressional votes on the basis of differing expectations of presidents versus members of Congress.[21]

Congressional Campaign Financing Raising the $900,000 it can take to win a House seat or the $5 to $10 million for a successful Senate campaign is a major job in and of itself (see "How Much Does It Cost to Get Elected?" in Chapter 8). Even incumbents who face little or no competition still work hard at fund raising, "banking" contributions against some future challenger. Large campaign chests, assembled well in advance of an election, can also be used to frighten off would-be challengers. Campaign funds can be used to build a strong personal organization back home, finance picnics and other festivities for constituents, expand the margin of victory, and develop a reputation for invincibility that may someday protect against an unknown challenger.[22]

Does money buy elections? In about 90 percent of all congressional races, the candidate who spends the most money wins. However, because most winning candidates are incumbents, the money probably reflects the expected political outcome rather than shapes it. But even in open-seat races, the candidate who spends the most money usually wins.

Party Fortunes in Congress

For forty years (1954–94) Democrats enjoyed an advantage in congressional races; in fact, the Democratic Party was said to have a "permanent majority" in the House of Representatives (see Figure 10.6). The Republican victory in the congressional election of 1994 was widely described as a political "earthquake." It gave the GOP control of the House for the first time in four decades, as well as control of the Senate. Republicans have remained in control of the House, and the Senate (except for a brief period in 2001–2002) through the 2004 elections.

The Historic Democratic Party Dominance of Congress The historic Democratic dominance of Congress was attributed to several factors. First, over those four decades more voters identified themselves with the Democratic Party than with the Republican Party (see Chapter 7). Party identification plays a significant role in congressional voting; it is estimated that 75 percent of those who

FIGURE 10.6 Party Control of the House and Senate

Except for two very brief periods, Democrats continuously controlled both the House of Representatives and the Senate for more than forty years. The Democratic Party's "permanent" control of Congress was ended in 1994, when Republicans won majorities in both houses. Republicans retained control of Congress despite President Clinton's victory in 1996, and retained control by a slim margin in the House in 1998, 2000, and 2002. President George W. Bush's reelection victory in 2004 increased Republican margins in both the House and Senate.

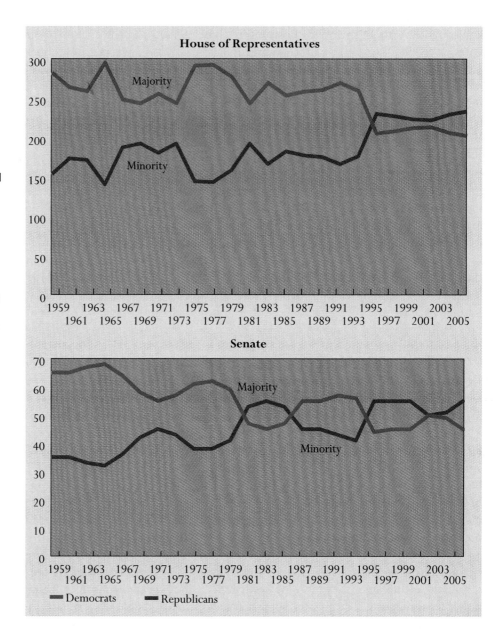

identify themselves with a party cast their vote for the congressional candidate of their party.[23] Second, the Democratic advantage was buttressed by the fact that many voters considered local rather than national conditions when casting congressional votes. Voters may have wanted to curtail overall federal spending in Washington (a traditional Republican promise), but they wanted a member of Congress who would "bring home the bacon." Although both Republican and Democratic congressional candidates usually promised to bring money and jobs to their districts, Democratic candidates appeared more creditable on such promises because their party generally supported large domestic-spending programs. Finally, Democratic congressional candidates over those years enjoyed the many advantages of incumbency. It was thought that only death or retirement would dislodge many of them from their seats.

The Republican "Revolution"? The sweeping Republican victory in 1994—especially the party's capturing control of the House of Representatives—surprised many analysts.[24] Just two years after a Democratic president won election and

Democrats won substantial majorities in both houses of Congress, the GOP gained its most complete victory in many years. How did it happen?

First of all, the Republican congressional candidates, under the leadership of Newt Gingrich, largely succeeded in *nationalizing* the midterm congressional election. That is, Republican candidates sought to exploit the voters' general skepticism about government and disenchantment with its performance. Voters were often unfamiliar with specific Republican promises, but they correctly sensed that the Republicans favored "less government."

The GOP's capture of control of both houses of Congress in 1994 for the first time in forty years raised conservatives' hopes of a "revolution" in public policy. The new Republican House Speaker, Newt Gingrich, was the acknowledged leader of the revolution, with Republican Senate Majority Leader Bob Dole in tow. But soon the revolution began to fizzle out. Two key Republican campaign promises failed to pass the Congress: the House failed to muster the necessary two-thirds majority for a constitutional amendment to impose congressional term limits, and the Senate failed to do so on behalf of a balanced budget amendment.

But worse was yet to come for the Republicans. Congress passed several budget resolutions aimed at balancing the federal budget in seven years, only to see them vetoed. Clinton positioned himself as the defender of popular programs—Medicare, Medicaid, education, and the environment—consistently referring to congressional efforts to reduce the rate of growth in these programs as "cuts." The failure of Congress and the president to agree on appropriations temporarily shut down the federal government in 1995. To the surprise of the Republican leadership, opinion polls reported that Americans blamed the GOP Congress for the gridlock. Clinton's approval ratings rose, and Newt Gingrich was portrayed as a mean-spirited "extremist."

Newt Gingrich (R-Ga.) led the Republican Party to victory in the House of Representatives in 1994 after forty years of Democratic control of that body.

The Democratic Revival Republicans succeeded in maintaining their control of Congress despite Clinton's reelection in 1996. But Democrats gained House seats in both the 1996 and 1998 congressional elections. Although the GOP retained a slim majority in the House of Representatives, the 1998 midterm election stunned Republicans. They had expected to benefit from Clinton's acknowledged sexual misconduct and the House impeachment investigation. But voters generally sided with Clinton. Democrats were encouraged because historically the party controlling the White House had *lost* seats in midterm elections.

Congress Divided The congressional elections of 2000 reflected the close partisan division of the nation. Republicans barely held on to their majority in the House of Representatives. The election produced a historic 50–50 tie in the Senate. Formal control of the Senate should have rested with Republicans, owing to the tie-breaking vote of Republican Vice President Dick Cheney. But in a precedent-shattering midsession shift of power, Democrats took control of the Senate in 2001, when Republican Senator Jim Jeffords from Vermont abandoned his party, declared himself an Independent, but gave his vote to the Democrats in the Senate. Other senators had defected from their party in the past, but no previous switch ever produced a change in party control. The new 51–49 Democratic majority took control of all Senate committees as well as the floor of that body.

Breaking with the Midterm Election Tradition Traditionally, the party that had won the White House in the previous presidential election *lost* seats in the following midterm congressional election. (Indeed, since Abraham Lincoln was president, the party holding the presidency lost House seats in every midterm election except three—1902, 1934, and 1998.) It was theorized that presidential popularity tended to wane after two years in office, and that voters usually sought to check presidential power in the following midterm election. It was also believed that even popular presidents had little impact on midterm congressional elections; these elections were thought to be decided by the popularity of individual candidates and local district issues.

But in 2002 President George W. Bush designated himself as "Campaigner-in-Chief," traveling about the country raising campaign money and lending his popularity to Republican House and Senate candidates. His continuing high approval rating throughout the year following the "9/11" terrorist attack on America made him a highly welcomed campaigner in districts and states across the nation. In his campaign stops, Bush talked about the war on terrorism and his need for "allies" in the Congress. Democratic candidates for Congress tried to shift the voters' focus to the weak economy. And indeed, most voters told pollsters that the economy was a more important issue than the war on terrorism and that Bush himself was not a major factor in determining their vote. Nonetheless, President Bush appeared to influence just enough voters in key districts and states to reverse the historic pattern of presidential midterm congressional losses. The GOP won back control of the U.S. Senate and strengthened their majority in the House of Representatives. Again in 2004 President Bush appeared to help GOP congressional candidates across the country. Republicans increased their control of the Senate from 51 to 55. They picked up several seats of retiring older-generation Southern Democrats. And they even succeeded in defeating the Democratic Senate Minority Leader, Tom Daschle of South Dakota. Nevertheless, Democrats retained sufficient strengths in the Senate (where a 3/5th "cloture" vote—60—is required to end a filibuster) to obstruct legislation and judicial nominations which they oppose. Senate Republican Majority Leader Bill Frist has threatened to revise the rules of the Senate regarding cloture votes, especially on judicial nominations. (He argues that the Constitution requires only a majority vote to "consent" for presidential nominations.) But support for the filibuster rule is strong. Supreme Court nominations are likely to generate heated controversy. The election also made the Senate slightly more "diverse": African-American Barack Obama was elected from Illinois, and Hispanic Mel Martinez was elected from Florida. In the House, Republicans also increased their margin of control. President Bush was quick to claim that winning the White House, the Senate, and the House of Representatives meant that the American People supported his "agenda."

Life in Congress

"All politics is local," declared former House Speaker Thomas P. "Tip" O'Neill, himself once the master of both Boston ward politics and the U.S. House of Representatives. Attention to the local constituency is the key to survival and success in congressional politics. If Congress often fails to deal responsibly with national problems, the explanation lies in part with the design of the institution. House members must devote primary attention to their districts and Senate members to their states. Only *after* their constituencies are served can they turn their attention to national policy making.

The "Representativeness" of Congress The Constitution requires only that members of the House of Representatives be (1) residents of the state they represent (they need not live in their congressional district, although virtually all do so); (2) U.S. citizens for at least seven years; and (3) at least twenty-five years old. Senators must also be residents of the state they represent, but they must be at least thirty years old and U.S. citizens for at least nine years.

■ *African Americans* African Americans were first elected to Congress following the Civil War—seven black representatives and one black senator served in 1875. But with the end of Reconstruction, black membership in Congress fell to a single seat in the House from 1891 to 1955. Following the Civil Rights Act of 1964 and the Voting Rights Act of 1965, black membership in Congress rose steadily. Redistricting following the 1990 census resulted in many new "majority-minority" congressional districts. After the 1992 elections, black membership in the House rose dramatically (see Figure 10.7), with most elected from predominantly African American districts.[25] As a result, although African Americans today make up a little more than 12 percent of the U.S. population, they make up less than 9 percent of the House membership. African American, Carol Mosely Brown of Illinois served in the Senate from 1993 to 1999, and Barack Obama won a Senate seat in the same state in 2004.

■ *Hispanics* Hispanics now comprise the nation's largest minority, with slightly more than 12 percent of the U.S. population. But Hispanic representation in the Congress lags considerably behind their population growth. Currently only about 5 percent of House members are Hispanic, and no Hispanics serve in the U.S. Senate. The Voting Rights Act of 1965 protects "language minorities" as well as racial and ethnic minorities. Prior to the 1990 census and the creation of many court-ordered "majority-minority" congressional districts, very few Hispanics served in the Congress. But with the creation of new Hispanic majority districts, Hispanic representation began to increase in the House of Representatives. Most Hispanic House members come from California, Florida, and Texas. In the 108th Congress, 23 Hispanics served in the House; 19 were Democrats, and 4 (all from Florida) were Republicans.

■ *Women* Women have made impressive gains in both the House and the Senate in the last decade. The "year of the woman" election in 1992 brought a significant increase in the number of women in the House of Representatives. Since then

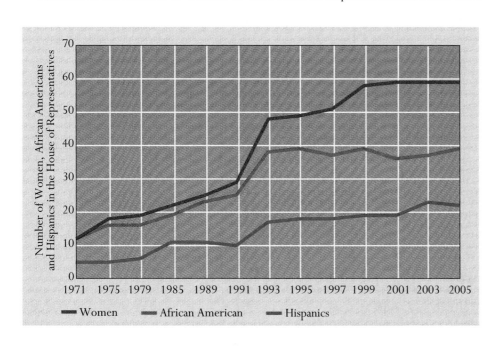

FIGURE 10.7 Women, African Americans, and Hispanics in the House of Representatives

Although the House of Representatives is still far short of "looking like America," in recent years the number of African Americans, Hispanics, and female members has risen noticeably. Particularly impressive advances were made in the 1992 elections, following court-ordered creation of "majority–minority" districts.

women's representation in the House continued upward, 59 women serve in the House in 108th Congress (2003–2005), divided between 38 Democrats and 21 Republicans. In the Senate, 14 women serve. California is represented by two Democratic women, Dianne Feinstein and Barbara Boxer. They are joined by seven other Democratic women Senators, including former First Lady Hillary Rodham Clinton. (See *People in Politics*: "Hillary Rodham Clinton in the Senate.") Five Republican women serve in the Senate: Elizabeth Dole from North Carolina, Kay Hutchinson from Texas, Olympia Snowe and Susan Collins from Maine, and Lisa Murkowski from Alaska. Although this is the largest delegation of women ever to serve together in the U.S. Senate, it is still only 14 percent of that body.

The number of women in Congress has grown as result of many factors, including strides that women have made in the workplace and other societal institutions. Yet stereotypes about women as politicians remain. Generally, voters view women as better able to handle "feminine" issues, such as health care, child care and education, but less able to handle "masculine" issues, including the economy and war. In the past, some women candidates tried to counter these stereotypes by emphasizing their toughness, especially on crime. But new evidence suggests that women candidates can use female stereotypes to their advantage by focusing the campaign on gender-owned issues—health, welfare, education, and other compassion issues.[26]

Congressional Staff Congress is composed of a great deal more than 535 elected senators and representatives. Congressional staff and other support personnel now total some 25,000 people. Each representative has a staff of twenty or more people, usually headed by a chief of staff or administrative assistant and including legislative assistants, communications specialists, constituent-service personnel, office managers, secretaries, and aides of various sorts. Senators frequently have staffs of thirty to fifty or more people. All representatives and senators are provided with offices both in Washington and in their home districts and states. In addition, representatives receive more than $500,000 apiece for office expenses, travel, and staff; and senators receive $2 million or more, depending on the size of their state's population. Overall, Congress spends more than $2 *billion* on itself each year.

Congressional staff people exercise great influence over legislation. Many experienced "Hill rats" have worked for the same member of Congress for many years. They become very familiar with "their" member's political strengths and vulnerabilities and handle much of the member's contacts with interest groups and constituents. Staff people, more than members themselves, move the legislative process—scheduling committee hearings, writing bills and amendments, and tracking the progress of such proposals through committees and floor proceedings. By working with the staff of other members of Congress or the staff of committees and negotiating with interest-group representatives, congressional staff are often able to work out policy compromises, determine the wording of legislation, or even outline "deals" for their member's vote (all subject to later approval by their member). With multiple demands on their time, members of Congress come to depend on their staff not only for information about the content of legislation but also for political recommendations about what position to take regarding it.

Support Agencies In addition to the thousands of personal and committee staff who are supposed to assist members of Congress in research and analysis, four congressional support agencies provide Congress with information:

Congresswoman Marge Roukema of New Jersey meets with a staff member at her offices in Washington, D.C. Congressional staff play a key role in the legislative process.

Hillary Rodham Clinton in the Senate

Hillary Rodham Clinton is the first First Lady ever elected to the Congress and the first woman senator from New York. Her celebrity attracts the media wherever she goes, sometimes causing resentment among her ninety-nine other Senate colleagues, all of whom think of themselves as stars in their own right. Her initial efforts in the Senate have been directed toward establishing herself as a serious, knowledgeable, and effective legislator. And she tries particularly hard to identify herself with the interests of her adopted state, New York.

Hillary Rodham grew up in suburban Chicago, the daughter of wealthy parents who sent her to the private, prestigious Wellesley College. A 1969 honors graduate with a counterculture image—hornrimmed glasses, long, straggling hair, no makeup—she was chosen by her classmates to give a commencement speech—a rambling statement about "more immediate, ecstatic, and penetrating modes of living."

At Yale Law School Hillary met a long-haired, bearded Rhodes scholar from Arkansas, Bill Clinton, who was just as politically ambitious as she was. Both Hillary and Bill received their law degrees in 1973. Bill returned to Arkansas to build a career in state politics, and Hillary went to Washington as an attorney—first for a liberal lobbying group, the Children's Defense Fund, and later on the staff of the House Judiciary Committee seeking to impeach President Richard Nixon. But Rodham and other Yale grads traveled to Arkansas to help Clinton run, unsuccessfully, for Congress in 1974. Hillary decided to stay with Bill in Little Rock: they married before his next campaign, a successful run for state attorney general in 1976. Hillary remained Hillary Rodham, even as her husband went on to the governorship in 1978.

Her husband's 1980 defeat for reelection as governor was blamed on his liberal leanings; therefore, in his 1982 comeback Bill repackaged himself as a moderate and centrist. Hillary cooperated by becoming Mrs. Bill Clinton, shedding her horn-rims for contacts, blonding her hair, and echoing her husband's more moderate line. These tactics helped propel them back into the governor's mansion. Hillary soon became a full partner in Little Rock's Rose law firm, regularly earning more than $200,000 a year (while Bill earned only $35,000 as Arkansas governor). She won national recognition as one of the "100 most influential lawyers in the United States," according to the *American National Law Journal*. She chaired the American Bar Association's Commission on Women and the Profession.

Hillary's steadfast support of Bill during the White House sex scandals and subsequent impeachment by the House of Representatives in all likelihood saved his presidency. Her approval ratings in public opinion polls skyrocketed during the affair. Whatever she thought in private, she never chastised her husband in public and blamed much of the scandal on "a vast right-wing conspiracy."

Her Senate race attracted national media attention as well as campaign contributions from supporters throughout the nation. When New York City's Mayor Rudolph Giuliani announced that he would *not* run for the Senate, Hillary was relieved to confront a little-known opponent, Congressman Rick Lazio. New York voters were unimpressed with charges that Hillary was not a true New Yorker. She studied New York problems diligently, and overwhelmed Lazio in the campaign. Over $85 million were spent by the candidates, making the campaign the most expensive congressional campaign in history.

Senator Clinton has developed a reputation as an advocate for children and families. Her early work with the Children's Defense Fund and Marian Wright Edelman (see *People in Politics:* "Marian Wright Edelman, Lobbying for the Poor" in Chapter 9) was carried forward in her book *It Takes a Village* in 1997. She was prominently mentioned in all of the early 2004 presidential polls, but she declined to run.

■ The Library of Congress and its Congressional Research Service (CRS) are the oldest congressional support agencies. Members of Congress can turn to the Library of Congress for references and information. The CRS responds to direct requests of members for factual information on virtually any topic. It tracks major bills in Congress and produces summaries of each bill introduced. This information is available on computer terminals in members' offices.

- The General Accounting Office (GAO) has broad authority to oversee the operations and finances of executive agencies, to evaluate their programs, and to report its findings to Congress. Established as an arm of Congress in 1921, the GAO largely confined itself to financial auditing and management studies in its early years but expanded to more than five thousand employees in the 1970s and undertook a broad agenda of policy research and evaluation. Most GAO studies and reports are requested by members of Congress and congressional committees, but the GAO also undertakes some studies on its own initiative.

- The Congressional Budget Office (CBO) was created by the Congressional Budget and Impoundment Act of 1974 to strengthen Congress's role in the budgeting process. It was designed as a congressional counterweight to the president's Office of Management and Budget (see Chapter 14). The CBO supplies the House and Senate budget committees with its own budgetary analyses and economic forecasts, sometimes challenging those found in the president's annual budget.

- The Government Printing Office (GPO), created in 1860 as the publisher of the *Congressional Record*, now distributes over 20,000 different government publications in U.S. government bookstores throughout the nation.

Note that the CBO was created at a time when Congress was growing in power relative to a presidency weakened by Vietnam and Watergate. In these same years, Congress encouraged the GAO to undertake a more active and critical role relative to executive agencies. Thus, the growth of congressional staff and supporting agencies is tied to the struggle for power between the legislative and executive branches.

Workload Members of Congress claim to work twelve- to fifteen-hour days: two to three hours in committee and subcommittee meetings; two to three hours on the floor of the chamber; three to four hours meeting with constituents, interest groups, other members, and staff in their offices; and two to three hours attending conferences, events, and meetings in Washington.[27] Members of Congress may introduce anywhere from ten to fifty bills in a single session of Congress. Most bills are introduced merely to exhibit the member's commitment to a particular group or issue. Cosigning a popular bill is a common practice; particularly popular bills may have 100 or 200 cosigners in the House of Representatives. Although thousands of bills are introduced, only 400 to 800 are passed in a session.

Members of Congress resent the notion that they are overpaid, underworked, pampered, self-seeking, corrupt, and ineffective. They respond to the bell calling them to the floor for a recorded vote 900 to 1,000 times a session. Each representative is a member of at least two standing committees and four subcommittees, and each senator may be a member of four committees and many more subcommittees. Thousands of committee and subcommittee meetings are scheduled each session.

Pay and Perks Taxpayers can relate directly to what members of Congress spend on themselves, even while millions—and even billions—of dollars spent on government programs remain relatively incomprehensible. Taxpayers thus were enraged when Congress, in a late-night session in 1991, raised its own pay from $89,500 to $129,000. Congress claimed the pay raise was a "reform," since it was coupled with a stipulation that members of Congress would no longer be allowed to accept honoraria from interest groups for their speeches and appearances, thus

Congressional Budget Office

The Web site of the CBO is an excellent source of data on federal finances, economic projections, and the budgetary process.
www.cbo.gov

supposedly reducing members' dependence on outside income. Many angry taxpayers saw only a 44 percent pay raise, in the midst of a national recession, for a Congress that was doing little to remedy the nation's problems. By 2004, automatic cost-of-living increases, also enacted by Congress, had raised members' pay to $154,700.

As the pay-raise debate raged in Washington, several states resurrected a constitutional amendment originally proposed by James Madison. Although passed by the Congress in 1789, it had never been ratified by the necessary three-quarters of the states. The 203-year-old amendment, requiring a House election to intervene before a congressional pay raise can take effect, was added as the Twenty-seventh Amendment when ratified by four states (for a total of thirty-nine) in 1992.

Home Style

Members of Congress spend as much time politically cultivating their districts and states as they do legislating. **Home style** refers to the activities of senators and representatives in promoting their images among constituents and personally attending to constituents' problems and interests.[28] These activities include members' allocations of their personnel and staff resources to constituent services; members' personal appearances in the home district or state to demonstrate personal attention; and members' efforts to explain their Washington activities to the voters back home.

THINK AGAIN

Do Congress members spend too much time in their home districts seeking re-election?

Casework Casework is really a form of "retail" politics. Members of Congress can win votes one at a time by helping constituents on a personal level. Casework can involve everything from tracing lost Social Security checks and Medicare claims to providing information about federal programs, solving problems with the Internal Revenue Service, and assisting with federal job applications. Over time, grateful voters accumulate, giving incumbents an advantage at election time. Congressional staff do much of the actual casework, but letters go out over the signature of the member of Congress. Senators and representatives blame the growth of government for increasing casework, but it is also clear that members solicit casework, frequently reminding constituents to bring their problems to their member of Congress.

The downside to extensive casework is that it may detract from Congress members' ability to deal effectively with national issues. Former U.S. Senator and vice president Walter Mondale observed:

> Constituent service can . . . be a bottomless pit. The danger is that a member of Congress will end up as little more than an ombudsman between citizens and government agencies. As important as this work is, it takes precious time away from Congress's central responsibilities as both a deliberative and a lawmaking body.[29]

Pork Barrel Pork barreling describes the efforts of senators and representatives to "bring home the bacon"—to bring federally funded projects, grants, and contracts that primarily benefit a single district or state to their home constituencies. Opportunities for pork barreling have never been greater: roads, dams, parks, and post offices are now overshadowed by redevelopment grants to city governments, research grants to universities, weapons contracts to local plants, "demonstration" projects of all kinds, and myriad other "goodies" tucked inside each year's annual appropriations bills. Members of Congress understand the importance of supporting each other's pork barrel projects, cooperating in the "incumbent-

home style Activities of Congress members specifically directed at their home constituencies.

casework Services performed by legislators or their staff on behalf of individual constituents.

pork barreling Legislation designed to make government benefits, including jobs and projects used as political patronage, flow to a particular district or state.

protection society." Even though pork barreling adds to the public's negative image of Congress as an institution, individual members gain local popularity for the benefits they bring to home districts and states.

Pressing the Flesh Senators and representatives spend a great deal of time in their home states and districts. Although congressional sessions last virtually all year, members of Congress find ways to spend more than a hundred days per year at home[30] It is important to be seen at home—giving speeches and attending dinners, fund-raising events, civic occasions, and so on. To accommodate this aspect of home style, Congress usually follows a Tuesday-to-Thursday schedule of legislative business, allowing members to spend longer weekends in their home districts. Congress also enjoys long recesses during the late summer and over holidays.

Puffing Images To promote their images back home, members make generous use of their **franking privilege** (free mailing) to send their constituents newsletters, questionnaires, biographical material, and information about federal programs. Newsletters "puff" the accomplishments of the members; questionnaires are designed more to flatter voters than to assess opinions; and informational brochures tout federal services members claim credit for providing and defending. Congress's penchant for self-promotion has also kept pace with the media and electronic ages. Congress now provides its members with television studios and support for making videotapes to send to local stations in home districts, and all members maintain Web sites on the Internet designed to puff their images.

Hill Styles and Home Styles Members of Congress spend their lives "moving between two contexts, Washington and home, and between two activities, governing and campaigning."[31] They must regularly ask themselves how much time they should spend at home with their constituents versus how much time they should spend on lawmaking assignments in Washington. It is no surprise that freshman legislators spend more time in their districts; indeed, very few first-termers move their families to Washington. Long-term incumbents spend more time in Washington, but all Congress members spend more time at home in an election year.

Much of the time spent at home—with small groups of constituents, among contributors, in public speeches, and appearances on radio and television—is devoted to explaining issues in justifying the member's vote on them. "Often members defend their own voting record by belittling Congress—portraying themselves as knights errant battling sinister forces and feckless colleagues."[32]

Members of Congress have even been known to change lifestyles between home and Washington. "The legendary Speaker Mr. Sam Rayburn represented his East Texas district for nearly 50 years (1913–61) as a plain dirt farmer. Once back in his hometown of Bonham, his drawl thickened; his tailored suits were exchanged for khakis, an old shirt and a slouch hat; and he traveled in a well-dented pickup truck, not the Speaker's limousine he used while in the Capitol."[33]

Organizing Congress: Party and Leadership

Congress is composed of people who think of themselves as leaders, not followers. They got elected without much help from their party. Yet they realize that their chances of attaining their personal goals—getting reelected and influencing policy—are enhanced if they cooperate with each other.

Congressional Quarterly (CQ)

The *Congressional Quarterly Weekly Report* provides the most comprehensive coverage of events in Congress, including key issues, House and Senate roll call votes, backgrounds of members, and political and election information. The CQ Press is a major publisher of books on politics and government. *www.cq.com*

franking privilege Free mail service afforded members of Congress.

Party Organizations in Congress The Democratic and Republican party organizations within the House of Representatives and the Senate are the principal bases for organizing Congress (see Figure 10.8). The leadership of each house of Congress, although nominally elected by the entire chamber, is actually chosen by secret ballot of the members of each party at a "conference" or caucus (see Table 10.4).

The parties and their leaders do not choose congressional candidates, nor can they deny them renomination; all members of Congress are responsible for their own primary and general election success. But party leadership in each chamber can help incumbents achieve their reelection goals. Each party in the House and Senate sponsors a campaign committee that channels some campaign funding to party members seeking reelection, although these Republican and Democratic congressional and senatorial campaign committees contribute less money than either PACs or individuals to the candidates.[34] Rather, good relations between members and their party's leadership are more important in the quest for power and influence in Washington.

Occasionally, congressional party leaders are urged to exercise more discipline over their members, to ensure that they support the party's position on key votes. Theoretically, party leaders in the House and Senate could do so by denying disloyal members appointment to preferred committees, by regularly burying their favorite bills, by cutting their pork barrel projects from the budget, or by denying them party campaign funds. But except in very extreme cases, party leaders have been reluctant to employ these punishments. Members of Congress cherish their independence. They respect each other's need to get reelected. A member's vote lost today may be won next week if the member is not alienated by disciplinary action.

Majority status confers great power on the party that controls the House and the Senate. The majority party chooses the leadership in each body, selects the chairs of every committee, and ensures that every committee has a majority of

TABLE 10.4 Leadership in Congress

Senate	
President Pro Tempore	An honorary post, usually the senior member of the majority party
Majority Leader	Top Senate post, elected by majority party members
Majority Whip	Second-ranking post in the majority party
Minority Leader	Leader of the minority opposition party
Minority Whip	Second-ranking post in the minority party
House	
Speaker	Powerful presiding officer, elected with the votes of the majority party
Majority Leader	Officially the leader of the majority party but second in power to the Speaker
Majority Whip	Third-ranking leader of the majority party
Minority Leader	Top post in the minority party
Minority Whip	Second-ranking post in the minority party

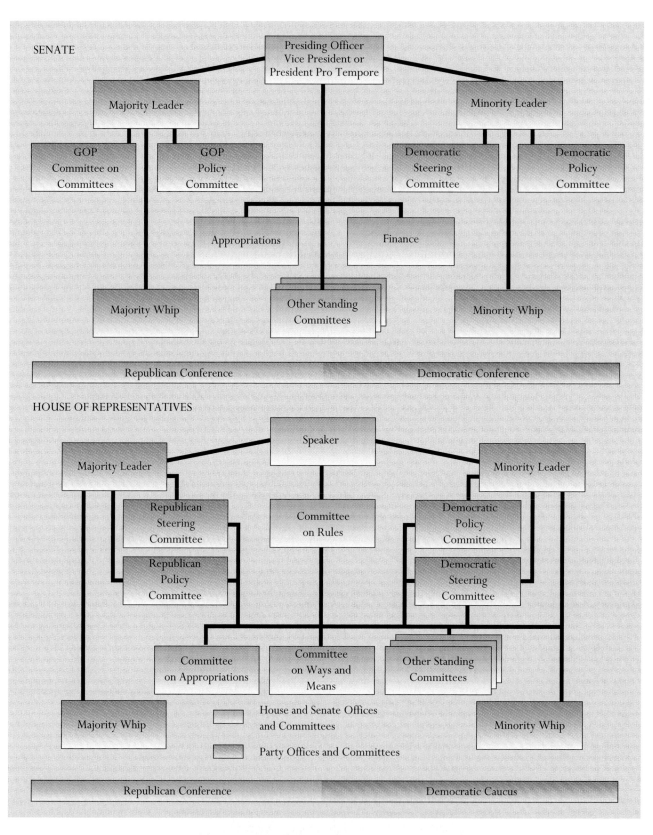

FIGURE 10.8 The Organization of Congress

Aside from naming the Speaker of the House as head of that body's operations and the vice president as overseer of Senate deliberations, the Constitution is silent on the organization of Congress. Political parties have filled this gap: both majority and minority parties have their own leadership, which governs the appointment of members to the various committees, where much of the work of Congress actually takes place.

members from the majority party. In other words, if Republicans are in the majority in either the House or the Senate or both, Republicans will occupy all leadership positions, chair every committee, and constitute a majority of the members of every committee, and, of course, the Democrats enjoy the same advantages when they capture a majority of either body. Majority-party members in each house even take in more campaign contributions than minority members.[35]

In the House: "Mr. Speaker" In the House of Representatives, the key leadership figure is the **Speaker of the House,** who serves as both presiding officer of the chamber and leader of the majority party. In the House, the Speaker has many powers. The Speaker decides who shall be recognized to speak on the floor and rules on points of order (with advice from the parliamentarian), including whether a motion or amendment is germane (relevant) to the business at hand. The Speaker decides to which committees new bills will be assigned and can schedule or delay votes on a bill. The Speaker appoints members of select, special, and conference committees and names majority-party members to the Rules Committee. And the Speaker controls both patronage jobs and office space in the Capitol. Although the norm of fairness requires the Speaker to apply the rules of the House consistently, the Speaker is elected by the majority party and is expected to favor that party.

Over the years, different Speakers have displayed different leadership styles. Republican Speaker Newt Gingrich was an ideological leader with a dramatic and aggressive agenda—a "Contract with America"—who contributed to partisan rancor in the House. In contrast, Republican Speaker Dennis Hastert has been a pragmatic leader who deals with his colleagues in an accommodating fashion.[36]

House Leaders and Whips The Speaker's principal assistant is the **majority leader.** The majority leader formulates the party's legislative program in consultation with other party leaders and steers the program through the House. The majority leader also must persuade committee leaders to support the aims of party leaders in acting on legislation before their committees. Finally, the majority leader arranges the legislative schedule with the cooperation of key party members.

The minority party in the House selects a **minority leader** whose duties correspond to those of the majority leader, except that the minority leader has no authority over the scheduling of legislation. The minority leader's principal duty has been to organize the forces of the minority party to counter the legislative program of the majority and to pass the minority party's bills. It is also the minority leader's duty to consult ranking minority members of House committees and to encourage them to adopt party positions and to follow the lead of the president if the minority party controls the White House (see *People in Politics:* "Nancy Pelosi, Leading House Democrats.")

In both parties, **whips** assist leaders in keeping track of the whereabouts of party members and in pressuring them to vote the party line. Whips are also responsible for ensuring the attendance of party members at important roll calls and for canvassing their colleagues on their likely support for or opposition to party-formulated legislation. Finally, whips are involved regularly in the formation of party policy and the scheduling of legislation.

In the Senate: "Mr. President" The Constitution declares the vice president of the United States to be the presiding officer of the Senate. But vice presidents seldom exercise this senatorial responsibility, largely because the presiding officer of the Senate has very little power. Having only 100 members, the Senate usually

Republican Speaker of the House Dennis Hastert leads the Republican majority.

Speaker of the House
Presiding officer of the House of Representatives.

majority leader In the House, the majority-party leader and second in command to the Speaker; in the Senate, the leader of the majority party.

minority leader In both the House and Senate, the leader of the opposition party.

whips In both the House and Senate, the principal assistants to the party leaders and next in command to those leaders.

Nancy Pelosi, Leading House Democrats

Nancy Pelosi is the first woman in the history of the U.S. Congress to lead a major party. In 2001 her Democratic colleagues elected her Minority Leader, the highest-ranking leadership position among Democratic members. Pelosi has represented her San Francisco district since her first election to the Congress in 1986.

Congresswoman Pelosi comes from a highly political family. Her father, Thomas D'Alesandro, served five terms in Congress and later 12 years as mayor of Baltimore. Pelosi's brother also served as mayor of Baltimore. Young Nancy grew up in Washington and graduated from that city's Trinity College in 1962. She served as a congressional intern to her Maryland sen- ator. She married Paul Pelosi, moved to his hometown of San Francisco, and raised five children. Prior to her election to Congress, she served on the National Democratic Committee.

In her years in Congress, Pelosi built a solid liberal reputation, serving on the powerful Appropriations Committee. She won the post as Democratic whip in 2001 in a close election against a more moderate Democrat. But Pelosi's real strength within the Democratic Party has long been her fund-raising ability. Her San Francisco district is the home of some of the party's wealthiest individual donors, and Democrats across the nation rely heavily upon money from California. Pelosi created her own leadership PAC and handed out over $1 million to her Democratic colleagues in 2000. She spends relatively little (about $400,000) on her own reelection races in her heavily Democratic district.

In 2002, Pelosi was reelected with an astonishing 80 percent of the vote in her California district. She topped that with 85 percent of the vote in 2004.

does not restrict debate and has fewer scheduling constraints than the House. The only significant power of the vice president is the right to cast a deciding vote in the event of a tie on a Senate roll call. In the usual absence of the vice president, the Senate is presided over by a *president pro tempore.* This honorific position is traditionally granted by the majority party to one of its senior stalwarts. The job of presiding over the Senate is so boring that neither the vice president nor the president pro tempore is found very often in the chamber. Junior senators are often asked to assume the chore. Nevertheless, speeches on the Senate floor begin with the salutation "Mr. President," referring to the president of the Senate, *not* the president of the United States.

Senate Majority and Minority Leaders Senate leadership is actually in the hands of the Senate majority leader, but the Senate majority leader is not as powerful in that body as the Speaker is in the House. With fewer members, all of whom perceive themselves as powerful leaders, the Senate is less hierarchically organized than the House. The Senate majority leader's principal power is scheduling the business of the Senate and recognizing the first speaker in floor debate. To be effective in policy making, the majority leader must be skilled in interpersonal persuasion and communication. Moreover, in the media age, the Senate majority leader must also be a national spokesperson for the party, along with the Speaker of the House. Republican Senate Leader Bill Frist and Republican Speaker of the House Dennis Hastert are their party's leading congressional spokesmen. The minority-party leader in the Senate represents the opposition in negotiations with the majority leader over Senate business. With the majority leader, the minority-party leader tends to dominate floor debate in the Senate.

TABLE 10.5 Top Congressional Leadership PACs, 2002

Name	Sponsor
Americans for a Republican Majority	Tom DeLay (R-Tex.)
HillPAC	Hillary Clinton (D-N.Y.)
Dedicated Americans	Tom Daschle (D-S.D.)
Responsible Opportunity PAC	Joseph Lieberman (D-Conn.)
Straight Talk America	John McCain (R-Ariz.)
New American Optimists	John Edwards (D-N.C.)
Keep Our Majority PAC	Dennis Hastert (R-Ill.)
Republican Majority Fund	Don Nickles (R-Okla.)
PAC to the Future	Nancy Pelosi (D-Ca.)
Majority Leaders Fund	Dick Army (R-Tex.)
Committee for a Democratic Majority	Ted Kennedy (D-Mass.)
Effective Government PAC	Richard Gephardt (D-Missouri)

Source: Center for Responsive Politics.

Career Paths within Congress Movement up the party hierarchy in each house is the most common way of achieving a leadership position. The traditional succession pattern in the House is from whip to majority leader to Speaker. In the Senate, Republicans and Democrats frequently resort to election contests in choosing their party leaders, yet both parties have increasingly adopted a two-step succession route from whip to leader.[37]

Leadership PACs House and Senate leaders, and members who aspire to become leaders, often ingratiate themselves to their colleagues by distributing campaign funds to them. In recent years, *leadership PACs* have proliferated on Capitol Hill. Table 10.5 lists the top leadership PACs by the size of their total contributions in the 2000 congressional elections.

In Committee

Much of the real work of Congress is done in committee. The floor of Congress is often deserted, C-SPAN focuses on the podium, not the empty chamber. Members dash to the floor when the bell rings throughout the Capitol signaling a roll-call vote. Otherwise they are found in their offices or in the committee rooms, where the real work of Congress is done.

Standing Committees The committee system provides for a division of labor in the Congress, assigning responsibility for work and allowing members to develop some expertise. The committee system is as old as the Congress itself: the very first Congress regularly assigned the task of wording bills to selected members who were believed to have a particular expertise. Soon a system of **standing committees**—permanent committees that specialize in a particular area of legislation—emerged. House committees have forty to sixty or more members and Senate committees fifteen to twenty-five members each. The proportions of Democrats and Republicans on each committee reflect the proportions of Democrats and Republicans in the House and Senate as a whole. Thus the majority party has a

Library of Congress
The Thomas system allows the tracing of bills from their introduction, through the committee system, floor schedule vote, etc. *http://thomas.loc.gov*

standing committee
Permanent committee of the House or Senate that deals with matters within a specified subject area.

majority of members on every committee; and every committee is chaired by a member of the majority party. The minority membership on each committee is led by the **ranking minority member**, the minority-party committee member with the most seniority.

The principal function of standing committees is the screening and drafting of legislation. With 8,000 to 10,000 or more bills introduced each session, the screening function is essential. The standing committees are the gatekeepers of Congress; less than 10 percent of the legislation introduced will pass the Congress. With rare exceptions, bills are not submitted to a vote by the full membership of the House or Senate without prior approval by the majority of a standing committee. Moreover, committees do not merely sort through bills assigned to them to find what they like. Rather, committees—or more often their subcommittees—draft (write) legislation themselves. Committees may amend, rewrite, or write their own bills. Committees are "little legislatures" within their own policy jurisdictions. Each committee guards its own policy jurisdiction jealously; jurisdictional squabbles between committees are common.

The Pecking Order of Committees The most powerful standing committees, and, therefore, the most sought-after committee assignments, are the Appropriations Committees in the House and the Senate. These committees hold the federal purse strings, arguably Congress's most important power. These committees are closely followed in influence and desirability by the Ways and Means Committee in the House and the Senate Finance Committee; these committees must pass on all tax matters, as well as Social Security and Medicare financing. In the House, the Rules Committee is especially powerful, owing to its control over floor consideration of every bill submitted to the full House. The Senate Judiciary Committee is especially influential because of its influence over all presidential nominees to the federal judiciary, including Supreme Court justices. Perhaps the least desirable committee assignments are those on the Senate Ethics Committee and the House Standards of Official Conduct Committee; these ethics panels are obliged to sit in judgment of their own colleagues.

Decentralization and Subcommittees Congressional **subcommittees** within each standing committee further decentralize the legislative process. At present, the House has about 90 subcommittees and the Senate about 70 subcommittees, each of which functions independently of its full committee (see Table 10.6). Subcommittees have fixed jurisdictions (for example, the House International Relations Committee has subcommittees on Africa, Asia and the Pacific, International Economic Policy, International Operations and Human Rights, and the Western Hemisphere); they meet and schedule their own hearings; and they have their own staffs and budgets. However, bills recommended by a subcommittee still require full standing-committee endorsement before being reported to the floor of the House or Senate. Full committees usually, but not always, ratify the decisions of their subcommittees.

Subcommittees decentralize power in Congress. Interest groups no longer concentrate their attention on a few senior standing-committee chairs and party leaders. Rather, they concentrate on those subcommittees dealing most directly with their concerns. Likewise, executive agencies must respond to subcommittees with policy oversight. Both lobbyists and bureaucrats must seek out "their" subcommittee and try to win the support of the chair and perhaps the ranking minority member. (For example, agents of the postal workers' union, the U.S. Postal Service,

ranking minority member
The minority-party committee member with the most seniority.

subcommittees Specialized committees within standing committees; subcommittee recommendations must be approved by the full standing committee before submission to the floor.

TABLE 10.6 Committees in Congress

Senate

Agriculture, Nutrition, and Forestry	Governmental Affairs
Appropriations	Indian Affairs
Armed Services	Judiciary
Banking, Housing, and Urban Affairs	Health, Education, Labor and Pensions
Budget	Rules and Administration
Commerce, Science, and Transportation	Small Business and Entrepreneurship
Energy and Natural Resources	Select Aging
Environment and Public Works	Select Ethics
Finance	Select Intelligence
Foreign Relations	Veterans Affairs

House

Agriculture	Resources
Appropriations	Rules
Armed Forces	Science
Budget	Small Business
Energy and Commerce	Standards of Official Conduct
Education and the Workforce	Transportation and Infrastructure
Financial Services	Veterans Affairs
Government Reform	Ways and Means
House Administration	Select Intelligence
International Relations	Select Homeland Security
Judiciary	

Joint Committees

Joint Economic Committee
Joint Taxation
Joint Committee on Printing
Joint Committee on the Library

and private competitors such as FedEx and United Parcel Service all converge on the Post Office and Civil Service Subcommittee of the Senate Governmental Affairs Committee.) The result has been hundreds of policy networks, each featuring subcommittee members and staff, lobbyists with an interest in the subcommittee's field, and bureaucrats in the executive branch charged with implementing congressional policy in that field.

Chairing a committee or subcommittee gives members of Congress the opportunity to exercise power, attract media attention, and thus improve their chances of reelection. Often committees have become "fiefdoms" over which their chairs exercise complete control and jealously guard their power. This situation allows a very small number of House and Senate members to block legislation. Many decisions are not really made by the whole Congress. Rather, they are made by subcommittee members with a special interest in the policy under consideration. Although the committee system may satisfy the desire of members to gain power, prestige, and reelection opportunities, it weakens responsible government in the Congress as a whole.

"Ted" Kennedy: Keeping Liberalism Alive in the U.S. Senate

To the American public, Massachusetts Senator, Edward M. "Ted" Kennedy is largely a symbol of his family's legendary triumphs and tragedies. But in the U.S. Senate, Kennedy has established himself over the years as the recognized leader of liberal Democrats and a highly effective legislator.

Ted Kennedy's father, Joseph P. Kennedy, was a wealthy banker and stock market manipulator who provided key financial backing for the 1932 presidential campaign of Franklin D. Roosevelt. FDR later appointed "Old Joe" as ambassador to England. The senior Kennedy fathered nine children, including Joseph P. Jr., who was killed in World War II; President John F. Kennedy, who was assassinated in 1963; Senator Robert F. Kennedy, who was assassinated in 1968; and youngest, Edward M. "Ted" Kennedy.

Although born to great wealth (he received his first communion from the Pope), Ted Kennedy acquired the sense of competition fostered in the large Kennedy household. In 1951, suspended from Harvard for cheating on an examination, he joined the Army and served two years in Germany. He was later readmitted to Harvard where he graduated in 1956. Rejected by Harvard Law School, he enrolled instead in the University of Virginia Law School and completed his law degree in 1959. When he was just 30 years old, the minimum age for a U.S. senator, he announced his candidacy for the Massachusetts Senate seat formerly held by his brother, who was then president. His 1962 election to the U.S. Senate reflected the esteem that Massachusetts voters have always held for his family.

Kennedy performed better in the Senate than many had expected. He worked hard learning about national health problems and problems of the elderly. In 1969 he was elected Senate Democratic whip by his colleagues. But his personal life was marred by accident, tragedy, and scandal. He nearly died in a 1964 plane crash in which he suffered a broken back. He was frequently the object of romantic gossip in Washington, In 1969, a young women died when the car Kennedy was driving plunged off a narrow bridge on Chappaquiddick Island after a late-night party. Missing for

Committee Membership Given the power of the committee system, it is not surprising that members of Congress have a very keen interest in their committee assignments. Members strive for assignments that will give them influence in Congress, allow them to exercise power in Washington, and ultimately improve their chances for reelection. For example, a member from a big city may seek a seat on Banking, Housing, and Urban Affairs, a member from a farm district may seek a seat on Agriculture, and a member from a district with a large military base may seek a seat on National Security or Veterans Affairs. Everyone seeks a seat on Appropriations, because both the House and the Senate Appropriations committees have subcommittees in each area of federal spending.[38]

Party leadership in both the House and the Senate largely determines committee assignments. These assignments are given to new Democratic House members by the Democratic Steering and Policy Committee; new Democratic senators receive their assignments from the Senate Democratic Steering Committee. New Republican members receive their committee assignments from the Republican Committee on Committees in both houses. The leadership generally tries to honor new members' requests and improve their chances for reelection, but because incumbent members of committees are seldom removed, openings on powerful committees are infrequent.

ten hours after the accident, Kennedy later made a dramatic national television appearance claiming that the tragedy had been an accident that he had been too confused to report until the next day. He pled guilty to the minor charge of leaving the scene of the accident. Senate Democrats removed Kennedy from his position as majority party whip.

Kennedy deliberately avoided Democratic presidential battles in both 1972 and 1976, believing that the public's memory of Chappaquiddick was still too fresh. However, in late 1979, with President Jimmy Carter standing in a near all-time low for presidents in opinion polls, Kennedy announced his presidential candidacy. But shortly thereafter, Soviet troops invaded neighboring Afghanistan. Support for the president was equated with support for America, and Carter benefited from this "rally round the flag" effect. Carter defeated Kennedy in the Democratic primaries, but Kennedy polished his own charismatic image with a dramatic inspiring speech at the 1980 Democratic national convention.

Kennedy avoided subsequent presidential races, citing family affairs as his reason. And indeed, family problems continued to plague him. He was divorced from his first wife, Joan, and stories were published in women's magazines portraying her as a victim of his heavy drinking and "womanizing." At the same time, he felt responsible for the many "third-generation" offspring of his deceased brother Robert, as well as his own children. One nephew died a drug-related death in a Miami motel in 1984, and another was found not guilty of rape charges in a nationally televised trial in 1992. That same year Kennedy married an accomplished Washington attorney and undertook to change his personal lifestyle. He delivered a moving eulogy on national television at the funeral of his nephew John F. Kennedy, Jr. after a plane crash in 1999 that killed JFK Jr., his wife, and sister-in-law.

As the ranking Democrat on the Senate Health, Education, and Labor Committee, Kennedy has undertaken the lead in a variety of important legislative issues. He helped pass the Family Leave Act of 1993, the Kennedy-Kasselbaum Act of 1996 that mandated health insurance "portability" (see Chapter 17), and increases in the minimum wage. While conservatives have frequently targeted Kennedy for his liberal politics, he has proven adept at working with Republicans in the Senate to win compromises in legislation. In 2000 he was elected to his seventh full term as U.S. senator from Massachusetts.

"50 Ways to Do the Job of Congress," *Congressional Quarterly*, October 30, 1999.

Seniority Committee chairs are elected in the majority-party caucus. But the **seniority system** governs most movement into committee leadership positions. The seniority system ranks all committee members in each party according to the length of time they have served on the committee. If the majority-party chair exits the Congress or leaves the committee, that position is filled by the next *ranking majority-party member*. New members of a committee are initially added to the bottom of the ranking of their party; they climb the seniority ranking by remaining on the committee and accruing years of seniority. Members who stay in Congress but "hop" committees are usually placed at the bottom of their new committee's list.

The seniority system has a long tradition in the Congress. The advantage is that it tends to reduce conflict among members, who otherwise would be constantly engaged in running for committee posts. It also increases the stability of policy direction in committees over time. Critics of the system note, though, that the seniority system grants greater power to members from "safe" districts—districts that offer little electoral challenge to the incumbent. (Historically in the Democratic Party, these districts were in the conservative South, and opposition to the seniority system developed among liberal northern Democrats. But in recent years, many liberal Democrats gained seniority and the seniority system again became entrenched (see *People in Politics:* "'Ted' Kennedy, Keeping Liberalism Alive in the

seniority system Custom whereby the member of Congress who has served the longest on the majority side of a committee becomes its chair and the member who has served the longest on the minority side becomes its ranking member.

Senator Joe Biden (left), of the Senate Foreign Relations Committee, speaks to reporters after meeting with President Bush about the arms treaty with Russia.

U.S. Senate"). The seniority rule for selecting committee chairs has been violated on only a few notable occasions.

Committee Hearings The decision of a congressional committee to hold public hearings on a bill or topic is an important one. It signals congressional interest in a particular policy matter and sets the agenda for congressional policy making. Ignoring an issue by refusing to hold hearings on it usually condemns it to oblivion. Public hearings allow interest groups and government bureaucrats to present formal arguments to Congress. Testimony comes mostly from government officials, lobbyists, and occasional experts recommended by interest groups or committee staff members. Hearings are usually organized by the staff under the direction of the chair. Staff members contact favored lobbyists and bureaucrats and schedule their appearances. Committee hearings are regularly listed in the *Washington Post* and are open to the public. Indeed, the purpose of many hearings is not really to inform members of Congress but instead to rally public support behind an issue or a bill. The media are the real target audience of many public hearings, with committee members jockeying in front of the cameras for a "sound bite" on the evening news.

Markup Once hearings are completed the committee's staff is usually assigned the task of writing a report and **drafting a bill**. The staff's bill generally reflects the chair's policy views. But the staff draft is subject to committee **markup**, a line-by-line consideration of the wording of the bill. Markup sessions are frequently closed to the public in order to expedite work. Lobbyists are forced to stand in the hallways, buttonholing members as they go into and out of committee rooms.

It is in markup that the detailed work of lawmaking takes place. Markup sessions require patience and skill in negotiation. Committee or subcommittee chairs may try to develop consensus on various parts of the bill, either within the whole committee or within the committee's majority. In marking up a bill, members of a subcommittee must always remember that the bill must pass both in the full committee and on the floor of the chamber. Although they have considerable freedom in writing their own policy preferences into law, especially on the details of the legislation, they must give some consideration to the views of these larger bodies. Consultations with party leadership are not infrequent.

Most bills die in committee. Some are voted down, but most are simply ignored. Bills introduced simply to reassure constituents or interest groups that a representative is committed to "doing something" for them generally die quietly. But House members who really want action on a bill can be frustrated by committee inaction. The only way to force a floor vote on a bill opposed by a committee is to get a majority (218) of House members to sign a **discharge petition**. Out of hundreds of discharge petition efforts, only a few dozen have succeeded. The Senate also can forcibly "discharge" a bill from committee by simple majority vote; but because senators can attach any amendment to any bill they wish, there is generally no need to go this route.

On the Floor

A favorable "report" by a standing committee of the House or Senate places a bill on the "calendar." The word *calendar* is misleading, because bills on the calendar are not considered in chronological order, and many die on the calendar without ever reaching the floor.

drafting a bill Actual writing of a bill in legal language.

markup Line-by-line revision of a bill in committee by editing each phrase and word.

discharge petition Petition signed by at least 218 House members to force a vote on a bill within a committee that opposes it.

House Rules Committee Even after a bill has been approved by a standing committee, getting it to the floor of the House of Representatives for a vote by the full membership requires favorable action by the Rules Committee. The Rules Committee acts as a powerful "traffic cop" for the House. In order to reach the floor, a bill must receive a rule from the Rules Committee. The Rules Committee can kill a bill simply by refusing to give it a rule. A **rule** determines when the bill will be considered by the House and how long the debate on the bill will last. More important, a rule determines whether amendments from the floor will be permitted and, if so, how many. A **closed rule** forbids House members from offering any amendments and speeds up consideration of the bill in the form submitted by the standing committee. A **restricted rule** allows certain specified amendments to be considered. An **open rule** permits unlimited amendments. Most key bills are brought to the floor of the House with fairly restrictive rules. In recent sessions, about three-quarters of all bills reaching the floor were restricted, and an additional 10 to 15 percent were fully closed. Only a few bills were open.

Senate Floor Traditions The Senate has no rules committee but relies instead on a **unanimous consent agreement** negotiated between the majority and minority leader to govern consideration of a bill. The unanimous consent agreement generally specifies when the bill will be debated, what amendments will be considered, and when the final vote will be taken. But as the name implies, a single senator can object to a unanimous consent agreement and thus hold up Senate consideration of a bill. Senators do not usually do so, because they know that a reputation for obstructionism will imperil their own favorite bills at a later date. Once accepted, a unanimous consent agreement is binding on the Senate and cannot be changed without another unanimous consent agreement. To get unanimous consent, Senate leaders must consult with all interested senators. Unanimous consent agreements have become more common in recent years as they have become more specific in their provisions.

The Senate cherishes its tradition of unrestricted floor debate. Senators may speak as long as they wish or even try to **filibuster** a bill to death by talking nonstop and tying up the Senate for so long that the leadership is forced to drop the bill in order to go on to other work. Senate rules also allow senators to place a "hold" on a bill, indicating their unwillingness to grant unanimous consent to its consideration. Debate may be ended only if *sixty* or more senators vote for **cloture**, a process of petition and voting that limits the debate. A cloture vote requires a petition signed by sixteen senators, two days must elapse between the petition's introduction and the cloture vote. If cloture passes, then each senator is limited to one hour of debate on the bill. But getting the necessary sixty votes for cloture is difficult. Recently Democrats, although a minority in the Senate, have defeated cloture motions in order to derail President Bush's nominees for federal judgeships (see Chapter 13).

Senate floor procedures also permit unlimited amendments to be offered, even those that are not "germane" to the bill. A **rider** is an amendment to a bill that is not germane to the bill's purposes.

These Senate traditions of unlimited debate and unrestricted floor amendments give individual senators considerably more power over legislation than individual representatives enjoy.

Floor Voting The key floor votes are usually on *amendments* to bills rather than on their final passage. Indeed, "killer amendments" are deliberately designed to

rule Stipulation attached to a bill in the House of Representatives that governs its consideration on the floor, including when and for how long it can be debated and how many (if any) amendments may be appended to it.

closed rule Rule that forbids adding any amendments to a bill under consideration by the House.

restricted rule Rule that allows specified amendments to be added to a bill under consideration by the House.

open rule Rule that permits unlimited amendments to a bill under consideration by the House.

unanimous consent agreement Negotiated by the majority and minority leaders of the Senate, it specifies when a bill will be taken up on the floor, what amendments will be considered, and when a vote will be taken.

filibuster Delaying tactic by a senator or group of senators, using the Senate's unlimited debate rule to prevent a vote on a bill.

cloture Vote to end debate—that is, to end a filibuster—which requires a three-fifths vote of the entire membership of the Senate.

rider Amendment to a bill that is not germane to the bill's purposes.

defeat the original purpose of the bill. Other amendments may water down the bill so much that it will have little policy impact. Thus the true policy preferences of senators or representatives may be reflected more in their votes on amendments than their vote on final passage. Members may later claim to have supported legislation on the basis of their vote on final passage, even though they earlier voted for amendments designed to defeat the bill's purposes.

Members may also obscure their voting records by calling for a voice vote—simply shouting "aye" or "nay"—and avoiding recording of their individual votes. In contrast, a **roll-call vote** involves the casting of individual votes, which are reported in the *Congressional Record* and are available to the media and the general public. Electronic voting machines in the House allow members to insert their cards and record their votes automatically. The Senate, truer to tradition, uses no electronic counters.

Conference Committees The Constitution requires that both houses of Congress pass a bill with identical wording. However, many major bills pass each house in different forms, not only with different wording but sometimes with wholly different provisions. Occasionally the House or the Senate will resolve these differences by reconsidering the matter and passing the other chamber's version of the bill. But about 15 percent of the time, serious differences arise and bills are assigned to **conference committees** to reach agreement on a single version for resubmission to both houses. Conference committees are temporary, with members appointed by the leadership in each house, usually from among the senior members of the committees that approved the bills.

Conference committees can be very powerful. Their final bill is usually (although not always) passed in both houses and sent to the president for approval. In resolving differences between the House and the Senate versions, the conference committee makes many final policy decisions. Although conference committees have considerable leeway in striking compromises, they focus on points of disagreement and usually do not change provisions already approved by both houses. Figure 10.9 on facing page summarizes the lawmaking process.

Decision Making in Congress

How do senators and representatives decide about how they will vote on legislation? From an almost limitless number of considerations that go into congressional decision making, a few factors recur across a range of voting decisions: party loyalty, presidential support or opposition, constituency concerns, interest-group pressures, and the personal values and ideologies of members themselves.

Party Voting Party appears to be the most significant influence on congressional voting. **Party votes** are roll-call votes on which a majority of voting Democrats oppose a majority of voting Republicans. Traditionally, party votes occurred on roughly *half* of all roll-call votes in Congress. Partisanship in Congress, as reflected in the percentage of party votes, rose during the 1990s but may be moderating somewhat today (see Figure 10.10 on page 356).

Party unity is measured by the percentage of Democrats and Republicans who stick by their party on party votes. Both Democratic and Republican Party unity has remained at fairly constant levels (75–85 percent) in both the House and the Senate over the past twenty years.

roll-call vote Vote of the full House or Senate on which all members' individual votes are recorded and made public.

conference committee Meeting between representatives of the House and Senate to reconcile differences over provisions of a bill passed by both houses.

party vote Majority of Democrats voting in opposition to a majority of Republicans.

party unity Percentage of Democrats and Republicans who stick with their party on party votes.

Bill Introduction

Subcommittee Hearings

Committee Action

Floor Action

Conference Action

Presidential Decision

HOUSE

Bill is introduced and assigned to a committee, which refers it to the appropriate subcommittee.

Subcommittee
Subcommittee holds hearings and "marks up" the bill. If the bill is approved in some form, it goes to the full committee.

Committee
Full committee considers the bill. If the bill is approved in some form, it is "reported" to the full House and placed on the House calendar.

Rules Committee
Rules Committee issues a rule to govern debate on the floor. Sends it to the full House.

Full House
Full House debates the bill and may amend it. If the bill passes and it is in a form different from the Senate version, it must go to a conference committee.

SENATE

Bill is introduced and assigned to a committee, which refers it to the appropriate subcommittee.

Subcommittee
Subcommittee holds hearings, debates provisions and "marks up" the bill. If a bill is approved, it goes to the full committee.

Committee
Full committee considers the bill. If the bill is approved in some form, it is "reported" to the full Senate and placed on the Senate calendar.

Leadership
Majority and minority leaders negotiate "unanimous consent" agreements scheduling full Senate debate and vote on the bill.

Full Senate
Full Senate debates the bill. Senate may amend it. If the bill passes and is in a form different from the House version, it must go to a conference committee.

Conference Committee
Conference committee of senators and representatives meets to reconcile differences between bills. When agreement is reached, a compromise bill is sent back to both the House and the Senate.

President
President signs or vetoes the bill. Congress can override a veto by a two-thirds majority vote in both the House and Senate.

LAW

FIGURE 10.9 How a Bill Becomes a Law

This diagram depicts the major hurdles a successful bill must overcome in order to be enacted into law. Few bills introduced travel this full path; less than 10 percent of bills introduced are passed by Congress and sent to the president for approval or veto. Bills fail at every step along the path, but most die in committees and subcommittees, usually from inaction rather than from being voted down.

FIGURE 10.10 **Party Voting in Congress**

Partisanship varies over time in Congress. For many years, between 30 and 40 percent of votes in the House and Senate were party votes—votes on which a majority of Democrats were in opposition to a majority of Republicans—but during the 1990s the percentage rose, indicating an increasingly partisan environment in Congress.

Note: Data indicate the percentage of all recorded votes on which a majority of voting Democrats opposed a majority of voting Republicans.

Source: Based on data from *Congressional Quarterly Weekly Report,* January 12, 2002, p. 136.

Sources of Partisanship

Why do Democrats and Republicans in Congress vote along party lines? First of all, the Democratic Party has become more liberal and the Republican Party has become more conservative over the years (see *Up Close:* "Polarization on Capitol Hill"). Conservative Democrats, once very common in southern politics, are rapidly disappearing. At the same time, the ranks of liberal Republicans, mostly from the Northeast, have thinned. Second, the decline in voter turnout, especially in primary elections, has added to the importance of well-organized and ideologically motivated groups. A reputation as a "moderate" is not much help in a low-voter-turnout primary election. In these elections Republicans must be more concerned with pleasing conservative activists (e.g., the Christian Coalition, National Right-to-Life Committee, National Rifle Association, etc.), and Democrats must be more concerned with pleasing liberal groups (National Education Association, American Federation of State, County, and Municipal Employees, EMILY's List, etc.). And third, the rising costs of campaigning make members ever more dependent upon the financial support of these interests.

Conflict between the parties occurs frequently on domestic social and economic issues—welfare, housing and urban affairs, health, business regulation, taxing, and spending. On civil rights issues, voting often follows party lines on amendments and other preliminary matters but then swings to **bipartisan** voting on a final bill. This pattern suggests that the parties tend to agree on the general goals of civil rights legislation but not on the means. Traditionally, bipartisanship was the goal of both presidents and congressional leaders on foreign and defense policy issues. Since the Vietnam War, however, Democrats in the House have been more critical of U.S. military involvements (and defense spending in general) than have Republicans.

bipartisan Agreement by members of both the Democratic and the Republican parties.

divided party government One party controls the presidency while the other party controls one or both houses of Congress.

Presidential Support or Opposition

Presidential influence in congressional voting is closely tied to party. Presidents almost always receive their greatest support from members of their own party (see Figure 10.11). Indeed, the policy gridlock associated with **divided party government**—in past decades, a Republican

Polarization on Capitol Hill

The Democratic and Republican parties in Congress are further apart ideologically than ever before. The Republicans are more uniformly conservative, and the Democrats more liberal, than in previous decades. "The proportion of political moderates—conservative Democrats or liberal Republicans—hovered at about 30 percent in the 1960s and 1970s. . . . Fewer than one in ten of today's lawmakers fall into this centrist category."[*] Conservative Southern Democrats once represented a third of their party's members, and a "conservative coalition" of Republicans and Southern Democrats was once a strong force in the Senate. Indeed, in the early 1980s President Ronald Reagan won the support of many moderate-to-conservative Democrats for his tax cutting measures. But today conservative Democrats account for less than ten percent of their party's membership in Congress; with the retirement of several Southern Democratic senators in 2004, conservative Democrats have practically disappeared from the Senate. And even rarer breed—liberal Republicans—are also nearing extinction.

Partisanship and ideology are closely connected in this polarization on Capitol Hill. The result is more conflict, less bipartisan cooperation, and more acrimony in the halls of Congress.

The most common explanation for this polarization is the realignment of Southern voters from the Democratic to the Republican party. Southern conservatives moved almost en bloc into the Republican Party in the 1980s. As conservatives in the Republican Party gained strength, liberal Republicans, mostly from the Northeast, lost ground. Geographically, the Republican Party became centered in the Mountain states and the South, while the Democratic Party held the Northeast and West Coast. Finally, more polarizing issues—abortion, term limits, budget balancing—and a more aggressive leadership style, notably speaker Newt Gingrich in the 1990s, also contributed to party polarization.[†]

---

[*]Roger H. Davidson and Usltard Oleszek *Congress and Its Members*. 9th ed. Washington, D.C.: CQ Press, 2004, p. 276.

[†]Jason M. Roberts and Steven S. Smith, "Procedure Contexts Party Strategy and Conditional Party Voting in the U.S. House of Representatives, 1971–2000." *American Journal of Political Science* 47 (April 2003): pp 305–317.

president and a Democratic-controlled Congress, but beginning in 1995 a Democratic president and a Republican-controlled Congress—arises directly from the tendency of the opposition party to obstruct the president's policy proposals.

The decentralization of power in the congressional committee system also limits the president's ability to influence voting. The president cannot simply negotiate with the leadership of the House and Senate but instead must deal with scores of committee and subcommittee chairs and ranking members. To win the support of so many members of Congress, presidents often music agree to insert pork into presidential bills, promise patronage jobs, or offer presidential assistance in campaign fund raising.

If negotiations break down, presidents can "go over the heads" of Congress, using the media to appeal directly to the people to support presidential programs and force Congress to act. The president has better access to the media than Congress has. But such threats and appeals can only be effective when (1) the president himself is popular with the public; and (2) the issue is one about which constituents can be made to feel intensely.

Finally, presidents can threaten to veto legislation. This threat, expressed or implied, confronts congressional leaders, committee chairs, and sponsors of a bill with several options. They must decide whether to (1) modify the bill to overcome the president's objections; (2) try to get two-thirds of both houses to commit to overriding the threatened veto; or (3) pass the bill and dare the president

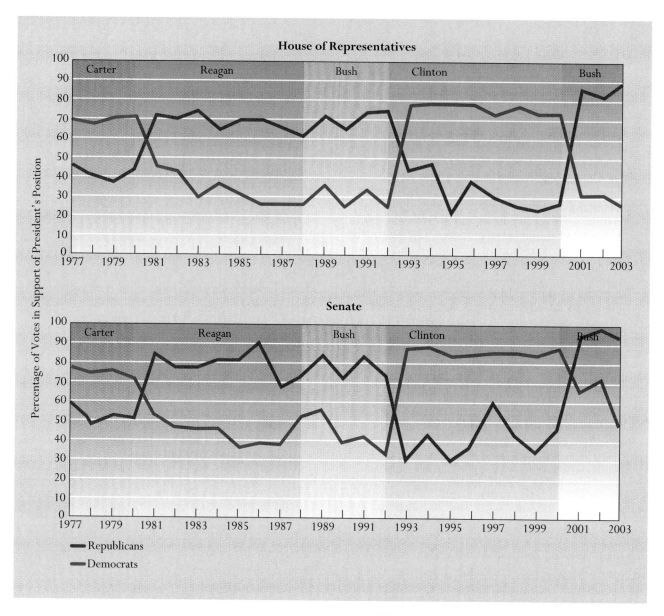

FIGURE 10.11 Congressional Voting in Support of the President

Presidents always receive more support in Congress from members of their own party. Democratic Presidents Jimmy Carter and Bill Clinton could count on winning large majorities of Democratic members' votes, Republican Presidents Ronald Reagan and George Bush won large majorities of GOP members' votes Percentages indicate congressional votes supporting the president on votes on which the president took a position.

Source: Norman J. Ornstein, Thomas E. Mann, and Michael J. Malbin, Vital Statistics on Congress 1999–2000 (Washington, D.C.: CQ Press, 2000), pp. 254–55; and Congressional Quarterly Weekly Report, December 11, 1999, p. 2987, January 12, 2002, p. 136; December 14, 2003, p. 3275 January 3, 2004.

to veto it, then make a political issue out of the president's opposition. Historically, less than 5 percent of vetoes have been overridden by the Congress. Unless the president is politically very weak (as Richard Nixon was during the Watergate scandal), Congress cannot count on overriding a veto. If members of Congress truly want to address an important problem and not just define a political issue, they must negotiate with the White House to write a bill the president will sign.

Constituency Influence Constituency influence in congressional voting is most apparent on issues that attract media attention and discussion and generate intense feelings among the general public. If many voters in the home state or district know about an issue and have intense feelings about it, members of Congress are likely to defer to their constituents' feeling, regardless of the position of their party's leadership or even their own personal feelings. Members of Congress from *safe seats* seem to be just as attuned to the interests of their constituents as members from competitive seats (see *Up Close:* "Tips on Lobbying Congress").

Constituency influence is particularly important on economic issues. Members from districts heavily dependent on a particular industry are routinely found protecting and advancing the interests of that industry. This kind of constituency representation is not unlike pork-barrel politics.

Constituencies may also exercise a subtle influence by conditioning the personal views of members. Many members were born, were raised, and continue to live in the towns they represent; over a lifetime they have absorbed and internalized the views of their communities. Moreover, some members of Congress feel an obligation to represent their constituents' opinions even when they personally disagree.

Members of Congress have considerable latitude in voting against their constituents' opinions if they choose to do so. Constituents, as noted earlier, lack information about most policy issues and the voting records of their senators and representatives. Even when constituents know about an issue and feel strongly about it, members can afford to cast a "wrong" vote from time to time. A long record of home-style politics—casework, pork barreling, visits, public appearances, and so on—can isolate members of Congress from the wrath generated by their voting records. Only a long string of "wrong" votes on issues important to constituents is likely to jeopardize an incumbent.

Interest-Group Influence Inside the Washington Beltway, the influence of interest groups, lobbyists, and fund raisers on members of Congress is well understood. This influence is seldom talked about back home or on the campaign trail, except perhaps by challengers. Lobbyists have their greatest effects on the *details* of public policy. Congressional decisions made in committee rooms, at markup sessions, and around conference tables can mean billions of dollars to industries and tens of millions to individual companies. Pressures from competing interest groups can be intense as lobbyists buttonhole lawmakers and try to win legislative amendments that can make or break business fortunes. One of the most potent tools in the lobbyist's arsenal is money. The prohibitive cost of modern campaigning has dictated that dollars are crucial to electoral victory, and virtually all members of Congress spend more time than they would like courting it, raising it, and stockpiling it for the next election.

Voters may be wrong when they think that all members of Congress are crooks, but they are not far off the mark when they worry that their own representatives may be listening to two competing sets of constituents—the real constituents back home in the district and the "cash constituents" who come calling in Washington.[39]

Personal Values It was the eighteenth-century English political philosopher Edmund Burke, himself a member of Parliament, who told his constituents; "You choose a member indeed; but when you have chosen him, he is not a member of Bristol, but he is a member of *Parliament*." Burke defended the classic notion of

THINK AGAIN

Are members of Congress obliged to vote the way their constituents wish, even if they personally disagree?

THINK AGAIN

Is it ethical for Congress members to pay special attention to requests for assistance by people who make large campaign contributions?

constituency The votes in a legislator's home district.

Tips on Lobbying Congress

YourCongress.com has some good suggestions about how to lobby Congress.

1. Keep it short and to the point. (Good lobbyists tell exactly what they want and why, in the least amount of words.)
2. Say thank you. (So few people say anything positive to members of Congress or their staff. If you know that they've done something good, say thank you. They'll remember it.)
3. Get to know the staff. (Good lobbyists don't complain when they don't get to meet the member of Congress. The staff does most of the work anyway, and has a knack for making requests disappear if given a reason to do so.)
4. Tell the whole story. (Good lobbyists don't patronize. They acknowledge when something is difficult and are up front about the opposition.)
5. Timing is everything. (Good lobbyists know the process of Congress, mention the proper deadlines, and don't ask for requests at the last minute.)
6. Always one page, and always written up in advance. (Good lobbyists have already written a draft of what they want before they ask for it, and are always happy to leave it or send it over.)
7. Capitol Hill is the last place to burn bridges. (Good lobbyists don't go ballistic when they are told no. They regroup and wait for another chance. D.C. is a very small place, and being a jerk will only mean you quickly get a reputation for being a jerk.)

representatives as **trustees** who feel obligated to use their own best judgment about what is good for the nation as a whole. In this theory, representatives are not obligated to vote the views of their constituents. This notion contrasts with the idea of representatives as **delegates** who feel obligated to vote according to the views of "the folks back home" regardless of their own personal viewpoint. Most legislators *claim* to be trustees, perhaps because of the halo effect generated by the independence implied in the term.

Democratic political philosophers have pondered the merits of trustee versus delegate representation over the centuries, but the question only rarely arises in actual congressional deliberations. In many cases, members' own personal views and those of their constituents are virtually identical. Moreover, members may overestimate the knowledge and issue-oriented tendencies of voters, since those most likely to communicate directly with their members of Congress are among the most knowledgeable and issue-oriented people in the district. Even when legislators perceive conflicts between their own views and those of their constituents, most attempt to find a compromise between these competing demands rather than choose one role or another exclusively. The political independence of members of Congress—their independence from party, combined with the ignorance of their constituents about most policy issues—allows members to give great weight to their own personal ideologies in voting.

Customs and Norms

trustees Legislators who feel obligated to use their own best judgment in decision making.

delegates Legislators who feel obligated to present the views of their home constituents.

Over time, institutions develop customs and norms of behavior to assist in their functioning. These are not merely quaint and curious folkways; they promote the purposes of the institution. Congressional customs and norms are designed to help members work together, to reduce interpersonal conflict, to facilitate bargaining and promote compromise, and in general to make life in Congress a little more pleasant.

Civility Traditionally members of Congress understood that uncivil behavior—expressions of anger, personal attacks on character, ugly confrontations, flaming rhetoric—undermined the lawmaking function. Indeed, civility was encouraged by the longstanding custom of members of Congress referring to each other in elaborately courteous terms: "my distinguished colleague from Ohio," "the honorable representative from Pennsylvania," and the like. By custom, even bitter partisan enemies in Congress were expected to avoid harsh personal attacks on each other. The purpose of this custom was to try to maintain an atmosphere in which people who hold very different opinions can nevertheless function with some degree of decorum. Unfortunately, many of these customs and norms of behavior are breaking down. Individual ambition and the drive for power and celebrity have led to a decline in courtesy, cooperation, and respect for traditional norms. One result is that it has become increasingly difficult for Congress to reach agreement on policy issues. Another result is that life in Congress is increasingly tedious, conflict-filled, and unpleasant (see *A Conflicting View:* "Congress Can Act Responsibly on Occasion").

The Demise of the Apprenticeship Norm Not too many years ago, "the first rule"[40] of congressional behavior was that new members were expected to be seen but not heard on the floor, to be studious in their committee work, and to be cooperative with party leaders. But the institutional norm of apprenticeship was swept aside in the 1970s as increasingly ambitious and independent senators and representatives arrived on Capitol Hill. Today new members of Congress feel free to grab the spotlight on the floor, in committee, and in front of television cameras. "The evidence is clear, unequivocal, and overwhelming: the [apprenticeship] norm is simply gone."[41] Nevertheless, experienced members are more active and influential in shaping legislation than are new members.[42]

Specialization and Deference The committee system encourages members of Congress to specialize in particular policy areas. Even the most independent and ambitious members can perceive the advantage of developing power and expertise in an area especially relevant to their constituents. Traditionally, members who developed a special expertise and accumulated years of service on a standing committee were deferred to in floor proceedings. These specialists were "cue givers" for party members when bills or amendments were being voted on. Members are still likely to defer to specialized committee members when the issues are technical or complicated, or when the issue is outside of their own area of policy specialization, but deference is increasingly rare on major public issues.

Bargaining Bargaining is central to the legislative process. Little could be achieved if individual members were unwilling to bargain with each other for votes both in committees and on the floor. A willingness to bargain is a longstanding functional norm of Congress.

Members of Congress are not expected to violate their consciences in the bargaining process. On the contrary, members respect one another's issues of conscience and receive respect in return. On most issues, however, members can and do bargain their support. "Horse trading" is very common in committee work. Members may bargain in their own personal interest, in the interests of constituents or groups, or even in the interests of their committee with members of other committees. Because most bargaining occurs in a committee setting, it is seldom a matter of public record. The success and reputation of committee chairs largely depend on their ability to work out bargains and compromises.

Congress Can Act Responsibly on Occasion

Congress is not always mired in partisanship, squabbling, and gridlock. On occasion it acts responsibly in the national interest. Indeed, consider the following congressional landmarks in U.S. history:

Louisiana Purchase (1803) President Thomas Jefferson offered to purchase from France nearly 830,000 square miles between the Mississippi and the Rockies for $15 million—about three cents an acre. There is no constitutional provision authorizing the federal government to buy foreign territory, but the Senate, accepting Jefferson's broad interpretation of the Constitution, approved the purchase. The House appropriated the money to consummate the deal. On December 29, 1803, the United States took possession of North America's heartland, doubling the nation's size with territory that would comprise thirteen states.

Homestead Act (1862) This Civil War–era legislation allowed any family head or adult male to claim 160 acres of prairie land for a $10 registration fee and a promise to live there continuously for five years. It opened up the midwestern United States for immediate settlement. The act drew thousands of English, Irish, Germans, Swedes, Danes, Norwegians, and Czechs to the United States, pushing settlement farther west.

Social Security Act (1935) The act was designed to secure "the men, women, and children of the nation against certain hazards and vicissitudes of life," explained President Franklin Roosevelt. The act's best-known measure is the social insurance system that provides monthly checks to the elderly.

National Labor Relations Act (1935) By declaring workers had a right to join unions and bargain collectively with employers for pay raises and improved working conditions, the act spurred the growth of the nation's major industrial unions. Labor's Magna Carta also provided workers with the legal weapons to improve plant conditions and protect themselves from employer harassment.

G.I. Bill of Rights (1944) The G.I. Bill of Rights, known officially as the Serviceman's Readjustment Act of 1944, offered to pay tuition for college or trade education to ex–World War II servicemen. It also mandated that they receive up to $500 a year for tuition, books, and supplies. Nearly 8 million veterans took advantage of this first G.I. Bill and American higher education expanded rapidly as a result. Veterans also made use of the bill's guaranteed mortgages and low interest rates to buy new homes in the suburbs, inspiring a development boom.

Truman Doctrine (1947) and NATO (1949) The Truman Doctrine initiated U.S. resistance to expansion of the Soviet Union into Western Europe following World War II, and the NATO treaty has provided the framework for European security for half a century. Truman declared to a joint session of Congress, "I believe that it must be the policy of the United States to support free people who are resisting attempted subjugation by armed minorities or by outside pressures."

Federal Highway Act (1956) President Dwight D. Eisenhower was right when he said, "More than any single action by the government since the end of the war, this one would change the face of America." The most expensive public-works project in U.S. history, the highway act built the 41,000 mile nationwide interstate highway system.

Civil Rights Act of 1964 Only Congress could end racial segregation in privately owned businesses and facilities. It did so by an overwhelming vote of both houses in the Civil Rights Act of 1964. Injustices endure, but the end of segregated restaurants, theaters, and drinking fountains provided new opportunities for African Americans and helped change white attitudes. In addition, Title VII of the act prohibits gender discrimination and serves as the legal bulwark for the women's rights.

Voting Rights Act of 1965 President Lyndon B. Johnson signed this act in the same room in the Capitol where Abraham Lincoln had penned the Emancipation Proclamation. This legislation guaranteed all Americans the most fundamental of all rights—the right to vote. Between the 1964 and 1968 presidential elections, black voter registration increased 50 percent across the nation, even in the reluctant southern states, giving African Americans newfound political clout.

Medicare and Medicaid (1965) Congress amended the Social Security Act of 1935 to provide for national health insurance for the aged (Medicare) and for the poor (Medicaid). In 2003 (28 years later) Congress added prescription drug coverage to Medicare.

Bargaining can assume different forms. Explicit trade-offs such as "If you vote for my bill, I'll vote for yours" are the simplest form of bargaining, but implicit understandings may be more common. Members may help other members in anticipation of receiving reciprocal help at some future unspecified time. Moreover, representatives who refuse to cooperate on a regular basis may find little support for their own bills. Mutual "back scratching" allows members to develop a reservoir of IOUs for the future. Building credit is good business for most members, one can never tell when one will need help in the future.

Bargaining requires a certain kind of integrity. Members of Congress must stick to their agreements. They must not consistently ask too high a price for their cooperation. They must recognize and return favors. They must not renege on promises. They must be trustworthy.

Conference-committee bargaining is essential if legislation acceptable to both houses is to be written. Indeed, it is expected that conferees from each house will bargain and compromise their differences. "Every House-Senate conference is expected to proceed via the methods of 'give and take,' 'trading back and forth,' 'pulling and hauling,' 'horse-trading and compromise,' 'splitting the difference,' etc."[43]

Reciprocity The norm of *reciprocity*—favors rendered should be repaid in kind— supports the bargaining process. Reciprocity may mean simply supporting a bill that is important to a colleague. But it may also extend to committees and subcommittees. In order to minimize intercommittee disputes over legislation, jurisdiction, or appropriations, "committees negotiate treaties of reciprocity ranging from 'I will stay out of your specialty if you will stay out of mine,' to 'I'll support your bill if you will support mine.' "[44]

The norm of reciprocity facilitates compromise and agreement and getting the work of Congress accomplished. Members who were willing to accept "half a loaf" traditionally accomplished more than those who insisted on a "whole loaf." But the norm of reciprocity may have weakened in recent years.

Logrolling Perhaps the most celebrated and reviled form of reciprocity, **logrolling** is mutual agreement to support projects that primarily benefit individual members of Congress and their constituencies. Logrolling is closely associated with pork-barrel legislation. Yet it can occur in virtually any kind of legislation. Even interest-group lobbyists may logroll with each other, promising to support each other's legislative agendas.

Leader-Follower Relations Because leaders have few means of disciplining members, they must rely heavily on their bargaining skills to solicit cooperation and get the work of Congress accomplished. Party leaders can appeal to members' concerns for their party image among the voters. Individual majority members want to keep their party in the majority—if for no other reason than to retain their committee and subcommittee chairs. Individual minority members would like their party to win control of their house in order to assume the power and privileges of committee and subcommittee chairs. Party leaders must appeal to more than partisanship to win cooperation, however.

To secure cooperation, leaders can grant—or withhold—some tangible benefits. A member of the House needs the Speaker's support to get recognition, to have a bill called up, to get a bill scheduled, to see to it that a bill gets assigned to a preferred committee, to get a good committee assignment, and to help a bill get out of the Rules Committee, for example.

logrolling Bargaining for agreement among legislators to support each other's favorite bills, especially projects that primarily benefit individual members and their constituents.

Bill Frist, M.D., Leading the Senate

At Senator Strom Thurmond's 100th birthday party, then Republican Majority Leader Trent Lott noted that the aged Thurmond had been the segregationist "Dixiecrat" candidate for president in 1948 and that Lott's state of Mississippi had voted for him. Then Lott went on: "If the rest of the country had followed our lead, we wouldn't have had all these problems over the years." This off-the-cuff remark was immediately denounced as racist and a political fire storm swept Washington. Lott apologized, but it was too late. President Bush declared, "Recent comments by Senator Lott do not reflect the spirit of our country." Lott was forced to resign as Majority Leader of the Senate.

Bill Frist, a highly respected heart surgeon first elected to the Senate in 1994, was viewed by his Republican colleagues as the remedy for the party's embarrassment. Born and raised in Nashville, Frist graduated from Princeton and went on to Harvard Medical School. (His father was the founder of the hospital chain, H.C.A.) Later at Vanderbilt University Medical Center, Frist performed over 150 heart and lung transplants and wrote more than a hundred medical research articles and several books.

Frist was a big winner in his first try at politics—defeating the three-term incumbent Tennessee Senator Jim Sasser. Frist spent nearly $10 million of his own money on his campaign. Upon arriving in Washington, he quickly won the respect of his Republican colleagues for his expertise on health-care issues. And he proved to be immensely popular with Tennessee voters, winning reelection in 2000 with 66 percent of the vote, the largest margin of victory in a statewide election in Tennessee history.

In December, 2002, Senate Republicans turned to Frist to provide respectability to the Majority Leader post. (Frist had served fewer years in the Senate than any Majority Leader in history.) Frist influenced his friend, President George Bush, to initiate a heavily-funded worldwide effort to fight AIDS. And Frist won a difficult fight to add a prescription drug benefit to Medicare, an issue that had plagued the Congress for years. Assuming that Frist continues to be popular and successful in his job, he is likely to emerge as a presidential candidate in 2008.

Party leaders may also seek to gain support from their followers by doing favors that ease their lives in Washington, advance their legislative careers, and help them with their reelection. Favors from party leaders oblige members to respond to leaders' requests at a later time. Members themselves like to build up a reservoir of good feeling and friendship with the leadership, knowing that eventually they will need some favors from the leadership (see *People in Politics:* Bill Frist, M.D., Leading the Senate).

Gridlock Congress is often criticized for legislative **gridlock**—the failure to enact laws, including appropriations acts, that are widely perceived to have merit. Indeed, much of the popular frustration with Congress relates to gridlock arising from policy and budgetary stalemates. Research has suggested that the following factors contribute to congressional gridlock:[45]

- Divided party control of the presidency and Congress

- Divided party control of the House and Senate

- Greater ideological polarization (liberal versus conservative) of the parties

- In the Senate, the willingness of members to filibuster against a bill, requiring 60 votes to overcome the opposition

In contrast, the factors that appear to lessen gridlock and encourage significant legislative accomplishment include:

gridlock The failure to enact laws that are widely perceived to have merit because of partisan or ideological bickering.

- Unified party control of the presidency, House, and Senate

- Larger numbers of moderates among Democrats and Republicans in Congress (as opposed to larger numbers of strong liberals and strong conservatives)

- Overwhelming public support for new legislation

Note that the constitutional structure of American government—separation of powers and checks and balances, as well as bicameralism—plays a major role in gridlock, as does the American two-party system. Overcoming gridlock requires a willingness of members of both parties in both houses of Congress, as well as the White House, to bargain and compromise over legislation. And it requires strong public opinion in support of congressional action.

Congressional Ethics

Although critics might consider the phrase *congressional ethics* to be an oxymoron, the moral climate of Congress today is probably better than in earlier eras of American history. Nevertheless, Congress as an institution has suffered from well-publicized scandals that continue to prompt calls for reform.

Ethics Rules Congress has an interest in maintaining the integrity of the institution itself and the trust of the people. Thus Congress has established its own rules of ethics. These rules include the following:

- *Financial disclosure:* All members must file personal financial statements each year.

- *Honoraria:* Members cannot accept fees for speeches or personal appearances.

- *Campaign funds:* Surplus campaign funds cannot be put to personal use. (A loophole allowed members elected before 1980 to keep such funds if they left office before January 1, 1993. A record number of House members resigned in 1992; many of them kept substantial amounts of campaign money.)

- *Gifts:* Members may not accept gifts worth more than $200 for representatives and $300 for senators (with annual increases in these amounts for inflation).

- *Free travel:* Members may not accept free travel from private corporations or individuals for more than four days of domestic travel and seven days of international travel per year. (Taxpayer-paid "junkets" to investigate problems at home or abroad or attend international meetings are not prohibited.)

- *Lobbying:* Former members may not lobby Congress for at least one year after retirement.

But these limited rules have not gone very far in restoring popular trust in Congress.

Gray Areas: Services and Contributions Congress members are expected to perform services for their political contributors. However, a direct *quid pro quo*—receiving a financial contribution specifically for the performance of official duty—is illegal. Few Congress members would be so foolish as to openly state a price to a potential contributor for a specific service, and most contributors know not to state a dollar amount that would be forthcoming if the member performed a particular service for them. But what if the contribution and the service occur close together? A Senate Ethics Committee once found that a close relationship between a service and a contribution to be an "impermissible pattern of conduct [that] violated established norms of behavior in the Senate . . . [and] was improper and repugnant."[46] But the Ethics Committee offered little in the way of a future guidance in handling services for campaign contributors.

Expulsion The Constitution gives Congress the power to discipline its own members. "Each House may . . . punish its Members for disorderly Behaviour, and, with the Concurrence of two thirds, expel a Member." But the Constitution fails to define *disorderly behavior*.

It seems reasonable to believe that criminal conduct falls within the constitutional definition of disorderly behavior. Bribery is a criminal act: it is illegal to solicit or receive anything of value in return for the performance of a government duty. During its notorious Abscam investigation in 1980, the Federal Bureau of Investigation set up a sting operation in which agents posing as wealthy Arabs offered bribe money to members of Congress while secretly videotaping the transactions. Six representatives and one senator were convicted. But criminal conviction does not automatically result in expulsion from Congress. In the Abscam case, only one defendant, Representative Michael Ozzie Myers (D-Pa.), was expelled, becoming the first member to be expelled since the Civil War. (Two other House members and the senator resigned rather than face expulsion, and the other three representatives were defeated for reelection. Perhaps the most interesting result of the Abscam investigation: only one member of Congress approached by the FBI, Democratic Senator Larry Presler of South Dakota, turned down the bribe.) The powerful chair of the House Ways and Means Committee, Democrat Dan Rostenkowski (Ill.), was indicted by a federal grand jury in 1994 for misuse of congressional office funds; he refused to resign from Congress, but his Chicago constituents voted him out of office. Democratic Representative Mel Reynolds (Ill.) resigned in 1995, following his criminal conviction on charges of sexual misconduct. (A special election to fill his vacated seat was won by Jesse Jackson, Jr., son of the popular preacher, commentator, and former Democratic presidential contender.) Republican Senator Robert Packwood (Oreg.) resigned in 1995 in order to avoid official expulsion following a Senate Ethics Committee report charging him with numerous counts of sexual harassment of female staff.

Censure A lesser punishment in the Congress than expulsion is official **censure**. Censured members are obliged to "stand in the well" and listen to the charges read against them. It is supposed to be a humiliating experience and fatal to one's political career. In 1983 two members of Congress were censured for sexual misconduct with teenage congressional pages. Both were obliged to "stand in the well." In 2002 New Jersey Democratic Senator Robert Torricelli was "severely admonished" by the Senate Ethics Committee for "at least the appearance of impropriety" for improperly accepting gifts and campaign contributions. Torricelli abruptly dropped out of his reelection race.

Lesser forms of censure included a public reprimand or admonition by the Ethics Committee expressing disapproval of the Congress member's behavior. And the Ethics Committee may also order a member to repay funds improperly received.

censure Public reprimand for wrongdoing, given to a member standing in the chamber before Congress.

■ The Constitution places all of the delegated powers of the national government in the Congress. The Founders expected Congress to be the principal institution for resolving national conflicts, balancing interests, and deciding who gets what. Today, Congress is a central battleground in the struggle over national policy. Congress generally does not initiate but responds to policy initiatives and budget requests originating from the president, the bureaucracy, and interest groups. Over time, the president and the executive branch, together with the Supreme Court and federal judiciary, have come to dominate national policy making.

■ The Congress represents local and state interests in policy making. The Senate's constituencies are the 50 states, and the House's constituencies are 435 separate districts. Both houses of Congress, but especially the House of Representatives, wield power in domestic and foreign affairs primarily through the "power of the purse."

■ Congressional powers include oversight and investigation. These powers are exercised primarily through committees. Although Congress claims these powers are a necessary part of lawmaking, their real purpose is usually to influence agency decision making, to build political support for increases or decreases in agency funding, to lay the political foundation for new programs and policies, and to capture media attention and enhance the power of members of Congress.

■ Congress is gradually becoming more "representative" of the general population in terms of race and gender. Redistricting, under federal court interpretations of the Voting Rights Act, has increased African American and Hispanic representation in Congress. And women have significantly increased their presence in Congress in recent years. Nevertheless, women and minorities do not occupy seats in Congress proportional to their share of the general population.

■ Members of Congress are independent political entrepreneurs. They initiate their own candidacies, raise their own campaign funds, and get themselves elected with very little help from their party. Members of Congress are largely career politicians who skillfully use the advantages of incumbency to stay in office. Incumbents outspend challengers by large margins. Interest-group political action committees and individual contributors strongly favor incumbents. Congressional elections are seldom focused on great national issues but rather on local issues and personalities and the ability of candidates to "bring home the bacon" from Washington and serve their constituents.

■ Congress as an institution is not very popular with the American people. Scandals, pay raises, perks, and privileges reported in the media have hurt the image of the institution. Nevertheless, individual members of Congress remain popular with their districts' voters.

■ Members of Congress spend as much time on "home-style" activities—promoting their images back home and attending to constituents' problems—as they do legislating. Casework wins votes one at a time, gradually accumulating political support back home, and members often support each other's "pork-barrel" projects.

■ Despite the independence of members, the Democratic and Republican party structures in the House and Senate remain the principal bases for organizing Congress. Party leaders in the House and Senate generally control the flow of business in each house, assigning bills to committees, scheduling or delaying votes, and appointing members to committees. But leaders must bargain for votes; they have few formal disciplinary powers. They cannot deny renomination to recalcitrant members.

■ The real legislative work of Congress is done in committees. Standing committees screen and draft legislation; with rare exceptions, bills do not reach the floor without approval by a majority of a standing committee. The committee and subcommittee system decentralizes power in Congress. The system satisfies the desires of members to gain power, prestige, and electoral advantage, but it weakens responsible government in the Congress as a whole. All congressional committees are chaired by members of the majority party. Seniority is still the major determinant of power in Congress.

■ In order to become law, a bill must win committee approval and withstand debate in both houses of Congress. The rules attached to a bill's passage in the House can significantly help or hurt its chances. Bills passed with differences in the two houses must be reworked in a conference committee composed of members of both houses and then passed in identical form in both.

■ In deciding how to vote on legislation, Congress members are influenced by party loyalty, presidential support or opposition, constituency concerns, interest-group pressures, and their own personal values and ideology. Party majorities oppose each other on roughly half of all roll-call votes in Congress. Presidents receive the greatest support in Congress from members of their own party.

■ The customs and norms of Congress help reduce interpersonal conflict, facilitate bargaining and compromise, and make life more pleasant on Capitol Hill. They include the recognition of special competencies of members, a willingness to bargain and compromise, mutual "back scratching" and logrolling, reciprocity, and deference toward the leadership. But traditional customs and norms have weakened over time as more members have pursued independent political agendas. And partisanship and incivility in Congress have risen in recent years.

■ Congress establishes its own rules of ethics. The Constitution empowers each house to expel its own members for "disorderly conduct" by a two-thirds vote, but expulsion has seldom occurred. Some members have resigned to avoid expulsion; others have been officially censured yet remained in Congress.

KEY TERMS

SUGGESTED READINGS

Bond, Jon R., and Richard Fleisher, eds. *Polarized Politics: Congress and the President in a Partisan Era.* Washington, D.C.: CQ Press, 2000. Essay on the rise of partisanship in Washington and its effect on congressional-presidential relations.

Congressional Quarterly. *How Congress Works.* 3rd ed. Washington, D.C.: CQ Press, 1998. A description and explanation of the rules and procedures that govern the House and the Senate.

Davidson, Robert H., and Walter J. Oleszek. *Congress and Its Members.* 9th ed. Washington, D.C.: CQ Press, 2004. Authoritative text on Congress covering the recruitment of members, elections, House styles and Hill styles, leadership, decision making, and relations with interest groups, presidency, and courts. Emphasizes tension between lawmaking responsibilities and desire to be reelected.

Fenno, Richard F. *Home Style.* Boston: Little, Brown, 1978. The classic description of how attention to constituency by members of Congress enhances their reelection prospects. Home-style activities, including casework, pork barreling, travel and appearances back home, newsletters, and surveys, are described in detail.

Herrnson, Paul S. *Playing Hardball: Campaigning for the U.S. Congress.* Upper Saddle River, N.J.: Prentice Hall, 2001. Congressional candidates' strategies, targeting, fund raising, and getting out the vote.

Herrson, Paul S. *Congressional Elections: Campaigning at Home and in Washington.* 4th ed. Washington, D.C.: CQ Press. Interviews with candidates, campaign aides, and political consultants to paint a comprehensive portrait of congressional campaigns.

Jones, Charles O. *Separate but Equal Branches: Congress and the Presidency.* 2nd ed. Washington, D.C.: CQ Press, 1999.

Presidential–congressional relations under Johnson, Nixon, Ford, Carter, Reagan, Bush, and Clinton.

Kaptur, Marcy. *Women of Congress.* Washington, D.C.: CQ Press, 1996. An account of the progress of women toward longer tenure, greater seniority, and more influential committee appointments and how women in Congress still differ from men on these factors.

Oleszek, Walter J. *Congressional Procedures and Policy Processes.* 6th ed. Washington, D.C.: CQ Press, 2003. The definitive work on congressional rules, procedures and traditions and their effect on the course and content of legislation.

Ornstein, Norman J., Thomas E. Mann, and Michael J. Malbin. *Vital Statistics on Congress.* Washington, D.C.: CQ Press, 2004. Published biennially. Excellent source of data on members of Congress, congressional elections, campaign finance, committees and staff, workload, and voting alignments.

Sinclair, Barbara. *Unorthodox Lawmaking.* 2nd ed. Washington, D.C.: CQ Press, 2000. A description of the various detours and shortcuts a major bill is likely to take in Congress, including five case studies.

Stathis, Stephen W. *Landmark Legislation 1774–2002.* Washington, D.C.: CQ Press, 2003. A summary of major congressional legislation over 225 years, in a single volume.

MAKE IT REAL

RUNNING FOR CONGRESS

You are a Republican or Democratic Party leader and the hottest campaign manager in American politics. You can have your pick of candidates you will work for in the upcoming congressional elections, but your help is most needed in Missouri. You will have to guide your candidate through the general election. You research the district and help your candidate raise money and create a strong media-based campaign. Good luck!

THE PRESIDENT:
WHITE HOUSE POLITICS

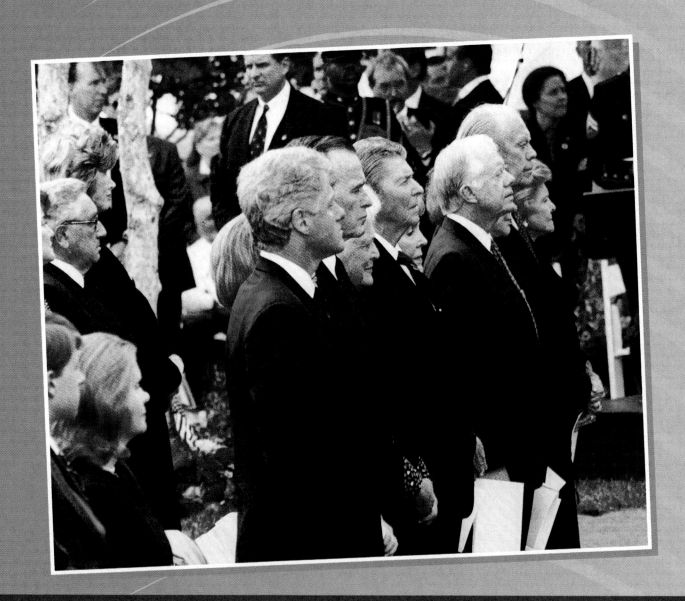

Presidential Power

Americans look to their president for "Greatness." The presidency embodies the popular "great man" view of history and public affairs—attributing progress in the world to the actions of particular individuals. Great presidents are those associated with great events: George Washington with the founding of the nation, Abraham Lincoln with the preservation of the Union, Franklin D. Roosevelt with the nation's emergence from economic depression and victory in World War II (see *What Do You Think?* "How Would You Rate the Presidents?"). People tend to believe that the president is responsible for "peace and prosperity" as well as for "change." They expect their president to present a "vision" of America's future and to symbolize the nation.

The Symbolic President The president personifies American government for most people. People expect the president to act decisively and effectively to deal with national problems. They expect the president to be "compassionate"—to show concern for problems confronting individual citizens.[1] The president, while playing these roles, is the focus of public attention and the nation's leading celebrity. Presidents receive more media coverage than any other person in the nation, for everything from their policy statements to their favorite foods to their dogs and cats.

Managing Crises In times of crisis, the American people look to their president to take action, to provide reassurance, and to protect the nation and its people. It is the president, not the Congress or the courts, who is expected to speak on behalf of the American people in times of national triumph and tragedy.[2] The president gives expression to the nation's pride in victory. The nation's heroes are welcomed and its championship sports teams are feted in the White House Rose Garden.

The president also gives expression to the nation's sadness in tragedy and strives to help the nation go forward. How presidents respond to crises often defines their place in history. Franklin D. Roosevelt raised public morale during the Great Depression of the 1930s by reassuring Americans that "the only thing we have to fear is fear itself." Later he led the nation into war following the Japanese attack on Pearl Harbor, December 7, 1941, "a day which will live in infamy." When the *Challenger* spaceship disintegrated before the eyes of millions of television viewers in 1986, Ronald Reagan gave voice to the nation's feelings about the disaster: "I want to say something to the school children of America who were watching the live

How Would You Rate the Presidents?

From time to time, historians have been polled to rate U.S. presidents (see table). The survey ratings given the presidents have been remarkably consistent. Abraham Lincoln, George Washington, and Franklin Roosevelt are universally recognized as the greatest American presidents. It is more difficult for historians to rate recent presidents; the views of historians are influenced by their own (generally liberal and reformist) political views. Richard Nixon once commented, "History will treat me fairly. Historians probably won't."

Historians may tend to rank activist presidents who led the nation through war or economic crisis higher than passive presidents who guided the nation in peace and prosperity. Initially Dwight Eisenhower, who presided in the relatively calm 1950s, was ranked low by historians. But later, after comparing his performance with those who came after him, his steadiness and avoidance of war raised his ranking dramatically.

Arthur M. Schlesinger (1948)	Arthur M. Schlesinger, Jr. (1962)	Robert Murray (1982)	Arthur M. Schlesinger, Jr. (1996)	W. J. Ridings, S. B. McIver (1997)
Great	**Great**	**Presidential Rank**	**Great**	**Overall Ranking**
1. Lincoln	1. Lincoln	1. Lincoln	1. Lincoln	1. Lincoln
2. Washington	2. Washington	2. F. Roosevelt	2. Washington	2. F. Roosevelt
3. F. Roosevelt	3. F. Roosevelt	3. Washington	3. F. Roosevelt	3. Washington
4. Wilson	4. Wilson	4. Jefferson		4. Jefferson
5. Jefferson	5. Jefferson	5. T. Roosevelt	**Near Great**	5. T. Roosevelt
6. Jackson		6. Wilson	4. Jefferson	6. Wilson
	Near Great	7. Jackson	5. Jackson	7. Truman
Near Great	6. Jackson	8. Truman	6. T. Roosevelt	8. Jackson
7. T. Roosevelt	7. T. Roosevelt	9. J. Adams	7. Wilson	9. Eisenhower
8. Cleveland	8. Polk	10. L. Johnson	8. Truman	10. Madison
9. J. Adams	Truman (tie)	11. Eisenhower	9. Polk	11. Polk
10. Polk	10. J. Adams	12. Polk		12. L. Johnson
	11. Cleveland	13. Kennedy	**High Average**	13. Monroe
Average		14. Madison	10. Eisenhower	14. J. Adams
11. J. Q. Adams	**Average**	15. Monroe	11. J. Adams	15. Kennedy
12. Monroe	12. Madison	16. J. Q. Adams	12. Kennedy	16. Cleveland
13. Hayes	13. J. Q. Adams	17. Cleveland	13. Cleveland	17. McKinley
14. Madison	14. Hayes	18. McKinley	14. L. Johnson	18. J. Q. Adams
15. Van Buren	15. McKinley	19. Taft	15. Monroe	19. Carter
16. Taft	16. Taft	20. Van Buren	16. McKinley	20. Taft
17. Arthur	17. Van Buren	21. Hoover		21. Van Buren
18. McKinley	18. Monroe	22. Hayes	**Average**	22. Bush
19. A. Johnson	19. Hoover	23. Arthur	17. Madison	23. Clinton
20. Hoover	20. B. Harrison	24. Ford	18. J. Q. Adams	24. Hoover
21. B. Harrison	21. Arthur	25. Carter	19. B. Harrison	25. Hayes
	Eisenhower (tie)	26. B. Harrison	20. Clinton	26. Reagan
Below Average	23. A. Johnson	27. Taylor	21. Van Buren	27. Ford
22. Tyler		28. Tyler	22. Taft	28. Arthur
23. Coolidge	**Below Average**	29. Fillmore	23. Hayes	29. Taylor
24. Fillmore	24. Taylor	30. Coolidge	24. Bush	30. Garfield
25. Taylor	25. Tyler	31. Pierce	25. Reagan	31. B. Harrison
26. Buchanan	26. Fillmore	32. A. Johnson	26. Arthur	32. Nixon
27. Pierce	27. Coolidge	33. Buchanan	27. Carter	33. Coolidge
	28. Pierce	34. Nixon	28. Ford	34. Tyler
Failure	29. Buchanan	35. Grant		35. W. Harrison
28. Grant		36. Harding	**Below Average**	36. Fillmore
29. Harding	**Failure**		29. Taylor	37. Pierce
	30. Grant		30. Coolidge	38. Grant
	31. Harding		31. Fillmore	39. A. Johnson
			32. Tyler	40. Buchanan
				41. Harding
			Failure	
			33. Pierce	
			34. Grant	
			35. Hoover	
			36. Nixon	
			37. A. Johnson	
			38. Buchanan	
			39. Harding	

Note: These ratings result from surveys of scholars ranging in number from 55 to 950.

Sources: Arthur Murphy, "Evaluating the Presidents of the United States," *Presidential Studies Quarterly* 14 (1984): 117–26; Arthur M. Schlesinger, Jr., "Rating the Presidents: Washington to Clinton," *Political Science Quarterly* 112 (1997): 179–90; William J. Ridings and Stuart B. McIver, *Rating the Presidents* (Secaucus, N.J.: Citadel Press, 1997).

The president and first lady personify government for many Americans. They become national celebrities and the focus of media attention.

coverage of the shuttle's takeoff. I know it is hard to understand, but sometimes painful things like this happen. The future doesn't belong to the faint-hearted. It belongs to the brave." And the terrorist attack on America, September 11, 2001, transformed President George W. Bush in the eyes of the nation:

> Tonight we are a country awakened to danger and called to defend freedom. Our grief has turned to anger, and anger to resolution. Whether we bring our enemies to justice, or bring justice to our enemies, justice will be done.[3]

Providing Policy Leadership The president is expected to set policy priorities for the nation. Most policy initiatives originate in the White House and various departments and agencies of the executive branch, then are forwarded to Congress with the president's approval. Presidential programs are submitted to Congress in the form of messages, including the president's annual State of the Union Address, and in the Budget of the United States Government, which the president presents each year to Congress.

As a political leader, the president is expected to mobilize political support for policy proposals. It is not enough for the president to send policy proposals to Congress. The president must rally public opinion, lobby members of Congress, and win legislative battles. To avoid being perceived as weak or ineffective, presidents must get as much of their legislative programs through Congress as possible. The president is responsible for "getting things done" in the policy arena.

Managing the Economy The American people hold the president responsible for maintaining a healthy economy. Presidents are blamed for economic downturns, whether or not governmental policies had anything to do with market conditions. The president is expected to "Do Something!" in the face of high unemployment, declining personal income, high mortgage rates, rising inflation, or even a stock market crash. Herbert Hoover in 1932, Gerald Ford in 1976, Jimmy Carter in 1980, and George Bush in 1992—all incumbent presidents defeated for reelection during recessions—learned the hard way that the general public holds the president responsible for hard economic times. Presidents must have an

The White House
This official White House site provides up-to-date information or news about the current president's policies, speeches, appointments, proclamations, and cabinet members.
www.whitehouse.gov

economic "game plan" to stimulate the economy—tax incentives to spur investments, spending proposals to create jobs, plans to lower interest rates (see Chapter 16).

Managing the Government As the chief executive of a mammoth federal bureaucracy with 2.8 million civilian employees, the president is responsible for implementing policy, that is, for achieving policy goals. Policy making does not end when a law is passed. Policy implementation involves issuing orders, creating organizations, recruiting and assigning personnel, disbursing funds, overseeing work, and evaluating results. It is true that the president cannot perform all of these tasks personally. But the ultimate responsibility for implementation—in the words of the Constitution, "to take Care that the Laws be faithfully executed"—rests with the president.

The Global President Nations strive to speak with a single voice in international affairs; for the United States, the global voice is that of the president. As Commander-in-Chief of the armed forces of the United States, the president is a powerful voice in foreign affairs. Efforts by Congress to speak on behalf of the nation in foreign affairs and to limit the war-making power of the president have been generally unsuccessful. It is the president who orders American troops into combat (see *People in Politics:* "George Bush, and the War on Terrorism").

Constitutional Powers of the President

Popular expectations of presidential leadership far exceed the formal constitutional powers granted to the president. Compared with the Congress, the president has only modest constitutional powers (see Table 11.1). Nevertheless, presidents have pointed to a variety of clauses in Article II to support their rights to do everything from doubling the land area of the nation (Thomas Jefferson) to routing out terrorists from Afghanistan and invading Iraq (George W. Bush).

Who May Be President? To become president, the Constitution specifies that a person must be a natural-born citizen at least thirty-five years of age and a resident of the United States for fourteen years.

Initially, the Constitution put no limit on how many terms a president could serve. George Washington set a precedent for a two-term maximum that endured until Franklin Roosevelt's decision to run for a third term in 1940 (and a fourth term in 1944). In reaction to Roosevelt's lengthy tenure, in 1947 Congress proposed the Twenty-second Amendment (ratified in 1951), which officially restricts the president to two terms (or one full term if a vice president must complete more than two years of the previous president's term). (See *Compared to What?* "Mexican President Vicente Fox.")

Presidential Succession Until the adoption of the Twenty-fifth Amendment in 1967, the Constitution had said little about presidential succession, other than designating the vice president as successor to the president "in Case of the Removal, . . . Death, Resignation, or Inability" and giving Congress the power to decide "what Officer shall then act as President" if both the president and vice president are removed. The Constitution was silent on how to cope with serious presidential illnesses. It contained no provision for replacing a vice president. The incapacitation issue was more than theoretical: James A. Garfield lingered months

American Presidents

Biographical facts and key events in the life of all U.S. presidents.
www.americanpresidents.org

TABLE 11.1 The Constitutional Powers of the President

Chief Administrator

Implement policy: "take Care that the Laws be faithfully executed" (Article II, Section 3)
Supervise executive branch of government
Appoint and remove executive officials (Article II, Section 2)
Prepare executive budget for submission to Congress (by law of Congress)

Chief Legislator

Initiate policy: "give to the Congress Information of the State of the Union, and recommend to their Consideration such Measures as he shall judge necessary and expedient" (Article II, Section 3)
Veto legislation passed by Congress, subject to override by a two-thirds vote in both houses
Convene special session of Congress "on extraordinary Occasions" (Article II, Section 3)

Chief Diplomat

Make treaties "with the Advice and Consent of the Senate" (Article II, Section 2)
Exercise the power of diplomatic recognition: "receive Ambassadors" (Article II, Section 3)
Make executive agreements (by custom and international law)

Commander-in-Chief

Command U.S. armed forces: "The president shall be Commander-in-Chief of the Army and Navy" (Article II, Section 2)
Appoint military officers

Chief of State

"The executive Power shall be vested in a President" (Article II, Section 1)
Grant reprieves and pardons (Article II, Section 2)
Represent the nation as chief of state
Appoint federal court and Supreme Court judges (Article II, Section 2)

after being shot in 1881; Woodrow Wilson was an invalid during his last years in office (1919–20); Dwight Eisenhower suffered major heart attacks in office; and Ronald Reagan was in serious condition following an assassination attempt in 1981.

The Twenty-fifth Amendment stipulates that when the vice president and a majority of the cabinet notify the Speaker of the House and the president pro tempore of the Senate in writing that the president "is unable to discharge the powers and duties of his office," then the vice president becomes *acting* president. To resume the powers of office, the president must then notify Congress in writing that "no inability exists." If the vice president and a majority of cabinet officers do not agree that the president is capable of resuming office, then the Congress "shall decide the issue" within twenty-one days. A two-thirds vote of both houses is required to replace the president with the vice president.

The disability provisions of the amendment have never been used, but the succession provisions have been. The Twenty-fifth Amendment provides for the selection of a new vice president by presidential nomination and confirmation by a majority vote of both houses of Congress. When Vice President Spiro Agnew resigned in the face of bribery charges in 1973, President Richard Nixon nominated the Republican leader of the House, Gerald Ford, as vice president; and when Nixon resigned in 1974, Ford assumed the presidency and made Nelson Rockefeller, governor of New York, his vice president. Thus Gerald Ford's two-year tenure in the White House marked the only time in history when the man serving as president had not been elected to either the presidency or the vice presidency. (If the offices of president and vice president are both vacated, then Congress by law has specified the next in line for the presidency as the Speaker

George Bush and the War on Terrorism

In times of crises for the nation, presidents matter. What they say, and what they do, create indelible images that determine how their presidencies are viewed by history. George W. Bush's place in history will likely be measured by his ability to inspire and mobilize the American public for the war on terrorism.

An Unpromising Start

George W. Bush was born into his family's tradition of wealth, privilege, and public service. (Bush's grandfather, investment banker Prescott Bush, was a U.S. senator from Connecticut and chairman of the Yale Corporation, the university's governing board.)

He grew up in Midland, Texas, where his father had established himself in the oil business before going into politics—first as a Houston congressman, then Republican National Chairman, director of the CIA, ambassador to China, and finally vice president and president of the United States. George W. followed in his father's footsteps to Yale University but he was not the scholar-athlete that his father had been. Rather, he was a friendly, likable, heavy-drinking president of his fraternity. Upon graduation in 1968, he joined the Texas Air National Guard, completed flight school, but never faced combat in Vietnam. He earned an MBA degree from the Harvard Business School and returned to Midland to enter the oil business himself. Later in his career he would acknowledge his "youthful indiscretions," including a drunk driving arrest in 1976.

Although his famous name attracted investors in a series of oil companies he managed, virtually all of them lost money. Even a deal with the government of oil-rich Bahrain, negotiated while his father was president, failed to bail out Bush's Harken Energy Company. But Bush was able to sell off his oil interests and reinvest the money in the Texas Rangers baseball team; he eventually sold his interest in the Rangers in a deal that netted him a substantial profit.

Texas Governor

George W. Bush had never held public office before running for governor of Texas in 1994. But he had gained valuable political experience serving as an unofficial adviser to his father during his presidential campaigns. He went up against the sharp-tongued incumbent Democratic Governor Ann Richards, who ridiculed him as the "shrub" (little Bush). Bush heavily outspent Richards and won 54 percent of the vote, to become Texas's second Republican governor in modern times.

George W.'s political style fit comfortably with the Texas "good old boys" in both parties. Although the Texas legislature was controlled by Democrats, Bush won most of his early legislative battles. Bush's style was to meet frequently and privately with his Democratic opponents and to remain on friendly personal terms with them. He easily won reelection as governor in 1998.

Running for President

Bush denies that his father ever tried to influence his decision to run for president, but many of his father's friends and political associates did, believing that only he could reclaim the White House for the GOP. They compared "Dubya" to Ronald Reagan—amiable, charming, and good-humored, even if a little vague on the details of public policy. His mother's 10,000-name Christmas card list of closest family friends helped in building a bankroll of more than $100 million before the campaign even began. And the GOP establishment stuck with him when he was challenged in the early primary elections by maverick Arizona Republican Senator and Vietnam war hero John McCain.

His Father's Friends

While "Dubya's" father remained in the background, the president's White House and cabinet appointments indicated his reliance on experienced people to run the government. People who served in the Reagan and earlier Bush administrations surround George W. Bush. Bush chose Richard Cheney as his vice president, even though Cheney, as a former small state (Wyoming) congressman, brought no significant electoral votes to the ticket. But Cheney had won the confidence of the Bushes as secretary of defense during the Gulf War. Bush also brought the former chairman of the Joint Chiefs of Staff, Colin Powell, into his administration as secretary of state. President Gerald Ford's secretary of defense, Donald Rumsfeld, was reappointed to his old job. National Security Adviser Condoleeza Rice brought a reputation for brilliance and independence to her position. It was clear that "Dubya" was not afraid of being overshadowed by "heavyweights" in his administration.

"9/11"

The terrorist attack on America, September 11, 2001, dramatically changed the political landscape in Washington and the nation. The attack became the defining moment in the presidency of George W. Bush. He grew in presidential stature, respect, and decisiveness. His public appearances and statements reassured the American people. He promptly declared a "War on Terrorism" against both the terrorist organizations themselves and in the nations that harbor and support them.

Military action in Afghanistan followed quickly. Bush showed no hesitation, no indecision, no willingness to negotiate with terrorists. His public approval ratings skyrocketed: 90 percent of Americans approved of the way he was handling his job, a figure that even exceeded his father's approval ratings during the Gulf War. The rapid collapse of the hated Taliban government in Afghanistan seems to confirm the wisdom of Bush's actions.

Good Versus Evil

George Bush convinced the American people that the war on terrorism is "a monumental struggle of good versus evil." In his 2002 State of the Union message he specifically identified an "axis of evil"— Iraq, Iran, and North Korea. While many in the media scoffed at Bush's portrayal of the war on terrorism as a struggle between good and evil, most Americans heralded what they saw as Bush's "moral clarity" and the firmness of his convictions. He tried to define the enemy as the terrorists and not Islam itself.

"The face of terror is not the true faith of Islam." Bush failed to win the support of the United Nations to oust Saddam Hussein from power in Iraq, but he succeeded in getting Congress to pass the joint resolution granting him authority to launch a preemptive military strike against Iraq. The early military phase of the war in Iraq went well; U.S. forces captured Baghdad in a mere 21 days, with precious few casualties. But remnants of Saddam's forces together with terrorists and other hard-line organizations began a guerrilla war against American and other coalition forces. Confronted with a prolonged struggle, costly lives and money, critics at home and abroad questioned American purposes in Iraq. Bush's high approval ratings began a slow decline. Throughout most of 2004, polls showed Bush running neck and neck with John Kerry in the presidential race. Kerry won the debates, but Bush remained "better at handling the war on terrorism." Election day brought the highest turnout in almost thirty years, and exit polls reported that "moral values" were the single most important concern of voters. These voters seemed to appreciate Bush's commitment to faith and family. He won a comfortable 51 percent of the popular vote.

After the September 11 terrorist attacks, U.S. troops moved quickly into Afghanistan to eliminate the Taliban.

Mexican President Vicente Fox

For the first time in nearly a century, Mexico's long-dominant PRI party (Partido Revolucionario institucional) lost a presidential election in 2000. The winner was a tall, charismatic, business-politician, Vicente Fox, leader of the PAN party (Partido Acción Nacional).

Mexico's president is elected by nationwide popular vote for a six-year term. The president cannot succeed himself. He must deal with a bicameral National Congress composed of a Senate (Cámera de Senatores) and a Chamber of Deputies (Cámera de Diputados). Mexico has a tradition of a strong presidency. The Mexican Revolution of 1911, ending the dictatorship of Porfirio Díaz, was followed for several years by fighting among contending forces, including those of Emiliano Zapata and Pancho Villa. (U.S. Army forces pursued Villa throughout northern Mexico for many months.) A new Mexican Constitution of 1917 established the current structure of government. The PRI laid claim to the popular revolutionary tradition, and Mexico was essentially a one-party system until the 1980s. But splits occurred within the PRI, and gradually a new party, the PAN, began to win local and state elections. The PAN promoted free enterprise and economic development and attacked the alleged corruption in the PRI. In 1997, for the first time the PRI lost its majority in the Chamber of Deputies.

In the July 2000 presidential elections three viable candidates competed for the job: Francisco Labastida of the PRI, Cuauhtemoc Cárdenas (who had earlier split with the PRI), and Vicente Fox of the PAN. The results: Fox—43 percent, Labastida—37 percent, Cárdenas—17 percent.

Fox studied business administration at the Ibero-American University (in Mexico City) and management at the Harvard University Business School. He worked his way up through the ranks of Coca-Cola de México to the position of president for Latin America. He was elected to the Chamber of Deputies in 1988, failed in his first run for governor of the state of Guanajuato in 1991, but then won that governorship overwhelmingly in 1995. He developed a friendship with a fellow governor across the border, George W. Bush.

Fox and Bush agree that the solution to many of Mexico's problems is economic development. Both are strong supporters of the North American Free Trade Agreement (NAFTA) and both have sought to normalize immigration and border problems along the 2,000-mile Mexican-American frontier. The terrorist "9/11" attack on America set back progress on immigration reform, and recession in the United States did little to help Mexico's economy. Fox's popularity in Mexico has slipped somewhat, but he has until 2006 to restore confidence in his policies and his party.

---

of the House of Representatives, followed by the president pro tempore of the Senate, then the cabinet officers, beginning with the secretary of state.)

Impeachment The Constitution grants Congress the power of **impeachment** over the president, vice president, and "all civil Officers of the United States" (Article II, Section 4). Technically, impeachment is a charge similar to a criminal indictment brought against an official. The power to bring charges of impeachment is given to the House of Representatives. The power to try all impeachments is given to the Senate, and "no Person shall be convicted without the Concurrence of two thirds of the Members present" (Article I, Section 3). Impeachment by the House and conviction by the Senate only remove an official from office; a subsequent criminal trial is required to inflict any other punishment.

The Constitution specifies that impeachment and conviction can only be for "Treason, Bribery, or other High Crimes and Misdemeanors." These words indicate that Congress is not to impeach presidents, federal judges, or any other officials simply because Congress disagrees with their decisions or policies. Indeed, the phrase implies that only serious criminal offenses, not political conflicts, can result in im-

impeachment Equivalent of a criminal charge against an elected official; removal of the impeached official from office depends on the outcome of a trial.

peachment. Nevertheless, politics was at the root of the impeachment of President Andrew Johnson in 1867. Johnson was a southern Democrat who had remained loyal to the Union. Lincoln had chosen him as vice president in 1864 as a gesture of national unity. A Republican House impeached him on a party-line vote, but after a month-long trial in the Senate, the "guilty" vote fell one short of the two-thirds needed for removal.[4] And partisan politics in the House impeachment and later Senate trial of Bill Clinton (see *Up Close:* "Sex, Lies, and Impeachment").

Presidential Pardons The Constitution grants the president the power to "grant Reprieves and Pardons." This power derives from the ancient right to appeal to the king to reverse errors of law or justice committed by the court system. It is absolute: the president may grant pardons to anyone for any reason. The most celebrated use of the presidential pardon was President Ford's blanket pardon of former President Nixon "for all offenses against the United States which he, Richard Nixon, has committed or may have committed or taken part in." Ford defended the pardon as necessary to end "the bitter controversy and divisive national debate," but his actions may have helped cause his defeat in the 1976 election.

Executive Power The Constitution declares that the "executive Power" shall be vested in the president, but it is unclear whether this statement grants the president any powers that are not specified later in the Constitution or given to the president by acts of Congress. In other words, does the grant of "executive Power" give presidents constitutional authority to act as they deem necessary *beyond* the actions specified elsewhere in the Constitution or specified in laws passed by Congress?

Contrasting views on this question have been offered over two centuries. President William Howard Taft provided the classic narrow interpretation of executive power:

> The true view of the executive function is, as I conceive it, that the president can exercise no power which cannot be fairly and reasonably traced to some specific grant of power or justly implied and included within such express grant as proper and necessary to its exercise. Such specific grants must be either in the federal constitution or in the pursuance thereof. There is no undefined residuum of power which can be exercised which seems to him to be in the public interest.[5]

Theodore Roosevelt, Taft's bitter opponent in a three-way race for the presidency in 1912, expressed the opposite view:

> I decline to adopt the view that what was imperatively necessary for the nation could not be done by the president unless he could find some specific authorization to do it. My belief was that it was not only his right but his duty to do anything that the needs of the nation demanded, unless such action was forbidden by the Constitution or by the laws.[6]

Although the constitutional question has never been fully resolved, history has generally sided with those presidents who have taken an expansive view of their powers. John F. Kennedy expressed the modern view of the constitutional presidency:

> The Constitution is a very wise document. It permits the president to assume just about as much power as he is capable of handling. . . . I believe that the president should use whatever power is necessary to do the job unless it is expressly forbidden by the Constitution.[7]

THINK AGAIN

Should presidents have the power to take actions not specifically authorized by law or the Constitution that they believe necessary for the nation's well-being?

Center for the Study of the Presidency

Studies of the presidency and publication of the scholarly journal *Presidential Studies Quarterly.*
www.thepresidency.org

Sex, Lies, and Impeachment

Bill Clinton is the second president in the nation's history (following Andrew Johnson in 1867) to be impeached by the U.S. House of Representatives. (President Richard Nixon resigned just prior to an impeachment vote in 1974.)

Clinton's impeachment followed a report to the House by Independent Counsel Kenneth Starr in 1998 that accused the president of perjury, obstruction of justice, witness tampering, and "abuse of power." The Starr Report describes in graphic and lurid detail Clinton's sexual relationship with young White House intern Monica Lewinsky.

Does engaging in extramartial sex and lying about it meet the Constitution's standard for impeachment? "Treason, Bribery, or other High Crimes and Misdemeanors"? Perjury—knowingly giving false testimony in a sworn legal proceeding—is a criminal offense. But does the Constitution envision more serious misconduct? According to Alexander Hamilton in the Federalist, No. 65, impeachment should deal with "the abuse or violation of some public trust." Is Clinton's acknowledged "inappropriate behavior" a private affair or a violation of the public trust?

How are such questions decided? Despite pious rhetoric in Congress about the "search for truth," "impartial investigation," and "unbiased constitutional judgment," the impeachment process, whatever the merits of the charges against a president, is *political,* not judicial.

The House vote to impeach Clinton on December 19, 1998 (228 to 205) was largely along partisan lines, with all but five Republicans voting "yes" and all but five Democrats voting "no." And the vote in Clinton's Senate "trial" on February 12, 1999, was equally partisan. Even on the strongest charge—that Clinton had tried to obstruct justice—the Senate failed to find the president guilty. Removing Clinton failed to win even a majority of Senate votes, far less than the required two-thirds. All forty-five Democrats were joined by five Republicans to create a 50–50 tie vote that left Clinton tarnished but still in office.

Most Americans believed the president had a sexual affair in the White House and subsequently lied about it, however, they also *approved* of the way Clinton was performing his job as president. Indeed, the public appeared to rally around the president following the allegations of sexual misconduct.

Various explanations have been offered for this apparent paradox—a public that believed the president had an affair in the White House and lied about it, yet gave the president the highest approval rat-

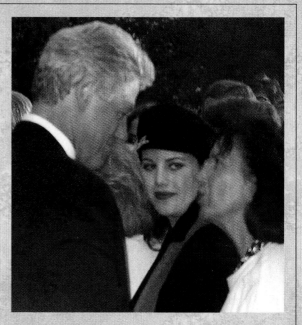

President Clinton greets well-wishers, including Monica Lewinsky, at a Democratic Party event in January 1996. Clinton's acknowledged "inappropriate behavior" and his efforts to conceal his relationship with Lewinsky were the subjects of the impeachment investigation opened against him by the House in 1998.

ings of his career. Many Americans believe that private sexual conduct is irrelevant to the performance of public duties. Private morality is viewed as a personal affair about which Americans should be nonjudgmental. Some people said, "If it's okay with Hillary, why should we worry?" Haven't we had adulterous presidents before, from Thomas Jefferson to John F. Kennedy, presidents who were ranked high in history? And many Americans believe that "they all do it."

Others argue, nonetheless, that private character counts in presidential performance, indeed, that it is a prerequisite for public trust. The president, in this view, performs a symbolic role that requires dignity, honesty, and respect. A president publicly embarrassed by sexual scandal, diminished by jokes, and laughed at by late-night television audiences cannot perform this role. The acceptance of a president's adulterous behavior, according to one commentator, lowers society's standards of behavior. "The president's legacy . . . will be a further vulgarization and demoralization of society."[*]

---

[*] Gertrude Himmelfarb, "Private Lives, Public Morality," *New York Times,* February 9, 1998.

Some Historical Examples U.S. history is filled with examples of presidents acting independently, beyond specific constitutional powers or laws of Congress. Among the most notable:

- George Washington issued a Proclamation of Neutrality during the war between France and Britain following the French Revolution, thereby establishing the president's power to make foreign policy.

- Thomas Jefferson, who prior to becoming president argued for a narrow interpretation of presidential powers, purchased the Louisiana Territory despite the fact that the Constitution contains no provision for the acquisition of territory, let alone authorizing presidential action to do so.

- Andrew Jackson ordered the removal of federal funds from the national bank and removed his secretary of the treasury from office, establishing the president's power to *remove* executive officials, a power not specifically mentioned in the Constitution.

- Abraham Lincoln, asking, "Was it possible to lose the nation yet preserve the Constitution?" established the precedent of vigorous presidential action in national emergencies: He blockaded southern ports, declared martial law in parts of the country, and issued the Emancipation Proclamation—all without constitutional or congressional authority.

- Franklin D. Roosevelt, battling the Great Depression during the 1930s, ordered the nation's banks to close temporarily. Following the Japanese attack on Pearl Harbor in 1941, he ordered the incarceration without trial of many thousands of Americans of Japanese ancestry living on the West Coast.

Checking Presidential Power President Harry Truman believed that "the president has the right to keep the country from going to hell," and he was willing to use means beyond those specified in the Constitution or authorized by Congress. In 1952, while U.S. troops were fighting in Korea, steelworkers at home were threatening to strike. Rather than cross organized labor by forbidding the strike under the terms of the Taft-Hartley Act of 1947 (which he had opposed), Truman chose to seize the steel mills by executive order and continue their operations under U.S. government control. The U.S. Supreme Court ordered the steel mills returned to their owners, however, acknowledging that the president may have inherent powers to act in a national emergency but arguing that Congress had provided a legal remedy, however distasteful to the president. Thus the president can indeed act to keep the country from "going to hell" but if Congress has already acted to do so, the president must abide by the law.[8]

The most dramatic illustration of the checking of presidential power was the forced resignation of Richard M. Nixon in 1974 (for details, see *Up Close:* "Watergate and the Limits of Presidential Power"). Nixon's conduct inspired the intense hostility of the nation's media, particularly the prestigious *Washington Post*. His high public approval ratings following the Vietnam peace agreement plummeted. A Democratic-controlled Senate created a special committee to investigate **Watergate** that produced damaging revelations almost daily. Congressional Republicans began to desert the embattled president. The Supreme Court ordered him to turn over White House audiotapes to a special investigator, tapes that implicated Nixon in cash payments to the men who had burglarized the Democratic National Committee offices during his 1972 reelection campaign. Facing the enmity of the media, the loss of public approval, opposition from his own party in the Congress, and

THINK AGAIN

Should Congress have the authority to call home U.S. troops sent by the president to engage in military actions overseas?

Watergate The scandal that led to the forced resignation of President Richard M. Nixon. Adding "gate" as a suffix to any alleged corruption in government suggests an analogy to the Watergate scandal.

Watergate and the Limits of Presidential Power

Richard Nixon was the only president ever to resign the office. He did so to escape certain impeachment by the House of Representatives and a certain guilty verdict in trial by the Senate. Yet Nixon's first term as president included a number of historic successes. He negotiated the first ever strategic nuclear arms limitation treaty, SALT I, with the Soviet Union. He changed the global balance of power in favor of the Western democracies by opening relations with the People's Republic of China and dividing the communist world. In his second term, he withdrew U.S. troops from Vietnam, negotiated a peace agreement, and ended one of America's longest and bloodiest wars. But his remarkable record is forever tarnished by his failure to understand the limits of presidential power.

On the night of June 17, 1972, five men with burglary tools and wiretapping devices were arrested in the offices of the Democratic National Committee in the Watergate Building in Washington. Also arrested were E. Howard Hunt, Jr., G. Gordon Liddy, and James W. McCord, Jr., all employed by the Committee to Reelect the President (CREEP). All pleaded guilty and were convicted, but U.S. District Court Judge John J. Sirica believed that the defendants were shielding whoever had ordered and paid for the operation.

Although there is no evidence that Nixon himself ordered or had prior knowledge of the break-in, he discussed with his chief of staff, H. R. Haldeman, and White House advisers John Ehrlichman and John Dean the advisability of payoffs to buy the defendants' silence. Nixon hoped his landslide electoral victory in November 1972 would put the matter to rest.

But a series of sensational revelations in the *Washington Post* kept the story alive. Using an inside source known only as Deep Throat, Bob Woodward and Carl Bernstein, investigative reporters for the *Post,* alleged that key members of Nixon's reelection committee, including its chairman, former Attorney General John Mitchell, and White House staff were actively involved in the break-in and, more important, in the subsequent attempts at a cover-up.

In February 1973 the U.S. Senate formed a Special Select Committee on Campaign Activities—the "Watergate Committee"—to delve into Watergate and related activities. The committee's nationally televised hearings enthralled millions of viewers with lurid stories of "the White House horrors." John Dean broke with the White House and testified before the committee that he had earlier warned Nixon the cover-up was "a cancer growing on the presidency." Then, in a dramatic revelation, the committee—and the nation—learned that President Nixon maintained a secret tape-recording system in the Oval Office. Hoping that the tapes would prove or disprove charges of Nixon's involvement in the cover-up, the committee issued a subpoena to the White House. Nixon refused to comply, arguing that the constitutional separation of powers gave the president an "executive privilege" to withhold his private conversations from Congress. However, the U.S. Supreme Court, voting 8 to 0 in *United States v. Richard M. Nixon* ordered Nixon to turn over the tapes.

Despite the rambling nature of the tapes, committee members interpreted them as confirming Nixon's involvement in the payoffs and cover-up. Informed by congressional leaders of his own party that impeachment by a majority of the House and removal from office by two-thirds of the Senate were assured, on August 9, 1974, Richard Nixon resigned his office.

On September 8, 1974, new President Gerald R. Ford pardoned former President Nixon "for all offenses against the United States which he, Richard Nixon, has committed or may have committed or taken part in" during his presidency. Upon his death in 1994, Nixon was eulogized for his foreign policy successes.

---

executive privilege Right of a president to withhold from other branches of government confidential communications within the executive branch; although posited by presidents, it has been upheld by the Supreme Court only in limited situations.

the failure of his constitutional claim of "executive privilege" in the Supreme Court, Nixon became the only president of the United States ever to resign that office.

Executive Privilege Over the years, presidents and scholars have argued that the Constitution's establishment of a separate executive branch of government entitles the president to **executive privilege**—the right to keep confidential communications from other branches of government. Public exposure of internal executive communications would inhibit the president's ability to obtain candid advice from subordinates and would obstruct the president's ability to conduct negotiations with foreign governments or to command military operations.

But Congress has never recognized executive privilege. It has frequently tried to compel the testimony of executive officials at congressional hearings. Presidents have regularly refused to appear themselves at congressional hearings and have frequently refused to allow other executive officials to appear or divulge specific information, citing executive privilege. The federal courts have generally refrained from intervening in this dispute between the executive and legislative branches. However, the Supreme Court has ruled that the president is not immune from court orders when illegal acts are under investigation. In *United States v. Nixon* (1974), the U.S. Supreme Court acknowledged that although the president might legitimately claim executive privilege where military or diplomatic matters are involved, such a privilege cannot be invoked in a criminal investigation. The Court ordered President Nixon to surrender tape recordings of White House conversations between the president and his advisors during the Watergate scandal.[9]

Presidential Impoundment The Constitution states that "no Money shall be drawn from the Treasury, but in Consequence of appropriations made by Law" (Article I, Section 9). Clearly the president cannot spend money *not* appropriated by Congress. But the Constitution is silent on whether the president must spend all of the money appropriated by Congress for various purposes. Presidents from Thomas Jefferson onward frequently refused to spend money appropriated by Congress, an action referred to as **impoundment**. But taking advantage of a presidency weakened by the Watergate scandal, the Congress in 1974 passed the Budget and Impoundment Control Act, which requires the president to spend all appropriated funds. The act does provide, however, that presidents may send Congress a list of specific **deferrals**—items on which they wish to postpone spending— and **rescissions**—items they wish to cancel altogether. Congress by *resolution* (which cannot be vetoed by the president) may restore the deferrals and force the president to spend the money. Both houses of Congress must approve a rescission; otherwise the government must spend the money.

Responsibility to the Courts The president is not "above the law"; that is, his conduct is not immune from judicial scrutiny. The president's official conduct must be lawful; federal courts may reverse presidential actions found to be unconstitutional or violative of laws of Congress. And presidents are not immune from criminal prosecution, they cannot ignore demands to provide information in criminal cases. However, the Supreme Court has held that the president has "absolute immunity" from civil suits "arising out of the execution of official duties."[10] In other words, the president cannot be sued for damages caused by actions or decisions that are within his constitutional or legal authority.

But can the president be sued for *private* conduct beyond the scope of his official duties? In 1994 Paula Corbin Jones sued William Jefferson Clinton in federal district court in Arkansas, alleging that he made "abhorrent" sexual advances toward her in Little Rock in 1991 while he was governor and she was a state employee. Clinton's defense lawyers argued that the president should be immune from civil actions, especially those arising from events alleged to occur before he assumed office. They argued that the president's constitutional responsibilities are so important and demanding that he must devote his undivided time and attention to them. He cannot be distracted by civil suits; otherwise a large volume of politically motivated frivolous litigation might undermine his ability to function effectively in office.

impoundment Refusal by a president to spend monies appropriated by Congress; outlawed except with congressional consent by the Budget and Impoundment Control Act of 1974.

deferrals Items on which a president wishes to postpone spending.

rescissions Items on which a president wishes to cancel spending.

However, in 1997 the U.S. Supreme Court rejected the notion of presidential immunity from civil claims arising from actions outside of the president's official duties. Although advising lower courts to give "utmost deference to Presidential responsibilities" in handling the case, the Court held that "the doctrine of separation of powers does not require federal courts to stay all private actions against the president until he leaves office."[11] Clinton was obliged to settle the case with a financial payment to Jones.

The Constitution's Congressional Tilt The Constitution, reflecting the Founders' view of the preeminence of the legislative branch, gives the last word to the Congress in disputes with the president:

- The Congress can override the president's veto of legislation if it can muster a two-thirds vote in both houses.

- The Congress can impeach and remove the president from office.

- Only the Congress can appropriate money.

- Major presidential appointments require Senate confirmation.

- The president is obliged by the Constitution to "take Care that the Laws be faithfully executed"—that is, the *laws of Congress*—regardless of any personal feelings about these laws.

Thus, Congress is *constitutionally* positioned to dominate American government. But it is the president who *politically* dominates the nation's public affairs.

Political Resources of the President

The real sources of presidential power are not found in the Constitution. The president's power is the *power to persuade.* As Harry Truman put it, "I sit here all day trying to persuade people to do things they ought to have sense enough to do without my persuading them. . . . That's all the powers of the president amount to."[12]

The president's political resources are potentially very great. The nation looks to the president for leadership, for direction, for reassurance. The president is the focus of public and media attention. The president has the capacity to mobilize public opinion, to communicate directly with the American people, and to employ the symbols of office to advance policy initiatives in both foreign and domestic affairs.

The Reputation for Power A reputation for power is itself a source of power. Presidents must strive to maintain the image of power in order to be effective. A president perceived as powerful can exercise great influence abroad with foreign governments and at home with the Congress, interest groups, and the executive bureaucracy. A president perceived as weak, unsteady, bumbling, or error prone will soon become unpopular and ineffective.

Presidential Popularity Presidential popularity with the American people is a political resource. Popular presidents cannot always transfer their popularity into foreign policy successes or legislative victories, but popular presidents usually have more success than unpopular presidents.

Presidential popularity is regularly tracked in national opinion polls. For more than forty years, national surveys have asked the American public: "Do you approve

THINK
AGAIN

Is presidential performance more related to character and personality than to policy positions?

or disapprove of the way _____ is handling his job as president?" (see Figures 11.1 and 11.2). Analyses of variations over time in these poll results suggest some generalizations about presidential popularity (see Figure 11.1).[13]

Presidential popularity is usually high at the beginning of a president's term of office, but this period can be very brief. The American public's high expectations for a new president can turn sour within a few months. A president's popularity will vary a great deal during a term in office, with sharp peaks and steep valleys in the ratings. But the general trend is downward.[14] Presidents usually recover some popularity at the end of their first term as they campaign for reelection.

Presidential popularity rises during crises. People "rally 'round the president" when the nation is confronted with an international threat or the president initiates a military action.[15] President George Bush, for example, registered the all-time high in presidential ratings during the Persian Gulf War. Likewise, the invasion of Grenada in 1983 and Panama in 1989 rallied support to the president. And the "9/11" terrorist attack on America rallied the American people behind George W. Bush (see Figure 11.2). But prolonged warfare and stalemate erode popular support. In both the Korean and the Vietnam wars, initial public approval of the president and support for the war eroded over time as military operations stalemated and casualties mounted.[16]

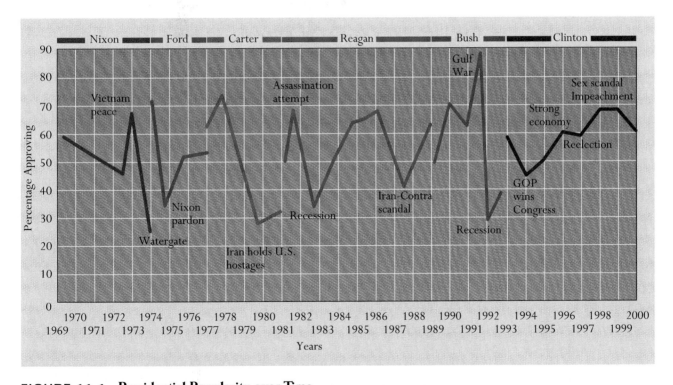

FIGURE 11.1 Presidential Popularity over Time

Americans expect a great deal from their presidents and are quick to give these leaders the credit—and the blame—for major events in the nation's life. In general, public approval (as measured by response to the question "Do you approve or disapprove of the way _____ is handling the job of president?") is highest at the beginning of a new president's term in office and declines from that point. Major military confrontations generally raise presidential ratings initially but can (as in the case of Lyndon Johnson) cause dramatic decline if the conflict drags on. In addition, public approval of the president is closely linked to the nation's economic health. When the economy is in recession, Americans tend to take a negative view of the president.

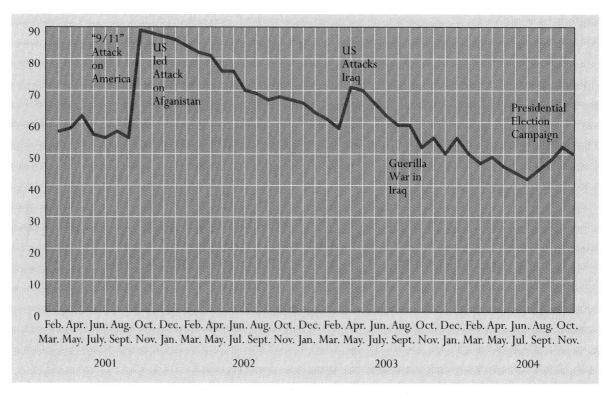

FIGURE 11.2   George W. Bush's Approval Ratings

Major scandals *may* also hurt presidential popularity and effectiveness. The Watergate scandal produced a low of 22 percent approval for Nixon just prior to his resignation. Reagan's generally high approval ratings were blemished by the Iran-Contra scandal hearings in 1987, although he ultimately left office with a high approval rate. But highly publicized allegations of sexual improprieties against President Clinton in early 1998 appeared to have the opposite effect; Clinton's approval ratings went *up*. Perhaps the public differentiates between private sexual conduct and performance in office. (see *What Do You Think?* "Should We Judge Presidents on Private Character or Performance in Office?").

Finally, economic recessions erode presidential popularity. Every president in office during a recession has suffered loss of popular approval, including President Reagan during the 1982 recession. But no president suffered a more precipitous decline in approval ratings than George Bush, whose popularity plummeted from its Gulf War high of 89 percent in 1991 to a low of 37 percent in only a year, largely as a result of recession.

Access to the Media   The president dominates the news more than any other single person. All major television networks, newspapers, and newsmagazines have reporters (usually their most experienced and skilled people) covering the "White House beat." The presidential press secretary briefs these reporters daily, but the president also may appear in person in the White House press room at any time. Presidents regularly use this media access to advance their programs and priorities.[17]

White House press corps
Reporters from both print and broadcast media assigned to regularly cover the president.

The **White House press corps** is an elite group of reporters assigned to cover the president. It includes the prestige press—the *New York Times, Washington Post, Wall Street Journal, Time, Newsweek, U.S. New and World Report,* as well as the television networks—ABC, CBS, NBC, CNN, FOX, and even the foreign press. Indeed, more

Should We Judge Presidents on Private Character or Performance in Office?

In evaluating presidents, should we consider their private moral conduct or should we focus on how they perform their public duties? Can private morality be divorced from public trust? The sex scandals surrounding Bill Clinton, not only those alleged to have occurred before he was elected president but also those alleged to have occurred in the Oval Office itself, brought these questions forcefully to the American people.

When allegations first emerged in January 1998 that Clinton had had an affair with a twenty-one-year-old intern working at the White House, President Clinton himself emphatically denied the allegations, saying, "I did not have sexual relations with that woman, Ms. Lewinsky!"

Most Americans (62 percent) believed the president had a sexual affair in the White House and subsequently lied abut it, however, they also approved of the way Clinton was performing his job as president. Indeed, the public appeared to rally around the president following the allegations of sexual misconduct. Clinton's job rating, already a healthy 60 percent at the beginning of 1998, experienced a "Lewinsky bounce" following lurid news stories of the affair. Indeed, many people blamed the independent counsel Kenneth Starr for investigating the private life of the president. And many people blamed the news media for focusing so much attention on the affair.

Various explanations have been offered for this apparent paradox—a public that believed the president had an affair in the White House and lied about it, yet gave the president the highest approval ratings of his career. Many Americans believe that private sexual conduct is irrelevant to the performance of public duties. Private morality is viewed as a personal affair about which Americans should be nonjudgmental. Some people said, "If it's okay with Hillary, why should we worry?" Haven't we had adulterous presidents before, from Thomas Jefferson to John F. Kennedy, presidents who were ranked high in history? And many Americans believe that "they all do it."

Others argue, nonetheless, that private character counts in presidential performance, indeed, that it is a prerequisite for public trust. The president, in this view, performs a symbolic role that requires dignity, honesty, and respect. A president publicly embarrassed by sexual scandal, diminished by jokes, and laughed at by late-night television audiences cannot perform this role. The acceptance of a president's adulterous behavior, according to one commentator, lowers society's standards of behavior. "The president's legacy . . . will be a further vulgarization and demoralization of society."[*]

---

[*]Gertrude Himmelfarb, "Private Lives, Public Morality," *New York Times*, February 9, 1998. Poll results reported in *The Polling Report*, February 9, 1998. See also George C. Edwards and Stephen J. Wayne, *Presidential Leadership*. 6th ed (Belmont, Calif.: Wadsworth, 2003). "How Important is Character?," p. 263.

---

than 1,800 journalists have White House press credentials. However, fortunately not all show up at once (there are only 48 seats in the White House briefing room, and attendance at press conferences is usually less than 300). The great majority of daily newspapers have no Washington correspondents, but instead rely on national news services such as the Associated Press.

Formal press conferences are a double-edged sword for the president. They *can* help mobilize popular support for presidential programs. Presidents often try to focus attention on particular issues, and they generally open press conferences with a policy statement on these issues. But reporters' questions and subsequent reporting often refocus the press conference in other directions. Often the lead media story emerging from a press conference has nothing to do with the president's purpose in holding the conference. The president cannot control questions or limit the subject matter of press conferences.

Presidents may also use direct television addresses from the White House. (President Reagan made heavy use of national prime time television appeals to mobi-

President George W. Bush answers questions during a press conference. These meetings with the press can be a double-edged sword. They give the president an opportunity to present his point of view to the public, but they also allow the press to raise issues a president might rather avoid.

lize support for his programs; he was exceptionally successful in generating telephone calls, wires, and letters to Congress in support of his programs.) President George Bush has used direct addresses to try to mobilize support the war on terrorism, including military actions in Afghanistan and Iraq.

Personality Versus Policy

A president with an engaging personality—warmth, charm, and good humor—can add to his political power. And, of course, a president who seems distant, uncaring, or humorless can erode his political resources. (Richard Nixon's seeming mean-spiritedness contributed to the collapse of his approval ratings during the Watergate scandal; Jimmy Carter's often cold and distant appearance failed to inspire much popular support for his programs; and George H. W. Bush appeared to be uncaring about the economic circumstances of ordinary Americans.) The public evaluates presidents as much on style as on policy substance.[18] (Perhaps no other president in recent times enjoyed such personal popularity while pursuing relatively unpopular policies as Ronald Reagan.) If the public thinks the president understands and cares about their problems, they may be willing to continue to approve of the job he is doing despite policy setbacks. In other words, the public evaluates the president by how much they like him as a person. (President Bill Clinton's likability kept his public approval ratings high during the sex scandal and impeachment effort.) Yet, as we have seen, public approval ratings of presidents can rise or fall based on wars and crises, scandals, and economic prosperity or recession, even while their personal style remains unaltered.

George Bush graduated from Yale two years ahead of John Kerry. Both were inducted into the prestigious leadership society, Scull and Bones, yet each displayed a distinctly different personality even in college. Bush was a hard-drinking fraternity man, a "regular guy." Kerry was hard-working, serious, austere, and eager to please his mentors (see *People in Politics* "John Kerry, War Hero and Anti-War Leader").

Bush's presidential campaigns, both against Al Gore in 2000 and John Kerry in 2004, rested largely on his personal appeal to voters—his perceived trustworthiness, warmth, good humor, and general "likeability." With a strong economy, budget surpluses, relative peace, and a popular president to follow, Al Gore should have won the 2000 presidential election. But compared to Bush, Gore seemed stiff, wooden, artificial, and out of touch with common people. Bush mangled his sentences (and even joked about it) and offered fewer details about public policy issues.

Bush never hid his religious faith. He admitted to giving up drinking and carousing and finding religion earlier in his life. Kerry seemed to be embarrassed by his Catholic faith and its stand on abortion, same-sex marriage, and stem-cell research. He also seemed conflicted about the war in Iraq: he had initially voted to give the president power to use military force, yet later he would talk of "the wrong war, in the wrong place, at the wrong time." He was a thoughtful, sensitive, and careful thinker; his position on issues was often qualified and nuanced. In the presidential debates Kerry appeared presidential, strong-voiced, articulate, and well-informed on the issues. He won the debates but failed to shed his image as aloof, austere, and lacking in strong commitment to issues that mattered. Bush was able to characterize him as a "waffler" and a "flip-flopper." Bush, despite all his flaws, was seen as strong, uncomplicated, and "willing to take a stand."

Party Leadership Presidents are leaders of their party, but this role is hardly a source of great strength. It is true that presidents select the national party chair, control the national committee and its Washington staff, and largely direct the national party convention. Incumbent presidents can use this power to help defeat challengers *within* their own parties. President Ford used this power to help defeat challenger Ronald Reagan in 1976; President Carter used it to help defeat challenger Ted Kennedy in 1980; and President Bush used it against challenger Pat Buchanan in 1992. But the role of party leader is of limited value to a president because the parties have few direct controls over their members (see Chapter 7).

Nevertheless, presidents enjoy much stronger support in Congress from members of their own party than from members of the opposition party (see "Decision Making in Congress" in Chapter 10). Some of the president's party support in Congress is a product of shared ideological values and policy positions. But Republican Congress members do have some stake in the success of a Republican president, as do Democratic members in the success of a Democratic president. Popular presidents may produce those few extra votes that make the difference for party candidates in close congressional districts.

Chief Executive

The president is the chief executive of the nation's largest bureaucracy: 2.8 million civilian employees, 60 independent agencies, 15 departments, and the large Executive Office of the President. The formal organizational chart of the federal government places the president at the head of this giant structure (see Figure 12.1, "The Federal Bureaucracy," in Chapter 12). But the president cannot command this bureaucracy in the fashion of a military officer or a corporation president. When Harry Truman was preparing to turn over the White House to Dwight Eisenhower, he predicted that the general of the army would not understand the presidency: "He'll sit here and say 'Do this! Do that!' and nothing will happen. Poor Ike—it won't be a bit like the army. He'll find it very frustrating." Truman vastly underestimated the political skills of the former general, but the crusty Missourian clearly understood the frustrations confronting the nation's chief executive. The president does not command the executive branch of government but rather stands at its center—persuading, bargaining, negotiating, and compromising to achieve goals (see *Up Close* Contrasting Presidential Styles).

The Constitutional Executive The Constitution is vague about the president's authority over the executive branch. It vests executive power in the presidency and

John Kerry, War Hero, Anti-War Leader

John Kerry was born into Boston's privileged elite. His father, Richard, was a Yale University and Harvard law school graduate who married into the internationally wealthy Forbes family. He served in various diplomatic posts in Europe while his son, John Forbes Kerry, attended boarding schools in France and Switzerland. Eventually, John returned to the United States to attend the private prestigious preparatory school St. Paul's in Concord, New Hampshire. He dated Janet Auchincloss, half-sister of Jackie Kennedy and was a frequent guest of the Kennedys. John F. Kennedy became his idol; young Kerry exulted in the fact that they shared initials.

At Yale, John Kerry played varsity soccer and was inducted into the prestigious leadership honorary Skull and Bones (only two years after George W. Bush). After graduation from Yale in 1966, Kerry sought to follow in his idol's footsteps by serving in the Navy. The war was still supported by most Americans. Kerry already envisioned a political career. Like JFK he volunteered for duty with small PT-like "swift boats" so that he could achieve a command as a relatively low ranking officer. But he soon found that swift boat duty was extremely dangerous, patrolling close inshore in Vietnam's Mekong Delta.

War Hero Kerry distinguished himself as an aggressive and courageous commander. He was directly engaged in many firefights, suffering three minor wounds for which he received Purple Hearts. When his boat was ambushed on the Mekong River, instead of fleeing, he beached the boat and personally led his sailors on an attack that destroyed an enemy machine gun position. He was awarded a Silver Star for his actions. Later he risked his own life to pull a Green Beret from the water while under enemy fire. He was awarded a Bronze Star for this action.

Anti-War Hero Like many Vietnam veterans, Kerry was shocked by anti-war protests upon his return to the United States. In 1970 he married Julia Thorne, the wealthy heiress, and immediately sought to run for Congress as a war hero. But with anti-war sentiment strong in Massachusetts, he failed even to win the Democratic nomination. He retreated to the Thorne's 200-acre estate on Long Island to replan his political career. His personal reservations about the wisdom of the Vietnam War began to involve him in the anti-Vietnam War movement. When he was approached by billionaire Edgar Bronfman, owner of Seagrams, and offered business support to create an anti-war organization, the Vietnam Veterans Against the War (VVAW), he accepted. In April, 1971, representing the VVAW, he appeared before the Senate Foreign Relations Committee dressed in green fatigues wearing his medals and angrily testified against the war. He became an overnight celebrity appearing on "60 Minutes" and other popular shows. But when he tried to run again for Congress in 1972 as an anti-war candidate, he again suffered defeat. Disappointed again, he decided to enter the Boston College of Law. Upon graduation in 1976 he became a prosecuting attorney for Middlesex County. He took up private practice in 1979.

Rapid Political Rise Kerry never really lost his ambition for high political office. When the Massachusetts lieutenant governorship post opened up in 1982, Kerry entered a crowded Democratic field. Arguments over the Vietnam war had faded, so Kerry's new rallying cry was opposition to Reagan's military buildup. He won a narrow victory to join the Democratic ticket with Michael Dukakis as the gu-

grants the president authority to appoint principal officers of the government "by and with the Advice and Consent of the Senate." Under the Constitution, the president may also "require the Opinion, in writing, of the principal Officer in each of the executive Departments, upon any Subject relating to the Duties of their respective Offices." This awkward phrase presumably gives the president the power to oversee operations of the executive departments. Finally, and perhaps most important, the president is instructed to "take Care that the Laws be faithfully executed."

At the same time, Congress has substantial authority over the executive branch. Through its lawmaking abilities, Congress can establish or abolish executive departments and regulate their operations. Congress's "power of the purse" allows it to determine the budget of each department each year and thus to limit or broaden or even "micromanage" the activities of these departments. Moreover, Congress can bernatorial nominee. In Democratic Massachusetts, they won easily.

When illness forced the popular Massachusetts Senator Paul Tsongas to leave office in 1984, Kerry again jumped into the Democratic primary for the open seat. He adopted the nuclear freeze movement as his campaign theme and brought thousands of liberal Democrats to his cause. He won the Democratic nomination by a paper thin margin and went on to represent Massachusetts in the U.S. Senate.

Senate Career Kerry's Senate career can at best be described as lackluster. He never sponsored any significant legislation and he was never selected for any significant leadership position by his fellow Democrats. His voting reflected that of his Massachusetts Senate colleague Ted Kennedy. Both regularly compiled the Senate's most liberal voting record. Kerry served on the Senate Foreign Relations Committee, the same committee before which he had testified as a young anti-war protester years earlier.

After years of separation, Kerry and his wife divorced in 1988. The divorce from the wealthy heiress left Kerry short of cash. He began accepting large campaign contributions from interest groups, and over time won the unwanted recognition as the largest recipient of interest group money in the Senate. In 1995 Kerry married Teresa Heinz, the widow of Pennsylvania Senator John Heinz who had died in a plane crash. Teresa Heinz inherited the bulk of the Heinz ketchup fortune, and is listed as one of the richest women in the country.

Kerry faced his first real reelection battle in 1996 when challenged by Massachusetts Governor William Weld, one of the few Republicans ever to win that state's governorship in modern times. Kerry spent heavily in the race, and with Clinton's sweep of the state, he managed a narrow reelection victory. Kerry was now ready to set his sights on higher office.

Running for President. Kerry was one of ten Democratic candidates to announce their intentions to seek their party's nomination in 2004. But in early debates Kerry stood out as taller, stronger-voiced, and more articulate. Only Vermont Governor Howard Dean appeared to offer a real challenge to Kerry. Dean vigorously opposed the war in Iraq; Kerry had voted for it. Dean appealed to many hardcore "hate Bush" Democratic activists. But Democratic primary voters chose Kerry as more "electable" than the boisterous Dean.

The political landscape seemed to favor Kerry. Polls reported that most Americans thought the country was going in the wrong direction; Bush's approval rating was barely 50 percent; the economy had not yet recovered as many jobs as it had when Bush entered office; Iraq was in chaos, American troops were dying every day, and there appeared to be no end to the conflict.

But Kerry failed to convince most Americans that he could do any better in resolving the war in Iraq than Bush. His contradictory comments on the war allowed Bush to label him a "waffler"; his position that the United States should have waited for approval from the United Nations before going into Iraq allowed Bush to characterize him as someone who would turn over America's national security to the U.N. Kerry won the debates, yet Bush was still perceived as a stronger leader for the war on terrorism.

The largest voter turnout in recent history rejected Kerry. Kerry won the voters that cited the economy, Iraq, health care, and education as most important to them. But most important to the largest number of voters was "moral values" and Bush won 79 percent of these voters. Kerry had focused on the issues but Bush had won the voters on a simple message of faith and family.

pressure executive agencies by conducting investigations, calling administrators to task in public hearings, and directly contacting agencies with members' own complaints or those of their constituents.

Executive Orders Presidents frequently use **executive orders** to implement their policies. Executive orders may direct specific federal agencies to carry out the president's wishes, or they may direct all federal agencies to pursue the president's preferred course of action. In any case, they must be based on either a president's constitutional powers or on powers delegated to the president by laws of Congress. Presidents regularly issue 50 to 100 executive orders each year, but some stand out. In 1942 President Franklin D. Roosevelt issued Executive Order 9066 for the internment of Japanese Americans during World War II. In 1948 President Harry

executive order Formal regulation governing executive branch operations issued by the president.

Contrasting Presidential Styles

Every president brings to the White House his own personal administrative style. Some presidents work almost constantly, putting in 12–14 hour days (Carter, Clinton). Others pursue a more leisurely schedule, leaving the Oval Office at 5 or 6 PM and spending weekends at the presidential retreat at Camp David or their home (Eisenhower, Reagan, Bush). Some presidents delegate a great deal of responsibility to Cabinet members and White House aides (Eisenhower, Reagan, Bush). Others closely monitor what is happening in executive departments and agencies (Johnson, Carter, Clinton). Some pursue a great many policy initiatives (Clinton), while others focus on a few key priorities (Reagan, Bush). Some are well informed about the specifics of public policy (Carter, Clinton), while others care more about overall goals and directions of their administration (Reagan, Bush). Some operate informally, communicating frequently with staff, Cabinet members, and others (Clinton). Other presidents function in a more business-like fashion, communicating mostly through their chief-of-staff (Eisenhower, Reagan). Below are the differences between the Bush and Clinton administrative styles as seen by two prominent political scientists:

Differences Between the Bush and Clinton Presidencies

George W. Bush	Bill Clinton
Disciplined White House	Less disciplined White House
Scripted presidency	Unscripted presidency
Strict focus on few key priorities	Wide-ranging policy focus
More reliance on vice president	Less reliance on vice president
Punctuality required for meetings with clear starting and ending times	Meetings start late and seldom end on time
Little use of the bully pulpit	More use of the bully pulpit
Direct public communicator	Skillful public communicator
Frequent reliance on experts to provide policy overviews	Well informed on policy issues
Somewhat more attentive to Congress and its members	Less attentive to Congress and its members
Large responsibilities delegated to aides	Close supervisory role maintained over all top aides
Preference for executive summaries	Enamored of thick briefing books
Regular working days observed insofar as practicable	A "24/7" president

Source: Roger H. Davidson and Walter J. Oleszak, *Congress and Its Members*. 9th ed. (Washington, D.C.: CQ Press, 2004), p. 302.

Truman issued Executive Order 9981 to desegregate the U.S. armed forces. In 1965 President Lyndon Johnson issued Executive Order 11246 to require that private firms with federal contracts institute affirmative action programs. A president can even declare a national emergency by executive order, a step that authorizes a broad range of unilateral actions.

Executive orders have legal force when they are based on the president's constitutional or statutory authority. And presidents typically take an expansive view of their own authority. (President George Washington issued an executive order declaring American neutrality in the war between France and England in 1793, while the Constitution gave the power to "declare war" to Congress, Washington assumed the authority to declare neutrality.) Federal courts have generally upheld presidential executive orders. However, the Supreme Court overturned an order by President Harry Truman in 1951 during the Korean War seizing the nation's steel mills.[19] Research on the frequency of executive orders suggests that: Democratic presidents issue more orders than Republican presidents; presidents may issue executive orders to circumvent Congress but only when they believe that Congress will not overturn their orders; and presidents issue more executive orders when they are running for reelection.[20]

Appointments Presidential power over the executive branch derives in part from the president's authority to appoint and remove top officials. Presidents can shape policy by careful attention to top appointments—cabinet secretaries, assistant secretaries, agency heads, and White House staff. The key is to select people who share the president's policy views and who have the personal qualifications to do an effective job. However, in cabinet appointments political considerations weigh heavily: unifying various elements of the party; appealing for interest-group support; rewarding political loyalty; providing a temporary haven for unsuccessful party candidates; achieving a balance of racial, ethnic, and gender representation.[21] The appointment power gives the president only limited control over the executive branch of government. Of the executive branch's 2.8 million civilian employees, the president actually appoints only about 3,000. The vast majority of federal executive branch employees are civil servants—recruited, paid, and protected under civil service laws—and are not easily removed or punished by the president. Cabinet secretaries and heads of independent regulatory agencies require congressional confirmation, but presidents can choose their own White House staff without the approval of Congress.

Presidents have only limited power to remove the heads of independent regulatory agencies. By law, Congress sets the terms of these officials. Federal Communications Commission members are appointed for five years; Securities and Exchange Commission members for five years; and Federal Reserve Board members, responsible for the nation's money supply, enjoy the longest term of any executive officials—fourteen years. Congress's responsibility for term length for regulatory agencies is supposed to insulate those agencies, in particular their quasijudicial responsibilities, from "political" influence.

Even having a presidential appointee at the helm of a department does not always guarantee the president control over that department. Many political appointees are stymied by the career bureaucrats in departments and agencies who have the knowledge, skills, and experience to function with little or no supervision from their nominal political chiefs. Rather than carrying out the president's policies, some appointees "go native": they yield to the career bureaucrats, adopt the prevailing customs and values of their agencies, and seek the support of the bureaucrats, interest groups, and congressional committees that determine the agencies' future. Republican presidents have an especially difficult task controlling the bureaucracy because the majority of career bureaucrats are Democrats.[22]

Budget Presidential authority also derives from the president's role in the budgetary process. The Constitution makes no mention of the president with regard to expenditures; rather, it grants the power of the purse to Congress. Indeed, for nearly 150 years, executive departments submitted their budget requests directly to the Congress without first submitting them to the president. But with the passage of the Budget and Accounting Act in 1921, Congress established the Office of Management and Budget (originally named the Bureau of the Budget) to assist the president in preparing an annual Budget of the United States Government for presentation to the Congress. The president's budget is simply a set of recommendations to the Congress. Congress must pass appropriations acts before the president or any executive department or agency may spend money. Congress can and frequently does alter the president's budget recommendations (see "The Politics of Budgeting" in Chapter 12).

Cabinet
The White House site provides the names of the current president's cabinet as well as those individuals with "cabinet-rank" status.
www.whitehouse.gov/ government/cabinet.html

cabinet The heads (secretaries) of the executive departments together with other top officials accorded cabinet rank by the president; only occasionally does it meet as a body to advise and support the president.

The Cabinet The **cabinet** is not mentioned in the U.S. Constitution; it has no formal powers. It consists of the secretaries of the executive departments and others the president may designate, including the vice president, the ambassador to the United Nations, the director of the Central Intelligence Agency, and the Special Trade Representative. According to custom, cabinet officials are ranked by the date their departments were created (see Table 11.2). Thus the secretary of state is the senior cabinet officer, followed by the secretary of the treasury. They sit next to the president at cabinet meetings, heads of the newest departments sit at the far ends of the table.

The cabinet rarely functions as a decision-making body. Cabinet officers in the United States are powerful because they head giant administrative organizations. The secretary of state, the secretary of defense, the secretary of the treasury, the attorney general, and, to a lesser extent, the other departmental secretaries are all people of power and prestige. But seldom does a strong president hold a cabinet meeting to decide important policy questions. More frequently, presidents know what they want and hold cabinet meetings only to help promote their views.

The Constitution requires that "Officers of the United States" be confirmed by the Senate. In the past, the Senate rarely rejected a presidential cabinet nomination; the traditional view was that presidents were entitled to pick their own peo-

TABLE 11.2 The Cabinet Departments

Department	Created
State	1789
Treasury	1789
Defense*	1947
Justice	1789
Interior	1849
Agriculture†	1889
Commerce	1913
Labor	1913
Health and Human Services‡	1953
Housing and Urban Development	1965
Transportation	1966
Energy	1977
Education	1979
Veterans' Affairs	1989
Homeland Security	2002

* Formerly the War and Navy Departments, created in 1789 and 1798, respectively.

†Agriculture Department created in 1862, made part of cabinet in 1889.

‡Originally Health, Education, and Welfare; reorganized in 1979, with the creation of a separate Department of Education.

President George W. Bush meets with his cabinet and advisers at Camp David on September 15, 2001.

ple and even make their own mistakes. In recent years, however, the confirmation process has become more partisan and divisive, with the Senate conducting lengthy investigations and holding public hearings on presidential cabinet nominees. In 1989 the Senate rejected President Bush's nomination of John Tower as secretary of defense in a partisan battle featuring charges that the former Texas senator was a heavy drinker. In 1993 President Clinton was obliged to withdraw the nomination of Zoe Baird as attorney general following Senate hearings featuring the charge that she had employed an illegal alien as a babysitter and had failed to pay the woman's Social Security taxes. The intense public scrutiny and potential for partisan attacks, together with financial disclosure and conflict-of-interest laws, may be discouraging some well-qualified people from accepting cabinet posts.

The National Security Council The **National Security Council (NSC)** is really an "inner cabinet" created by law in 1947 to advise the president and coordinate foreign, defense, and intelligence activities. The president is chair, and the vice president, secretary of state, and secretary of defense are participating members. The chair of the Joint Chiefs of Staff and the director of the Central Intelligence Agency serve as advisers to the NSC, which is headed by the special assistant to the president for national security affairs. The purposes of the council are to advise and coordinate policy; but in the Iran-Contra scandal in 1987, a staff member of the NSC, Lt. Col. Oliver North, undertook to *implement* security policy by directly channeling funds and arms to Nicaraguan "contras" fighting a communist-dominated government. Various investigative committees strongly recommended that the NSC staff confine itself to an advisory role.

White House Staff Today, presidents exercise their powers chiefly through the White House staff.[23] This staff includes the president's closest aides and advisers. Over the years, the White House staff has grown from Roosevelt's small "brain trust" of a dozen advisers to several hundred people, many with impressive titles, such as assistant to the president, deputy assistant to the president, special assistant to the president, and counsel to the president.

Senior White House staff members are trusted political advisers, often personal friends and long-time associates of the president. Some enjoy office space in the White House itself and daily contact with the president (see Figure 11.3). Appointed without Senate confirmation, they are loyal to the president alone, not to departments, agencies, or interest groups. Their many tasks include the following:

National Security Council
Site provides brief history of NSC plus new releases dealing with national security
www.whitehouse.gov/nsc

National Security Council (NSC) "Inner cabinet" that advises the president and coordinates foreign, defense, and intelligence activities.

FIGURE 11.3 The White House Corridors of Power

Presidents allocate office space in the White House according to their own desires. An office located close to the president's is considered an indication of the power of the occupant. This diagram shows the office assignments during the Clinton Administration.

- Providing the president with sound advice on everything from national security to congressional affairs, policy development, and electoral politics.

- Monitoring the operations of executive departments and agencies and evaluating the performance of key executive officials.

- Setting the president's schedule, determining whom the president will see and call, where and when the president will travel, and where and to whom the president will make personal appearances and speeches.

- Above all, the staff must protect their boss, steering the president away from scandal, political blunders, and errors of judgment.

The senior White House staff normally includes a chief of staff, the national security adviser, a press secretary, the counsel to the president (an attorney), a director of personnel (patronage appointments), and assistants for political affairs, legislative liaison, management, and domestic policy. Staff organization depends on each president's personal taste. Some presidents have organized their staffs hierarchically, concentrating power in the chief of staff. Others have maintained direct contact with several staff members.

Chief Legislator and Lobbyist

The president has the principal responsibility for the initiation of national policy. Indeed, about 80 percent of the bills considered by Congress originate in the executive branch. Presidents have a strong incentive to fulfill this responsibility: the American people hold them responsible for anything that happens in the nation during their term of office, whether or not they have the authority or capacity to do anything about it.

Policy Initiation The Founders understood that the president would be involved in policy initiation. The Constitution requires the president to "give to the Congress Information of the State of the Union," to "recommend to their Consideration such Measures as he shall judge necessary and expedient" (Article II, Section 3). "On extraordinary Occasions" the president may call a recessed Congress into special session. Each year the principal policy statement of the president comes in the State of the Union message to Congress. It is followed by the president's Budget of the United States Government, which sets forth the president's programs with price tags attached. Many other policy proposals are developed by executive departments and agencies, transmitted to the White House for the president's approval or "clearance," and then sent to Congress.

Congress may not accept all or even most of the president's proposals. Indeed, from time to time it may even try to develop its own legislative agenda in competition with the president's. But the president's legislative initiatives usually set the agenda of congressional decision making. As one experienced Washington lobbyist put it, "Obviously when the president sends up a bill, it takes first place in the queue. All other bills take second place."[24]

White House Lobbying Presidents do not simply send their bills to Congress and then await the outcome. The president is also expected to be the chief lobbyist on behalf of the administration's bills as they make their way through the legislative labyrinth. The White House staff includes "legislative liaison" people—lobbyists for the president's programs. They organize the president's legislative proposals, track them through committee and floor proceedings, arrange committee appearances by executive department and agency representatives, count votes, and advise the president on when and how to "cut deals" and "twist arms."

Presidents are not without resources in lobbying Congress. They may exchange many favors, large and small, for the support of individual members. They can help direct "pork" to a member's district, promise White House support for a member's pet project, and assist in resolving a member's problems with the bureaucracy. Presidents also may issue or withhold invitations to the White House for prestigious ceremonies, dinners with visiting heads of state, and other glittering social occasions—an effective resource because most members of Congress value the prestige associated with close White House "connections."

The president may choose to "twist arms" individually—by telephoning and meeting with wavering members of Congress. Arm twisting is generally reserved for the president's most important legislative battles. There is seldom time for a president to contact individual members of Congress personally about many bills in various stages of the legislative process—in subcommittee, full committee, floor consideration, conference committee, and final passage—in both the House and the Senate. Instead, the president must rely on White House staff for most legislative contacts and use personal appeals sparingly.

The Honeymoon The **honeymoon period** at the very start of a president's term offers the best opportunity to get the new administration's legislative proposals enacted into law. Presidential influence in Congress is generally highest at this time both because the president's personal popularity is typically at its height and because the president can claim the recent election results as a popular mandate for key programs. Sophisticated members of Congress know that votes cast for a presidential candidate are not necessarily votes cast for that candidate's policy position (see "The Voter Decides" in Chapter 8). But election results signal members of Congress, in a language they understand well, that the president is politically popular and that they must give the administration's programs careful consideration. President Lyndon Johnson succeeded in getting the bulk of his Great Society program enacted in the year following his landslide victory in 1964. Ronald Reagan pushed through the largest tax cut in American history in the year following his convincing electoral victory over incumbent president Jimmy Carter in 1980. Bill Clinton was most successful with the Congress during his first year in office, in 1993, even winning approval for a major tax increase as part of a deficit-reduction package. And George W. Bush succeeded in getting a tax cut through Congress in his first six months in office. Both Democrat Clinton and Republican Bush benefited from having their party control the Congress during their first months in office.

Presidential "Box Scores" How successful are presidents in getting their legislation through Congress? *Congressional Quarterly* regularly compiles "box scores" of presidential success in Congress—percentages of presidential victories on congressional votes on which the president took a clear-cut position. The measure does not distinguish between bills that were important to the president and bills that may have been less significant. But viewed over time (see Figure 11.4), the presidential box scores provide interesting insights into the factors affecting the president's legislative success.

The most important determinant of presidential success in Congress is party control. Presidents are far more successful when they face a Congress controlled

honeymoon period Early months of a president's term in which his popularity with the public and influence with the Congress are generally high.

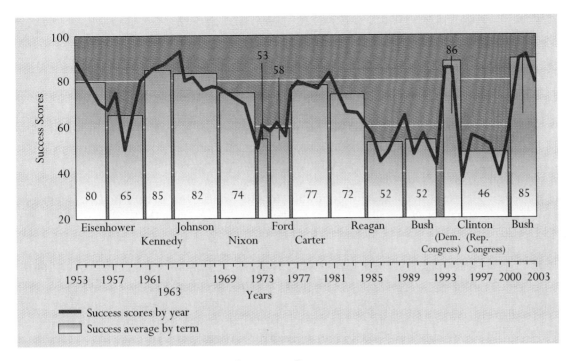

FIGURE 11.4   Presidential Success Scores in Congress

Presidential "box scores"—the percentage of times that a bill endorsed by the president is enacted by Congress—are closely linked to the strength of the president's party in Congress. For example, both Dwight D. Eisenhower and Ronald Reagan benefited from having a Republican majority in the Senate in their first terms and suffered when Democrats gained control of the Senate in their second terms. Democratic control of both houses of Congress resulted in significantly higher box scores for Democratic presidents John Kennedy, Lyndon Johnson, and Jimmy Carter than for Republicans Richard Nixon, Gerald Ford, and George Bush. Clinton was very successful in his first two years, when the Democrats controlled Congress, but when the Republicans won control following the 1994 midterm election, Clinton's box score plummeted.

by their own party. Democratic presidents John F. Kennedy and Lyndon Johnson enjoyed the support of Democratic-controlled Congresses and posted average success scores over 80 percent. Jimmy Carter was hardly a popular president, but he enjoyed the support of a Democratic Congress and an average of 76.8 percent presidential support. Republican presidents Richard Nixon and Gerald Ford fared poorly with Democratic-controlled Congresses. Republican president Ronald Reagan was very successful in his first term when he faced a Democratic House and a Republican Senate, but after Democrats took over both houses of Congress, Reagan's success rate plummeted. During the Reagan and Bush presidencies, divided party control of government (Republicans in the White House and Democrats controlling one or both houses of Congress) was said to produce **gridlock**, the political inability of the government to act decisively on the nation's problems. President Bill Clinton's achievements when Democrats controlled the Congress (1993–94), contrasted with his dismal record in dealing with Republican-controlled Congresses (1995–99), provide a vivid illustration of the importance of party in determining a president's legislative success.

The Veto Power   The **veto** is the president's most powerful weapon in dealing with Congress. The veto is especially important to a president facing a Congress controlled by the opposition party. Even the *threat* of a veto enhances the president's

gridlock   Political stalemate between the executive and legislative branches arising when one branch is controlled by one major political party and the other branch by the other party.

veto   Rejection of a legislative act by the executive branch; in the U.S. federal government, overriding of a veto requires a two-thirds majority in both houses of Congress.

bargaining power with Congress.[25] Confronted with such a threat, congressional leaders must calculate whether they can muster a two-thirds vote of both houses to override the veto.

To veto a bill passed by the Congress, the president sends to Congress a veto message specifying reasons for not signing it. If the president takes no action for ten days (excluding Sundays) after a bill has been passed by Congress, the bill becomes law without the president's signature. However, if Congress has adjourned within ten days of passing a bill and the president has not signed it, then the bill does not become law; this outcome is called a **pocket veto**.

A bill returned to Congress with a presidential veto message can be passed into law over the president's opposition by a two-thirds vote of both houses. (A bill that has received a pocket veto cannot be overridden because the Congress is no longer in session.) In other words, the president needs only to hold the loyalty of more than one-third of *either* the House or the Senate to sustain a veto. If congressional leaders cannot count on the votes to **override**, they are forced to bargain with the president. "What will the president accept?" becomes a key legislative question.

The president's bargaining power with Congress has been enhanced over the years by a history of success in sustaining presidential vetoes.[26] From George Washington to Bill Clinton, more than 96 percent of all presidential vetoes have been sustained (see Table 11.3). For example, although Bush was unable to achieve much success in getting his own legislative proposals enacted by a Democratic Congress, he was extraordinarily successful in saying no. Of Bush's many vetoes, only one (regulation of cable TV) was overridden by Congress. Clinton did not veto any bills when Democrats controlled Congress, but he began a series of vetoes in his struggle with the Republican Congress elected in 1994. He was able to sustain almost all of his vetoes because Republicans did not have two-thirds of the seats in both houses and most Democratic Congress members stuck with their president.

pocket veto Effective veto of a bill when Congress adjourns within ten days of passing it and the president fails to sign it.

override Voting in Congress to enact legislation vetoed by the president; requires a two-thirds vote in both the House and Senate.

TABLE 11.3 Presidential Vetoes

President	Total Vetoes*	Vetoes Overridden	Percentage of Vetoes Sustained
F. Roosevelt	633	9	99%
Truman	250	12	95
Eisenhower	181	2	99
Kennedy	21	0	100
L. Johnson	30	0	100
Nixon	43	5	90
Ford	66	12	85
Carter	31	2	94
Reagan	78	8	91
Bush	46	1	98
Clinton	37	2	95
Bush	0	0	—

*Regular vetoes plus pocket vetoes.

Source: Harold W. Stanley and Richard G. Niemi, *Vital Statistics on American Politics, 1999–2000* (Washington, D.C.: CQ Press, 2000), p. 256. Updated by author.

Line-Item Veto Power Denied For many years, presidents, both Democratic and Republican, petitioned Congress to give them the **line-item veto**, the ability to veto some provisions of a bill while accepting other provisions. The lack of presidential line-item veto power was especially frustrating when dealing with appropriations bills because the president could not veto specific pork-barrel provisions from major spending bills for defense, education, housing, welfare, and so on. Finally, in 1996 Congress granted the president authority to "cancel" spending items in any appropriation act and any limited tax benefit. Such cancellation would take effect immediately unless blocked by a special "disapproval bill" passed by Congress. The president could veto the disapproval bill, and a two-thirds vote of both houses would be required to override the veto.

However, opponents of the line-item veto successfully challenged its constitutionality, arguing that it transfers legislative power—granted by the Constitution only to Congress—to the president. The U.S. Supreme Court agreed: "There is no provision in the Constitution that authorizes the president to enact or amend or repeal statutes." The line-item veto, the Court said, "authorizes the president himself to elect to repeal laws, for his own policy reasons" and therefore violates the law-making procedures set forth in Article I of the Constitution.[27]

Global Leader

The president of the United States is the leader of the world's largest and most powerful democracy. During the Cold War, the president of the United States was seen as the leader of the "free world." The threat of Soviet expansionism, the huge military forces of the Warsaw Pact, and Soviet-backed guerrilla wars around the world all added to the global role of the American president as the defender of democratic values. In today's post—Cold War world, Western Europe and Japan are formidable economic competitors and no longer routinely defer to American political leadership. But if a new stable world order based on democracy and self-determination is to emerge, the president of the United States must provide the necessary leadership.

Global leadership is based on a president's powers of persuasion. Presidents are more persuasive when the American economy is strong, when American military forces are perceived as ready and capable, and when the president is seen as having the support of the American people and Congress. America's allies as well as its enemies perceive the president as the controlling force over U.S. foreign and military policy. Only occasionally do they seek to bypass the president and appeal to the Congress or to American public opinion.

Presidents sometimes prefer their global role to the much more contentious infighting of domestic politics. Abroad, presidents are treated with great dignity as head of the world's most powerful state. In contrast, at home presidents must confront hostile and insulting reporters, backbiting bureaucrats, demanding interest groups, and contentious members of Congress.

Foreign Policy As the nation's chief diplomat, the president has the principal responsibility for formulating U.S. foreign policy. The president's constitutional powers in foreign affairs are relatively modest. Presidents have the power to make treaties with foreign nations "with the Advice and Consent of the Senate." Presidents may negotiate with nations separately or through international organizations such as the North Atlantic Treaty Organization (NATO) or the United Nations, where the president determines the U.S. position in that body's

line-item veto Power of the chief executive to reject some portions of a bill without rejecting all of it.

deliberations. The Constitution also empowers the president to "appoint Ambassadors, other public Ministers, and Consuls" and to "receive Ambassadors." This power of **diplomatic recognition** permits a president to grant legitimacy to or withhold it from ruling groups around the world (to declare or refuse to declare them "rightful"). Despite controversy, President Franklin Roosevelt officially recognized the communist regime in Russia in 1933, Richard Nixon recognized the communist government of the People's Republic of China in 1972, and Carter recognized the communist Sandinistas' regime in Nicaragua in 1979. To date, all presidents have withheld diplomatic recognition of Fidel Castro's government in Cuba.

Presidents have expanded on these modest constitutional powers to dominate American foreign policy making. In part, they have done so as a product of their role as Commander-in-Chief. Military force is the ultimate diplomatic language. During wartime, or when war is threatened, military and foreign policy become inseparable. The president must decide on the use of force and, equally important, when and under what conditions to order a cease-fire or an end to hostilities.

Presidents have also come to dominate foreign policy as a product of the customary international recognition of the head of state as the legitimate voice of a government. Although nations may also watch the words and actions of the American Congress, the president's statements are generally taken to represent the official position of the U.S. government.

Treaties Treaties the president makes "by and with the Advice and Consent of the Senate" are legally binding upon the United States. The Constitution specifies that "all Treaties made . . . under the Authority of the United States, shall be the supreme Law of the Land, and the Judges in every State shall be bound thereby" (Article VI). Thus treaty provisions are directly enforceable in federal courts.

Although presidents may or may not listen to "advice" from the Senate on foreign policy, no formal treaty is valid unless "two-thirds of the Senators present concur" to its ratification. Although the Senate has ratified the vast majority of treaties, presidents must be sensitive to Senate concerns. The Senate defeat of the Versailles Treaty in 1920, which formally ended World War I and established the League of Nations, prompted Presidents Roosevelt and Truman to include prominent Democratic and Republican members of the Senate Foreign Relations Committee in the delegation that drafted the United Nations Charter in 1945 and the NATO Treaty in 1949.

President Clinton was sharply reminded of the need to develop bipartisan support for treaties in the Senate in 1999 when that body rejected the Comprehensive Test Ban Treaty. This treaty would have prohibited all signatory nations from conducting any tests of nuclear weapons. Most Western European nations had already signed and ratified the nuclear test ban, but North Korea, Iraq, Iran, India, and Pakistan, among other nations, had rejected it. China and Russia appeared to be waiting for the United States to act first. The president argued that the United States should take moral leadership in worldwide nonproliferation of nuclear weapons. His opponents in the Senate argued that too many rogue nations would ignore the treaty and continue their own nuclear testing. Despite the Senate's rejection of the treaty, Clinton continued by executive order his own moratorium on nuclear testing by the United States (see Chapter 18).

Executive Agreements Over the years, presidents have come to rely heavily on **executive agreements** with other governments rather than formal treaties. An executive agreement signed by the president of the United States has much the

diplomatic recognition
Power of the president to grant "legitimacy" to or withhold it from a government of another nation (to declare or refuse to declare it "rightful").

executive agreement
Agreement with another nation signed by the president of the United States but less formal (and hence potentially less binding) than a treaty because it does not require Senate confirmation.

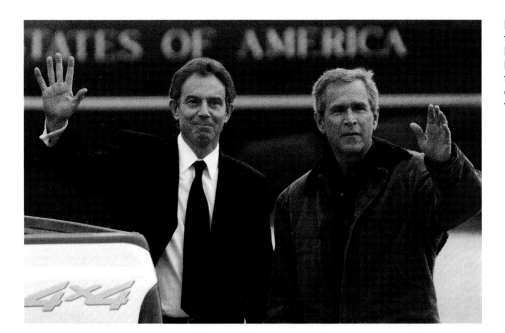

President Bush, acting as the United States' "Chief Diplomat," with British Prime Minister Tony Blair as they begin two days of talks dominated by the rise of violence in the Middle East.

same effect in international relations as a treaty. However, an executive agreement does not require Senate ratification. Presidents have asserted that their constitutional power to execute the laws, command the armed services, and determine foreign policy gives them the authority to make agreements with other nations and heads of state without obtaining approval of the U.S. Senate. However, unlike treaties, executive agreements do not supersede laws of the United States or of the states with which they conflict, but they are otherwise binding on the United States.

The use of executive agreements in important foreign policy matters was developed by President Franklin Roosevelt. Prior to his administration, executive agreements had been limited to minor matters. But in 1940, Roosevelt agreed to trade fifty American destroyers to England in exchange for naval bases in Newfoundland and the Caribbean. Roosevelt was intent on helping the British in their struggle against Nazi Germany, but before the Japanese attack on Pearl Harbor in 1941, isolationist sentiment in the Senate was too strong to win a two-thirds ratifying vote for such an agreement. Toward the end of World War II, Roosevelt at the Yalta Conference and Truman at the Potsdam Conference negotiated secret executive agreements dividing the occupation of Germany between the Western Allies and the Soviet Union.

Congress has sometimes objected to executive agreements as usurping its own powers. In the Case Act of 1972, Congress required the president to inform Congress of all executive agreements within sixty days, but the act does not limit the president's power to make agreements. It is easier for Congress to renege on executive agreements than on treaties that the Senate has ratified. In 1973 President Nixon signed an executive agreement with South Vietnamese President Nguyen Van Thieu pledging that the United States would "respond with full force" if North Vietnam violated the Paris Peace Agreement that ended American participation in the Vietnam War. But when North Vietnam reinvaded the south in 1975, Congress rejected President Gerald Ford's pleas for renewed military aid to the South Vietnamese government, and Ford knew that it had become politically impossible for the United States to respond with force.

Intelligence The president is responsible for the intelligence activities of the United States. Presidents have undertaken intelligence activities since the founding of the nation. During the Revolutionary War, General George Washington nurtured small groups of patriots living behind British lines who supplied him with information on Redcoat troop movements.[28] Today, the director of central intelligence (DCI) is appointed by the president (subject to Senate confirmation) and reports directly to the president.

The DCI coordinates the activities of the "intelligence community" (see Figure 11.5). Some elements of the intelligence community—the Central Intelligence Agency, the Defense Intelligence Agency, the National Security Agency, the Na-

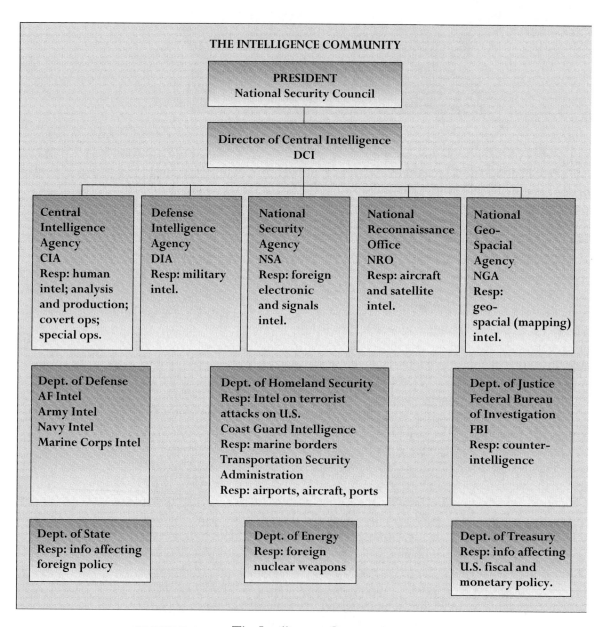

FIGURE 11.5 The Intelligence Community

Note: The CIA, DIA, NSA, NRO, and NGA are concerned exclusively with intelligence. The Departments of Defense, Homeland Security, Justice, State, Energy, and Treasury are concerned primarily with other missions, but do have intelligence responsibilities.

tional Reconnaissance Office, and the National Geo-Spacial Agency—deal exclusively with intelligence collection, analysis and distribution. Other elements of the intelligence community are located in the Department of Defense, Department of Homeland Security, Federal Bureau of Investigation, Department of State, Department of Energy, and the Department of Treasury. The DCI has no direct supervision over any of these agencies other than the Central Intelligence Agency. Indeed, the fragmentation of the intelligence community may be its principal weakness.[29]

The Central Intelligence Agency The CIA is directly supervised by the DCI. It provides intelligence on national security to the president, the National Security Council, and other top Washington decision makers. The CIA is responsible for (1) assembly, analysis, and dissemination of intelligence information from all agencies in the intelligence community; (2) collection of human intelligence from abroad; (3) with specific "presidential findings," the conduct of **covert actions**, including paramilitary special operations.

Covert actions refer to activities in support of the national interest of United States that would be ineffective if their sponsorship were made public. For example, one of the largest covert actions ever undertaken by the United States was the support, for nearly ten years, of the Afghan rebels fighting Soviet occupation of their country during the Afghanistan war (1978–88). Public acknowledgment of such aid would have assisted the Soviet-backed regime in Afghanistan to claim that the rebels were not true patriots but rather "puppets" of the United States. The rebels themselves did not wish to acknowledge U.S. aid publicly, even though they knew it was essential to the success of their cause. Hence Presidents Carter and Reagan aided the Afghan rebels through covert action.

Covert action is, by definition, secret. And secrecy spawns elaborate conspiracy theories and flamboyant tales of intrigue and deception. In fact, most covert actions consist of routine transfers of economic aid and military equipment to pro-U.S. forces that do not wish to acknowledge such aid publicly. Although most covert actions would have widespread support among the American public if they

Central Intelligence Agency

The CIA site provides information about the agency's mission, organization, values, press releases, and congressional testimony along with employment possibilities.
www.CIA.gov

covert action Secret intelligence activity outside U.S. borders undertaken with specific authorization by the president; acknowledgment of U.S. sponsorship would defeat or compromise its purpose.

Although still part of the "Big Three," along with Prime Minister Winston Churchill of Great Britain (right) and Marshal Josef Stalin of the Soviet Union (left), it was a gravely ill President Franklin Roosevelt (middle) who traveled to Yalta, a port on Russia's Crimean peninsula, and negotiated secret executive agreements dividing Germany among the Allies in 1945. Germany remained divided until 1989, when protesters tore down the Berlin Wall and the Soviet Union under Mikhail Gorbachev acquiesced in the unification of Germany under a democratic government.

were done openly, secrecy opens the possibility that a president will undertake to do by covert action what would be opposed by Congress and the American people if they knew about it.

In the atmosphere of suspicion and distrust engendered by the Watergate scandal, Congress passed intelligence oversight legislation in 1974 requiring a written "presidential finding" for any covert action and requiring that members of the House and Senate Intelligence Committees be informed of all covert actions. The president does not have to obtain congressional approval for covert actions; but Congress can halt such actions if it chooses to do so.

Commander-in-Chief

Global power derives primarily from the president's role as Commander-in-Chief of the armed forces of the United States. Presidential command over the armed forces is not merely symbolic; presidents may issue direct military orders to troops in the field. As president, Washington personally led troops to end the Whiskey Rebellion in 1794; Abraham Lincoln issued direct orders to his generals in the Civil War, Lyndon Johnson personally chose bombing targets in Vietnam; and George Bush personally ordered the Gulf War cease-fire after 100 hours of ground fighting. All presidents, whether they are experienced in world affairs or not, soon learn after taking office that their influence throughout the world is heavily dependent upon the command of capable military forces.

War-making Power Constitutionally, war-making power is divided between the Congress and the president. Article I, Section 8, says, "The Congress shall have Power . . . to . . . provide for the common Defence . . . to declare War . . . to raise and support Armies . . . to provide and maintain a Navy . . . to make Rules for the Government and Regulation of the land and naval forces." However, Article II, Section 2, says, "The President shall be Commander-in-Chief of the Army and Navy of the United States." In defending the newly written Constitution, the *Federalist Papers* construed the president's war powers narrowly, implying that the war-making power of the president was little more than the power to defend against imminent invasion when Congress was not in session.

In reality, however, presidents have exercised their powers as Commander-in-Chief to order U.S. forces into military action overseas on many occasions—from John Adams's ordering of U.S. naval forces to attack French ships (1789–99) to Harry Truman's decision to intervene in the Korean War (1951–53) to Lyndon Johnson's and Richard Nixon's conduct of the Vietnam War (1965–73), to George Bush's Operation Desert Storm (1991), to Bill Clinton's interventions in Bosnia and Kosovo (1998–99), to George W.'s military actions in Afghanistan (2001) and Iraq (2003). The Supreme Court has consistently refused to hear cases involving the war powers of the president and Congress.[30]

Thus, although Congress retains the formal power to "declare war," in modern times wars are seldom "declared." Instead, they begin with direct military actions, and the president, as Commander-in-Chief of the armed forces, determines what those actions will be. Historically, Congress accepted the fact that only the president has the information-gathering facilities and the ability to act with the speed and secrecy required for military decisions during the periods of crisis. Not until the Vietnam War was there serious congressional debate over whether the president has the power to commit the nation to war.

DefenseLink
Official site of U.S. Department of Defense, with news and links to Army, Navy, Air Force, and Marine Corps Web sites and other defense agencies and commands.
www.defenselink.gov

War Powers Act In the early days of the Vietnam War, the liberal leadership of the nation strongly supported Democratic President Lyndon Johnson's power to commit the nation to war. By 1969, however, many congressional leaders had withdrawn their support of the war. With a new Republican president, Richard Nixon, and a Democratic Congress, congressional attacks on presidential policy became much more partisan.

Antiwar members of Congress made several attempts to end the war by cutting off money for U.S. military activity in Southeast Asia. Such legislation only passed after President Nixon announced a peace agreement in 1973, however. It is important to note that Congress has *never* voted to cut off funds to support American armies while they were in the field.

Congress also passed the **War Powers Act,** designed to restrict presidential war-making powers, in 1973. (President Nixon vetoed the bill, but the Watergate affair undermined his support in Congress, which overrode his veto.) The act has four major provisions:

1. In the absence of a congressional declaration of war, the president can commit armed forces to hostilities or to "situations where imminent involvement in hostilities is clearly indicated by the circumstances" *only*:

   - To repel an armed attack on the United States or to forestall the "direct and imminent threat of such an attack."

   - To repel an armed attack against U.S. armed forces outside the United States or to forestall the threat of such attack.

   - To protect and evacuate U.S. citizens and nationals in another country if their lives are threatened. To

2. The president must report promptly to Congress the commitment of forces for such purposes.

3. Involvement of U.S. forces must be no longer than sixty days unless Congress authorizes their continued use by specific legislation.

4. Congress can end a presidential commitment by resolution, an action that does not require the president's signature.

Presidential Noncompliance The War Powers Act raises constitutional questions. A Commander-in-Chief clearly can order U.S. forces to go anywhere. Presumably, Congress cannot constitutionally command troops, yet that is what the act attempts to do by specifying that troops must come home if Congress orders them to do so or if Congress simply fails to endorse the president's decision to commit them. No president—Democrat or Republican—can allow Congress to usurp this presidential authority. Thus, since the passage of the War Powers Act, presidents have continued to undertake military actions on their own initiative (see Table 18.1 in Chapter 18).

The War Powers Act is not only constitutionally questionable but also politically weak. The president almost always enjoys great popular support in the initial stages of an international conflict. At this point, members of Congress are likely to be swept along and to endorse the president's action rather than invoking the War Powers Act and appearing unsupportive of U.S. troops. Only if the fighting goes badly, becomes protracted, or fails to produce decisive results is the War Powers Act likely to be invoked by Congress. Thus the War Powers Act

THINK AGAIN

Should Congress have the authority to call home U.S. troops sent by the president to engage in military actions overseas?

War Powers Act Bill passed in 1973 to limit presidential war-making powers; it restricts when, why, and for how long a president can commit U.S. forces and requires notification of and, in many cases, approval by Congress.

George Bush and "Operation Iraqi Freedom"

At the end of the Gulf War in 1991, the Iraqi regime of Saddam Hussein agreed to destroy all of its chemical and biological weapons and end his efforts to acquire nuclear weapons. United Nations inspectors were to verify Iraqi compliance with these conditions. But Saddam refused to cooperate. U.N. inspectors were hindered and harassed, and finally in 1998 they were ordered out of the country. Over a twelve-year period Iraq violated at least a dozen U.N. resolutions. Following a U.S. military buildup in the region in late 2002, Saddam allowed U.N. inspectors to return but continued to obstruct their work.

President Bush did not believe that the Constitution required him to obtain congressional authorization to use military force against Iraq. But he believed that a congressional resolution would put added political pressure on the United Nations Security Council to authorize military force, and that such a Security Council resolution would compel Saddam to allow open inspections for the presence of weapons of mass destruction. In October 2002 Congress passed a resolution authorizing the president "to use the Armed Forces of the United States as he determines to be necessary and appropriate in order to (1) defend the national security of the United States against the continuing threat posed by Iraq; and (2) enforce all relevant United Nations Security Council resolutions regarding Iraq." The resolution passed overwhelmingly in both the House and Senate.

At different times President Bush stated the purposes of "Operation Iraqi Freedom" as (1) the elimination of Iraq's weapons of mass destruction, (2) a "regime change" in Iraq to end the threat that Saddam posed for his neighbors and to free the Iraqi people from his oppressive rule, and (3) to ensure that Saddam would not harbor or assist terrorist organizations. But President Bush and Secretary of State Colin Powell failed to secure U.N. Security Council approval for military action. Among the permanent members of the Security Council, only the British, with the strong support of Prime Minister Tony Blair, were prepared to offer significant military support for the war against Saddam. Public opinion in America supported military action, but public opinion in Europe opposed it. France and Germany led the diplomatic opposition; Turkey refused to let U.S. troops use its territory to attack Iraq.

On March 19, 2003, after giving Saddam a forty-eight hour warning to leave Iraq, United States and Great Britain launched airstrikes designed to eliminate Saddam in his top command. Baghdad was captured in just 21 days, with precious few Allied casualties.

But Bush's critics at home and abroad complained of the president's "unilateralism"—his willingness to go it alone, without the support of United Nations. Bush's actions clearly alienated our traditional allies—France and Germany—and were strongly opposed by Russia and China and most of the Muslim world. Bush's critics also charged that he misled the Congress and the American people about the existence of weapons of mass destruction in Iraq and the immediacy of any threat to United States. While most Americans believed that Saddam was allied with Al Qaeda, no real evidence of such an alliance emerged.

remains largely a symbolic reminder to presidents that if things go badly, the Congress will desert them.

Politically, it is often important for the president to show the world, and especially enemies of the United States, that he has congressional support for going to war. For this reason, presidents have asked Congress for resolutions in support of using military means to achieve specific goals. President George H. W. Bush asked for and received (by a close vote) a resolution of support to use military force to oust Iraqi forces from Kuwait in 1991. President George W. Bush won strong support for a congressional resolution in 2002 to allow him to use military force to make Saddam Hussein comply with U.N. resolutions. Both presidents claimed that they had the constitutional authority as Commander-in-Chief to use military force even without such resolutions. But politically such resolutions strengthen the president when he chooses to use military force. (See *Up Close*, "George Bush and 'Operation Iraqi Freedom'.")

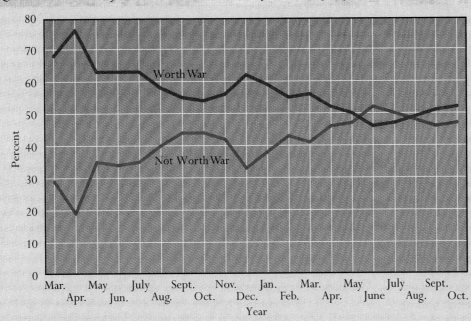

Question: *All in all, do you think the situation in Iraq was worth going to war over, or not?*

Support for the War in Iraq

Finally, critics charge that Bush had "no plan" for the reconstruction of Iraq after the fall of Saddam. Continuing attacks on American troops in Iraq resulted in a continuing stream of casualties. But the capture of Saddam Hussein in December 2003 was widely hailed throughout the world. Evidence of his oppressive rule was found in mass graves and torture chambers. Few people regretted the "regime change" in Baghdad. Overall, the American people initially supported going to war in Iraq (see figure above). But support fell with the prolonged guerilla war that followed U.S. occupation of that country. By the summer of 2004 a majority of Americans thought Iraq was not worth going to war over. The presidential campaign raised support for the war slightly, but Americans were fairly evenly divided.

Presidential Use of Military Force in Domestic Affairs Democracies are generally reluctant to use military force in domestic affairs. Yet the president has the constitutional authority to "take Care that the Laws be faithfully executed" and, as Commander-in-Chief of the armed forces, can send them across the nation as well as across the globe. The Constitution appears to limit presidential use of military forces in domestic affairs to protecting states "against domestic Violence" and only "on Application of the [state] Legislature or the [state] Executive (when the Legislature cannot be convened)" (Article IV, Section 4). Although this provision would seem to require states themselves to request federal troops before they can be sent to quell domestic violence, historically presidents have not waited for state requests to send troops when federal laws, federal court orders, or federal constitutional guarantees are being violated.

Relying on their constitutional duty to "faithfully execute" federal laws and their command over the nation's armed forces, presidents have used military force in do-

Despite a Supreme Court ruling that segregation in education was illegal, many southern states continued to try to keep their schoolhouse doors closed to black students. Here Elizabeth Eckford, a fifteen-year-old resident of Little Rock, Arkansas, is denied entry to Central High School by a member of the National Guard under the orders of Governor Orval Faubus. Not until President Dwight Eisenhower sent the 101st Airborne Division to Little Rock were the high court's desegregation orders enforced.

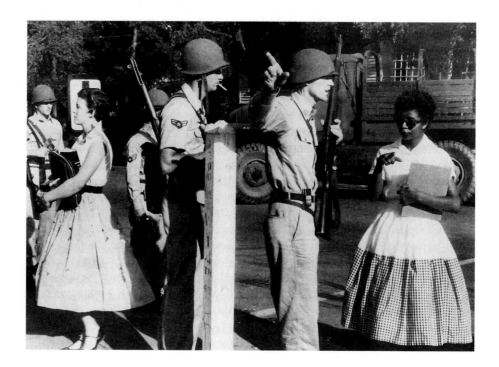

mestic disputes since the earliest days of the Republic. Perhaps the most significant example of a president's use of military force in domestic affairs was Dwight Eisenhower's 1957 dispatch of U.S. troops to Little Rock, Arkansas, to enforce a federal court's desegregation order. In this case, the president acted directly *against* the expressed wishes of the state's governor, Orval Faubus, who had posted state units of the National Guard at the entrance of Central High School to prevent the admission of black students who had been ordered by the federal court. Eisenhower officially called Arkansas's National Guard units into federal service, took personal command of them, and then ordered them to leave the high school. Ike then replaced the Guard units with U.S. federal troops under orders to enforce desegregation. Eisenhower's action marked a turning point in the struggle over school desegregation. The Supreme Court's historic desegregation decision in *Brown v. Board of Education of Topeka* might have been rendered meaningless had not the president chosen to use military force to secure compliance.

The Vice Presidential Waiting Game

Historically, the principal responsibility of the vice president is to be prepared to assume the responsibilities of the president. Eight vice presidents have become president following the death of their predecessor. But vice presidents have not always been well prepared: Harry Truman, who succeeded Franklin Roosevelt while World War II still raged, had never even been informed about the secret atomic bomb project.

Political Selection Process The political process surrounding the initial choice of vice presidential candidates does not necessarily produce the persons best qualified to occupy the White House. It is, indeed, a "crap shoot"[31]; if it produces a person well qualified to be president, it is only by luck. Candidates may *claim* that they select running mates who are highly qualified to take over as president, but this claim is seldom true.

Traditionally, vice presidential candidates have been chosen to give political "balance" to the ticket, to attract voters who might otherwise desert the party or stay home. Democratic presidential candidates sought to give ideological and geographical balance to the ticket. Northern liberal presidential candidates (Adlai Stevenson, John Kennedy) selected southern conservatives (John Sparkman, Estes Kefauver, Lyndon Johnson) as their running mates. Walter Mondale selected New York Congresswoman Geraldine Ferraro in a bold move to exploit the gender gap. Liberal Massachusetts Governor Michael Dukakis returned to the earlier Democratic tradition, choosing to run with conservative Texas Senator Lloyd Bentsen. Bill Clinton sought a different kind of balance: Al Gore's military service in Vietnam and his unimpeachable family life helped offset reservations about Clinton's avoidance of the draft and his past marital troubles. Massachusetts Senator John Kerry was viewed as serious, sober, and reserved; so the choice of the cheerful, enthusiastic, and outgoing North Carolinian John Edwards seemed to balance the ticket in both image and geography.

Republican presidential candidates sought to accommodate either the conservative or moderate wing of their party in their vice presidential selections. Moderate Eisenhower chose conservative Nixon. Conservative Barry Goldwater's selection of William Miller, an unknown conservative member of the House, ensured his loss of moderate support in 1964. In 1980 conservative Reagan first asked his moderate predecessor, Gerald Ford, to join him on the ticket before turning to his moderate primary opponent George Bush, who in 1988 tapped conservative Senator Dan Quayle. In 1996 Bob Dole gambled big in choosing the popular and charismatic—but opinionated and unpredictable—Jack Kemp as his running mate. Far behind in the polls, Dole could not afford a "safe" choice. He needed the former star quarterback of the Buffalo Bills to add excitement to the ticket, even at the risk of seeing Kemp call plays not approved by the coach.

Running behind in the polls prior to the 2000 Democratic convention, Al Gore believed he needed a dramatic choice of a running mate to stir interest in his campaign. Connecticut Senator Joe Lieberman would make history as the first Jew to run on a major party national ticket. Moreover, his moderate voting record balanced Gore's appeal to liberals.

Bush's dream running mate, General Colin Powell, turned down the offer. So Bush turned to Dick Cheney, secretary of defense in his father's administration during the Gulf War. It was hoped that Cheney would add *gravitas* (experience and wisdom) to the ticket. And Cheney's conservative voting record, as a former Congressman from Wyoming, helped reassure conservatives in the Republican Party that Bush was not overlooking them. Cheney's public approval ratings dropped as the Iraq war lengthened. Bush was urged to replace him with the popular former New York City Mayor Rudolph Giuliani. But Bush remained loyal to his family's old adviser.

Vice Presidential Roles   Presidents determine what role their vice presidents will play in their administration. Constitutionally, the only role given the vice president is to preside over the Senate and to vote in case of a tie in that body. Presiding over the Senate is so tiresome that vice presidents perform it only on rare ceremonial occasions, but they have occasionally cast important tie-breaking votes. If the president chooses not to give the vice president much responsibility, the vice presidency becomes what its first occupant, John Adams, described as "the most insignificant office that ever the invention of man contrived or his imagination conceived." One of Franklin Roosevelt's three vice presidents, the salty Texan

Dick Cheney, Presidential Confidant

For many weeks after the "9/11" attack on America, Vice President Dick Cheney remained out of sight "in a secure undisclosed location." A direct attack on the White House was viewed as a distinct possibility, and Cheney's absence from Washington was designed to ensure "continuity of government."

Yet during the crisis—indeed, throughout George W. Bush's presidency—Dick Cheney has been his chief's closest adviser—a prime minister, a *consigliore*, pal, tutor, and big brother to the president. Reportedly, Cheney and Bush confer several times a day, and Cheney's recommendations are seldom ignored. Cheney exercises more influence in the White House than perhaps any previous vice president.

Why does Bush place so much trust in his vice president? Cheney served as secretary of defense for Bush's father, and also served in the Nixon and Ford administrations. He also served as a Republican Congress member from Wyoming and a leader of the conservatives in the House of Representatives. But perhaps his most valued characteristic as vice president is his absence of political ambition. Unlike any other recent vice president. Cheney has no plans to run for president, no personal agenda other than to give his best advice to his president. This elevates the level of trust between the two men.

Dick Cheney has experienced four heart attacks and quadruple bypass heart surgery, and wears a surgically implanted heart pacemaker. Yet he follows a very demanding schedule, including lengthy trips to the Middle East and elsewhere in the world.

Cheney was reported to be a strong supporter of the Iraq invasion, and his public approval ratings tumbled as the war lengthened. But he remained Bush's closest advisor.

John Nance Garner, put it more pithily, saying that the job "ain't worth a bucket of warm spit" (reporters of that era may have substituted "spit" for Garner's actual wording).

The political functions of vice presidents are more significant than their governmental functions. Vice presidents are obliged to support their president and the administration's policies. But sometimes a president will use the vice president to launch strongly partisan political attacks on opponents while the president remains "above" the political squabbles and hence more "presidential." Richard Nixon served as a partisan "attack dog" for Eisenhower, then gave Spiro Agnew this task in his own administration. George Bush was a much more reserved vice president, but Dan Quayle renewed the tradition of the vice president as political "hit man." The attack role allows the vice president also to help cement political support for the president among highly partisan ideologues. Vice presidents are also useful in campaign fund raising. Large contributors expect a personal touch; the president cannot be everywhere at once, so the vice president is frequently a guest at political fund-raising events. Presidents also have traditionally sent their vice presidents to attend funerals of world leaders and placed them at the head of governmental commissions.

Vice presidents themselves strive to play a more significant policy-making role, often as senior presidential adviser and confidant. Recent presidents have encouraged the development of the vice presidency along these lines. Walter Mondale, the first modern vice president to perform this function, had an office in the White House next to the president's, had access to all important meetings and policy decisions, and was invited to lunch privately each week with President Carter. Vice President Al Gore was routinely stationed behind President Clinton during major policy pronouncements. Clinton reportedly gave great weight to Gore's views on the environment, on cost savings in government, and on information technology. Gore also spoke out aggressively in defense of Clinton's policies. Thus the senior advisory role is becoming institutionalized over time (see *People in Politics:* "Dick Cheney, Presidential Confidant").

The Waiting Game Politically ambitious vice presidents are obliged to play a torturous waiting game. They can use their time in office to build a network of contacts that can later be tapped for campaign contributions, workers, and support in their own race for the presidency, should they decide to run. But winning the presidency following retirement of their former boss requires a delicate balance. They must show loyalty to the president in order to win the president's endorsement and also to help ensure that the administration in which they participated is judged a success by voters. At the same time, vice presidents must demonstrate that they have independent leadership qualities and a policy agenda of their own to offer voters. This dilemma becomes more acute as their boss's term nears its end.

Historically, only a few sitting vice presidents have won election to the White House: John Adams (1797), Thomas Jefferson (1801), Martin Van Buren (1837), and George Bush (1988). In addition, four vice presidents won election in their own right after entering the Oval Office as a result of their predecessors' death: Theodore Roosevelt (1901), Calvin Coolidge (1923), Harry Truman (1945), and Lyndon Johnson (1963). Only one nonsitting former vice president has been elected president: Richard Nixon (1968, after losing to Kennedy in 1960). Thus, out of the forty-seven men who served the nation as vice president through 2000, only nine were ever elected to higher office.

SUMMARY NOTES

- The American presidency is potentially the most powerful office in the world. As head of state, the president symbolizes national unity and speaks on behalf of the American people to the world. And as Commander-in-Chief of the armed forces, the president has a powerful voice in national and international affairs. The president also symbolizes government for the American people, reassuring them in times of hardship and crises.

- As head of the government, the president is expected to set forth policy priorities for the nation, to manage the economy, to mobilize political support for the administration's programs in Congress, to manage the giant federal bureaucracy, and to recruit people for policy-making positions in both the executive and judicial branches of government.

- Popular expectations of presidential leadership far exceed the formal constitutional powers of the president: chief administrator, chief legislator, chief diplomat, Commander-in-Chief, and chief of state. The vague reference in the Constitution to "executive Power" has been used by

- presidents to justify actions beyond those specified elsewhere in the Constitution or in laws of Congress.

- It is the president's vast political resources that provide the true power base of the presidency. These include the president's reputation for power, personal popularity with the public, access to the media, and party leadership position.

- Presidential popularity and power are usually highest at the beginning of the term of office. Presidents are more likely to be successful in Congress during this honeymoon period. Presidents' popularity also rises during crises, especially during international threats and military actions. But prolonged indecision and stalemate erode popular support, as do scandals and economic recessions.

- As chief executive, the president oversees the huge federal bureaucracy. Presidential control of the executive branch is exercised through executive orders, appointments and removals, and budgetary recommendations to Congress. But the president's control of the executive branch is heavily circumscribed by Congress, which establishes executive departments and agencies, regulates their activities by law, and determines their budgets each year.

- Presidents are expected not only to initiate programs and policies but also to shepherd them through Congress. Presidential success scores in Congress indicate that presidents are more successful early in their term of office. Presidents who face a Congress controlled by the opposition party are far less successful in winning approval for their programs than presidents whose party holds a majority.

- The veto is the president's most powerful weapon in dealing with Congress. The president needs to hold the loyalty of only one more than one-third of either the House or the Senate to sustain a veto. Few vetoes are overridden. The threat of a veto enables the president to bargain in Congress for more acceptable legislation.

- During the long years of the Cold War, the president of the United States was the leader of the "free world." In the post—Cold War world, the president is still the leader of the world's most powerful democracy and is expected to exercise global leadership on behalf of a stable world order.

- Presidents have come to dominate foreign policy through treaty making, executive agreements, control of intelligence activities, and international recognition of their role as head of state. Above all, presidents have used their power as Commander-in-Chief of the armed forces to decide when to make war and when to seek peace.

- The global power of presidents derives primarily from this presidential role as Commander-in-Chief. Constitutionally, war-making power is divided between Congress and the president, but historically, it has been the president who has ordered U.S. military forces into action. In the War Powers Act, Congress tried to reassert its war-making power after the Vietnam War, but the act has failed to restrain presidents. Presidents have also used the armed forces in domestic affairs to "take Care that the Laws be faithfully executed."

- The principal responsibility of the vice president is to be prepared to assume the responsibilities of the president. However, the selection of the vice president is dominated more by political concerns than by consideration of presidential qualifications. Aside from officially presiding over the U.S. Senate, vice presidents perform whatever roles are assigned them by the president.

KEY TERMS

impeachment   378
Watergate   381
executive privilege   382
impoundment   383
deferrals   383
rescissions   383

White House press corps   386
executive order   391
cabinet   394
National Security Council   (NSC)   395

honeymoon period   398
gridlock   399
veto   399
pocket veto   400
override   400
line-item veto   401

diplomatic recognition   402
executive agreement   402
covert action   405
War Powers Act   407

SUGGESTED READINGS

Barber, James David. *The Presidential Character; Predicting Performance in the White House.* 4th ed. Upper Saddle River, N.J.: Prentice Hall, 1992. Barber's original thesis that a president's performance in office is largely a function of active/passive and positive/negative character; includes classifications of twentieth-century presidents through Reagan.

Brace, Paul, and Barbara Hinckley. *Follow the Leader.* New York: Basic Books, 1992. The most marked increases in public approval of the president come on the heels of international crises, especially when the president responds with bold and decisive action.

Brody, Richard A. *Assessing Presidents: The Media, Elite Opinion, and Public Support.* Stanford, Calif.: Stanford University Press, 1991. Develops the thesis that media and elite interpretations of presidential actions shape public evaluations of the president; includes analysis of the president's "honeymoon," "rally round the president" events, and the rise and fall of public approval ratings.

DiClerico, Robert E. *The American President.* 5th ed. Upper Saddle River, N.J.: Prentice Hall, 2000. Comprehensive text on the presidency, focusing on selection, power, accountability, decision making, personality, and leadership.

Edwards, George C. and Stephen J. Wayne. *Presidential Leadership.* 6th ed. Belmont, Calif.: Wadsworth, 2003. Comprehensive text covering nomination and election of the president, relations with the public, the media, the bureaucracy, Congress and the courts.

Lowi, Theodore. *The Personal President.* Ithaca, N.Y.: Cornell University Press, 1987. An examination of the presidency from the perspective of the public and its reliance on the president for reassurance in crises.

Milkus, Stanley, and Michael Nelson. *The American Presidency: Origins and Development, 1776–2002* 4th ed. Washington, D.C.: CQ Press, 2003. A comprehensive history of the presidency which argues that the institution is best understood by examining its development over time, describes the significant presidential actions in the early days of the Republic that shaped the office, as well as the modern era in which the president has replaced Congress and the political parties as the leading instrument of popular rule.

Neustadt, Richard E. *Presidential Power.* New York: Wiley, 1960. The classic argument that the president's power is the power to persuade, that the formal constitutional powers of the presidency provide only a framework for the president's use of persuasion, public prestige, reputation for power, and other personal attributes to exercise real power.

Pika, Joseph A., John Maltese, and Norman C. Thomas. *The Politics of the Presidency.* 6th ed. Washington, D.C.: CQ Press, 2003. An overview of the institution of the presidency.

Schultz, Jeffrey D. *Presidential Scandals.* Washington, D.C.: CQ Press, 1999. An historical survey of scandals in presidential administrations, from George Washington to Bill Clinton.

Van Tassel, Emily Field, and Paul Finkelman. *Impeachable Offenses.* Washington, D.C.: CQ Press, 1999. A documentary history of impeachment from 1787 to the present.

MAKE IT REAL

WHO'S GOT THE POWER?

Although presidents share with Congress the responsibility for making foreign policy, in practice a president has the primary responsibility to shape foreign policy. Presidents can bargain, negotiate, persuade, apply economic pressures, threaten, or even use armed force. In addition, the agencies that carry out foreign policy report directly or indirectly to the president. However, Congress can block the president's foreign policy and undermine the chief executive's decisions. In this simulation, as the president of the United States, you are expected to provide strong leadership in foreign policy matters. This will entail choosing policies and responding to international events. You will make decisions regarding three policies and respond to one international crisis. Your success or failure depends on which issues you choose to address and how well you can gain the support of the U.S. Senate.

PRESIDENTIAL GREATNESS: HOW DO WE JUDGE THEM?

Most Americans judge contemporary presidents against the standard of the Mount Rushmore presidents. We want presidents who can summon us to live up to our shared ideals about liberty and freedom and who will pay close attention to our immediate needs. In sum, we use varying and sometimes unfair standards when we judge presidents. The opinions of historians differ from what the general public believes. They rate presidents as outstanding, great, or near great on the basis of whether they brought about desirable changes and acted wisely to guide the nation through turbulent times. But why should historians have all the fun? In this simulation, we ask you to rate the last nine presidents—from Dwight D. Eisenhower to William J. Clinton. Do some research first, to refresh your memory, then see how your opinions rate against some of the most respected presidential historians of our time.

12

THE BUREAUCRACY:
BUREAUCRATIC POLITICS

THINK
ABOUT POLITICS

1 Do bureaucrats in Washington have too much power?
Yes ● No ●

2 Should the federal bureaucracy be managed by nonpartisan professionals rather than people politically loyal to the president?
Yes ● No ●

3 Should the federal bureaucracy at all levels reflect the gender and minority ratios of the total civilian work force?
Yes ● No ●

4 Do you believe the bureaucrats in Washington waste a lot of the money we pay in taxes?
Yes ● No ●

5 Do you believe the federal government is spending more money but delivering less service?
Yes ● No ●

6 Do you believe that the overall costs of federal regulatory activity are justified by the benefits?
Yes ● No ●

7 Do you believe bureaucratic regulations of all kinds are hurting America's competitiveness in the global economy?
Yes ● No ●

Power in Washington is not only exercised by the president, Congress, and courts, but also by 2.8 million federal bureaucrats—neither elected nor accountable to ordinary citizens—who determine in large measure who gets what in America.

Bureaucratic Power

Political conflict does not end after a law has been passed by Congress and signed by the president. The arena for conflict merely shifts from Capitol Hill and the White House to the **bureaucracy**—to the myriad departments, agencies, and bureaus of the federal executive branch that implement the law. Despite the popular impression that policy is decided by the president and Congress and merely implemented by the federal bureaucracy, in fact policy is also made by the bureaucracy. Indeed, it is often remarked that "implementation is the continuation of policy making by other means." The Washington bureaucracy is a major base of power in the American system of government—independent of Congress, the president, the courts, and the people. Indeed, controlling the bureaucracy has become a major challenge of democratic government.

The Nature of Bureaucracy "Bureaucracy" has become a negative term equated with red tape,[1] paper shuffling, duplication of effort, waste and inefficiency, impersonality, senseless regulations, and unresponsiveness to the needs of "real" people. But bureaucracy is really a form of social organization found not only in governments but also in corporations, armies, schools, and many other societal institutions. The German sociologist Max Weber described bureaucracy as a "rational" way for society to organize itself that has the following characteristics: a **chain of command** (hierarchical structure of authority in which command flows downward); a **division of labor** (work divided among many specialized workers in an effort to improve productivity); and **impersonality** (all persons within the bureaucracy treated on "merit" principles, and all "clients" served by the bureaucracy treated equally according to rules; all activities undertaken according to rules; records maintained to assure rules are followed).[2] Thus, according to Weber's definition, General Motors and IBM, the U.S. Marine Corps, the U.S. Department of Education, and all other institutions organized according to these principles are "bureaucracies."

The Growth of Bureaucratic Power Bureaucratic power has grown with advances in technology and increases in the size and complexity of society. There is a variety of explanation for this growth of power.

417

THINK AGAIN

Do bureaucrats in
Washington have too much
power?

bureaucracy Departments,
agencies, bureaus, and offices
that perform the functions of
government.

chain of command
Hierarchical structure of
authority in which command
flows downward; typical of a
bureaucracy.

division of labor Division of
work among many
specialized workers in a
bureaucracy.

impersonality Treatment of
all persons within a
bureaucracy on the basis of
"merit" and of all "clients"
served by the bureaucracy
equally according to rules.

implementation
Development by the federal
bureaucracy of procedures
and activities to carry out
policies legislated by
Congress; it includes
regulation as well as
adjudication.

1. *Needed Expertise and Technological Advances* Congress and the president do not have the time, energy, or expertise to handle the details of policy making. A related explanation is that the increasing complexity and sophistication of technology require technical experts ("technocrats") to actually carry out the intent of Congress and the president. Neither the president nor the 535 members of Congress can look after the myriad details involved in environmental protection, occupational safety, air traffic control, or thousands of other responsibilities of government. So the president and Congress create bureaucracies, appropriate money for them, and authorize them to draw up detailed rules, regulations, and "guidelines" that actually govern the nation. Bureaucratic agencies receive only vague and general directions from the president and Congress. Actual governance is in the hands of the Environmental Protection Agency, the Occupational Safety and Health Administration, the Federal Aviation Administration, and hundreds of similar agencies (see Figure 12.1).

2. *Symbolic Politics* But there are also political explanations for the growth of bureaucratic power. Congress and the president often deliberately pass vague and ambiguous laws. These laws allow elected officials to show symbolically their concerns for environmental protection, occupational safety, and so on, yet avoid the controversies surrounding actual application of those lofty principles. Bureaucracies must then give practical meaning to these symbolic measures by developing specific rules and regulations. If the rules and regulations prove unpopular, Congress and the president can blame the bureaucrats and pretend that these unpopular decisions are a product of an "ungovernable" Washington bureaucracy (see *What Do You Think?* "How Would You Rate These Federal Agencies?")

3. *Bureaucratic Explanation* There is also a bureaucratic explanation of the growth in the size and influence of government agencies. Bureaucracy has become its own source of power. Bureaucrats have a personal stake in expanding the size of their own agencies and budgets and adding to their own regulatory authority. They can mobilize their "client" groups (interest groups that directly benefit from the agency's programs, such as environmental groups on behalf of the Environmental Protection Agency, farm groups for the Department of Agriculture, the National Education Association for the Department of Education) in support of larger budgets and expanded authority.

4. *Popular Demands* Finally, it has been argued that "big government" is really an expression of democratic sentiments. People want to use the power of government to improve their lives—to regulate and develop the economy, to guarantee civil rights, to develop their communities, and so on. Conservative opponents of the government are really expressing their disdain for popular demands.[3]

Bureaucratic Power: Implementation Bureaucracies are not *constitutionally* empowered to decide policy questions. But they do so, nevertheless, as they perform their tasks of implementation, regulation, and adjudication.

Implementation is the development of procedures and activities to carry out policies legislated by Congress. It may involve creating new agencies or bureaus or assigning new responsibilities to old agencies. It often requires bureaucracies to translate laws into operational rules and regulations and usually to allocate resources—money, personnel, offices, supplies—to the new function. All of these

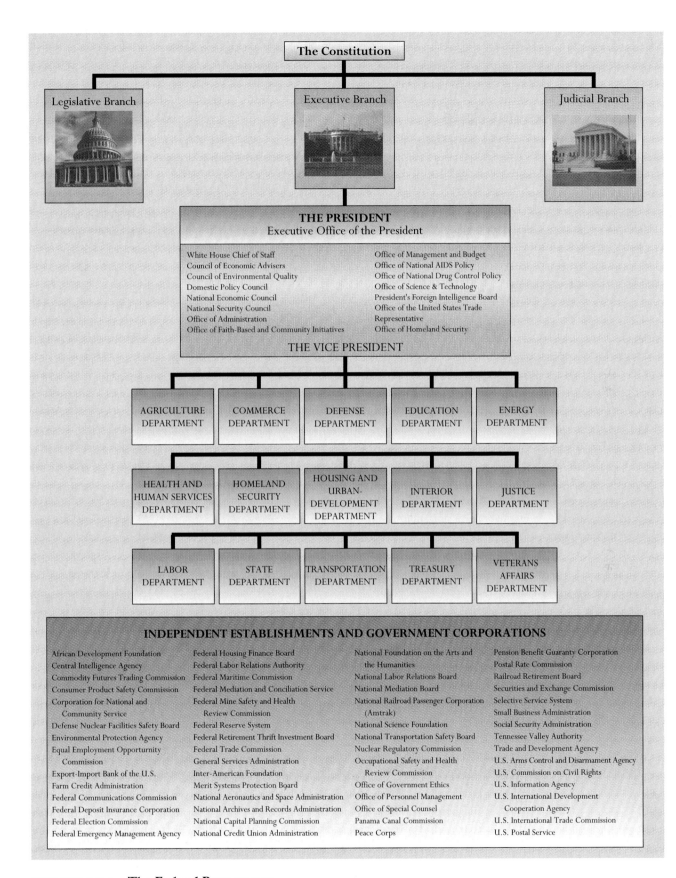

The Constitution

Legislative Branch

Executive Branch

Judicial Branch

THE PRESIDENT
Executive Office of the President

White House Chief of Staff
Council of Economic Advisers
Council of Environmental Quality
Domestic Policy Council
National Economic Council
National Security Council
Office of Administration
Office of Faith-Based and Community Initiatives

Office of Management and Budget
Office of National AIDS Policy
Office of National Drug Control Policy
Office of Science & Technology
President's Foreign Intelligence Board
Office of the United States Trade
Representative
Office of Homeland Security

THE VICE PRESIDENT

AGRICULTURE DEPARTMENT

COMMERCE DEPARTMENT

DEFENSE DEPARTMENT

EDUCATION DEPARTMENT

ENERGY DEPARTMENT

HEALTH AND HUMAN SERVICES DEPARTMENT

HOMELAND SECURITY DEPARTMENT

HOUSING AND URBAN-DEVELOPMENT DEPARTMENT

INTERIOR DEPARTMENT

JUSTICE DEPARTMENT

LABOR DEPARTMENT

STATE DEPARTMENT

TRANSPORTATION DEPARTMENT

TREASURY DEPARTMENT

VETERANS AFFAIRS DEPARTMENT

INDEPENDENT ESTABLISHMENTS AND GOVERNMENT CORPORATIONS

African Development Foundation
Central Intelligence Agency
Commodity Futures Trading Commission
Consumer Product Safety Commission
Corporation for National and
     Community Service
Defense Nuclear Facilities Safety Board
Environmental Protection Agency
Equal Employment Opporturnity
     Commission
Export-Import Bank of the U.S.
Farm Credit Administration
Federal Communications Commission
Federal Deposit Insurance Corporation
Federal Election Commission
Federal Emergency Management Agency

Federal Housing Finance Board
Federal Labor Relations Authority
Federal Maritime Commission
Federal Mediation and Conciliation Service
Federal Mine Safety and Health
     Review Commission
Federal Reserve System
Federal Retirement Thrift Investment Board
Federal Trade Commission
General Services Administration
Inter-American Foundation
Merit Systems Protection Board
National Aeronautics and Space Administration
National Archives and Records Administration
National Capital Planning Commission
National Credit Union Administration

National Foundation on the Arts and
     the Humanities
National Labor Relations Board
National Mediation Board
National Railroad Passenger Corporation
     (Amtrak)
National Science Foundation
National Transportation Safety Board
Nuclear Regulatory Commission
Occupational Safety and Health
     Review Commission
Office of Government Ethics
Office of Personnel Management
Office of Special Counsel
Panama Canal Commission
Peace Corps

Pension Benefit Guaranty Corporation
Postal Rate Commission
Railroad Retirement Board
Securities and Exchange Commission
Selective Service System
Small Business Administration
Social Security Administration
Tennessee Valley Authority
Trade and Development Agency
U.S. Arms Control and Disarmament Agency
U.S. Commission on Civil Rights
U.S. Information Agency
U.S. International Development
     Cooperation Agency
U.S. International Trade Commission
U.S. Postal Service

FIGURE 12.1 **The Federal Bureaucracy**

Although the president has constitutional authority over the operation of the executive branch, Congress creates departments and agencies and appropriates their funds, and Senate approval is needed for presidential appointees to head departments. The new Department of Homeland Security will be the 15th department in the executive branch.

How Would You Rate These Federal Agencies?

Many federal agencies have come under close scrutiny following the devastating terrorist attacks of 9/11, deadly anthrax letters, and economic recession, the threat of a SARS epidemic, and a space shuttle explosion. A poll near the end of 2003 asked Americans to rate some of the key government agencies charged with protecting the American public. While the poll did not ask about all government agencies, it does give a sense of how the public views some of the more prominent of them.

Overall, Americans rate individual agencies fairly highly. Even though the opinion polls regularly report that Americans believe "the federal government in Washington" has "too much power" (60 percent), individual agencies are given reasonably good marks.

Q. How would you rate the job being done by _____ *? Would you say it is doing an excellent, good, only fair, or poor job?*

Percent saying "excellent" or "good"

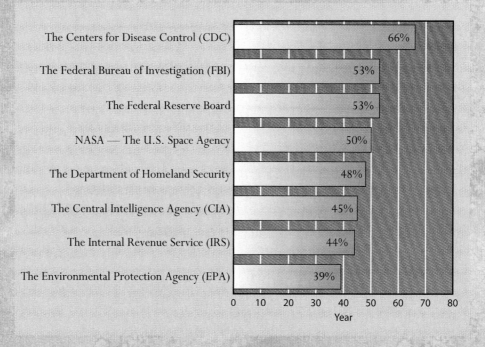

Agency	Percent
The Centers for Disease Control (CDC)	66%
The Federal Bureau of Investigation (FBI)	53%
The Federal Reserve Board	53%
NASA — The U.S. Space Agency	50%
The Department of Homeland Security	48%
The Central Intelligence Agency (CIA)	45%
The Internal Revenue Service (IRS)	44%
The Environmental Protection Agency (EPA)	39%

Year

Source: Gallup poll, September 30, 2003. Copyright © 1996–2004 by The Gallup Organization.

tasks involve decisions by bureaucrats, decisions that drive how the law will actually affect society. In some cases, bureaucrats delay the development of regulations based on a new law, assign enforcement responsibility to existing offices with other higher priority tasks, and allocate few people with limited resources to the task. In other cases, bureaucrats act forcefully in making new regulations, insist on strict enforcement, assign responsibilities to newly created aggressive offices with no other assignments, and allocate a great deal of staff time and agency resources to the task. Interested groups have a strong stake in these decisions, and they actively seek to influence the bureaucracy.

Bureaucratic Power: Regulation Regulation involves the development of formal rules for implementing legislation. The federal bureaucracy publishes about 60,000 pages of rules in the *Federal Register* each year. The Environmental Protection Agency (EPA) is especially active in developing regulations governing the handling of virtually every substance in the air, water, or ground. The rule-making process for federal agencies is prescribed by an Administrative Procedures Act, first passed in 1946 and amended many times. Generally, agencies must:

1. Announce in the *Federal Register* that a new regulation is being considered.
2. Hold hearings to allow interested groups to present evidence and arguments regarding the proposed regulation.
3. Conduct research on the proposed regulation's economic and environmental impacts.
4. Solicit "public comments" (usually the arguments of interest groups).
5. Consult with higher officials, including the Office of Management and Budget.
6. Publish the new regulation in the *Federal Register*.

Regulatory battles are important because formal regulations that appear in the *Federal Register* have the effect of law. Congress can amend or repeal a regulation only by passing new legislation and obtaining the president's signature. Controversial bureaucratic regulations often remain in place because Congress is slow to act, because key committee members block corrective legislation, or because the president refuses to sign bills overturning the regulation.

Bureaucratic Power: Adjudication Adjudication involves bureaucratic decisions about individual cases. Rule making resembles the legislative process, and adjudication resembles the judicial process. In adjudication, bureaucrats decide whether a person or firm is failing to comply with laws or regulations and, if so, what penalties or corrective actions are to be applied. Regulatory agencies and commissions—for example, the National Labor Relations Board, the Federal Communications Commission, the Equal Employment Opportunity Commission, the Federal Trade Commission, the Securities and Exchange Commission—are heavily engaged in adjudication. Their elaborate procedures and body of previous decisions closely resemble the court system. Losers may appeal to the federal courts, but the record of agency success in the federal courts discourages many appeals.

Bureaucratic Power: Administrative Discretion Much of the work of bureaucrats is administrative routine—issuing Social Security checks, printing forms, delivering the mail. Routines are repetitive tasks performed according to established rules and procedures. Yet bureaucrats almost always have some discretion in performing even the most routine tasks. Discretion is greatest when cases do not exactly fit established rules, or when more than one rule might be applied to the same case, resulting in different outcomes. The Internal Revenue Service administers the hundreds of thousands of rules developed to implement the U.S. Tax Code, but each IRS auditing agent has wide discretion in deciding which rules to apply to a taxpayer's income, deductions, business expenses, and so on. Indeed, identical tax information submitted to different IRS offices almost always results in different estimates of tax liability. But even in more routine tasks, from processing Medicare applications to forwarding mail, individual bureaucrats can be friendly and helpful or hostile and obstructive.[4]

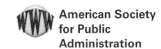

American Society for Public Administration
Organization of scholars and practitioners in public administration. Site includes information on careers, job listings, etc. *www.apsanet.org*

regulation Development by the federal bureaucracy of formal rules for implementing legislation.

adjudication Decision making by the federal bureaucracy as to whether or not an individual or organization has complied with or violated government laws and/or regulation.

An Internal Revenue Service processing center. The IRS administers the nation's complex tax code, leaving wide discretion to its agents to determine how to apply the rules to individual taxpayers.

Bureaucratic Power and Budget Maximization Bureaucrats generally believe strongly in the value of their programs and the importance of their tasks. Senior military officers and civilian officials of the Department of Defense believe in the importance of a strong national defense, and top officials in the Social Security Administration are committed to maintaining the integrity of the retirement system and serving the nation's senior citizens. Beyond these public-spirited motives, bureaucrats, like everyone else, seek higher pay, greater job security, and added power and prestige for themselves.

These public and private motives converge to inspire bureaucrats to seek to expand the powers, functions, and budgets of their departments and agencies. Rarely do bureaucrats request a reduction in authority, the elimination of a program, or a decrease in their agency's budget. Rather, over time, **budget maximization**—expanding the agency's budget, staff, and authority as much as possible—becomes a driving force in government bureaucracies. This is especially true of discretionary funds. **Discretionary funds** are those that bureaucrats have flexibility in deciding how to spend, rather than money committed by law to specific purposes.[5] Thus, bureaucracies continually strive to add new functions, acquire more authority and responsibility, and increase their budgets and personnel. Bureaucratic expansion is just one of the reasons that government grows over time (see *Up Close:* "Why Government Grows, and Grows, and Grows").

The Federal Bureaucracy

The federal bureaucracy—officially the executive branch of the U.S. government—consists of about 2.7 million civilian employees (plus 1.4 million persons in the armed forces) organized into 15 cabinet departments, more than 60 independent agencies, and a large Executive Office of the President (see Figure 12.2). The expenditures of *all* governments in the United States—the federal government, the 50 state governments, and some 86,000 local governments—now amount

budget maximization
Bureaucrats' tendencies to expand their agencies' budgets, staff, and authority.

discretionary funds
Budgeted funds not earmarked for specific purposes but available to be spent in accordance with the best judgment of a bureaucrat.

Why Government Grows, and Grows, and Grows

What accounts for the growth of government activity? Many theories offer explanations. The theories listed below are not mutually exclusive; indeed, probably all of the forces they identify contribute to government growth.

Societal Demands: Wagner's Law

In the nineteenth century, economist Adolf Wagner proposed a "law of increasing state activity"—the notion that government activity increased faster than economic output in all developing societies.[*] He attributed this growth to a variety of factors, including increasing demands in a developed society for social services such as education, welfare, and public health.

Wars and Crises

Another theory is based on the fact that during periods of social upheaval, especially war or economic turmoil, people willingly accept higher-than-normal levels of taxation. During these periods, then, government grows. But after the stressful period is over, government size does not return to its previous levels. Instead, governments substitute new expenditures for those accepted during the crisis. Thus expenditures increase during crisis periods but never return to the precrisis levels after the crisis passes.

Fiscal "Illusion"

This explanation assumes that government officials can increase revenues, and then expenditures, by altering tax-collecting devices so that voters do not realize how much money government is actually taking from them. The federal income tax grew very rapidly *after* the introduction of federal tax "withholding" in 1943. Since that time, wage earners have not received all of the money they earn and have come to perceive the missing portion as "belonging" to the federal government. This illusion is also aided by government-mandated withholding of Social Security taxes.

Bureaucratic Expansionism

Bureaucrats and legislators have a personal interest in expanding government budgets. Bureaucrats want to increase the amount of money they can spend and the number of employees under their supervision. Legislators want to increase the resources over which they have jurisdiction and to enhance the government benefits bestowed on their constituents.

Interest-Group Pressures

This explanation assumes that interest groups want to increase the size of government programs that benefit their own members. Benefits are visible and concentrated. Costs are invisible in many cases or are of less significance to those who will clearly benefit. As each interest group is motivated to act on behalf of its own members, largely ignoring the associated costs, government grows.

Politicians Seeking Votes

Politicians in competitive elections frequently promise their constituents visible and exaggerated benefits while hiding or minimizing the costs to other voters. When these promises become policies, government grows.

Cumulative Unintended Consequences

The current size of the government is the result of previous efforts to solve earlier problems. Once established, bureaucracies and programs live on, even when their original tasks no longer need doing. Over the years, the effects of all these decisions accumulate beyond what anyone originally intended.

Incrementalism

Governments expand because decision making is incremental. Presidents and members of Congress focus on a narrow range of new policy proposals and *increases* or *decreases* in the budget. Old programs are never reviewed as a whole every year. The value of existing programs is seldom reconsidered.

---

[*]Adolf Wagner's major work is *Grundlegung der Politischen Ökonomie* (Leipzig, 1883). This work is discussed at length in Alan T. Peacock and Jack Wiseman, *The Growth of Public Expenditures in the United Kingdom* (Princeton, N.J.: Princeton University Press, 1961).

FIGURE 12.2 Corridors of Power in the Bureaucracy

This map shows the Capitol, the White House, and the major departments of the federal bureaucracy in Washington, D.C.

to more than $3.0 *trillion* (roughly 30 percent of the U.S. gross domestic product, or GDP of $10.4 *trillion*). About two-thirds of this—about $2.2 *trillion* a year (about 20 percent of GDP)—is spent by the *federal* government. Government spending in the United States remains relatively modest compared to that of many nations (see *Compared to What?* "The Size of Government in Other Nations" on the facing page).

The Size of Government in Other Nations

How does the size of the public sector in the United States compare with the size of the public sector in other economically advanced, democratic countries? There is a great deal of variation in the size of government across countries. Government spending accounts for nearly two-thirds of the total output in Sweden. Government spending exceeds one-half of the total output of Denmark, Netherlands, Finland, Germany, Italy, Austria, Belgium, and France. The high level of government spending in these countries primarily reflects greater public-sector involvement in the provision of housing, health care, retirement insurance, and aid to the unemployed. The sizes of the public sectors in Australia, Japan, and Switzerland are only slightly higher than that of United States.

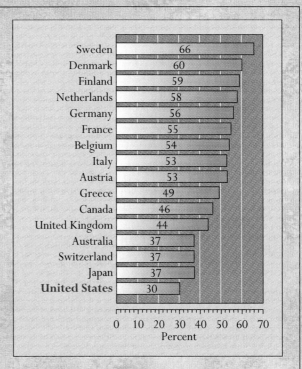

Governmental Percentage of Gross Domestic Product

Source: Joint Economic Committee of Congress, "The Size and Function of Government" (Washington, D.C.: 1998). United States updated to 2002.

Cabinet Departments Cabinet departments employ about 60 percent of all federal workers (see Table 12.1). Each department is headed by a secretary (with the exception of the Justice Department, which is headed by the attorney general) who is appointed by the president and must be confirmed by the Senate. Each department is hierarchically organized; each has its own organization chart. Although organizational patterns differ among departments, the chart for the Department of Health and Human Services shown in Figure 12.3 is typical.

Cabinet status confers great legitimacy on a governmental function and prestige on the secretary, thus strengthening that individual's voice in the government. Therefore the elevation of an executive department to cabinet level often reflects political considerations as much as or more than national needs. Strong pressures from "client" interest groups (groups principally served by the department), as well as presidential and congressional desires to pose as defenders and promoters of particular interests, account for the establishment of all of the newer departments. President Woodrow Wilson appealed to the labor movement in 1913 when he separated out a Department of Labor from the earlier business-dominated Department of Commerce and Labor. In 1965 President Lyndon Johnson created the Department of Housing and Urban Development to demonstrate his concern for urban problems. Seeking support from teachers and educational administrators,

Fed World
Run by the U.S. Commerce Department, this site contains information about federal/state–local agency links, government jobs, IRS forms, Supreme Court decisions, and the vast array of governmental services. *www.fedworld.gov*

TABLE 12.1 Cabinet Departments and Functions

Department and Date Created	Function
State (1789)	Advises the president on the formation and execution of foreign policy; negotiates treaties and agreements with foreign nations; represents the United States in the United Nations and in the more than fifty major international organizations and maintains U.S. embassies abroad; issues U.S. passports and, in foreign countries, visas to the United States.
Treasury (1789)	Serves as financial agent for the U.S. government; issues all payments of the U.S. government according to law; manages the debt of the U.S. government by issuing and recovering bonds and paying their interest; collects taxes owed to the U.S. government; collects taxes and enforces laws on alcohol, tobacco, and firearms and on customs duties; manufactures coins and currency.
Defense (1947: formerly the War Department, created in 1789, and the Navy Department, created in 1798)	Provides the military forces needed to deter war and protect the national security interest; includes the Departments of the Army, Navy, and Air Force.
Justice (1789)	Enforces all federal laws, including consumer protection, antitrust, civil rights, drug, and immigration and naturalization; maintains federal prisons.
Interior (1849)	Has responsibility for public lands and natural resources, for American Indian reservations, and for people who live in island territories under U.S. administration; preserves national parks and historical sites.
Agriculture (1889)	Works to improve and maintain farm income and to develop and expand markets abroad for agricultural products; safeguards standards of quality in the food supply through inspection and grading services; administers rural development, credit, and conservation programs; administers food stamp program.
Commerce (1913)	Encourages the nation's international trade, economic growth, and technological advancement; conducts the census; provides social and economic statistics and analyses for business and government; maintains the merchant marine; grants patents and registers trademarks.
Labor (1913)	Oversees working conditions; administers federal labor laws; protects workers' pension rights; sponsors job training programs; keeps track of changes in employment, price, and other national economic indicators.
Health and Human Services (1953 as Health, Education, and Welfare; reorganized with Education as a separate department in 1979)	Administers to social welfare programs for the elderly, children, and youths; protects the health of the nation against impure and unsafe foods, drugs, and cosmetics; operates the Centers for Disease Control; funds the Medicare and Medicaid programs.
Housing and Urban Development (1965)	Is responsible for programs concerned with housing needs, fair housing opportunities, and the improvement and development of the nation's communities; administers mortgage insurance programs, rental subsidy programs, and neighborhood rehabilitation and preservation programs.
Transportation (1966)	Is responsible for the nation's highway planning, development, and construction; also urban mass transit, railroads, aviation, and the safety of waterways, ports, highways, and oil and gas pipelines.
Energy (1977)	Is responsible for the research, development, and demonstration of energy technology; marketing of federal electric power; energy conservation; the nuclear weapons program; regulation of energy production and use; and collection and analysis of energy data.
Education (1979)	Administers and coordinates most federal assistance to education.
Veterans Affairs (1989)	Operates programs to benefit veterans and members of their families.
Homeland Security (2002)	Prevent terrorist attacks within the United States, reduce the vulnerability of the nation to terrorism, and minimize the damage and assist in recovery from terrorist attacks.

Source: The United States Government Manual 2002/03 (Washington, D.C.: Government Printing Office, 2003).

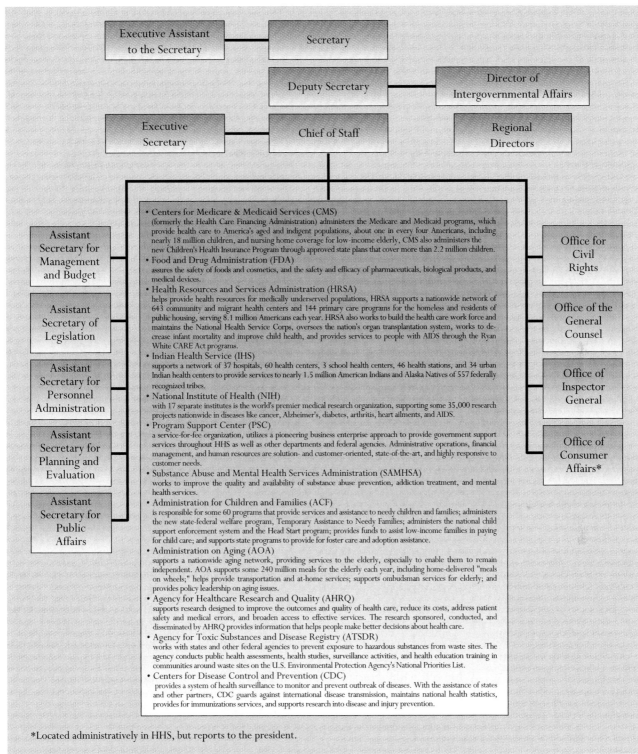

*Located administratively in HHS, but reports to the president.

FIGURE 12.3 Department of Health and Human Services

The internal structures of various cabinet-level departments differ somewhat in specifics, but this chart of the Department of Health and Human Services (HHS) is typical of most. It includes secretary, deputy secretary, assistant secretaries, and multiple "administrations" (subdepartments), agencies, offices, and services. The Social Security Administration became an independent agency in 1995.

The Department of Homeland Security

Presidents often create new bureaucratic organizations to symbolize their commitment to a policy direction. On October 8, 2001, less than one month after the "9/11" terrorist attack on America, President George W. Bush issued an executive order establishing the Office of Homeland Security and naming

HOMELAND SECURITY ADVISORY SYSTEM

SEVERE
SEVERE RISK OF TERRORIST ATTACKS

HIGH
HIGH RISK OF TERRORIST ATTACKS

ELEVATED
SIGNIFICANT RISK OF TERRORIST ATTACKS

GUARDED
GENERAL RISK OF TERRORIST ATTACKS

LOW
LOW RISK OF TERRORIST ATTACKS

Director Tom Ridge speaks to the newly created Department of Homeland Security.

President Jimmy Carter created a separate Department of Education in 1979 and changed the name of the former Department of Health, Education, and Welfare to the Department of Health and Human Services (perhaps finding the phrase "human services" more politically acceptable than "welfare"). President Ronald Reagan tried, and failed, to "streamline" government by abolishing the Department of Education. But Reagan himself added a cabinet post, elevating the Veterans Administration to the Department of Veterans Affairs in an attempt to ingratiate himself with veterans. President George W. Bush created a new Department of Homeland Security in 2002 in response to the "9/11" terrorist attack on America and the threat of future attacks directly on the soil of the United States (see *Up Close: "The Department of Homeland Security"*).

Cabinet Department Functions The relative power and prestige of each cabinet-level department is a product not only of its size and budget but also of the importance of its function. By custom, the "pecking order" of departments—and therefore the prestige ranking of their secretaries—is determined by their years of origin. Thus the Departments of State, Treasury, Defense (War), and Justice, created by the First Congress in 1789, head the protocol list of departments. Overall, the duties of the fifteen cabinet-level departments of the executive branch

Pennsylvania's popular governor Tom Ridge as its director with "cabinet-level" status. The announced mission of the new office: "to develop a comprehensive national strategy to strengthen protection against terrorist threats or attacks on the United States . . . and to coordinate the executive branch's efforts to detect, prepare for, prevent, protect against, respond to, and recover from terrorist attacks within the United States."

But Ridge was given very little direct authority to carry out these monumental tasks. Working out of a small White House office, Ridge is expected to coordinate the counterterrorism activities of 46 separate bureaucracies, including the Federal Bureau of Investigation, the Central Intelligence Agency, the Department of Defense, the State Department, the Immigration and Naturalization Service, the Federal Aviation Administration, the Department of Transportation, and the Federal Emergency Management Administration, as well as many state and local government agencies. The authority to "coordinate" did *not* give Ridge or his office direct control over any government department or agency.

In 2002, in response to growing concerns that he had not done enough to reassure the American public of the federal government's commitment to pro-tect them from terrorism, President George W. Bush proposed a new Department of Homeland Security. Its mission is to prevent terrorist attacks within the United States, to reduce vulnerability of the United States to terrorism, and to minimize damage and assist recovery when and if terrorist attacks occur within the country.

The new department does more than just "coordinate" other federal agencies. In a major reorganization, the Department of Homeland Security has been given direct responsibility over agencies concerned with border protection, transportation security, and emergency preparedness, including the U.S. Border Patrol, the U.S. Customs Service, the Immigration and Naturalization Service, the U.S. Coast Guard, the Secret Service, the Federal Emergency Management Agency, and a newly created Transportation Security Administration.

But the Department of Homeland Security does *not* have authority over the Federal Bureau of Investigation in the Justice Department or the independent Central Intelligence Agency. So questions remain as to whether these two law enforcement and intelligence organizations can coordinate information among themselves and with the new Department of Homeland Security.

cover an enormous range—everything from providing mortgage insurance to overseeing the armed forces of the United States (see Table 12.1).

Cabinet Appointments The Constitution requires that "Officers of the United States" be confirmed by the Senate. In the past, the Senate rarely rejected a presidential cabinet nomination; the traditional view was that presidents were entitled to pick their own people and even make their own mistakes. In recent years, however, the confirmation process has become more partisan and divisive, with the Senate conducting lengthy investigations and holding public hearings on presidential cabinet nominees. In 1989 the Senate rejected President Bush's nomination of John Tower as secretary of defense in a partisan battle featuring charges that the former Texas senator was a heavy drinker. The intense public scrutiny and potential for partisan attacks, together with financial disclosure and conflict-of-interest laws, may be discouraging some well-qualified people from accepting cabinet posts.

Independent Regulatory Commissions Independent regulatory commissions differ from cabinet departments in their function, organization, and accountability to the president. Their function is to *regulate* a sector of

Internal Revenue Service

The tax-collecting IRS is potentially the most powerful of all government agencies with financial records on every tax-paying American. ***www.irs.gov***

Food and Drug Administration

The Food and Drug Administration site is a reflection of the agency's mission "to promote and protect the public health by helping safe and effective products reach the market in a timely way." ***www.fda.gov***

society—transportation, communications, banking, labor relations, and so on (see Table 12.2). These commissions are empowered by Congress both to make and to enforce rules, and they thus function in a quasi-judicial fashion. To symbolize their impartiality, many of these organizations are headed by *commissions*, usually with five to ten members, rather than by a single secretary. Major policy decisions are made by majority vote of the commission. Finally, these agencies are more independent of the president than are cabinet departments. Their governing commissions are appointed by the president and confirmed by the Senate in the same fashion as cabinet secretaries, but their terms are fixed; they cannot be removed by the president.[6] These provisions are designed to insulate regulators from direct partisan or presidential pressures in their decision making.

A few powerful regulatory agencies remain inside cabinet departments. The most notable are the Food and Drug Administration (FDA), which remains in the Department of Health and Human Services and has broad authority to prevent the sale of drugs not deemed by the agency to be both "safe" and "effective"; the Occupational Health and Safety Administration (OSHA) in the Department of Labor, with authority to make rules governing any workplace in America; and the most powerful government agency of all, the Internal Revenue Service in the Treasury Department, with its broad authority to interpret the tax code, maintain records on every American, and investigate and punish alleged violations of the tax code.

Independent Agencies Congress has created a number of independent agencies outside of any cabinet department. Like cabinet departments, these agencies are hierarchically organized with a single head—usually called an "administrator"—who is appointed by the president and confirmed by the Senate. Administrators have no fixed terms of office and can be dismissed by the president; thus they are independent only insofar as they report directly to the president rather than through a cabinet secretary. Politically, this independence ensures that their interests and budgets will not be compromised by other concerns, as may occur in agencies located within departments. (For more on their operations, see "Regulatory Battles" later in this chapter.)

One of the most powerful independent agencies is the Environmental Protection Agency (EPA), which is responsible for implementing federal legislation dealing with clean air, safe drinking water, solid waste disposal, pesticides, radiation, and toxic substances. EPA establishes and enforces comprehensive and complex standards for thousands of substances in the environment. It enjoys the political support of influential environmental interest groups, including the Environmental Defense Fund, Friends of the Earth, National Audubon Society, National Wildlife Federation, Natural Resources Defense Council, Sierra Club, and the Wilderness Society.

The Federal Reserve System is the most independent of all federal government agencies. The function of the "Fed" is to regulate the supply of money and thereby avoid both inflation and recession (see Chapter 16). The Federal Reserve System is independent of either the president or Congress. Its seven-member Board of Governors is appointed for *14-year terms*. Members are appointed by the president, with the consent of the Senate, but they may not be removed from the board except for "cause." No member has ever been removed since the creation of the board in 1913. The chairman of the board serves only a four-year term, but the chairman's term overlaps that of president, so that new presidents cannot immediately name

Cleaning up an oil spill on a California beach. The Environmental Protection Agency is perhaps the most powerful independent agency in the bureaucracy.

TABLE 12.2 Major Regulatory Bureaucracies

Commission	Date Created	Primary Functions
Federal Communications Commission (FCC)	1934	Regulates interstate and foreign communications by radio, television, wire, and cable.
Food and Drug Administration (FDA)	1930	Sets standards of safety and efficacy for foods, drugs, and medical devices.
Federal Home Loan Bank	1932	Regulates savings and loan associations that specialize in making home mortgage loans.
Federal Maritime Commission	1961	Regulates the waterborne foreign and domestic offshore commerce of the United States.
Federal Reserve Board (FRB)	1913	Regulates the nation's money supply by making monetary policy, which influences the lending and investing activities of commercial banks and the cost and availability of money and credit.
Federal Trade Commission (FTC)	1914	Regulates business to prohibit unfair methods of competition and unfair or deceptive acts or practices.
National Labor Relations Board (NLRB)	1935	Protects employees' rights to organize; prevents unfair labor practices.
Securities and Exchange Commission (SEC)	1934	Regulates the securities and financial markets (such as the stock market).
Occupational Safety and Health Administration (OSHA)	1970	Issues workplace regulations; investigates, cites, and penalizes for noncompliance.
Consumer Product Safety Commission (CPSC)	1972	Protects the public against product-related deaths, illnesses, and injuries.
Commodity Futures Trading Commission	1974	Regulates trading on the futures exchanges as well as the activities of commodity exchange members, public brokerage houses, commodity salespersons, trading advisers, and pool operators.
Nuclear Regulatory Commission (NRC)	1974	Regulates and licenses the users of nuclear energy.
Federal Energy Regulatory Commission (formerly Federal Power Commission)	1977	Regulates the transportation and sale of natural gas, the transmission and sale of electricity, the licensing of hydroelectric power projects, and the transportation of oil by pipeline.
Equal Employment Opportunity Commission (EEOC)	1964	Investigates and rules on charges of racial, gender, and age discrimination by employers and unions, in all aspects of employment.
Environmental Protection Agency (EPA)	1970	Issues and enforces pollution control standards regarding air, water, solid waste, pesticides, radiation, and toxic substances.

Source: The United States Government Manual 2001/02 (Washington, D.C.: Government Printing Office, 2002).

their own chair (see *People and Politics:* "Alan Greenspan, Managing the Nation's Economy").

Government Corporations Government corporations are created by Congress to undertake independent commercial enterprises. They resemble private corporations in that they typically charge for their services. Like private corporations, too, they are usually governed by a chief executive officer and a board of directors, and they can buy and sell property and incur debts.

Occupational Safety and Health Administration

This site covers news and information directly related to OSHA's mission "to ensure safe and healthful workplaces in America." ***www.osha.gov***

Alan Greenspan, Managing the Nation's Economy

The Federal Reserve System regulates the nation's monetary policy and credit conditions, supervises and regulates all banking activity, and provides various services to banks. Federal Reserve Banks are banks' banks. There are 12 Federal Reserve Banks serving the nation's nearly 8,000 commercial banks. The "Fed" requires all banks to maintain a reserve in deposits with a Federal Reserve Bank. The Fed also makes loans to banks, allowing them to add to their reserve and therefore allowing them to make more loans to customers. But the Fed charges banks an interest rate on these loans, called the "discount rate." By raising the discount rate, the Fed forces banks to raise their own interest rates and thereby contract the nation's money supply; lowering the discount rate encourages banks to expand the money supply. Interest rates generally—on loans to businesses, mortgages, car loans, and so on—rise and fall with rises and falls in the Fed's discount rate. Lowering rates encourages economic expansion; raising rates dampens inflation. These decisions by the Fed, referred to as monetary policy (see Chapter 16), have a vital impact on the economy.

Economist Alan Greenspan is the chairman of the Board of Governors of the Federal Reserve System. He was appointed in 1987 by President Ronald Reagan.

Born in New York City, Alan Greenspan studied music at the prestigious Julliard School and enjoyed a brief but successful career as a professional saxophone player in a big swing band before returning to the classroom at New York University. He received an M.A. in economics in 1950 under the tutelage of Arthur F. Burns, who served as chair of the Federal Reserve from 1970 to 1978. After graduation, Greenspan formed his own economic consulting company, Townsend-Greenspan, which provided economic forecasts for some of America's largest corporations. In his spare time, Greenspan completed his Ph.D. at New York University.

Greenspan began his public service in the Nixon Administration, serving on commissions and task forces, including the Commission on an All-Volunteer Armed Force. In 1974 President Nixon appointed Greenspan to chair the Council of Economic Advisers, a position Greenspan continued to hold under President Gerald Ford. When the Carter Administration came to Washington in 1977, Republican Greenspan returned to running his private company.

As Fed chairman under four presidents—Reagan, Bush, Clinton, and Bush — Greenspan has often acted independently and disagreed with the administration over the money supply. Yet his management of the Fed has been widely praised by both Democrats and Republicans. He has earned credibility with his fellow economists by avoiding the Washington political game. He is credited for his quick reaction to the stock market crash on October 19, 1987, when he ensured that Federal Reserve Banks would have enough cash on hand to prevent panic following the record drop in stock prices.

Greenspan successfully fought inflationary trends during the nation's economic expansion in the 1990s by raising interest rates. When recession threatened in 2001, he led the Fed in bringing down interest rates to an all-time low, preventing a deep recession. When Greenspan testifies before Congress, as he frequently does, stock traders closely monitor every word, and stock prices usually react to his mood. Arguably, the Fed chairman has more power over the nation's economy than any other single individual, including the president.

Federal Reserve System

This Federal Reserve System site covers general information about "Fed" operations, including monetary policy, reserve bank services, international banking, and supervisory and regulatory functions.
www.federalreserve.gov

Presumably, government corporations perform a service that the private enterprise system has been unable to carry out adequately. The first government corporation was the Tennessee Valley Authority, created by President Franklin Roosevelt during the Depression to build dams and sell electricity at inexpensive rates to impoverished citizens in the mid-South. In 1970 Congress created Amtrak to restore railroad passenger service to the United States. The U.S. Post Office had originally been created as a cabinet-level department, but in 1971 it became the U.S. Postal Service, a government corporation with a mandate from Congress to break even.

Contractors and Consultants How has the federal government grown enormously in power and size, yet kept its number of employees at roughly the same level in recent years? The answer is found in the spectacular growth of private firms that live off federal contracting and consulting fees. Nearly one-fifth of all federal government spending flows through private contractors: for supplies, equipment, services, leases, and research and development. An army of scientists, economists, education specialists, management consultants, transportation experts, social scientists, and others are scattered across the country in universities, think tanks, consulting firms, and laboratories. Many are concentrated in the "beltway bandit" firms surrounding Washington, D.C.

The federal grant and contracting system is enormously complex; an estimated 150,000 federal contracting offices in nearly 500 agencies oversee thousands of outside contractors and consultants[7] Although advertised bidding is sometimes required by law, most contracts and grants are awarded without competition through negotiation with favored firms or "sole source contracts" with organizations believed by bureaucrats to be uniquely qualified. Even when federal agencies issue public requests for proposals (RFPs), often a favored contractor has been alerted and advised by bureaucrats within the agency about how to win the award.

Bureaucracy and Democracy

Traditionally, conflict over government employment centered on the question of partisanship versus competence. Should the federal bureaucracy be staffed by people politically loyal to the president, the president's party, or key members of Congress? Or should it be staffed by nonpartisan people selected on the basis of merit and protected from "political" influence?

The Spoils System Historically, government employment was allocated by the **spoils system**—selecting employees on the basis of party loyalty, electoral support, and political influence. Or, as Senator William Marcy said in 1832, "They see nothing wrong in the rule that to the victors belong the spoils of the enemy."[8] The spoils system is most closely associated with President Andrew Jackson, who viewed it as a popular reform of the earlier tendency to appoint officials on the basis of kinship and class standing. Jackson sought to bring into government many of the common people who had supported him. Later in the nineteenth century, the bartering and sale of government jobs became so scandalous and time-consuming that presidents complained bitterly about the task. When President James Garfield was shot and killed in 1881 by a disgruntled job seeker, the stage was set for reform.

The Merit System The **merit system**—government employment based on competence, neutrality, and protection from partisanship—was introduced in the Pendleton Act of 1883. The act created the Civil Service Commission to establish a system for selecting government personnel based on merit, as determined by competitive examinations. In the beginning, "civil service" coverage included only about 10 percent of total federal employees. Over the years, however, more and more positions were placed under civil service, primarily at the behest of presidents who sought to "freeze in" their political appointees. By 1978 more than 90 percent of federal employees were covered by civil service or other merit systems.

The civil service system established a uniform General Schedule (GS) of job grades from GS 1 (lowest) to GS 15 (highest), with an Executive Schedule added

WWW **Amtrak**
The Amtrak Web site provides valuable information about trip planning, reservations, train schedules, and respective train fares. ***www.amtrak.com***

THINK AGAIN

Should the federal bureaucracy be managed by nonpartisan professionals rather than people politically loyal to the president?

spoils system Selection of employees for government agencies on the basis of party loyalty, electoral support, and political influence.

merit system Selection of employees for government agencies on the basis of competence, with no consideration of an individual's political stance and/or power.

later for top managers and pay ranges based on an individual's time in the grade. Each grade has specific educational requirements and examinations. College graduates generally begin at GS 5 or above; GS 9 through GS 12 are technical and supervisory positions; and GS 13, 14, and 15 are midlevel management and highly specialized positions. The Executive Schedule (the "supergrades") are reserved for positions of greatest responsibility. (In 2004 annual pay ranged from roughly $25,000 to $42,000 for Grades 5–8, up to $62,000 to $112,000 for Grades 13–15, and $175,000 for some Executive Schedule positions.) When a position in a federal agency opens up, the agency is supposed to receive the names of the three people earning the highest examination scores for that position grade. The agency is supposed to hire one of the three, with the other two remaining at the top of the register for the next opening. But agencies often set highly specialized job qualifications that relatively few applicants possess, and special preferences abound in federal employment regulations.

About two-thirds of all federal civilian jobs come under the General Schedule system, with its written examinations and/or training, experience, and educational requirements. Most of the other one-third of federal civilian employees are part of the "excepted services"; they are employed by various agencies that have their own separate merit systems, such as the Federal Bureau of Investigation, the Central Intelligence Agency, the U.S. Postal Service, and the State Department Foreign Service. The military also has its own system of recruitment, promotion, and pay.

Political Involvement Congress passed the Hatch Act in 1939, a law that prohibited federal employees from engaging in partisan political activity, including running for public office, soliciting campaign funds, or campaigning for or against a party or candidate. It also protected federal merit system employees from dismissal for partisan reasons. But over the years many federal employees came to believe that the Hatch Act infringed on their rights as citizens. In 1993, a Democratic-controlled Congress repealed major portions of the Hatch Act, allowing civil servants to hold party positions and involve themselves in political fund raising and campaigning. They still may not be candidates for public office in partisan elections, or solicit contributions from subordinate employees or people who do business with—or have cases before—their agencies.

The Problem of Responsiveness The civil service system, like most "reforms," eventually created problems at least as troubling as those in the system it replaced. First of all, there is the problem of a *lack of responsiveness* to presidential direction. Civil servants, secure in their protected jobs, can be less than cooperative toward their presidentially appointed department or agency heads. They can slow or obstruct policy changes with which they personally disagree. Each bureau and agency develops its own "culture," usually in strong support of the governmental function or client group served by the organization. Changing the culture of an agency is extremely difficult, especially when a presidential administration is committed to reducing its resources, functions, or services. Bureaucrats' powers of policy obstruction are formidable: they can help mobilize interest-group support against the president's policy; they can "leak" damaging information to sympathizers in Congress or the media to undermine the president's policy; they can delay and/or "sabotage" policies with which they disagree.

The Problem of Productivity Perhaps the most troublesome problem in the federal bureaucracy has involved *productivity*—notably the inability to improve job performance because of the difficulties in rewarding or punishing civil servants.

During the administration of Andrew Jackson, the spoils system was perhaps more overt than at any other time in the history of the U.S. federal government. Jackson claimed he was trying to involve more of the "common folk" in the government, but his selection of advisers on the basis of personal friendship rather than qualifications sometimes caused him difficulties.

"Merit" salary rewards have generally proven ineffective in rewarding the performance of federal employees. More than 99 percent of federal workers regularly receive annual "merit" pay increases. Moreover, over time, federal employees have secured higher grade classifications and hence higher pay for most of the job positions in the General Schedule. This "inflation" in GS grades, combined with regular increases in salary and benefits, has resulted in many federal employees enjoying higher pay and benefits than employees in the private sector performing similar jobs.

At the same time, very poor performance often goes largely unpunished. Once hired and retained through a brief probationary period, a federal civil servant cannot be dismissed except for "cause." Severe obstacles to firing a civil servant result in a rate of dismissal of about one-tenth of 1 percent of all federal employees (see Table 12.3). It is doubtful that only such a tiny fraction are performing unsatisfactorily. A federal executive confronting a poorly performing or nonperforming employee must be prepared to spend more than a year in extended proceedings to secure a dismissal. Often costly substitute strategies are devised to work around or inspire the resignation of unsatisfactory federal employees—assigning them meaningless or boring tasks, denying them promotions, transferring them to distant or undesirable locations, removing secretaries or other supporting resources, and the like.

Civil Service Reform Presidents routinely try to remedy some of the problems in the system. The Civil Service Reform Act of 1978, initiated by President Jimmy Carter, replaced the Civil Service Commission with the Office of Personnel Management (OPM) and made OPM responsible for recruiting, examining, training, and promoting federal employees. Unlike the Civil Service Commission, OPM is headed by a single director responsible to the president. The act also sought to (1) streamline procedures through which individuals could be disciplined for poor performance; (2) establish merit pay for middle-level managers; and (3) create a Senior Executive Service (SES) composed of about 8,000 top people designated for higher Executive Schedule grades and salaries who also might be given salary bonuses, transferred among agencies, or demoted, based on performance.

But like many reforms, this act failed to resolve the major problems—the responsiveness and productivity of the bureaucracy. No senior executives were fired,

TABLE 12.3 Firing a Bureaucrat: What Is Required to Dismiss a Federal Employee

- Written notice at least thirty days in advance of a hearing to determine incompetence or misconduct.
- A statement of cause, indicating specific dates, places, and actions cited as incompetent or improper.
- The right to a hearing and decision by an impartial official, with the burden of proof falling on the agency that wishes to fire the employee.
- The right to have an attorney and to present witnesses in the employee's favor at the hearing.
- The right to appeal any adverse action to the Merit Systems Protection Board.
- The right to appeal any adverse action by the board to the U.S. Court of Appeals.
- The right to remain on the job and be paid until all appeals are exhausted.

TABLE 12.4 Women and Minorities in the Federal Bureaucracy

	Percentage Female	Percentage White, Non-Hispanic	Percentage African American	Percentage Hispanic
Overall	48.7%	74.7%	18.2%	7.0%
By pay grade				
Lowest GS 1–4	74.8	55.5	29.7	9.8
GS 5–8	53.5	65.5	27.0	8.6
GS 9–12	32.9	77.1	15.8	7.1
GS 13–15	17.0	85.6	10.1	4.3
Executive	9.1	87.5	7.5	3.0
U.S. population				
(2000)	50.9	75.2	12.3	12.5

Table excludes American Indians, Alaska Natives, and Asian and Pacific Islanders.

Source: Statistical Abstract of the United States, 2001, p. 320.

demoted, or involuntarily transferred. The bonus program proved difficult to implement: there are few recognized standards for judging meritorious work in the public service, and bonuses often reflect favoritism as much as merit.[9] Because the act creates a separate Merit Systems Protection Board to hear appeals by federal employees from dismissals, suspensions, and demotions, rates of dismissal for all grades have not changed substantially from earlier days.

THINK AGAIN

Should the federal bureaucracy at all levels reflect the gender and minority ratios of the total civilian work force?

Bureaucracy and Representation In addition to the questions of responsiveness and productivity, there is also the question of the representativeness of the federal bureaucracy. Today, the federal bureaucracy *as a whole* reflects fairly well the gender and minority ratios of the U.S. population. Nearly half of the total civilian work force is female, 18.2 percent is black, and 7.0 is Hispanic. However, a close look at *top* bureaucratic positions reveals a somewhat different picture. As Table 12.4 shows, only 9.1 percent of federal "executive" positions (levels GS 16–18) are filled by women, only 7.5 percent by blacks, and only 3.0 percent by Hispanics. Thus the federal bureaucracy, like other institutions in American society, is *un*representative of the general population in its top executive positions.

Bureaucratic Politics

To whom is the federal bureaucracy really accountable? The president, Congress, or itself? Article II, Section 2, of the Constitution places the president at the head of the executive branch of government, with the power to "appoint Ambassadors, other public Ministers and Consuls, Judges of the Supreme Court, and all other Officers of the United States . . . which shall be established by Law." Appointment of these officials requires "the Advice and Consent of the Senate"—that is, a majority vote in the Senate. The Constitution also states that "the Congress may by Law vest the Appointment of such inferior Officers, as they think proper, in the President alone." If the bureaucracy is to be made accountable to the president, we would expect the president to directly appoint *policy-making* executive officers. But it is difficult to determine exactly how many positions are truly "policy making."

Presidential "Plums" The president retains direct control over about 3,000 federal jobs. Some 700 of these jobs are considered policy-making positions. They include presidential appointments authorized by law—cabinet and subcabinet officers, judges, U.S. marshals, U.S. attorneys, ambassadors, and members of various boards and commissions. The president also appoints a large number of "Schedule C" jobs throughout the bureaucracy, described as "confidential or policy-determining" in character. Each new administration goes through many months of high-powered lobbying and scrambling to fill these posts. Applicants with congressional sponsors, friends in the White House, or a record of loyal campaign work for the president compete for these "plums." Political loyalty must be weighed against administrative competence.

Rooms at the Top The federal bureaucracy has "thickened" at the top, even as total federal employment has declined. Over time, departments and agencies have added layers of administrators, variously titled "deputy secretary," "undersecretary," "assistant secretary," "deputy assistant secretary," and so on. Cabinet departments have become top-heavy with administrators, and the same multiplication of layers of executive management has occurred in independent agencies as well.[10]

Whistle-Blowers The question of bureaucratic responsiveness is complicated by the struggle between the president and Congress to control the bureaucracy. Congress expects federal agencies and employees to respond fully and promptly to its inquiries and to report candidly on policies, procedures, and expenditures. **Whistle-blowers** are federal employees (or employees of a firm supplying the government) who report government waste, mismanagement, or fraud to the media or to congressional committees or who "go public" with their policy disputes with their superiors. Congress generally encourages whistle-blowing as a means of getting information and controlling the bureaucracy, but the president and agency heads whose policies are under attack are often less kindly disposed toward whistle-blowers. In 1989 Congress passed the Whistleblower Protection Act, which established an independent agency to guarantee whistle-blowers protection against unjust dismissal, transfer, or demotion.

Center for Public Integrity

Reform organization committed to "exposing" corruption, mismanagement, and waste in government.
www.publicintegrity.org

Agency Cultures Over time, every bureaucracy tends to develop its own "culture"—beliefs about the values of the organization's programs and goals and close associations with the agency's client groups and political supporters. Many government agencies are dominated by people who have been in government service most of their lives, and most of these people have worked in the same functional field most of their lives. They believe their work is important, and they resist efforts by either the president or Congress to reduce the activities, size, or budget of their agency. Career bureaucrats tend to support enlargement of the public sector—to enhance education, welfare, housing, environmental and consumer protection, and so on. Bureaucrats not only share a belief in the need for government expansion but also stand to benefit directly from increased authority, staffing, and funding as government takes on new and enlarged responsibilities.

Friends and Neighbors Bureaucracies maintain their own cultures in part by staffing themselves. Informal practices in recruitment often circumvent civil service procedures. Very few people ever get hired by taking a federal civil service examination administered by OPM and then sitting and waiting to be called for an interview by an agency. Most bureaucratic hiring actually comes about through

whistle-blower Employee of the federal government or of a firm supplying the government who reports waste, mismanagement, and/or fraud by a government agency or contractor.

"networks" of personal friends and professional associates. People inside an agency contact their friends and associates when a position first becomes vacant; they then send their friends to OPM to formally qualify for the job. Thus inside candidates learn about an opening well before it appears on any list of vacant positions and can tailor their applications to the job description. Agencies may even send a "name request" to OPM, ensuring that the preselected person will appear on the list of qualified people. In this way, individuals sometimes move through many jobs within a specific policy network—for example, within environmental protection, within transportation, or within social welfare—shifting between the federal bureaucracy, state or local government, and private firms or interest groups in the same field. Network recruiting generally ensures that the people entering a bureaucracy will share the same values and attitudes of the people already there.

"Reinventing" Government Reformers lament "the bankruptcy of bureaucracy"—the waste, inefficiency, impersonality, and unresponsiveness of large government organizations. They decry "the routine tendency to protect turf, to resist change, to build empires, to enlarge one's sphere of control, to protect projects and programs regardless of whether or not they are any longer needed."[11] Many bureaucratic reform efforts have foundered, from Hoover Commission studies in the Truman and Eisenhower years to the Grace Commission work in the Reagan Administration. Clinton assigned a "reinventing government" task to Vice President Al Gore. Gore produced a report designed to put the "customer" (U.S. citizen) first, to "empower" government employees to get results, to cut red tape, to introduce competition and a market orientation wherever possible, and to decentralize government decision making.[12] The most impressive result was the overall decline in federal employment during the Clinton Administration, from 3.1 million to 2.7 million civilian employees.

Presidential Initiative Presidents can create some new agencies by executive order. Often Congress gives presidents the authority to reorganize agencies by legislation. But presidents have also acted on their own to create new agencies. Indeed, one study concludes that presidents have created about 40 percent of all new agencies[13]—perhaps the most famous was President Kennedy's Peace Corps. Of course, Congress has the last word, inasmuch as the continuation of a presidentially created agency requires funding and Congress controls the purse strings. It can end an agency's existence by cutting off its funds.

The Budgetary Process

THINK
AGAIN

Do you believe the bureaucrats in Washington waste a lot of the money we pay in taxes?

The federal government's annual budget battles are the heart of political process. Budget battles decide who gets what and who pays the cost of government. The budget is the single most important policy statement of any government.

The president is responsible for submitting the annual *Budget of the United States Government*—with estimates of revenues and recommendations for expenditures—for consideration, amendment, and approval by the Congress. But the president's budget reflects the outcome of earlier bureaucratic battles over who gets what. Despite highly publicized wrangling between the president and Congress each year—and occasional declarations that the president's budget is "DOA" (dead on arrival)—final congressional appropriations rarely deviate by more than 2 or 3 percent from the original presidential budget. Thus the president and the Office of Management and Budget in the Executive Office of the President have real budgetary power.

The Office of Management and Budget The Office of Management and Budget (OMB) has the key responsibility for budget preparation. In addition to this major task, OMB has related responsibilities for improving the organization and management of the executive agencies, for coordinating the extensive statistical services of the federal government, and for analyzing and reviewing proposed legislation.

Preparation of the budget begins when OMB, after preliminary consultations with the executive agencies and in accord with presidential policy, develops targets or ceilings within which the agencies are encouraged to build their requests (see Figure 12.4). Budget materials and instructions then go to the agencies, with the request that the forms be completed and returned to OMB. This request is followed by about three months of arduous work by agency budget officers, department heads, and the "grass-roots" bureaucracy in Washington, D.C., and out in the field. Budget officials at the bureau and departmental levels check requests from the smaller units, compare them with previous years' estimates, hold conferences, and make adjustments. The heads of agencies are expected to submit their completed requests to OMB by July or August. Although these requests usually remain within target levels, occasionally they include some "overceiling" items (requests above the suggested ceilings). With the requests of the spending agencies at hand, OMB begins its own budget review, including hearings at which top agency officials support their requests as convincingly as possible. Frequently OMB must say "no," that is, reduce agency requests. On rare occasions, dissatisfied agencies may ask the budget director to take their cases to the president.

The President's Budget In December, the president and the OMB director devote much time to the key document, *The Budget of the United States Government*, which by now is approaching its final stages of assembly. Each budget is named for the **fiscal year** in which it *ends*. The federal fiscal year begins on October 1 and ends the following September 30. (Thus *The Budget of the United States Government Fiscal Year* 2006 begins October 1, 2005, and ends September 30, 2006.) Although the completed document includes a revenue plan with general estimates for taxes and other income, it is primarily an expenditure budget. (Revenue and tax policy staff work centers in the Treasury Department, not in the Office of Management and Budget.) In late January, the president presents Congress with *The Budget of the United States Government* for the fiscal year beginning October 1. After the budget is in legislative hands, the president may recommend further alterations as needs dictate.

House and Senate Budget Committees The Constitution gives Congress the authority to decide how the government should spend its money: "No money shall be drawn from the Treasury, but in Consequence of Appropriations made by Law" (Article 1, Section 9). The president's budget is sent initially to the House and Senate Budget Committees, which rely on their own bureaucracy, the Congressional Budget Office (CBO), to review the president's budget. Based on the CBO's assessment, these committees draft a first **budget resolution** (due May 15) setting forth target goals to guide congressional committees regarding specific appropriations and revenue measures. If proposed spending exceeds the targets in the budget resolution, the resolution comes back to the floor in a reconciliation measure. A second budget resolution (due September 15) sets

Office of Management and Budget

The OMB site includes all budget documents and information on regulatory oversight. *www.omb.gov*

fiscal year Yearly government accounting period, not necessarily the same as the calendar year. The federal government's fiscal year begins October 1 and ends September 30.

budget resolution Congressional bill setting forth target budget figures for appropriations to various government departments and agencies.

WHO	WHAT	WHEN
Presidential budget making		
President and OMB	OMB presents long-range forecasts for revenues and expenditures to the president. President and OMB develop general guidelines for all federal agencies. Agencies are sent guidelines and forms for their budget requests.	January February March
Executive agencies	Agencies prepare and submit budget requests to OMB.	April May June July
OMB and agencies	OMB reviews agency requests and holds hearings with agency officials.	August September October
OMB and president	OMB presents revised budget to president. President and OMB write budget message for Congress.	November December January
President	President presents budget for the next fiscal year to Congress.	February
Congressional budget process		
CBO and congressional committees	CBO reviews taxing and spending proposals and reports to House and Senate budget committees.	February-April
Congress; House and Senate budget committees	Committees present first concurrent resolution, which sets overall total for budget outlays in major categories. Full House and Senate vote on resolution. Committees are instructed to stay within Budget Committee's resolution.	May June
Congress; House and Senate appropriations committees and budget committees	Appropriations committees and subcommittees draw up detailed appropriations bills and submit them to budget committees for second concurrent resolution. The full House and Senate vote on "reconciliations" and second (firm) concurrent resolution.	July August September
Congress and president	House and Senate pass various appropriations bills (nine to sixteen bills, by major functional category, such as "defense"). Each is sent to president for signature. (If successfully vetoed, a bill is revised and resubmitted to the president.)	September October
Executive budget implementation		
Congress and president	Fiscal year for all federal agencies begins October 1. If no appropriations bill for an agency has been passed by Congress and signed by the president, Congress must pass and the president sign a continuing resolution to allow the agency to spend at last year's level until a new appropriations bill is passed. If no continuing resolution is passed, the agency must officially cease spending government funds and must officially shut down.	After October 1

FIGURE 12.4 The Budget Process

Development, presentation, and approval of the federal budget for any fiscal year takes almost two full years. The executive branch spends more than a year on the process before Congress even begins its review and revision of the president's proposals. The problems of implementing the budgeted programs then fall to the federal bureaucracy.

binding budget figures for committees and subcommittees considering appropriations. In practice, however, these two budget resolutions are often folded into a single measure because Congress does not want to argue the same issues twice.

Congressional Appropriations Committees Congressional approval of each year's spending is usually divided into thirteen separate appropriations bills (acts), each covering separate broad categories of spending (for example, defense, labor, human services and education, commerce, justice). These appropriations bills are drawn up by the House and Senate Appropriations Committees and their specialized subcommittees, which function as overseers of agencies included in their appropriations bills. Committee work in the House of Representatives is usually more thorough than it is in the Senate; the committee in the Senate tends to be a "court of appeal" for agencies opposed to House action. Each committee, moreover, has about ten largely independent subcommittees, each reviewing the requests of a particular agency or a group of related functions. Specific appropriations bills are taken up by the subcommittees in hearings. Departmental officers answer questions on the conduct of their programs and defend their requests for the next fiscal year; lobbyists and other witnesses testify. Although committees and subcommittees have broad discretion in allocating funds to the agencies they monitor, they must stay within overall totals set forth in the second budget resolution adopted by Congress.

Appropriations Acts In examining the interactions between Congress and the federal bureaucracy over spending, it is important to distinguish between appropriations and authorization. An **authorization** is an act of Congress that establishes a government program and defines the amount of money it may spend. Authorizations may be for one or several years. However, an authorization does not actually provide the money that has been authorized; only an **appropriations act** can do that. In fact, appropriations acts, which are usually for a single fiscal year, are almost always *less* than authorizations; deciding how much less is the real function of the Appropriations Committees and subcommittees. (By its own rules, Congress cannot appropriate money for programs it has not already authorized.) Appropriations acts include both obligational authority and outlays.

Obligational authority permits a government agency to enter into contracts that will require the government to make payments beyond the fiscal years in question. **Outlays** must be spent in the fiscal year for which they are appropriated.

Continuing Resolutions and "Shutdowns" All appropriations acts *should* be passed by both houses and signed by the president into law before October 1, the date of the start of the fiscal year. However, it is rare for Congress to meet this deadline, so the government usually finds itself beginning a new fiscal year without a budget. Constitutionally, any U.S. government agency for which Congress does not pass an appropriations act may not draw money from the Treasury and thus is obliged to shut down. To get around this problem, Congress usually adopts a **continuing resolution** that authorizes government agencies to keep spending money for a specified period at the same level as in the previous fiscal year.

A continuing resolution is supposed to grant additional time for Congress to pass, and the president to sign, appropriations acts. But occasionally this process has broken down in the heat of political combat over the budget: the time period specified in a continuing resolution has expired without agreement on appropriations acts or even on a new continuing resolution. Shutdowns occurred during the bitter battle between President Bill Clinton and the Republican-controlled

authorization Act of Congress that establishes a government program and defines the amount of money it may spend.

appropriations act Congressional bill that provides money for programs authorized by Congress.

obligational authority Feature of some appropriations acts by which an agency is empowered to enter into contracts that will require the government to make payments beyond the fiscal year in question.

outlays Actual dollar amounts to be spent by the federal government in a fiscal year.

continuing resolution Congressional bill that authorizes government agencies to keep spending money for a specified period at the same level as in the previous fiscal year; passed when Congress is unable to enact final appropriations measures by October 1.

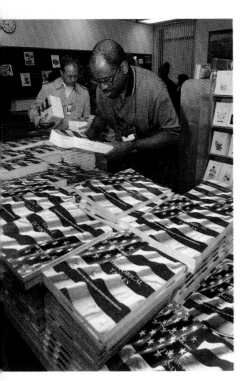

The 2005 Budget of the United States government shows total outlays of $2.4 trillion, with a deficit of nearly $365 billion. The deficit is in part a product of increased spending for defense and home security.

Congress over the Fiscal Year 1996 budget. In theory, the absence of either appropriations acts or a continuing resolution should cause the entire federal government to "shut down," that is, to cease all operations and expenditures for lack of funds. But in practice, such shutdowns have been only partial, affecting only "nonessential" government employees and causing relatively little disruption.

The Politics of Budgeting

Budgeting is very political. Being a good "bureaucratic politician" involves (1) cultivating a good base of support for requests among the public at large and among people served by the agency; (2) developing interest, enthusiasm, and support for one's program among top political figures and congressional leaders; (3) winning favorable coverage of agency activities in the media; and (4) following strategies that exploit opportunities.[14] (see *Up Close*: "Bureaucratic Budget Strategies").

Budgeting Is "Incremental" The most important factor determining the size and content of the budget each year is last year's budget. Decision makers generally use last year's expenditures as a *base*; active consideration of budget proposals generally focuses on new items and requested increases over last year's base. The budget of an agency is almost never reviewed as a whole. Agencies are seldom required to defend or explain budget requests that do *not* exceed current appropriations; but requested increases *do* require explanation and are most subject to reduction by OMB or Congress.

The result of **incremental budgeting** is that many programs, services, and expenditures continue long after there is any real justification for them. When new needs, services, and functions arise, they do not displace older ones but rather are *added* to the budget. Budget decisions are made incrementally because policy makers do not have the time, energy, or information to review every dollar of every budget request every year. Nor do policy makers wish to refight every political battle over existing programs every year. So they generally accept last year's base spending level as legitimate and focus attention on proposed increases for each program.

Reformers have proposed "sunset" laws requiring bureaucrats to justify their programs every five to seven years or else the programs go out of existence, as well as **zero-based budgeting** that would force agencies to justify every penny requested—not just requested increases. In theory, sunset laws and zero-based budgeting would regularly prune unnecessary government programs, agencies, and expenditures and thus limit the growth of government and waste in government (see *What Do You Think?* "How Much Money Does the Government Waste?"). But in reality, sunset laws and zero-based budgeting require so much effort in justifying already accepted programs that executive agencies and legislative committees grow tired of the effort and return to incrementalism.

The "incremental" nature of budgetary politics helps reduce political conflicts and maintain stability in governmental programs. As bruising as budgetary battles are today, they would be much worse if the president or Congress undertook to review the value of *all* existing expenditures and programs each year. Comprehensive budgetary review would "overload the system" with political conflict by refighting every policy battle every year.

Budgeting Is Nonprogrammatic Budgeting is *nonprogrammatic* in that an agency budget typically lists expenditures under ambiguous phrases: "personnel ser-

incremental budgeting
Method of budgeting that focuses on requested increases in funding for existing programs, accepting as legitimate their previous year's expenditures.

zero-based budgeting
Method of budgeting that demands justification for the entire budget request of an agency, not just its requested increase in funding.

Bureaucratic Budget Strategies

How do bureaucrats go about "maximizing" their resources? Some of the most common budgetary strategies of bureaucrats are listed here. Remember that most bureaucrats believe strongly in the importance of their tasks; they pursue these strategies not only to increase their own power and prestige but also to better serve their client groups and the entire nation.

- **Spend it all:** Spend all of your current appropriation. Failure to use up an appropriation indicates the full amount was unnecessary in the first place, which in turn implies that your budget should be cut next year.
- **Ask for more:** Never request a sum less than your current appropriation. It is easier to find ways to spend up to current appropriation levels than it is to explain why you want a reduction. Besides, a reduction indicates your program is not growing, an embarrassing admission to most government administrators. Requesting an increase, at least enough to cover "inflation," demonstrates the continued importance of your program.
- **Put vital programs in the "base":** Put top priority programs into the basic budget—that is, that part of the budget within current appropriation levels. The Office of Management and Budget (OMB) and legislative committees seldom challenge programs that appear to be part of existing operations.
- **Make new programs appear "incremental":** Requested increases should appear to be small and should appear to grow out of existing operations. Any appearance of a fundamental change in a budget should be avoided.
- **Give them something to cut:** Give the OMB and legislative committees something to cut. Normally it is desirable to submit requests for substantial increases in existing programs and many requests for new programs, in order to give higher political authorities something to cut. This approach enables authorities to "save" the public untold millions of dollars and justify their claim of promoting "economy" in government. Giving them something to cut also diverts attention from the basic budget with its vital programs.
- **Make cuts hurt:** If your agency is faced with a real budget cut—that is, a reduction from last year's appropriation—announce pending cuts in vital and popular programs in order to stir up opposition to the cut. For example, the National Park Service might announce the impending closing of the Washington Monument. Never acknowledge that cuts might be accommodated by your agency without reducing basic services.

---

vices," "contractual services," "travel," "supplies," "equipment." It is difficult to tell from such a listing exactly what programs the agency is spending its money on. Such a budget obscures policy decisions by hiding programs behind meaningless phrases. Even if these categories are broken down into line items (for example, under "personnel services," the line-item budget might say, "John Doaks, Assistant Administrator, $85,000"), it is still next to impossible to identify the costs of various programs.

For many years, reformers have called for budgeting by programs. **Program budgeting** would require agencies to present budgetary requests in terms of the end products they will produce or at least to allocate each expense to a specific program. However, bureaucrats are often unenthusiastic about program budgeting; it certainly adds to the time and energy devoted to budgeting, and many agencies are reluctant to describe precisely what it is they do and how much it really costs to do it. Moreover, some political functions are best served by *non*program budgeting. Agreement comes more easily when the items in dispute can be treated in dollars instead of programmatic differences. Congressional Appropriations Committees can focus on increases or decreases in overall dollar amounts for agencies

program budgeting
Identifying items in a budget according to the functions and programs they are to be spent on.

How Much Money Does the Government Waste?

Bureaucracy is often associated in the public's mind with waste and inefficiency. But it is very difficult to determine objectively how much money government really wastes. People disagree on the value of various government programs. What is "waste" to one person may be a vital governmental function to another. But even those who believe a government program is necessary may still believe some of the money going to that program is wasted by the bureaucracy.

Indeed, over the last twenty years, nearly two-thirds of Americans have described the government as wasting "a lot" of money rather than "some" or "not very much" (see graph). Americans believe that there is more waste in domestic spending than in military spending.

Is public opinion correct in estimating that "a lot" of money is wasted? The General Accounting Office is an arm of Congress with broad authority to audit the operations and finances of federal agencies. GAO audits have frequently found fraud and mismanagement amounting to 10 percent or more of the spending of many agencies it has reviewed, which suggests that *$200 billion* of the overall federal budget of $2.1 trillion may be wasted.[*] Citizens' commissions studying the federal bureaucracy

place an even higher figure on waste. The Grace Commission estimated waste at more than 20 percent of federal spending.[†]

[*] General Accounting Office, *Federal Evaluation Issues* (Washington, D.C., 1989).

[†] *President's Private Sector Survey on Cost Control* (Grace Commission Report) (Washington, D.C.: Government Printing Office, 1984).

Question: *How much waste would you say there is in various spending by the United States government: a great deal, some, not not very much, or none at all?*

In domestic spending

Great deal	61%
Some	32%
Not very much	5%
None at all	1%

In military spending

Great deal	43%
Some	41%
Not very much	10%
None at all	3%

Source: Copyright © 2001, *The Washington Post,* Reprinted with permission.

---

rather than battle over even more contentious questions of which individual programs are worthy of support.

Regulatory Battles

Bureaucracies regulate virtually every aspect of American life. Interest rates on loans are heavily influenced by the Federal Reserve Board. The National Labor Relations Board protects unions and prohibits "unfair labor practices." Safety in automobiles and buses is the responsibility of the National Transportation Safety Board. The Federal Deposit Insurance Corporation insures bank accounts. The Federal Trade Commission orders cigarette manufacturers to place a health warning on each pack. The Equal Employment Opportunity Commission investigates complaints about racial and sexual discrimination in jobs. The Consumer Product Safety Commission requires that toys be large enough that they cannot be swallowed by children. The Federal Communications Commission bans tobacco advertisements on television. The Environmental Protection Agency requires

THINK AGAIN

Do you believe that the overall costs of federal regulatory activity are justified by the benefits?

THINK AGAIN

Do you believe bureaucratic regulations of all kinds are hurting America's competitiveness in the global economy?

automobile companies to limit exhaust emissions. The Occupational Safety and Health Administration requires construction firms to place portable toilets at work sites. The Food and Drug Administration decides what drugs your doctor can prescribe. The list goes on and on. Indeed, it is difficult to find an activity in public or private life that is not regulated by the federal government (see *A Conflicting View:* "Bureaucratic Regulations Are Suffocating America").

Federal regulatory bureaucracies are legislators, investigators, prosecutors, judges, and juries—all wrapped into one. They issue thousands of pages of rules and regulations each year, they investigate thousands of complaints and conduct thousands of inspections; they require businesses to submit hundreds of thousands of forms each year; they hold hearings, determine "compliance" and "noncompliance," issue corrective orders, and levy fines and penalties. Most economists agree that regulation adds to the cost of living, is an obstacle to innovation and productivity, and hinders economic competition. Most regulatory commissions are independent; they are not under an executive department, and their members are appointed for long terms by a president who has little control over their activities.

Traditional Agencies: Capture Theory

The **capture theory of regulation** describes how some regulated industries come to benefit from government regulation and how some regulatory commissions come to represent the industries they are supposed to regulate rather than representing "the people." Historically, regulatory commissions have acted against only the most wayward members of an industry. By attacking those businesses that gave the industry bad publicity, the commissions actually helped improve the public's opinion of the industry as a whole. Regulatory commissions provided symbolic reassurance to the public that the behavior of the industry was proper. Among the traditional regulatory agencies that have been accused of becoming too close to their regulated industry are the Federal Communications Commission (FCC, the communications industry, including the television networks), the Securities and Exchange Commission (SEC, the securities industry and stock exchanges), the Federal Reserve Board (FRB, the banking industry), and National Labor Relations Board (NLRB, unions).

Commission members often come from the industry they are supposed to regulate, and after a few years in government, the "regulators" return to high-paying jobs in the industry, creating the *revolving door problem* described in Chapter 9. In addition, many regulatory commissions attract young attorneys fresh from law school to their staffs. Industry siphons off the "best and the brightest" of these, offering them much higher paying jobs as defenders against government regulation. Over the years, then, some industries have come to support their regulatory bureaucracies. Industries have often strongly opposed proposals to reduce government controls. Proposals to deregulate railroads, interstate trucking, and airlines have met with substantial opposition from both the regulatory bureaucracies and the regulated industries, working together.

The Newer Regulators: The Activists

In recent decades, Congress created several new "activist" regulatory agencies in response to the civil rights movement, the environmental movement, and the consumer protection movement. Unlike traditional regulatory agencies, the activist agencies do not regulate only a single industry; rather, they extend their jurisdiction to all industries. The Equal Employment Opportunity Commission (EEOC), the Environmental Protection Agency (EPA), and the Occupational Safety and Health Administration (OSHA) pose serious challenges to the business community. Many businesspeople argue that

capture theory of regulation
Theory describing how some regulated industries come to benefit from government regulation and how some regulatory commissions come to represent the industries they are supposed to regulate rather than representing "the people."

Bureaucratic Regulations Are Suffocating America

Today, bureaucratic regulations of all kinds—environmental controls, workplace safety rules, municipal building codes, government contracting guidelines—have become so numerous, detailed, and complex that they are stifling initiative, curtailing economic growth, wasting billions of dollars, and breeding popular contempt for law and government.

Consider, for example, the Environmental Protection Agency's rules and regulations, now *seventeen volumes* of fine print. Under one set of rules, before any land on which "toxic" waste was once used can be reused by anyone for any purpose, it must be cleaned to near perfect purity. The dirt must be made cleaner than soil that has never been used for anything. The result is that most new businesses choose to locate on virgin land rather than incur the enormous expense of cleaning dirt, and a great deal of land previously used by industry sits vacant while new land is developed.

These and similar examples of "the death of common sense" in bureaucratic regulations are set forth by critic Philip K. Howard, who argues, "We have constructed a system of regulatory law that basically outlaws common sense."* The result is that we direct our energy and wealth into defensive measures, designed not to improve our lives but to avoid tripping over senseless rules. People come to see government as their adversary and government regulations as obstacles in their lives.

The explosive growth in federal regulations in the last two decades has added heavy costs to the American economy. The costs of regulations do not appear in the federal budget: rather, they are paid for by businesses, employees, and consumers. Indeed, politicians prefer a regulatory approach to the environment, health, and safety precisely because it forces costs on the private sector—costs that are largely invisible to voters and taxpayers. Yet as the costs of regulation multiply for American businesses, the prices of their products rise in world markets.

How large is the regulatory bill? Proponents of a regulatory activity usually object to estimating its cost. Politicians who wish to develop an image as protectors of the environment, of consumers, of the disabled, and so on, do not want to call attention to the costs of their legislation. Only recently has the Office of Management and Budget (OMB) even attempted to estimate the costs of federal regulatory activity. Overall, regulatory activity costs Americans between $300 billion (OMB estimate) and $700 billion a year (estimate by Center for the Study of American Business), an amount equal to over one-third of the total federal budget. If the $700 billion estimate is correct, it means that each of America's 100 million households pays about $7,000 per year in the hidden costs of regulation. Paperwork requirements consume more than 5 billion hours of people's time, mostly to comply with the administration by the Internal Revenue Service of the tax laws. However, the costs of environmental controls, including the Environmental Protection Agency's enforcement of clean air and water and hazardous waste disposal regulations, are the fastest growing regulatory costs.

The real question is whether the *benefits* of this regulatory activity—for example, cleaner air and water, safer disposal of toxic wastes, safer consumer products, fewer workplace injuries, fewer highway deaths, protections against discrimination, improved access for disabled, and so on—are greater or less than the costs. But assessing the value of benefits is extraordinarily difficult. Many people object on ethical grounds to economic estimates of the value of a human life saved.

Regulation also places a heavy burden on innovations and productivity. The costs and delays in winning permission for a new product tend to discourage invention and to drive up prices. For example, new drugs are difficult to introduce in the United States because the Food and Drug Administration (FDA) typically requires up to ten years of testing. Western European nations are many years ahead in their number of life-saving drugs available; they speak of the "drug lag" in the United States. Critics charge that if aspirin were proposed for marketing today, it would not be approved by the FDA. Recently activists have succeeded in speeding up FDA approval of drugs to treat AIDS, but the agency has continued to delay the introduction of drugs to treat other diseases.

*Philip K. Howard. *The Death of Common Sense: How Law Is Suffocating America* (New York: Random House, 1995), pp. 10–11.

EEOC rules designed to prevent racial and sexual discrimination in employment and promotion (affirmative action guidelines) ignore the problems of their industry or their labor market and overlook the costs of training or the availability of qualified minorities. Likewise, many of OSHA's thousands of safety regulations appear costly and ridiculous to people in industry. The complaint about EPA is that it seldom considers the cost of its rulings to business or the consumer. Industry representatives contend that EPA should weigh the costs of its regulations against the benefits to the environment.

Deregulation The demand to deregulate American life was politically very popular during President Ronald Reagan's administration in the 1980s. But **deregulation** made only limited progress in curtailing the power of the regulatory bureaucracies. Arguments for deregulation centered on the heavy costs of compliance with regulations, the burdens these costs imposed on innovation and productivity, and the adverse impact of regulatory activity on the global competitiveness of American industry. In 1978 Jimmy Carter succeeded in getting Congress to deregulate the airline industry. Against objections by the industry itself, which *wanted* continued regulation, the Civil Aeronautics Board was stripped of its powers to allocate airline routes to various carriers and to set rates. At the end of 1984, the board went out of existence, the first major regulatory agency ever to be abolished. With the airlines free to choose where to fly and what to charge, competition on heavily traveled routes (such as from New York to Los Angeles) reduced fares dramatically while prices rose on less traveled routes served by a single airline. Overall the cost of airline travel declined by 25 to 30 percent.[15] Competition caused airline profits to decline and financially weak airlines to declare bankruptcy. Also, during the 1980s the Interstate Commerce Commission (ICC), the first regulatory commission ever established by the federal government, dating from 1887, was stripped of most of its power to set railroad and trucking rates. The ICC itself was finally abolished in 1995. Prices to consumers of railroad and trucking services declined dramatically.

Reregulation Deregulation threatens to diminish politicians' power and to eliminate bureaucrats' jobs. It forces industries to become competitive and diminishes the role of interest group lobbyists. So in the absence of strong popular support for deregulation, pressures to continue and expand regulatory activity will always be strong in Washington.

Airline deregulation brought about a huge increase in airline travel. The airlines doubled their seating capacity and made more efficient use of their aircraft through the development of "hub-and-spoke" networks. Air safety continued to improve; fatalities per millions of miles flown declined; and by taking travelers away from far more dangerous highway travel, overall transportation safety was enhanced. But these favorable outcomes were overshadowed by complaints about congestion at major airports and increased flight delays, especially at peak hours. The major airports are publicly owned, and governments have been very slow in responding to increased air traffic. Congestion and delays are widely publicized, and politicians respond to complaints by calling for reregulation of airline travel.

The political incentives to create new regulatory agencies, grant additional powers to existing agencies, and add to the accumulation of federal regulations are great. Politicians want to be seen "doing something" about any well-publicized problem in America. When the media reports accidents, health scares, environmental dangers, etc., politicians are interviewed for their response, and most feel

The deregulation of the airline industry contributed to the development of the hub-and-spoke system currently used by most airlines to reduce their costs. Here American Airlines aircraft congregate at the airline's hub in Dallas/Fort Worth. Although deregulation has caused fares to decrease on heavily competitive routes, critics charge that it has contributed to higher rates on non-competitive routes.

deregulation Lifting of government rules and bureaucratic supervision from business and professional activity.

obliged to call for new laws and regulations, with little regard to their likely costs or effectiveness.

Regulating America

WWW **Code of Federal Regulations**

All 50 titles of federal regulations can be found at the Cornell Law School site. *www.cfr.law.cornell.edu*

Federal regulatory agencies continually add more rules to American life. Roughly 4,000 new rules, all with the force of law, are issued by regulatory agencies each year. The Environmental Protection Agency (EPA) leads in making new rules, closely followed by the Internal Revenue Service (IRS) and the Federal Communications Commission (FCC).

Over 50 federal agencies have rule-making power. These agencies must publish proposed rules in the *Federal Register* and allow time for interested groups to "comment" on them. "Major rules," those estimated to cost Americans at least $100 or more per year in compliance, are sent to the Office of Management and Budget before being finalized. In the five-year period 1996–2001, the General Accounting Office of Congress reported that 21,653 *new* final rules were issued. Some 335 of these new rules were listed as "major rules."[16]

Multiplying Regulations Inasmuch as proposed new regulations must be published in the *Federal Register,* the size of this publication is often used as an indicator of overall federal regulatory activity. In 1970, the *Federal Register* included roughly 20,000 pages; by 1980 it had expanded to over 73,000 pages. Only during the presidency of Ronald Reagan, who promised to reduce federal regulatory activity, did the size of the *Federal Register* decline somewhat (see Figure 12.5). But by 2000 it was again over 80,000 pages.

The accumulated regulations of federal government are published in the Code of Federal Regulations. The Code includes all regulations currently in effect. The Code has now expanded to over 144,000 pages in 205 volumes.

The Costs of Regulation Regulatory activity incurs costs for American businesses, employers, and consumers—costs which do not appear in federal budget.

FIGURE 12.5
Regulating America

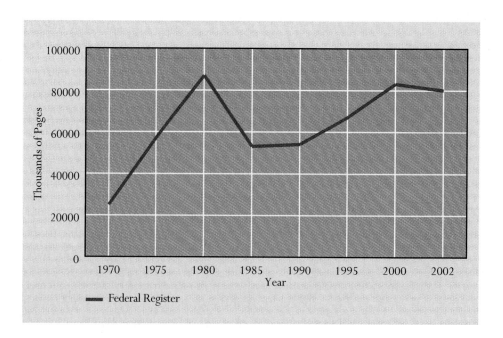

(The official budgets of all federal regulatory agencies combined add up to "only" about $15 billion.) Indeed, it is precisely because these costs do not appear in the federal budget that politicians prefer a regulatory approach to many of the nation's problems. Regulation shifts costs from the government itself onto the private sector, costs that are largely invisible to voters and taxpayers. Even when agencies themselves are supposed to calculate the costs of their regulations, their calculations vary in quality and almost always underestimate the true costs. One independent estimate of the total costs of federal regulation sets the figure at $700 *billion*, or about 7 percent of the nation's Gross Domestic Product.[17]

Regulations impose costs on Americans in a variety of ways. First of all, there are the direct costs of compliance. Direct costs include everything from adding pollution control devices and making businesses accessible to the disabled, to the overhead costs of paperwork, attorney and accounting fees, and staff time needed to negotiate the federal regulatory maze. Secondly, there are indirect economic costs—costs incurred by devoting resources to compliance that otherwise would be used to increase productivity. This lost economic output may amount to *$1 trillion* per year.[18] All of these costs, which typically are imposed on businesses, are ultimately passed onto American consumers in the form of higher prices.

Congressional Constraints on the Bureaucracy

Bureaucracies are unelected hierarchical organizations, yet they must function within democratic government. To wed bureaucracy to democracy, ways must be found to ensure that bureaucracy is responsible to the people. Controlling the bureaucracy is a central concern of democratic government. The federal bureaucracy is responsible to all three branches of government—the president, the Congress, and the courts. Although the president is the nominal head of the executive agencies, Congress—through its power to create or eliminate and fund or fail to fund these agencies—exerts its full share of control. Most of the structure of the executive branch of government (see Figure 12.1) is determined by laws of Congress. Congress has the constitutional power to create or abolish executive departments and independent agencies, or to transfer their functions, as it wishes. Congress can by law expand or contract the discretionary authority of bureaucrats. It can grant broad authority to agencies in vaguely written language, thereby adding to the power of bureaucracies, which can then determine themselves how to define and implement their own authority. In contrast, narrow and detailed laws place constraints on the bureaucracy.

In addition to specific constraints on particular agencies, Congress has placed a number of general constraints on the entire federal bureaucracy. Among the more important laws governing bureaucratic behavior are these:

- *Administrative Procedures Act (1946):* Requires that agencies considering a new rule or policy give public notice in the *Federal Register,* solicit comments, and hold public hearings before adopting the new measures.

- *Freedom of Information Act (1966):* Requires agencies to allow citizens (and the media) to inspect all public records, with some exceptions for intelligence, current criminal investigations, and personnel actions (see *Up Close:* "How to Use the Freedom of Information Act").

- *Privacy Act (1974):* Requires agencies to keep confidential the personal records of individuals, notably their Social Security files and income tax records.

The Director of the Office of Management and Budget is one of the most influential bureaucrats in Washington. Yet he is seldom seen on national television. Here, President Bush's OMB Director Joshua B. Bolten testifies before a congressional committee.

How to Use the Freedom of Information Act

The Freedom of Information Act (FOIA) of 1966 requires agencies of the federal government to provide any member of the public records of the agencies. As amended by the Privacy Act of 1974, individuals can obtain personal records held by government agencies and are given the right to correct information that is inaccurate. The FOIA does not apply to Congress, the federal courts, state and local government agencies (unless a state has similar law), military plans and weapons, law enforcement investigations, records of financial institutions, or records which would invade the privacy of others. An agency must respond within ten days to an FOIA request, but it may charge fees for the costs of searching for the documents and duplicating them.

A good request must "reasonably describe" the records that are being sought; it must be specific enough that an agency employee will be able to locate the records within a reasonable amount of time. A good FOIA request letter includes:

Attention: Freedom of Information/Privacy Request Name and Address of Agency

This is a request under the Freedom of Information Act, 5 U.S.C. Sec.552

I request a copy of the following documents be provided for me.

_____

_____

I am aware that if my request is denied I am entitled to know the grounds for this denial and make an administrative appeal.

I am willing to pay fees for this request up to a maximum of $___. If you estimate that fees will succeed this limit, please inform me first.

Thank you for your prompt attention.

Signature

Address

Senate Confirmation of Appointments The U.S. Senate's power to confirm presidential appointments gives it some added influence over the bureaucracy.[19] It is true that once nominated and confirmed, cabinet secretaries and regulatory commission members can defy the Congress; only the president can remove them from office. Senators usually try to impress their own views on presidential appointees seeking confirmation, however. Senate committees holding confirmation hearings often subject appointees to lengthy lectures on how the members believe their departments or agencies should be run. In extreme cases, when presidential appointees do not sufficiently reflect the views of Senate leaders, their confirmation can be held up indefinitely or, in very rare cases, defeated in a floor vote on confirmation.

Congressional Oversight Congressional oversight of the federal bureaucracy is a continuing activity.[20] Congress justifies its oversight activities on the ground that its lawmaking powers require it to determine whether the purposes of the laws it passed are being carried out. Congress has a legitimate interest in communicating legislative *intent* to bureaucrats charged with the responsibility for implementing laws of Congress. But often oversight activities are undertaken to influence bureaucratic decision making. Members of Congress may seek to secure favorable treatment for friends and constituents, try to lay the political groundwork for increases or decreases in agency appropriations, or simply strive to enhance their own power or the power of their committees or subcommittees over the bureaucracy.

Oversight is lodged primarily in congressional committees and subcommittees (see "In Committee" in Chapter 10) whose jurisdictions generally parallel those of executive departments and agencies. However, all too frequently, agencies are required to respond to multiple committee inquiries in both the House and the Senate.

Congressional Appropriations The congressional power to grant or to withhold the budget requests of bureaucracies and the president is perhaps Congress's most potent weapon in controlling the bureaucracy. Spending authorizations for executive agencies are determined by standing committees with jurisdiction in various policy areas, such as armed services, judiciary, education, and labor (see Table 10.4 in Chapter 10), and appropriations are determined by the House and Senate Appropriations Committees and, more specifically, their subcommittees with particular jurisdictions. These committees and subcommittees exercise great power over executive agencies. The Defense Department, for example, must seek *authorizations* for new weapons systems from the House and Senate Armed Services Committees and *appropriations* to actually purchase these weapons from the House and Senate Appropriations Committees, especially their Defense Appropriations subcommittees.

Congressional Investigation Congressional investigations offer yet another tool for congressional oversight of the bureaucracy. Historically, congressional investigations have focused on scandal and wrongdoing in the executive branch (see "Oversight of the Bureaucracy" in Chapter 10). Occasionally, investigations even produce corrective legislation, although they more frequently produce changes in agency personnel, procedures, or policies. Investigations are more likely to follow media reports of waste, fraud, or scandal than to uncover previously unknown problems. In other words, investigations perform a political function for Congress—assuring voters that the Congress is taking action against bureaucratic abuses. Studies of routine bureaucratic performance are likely to be undertaken by the General Accounting Office (GAO), an arm of Congress and frequent critic of executive agencies. GAO may undertake studies of the operations of executive agencies on its own initiative but more often responds to requests for studies by specific members of Congress.

Casework Perhaps the most frequent congressional oversight activities are calls, letters, and visits to the agencies by individual members of Congress seeking to influence particular actions on behalf of themselves or their constituents. A great deal of congressional **casework** involves intervening with executive agencies on behalf of constituents[21] (see Chapter 10). Executive departments and agencies generally try to deal with congressional requests and inquiries as favorably and rapidly as the law allows. Pressure from a congressional office will lead bureaucrats to speed up an application, correct an error, send information, review a case, or reinterpret a regulation to favor a client with congressional contacts. But bureaucrats become very uncomfortable when asked to violate established regulations on behalf of a favored person or firm. The line between serving constituents and unethical or illegal attempts to influence government agencies is sometimes very difficult to discern.

Lobbying Washington can take many forms. Although most professional lobbyists operate quietly within the balls of the nation's capital, groups of private citizens often take to the streets to get their message across. Demonstrations may capture the attention of the media and thus may force bureaucrats and politicians at least to consider a group's cause, but the attention span of both media and Washington power brokers can be extremely short. Here people protest in front of the White House against President Clinton's decision to back NATO air attacks on Serbia.

casework Services performed by legislators and their staffs on behalf of individual constituents.

Interest Groups and Bureaucratic Decision Making

Interest groups understand that great power is lodged in the bureaucracy. Indeed, interest groups exercise an even closer oversight of bureaucracy than do the president, Congress, and courts, largely because their interests are directly affected by day-to-day bureaucratic decisions. Interest groups focus their attention on the particular departments and agencies that serve or regulate their own members or that function in their chosen policy field. For example, the American Farm Bureau Federation monitors the actions of the Department of Agriculture; environmental lobbies—such as the National Wildlife Federation, the Sierra Club, and the Environmental Defense Fund—watch over the Environmental Protection Agency as well as the National Park Service; the American Legion, Veterans of Foreign Wars, and Vietnam Veterans "oversee" the Department of Veterans Affairs. Thus, specific groups come to have a proprietary interest in "their" specific departments and agencies. Departments and agencies understand that their "client" groups have a continuing interest in their activities.

Many bureaucracies owe their very existence to strong interest groups that successfully lobbied Congress to create them. The Environmental Protection Agency owes its existence to the environmental groups, just as the Equal Employment Opportunity Commission owes its existence to civil rights groups. Thus, many bureaucracies nourish interest groups' support to aid in expanding their authority and increasing their budgets (see "Iron Triangles and Policy Networks" in Chapter 9).

Interest groups can lobby bureaucracies directly by responding to notices of proposed regulations, testifying at public hearings, and providing information and commentary. Or interest groups can lobby Congress either in support of bureaucratic activity or to reverse a bureaucratic decision. Interest groups may also seek to "build fires" under bureaucrats by holding press conferences, undertaking advertising campaigns, and soliciting media support for agency actions. Or interest groups may even seek to influence bureaucracies through appeals to the federal courts.

Judicial Constraints on the Bureaucracy

Judicial oversight is another source of restraint on the bureaucracy. Bureaucratic decisions are subject to review by the federal courts. Federal courts can even issue *injunctions* (orders) to an executive agency *before* it issues or enforces a regulation or undertakes a particular action. Thus, the judiciary poses a check on bureaucratic power.

Judicial Standards for Bureaucratic Behavior Historically, the courts have stepped in when agency actions have violated laws passed by Congress, when agencies have exceeded the authority granted them under the laws, when the agency actions have been adjudged "arbitrary and unreasonable," and when agencies have failed in their legal duties under the law. The courts have also restrained the bureaucracy on procedural grounds—ensuring proper notice, fair hearings, rights of appeal, and so on. In short, appeal to the courts must cite failures of agencies to abide by substantive or procedural laws.

Judicial oversight tends to focus on (1) whether or not agencies are acting beyond the authority granted them by Congress; and (2) whether or not they are abiding by rules of procedural fairness. It is important to realize that the courts do not usually involve themselves in the *policy* decisions of bureaucracies. If policy decisions are made in accordance with the legal authority granted agencies by Congress, and if they are made with procedural fairness, the courts generally do not intervene.

Bureaucrats' Success in Court Bureaucracies have been very successful in defending their actions in federal courts.[22] individual citizens and interest groups seeking to restrain or reverse the actions or decisions of executive agencies have been largely *unsuccessful*. What accounts for this success? Bureaucracies have established elaborate administrative processes to protect their decisions from challenge on procedural grounds. Regulatory agencies have armies of attorneys, paid for out of tax monies, who specialize in these narrow fields of law. It is very expensive for individual citizens to challenge agency actions. Corporations and interest groups must weigh the costs of litigation against the costs of compliance before undertaking a legal challenge of the bureaucracy. Excessive delays in court proceedings, sometimes extending to several years, add to the time and expense of challenging bureaucratic decisions.

SUMMARY NOTES

- The Washington bureaucracy—the departments, agencies, and bureaus of the executive branch of the federal government—is a major base of power in American government. Political conflict does not end when a law is passed by Congress and signed by the president. The arena merely shifts to the bureaucracy.

- Bureaucratic power has grown with increases in the size of government, advances in technology, and the greater complexity of modern society. Congress and the president do not have the time, resources, or expertise to decide the details of policy across the wide range of social and economic activity in the nation. Bureaucracies must draw up the detailed rules and regulations that actually govern the nation. Often laws are passed for their symbolic value; bureaucrats must give practical meaning to these laws. And the bureaucracy itself is now sufficiently powerful to get laws passed adding to its authority, size, and budget.

- Policy implementation is the development of procedures and activities and the allocation of money, personnel, and other resources to carry out the tasks mandated by law. Implementation includes regulation—the making of detailed rules based on the law—as well as adjudication—the application of laws and regulations to specific cases. Bureaucratic power increases with increases in administrative discretion.

- Bureaucracies usually seek to expand their own powers, functions, and budgets. Most bureaucrats believe strongly in the value of their own programs and the importance of their tasks. And bureaucrats, like everyone else, seek added power, pay, and prestige. Bureaucratic expansion contributes to the growth of government.

- The federal bureaucracy consists of 2.8 million civilian employees in 14 cabinet departments and more than 60 independent agencies, as well as a large Executive Office of the President. Federal employment is not growing, but federal spending, especially for Social Security, Medicare, and Medicaid, is growing rapidly.

- Today federal spending amounts to about 20 percent of GDP, and federal, state, and local government spending combined amounts to about 30 percent of GDP.

- Historically, political conflict over government employment centered on the question of partisanship versus competence. Over time, the "merit system" replaced the "spoils system" in federal employment, but the civil service system raised problems of responsiveness and productivity in the bureaucracy. Civil service reform efforts have not really resolved these problems.

- The president's control of the bureaucracy rests principally on the powers to appoint and remove policy-making officials, to recommend increases and decreases in agency budgets, and to recommend changes in agency structure and function.

- But the bureaucracy has developed various means to insulate itself from presidential influence. Bureaucrats have many ways to delay and obstruct policy decisions with which they disagree. Whistle-blowers may inform Congress or the media of waste, mismanagement, or fraud. A network of friends and professional associates among bureaucrats, congressional staffs, and client groups helps create a "culture" within each agency and department. The bureaucratic culture is highly resistant to change.

- Women and minorities are represented in overall federal employment in proportion to their percentages of the U.S. population. However, women and minorities are not proportionately represented in the higher levels of the bureaucracy.

- Budget battles over who gets what begin in the bureaucracy as departments and agencies send their budget requests forward to the president's Office of Management and Budget. OMB usually reduces agency requests in line with the president's priorities. The president submits spending recommendations to Congress early each year in *The Budget of the United States Government.* Congress is supposed to pass its appropriations acts prior to the beginning of the fiscal year, October 1, but frequently falls behind schedule.

- Budgeting is incremental, in that last year's agency expenditures are usually accepted as a base and attention is focused on proposed increases. Incrementalism saves time and effort and reduces political conflict by not requiring agencies to justify every dollar spent, only proposed increases each year. Nonprogrammatic budgeting also helps reduce conflict over the value of particular programs. The result, however, is that many established pro-grams continue long after the need for them has disappeared.

- Bureaucracies regulate virtually every aspect of our lives. The costs of regulation are borne primarily by business and consumers; they do not appear in the federal budget. In part for this reason, a regulatory approach to national problems appeals to elected officials who seek to obscure the costs of government activity. It is difficult to calculate the true costs and benefits of much regulatory activity. After a brief period of deregulation in the 1980s, regulation has regained popular favor.

- Congress can exercise control over the bureaucracy in a variety of ways: by creating, abolishing, or reorganizing departments and agencies; by altering their authority and functions; by requiring bureaucrats to testify before congressional committees; by undertaking investigations and studies through the General Accounting Office; by intervening directly on behalf of constituents; by instructing presidential nominees in Senate confirmation hearings and occasionally delaying or defeating nominations; and especially by withholding or threatening to withhold agency appropriations or by writing very specific provisions into appropriations acts.

- Interest groups also influence bureaucratic decision making directly by testifying at public hearings and providing information and commentary, and indirectly by contacting the media, lobbying Congress, and initiating lawsuits.

- Judicial control of the bureaucracy is usually limited to determining whether agencies have exceeded the authority granted them by law or have abided by the rules of procedural fairness. Federal bureaucracies have a strong record of success in defending themselves in court.

KEY TERMS

bureaucracy   417
chain of command   417
division of labor   417
impersonality   417
implementation   418
regulation   421
adjudication   421

budget maximization   422
discretionary funds   422
spoils system   433
merit system   433
whistle-blower   437
fiscal year   439
budget resolution   439

authorization   441
appropriations act   441
obligational authority   441
outlays   441
continuing resolution   441
incremental budgeting   442

zero-based budgeting   442
program budgeting   443
capture theory of regulation   445
deregulation   447
casework   451

SUGGESTED READINGS

Gore, Al. *Creating a Government That Works Better and Costs Less.* Washington, D.C.: Government Printing Office, 1993. Specific recommendations for "reinventing" government by making citizens "customers," introducing competition, cutting red tape, and privatizing government services.

Henry, Nicholas. *Public Administration and Public Affairs.* 9th ed. Upper Saddle River, N. J.: Prentice Hall, 2003. Authoritative introductory textbook on public organizations (bureaucracies), public management, and policy implementation.

Howard, Philip K. *The Death of Common Sense: How Law Is Suffocating America.* New York: Random House, 1995. Outrageous stories of bureaucratic senselessness coupled with a plea to allow bureaucrats flexibility in achieving the purposes of laws and holding them accountable for outcomes.

Maxwell, Bruce. *CQ's Insider's Guide to Finding a Job in Washington.* Washington, D.C.: CQ Press, 2000. How to locate job vacancies, make contacts, "market" oneself, and build a career in the Washington bureaucracy.

Neiman, Max. *Defending Government: Why Big Government Works.* Upper Saddle River, N. J.: Prentice Hall, 2000. A spirited defense of big government as a product of people's desire to improve their lives.

Osborne, David, and Ted Gaebler. *Reinventing Government.* New York: Addison-Wesley, 1992. The respected manual of the "reinventing government" movement with recommendations to overcome the routine tendencies of bureaucracies and inject "the entrepreneurial spirit" in them.

Radin, Beryl. *The Accountable Juggler: The Art of Leadership in a Federal Agency.* Washington, D.C.: CQ Press, 2002. A close-up look at managers in the Department of Health and Human Services, how they juggle competing accountability demands.

Schick, Allen. *The Federal Budget: Politics, Policy, Process.* Rev. ed. Washington, D.C.: Brookings Institution, 2000. A comprehensive explanation of the federal budgetary process.

Shafvitz, Jay M. and E.W. Russell. *Introducing Public Administration.* 3rd ed. New York: Pearson Longman, 2002. Comprehensive introductory textbook in public administration.

Wilson, James Q. *Bureaucracy: What Government Agencies Do and Why They Do It.* New York: Basic Books, 1989. In the author's words, "an effort to depict the essential features of bureaucratic life in the government agencies of the United States." Examining what really motivates middle-level public servants, Wilson argues that congressional attempts to "micromanage" government activities hamper the ability of bureaucrats to do their jobs.

MAKE IT REAL

BUREAUCRACY: A PLACE WHERE IDEALS MEET REALITY

Congratulations on your appointment as Deputy Director of the Census Bureau! With the change in administration you will help to rebuild a bureaucracy that was shaken up during the transition from the previous administration. One of your responsibilities is to shield the Director from the routine problems that arise in any bureaucratic organization. As bureaucratic problems arrive on your desk you must make the decisions that will establish you as a seasoned administrator.

CHAPTER *13*

COURTS:
JUDICIAL POLITICS

THINK
ABOUT POLITICS

Judicial Power

"There is hardly a political question in the United States which does not sooner or later turn into a judicial one."[1] This observation by French diplomat and traveler Alexis de Tocqueville, although made in 1835, is even more accurate today. It is the Supreme Court and the federal judiciary, rather than the president or Congress, that has taken the lead in deciding many of the most heated issues of American politics. It has undertaken to:

■ Eliminate racial segregation and decide about affirmative action.

■ Ensure separation of church and state and decide about prayer in public schools.

■ Determine the personal liberties of women and decide about abortion.

■ Define the limits of free speech and free press and decide about obscenity, censorship, and pornography.

■ Ensure equality of representation and require legislative districts to be equal in population.

■ Define the rights of criminal defendants, prevent unlawful searches, limit the questioning of suspects, and prevent physical or mental intimidation of suspects.

■ Protect private homosexual acts between consenting adults from criminal prosecution.

■ Decide the life-or-death issue of capital punishment.

Courts are "political" institutions. Like Congress, the president, and the bureaucracy courts decide who gets what in American society. Judges do not merely "apply" the law to specific cases. Years ago, former Supreme Court Justice Felix Frankfurter explained why this mechanistic theory of judicial objectivity fails to describe court decision making.

> The meaning of "due process" and the content of terms like "liberty" are not revealed by the Constitution. It is the Justices who make the meaning. They read into the neutral language of the Constitution their own economic and social views. . . . Let us face the fact that five Justices of the Supreme Court are the molders of policy rather than the impersonal vehicles of revealed truth.[2]

Constitutional Power of the Courts The Constitution grants "the judicial Power of the United States" to the Supreme Court and other "inferior Courts" that Congress may establish. The Constitution guarantees that the Supreme Court and federal judiciary will be politically independent: judges are appointed, not elected, and hold their appointments for life (barring commission of any impeachable offenses). It also guarantees that their salaries will not be reduced during their time in office. The Constitution goes on to list the kinds of cases and controversies that the federal courts may decide. Federal judicial power extends to any case arising under the Constitution and federal laws and treaties, to cases in which officials of the federal government or of foreign governments are a party, and to cases between states or between citizens of different states.

Interpreting the Constitution: Judicial Review The Constitution is the "supreme Law of the Land" (Article VI). Judicial power is the power to decide cases and controversies and, in doing so, to decide what the Constitution and laws of Congress really mean. This authority—together with the guaranteed independence of judges—places great power in the Supreme Court and the federal judiciary. Indeed, because the Constitution takes precedence over laws of Congress as well as state constitutions and laws, it is the Supreme Court that ultimately decides whether Congress, the president, the states, and their local governments have acted constitutionally.

The power of **judicial review** is the power to invalidate laws of Congress or of the states that conflict with the U.S. Constitution. Judicial review is not specifically mentioned in the Constitution but has long been inferred from it. Even before the states had approved the Constitution, Alexander Hamilton wrote in 1787 that "limited government . . . can be preserved in practice no other way than through the medium of courts of justice, whose duty it is to declare all acts contrary to the manifest tenor of the Constitution void."[3] But it was the historic decision of *Marbury v. Madison* (1803)[4] that officially established judicial review as the most important judicial check on congressional power (see *People in Politics:* "John Marshall and Early Supreme Court Politics"). Writing for the majority, Chief Justice Marshall constructed a classic statement in judicial reasoning as he proceeded step by step to infer judicial review from the Constitution's Supremacy (Article VI) and Judicial Power (Article III, Section 1) clauses:

- The Constitution is the supreme law of the land, binding on all branches of government: legislative, executive, and judicial.

- The Constitution deliberately establishes a government with limited powers.

- Consequently, "an act of the legislature repugnant to the Constitution is void." If this were not true, the government would be unchecked and the Constitution would be an absurdity.

- Under the judicial power, "It is emphatically the province and duty of each of the judicial departments to say what the law is."

- "So if a law be in opposition to the Constitution . . . the court must determine which of these conflicting rules governs the case. This is the very essence of judicial duty."

- "If, then, the courts are to regard the Constitution, and the Constitution is superior to any ordinary act of the legislature, the Constitution, and not such ordinary act, must govern the case to which they both apply."

judicial review Power of the courts, especially the Supreme Court, to declare laws of Congress, laws of the states, and actions of the president unconstitutional and invalid.

John Marshall and Early Supreme Court Politics

John Marshall was a dedicated Federalist. A prominent Virginia lawyer, he was elected a delegate to Virginia's Constitution-ratifying convention, where he was instrumental in winning his state's approval of the document in 1788. Later Marshall served as secretary of state in the administration of John Adams, where he came into conflict with Adams's vice president, Thomas Jefferson.

In the election of 1800, Jefferson's Democratic-Republicans crushed Adams's Federalist Party. But Adams, taking advantage of the fact that his term of office would not expire until the following March,[*] sought to pack the federal judiciary with Federalists. The lame duck Federalist majority in the Senate confirmed the appointments, and John Marshall was sworn in as Chief Justice of the Supreme Court on February 4, 1801. Many of these "midnight appointments" came at the very last hours of Adams's term of office.

At that time, a specified task of the secretary of state was to deliver judicial commissions to new judges. When Marshall left his position as secretary of state to become Chief Justice, several of these commissions were still undelivered. Jefferson and the Democratic-Republicans were enraged over this last-minute Federalist chicanery, so when Jefferson assumed office in March, he ordered his new secretary of state, James Madison, not to deliver the remaining commissions. William Marbury, one of the disappointed Federalist appointees, brought a lawsuit to the Supreme Court, asking it to issue a writ of mandamus ("we command") to James Madison, ordering him to do his duty and deliver the valid commission.

The Judiciary Act of 1789, which established the federal court system, had included a provision granting original jurisdiction to the Supreme Court to issue writs of mandamus. The case, therefore, came directly to new Chief Justice John Marshall, who had failed to deliver the commission in the first place. (Today, we expect justices who are personally involved in a case to "recuse" themselves—that is, not to participate in that case, allowing the other justices to make the decision—but Marshall's actions were typical of his time.)

John Marshall realized that if he issued a direct order to Madison to deliver the commission, Madison would probably ignore it. The Court had no way to enforce such an order, and Madison had the support of President Jefferson. Issuing the writ would create a constitutional crisis in which the Supreme Court would most likely lose power. But if the Court failed to pronounce Madison's actions unlawful, it would lose legitimacy.

Marshall resolved his political dilemma with a brilliant judicial ploy. Writing for the majority in *Marbury v. Madison,* he announced that Madison was wrong to withhold the commission but that the Supreme Court could not issue a writ of mandamus because Section 13 of the Judiciary Act of 1789, which gave the Court *original* jurisdiction in the case, was unconstitutional. Giving the Supreme Court *original* jurisdiction conflicted with Article III, Section 2, of the Constitution, which gives the Supreme Court original jurisdiction only in cases affecting "Ambassadors, other public Ministers and Consuls, and those in which a State shall be a Party." "In all other Cases," the Constitution states that the Court shall have appellate jurisdiction. Thus Section 13 of the Judiciary Act was unconstitutional.

By declaring part of an act of Congress unconstitutional, Marshall accomplished multiple political objectives. He avoided a showdown with the executive branch that would undoubtedly have weakened the Court. He left Jefferson and Madison with no Court order to disobey. At the same time, Marshall forced Jefferson and the Democratic-Republicans to acknowledge the Supreme Court's power of judicial review—the power to declare an act of Congress unconstitutional. (To do otherwise would have meant acknowledging Marbury's claim.) Thus Marshall sacrificed Marbury's commission to a greater political goal, enhancing the Supreme Court's power.

---

[*] Not until the adoption of the Twentieth Amendment in 1933 was the president's inauguration moved up to January.

■ Hence, if a law is repugnant to the Constitution, the judges are duty bound to declare that law void in order to uphold the supremacy of the Constitution.

Arguments over Judicial Review The power of the federal courts to invalidate *state* laws and constitutions that conflict with federal laws or the federal Constitution is easily defended. Article VI states that the Constitution and federal laws and treaties are the supreme law of the land, "any Thing in the Constitution or Laws of any State to the Contrary notwithstanding." Indeed, the Constitution specifically obligates state judges to be "bound" by the Constitution and federal laws and to give these documents precedence over state constitutions and laws in rendering decisions. Federal court power over state decisions is probably essential to maintaining national unity: fifty different state interpretations of the meaning of the Constitution or of the laws and treaties of Congress would create unimaginable confusion. Thus the power of federal judicial review over state constitutions, laws, and court decisions is seldom questioned.

Today, the power of federal courts to invalidate laws of Congress and actions of the president is also widely accepted. No serious challenge to the power of judicial review has emerged in American politics. But we still might ask: Why should an appointed court's interpretation of the Constitution prevail over the views of an elected Congress and an elected president? Members of Congress and presidents swear to uphold the Constitution, and we can assume they do not pass laws they believe to be unconstitutional. Because both houses of Congress and the president must approve laws, why should federal courts be allowed to set aside these decisions? Is not judicial review, especially by unelected justices appointed for life, undemocratic?

Judicial Review of Laws of Congress Judicial review is potentially the most powerful weapon in the hands of the Supreme Court. It enables the Court to assert its power over the Congress, the president, and the states and to substitute its own judgment for that of other branches of the federal government and the states. However, the Supreme Court has been fairly restrained in its use of judicial review to void acts of Congress. Prior to the Civil War, the Supreme Court invalidated very few laws of any kind. Since that time, however, the general trend has been for the U.S. Supreme Court to strike down more *state* laws as unconstitutional. In contrast, the Court has been relatively restrained in its rejection of *federal* laws; over two centuries the Court has struck down fewer than 150 of the more than 60,000 laws passed by Congress.

Nevertheless, some of the laws overturned by the Supreme Court have been very important. In *Buckley v. Valeo* (1976)[5] the Court struck down provisions of the Federal Election Campaign Act that had limited the amount individuals could spend to finance their own campaigns or express their own independent political views. In *United States v. Morrison* (2000), the Supreme Court struck down Congress's Violence Against Women Act[6] as an unconstitutional expansion of the interstate commerce power and an invasion of powers reserved to the states (see *Up Close:* "Is Violence Against Women a Federal Crime?" in Chapter 4). Overall, however, the Supreme Court's use of judicial review against the Congress has been restrained.

Judicial Review of Presidential Actions The Supreme Court has only rarely challenged presidential power. The Court has overturned presidential policies both on the grounds that they conflicted with laws of Congress and on the grounds that they conflicted with the Constitution. In *Ex parte Milligan* (1866)[7] for example, the Court held (somewhat belatedly) that President Abraham Lincoln could not suspend the writ of habeas corpus in rebellious states during the Civil

William Jefferson Clinton Versus Paula Corbin Jones

The president is not "above the law"; that is, his conduct is not immune from judicial scrutiny. The president's official conduct must be lawful; federal courts may reverse presidential actions found to be unconstitutional or violative of laws of Congress. And presidents are not immune from criminal prosecution; they cannot ignore demands to provide information in criminal cases.[*] However, the Supreme Court has held that the president has "absolute immunity" from civil suits "arising out of the execution of official duties."[†] In other words, the president cannot be sued for damages caused by actions or decisions that are within his constitutional or legal authority.

But can the president be sued for *private* conduct beyond the scope of his official duties? In 1994 Paula Corbin Jones sued William Jefferson Clinton in federal district court in Arkansas, alleging that he made "abhorrent" sexual advances toward her in Little Rock in 1991 while he was governor and she was a state employee.

The president's lead attorney, Robert Bennett (brother of conservative commentator and former Reagan cabinet official William Bennett), stated that Clinton "has no recollection of ever meeting this woman" and "did not engage in any inappropriate or sexual conduct with this woman." But the president's defense team also argued that the president should be immune from civil actions, especially those arising from events alleged to occur *before* he assumed office. They argued that the president's constitutional responsibilities are so important and demanding that he must devote his undivided time and attention to them. He cannot be distracted by civil suits; otherwise a large volume of politically motivated frivolous litigation might undermine his ability to function effectively in office. At the very least, the president's attorney argued, the president should be given "temporary immunity" by postponing the case until after he leaves office.

However, in 1997 the U.S. Supreme Court rejected the notion of presidential immunity (as well as temporary immunity) from civil claims arising from actions outside of the president's official duties. Although advising lower courts to give "utmost deference to Presidential responsibilities" in handling the case, the Court held that "the doctrine of separation of powers does not require federal courts to stay all private actions against the president until he leaves office."[‡]

Subsequently, after reviewing the case, federal district judge Susan Wright dismissed Jones's charges as insufficient to prove sexual assault or harassment.[§] Clinton later settled the case with a financial payment to Jones, but with no admission or apology. The settlement ended Jones's appeals and avoided possible reopening of the case.

---

[*] *United States v. Nixon* (1974).
[†] *Nixon v. Fitzgerald* (1982).
[‡] *Clinton v. Jones*, May 27, 1997.
[§] *Jones v. Clinton*, April 1, 1998.

War. In *Youngstown Sheet and Tube Co. v. Sawyer*, in 1952,[8] it declared President Harry Truman's seizure of the nation's steel mills during the Korean War to be illegal. In 1974 it ordered President Richard Nixon to turn over taped White House conversations to the special Watergate prosecutor, leading to Nixon's forced resignation.[9] And in 1997 the Court held that President Bill Clinton was obliged to respond to a civil suit even while serving in the White House.[10] (See *Up Close:* "William Jefferson Clinton Versus Paula Corbin Jones.")

Judicial Review of State Laws The Supreme Court has used its power of judicial review far more frequently to invalidate state laws. Some of these decisions had impact far beyond the individual states on trial. For example, the historic 1954 decision in *Brown v. Board of Education of Topeka*, declaring segregation of the races in public schools to be unconstitutional, struck down the laws of twenty-one states[11] (see Chapter 12). The 1973 *Roe v. Wade* decision, establishing the constitutional right to abortion, struck down anti-abortion laws in more than forty states.[12] In 2003 the Court again struck down the laws of more than forty states by holding that private homosexual acts by consenting adults were protected by the constitution.[13]

Interpreting Federal Laws The power of the Supreme Court and the federal judiciary does not rest on judicial review alone. The courts also make policy in their interpretation of **statutory laws**—the laws of Congress. Frequently, Congress decides that an issue is too contentious to resolve. Members of Congress cannot themselves agree on specific language, so they write, sometimes deliberately, vague, symbolic language into the law—words and phrases like "fairness," "equitableness," "good faith," "good cause," and "reasonableness"—effectively shifting policy making to the courts by giving courts the power to read meaning into these terms.

THINK AGAIN

Is it really democratic to allow federal court judges, who are appointed, not elected, and who serve for life, to overturn laws of an elected Congress and president?

Activism Versus Self-Restraint

Supreme Court Justice Felix Frankfurter once wrote: "The only check upon our own exercise of power is our own sense of self-restraint. For the removal of unwise laws from the statute books, appeal lies not to the courts but to the ballot and to the processes of democratic government."[14]

Judicial Self-Restraint The idea behind **judicial self-restraint** is that judges should not read their own philosophies into the Constitution and should avoid direct confrontations with Congress, the president, and the states whenever possible. The argument for judicial self-restraint is that federal judges are not elected by the people and therefore should not substitute their own views for the views of elected representatives. The courts should defer to the judgments of the other branches of government unless there is a clear violation of constitutional principle. The benefit of the doubt should be given to actions taken by elected officials. Courts should only impose remedies that are narrowly tailored to correct specific legal wrongs. As Justice Sandra Day O'Connor (see *People in Politics:* "Sandra Day O'Connor, Holding the Middle Ground") argued in her Senate confirmation hearings, "The courts should interpret the laws, not make them. . . . I do not believe it is a function of the Court to step in because times have changed or social mores have changed."[15]

Wisdom versus Constitutionality A law may be unwise, unjust, or even stupid and yet still be constitutional. One should not equate the wisdom of a law with its constitutionality, and the Court should decide only the constitutionality and not the wisdom of a law. Justice Oliver Wendell Holmes once lectured a younger colleague, sixty-one-year-old Justice Harlan Stone, on this point:

> Young man, about 75 years ago I learned that I was not God. And so, when the people . . . want to do something I can't find anything in the Constitution expressly forbidding them to do, I say, whether I like it or not, "Goddamn it, let 'em do it."[16]

statutory laws Laws made by act of Congress or the state legislatures, as opposed to constitutional law.

judicial self-restraint Self-imposed limitation on judicial power by judges deferring to the policy judgments of elected branches of government.

However, the actual role of the Supreme Court in the nation's power struggles suggests that the Court indeed often equates wisdom with constitutionality. People frequently cite broad phrases in the Fifth and Fourteenth Amendments establishing constitutional standards of "due process of law" and "equal protection of the laws" when attacking laws they believe are unfair or unjust. Most Americans have come to believe that unwise laws must be unconstitutional. If so, then the courts must be the final arbiters of fairness and justice.

Original Intent Should the Constitution be interpreted in terms of the intentions of the Founders or according to the morality of society today? Most jurists

Sandra Day O'Connor, Holding the Middle Ground

For nearly two hundred years, the U.S. Supreme Court was America's most exclusive all-male club. After 101 male justices, Sandra Day O'Connor was named to the Supreme Court by President Ronald Reagan in 1981. On the high court, O'Connor has succeeded in molding a moderate bloc of votes that holds the balance of power on the Supreme Court between liberal and conservative blocs. More important, perhaps, O'Connor has taken the lead in shaping Court policy on women's issues, including the most controversial issue of all—abortion.

Sandra Day grew up on her family's large Arizona ranch, graduated from Stanford with honors, and went on to Stanford Law School, where she finished near the top of her class (along with now Chief Justice of the Supreme Court William Rehnquist, who was first in the class). After graduation, she married John Jay O'Connor, a Phoenix attorney, and had three sons. She entered Arizona politics about the time her youngest son entered school. In 1969 she was appointed to fill a vacancy in the Arizona state senate and was later elected twice to that body, where she rose to become majority leader in 1973. She left the Arizona legislature in 1975 to become a Phoenix trial judge and in 1979 was appointed by a Democratic governor to the Arizona Court of Appeals, an intermediate court that does not hear major constitutional issues.

O'Connor had some business experience: she was formerly a director of the First National Bank of Arizona and Blue Cross/Blue Shield of Arizona. But until her appointment to the U.S. Supreme Court, she was an obscure state court judge. Her service as a Republican leader in the Arizona state senate qualified her as a moderately conservative party loyalist. However, it appears that her professional and political friendships had more to do with bringing her to President Ronald Reagan's attention than her record as a jurist. She had known both Justice Rehnquist and former Chief Justice Warren Burger for many years, and Barry Goldwater, Arizona's senior U.S. senator and Republican warhorse, had been her mentor in Arizona Republican politics. When Reagan's political advisers told him during the presidential campaign that he was not doing well among women voters (he opposed the Equal Rights Amendment), he responded by pledging to appoint a woman to the Supreme Court. Reagan's fulfillment of his campaign pledge was a politically popular decision. Feminist groups felt forced to support the appointment, even though O'Connor's record in Arizona was moderately conservative.

In her early Court deliberations, Justice O'Connor generally reflected the moderate conservatism of recent Republican appointees, but on gender questions she took an independent role from the beginning. Over time, her independent course has made her a swing vote on many key policy issues, from affirmative action to abortion. Indeed, her leadership of the Court on the abortion issue has preserved the constitutional right to abortion.

---

agree the Constitution is a living document, that it must be interpreted by each generation in the light of current conditions, and to do otherwise would soon render the document obsolete. But in interpreting the document, whose values should prevail—the values of the judges or the values of the Founders? The doctrine of **original intent** takes the values of the Founders as expressed in the text of the Constitution and attempts to apply these values to current conditions. Defenders of original intent argue that the words in the document must be given their historical meaning and that meaning must restrain the courts as well as the legislative and executive branches of government. That is, the Supreme Court should not set aside laws made by elected representatives unless they conflict with the original intent of the Founders. Judges who set aside laws that do not accord with their personal views of today's moral standards are simply substituting their own morality for that of elected bodies. Such decisions lack democratic legitimacy because there is no reason why judges' moral views should prevail over those of elected representatives.

original intent Judicial philosophy under which judges attempt to apply the values of the Founders to current issues.

Judicial Activism However, the doctrine of original intent carries little weight with proponents of judicial activism. The idea behind **judicial activism** is that the Constitution is a living document whose strength lies in its flexibility, and judges should shape constitutional meaning to fit the needs of contemporary society. The argument for judicial activism is that viewing the Constitution as a broad and flexible document saves the nation from having to pass dozens of new constitutional amendments to accommodate changes in society. Instead, the courts need to give contemporary interpretations to constitutional phrases, particularly general phrases such as "due process of law" (Fifth Amendment), "equal protection of the laws" (Fourteenth Amendment), "establishment of religion" (First Amendment), and "cruel and unusual punishment" (Eighth Amendment). Courts have the responsibility to review the actions of other branches of government vigorously, to strike down unconstitutional acts, and to impose far-reaching remedies for legal wrongs whenever necessary.[17]

Stare Decisis Conflicts between judicial activism and judicial self-restraint are underscored by questions of whether to let past decisions stand or to find constitutional support for overturning them. The principle of **stare decisis**, which means the issue has already been decided in earlier cases, is a fundamental notion in law. Reliance on **precedent** gives stability to the law; if every decision were new law, then no one would know what the law is from day to day. Yet the Supreme Court has discarded precedent in many of its most important decisions: *Brown v. Board of Education* (1954), which struck down laws segregating the races; *Baker v. Carr* (1962), which guaranteed equal representation in legislatures; *Roe v. Wade* (1973), which made abortion a constitutional right; and many other classic cases. Former Justice William O. Douglas, a defender of judicial activism, justified disregard of precedent as follows:

> The decisions of yesterday or of the last century are only the starting points. . . . A judge looking at a constitutional decision may have compulsions to revere the past history and accept what was once written. But he remembers above all else that it is the Constitution which he swore to support and defend, not the gloss which his predecessors may have put on it. So he comes to formulate his own laws, rejecting some earlier ones as false and embracing others. He cannot do otherwise unless he lets men long dead and unaware of the problems of the age in which he lives do his thinking for him.[18]

Rules of Restraint Even an activist Supreme Court adheres to some general rules of judicial self-restraint, however, including the following:

■ The Court will pass on the constitutionality of legislation only in an actual case; it will not advise the president or Congress on constitutional questions.

■ The Court will not anticipate a question on constitutional law; it does not decide hypothetical cases.

■ The Court will not formulate a rule of constitutional law broader than that required by the precise facts to which it must be applied.

■ The Court will not decide on a constitutional question if some other ground exists on which it may dispose of the case.

■ The Court will not decide on the validity of a law if the complainants fail to show that they have been injured by the law.

■ When doubt exists about the constitutionality of a law, the Court will try to interpret the law so as to give it a constitutional meaning and avoid the necessity of declaring it unconstitutional.

judicial activism Making of new law through judicial interpretations of the Constitution.

stare decisis Judicial precept that the issue has already been decided in earlier cases and the earlier decision need only be applied in the specific case before the bench; the rule in most cases, it comes from the Latin for "the decision stands."

precedent Legal principle that previous decisions should determine the outcome of current cases; the basis for stability in law.

- Complainants must have exhausted all remedies available in lower federal courts or state courts before the Supreme Court will accept review.

- The Court will invalidate a law only when a constitutional issue is crucial to the case and is substantial, not trivial.

- Occasionally the Court defers to Congress and the president, classifies an issue as a political question, and refuses to decide it. The Court has generally stayed out of foreign and military policy areas.

- If the Court holds a law unconstitutional, it will confine its decision to the particular section of the law that is unconstitutional, the rest of the statute stays intact.

Structure and Jurisdiction of Federal Courts

The federal court system consists of three levels of courts—the Supreme Court, the Courts of Appeals, and the district courts—together with various special courts (see Figure 13.1). Only the Supreme Court is established by the Constitution, although the number of justices is determined by Congress. Article III authorizes Congress to establish such "inferior Courts" as it deems appropriate. Congress has designed a hierarchical system with a U.S. Court of Appeals divided into 12 regional circuit courts, a federal circuit, and 94 district courts in the 50 states and one each in Puerto Rico and the District of Columbia. Table 13.1 describes their **jurisdiction** and distinguishes between **original jurisdiction**—where cases are begun, argued, and initially decided—and **appellate jurisdiction**—where cases begun in lower courts are argued and decided on **appeal**.

The Supreme Court is the "court of last resort" in the United States, but it hears only a very small number of cases each year. In a handful of cases, the Supreme Court has original jurisdiction; these concern primarily disputes between states (or states and residents of other states), disputes between a state and the federal government, and disputes involving foreign dignitaries. However, most Supreme Court cases are appellate decisions involving cases from state supreme courts or cases tried first in a U.S. district court.

District Courts District courts are the original jurisdiction trial courts of the federal system. Each state has at least one district court, and larger states have more (New York, for example, has four). There are about eight hundred federal district judges, each appointed for life by the president and confirmed by the Senate. The president also appoints a U.S. marshall for each district to carry out orders of the court and maintain order in the courtroom. District courts hear criminal cases prosecuted by the Department of Justice as well as civil cases. As trial courts, the district courts make use of both **grand juries** (called to hear evidence and, if warranted, to indict a defendant by bringing formal criminal charges) and **petit (regular) juries** (which determine guilt or innocence). District courts may hear more than 250,000 cases in a year, including 70,000 criminal cases.

Courts of Appeals Federal **circuit courts** (see *Across the USA:* "Geographic Boundaries of Federal Courts") are appellate courts. They do not hold trials or accept new evidence but consider only the records of the trial courts and oral or written arguments (**briefs**) submitted by attorneys. Federal law guarantees everyone the right to appeal, so the Court of Appeals has little discretion in this regard. Appellate judges themselves estimate that more than 80 percent of all appeals are frivolous—that is, without any real basis. There are more than a hundred circuit

jurisdiction Power of a court to hear a case in question.

original jurisdiction Refers to a particular court's power to serve as the place where a given case is initially argued and decided.

appellate jurisdiction Particular court's power to review a decision or action of a lower court.

appeal In general, requests that a higher court review cases decided at a lower level. In the Supreme Court, certain cases are designated as appeals under federal law; formally, these must be heard by the Court.

WWW **U.S. Courts**
The goal of this site is "to function as a clearinghouse for information from and about the Judicial Branch of the U.S. government." The site covers the U.S. Supreme Court, U.S. Courts of Appeals, U.S. District Courts, and U.S. Bankruptcy courts.
www.uscourts.gov

district courts Original jurisdiction trial courts of the federal system.

grand juries Juries called to hear evidence and decide whether defendants should be indicted and tried.

petit (regular) juries Juries called to determine guilt or innocence.

circuit courts The twelve appellate courts that make up the middle level of the federal court system.

briefs Documents submitted by an attorney to a court, setting out the facts of the case and the legal arguments in support of the party represented by the attorney.

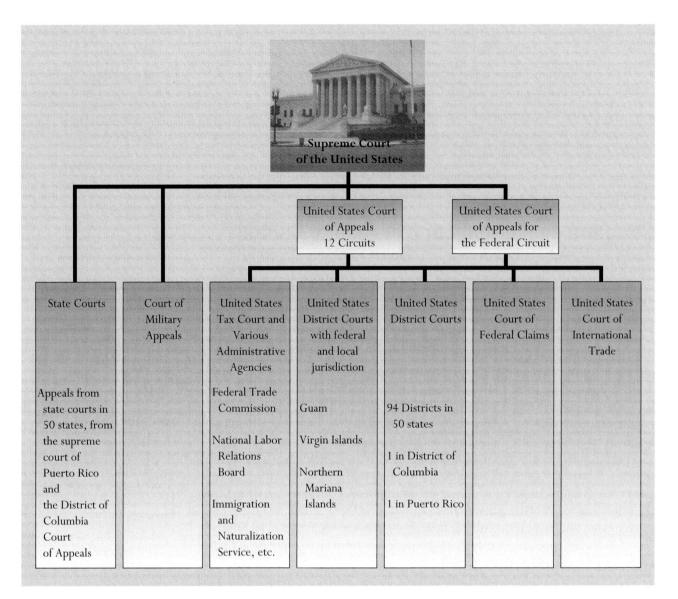

FIGURE 13.1 Structure of Federal Courts

The federal court system of the United States is divided into three levels: the courts of original jurisdiction (state courts, military courts, tax courts, district courts, claims courts, and international trade courts), U.S. Courts of Appeals (which hear appeals from all lower courts except state and military panels), and the U.S. Supreme Court, which can hear appeals from all sources.

judges, each appointed for life by the president subject to confirmation by the Senate. Normally, these judges serve together on a panel to hear appeals. More than 90 percent of the cases decided by the Court of Appeals end at this level. Further appeal to the Supreme Court is not automatic; it must be approved by the Supreme Court itself. Because the Supreme Court hears very few cases, in most cases the decision of the circuit court becomes law.

Supreme Court The Supreme Court of the United States is the final interpreter of all matters involving the Constitution and federal laws and treaties, whether the case began in a federal district court or in a state court. Appeals to the U.S. Supreme Court may come from a state court of last resort (usually a state's supreme court) or from lower federal courts. The Supreme Court determines

TABLE 13.1 Jurisdiction of Federal Courts		
Supreme Court of the United States	**United States Courts of Appeals**	**United States District Courts**
Appellate jurisdiction (cases begin in a lower court); hears appeals, at its own discretion, from:	No original jurisdiction; hear only appeals from:	Original jurisdiction over cases involving:
1. Lower federal courts	1. Federal district courts	1. Federal crimes
2. Highest state courts	2. U.S. regulatory commissions	2. Civil suits under the federal law
Original jurisdiction (cases begin in the Supreme Court) over cases involving:	3. Certain other federal courts	3. Civil suits between citizens of states where the amount exceeds $50,000
1. Two or more states		4. Admiralty and maritime cases
2. The United States and a state		5. Bankruptcy cases
3. Foreign ambassadors and other diplomats		6. Review of actions of certain federal administrative agencies
4. A state and a citizen of a different state (if begun by the state)		7. Other matters assigned to them by Congress

whether to accept an appeal and consider a case. It may do so when there is a "substantial federal question" presented in a case or when there are "special and important reasons," or it may reject a case—with or without explaining why.

In the early days of the Republic, the size of the Supreme Court fluctuated, but since 1869 the membership has remained at nine: the Chief Justice and eight associate justices. The Supreme Court is in session each year from October through June, hearing oral arguments, accepting written briefs, conferring, and rendering opinions.

Appeals from State Courts Each of the fifty states maintains its own courts. The federal courts are not necessarily superior to those courts; state and federal courts operate independently. State courts have original jurisdiction in most criminal and civil cases. Because the U.S. Supreme Court has appellate jurisdiction over state supreme courts as well as over lower federal courts, the Supreme Court oversees the nation's entire judicial system, but the great bulk of cases begin and end in the state court systems. The federal courts do not interfere once a case has been started in a state court except in very rare circumstances. And Congress has stipulated that legal disputes between citizens of different states must involve $50,000 or more to be heard in federal courts. Moreover, parties to cases in state courts must "exhaust their remedies"—that is, appeal their case all the way through the state court system—before the federal courts will hear an appeal. Appeals from state supreme courts go directly to the U.S. Supreme Court and not to a federal district or circuit court. Such appeals are usually made on the grounds that a federal question is involved in the case—that is, a question has arisen regarding the application of the Constitution or a federal law.

Federal Cases Some 10 million civil and criminal cases are begun in the nation's courts each year (see *A Conflicting View:* "America Is Drowning Itself in a Sea of Lawsuits" on page 469). Fewer than 300,000 (3 percent) of the cases are begun in the federal courts. About 8,000 are appealed to the Supreme Court each year, but

 Supreme Court Cases

This Cornell Law School's Legal Information Institute site contains up-to-date information about important legal decisions rendered by federal and state courts along with an exhaustive online law library available to researchers.
www.law.cornell.edu

 The U.S. Supreme Court

Official site provides recent decisions, case dockets, oral arguments, public information, etc.
www.supremecourtus.gov

Geographic Boundaries of Federal Courts

For administrative convenience, the U.S. District Courts are organized into twelve circuits (regions), plus the Federal Circuit (Washington, D.C.). Within each region, circuit court judges form panels to hear appeals from district courts. U.S. Circuit Courts of Appeals are numbered. U.S. District Courts are named for geographic regions of the states (East, West, North, South, Middle), for example, U.S. District Court for Northern California.

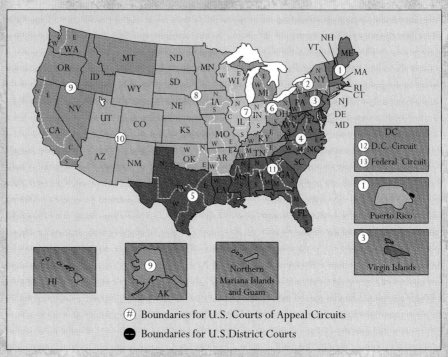

(#) Boundaries for U.S. Courts of Appeal Circuits
(-) Boundaries for U.S. District Courts

FIGURE 13.2
Caseloads in Federal Courts

Increasing caseloads in the federal courts have placed a heavy burden on prosecutors and judges. Although the increase in civil suits in the federal courts is the result of more plaintiffs insisting on taking their cases to the federal level both originally and on appeal, the increase in criminal cases is the result of Congress's decision to make more crimes—especially drug-related crimes—federal offenses and to pursue such criminals more vigorously.

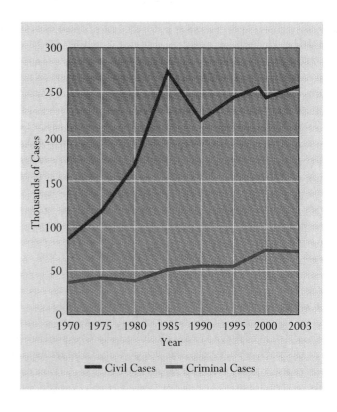

America Is Drowning Itself in a Sea of Lawsuits

America is threatening to drown itself in a sea of lawsuits. Civil suits in the nation's courts exceed *10 million* per year. There are more than 805,000 lawyers in the United States (compared to about 650,000 physicians). These lawyers are in business, and their business is litigation. Generating business means generating lawsuits. And just as businesses search for new products, lawyers search for new legal principles on which to bring lawsuits. They seek to expand legal liability for civil actions—that is, to expand the definition of civil wrongdoings, or torts.

Unquestionably, the threat of lawsuits is an important safeguard for society, compelling individuals, corporations, and government agencies to behave responsibly toward others. Because victims require compensation for *actual* damages incurred by the wrongdoing of others, liability laws protect all of us.

But we need to consider the social costs of frivolous lawsuits, especially those brought without any merit but initiated in the hope that individuals or firms will offer a settlement just to avoid the expenses of defending themselves. Legal expenses and excessive jury awards leveled against corporations increase insurance premiums for businesses and service providers. The Insurance Information Institute estimates that the overall costs of civil litigation in America is many times more than that of other industrial nations, perhaps amounting to over 2 percent of our nation's GDP. For example, the risk of lawsuits forces physicians to practice "defensive medicine," ordering expensive tests, multiple consultations with specialists, and expensive procedures, not because they are adjudged medically necessary, but rather to protect themselves from the possibility of a lawsuit.

Insurance premiums have risen sharply for physicians seeking malpractice insurance, as have premiums for recreation facilities, nurseries and day-care centers, motels, and restaurants.

Product Liability

The threat of lawsuits discourages new products from entering the marketplace. Virtually any accident involving a commercial product can inspire a product liability suit. An individual who gets cut opening a can of peas can sue the canning company. A woman who spills hot coffee on herself while driving sues the fast-food restaurant for making the coffee too hot. Hotels pay damages to persons raped in their rooms.

Third-Party Suits

Defendants in civil cases are not necessarily the parties directly responsible for damages to the plaintiff. Instead, wealthier third parties, who may indirectly contribute to an accident, are favorite targets of lawsuits. For example, if a drunk driver injures a pedestrian but the driver has only limited insurance and small personal wealth, a shrewd attorney will sue the bar that sold the driver the drinks instead of the driver.

"Pain and Suffering" Awards

High jury awards in liability cases, sometimes running into tens of millions of dollars, cover much more than the doctor bills, lost wages, and cost of future care for injured parties. Most large damage awards are for *pain and suffering*. Pain and suffering awards are *added* compensation for the victim, beyond actual costs for medical care and lost wages.

"Joint and Severable" Liability

A legal rule known as *joint and severable liability* allows a plaintiff to collect the entire award from any party that contributed in any way to an accident if other defendants cannot pay. If, for example, a drunk driver crosses a median strip and crashes into another car, leaving its driver crippled, the victim may sue the city for not placing a guard railing in the median strip. The rule encourages trial lawyers to sue the party "with the deepest pockets," that is, the wealthiest party rather than the party most responsible for the accident.

Reform Politics

Reforming the nation's liability laws presents major challenges to the political system. The reform movement can count on support from some normally powerful interest groups—insurance companies, manufacturers, drug companies, hospitals, and physicians. But legal reform is an anathema to the legal profession itself, notably the powerful Association of Trial Lawyers. And lawyers compose the single largest occupational background of Congress members—indeed, of politicians generally.

only about 125 of them are openly argued and decided by signed opinions. The Constitution "reserves" general police powers to the states. That is, civil disputes and most crimes—murder, robbery, assault, and rape—are normally state offenses rather than federal crimes and thus are tried in state and local courts.

Federal court caseloads have risen in recent years (see Figure 13.2), in part because more civil disputes are being brought to federal courts. In addition, the U.S. Justice Department is prosecuting more criminal cases as federal law enforcement agencies—such as the Federal Bureau of Investigation (FBI), Drug Enforcement Administration (DEA), Internal Revenue Service (IRS), and Bureau of Alcohol, Tobacco and Firearms (ATF)—have stepped up their investigations. Most of this recent increase is attributable to enforcement of federal drug laws.

Traditionally, federal crimes were offenses directed against the U.S. government, its property, or its employees or were offenses involving the crossing of state lines. Over the years, however, Congress has greatly expanded the list of federal crimes so that federal and state criminal court jurisdictions often overlap, as they do, for example, in most drug violations.

The Special Rules of Judicial Decision Making

Courts are political institutions that resolve conflict and decide about public policy. But unlike Congress, the presidency, and the bureaucracy, the courts employ highly specialized rules in going about their work.

Cases and Controversies Courts do not initiate policy but rather wait until a case or controversy is brought to them for resolution. A case must involve two disputing parties, one of which must have incurred some real damage as a result of the action or inaction of the other. They do *not* issue policy declarations or decide hypothetical cases. Rather, the courts wait until disputing parties bring a case to them that requires them to interpret the meaning of a law or determine its constitutionality in order to resolve the case. Only then do courts render opinions.

The vast majority of cases do *not* involve important policy issues. Courts determine the guilt or innocence of criminal defendants. Courts enforce contracts and award damages to victims of negligence in **civil cases**. And courts render these decisions on the basis of established law. Only occasionally do courts make significant policy decisions.

civil cases Noncriminal court proceedings in which a plaintiff sues a defendant for damages in payment for harm inflicted.

adversarial system Method of decision making in which an impartial judge or jury or decision maker hears arguments and reviews evidence presented by opposite sides.

standing Requirement that the party who files a lawsuit have a legal stake in the outcome.

Adversarial Proceedings Underlying judicial decision making is the assumption that the best way to decide an issue is to allow two disputing parties to present arguments on each side. Judges in the United States do not investigate cases, question witnesses, or develop arguments themselves (as they do in some European countries). This **adversarial system** depends on quality of argument on each side, which means it often depends on the capabilities of attorneys. There is no guarantee that the adversarial process will produce the best policy outcomes.

Standing To bring an issue into court as a case, individuals or firms or interest groups must have **standing**; that is, they must be directly harmed by a law or action. People cannot "go to court" simply because they do not like what the government is doing. Merely being taxpayers does not entitle people to claim that they are damaged by government actions.[19] Individuals or firms automatically have standing when they are prosecuted by the government for violation of laws or regulations. Thus one way to gain standing in order to challenge the legality of a regulation or the constitutionality of a law is to violate the regulation or law and invite the government to prosecute.

To sue the government, plaintiffs must show they have suffered financial damages, loss of property, or physical or emotional harm as a direct result of the government's action. (The party initiating a suit and claiming damages is the **plaintiff**; the party against whom a suit is brought is the **defendant**.) The ancient legal doctrine of **sovereign immunity** means that one cannot sue the government without the government's consent. But by law, the U.S. government allows itself to be sued in a wide variety of contract and negligence cases. A citizen can also personally sue to force government officials to carry out acts that they are required by law to perform or for acting contrary to law. The government does not allow suits for damages as a result of military actions.

Class Action Suits **Class action suits** are cases brought into court by individuals on behalf not only of themselves but also of all other persons "similarly situated." That is, the party bringing the case is acting on behalf of a "class" of people who have suffered the same damages from the same actions of the defendant. One of the most famous and far-reaching class action suits was *Brown v. Board of Education of Topeka* (1954). The plaintiff, Linda Brown of Topeka, Kansas, sued her local board of education on behalf of herself and all other black pupils who were forced to attend segregated schools, charging that such schools violated the Equal Protection Clause of the Fourteenth Amendment. When she won the case, the Court's ruling affected not only Linda Brown and the segregated public schools in Topeka but also all other black pupils similarly situated across the nation (see Chapter 12).

Class action suits have grown in popularity. These suits have enabled attorneys and interest groups to bring multimillion-dollar suits against corporations and governments for damages to large numbers of people, even when none of them has

plaintiffs Parties initiating suits and claiming damages. In criminal cases, the state acts as plaintiff on behalf of an injured society and requests fines and/or imprisonment as damages. In civil suits, the plaintiff is the injured party and seeks monetary damages.

defendants Parties against whom a criminal or civil suit is brought.

sovereign immunity Legal doctrine that individuals can sue the government only with the government's consent.

class action suits Cases initiated by parties acting on behalf of themselves and all others similarly situated.

THINK AGAIN

Are the costs of lawsuits in America becoming too burdensome on the economy?

Justices of the Supreme Court. Front row, from the left: Antonin Scalia, John Paul Stevens, Chief Justice William Rehnquist, Sandra Day O'Connor, and Anthony Kennedy. Back row, from the left: Ruth Bader Ginsburg, David Souter, Clarence Thomas, and Stephen Breyer.

individually suffered sufficient harm to merit bringing a case to court. For example, an individual overcharged by an electric utility would not want to incur the expense of suing for the return of a few dollars. But if attorneys sue the utility on behalf of a large number of customers similarly overcharged, the result may be a multimillion-dollar settlement from which the attorneys can deduct their hefty fees.

Legal Fees Going to court requires financial resources. Criminal defendants are guaranteed an attorney, without charge if they are poor, by the Sixth Amendment's guarantee of "Assistance of Counsel" (see Chapter 12).[20] However, persons who wish to bring a *civil* suit against governments or corporations must still arrange for the payment of legal fees. The most common arrangement is the **contingency fee**, in which plaintiffs agree to pay expenses and share one-third or more of the money damages with their lawyers if the case is won. If the case is lost, neither plaintiffs nor their lawyers receive anything for their labors. Lawyers do not usually participate in such arrangements unless the prospects for winning the case are good and the promised monetary reward is substantial. Civil suits against the government have increased since Congress enacted a law requiring governments to pay the attorneys' fees of citizens who successfully bring suit against public officials for violation of their constitutional rights.

Remedies and Relief Judicial power has vastly expanded through court determination of **remedies and relief**. These are the orders of a court following a decision that are designed to correct a wrong. In most cases, judges simply fine or sentence criminal defendants to jail or order losing defendants in civil suits to pay monetary damages to the winning plaintiffs. In recent years, however, federal district court judges have issued sweeping orders to governments to correct constitutional violations. For example, a federal district judge took over operation of the Boston public schools for more than ten years to remedy *de facto* (an existing, although not necessarily deliberate, pattern of) racial segregation. A federal district judge ordered the city of Yonkers, New York, to build public housing in white neighborhoods. A federal district judge took over the operation of the Alabama prison system to ensure proper prisoner treatment. A federal district judge ordered the Kansas City, Missouri, school board to increase taxes to pay for his desegregation plan.[21]

Independent Counsels? The Ethics in Government Act of 1978 (passed in the wake of the Watergate scandal) granted federal courts the power, upon request of the attorney general, to appoint an **independent counsel**, or "**special prosecutor**," to investigate and prosecute violations of federal law by the president and other high officials. This act was challenged in the U.S. Supreme Court as a transferral of executive power ("to take care that the laws be faithfully executed"—Article II) to the judicial branch of government in violation of the separation of powers in the U.S. Constitution. But the Court upheld the law, noting that the attorney general, an executive branch official appointed by the president, had to request the judiciary to appoint the independent counsel.[22]

Whatever the original intent of the act, special prosecutors were often accused of *bringing politics into* the criminal justice system. Indeed, special prosecutor Kenneth Starr's dogged pursuit of Bill and Hillary Clinton (in "Whitewater" real estate deals and later the Monica Lewinsky sex scandal) was deemed a "witch hunt" by friends of the president. The First Lady linked Starr to "a vast right-wing conspiracy" trying to reverse the outcome of two presidential elections.

contingency fees Fees paid to attorneys to represent the plaintiff in a civil suit and receive in compensation an agreed-upon percentage of damages awarded (if any).

remedies and reliefs Orders of a court to correct a wrong, including a violation of the Constitution.

independent counsel ("special prosecutor") A prosecutor appointed by a federal court to pursue charges against a president or other high official. This position was allowed to lapse by Congress in 1999 after many controversial investigations by these prosecutors.

Class action suits initiated by attorneys or interest groups on behalf of large numbers of people are increasingly popular. Here an attorney announces a suit against the nation's tobacco companies on behalf of flight attendants previously subjected to smoke.

Congress allowed the independent counsel law to lapse in 1999. Democrats, infuriated by Starr's investigations, joined Republicans, who had earlier complained when Reagan and Bush administration officials were the targets of prosecution, in killing the act. Getting rid of the law, said its opponents, will help to "decriminalize" politics in Washington.

The Politics of Selecting Judges

The Constitution specifies that all federal judges, including justices of the Supreme Court, shall be appointed by the president and confirmed by a majority vote of the Senate. Judicial recruitment is a political process: presidents almost always appoint members of their own party to the federal courts. More than 80 percent of federal judges have held some political office prior to their appointment to the court. More important, political philosophy now plays a major role in the selection of judges. Thus the appointment of federal judges has increasingly become an arena for conflict between presidents and their political opponents in the Senate.

The Politics of Presidential Selection Presidents have a strong motivation to select judges who share their political philosophy. Judicial appointments are made for life. The Constitution stipulates that federal judges "shall hold their Offices during good Behaviour." Although a rather vague phrase, it has come to mean a virtually guaranteed life term. A president cannot remove a judge for any reason, and Congress cannot impeach judges just because it dislikes their decisions.

This independence of the judiciary has often frustrated presidents and Congresses. Presidents who have appointed people they thought were liberals or conservatives to the Supreme Court have sometimes been surprised by the decisions of their appointees. An estimated one-quarter of the justices of the Supreme Court have deviated from the political expectations of the presidents who appointed them.[23]

It is important to recognize that presidents' use of political criteria in selecting judges has a democratic influence on the courts. Presidents can campaign on the pledge to make the courts more liberal or conservative through their appointive powers, and voters are free to cast their ballots on the basis of this pledge.

THINK AGAIN

Should presidents appoint only judges who agree with their judicial philosophy?

Political Litmus Test Traditionally, presidents and senators have tried to discern where a Supreme Court candidate fits on the continuum of liberal activism versus conservative self-restraint. Democratic presidents and senators usually prefer liberal judges who express an activist philosophy. Republican presidents usually prefer conservative judges who express a philosophy of judicial self-restraint. Until very recently, both the president and the Senate denied using any political "litmus test" in judicial recruitment. A **litmus test** generally refers to recruitment based on a nominee's stand on a single issue. Since the Supreme Court ruling on *Roe v. Wade* (1973), however, the single issue of abortion has come to dominate the politics of judicial recruitment. President Clinton was forthright in his pledge to nominate only justices who specifically support the *Roe v. Wade* decision. Republican presidents have denied using a litmus test, but they have insisted that nominees generally support a philosophy of judicial self-restraint.

The Politics of Senate Confirmation All presidential nominations for the federal judiciary, including the Supreme Court, are sent to the Senate for confirmation. The Senate refers them to its powerful Judiciary Committee, which holds hearings, votes on the nomination, and then reports to the full Senate, where floor debate may precede the final confirmation vote.

The Senate's involvement in federal district judgeships traditionally centered on the practice of **senatorial courtesy**. If senators from the president's party from the same state for which an appointment was being considered disapproved of a nominee, their Senate colleagues would defeat the nomination. But if the president and senators from that party agreed on the nomination, the full Senate, even if controlled by the opposition, customarily confirmed the nomination. During the Reagan-Bush years, however, partisan divisions between these Republican presidents and Senate Democrats eroded the tradition of senatorial courtesy.

Supreme Court nominations have always received close political scrutiny in the Senate. Over the last two centuries, the Senate has rejected or refused to confirm about 20 percent of presidential nominees to the high court, but only five nominees in this century (see Table 13.2). In the past, most senators believed that presidents deserved to appoint their own judges; the opposition party would get its own opportunity to appoint judges when it won the presidency. Only if the Senate found some personal disqualification in a nominee's background (for example, financial scandal, evidence of racial or religious bias, judicial incompetence) would a nominee likely be rejected. But publicity and partisanship over confirmation of Supreme Court nominees have increased markedly in recent years.[24]

The Bork Battle The U.S. Senate's rejection of President Ronald Reagan's nomination of Judge Robert H. Bork in 1987 set a new precedent in Senate confirmation of Supreme Court nominees. The Senate rejected Bork because of his views, not because he lacked judicial qualifications. Bork had a reputation for "conservative activism"—a desire better to reflect the "original intent" of the Constitution's framers by rolling back some of the Supreme Court's broad interpretations of privacy rights, free speech, and equal protection of the law. Perhaps most controversial were his views on *Roe v. Wade;* he had labeled the Court's striking down of state laws prohibiting abortion as "wholly unjustifiable judicial usurpation of state legislative authority."

Unlike previous nominees, Bork was subjected by the Senate Judiciary Committee to extensive case-by-case questioning in nationally televised confirmation hearings, during which the bearded, scholarly Bork presented a poor TV image. The Democrat-controlled U.S. Senate rejected his nomination. Victory in the Bork battle encouraged liberal interest groups to closely scrutinize the personal lives

litmus test In political terms, a person's stand on a key issue that determines whether he or she will be appointed to public office or supported in electoral campaigns.

senatorial courtesy Custom of the U.S. Senate with regard to presidential nominations to the judiciary to defer to the judgment of senators from the president's party from the same state as the nominee.

Nominee	President	Year	Vote
Earl Warren	Eisenhower	1954	NRV*
John Marshall Harlan	Eisenhower	1955	71–11
William J. Brennan	Eisenhower	1957	NRV
Charles Whittaker	Eisenhower	1957	NRV
Potter Stewart	Eisenhower	1959	70–17
Byron White	Kennedy	1962	NRV
Arthur Goldberg	Kennedy	1962	NRV
Abe Fortas	Johnson	1965	NRV
Thurgood Marshall	Johnson	1967	69–11
Abe Fortas[†]	Johnson	1968	Withdrawn[‡]
Homer Thornberry	Johnson	1968	No action
Warren Burger	Nixon	1969	74–3
Clement Haynsworth	Nixon	1969	Defeated 45–55
G. Harrold Carswell	Nixon	1970	Defeated 45–51
Harry Blackmun	Nixon	1970	94–0
Lewis Powell	Nixon	1971	89–1
William Rehnquist	Nixon	1971	68–26
John Paul Stevens	Nixon	1975	98–0
Sandra Day O'Connor	Reagan	1981	99–0
William Rehnquist[†]	Reagan	1986	65–33
Antonin Scalia	Reagan	1986	98–0
Robert Bork	Reagan	1987	Defeated 42–58
Douglas Ginsburg	Reagan	1987	Withdrawn
Anthony Kennedy	Reagan	1988	97–0
David Souter	Bush	1990	90–9
Clarence Thomas	Bush	1991	52–48
Ruth Bader Ginsburg	Clinton	1993	96–3
Stephen G. Breyer	Clinton	1994	87–9

* No recorded vote.

[†] Elevation to Chief Justice.

[‡] Nomination withdrawn after Senate vote failed to end filibuster against nomination; vote was 45 to 43 to end filibuster, and two-thirds majority was required.

Source: Congressional Quarterly, *The Supreme Court: Justice and the Law* (Washington, D.C.: Congressional Quarterly, 1983), p. 179; updated by the author.

and political views of subsequent nominees. Indeed, the Bork battle set the stage for an even more controversial political struggle—the confirmation of Justice Clarence Thomas (see *Up Close:* "The Confirmation of Clarence Thomas").

Filibustering Court Nominees The Constitution requires only a majority vote of the Senate to "advise and consent" to a presidential nominee for a federal court judgeship, including a seat on the Supreme Court. However recent partisan battles over nominees have centered on the Senate's filibuster rule and the 60 votes required for cloture to end a filibuster (see "Senate Floor Traditions" in Chapter 8). The Democrats in the Senate control more than 40 votes, so they can deny the majority the ability to end debate: This means they can deny the vote on a federal court nominee indefinitely and thereby effectively kill the nomination. The president cannot force an up-or-down vote on a court nominee.[25]

President George W. Bush has suffered several key defeats of judicial nominees for seats on the U.S. Court of Appeals by failing to get 60 votes to end filibusters over their nominations. All of his nominations were qualified from a judicial point of view, but all were considered conservatives by leading Democrats in the Senate. And Democrats wished to warn President Bush that a nomination of a conservative to the Supreme Court would bring about the same stalemate and failure at confirmation.

Republican Majority Leader Bill Frist has threatened to try to end the filibuster rule for judicial nominations. He argues that the Constitution itself specifies a "majority vote of the Senate", not a 3/5ths (60) vote for confirmation. But Senators of both parties are reluctant to give up the filibuster rule.

Who Is Selected?

What background and experiences are brought to the Supreme Court? Despite often holding very different views on the laws, the Constitution, and their interpretation, the justices of the U.S. Supreme Court tend to share a common background of education at the nation's most prestigious law schools and prior judicial experience.

Law Degrees There is no constitutional requirement that Supreme Court justices be attorneys, but every person who has ever served on the High Court has been trained in law. Moreover, a majority of the justices have attended one or another of the nation's most prestigious law schools—Harvard, Yale, and Stanford (see Table 13.3).

Judicial Experience Historically, about half of all Supreme Court justices have been federal or state court judges. Many justices have served some time as U.S. attorneys in the Department of Justice early in their legal careers. Relatively few have held elected political office; among today's justices, only Sandra Day O'Connor ever won an election (to the Arizona state legislature), but one chief justice—William Howard Taft—previously held the nation's highest elected post, the presidency.

Age Most justices have been in their fifties when appointed to the Court. Presumably this is the age at which people acquire the necessary prominence and experience to bring themselves to the attention of the White House and Justice Department as potential candidates. At the same time, presidents seek to make a lasting imprint on the Court, and candidates in their fifties can be expected to serve on the Court for many more years than older candidates with the same credentials.

Race and Gender No African American had ever served on the Supreme Court until President Lyndon Johnson's appointment of Thurgood Marshall in 1967. A Howard University Law School graduate, Marshall had served as counsel for the National Association for the Advancement of Colored People Legal Defense Fund and had personally argued the historic *Brown v. Board of Education* case before the Supreme Court in 1954. He served as solicitor general of the United States under President Lyndon Johnson before his elevation to the high court. Upon Marshall's retirement in 1991, President George Bush sought to retain minority representation on the Supreme Court, yet at the same time to reinforce conservative judicial views, with his selection of Clarence Thomas.

No woman had served on the Supreme Court prior to the appointment of Sandra Day O'Connor by President Ronald Reagan in 1981. O'Connor was Reagan's first Supreme Court appointment. Although a relatively unknown Arizona state court judge, she had the powerful support of Arizona Republican Senator Barry

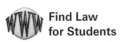
Find Law for Students
Law school information for schools A–Z, state bar information, job listings, law school rankings, etc.
http://stu.findlaw.com

The Confirmation of Clarence Thomas

Television coverage of Senate confirmation hearings on Clarence Thomas's appointment to the Supreme Court in 1991 captivated a national audience. The conflict raised just about every "hot-button" issue in American politics, from abortion rights and affirmative action to sexual harassment.

Born to a teenage mother who earned $10 a week as a maid, Clarence Thomas and his brother lived in a dirt-floor shack in Pin Point, Georgia, where they were raised by strict, hardworking grandparents who taught young Clarence the value of education and sacrificed to send him to a Catholic school. He excelled academically and went on to mostly white Immaculate Conception Seminary College in Missouri to study for the Catholic priesthood. But when he overheard a fellow seminarian express satisfaction at the assassination of Dr. Martin Luther King, Jr., Thomas left the seminary in anger and enrolled at Holy Cross College, where he helped found the college's Black Student Union, and went on to graduate with honors and to win admission to Yale Law School.

Upon graduating from Yale, Thomas took a job as assistant attorney general in Missouri and later became a congressional aide to Republican Missouri Senator John Danforth. In 1981 he accepted the post as head of the Office of Civil Rights in the Department of Education. In 1982 he was named chair of the Equal Employment Opportunity Commission (EEOC), where he successfully eliminated much of that agency's financial mismanagement and aggressively pursued individual cases of discrimination. But at the same time, he spoke out against racial "quotas." In 1989 President Bush nominated him to the U.S. Court of Appeals, and he was easily confirmed by the Senate.

In tapping Thomas for the Supreme Court, the White House reasoned that the liberal groups who had blocked the earlier nomination of conservative Robert Bork would be reluctant to launch personal attacks on an African American. With the opposition fractured, the White House saw an opportunity to push a strong conservative nominee through the Democrat-dominated Senate Judiciary Committee and win confirmation by the full Senate.

But behind the scenes, liberal interest groups, including the National Abortion Rights Action League, People for the American Way, and the National Organization for Women, were searching for evidence to discredit Thomas. A University of Oklahoma law professor, Anita Hill, a former legal assistant to Thomas both at the Department of Education and later at the Equal Employment Opportunity Commission, charged, in a nationally televised press conference, that Thomas had sexually harassed her in both jobs. Thomas himself flatly denied the charges.

Democrats on the committee treated Hill with great deference, asking her to talk about her feelings and provide even more explicit details of Thomas's alleged misconduct. Given an opportunity to rebut Hill's charges, Thomas did so very emphatically: "This is a circus. It's a national disgrace. And from my standpoint as a black American, as far as I'm concerned, it is a high-tech lynching for uppity blacks who in any way deign to think for themselves."

In the end, there was no way to determine who was telling the truth, and "truth" in Washington is, at any rate, often determined by opinion polls. A majority of blacks as well as whites, and a majority of women as well as men, sided with the nominee.[*] In a fitting finale to the bitter and sleazy conflict, the final Senate confirmation vote was 52 to 48, the closest vote in the history of such confirmations. The best that can be said about the affair was that it placed the issue of sexual harassment on the national agenda.

---

[*]*Gallup Opinion Reports*, October 15, 1991, p. 209.

TABLE 13.3 The Supreme Court

Justice	Age at Appointment	President Who Appointed	Law School	Position at Time of Appointment	Years as a Judge before Appointment
William H. Rehnquist					
Original appointment	47	Nixon (1971)	Stanford	Assistant Attorney	0
Chief Justice	61	Reagan (1986)		General	15
John Paul Stevens	50	Ford (1976)	Northwestern	U.S. Court of Appeals	5
Sandra Day O'Connor	51	Reagan (1981)	Stanford	State Court	6
Antonin Scalia	50	Reagan (1988)	Harvard	U.S. Court of Appeals	4
Anthony M. Kennedy	51	Reagan (1988)	Harvard	U.S. Court of Appeals	12
David H. Souter	50	Bush (1990)	Harvard	State Supreme Court	13
Clarence Thomas	43	Bush (1991)	Yale	U.S. Court of Appeals	2
Ruth Bader Ginsburg	60	Clinton (1993)	Columbia	U.S. Court of Appeals	13
Stephen G. Breyer	56	Clinton (1994)	Harvard	U.S. Court of Appeals	14

Women and the Courts

When Myra Bradwell applied for an attorney's license in Illinois in 1869, the state refused her application. Ms. Bradwell appealed to the U.S. Supreme Court which denied her claim, adding that:

> The paramount destiny and mission of women are to fulfill the noble and benign offices of wife and mother. This is the law of the Creator, *Bradwell vs. Illinois* 83 U.S. 130 (1873).

But states gradually began to accept women as lawyers. President Franklin D. Roosevelt appointed Florence Allen to the U.S. Court of Appeals in 1934, the first woman ever appointed to a federal court of general jurisdiction. Yet Harvard did not admit women to their law school prior to 1950 and continued to restrict women's applications until the 1960s.

Today women constitute about half of all law school admissions in the country. However, after graduation women are less likely to enter private practice than men and disproportionately tend to become government lawyers.[*] It is reported that fewer than 20 percent of senior partners in law firms are women.

Women judges are increasingly taking their seats on state and federal court benches. As of 2000, women made up about 15 percent of federal judges on both district courts and courts of appeal. And two women, Sandra Day O'Connor, first appointed by President Ronald Reagan in 1981, and Ruth Bader Ginsburg, first appointed by President Bill Clinton in 1993, currently serve on the U.S. Supreme Court.

[*] See Barbara Palmer " 'To Do Justly': The Integration of Women into the American Judiciary," *P.S. Political Science and Politics* (June 2001): 235–38.

Goldwater and Stanford classmate Justice William Rehnquist. The second woman to serve on the High Court, Ruth Bader Ginsburg, had served as an attorney for the American Civil Liberties Union while teaching at Columbia Law School and had argued and won several important gender discrimination cases. President Jimmy Carter appointed her in 1980 to the U.S. Court of Appeals; President Bill Clinton elevated her to the Supreme Court in 1993 (see *Up Close:* "Women and the Court).

Supreme Court Decision Making

The Supreme Court sets its own agenda: it decides what it wants to decide. Of the more than 8,000 requests for hearing that come to its docket each year, the Court issues opinions on only about 150 cases. Another 150 or so cases are decided *summarily* (without opinion) by a Court order either affirming or reversing the lower court decision. The Supreme Court refuses to rule at all on the vast majority of cases that are submitted to it. Thus the rhetorical threat to "take this all the way to the Supreme Court" is usually an empty one. It is important, however, to realize that a refusal to rule also creates law by allowing the decision of the lower court to stand. That is why the U.S. Circuit Courts of Appeals are powerful bodies.

Setting the Agenda: Granting Certiorari Most cases reach the Supreme Court when a party in a case appeals to the Court to issue a **writ of certiorari** (literally to "make more certain"), a decision by the Court to require a lower federal or state court to turn over its records on a case.[26] To "grant certiorari"—that is, to decide to hear arguments in a case and render a decision—the Supreme Court relies on its **rule of four**: four justices must agree to do so. Deciding which cases to hear takes up a great deal of the Court's time.

What criteria does the Supreme Court use in choosing its policy agenda—that is, in choosing the cases it wishes to decide? The Court rarely explains why it accepts or rejects cases, but there are some general patterns. First, the Court accepts cases involving issues that the justices are interested in. The justices are clearly interested in the area of First Amendment freedoms—speech, press, and religion. Members of the Court are also interested in civil rights issues under the Equal Protection Clause of the Fourteenth Amendment and the civil rights laws and in overseeing the criminal justice system and defining the Due Process Clauses of the Fifth and Fourteenth Amendments.

In addition, the Court seems to feel an obligation to accept cases involving questions that have been decided differently by different circuit courts of appeals. The Supreme Court generally tries to see to it that "the law" does not differ from one circuit to another. Likewise, the Supreme Court usually acts when lower courts have made decisions clearly at odds with Supreme Court interpretations in order to maintain control of the federal judiciary. Finally, the Supreme Court is more likely to accept a case in which the U.S. government is a party and requests a review, especially when an issue appears to be one of overriding importance to the government. In fact, the U.S. government is a party in almost half of the cases decided by the Supreme Court.

Hearing Arguments Once the Supreme Court places a case on its decision calendar, attorneys for both sides submit written briefs on the issues. The Supreme Court may also allow interest groups to submit **amicus curiae** (literally, "friend of the court") briefs. This process allows interest groups direct access to the Supreme

writ of certiorari Writ issued by the Supreme Court, at its discretion, to order a lower court to prepare the record of a case and send it to the Supreme Court for review. Most cases come to the Court as petitions for writs of certiorari.

rule of four At least four justices must agree to hear an appeal (writ of certiorari) from a lower court in order to get a case before the Supreme Court.

amicus curiae Literally, "friend of the court"; a person, private group or institution, or government agency that is not a party to a case but participates in the case (usually through submission of a brief) at the invitation of the court or on its own initiative.

Court. In the affirmative action case of *University of California Regents v. Bakke* (1978)[27] the Court accepted 59 amicus curiae briefs representing more than 100 interest groups. The U.S. government frequently submits amicus curiae arguments in cases in which it is not a party. The **solicitor general** of the United States is responsible for presenting the government's arguments both in cases in which the government is a party and in cases in which the government is merely an amicus curiae.

Oral arguments before the Supreme Court are a time-honored ritual of American government. They take place in the marble "temple"—the Supreme Court building across the street from the U.S. Capitol in Washington, D.C. (see Figure 13.3). The justices, clad in their black robes, sit behind a high "bench" and peer down at the attorneys presenting their arguments. Arguing a case before the Supreme Court is said to be an intimidating experience. Each side is usually limited to either a half-hour or an hour of argument, but justices frequently interrupt with their own pointed questioning. Court watchers sometimes try to predict the Court's decision from the tenor of the questioning. Oral argument is the most public phase of Supreme Court decision making, but no one really knows whether these arguments ever change the justices' minds.

In Conference   The actual decisions are made in private conferences among the justices. These conferences usually take place on Wednesdays and Fridays and cover the cases argued orally during the same week. The Chief Justice (currently William Rehnquist) presides, and only justices (no law clerks) are present. It is customary for the Chief Justice to speak first on the issues, followed by each associate justice in order of seniority. A majority must decide which party wins or loses and whether a lower court's decision is to be affirmed or reversed.

Writing Opinions   The *written* opinion determines the actual outcome of the case (votes in conference are not binding). When the decision is unanimous, the Chief Justice traditionally writes the opinion. In the case of a split decision, the Chief Justice may take on the task of writing the **majority opinion** or assign it to another

solicitor general   Attorney in the Department of Justice who represents the U.S. government before the Supreme Court and any other courts.

majority opinion   Opinion in a case that is subscribed to by a majority of the judges who participated in the decision.

FIGURE 13.3
Corridors of Power in the Supreme Court

This cutaway shows the location of the principal offices and chambers of the Supreme Court building.

THE SUPREME COURT

1. Courtyards
2. Solicitor General's Office
3. Lawyers' Lounge
4. Marshall's Office
5. Main Hall
6. Courtroom
7. Conference and Reception Rooms

justice in the majority. If the Chief Justice is in the minority, the senior justice in the majority makes the assignment. Writing the opinion of the Court is the central task in Supreme Court policy making. Broadly written opinions may effect sweeping policy changes; narrowly written opinions may decide a particular case but have very little policy impact. The reasons cited for the decision become binding law, to be applied by lower courts in future cases. Yet despite the crucial role of opinion writing in Court policy making, most opinions are actually written by law clerks who are only recent graduates of the nation's prestigious law schools. The justices themselves read, edit, correct, and sometimes rewrite drafts prepared by clerks, but clerks may have a strong influence over the position taken by justices on the issues.

In addition, the views of the legal profession itself—as reflected by the American Bar Association (ABA) as well as the numerous law reviews published by law schools—influence the Court in subtle yet important ways. Often new interpretations of laws or the Constitution first appear in prestigious law journals, then are borrowed by Supreme Court clerks preparing drafts of opinions by justices, and finally become law when incorporated into majority opinions.

A draft of the opinion is circulated among members of the majority. Any majority member who disagrees with the reasoning in the opinion, and thus disagrees with the policy that is proposed, may either negotiate changes in the opinion with others in the majority or write a concurring opinion. A **concurring opinion** agrees with the decision about which party wins the case but sets forth a different reason for the decision, proposing, in fact, a different policy position.

Justices in the minority often agree to present a **dissenting opinion**. The dissenting opinion sets forth the views of justices who disagree with both the decision and the majority reasoning. Dissenting opinions do not have the force of law. They are written both to express opposition to the majority view and to appeal to a future Court to someday modify or reverse the position of the majority. Occasionally, the Court is unable to agree on a clear policy position on particularly vexing questions. If the majority is strongly divided over the reasoning behind their decision and as many as four justices dissent altogether from the decision, lower courts will lack clear guidance and future cases will be decided on a case-by-case basis, depending on multiple factors occurring in each case (see, for example, "Affirmative Action in the Courts" in Chapter 12). The absence of a clear opinion of the Court, supported by a unified majority of the justices, invites additional cases, keeping the issue on the Court's agenda until such time (if any) as the Court establishes a clear policy on the issue.

Politics and the Supreme Court

The political views of Supreme Court justices have an important influence on Court decisions. Justices are swayed primarily by their own ideological views; but public opinion, the president's position, and the arguments of interest groups all contribute to the outcome of cases.

Liberal and Conservative Voting Blocs
Although liberal and conservative voting blocs on the Court are visible over time, on any given case particular justices may deviate from their perceived ideological position. Many cases do not present a liberal-conservative dimension. Each case presents a separate set of facts, and even justices who share a general philosophy may perceive the central facts of a case differently. Moreover, the liberal-versus-conservative dimension sometimes clashes with the activist-versus-self-restraint dimension. Although we

American Bar Association

ABA news and views; information for law students.
www.abanet.org

concurring opinion
Opinion by a member of a court that agrees with the result reached by the court in the case but disagrees with or departs from the court's rationale for the decision.

dissenting opinion
Opinion by a member of a court that disagrees with the result reached by the court in the case.

generally think of liberals as favoring activism and conservatives self-restraint, occasionally those who favor self-restraint are obliged to approve of legislation that violates their personal conservative beliefs because opposing it would substitute their judgment for that of elected officials. So ideological blocs are not always good predictors of voting outcomes on the Court.

Over time, the composition of the Supreme Court has changed, as has the power of its various liberal and conservative voting blocs (see Table 13.4). The liberal bloc, headed by Chief Justice Earl Warren, dominated Court decision making from the mid-1950s through the end of the 1960s. The liberal bloc gradually weakened following President Richard Nixon's appointment of Warren Burger as Chief Justice in 1969, but not all of Nixon's appointees joined the conservative bloc; Justice Harry Blackmun and Justice Lewis Powell frequently joined in voting with the liberal bloc. Among Nixon's appointees, only William Rehnquist has consistently adopted conservative positions. President Gerald Ford's only appointee to the Court, John Paul Stevens, began as a moderate and drifted to the liberal bloc. As a result, the Burger Court, although generally not as activist as the Warren Court, still did not reverse any earlier liberal holdings.

President Ronald Reagan, who had campaigned on a pledge to restrain the liberal activism of the Court, tried to appoint conservatives. His first appointee, Sandra Day O'Connor, turned out to be less conservative than expected, especially on women's issues and abortion rights. When Chief Justice Burger retired in 1986, Reagan seized on the opportunity to strengthen the conservative bloc by elevating Rehnquist to Chief Justice. Reagan also appointed Antonin Scalia, another strong conservative, to the Court. Reagan added Anthony Kennedy to the Court in 1988, hoping to give Rehnquist and the conservative bloc the opportunity to form a majority. Had President Reagan succeeded in getting the powerful conservative voice of Robert Bork on the Court, it is possible that many earlier liberal decisions, including *Roe v. Wade*, would have been reversed. But the Senate rejected Bork, David Souter, the man ultimately confirmed, compiled a moderate record.

Liberals worried that the appointment of conservative Clarence Thomas as a replacement for the liberal Thurgood Marshall would give the conservative bloc a

TABLE 13.4 Liberal and Conservative Voting Blocs on the Supreme Court

	Warren Court	The Burger Court	The Rehnquist Court
	1968	1975	2004
Liberal	Earl Warren	William O. Douglas	John Paul Stevens
	Hugo Black	Thurgood Marshall	Ruth Bader Ginsburg
	William O. Douglas	William J. Brennan	Stephen G. Breyer
	Thurgood Marshall		
	William J. Brennan		
	Abe Fortas		
Moderate	Potter Stewart	Potter Stewart	Anthony Kennedy
	Byron White	Byron White	Sandra Day O'Connor
		Lewis Powell	David Souter
		Harry Blackmun	
Conservative	John Marshall Harlan	Warren Burger	William Rehnquist
		William Rehnquist	Antonin Scalia
			Clarence Thomas

commanding voice in Supreme Court policy making. But no solid conservative majority emerged. Justices Rehnquist, Scalia, and Thomas are considered the core of the conservative bloc, but they must win over at least two of the more moderate justices in order to form a majority in a case. President Bill Clinton's appointees, Ruth Bader Ginsburg and Stephen G. Breyer, have consistently supported liberal views on the Supreme Court. On key questions, the moderate bloc has the deciding vote.

While the moderate bloc currently holds the balance of power on the Court, the Court as a whole has moved in a conservative direction since the high watermark of judicial liberalism during the era of Chief Justice Earl Warren (1953–68). Liberalism on the Court—as measured by pro-individual rights decisions against the government in civil liberties cases, pro-defendant decisions in criminal cases, and pro-women and minorities in civil rights cases—has declined significantly since the 1960s (see Table 13.5).

Public Opinion "By all arguable evidence of the modern Supreme Court, Court appears to reflect public opinion about as accurately as other policy makers."[28] And indeed, on the liberal-conservative dimension, it can be argued that Supreme Court decisions have generally followed shifts in American public opinion. However, the Court appears to lag behind public opinion. It is doubtful that the justices read opinion polls; their jobs do not depend on public approval ratings. Rather, it is more likely that the justices, whose nomination and confirmation depended on an elected president and Senate, generally share the views of those who put them on the bench. Thus, public opinion affects the Court only indirectly, through the nomination and confirmation process.

Presidential Influence Even after a president's initial appointment of a Justice to the High Court, a president may exercise some influence over judicial decision making. The Office of the U.S. Solicitor General is charged with the responsibility of presenting the government's (the president's) views in cases not only to which the U.S. government is a party, but also in cases in which the president and the Attorney General have a strong interest and present their arguments in amicus curiae briefs. The Solicitor General's Office, in both Democratic and Republican presidential administrations, has compiled an enviable record in Supreme Court cases. When representing federal agencies that are parties to cases, the Solicitor General has won two-thirds of their cases before the Supreme Court over

TABLE 13.5 Liberalism in the Supreme Court

Type of Case	Percent Liberal Decisions		
	Warren Court	**Burger Court**	**Rehnquist Court**
Civil Liberties	67.7	43.6	42.8
Civil Rights	76.3	51.8	55.3
Criminal Procedures	59.4	34.2	33.2
First Amendment	69.0	48.6	48.5

Note: First Amendment includes all First Amendment guarantees plus due process and privacy; Criminal Procedures includes rights of persons accused of crime except due process; Civil Rights includes non-First Amendment cases pertaining to race, sex, age, and other individual characteristics. Civil Liberties combines all three of these types of cases.

Source: Derived from Lee Epstein et al., *The Supreme Court Compendium,* 3rd ed. (Washington, D.C.: CQ Press, 2002).

Bush v. Gore, Majority and Dissenting Opinions

From the Majority Opinion

With respect to the equal protection question, we find a violation of the Equal Protection Clause. . . .

Much of the controversy seems to revolve around ballot cards designed to be perforated by a stylus but which, either through error or deliberate omission, have not been perforated with sufficient precision for a machine to count them.

In some cases a piece of the card—a chad—is hanging, say by two corners. In other cases there is no separation at all, just an indentation. The Florida Supreme Court has ordered that the intent of the voter be discerned from such ballots. . . .

The recount mechanisms implemented in response to the decisions of the Florida Supreme Court do not satisfy the minimum requirement for non-arbitrary treatment of voters necessary to secure the

fundamental right (of equal protection). Florida's basic command for the count of legally cast votes is to consider the "intent of the voter." . . . This is unobjectionable as an abstract proposition and a starting principle. The problem inheres in the absence of specific standards to ensure its equal application.

From Justices Rehnquist, Scalia, and Thomas Concurring with the Majority

Moreover, the [Florida] court's interpretation of "legal vote," and hence its decision to order a contest-period recount, plainly departed from the legislative scheme. Florida statutory law cannot reasonably be thought to require the counting of improperly marked ballots. Each Florida precinct before election day provides instructions on how properly to cast a vote; each polling place on election day contains a working model of the voting machine it uses; and each voting booth contains a sample ballot. In precincts using punch-card ballots, voters are instructed to punch out the ballot cleanly:

Kweisi Mfume resigned from a Maryland congressional seat that he had held for ten years in order to assume the leadership of the NAACP, the nation's oldest and largest civil rights organization.

the years. And in cases where the Solicitor General has offered an amicus curiae brief, it has won about three-quarters of its cases. In contrast, the states have won fewer than half of the cases before the Supreme Court in which a state has been a party.

Interest-Group Influence Interest groups have become a major presence in Supreme Court cases. First of all, interest groups (for example, Planned Parenthood, National Association for the Advancement of Colored People, American Civil Liberties Union) sponsor many cases themselves. They find persons they believe to be directly damaged by a public policy, initiate litigation on their behalf, and provide the attorneys and money to pursue these cases all the way to the Supreme Court. Secondly, it is now a rare case that comes to the Court without multiple amicus curiae briefs filed by interest groups.

How influential are interest groups in Supreme Court decisions? Certainly interest groups have a significant influence in bringing issues before the Supreme Court through their sponsorship of cases. It is unlikely that the Court would have acted when it did on many key issues from racial segregation in 1954 (*Brown v. Board of Education* sponsored by the NAACP) to abortion in 1992 (*Planned Parenthood v. Casey* sponsored by Planned Parenthood) in the absence of interest-group activity. And interest-group amicus curiae briefs are now mentioned (cited) in about two-thirds of the written decisions of the Court. However, these briefs may not have much *independent* effect on decisions, that is, they may not have convinced the justices to decide a case one way or another. Several studies have found that interest-group briefs have had very little effect on Supreme Court decisions.[29]

"AFTER VOTING, CHECK YOUR BALLOT CARD TO BE SURE YOUR VOTING SELECTIONS ARE CLEARLY AND CLEANLY PUNCHED AND THERE ARE NO CHIPS LEFT HANGING ON THE BACK OF THE CARD."

From Dissenting Opinions, Justice Stevens

It is confidence in the men and women who administer the judicial system that is the true backbone of the rule of law. Time will one day heal the wound to that confidence that will be inflicted by today's decision. One thing, however, is certain. Although we may never know with complete certainty the identity of the winner of this year's presidential election, the identity of the loser is perfectly clear. It is the nation's confidence in the judge as an impartial guardian of the rule of law.

Source: Bush v. Gore.

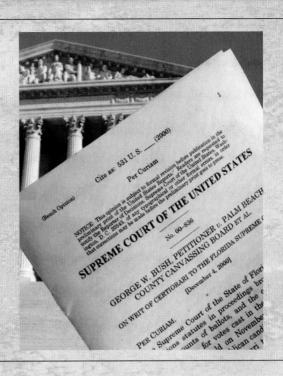

Bush v. Gore in the U.S. Supreme Court

The presidential election of 2000 was unique in American history in that the outcome was decided by the Supreme Court of the United States. The Supreme Court's decision on December 12, 2000, in *Bush v. Gore*, rested on constitutional issues, but the 5–4 decision of the justices raised the question of the High Court's political partisanship.[30]

"Too Close to Call" On the morning after Election Day, it became clear that the outcome of the presidential election depended on Florida's twenty-five electoral votes. Florida's Secretary of State (separately elected Republican Katherine Harris) initially reported a margin of 1,784 for Bush out of over 6 million votes cast in the state. But because Florida law provides for a recount when the margin of victory is less than one-half of 1 percent, the recount of machine votes was conducted as well as a count of absentee ballots. Bush's lead was reduced to a slim 930 votes. The Florida Secretary of State declined to accept any recount returns from the counties after November 14, the date set by Florida law as the final date for submission of returns to the Secretary.

Judicial Maneuvering But immediately after Election Day armies of lawyers descended on Florida's capital city, Tallahassee. The stakes were high—the presidency of the United States. Gore's legal team was headed by former Secretary of State Warren Christopher, and the Bush team by former Secretary of State James Baker (although neither argued directly before the courts). The Gore team demanded *manual* recounts of the ballots in the state's three largest (and most

 Southeastern Legal Foundation

Public interest law firm advocating limited government, individual freedom, and the free enterprise system.
www.southeasternlegal.org

 Southern Poverty Law Center

Civil rights law firm opposing death penalty, hate groups, display of religion in public places, etc. *www.splcenter.org*

Democratic) counties—Miami-Dade, Broward (Fort Lauderdale), and Palm Beach. The case was first argued before a Leon County (Tallahassee) trial judge, who dismissed Gore's petition. But the case was quickly appealed to the Florida Supreme Court (with its seven justices, all appointed by Democratic governors). That Court set aside the state's legal deadline for recounts, and county canvassing boards began a tedious hand count of punch card ballots.

The Bush legal team appealed directly to the U.S. Supreme Court arguing, first of all, that the U.S. Constitution gives the power to appoint presidential electors "in such Manner as the *Legislature* thereof may direct" (Article II, Section 1), and that the Florida Supreme Court overreached its authority when it set aside legislative-enacted provisions of the election laws of the state, including the deadline for recounts. They also argued that hand counts in counties were late, unreliable, subjective, and open to partisan bias. The U.S. Supreme Court responded initially by ordering a halt to the recounts and remanding (sending back) the case to the Florida Supreme Court for clarification as to the grounds on which it had been decided.

The Florida Supreme Court was apparently not intimidated by the U.S. Supreme Court's implied judgment that it had erred in its decision. It ordered a manual recount of all legal votes in the state, especially undercounts (where ballots failed to register a vote for president). It specified that "the intent of the voter" should be the criterion for deciding how to count a ballot. The Florida Supreme Court decision, *Gore v. Harris*,[31] was immediately appealed to the U.S. Supreme Court.

By now more than a month had passed with the nation not knowing who would be its next president. It became clear that Al Gore had won the nationwide popular vote. But most Americans acknowledged that the popular vote was of secondary importance to the Constitution of the United States in its provisions for choosing the president by state electoral votes. (Indeed, nationwide polls indicated that 73 percent of Americans said they would accept the U.S. Supreme Court's decision as "the legitimate outcome no matter which candidate it favors."[32]) Only the U.S. Supreme Court seemed to possess sufficient legitimacy to resolve the first contested presidential election in over a century.

A Divided Supreme Court The Supreme Court held that "the use of standardless manual recounts violates the Equal Protection and Due Process Clauses [of the U.S. Constitution] . . . The judgment of the Supreme Court of Florida is reversed." (See *Up Close: "Bush v. Gore*, Majority and Dissenting Opinions.")

The narrow 5–4 decision appeared to follow partisan lines, with Justices O'Connor, Kennedy, Rehnquist, Scalia, and Thomas voting in the majority to allow Florida's Secretary of State to certify that state's electoral votes for Bush. Justices Souter, Stevens, Ginsburg, and Breyer dissented, arguing that the U.S. Supreme Court should not interfere with the Florida Supreme Court's order for a manual recount. Indeed, Justice Stevens implied that the Supreme Court's decision would undermine "the nation's confidence in the judge as an impartial guardian of the rule of law."

Checking Court Power

Many people are concerned about the extent to which we now rely on a nonelected judiciary to decide key policy issues rather than depending on a democratically elected president or Congress.

Legitimacy as a Restraint in the Judiciary Court authority derives from legitimacy rather than force. By that we mean that the courts depend on their au-

Do You Have Confidence in the Supreme Court?

The Supreme Court has issued many controversial rulings throughout its history, yet public confidence in the Court has remained fairly high. While many Americans disagree with specific Supreme Court decisions, they remain supportive of the Court itself. For example, in *Bush vs. Gore* many opponents of the decision claimed that the Court reached its decision based on "politics" and "partisanship." Yet most Americans accepted the decision as the final word on the election. The Supreme Court's institutional legitimacy appeared to be sufficient to persuade people to go along with the decision, even if they strongly disagreed with it. In short, Americans appear to distinguish between the Court's specific decisions and the legitimacy of the Court as a political institution.

However, the willingness of Americans to trust the Supreme Court has become more closely tied to party preferences than in the past. In recent years Republicans have been much more confident of the Supreme Court than Democrats. Perhaps this disparity is a result of the Court's decision in *Bush vs. Gore*. Partisanship, together with such highly contentious issues as abortion, the death penalty, and affirmative-action, will likely lead to huge battles in Washington over the replacement of any retiring justices.

Question: Now I am going to read you a list of institutions in American society. Please tell me how much confidence you, yourself, have in each one—a great deal, quite a lot, some, or very little? . . . The U.S. Supreme Court.

Source: Copyright © 2003 by The Gallup Organization.

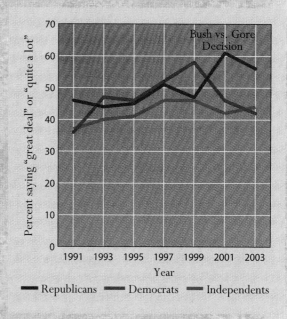

thority being seen as rightful, on people perceiving an obligation to abide by court decisions whether they agree with them or not. The courts have no significant force at their direct command. Federal marshals, who carry out the orders of federal courts, number only a few thousand. Courts must rely primarily on the executive branch for enforcement of their decisions.

Today most Americans believe that Supreme Court decisions are authoritative statements about the Constitution and that people have an obligation to obey these decisions whether they agree with them or not.[33] Thus public opinion constrains other public officials—from the president, to governors, to school superintendents, to law enforcement officials—to obey Supreme Court decisions. Their constituents do not hold them personally responsible for unpopular actions ordered by the Supreme Court or federal judges. On the contrary, their constituents generally expect them to comply with court decisions (see *What Do You Think?: "Do You Have Confidence in the Supreme Court?"*)

Compliance with Court Policy Federal and state court judges must apply Supreme Court policies when ruling on cases in their own courts. Occasionally lower courts express their disagreement with the Supreme Court in an opinion, even when they feel obliged to carry out the High Court's policy. At times, lower federal and state courts try to give a narrow interpretation to a Supreme Court decision with which they disagree. But judges who seek to defy the Supreme Court face the ultimate sanction of reversal on appeal by the losing party. Professional pride usually inspires judges to avoid reversals of their judgments by higher courts even though a long record of reversals is not grounds for impeachment or removal of a federal judge.

Public officials who defy Supreme Court rulings risk lawsuits and court orders mandating compliance. Persons injured by noncompliance are likely to file suit against noncomplying officials, as are interest groups that monitor official compliance with the policies they support. These suits are expensive, time consuming, and potentially embarrassing to government officials and agencies. Once a court order is issued, continued defiance can result in fines and penalties for contempt of court.

The president of the United States is subject to federal court orders. Historically, this notion has been challenged: early presidents believed they were separate and at least co-equal to the courts and that their own determination about the legality or constitutionality of their own acts could not be overturned by the courts. President Andrew Jackson could—and did—say: "John Marshall has made his decision. Now let him enforce it," expressing the view that the president was not obliged to enforce court decisions he disagreed with.[34] But in the course of 200 years, the courts—not the president—have gained in legitimacy as the final authority on the law and the Constitution. Today a president who openly defied the Supreme Court would lose any claims to legitimacy and would risk impeachment by Congress.

The case of Richard Nixon illustrates the weakness of a modern president who would even consider defying the Supreme Court. When Nixon sought to invoke executive privilege to withhold damaging tapes of White House conversations in the Watergate investigation (see *Up Close:* "Watergate and the Limits of Presidential Power" in Chapter 9), federal district judge John Sirica rejected his claim and ordered that the tapes be turned over to the special prosecutor in the case. In arguments before the Supreme Court, Nixon's lawyers contended that the president would not have to comply with a Supreme Court decision to turn over the tapes. Yet when the Court ruled unanimously against him, Nixon felt bound to comply and released tapes that were very damaging to his cause. But Nixon understood that refusal to abide by a Supreme Court decision would most assuredly have resulted in impeachment. Under the circumstances, compliance was the better of two unattractive choices.

Presidential Influence on Court Policy The president and Congress can exercise some restraint over court power through the checks and balances built into the Constitution. Using the office's powers of appointment, presidents have effectively modified the direction of Supreme Court policy and influenced lower federal courts as well. Certainly presidents must await the death or retirement of Supreme Court justices and federal judges, and presidents are constrained by the need to secure Senate confirmation of their appointees. However, over time presidential influence on the courts can be significant. During their combined twelve years in the White House, Ronald Reagan and George Bush were able to fill 70 percent of federal district and appellate court judgeships and six of nine Supreme Court positions with their own appointees. As noted earlier, however, their appointees did not always reflect these presidents' philosophy of judicial self-restraint in rendering decisions. Nevertheless, the federal courts tilted in a somewhat more conservative direction. President Bill Clinton's appointments generally strengthened liberal, activist impulses throughout the federal judiciary.

Congressional Checks on the Judiciary The Constitution gives Congress control over the structure and jurisdiction of federal district and appellate courts, but congressional use of this control has been restrained. Only the Supreme Court is established by the Constitution; Article III gives Congress the power to "ordain and establish" "inferior" courts. In theory, Congress could try to limit court jurisdiction to hear cases that Congress did not wish it to decide. Congress has used this power to lighten the federal courts' workload; for example, Congress has limited the jurisdiction of federal courts in cases between citizens of different states by requiring that the dispute involve more than $50,000. But Congress has never used this power to change court policy—for example, by removing federal court jurisdiction over school prayer cases or desegregation cases. Indeed federal courts would probably declare unconstitutional any congressional attempt to limit their power to interpret the Constitution by limiting jurisdiction.

Likewise, although Congress could, in theory, expand membership on the Supreme Court, the custom of a nine-member Supreme Court is now so deeply ingrained in American government that "court packing" is politically unthinkable. Franklin Roosevelt's unsuccessful 1937 attempt to expand the Supreme Court was the last serious assault on its membership. However, President Jimmy Carter succeeded in getting Congress to add a large number of federal district judgeships, and he used these new posts to appoint more women and minorities to the federal judiciary.

A more common congressional constraint on the Supreme Court is amending statutory laws to reverse federal court interpretations of these laws that Congress believes are in error. Thus when the Supreme Court decided that civil rights laws did not mandate a cutoff of all federal funds to a college upon evidence of discrimination in a single program but only the funds for that program.[35] Congress amended its own laws to require the more sweeping remedy. Although members of Congress frequently berate the Court for what they see as misreading of the laws, all Congress needs to do to reverse a Court interpretation of those laws is to pass amendments to them.

Constitutional amendment is the only means by which the Congress and the states can reverse a Supreme Court interpretation of the Constitution itself. After the Civil War, the Thirteenth Amendment abolishing slavery reversed the Supreme Court's *Dred Scott* decision (1857) that slavery was constitutionally protected. The Sixteenth Amendment (1913) gave Congress the power to impose an income tax, thus reversing the Supreme Court's earlier decision in *Pollock v. Farmer's Loan*[36] holding income taxes unconstitutional (1895). But recent attempts to reverse Supreme Court interpretations of the Constitution by passing constitutional amendments on the issues of prayer in public schools, busing, and abortion have all failed to win congressional approval. The barriers to a constitutional amendment are formidable: a two-thirds vote of both houses of Congress and ratification by three-quarters of the states. Thus, for all practical purposes, the Constitution is what the Supreme Court says it is.

Congress can impeach federal court judges, but only for "cause" (committing crimes), not for their decisions. Although impeachment is frequently cited as a constitutional check on the judiciary, it has no real influence over judicial policy making. Only five federal court judges have ever been impeached by the House, convicted by the Senate, and removed from office, although two others were impeached and another nine resigned to avoid impeachment. In 1989 Federal District Court Judge Alcee Hastings became the first sitting judge in more than fifty years to be impeached, tried, and found guilty by the Congress. He was convicted by the Senate of perjury and conspiracy to obtain a $150,000 bribe; but a federal district court judge later ruled that he should have been tried by the full Senate, not a special committee of the Senate. Hastings declared the ruling a vindication; in 1992 he won a congressional seat in Florida, becoming the first person ever to become a member of the House after being impeached by that same body. Even criminal convictions do not ensure removal from office, although judges have resigned under fire.

SUMMARY NOTES

- Great power is lodged in the Supreme Court of the United States and the federal judiciary. These courts have undertaken to resolve many of the most divisive conflicts in American society. The judicial power is the power to decide cases and controversies, and in so doing to decide the meaning of the Constitution and laws of Congress.

- The power of judicial review is the power to invalidate laws of Congress or of the states that the federal courts believe conflict with the U.S. Constitution. This power is not specifically mentioned in the Constitution but was derived by Chief Justice John Marshall from the Supremacy Clause and the meaning of judicial power in Article III.

- The Supreme Court has been fairly restrained in its use of judicial review with regard to laws of Congress and actions of presidents; it has more frequently overturned state laws. The federal courts also exercise great power in the interpretation of the laws of Congress, especially when statutory language is vague.

- Arguments over judicial power are reflected in the conflicting philosophies of judicial activism and judicial self-restraint. Advocates of judicial restraint argue that judges must not substitute their own views for those of elected representatives and the remedy for unwise laws lies in the legislature, not the courts. Advocates of judicial activism argue that the courts must view the Constitution as a living document and its meaning must fit the needs of a changing society.

- The federal judiciary consists of three levels of courts—the Supreme Court, the U.S. Courts of Appeals, and the U.S. District Courts. The district courts are trial courts that hear both civil and criminal cases. The courts of appeals are appellate courts and do not hold trials but consider only the record of trial courts and the arguments (briefs) of attorneys. More than 90 percent of federal cases end in appeals courts. The Supreme Court can hear appeals from state high courts as well as lower federal courts. The Supreme Court hears only about 200 cases a year.

- Courts function under general rules of restraint that do not bind the president or Congress. The Supreme Court does not decide hypothetical cases or render advisory opinions. The principle of stare decisis, or reliance on precedent, is not set aside lightly.

- The selection of Supreme Court justices and federal judges is based more on political considerations than legal qualifications. Presidents almost always appoint judges from their own party, and presidents increasingly have sought judges who share their ideological views. However, because of the independence of judges once they are appointed, presidents have sometimes been disappointed in the decisions of their appointees. In addition, Senate approval of nominees has become increasingly politicized, with problems most evident when different parties control the White House and the Senate.

- The Supreme Court sets its own agenda for policy making, usually by granting or withholding certiorari. Generally four justices must agree to grant certiorari for a case to be decided by the Supreme Court. The Supreme Court has been especially active in policy making in interpreting the meaning of the Fourteenth Amendment's guarantee of "equal protection of the laws," as well as of the civil rights and voting rights acts of Congress. It has also been active in defining the meaning of freedom of press, speech, and religion in the First Amendment and "due process of law" in the Fifth Amendment. The federal courts are active in overseeing government regulatory activity. But federal courts have generally left the areas of national security and international relations to the president and Congress. In addition, the Court tends to accept cases involving questions decided differently by different courts of appeal, cases in which lower courts have challenged Supreme Court interpretations, and cases in which the U.S. government is a party and it requests review.

- Liberal and conservative blocs on the Supreme Court can be discerned over time. Generally, liberals have been judicial activists and conservatives have been restraintists. Today a moderate bloc appears to hold the balance of power.

- The Supreme Court risked its reputation for political impartiality when it intervened in the 2000 presidential election, and issued a decision that in effect gave Florida's

25 electoral votes to George W. Bush and by so doing won him a majority in the Electoral College.

■ Court power derives primarily from legitimacy rather than force. Most Americans believe that Supreme Court decisions are authoritative statements about the Constitution and people have an obligation to obey these decisions whether they agree with them or not. Although early presidents thought of themselves as constitutional co-equals with the Supreme Court and not necessarily bound by Court decisions, today it would be politically unthinkable for a president to ignore a court order.

■ There are very few checks on Supreme Court power. Presidents may try to influence Court policy through judicial nominations, but once judges are confirmed by the Senate they can pursue their own impulses. Congress has never used its power to limit the jurisdiction of federal courts in order to influence judicial decisions.

■ Only by amending the Constitution can Congress and the states reverse a Supreme Court interpretation of its meaning. Congress can impeach federal judges only for committing crimes, not for their decisions.

KEY TERMS

judicial review   458
statutory laws   462
judicial self-restraint   462
original intent   463
judicial activism   464
stare decisis   464
precedent   4640
jurisdiction   465
original jurisdiction   465
appellate jurisdiction   465

appeal   465
district courts   465
grand juries   465
petit (regular) juries   465
circuit courts   465
briefs   465
civil cases   470
adversarial system   470
standing   470

plaintiffs   471
defendants   471
sovereign immunity   471
class action suits   471
contingency fees   472
remedies and reliefs   472
independent counsel ("special prosecutor")   472

litmus test   474
senatorial courtesy   474
writ of certiorari   479
rule of four   479
amicus curiae   479
solicitor general   480
majority opinion   480
concurring opinion   481
dissenting opinion   481

SUGGESTED READINGS

Baum, Lawrence. *The Supreme Court.* 8th ed. Washington, D.C.: CQ Press, 2003. Readable introduction to the Supreme Court as a political institution, covering the selection and confirmation of judges, the nature of the issues decided by courts, the process of judicial decision making, and the impact of Supreme Court decisions.

Bork, Robert H. *Coercing Virtue.* Washington DC: AEI Press, 2003. An argument that judges, rather than legislators, are making and repealing law and deciding cases with partisan and ideological subjectivity.

Carp, Robert A., and Ronald Stidham. *The Federal Courts.* 4th ed. Washington, D.C.: CQ Press, 2001. Overview of the federal judicial system, arguing that federal judges and Supreme Court justices function as part of the political system and engage in policy making that influences all our lives.

Epstein, Lee, and Thomas G. Walker. *Constitutional Law for a Changing America: Institutional Power and Constraints.* 4th ed. Washington, D.C.: CQ Press, 2001. Commentary and selected excerpts from cases dealing with the structure and powers of government.

Johnson, Charles, and Danette Buickman. *Independent Counsel: The Law and the Investigations.* Washington, D.C.: CQ Press, 2001. A comprehensive history of the independent counsel law and the investigations conducted under it since 1978, from Watergate to Whitewater.

Neubauer, David W. and Stephen S. Weinhold. *Judicial Politics: Law, Courts, and Politics in the United States.* Belmont, Calif.: Wadsworth, 2004. Introduction to the judicial process with controversial cases in each chapters.

U.S. Supreme Court decisions are available at most public and university libraries as well as at law libraries in volumes of *United States Reports.* Court opinions are cited by the names of the parties, for example, *Brown v. Board of Education of Topeka,* followed by a reference number such as 347 U.S. 483 (1954). The first number in the citation (347) is the volume number; "U.S." refers to *United States Reports;* the subsequent number is the page on which the decision begins; the year the case was decided is in parentheses.

14

POLITICS AND
PERSONAL LIBERTY

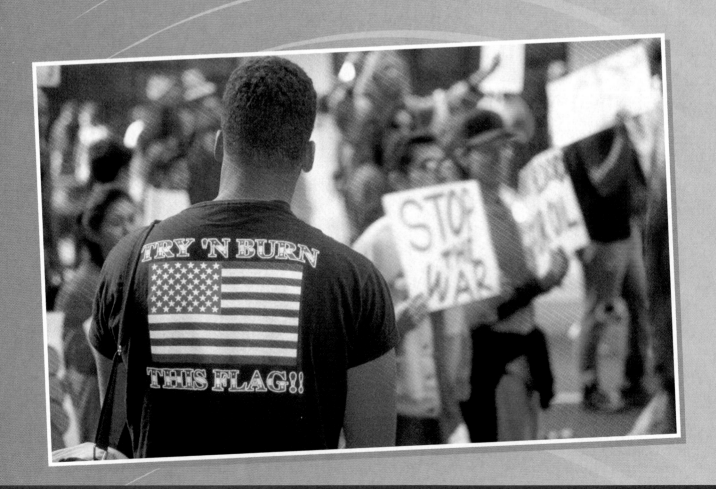

Power and Individual Liberty

To the authors of the Declaration of Independence, individual liberty was inherent in the human condition. It was not derived from governments or even from constitutions. Rather, governments and constitutions existed to make individual liberty more secure.

> We hold these truths to be self-evident, that all men are created equal, that they are endowed by their Creator with certain unalienable Rights, that among these are Life, Liberty and the pursuit of Happiness. That to secure these rights, Governments are instituted among Men, deriving their just powers from the consent of the governed.

The authors of the Bill of Rights (the first ten amendments to the Constitution) did *not* believe that they were creating individual rights, but rather that they were recognizing and guaranteeing rights that belonged to individuals by virtue of their humanity.

Authority and Liberty To avoid the brutal life of a lawless society, where the weak are at the mercy of the strong, people form governments and endow them with powers to secure peace and self-preservation. People voluntarily relinquish some of their individual freedom to establish a government that is capable of protecting them from their neighbors as well as from foreign aggressors. This government must be strong enough to maintain its own existence or it cannot defend the rights of its citizens.

But what happens when a government becomes too strong and infringes on the liberties of its citizens? How much liberty must individuals surrender to secure an orderly society? This is the classic dilemma of free government: people must create laws and governments to protect their freedom, but the laws and governments themselves restrict freedom.

Democracy and Personal Liberty When democracy is defined only as a *decision-making process*—widespread popular participation and rule by majority—it offers little protection for individual liberty. Democracy must also be defined to include *substantive values*—a recognition of the dignity of all individuals and their equality under law. Otherwise, some people,

THINK
ABOUT POLITICS

1 Do you think the government has become so large and powerful that it poses a threat to the rights and freedoms of ordinary citizens?
Yes ● No ●

2 Do you believe that using tax funds to pay tuition at church-affiliated schools violates the separation of church and state?
Yes ● No ●

3 Do we have a constitutional right to physician-assisted suicide?
Yes ● No ●

4 Do law-abiding citizens have a constitutional right to carry a handgun for self-protection?
Yes ● No ●

5 Should persons captured on a foreign battlefield in the war on terrorism be entitled to constitutional protections?
Yes ● No ●

6 Do you believe that the seizure of property believed by police to be used in drug trafficking, without a judicial hearing or trial, violates civil liberty?
Yes ● No ●

7 Is the death penalty a "cruel and unusual" punishment?
Yes ● No ●

Government power defends your most basic rights to life, liberty, and the pursuit of happiness while at the same time ensuring that all other Americans have the same rights. The Founders guaranteed individual liberty in the earliest days of our nation through the first ten amendments to the Constitution—our Bill of Rights.

First Amendment Center

Vanderbilt University center provides sources of information on First Amendment issues.
www.firstamendmentcenter.org

incorporation In constitutional law, the application of almost all of the Bill of Rights to the states and all of their subdivision through the Fourteenth Amendment.

In 1990 the Supreme Court ruled against two Native Americans who had been fired from their jobs as drug counselors for taking peyote during religious ceremonies of the Native American Church. The Court maintained that the Free Exercise Clause does not exempt individuals from complying with valid laws regulating conduct. In this picture, a Native American holy man performs a ceremony outside the Court as it hears arguments on the case.

particularly "the weaker party, or an obnoxious individual" would be vulnerable to deprivations of life, liberty, or property simply by decisions of majorities (see "The Paradox of Democracy" in Chapter 1). Indeed, the "great object" of the Constitution, according to James Madison, was to preserve popular government yet at the same time to protect individuals from "unjust" majorities.[1]

The purpose of the Constitution—and especially its Bill of Rights, passed by the First Congress in September 1789—is to limit governmental power over the individual, that is, to place personal liberty beyond the reach of government (see Table 14.1 on page 495). Each individual's rights to life, liberty, and property, due process of law, and equal protection of the law are not subject to majority vote. Or, as Supreme Court Justice Robert Jackson once declared, "One's right to life, liberty, and property, to free speech, a free press, freedom of worship and assembly, and other fundamental rights may not be submitted to vote: they depend on the outcome of no elections."[2]

Nationalizing the Bill of Rights The Bill of Rights begins with the words *"Congress* shall make no law . . .," indicating that it was originally intended to limit only the powers of the federal government. The Bill of Rights was added to the Constitution because of fear that the *federal* government might become too powerful and encroach on individual liberty. But what about encroachments by state and local governments and their officials?

The Fourteenth Amendment includes the words "No State shall . . ."; its provisions are directed specifically at states. Initially, the U.S. Supreme Court rejected the argument that the Fourteenth Amendment's Privileges or Immunities Clause[3] and the Due Process Clause[4] incorporated the Bill of Rights. But beginning in the 1920s, the Court handed down a long series of decisions that gradually brought about the **incorporation** of almost all of the protections of the Bill of Rights into the "liberty" guaranteed against state actions by the Due Process Clause of the Fourteenth Amendment. In *Gitlow v. New York* (1925), the Court ruled that "freedom of speech and of the press—which are protected by the First Amendment from abridgment by Congress—are among the fundamental personal rights and liberties protected by the due process clause of the Fourteenth Amendment from impairment by the states."[5] Over time, the Court applied the same reasoning in incorporating almost all provisions of the Bill of Rights into the Fourteenth Amendment's Due Process Clause. States and all of their subdivisions—cities, counties, townships, school districts, etc.—are bound by the Bill of Rights.

Freedom of Religion

Americans are a very religious people. Belief in God and church attendance are more widespread in the United States than in any other advanced industrialized nation. Although many early American colonists came to the new land to escape religious persecution, they frequently established their own government-supported churches and imposed their own religious beliefs on others. Puritanism was the official faith of colonial Massachusetts, and Virginia officially established the Church of England. Only two colonies (Maryland and Rhode Island) provided for full religious freedom. In part to lessen the potential for conflict among the states, the framers of the Bill of Rights sought to prevent the new national government from establishing an official religion or interfering with religious exercises.[6] The very first words of the First Amendment set forth two separate prohibitions on government: "Congress shall

TABLE 14.1   **Constitutionally Protected Rights**

The Bill of Rights

The first ten amendments to the Constitution of the United States, passed by the First Congress of the United States in September 1789 and ratified by the states in December 1791.

Amendments	Protections
First Amendment: Religion, Speech, Press, Assembly, Petition	
Congress shall make no law respecting an establishment of religion, or prohibiting the free exercise thereof, or abridging the freedom of speech, or of the press; or the right of the people peaceably to assemble, and to petition the Government for a redress of grievances.	Prohibits government establishment of religion. Protects the free exercise of religion. Protects freedom of speech. Protects freedom of the press. Protects freedom of assembly. Protects the right to petition government "for a redress of grievances."
Second Amendment: Right to Bear Arms	
A well regulated Militia, being necessary to the security of a free State, the right of the people to keep and bear Arms, shall not be infringed.	Protects the right of people to bear arms and states to maintain militia (National Guard) units
Third Amendment: Quartering of Soldiers	
No Soldier shall, in time of peace, be quartered in any house, without the consent of the Owner, nor in time of war, but in a manner to be prescribed by law.	Prohibits forcible quartering of soldiers in private homes in peacetime, or in war without congressional authorization.
Fourth Amendment: Searches and Seizures	
The right of the people to be secure in their persons, houses, papers, and effects, against unreasonable searches and seizures, shall not be violated, and no Warrants shall issue, but upon probable cause, supported by Oath or affirmation, and particularly describing the place to be searched, and the persons or things to be seized.	Protects against "unreasonable searches and seizures." Requires warrants for searches of homes and other places where there is a reasonable expectation of privacy. Judges may issue search warrants only with "probable cause," and such warrants must be specific regarding the place to be searched and the things to be seized.
Fifth Amendment: Grand Juries, Double Jeopardy, Self-Incrimination, Due Process, Protection against Government Takings of Property	
No person shall be held to answer for a capital, or otherwise infamous crime, unless on a presentment or indictment of a Grand jury, except in cases arising in the land or naval forces, or in the Militia, when in actual service in time of war or public danger; nor shall any person be subject for the same offence to be twice put in jeopardy of life or limb, nor shall he be compelled in any criminal case to be a witness against himself, nor be deprived of life, liberty, or property, without due process of law; nor shall private property be taken for public use, without just compensation.	Requires that, before trial for a serious crime, a person (except military personnel) must be indicted by a grand jury. Prohibits double jeopardy (trial for the same offense a second time after being found innocent). Prohibits the government from forcing any person in a criminal case to be a witness against himself or herself. Prohibits the government from taking life, liberty, or property "without due process of law." Prohibits government from taking private property without paying "just compensation."

(continued)

TABLE 14.1 **Constitutionally Protected Rights (continued)**

Amendments	Protections
Sixth Amendment: Fair Trial	
In all criminal prosecutions, the accused shall enjoy the right to a speedy and public trial, by an impartial jury of the State and district wherein the crime shall have been committed, which district shall have been previously ascertained by law, and to be informed of the nature and cause of the accusation; to be confronted with the witnesses against him; to have compulsory process for obtaining witnesses in his favor, and to have the Assistance of Counsel for his defense.	Requires that the accused in a criminal case be given a speedy and public trial, and thus prohibits prolonged incarceration without trial or secret trials. Requires that trials be by jury and take place in the district where the crime was committed. Requires that the accused be informed of the charges, have the right to confront witnesses, have the right to force supporting witnesses to testify, and have the assistance of counsel.
Seventh Amendment: Trial by Jury in Civil Cases	
In Suits at common law, where the value in controversy shall exceed twenty dollars, the right of trial by jury shall be preserved, and no fact tried by a jury, shall be otherwise reexamined in any Court of the United States, than according to the rules of the common law.	Requires a jury trial in civil cases involving more than $20. Limits the degree to which factual questions decided by a jury may be reviewed by another court.
Eighth Amendment: Bail, Fines and Punishment	
Excessive bail shall not be required, nor excessive fines imposed, nor cruel and unusual punishments inflicted.	Prohibits excessive bail. Prohibits excessive fines. Prohibits cruel and unusual punishment.
Ninth Amendment: Unspecified Rights Retained by People	
The enumeration in the Constitution, of certain rights, shall not be construed to deny or disparage others retained by the people.	Protection of unspecified rights (including privacy) that are not listed in the Constitution. The Constitution shall not be interpreted to be a complete list of rights retained by the people.
Tenth Amendment: Rights Reserved to the States	
The powers not delegated to the United States by the Constitution, nor prohibited by it to the States, are reserved to the States respectively, or to the people.	States retain powers that are not granted by the Constitution to the national government or prohibited by it to the states.

Rights in the Text of the Constitution

Several rights were written into the text of the Constitution in 1787 and thus precede in time the adoption of the Bill of Rights.

Article 1 Section 9: Habeas Corpus, Bills of Attainder, and Ex Post Facto Laws	
The privilege of the Writ of Habeas Corpus shall not be suspended, unless when in Cases of Rebellion or Invasion the public Safety may require it. No Bill of Attainder or ex post facto Law shall be passed.	Habeas corpus prevents imprisonment without a judge's determination that a person is being lawfully detained. Prohibition of bills of attainder prevents Congress (and states) from deciding people guilty of a crime and imposing punishment without trial. Prohibition of ex post facto laws prevents Congress (and states) from declaring acts to be criminal that were committed before the passage of a law making them so.

(continued)

TABLE 14.1 **Constitutionally Protected Rights (continued)**

Thirteenth and Fourteenth Amendments

The Bill of Rights begins with the words "Congress shall make no law . . ." indicating that it initially applied only to the *federal* government. Although states had their own constitutions that guarantee many of the same rights, for more than a century the Bill of Rights did not apply to state and local governments. Following the Civil War, the Thirteenth, Fourteenth, and Fifteenth (voting rights) Amendments were passed, restricting *state* governments and their local subdivisions. But not until many years later did the U.S. Supreme Court, in a long series of decisions, apply the Bill of Rights against the states.

Thirteenth Amendment

Neither slavery nor involuntary servitude, except as a punishment for crime whereof the party shall have been duly convicted, shall exist within the United States, or any place subject to their jurisdiction.	Prohibits slavery or involuntary servitude except for punishment by law; applies to both governments and private citizens.

Fourteenth Amendment

All persons born or naturalized in the United States, and subject to the jurisdiction thereof, are citizens of the United States and of the State wherein they reside. No State shall make or enforce any law which shall abridge the privileges or immunities of citizens of the United States; nor shall any State deprive any person of life, liberty, or property, without due process of law; nor deny to any person within its jurisdiction the equal protection of the laws.	Protects "privileges and immunities of citizenship." Prevents deprivation of life, liberty, or property "without due process of law"; this phrase incorporates virtually all of the rights specified in the Bill of Rights. Prevents denial of "equal protection of the laws" for all persons.

make no law respecting an *establishment of religion,* or prohibiting the *free exercise* thereof." These two restrictions on government power—the Free Exercise Clause and the No Establishment Clause—guarantee separate religious freedoms.

Free Exercise of Religion The **Free Exercise Clause** prohibits government from restricting religious beliefs or practices. Although the wording of the First Amendment appears absolute ("Congress shall make no law . . ."), the U.S. Supreme Court has never interpreted the phrase to protect any conduct carried on in the name of religion. In the first major decision involving this clause, the Court ruled in 1879 that polygamy could be outlawed by Congress in Utah Territory even though some Mormons argued that it was part of their religious faith. The Court distinguished between belief and behavior, saying that "Congress was deprived of all legislative power over mere opinion [by the First Amendment], but was left free to reach actions which were in violation of social duties."[7] The Court also employed the Free Exercise Clause to strike down as unconstitutional an attempt by a state to prohibit private religious schools and force all children to attend public schools.[8] This decision protects the entire structure of private religious schools in the nation.

Later, the Supreme Court elaborated on its distinction between religious belief and religious practice. *Beliefs* are protected absolutely, but with regard to religious *practices,* the Court has generally upheld governmental restrictions when enacted for valid secular purposes.[9] Thus the government can outlaw religious practices that threaten health, safety, or welfare. The Free Exercise Clause does *not* confer the *right* to practice human sacrifice or even the ceremonial use of illegal drugs.[10]

Free Exercise Clause Clause in the First Amendment to the Constitution that prohibits government from restricting religious beliefs and practices.

Individuals must comply with valid and neutral laws even if these laws restrict religious practices.

But the Supreme Court has continued to face many difficulties in applying its "valid secular test" to specific infringements of religious freedom. When some Amish parents refused to allow their children to attend any school beyond the eighth grade, the state of Wisconsin argued that its universal compulsory school attendance law had a valid purpose: the education of children. The Amish parents argued that high school exposed their children to worldly influences and values contrary to their religious beliefs. The Supreme Court sided with the Amish, deciding that their religious claims outweighed the legitimate interests of the state in education.[11] When a Florida city attempted to outlaw the Santeria (a mix of Catholicism and voodoo) practice of slaughtering animals in religious ceremonies, the Supreme Court held that the city's ordinance was "not neutral" and "targeted" a particular religious ceremony and was therefore unconstitutional.[12]

Yet the Supreme Court has upheld government actions that were challenged as infringements of religious freedom in several key cases. The Court approved of an Internal Revenue Service action revoking the tax-exempt status of Bob Jones University because of its rules against interracial dating or marriage among its students. The school argued that its rule was based on religious belief, but the Court held that the government had "an overriding interest in eradicating racial discrimination in education."[13] And the Court upheld an Oregon law that prohibited the possession of peyote (a hallucinogenic drug made from cactus plants) against the claims of a Native American church that its use was a religious sacrament.[14] The Court also upheld an Air Force dress code regulation that prevented Orthodox Jews from wearing a yarmulke while in uniform. The Court rejected the argument that the regulation violated the Free Exercise Clause, holding instead that "the mission of the military . . . [included fostering] obedience, unity, commitment and esprit de corps" overrides the individual freedom that would protect civilians from such a government regulation.[15]

No Establishment of Religion
Various meanings have been ascribed to the First Amendment's **No Establishment Clause.**

1. The first meaning—what the writers of the Bill of Rights had in mind—is that it merely prohibits the government from officially recognizing and supporting a national church, like the Church of England in that nation.

2. A second meaning is somewhat broader: the government may not prefer one religion over another or demonstrate favoritism toward or discrimination against any particular religion, but it might recognize and encourage religious activities in general.

3. The most expansive meaning is that the clause creates "a wall of separation between church and state" that prevents government from endorsing, aiding, sponsoring, or encouraging any or all religious activities.

The phrase "separation of church and state" does *not* appear in the constitution. It was first used by Thomas Jefferson in a letter to a Baptist Church in 1802 assuring them that the federal government would not establish a national church. The current meaning derives from a 1947 decision by Justice Hugo Black, who, writing for the Supreme Court majority, gave the following definition of the **wall-of-separation doctrine:**

No Establishment Clause
Clause in the First Amendment to the Constitution that is interpreted to require the separation of church and state.

Wall-of-separation doctrine
The Supreme Court's interpretation of the No Establishment Clause that laws may not have as their purpose aid to one religion or aid to all religions.

Neither a state nor the Federal Government can set up a church. Neither can pass laws which aid one religion, aid all religions, or prefer one religion over another. Neither can force nor influence a person to go to or to remain away from church . . . or force him to profess a belief or disbelief in any religion. . . . No tax in any amount, large or small, can be levied to support any religious activities or institutions, whatever they may be called, or whatever form they may adopt to teach or practice religion.[16]

Although the Supreme Court has generally voiced its support for the wall-of-separation doctrine, on several occasions it has permitted cracks to develop in the wall. In allowing public schools to give pupils regular releases from school to attend religious instructions given outside of the school, Justice William O. Douglas wrote that the state and religion need not be "hostile, suspicious or even unfriendly."[17]

What Constitutes "Establishment"? It has proven difficult for the Supreme Court to reconcile this wall-of-separation interpretation of the First Amendment with the fact that religion plays an important role in the life of most Americans. Public meetings, including sessions of the Congress, often begin with prayers;[18] coins are inscribed with the words "In God We Trust"; and the armed forces provide chaplains for U.S. soldiers.

The Supreme Court has set forth a three-part **Lemon test** for determining whether a particular state law constitutes "establishment" of religion and thus violates the First Amendment. To be constitutional, a law affecting religious activity:

1. Must have a secular purpose.
2. As its primary effect, must neither advance nor inhibit religion.
3. Must not foster "an excessive government entanglement with religion."[19]

Using this three-part test, the Supreme Court held that it was unconstitutional for a state to pay the costs of teachers' salaries or instructional materials in parochial schools. The justices argued that this practice would require excessive government controls and surveillance to ensure that funds were used only for secular instruction and thus involved "excessive entanglement between government and religion."

However, the Court has upheld the use of tax funds to provide students attending church-related schools with nonreligious textbooks, lunches, transportation, sign-language interpreting, and special education teachers. And the Court has upheld a state's granting of tax credits to parents whose children attend private schools, including religious schools.[20] The Court has also upheld government grants of money to church-related colleges and universities for secular purposes.[21] The Court has ruled that if public buildings are open to use for secular organizations, they must also be opened to use by religious organizations.[22] And the Court has held that a state institution (the University of Virginia) not only can but must grant student activity fees to religious organizations on the same basis as it grants these fees to secular organizations.[23]

The Supreme Court has upheld tax exemptions for churches on the grounds that "the role of religious organizations as charitable associations, in furthering the secular objectives of the state, has become a fundamental concept in our society."[24] It held that schools must allow after-school meetings on school property by religious groups if such a privilege is extended to nonreligious groups.[25]

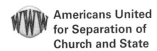

Americans United for Separation of Church and State

Organization advocating elimination of religious activity from public life.
www.au.org

Lemon test To be constitutional, a law must have a secular purpose; its primary effect must neither advance nor inhibit religion; and it must not foster excessive government entanglement with religion.

A Menorah lighting ceremony celebrating Chanukah on public property near the White House. The Supreme Court is divided over whether such public displays violate the No Establishment Clause of the First Amendment.

 Anti Defamation League

Organization opposing anti-Semitism and securing justice for the Jewish people.
www.adl.org

Although the Supreme Court ruled in 1962 (*Engle v. Vitale*) that even voluntary prayer in public schools was an unconstitutional violation of the separation of church and state under the First Amendment, the question of prayer in the schools remains a heated one. Indeed, recent court rulings regarding nondenominational prayers at graduation ceremonies and sporting events have, if anything, further confused the issue.

Deductions on federal income tax returns for church contributions are also constitutional. The Supreme Court allows states to close stores on Sundays and otherwise set aside that day, as long as there is a secular purpose—such as "rest, repose, recreation and tranquility"—in doing so.[26]

But the Court has not always acted to "accommodate" religion. In a controversial case, the Court held that a Christmas nativity scene sitting alone on public property was an official "endorsement" of Christian belief and therefore violated the No Establishment Clause. However, if the Christian display was accompanied by a Menorah, a traditional Christmas tree, Santa Claus and reindeer, it would simply be "taking note of the season" and not an unconstitutional endorsement of religion.[27] And in another case, the Supreme Court held that a Louisiana law requiring the teaching of "creationism" along with evolution in the public schools was an unconstitutional establishment of a religious belief.[28]

Prayer in the School The Supreme Court's most controversial interpretation of the No Establishment Clause involved the question of prayer and Bible-reading ceremonies conducted by public schools. The practice of opening the school day with prayer and Bible-reading ceremonies was once widespread in American public schools. To avoid the denominational aspects of these ceremonies, New York State's Board of Regents substituted the following nondenominational prayer, which it required to be said aloud in each class in the presence of a teacher at the beginning of each school day: "Almighty God, we acknowledge our dependence upon Thee, and we beg Thy blessings upon us, our parents, our teachers, and our country." New York argued that this brief prayer did not violate the No Establishment Clause, because the prayer was denominationally neutral and because student participation in the prayer was voluntary. However, in *Engle v. Vitale* (1962), the Supreme Court stated that "the constitutional prohibition against laws respecting an establishment of a religion must at least mean in this country it is no part of the business of government to compose official prayers for any group of the American people to recite as part of a religious program carried on by government." The Court pointed out that making prayer voluntary did not free it from the prohibitions of the No Establishment Clause, and that clause prevented the *establishment* of a religious ceremony by a government agency regardless of whether the ceremony was voluntary.[29]

One year later, in the case of *Abington Township v. Schempp*, the Court considered the constitutionality of Bible-reading ceremonies in the public schools. Here again, even though the children were not required to participate, the Court found that Bible reading as an opening exercise in the schools was a religious ceremony. The justices went to some trouble in the majority opinion to point out that they were not "throwing the Bible out of the schools." They specifically stated that the *study* of the Bible or of religion, when presented objectively and as part of a secular program of education, did not violate the First Amendment; but religious *ceremonies* involving Bible reading or prayer established by a state or school did.[30]

"Voluntary" Prayer State efforts to encourage "voluntary prayer" in public schools have also been struck down by the Supreme Court as unconstitutional. When the state of Alabama authorized a period of silence for "meditation or voluntary prayer" in public schools, the Court ruled that this action was an "establishment of religion." The Court said the law had no secular purpose, that it conveyed "a message of state endorsement and promotion of prayer," and that its real intent was to encourage prayer in public schools.[31] In a stinging dissenting opinion, Justice William Rehnquist noted that the Supreme Court itself opened its session with a prayer and that both houses of Congress opened every session with prayers led by official chaplains paid by the government. In 1992 the Court held that invocations and benedictions at public high school graduation ceremonies were an unconstitutional establishment of religion.[32] And in 2000 the Court ruled that student-led "invocations" at football games were unconstitutional. A Texas school district that allowed students to use its public address system at football games "to solemnize the event" was violating the No Establishment Clause. "The Constitution demands that schools not force on students the difficult choice between whether to attend these games or to risk facing a personally offensive religious ritual."[33]

State Vouchers to Attend Religious Schools Another important issue arising under the No Establishment Clause is the granting of educational vouchers to parents to spend at any school they choose, including religious schools. State governments redeem the vouchers submitted by schools by paying specific amounts for each student enrolled. When Ohio initiated a "Scholarship Program" that provided tuition aid to certain students in the Cleveland City School District who could choose to use this aid to attend either public or private or religious schools of their parents' choosing, opponents challenged the program in federal court arguing that it "advanced a religious mission" in violation of the No Establishment Clause. Although parents could use the vouchers to send their children to other public schools or nonreligious private schools, over 90 percent of the students participating in the scholarship program were enrolled in religiously affiliated schools. In 2002 the U.S. Supreme Court held (in a narrow 5–4 decision) that the program did *not* violate the Constitution. The Court reasoned that the program was neutral with respect to religion and provided assistance directly to citizens who, in turn, directed this aid to religious schools wholly as a result of their own independent private choices. The incidental advancement of a religious mission is reasonably attributed to the indi-

Christian Coalition Organization dedicated to "take America back" from the "judicial tyranny" that would remove religion from public life.
www.cc.org

vidual recipients not the government, "whose role ends with the distribution of benefits."[34]

Freedom of Speech

THINK AGAIN

Do you believe that using tax funds to pay tuition at church-affiliated schools violates the separation of church and state?

Although the First Amendment is absolute in its wording ("Congress shall pass no law . . . abridging the freedom of speech"), the Supreme Court has never been willing to interpret this statement as a protection of *all* speech. What kinds of speech does the First Amendment protect from government control, and what kinds of speech may be constitutionally prohibited?

Clear and Present Danger Doctrine The classic example of speech that can be prohibited was given by Justice Oliver Wendell Holmes in 1919: "The most stringent protection of free speech would not protect a man in falsely shouting 'fire' in a theater and causing a panic."[35] Although Holmes recognized that the government may prevent speech that creates a serious and immediate danger to society, he objected to government attempts to stifle critics of its policies, such as the Espionage Act of 1917 and the Sedition Act of 1918. The Sedition Act prohibited, among other things, speech that was meant to discourage the sale of war bonds; "disloyal" speech about the government, the Constitution, the military forces, or the flag of the United States; and speech that urged the curtailment of war production. In the case of *Gitlow v. New York,* the majority supported the right of the government to curtail any speech that "tended to subvert or imperil the government," but Holmes dissented, arguing that "every idea is an incitement. It offers itself for belief and if believed it is acted on unless some other belief outweighs it."[36] Unless the expression of an idea created a *serious and immediate danger,* Holmes argued that it should be tolerated and combated or defeated only by the expression of better ideas. This standard for determining the limits of free expression became known as the **clear and present danger doctrine**. Government should not curtail speech merely because it *might tend* to cause a future danger: "The question in every case is whether the words used are used in such circumstances and are of such a nature as to create a clear and present danger that they will bring about the substantive evils that Congress has a right to prevent."[37] Holmes's dissent inspired a long struggle in the courts to strengthen constitutional protections for speech and press (see *Up Close:* "The American Civil Liberties Union").

Although Holmes was the first to use the phrase "clear and present danger," it was Justice Louis D. Brandeis who later developed the doctrine into a valuable constitutional principle that the Supreme Court gradually came to adopt. Brandeis explained that the doctrine involved two elements: (1) the clearness or seriousness of the expression; and (2) the immediacy of the danger flowing from the speech. With regard to immediacy he wrote,

> No danger flowing from speech can be deemed clear and present, unless the incidence of the evil apprehended is so imminent that it may befall before there is opportunity for full discussion. If there be time to expose through discussion the falsehood and fallacies, to avert the evil by the processes of education, the remedy to be applied is more speech, not enforced silence.

And with regard to seriousness he wrote,

> Moreover, even imminent danger cannot justify resort to prohibition [of speech] . . . unless the evil apprehended is relatively serious. Prohibition of free speech and assembly

clear and present danger doctrine Standard used by the courts to determine whether speech may be restricted; only speech that creates a serious and immediate danger to society may be restricted.

The American Civil Liberties Union

The American Civil Liberties Union (ACLU) is one of the largest and most active interest groups devoted to litigation. Its Washington offices employ a staff of several hundred people; it counts on some five thousand volunteer lawyers across the country; and it has affiliates in every state and most large cities. The ACLU claims that its sole purpose is defense of civil liberty, that it has no other political agenda, that it defends the Communist Party and the Ku Klux Klan alike—not because it endorses their beliefs but because "the Bill of Rights is the ACLU's only client."* And indeed on occasion it has defended the liberties of Nazis, Klansmen, and other right-wing extremists to express their unpopular views. But most ACLU work has involved litigation on behalf of liberal causes, such as abortion rights, resistance to military service, support for affirmative action, and opposition to the death penalty.

The ACLU was founded in 1920 by Roger Baldwin, a wealthy radical activist who opposed both capitalism and war. Baldwin graduated from Harvard University and briefly taught sociology at Washington University in St. Louis. He refused to be drafted during World War I and served a year's imprisonment for draft violation. In prison, Baldwin joined the Industrial Workers of the World (IWW, or the "Wobblies"), a radical labor union that advocated violence to achieve its goals. In the early 1920s, the ACLU defended socialists, "Bolsheviks," labor organizers, and pacifists against government coercion, including those arrested in the "Red Scare" raids of Attorney General Alexander Mitchell Palmer.

Later the ACLU concentrated its efforts on the defense of First Amendment freedoms of speech, press, religion, and assembly. ACLU member Felix Frankfurter, later a Supreme Court justice, set the tone: "Civil liberty means liberty for those whom we do not like or even detest." In the famous "Monkey Trial" of 1925, the ACLU helped defend school-teacher John Scopes for having taught the theory of evolution in violation of Tennessee state law. Later, it played a supporting role in the litigation efforts of the National Association for the Advancement of Colored People in the elimination of segregation; it defended Vietnam War protesters; it brought cases to court to ban prayer and religious exercise in public schools; it has opposed the death penalty and fought for abortion rights; and it de-

In 1978 the ACLU defended the right of American Nazis to march in the Chicago suburb of Skokie, Illinois, home to many survivors of the Nazi holocaust in Europe.

fended the rights of people to burn the American flag as a form of symbolic speech.

The ACLU's decision to defend the right of the American Nazi Party to march through Skokie, Illinois, a Chicago suburb with a large Jewish population, including some Holocaust survivors, created a crisis in the organization. The ACLU had defended Nazis and Klansmen before, but the Skokie case engendered more publicity than any earlier cases involving right-wing extremists. Many members quit the organization and financial contributions temporarily declined.

Today, the ACLU is racked by internal arguments over politically correct speech codes and over whether "hate crimes" (crimes committed with racist, sexist, antihomosexual, and similar motives) should invoke harsher sentences than the same crimes committed for other motives. "Pure" First Amendment defenders in the organization oppose speech codes and hate crime legislation, while many liberal members rationalize these penalties on speech and thought.

Former Supreme Court Chief Justice Earl Warren once said of the ACLU, "It is difficult to appreciate how far our freedoms might have eroded had it not been for the Union's valiant representation in the courts of the constitutional rights of people of all persuasions."†

---

* William A. Donohue. *The Politics of the American Civil Liberties Union* (New Brunswick: Transaction Books, 1985), p. 3.
† Quoted in *ACLU Annual Report*, 1977, cited in ibid., p. 2.

is a measure so stringent that it would be inappropriate as the means for averting a relatively trivial harm to society. . . . There must be the probability of serious injury to the State.[38]

Preferred Position Doctrine Over the years, the Supreme Court has given the First Amendment freedom of speech, press, and assembly a special **preferred position** in constitutional law. These freedoms are especially important to the preservation of democracy. If speech, press, or assembly are prohibited by government, the people have no way to correct the government through democratic processes. Thus the burden of proof rests on the *government* to justify any restrictions on speech, writing, or assembly.[39] In other words, any speech or writing is presumed constitutional unless the government proves that a serious and immediate danger would ensue if the speech were allowed.

The Cold War Challenge Despite the Supreme Court's endorsement of the clear and present danger and preferred position doctrines, in times of perceived national crisis the courts have been willing to permit some government restrictions of speech, press, and assembly. At the outbreak of World War II, just prior to U.S. entry into that world conflict, Congress passed the Smith Act, which stated,

> It shall be unlawful for any person to knowingly or willfully advocate, abet, advise, or teach the duty, necessity, desirability, or propriety of overthrowing or destroying any government in the United States by force or violence, or by the assassination of any officer of any such government.

Congress justified its action in terms of national security, initially as a protection against fascism during World War II, then later as a protection against communist revolution in the early days of the Cold War.

In 1949 the Department of Justice prosecuted Eugene V. Dennis and ten other top leaders of the Communist Party of the United States for violation of the Smith Act. A jury found them guilty of violating the act, and the party leaders were sentenced to jail terms ranging from one to five years. In 1951 the case of *Dennis v. United States* came to the Supreme Court on appeal. In upholding the conviction of the Communist Party leaders, the Court seemed to abandon Brandeis's idea that "present" meant "before there is opportunity for full discussion."[40] It seemed to substitute clear and *probable* for clear and *present*.

Since that time, however, the Supreme Court has returned to a policy closer to the original clear and present danger doctrine. As the Cold War progressed, Americans grew to view communism as a serious threat to democracy, but not a *present* danger. The overthrow of the American government advocated by communists was not an incitement to *immediate* action. A democracy must not itself become authoritarian to protect itself from authoritarianism. In later cases, the Supreme Court held that the mere advocacy of revolution, apart from unlawful action, is protected by the First Amendment.[41] It struck down federal laws requiring communist organizations to register with the government,[42] laws requiring individuals to sign "loyalty oaths,"[43] laws prohibiting communists from working in defense plants,[44] and laws stripping passports from Communist Party leaders.[45] In short, once the perceived Cold War crisis began to fade, the Supreme Court reasserted the First Amendment rights of individuals and groups.

Symbolic Speech The First Amendment's guarantees of speech, press, and assembly are broadly interpreted to mean **freedom of expression**. Political expres-

preferred position Refers to the tendency of the courts to give preference to the First Amendment rights to speech, press, and assembly when faced with conflicts.

freedom of expression Collectively, the First Amendment rights to free speech, press, and assembly.

sion encompasses more than just words. For example, when Mary Beth Tinker and her brothers were suspended for wearing black armbands to high school to protest the Vietnam War, they argued that the wearing of armbands constituted **symbolic speech** protected by the First Amendment. The Supreme Court agreed, noting that the school did not prohibit all wearing of symbols but instead singled out this particular expression for disciplinary action.[46]

The Supreme Court continues to wrestle with the question of what kinds of conduct are symbolic speech protected by the First Amendment and what kinds of conduct are outside of this protection (see *Up Close:* "We Can Burn the Flag But Not the Cross"). Symbolic speech, like speech itself, cannot be banned just because it offends people. "If there is only one bedrock principle underlying the First Amendment, it is that the Government may not prohibit the expression of an idea simply because society finds the idea itself offensive or disagreeable."[47]

Speech and Public Order The Supreme Court has wrestled with the question of whether speech can be prohibited when it stirs audiences to public disorder, not because the speaker urges lawless action but because the audience reacts to the speech with hostility. In short, can a speaker be arrested because of the *audience's* disorderly behavior? In an early case, the Supreme Court fashioned a *fighting words doctrine*, to the effect that words that "ordinary men know are likely to cause a fight" may be prohibited.[48] But later the Court seemed to realize that this doctrine, if broadly applied, could create a huge constitutional hole in the First Amendment guarantee of free speech. Authorities could curtail speech simply because it met with audience hostility. The Court recognized that "speech is often provocative and challenging. It may . . . have profound unsettling effects. . . . That is why freedom of speech, while not absolute, is nevertheless protected against censorship."[49] The Court has also held that the First Amendment protects the use of four-letter words when used to express an idea: "One man's vulgarity may be another's lyric."[50] And the Court has consistently refused to allow government authorities to ban speech *before* it has occurred simply because they believe it *may* create a disturbance.

Campus Speech Many colleges and universities have undertaken to ban speech that is considered racist, sexist, homophobic, or otherwise "insensitive" to the feelings of women and minorities. Varieties of "speech codes," "hate codes," and sexual harassment regulations that prohibit verbal expressions raise serious constitutional questions, especially at state-supported colleges and universities. The First Amendment does not exclude insulting or offensive racist or sexist words or comments from its protection (see *Up Close:* "Political Correctness Versus Free Speech on Campus"). Many of these college and university regulations would not withstand a judicial challenge if students or faculty undertook to oppose them in federal court.

Hate Speech and Hate Crimes "Hate" speech is usually defined as hostile or prejudicial attitudes expressed toward another person's or group's characteristics, notably sex, race, ethnicity, religion, or sexual orientation. Banning hate speech is now common at colleges and universities, in business employment and sports enterprises, on radio and television, and in the press. But do *government* prohibitions on hate speech violate the First Amendment?

The Supreme Court ruled in 2003 that cross burning was meant to intimidate and was therefore *not* protected as symbolic speech by the First Amendment.

 American Civil Liberties Union

This American Civil Liberties Union Web site provides ample information about the ACLU as an organization and the issues it deals with. ***www.aclu.org***

 National Association of Scholars

Advocacy organization opposing speech codes and other PC violations of individual freedom on campuses. ***www.nas.org***

symbolic speech Actions other than speech itself but protected by the First Amendment because they constitute political expression.

We Can Burn the Flag But Not the Cross

Symbolic speech continues to create difficulties for the Supreme Court. Two separate cases illustrate the problems in protecting symbolic speech.

Burning the Flag

Flag desecration is a physical act, but it also has symbolic meaning—for example, hatred of the United States or opposition to government policies. At the 1984 Republican national convention in Dallas, Gregory Lee Johnson joined a protest march against Reagan Administration policies, then doused an American flag with kerosene and set fire to it. As it burned, he and others chanted, "America, the red, white, and blue, we spit on you." Police arrested Johnson and charged him with violating a Texas law against flag desecration. The American Civil Liberties Union came to Johnson's defense, arguing that flag burning is "symbolic speech" protected by the First Amendment.

In the case of *Texas v. Johnson* (1989), a majority of Supreme Court justices argued that "Johnson's burning of the flag was conduct sufficiently imbued with elements of communication to implicate the First Amendment." They declared that when speech and conduct are combined in the same expressive act, the government must show that it has "a sufficiently important interest in regulating the non-speech element to justify incident limitations on First Amendment freedoms." In this case, "preserving the flag as a symbol of nationhood and national unity" was not deemed sufficiently important to justify limiting Johnson's freedom of expression.*

Burning the Cross

The Supreme Court has long recognized that threats to commit unlawful violence on a particular individual or group of individuals is unlawful speech. In an early case the Court had held that wearing Ku Klux Klan hoods and gathering to burn a cross were protected symbolic speech. However, in 2003 the Court upheld a Virginia statute that prohibited the burning of a cross "with the intent of intimidating any person or group" and asserting that "any such burning . . . shall be prima facie evidence of an intent to intimidate." The Supreme Court cited the long history of cross burnings as a form of intimidation and a threat of impending violence. "As the history of cross burning in this country shows, that act is often intimidating, intended to create a pervasive fear in victims that they are a target of violence." Therefore, "The First Amendment permits Virginia to outlaw cross burnings done with the intent to intimidate because burning a cross is a particularly virulent form of intimidation."†

Texas v. Johnson, 491 U.S. 397 (1989).
†*Virginia v. Black*, April 7, 2003.

Historically the Supreme Court viewed prohibitions on offensive speech as unconstitutional infringements of First Amendment freedoms. "The remedy to be applied is more speech, not enforced silence."[51]

The Supreme Court was called upon to review prohibitions on hate speech in 1992 when the city of St. Paul, Minnesota, enacted an ordinance prohibiting any communication that "arouses anger, alarm, or resentment among others on the basis of race, color, creed, religion, or gender." The ordinance defined such expressions as "disorderly conduct" and made them misdemeanors punishable by law. But the Supreme Court, in a unanimous decision, struck down the city's effort to prohibit expressions only because they cause "hurt feelings, offense, or resentment." Speech expressing racial, gender, or religious intolerance is still speech, and it is protected by the First Amendment.[52]

However, the Supreme Court is willing to recognize that bias-motivated crimes—crimes intentionally directed at a victim because of his or her race, religion, disability, national origin, or sexual orientation—may be more heavily punished than the same crimes inspired by other motives. The Court held that a criminal defendant's "abstract beliefs, however obnoxious to most people, may not be taken into consideration by a sentencing judge."[53] But a defendant's *motive* for

Political Correctness Versus Free Speech on Campus

Universities have a very special responsibility to protect freedom of expression. The free and unfettered exchange of views is essential to the advancement of knowledge—the very purpose of universities. For centuries universities have fought to protect academic freedom from pressures arising from the world *outside* of the campus—governments, interest groups, financial contributors—arguing that the university must be a protected enclave for free expression of ideas. But today's threat to academic freedom arises from *within* universities—from efforts by administrations, faculty, and campus groups to suppress ideas, opinions, and language that are not "politically correct" (PC). PC activists seek to suppress opinions and expressions they consider to be racist, sexist, "homophobic," or otherwise "insensitive" to specified groups.*

Speech Codes

The experience at the University of Michigan with its "Policy on Discrimination and Discriminatory Harassment" illustrates the battles occurring on many campuses over First Amendment rights. In 1988 a series of racial incidents on campus prompted the university to officially ban "any behavior verbal or physical" that "stigmatized" an individual "on the basis of race, ethnicity, religion, sex, sexual orientation, creed, national origin, ancestry, age, marital status, handicap, or Vietnam-era veteran status" or that created "an intimidating, hostile, or demeaning environment for educational pursuits." A published guide provided examples of banned activity, which included the following:

- A male student makes remarks in class like "women just aren't as good in this field as men."
- Jokes about gay men and lesbians.
- Commenting in a derogatory way about a particular person or group's physical appearance or sexual orientation, or their cultural origins, or religious beliefs.

Free Speech

In 1989 "John Doe," a psychology graduate student studying gender differences in personality traits and mental functions, filed suit in federal court requesting that the University of Michigan policy be declared a violation of the First Amendment. (He was permitted by the court to remain anonymous because of fear of retribution.) He was joined in his complaint against the university by the American Civil Liberties Union.

In its decision, the court acknowledged that the university had a legal responsibility to prevent racial or sexual discrimination or harassment. However, it did not have a right to

> establish an anti-discrimination policy which had the effect of prohibiting certain speech because it disagreed with ideas or messages sought to be conveyed. . . . Nor could the University proscribe speech simply because it was found to be offensive, even gravely so, by large numbers of people. . . . These principles acquire a special significance in the University setting, where the free and unfettered interplay of competing views is essential to the institution's educational mission. . . . While the Court is sympathetic to the University's obligation to ensure educational opportunities for all of its students, such efforts must not be at the expense of free speech.[†]

It seems ironic that students and faculty now must seek the protection of the federal courts from attempts by universities to limit speech. Traditionally, universities themselves fought to protect academic freedom. Academic freedom included the freedom of faculty and students to express themselves in the classroom, on the campus, and in writing, on controversial and sensitive topics, including race and gender. It was recognized that students often express ideas that are biased or ill informed, immature, or crudely expressed. But students were taught that the remedy for offensive language or off-color remarks or ill-chosen examples was more enlightened speech, not the suppression of speech.

---

*Dinesh D'Souza, *Illiberal Education: The Politics of Race and Sex on Campus* (New York: Vintage Books, 1992).

[†]*John Doe v. University of Michigan,* 721 F. Supp. 852 (1989).

committing a particular criminal act has traditionally been a factor in sentencing, and a defendant's verbal statements can be used to determine motive.

Commercial Speech Do First Amendment freedoms of expression apply to commercial advertising? The Supreme Court has frequently asserted that **commercial speech** is protected by the First Amendment. The Court held that states cannot outlaw price advertising by pharmacists[54] or advertising for services by attorneys[55] and that cities cannot outlaw posting "For Sale" signs on property, even in the interests of halting white flight and promoting racially integrated neighborhoods. Advertising is the "dissemination of information" and is constitutionally protected.[56]

However, the Court has also been willing to weigh the First Amendment rights of commercial advertisers against the public interest served by regulation. In other words, the Court seems to suspend its preferred position doctrine with regard to commercial advertising and to call for a "balancing of interests." Thus, the Supreme Court has allowed the Federal Communications Commission to regulate the contents of advertising on radio and television and even to ban advertising for cigarettes. The Federal Trade Commission enforces "truth" in advertising by requiring commercial packages and advertisers to prove all claims for their products.

Libel and Slander Libel and slander have never been protected by the First Amendment against subsequent punishment (see "Libel and Slander" in Chapter 6). Once a communication is determined to be libelous or slanderous, it is outside of the protection of the First Amendment. The courts have traditionally defined "libel" as a "damaging falsehood." However, if plaintiffs are public officials they must prove that the statements made about them are not only false and damaging but also "made with actual malice"—that is, with knowledge that they are false or with "reckless disregard" of the truth—in order to prove libel.[57]

Privacy, Abortion, and the Constitution

A right of "privacy" is not expressly provided for anywhere in the Constitution. But does the word *liberty* in the First and Fourteenth Amendments include a constitutional right to privacy?

Finding a Right to Privacy The U.S. Supreme Court found a right of privacy in the Constitution when it struck down a Connecticut law prohibiting the use of contraceptives in 1965. Estelle Griswold had opened a birth control clinic on behalf of the Planned Parenthood League of that state and was distributing contraceptives in violation of the state statute prohibiting their use. She challenged the constitutionality of the statute, even though there is no direct reference to birth control in the Bill of Rights. The Supreme Court upheld Griswold's challenge, finding a right of privacy, according to Justice William O. Douglas, in the "penumbras formed by the emanations from" the First, Third, Fourth, Fifth, Ninth, and Fourteenth Amendments. "Various guarantees create a zone of privacy. . . . Would we allow the police to search the sacred precincts of marital bedrooms for telltale signs of the use of contraceptives? The very idea is repulsive to the notion of privacy surrounding the marriage relationship." In concurrent opinions, other justices found the right of privacy in the Ninth Amendment: "The enumeration in the

commercial speech
Advertising communications given only partial protection under the First Amendment to the Constitution.

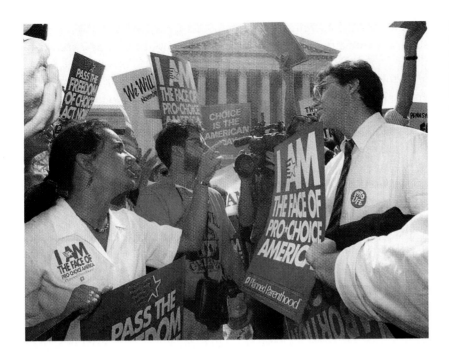

Pro-life and pro-choice activists confront each other outside the Supreme Court in 1992 after the justices issued their ruling in *Planned Parenthood of Pennsylvania v. Casey.*

Constitution of certain rights, shall not be construed to deny or disparage others retained by the people."[58]

Roe v. Wade The fact that *Griswold* dealt with reproduction gave encouragement to groups advocating abortion rights. In 1969 Norma McCorvey sought an abortion in Texas, but was refused by doctors who cited a state law prohibiting abortion except to save a woman's life. McCorvey challenged the Texas law in federal courts on a variety of constitutional grounds, including the right to privacy. McCorvey became "Jane Roe," and the case became one of the most controversial in the Supreme Court's history.[59]

The Supreme Court ruled that the constitutional right of privacy as well as the Fourteenth Amendment's guarantee of "liberty" included a woman's decision to bear or not to bear a child. The Court held that the word "person" in the Constitution did *not* include the unborn child; therefore, the Fifth and Fourteenth Amendments' guarantee of "life, liberty, or property" did not protect the "life" of the fetus. The Court also ruled that a state's power to protect the health and safety of the mother could not justify any restriction on abortion in the first three months of pregnancy. Between the third and sixth months of pregnancy, a state could set standards for abortion procedures in order to protect the health of women, but a state could not prohibit abortions. Only in the final three months could a state prohibit or regulate abortion to protect the unborn.

Rather than end the political controversy over abortion, *Roe v. Wade* set off a conflagration. Congress defeated efforts to pass a constitutional amendment restricting abortion or declaring that life begins at conception. However, when Congress banned the use of federal funds under Medicaid (medical care for the poor) for abortions except to protect the life of a woman, the Supreme Court upheld the ban, holding that there was no constitutional obligation for governments to pay for abortions.[60]

Reaffirming Roe v. Wade Abortion has become such a polarizing issue that "pro-choice" and "pro-life" groups are generally unwilling to search out a middle

Pro-Choice America
Formerly the National Abortion Rights Action League (NARAL), with information on current legislation and court cases.
www.prochoiceamerica.org

National Right to Life
Leading anti-abortion organization with information on current legislation and court cases.
www.nrlc.org

ground. Yet the current Supreme Court appears to have chosen a policy of affirming a woman's right to abortion while upholding modest restrictions, as evidenced by the Court's ruling in *Planned Parenthood of Pennsylvania v. Casey* (1992).[61]

In this case, the Supreme Court considered a series of restrictions on abortion enacted by Pennsylvania: that physicians must inform women of risks and alternatives; that women must wait twenty-four hours after requesting an abortion before having one; and that the parents of minors must be notified. It struck down a requirement that spouses be notified.

Justice Sandra Day O'Connor took the lead in forming a moderate, swing bloc on the Court. Her majority opinion strongly reaffirmed the fundamental right of abortion, both on the basis of the Fourteenth Amendment and on the principle of stare decisis. But the majority also upheld states' rights to protect any fetus that reached the point of "viability." The Court went on to establish a new standard for constitutionally evaluating restrictions: they must not impose an "undue burden" on women seeking abortion or place "substantial obstacles" in her path. All of Pennsylvania's restrictions met this standard and were upheld except spousal notification.

"Partial Birth Abortion" A number of states have attempted to outlaw an abortion procedure known as "intact dilation and evacuation" or "partial birth" abortion. This procedure, which is used in less than one percent of all abortions, involves partial delivery of the fetus feet-first, then vacuuming out the brain and crushing the skull to ease complete removal. In a surprise 5 to 4 decision, with Justice O'Connor supporting the majority, the Supreme Court declared a Nebraska law prohibiting the procedure to be an unconstitutional "undue burden" on a woman's right to an abortion. The Nebraska law failed to make an exception in its prohibition of the procedure "for the preservation of the health of the mother."[62]

Congress passed a ban on partial birth abortions in 2003 and President George Bush signed it into law. (Earlier bans passed by Congress had been vetoed by President Bill Clinton.) The new law provides an exception—allowing the method if it is necessary to save a mother's life. Proponents of the law hope that this exception will make it acceptable to a majority of the Supreme Court.

Sexual Conduct "Liberty gives substantial protection to adult persons in deciding how to conduct their lives in matters pertaining to sex." This Supreme Court ruling in *Lawrence vs. Texas* (2003) struck down a state law against homosexual sodomy. The ruling overturned an earlier case in which the Court held that the Constitution granted no "fundamental right to homosexuals to engage in acts of consensual sodomy."[63] Rather, the Supreme Court decided that "The liberty protected by the Constitution allows homosexual persons the right to choose to enter upon relationships in the confines of their homes and their own private lives and still retain their dignity as free persons."[64]

Other Private Activities How far does the right of privacy extend? The Supreme Court appears to have left this question open to argument. In 1969 the Court held that privacy may be constitutionally protected where there is a "reasonable expectation of privacy," notably in one's own home. The Court overturned a criminal conviction for the "mere private possession of obscene material," that is, the possession and viewing of pornography at home.[65]

Gay Marriage The Supreme Court has not yet spoken out on gay marriages—marriages between persons of the same sex. Several state courts, including the

Should We Amend the Constitution to Ban Gay Marriages?

President George W. Bush asked Congress to pass a constitutional amendment to be sent to the states for ratification, an amendment that would ban gay marriages: "After more than two centuries of American jurisprudence and a millennium of human experience, a few judges and local authorities are presuming to change the most fundamental institution of civilization." Congress has before it an amendment which says: "Marriage in the United States shall consist only of the union of a man and a woman. Neither this Constitution or the Constitution of any state, nor state or federal law, shall be construed to require that marital status or the legal incidents thereof be conferred upon unmarried couples or groups."

In general, Americans oppose same-sex marriages. Various polls over time indicate that almost two-thirds of the public opposes gay marriages.

Should same-sex marriages be recognized by law as valid with the same rights as traditional marriages?

Yes 32% No 64%

However, many Americans are reluctant to amend the Constitution to define marriage as strictly between a man and a woman.

Do you favor a constitutional amendment that would define marriage as being between a man and a woman, thus barring same-sex marriages?

Yes 53% No 44%

And Americans are divided over whether federal or state laws should govern same-sex marriage.

Do you think laws regarding same-sex marriage should be determined by the federal government or individual state governments?

Federal 48% State 46%

Source: As reported in *USA Today*, February 25, 2004.

Supreme Court of Massachusetts, have held that the Equal Protection Clause of the Fourteenth Amendment entitles gay couples to marry, that to deny them marriage rights while recognizing heterosexual marriages amounts to discrimination. The issue is complicated by the constitutional provision that requires all states to give "Full Faith and Credit" to judicial proceedings of other states (see "State Obligations to Each Other" in Chapter 4). This provision implies that gay marriages in any state must be recognized in all states. Congress passed a Defense of Marriage Act in 1996 declaring that no state need recognized a gay marriage. But Congress failed to pass a constitutional amendment banning same-sex marriage (see *What Do You Think?*: "Should We Amend the Constitution to Ban Gay Marriages?").

A Right to Die? In most states, for most of the nation's history, it has been a crime to help another person to commit suicide. Michigan's prosecution of Dr. Jack Kevorkian for publicly participating in physician-assisted suicides launched a nation-wide debate on the topic. More important, a group of physicians in Washington, along with their gravely ill patients, filed suit in federal court seeking a declaration that their state's law banning physician-assisted suicide violated the "liberty" guaranteed by the Fourteenth Amendment. They argued that mentally competent, terminally ill patients had the "right to die"; that is, they had a privacy right to request and receive aid in ending their life. They relied on the Supreme Court's previous rulings on abortion, contending that Washington's law placed an undue burden on the exercise of a privacy right. But the U.S. Supreme Court held that there is no *constitutional right* to physician-assisted suicide.[66] The Court implied that if the laws governing the practice are to be changed, they must be changed by legislatures, not by reinterpreting the Constitution.

Obscenity and the Law

Obscene materials of all kinds—words, publications, photos, videotapes, films—are *not* protected by the First Amendment. Most states ban the publication, sale, or possession of obscene material, and Congress bans its shipment in the mails. Because obscene material is not protected by the First Amendment, it can be banned without even an attempt to prove that it results in antisocial conduct. In other words, it is not necessary to show that obscene material would result in a clear and present danger to society, the test used to decide the legitimacy of *speech*. In order to ban obscene materials, the government need only prove that they are *obscene*.

Defining "obscenity" has confounded legislatures and the courts for years, however. State and federal laws often define pornography and obscenity in such terms as "lewd," "lascivious," "filthy," "indecent," "disgusting"—all equally as vague as "obscene." "Pornography" is simply a synonym for "obscenity." *Soft-core pornography* usually denotes nakedness and sexually suggestive poses; it is less likely to confront legal barriers. *Hard-core pornography* usually denotes explicit sexual activity. After many fruitless efforts by the Supreme Court to come up with a workable definition of "pornography" or "obscenity," a frustrated Justice Potter Stewart wrote in 1974, "I shall not today attempt further to define [hard-core pornography]. . . . But *I know it when I see it.*"[67]

Slackening Standards: *Roth v. United States* The Court's first comprehensive effort to define "obscenity" came in *Roth v. United States* (1957). Although the Court upheld Roth's conviction for distributing pornographic magazines through the mails, it defined "obscenity" somewhat narrowly: "Whether to the average person applying contemporary community standards, the dominant theme of the material, taken as a whole, appeals to prurient interests."[68]

Note that the material must be obscene to the *average* person, not to children or particular groups of adults who might be especially offended by pornography. The standard is "contemporary," suggesting that what was once regarded as obscene might be acceptable today. Later, the *community standard* was clarified to mean the "society at large," not a particular state or local community.[69] The material must be "considered as a whole," meaning that even if a work includes some obscene material, it is still acceptable if its "dominant theme" is something other than "prurient." The Court added that a work must be "utterly without redeeming social or literary merit" in order to be judged obscene.[70] The Court never really said what a "prurient" interest was but reassured everyone that "sex and obscenity are not synonymous."[71]

Tightening Standards: *Miller v. California* The effect of the Roth decision, and the many and varied attempts by lower courts to apply its slippery standards, tended to limit law enforcement efforts to combat pornography during the 1960s and 1970s. The Supreme Court itself came under ridicule when it was learned that the justices had set up a movie room in the basement of the Supreme Court building to view films that had been brought before them in obscenity cases.[72]

Child Pornography

In 1982 the U.S. Supreme Court struck a hard blow against child pornography—the "dissemination of material depicting children engaged in sexual conduct regardless of whether the material is obscene."* Such material includes any visual depiction of children performing sexual acts or lewdly exhibiting their genitals. The Court reasoned that films or photographs of sexual exploitation and abuse of children were "intrinsically related" to criminal activity; such material was evidence that crime has been committed. Thus the test for *child* pornography was much stricter than the standards set for obscene material. It is not necessary to show that the sexual depiction of children is "obscene" (under the *Miller* standards) in order to ban such material; it is only necessary to show that children were used in the production of the material.

But what if the images of children involved in sexual activity are produced by means other than using real children, such as the use of youthful-looking adults or computer-imaging technology? In the Child Pornography Prevention Act of 1996, Congress tried to prohibit "any visual depiction, including any photograph, film, video, picture, or computer or computer-generated image . . . [that] is, or appears to be, of a minor engaging in sexually explicit conduct." Congress did not construct this act to meet the *Miller* standards; it prohibited *any* depictions of sexually explicit activity by children, whether or not they contravened community standards or had serious redeeming value.

But the Supreme Court, in a highly controversial (6–3) decision, held that there was an important distinction between actual and virtual child pornography. Virtual child pornography and adults posing as minors do not directly involve the exploitation or abuse of children. The Court held that the congressional definition of child pornography was overly broad; the mere assertion that such material might encourage pedophiles to seduce children was not sufficient to prohibit it. "The First Amendment requires a more precise restriction."[†]

---

* *New York v. Ferber*, 458 U.S. 747 (1982).

[†] *Ashcraft v. Free Speech Coalition*, April 16, 2002.

So the Supreme Court tried again, in *Miller v. California* (1973), to give law-enforcement officials some clearer standards in determining obscenity. Although the Court retained the "average person" and "contemporary" standards, it redefined "community" to mean the *local* community rather than the society at large. It also defined "prurient" as "patently offensive" representations or descriptions of "ultimate sex acts, normal or perverted, actual or simulated," as well as "masturbation, excretory functions, and lewd exhibition of the genitals." It rejected the earlier requirement that the work had to be "utterly without redeeming social value" in order to be judged obscene, and it substituted instead "lacks serious literary, artistic, political, or scientific value."[73]

The effect of the Supreme Court's *Miller* standards has been to increase the likelihood of conviction in obscenity-pornography cases. It is easier to prove that a work lacks serious value than to prove that it is utterly without redeeming merit. Moreover, the *local community standard* allows prosecution of adult bookstores and X-rated video stores in some communities, while allowing the same stores to operate in other communities. The Supreme Court has also upheld local ordinances that ban nudity in public places, including bars and lounges. The Court rejected the argument that nude dancing was "expressive" conduct.[74]

Porn on the Internet New technologies continue to challenge courts in the application of First Amendment principles. Currently the Internet, the global computer communication network, allows users to gain access to information worldwide. Thousands of electronic bulletin boards give computer users access to

Internet Freedom
Organization opposed to all forms of censorship and content regulation on the Internet.
www.netfreedom.org

everything from bomb-making instructions and sex conversations to obscene photos and even child pornography. Many commercial access services ban obscene messages and exclude bulletin boards with sexually offensive commentary. Software programs that screen out pornography Web sites are readily available to consumers. But can *government* try to ban such material from the Internet without violating First Amendment freedoms?

Congress tried unsuccessfully to ban "indecent" and "patently-offensive" communications from the Internet in its Communications Decency Act of 1996. Proponents of the law cited the need to protect children from pornography. But in 1997 the Supreme Court held the act unconstitutional: "Notwithstanding the legitimacy and importance of the Congressional goal of protecting children from harmful materials, we agree that the statute abridges freedom of speech protected by the First Amendment." Government cannot limit Internet messages "to only what is fit for children." The Supreme Court agreed with the assertion that "as the most participatory form of mass speech yet developed [the Internet] deserves the highest protection from government intrusion."[75] (See also *Up Close:* "Child Pornography").

Freedom of the Press

Democracy depends on the free expression of ideas. Authoritarian regimes either monopolize the media or subject them to strict licensing and censorship of their content. The idea of a free and independent press is deeply rooted in the evolution of democratic government.

No-Prior-Restraint Doctrine Long before the Bill of Rights was written, English law protected newspapers from government restrictions or licensing prior to publication—a practice called **prior restraint**. This protection, however, does not mean that publishers are exempt from *subsequent punishment* for libelous, obscene, or other illegal publications. Prior restraint is more dangerous to free expression because it allows the government to censor the work prior to publication and forces the defendants to *prove* that their material should *not* be censored. In contrast, subsequent punishment requires a trial in which the government must prove that the defendant's published materials are unlawful.

In *Near v. Minnesota* (1931), a muckraking publication that accused local officials of trafficking with gangsters was barred from publishing under a Minnesota law that prohibited the publication of a "malicious, scandalous or defamatory newspaper." The Supreme Court struck down the law as unconstitutional, affirming the *no-prior-restraint doctrine.* However, a close reading of the majority opinion reveals that the doctrine is not absolute. Chief Justice Charles Evans Hughes noted that prior government censorship might be constitutional "if publication . . . threatened the country's safety in times of war."[76]

Yet the question of whether or not the government can restrain publication of stories that present a serious threat to national security remains unanswered. For example, can the government restrain the press from reporting in advance on the time and place of an impending U.S. military action, thereby warning an enemy and perhaps adding to American casualties? In the most important case on this question, *New York Times v. United States* (1971), the Supreme Court upheld the right of the newspaper to publish secret documents that had been stolen from State Department and Defense Department files. The material covered U.S. policy decisions in Vietnam, and it was published while the war was still being waged. But five

prior restraint Government actions to restrict publication of a magazine, newspaper, or books on grounds of libel, obscenity, or other legal violations prior to actual publication of the work.

separate (concurring) opinions were written by justices in the majority as well as two dissenting opinions. Only two justices argued that government can *never* restrain any publication regardless of the seriousness or immediacy of the harm. Others in the majority cited the government's failure to show proof in this case that publication "would surely result in direct, immediate, and irreparable damage to our nation or its people."[77] Presumably, if the government had produced such proof, the case might have been decided differently. The media interpret the decision as a blanket protection to publish anything they wish regardless of harm to government or society.

Film Censorship The no-prior-restraint doctrine was developed to protect the print media—books, magazines, newspapers. When the motion picture industry was in its infancy, the Supreme Court held that films were "business, pure and simple" and were not entitled to the protection of the First Amendment.[78] But as films grew in importance, the Court gradually extended First Amendment freedoms to cover motion pictures.[79] However, the Supreme Court has not given the film industry the same strong no-prior-restraint protection it has given the press. The Court has approved government requirements for prior submission of films to official censors, so long as (1) the burden of proof that the film is obscene rests with the censor; (2) a procedure exists for judicial determination of the issue; and (3) censors are required to act speedily.[80] To avoid government-imposed censorship the motion picture industry adopted its own system of rating films:

G: suitable for all audiences

PG: parental guidance suggested

PG-13: parental guidance strongly suggested for children under thirteen

R: restricted to those seventeen or older unless accompanied by a parent or guardian

NC-17: no one under seventeen admitted

Some city governments have sought to restrict showing of NC-17 films, and their restrictions have been upheld by the Courts.[81]

Radio and Television Censorship The Federal Communications Commission was created in 1934 to allocate broadcast frequencies and to license stations. The exclusive right to use a particular frequency is a "public trust." Thus, broadcasters, unlike newspapers and magazines, are licensed by the government and subject to government rules. Although the First Amendment protects broadcasters, the Supreme Court has recognized the special obligations that may be imposed on them in exchange for the exclusive right to use a broadcast frequency. "No one has a First Amendment right to a license or to monopolize a radio frequency; to deny a station license because 'the public interest' requires it, is not a denial of free speech."[82] Thus the Court has upheld FCC-imposed "equal time" and "fairness" rules against broadcasters, even while striking down government attempts to impose the same rules on newspapers.[83]

Media Claims for Special Rights The news media make various claims to special rights arising out of the First Amendment's guarantee of a free press. Reporters argue, for example, that they should be able to protect their news sources and are not obliged to give testimony in criminal cases when they have obtained evidence in confidence. However, the only witnesses the Constitution exempts

Television networks hope to avoid government-imposed censorship by offering warnings such as "viewer discretion advised."

from compulsory testimony are defendants themselves, who enjoy the Fifth Amendment's protection against "self-incrimination." The Supreme Court has flatly rejected reporters' claims to a privilege against compulsory testimony. "We cannot seriously entertain the notion that the First Amendment protects a newsman's agreement to conceal the criminal conduct of his source, or evidence thereof, on the theory that it is better to write about a crime than to do something about it."[84]

Despite these rulings, reporters regularly boast of their willingness to go to jail to protect sources, and many have done so. But the media have also pressured the nation's legislatures for protection. Congress has passed the Privacy Protection Act, which sharply limits the ability of law-enforcement officials to search press offices, and many states have passed **shield laws** specifically protecting reporters from giving testimony in criminal cases.

Conflicting "Rights" The conflict between reporters' "rights" to protect their sources under shield laws and the constitutional right of individuals to face their accusers when on trial is just one example of the many conflicts over "rights" in American life. In the case of shield laws, the courts have ruled that "rights" granted by law are not equal to rights granted by the Constitution and have imprisoned those who try to hide behind these laws. Sometimes, however, conflict pits two constitutional rights against one another, as when a judge places a **gag order** on individuals involved in a case. In such cases, the court has essentially decreed that the First Amendment rights of free speech and freedom of the press must be postponed so that the right of an individual to receive a fair and impartial trial is not destroyed.

Freedom of Assembly and Petition

The First Amendment guarantees "the right of the people peaceably to assemble, and to petition the government for redress of grievances." The right to organize political parties and interest groups derives from the right of assembly. And freedom of petition protects most lobbying activities.

The Right of Association Freedom of assembly includes the right to form and join organizations and associations. In an important case during the early civil rights movement, the state of Alabama attempted to harass the National Association for the Advancement of Colored People by requiring it to turn over its membership lists to authorities. The Supreme Court held the state's action to be an unconstitutional infringement of the freedom of association.[85]

shield laws Laws in some states that give reporters the right to refuse to name their sources or to release their notes in court cases; may be overturned by the courts when such refusals jeopardize a fair trial for a defendant.

gag order Order by a judge banning discussion or reporting of a case in order to ensure a fair and impartial trial.

The Supreme Court has also protected the right of students to form organizations. "First Amendment rights . . . are available to teachers and students. It can hardly be argued that either teachers or students shed their constitutional rights at the school house gate."[86] Attempts by a college or university to deny official recognition to a student organization based on its views violates the right of association.

Protests, Parades, and Demonstrations Freedom of assembly includes the right to peacefully protest, parade, and demonstrate. Authorities may, within reasonable limits, enact restrictions regarding the "time, place, and manner" of an assembly so as to preserve public order, smooth traffic flow, freedom of movement, and even peace and quiet. But these regulations cannot be unevenly applied to groups with different views. Thus authorities may require a permit to parade, but they cannot deny a permit to a group because of the nature of their views or content of their message. For example, the Supreme Court held that city authorities in Skokie, Illinois, acted unconstitutionally in prohibiting the American Nazi Party from holding a march in that city even though it was populated with large numbers of Jewish survivors of the Holocaust.[87]

Picketing Assemblies of people have a high potential for creating a public disturbance. Parades block traffic and litter the streets; loudspeakers assault the ears of local residents and bystanders; picket lines may block the free passage of others. Although the right of assembly is protected by the First Amendment, its exercise involves conduct as well as expression, and therefore it is usually subject to greater government regulation than expression alone. The Court has generally upheld reasonable use of public property for assembly, but it has not forced *private* property owners to accommodate speeches or assemblies. Airport terminals, shopping malls, and other open forums, which may or may not be publicly owned, have posed problems for the courts.

Freedom of assembly is currently being tested by opponents of abortion who picket abortion clinics, hoping to embarrass and dissuade women from entering

No rights are absolute. The freedom to assemble does not include the right to block public access to buildings. Congress reaffirmed this limitation in 1994 in a law guaranteeing access to abortion clinics.

them. Generally the courts have allowed limits on these demonstrations to ensure that people can move freely in and out of the clinics. Freedom of assembly does not include the right to block access to public or private buildings. And when abortion opponents demonstrated at the residence of a physician who performed abortions, the Supreme Court upheld a local ordinance barring assemblies in residential neighborhoods.[88] Physically obstructing access to buildings almost always violates state or local laws, as does the threat or use of force by picketers. The Supreme Court made a distinction between a "fixed buffer zone," prohibiting assembly around a building entrance, and a "floating buffer zone" (of 15 feet), prohibiting demonstrators from approaching individuals in public places. The "fixed" zone was held to be a constitutional limit on assembly but the "floating" zone was held to be an unconstitutional limit on free speech.[89] In 1994 Congress passed a federal law guaranteeing access to abortion clinics, arguing that the federal government should act to guarantee a recognized constitutional right.

The Right to Bear Arms

The Second Amendment to the U.S. Constitution states: "A well regulated Militia, being necessary to the security of a free State, the right of the people to keep and bear Arms, shall not be infringed."

Bearing Arms What is meant by the right of the people "to keep and bear arms"? One view is that the Second Amendment confers on Americans an *individual* constitutional right, like the First Amendment freedom of speech or press. The history surrounding the adoption of the Second Amendment reveals the concern of colonists with attempts by despotic governments to confiscate the arms of citizens and render them helpless to resist tyranny. James Madison wrote in the *Federalist Papers*, No. 46 that "the advantage of being armed which the Americans possess over the people of almost every other nation, forms a barrier against the enterprise of [tyrannical] ambition.[90] The Second Amendment was adopted with little controversy; most state constitutions at the time, like Pennsylvania's, declared that "the people have a right to bear arms for the defense of themselves and the state." Early American political rhetoric was filled with praise for an armed citizenry able to protect its freedoms by force if necessary.

State Militias But many constitutional scholars argue that the Second Amendment protects only the *collective* right of the states to form militias—that is, their right to maintain National Guard units. They focus on the qualifying phrase "a well-regulated Militia, being necessary to the security of a free State." The Second Amendment merely prevents Congress from denying the states the right to organize their own military units. If the Founders had wished to create an individual right to bear arms, they would not have inserted the phrase about a "well-regulated militia." (Opponents of this view argue that the original definition of a militia included all free males over eighteen.) Interpreted in this fashion, the Second Amendment does *not* protect private groups who form themselves into militias, nor does it guarantee citizens the right to own guns.

Citizen "Militias" In recent years, self-styled citizen "militias" have cropped up across the nation. They are armed groups who more or less regularly get together

THINK AGAIN

Do law-abiding citizens have a constitutional right to carry a handgun for self-protection?

Right to Keep and Bear Arms

Organizations advocating self-defense rights with information on legislation, court cases, etc.
www.rkba.org

Brady Campaign

The nation's leading gun control organization, with facts, legislation, and a "report card" on each state.
www.bradycampaign.org

The violent conclusion of the attempt by the Bureau of Alcohol, Tobacco and Firearms to enforce federal gun laws against the Branch Davidians in Waco, Texas. Members of citizen militia groups regard the ATF as a threat to their freedom to bear arms.

dressed in camouflage to engage in military tactics and training. They generally view federal government agencies, and often the United Nations, as potential threats to their freedom. They view themselves as modern-day descendants of the American patriot militias who fought in the Revolutionary War. Indeed, the Militia Act of 1792 *required* "every free white male citizen of the respective states, resident therein, who is or shall be of the age of 18 years and under the age of 45 years" to be enrolled in the militia and equipped with "a good musket," a bayonet, and "24 rounds of ammunition." This law was not changed until 1912, when National Guard units replaced state militia.

Citizen militia groups frequently come into conflict with federal firearms regulations. Enforcement of these regulations is the responsibility of the Bureau of Alcohol, Tobacco and Firearms. It was the ATF's violent efforts to enforce federal gun laws that led to the deaths of more than seventy people at the Branch Davidian compound in Waco, Texas, in 1993.

Rights of Criminal Defendants

While society needs the protection of the police, it is equally important to protect society from the police. Arbitrary searches and arrests, imprisonment without trial, forced confessions, beatings and torture, secret trials, tainted witnesses, excessive punishments, and other human rights violations are all too common throughout the world. The U.S. Constitution limits the powers of the police and protects the rights of the accused (see Table 14.2). (See also *What Do You Think?:* "Should Victims' Rights Be Added to the Constitution?")

The Guarantee of the Writ of Habeas Corpus One of the oldest and most revered rights in English common law is the right to obtain a **writ of habeas corpus,** which is a court order directing public officials who are holding a person in custody to bring the prisoner into court and explain the reasons for confinement. If a judge finds that the prisoner is being unlawfully detained, or finds insufficient evidence that a crime has been committed or that the prisoner could have committed it, the judge must order the prisoner's release. Thus the writ of habeas

Bureau of Alcohol, Tobacco, and Firearms

Federal agency responsible for regulation of alcohol, tobacco, firearms, and explosives; site includes publications on gun crimes. *www.atf.gov*

THINK AGAIN

Do you believe that the seizure of property believed by police to be used in drug trafficking, without a judicial hearing or trial, violates civil liberty?

writ of habeas corpus
Court order directing public officials who are holding a person in custody to bring the prisoner into court and explain the reasons for confinement; the right to habeas corpus is protected by Article I of the Constitution.

TABLE 14.2 Individual Rights in the Criminal Justice Process

Rights	Process
Fourth Amendment: Protection against unreasonable searches and seizures Warranted searches for sworn "probable cause." Exceptions: consent searches, safety searches, car searches, and searches incident to a valid arrest.	**Investigation by law-enforcement officers** Expectation that police act lawfully.
Fifth Amendment: Protection against self-incrimination Miranda rules (see Figure 14.1, p. 528).	**Arrest** Arrests based on warrants issued by judges and magistrates. Arrests based on crimes committed in the presence of law enforcement officials. Arrests for "probable cause."
Habeas corpus Police holding a person in custody must bring that person before a judge with cause to believe that a crime was committed and the prisoner committed it.	
Eighth Amendment: No excessive bail Defendant considered innocent until proven guilty; release on bail and amount of bail depends on seriousness of crime, trustworthiness of defendant, and safety of community.	**Hearing and bail** Preliminary hearing in which prosecutor presents testimony that a crime was committed and probable cause for charging the accused.
Fifth Amendment: Grand jury (federal) Federal prosecutors (but not necessarily state prosecutors) must convince a grand jury that a reasonable basis exists to believe the defendant committed a crime and he or she should be brought to trial.	**Indictment** Prosecutor, or a grand jury in federal cases, issues formal document naming the accused and specifying the charges.
Sixth Amendment: Right to counsel Begins in investigation stage, when officials become "accusatory"; extends throughout criminal justice process. Free counsel for indigent defendants.	**Arraignment** Judge reads indictment to the accused and ensures that the accused understands charges and rights and has counsel. Judge asks defendant to choose a plea: Guilty, *nolo contendere* (no contest), or not guilty. If defendant pleads guilty or no contest, a trial is not necessary and defendant proceeds to sentencing.
Sixth Amendment: Right to a speedy and public trial Impartial jury. Right to confront witnesses. Right to compel favorable witnesses to testify.	**Trial** Impartial judge presides as prosecuting and defense attorneys present witnesses and evidence relevant to guilt or innocence of defendant and make arguments to the jury. Jury deliberates in secret and issues a verdict.
Fourth Amendment: Exclusionary rule Illegally obtained evidence cannot be used against defendant.	
Eighth Amendment: Protection against cruel and unusual punishments	**Sentencing** If the defendant is found not guilty, the process ends. Defendants who plead guilty or no contest and defendants found guilty by jury are sentenced by fine, imprisonment, or both by the judge. Sentences imposed must be commensurate to the crimes committed.
Fifth Amendment: Protection against double jeopardy Government cannot try a defendant again for the same offense.	**Appeal** Defendants found guilty may appeal to higher courts for reversal of verdict or a new trial based on errors made anywhere in the process.

Should Victims' Rights Be Added to the Constitution?

The U.S. Constitution includes fifteen specific guarantees of the rights of the accused. It makes no mention of victims' rights.

Liberal California Democratic U.S. Senator Dianne Feinstein and conservative Arizona Republican U.S. Senator Jon Kyl have co-sponsored an amendment to the Constitution that would guarantee to victims of violent crime:

- To be informed of and not be excluded from critical proceedings including:
  arraignment
  preliminary hearing
  trial
  sentencing
  appeals hearing
  parole hearings
- To be heard at proceedings involving a release from custody, sentencing, or acceptance of a negotiated plea
- To notice of any release or escape of the offender
- To a disposition free from unreasonable delay
- To an order of restitution from the convicted offender
- To have the safety of the victims considered in determining a release from custody
- To notice of the victim's rights.

Supporters of a constitutional amendment, a "Crime Victims' Bill of Rights," argue that each year there are millions of victims of violent crime, many of whom are victimized a second time by the criminal justice system itself. They are not notified of the arrest, arraignment, or trial of the person accused of harming them, nor are they guaranteed a hearing at crucial stages of the judicial process—plea-bargaining, sentencing, or parole. Polls show that victims' rights are overwhelmingly supported by the American people. The Senate Judiciary Committee has approved of the victims' rights amendment to the Constitution, and it has the support of President George W. Bush.

But to date the sponsors of the amendment have failed to gather the necessary two-thirds vote of both houses of Congress to send the amendment to the states for ratification. Opponents argue that more than half the states already have added victims' rights amendments to their state constitutions. They argue that it is unnecessary to further clutter the U.S. Constitution with a lengthy amendment that is likely to cause additional litigation and delay in criminal cases.

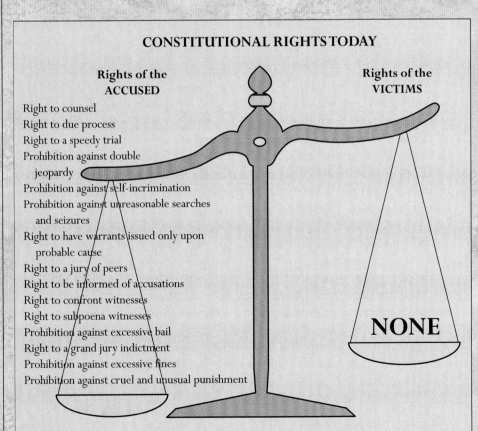

CONSTITUTIONAL RIGHTS TODAY

Rights of the ACCUSED

Right to counsel
Right to due process
Right to a speedy trial
Prohibition against double jeopardy
Prohibition against self-incrimination
Prohibition against unreasonable searches and seizures
Right to have warrants issued only upon probable cause
Right to a jury of peers
Right to be informed of accusations
Right to confront witnesses
Right to subpoena witnesses
Prohibition against excessive bail
Right to a grand jury indictment
Prohibition against excessive fines
Prohibition against cruel and unusual punishment

Rights of the VICTIMS

NONE

The Need for a Victims' Rights Amendment

Source: From the Office of U.S. Senator Dianne Feinstein.

Are Persons Captured on the Battlefields of Afghanistan and Iraq Entitled to the Protections of the U.S. Constitution?

The United States has held 6,000 or more "enemy combatants" captured on the battlefields of Afghanistan and Iraq for several years. Many are held at the U.S. base in Guantanamo Bay, Cuba.

Prisoners of war have never been entitled to constitutional protection. Prisoners of war are uniformed members of the military forces of a nation. (The U.S. held tens of thousands of German and Japanese prisoners of war during World War II.) They are entitled only to "humane treatment" under the Geneva Accords. They are not released until the war is ended.

"Detainees" from the war on terrorism are not officially prisoners of war, inasmuch as they are not uniformed soldiers of any nation. The U.S. has pledged humane treatment even though it is not clear that these detainees are protected by the Geneva Accords. They are not citizens of the United States and they are not held on U.S. soil. As military detainees, they are not given lawyers or access to courts or in most cases, even identified by name. The U.S. military itself decides whether or not they will face a military tribunal or be released to their home countries.

But in a controversial decision in 2004 the Supreme Court held that enemy combatants captured on the battlefield and "imprisoned in territory over which the United States exercises an exclusive jurisdiction and control" are entitled to constitutional rights including habeas corpus—the right to bring their case to U.S. courts. "The fact that petitioners are being held in military custody is immaterial."* The Court reasoned that by agreement with Cuba, the U.S. exercises complete jurisdiction over its Guantanamo base where detainees were being held. The Court was vague about whether enemy combatants held elsewhere in the world were entitled to constitutional protections.

*Rasul v. Bush June 28, 2004.

corpus is a means to test the legality of any imprisonment (see *What Do You Think?:* "Are Persons Captured on the Battlefields of Afghanistan and Iraq Entitled to Protections of the U.S. Constitution?").

The writ of habeas corpus was considered so fundamental to the framers of the Constitution that they included it in the original text of Article I: "The privilege of the Writ of Habeas Corpus shall not be suspended, unless when in Cases of Rebellion or Invasion the public Safety may require it." Despite the qualifying phrase, the Supreme Court has never sanctioned suspension of the writ of habeas corpus even during wartime. President Abraham Lincoln suspended the writ of habeas corpus in several areas during the Civil War, but in the case of *Ex parte Milligan* (1866), the Supreme Court ruled that the president had acted unconstitutionally.[91] (With the war over, however, the Court's decision had no practical effect.) Again, in 1946, the Supreme Court declared that the military had had no right to substitute military courts for ordinary courts in Hawaii during World War II, even though Hawaii was in an active theater of war.[92] State courts cannot issue writs of habeas corpus to federal officials, but federal judges may issue such writs to state officials whenever there is reason to believe that a person is being held in violation of the Constitution or laws of the United States.

The Prohibition of Bills of Attainder and Ex Post Facto Laws Like the guarantee of habeas corpus, protection against bills of attainder and ex post facto laws was considered so fundamental to individual liberty that it was included in the original text of the Constitution. A **bill of attainder** is a legislative act inflicting punishment without judicial trial. An **ex post facto law** is a retroactive criminal law that works against the accused—for example, a law that makes an act criminal after the act is committed or a law that increases the punishment for a crime and applies it retroactively. Both the federal government and the states are prevented from passing such laws.

The fact that relatively few cases of bills of attainder or ex post facto laws have come to the federal courts does not diminish the importance of these protections. Rather, it testifies to the widespread appreciation of their importance in a free society.

Unreasonable Searches and Seizures Individuals are protected by the Fourth Amendment from "unreasonable searches and seizures" of their private "persons, houses, papers, and effects." The Fourth Amendment lays out specific rules for searches and seizures of evidence: "No warrants shall issue, but upon probable cause, supported by Oath or affirmation, and particularly describing the place to be searched, and the persons or things to be seized." Judges cannot issue a **search warrant** just to let police see *if* an individual has committed a crime; there must be "probable cause" for such issuance. The indiscriminate searching of whole neighborhoods or groups of people is unconstitutional and is prevented by the Fourth Amendment's requirement that the place to be searched must be specifically described in the warrant. The requirement that the things to be seized must be described in the warrant is meant to prevent "fishing expeditions" into an individual's home and personal effects on the possibility that some evidence of unknown illegal activity might crop up. The only exception is if police, in the course of a valid search for a specified item, find other items whose very possession is a crime—for example, illicit drugs.

But the courts also permit police to undertake various other "reasonable" searches *without* a warrant: searches in connection with a valid arrest; searches to protect the safety of police officers; searches to obtain evidence in the immediate vicinity and in the suspect's control; searches to preserve evidence in danger of being immediately destroyed; and searches with the consent of a suspect. Indeed, most police searches today take place without warrant under one or another of these conditions. The Supreme Court has also allowed automobile searches and searches of open fields without warrants in many cases. The requirement of "probable cause" has been very loosely defined; even a "partially corroborated anonymous informant's tip" qualifies as "probable cause" to make a search, seizure, or arrest.[93] And if the police, while making a warranted search, or otherwise lawfully on the premises, see evidence of a crime "in plain view," they may seize such evidence without further authorization.[94] However, the Court has held that merely stopping a car for a traffic violation does not give police excuse for a search of the car for drugs.[95]

Wiretapping and Electronic Surveillance For many years the Supreme Court refused to view wiretapping as a search and seizure within the meaning of the Fourth Amendment.[96] However, over time as electronic surveillance techniques became more common and more sophisticated, the Court changed its position. The Court began to view wiretapping and electronic surveillance as a challenge to privacy rights implied by the Fourth Amendment; the Court held that such law enforcement techniques required "probable cause" and a warrant. The government may not undertake to eavesdrop where a person has "a reasonable ex-

bill of attainder Legislative act inflicting punishment without judicial trial; forbidden under Article I of the Constitution.

ex post facto law Retroactive criminal law that works against the accused; forbidden under Article I of the Constitution.

search warrant Court order permitting law-enforcement officials to search a location in order to seize evidence of a crime; issued only for a specified location, in connection with a specific investigation, and on submission of proof that "probable cause" exists to warrant such a search.

New technologies continuously challenge the right of privacy implied by the Fourth Amendment. Here, a video camera monitors a Connecticut preschool.

pectation of privacy," without first showing probable cause and obtaining a warrant.[97] Congress has also enacted a law prohibiting federal agents from intercepting a wire, oral, or electronic communication without first obtaining a warrant (see also *A Conflicting View:* "Terrorism Requires Restrictions on Civil Liberties").

Drug Testing "Unreasonable" drug testing violates the Fourth Amendment. But the Supreme Court has held that it is reasonable to impose mandatory drug testing on railroad workers, federal law-enforcement agents, and even students participating in athletics.[98] However, when the state of Georgia enacted a law requiring drug testing for candidates for public office, the Court found it to be an "unreasonable" search in violation of the Fourth Amendment.[99] Apparently mandatory drug testing in occupations affecting public safety and drug testing in schools to protect children are reasonable, while suspicionless drug testing of the general public is not.

Arrests The Supreme Court permits *arrests without warrants* (1) when a crime is committed in the presence of an officer; and (2) when an arrest is supported by "probable cause" to believe that a crime has been committed by the person apprehended.[100] However, the Court has held that police may not enter a home to arrest its occupant without either a warrant for the arrest or the consent of the owner.[101]

Indictment The Fifth Amendment requires that an **indictment** be issued by a **grand jury** before a person may be brought to trial on a felony offense. This provision was designed as a protection against unreasonable and harassing prosecutions by the government. In principle, the grand jury is supposed to determine whether the evidence submitted to it by government prosecutors is sufficient to place a person on trial. In practice, however, grand juries spend very little time deliberating on the vast majority of cases. Neither defendants nor their attorneys are permitted to testify before grand juries without the prosecution's permission, which is rarely given. Thus the prosecutor controls the information submitted to

indictment Determination by a grand jury that sufficient evidence exists to warrant trial of an individual on a felony charge; necessary before an individual can be brought to trial.

grand jury Jury charged only with determining whether sufficient evidence exists to support indictment of an individual on a felony charge; the grand jury's decision to indict does not represent a conviction.

Terrorism Requires Restrictions on Civil Liberties

The terrorist attack on America of September 11, 2001 was the most horrific violence committed against innocent American citizens in recent times. It created a new examination of Americans' commitment to personal freedoms and their willingness to trade these freedoms for the safety and security of society. All of the polls taken shortly after the attack indicated that Americans were prepared to accept many new restrictions on their freedom—more surveillance of their papers and communications, more searches of their belongings, roundups of suspected immigrants, and even prolonged detention without recourse to the courts. As time passed, however, fewer Americans expressed a willingness to sacrifice basic civil liberties to prevent additional acts of terrorism.*

Following the attack, Congress moved swiftly to enact the "Patriot" Act, officially the Uniting and Strengthening America Act by Providing Appropriate Tools Required to Intercept and Obstruct Terrorism of 2001. President Bush and Attorney General John Ashcroft successfully lobbied Congress to increase the federal government's powers of searches, seizures, surveillance, and detention of suspects. The concerns of civil libertarians were largely swept aside. The Act was passed nearly unanimously in the Senate (98–1) and overwhelmingly in the House (357–66), with the support of both Democrats and Republicans.

Among the key provisions of the Patriot Act:

- *Roving wiretaps:* Allows wiretaps of any telephones that suspects might use instead of requiring separate warrants for each line.
- *Internet tracking:* Allows law enforcement authorities to track Internet communications, that is, to "surf the Web" without obtaining warrants.
- *Business records:* Allows investigators to obtain information from credit cards, bank records, consumer purchases, libraries, schools and colleges, etc.
- *Foreign Intelligence Surveillance Court:* A special Foreign Intelligence Surveillance Court may issue search warrants on an investigator's assertion that the information sought is relevant to a terrorist investigation. No showing of "probable cause" is required. The warrant is not made public, in order to avoid "tipping off" the subject.
- *Property seizure:* Authorizes the seizure of the property of suspected terrorists. Persons whose property is seized bear the burden of proof that the property was not used for terrorist purposes in order to secure the return of their property.
- *Detention:* Allows the detention of suspected terrorists for lengthy periods without judicial recourse.
- *Aliens reporting and detention:* Authorizes the Immigration and Naturalization Service to require reporting by aliens of selected nations and indefinite detention of illegal aliens suspected of terrorist connections.
- *Prohibits harboring of terrorists:* Creates a new federal crime—knowingly harboring persons who have committed, or are about to commit, a terrorist act.

What factors affect Americans' willingness to trade off restrictions on civil liberties in order to provide for safety and security from terrorism? Political science research suggests that the greater people's sense of threat, the greater their support for restrictions on civil liberties. The lower people's trust in government, the less willing they are to trade off civil liberties for security. Liberals are less willing to trade off civil liberties than moderates or conservatives. Overall it seems clear that Americans' commitment to civil liberties is highly contingent on their concerns about threats to national or personal security.

---

* Darren W. Davis and Brian D. Silver, "Civil Liberties vs. Security: Public Opinion in the Context of the Terrorist Attacks on America," *American Journal of Political Science* 48 (January 2004): 28–46.

grand juries and instructs them in their duties. In almost all cases, grand juries accept the prosecution's recommendations with little or no discussion. Thus grand juries, whose hearings are secret, do not provide much of a check on federal prosecutors, and their refusal to indict is very rare.

Self-Incrimination and the Right to Counsel Freedom from self-incrimination had its origin in English common law; it was originally designed to prevent persons from being tortured into confessions of guilt. It is also a logical extension of the notion that individuals should not be forced to contribute to their own prosecution, that the burden of proof rests on the state. The Fifth Amendment protects people from both physical and psychological coercion.[102] It protects not only accused persons at their own trial but also witnesses testifying in trials of other persons, civil suits, congressional hearings, and so on. Thus "taking the Fifth" has become a standard phrase in our culture: "I refuse to answer that question on the grounds that it might tend to incriminate me." The protection also means that judges, prosecutors, and juries cannot use the refusal of people to take the stand at their own trial as evidence of guilt. Indeed, a judge or attorney is not even permitted to imply this to a jury, and a judge is obligated to instruct a jury not to infer guilt from a defendant's refusal to testify.

It is important to note that individuals may be forced to testify when they are not themselves the object of a criminal prosecution. Government officials may also extend a **grant of immunity from prosecution** to a witness in order to compel testimony. Under a grant of immunity, the government agrees not to use any of the testimony against the witness; in return, the witness provides information that the government uses to prosecute others who are considered more dangerous or more important than the immune witness. Because such grants ensure that nothing the witnesses say can be used against them, immunized witnesses cannot refuse to answer under the Fifth Amendment.

The Supreme Court under Chief Justice Earl Warren greatly strengthened the Fifth Amendment protection against self-incrimination and the right to counsel in a series of rulings in the 1960s:

- *Gideon v. Wainwright* (1963): Equal protection under the Fourteenth Amendment requires that free legal counsel be appointed for all indigent defendants in all criminal cases.[103]

- *Escobedo v. Illinois* (1964): Suspects are entitled to confer with counsel as soon as police investigation focuses on them or once "the process shifts from investigatory to accusatory."[104]

- *Miranda v. Arizona* (1966): Before questioning suspects, a police officer must inform them of all their constitutional rights, including the right to counsel (appointed at no cost to the suspect if necessary) and the right to remain silent. Although suspects may knowingly waive these rights, the police cannot question anyone who at any point asks for a lawyer or declines "in any manner" to be questioned. If the police commit an error in these procedures, the accused goes free, regardless of the evidence of guilt.[105] Figure 14.1 shows a typical **Miranda warning** card carried by police to ensure that they issue the proper warnings to those under arrest.

The Exclusionary Rule Illegally obtained evidence and confessions may not be used in criminal trials. If police find evidence of a crime in an illegal search or

grant of immunity from prosecution Grant by the government to an individual of freedom from prosecution on a particular charge in return for testimony by that individual that might otherwise be self-incriminating.

Miranda warning Requirement that persons arrested be informed of their rights immediately after arrest.

METROPOLITAN POLICE DEPARTMENT	WAIVER
Warning As To Your Rights	

METROPOLITAN POLICE DEPARTMENT
Warning As To Your Rights

You are under arrest. Before we ask you any questions you must understand what your rights are.

You have the right to remain silent. You are not required to say anything to us at any time or to answer any questions. Anything you say can be used against you in court.

You have the right to talk to a lawyer for advice before we question you and to have him with you during questioning.

If you cannot afford a lawyer and want one, a lawyer will be provided for you.

If you want to answer questions now without a lawyer present, you will still have the right to stop answering at any time. You also have the right to stop answering at any time until you talk to a lawyer.

WAIVER

1. Have you read or had read to you the warning as to your rights?_____

2. Do you understand these rights? _____

3. Do you wish to answer any questions? _____

4. Are you willing to answer questions without having an attorney present? _____

5. Signature of defendant on line below.

_____

6. Time _____   Date _____

7. Signature of officer _____

8. Signature of witness _____

FIGURE 14.1   The Miranda Warning Since the U.S. Supreme Court's ruling in the case of *Miranda v. Arizona* in 1966, law-enforcement officials at all levels have routinely carried "Miranda rights" cards, which they read to accused individuals immediately after their arrest. This procedure has largely eliminated defendants' abilities to obtain dismissals and/or acquittals on the basis of ignorance of their rights or lack of proper counsel. The Supreme Court reaffirmed the *Miranda* rule in 2000.

if they elicit statements from suspects without informing them of their rights to remain silent or to have counsel, the evidence or statements produced are not admissible in a trial. This **exclusionary rule** is one of the more controversial procedural rights that the Supreme Court has extended to criminal defendants. The rule is also unique to the United States: in Great Britain evidence obtained illegally may be used against the accused, although the accused may bring charges against the police for damages.

The rule provides *enforcement* for the Fourth Amendment guarantee against unreasonable searches and seizures, as well as the Fifth Amendment guarantee against compulsory self-incrimination and the guarantee of counsel. Initially applied only in federal cases, in *Mapp v. Ohio* (1961) the Supreme Court extended the exclusionary rule to all criminal cases in the United States.[106] A *good faith exception* is made "when law enforcement officers have acted in objective good faith or their transgressions have been minor."[107] And police are *not* prohibited from tricking a suspect into giving them incriminating evidence.[108] But the exclusionary rule is frequently attacked for the high price it extracts from society—the release of guilty criminals. Why punish society because of the misconduct of police? Why not punish police directly, perhaps with disciplinary measures imposed by courts that discover errors, instead of letting guilty persons go free?

exclusionary rule Rule of law that evidence found in an illegal search or resulting from an illegally obtained confession may not be admitted at trial.

Bail Requirements The Eighth Amendment says only that *"excessive* bail shall not be required." This clause does not say that pretrial release on **bail** will be available to all. The Supreme Court has held that "in our society liberty is the norm, and detention prior to trial or without trial is the carefully limited exception." Pretrial release on bail can be denied on the basis of the seriousness of the crime (bail is often denied in murder cases), the trustworthiness of the defendant (bail is often denied when the prosecution shows that the defendant is likely to flee before trial), or, in a more controversial exception, when release would threaten "the safety of any other person or the community."[109] If the court does not find any of these exceptions, it must set bail no higher than an amount reasonably calculated to ensure the defendant's later presence at trial.

Most criminal defendants cannot afford the bail money required for pretrial release. They must seek the services of a bail bondsman, who charges a heavy fee for filing the bail money with the court. The bail bondsman receives all of the bail money back when the defendant shows up for trial. But even if the defendant is found innocent, the bail bondsman retains the charge fee. (Thus the system is said to discriminate against poor defendants who cannot afford the bondsman's fee.) The failure of a criminal defendant to appear at his or her trial is itself a crime and subjects the defendant to immediate arrest as well as forfeiture of bail. Most states authorize bail bondsmen to find and arrest persons who have "jumped bail," return them to court, and thereby recover the bail money.

Fair Trial The original text of the Constitution guaranteed jury trials in criminal cases, and the Sixth Amendment went on to correct weaknesses the framers saw in the English justice system at that time—closed proceedings, trials in absentia (where the defendant is not present), secret witnesses, long delays between arrest and trial, biased juries, and the absence of defense counsel. Specifically, the Sixth Amendment guarantees the following:

- The right to a speedy and public trial. ("Speedy" refers to the time between arrest and trial, not the time between the crime itself and trial,[110] but the Supreme Court has declined to set a specific time limit that defines speedy.[111])

bail Release of an accused person from custody in exchange for promise to appear at trial, guaranteed by money or property that is forfeited to court if defendant does not appear.

Dollree Mapp was arrested in 1957 but police seized vital evidence against her during an unwarranted, unconstitutional search. In *Mapp v. Ohio* (1961), the U.S. Supreme Court held that evidence obtained illegally could not be used in a criminal trial.

- An impartial jury chosen from the state or district where the crime was committed.

- The right to confront (cross-examine) witnesses against the accused.

- The right of the accused to compel (subpoena) favorable witnesses to appear.

- The right of the accused to be represented by counsel.

Over the years the courts have elaborated on these elements of a fair trial so that today trial proceedings follow a rigidly structured format. First, attorneys make opening statements. The prosecution describes the crime and how it will prove beyond a reasonable doubt that the defendant committed it. The defense attorney argues either that the crime did not occur or that the defendant did not do it. Next, each side, again beginning with the prosecution, calls witnesses who first testify on "direct examination" for their side, then are cross-examined by the opposing attorney. Witnesses may be asked to verify evidence that is introduced as "exhibits." Defendants have a right to be present during their own trials (although an abusive and disruptive defendant may be considered to have waived his or her right to be present and be removed from the courtroom).[112] Prosecution witnesses must appear in the courtroom and submit to cross-examination (although special protection procedures, including videotaped testimony, may be used for children).[113] Prosecutors are obliged to disclose any information that might create a reasonable doubt about the defendant's guilt,[114] but the defendant may not be compelled to disclose incriminating information.

After all of the witnesses offered by both sides have been heard and cross-examined, prosecution and defense give their closing arguments. The burden of proof "beyond a reasonable doubt" rests with the prosecution; the defense does not need to prove that the accused is innocent, only that reasonable doubt exists regarding guilt. (However, see *A Conflicting View:* "The War on Drugs Threatens Individual Liberty.")

Juries must be "impartial": they must not have prejudged the case or exhibit bias or prejudice or have a personal interest in the outcome. Judges can dismiss jurors for "cause." During jury selection, attorneys for the prosecution and defense are allowed a fixed number of "peremptory" challenges of jurors (although they cannot do so on the basis of race).[115] Jury selection is often regarded by attorneys as the key to the outcome of a case; both sides try to get presumed sympathetic people on the jury. In well-publicized cases, judges may "sequester" a jury (keep them in a hotel away from access to the mass media) in order to maintain impartiality. Judges may exclude press or television to prevent trials from becoming spectacles if they wish.[116] By tradition, English juries have had twelve members; however, the Supreme Court has allowed six-member juries in non-death-penalty cases.[117] Also by tradition, juries should arrive at a unanimous decision. If a jury cannot do so, judges declare a "hung" jury and the prosecutor may schedule a retrial. Only a "not guilty" prevents retrial of a defendant. Traditionally, it was believed that a lack of unanimity raised "reasonable doubt" about the defendant's guilt. But the Supreme Court has permitted nonunanimous verdicts in some cases.[118]

Plea Bargaining Few criminal cases actually go to trial. More than 90 percent of criminal cases are plea bargained.[119] In **plea bargaining**, the defendant agrees to plead guilty and waives the right to a jury trial in exchange for concessions made by the prosecutor, perhaps the dropping of more serious charges against the

plea bargaining Practice of allowing defendants to plead guilty to lesser crimes than those with which they were originally charged in return for reduced sentences.

The War on Drugs Threatens Individual Liberty

Drug offenses currently account for over half of all prison sentences meted out by federal courts. The average federal sentence for drug crimes—possession, trafficking, or manufacturing of illegal substances—is seven years; the federal minimum sentence for possession of illegal drugs is five years. Nearly 1 million persons are arrested each year for drug violations.* The United States imprisons a larger proportion of its population than any other advanced nation.

The greatest threat arising from the "war on drugs," however, is the loss of personal liberty that has accompanied efforts to "take the profit out of crime." Congress passed a Racketeer influenced and Corrupt Organizations Act (RICO) in 1970, following a 1968 presidential campaign in which President Richard Nixon made "getting tough on crime" a key issue. RICO authorizes federal agents to seize cash, bank accounts, homes, cars, boats, businesses, and other assets on "probable cause" to believe that they were used in criminal activity or were obtained with profits from criminal activity. People may be stopped in an airport terminal, a bus station, or on the street, on suspicion of drug trafficking, and have their cash and cars seized by law enforcement agencies. Boats and airplanes are also favored targets of seizure, but RICO also allows the seizure of bank accounts, homes, and businesses. Assets seized by federal law-enforcement agencies—FBI, DEA, Customs Service, Treasury and Justice Departments—are usually retained by these agencies (or the profits of selling these assets at auction), and proceeds are often shared with state and local law-enforcement agencies that cooperated in the investigation. Thus, there is a strong bureaucratic incentive for agencies to concentrate on cases likely to result in forfeiture of these assets—primarily drug cases—and to overlook other law-enforcement activities.

RICO permits the government to seize property *before* any adjudication of guilt. Indeed a subsequent guilty verdict in a criminal trial is not necessary for the government to retain possession of the property seized. The only requirement is that government agents have "probable cause" to believe that the property was used in a crime or was purchased with the profits of crime. People whose property is seized under RICO must initiate a suit against the government. They have the burden of proving that they are innocent of any crime and, more importantly, that officers had no probable cause to seize their property. The proceedings are considered a civil suit by an individual against the government, not a criminal case by the government against the individual. The government, therefore, need not prove "beyond a reasonable doubt" that the person was involved in criminal activity or the property was used in commission of a crime. Rather, the person must prove his or her own innocence and the government's lack of probable cause to seize the property.

In a decision that seriously endangers personal liberty in America, the Supreme Court upheld RICO.[†] The Court ruled that the government's seizure of property is a civil and not a criminal punishment. This means that individuals whose property is seized are not afforded the constitutional rights of criminal defendants. They have no right to "due process of law" (Fifth Amendment), protection against double jeopardy (Fifth Amendment), or protection against "excessive fines" (Eighth Amendment).

Efforts in Congress to reform RICO have consistently failed. Members of Congress wish to avoid being labeled "soft on crime." And law-enforcement agencies—federal, state, and local—lobby heavily against reform.

---

* *Statistical Abstract of the United States, 1999.* p. 232.

† *U.S. v. Ursery* 518 U.S. 267 (1996).

---

defendant or a pledge to seek a reduced sentence or fine. Some critics of plea bargaining view it as another form of leniency in the criminal justice system that reduces its deterrent effects. Other critics view plea bargaining as a violation of the Constitution's protection against self-incrimination and guarantee of a fair jury trial. Prosecutors, they say, threaten defendants with serious charges and stiff penalties in order to force a guilty plea. Still other critics see plea bargaining as an "under-the-table" process that undermines respect for the criminal justice system.

Yet it is vital to the nation's court system that most defendants plead guilty. The court system would quickly break down from overload if any substantial proportion of defendants insisted on jury trials.

Double Jeopardy The Constitution appears to bar multiple prosecutions for the same offense: "Nor shall any person be subject for the same offense to be twice put in jeopardy of life or limb" (Fifth Amendment). But very early the Supreme Court held that this clause does not protect an individual from being tried a second time if jurors are deadlocked and cannot reach a verdict in the first trial (a "hung" jury).[120] Moreover, the Supreme Court has held that federal and state governments may separately try a person for the same offense if it violates both federal and state laws.[121] Thus, in the well-publicized Rodney King case in 1992, in which police officers were videotaped beating King, a California court found the officers not guilty of assault, but later the U.S. Justice Department won convictions against the officers in a federal court for violating King's civil rights. Finally, a verdict of guilt or innocence in a criminal trial does not preclude a civil trial in which plaintiffs (private citizens) sue for damages inflicted by the accused. Thus, O.J. Simpson was found not guilty of murder in a criminal trial but later found to be responsible for the deaths of two people in a civil trial. Civil courts, of course, can only impose monetary awards; they cannot impose criminal penalties.

The Death Penalty

Perhaps the most heated debate in criminal justice policy today concerns capital punishment. Opponents of the death penalty argue that it violates the prohibition against "cruel and unusual punishments" in the Eighth Amendment to the Constitution. They also argue that the death penalty is applied unequally. A large proportion of those executed have been poor, uneducated, and nonwhite. In contrast, many Americans feel that justice demands strong retribution for heinous crimes—a life for a life. A mere jail sentence for a multiple murderer or rapist-murderer seems unjust compared with the damage inflicted on society and the victims. In many cases, a life sentence means less than ten years in prison under the current early-release and parole policies in many states. Convicted murderers have been set free, and some have killed again.

Prohibition against Unfair Application Prior to 1971, the death penalty was officially sanctioned by about half of the states. Federal law also retained the death penalty. However, no one had actually suffered the death penalty since 1967 because of numerous legal tangles and direct challenges to the constitutionality of capital punishment.

In *Furman v. Georgia* (1972), the Supreme Court ruled that capital punishment, as then imposed, violated the Eighth and Fourteenth Amendment prohibitions against cruel and unusual punishment and due process of law. The justices' reasoning in the case was very complex. Only Justices William J. Brennan and Thurgood Marshall declared that capital punishment itself is cruel and unusual. The other justices in the majority felt that death sentences had been applied unfairly; some individuals received the death penalty for crimes for which many others

THINK AGAIN

Is the death penalty a "cruel and unusual" punishment?

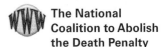
The National Coalition to Abolish the Death Penalty

This site provides information about public policies, institutions, and individuals that collectively work toward the "unconditional rejection of capital punishment."
www.ncadp.org

received much lighter sentences. These justices left open the possibility that capital punishment would be constitutional if it was specified for certain kinds of crime and applied uniformly.[122]

After this decision, a majority of states rewrote their death penalty laws to try to ensure fairness and uniformity of application. Generally, these laws mandate the death penalty for murders committed during rape, robbery, hijacking, or kidnapping; murder of prison guards; murder with torture; and multiple murders. They call for two trials to be held—one to determine guilt or innocence and another to determine the penalty. At the second trial, evidence of "aggravating" and "mitigating" factors must be presented; if there are aggravating factors but no mitigating factors, the death penalty is mandatory.

Death Penalty Reinstated The revised death penalty laws were upheld in a series of cases that came before the Supreme Court in 1976. The Court concluded that "the punishment of death does *not* invariably violate the Constitution." The majority decision noted that the framers of the Bill of Rights had accepted death as a common penalty for crime. Although acknowledging that the Constitution and its amendments must be interpreted in a dynamic fashion, reflecting changing moral values, the Court's majority noted that most state legislatures have been willing to reenact the death penalty and hundreds of juries have been willing to impose that penalty. Thus "a large proportion of American society continues to regard it as an appropriate and necessary criminal sanction." Moreover, the Court held that the social purposes of retribution and deterrence justify the use of the death penalty; this ultimate sanction is "an expression of society's moral outrage at particularly offensive conduct."[123]

The Court reaffirmed that *Furman v. Georgia* struck down the death penalty only where it was invoked in "an arbitrary and capricious manner." A majority of the justices upheld the death penalty in states where the trial is a two-part proceeding, provided that during the second part the jury is given relevant information and standards for deciding whether to impose the death penalty. The Court approved the consideration of "aggravating and mitigating circumstances." Later

Bureau of Justice Statistics

Federal statistics on jails, prisons, probation, and capital punishment. Click to capital punishment for numbers of executions and persons under sentence of death. *www.ojp.usdoj.gov/bjs*

Do retribution and deterrence justify the use of the death penalty? Perhaps the most heated debate in criminal justice policy today concerns capital punishment.

the Court held that the jury, not a judge acting alone, must find aggravating circumstances in order to impose the death sentence.[124] The Court also called for automatic review of all death sentences by state supreme courts to ensure that none is imposed under the influence of passion or prejudice, that aggravating factors are supported by the evidence, and that the sentence is not disproportionate to the crime. However, the court disapproved of state laws making the death penalty mandatory in all first-degree murder cases, holding that such laws were "unduly harsh and unworkably rigid." And the Court has held that executions of the mentally retarded are "cruel and unusual punishments" prohibited by the Eighth Amendment.[125]

Racial Bias The death penalty has been challenged as a violation of the Equal Protection Clause of the Fourteenth Amendment because of racial bias in the application of the punishment. White murderers are just as likely to receive the death penalty as black murderers. However, some statistics show that if the *victim* is white there is a greater chance that the killer will be sentenced to death than if the victim is black. Nevertheless, the U.S. Supreme Court has ruled that statistical disparities in the race of victims by itself does not bar the use of the death penalty in all cases. There must be evidence of racial bias against a particular defendant in order for the Court to reverse a death sentence.[126]

Delays Once imposed, the death penalty is, of course, irreversible. It is the ultimate punishment, and it must not be imposed if there is any doubt whatsoever about the defendant's guilt. Yet how many opportunities should death row inmates have to challenge their convictions and sentences? The writ of habeas corpus is guaranteed in the Constitution, but how many habeas corpus petitions should federal courts allow a condemned prisoner to submit? Attorneys for prisoners often generate new claims for last-minute appeals, expecting that federal courts will delay executions for future hearings and adjudications. Sometimes these claims are repetitive and frivolous. Multiple appeals and writs by prisoners mean more than a decade between death sentence and execution.

In recent years, the Supreme Court has limited habeas corpus petitions of prisoners who have already exhausted their appeals and filed one claim in federal court and lost, and prisoners who failed to follow state rules of appeal. And the Congress in 1996, directed that claims raised in earlier habeas corpus petitions must be dismissed when raised again, unless they are accompanied by new evidence not knowable at the time of the earlier petition. The Supreme Court held this Act to be constitutional.[127] So what if genuine new evidence is uncovered after all appeals have been exhausted? Prisoners must then rely on governors' pardons (or, in federal cases, a presidential pardon). Recently, some state governors have declared a moratorium (temporary halt) on all executions, fearing that some innocent persons may be put to death.

- Laws and government are required to protect individual liberty. Yet laws and governments themselves restrict liberty. To resolve this dilemma, constitutions seek to limit governmental power over the individual. In the U.S. Constitution, the Bill of Rights is designed to place certain liberties beyond the reach of government.

- Initially the Bill of Rights applied against only the federal government, not state or local governments. But over time, the Bill of Rights was nationalized, as the Supreme Court applied the Due Process Clause of the Fourteenth Amendment to all governments in the United States.

- Freedom of religion encompasses two separate restrictions on government: government must not establish religion or prohibit its free exercise. Although the wording of the First Amendment is absolute ("Congress shall make no law . . ."), the Supreme Court has allowed some restrictions on religious practices that threaten health, safety, or welfare.

- The Supreme Court's efforts to maintain "a wall of separation" between church and state have proven difficult and controversial. The Court's banning of prayer and religious ceremony in public schools more than thirty years ago remains politically unpopular today.

- The Supreme Court has never adopted the absolutist position that all speech is protected by the First Amendment. The Court's clear and present danger doctrine and its preferred position doctrine recognize the importance of free expression in a democracy, yet the Court has permitted some restrictions on expression, especially in times of perceived national crisis.

- The Supreme Court has placed obscenity outside of the protection of the First Amendment, but it has encountered considerable difficulty in defining "obscenity."

- Freedom of the press prevents government from imposing prior restraints (censorship) on the news media except periodically in wartime, when it has been argued that publication would result in serious harm or loss of life. The Supreme Court has allowed greater government authority over radio and television than over newspapers, on the grounds that radio and television are given exclusive rights to use specific broadcast frequencies.

- The First Amendment guarantee of the right of assembly and petition protects the organization of political parties and interest groups. It also protects the right of people to peacefully protest, parade, and demonstrate. Governments may, within reasonable limits, restrict these activities for valid reasons but may not apply different restrictions to different groups based on the nature of their views.

- The Second Amendment guarantees "the right of the people to keep and bear arms." However, it is frequently argued that this is not an individual right to possess a gun, but rather a collective right of the states to maintain National Guard units.

- Crime rates in the United States are currently declining. Yet a free society must balance any remedies to the crime problem against potential infringements of the rights of its citizens.

- The Constitution includes a number of important procedural guarantees in the criminal justice system: the writ of habeas corpus; prohibitions against bills of attainder and ex post facto laws; protection against unreasonable searches and seizures; protection against self-incrimination; guarantee of legal counsel; protection against excessive bail; guarantee of a fair public and speedy trial by an impartial jury; the right to confront witnesses and to compel favorable witnesses to testify; and protection against cruel or unusual punishment.

- The Supreme Court's exclusionary rule helps to enforce some of these procedural rights by excluding illegally obtained evidence and self-incriminating statements from criminal trials. In the 1960s, Court interpretations of the Fourth and Fifth Amendments strengthened the rights of criminal defendants. Police procedures adjusted quickly, and today there is little evidence that procedural rights greatly hamper law enforcement.

- Few criminal cases go to trial. Most are plea bargained, with the defendant pleading guilty in exchange for reduced charges and/or a lighter sentence. Although this practice is frequently criticized, without plea bargaining the nation's criminal court system would break down from case overload.

- The Supreme Court has ruled that the death penalty is not a "cruel and unusual punishment," but the Court has insisted on fairness and uniformity of application.

incorporation   494
Free Exercise Clause   497
No Establishment Clause   498
wall-of-separation doctrine   498
Lemon test   499

clear and present danger doctrine   502
preferred position   504
freedom of expression   504
symbolic speech   505
commercial speech   508
prior restraint   514

shield laws   516
gag order   516
writ of habeas corpus   519
bill of attainder   523
ex post facto law   523
search warrant   523
indictment   524

grand jury   524
grant of immunity from prosecution   526
Miranda warning   526
exclusionary rule   527
bail   528
plea bargaining   529

SUGGESTED READINGS

Bruce, Tammy. *The New Thought Police.* New York: Prima Lyfestyles, 2003. A liberal feminist confronts the Left's assault on free speech.

Epstein, Lee, and Thomas G. Walker. *Constitutional Law for a Changing America: Rights, Liberties and Justice.* 5th ed. Washington, D.C.: CQ Press, 2003. An authoritative text on civil liberties and the rights of the criminally accused. It describes the political context of Supreme Court decisions and provides key excerpts from the most important decisions.

Etzioni, Amitai. *The Limits of Privacy.* New York: Basic Books, 1999. A "communitarian" argument that Americans' focus on individual rights, including the right of privacy, should be balanced against the legitimate needs of the community.

Garrow, David. *Liberty and Sexuality: The Right to Privacy and the Making of Roe v. Wade.* New York: Macmillan, 1994. Historical account of the background and development of the right to sexual privacy.

Hentoff, Nat. *Free Speech for Me—But Not for Thee.* New York: HarperCollins, 1992. Account of how both the right and the left in America try to suppress the opinions of those who disagree with them.

Kobylka, Joseph F. *The Politics of Obscenity.* Westport, Conn.: Greenwood Press, 1991. Comprehensive review of Supreme Court obscenity decisions, arguing that the *Miller* case in 1973 was a turning point away from a more permissive to a more restrictive approach toward sexually oriented material. It examines the litigation strategies of the American Civil Liberties Union and other groups in obscenity cases.

Lewis, Anthony. *Gideon's Trumpet.* New York: Random House, 1964. The classic story of Clarence Gideon and how his handwritten habeas corpus plea made its way to the U.S. Supreme Court, resulting in the guarantee of free legal counsel for poor defendants in felony cases.

Shiell, Timothy C. *Campus Hate Speech on Trial.* Lawrence: University of Kansas Press, 1998. Traditional academic values emphasizing the free exchange of ideas are being sacrificed on campus by anti-hate speech codes.

Sullivan, Harold J. *Civil Rights and Liberties: Provocative Questions and Evolving Answers.* Upper Saddle River, N.J.: Prentice Hall, 2001. Contemporary issues in civil liberties discussed in a question-and-answer format.

MAKE IT REAL

CIVIL LIBERTIES: THE GREAT BALANCING ACT

In this simulation you are the Mayor of the City. You will have to make decisions and policies for a number of situations dealing with civil liberties. The City has been in an uproar over political events lately. When political conflict occurs, you are expected to keep public order and at the same time respect the civil liberties of the people involved. The toughest part about being the Mayor of the City is that the City newspaper has little to write about other than your latest actions, especially the mistakes. Good luck trying to control conflict while guarding everyone's rights.

15

POLITICS AND CIVIL RIGHTS

The Politics of Equality

Equality has been the central issue of American politics throughout the history of the nation. It is the issue that sparked the nation's only civil war, and it continues today to be the nation's most vexing political concern.

Conflict begins over the very definition of "equality" (see "Dilemmas of Equality" in Chapter 2). Although Americans agree in the abstract that everyone is equal, they disagree over what they mean by "equality." Traditionally, equality meant "equality of *opportunity*": an equal opportunity to develop individual talents and abilities and to be rewarded for work, initiative, merit, and achievement. Over time, the issue of equality has shifted to "equality of *results*": an equal sharing of income and material rewards. With this shift in definition has come political conflict over the question of what, if anything, government should do to narrow the gaps between rich and poor, men and women, blacks and whites, and all other groups in society.

The nation's long struggle over equality has produced a number of constitutional and legal milestones in civil rights. These are summarized in Table 15.1. Much of the politics of civil rights centers on the development and interpretation of these guarantees of equality.

Slavery, Segregation, and the Constitution

In penning the Declaration of Independence in 1776, Thomas Jefferson affirmed that "All men are created equal." Yet from 1619, when the first slaves were brought to Jamestown, Virginia, until 1865, when the Thirteenth Amendment to the Constitution outlawed the practice, slavery was a way of life in the United States. Africans were captured, enslaved, transported to America, bought and sold, and used as personal property.

Slavery and the Constitution The Constitution of 1787 recognized and protected slavery in the United States. Article I stipulated that slaves were to be counted as three-fifths of a person for purposes of

TABLE 15.1 **Guarantees of Civil Rights**

Thirteenth Amendment (1865)

Neither slavery nor involuntary servitude, except as a punishment for crime whereof the party shall have been duly convicted, shall exist within the United States, or any place subject to their jurisdiction.

Fourteenth Amendment (1868)

No State shall make or enforce any law which shall abridge the privileges or immunities of citizens of the United States; nor shall any State deprive any person of life, liberty, or property, without due process of law; nor deny to any person within its jurisdiction the equal protection of the laws.

Fifteenth Amendment (1870)

The rights of the citizens of the United States to vote shall not be denied or abridged by the United States or by any State on account of race, color, or previous condition of servitude.

Nineteenth Amendment (1920)

The right of the citizens of the United States to vote shall not be denied or abridged by the United States or by any State on account of sex.

Civil Rights Acts of 1866, 1871, and 1875

Acts passed by the Reconstruction Congress following the Civil War. The Civil Rights Act of 1866 guaranteed newly freed persons the right to purchase, lease, and use real property. The Civil Rights Act of 1875 outlawed segregation in privately owned businesses and facilities, but in the Civil Rights Cases (1883), the Supreme Court declared the act an unconstitutional expansion of federal power, ruling that the Fourteenth Amendment limits only "State" actions. Other provisions of these acts were generally ignored for many decades. But the Civil Rights Act of 1871 has been revived in recent decades; the act makes it a federal crime for any person acting under the authority of state law to deprive another of rights protected by the Constitution.

Civil Rights Act of 1957

The first civil rights law passed by Congress since Reconstruction. It empowers the U.S. Justice Department to enforce voting rights, established the Civil Rights Division in the Justice Department, and created the Civil Rights Commission to study and report on civil rights in the United States.

Civil Rights Act of 1964

A comprehensive enactment designed to erase racial discrimination in both public and private sectors of American life. Major titles of the act: I. outlaws arbitrary discrimination in voter registration and expedites voting rights suits; II. bars discrimination in public accommodations, such as hotels and restaurants, that have a substantial relation to interstate commerce; III. and IV. authorize the national government to bring suits to desegregate public facilities and schools; V. extends the life and expands the power of the Civil Rights Commission; VI. provides for withholding federal funds from programs administered in a discriminatory manner; VII. establishes the right to equality in employment opportunities.

Civil Rights Act of 1968

Prohibits discrimination in the advertising, financing sale, or rental of housing, based on race, religion, or national origin and, as of 1974, sex. A major amendment to the act in 1988 extended coverage to the handicapped and to families with children.

Voting Rights Act

Enacted by Congress in 1965 and renewed and expanded in 1970, 1975, and 1982, this law has sought to eliminate restrictions on voting that have been used to discriminate against blacks and other minority groups. Amendments in 1975 (1) required bilingual ballots in all states; (2) required approval by the Justice Department or a federal court of any election law changes in states covered by the act; (3) extended legal protection of voting rights to Hispanic Americans, Asian Americans, and Native Americans. The 1982 act provides that *intent* to discriminate need not be proven if the *results* demonstrate otherwise. Although the 1982 extension does not require racial quotas for city councils, school boards, or state legislatures, a judge may under the law redraw voting districts to give minorities maximum representation.

THINK AGAIN

Does the U.S. Constitution require the government to be color blind with respect to different races in all its laws and actions?

representation and taxation; it also prohibited any federal restriction on the importation of slaves until 1808. Article IV even guaranteed the return of escaped slaves to their owners. The Founders were aware that the practice of slavery contradicted their professed belief in "equality," and this contradiction caused them some embarrassment. Thus they avoided the word "slave" in favor of the euphemism "person held to Service or Labour" in writing the Constitution.

Supreme Court Chief Justice Roger Taney, ruling in the notorious case of *Dred Scott v. Sandford* in 1857, reflected the racism that prevailed in early America:

> They had for more than a century before been regarded as beings of an inferior order, and altogether unfit to associate with the white race, either in social or political relations; and so far inferior, that they had no rights which the white man was bound to respect; and that the negro might justly and lawfully be reduced to slavery for his benefit.[1]

Taney's decision in this case interpreted the Constitution in terms of the *original intent* of the Founders. The ruling upheld slavery and the constitutional guarantee given slave owners for the return of slaves escaping to nonslave states.

Emancipation and Reconstruction A growing number of Americans, especially members of the **abolition movement**, disagreed with Taney. In 1860 internal party divisions over the slavery issue led to a four-way race for the presidency and the election of Abraham Lincoln. Although personally opposed to slavery, Lincoln had promised during the campaign not to push for abolition of slavery where it existed. Many southerners were unconvinced, however, and on December 20, 1860 (three months before Lincoln's inauguration), South Carolina became the first state to secede from the Union, touching off the Civil War.

The Civil War was the nation's bloodiest war. (Combined deaths of Union and Confederate forces matched the nation's losses in World War II, even though the nation's population in 1860 was only 31 million compared to 140 million during World War II.) Very few families during the Civil War did not experience a direct loss from that conflict. As casualties mounted, northern Republicans joined abolitionists in calling for emancipating, or freeing, the slaves simply to punish the Rebels. They knew that much of the South's power depended on slave labor. Lincoln also knew that if he proclaimed the war was being fought to free the slaves, military intervention by the British on behalf of the South was less likely. Accordingly, on September 22, 1862, Lincoln issued his **Emancipation Proclamation**. Claiming his right as Commander-in-Chief of the army and navy, he declared that, as of January 1, 1863, "all persons held as slaves within any State, or designated part of a State, the people whereof shall then be in rebellion against the United States, shall be then, thenceforward, and forever free." The Emancipation Proclamation did not come about as a result of demands by the people. It was a political and military action by the president intended to help preserve the Union.

The Emancipation Proclamation freed slaves in the seceding states, and the Thirteenth Amendment in 1865 abolished slavery everywhere in the nation. But freedom did not mean civil rights. The post–Civil War Republican Congress attempted to "reconstruct" southern society. The Fourteenth Amendment, ratified in 1868, made "equal protection of the laws" a command for every state to obey The Fifteenth Amendment, passed in 1869 and ratified in 1870, prohibited federal and state governments from abridging the right to vote "on account of race, color, or previous condition of servitude." In addition, Congress passed a series of civil rights laws in the 1860s and 1870s guaranteeing the newly freed slaves protection in the exercise of their constitutional rights. Between 1865 and the early 1880s, the success of Reconstruction was evident in widespread black voting throughout the South, the presence of many blacks in federal and state offices, and the admission of blacks to theaters, restaurants, hotels, and public transportation.[2]

The Imposition of Segregation But political support for Reconstruction policies soon began to erode. In the Compromise of 1877, the national

abolition movement Social movement before the Civil War whose goal was to abolish slavery throughout the United States.

Emancipation Proclamation Lincoln's 1862 Civil War declaration that all slaves residing in rebel states were free. It did not abolish all slavery; that would be done by the Thirteenth Amendment in 1865.

The Thirteenth, Fourteenth, and Fifteenth Amendments to the Constitution, as well as other legislation passed during Reconstruction, opened the ballot box and access to political office to the freedmen of the South. However, these gains were soon largely reversed by Jim Crow laws and segregation.

Jim Crow   Second-class-citizen status conferred on blacks by southern segregation laws; derived from a nineteenth-century song-and-dance act (usually performed by a white man in blackface) that stereotyped blacks

separate but equal   Ruling of the Supreme Court in the case of *Plessy v. Ferguson* (1896) to the effect that segregated facilities were legal as long as the facilities were equal.

government agreed to end military occupation of the South, give up its efforts to rearrange southern society, and lend tacit approval to white supremacy in that region. In return, the southern states pledged their support to the Union, accepted national supremacy, and agreed to permit the Republican presidential candidate, Rutherford B. Hayes, to assume the presidency, although the Democratic candidate, Samuel Tilden, had received more popular votes in the disputed election of 1876.

As white southerners regained political power and blacks lost the protection of federal forces, the Supreme Court moved to strike down Reconstruction laws. In the Civil Rights Cases of 1883, the Supreme Court declared federal civil rights laws preventing discrimination by private individuals to be unconstitutional.[3] By denying Congress the power to protect blacks from discrimination by businesses and individuals, the Court paved the way for the imposition of segregation as the prevailing social system of the South. In the 1880s and 1890s, white southerners imposed segregation in public accommodations, housing, education, employment and almost every other sector of private and public life. By 1895 most southern states had passed laws *requiring* racial segregation in education and in public accommodations. At the time, more than 90 percent of the African American population of the United States lived in these states.

Segregation became the social instrument by which African Americans were "kept in their place"—that is, denied social, economic, educational, and political equality. In many states, **Jim Crow** followed them throughout life: birth in segregated hospital wards, education in segregated schools, residence in segregated housing, employment in segregated jobs, eating in segregated restaurants, and burial in segregated graveyards. Segregation was enforced by a variety of public and private sanctions, from lynch mobs to country club admission committees. But government was the principal instrument of segregation in both the southern and the border states of the nation. (For a look at the political reactions of African Americans to segregation, see *Up Close:* "African American Politics in Historical Perspective" on page 544.)

Early Court Approval of Segregation   Segregation was imposed despite the Fourteenth Amendment's guarantee of "equal protection of the laws." In the 1896 case of *Plessy v. Ferguson*, the Supreme Court upheld state laws requiring segregation. Although segregation laws involved state action, the Court held that segregation of the races did not violate the Equal Protection Clause of the Fourteenth Amendment so long as people in each race received equal treatment. Schools and other public facilities that were **separate but equal** were constitutional, the Court ruled.

> The object of the amendment was undoubtedly to enforce the absolute equality of the two races before the law, but in the nature of things it could not have been intended to abolish distinctions based upon color, or to enforce social, as distinguished from political, equality, or a commingling of the two races upon terms unsatisfactory to either. Laws permitting, and even requiring, their separation in places where they are liable to be brought into contact do not necessarily imply the inferiority of either race to the other, and have been generally, if not universally, recognized as within the competency of the state legislatures in the exercise of their police power.[4]

The effect of this decision was to give constitutional approval to segregation; the decision was not reversed until 1954.

Equal Protection of the Laws

The initial goal of the civil rights movement was to eliminate segregation laws, especially segregation in public education. Only after this battle was well under way could the civil rights movement turn to the fight against segregation and discrimination in all sectors of American life, *private* as well as *governmental*.

The NAACP and the Legal Battle The National Association for the Advancement of Colored People (NAACP) and its Legal Defense and Education Fund led the fight to abolish lawful segregation. As chief legal counsel to the fund, Thurgood Marshall, later to become the first African American to sit on the U.S. Supreme Court, began a long legal campaign to ensure equal protection of the law for African Americans. Initially, the NAACP's strategy focused on achieving the "equal" portion of the separate-but-equal doctrine. Segregated facilities, including public schools, were seldom "equal," even with respect to physical conditions, teachers' salaries and qualifications, curricula, and other tangible factors. In other words, southern states failed to live up even to the segregationist doctrine of separate but equal. In a series of cases, Marshall and other NAACP lawyers convinced the Supreme Court to act when segregated facilities were clearly unequal. For example, the Court ordered the admission of individual blacks to white public universities where evidence indicated that separate black institutions were inferior or nonexistent.[5]

But Marshall's goal was to prove that segregation *itself* was inherently unequal whether or not facilities were equal in all tangible respects. In other words, Marshall sought a reversal of *Plessy v. Ferguson* and a ruling that separation of the races was unconstitutional. In 1952 Marshall led a team of NAACP lawyers in a suit to admit Linda Brown to the white public schools of Topeka, Kansas, one of the few segregated school systems where white and black schools were equal with respect to buildings, curricula, teachers' salaries, and other tangible factors. In choosing the *Brown* suit, the NAACP sought to prevent the Court from simply ordering the admission of black pupils because tangible facilities were not equal and to force the Court to review the doctrine of segregation itself.

Brown v. Board of Education of Topeka On May 17, 1954, the Court rendered its historic decision in the case of *Brown v. Board of Education of Topeka*:

> Segregation of white and colored children in public schools has a detrimental effect upon the colored children. The impact is greater when it has the sanction of law, for the policy of separating the races is usually interpreted as denoting the inferiority of the Negro group. A sense of inferiority affects the motivation of a child to learn. Segregation with the sanction of law, therefore, has a tendency to retard the educational and mental development of Negro children and to deprive them of some of the benefits they would receive in a racially integrated school system. Whatever may have been the extent of psychological knowledge of the time of *Plessy v. Ferguson*, this finding is amply supported by modern authority. Any language in *Plessy v. Ferguson* contrary to this source is rejected. . . . We conclude that in the field of public education the doctrine of "separate but equal" has no place. Separate educational facilities are inherently unequal.[6]

The Supreme Court decision in *Brown* was symbolically very important. Although it would be many years before any significant number of black children would attend previously all-white schools in the South, the decision by the nation's

NAACP Legal Defense Fund

Founded in 1940 by Thurgood Marshall to provide legal assistance to poor African Americans. Originally affiliated with the NAACP; now a separate organization.
www.naacpldf.org

THINK AGAIN

If a city's schools are mostly black and the surrounding suburban schools are mostly white, should busing be used to achieve a better racial balance?

Brown Matters
Chronology of *Brown vs. Board of Education*, 1957.
www.brownmatters.org

African American Politics in Historical Perspective

Many early histories of Reconstruction paid little attention to the political responses of African Americans to the imposition of segregation. But there were at least three distinct types of response: accommodation to segregation; the formation of a black protest movement and resort to legal action; and migration out of the South (to avoid some of the worst consequences of white supremacy) coupled with political mobilization of black voters in large northern cities.

Accommodation

The foremost African American advocate of accommodation to segregation was well-known educator Booker T. Washington (1856–1915). Washington enjoyed wide popularity among both white and black Americans. An adviser to two presidents (Theodore Roosevelt and William Howard Taft), he was highly respected by white philanthropists and government officials. In his famous Cotton States' Exposition speech in Atlanta in 1895, Washington assured whites that blacks were prepared to accept a separate position in society: "In all things that are purely social we can be as separate as the fingers, yet one as the hand in all things essential to mutual progress."*

Washington's hopes for black America lay in a program of self-help through education. He himself had attended Hampton Institute in Virginia, where the curriculum centered around practical trades for African Americans. Washington obtained some white philanthropic support in establishing his own Tuskegee Institute in Tuskegee, Alabama, in 1881. His first students helped build the school. Early curricula at Tuskegee emphasized immediately useful vocations, such as farming, teaching, and blacksmithing. One of Tuskegee's outstanding faculty members, George Washington Carver, researched and developed uses for southern crops. Washington urged his students to stay in the South, to acquire land, and to build homes, thereby helping to eliminate ignorance and poverty.

Protest

While Booker T. Washington was urging African Americans to make the best of segregation, a small group was organizing in support of a declaration of black resistance and protest that would later rewrite American public policy. The leader of this group was W.E.B. Du Bois (1868–1963), a historian and sociologist at Atlanta University. In 1905 Du Bois and a few other black intellectuals met in Niagara Falls, Canada, to draw up a platform intended to "assail the ears" and sear the consciences of white Americans. The Niagara Statement listed the major injustices perpetrated against African Americans since Reconstruction: the loss of voting rights, the imposition of Jim Crow laws and segregated public schools, the denial of equal job opportunities, the

Booker T. Washington

highest court stimulated black hopes and expectations. Indeed, *Brown* started the modern civil rights movement. As the African American psychologist Kenneth Clark wrote, "This [civil rights] movement would probably not have existed at all were it not for the 1954 Supreme Court school desegregation decision, which provided a tremendous boost to the morale of blacks by its clear affirmation that color is irrelevant to the rights of American citizens."[7]

W.E.B. Du Bois

existence of inhumane conditions in southern prisons, the exclusion of blacks from West Point and Annapolis, and the federal government's failure to enforce the Fourteenth and Fifteenth Amendments. Out of the Niagara meeting came the idea of a nationwide organization dedicated to fighting for African Americans, and on February 12, 1909, the one hundredth anniversary of Abraham Lincoln's birth, the National Association for the Advancement of Colored People (NAACP) was founded.

Du Bois himself was on the original board of directors of the NAACP, although a majority of the early board members and financial contributors were white. Du Bois was also the NAACP's first director of research and the editor of its magazine, *Crisis.* The NAACP began a long and eventually successful campaign to establish black rights through legal action. Over the years, this organization brought hundreds of court cases at the local, state, and federal court levels on behalf of African Americans denied their constitutional rights.

Migration and Political Mobilization

World War I provided an opportunity for restive blacks in the South to escape the worst abuses of white supremacy by migrating en masse to northern cities. Between 1916 and 1918, an estimated half-million African Americans moved north to fill the labor shortage caused by the war effort. Most arrived in big northern cities only to find more poverty and segregation, but at least they could vote, and they did not encounter laws requiring segregation in public places.

The progressive "ghettoization" of African Americans—their migration from the rural South to the urban North and their increasing concentration in central cities—had profound political, as well as social, implications. The ghetto provided an environment conducive to political mobilization. As early as 1928, African Americans in Chicago were able to elect one of their own to the U.S. House of Representatives. The election of Oscar de Priest, the first black member of Congress from the North, signaled a new turn in American urban politics by announcing to white politicians that they would have to reckon with the black vote in northern cities. The black ghettos would soon provide an important element in a new political coalition that was about to take form: the Democratic Party of Franklin Delano Roosevelt.

The increasing concentration of African Americans in large, politically competitive, "swing" states provided black voters with new political power—not only to support the Democratic Party coalition in national politics but also to elect African Americans to local public office. Today African American mayors serve, or have served, in cities as diverse as New York, Chicago, Los Angeles, Detroit, Philadelphia, Atlanta, and New Orleans.

---

*Quoted in Henry Steele Commager, ed., *The Struggle for Racial Equality* (New York: Harper & Row 1967), p. 19.

Enforcing Desegregation The *Brown* ruling struck down the laws of twenty-one states as well as congressional laws segregating the schools of the District of Columbia.[8] Such a far-reaching exercise of judicial power was bound to meet with difficulties in enforcement, and the Supreme Court was careful not to risk its own authority. It did not order immediate national desegregation but rather required state and local authorities, under the supervision of federal district courts, to proceed with "all deliberate speed" in desegregation.[9] For more than fifteen years, state and school districts in the South waged a campaign of resistance to desegregation. Delays in implementing school desegregation continued until 1969, when the Supreme Court rejected a request by Mississippi officials for further delay, declaring that all school districts were obligated to end their dual school systems "at once" and "now and hereafter" to operate only integrated schools.[10]

Busing and Racial Balancing Federal district judges enjoy wide freedom in fashioning remedies for past or present discriminatory practices by governments. If a federal district court anywhere in the United States finds that any actions by governments or school officials have contributed to racial imbalances (for example, drawing school district attendance lines that separate black and white pupils), the judge may order the adoption of a desegregation plan to overcome racial imbalances produced by official action. A large number of cities have come under federal district court orders to improve racial balances in their schools through busing.

In the important case of *Swann v. Charlotte-Mecklenburg County Board of Education* (1971), the Supreme Court upheld the following:

- The use of racial balance requirements in schools and the assignment of pupils to schools based on race.

- "Close scrutiny" by judges of schools that are predominantly of one race.

- Gerrymandering of school attendance zones as well as "clustering" or "grouping" of schools to achieve racial balance.

- Court-ordered busing of pupils to achieve racial balance.[11]

The Court was careful to note, however, that racial imbalance in schools is not itself grounds for ordering these remedies unless it is also shown that some present or past governmental action contributed to the imbalance.

De Facto Segregation However, in the absence of any past or present governmental actions contributing to racial imbalance, states and school districts are not required by the Fourteenth Amendment to integrate their schools. For example, where central-city schools are predominantly black and suburban schools are predominantly white owing to residential patterns, cross-district busing is not required unless some official action brought about these racial imbalances. Thus in 1974 the Supreme Court threw out a lower federal court order for massive busing of students between Detroit and fifty-two suburban school districts.[12] Although Detroit city schools were 70 percent black and the suburban schools almost all white, none of the area school districts segregated students within their own boundaries. This important decision means that largely black central cities surrounded by largely white suburbs will remain segregated in practice because there are not enough white students living within the city boundaries to achieve integration.

De facto segregation is more common in the northern metropolitan areas than in the South. The states with the largest percentages of African American students attending schools that have 90 to 100 percent minority enrollments are Illinois (62 percent), Michigan (60 percent), New York (57 percent), and New Jersey (54 percent). The persistence of de facto segregation, together with a renewed interest in the quality of education, has caused many civil rights organizations to focus their attention on improving the quality of schools in urban areas rather than trying to desegregate these schools.

de facto segregation Racial imbalances not directly caused by official actions but rather by residential patterns.

Although the first conflicts over integration in the public schools erupted in the segregated southern states, northern cities later became the focus of unrest over school integration. When federal judges ordered the busing of schoolchildren outside their neighborhoods in order to achieve racial balances citywide, parents and politicians in some northern cities responded with a ferocity equal to earlier southern protests. In Boston, many parents initially boycotted a busing order in 1974, refusing to send their children to school at all or establishing private schools and even attacking busloads of minority children arriving at formerly white schools.

Many school districts in the South and elsewhere have operated under federal court supervision for many years. How long should court supervision continue, and what standards are to be used in determining when desegregation has been achieved once and for all? The Rehnquist-led Supreme Court in recent years has undertaken to free some school districts from direct federal court supervision. Where the last vestiges of state-sanctioned discrimination have been removed "as far as practicable," the Supreme Court has allowed lower federal courts to dissolve racial balancing plans even though imbalances due to residential patterns may continue to exist.[13]

The Civil Rights Acts

The early goal of the civil rights movement was to eliminate discrimination and segregation practiced by *governments*, particularly states and school districts. When the civil rights movement turned to *private* discrimination—discrimination practiced by private owners of restaurants, hotels, motels, and stores; private employers, landlords, and real estate agents; and others who were not government officials—it had to take its fight to the Congress. The Constitution does not govern the activities of private individuals. Only Congress at the national level could outlaw discrimination in the private sector. Yet prior to 1964, Congress had been content to let the courts struggle with the question of civil rights. New political tactics and organizations were required to put the issue of equality on the agenda of Congress.

Martin Luther King, Jr., and Nonviolent Direct Action Leadership in the struggle to eliminate discrimination and segregation from private life was provided by a young African American minister, Martin Luther King, Jr. (see *People in Politics:* "Martin Luther King, Jr., 'I Have a Dream' "). Under King, the civil rights movement developed and refined political techniques for use by American minorities, including **nonviolent direct action**. Nonviolent direct action is a form of protest that involves breaking "unjust" laws in an open, "loving," nonviolent

The King Center
Biography of M. L. K., Jr., together with news and information from Atlanta King Center.
http://thekingcenter.com

nonviolent direct action
Strategy used by civil rights leaders such as Martin Luther King, Jr., in which protesters break "unjust" laws openly but in a "loving" fashion in order to bring the injustices of such laws to public attention.

Martin Luther King, Jr., "I Have a Dream"

"If a man hasn't discovered something he will die for, he isn't fit to live."[*]

For Martin Luther King, Jr. (1929–1968), civil rights was something to die for, and before he died for the cause, he would shatter a century of southern segregation and set a new domestic agenda for the nation's leaders. King's contributions to the development of nonviolent direct action won him international acclaim and the Nobel Peace Prize.

King's father was the pastor of one of the South's largest and most influential African American congregations, the Ebenezer Baptist Church in Atlanta, Georgia. Young Martin was educated at Morehouse College in Atlanta and received a Ph.D. in religious studies at Boston University. Shortly after beginning his career as a Baptist minister in Montgomery, Alabama, in 1955, a black woman, Rosa Parks, refused to give up her seat to whites on a Montgomery bus, setting in motion a year-long bus boycott in that city. Only twenty-six years old, King was thrust into national prominence as the leader of that boycott, which ended in the elimination of segregation on the city's buses. In 1957 King founded the Southern Christian Leadership Conference (SCLC) to provide encouragement and leadership to the growing nonviolent protest movement against segregation.

Perhaps the most dramatic application of nonviolent direct action occurred in Birmingham, Alabama, on the spring of 1963. Thousands of African Americans, ranging from schoolchildren to senior citizens, marched in protest. Although the demonstrators conducted themselves in a nonviolent fashion, police and firefighters attacked the demonstrators with fire hoses, cattle prods, and police dogs, all in clear view of national television cameras. Thousands of demonstrators were dragged off to jail, including King. (It was at this time that King wrote his "Letter from Birmingham Jail," explaining and defending nonviolent direct action.) Pictures of police brutality flashed throughout the nation and the world, touching the consciences of many white Americans.

King was also the driving force behind the most massive application of nonviolent direct action in U.S. history: the great "March on Washington" in August 1963, during which more than 200,000 black and white marchers converged on the nation's capital. The march ended at the Lincoln Memorial, where King delivered his most eloquent appeal, entitled "I Have a Dream."

> I still have a dream. It is a dream deeply rooted in the American dream. I have a dream that one day this nation will rise up and live out the true meaning of its creed: "We hold these truths to be self-evident, that all men are created equal."[†]

It was in the wake of the March on Washington that President John F. Kennedy sent to the Congress a strong civil rights bill that would be passed after his death—the Civil Rights Act of 1964. That same year, King received the Nobel Peace Prize.

White racial violence in the early 1960s, including murders and bombings of black and white civil rights workers, shocked and disgusted many whites in both the North and the South. In 1963 Medgar Evers, the NAACP's state chair for Mississippi, was shot to death by a sniper as he entered his Jackson home. That same year, a bomb killed four young black girls attending Sunday school in Birmingham. On the evening of April 3, 1968, King spoke to a crowd in Memphis, Tennessee, in eerily prophetic terms. "I just want to do God's will. And He's allowed me to go to the mountain. And I've looked over, and I've seen the promised land. I may not get there with you. But I want you to know tonight, that we, as a people will get to the promised land. So I'm happy tonight. I'm not worried about anything. I'm not fearing any man." On the night of April 4, 1968, the world's leading exponent of nonviolence was killed by an assassin's bullet.[‡]

---

[*]Martin Luther King, Jr., speech, June 23, 1963, Detroit, Michigan.

[†]Martin Luther King, Jr., "I Have a Dream" speech, August 28, 1963, at the Lincoln Memorial, Washington, D.C., printed in David J. Garrow, *Bearing the Cross: Martin Luther King, Jr., and the Southern Christian Leadership Conference* (New York: Vintage Books, 1988), pp. 283–84.

[‡]Martin Luther King, Jr., speech, April 3, 1968, Memphis, Tennessee, ibid., p. 621.

fashion. The purpose of nonviolent direct action is to call attention—to "bear witness"—to the existence of injustice. In the words of Martin Luther King, Jr., such civil disobedience "seeks to dramatize the issue so that it can no longer be ignored"[14] (see also *A Conflicting View:* "Sometimes It's Right to Disobey the Law" in Chapter 1).

King formed the Southern Christian Leadership Conference (SCLC) in 1957 to develop and direct the growing nonviolent direct action movement. During the next few years, the SCLC overshadowed the older NAACP in leading the fight against segregation. Where the NAACP had developed its strategy of court litigation to combat discrimination by *governments*, now the SCLC developed nonviolent direct action tactics to build widespread popular support and to pressure Congress to outlaw discrimination by *private businesses*.

The year 1963 was perhaps the most important for nonviolent direct action. The SCLC focused its efforts in Birmingham, Alabama, where King led thousands of marchers in a series of orderly and peaceful demonstrations. When police attacked the marchers with fire hoses, dogs, and cattle prods—in full view of national television cameras—millions of viewers around the country came to understand the injustices of segregation. The Birmingham action set off demonstrations in many parts of the country. The theme remained one of nonviolence, and it was usually whites rather than blacks who resorted to violence in these demonstrations. Responsible black leaders remained in control of the movement and won widespread support from the white community.

The culmination of King's nonviolent philosophy was a huge yet orderly march on Washington, D.C., held on August 28, 1963. More than 200,000 blacks and whites participated in the march, which was endorsed by many civic leaders, religious groups, and political figures. The march ended at the Lincoln Memorial, where Martin Luther King, Jr., delivered his most eloquent appeal, entitled "I Have a Dream." Congress passed the Civil Rights Act of 1964 by better than a two-thirds favorable vote in both houses; it won the overwhelming support of both Republican and Democratic members of Congress.

In the civil rights march of 1963 more than 200,000 people marched peacefully on Washington, D.C., to end segregation. It was here that Martin Luther King, Jr., delivered his famous "I Have a Dream" speech.

The Civil Rights Act of 1964 Signed into law on July 4, 1964, the Civil Rights Act of 1964 ranks with the Emancipation Proclamation, the Fourteenth Amendment, and the *Brown* case as one of the most important steps toward full equality for African Americans. Among its most important provisions are the following:

Title II: It is unlawful to discriminate or segregate persons on the grounds of race, color, religion, or national origin in any public accommodation, including hotels, motels, restaurants, movies, theaters, sports arenas, entertainment houses, and other places that offer to serve the public. This prohibition extends to all business establishments whose operations affect interstate commerce or whose discriminatory practices are supported by state action.

Title VI: Each federal department and agency is to take action to end discrimination in all programs or activities receiving federal financial assistance in any form. This action may include termination of financial assistance to persistently discriminatory agencies.

Title VII: It is unlawful for any employer or labor union to discriminate against any individual in any fashion in employment because of the individual's race, color, religion, sex, or national origin. The Equal Employment Opportunity Commission is established to enforce this provision by investigation, conference, conciliation, persuasion, and, if need be, civil action in federal court.

The Civil Rights Act of 1968 For many years "fair housing" had been considered the most sensitive area of civil rights legislation. Prospects for a fair housing law were poor at the beginning of 1968. However, when Martin Luther King, Jr., was assassinated on April 4, the mood of Congress and the nation changed dramatically. Congress passed a fair housing law as tribute to the slain civil rights leader. The Civil Rights Act of 1968 prohibited discrimination in the sale or rental of a dwelling to any person on the basis of race, color, religion, or national origin.

Equality: Opportunity Versus Results

Although the gains of the civil rights movement were immensely important, these gains were primarily in *opportunity* rather than in *results*. The civil rights movement of the 1960s did not bring about major changes in the conditions under which most African Americans lived in the United States. Racial politics today center around the *actual* inequalities between blacks and whites in incomes, jobs, housing, health, education, and other conditions of life.

Continuing Inequalities The issue of inequality today is often posed as differences in the "life chances" of blacks and whites. Figures can reveal only the bare outline of an African American's "life chances" in this society (see Table 15.2). The average income of a black family is 62 percent of the average white family's income. Over 20 percent of all black families live below the recognized poverty line, whereas less than 10 percent of white families do so. The black unemployment rate is more than twice as high as the white unemployment rate. Blacks are less likely to hold prestigious executive jobs in professional, managerial, clerical, or sales work. They do not hold many skilled craft jobs in industry but are concentrated in operative, service, and laboring positions. The civil rights movement opened up new opportunities for African Americans. But equality of *opportunity* is not the same as equality of *results*.

U.S. Department of Justice, Civil Rights Division

Responsible for enforcement of U.S. civil rights laws. Site includes information on cases. *www.usdoj.gov/crt*

U.S. Commission on Civil Rights

National clearinghouse on information regarding discrimination because of race, color, religion, sex, age, disability, or national origin. Publishes reports, findings and recommendations. *www.usccr.gov*

TABLE 15.2 Minority Life Chances

Median Income of Families

	1970	1975	1980	1985	2002
White	$10,236	$14,268	$21,904	$29,152	$46,900
Black	6,279	8,779	12,674	16,786	29,026
Hispanic	(NA)	9,551	14,716	19,027	33,103

Percentage of Persons below Poverty Level

	1975	1980	1985	2002
White	9.7%	10.2%	11.4%	10.3%
Black	31.3	32.5	31.3	24.1
Hispanic	26.9	25.7	29.0	21.8

Unemployment Rate

	1980	1985	2003
White	6.3%	6.2%	4.9%
Black	14.3	15.1	9.9
Hispanic	10.1	10.5	6.5

Education: Percentage of Persons over Twenty-Five Completing High School

	1960	1970	1980	1990	2000
White	43%	55%	69%	79%	85%
Black	20	31	51	66	79
Hispanic	(NA)	32	44	51	57

Education: Percentage of Persons over Twenty-Five Completing College

	1960	1970	1980	1990	2000
White	8%	11%	17%	22%	26%
Black	3	4	8	11	17
Hispanic	(NA)	4	8	9	11

Source: Statistical Abstract of the United States, various issues; U.S. Census Bureau, *Income in the United States* 2002. Washington: Government Printing Office, 2003.

Explaining Inequalities African American and Hispanic minorities have improved their economic condition in recent years. However, the income *disparity* between whites and minorities has remained about the same. Note that in 1970 black median family income was approximately 61 percent of white median family income, almost the same percentage as in 2000. This income gap remains despite a significant narrowing of differences in educational levels between whites and minorities.

Much, but certainly not all, of the disparity in income between whites and minorities disappears when educational levels are taken into account. Comparing the income of whites and minorities *at same educational levels* suggests that some discrimination may remain. Black college graduates on average earn about 77 percent of the income of white college graduates; black high school graduates earn about 80 percent of the income of white high school graduates. The average income of

THINK AGAIN

Are differences between blacks and whites in average income mainly a product of discrimination?

TABLE 15.3 White and Minority Income by Educational Attainment

		Annual Mean Income			
	White	**Black**	**Hispanic**	**Black/White Ratio**	**Hispanic/White Ratio**
Graduate Degree	$52,475	$40,610	$46,556	77%	89%
Bachelor's Degree	41,439	32,062	33,465	77	81
High School Degree	23,618	18,930	19,558	80	81
No High School Degree	16,596	13,185	15,069	79	91

Source: U.S. Bureau of the Census, 2000. Data for 1998.

Hispanics is even closer to that of whites at the same educational levels. But neither African Americans nor Hispanics earn the same income as whites with the same educational background (see Table 15.3).

Policy Choices What public policies should be pursued to achieve equality in America? Is it sufficient that government eliminate discrimination, guarantee equality of opportunity, and apply color-blind standards to both blacks and whites? Or should government take **affirmative action** to overcome the results of past unequal treatment of blacks—preferential or compensatory treatment to assist black applications for university admissions and scholarships, job hiring and promotion, and other opportunities for advancement in life?

Shifting Goals in Civil Rights Policy For decades, the emphasis of government policy was on equal *opportunity*. This early nondiscrimination approach began with President Harry Truman's decision to desegregate the armed forces in 1948 and carried through to Title VI and Title VII of the Civil Rights Act of 1964, which eliminated discrimination in federally aided projects and private employment. Gradually, however, the goal of the civil rights movement shifted from the traditional aim of equality of opportunity through nondiscrimination alone to affirmative action involving the establishment of "goals and timetables" to achieve greater equality of results between blacks and whites. While avoiding the term **quota**, the notion of affirmative action tests the success of equal opportunity by observing whether blacks achieve admissions, jobs, and promotions in proportion to their numbers in the population.

Affirmative Action Affirmative action programs were initially developed in the federal bureaucracy. Federal executive agencies were authorized by the Civil Rights Act of 1964 to develop "rules and regulations" for desegregating any organization or business receiving federal funds. In 1965 President Lyndon B. Johnson signed Executive Order 11246, requiring all federal agencies and businesses contracting with the federal government to practice affirmative action. In 1972 the U.S. Office of Education issued guidelines that mandated "goals" for university admissions and faculty hiring of minorities and women. The Equal Employment Opportunity Commission (EEOC), established by the Civil Rights Act of 1964, is responsible for monitoring affirmative action programs in private employment.

Federal officials generally measure "progress" in affirmative action in terms of the number of disadvantaged group members admitted, employed, or promoted. The

affirmative action Any program, whether enacted by a government or by a private organization, whose goal is to overcome the results of past unequal treatment of minorities and/or women by giving members of these groups preferential treatment in admissions, hiring, promotions, or other aspects of life.

quota Provision of some affirmative action programs in which specific numbers or percentages of positions are open only to minorities and/or women.

 Equal Employment Opportunity Commission

Federal EEOC site with information on what constitutes discrimination by age, disability, race, ethnicity, religion, gender; how to file a charge; and guidance for employers. *www.eeoc.gov*

Harvard University's graduating class is racially diversified. The nation's most prestigious colleges and universities actively recruit quality minority students. While these graduates can look forward to high rewards, on average throughout the nation minority college graduates do not earn the same income as nonminority college graduates.

pressure to show "progress" can result in relaxation of traditional measures of qualifications, such as test scores and educational achievement. Advocates of affirmative action argue that these measures are not good predictors of performance on the job or in school and are biased in favor of white culture. State and local governments, schools, colleges and universities, and private employers are under pressure to revise these standards.

Affirmative Action in the Courts

The constitutional question posed by affirmative action programs is whether or not they discriminate against whites in violation of the Equal Protection Clause of the Fourteenth Amendment. A related question is whether or not affirmative action programs discriminate against whites in violation of the Civil Rights Act of 1964, which prohibits discrimination "on account of race," not just discrimination against blacks. Clearly, these are questions for the Supreme Court to resolve.

The Bakke Case In the absence of a history of racial discrimination, the Supreme Court has been willing to scrutinize affirmative action programs to ensure that they do not directly discriminate against whites. In *University of California Regents v. Bakke* (1978), the Supreme Court struck down a special admissions program for minorities at a state medical school on the grounds that it excluded a white applicant because of his race and violated his rights under the Equal Protection Clause.[15] Allan Bakke applied to the University of California Davis Medical School two consecutive years and was rejected; in both years, black applicants with significantly lower grade point averages and medical aptitude test scores were accepted through a special admissions program that reserved sixteen minority places in a class of one hundred.[16] The University of California did not deny that its admissions decisions were based on race. Instead, it argued that its racial classification was "benign," that is, designed to assist minorities. The special admissions program was designed to (1) "reduce the historical deficit of traditionally disfavored minorities in medical schools and the medical profession"; (2) "counter the effects

Do you generally favor affirmative action programs for women and minorities?

The Reverend Jesse Jackson leads a group of marchers protesting California's anti-affirmative action policies. Pictured alongside Jackson are radio personality Kasey Kasem and Delores Huerta, co-founder of the United Farm Workers' Union.

of societal discrimination"; (3) "increase the number of physicians who will practice in communities currently underserved"; and (4) "obtain the educational benefits that flow from an ethnically diverse student body."

The Supreme Court held that these objectives were legitimate and that race and ethnic origin *may* be considered in reviewing applications to a state school without violating the Fourteenth Amendment's Equal Protection Clause. However, the Court also held that a separate admissions program for minorities with a specific quota of openings which were unavailable to white applicants *did* violate the Equal Protection Clause. The Court ordered the university to admit Bakke to its medical school and to eliminate the special admissions program. It recommended that California consider an admissions program developed at Harvard, which considered disadvantaged racial or ethnic background as a "plus" in an overall evaluation of an application but did not set numerical quotas or exclude any person from competing for all positions.

Reaction to the decision was predictable: supporters of affirmative action emphasized the Supreme Court's willingness to allow minority status to be considered a positive factor; opponents emphasized the Supreme Court's unwillingness to allow quotas that exclude whites from competing for some positions. Because **Bakke** had "won" the **case**, many observers felt that the Supreme Court was not going to permit racial quota systems.

Affirmative Action as a Remedy for Past Discrimination

The Supreme Court has continued to approve of affirmative action programs where there is evidence of past discriminatory practices. In *United Steelworkers of America v. Weber* (1979), the Supreme Court approved a plan developed by a private employer and a union to reserve 50 percent of higher paying, skilled jobs for minorities. The Court held that "employers and unions in the private sector [are] free to take such race-conscious steps to eliminate manifest racial imbalances in traditionally segregated job categories. We hold that Title VII does not prohibit such . . . affirmative action plans." According to the Court, it would be "ironic indeed" if the Civil Rights Act were used to prohibit voluntary private race-conscious efforts to over-come the past effects of discrimination.[17] In *United States v. Paradise* (1987), the Court upheld a rigid 50 percent black quota system for promotions in the Alabama Department of Safety, which had excluded blacks from the ranks of state troopers prior to 1972 and had not promoted any blacks higher than corporal prior to 1984. In a 5 to 4 decision, the majority stressed the long history of discrimination in the agency as a reason for upholding the quota system. Whatever burdens imposed on innocent parties were outweighed by the need to correct the effects of past discrimination.[18]

Cases Questioning Affirmative Action

However, the Supreme Court has continued to express concern about whites who are directly and adversely affected by government action solely because of their race. In *Firefighters Local Union 1784 v. Stotts* (1984), the Court ruled that a city could not lay off white fire fighters in favor of black fire fighters with less seniority.[19] In *City of Richmond v. Crosen Co.* (1989), the Supreme Court held that a minority **set-aside program** in Richmond, Virginia, which mandated that 30 percent of all city construction contracts must go to "blacks, Spanish-speaking, Orientals, Indians, Eskimos, or Aleuts," violated the Equal Protection Clause of the Fourteenth Amendment.[20]

Moreover, the Court has held that racial classifications in law must be subject to "strict scrutiny." This means that race-based actions by government—any disparate treatment of the races by federal, state, or local public agencies—must be

Bakke case U.S. Supreme Court case challenging affirmative action.

set-aside program Program in which a specified number or percentage of contracts must go to designated minorities.

found necessary to remedy past proven discrimination, or to further clearly identified, legitimate and "compelling" government interests. Moreover, race-based actions must be "narrowly tailored" and "least restrictive" so as to minimize adverse effects on rights of other individuals. In striking down a federal construction contract set-aside program for small businesses owned by racial minorities, the Court expressed skepticism about governmental racial classifications: "There is simply no way of determining what classifications are 'benign' and 'remedial' and what classifications are in fact motivated by illegitimate notions of racial inferiority or simple racial politics."[21]

Affirmative Action in the Workplace The Civil Rights Act of 1964, Title VII, bars racial or sexual discrimination in employment. But how can persons who feel they have been passed over for jobs or promotions go about the task of proving that discrimination was involved? Evidence of direct discrimination is often difficult to obtain. Can underrepresentation of minorities or women in a work force be used as evidence of discrimination in the absence of any evidence of direct discriminatory practices? If an employer uses a requirement or test that has a disparate effect on minorities or women, who has the burden of proof of showing that the requirement or test is relevant to effective job performance?

The Supreme Court responded to both of these questions in its interpretation of the Civil Rights Act in *Wards Cove Packing Co., Inc. v. Antonio* in 1989.[22] In a controversial 5 to 4 decision, the Court held that statistical imbalances in race or gender in the workplace were not sufficient evidence by themselves to prove discrimination. And the Court ruled it was up to plaintiffs to prove that an employer had no business reason for requirements or tests which had an adverse impact on minorities or women. This decision clearly made it more difficult to prove job discrimination.

Civil rights groups were highly critical of what they regarded as the Supreme Court's "narrowing" of the Civil Rights Act protections in employment. They turned to Congress to rewrite portions of the Civil Rights Act to "restore" these protections. Business lobbies, however, believed that accepting statistical imbalances as evidence of discrimination or that shifting the burden of proof to employers would result in hiring by "quotas" simply to avoid lawsuits. After nearly two years of negotiations on Capitol Hill and a reversal of President George Bush's initial opposition, Congress produced the Civil Rights and Women's Equity Act of 1991. Among the more important provisions of the act were these:

■ *Statistical imbalances:* The mere existence of statistical imbalance in an employer's work force is not, by itself, sufficient evidence to prove discrimination. However, statistical imbalances may be evidence of employment practices (rules, requirements, academic qualifications, tests) that have a "disparate impact" on minorities or women.

■ *Disparate employment practices:* Employers bear the burden of proof that any practice which has a "disparate impact" is necessary and has "a significant and manifest relationship to the requirements for effective job performance."

Affirmative Action and "Diversity" in Higher Education

Most colleges and universities in United States—public as well as private—identify "diversity," a term that refers to racial and ethnic representation in the student body and faculty, as an institutional goal.

University administrators argue that students benefit when they interact with others from different cultural heritages. "Students must be engaged with diverse peers if we expect learning and development to occur," and the existence of a racially and ethnically diverse student body is "a necessary condition" for such engagement. There is some evidence that students admitted under policies designed to increase diversity do well in their post-college careers. And there are claims that racial and ethnic diversity on the campus improve students' "self-evaluation," "social-historical thinking," and "intellectual engagement."

But despite numerous efforts to develop scientific evidence that racial or ethnic diversity on the campus improves learning no definitive conclusions have emerged. Educational research on this topic is clouded by political and ideological conflict. There is no evidence that racial diversity does in fact promote the expression of ideas on the campus or change perspectives or viewpoints of students.

Diversity and Affirmative Action Even if diversity provides educational benefits, the question arises as to how to achieve it. Diversity is closely linked to affirmative action programs on campuses throughout the nation. When affirmative action programs are designed as special efforts to recruit and encourage qualified minority students to attend college, they enjoy widespread public support. But when affirmative action programs include preferences for minority applicants over equally or better qualified nonminorities, public support falters and constitutional questions arise.

Diversity as a Constitutional Question The U.S. Supreme Court has held that the Equal Protection Clause of the Fourteenth Amendment requires that racial classifications be subject to "strict scrutiny." This means that race-based actions by governments—any disparate treatment of the racial or ethnic group by federal, state, or local public agencies, including colleges and universities—must be found necessary to advance a "compelling government interest" and must be "narrowly tailored" to further that interest.[23]

The U.S. Supreme Court held in 2003 that diversity may be a compelling government interest because it "promotes cross-racial understanding, helps to break down racial stereotypes, and enables [students] to better understand persons of different races." This opinion was written by Justice Sandra Day O'Connor in a case involving the University of Michigan Law School's affirmative action program. In a 5–4 decision, O'Connor, writing for the majority, said the Constitution "does not prohibit the law school's narrowly tailored use of race in admissions decisions to further a compelling interests in obtaining the educational benefits that flow from a diverse student body."[24]

However, in a case involving the University of Michigan's affirmative action program for undergraduate admissions, the Supreme Court held that the admissions policy was "not narrowly tailored to achieve respondents' asserted interest in diversity" and therefore violated the Equal Protection Clause of the Fourteenth Amendment. The Court again recognized that diversity may be a compelling interest, but rejected an affirmative action plan that made race the decisive factor for even minimally qualified minority applicants. Yet the Supreme Court restated its support for limited affirmative action programs that use race as a "plus" factor, the position the court has held since the *Bakke* case in 1978.[25]

Race-Neutral Approaches to Diversity There is a variety of ways in which diversity can be achieved without using racial preferences in the admission of students. The U.S. Department of Education recommends (1) preferences based on

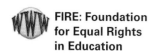

FIRE: Foundation for Equal Rights in Education

Advocacy organization defending individual rights on campus and opposing racial preferences.
www.thefire.org

socioeconomic status; (2) recruitment outreach efforts targeted at students from traditionally low-performing schools; and (3) the admission plans for students to finish at the top of their high school classes without regard to SAT or ACT scores.[26] California, Texas, and Florida currently give preference to students who stand at or near the top of their class in each of the states' high schools. All three states officially abandoned racial preferences. Yet currently all three states enroll roughly the same numbers of minorities in their colleges and universities that they did before abandoning racial preferences.

The Absence of a Clear Constitutional Principle The Supreme Court's decisions on affirmative action have not yet established a clear and coherent interpretation of the Constitution. No clear rule of law or constitutional principle tells us exactly what is permissible and what is prohibited in the way of racially conscious laws and practices. Nevertheless, over time some general tendencies in Supreme Court policy can be identified. Affirmative action programs are *more likely to be found constitutional* when:

■ They are adopted in response to a past proven history of discrimination.

■ They do not absolutely bar whites or ban them from competing or participating.

■ They serve a clearly identified, legitimate, and "compelling governmental interest."

■ They are "narrowly tailored" to achieve the government's compelling interest and represent the "least restrictive" means of doing so.

It is important to note that the Supreme Court has never adopted the color-blind doctrine, first espoused by Justice Harlan in his *dissent* from *Plessy v. Ferguson,* that "Our Constitution is color-blind, and neither knows nor tolerates classes among the citizens." If the Equal Protection Clause required the laws of the United States and the states to be truly color-blind, then no racial guidelines, goals, or quotas would be tolerated. Occasionally this view has been expressed in recent minority dissents (see *A Conflicting View:* "The Constitution Should Be Color-blind").

The California Civil Rights Initiative National rethinking of affirmative action was inspired by a citizen's initiative placed on the ballot in California by popular petition and approved by 54 percent of the state's voters in 1996. The California Civil Rights Initiative added the following phrase to that state's constitution:

> Neither the state of California nor any of its political subdivisions or agents shall use race, sex, color, ethnicity or national origin as a criterion for either discriminating against, or granting preferential treatment to, any individual or group in the operation of the State's system of public employment, public education or public contracting.[27]

The key words are "or granting preferential treatment to . . . ." Opponents argued that a constitutional ban on preferential treatment of minorities and women eliminates affirmative action programs in government, prevents governments from acting to correct historic racial or gender imbalances, and denies minorities and women the opportunity to seek legal protections in education and employment. Opponents challenged the California Civil Rights Initiative in federal courts arguing that by preventing minorities and women from seeking preferential treatment under law, the initiative violated the Equal Protection Clause of the Fourteenth

Demonstrators at the Florida state capitol in Tallahassee chant "Shame on Bush" over Governor Jeb Bush's effort to ban racial preferences in university admissions and state contracting.

The Constitution Should Be Color-Blind

In 1896 a single voice spoke out against *all* racial classifications—Supreme Court Justice John Harlan opposing segregation: "Our Constitution is color-blind and neither knows nor tolerates classes among the citizens." He was *dissenting* from the Supreme Court's majority opinion in the infamous case of *Plessy v. Ferguson,* which approved the segregationist doctrine of "separate but equal." Unfortunately, the ideal of a color-blind society remains almost as elusive today as it was more than a hundred years ago.

Martin Luther King, Jr., had a dream that "our children will one day live in a nation where they will not be judged by the color of their skin but by the content of their character." Can that dream be made a reality?

Over time, the civil rights movement shifted its focus from *individual rights* to *group benefits.* Affirmative action programs classify people by group membership, thereby challenging a belief widely held in the United States—that people be judged on individual attributes like character and achievement, rather than on race or gender. Racial and gender preferences are currently encountered in hiring and promotion practices in private and public employment and in college in university admissions, scholarships, and faculty recruitment.

Affirmative action programs divide Americans into two classes—those who enjoy legally mandated preferential treatment and those who do not. Majority support for civil rights laws is weakening under growing resentment among those who are denied preferential treatment.

Some early supporters of affirmative action have come to view race-conscious programs as no longer necessary. They argue that disadvantages in society today are based more on class than on race. If preferences are to be granted at all, in their view, they should be based on economic disadvantage, not race.

Misgivings also have been expressed by a few African American scholars about the unfair stigmatizing of the supposed beneficiaries of affirmative action—a resulting negative stereotyping of blacks as unable to advance on merit alone. Race-conscious government policies, they argue, have done more harm than good. African American economist Glenn Loury claims that proponents of affirmative action have an inferiority complex: "When blacks say we have to have affirmative action, please don't take it away from us, it's almost like saying, you're right, we can't compete on merit. But I know that we can compete." Conservative columnist William Bennett says that "toxic" race relations, aggravated by affirmative action, have led to damaging forms of new segregation: "Affirmative action has not brought us what we want—a color-blind society. It has brought us an extremely color-conscious society. In our universities we have separate dorms, separate social centers. What's next—water fountains? That's not good and everybody knows it."

Many argue that affirmative action has caused the civil rights movement to lose widespread public support and instead become contentious and divisive. In fact, civil rights has become such a hot topic that most elected officials now prefer to avoid it. As one anonymous member of Congress put it, "The problem is political correctness—you can't talk openly."

Source: Quotations reported in *Newsweek,* February 13, 1996.

Amendment. But a Circuit Court of Appeals held, and the U.S. Supreme Court affirmed that "[A] ban on race or gender preferences, as a matter of law or logic does not violate the Equal Protection Clause in any conventional sense. . . Impediments to preferential treatment do not deny equal protection."[28] The Court reasoned that the Constitution allows some race-based preferences to correct past discrimination, but it does not prevent states from banning racial preferences altogether.

The California citizens initiative barring racial and gender preferences has inspired similar movements in other states. In 1998 voters in the state of Washington adopted a similarly worded state constitutional amendment by a large margin. In 2000 Florida's Governor Jeb Bush issued an executive order banning racial preference in state contracting and university admissions.

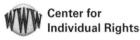

Center for Individual Rights
Advocacy organization opposing racial preferences.
www.cir-usa.org

Hispanics in America

Hispanics—a term the U.S. Census Bureau uses to refer to Mexican Americans, Puerto Ricans, Cubans, and others of Spanish-speaking ancestry and culture—are now the nation's largest minority (see Table 15.4). The largest Hispanic subgroup is Mexican Americans. Some are descendants of citizens who lived in the Mexican territory annexed to the United States in 1848, but most have come to the United States in accelerating numbers in recent years. The largest Mexican American populations are found in Texas, Arizona, New Mexico, and California. Puerto Ricans constitute the second largest Hispanic subgroup. Many still retain ties to the commonwealth and move back and forth from Puerto Rico to New York. Cubans make up the third largest subgroup; most have fled from Fidel Castro's Cuba and live mainly in the Miami metropolitan area. Each of these Hispanic groups has encountered a different experience in American life. Indeed, some evidence indicates that these groups identify themselves separately, rather than as Hispanics.[29]

If all Hispanics are grouped together for statistical comparisons, their median family income level is well below that of whites (see Table 15.2). Hispanic poverty and unemployment rates are also higher than those of whites. The percentage of Hispanics completing high school and college education is well below that of both whites and blacks, suggesting language or other cultural obstacles in education. Yet within these overall racial comparisons, there are wide disparities among subgroups as well as among individuals.

Mexican Americans The Mexican American population in the southwestern United States is growing very rapidly; it doubled in size between 1980 and 1990. For many years, agricultural business encouraged immigration of Mexican farm laborers willing to endure harsh conditions for low pay. Many others came to the United States as *indocumentados*—undocumented, or illegal, aliens. In the Immigration Reform Act of 1986 Congress offered amnesty to all undocumented workers who had entered the United States prior to 1982.

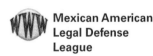

Mexican American Legal Defense League

Advocacy and litigation on behalf of Latinos, with information on cases dealing with immigration rights.
www.maldef.org

Economic conditions in Mexico and elsewhere in Central America continue to fuel immigration, legal and illegal, to the United States. But with lower educational levels, average incomes of Mexican American families in the United States are lower and the poverty rate is higher than the general population. Although Mexican Americans have served as governors of Arizona and New Mexico and

TABLE 15.4   Minorities in America, 2000

	Number	Percentage of Population
African Americans	34,658,000	12.3
Hispanic Americans	35,306,000	12.5
Asian or Pacific Islander Americans	10,643,000	3.7
Native Americans, Eskimos, Aleuts	2,476,000	0.9
Total Population	281,422,000	100.0*

*In the 2000 census, for the first time, some people were recognized as "two or more races" (2.4%).

Source: Census of Population, 2000.

have won election to the U.S. Congress, their political power does not yet match their population percentages. Mexican American voter turnout is lower than other ethnic groups, perhaps because many are resident aliens or illegal immigrants not eligible to vote, or perhaps because of cultural factors that discourage political participation.[30]

Puerto Ricans Residents of Puerto Rico are American citizens because Puerto Rico is a commonwealth of the United States. Puerto Rico's commonwealth government resembles that of a state, with a constitution and elected governor and legislature, but the island has no voting members of the U.S. Congress and no electoral votes for president. As citizens, Puerto Ricans can move anywhere in the United States; many have immigrated to New York City.

Median family income in Puerto Rico is higher than anywhere else in the Caribbean but only half that of the poorest state in the United States. Puerto Ricans have not fared as well economically as other Hispanic groups within the United States: Puerto Ricans have lower median family incomes and higher poverty percentages, in part perhaps because of lower work force participation. One explanation centers on the history of access to federal welfare programs on the island and the resulting social dependency it fostered among some Puerto Rican families.[31]

Puerto Ricans have long debated whether to remain a commonwealth of the United States, apply for statehood, or seek complete independence from the United States. As citizens of a commonwealth, Puerto Ricans pay no U.S. income tax (although their local taxes are substantial) while receiving all the benefits that U.S. citizens are entitled to—Social Security, welfare assistance, food stamps, Medicaid, Medicare, and so forth. If Puerto Rico chose to become a state, its voters could participate in presidential and congressional elections, but its taxpayers would not enjoy the same favorable cost-benefit ratio they enjoy under commonwealth status. Some Puerto Ricans also fear that statehood would dilute the island's cultural identity and force English on them as the national language.

As a state, Puerto Rico would have two U.S. senators and perhaps six U.S. representatives. The island's majority party, the Popular Democratic Party, is closely identified with the Democratic Party, so most of these new members would likely be Democrats. But the island's New Progressive Party, identified with the Republican Party, supports statehood, and many GOP leaders believe their party should appeal to Hispanic voters. If Puerto Ricans were to choose independence, a new constitution for the Republic of Puerto Rico would be drawn up by the islanders themselves.

Only Congress can admit a new state, but Congress is unlikely to act without the full support of Puerto Ricans themselves. Several nonbinding referenda votes have been held in Puerto Rico over the years, the most recent in 1998. Opinion today appears to be closely divided, with commonwealth status edging out statehood by a small margin; independence has never received more than one percent of the vote.

Cuban Americans Many Cuban Americans, especially those in the early waves of refugees from Castro's revolution in 1959, were skilled professionals and businesspeople, and they rapidly set about building Miami into a thriving economy. Although Cuban Americans are the smallest of the Hispanic subgroups, today they are better educated and enjoy higher incomes than the others. They are well organized politically, and they have succeeded in electing Cuban Americans to local office in Florida and to the U.S. Congress.

Hispanic Politics

Mexican Americans constitute the largest portion, nearly three-quarters, of the nation's Hispanic population. Most reside in the southwestern United States— California, Texas, Arizona, New Mexico, and Colorado. Puerto Ricans in New York, and Cubans and other Central and South Americans in Florida, constitute only about one-quarter of the Hispanic population. Thus, generalizations about Hispanic politics are heavily influenced by Mexican Americans.

Organizing for Political Activity For many decades American agriculture encouraged Mexican American immigration, both legal and illegal, to labor in fields as *braceros*. Most of these migrant farm workers lived and worked under very difficult conditions; they were paid less than minimum wages for backbreaking labor. Farm workers were not covered by the federal National Labor Relations Act and therefore not protected in the right to organize labor unions. But civil rights activity among Hispanics, especially among farm workers, grew during the 1960s under the leadership of Cesar Chavez and his United Farm Workers union. Chavez organized a national boycott of grapes from California vineyards that refused to recognize the union or improve conditions. *La Raza*, as the movement was called, finally ended in a union contract with the growers and later a California law protecting the right of farm workers to organize unions and bargain collectively with their employers. More importantly, the movement galvanized Mexican Americans throughout the Southwest to engage in political activity.[32]

However, inasmuch as many Mexican American immigrants were noncitizens, and many were *indocumentados* (undocumented residents of the United States), the voting strength of Mexican Americans never matched their numbers in the population. The Immigration Reform and Control Act of 1986 granted amnesty to illegal aliens living in the United States in 1982. But the same act also imposed penalties on employers who hired illegal aliens. The effect of these threatened penalties on many employers was to make them wary of hiring Hispanics, especially as permanent employees. At the same time, industries in need of cheap labor—agriculture, health and hospitals, restaurants, clothing manufacturers, etc.— continued to encourage legal and illegal immigration to fill minimum and even subminimum wage level jobs with few if any benefits.

Hispanic Political Power Most Hispanics today believe that they confront less prejudice and discrimination than their parents. Nonetheless, in 1994 California voters approved a referendum, Proposition 187, that would have barred welfare and other benefits to persons living in the state illegally. Most Hispanics opposed the measure, believing that it was motivated by prejudice. A federal court later declared major portions of Proposition 187 unconstitutional. And the U.S. Supreme Court has held that a state may not bar the children of illegal immigrants from attending public schools.[33]

Mexican American voter turnout remains weak. Various explanations have been advanced for the lower voter participation of Mexican Americans. Language barriers may still discourage some voters, even though ballots in many states are now available in Spanish language. Illegal immigrants, of course, cannot vote. Lower education and income levels are also associated with lower voter turnout. Nonetheless, Hispanic voting is on the increase throughout the nation and both Democratic and Republican candidates are increasingly aware of the importance of the Hispanic vote.

La Raza
National Council of La Raza. Issue positions, programs, news, dedicated to improving life experiences of Hispanic Americans.
www.nclr.org

TABLE 15.5 **Hispanic Politics**

	Total	Mexican	Puerto Rican	Cuban	Other
"In politics today do you consider yourself a Republican, a Democrat, an Independent, or something else?"					
Democrat	37%	33%	52%	29%	39%
Republican	16	15	17	34	12
Independent	33	37	17	27	35
"Do you think abortion should be legal in all cases, illegal in most cases, or illegal in all cases?"					
Legal	40	36	60	49	32
Illegal	58	61	39	49	66
"Do you think the government should provide health insurance for Americans without insurance, or is this something the government should not do?"					
Should	83	83	84	87	86
Should not	14	14	15	11	11
"Should colleges sometimes take a student's racial and ethnic background into consideration when they decide which students to admit, or should they select students without considering their racial or ethnic backgrounds?					
Consider	22	21	17	17	21
Don't consider	75	76	78	82	76
"Do you favor or oppose offering government financial aid or 'vouchers' to pay parents some of the cost of sending their children to private and parochial schools?					
Favor	40	40	46	49	37
Oppose	18	16	12	22	23

Source: Copyright © *Public Perspective,* a publication of the Roper Center for Public Opinion Research, University of CT, Storrs. Reprinted by permission of Roper Center for Public Opinion Research.

Overall, most Hispanics identify with the Democratic Party (see Table 15.5). Mexican Americans in the southwestern states and Puerto Ricans in New York have traditionally supported Democratic candidates, while the strong anticommunist heritage among Cuban Americans has fostered a Republican voting tradition in Florida. Hispanics are generally conservative on social issues (opposing abortion, opposing racial preferences, favoring government vouchers to pay parochial school tuitions) but liberal on economic issues (favoring government provision of health insurance for all, favoring a larger federal government with many services).

The Voting Rights Act of 1965, as later amended and as interpreted by the U.S. Supreme Court, extends voting rights protections to "language minorities," including Hispanics (see "Congressional Apportionment and Redistricting" in Chapter 10). Following redistricting after the 1990 census, Hispanic representation in Congress rose substantially; today there are nineteen Hispanic members of the House of Representatives—about 4 percent, still well below the 11 percent of the U.S. population which is Hispanic. Hispanics had been elected governors of Arizona, New Mexico, and Florida.

Native Americans: Trail of Tears

Christopher Columbus, having erred in his estimate of the circumference of the globe, believed he had arrived in the Indian Ocean when he first came to the Caribbean. He mistook the Arawaks there for people of the East Indies, calling them *Indios,* and this Spanish word passed into English as "Indians"—a word that came to refer to all Native American peoples. But at the time of the first European contacts, these peoples had no common ethnic identity; hundreds of separate cultures and languages were thriving in the Americas. Although estimates vary, most historians believe 7 million to 12 million people lived in the land that is now the United States and Canada; 25 million more lived in Mexico; and as many as 60 million to 70 million in all lived in the Western Hemisphere, a number comparable to Europe's population at the time.

In the centuries that followed, the Native American population of the Western Hemisphere was devastated by warfare, by famine, and, most of all, by epidemic diseases brought from Europe. Overall, the Native population fell by 90 percent, the greatest known human disaster in world history. In the Europeans' conquest of the Americas, smallpox wreaked the greatest havoc, followed by measles, bubonic plague, influenza, typhus, diphtheria, and scarlet fever. Superior military technology, together with skill in exploiting hostilities between Native nations, gradually overcame the resistance of Native peoples. By 1910 only 210,000 Native Americans lived in the United States. Their population has slowly recovered to the current 2.2 million (less than 1 percent of the U.S. population). Many live on reservations and trust lands, the largest of which is the Navajo and Hopi enclave in the southwestern United States (see *Across the USA:* "Native American Peoples").

The Trail of Broken Treaties In the Northwest Ordinance of 1787, Congress, in organizing the western territories of the new nation, declared, "The utmost good faith shall always be observed toward the Indians. Their lands and property shall never be taken from them without their consent." And later, in the Intercourse Act of 1790, Congress declared that public treaties between the United States government and the independent Native nations would be the only legal means of obtaining "Indian" land.

As president, George Washington forged a treaty with the Creeks: in exchange for land concessions, the United States pledged to protect the boundaries of the Creek nation and to allow the Creeks themselves to punish all violators of their laws within these boundaries. This semblance of legality was reflected in hundreds of treaties that followed. (Indeed, in recent years some Native American nations have successfully sued in federal court for reparations and return of lands obtained in violation of the Intercourse Act of 1790 and subsequent treaties.) Yet Native lands were constantly invaded by whites. The resulting Native resistance typically led to wars that ultimately resulted in great loss of life among warriors and their families and the further loss of Native land. The cycle of invasion, resistance, military defeat, and further land concessions continued for a hundred years.

"Indian Territories" Following the purchase of the vast Louisiana Territory in 1803, President Thomas Jefferson sought to "civilize" the Natives by promoting farming in "reservations" that were located west of the Mississippi River. But soon, peoples who had been forced to move from Ohio to Missouri were forced to move again to survive the relentless white expansion. President James Monroe designated as "Indian territory" most of the Great Plains west of the Missouri River. Native peoples increasingly faced three unattractive choices: assimilation, removal, or extinction.

In 1814 the Creeks, encouraged by the British during the War of 1812 to attack American settlements, faced an army of Tennessee volunteer militia led by Andrew Jackson. At the Battle of Horseshoe Bend, Jackson's cannon fire decimated

Native American Peoples

This map shows the locations of the principal Native American reservations in the United States. Tribal governments officially govern these reservations. (Alaska Natives, including Aleuts and Eskimos, live mostly in 200 villages widely scattered across rural Alaska, twelve regional Native American corporations administer property and mineral rights on behalf of Native peoples in that state.)

the Creek warriors. In the uneven Treaty of Fort Jackson, the Creeks, Choctaws, and Cherokees were forced to concede millions of acres of land.

By 1830 the "Five Civilized Tribes" of the southeastern United States (Cherokees, Chickasaws, Choctaws, Creeks, and Seminoles) had ceded most but not all of their lands. When gold was discovered on Cherokee land in northern Georgia in 1829, whites invaded their territory. Congress, at the heeding of the old "Indian fighter" President Andrew Jackson, passed the Removal Act, ordering the forcible relocation of the Natives to Oklahoma Indian Territory. The Cherokees tried to use the whites' law to defend their land, bringing their case to the U.S. Supreme Court. When Chief Justice John Marshall held the Cherokees were a "domestic dependent nation" that could not be forced to give up its land, President Jackson replied scornfully, "John Marshall has made his decision. Now let him enforce it." He sent a 7,000-strong army to pursue Seminoles into the huge Florida Everglades swamp and forced 16,000 Cherokees and other peoples on the infamous "Trail of Tears" march to Oklahoma in 1838.

Encroachment on the Indian Territory of the Great Plains was not long in coming. First, the territory was crossed by the Santa Fe and Oregon Trails, and a series of military forts were built to protect travelers. In 1854, under pressure from railroad interests, the U.S. government abolished much of the Indian Territory to create the Kansas and Nebraska territories, which were immediately opened to white settlers. The Native peoples in these lands—including Potawatomis, Kickapoos, Delawares, Shawnees, Miamis, Omahas, and Missouris—were forced to sign treaties accepting vastly reduced land reservations. But large, warlike buffalo-hunting nations remained in the northern Dakotas and western Great Plains: the Sioux, Cheyennes, Arapahoes, Comanches, and Kiowas. (Other smaller peoples inhabited the Rockies to California and the Pacific Northwest; the sedentary Pueblos, Hopis, and Pimas and the migrating Apaches and Navajos occupied the Southwest.) The Plains peoples took pride in their warrior status, often fighting among themselves.

"Indian Wars" The "Indian Wars" were fought between the Plains nations and the U.S. Army between 1864 and 1890. Following the Civil War, the federal government began to assign boundaries to each nation and authorized the Bureau of Indian Affairs (BIA) to "assist and protect" Native peoples on their "reservations." But the reservations were repeatedly reduced in size until subsistence by hunting became impossible. Malnutrition and demoralization of the Native peoples were accelerated by the mass slaughter of the buffalo; vast herds, numbering perhaps as many as 70 million, were exterminated over the years. The most storied engagement of the long war occurred at the Little Bighorn River in Montana on June 25, 1876, where Civil War hero General George Armstrong Custer led elements of the U.S. Seventh Cavalry to destruction at the hands of Sioux and Cheyenne warriors led by Chief Crazy Horse, Sitting Bull, and Gall. But "Custer's last stand" inspired renewed army campaigns against the Plains peoples; the following year, Crazy Horse was forced to surrender. In 1881 destitute Sioux under Chief Sitting Bull returned from exile in Canada to surrender themselves to reservation life. Among the last peoples to hold out were the Apaches, whose famous warrior Geronimo finally surrendered in 1886. Sporadic fighting continued until 1890, when a small malnourished band of Lakota Sioux were wiped out at Wounded Knee Creek.

The Attempted Destruction of Traditional Life The Dawes Act of 1887 governed federal Native American policy for decades. The thrust of the policy was to break up Native lands, allotting acreage for individual homesteads in order to assimilate Natives into the white agricultural society. Farming was to replace hunting, and traditional Native customs were to be shed for English language and schooling. But this effort to destroy culture never really succeeded. Although Native peoples lost more than half of their 1877 reservation land, few lost their communal ties or accumulated much private property. Life on the reservations was often desperate. Natives suffered the worst poverty of any group in the United States, with high rates of infant mortality, alcoholism, and other diseases. The Federal Bureau of Indian Affairs (BIA), notoriously corrupt and mismanaged, encouraged dependency and regularly interfered with religious affairs and customs.

Bureau of Indian Affairs
Government agency with responsibility for administration of 562 federally recognized tribal governments in the U.S.
www.doi.gov/ bureau-Indian-affairs

The New Deal The New Deal under President Franklin D. Roosevelt came to Native Americans in the form of the Indian Reorganization Act of 1934. This act sought to restore Native tribal structures by recognizing these nations as instruments of the federal government. Landownership was restored, and elected Native tribal councils were recognized as legal governments. Efforts to force assimilation were largely abandoned. The BIA became more sensitive to Native culture and began employing Native Americans in larger numbers.

Yet the BIA remained "paternalistic," frequently interfering in tribal "sovereignty." Moreover, in the 1950s Congress initiated a policy of "termination" of sovereignty rights for specific nations that consented to relinquish their lands in exchange for cash payments. Although only a few nations chose this course, the results were often calamitous: after the one-time cash payments were spent, Native peoples became dependent on state social welfare services and often slipped further into poverty and alcoholism.

The American Indian Movement The civil rights movement of the 1960s inspired a new activism among Native American groups. The American Indian Movement (AIM) was founded in 1968 and attracted national headlines by occupying Alcatraz Island in San Francisco Bay. Violence flared in 1972 when AIM activists took over the site of the Wounded Knee battle and fought with FBI agents. Several Native nations succeeded in federal courts and Congress to win back lands and/or compensation for lands taken from them in treaty violations. Native culture was revitalized, and Vine Deloria's *Custer Died for Your Sins* (1969) and Dee Brown's *Bury My Heart at Wounded Knee* (1971) became nationally best-selling books.

Native Americans Today The U.S. Constitution (Article I, Section 8) grants Congress the full power "to regulate Commerce . . . with the Indian Tribes." States are prevented from regulating or taxing Native peoples or extending their courts' jurisdiction over them unless authorized by Congress. The supreme Court recognizes Native Americans "as members of quasi-sovereign tribal entities"[34] with powers to regulate their own internal affairs, establish their own courts, and enforce their own laws, all subject to congressional supervision. Thus, for example, many Native peoples chose to legalize gambling, including casino gambling, on reservations in states that otherwise prohibited the activity. As citizens, Native Americans have the right to vote in state as well as national elections. Those living off reservations have the same rights and responsibilities as other citizens. Ben Nighthorse Campbell, U.S. senator from Colorado, is the only tribal member (Northern Cheyenne) currently serving in Congress.

The Bureau of Indian Affairs in the Department of the Interior continues to supervise reservation life, and Native Americans enrolled as members of nations and living on reservations are entitled to certain benefits established by law and treaty. Nevertheless, these peoples remain the poorest and least healthy in the United States, with high incidences of infant mortality, suicide, and alcoholism. Approximately half of all Native Americans live below the poverty line.

The Rights of Disabled Americans

Disabled Americans were *not* among the classes of people protected by the landmark Civil Rights Act of 1964. Throughout most of the nation's history, little thought was given to making public or private buildings or facilities accessible to blind, deaf, or mobility-impaired people.[35] Not until the Education of Handicapped Children Act of 1975 did the federal government mandate that the nation's public schools provide free education to handicapped children.

Americans with Disabilities Act The Americans with Disabilities Act (ADA) of 1990 is a sweeping law that prohibits discrimination against disabled people in private employment, government programs, public accommodations, and telecommunications. The act is vaguely worded in many of its provisions, requiring "reasonable accommodations" for disabled people that do not involve "undue hardship." This means disabled Americans do not have exactly the same standard of protection as minorities or women, who are protected from discrimination *regardless* of hardship or costs. (It also means that attorneys, consultants, and bureaucrats will make handsome incomes over the years interpreting the meaning of these phrases.) Specifically the ADA includes the following protections:

- *Employment*: Disabled people cannot be denied employment or promotion if, with "reasonable accommodation," they can perform the duties of the job. Rea-

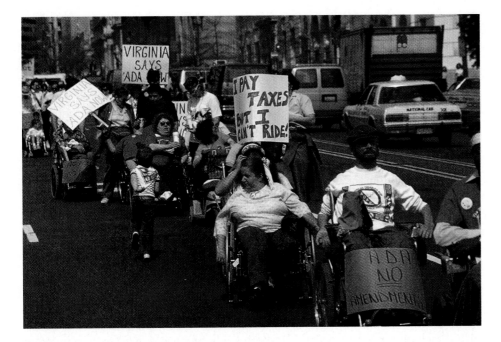

The most recent Americans to pressure Congress and the courts for protection of rights long denied them are the nation's disabled citizens. In 1990 disability rights activists succeeded in getting Congress to pass the Americans with Disabilities Act, which mandates the removal of many barriers that have kept handicapped people from working, traveling, and enjoying leisure activities. Nevertheless, many obstacles remain. Here, activists demonstrate in favor of the act.

sonable accommodation need not be made if doing so would cause "undue hardship" on the employer.

■ *Government programs:* Disabled people cannot be denied access to government programs or benefits. New buses, taxis, and trains must be accessible to disabled persons, including those in wheelchairs.

■ *Public accommodations:* Disabled people must enjoy "full and equal" access to hotels, restaurants, stores, schools, parks, museums, auditoriums, and the like. To achieve equal access, owners of existing facilities must alter them "to the maximum extent feasible"; builders of new facilities must ensure that they are readily accessible to disabled persons unless doing so is structurally impossible.

■ *Communications:* The Federal Communications Commission is directed to issue regulations that will ensure telecommunications devices for hearing- and speech-impaired people are available "to the extent possible and in the most efficient manner."

Mental and Learning Disabilities The ADA protects the rights of people with learning and psychiatric disabilities, as well as physical disabilities. The U.S. Equal Employment Opportunity Commission has received almost as many complaints about workplace discrimination against the mentally disabled as it has received from people claiming back injuries.[36] But it is far more difficult for employers to determine how to handle a depressed or anxiety-ridden employee than an employee with a visible physical disability. How can employers distinguish uncooperative employees from those with psychiatric disorders?

The American Council on Education reports that the percentage of students in colleges and universities claiming a "learning disability" has jumped from 3 to 10 percent.[37] A recent decision by the U.S. Department of Education that "attention deficit disorder" is covered by the ADA is expected to result in another significant rise in students claiming disabilities. Colleges and universities are required to provide special accommodations for students with disabilities, including tutors, extra time on examinations, oral rather than written exams, and the like.

 ADA Home Page
Federal agency site with guide to disability rights laws. *www.usdoj.gov/crt/ada*

American Council on Education
Information on a wide range of educational issues, including diversity, testing, admissions, etc.
www.acenet.edu

Gender Equality and the Fourteenth Amendment

THINK AGAIN

Should gender equality receive the same level of legal protection as racial equality?

The historical context of the Fourteenth Amendment implies its intent to guarantee equality for newly freed slaves, but the wording of its Equal Protection Clause applies to "any person." Thus the text of the Fourteenth Amendment could be interpreted to bar any gender differences in the law, in the fashion of the once proposed yet never ratified Equal Rights Amendment. But the Supreme Court has not interpreted the Equal Protection Clause to give the same level of protection to gender equality as to racial equality. Indeed, in 1873 the Supreme Court specifically rejected arguments that this clause applied to women. The Court once upheld a state law banning women from practicing law, arguing that "the natural and proper timidity and delicacy which belongs to the female sex evidently unfits it for many of the occupations of civil life. . . . The paramount destiny and mission of women are to fulfill the noble and benign offices of wife and mother. This is the law of the Creator."[38]

Early Feminist Politics The earliest active feminist organizations grew out of the pre–Civil War antislavery movement. There the first generation of feminists—including Lucretia Mott, Elizabeth Cady Stanton, Lucy Stone, and Susan B. Anthony—learned to organize, hold public meetings, and conduct petition campaigns. After the Civil War, women were successful in changing many state laws that abridged the property rights of married women and otherwise treated them as "chattel" (property) of their husbands. By the early 1900s activists were also successful in winning some protections for women in the workplace, including state laws limiting women's hours of work, working conditions, and physical demands. At the time, these laws were regarded as "progressive."

The most successful feminist efforts of the 1800s centered on protection of women in families. The perceived threats to women's well-being were their husbands' drinking, gambling, and consorting with prostitutes. Women led the Anti-Saloon League, succeeded in outlawing gambling and prostitution in every state except Nevada, and provided the major source of moral support for the Eighteenth Amendment (Prohibition).

In the early twentieth century, the feminist movement concentrated on women's suffrage—the drive to guarantee women the right to vote. The early suffragists employed mass demonstrations, parades, picketing, and occasional disruption and civil disobedience—tactics similar to those of the civil rights movement of the 1960s. The culmination of their efforts was the 1920 passage of the Nineteenth Amendment to the Constitution: "The right of citizens of the United States to vote shall not be denied or abridged by the United States or by any State on account of sex." The suffrage movement spawned the League of Women Voters; in addition to women's right to vote, the League has sought protection of women in industry, child welfare laws, and honest election practices.

Judicial Scrutiny of Gender Classifications In the 1970s, the Supreme Court became responsive to arguments that sex discrimination might violate the Equal Protection Clause of the Fourteenth Amendment. In *Reed v. Reed* (1971), it ruled that sexual classifications in the law "must be reasonable and not arbitrary, and must rest on some ground of difference having fair and substantial relation to . . . important governmental objectives."[39] This is a much more relaxed level of scrutiny than the Supreme Court gives to racial classification in the law. Since then, the Court has also made these rulings:

Elizabeth Cady Stanton addresses a meeting. Stanton, with Lucretia Mott and others, organized one of the defining moments in feminist politics in the United States—the Seneca Falls convention of 1848. Participants at the convention approved a Declaration of Sentiments, modeled on the Declaration of Independence, that demanded legal and political rights for women, including the right to vote.

- A state can no longer set different ages for men and women to become legal adults[40] or purchase alcoholic beverages.[41]

- Women cannot be barred from police or fire-fighting jobs by arbitrary height and weight requirements.[42]

- Insurance and retirement plans for women must pay the same monthly benefits (even though women on the average live longer).[43]

- Schools must pay coaches in girls' sports the same as coaches in boys' sports.[44]

Continuing Gender Differences The Supreme Court continues to wrestle with the question of whether some gender differences can be recognized in law. The question is most evident in laws dealing with sexual activity and reproduction. The Court has upheld statutory rape laws that make it a crime for an adult male to have sexual intercourse with a female under the age of eighteen, regardless of her consent. "We need not to be medical doctors to discern that young men and young women are not similarly situated with respect to the problems and the risks of sexual intercourse. Only women may become pregnant, and they suffer disproportionately the profound physical, emotional and psychological consequences of sexual activity."[45]

Women's participation in military service, particularly combat, raises even more controversial questions regarding permissible gender classifications. The Supreme Court appears to have bowed out of this particular controversy. In upholding Congress's draft registration law for men only, the Court ruled that "the constitutional power of Congress to raise and support armies and to make all laws necessary and proper to that end is broad and sweeping."[46] Congress and the Defense Department are responsible for determining assignments for women in the military. Women have won assignments to air and naval combat units but remain excluded from combat infantry, armor, artillery, special forces, and submarine duty.

National Organization of Women (NOW)

Advocacy organization for feminist activists working to protect abortion rights, end discrimination against women, and "eradicate racism, sexism, and homophobia." *www.now.org*

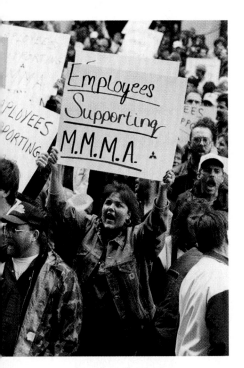

Employees of the Mitsubishi automobile plant in Normal, Illinois, demonstrated outside the offices of the Equal Employment Opportunity Commission in Chicago in April 1996 in support of the company after it became the target of a sexual harassment investigation. The company provided transportation to the demonstration and paid the workers for the day.

direct discrimination Now illegal practice of differential pay for men versus women even when those individuals have equal qualifications and perform the same job.

Aims of the Equal Rights Amendment The proposed Equal Rights Amendment to the U.S. Constitution, passed by Congress in 1972 but never ratified by the states, was worded very broadly: "Equality of rights under the law shall not be denied or abridged by the United States or any State on account of sex." Had it been ratified by the necessary thirty-eight states, it would have eliminated most, if not all, gender differences in the law. Without ERA, many important guarantees of equality for women rest on laws of Congress rather than on the Constitution.

Gender Equality in the Economy

As cultural views of women's roles in society have changed and economic pressures on family budgets have increased, women's participation in the labor force has risen. The gap between women's and men's participation in the nation's work force is closing over time.[47] With the movement of women into the work force, feminist political activity has shifted toward economic concerns—gender equality in education, employment, pay, promotion, and credit.

Gender Equality in Civil Rights Laws Title VII of the Civil Rights Act of 1964 prevents sexual (as well as racial) discrimination in hiring, pay, and promotions. The Equal Employment Opportunity Commission, the federal agency charged with eliminating discrimination in employment, has established guidelines barring stereotyped classifications of "men's jobs" and "women's jobs." The courts have repeatedly struck down state laws and employer practices that differentiate between men and women in hours, pay, retirement age, and so forth.

The Federal Equal Credit Opportunity Act of 1974 prohibits sex discrimination in credit transactions. Federal law prevents banks, credit unions, savings and loan associations, retail stores, and credit card companies from denying credit because of sex or marital status. However, these businesses may still deny credit for a poor or nonexistent credit rating, and some women who have always maintained accounts in their husband's name may still face credit problems if they apply in their own name.

Title IX of the Education Act Amendment of 1972 deals with sex discrimination in education. This federal law bars discrimination in admissions, housing, rules, financial aid, faculty and staff recruitment and pay, and—most troublesome of all—athletics. The latter problem has proven very difficult because men's football and basketball programs have traditionally brought in the money to finance all other sports, and men's football and basketball have received the largest share of school athletic budgets.

The Earnings Gap Despite protections under federal laws, women continue to earn substantially less than men do. Today women, on average, earn about 76 percent of what men do (see Figure 15.1). This earnings gap has been closing very slowly: In 1985 women earned an average 68 percent of men's earnings. The earnings gap is not primarily a product of **direct discrimination**; women in the same job with the same skills, qualifications, experience, and work record are not generally paid less than men. Such direct discrimination has been illegal since the Civil Rights Act of 1964. Rather, the earnings gap is primarily a product of a division in the labor market between traditionally male and female jobs, with lower salaries paid in traditionally female occupations.

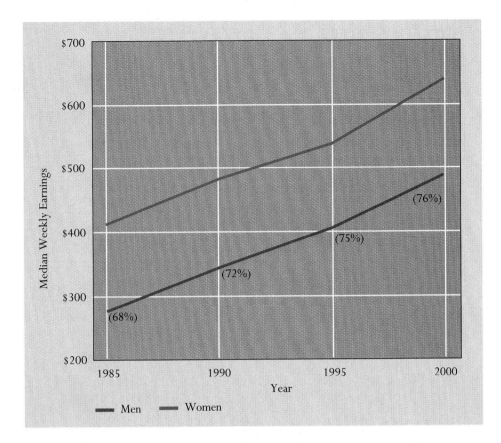

FIGURE 15.1 The Earnings Gap: Median Weekly Earnings of Men and Women

The continuing "earnings gap" between men and women reflects a division in the labor market between traditionally male higher paying occupations and traditionally female lower paying positions.

Note: Figures in parentheses indicate the ratio of women's to men's median weekly earnings.

Source: Statistical Abstract of the United States, 2001, p. 403.

The Dual Labor Market and "Comparable Worth" The existence of a "dual" labor market, with male-dominated "blue-collar" jobs distinguishable from female-dominated "pink-collar" jobs, continues to be a major obstacle to economic equality between men and women. These occupational differences result from cultural stereotyping, social conditioning, and training and education—all of which narrow the choices available to women. Although significant progress has been made in reducing occupational sex segregation (see Figure 15.2), many observers nevertheless doubt that sexually differentiated occupations will be eliminated in the foreseeable future.

As a result of a growing recognition that the wage gap is more a result of occupational differentiation than direct discrimination, some feminist organizations have turned to a new approach—the demand that pay levels in various occupations be determined by **comparable worth** rather than by the labor market. Comparable worth goes beyond paying men and women equally for the same work and calls for paying the same wages for jobs of comparable value to the employer. Advocates of comparable worth argue that governmental agencies or the courts should evaluate traditionally male and female jobs to determine their "worth" to the employer, perhaps by considering responsibilities, effort, knowledge, and skill requirements. Jobs adjudged to be "comparable" would be paid equal wages. Government agencies or the courts would replace the labor market in determining wage rates.

The "Glass Ceiling" The barriers to women's advancement to top positions in the corporate and financial worlds are often very subtle, giving rise to the phrase **glass ceiling.** In explaining "why women aren't getting to the top," one observer argues that "at senior management levels competence is assumed. What you're looking for is someone who fits, someone who gets along, someone you trust. Now that's subtle

comparable worth
Argument that pay levels for traditionally male and traditionally female jobs should be equalized by paying equally all jobs that are "worth about the same" to an employer.

Feminist.Com
Web site promoting women's business development, with information and advice.
www.feminist.com

glass ceiling "Invisible" barriers to women rising to the highest positions in corporations and the professions.

FIGURE 15.2 Gender Differentiation in the Labor Market

Most of the earnings gap between men and women in the U.S. labor force today is the result of the different job positions held by the two sexes. Although women are increasingly entering "white-collar" occupations long dominated by men, they continue to be disproportionately concentrated in "pink-collar" service positions. "Blue-collar" jobs have been the most resistant to change, remaining a male bastion, although women bartenders now outnumber men.

Sources: Statistical Abstract of the United States, 2001, pp. 380–82.

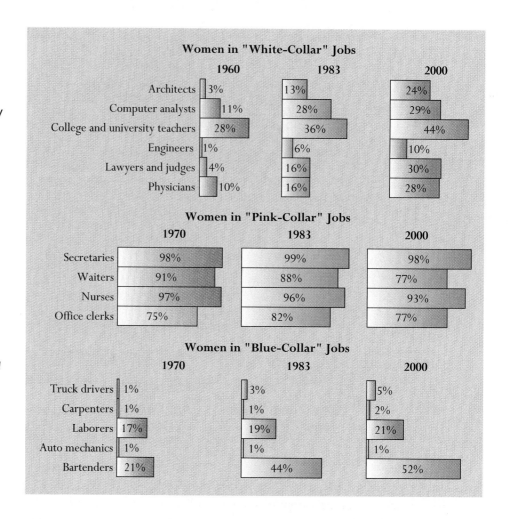

Women in "White-Collar" Jobs

	1960	1983	2000
Architects	3%	13%	24%
Computer analysts	11%	28%	29%
College and university teachers	28%	36%	44%
Engineers	1%	6%	10%
Lawyers and judges	4%	16%	30%
Physicians	10%	16%	28%

Women in "Pink-Collar" Jobs

	1970	1983	2000
Secretaries	98%	99%	98%
Waiters	91%	88%	77%
Nurses	97%	96%	93%
Office clerks	75%	82%	77%

Women in "Blue-Collar" Jobs

	1970	1983	2000
Truck drivers	1%	3%	5%
Carpenters	1%	1%	2%
Laborers	17%	19%	21%
Auto mechanics	1%	1%	1%
Bartenders	21%	44%	52%

stuff. How does a group of men feel that a woman is going to fit? I think it's very hard." Or, as a woman bank executive says, "The men just don't feel comfortable."[48]

There are many other explanations for the glass ceiling, all controversial: Women choose staff assignments rather than fast-track, operating-head assignments. Women are cautious and unaggressive in corporate politics. Women have lower expectations about peak earnings and positions, and these expectations become self-fulfilling. Women bear children, and even during relatively short maternity absences they fall behind their male counterparts. Women are less likely to want to change locations than men, and immobile executives are worth less to a corporation than mobile ones. Women executives in sensitive positions come under even more pressure than men in similar posts. Women executives believe they get much more scrutiny than men and must work harder to succeed. And at all levels, increasing attention has been paid to sexual harassment (see *What Do You Think?* "What Constitutes Sexual Harassment?"). Finally, it is important to note that affirmative action efforts by governments—notably the EEOC—are directed primarily at entry-level positions rather than senior management posts.

Inequality and the Constitution

Americans frequently claim "rights" that have no basis in the U.S. Constitution—for example, the "right" to an education, to medical care, to decent housing, to retirement benefits, to a job. The U.S. Constitution *limits* government; it protects individuals *from* government oppression. The U.S. Constitution does not mandate that governments act wisely or compassionately.

Constitutional versus Legal Rights There is no requirement in the U.S. Constitution that governments establish education, welfare, or social security programs or provide housing, job training, or unemployment compensation. Whatever benefits individuals derive from these government programs, they do so as a matter of law, not as a constitutional right.

> The importance of a service performed by the State does not determine whether it must be regarded as fundamental for purposes of examination under the equal protection clause. . . . Education, of course, is not among the rights afforded explicit protection under our federal Constitution. Nor do we find any basis for saying it is implicitly so protected.[49]

"Reasonable" Classifications Governments by law may classify people according to income, age, illness, disability, or any other "reasonable" standard in administering its programs. However, the Supreme Court has interpreted the Equal Protection Clause to mean only that governments may not practice "invidious" discrimination—that is, establish discriminatory classifications in the law which are "arbitrary and unreasonable" and have "no rational basis."[50] *Reasonable* classifications of individuals by law—those that serve a legitimate government purpose— are *not* unconstitutional. Yet the Equal Protection Clause obligates governments to treat equally all persons who are "similarly situated"—to treat every person who falls into a particular class in the same fashion as every other person in that class. Thus all persons who meet the eligibility requirements stated in the law must receive the same benefits. For example, if Congress establishes a public health care program for people sixty-five years of age and over (Medicare), then everyone in that age classification is entitled to the benefits of the program. Because the benefits of these programs are *legal* entitlements, not *constitutional* rights, however, Congress may choose to change the benefits or eligibility requirements at any time.

Protections for Poor Americans The Constitution ensures that poor people are protected in their legal and political rights. Included among the specific protections given indigent persons are these:

■ *Free legal counsel in criminal cases:* "From the very beginning, our state and national constitutions have laid great emphasis on procedures and substantial safeguards designed to assure fair trials before impartial tribunals in which every defendant stands equal before the law. This noble ideal cannot be realized if the poor man charged with a crime has to face his accusers without the lawyer to assist him."[51]

■ *No tax or financial requirement for voting:* "A state violates the equal protection clause of the Fourteenth Amendment whenever it makes the affluence of the voter or payment of any fee an electoral standard."[52] This decision extended the Twenty-fourth Amendment's ban on poll taxes for national elections to state elections as well.

But the poor cannot demand government funding as a matter of constitutional right in order to exercise other recognized rights. For example, freedom of the press does not mean that the government must buy a printing press for anyone unable to afford one. Congress, in the controversial Hyde Amendment in 1977, denied the use of Medicaid funds for poor women seeking abortions, and the Supreme Court rejected arguments that federal funding of abortions was required by the

What Constitutes Sexual Harassment?

Various surveys report that up to one-third of female workers say they have experienced sexual harassment on the job.* But it is not always clear exactly what kind of behavior constitutes "sexual harassment."

The U.S. Supreme Court has provided some guidance in the development of sexual harassment definitions and prohibitions. Title VII of the Civil Rights Act of 1964 makes it "an unlawful employment practice to discriminate against any individual with respect to his [sic] compensation, terms, conditions or privileges of employment because of such individual's race, color, religion, sex, or national origin." In the employment context, the U.S. Supreme Court has approved the following definition of sexual harassment:

> Unwelcome sexual advances, requests for sexual favors, and other verbal or physical conduct of a sexual nature constitute sexual harassment when (1) submission to such conduct is made either explicitly or implicitly a term or condition of an individual's employment; (2) submission to or rejection of such conduct by an individual is used as the basis for employment decisions affecting such individual; or (3) such conduct has the purpose or effect of unreasonably interfering with an individual's work performance or creating an intimidating, hostile, or offensive working environment.†

There are no great difficulties in defining sexual harassment when jobs or promotions are conditional on the granting of sexual favors. But several problems arise in defining a "hostile working environment." This phrase may include offensive utterances, sexual innuendoes, dirty jokes, the display of pornographic material, and unwanted proposals for dates. First, it would appear to include speech and hence raise First Amendment questions regarding how far speech may be curtailed by law in the workplace. Second, the definition depends more on the subjective feelings of the individual employee about what is "offensive" and "unwanted" than on an objective standard of behavior easily understood by all. Justice Sandra Day O'Connor wrestled with the definition of a "hostile work environment" in *Harris v. Forklift* in 1993. She held that a plaintiff need not show that the utterances caused psychological injury but that a "reasonable person," not just the plaintiff, must perceive the work environment to be hostile or abusive. Presumably a single incident would not constitute harassment; rather, courts should consider "the frequency of the discriminatory conduct," "its severity," and whether it "unreasonably interferes with an employee's work performance."‡

What behaviors does a "reasonable person" believe to be sexual harassment? Some polls indicate that women are somewhat more likely to perceive sexual harassment in various behaviors than men (see figure). But neither women nor men are likely to perceive it to include repeated requests for a date, the telling of dirty jokes, or comments on attractiveness—even though these behaviors often inspire formal complaints.

Many university policies go well beyond both Supreme Court rulings and opinion polls in defining what constitutes sexual harassment, including the following: "remarks about a person's clothing" "suggestive or insulting sounds," and "leering at or ogling of a person's body."

---

* *Washington Post National Weekly Edition:* March 7, 1993.
† *Mentor Savings Bank v. Vinson,* 477 U.S. 57 (1986).
‡ *Harris v. Forklift Systems,* 126 L. Ed. 2d 295 (1993).

Question: *Here is a list of some different situations. We're interested in knowing whether you think they are forms of sexual harassment—not just inappropriate or in bad taste, but sexual harassment.*

Definitely is sexual harassment...

Situation	Men	Women
If a male boss makes it clear to a female employee that she must go to bed with him for a promotion	91%	92%
If a male boss asks very direct questions of a female employee about her personal sexual practices and preferences	59%	68%
If a female boss asks very direct questions of a male employee about his personal sexual practices and preferences	47%	57%
If a man once in a while asks a female employee of his to go out on dates, even though she has said no in the past	15%	21%
If a man once in a while tells dirty jokes in the presence of female employees	15%	16%
If a male boss tells a female employee that she looks very attractive today	3%	5%

☐ Men ☐ Women

Source: Roper Organization as reported in *American Enterprise.* September/October 1993, p. 93.

Constitution. Even though the Court reaffirmed that abortion was a constitutional right, "it simply does not follow that a woman's freedom of choice carries with it a constitutional entitlement to the financial means to avail herself of the protected choices. . . . Although the government may not place obstacles in the path of a woman's exercise of her freedom of choice, it need not remove those not of its own creation."[53]

Income Inequality Governments in the United States are not under any constitutional requirement to eliminate inequality of income or wealth. (The Founders believed that "dangerous leveling" was a violation of the right to property and to use and dispose of the fruits of one's own labors.) For example, representatives of poor, black, and Hispanic groups have charged that differences in public school spending per pupil among school districts in a state discriminate unconstitutionally against poor children. Although the state governments do not discriminate against the poor in their funding (on the contrary, most states have equalization programs written into state law giving more aid to schools serving poor students), it is argued that spending differences among local school districts violate the Equal Protection Clause of the Fourteenth Amendment. But the Supreme Court has ruled that disparities in school funding created by dependence on local property tax revenue and inequalities among districts in the value of property and amount of revenue raised do not violate the Equal Protection Clause. "We cannot say that such disparities are the product of a system that is so irrational as to be invidiously discriminatory."[54] Some *state* courts, however, have ruled that these same disparities violate *state* constitutional guarantees of equal protection.[55]

SUMMARY NOTES

■ Equality has long been the central issue of American politics. Today, most Americans agree that all individuals should have an equal opportunity to make of their lives whatever they can without artificial barriers of race, class, gender, or ethnicity. Political conflict arises over what, if anything, government should do to achieve greater equality of results—the reduction of gaps between rich and poor, men and women, blacks and whites, and other groups in society.

■ The original Constitution of 1787 recognized and protected slavery. Not until after the Civil War did the Thirteenth Amendment (1865) abolish slavery. But the Fourteenth Amendment's guarantee of "equal protection of the laws" and the Fifteenth Amendment's guarantee of voting rights were largely ignored in southern states after the federal government's Reconstruction efforts ended. Segregation was held constitutional by the U.S. Supreme Court in its "separate but equal" decision in *Plessy v. Ferguson* in 1896.

■ The NAACP led the long legal battle in the federal courts to have segregation declared unconstitutional as a violation of the Equal Protection Clause of the Fourteenth Amendment. Under the leadership of Thurgood Marshall, a major victory was achieved in the case of *Brown v. Board of Education of Topeka* in 1954.

■ The struggle over school desegregation continues even today. Federal courts are more likely to issue desegregation orders (including orders to bus pupils to achieve racial balance in schools) in school districts where present or past actions by government officials contributed to racial imbalances. Courts are less likely to order desegregation where racial imbalances are a product of residential patterns.

■ The courts could eliminate *governmental* discrimination by enforcing the Fourteenth Amendment of the Constitution; but only Congress could end private discrimination through legislation. Martin Luther King, Jr.'s campaign of nonviolent direct action helped bring remaining racial injustices to the attention of Congress. Key legislation includes the Civil Rights Act of 1964, which bans discrimination in public accommodations, government-funded programs, and private employment; the Voting

Rights Act of 1965, which authorizes strong federal action to protect voting rights; and the Civil Rights Act of 1968, which outlaws discrimination in housing.

- Today, racial politics center around continuing inequalities between blacks and whites in the areas of income, jobs, housing, health, education, and other conditions of life. Should the government concentrate on "equality of opportunity" and apply "color-blind" standards to both blacks and whites? Or should government take "affirmative action" to assist blacks and other minorities to overcome the results of past unequal treatment?

- Generally the Supreme Court is likely to approve of affirmative action programs when these programs have been adopted in response to a past proven history of discrimination, when they are narrowly tailored so as not to adversely affect the rights of individuals, when they do not absolutely bar whites from participating, and when they serve clearly identified, compelling, and legitimate government objectives.

- Economic conditions in Mexico and other Spanish-speaking nations of the Western Hemisphere continue to fuel large-scale immigration, both legal and illegal, into the United States. But the political power of Mexican Americans, the nation's largest Hispanic group, does not yet match their population percentage. Their voter turnout remains lower than that of other ethnic groups in the United States.

- Since the arrival of the first Europeans on this continent, Native American peoples have experienced cycles of invasion, resistance, military defeat, and land concessions. Today Native American peoples collectively remain the poorest and least healthy of the nation's ethnic groups.

- The most recent major civil rights legislation is the Americans with Disabilities Act of 1990, which prohibits discrimination against disabled persons in private employment, government programs, public accommodations, and communications.

- The Equal Protection Clause of the Fourteenth Amendment applies to "any person," but traditionally the Supreme Court has recognized gender differences in laws. Nevertheless, in recent years the Court has struck down gender differences where they are unreasonable or arbitrary and unrelated to legitimate government objectives.

- Gender discrimination in employment has been illegal since the passage of the Civil Rights Act of 1964. Nevertheless, differences in average earnings of men and women persist, although these differences have narrowed somewhat over time. The earnings gap appears to be mainly a product of lower pay in occupations traditionally dominated by women and higher pay in traditionally male occupations. Although neither Congress nor the courts have mandated wages based on comparable worth of traditional men's and women's jobs in private employment, many governmental agencies and some private employers have undertaken to review wage rates to eliminate gender differences.

- The Equal Protection Clause does not bar government from treating persons in various income classes differently. However, governments must treat every individual in a class equally, and the classifications must not be "arbitrary" or "unreasonable." The poor cannot demand benefits or services as a matter of constitutional rights; but once government establishes a social welfare program by law, it must provide equal access to all persons "similarly situated."

KEY TERMS

abolition movement 539
Emancipation Proclamation 539
Jim Crow 540

separate but equal 540
de facto segregation 546
nonviolent direct action 545

affirmative action 550
quota 550
Bakke case 552
set-aside program 552

direct discrimination 568
comparable worth 569
glass ceiling 569

SUGGESTED READINGS

Barker, Lucius J., and Mack H. Jones. *African Americans and the American Political System*. 4th ed. Upper Saddle River, N.J.: Prentice Hall, 1999. Comprehensive analysis of African American politics, examining access to the judicial arena, the interest-group process, political parties, Congress, and the White House.

Bowen, William G., and Derek Curtis Bok. *The Shape of the River*. Princeton, N.J.: Princeton University Press, 1999. An argument by two university presidents that preferential treatment of minorities in admissions to prestigious universities has led to the subsequent success in life by the beneficiaries of the preferences.

Conway, M. Margaret, Gertrude A. Steurnagel, and David W. Ahern. *Women and Political Participation*. Washington, D.C.: CQ Press, 1997. A wide-ranging review of changes in American political culture brought about by women's increasing political clout. Continuing gender differences in representation are explored.

Fox-Genovese, Elizabeth. *Feminism Is Not the Story of My Life*. New York: Doubleday, 1995. Critique of radical feminism for failing to understand the central importance of marriage and motherhood in women's lives, and a discussion of how public policy could ease the clashing demands of work and family on women.

Harrison, Brigid C. *Women in American Politics*. Belmont, Calif.: 2003. Comprehensive text on role of women in interest groups, parties, elections, Congress, the executive branch, and the judiciary.

Hero, Rodney E. *Latinos and the U.S. Political System*. Philadelphia: Temple University Press, 1992. General history of political participation of major Latino groups, arguing that different cultural behaviors limit their ability to participate in the interest-group system and policy-making process as currently structured.

Kluegel, James R., and Eliot R. Smith. *Beliefs about Inequality*. New York: Aldine de Gruyter, 1986. Comprehensive description of Americans' beliefs and attitudes about inequality, based on extensive survey data, including evidence of changes in beliefs over time as well as inconsistencies and contradictions.

McGlen, Nancy E., and Karen O'Conner. *Women, Politics, and American Society*. Upper Saddle River, N.J.: Prentice Hall, 1996. Comprehensive text contrasting women's rights and realities in politics, employment, education, reproduction, and family.

Sigelman, Lee, and Susan Welch. *Black Americans' Views of Racial Inequality*. Cambridge, Mass.: Cambridge University Press, 1991. Analysis of survey research showing that black perceptions of racial inequality in America are considerably different from white perceptions. Although remaining optimistic about the future, blacks see discrimination as commonplace and are much more likely than whites to attribute black-white differences in education, occupation, and income to racism.

Thernstrom, Stephen, and Abigail Thernstrom. *America in Black and White*. New York: Simon & Schuster, 1997. Information-rich analysis tracing social and economic progress of African Americans and arguing that gains in education and employment were greater *before* the introduction of affirmative action programs.

MAKE IT REAL

TRAVEL THE CIVIL RIGHTS TIMELINE

Using this timeline of significant events in the civil rights struggle, you will access a wealth of information and multimedia to further explain the struggle. In addition the timeline will highlight all major events (good and bad), speeches, conflicts that are part of the civil rights story including constitutional disputes on slavery, abolition women's suffrage, Jim Crow laws, and major sociological changes, to name a few.

16

POLITICS AND THE ECONOMY

THINK
ABOUT POLITICS

1 Do you believe government efforts to manage the economy usually make things better or worse?
Better ● Worse ●

2 Do you believe the government should spend more during recessions to ease economic hardship even if it means larger government deficits?
Yes ● No ●

3 Do you think the trend toward a global economy is a good thing or a bad thing for the United States?
Good thing ● Bad thing ●

4 Which is more important holding down the size of government or providing needed services?
Holding down the size of government ●
Providing needed services ●

5 Do you think the federal government should increase spending on Social Security and Medicare for the elderly?
Yes ● No ●

6 Do you believe all wage earners should pay the same percentage of income in taxes (a flat tax)?
Yes ● No ●

7 Would you favor ending all deductions if income taxes could be lowered to no more than 19 percent?
Yes ● No ●

What is the proper relationship between government and the economy? How much influence should the government exercise over the production and distribution of goods and services in this country?

Politics and Economics

Earlier, we observed that one of America's foremost political scientists, Harold Lasswell, defined "politics" as "who gets what, when, and how." One of America's foremost economists, Paul Samuelson, defined "economics" as "deciding what shall be produced, how, and for whom."[1] The similarity between these definitions is based on the fact that both the political system and the economic system provide society with means for deciding about the production and distribution of goods and services. The political system involves *collective* decisions—choices made by communities, states, or nations—and relies on government coercion through laws, regulations, taxes, and so on to implement them. A free-market economic system involves *individual* decisions—choices made by millions of consumers and thousands of firms—and relies on *voluntary exchange* through buying, selling, borrowing, contracting, and trading to implement them (see *People in Politics:* "Milton Friedman, In Defense of Free Markets"). Both politics and markets function to transform popular demands into goods and services, to allocate costs, and to distribute goods and services.

One of the key questions in any society is how much to rely on government versus the marketplace to provide goods and services. This question of the proper relationship between governments and markets—that is, between politics and economics—is the subject of political economy. The United States is primarily a free-market economy, but the federal government strongly influences economic activity.

Economic Decision Making

Economic decision making involves both fiscal and monetary policy. **Fiscal policy** refers to the taxing, spending, and borrowing activities of the national government. Fiscal policy making takes place within the same system of separated powers and checks and balances that governs other areas of federal policy making (see "Separation of Powers and Checks and Balances" in Chapter 3), with both the Congress and the president sharing responsibility.

Monetary policy refers to decisions regarding the supply of money in the economy, including private borrowing, interest rates, and banking activity. Monetary policy is a principal responsibility of the powerful and independent Federal Reserve Board. Congress established the Federal Reserve Board in 1913 and its power rests on congressional legislation. Congress could, if it wished, reduce its power or even abolish the Fed. But no serious effort has ever been undertaken to do so.

Milton Friedman, In Defense of Free Markets

Economist Milton Friedman is perhaps the world's most influential spokesperson on behalf of free-market economics. He has spent a lifetime arguing that free markets are indispensable for human freedom and dignity. In 1976 Friedman was awarded a Nobel Prize in economics for his work in monetary policy.

Friedman was born in Brooklyn, New York, the son of working-class immigrants who stressed the importance of education. Young Friedman was an excellent high school student who went on to major in economics at Rutgers University, where he worked his way through college with a number of odd jobs. Upon graduation in 1932, Friedman was awarded a scholarship to attend graduate school at the University of Chicago. After earning his M.A. in economics, he worked in Washington, D.C., at various posts before returning to Columbia University for his Ph.D. In 1943. In 1946 he joined the faculty at the University of Chicago.

In his book *Studies in the Quantity Theory of Money* (1956) and in testimony before the Joint Congressional Economic Committee, Friedman argued against the prevailing economic philosophy of John Maynard Keynes and its prescription of increased government borrowing and spending to stimulate the economy. Friedman contended that a gradual, steady, continuous rate of increase in the money supply would be the best policy for achieving stable economic growth. Friedman and other economists who support this theory are known as *monetarists*.

In Friedman's view, the chief cause of recession and inflation is fluctuation in the nation's money supply. In an influential book, *A Monetary History of the United States* (1963), Friedman presented extensive historical evidence of the effect of money supply on the economic health of the nation. But Friedman's most widely read works are his cogent defenses of individual freedom and dignity. In *Capitalism and Freedom* (1962), he argued convincingly that free markets are essential to individual freedom and that government intervention in the marketplace inevitably curtails individual liberty and substitutes the judgment of a privileged few for the decisions of the people. In his television series *Free to Choose*, he brought his free-market ideas to a wide audience. According to Friedman, "The preservation of freedom requires limiting narrowly the role of government and placing primary reliance on private property, free markets and voluntary arrangements."

fiscal policy Economic policies involving taxing, spending, and deficit levels of the national government.

monetary policy Economic policies involving the money supply, interest rates, and banking activity.

Congress, the President, and Fiscal Policy The Constitution of the United States places all taxing, borrowing, and spending powers in the hands of Congress. Article I grants Congress the "Power to lay and collect Taxes, Duties, Imposts and Excises, to pay the Debts and provide for the common Defence and general Welfare of the United States," and "to borrow Money on the Credit of the United States." It also declares that "No Money shall be drawn from the Treasury, but in Consequence of Appropriations made by Law." For nearly 150 years the power to spend was interpreted in a limited fashion: Congress could only spend money to perform powers specifically enumerated in Article I, Section 8, of the Constitution. But the Supreme Court has since ruled that the phrase "to pay the Debts and provide for the common Defence and general Welfare" may be broadly interpreted to authorize congressional spending for any purpose that serves the general welfare. Thus today there are no constitutional limits on Congress's spending power. Congress's borrowing power has always been unlimited constitutionally; and as yet there is no constitutional requirement for a balanced budget.

The Constitution gives the president no formal powers over taxing and spending or borrowing, stating only that the president shall . . . recommend to [Congress's] Consideration such Measures as he shall judge necessary and expedient"

(Article II, Section 3). From this meager constitutional grant of power, however, presidents have gradually acquired leadership over national economic policy. The principal instrument of executive economic policy making is the Budget of the United States Government, which the president submits annually to Congress. The budget sets forth the president's recommendations for spending for the forthcoming fiscal year; revenue estimates, based on existing taxes or recommendations for new or increased tax levels; and estimates of projected deficits and the need for borrowing when, as has usually been the case of late, spending recommendations exceed revenue estimates (see Figure 12.4, "The Budgetary Process," for more detail).

The President's Economic Team The *president's* recommendations to Congress regarding taxing, spending, and borrowing are influenced by advice received from three sources:

1. The Office of Management and Budget (OMB), responsible for preparing the Budget of the United States Government, exerts a powerful influence on the expenditure side of the budget. OMB supervises the year-long process of checking, reviewing, and modifying the budget requests of every federal department and agency.

2. The Department of the Treasury and the secretary of the Treasury have the principal responsibility for estimating revenues and, if requested by the president, for drawing up new tax proposals and forecasting how much revenue they might produce. The Treasury Department also manages the nation's huge national debt—the result of past annual deficits. The Treasury must continually sell **government bonds** to banks and other investors, both foreign and domestic, in order to cover payments on previous deficits as well as to fund current deficits. In doing so, the Treasury Department determines interest rates on federal bonds, and it pays out interest charges on the national debt—charges that now amount to 12 percent of all federal spending.

3. The Council of Economic Advisers (CEA), which forecasts economic conditions and recommends economic policies, is composed of three professional economists and a small staff. In theory, the CEA gives the president unbiased forecasts of economic trends and impartial analyses of economic issues. It does so principally in the annual Economic Report of the President, which the CEA prepares. But because the president chooses the members of the CEA, it often produces economic reports that reflect the president's thinking.

The Fed and Monetary Policy Most economically advanced democracies have central banks whose principal responsibility is to regulate the supply of money, both currency in circulation and bank deposits. And most of these democracies have found it best to remove this responsibility from the direct control of elected politicians. Politicians everywhere are sorely tempted to inflate the supply of money in order to fund projects and programs with newly created money instead of new taxes. Nations pay for this approach with a general rise in prices and a reduction in goods and services available to private firms and individuals—inflation. Indeed, nations whose control of the money supply has fallen victim to irresponsible governments have experienced inflation rates of 500 to 1,000 percent per year, which is to say that their money became worthless.

Council of Economic Advisors
Official CEA site, with latest *Economic Report of the President* and mostly economic indicators.
www.whitehouse.gov/cea

Federal Reserve System
Official site of the Fed, with data on money supply, interest rates, and banking regulation.
www.federalreserve.gov

government bonds
Certificates of indebtedness that pay interest and promise repayment on a future date.

The Federal Reserve System of the United States is largely independent of either the president or Congress. Its independent status is a result not only of law but also of its structure. It is run by a seven-member board of governors who are appointed by the president, with the consent of the Senate, for fourteen-year terms. Members may not be removed from the board except for "cause"; no member has ever been removed since the creation of the board in 1913. The board's chair serves only a four-year term, but the chair's term overlaps that of the president, so that new presidents cannot immediately name their own chair (see *People in Politics:* "Alan Greenspan, Managing the Nation's Economy" in Chapter 12).

The task of the **Federal Reserve Board (the Fed)** is to regulate the money supply and by so doing to help avoid both inflation and recession. The Fed oversees the operation of the nation's twelve Federal Reserve Banks, which actually issue the nation's currency, called "Federal Reserve Notes." The Federal Reserve Banks are bankers' banks; they do not directly serve private citizens or firms. They hold the deposits, or "reserves," of banks; lend money to banks at "discount rates" that the Fed determines; buy and sell U.S. Government Treasury bonds; and assure regulatory compliance by private banks and protection of depositors against fraud. The Fed determines the reserve requirements of banks and otherwise monitors the health of the banking industry. The Fed also plays an important role in clearing checks throughout the banking system.

The Fed's influence over the economy is mainly through monetary policy—increasing or decreasing the supply of money and hence largely determining interest rates. When **inflation** threatens, the Fed typically acts to limit ("tighten") the supply of money and raise interest rates by (1) raising the reserve requirement of banks and thereby reducing the amount of money they have to loan out; or (2) raising the discount rate and thereby the cost of borrowing by banks; or (3) selling off government bonds to banks and others in "open market operations," thereby reducing the funds banks can lend to individuals and businesses. When **recession** threatens, the Fed typically acts to expand ("ease") the money supply and lower interest rates by taking the opposite of each action just described.

Politics and Monetary Policy Although it is the Fed that makes monetary policy, voters typically hold the president responsible for recessions. Hence presidents frequently try to persuade ("jawbone") the independent Fed into lowering interest rates, especially in an election year, believing a temporary stimulus to help win the election is worth whatever inflationary effects it might create after the election.[2] Congress, too, is usually aligned on the side of "easy" money. But Fed members are mainly bankers and economists who understand the threats posed by inflation; so are the members of the Federal Advisory Council, presidents of the twelve Federal Reserve Banks who advise the Fed. Thus tension frequently arises between the Fed, with its concern about inflation, and the president and Congress, with their concern about recession.

When the Fed deviates from the desires of the president and Congress, the Fed's independence often comes under attack. Congress frequently threatens to curtail the independence of the Fed by shortening the terms of members or otherwise bringing them under the direction of the president or Congress. Despite these attempts to intimidate the Fed into abandoning its own judgment and following the lead of the president and Congress, over the years the Fed has established itself as a strong independent guardian of the nation's money supply.

Federal Reserve Board (the Fed) Independent agency of the executive branch of the federal government charged with overseeing the nation's monetary policy.

inflation Rise in the general level of prices; not just the prices of some products.

recession Decline in the general level of economic activity.

The Performance of the American Economy

Underlying the power of nations and the well-being of their citizens is the strength of their economy—their total productive capacity. The United States produces about $12 *trillion* worth of goods and services in a single year for its 281 million people—more than $40,000 worth of output for every person.

Economic Growth Gross domestic product (GDP) is a widely used measure of the performance of the economy.[3] GDP is a nation's total production of goods and services for a single year valued in terms of market prices. It is the sum of all the goods and services that people have been willing to pay for, from wheat production to bake sales, from machine tools to maid service, from aircraft manufacturing to bus rides, from automobiles to chewing gum. GDP counts only final purchases of goods and services (that is, it ignores the purchase of steel by car makers until it is sold as a car) to avoid double counting in the production process. GDP also excludes financial transactions (such as the sale of bonds and stocks) and income transfers (such as Social Security, welfare, and pension payments) that do not add to the production of goods and services. Although GDP is expressed in current dollar prices, it is often recalculated in constant dollar terms to reflect real values over time, adjusting for the effect of inflation. GDP estimates are prepared each quarter by the U.S. Department of Commerce; these figures are widely reported and closely watched by the business and financial community.

Growth in real (constant dollar) GDP measures the performance of the overall economy. Economic recessions and recoveries are measured as fluctuations or swings in the growth of GDP. For example, a recession is usually defined as negative GDP growth in two or more consecutive quarters. Historical data reveal that periods of economic growth have traditionally been followed by periods of contraction, giving rise to the notion of *economic cycles*. Prior to 1950, economic cycles in the United States produced extreme ups and downs, with double-digit swings in real GDP. In recent decades, however, economic fluctuations have been more moderate. The United States still experiences economic cycles, but many economists believe that countercyclical government fiscal and monetary policy has succeeded in achieving greater stability (see Figure 16.1).

Unemployment From a political standpoint, the **unemployment rate** may be the most important measure of the economy's performance. The unemployment rate is the percentage of the civilian labor force who are looking for work or waiting to return to or begin a job. Unemployment is different from not working; people who have retired or who attend school and people who do not work because of sickness, disability, or unwillingness are not considered part of the labor force and so are not counted as unemployed. People who are so discouraged about finding a job that they have quit looking for work are also not counted in the official unemployment rate. The unemployed do include people who have been terminated from their last job or temporarily laid off from work, as well as people who voluntarily quit and those who have recently entered or reentered the labor force and are now seeking employment.

The unemployment rate is measured each month by the U.S. Department of Labor. It does so by contacting a random sample of more than 50,000 households in many locations throughout the country. Trained interviewers ask a variety of questions to determine how many (if any) members of the household are either

Bureau of Economic Analysis
Source of official economic statistics, listed A–Z.
www.bea.gov

gross domestic product (GDP) Measure of economic performance in terms of the nation's total production of goods and services for a single year, valued in terms of market prices.

unemployment rate
Percentage of the civilian labor force who are not working but who are looking for work or waiting to return to or to begin a job.

FIGURE 16.1 Economic Growth

The tendency for periods of economic growth to alternate with periods of contraction has led to the concept of the business cycle—the idea that at least some fluctuation is normal, even healthy, helping to keep the economy growing in the long run by keeping prices from getting too high. In recent decades, government intervention in the economy appears to have succeeded in reducing, although not in altogether eliminating, the depths of recessions to which the nation was formerly prone.

Source: Data from Council of Economic Advisers, Economic Indicators, August 2004.

 Bureau of Labor Statistics

The U.S. Department of Labor's Bureau of Labor Statistics site contains monthly information about the nation's employment rate plus a wealth of supporting data. *www.bls.gov*

working or have a job but did not work at it because of sickness, vacation, strike, of personal reasons (employed); or whether they have no job but are available for work and actively seeking a job (unemployed). The unemployment rate fluctuates with the business cycle, reflecting recessions and recoveries (see Figure 16.2). Generally, unemployment lags behind GDP growth, going down only after the recovery has begun. Following years of economic growth in the 1990s, the nation's unemployment rate fell to near record lows, below 5 percent. The economic slowdown of 2001–2002 pushed up unemployment above 5 percent again.

Inflation Inflation erodes the value of the dollar because higher prices mean that the same dollars can now purchase fewer goods and services. Thus inflation erodes

FIGURE 16.2 Unemployment and Inflation

Economic growth during the 1980s lowered both the inflation and unemployment rates, freeing the nation from the stagflation (combined inflation and high unemployment) that had characterized much of the 1970s. Unemployment rose during the recession of 1990–91 and again in 2002–2003. Inflation has remained relatively low in recent years.

Source: Data from Council of Economic Advisers, 2004.

Just how bad can inflation get? Between the two world wars, inflation in Germany reached such levels that the nation's currency was often weighed, rather than counted, in order to speed transactions.

the value of savings, reduces the incentive to save, and hurts people who are living on fixed incomes. When banks and investors anticipate inflation, they raise interest rates on loans in order to cover the anticipated lower value of repayment dollars. Higher interest rates, in turn, make it more difficult for new or expanding businesses to borrow money, for home buyers to acquire mortgages, and for consumers to make purchases on credit. Thus inflation and high interest rates slow economic growth.

In recent years the Fed has been very successful in keeping down the rate of inflation, and as a result, keeping down overall interest rates as well. Low interest rates contributed to the nation's booming economy in the 1990s by encouraging businesses to borrow money for expansion and consumers to buy more on credit. The "soft" economy in 2001–2002 inspired the Fed to lower interest rates even farther.

Economic Globalization

The American economy is a major force in the global economy. International trade—the buying and selling of goods and services between individuals and firms located in different countries—has expanded rapidly in recent decades. Today almost one-quarter of the world's total output is sold in a country other than the one in which it was produced. The United States exports about 11 percent of the value of its gross domestic product (GDP) and imports about 12 percent. As late as 1970, exports and imports were only about 3 percent of GDP (see Figure 16.3)

Historic Protectionism Historically, American business supported high tariffs—taxes on foreign imports. Prior to World War II, U.S. tariffs on imported goods averaged 30 to 50 percent in various decades. This eliminated most foreign competition from U.S. markets. American firms could raise prices to levels just below the price of imported goods with their high tariffs attached. Not only did this improve the profit margins of American manufacturers, it also allowed them to be less efficient than foreign producers and yet survive and prosper under the protection of tariffs. The pressure to cut wages and downsize work forces was less

THINK AGAIN

Do you think the trend toward a global economy is a good thing or a bad thing for the United States?

FIGURE 16.3 U.S. World Trade

Source: U.S. Bureau of Economic Analysis, December, 2003.

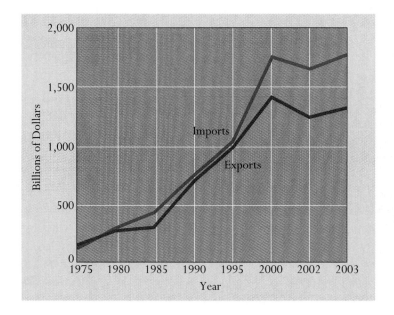

than it would be if U.S. firms had to face foreign competition directly. American consumers, of course, paid higher prices than they otherwise would if foreign goods could come into the country without tariffs. The policy of high tariffs and quotas—limits on the number of units of specific goods imported into the country—was referred to as **protectionism**.

Free Trade But after World War II, the American economy became the most powerful in the world, and American businesses sought to expand their markets overseas. In order to lower trade barriers in other countries, the United States reduced or eliminated almost all of its own tariffs and import quotas. In effect, the United States became an open market. "Free trade" became a byword of American business, and "protectionism" became a derogatory term.

The argument for **free trade** is that it lowers the price of goods and improves the standard of living in nations that choose to trade with each other. Trade shifts resources (investment capital, jobs, technology, raw materials, etc.) in each nation toward what each does best. If one nation is much better producing aircraft and another better at producing clothing, then each nation will benefit more from trading than from trying to produce both airplanes and clothing. The efficiencies achieved by trading are said to directly benefit consumers by making available cheaper imported goods. Export industries also benefit when world markets are opened to their products. It is also argued that the pressure from competition from foreign-made goods in the American marketplace forces our own industries to become more efficient—cutting their costs and improving the quality of their goods. Finally, trade expands the menu of goods and services available to trading countries. American consumers gain access to everything from exotic foods and foreign-language movies to Porsches, BMWs, and Jaguars.

protectionism A policy of high tariffs and quotas on imports to protect domestic industries.

free trade A policy of reducing or eliminating tariffs and quotas on imports to stimulate international trade.

Uneven Benefits of Globalization While the U.S. economy has performed very well in recent years, the benefits of that performance have been unevenly distributed. A global economy inspires worldwide competition not only among corporations and businesses but also among workers. America's best educated and most highly skilled workers compete well in the global economy. U.S. export industries have thrived on international trade expansion, adding jobs to the American economy and raising the incomes of their executives, professionals, and skilled high-tech workers. But the global economy offers a huge supply of unskilled and semiskilled workers at very low wages. Increased trade, especially with less developed economies such as Mexico, China, and India, with their huge numbers of low-wage workers, creates competition with America's unskilled and semiskilled workers. It is difficult to maintain the wage levels of American jobs, especially in labor-intensive industries, in the face of competition from low-wage countries. And U.S. corporations can move their manufacturing plants to low-wage countries, for example to northern Mexico, where the transportation costs of moving these products back into the United States are minimal. Harvard economist Richard B. Freeman summarizes the problem:

> An economic disaster has befallen low-skilled Americans, especially young men. Researchers using several data sources—including household survey data from the Current Population Survey, other household surveys, and establishment surveys—have documented that wage inequality and skill differentials in earnings and employment increased sharply in the United States from the mid-1970s through the 1980s and into the 1990s. The drop in the relative position of the less skilled shows up in a number of ways: greater earnings differentials between those with more and less education; greater earnings differentials between older and younger workers; greater differentials between high-skilled and low-skilled occupations; in a wider earnings distribution overall and within demographic and skill groups; and in less time worked by low-skill and low-paid workers.[4]

Income inequality has worsened in America along with the growth of international trade (see "Inequality of Wealth and Income" in Chapter 2). Figure 16.4 shows the percentage of losses and gains between 1980 and 2000 for American

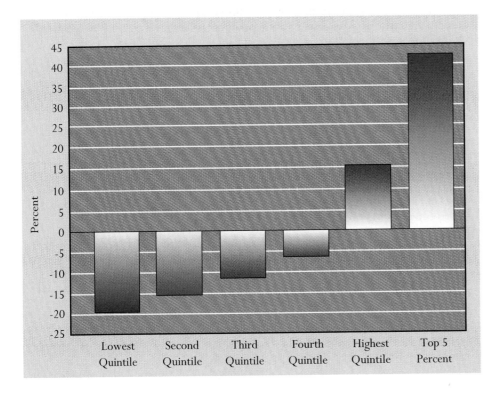

FIGURE 16.4
Worsening Inequality

Change in percent distribution of family income by quintile, 1980–2000.

Source: Statistical Abstract of the United States, 2002 p. 437.

families in each income class. The nation's lowest income families lost 22 percent of their real income over these years, while the highest income families gained 33 percent in real income. Not all of this increase in inequality can be attributed to the growth of international trade. But, clearly, America's less educated and less skilled workers are at a disadvantage in global competition.

The Politics of Free Trade Over the years both Democratic and Republican presidential administrations have advanced free trade. And Congress has approved the major treaties and organizations designed to institutionalize the global economy (see Table 16.1). The task of the cabinet-level position, International Trade

World Trade Organization
Official WTO site, with trade agreements, including General Agreement on Tariff and Trade (GATT).
www.wto.org

TABLE 16.1 Major International Trade Agreements

The World Trade Organization and GATT.

The World Trade Organization was created in 1993. Today the WTO includes 130 nations that agree to a governing set of global trade rules. (China and Russia have applied to join.) The WTO is given power to adjudicate trade disputes among countries and monitor and enforce trade agreements, including GATT. GATT, the multinational General Agreement on Tariffs and Trade, was created following World War II for the purpose of encouraging international trade. Over the years GATT has been dominated by banking, business, and commercial interests in Western nations seeking multilateral tariff reductions and the relaxation of quotas. In 1993 the GATT "Uruguay Round" eliminated quotas on textile products; established more uniform standards for proof of dumping; set rules for the protection of intellectual property rights (patents and copyrights on books, movies, videos, and so on); reduced tariffs on wood, paper, and some other raw materials; and scheduled a gradual reduction of government subsidies for agricultural products.

The International Monetary Fund and the World Bank.

The IMF's purpose is to facilitate international trade, allowing nations to borrow to stabilize their balance of trade payments. When economically weak nations, however, incur chronic balance of trade deficits and perhaps face deferral or default on international debts, the IMF may condition its loans on changes in a nation's economic policies. It may require a reduction in a nation's government deficits by reduced public spending and/or higher taxes; or it may require a devaluation of its currency, making its exports cheaper and imports more expensive. It may also require the adoption of noninflationary monetary policies. Currently, the IMF as well as the World Bank are actively involved in assisting Russia and other states of the former Soviet Union to convert to free-market economies.

The World Bank makes long-term loans, mostly to developing nations, to assist in economic development. It works closely with the IMF in investigating the economic conditions of nations applying for loans and generally imposes IMF requirements on these nations as conditions for loans.

NAFTA.

In 1993 the United States, Canada, and Mexico signed the North American Free Trade Agreement. Objections by labor unions in the United States (and independent presidential candidate Ross Perot) were drowned out in a torrent of support by the American corporate community, Democrats and Republicans in Congress, President Bill Clinton, and former President George Bush. NAFTA envisions the removal of tariffs on virtually all products by all three nations over a period of ten to fifteen years. It also allows banking, insurance, and other financial services to cross these borders.

Does Globalization Help or Hurt America?

While Democratic and Republican presidents and Congresses have supported free trade and given their approval to two major trade agreements, the American public appears to be divided over the benefits of economic globalization.

Q. Based on what you know or may have heard, do you think the globalization of the world economy is mostly good for the United States, mostly bad for the United States, or doesn't make much difference?

Bad	22%
Good	38
No difference	25
Haven't heard/don't know	14

More Americans believe that free trade agreements cost U.S. jobs rather than create U.S. jobs.

Q. Do you think the trade agreements between the United States and other countries have helped create more jobs in the United States, or have they cost the U.S. jobs, or haven't they made much of a difference?

Cost U.S. jobs	49%
Haven't made much difference	23
Helped create more U.S. jobs	21
Don't know	7

It comes as no surprise that higher-income Americans voice greater support for globalization than lower-income Americans. Nor is it much of a surprise that public policy more closely reflects the views of higher-income Americans.

Question: *Do you think the trend toward a global economy is a good thing or a bad thing for the country?*

	Good thing	Bad thing
$75,000 and up	69%	31%
$50-75,000	65%	35%
$30-49,000	61%	39%
$20-29,000	60%	40%
Under $20,000	56%	44%
Total	61%	39%

Sources: Washington Post/Newsweek survey, October 2000 (for first and second questions); Princeton Survey Research, September 1998 (for third question). See Public Agenda Online at www.publicagenda.org

---

Representative, has been to open up foreign markets to American products. Occasionally the United States has threatened to limit the importation of foreign products in order to force other nations to open up their own markets. And occasionally in Congress members from districts adversely affected by foreign competition have opposed specific trade arrangements or, alternatively, called upon the federal government to assist workers displaced by foreign competition. But the thrust of U.S. policy has been to expand free trade.

Democrats in Congress have expressed more reservations about free trade than Republicans. (Democrats often call for "fair trade" in lieu of "free trade.") Democratic Congress members often reflect the views of their party's core constituencies, including labor unions, that fear the adverse effect on wages created by globalization. Environmentalists also complain that foreign corporations are not governed by strong or well-enforced environmental laws in their own countries. An array of other groups frequently demonstrates against globalization at meetings of the World Trade Organization and other international bodies (see *What Do You Think?*: "Does Globalization Help or Hurt America?").

THINK AGAIN

Which is more important holding down the size of government or providing needed services?

Government Spending, Budget Priorities, and Debt

The expenditures of all governments in the United States—federal, state, and local governments combined—today amount to about 30 percent of GDP. The federal government itself spends more than $2.4 trillion each year—about 20 percent of GDP.

"Mandatory" Spending Much of the growth of federal government spending over the years is attributed to **mandatory spending** items in the federal budget. These "uncontrollables" are budget items committed to by past policies of Congress that are not easily changed in annual budget making. Sources of mandatory spending include the following:

- *Entitlement programs:* Federal programs that provide classes of people with a legally enforceable right to benefits are called **entitlement programs.** Entitlement programs account for more than half of all federal spending, including Social Security, Medicare and Medicaid, food stamps, federal employees' retirement pensions, and veterans' benefits (see *Up Close:* "Transfers and Entitlements Drive Government Spending" on page 591). These entitlements are benefits that past Congresses have pledged the federal government to pay. Entitlements are not really uncontrollable. Congress can always amend the basic laws that established them, but doing so is politically difficult and might be regarded as abandonment of a public trust. As more people become "entitled" to government benefits—for example, as more people reach retirement ages and claim Social Security benefits—federal spending increases.

- *Indexing of benefits:* Another reason that spending increases each year is that Congress has authorized automatic increases in benefits to match inflation. Benefits under such programs as Social Security are tied to the Consumer Price Index. This **indexing** pushes up the cost of entitlement programs each year, even when the number of recipients stays the same, thus running counter to federal efforts to restrain inflation. Moreover, because the Consumer Price Index includes interest payments for new housing and the cost of new cars and appliances, it generally overestimates the needs of older recipients for cost-of-living increases.

- *Increasing costs of in-kind benefits:* Rises in the cost of major **in-kind (noncash) benefits,** particularly the medical costs of Medicaid and Medicare, also guarantee growth in federal spending. These in-kind benefit programs have risen faster in cost than cash benefit programs.

- *Interest on the national debt:* The federal government has a long history of deficits. In 1998 the president sent the first **balanced budget** to the Congress in thirty years. Deficit spending resumed in 2002. The accumulated deficits leave the government with a national debt of over $8.0 trillion. Interest payments on this debt now make up about 8 percent of total federal spending.

- *Backdoor spending and loan guarantees:* Some federal spending does not appear on the budget. For example, spending by the Postal Service is not included in the federal budget. No clear rule explains why some agencies are in the budget and others are not, but "off-budget" agencies have the same economic effects as other government agencies. Another form of **backdoor spending** is found in government-guaranteed loans. Initially government guarantees for loans—Federal

mandatory spending
Spending for program committments made by past congresses.

entitlement programs
Social welfare programs that provide classes of people with legally enforceable rights to benefits.

indexing Tying of benefit levels in social welfare programs to the general price level.

in-kind (noncash) benefits
Benefits of a social welfare program that are not cash payments, including free medical care, subsidized housing, and food stamps.

balanced budget
Government budget in which expenditures and revenues are equal, so that no deficit or surplus exists.

backdoor spending
Spending by agencies of the federal government whose operations are not included in the federal budget.

Transfers and Entitlements Drive Government Spending

Traditionally, governments in the United States have provided for national defense, police and fire protection, roads, education, and other public goods and services. These "public goods" cannot readily be provided by private markets because if one individual or firm purchased them, everyone else would get a "free ride"—that is, would use them without paying. Government involvement in these areas is not surprising. But these traditional public functions are not responsible for the growth of government in recent years.

Income Transfers

Expansion in the relative size of government over the years has been the result of increased governmental involvement in "income transfer" activities. The government has become a redistributor of income from one group to another—from the working population to retirees, from the employed to the unemployed, from the taxpayers to the disadvantaged (such as low-income households with dependent children).

Entitlements

Entitlement spending—payments to people entitled by law to receive them—account for about 6 percent of all federal spending. Note that most entitlement payments do not go to the poor. The largest share of entitlements—Social Security, Medicare, veterans' and federal retirement—goes to retirees. These programs alone account for two-thirds of all entitlement payments. Payments to the poor and unemployed—welfare, Medicaid, and unemployment insurance—account for less than one-third of federal entitlement spending.

Entitlements in the Federal Budget

	Billions of Dollars	Percentage
Entitlement, Total	$1,470	61.2
Social Security	515	21.5
Medicare	294	12.2
Medicaid	253	10.5
Federal retirement	93	3.9
Welfare entitlement (housing, food, cash assistance)	205	8.5
Veterans' benefits	67	2.8
Unemployment insurance	43	1.8
Defense	450	18.7
Domestic	264	11.1
Interest	178	7.4
International	38	1.6
Total Federal Spending	2,400	100.0

Source: Budget of the United States Government, 2005.

Housing Administration (FHA) housing loans, Guaranteed Student Loans, veterans' loans, and so forth—do not require federal money. The government merely promises to repay the loan if the borrower fails to do so. Yet these loans create an obligation against the government.

Federal Budget Priorities Federal budget shares (the percentage of outlays devoted to various functions) reflect the spending priorities of the national

Center on Budget and Policy Priorities

Data on budget items, projected costs of federal programs, etc. *www.cbpp.org*

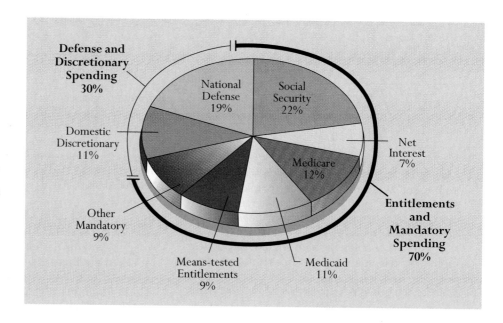

FIGURE 16.5 Federal Budget Shares

Mandatory spending—spending commitments in existing laws, notably Social Security, Medicare, Medicaid, and other entitlements, plus interest on the national debt—accounts for about two-thirds of the federal budget. Discretionary spending, including defense, accounts for only a little over one-third of the budget.

Source: Budget of the United States Government, 2005.

government. Entitlements and other mandatory spending (principally interest on the national debt) heavily outweighs defense and **discretionary spending** combined (see Figure 16.5). Spending on programs designed to assist senior citizens (Social Security and Medicare) heavily outweighs defense spending, welfare spending, and all discretionary spending. Today Social Security payments are the largest single item in the federal budget. Over time defense spending declined from over 50 percent of the federal budget at the height of the Cold War in the early 1960s to 14 percent in the 1990s. The war on terror, including military operations in Iraq and Afganistan, have increased defense spending to about 19 percent of the budget. Medical costs—Medicare for elderly and Medicaid for the poor—are currently the fastest growing items in the federal budget.

The Debt Burden The U.S. federal government incurred a **deficit** every year from 1969 to 1998—that is, its expenditure exceeded its revenues (see Figure 16.6). The accumulated **national debt** is over $5 trillion, or $20,000 for every man, woman, and child in the nation. This government debt is owed mostly to U.S. banks and financial institutions and private citizens who buy Treasury bonds. Only about 13 percent of the debt is owed to foreign banks and individuals. As old debt comes due, the U.S. Treasury Department sells new bonds to pay off the old; that is, it continues to "roll over" or "float" the debt. Despite its size in dollars, the debt today is smaller as a percentage of GDP than at some periods in U.S. history. For example, to pay the costs of fighting World War II, the U.S. government ran up a debt equivalent to over 100 percent of GDP. The current $5 trillion debt, although the highest in history in dollar terms, is equal to about 42 percent of GDP.

The ability to float such a huge debt depends on public confidence in the U.S. government—confidence that it will continue to pay interest on its debt, that it will pay off the principal of bonds when they come due, and that the value of the bonds will not decline over time because of inflation.

discretionary spending
Spending for programs not previously mandated by law.

deficit Imbalance in the annual federal budget in which spending exceeds revenues.

national debt Total debt accumulated by the national government over the years.

Interest Burden for Future Generations Interest payments on the national debt come from current taxes and so divert money away from *all* other government programs. Even if the federal government manages to balance future

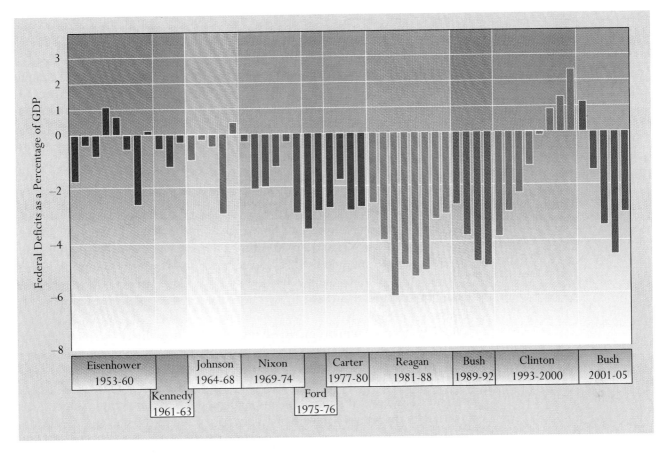

FIGURE 16.6 Deficits through the Years

This figure shows annual federal deficits as percentages of the GDP. Note that the federal government incurred deficits for thirty years, under both Republican and Democratic presidential administrations. A strong economy, and resulting increases in revenues flowing to the federal government, created budget surpluses from 1998 to 2001. An economic slowdown, and added security costs after the 9/11 attack on America put the federal budget back in the red.

Source: Budget of the United States Government, 2005.

budgets, these payments will remain obligations of the children and grandchildren of the current generation of policy makers and taxpayers. Interest payments on the national debt, currently about 9 percent of the federal budget, do not purchase any government goods or services. This means that for every dollar paid in federal taxes, taxpayers currently receive only 91 cents in government goods and services.

The Long-Sought Balanced Budget Economic growth began to shrink annual deficits after the 1991–92 recession. The nation's booming economy increased tax revenues. And in 1993, President Clinton succeeded in getting a Democratic-controlled Congress to pass a major increase in tax rates (see "Tax Politics," later in this chapter). After 1994, a Republican-controlled Congress slowed the growth of federal spending. Budget "caps" were enacted by Congress and worked surprisingly well during the 1990s in holding down overall spending. President Clinton did not introduce any major new spending programs after his comprehensive health care program failed to pass Congress in 1993 (see Chapter 17). So both Democrats and Republicans claimed credit for reducing annual deficits.

Concord Coalition
Nonpartisan advocacy organization promoting fiscal responsibility and balanced federal budget.
www.concordcoalition.org

Politics, Deficits, and Spending Federal budget surpluses lasted for only four years, 1998–2001. During those years, Democrats and Republicans in Washington fought over what to do with the surplus revenues. Both parties pledged to use part of the surplus to strengthen Social Security and Medicare for the coming retirement of the "baby-boom" generation. But Republicans and conservatives argued that surpluses should also be used to reduce taxes or to pay off part of the national debt, or some combination of both. In contrast, Democrats argued that the surpluses should be used for investment in education, job skills, federal health insurance, and environmental protection. The result of the stalemate was a modest automatic reduction in the national debt.

But an economic slowdown, combined with the added security spending after the 9/11 attack on America, brought a return of red ink to federal budgets. Outlays for national defense increased dramatically, as the spending for homeland security increased—border and airport security, terrorism preparedness, aid to police, fire, and rescue teams, and the like. Democrats also blamed the return of deficits on Bush's tax cuts of 2001 and 2003 (see "Bush Tax Cuts" later in this chapter). But Republicans argued that these tax cuts helped avoid an even deeper economic recession.

Both parties now support increased spending for the military and for homeland security. Both seem willing to set aside the goal of a balanced budget in order to do so. But it is likely that conflict between Democrats, who seek to spend more on social programs, and Republicans, who seek further tax reductions, is likely to continue. The general public remains ambiguous over conflicting budget goals they want both increased government services *and* reduced taxes (see *What Do You Think?* "Should We Increase Government Services or Reduce Taxes?" on page 595).

The Tax Burden

The tax burden in the United States is modest compared to burdens in other advanced democracies (see *Compared to What?*: "Tax Burdens in Advanced Democracies" on page 596). Federal revenues are derived mainly from (1) individual income taxes, (2) corporate income taxes, (3) Social Security payroll taxes, (4) estate and gift taxes, and (5) excise taxes and custom duties.

Individual Income Taxes The **individual income tax** is the federal government's largest source of revenue (see Figure 16.7). Following tax cuts enacted by Congress in 2001 and 2003, individual income is now taxed at six rates: 10, 15, 25, 28, 33, and 35 percent. These are *marginal rates*, a term that economists use to mean additional. That is, income up to the top of the lowest bracket is taxed at 10 percent; additional income in the next bracket is taxed at 15 percent, up to a top marginal rate of 35 percent on income over $311,950 (in 2003). A personal exemption for each taxpayer and dependent, together with a standard deduction for married couples and a refundable earned income tax credit, ensure that low income earners pay no income tax. (However, they still must pay Social Security taxes on wages.) Tax brackets, as well as the personal exemption and standard deduction, are indexed annually to protect against inflation.

The income tax is automatically deducted from the paychecks of employees. This "withholding" system is the backbone of the individual income tax. There is no withholding of nonwage income such as dividends on investments, but taxpayers with such income must file a "Declaration of Estimated Taxes" and pay this estimate in quarterly installments. Before April 15 of each year, all income-

THINK AGAIN

Do you believe all wage earners should pay the same percentage of income in taxes (a flat tax)?

individual income tax
Taxes on individuals' wages and other earned income, the primary source of revenue for the U.S. federal government.

Should We Increase Government Services or Reduce Taxes?

Americans want both increased services from government *and* a smaller government and lower taxes. They say they want a smaller government, but at the same time they say that "providing needed services" is more important than holding down the size of government. In other words, people want more for less. Consider the responses to two separate questions regularly asked in national polls.

Q. Do you favor smaller government with fewer services, or larger government with many services?

Smaller government, fewer services	54%
Larger government, many services	41
No opinion	5

Q. Which of these is more important to you: holding down the size of government of providing needed services?

Providing needed services	64%
Holding down size of government	33
Both (volunteered)	3

On the surface these responses appear to be contradictory. Yet one could argue that citizens really want a small, efficient government that provides for all of their needs.

The American public wants a balanced federal budget, but apparently this is not its highest priority. On the contrary, a number of issues are considered more important than a balanced budget, including the War on Terrorism, economic stimulus, improving education, providing for national defense, improving health care, and providing the elderly with prescription drugs.

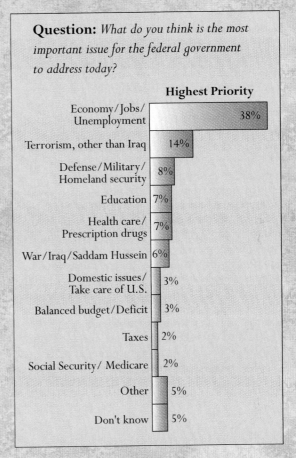

Question: *What do you think is the most important issue for the federal government to address today?*

Highest Priority

- Economy/Jobs/Unemployment — 38%
- Terrorism, other than Iraq — 14%
- Defense/Military/Homeland security — 8%
- Education — 7%
- Health care/Prescription drugs — 7%
- War/Iraq/Saddam Hussein — 6%
- Domestic issues/Take care of U.S. — 3%
- Balanced budget/Deficit — 3%
- Taxes — 2%
- Social Security/Medicare — 2%
- Other — 5%
- Don't know — 5%

Source: First questions based on data from ABC News/*Washington Post*, February 2002 as reported in *Public Agenda Online*, questions on priorities based on data from Fox News poll (September, 2003).

---

earning Americans must report their taxable income for the previous year to the Internal Revenue Service on its 1040 Form.

Americans are usually surprised to learn that half of all personal income is not taxed. To understand why, we must know how the tax laws distinguish between *adjusted gross income* (an individual's total money income minus expenses incurred in earning that income) and *taxable income* (that part of adjusted gross income subject to taxation). Federal tax rates apply only to *taxable* income.

Tax expenditures are tax revenues lost to the federal government because of exemptions, exclusions, deductions, and special treatments in tax laws. Federal government revenues from individual and business income taxes would be substantially

tax expenditures Revenues lost to the federal government because of exemptions, exclusions, deductions, and special-treatment provisions in tax laws.

Tax Burdens in Advanced Democracies

Americans complain a lot about taxes. But from a global perspective, overall tax burdens in the United States are relatively low (see figure). Federal, state, and local taxes in the United States amount to about 30 percent of the gross domestic product (GDP), slightly below the burden carried by the nation's leading competitors, Japan and Germany. U.S. taxes are well below the burdens imposed in Sweden, Denmark, and other nations with highly developed welfare systems.

Top marginal tax rates in many nations were reduced during the 1980s and 1990s. For example, the top rate in Great Britain was lowered from 60 to 40 percent, in Japan from 70 to 50 percent, and in Sweden from 80 to 65 percent. Both in the United States and abroad, the notion that excessively high tax rates discourage work, savings, and investment, as well as slow economic growth, won acceptance (although how high is "excessive" is obviously open to different interpretations). Moreover, in a global economy, with increased mobility of individuals and firms, pressures push nations to keep their top tax rates within reasonable limits. Corporations can shift their assets to low-tax jurisdictions, and high personal income tax rates can even threaten a "brain drain" of talented individuals.

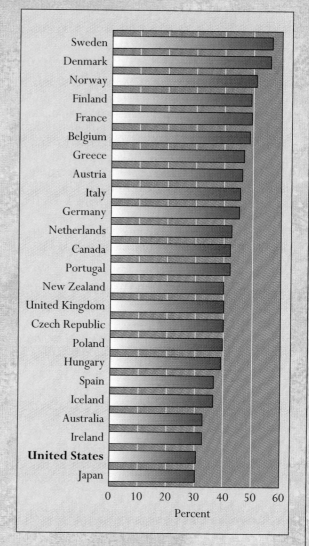

Government Revenues as a Percentage of GDP

Source: OECD, *Economic Outlook.* 1999.

 Internal Revenue Service

Official IRS site, with downloadable tax forms, information on tax laws, and tax statistics. **www.irs.gov**

higher were it not for special provisions in tax laws that enable taxpayers to avoid paying taxes on often substantial sums of income. Although each of these "loopholes" supposedly has a larger social goal behind it (for example, the deductibility of mortgage interest is supposed to stimulate the purchase—and construction—of homes, keeping up the value of those assets for current homeowners and keeping the construction industry employed), critics charge that many cost far more than they are worth to society. These are the major tax expenditures in federal tax law:

■ Personal exemptions for taxpayer, spouse, and children

■ Deductibility of mortgage interest on homes

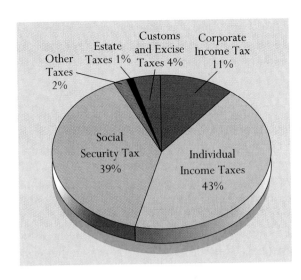

FIGURE 16.7 Sources of Federal Income

Individual income taxes make up the largest portion of the federal government's revenues (43 percent). The government also relies heavily on the second largest source of its revenues, Social Security taxes.

Source: Budget of the United States Government, 2005.

- Deductibility of property taxes on first and second homes

- Deferral of capital gains on home sales

- Deductibility of charitable contributions

- Credit for child-care expenses

- Tax-free deposits for educational savings accounts

- Exclusion of employer contributions to pension plans and medical insurance

- Partial exclusion of Social Security benefits

- Exclusion of interest on public-purpose state and local bonds

- Deductibility of state and local income taxes

- Exclusion of income earned abroad

- Accelerated depreciation of machinery, equipment, and structure

- Deductible contributions to IRAs and 401(K) retirement plans, and accrued interest and profits in these plans. (But taxes must be paid when cash is taken from these plans.)

There is a continual struggle between proponents of special tax exemptions to achieve social goals and those who believe the tax laws should be simplified and social goals met by direct government expenditures. Much of the political infighting in Washington involves the efforts of interest groups to obtain exemptions, exclusions, deductions, and special treatments in tax laws.[5]

In addition to these multiple means of tax *avoidance* (legal means), an "underground economy" that facilitates tax *evasion* (illegal means of dodging taxes) costs the federal government many billions of dollars. The federal Internal Revenue Service itself estimates that it is losing about $200 billion per year in revenue due to the failure of people to report income and pay taxes on it. Independent estimates of the size of the underground economy are much higher, perhaps $350 billion, or 15 percent of all taxes due.[6] Many citizens receive cash for goods and services they provide, and it simply does not occur to them to report these amounts as income in addition to the wage statements they receive from their employer. Many others receive all or most of their income from cash transactions; they have a strong incentive to underreport their income. And, of course, illegal criminal transactions such as drug dealing are seldom reported on personal income tax forms. As tax rates rise, hiding income becomes more profitable.

Corporate Income Taxes The corporate income tax provides only about 10 percent of the federal government's total revenue. The Tax Reform Act of 1986 reduced the top corporate income tax from 46 to 34 percent (raised to 35 percent in 1993). However, corporations find many ways of reducing their taxable income often to zero. The result was that many very large and profitable corporations pay little in taxes. Religious, charitable, and educational organizations as well as labor unions, are exempt from corporate income taxes except for income they may derive from "unrelated business activity."

Who really bears the burden of the corporate income tax? Economists differ over whether the corporate income tax is "shifted" to consumers or whether corporations and their stockholders bear its burden. The evidence on the **incidence**—that is, who actually bears the burden—of this tax is inconclusive.[7]

Social Security Taxes The second largest source of federal revenue is the Social Security tax. It is withheld from paychecks as the "FICA" deduction an acronym that helps hide the true costs of Social Security and Medicare from wage earners. To keep up with the rising number or beneficiaries and the higher levels of benefits voted for by Congress, including generous automatic cost-of-living increases each year, the Social Security taxes rose to 15.3 percent. (The Social Security tax is 12.4 percent and the Medicare tax is 2.9 percent all wage income is subject to the Medicare tax, but wage income above a certain level $87,900 in 2004—is not subject to the Social Security tax.)

Taxes collected under FICA are earmarked (by Social Security number) for the account of each taxpayer. Workers thus feel they are receiving benefits as a right rather than as a gift of the government. However, less than 15 percent of the benefits being paid to current recipients of Social Security can be attributed to their prior contributions. Current taxpayers are paying more than 85 percent of the benefits received by current retirees.

Today a majority of taxpayers pay more in Social Security taxes than income taxes. Indeed, combined employer and employee Social Security taxes now amount to over $13,500 for each worker at the top of the wage base. If we assume that the employer's share of the tax actually comes out of wages that would otherwise be paid to the employee, then more than 75 percent of all taxpayers pay more in Social Security taxes than in income taxes.

Estate and Gift Taxes Taxation of property left to heirs is one of the oldest forms of taxation in the world. Federal estate taxes begin on estates of $650,000 (scheduled to rise to $1 million in 2006) and levy a tax rate that starts at 18 percent and rises to 49 percent for estates worth more than $3 million. (This top rate is scheduled to decrease one percent each year to 45% in 2007). Because taxes at death otherwise could be avoided by simply giving estates to heirs while the giver is still alive, a federal gift tax is also levied on anyone who gives gifts in excess of $10,000 annually.

Excise Taxes and Custom Duties Federal excise taxes on the consumption of liquor, tobacco, gasoline, telephones, air travel, and other so-called luxury items, together with custom taxes on imports, provide about 3 percent of total federal revenues.

incidence Actual bearer of a tax burden.

Tax Politics

The politics of taxation centers around the question of who actually bears the heaviest burden of a tax—especially which income groups must devote the largest proportion of their income to taxes. **Progressive taxation** requires high-income groups to pay a larger percentage of their incomes in taxes than low-income groups. **Regressive taxation** takes a larger share of the income of low-income groups. **Proportional (flat) taxation** requires all income groups to pay the same percentage of their income in taxes. Note that the *percentage of income* paid in taxes is the determining factor. Most taxes take more money from the rich than the poor, but a progressive or regressive tax is distinguished by the percentages of income taken from various income groups.

The Argument for Progressivity
Progressive taxation is generally defended on the principle of ability to pay; the assumption is that high-income groups can afford to pay a larger percentage of their incomes into taxes at no more of a sacrifice than that required of lower income groups to devote a smaller proportion of their income to taxation. This assumption is based on what economists call *marginal utility theory* as it applies to money; each additional dollar of income is slightly less valuable to an individual than preceding dollars. For example, a $5,000 increase in the income of an individual already earning $100,000 is much less valuable than a $5,000 increase to an individual earning only $10,000 or to an individual with no income at all. Hence, it is argued that added dollars of income can be taxed at higher rates without violating equitable principles.

The Argument for Proportionality
Opponents of progressive taxation generally assert that equity can only be achieved by taxing everyone at the same percentage of their income, regardless of the size of their income. Progressivity penalizes initiative, enterprise, and the risk taking necessary to create new products and businesses. It also reduces incentives to expand and develop the nation's economy. Highly progressive taxes curtail growth and make everyone poorer (see *A Conflicting View*: "We Should Enact a Flat Tax").

Reagan's Reductions in Progressivity
Certainly the most dramatic change in federal tax laws during the Reagan years was the reduction in the progressivity of individual income tax rates (see Figure 16.8). The top marginal tax rate fell from 70 percent when President Reagan took office to 28 percent following enactment of tax reform in 1986. The Tax Reform Act of 1986 reduced fourteen rate brackets to only two rate brackets, 15 and 28 percent.

"Read My Lips"
At the Republican national convention in 1988, presidential nominee George Bush made a firm pledge to American voters that he would veto any tax increases passed by the Democratic-controlled Congress: "Read my lips! No new taxes." Yet in a 1990 budget summit with Democratic congressional leaders, President Bush agreed to add a top marginal rate of 31 percent to the personal income tax. Breaking his solemn pledge on taxes contributed heavily to Bush's defeat in the 1992 presidential election.

"Soak the Rich"
Proposals to "soak the rich" are always politically very popular. President Clinton pushed Congress to raise the top marginal tax rates to 36 percent for families earning $140,000, and to 39.6 percent for families earning

National Taxpayers Union

Advocacy organization for taxpayers "to keep what they have earned," with policy papers and data on tax burdens. ***www.ntu.org***

progressive taxation
System of taxation in which higher income groups pay a larger percentage of their incomes in taxes than do lower income groups.

regressive taxation System of taxation in which lower income groups pay a larger percentage of their incomes in taxes than do higher income groups.

proportional (flat) taxation
System of taxation in which all income groups pay the same percentage of their income in taxes.

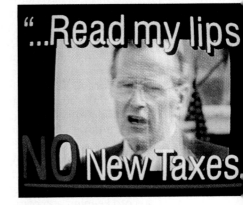

George Bush's pledge "Read my lips, no new taxes" helped him to victory in 1988. But breaking the pledge in 1990 contributed heavily to his defeat in 1992.

We Should Enact a Flat Tax

More than a hundred years ago, Supreme Court Justice Stephen J. Field, in striking down as unconstitutional a progressive income tax enacted by Congress, predicted that such a tax would lead to class wars: "Our political contests will become a war of the poor against the rich, a war constantly growing in intensity and bitterness."[*] But populist sentiment in the early twentieth century—the anger of midwestern farmers toward eastern rail tycoons and the beliefs of impoverished southerners that they would never have incomes high enough to pay an income tax—helped secure the passage of the Sixteenth Amendment to the U.S. Constitution. The federal income tax passed by Congress in 1914 had a top rate of 7 percent; less than 1 percent of the population had incomes high enough to be taxed. Today the top rate is 39.6 percent (actually over 42 percent when mandated phaseouts of deductions are calculated); about half of the population pays income taxes.

The current income tax progressively penalizes all the behaviors that produce higher incomes—work, savings, investment, and initiative. And whenever incomes are taxed at different rates, people will figure out ways to take advantage of the differential. They will hire lawyers, accountants, and lobbyists to find or create exemptions, exclusions, deductions, and preferential treatments for their own sources of income. The tax laws will become increasingly lengthy and complex. Today about half of all personal income is excluded from federal income taxation.

The Internal Revenue Service (IRS) is the most intrusive of all government agencies, overseeing the finances of every tax-paying citizen and corporation in America. It maintains personal records on more than 100 million Americans and requires them to submit more than a billion forms each year. It may levy fines and penalties and collect taxes on its own initiative; in disputes with the IRS, the burden of proof falls on the taxpayer, not the agency. Its 110,000 employees spend $8 billion per year reviewing tax returns, investigating taxpayers, and collecting revenue. Americans pay an additional $30 billion for the services of tax accountants and preparers, and they waste some $200 billion in hours of record keeping and computing their taxes.

We should replace the current federal income tax system with a simple flat tax that could be calculated on a postcard. The elimination of all exemptions, exclusions, deductions, and special treatment, and the replacement of current progressive tax rates with a flat 19 percent tax on all forms of income, even excluding family incomes under $25,000, would produce just as much revenue as the current complicated system. It would sweep away the nation's army of tax accountants and lawyers and lobbyists, and increase national productivity by relieving taxpayers of millions of hours of record keeping and tax preparation. A flat tax could be filed on a postcard form (see below). Removing progressive rates would create incentives to work, save, and invest in America. It would lead to more rapid economic growth and improve efficiency by directing investments to their most productive uses rather than to tax avoidance. It would eliminate current incentives to underreport income, overstate exemptions, and avoid and evade taxation. Finally, by exempting a generous personal and family allowance, the flat tax would be made fair.

---

[*]*Pollock v. Farmer's Loan*, 158 U.S. 601 (1895).

Form 1	Individual Wage Tax		2000
Your first name and initial (if joint return, also give spouse's name and initial)	Last name		Your social security number
Home address (number and street including apartment number or rural route)			Spouse's social security number
City, town, or post office, state, and ZIP code			Your occupation
			Spouse's occupation
1 Wages and salary		1	
2 Pension and retirement benefits		2	
3 Total compensation (*line 1 plus line 2*)		3	
4 Personal allowance			
(a) 0 $16,500 for married filing jointly		4a	
(b) 0 $9,500 for single		4b	
(c) 0 $14,000 for single head of household		4c	
5 Number of dependents, not including spouse		5	
6 Personal allowances for dependents (*line 5 multiplied by $4,500*)		6	
7 Total personal allowances (*line 4 plus line 6*)		7	
8 Taxable compensation (*line 3 less line 7, if positive; otherwise zero*)		8	
9 Tax (*19% of line 8*)		9	
10 Tax withheld by employer		10	
11 Tax due (*line 9 less line 10, if positive*)		11	
12 Refund due (*line 10 less line 9, if positive*)		12	

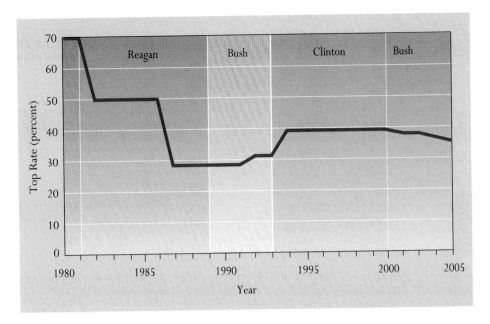

FIGURE 16.8 Top Personal Income Tax Rates

The top marginal personal income tax rate fell dramatically during the Reagan Administration, then began to creep upward again under Presidents Bush and Clinton. George W. Bush lowered the top rate in 2001 and again in 2003.

$250,000. But these new top rates do not raise much revenue, partly because very few people have annual incomes in these categories. Moreover, high rates encourage people to seek tax-sheltered investments—to use their capital less efficiently to create tax breaks for themselves rather than to promote new business and new jobs.

Bush Tax Cuts George W. Bush came into office vowing *not* to make the same mistake as his father, raising tax rates in an effort to compromise with the Democrats. On the contrary, Bush was strongly committed to lowering taxes, arguing first in 2001 that the American people should receive some part of the government's surpluses. Congress responded with a small tax cut, bringing the top marginal rate from 39.6 percent to 38.6 percent.

By 2003 the economy appeared to be in a slide. Bush argued that an "economic stimulus" package of additional tax cuts would revive the economy. He believed that federal deficits were the result of slow economic growth; tax reductions might temporarily add to deficits but eventually the economic growth inspired by lower taxes would increase government revenues and eliminate deficits.

Bush moved the Republican-controlled Congress to lower the top marginal rate to 35 percent, and restructure rates through six brackets—10, 15, 25, 28, 33, and 35 percent. (see Table 16.2). And the Bush 2003 tax package also contained a variety of new credits and special treatments:

Dividends: Corporate stock dividends are to be taxed at a low 15 percent rather than at the same rate as earned income. Bush and the Republicans in Congress initially proposed eliminating all taxes on dividends. They argued that corporations already paid taxes on corporate profits, and inasmuch as dividends come out of profits, taxing them as personal income amounted to "double taxation." They also recognized that nearly one-half of all American families now own stock or mutual funds, and they hoped that this new tax break would be politically popular. The 15 percent tax rate on dividends is less than half of the top marginal rate of 35 percent on earned income.

TABLE 16.2 Marginal Individual Income Tax Rates

	Before 2001	2001	2005
Lowest	15%	10%	10%
to	28	15	15
Highest	31	27	25
Income	36	30	28
Brackets	39.6	35	33
		38.6	35

Marriage penalty: For married couples the new law made the standard personal deduction twice that of a single person. This change corrected a flaw in the tax law that had long plagued married persons filing joint returns.

Child tax credit: The per child tax credit was raised to $1,000 (from $600). This was a politically popular change supported by many Democrats as well as Republicans.

Capital gains: Finally, the Bush tax package chipped away again at the tax on capital gains—profits from the sale of investments held at least one year. The capital gains tax was reduced from 20 to 15 percent, a rate less than half of the top marginal rate on earned income of 35 percent.

The Bush tax package was approved in the Republican-controlled House and Senate on largely party line votes. Most Democrats were opposed to the package, arguing that it primarily benefited the rich, that it would do little to help the economy, and that it would add to the already huge annual federal deficits. Republicans argued that the package benefited all taxpayers, and inasmuch as the rich pay most of the taxes it is only fair that they should benefit from tax reductions. And they argued that the child credit and marriage penalty breaks would continue to ensure that families with incomes under $40,000 would pay little or no federal income taxes.

Democrats in opposition to the Bush package managed to limit it to two years. The effect was to require a congressional renewal in 2005 or a vote to make the cuts permanent as urged by President Bush.

Who Pays the Federal Income Tax?
The federal income tax continues to be highly progressive. Progressive rates, together with the personal and standard deductions for families and the earned income tax credit for low-income earners, combined to remove most of the income tax burden on middle- and low-income Americans. Indeed, the lower half of the nation's taxpayers pay only about 4 percent of total income taxes paid to the federal government. The top 10 percent of income earners pay 69 percent of all individual income taxes (see Figure 16.9). Politically, this means that most proposals to reduce income taxes can be branded by opponents as "favoring the rich" inasmuch as the rich pay most of the income tax bill.

Capital Gains Taxation
All income is *not* taxed equally under federal income tax laws. (Indeed, interest income from municipal bonds is totally tax free, encouraging many wealthy investors to put their money into these "munies.") The Tax

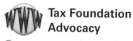

Tax Foundation Advocacy

Organization devoted to making the public "tax conscious," with information, "fiscal facts," and "tax freedom day." **www.taxfoundation.org**

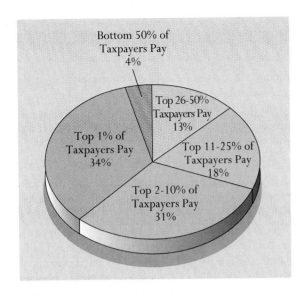

FIGURE 16.9   Who Pays the Federal Personal Income Tax?

Percentage of Total Federal Income Taxes Paid by Income Levels

Source: Based on data from The Tax Foundation at http://www.taxfoundation.org .html.

Bottom 50% of Taxpayers Pay 4%

Top 26-50% Taxpayers Pay 13%

Top 1% of Taxpayers Pay 34%

Top 11-25% of Taxpayers Pay 18%

Top 2-10% of Taxpayers Pay 31%

Code distinguishes between earned income and **capital gains**—profits from the buying and selling of property, including stocks, bonds, and real estate. Currently capital gains are taxed at a top marginal rate of 15 percent, compared to the top marginal rate of 35 percent for earned income in 2005.

Why should income earned from *working* be taxed at a higher rate than income earned from *investing*? The real estate industry, together with investment firms and stockbrokers, argue that high tax rates on capital gains discourage investment and economic growth. (But if it is true that high taxes discourage investment, high taxes must also discourage work, and both capital and labor are required for economic growth.) But the political power of investors, especially in the Republican Party, places heavy downward pressure on capital gains tax rates.

A major goal of tax reform has been to treat all income equally. The Tax Reform Act of 1986 eliminated preferential treatment for capital gains, but this preference was restored by President Bush and Congress in 1991: the top rate on earned income was pushed to 31 percent while the capital gains rate stayed at 28 percent. And again in 1993, when President Clinton raised the top rate on earned income to 39.6 percent, he quietly allowed the lower capital gains rate to remain the same. But the Republican Congress lowered capital gains taxation even further, granting additional preferential treatment for capital gains that brings the effective tax rate on such income to 15 percent.

capital gains Profits from buying and selling property including stocks, bonds, and real estate.

- A central policy issue is deciding how much to rely on government versus the marketplace to produce and distribute goods and services. The United States is primarily a free-market economy, but federal fiscal and monetary policies exercise a strong influence over economic activity.

- Fiscal policy—decisions about government taxing, spending, and deficits or surpluses—is decided in the president's budget recommendations and in the appropriations acts passed by Congress. Monetary policy is largely decided by the independent Federal Reserve Board.

- The performance of the economy can be measured by GDP growth and the unemployment and inflation rates. Politically the unemployment rate may be the most important of these measures of economic performance.

- Imports and exports grow each year as a percentage of the gross domestic product of the United States. This trend toward globalization has been fostered by U.S. participation in the World Trade Organization, the International Monetary Fund, the World Bank, the North American Free Trade Agreement, and other agreements and treaties in support of free trade. Free trade may benefit the economy as a whole, but it appears to disadvantage poorly educated, low-skilled American workers.

- Annual federal budget deficits over thirty years led to a national debt of more than $5 trillion, an amount equal almost half the nation's GDP. A strong economy produced budget surpluses from 1998 through 2001, but an economic slowdown combined with the effects of the 9/11 terrorist attack, and perhaps also the effects of tax cuts enacted by the Republican-controlled Congress and President George W. Bush, led to a return of annual budget deficits.

- Tax politics centers on the question of who actually bears the burden of a tax. The individual income tax, the largest source of federal government revenue, is progressive, with higher rates levied at higher income levels. Progressive taxation is defended on the ability-to-pay principle. But half of all personal income, and a great deal of corporate income, is untaxed, owing to a wide variety of exemptions, exclusions, deductions, and special treatments on tax laws. These provisions are defended in Washington by a powerful array of interest groups.

- The Reagan Administration reduced top income tax rates from 70 to 28 percent, believing high rates discouraged work, savings, and investment, and thereby curtailed economic growth. But George Bush agreed to an increase in the top rate to 31 percent. Bill Clinton pushed Congress to raise the top rates to 36 and 39.6 percent, arguing that rich people had benefited from Reagan's "trickle down" policies and must now be forced to bear their "fair share." George W. Bush succeeded in getting two tax cut bills through Congress in 2001 and 2003. The bills lower the top marginal income tax rate to 35 percent, and the individual penalty, increase child exemptions, and lower the capital gain rate to 15 percent.

KEY TERMS

Wolff, Edward N. *Top Heavy* (updated edition). New York: Century Foundation, 2002. The study of the increasing inequality of wealth in United States and an argument for taxing financial wealth (bank accounts, stocks, bonds, property, houses, cars, etc.) as well as income.

Langren, Robert and Martin Snitzer. *Government, Business and the American Economy.* Upper Saddle River, N.J.: Prentice Hall, 2001. Comprehensive text on the government's role in the economy.

Sowell, Thomas. *Basic Economics: A Citizen's Guide to the Economy.* New York: Basic Books, 2003. Introduction to economics with an emphasis on public policy. No jargon or equations.

Rothgeb, John M. Jr. *U.S. Trade Policy.* Washington, D.C.: CQ Press, 2001. Concise text on international trade, including history of GATT, WTO, and NAFTA.

Steger, Manfred B. *Globalism.* Boston: Rowman & Littlefield, 2002. The politics of pro- and anti-globalist groups, with a sharp critique of the ideology of globalism.

Ryscavage, Paul. *Income Inequality in America.* Armonk, N.Y.: M.E. Sharpe, 1999. An analysis of the trend toward growing income inequality in United States since the early 1970s.

MAKE IT REAL

BALANCING THE NATION'S CHECKBOOK: WHAT CAN YOU GET FOR $4 TRILLION?

The federal government's budget process begins nearly two years in advance, when the various departments and agencies estimate their needs and propose their budgets to the president. Agency officials take into account not only their needs but also the overall presidential program and the prob- able reactions of Congress. In this simulation you are the director of the Office of Management and Budget and need to make recommendations for budget cuts to make up for the president's tax.

POLITICS AND SOCIAL WELFARE

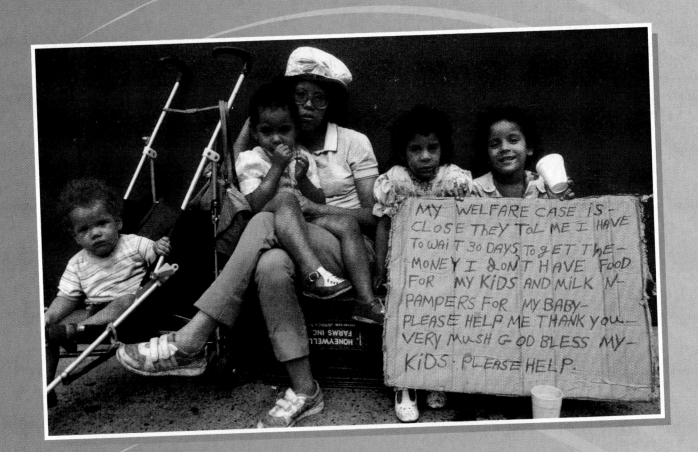

Power and Social Welfare

Social welfare policy largely determines who gets what from government—who benefits from government spending on its citizens and how much they get. This vast power has made the federal government a major *redistributor* of income from one group to another—from the working population to retirees, from the employed to the unemployed, from taxpayers to poor people. Direct payments to individuals—Social Security, welfare, pension, and other **transfer payments**—now account for about 60 percent of all federal government outlays.

When most Americans think of social welfare programs, they think of poor people. An estimated 35 million to 40 million people in the United States (11 to 15 percent of the population) have incomes below the official **poverty line**—that is, their annual cash income falls below what is required to maintain a decent standard of living (see Figure 17.1). If the approximately $1 trillion spent per year for social welfare were directly distributed to the nation's poor people, each poor person—man, woman, and child—would receive $25,000 per year.

Why does poverty persist in a nation where total social welfare spending is more than four times the amount needed to eliminate poverty? Because poor people are not the principal beneficiaries of social welfare spending. Most social welfare spending, including the largest programs—Social Security and Medicare—goes to the *non*poor (see Figure 17.2). Less than one-third of federal social welfare spending is **means-tested spending**—that is, distributed on the basis of the recipient's income. The middle classes, not the poor, are the major beneficiaries of the nation's social welfare system.

Poverty in the United States

How much poverty really exists in the United States? It depends on how you define the term "poverty." The official definition used by the federal government focuses on the cash income needed to maintain a "decent standard of living." The official poverty line is only a little more than one-third of the median income of all American families. It takes into account the effects of inflation, rising each year with the rate of inflation. (For example, in 1990, the official poverty line for an urban family of four was $13,359 per year; by 2004 the poverty line had risen to about $19,000.)

Temporary Poverty Poor people are often envisioned as a permanent "underclass" living most of their lives in poverty. But most poverty is not long term. Tracing poor families over time presents a different picture of the

FIGURE 17.1 Number of Poor and Poverty Rate

Source:
http://www.census.gov/hhes/poverty00/pov00.html.

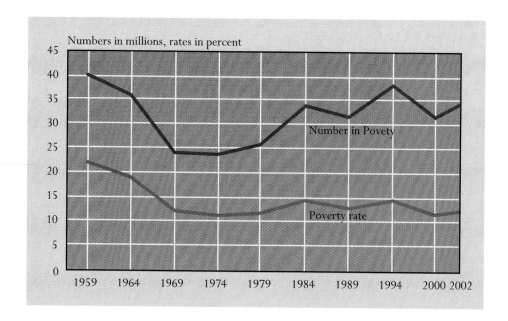

Numbers in millions, rates in percent

Number in Poverty

Poverty rate

National Center for Children in Poverty

Columbia University Center with studies and data on children in poverty.
www.nccp.org

transfer payments Direct payments (either in cash or in goods and/or services) by governments to individuals as part of a social welfare program, not as a result of any service or contribution rendered by the individual.

poverty line Official standard regarding what level of annual cash income is sufficient to maintain a "decent standard of living"; those with incomes below this level are eligible for most public assistance programs.

means-tested spending Spending for benefits that is distributed on the basis of the recipient's income.

underclass People who have remained poor and dependent on welfare over a prolonged period of time.

nature of poverty from the "snapshot" view taken in any one year. For example, over the last decade 11 to 15 percent of the nation's population has been officially classified as poor in any one year. However, only *some* poverty is persistent: about 6 to 8 percent of the population remains in poverty for more than five years. Thus about half of the people who are counted as poor are experiencing poverty for only a short period of time. For these temporary poor, welfare is a "safety net" that helps them through hard times.

Persistent Poverty About half of the people on welfare rolls at any one time are *persistently poor*, that is, likely to remain on welfare for five or more years. For these people, welfare is a more permanent part of their lives.

Because they place a disproportionate burden on welfare resources, persistently poor people pose serious questions for social scientists and policy makers. Prolonged poverty and welfare dependency create an **underclass** that suffers from many social ills—teen pregnancy, family instability, drugs, crime, alienation, apathy, and irresponsibility.[1] Government educational, training, and jobs programs, as well as many other social service efforts, fail to benefit many of these people.

Family Structure Poverty and welfare dependency are much more frequent among female-headed households with no husband present than among husband-wife households (see *Up Close:* "Who Are the Poor?"). Traditionally, "illegitimacy" was held in check by powerful religious and social structures. But these structures weakened over time (see Figure 17.3), and the availability of welfare cash benefits, food stamps, medical care, and government housing removed much of the economic hardship once associated with unwed motherhood. Indeed, it was sometimes argued that government welfare programs, however well meaning, ended up perpetuating poverty and social dependency. This argument inspired welfare reform in 1996 (see "Politics and Welfare Reform" later in this chapter).

Teen Pregnancy Teenage motherhood is usually a path to poverty. "Babies having babies" is closely associated with social welfare dependency. But births to teenage mothers—the number of births per 1,000 women fifteen to nineteen years of age—has actually *declined* in recent years. Liberals claim that this modest victory

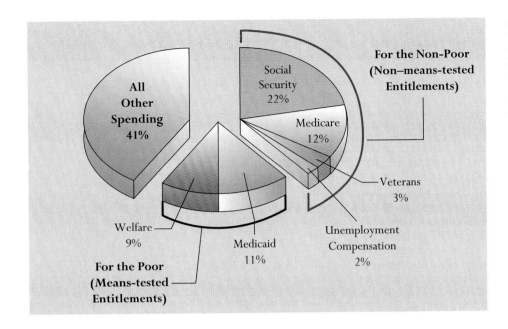

FIGURE 17.2 Social Welfare Entitlement Programs in the Federal Budget

Source: Budget of the United States Government, 2005.

is a product of better sex education and condom distribution in schools. Conservatives claim that it is a result of teaching abstinence, as well as welfare reforms requiring teenagers to reside with their parents and continue schooling as conditions for cash payments. According to federal survey data, teenage girls are having less sex *and* making more use of birth control.

The "Truly Disadvantaged" The nation's largest cities have become the principal location of virtually all of the social problems confronting our society—poverty, homelessness (see *Up Close:* "Homelessness in America"), racial tension, drug abuse, delinquency, and crime. These problems are all made worse by their concentration in large cities. Yet the concentration of social ills in cities is a relatively recent occurrence; as late as 1970, there were higher rates of poverty in rural America than in the cities.

Why has the inner city become the locus of social problems? Some observers argue that changes in the labor market from industrial goods—producing jobs to professional, financial, and technical service—producing jobs have increasingly

Institute for Research on Poverty

University of Wisconsin Institute leads in research on extent and causes of poverty.
www.ssc.wsc.edv/irp

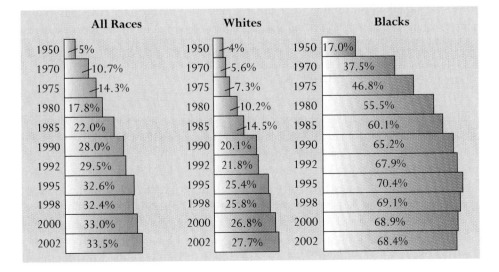

FIGURE 17.3 Births to Unmarried Women

The rate of children born to unmarried women rose through 1995. Recent reports indicate a leveling off of births to unmarried women, at approximately one-third of all births.

Source: Statistical Abstract of the United States, 2003, p. 77.

Who Are the Poor?

Poverty occurs in many kinds of families and in all races and ethnic groups. However, some groups experience poverty (low income) in greater proportions than the national average (see figure).

Poverty is most common among families headed by women. The incidence of poverty among these families is four times greater than that for married couples. These women and their children constitute over two-thirds of all of the persons living in poverty in the United States. About one of every five children in the United States lives in poverty. These figures describe what has been labeled the "feminization of poverty" in the United States. Clearly, poverty is closely related to family structure. The disintegration of the traditional husband-wife family is the single most influential factor contributing to poverty today.

Blacks also experience poverty in much greater proportions than whites. Over the years, the poverty rate among blacks in the United States has been almost three times higher than the poverty rate among whites. Poverty among Hispanics is also significantly greater than among whites.

In contrast, elderly people in America experience less poverty than the nonaged. The aged are not poor, despite the popularity of the phrase "the poor and the aged." The percentage of persons over sixty-five years of age with low incomes is below the national average. Moreover, elderly people are much

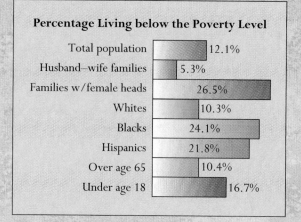

Percentage Living below the Poverty Level

Total population	12.1%
Husband–wife families	5.3%
Families w/female heads	26.5%
Whites	10.3%
Blacks	24.1%
Hispanics	21.8%
Over age 65	10.4%
Under age 18	16.7%

wealthier in terms of assets and have fewer expenses than the nonaged. They are more likely than younger people to own homes with paid-up mortgages. Medicare pays a large portion of their medical expenses. With fewer expenses, elderly people, even with relatively smaller cash incomes, experience poverty differently from the way a young mother with children experiences it. The declining poverty rate among elderly people is a relatively recent occurrence, however. Continuing increases in Social Security benefits over the years are largely responsible for this singular "victory" in the war against poverty.

Source: U.S. Bureau of the Census, 2004.

divided the labor market into low-wage and high-wage sectors.[2] The decline in manufacturing jobs, together with a shift in remaining manufacturing jobs and commercial (sales) jobs to the suburbs, has left inner-city residents with fewer and lower paying job opportunities. The rise in joblessness in the inner cities has in turn increased the concentration of poor people, added to the number of poor single-parent families, and increased welfare dependency.

Social Welfare Policy

Public welfare has been a recognized responsibility of government in English-speaking countries for many centuries. As far back as the Poor Relief Act of 1601, the English Parliament provided workhouses for the "able-bodied poor" (the unemployed) and poorhouses for widows and orphans, elderly and handicapped people.[3] Today, nearly one-third of the U.S. population receives some form of government benefits: Social Security, Medicare or Medicaid, disability insurance, unemployment compensation, government employee retirement, veterans' benefits, food stamps, school lunches, job training, public housing, and cash public assistance payments (see Table 17.1). More than half of all families in the United

Homelessness in America

The most visible social welfare problem in the United States is the nation's homeless people, who wander about in the larger cities suffering exposure, alcoholism, drug abuse, and chronic mental illness.

The issue of homelessness has become so politicized that in accurate assessment of the problem and a rational strategy for dealing with it have become virtually impossible. The term "homeless" is used to describe many different situations.* Many are street people who sleep in subways, bus stations, parks, or the streets. Some of them are temporarily traveling in search of work; some have left home for a few days or are youthful runaways; others have roamed the streets for months or years. In contrast sheltered homeless people have obtained housing in shelters operated by local governments or private charities. As the number of shelters has grown over the years, the number of sheltered homeless people has also grown. But most of the sheltered homeless people come from other housing, not the streets. These are people who have recently been evicted from rental units or have previously lived with family or friends. They often include families with children; the street people are virtually all single persons.

About half of all street people are chronic alcoholic and drug abusers; an additional one-fourth to one-third are mentally ill.[†] Moreover, homeless people who are alcohol and drug abusers and/or mentally ill are by far the most likely to remain on the streets for long periods of time.

The current plight of homeless people is primarily a result of various "reforms" in public policy, notably the "deinstitutionalization" of care for the mentally ill and the newly recognized rights of individuals to refuse treatment; the "decriminalization" of vagrancy and public intoxication; and urban renewal, which has eliminated many low-rent apartments and cheap hotels.

Deinstitutionalization, a policy advanced by mental health care professionals and social welfare activists in the 1960s and 1970s after the introduction of new psychotropic drug therapies, has resulted in the release of all but the most dangerous mental patients from state-run mental hospitals.

Decriminalization of public intoxication has also added to the numbers of street people. Involuntary confinement of substance abusers is now banned

A family eating a Christmas Eve lunch for the needy and homeless, prepared by a Washington, D.C., mission.

unless a person is arrested while possessing an illegal substance or is found in court to be "a danger to himself or others," which means a person must commit a serious act of violence before the courts will intervene.

Community-based care has failed for many substance abusers and chronically mentally ill street people. Many are "uncooperative"; they are isolated from society; they have no family members or doctors or counselors to turn to for help. The nation's vast social welfare system provides them little help. They cannot handle forms, appointments, or interviews; the welfare bureaucracy is intimidating. Lacking a permanent address, many receive no Social Security, welfare, or disability checks. Shelters provided by private charities, such as the Salvation Army, or by city governments are more helpful to the temporarily homeless than to chronic alcohol or drug abusers or mentally ill people. Few shelters offer treatment for alcohol or drug abusers, and some refuse disruptive people.

---

*Peter H. Rossi, *Down and Out in America* (Chicago: University of Chicago Press, 1989).

[†] As reported in a twenty-seven-city survey by the U.S. Conference of Mayors. See *U.S. News & World Report*, January 15, 1990, pp. 27–29.

social insurance programs
Social welfare programs to which beneficiaries have made contributions so that they are entitled to benefits regardless of their personal wealth.

public assistance programs
Those social welfare programs for which no contributions are required and only those living in poverty (by official standards) are eligible; includes food stamps, Medicaid, and Family Assistance.

entitlements Any social welfare program for which there are eligibility requirements, whether financial or contributory.

States include at least one person who receives a government check. Thus the "welfare state" now encompasses a very large part of our society.

The major social welfare programs can be classified as either **social insurance** or **public assistance**. This distinction is an important one that has on occasion become a major political issue. If the beneficiaries of a government program are required to have made contributions to it before claiming any of its benefits, and if they are entitled to the benefits regardless of their personal wealth—as in Social Security and Medicare—then the program is said to be financed on the social insurance principle. If the program is financed out of general tax revenues and if recipients are required to show that they are poor before claiming its benefits—as in Temporary Assistance to Needy Families, Supplemental Security Income, and Medicaid—then the program is said to be financed on the public assistance principle. Public assistance programs are generally labeled as "welfare."

Entitlements Entitlements are government benefits for which Congress has set eligibility criteria—age, income, retirement, disability, unemployment, and so on. Everyone who meets the criteria is "entitled" to the benefit.

Most of the nation's major entitlement programs were launched either in the New Deal years of the 1930s under President Franklin D. Roosevelt (Social Security, Un-

TABLE 17.1 Beneficiaries of Major Federal Social Welfare Programs

Social Insurance Programs	Beneficiaries (millions)	Public Assistance Programs	Beneficiaries (millions)
Social Security		**Cash Aid**	
Retirement	29.2	Assistance to Families	6.0
Survivors	11.7	Supplemental Security Income (SSI)	6.6
Disabled	5.5	**Medical Care**	
Total	46.4	Medicaid	42.0
Unemployment Compensation		Veterans	1.1
Total	10.1	Indians	1.5
Government and Military Retirement		Maternal and child health	27.0
Military	3.4	**Food Benefits**	
Federal employees	3.5	Food stamps	18.2
State and local	7.3	School lunches	15.1
Medicare		Women, Infants, Children (WIC)	7.2
Total	38.0	Child and adult care food	1.9
		Housing Benefit	
		Total	3.2
		Education Aid	
		Pell Grants	3.8
		Stafford Loans	5.4
		Head Start	0.8
		Job Training	
		Total	1.0
		Energy Assistance	
		Total	4.1

Source: U.S. Bureau of the Census, *Statistical Abstract of the United States,* 2004, pp. 114, 360, 362, 368.

employment Compensation, Aid to Families with Dependent Children, now called Temporary Assistance to Needy Families, and Aid to Aged, Blind, and Disabled, now called Supplemental Security Income) or in the Great Society years of the 1960s under President Lyndon B. Johnson (food stamps, Medicare, Medicaid).

Social Security Begun during the Depression (1935), **Social Security** is now the largest of all entitlements; it comprises two distinct programs. The Old Age and Survivors Insurance program provides monthly cash benefits to retired workers and their dependents and to survivors of insured workers. The Disability Insurance program provides monthly cash benefits for disabled workers and their dependents. An automatic, annual cost-of-living adjustment (COLA) for both programs matches any increase in the annual inflation rate.

With more than 44 million beneficiaries, Social Security is the single largest spending program in the federal budget. About 96 percent of the nation's paid work force is covered by the program, which is funded by a payroll tax on employers and employees. Retirees can begin receiving benefits at age sixty-two (full benefits at age sixty-five), regardless of their personal wealth or income (see "Senior Power" later in this chapter).

Unemployment Compensation **Unemployment compensation** temporarily replaces part of the wages of workers who lose their jobs involuntarily and helps stabilize the economy during recessions. The U.S. Department of Labor oversees the system, but states administer their own programs, with latitude within federal guidelines to define weekly benefits and other program features. Benefits are funded by a combination of federal and state unemployment taxes on employers.

Supplemental Security Income **Supplemental Security Income (SSI)** is a means-tested, federally administered income assistance program that provides monthly cash payments to needy elderly (sixty-five or older), blind, and disabled people. A loose definition of "disability"—including alcoholism, drug abuse, and attention deficiency among children—has led to a rapid growth in the number of SSI beneficiaries.

Family Assistance **Family Assistance**, officially Temporary Assistance to Needy Families (formerly AFDC, or Aid to Families with Dependent Children), is a grant program to enable the states to assist needy families. States now operate the program and define "need"; they set their own benefit levels and establish (within federal guidelines) income and resource limits. Prior to welfare reform in 1996, AFDC was a *federal* entitlement program. The federal government now mandates a two-year limit on benefits, a five-year lifetime limit, and other requirements (see "Politics and Welfare Reform" later in this chapter).

Food Stamps The **Food Stamp program** provides low-income household members with coupons that they can redeem for enough food to provide a minimal nutritious diet. The program is overseen by the federal government but administered by the states.

Earned Income Tax Credit The **Earned Income Tax Credit (EITC)** is designed to assist the working poor. It not only refunds their payroll taxes but also provides larger refunds than they actually paid during the previous tax year. Thus, the EITC is in effect a "negative" income tax. It was originally passed by a Democratic-controlled Congress and signed by Republican President Gerald Ford

Food Stamp Program

This U.S. Department of Agriculture's Food Stamp program site contains information about application procedures, recipient eligibility guidelines, and other relevant informational materials.
www.fns.usda.gov/fsp/

Most of America's social welfare programs began in either the Great Depression of the 1930s or the War on Poverty in the 1960s. At the outset of the Depression, millions of unemployed Americans, like the New Yorkers in a bread line in the photo at left, had only private charities to turn to for survival. The War on Poverty of the 1960s was a reaction to the presistence of extreme poverty, like that of the rural family in the photograph at right in the midst of the prosperity that followed World War II.

in 1975. Over the years EITC payments have increased substantially. However, the program applies only to those poor who actually work and who apply for the credit when filing their income tax.

Medicaid Medicaid is a joint federal-state program providing health services to low-income Americans. Most Medicaid spending goes to elderly and nonelderly disabled people. However, women and children receiving benefits under AFDC automatically qualify for Medicaid, as does anyone who gets cash assistance under SSI. States can also offer Medicaid to the "medically needy"—those who face crushing medical costs but whose income or assets are too high to qualify for SSI or Family Assistance, including pregnant women and young children not receiving Family Assistance. Medicaid also pays for long-term nursing home care, but only after beneficiaries have used up virtually all of their savings and income.

Senior Power

Senior citizens are the most politically powerful age group in the population. They constitute 28 percent of the voting-age population, but, more important, because of their high voter turnout rates, they constitute more than one-third of the voters on election day. Persons over age sixty-five average a 68 percent turnout rate in presidential elections and a 61 percent rate in congressional elections. By comparison, those aged eighteen to twenty-one have a turnout rate of 36 percent in presidential elections and 19 percent in congressional elections, so the voting power of senior citizens is twice that of young people. Moreover, seniors are well represented in Washington; the American Association of Retired Persons (AARP) is the nation's largest organized interest group (see *Up Close:* "AARP: The Nation's Most Powerful Interest Group" in Chapter 9). No elected officials can afford to offend seniors, and seniors strongly support generous Social Security benefits.

The Aged in the Future The baby boom from 1945 to 1960 produced a large generation of people who crowded schools and colleges in the 1960s and 1970s and

THINK
AGAIN

Should all retirees receive Social Security benefits regardless of their personal wealth or income?

THINK
AGAIN

Do you believe the Social Security system will still be solvent when you retire?

THINK
AGAIN

Should the government pay for nursing home care without forcing beneficiaries to use up all their savings and income?

Medicaid Public assistance program that provides health care to the poor.

Senior citizens enjoy enormous influence over the nation's politicians. Social Security is sancrosanct to the elderly. Any proposed changes in it bring about powerful reactions. Even a proposal to allow workers to allocate part of their Social Security taxes to stock market investments generates controversy.

encountered stiff competition for jobs in the 1980s. During the baby boom, women averaged 3.5 births during their lifetime. Today, the birthrate is only 1.8 births per woman, less than the 2.1 figure required to keep the population from declining. (Current U.S. population growth is a product of immigration.) The baby-boom generation will be retiring beginning in 2010, and by 2030 they will constitute more than 80 million people, 20 percent of the population (see Figure 17.4). Changes in lifestyle—less smoking, more exercise, better weight control—may increase the aged population even more. Medical advances may also extend life expectancy.

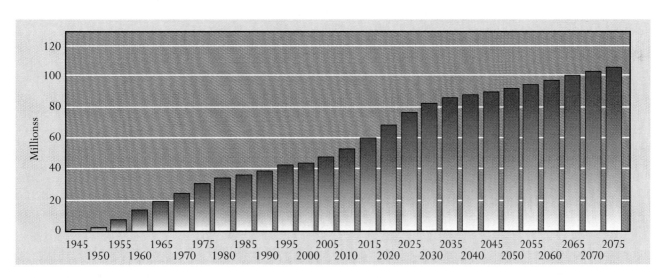

FIGURE 17.4 Growing Number of Social Security Beneficiaries

Millions of Old-Age, Survivors, and Disability Insurance (OASDI) recipients, 1945–2075.

Note: Numbers for 2000 onwards are estimates based on intermediate assumptions.

Source: "2000 Annual Report." March 2000, Board of Trustees, Federal Old-Age and Survivors Insurance and Disability Insurance Trust Funds.

The Generational Compact The framers of the Social Security Act of 1935 created a "trust fund" with the expectation that a reserve would be built up from social insurance taxes paid by working persons. The reserve would earn interest, and the interest and principal would be used in later years to pay benefits. In theory, Social Security is an insurance program. (Payments are recorded by name and Social Security number.) Many people believe that they get back what they paid during their working years. Reality, however, has proven much different.

Social Security is now financed on a pay-as-you-go system, rather than a reserve system. Today, the income from all social insurance premiums (taxes) pays for current Social Security benefits. This generation of workers is paying for the benefits of the last generation, and this generation must hope that its future benefits will be financed by the next generation of workers. Taxing current workers to pay benefits to current retirees may be viewed as a compact between generations. Each generation of workers in effect agrees to pay benefits to an earlier generation of retirees and expects the next generation will pay for its retirement.

The Rising Dependency Ratio Because current workers must pay for the benefits of current retirees and other beneficiaries, the **dependency ratio** becomes an important component of evaluating the future of Social Security. The dependency ratio for Social Security is the number of recipients as a percentage of the number of contributing workers. Americans are living longer and increasing the dependency ratio. A child born in 1935, when the Social Security system was created, could expect to live only to age sixty-one, four years *less* than the retirement age of sixty-five. The life expectancy of a child born in 1990 is seventy-four years, nine years beyond the retirement age. In the early years of Social Security, there were ten workers supporting each retiree—a dependency ratio of 10 to 1. But today, as the U.S. population grows older—due to lower birthrates and longer life spans—there are only three workers for each retiree, and by 2010 the dependency ratio will be two workers for each retiree.

Social Security Taxes Social Security taxes are levied on workers' earnings. Combined Social Security and Medicare taxes amount to 15.3 percent of wage earnings. (The Social Security tax is 12.4 percent and the Medicare tax is 2.9 percent.) Half is paid directly by the employer, and half is deducted from the employees' check as the FICA deduction. All wage income is subject to the Medicare tax, but wage income above a certain level—$84,900 in 2002—is not taxed. This wage limit increases every year.

Burdens on Generation X With fewer workers to support each retiree, the burdens of Social Security on the current generation of young Americans will become unsupportable. Members of Generation X will pay many times more into Social Security than they will ever get out of it.

Cost-of-Living Increases Currently, the annual Social Security cost-of-living adjustments (**COLAs**) are based on the Consumer Price Index, which estimates the cost of all consumer items each year. These costs include home buying, mortgage interest, child rearing, and other costs that many retirees do not confront. Moreover, most workers do not have the same protection against inflation as retirees; average wage rates do not always match increases in the cost of living. Hence, over the years, COLAs have improved the economic well-being of Social Security recipients relative to all American workers.

dependency ratio In the Social Security system, the number of recipients as a percentage of the number of contributing workers.

COLAs Annual cost-of-living adjustments mandated by law in Social Security and other welfare benefits.

Wealthy Retirees Social Security benefits are paid to *all* eligible retirees, regardless of whatever other income they may receive. There is no means test for Social Security benefits. As a result, large numbers of affluent Americans receive government checks each month. They paid into Social Security during their working years, and they can claim these checks as an entitlement under the social insurance principle. But currently their benefits far exceed their previous payments.

Because elderly people experience less poverty than today's workers (see *Up Close:* "Who Are the Poor?" on page 616) and possess considerably more wealth, Social Security benefits constitute a "negative" redistribution of income—that is, a transfer of income from poorer to richer people. The elderly are generally better off than the people supporting them.

"Saving" Social Security The income from Social Security taxes *currently* exceeds payments to beneficiaries—that is, it produces a "surplus." But Social Security taxes are lumped together with general tax revenues in federal budgets; the Social Security surplus is used to hide a portion of overall federal deficits. Democrats and Republicans alike have promised to create a "lock box" and not "dip into Social Security" in order to fund current programs. But the Social Security "trust fund" is merely an accounting gimmick: current Social Security taxes are used to fund current government spending and future retirement benefits will be paid from future revenues.

The Social Security system appears to be adequately financed for the next several decades. (In 1983 a National Commission on Social Security Reform, appointed by President Reagan, recommended an increase in Social Security taxes and a gradual increase in the retirement age from sixty-five to sixty-seven beginning in 2000. Congress adopted these recommendations.) But with the aging of the population and the resulting increases in the dependency ratio expected in the twenty first century, Social Security will become a heavy burden on working Americans.

"Saving" Social Security is a popular political slogan in Washington. But agreement on exactly how to reform the system continues to evade lawmakers. In theory, Congress could reform Social Security by limiting COLAs to the true increases in the cost of living for retirees, or it could introduce means tests to deny benefits to high-income retirees. But politically these reforms are very unlikely. Yet another approach to reform is to allow the Social Security trust fund to invest in the private stock market with the expectation that stock values will increase over time. But if stock market investment decisions were made by the government itself, presumably the Social Security Administration, controversies would be bound to arise over these decisions. And critics object to the idea of the government making private investment decisions for Americans. Another reform frequently recommended is to allow American workers to deposit all or part of their Social Security payroll tax into an individual retirement account to buy securities of their own choosing. But such a plan would expose those individuals to the risk of bad investment decisions. (See *What Do You Think?:* "How Should We Reform Social Security?")

Politics and Welfare Reform

Americans confront a clash of values in welfare policy. Americans are a generous people; they believe government should aid those who are unable to take care of themselves, especially children, disabled people, and elderly people. But Americans are worried that welfare programs encourage dependency, undermine the work ethic, and contribute to illegitimate births and the breakup of families. Although social

THINK AGAIN

Do you think government welfare programs perpetuate poverty?

THINK AGAIN

Should the states rather than the federal government decide about welfare policy?

THINK AGAIN

Should there be a time limit on how long a person can receive welfare payments?

How Should We Reform Social Security?

Politicians want to make Social Security reform as painless as possible. The topic of Social Security reform in Washington is so sensitive that Congress has been unable to adopt any long-term reform proposals since 1983, when a presidential commission recommended a gradual increase in the retirement age. But most Americans do recognize the seriousness of the problem. Polls show that fewer than half of the American public believes the Social Security system will have money to provide benefits when they retire. Yet despite their skepticism about the future of Social Security, relatively few Americans save enough for retirement.

Specific proposals for reforming Social Security receive mostly negative, or at best only lukewarm, support among the general public (see below). Americans do not want to cut Social Security benefits, or increase taxes, or raise the eligibility age; and they give only lukewarm support for allowing individuals to invest part of their Social Security taxes in private investments (stocks or bonds) with the expectation of higher returns over the long run.

	Favor	Oppose	Neither/ Don't Know
Changing Social Security from a system where the government collects the taxes to a system where individuals invest some of their payroll tax contributions themselves	48%	37%	15%
Reducing Social Security benefits for people who have retirement incomes over about $60,000 per year	42%	49%	9%
Gradually increasing the early retirement age for collecting reduced benefits from 62 to 65	37%	54%	9%
Increasing the payroll tax that workers and employees each pay into the Social Security system from 6.2% to 6.7%	36%	54%	10%
Cutting the amount that Social Security benefits go up each year for changes in the cost of living	35%	55%	10%
Changing Social Security from a system where the money in the trust is invested in government bonds to a system where some of the money is invested in the stock market	30%	53%	17%
Gradually raising the age when a person can collect full Social Security benefits to age 70	17%	78%	5%

Source: Based on International Communications Research for the Kaiser Family Foundation. February 2001, as reported at *Public Agenda Online*, 2002.

insurance programs (Social Security, Medicare, and Unemployment Compensation) are politically popular and enjoy the support of large numbers of active beneficiaries, public assistance programs (Family Assistance, SSI, Medicaid) are far less popular. A variety of controversies surround welfare policy in the United States.

Conflict Over What Causes Poverty Americans have different ideas about what causes poverty (see Table 17.2). Some attribute poverty to characteristics of individuals—drug use, declining moral values, lack of motivation. Others blame the economy—too many part-time and low-wage jobs and a shortage of good jobs. Still others place blame on the welfare system itself. Indeed, prior to welfare reform in 1996, some scholars argued that government itself was a major cause of poverty—that social welfare programs destroyed incentives to work, encouraged teenage pregnancies, and made people dependent on government handouts.[4] They

TABLE 17.2 Public Opinion about the Causes of Poverty

Question: For each of the following, please tell me if this is a major cause of poverty, a minor cause of poverty, or not a cause at all.

	Major	Minor	Not a Cause	Don't Know
Drug abuse	70%	24%	5%	2%
Medical bills	58%	32%	7%	2%
Decline in moral values	57%	29%	12%	3%
Too many part-time or low-wage jobs	54%	32%	10%	4%
Too many single parents	54%	32%	12%	2%
Poor people lacking motivation	52%	35%	9%	4%
Poor public schools	47%	38%	13%	4%
The welfare system	46%	37%	11%	7%
A shortage of jobs	34%	41%	23%	2%

Source: Data copyrighted by International Communications Research for the Kaiser Family Foundation. Graphic copyright © 2002 by Public Agenda. www.publicagenda.org. Reprinted by permission of Public Agenda.

argued that the combination of cash-payments, food stamps, Medicaid, and housing assistance unintentionally discouraged people from forming families, taking low-paying jobs, and, perhaps, with hard work and perseverance, gradually pulling themselves and their children into the mainstream of American life.

There is little doubt that poverty and welfare dependency are closely related to family structure. As noted earlier, poverty is much more frequent among female headed households with no husband present than among husband-wife households. As births to unmarried women rose, poverty and social dependency increased. (In 1970 only 11 percent of births were to unmarried women by 2000 this figure had risen to 33 percent of all births and 69 percent of minority births.) The troubling question was whether the welfare system ameliorated some of the hardships confronting unmarried mothers and their children, or whether it actually contributed to social dependency by mitigating the consequences of unmarried motherhood. For example, were teenage pregnancies more common because teenagers knew that government benefits were available to young mothers and their children?

The Politics of Welfare Reform

A political consensus grew over the years that long-term social dependency had to be addressed in welfare policy. The fact that most nonpoor mothers work convinced many *liberals* that welfare mothers had no special claim to stay at home with their children. And many *conservatives* acknowledged that some transitional assistance—education, job training, continued health care, and day care for children—might be necessary to move welfare mothers into the work force.

Although President Clinton had once promised "to end welfare as we know it," it was the Republican-controlled Congress elected in 1994 that proceeded to do so. The Republican-sponsored welfare reform bill ended the sixty-year-old federal "entitlement" for low-income families with children—the venerable AFDC program. In its place the Republicans devised a "devolution" of responsibility to the states through federal block grants—**Temporary Assistance to Needy Families**—lump sum allocations to the states for cash welfare payments with benefits and eligibility requirements decided by the states. Conservatives in Congress imposed

Temporary Assistance to Needy Families Welfare reform program replacing federal cash entitlement with grants to the states for welfare recipients.

tough-minded "strings" to state aid, including a two-year limit on continuing cash benefits and a five-year lifetime limit; a "family cap" that would deny additional cash benefit to women already on welfare who bear more children; the denial of cash welfare to unwed parents under 18 years of age unless they live with an adult and attend school. President Clinton vetoed the first welfare reform bill passed by Congress in early 1996, but as the presidential election neared, he reversed himself and signed the welfare reform act, establishing the Temporary Assistance to Needy Families program. Food stamps, SSI, and Medicaid were continued as federal "entitlements" (see *Up Close:* "Is Welfare Reform Working?").

More Reform? Public sentiment is strongly behind the concept of working in exchange for receiving public assistance. It is unlikely that public policy will ever return to welfare as we used to know it. But Democrats and liberals and Republicans and conservatives continue to argue over additional reforms. Democrats and liberals argue for expanded subsidized day care, increases in the minimum wage, spending more on medical care for the poor, and making food stamps more available. Republicans and conservatives propose toughening the work requirements for cash welfare assistance and closing many of the loopholes that allow states to continue paying benefits to persons whose time limit has expired.

President George W. Bush established an Office of Faith-Based and Community Initiatives in the White House to eliminate "federal barriers to churches, synagogues, mosques and charities" from receiving federal grants to assist them in providing food, job training and counseling, substance abuse programs, and other aid. The Office is supposed to "identify and act to remedy statutes, regulations, and bureaucratic barriers that stand in the way of defective faith-based and community programs." But it is not supposed to direct government funds toward "inherently religious activities like sectarian worship or proselytizing." Public opinion generally approves (63 percent) rather than disapproves (29 percent) of "religious organizations receiving governments funds to provide services to the poor."[5] But critics worry that government-funded faith-based organizations promote religious messages and violate the No Establishment Clause of the First Amendment.

"As far as I'm concerned, they can do what they want with the minimum wage, just as long as they keep their hands off the maximum wage."

Source: © *The New Yorker Collection 1989.* Robert Mankoff from cartoonbank.com. All rights reserved.

Is Welfare Reform Working?

Welfare reform, officially Temporary Assistance to Needy Families, was passed by Congress in 1996; its provisions took effect in 1997. By early 1998 the Clinton Administration, as well as Republican congressional sponsors of welfare reform, was declaring it a success.

The number of cash welfare recipients in the nation has dropped below 6 million—the lowest number in more than twenty-five years. Only about 2 percent of Americans are now on cash welfare—the smallest proportion since 1970. No doubt some of this decline is attributable to strong growth of the economy: declines in welfare rolls began *before* Congress passed its welfare reform law, and some decline may have occurred without reform. Many states had initiated their own reforms under "waivers" from the federal government even before Congress acted.

All states have now developed work programs for welfare recipients. Applicants for welfare benefits are now generally required to enter job-search programs, to undertake job training, and to accept jobs or community service positions.

Yet, although nearly everyone agrees that getting people off welfare rolls and onto payrolls is the main goal of reform, there are major obstacles to the achievement of this goal. First of all, a substantial portion (perhaps 25 to 40 percent) of long-term welfare recipients have handicaps—physical disabilities, chronic illnesses, learning disabilities, alcohol or drug abuse problems—that prevent them from holding a full-time job. Many long-term recipients have no work experience (perhaps 40 percent), and two-thirds of them did not graduate from high

Source: Department of Health and Human Services, 2004.

school. Almost half have three or more children, making day-care arrangements a major obstacle. It is unlikely that any counseling, education, job training, or job placement programs could ever succeed in getting these people into productive employment.

Early studies of people who left the welfare rolls following welfare reform suggest that over half and perhaps as many as three-quarters have found work, although most at minimum or near-minimum wages.[*] But it is likely that the early dramatic reductions in welfare caseloads (see figure) will begin to level off after 2000.

---

[*]*Governing* April 1999, pp. 21–26.

Programs such as this Riverside, California. "Jobs Club" try to help welfare recipients find jobs in the wake of reforms intended to reduce welfare dependency.

THINK AGAIN

Should government provide health care insurance for all Americans?

Health Care in America

The United States spends more of its resources on health care than any other nation (see *Compared to What?* "Health and Health Care Costs in Advanced Democracies"). Nevertheless, the United States ranks well below other advanced democracies in key measures of the health of its people such as life expectancy and infant death rate. Moreover, unlike most other advanced democracies, which make provision for health care for all citizens, Americans have no guarantee of access to medical care. In short, the American health care system is the most expensive and least universal in its coverage in the world.

The Health of Americans Historically, most reductions in death rates have resulted from public health and sanitation improvements, including immunizations, clean public water supplies, sanitary sewage disposal, improved diets, and increased standards of living. Many of the leading causes of death today (see Table 17.3), including heart disease, cancer, stroke, and AIDS, are closely linked to heredity, personal habits and lifestyles (smoking, eating, drinking, exercise, stress, sexual practices), and the physical environment—factors over which doctors and hospitals have no direct control. Thus some argue that the greatest contribution to better health is likely to be found in altered personal habits and lifestyles rather than in more medical care. Thanks to improved health care habits as well as breakthroughs in medical technology, Americans are living longer than ever before.

Access to Care A major challenge in health care is to extend coverage to all Americans. Today, about 85 percent of the nation's population is covered by either government or private health insurance. Government pays about 43 percent of all health care costs—through Medicare for the aged, Medicaid for the poor, and other government programs, including military and veterans' care. Private insurance pays for about 40 percent of the nation's health costs (see Figure 17.5).

But about 15 percent of the U.S. population—an estimated 42 million Americans—have *no* medical insurance. These include workers and their dependents whose employers do not offer a health insurance plan as well as unemployed people who are not eligible for Medicare or Medicaid. People who lack health insurance may postpone or go without needed medical care or may be denied medical care by hospitals and physicians in all but emergency situations. Confronted with serious illness, they may be obliged to impoverish themselves in order to become eligible for Medicaid. Any unpaid medical bills must be absorbed by hospitals or shifted to paying patients and their insurance companies.

Coverage Gaps Even people who *do* have health insurance often confront serious financial problems in obtaining medical care owing to inadequate coverage. Medicare, like most private insurance plans, requires patients to pay some *initial* charges called **deductibles**. The purpose of deductibles is to discourage unnecessary treatment. Patients must also make up any difference between doctors' actual charges and the rates allowed by their insurance plans. Indeed, only an estimated half of the doctors in the nation accept Medicare rates as payment in full. In addition, Medicare and many private insurance plans do not pay for eyeglasses, hearing aids, or routine physical examinations.

More important, perhaps, Medicare does *not* pay for long-term care or catastrophic illness. Medicare covers only the first 60 days of hospitalization; it covers nursing home care for 100 days only if the patient is sent there from a hospital. Yet

deductibles Initial charges in insurance plans, paid by beneficiaries.

Health and Health Care Costs in Advanced Democracies

Americans spend more than any other nation in the world for health care (see figure). They spend over 50 percent more than Canadians and nearly 100 percent more than Japanese. Few people object to heavy spending for health care if they get their money's worth. But cross-national comparisons of health statistics indicate that Americans on the average are less healthy than citizens in other advanced democracies. The United States ranks *below* many other advanced nations in life expectancy and infant death rates—two commonly used measures of national health.

The United States offers some of the most advanced and sophisticated medical care in the world, attracting patients from the countries that rank well ahead of it in various health measures. The United States is the locus of some of the most advanced medical research, attracting medical researchers from throughout the world. But the high quality of medical care available in the United States, combined with the poor health statistics of the general public, suggests that the nation's health care problems center more on access to care and education and prevention of health problems than on the quality of care available.

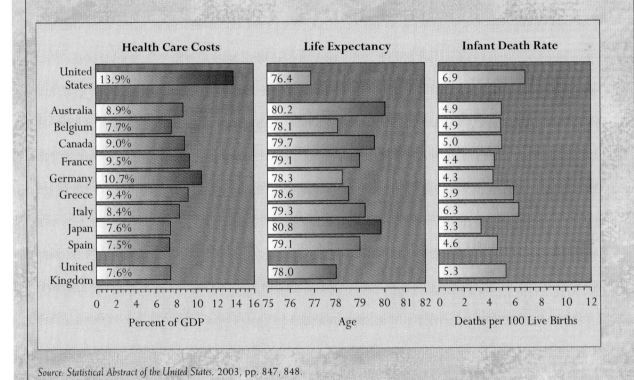

Source: Statistical Abstract of the United States, 2003, pp. 847, 848.

as the number and proportion of the elderly population grows in the United States (eighty years and over is the fastest growing age group in the nation), the need for long-term nursing home care grows. Medicaid assistance to needy people is paid for nursing home patients, but middle-class people cannot qualify for Medicaid without first "spending down" their savings. Long-term nursing home care threatens their assets and their children's inheritance. Private insurance policies covering long-term care are said to be too expensive. So senior citizen groups have lobbied heavily for long-term nursing home care to be paid for by taxpayers under Medicare.

TABLE 17.3 Leading Causes of Death

	Deaths per 100,000 Population per Year				
	1960	**1970**	**1980**	**1990**	**2002**
All causes	954.7	945.3	883.4	863.8	848.5
Heart disease	369.0	362.0	336.0	368.3	245.8
Stroke (cerebrovascular)	108.0	101.9	75.5	57.9	57.4
Cancer	149.2	162.8	183.9	203.2	194.4
Accidents	52.3	56.4	46.7	37.0	35.7
Pneumonia/Influenza	37.3	30.9	24.1	32.0	43.2
Diabetes	16.7	18.9	15.5	19.2	25.1
AIDS	N.A.	N.A.	N.A.	17.6	5.0
Suicide	10.6	11.6	11.9	12.4	10.8
Homicide	4.7	8.3	10.7	10.0	7.1

Source: Statistical Abstract of the United States, 2003, p. 95.

Health Care Costs No system of health care can provide as much as people will use. Anyone whose health and life may be at stake will want the most thorough diagnostic testing, the most constant care, the most advanced treatment. Sworn to preserve life, doctors, too, want the most advanced diagnostic and treatment facilities available for their patients. Under conditions of uncertainty in a medical situation—and there is always some uncertainty—physicians are trained to seek more consultations, run more tests, and try new therapeutic approaches. Any tendency for doctors to limit testing and treatment is countered by the threat of malpractice suits; it is always easier to order one more test or procedure than to risk even the tiniest chance

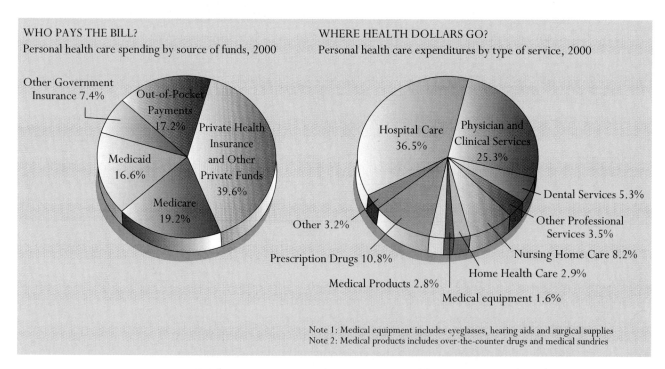

FIGURE 17.5 Health Care Costs in America

Source: "National Health Expenditures Tables." Health Care Financing Administration.

that failing to do so will some day be cause for a court suit. So in the absence of restraints, both patients and doctors will push up the costs of health care. Currently, health care costs appeared to have stabilized at about 13 percent of the nation's GDP.

Managed Care Controversies Both private and government insurers have made efforts to counter rising costs through **managed care**. Private insurers have negotiated discounts with groups of physicians and with hospitals—**preferred provider organizations (PPOs)**—and have implemented rules to guide physicians about when patients should and should not receive costly diagnostic and therapeutic procedures. Medicare no longer pays hospitals based on costs incurred; instead it pays fixed fees based on primary and secondary diagnoses at the time of admission. Both government and private insurers have encouraged the expansion of **health maintenance organizations (HMOs)**, groups that promise to provide a stipulated list of services to patients for a fixed fee and that are able to provide care at lower total costs than can other providers. Today over 30 percent of Americans are enrolled in HMOs.

But many of the efforts by both private insurers and governments to control costs have created new problems. These include cost-control regulations and restrictions that add to administrative costs and create a mountain of paperwork for physicians and hospitals, and frustration and anger among both health care workers and patients. Doctors and hospitals argue that the *administrative* costs imposed by these cost-control measures far exceed whatever savings are achieved. Patients and doctors complain that preapproval of treatment by insurance companies often removes medical decisions from the physician and patient and places them in the hands of insurance company employees.

Medicare Medicare is a two-part program that helps elderly and disabled people pay acute-care (as opposed to long-term-care) health costs. Hospital insurance (Part A) helps pay the cost of hospital inpatient and skilled nursing care. Anyone sixty-five or older who is eligible for Social Security is automatically eligible for Part A benefits. Also eligible are people under sixty-five who receive Social Security disability or railroad retirement disability and people who have end-stage kidney disease. Part A is financed primarily by the 1.45 percent payroll tax collected with Social Security (FICA) withholding. Supplemental Medical Insurance (Part B) is an optional add-on taken by virtually all those covered by Part A. It pays 80 percent of covered doctor and outpatient charges. Small monthly premiums are deducted from Social Security benefit checks to finance it.

Medicare has tried to control rising costs in a variety of ways. Currently Medicare offers beneficiaries:

- *Original Medicare plan (fee-for-services)*. Patients choose any physician or specialist, but pay a higher patient co-payment.

- *Managed care plans*. Patients join an HMO that receives the patient's monthly Medicare premiums from the government in exchange for an insurance plan that covers many items not covered by original Medicare, for example, eye exams, hearing aids, routine physicals, and (until newly enacted for 2006) prescription drugs. However, patients must see only HMO doctors and obtain their recommendation before seeing specialists.

- *Medicare plus Medigap plans*. Patients remain in original Medicare plan, choosing their own physicians and specialists, but purchase a separate "medigap" plan from a private insurer to cover most of the gaps in Medicare.

managed care Programs designed to keep health care costs down by the establishment of strict guidelines regarding when and what diagnostic and therapeutic procedures should be administered to patients under various circumstances.

Medicare
Official government site explaining eligibility, plan options appeals, etc.
www.medicare.gov

preferred provider organizations (PPOs)
Groups of hospitals and physicians who have joined together to offer their services to private insurers at a discount.

health maintenance organizations (HMOs)
Health care provider groups that provide a stipulated list of services to patients for a fixed fee that is usually substantially lower than such care would otherwise cost.

Medicare Social insurance program that provides health care insurance to elderly and disabled people.

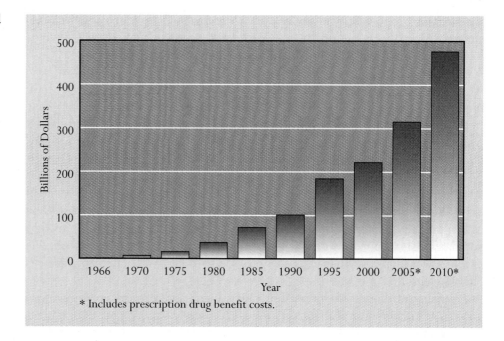

* Includes prescription drug benefit costs.

But Medicare costs are expected to rise dramatically in future years as the baby boom generation expands the population age sixty-five and over and people live longer (see Figure 17.6). The addition of prescription drug coverage will add even more to Medicare costs.

Politics and Health Care Reform

Health care reform centers on two central problems: controlling costs and expanding access. These problems are related: expanding access to Americans who are currently uninsured and closing gaps in coverage requires increased costs, even while a central thrust of reform is to control overall health care costs.

National Health Insurance Plans Liberals have long sought the creation of a Canadian-style health care system in which the federal government would provide health insurance for all Americans in a single national plan paid for by general tax increases. Under **national health insurance** all Americans would be entitled to a stipulated list of services from physicians, hospitals, and nursing homes, regardless of their employment, age, medical status, or income level. The federal government would be the "single payer" of health care costs through increased taxes. Hospitals would operate on budgets periodically negotiated with the government. Government fee schedules would dictate payments to physicians. Patients also might have to pay some share of the costs at the time of illness. This approach to health care would shift most costs from the private to the public sector. Although these plans are generally popular in Canada and Western Europe, proposals for federal nationwide insurance systems have consistently failed to win political support in Washington (see *What Do You Think?:* "Should We Enact a National Health Care System Covering All Americans?").

national health insurance
Government-provided
insurance to all citizens paid
from tax revenues.

Employer-Based Plans Others have advanced the notion of universal coverage through mandated employer-based insurance for most workers combined with government subsidies to pay the insurance costs for people living below the poverty line and to assist others in purchasing insurance.

Should We Enact a National Health Care System Covering All Americans?

Most Americans say that they would support a government-run universal health-care system covering all Americans, not just the aged and the poor. Presumably such a program would resemble the Canadian health-care system. However, when confronted with some of the common difficulties encountered in such programs—for example, long lines for non-emergency treatment and little choice of doctors—support for a Canadian-style system plummets among Americans.

Question: *Which would you prefer — the current health insurance system in the U.S., in which most people get their health insurance from private employers but some people have no insurance, or a universal health insurance program, in which everyone is covered under a program like Medicare that's run by the government and financed by taxpayers?*

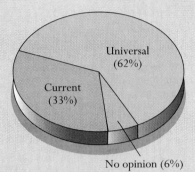

Universal (62%)

Current (33%)

No opinion (6%)

[Asked of those who said they support universal health care coverage] Would you support a universal health insurance program if it:

Percentage saying yes

Limited your choice of doctors — 35%

Meant there were waiting lists for some non-emergency medical treatments — 38%

Source: Derived from *ABC News/Washington Post* poll, October, 2003.

A majority of American employees are currently enrolled in employer-based plans, but these plans vary a great deal in coverage and cost to employees. And, of course, they do not cover the self-employed or unemployed. The federal government has never *mandated* employers to provide health insurance to their workers.

Modest Reforms Some modest reforms were enacted in 1996 in the Kennedy–Kassebaum Act, named for its bipartisan sponsorship by liberal Democratic Senator Edward M. Kennedy and moderate Republican Senator Nancy Kassebaum. This act guarantees the "portability" of health insurance—allowing workers to maintain their insurance coverage if they lose or change jobs. Their new employers health insurance company cannot deny them insurance for "preexisting conditions."

Adding prescription drugs to the benefits provided under Medicare has been long soughtly the nation's elderly.

A Patients' Bill of Rights The growth of managed care health plans, and their efforts to control costs, have fueled a drive for a "patients' bill of rights." Various proposals have been put forward for inclusion in a patients' bill of rights. The most common proposals are those allowing patients to see specialists without first obtaining permission from a representative of their health plan; providing emergency care without securing prior approval from a health plan representative; allowing immediate appeals when a patient is denied coverage for a particular treatment; and giving patients the right to sue their health plans for medical mistakes. The health insurance industry, including HMOs, argue that these proposals would significantly increase costs of health insurance. They oppose giving the federal government such a large role in overseeing health care plans. And they are particularly concerned about opening themselves to patients' lawsuits—"just a lawyers' bill of rights."

Prescription Drug Coverage under Medicare The long battle over adding prescription drug coverage to Medicare reached a turning point in 2004 when Congress finally passed by wide margins and President Bush signed such a bill. Americans have long supported the addition of prescription drug benefits to Medicare. And in every election over the previous twenty years both Democrats and Republicans had pledged their support for such a benefit. But it was not until after a prolonged battle over the details of legislation did Congress finally add the long awaited prescription drug benefit to Medicare.

The bill is lengthy and leaves many gaps in coverage (see Table 17.4). It was passed by a Republican-controlled Congress and by a Republican president; most Democrats in Congress opposed the bill, claiming that it failed to go far enough in protecting seniors. The AARP provided crucial support for the bill, arguing that later amendments could cure any defects.

Note that the government pays no part of health coverage costs between $2,250 and $5,100. This $3,600 gap in coverage is one of the principal objections to the act. Democrats and the AARP have promised to close this gap. Further, the government is barred from trying to negotiate with drug companies to force down prices.

Lack of health insurance forces many Americans to postpone regular visits to a doctor and to rely on crowded hospital emergency rooms when they become sick.

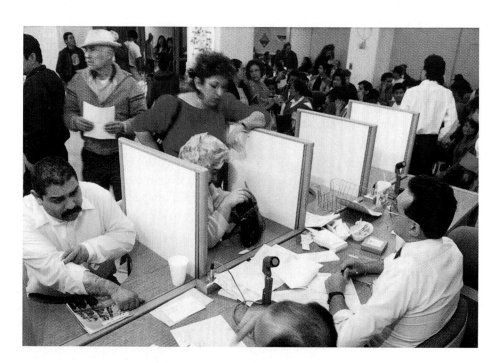

TABLE 17.4 Prescription Drug Benefits Under Medicare Major Provisions

Prescription drug benefits (beginning in 2006)

- The government will pay 75 percent of annual health insurance coverage up to $2,250. Once the beneficiary has paid the next $5,100 out of pocket, the government will pick up 95 percent of the coverage.
- Beneficiaries must pay a $250 annual deductible in an average monthly premium of $35.
- Beneficiaries will be guaranteed access to at least two competing insurance plans. If no private plans bid in a region, the government will offer a fall-back plan.
- Beneficiaries with incomes near the poverty level will get benefits with no gaps in coverage but will be subject to premiums based on a sliding scale.
- Companies already providing drug benefits to retirees will receive tax breaks to encourage them to continue to do so.

Drug discount cards (beginning in 2004)

- Medicare beneficiaries will receive discount cards in 2004. These cards are expected to provide savings of 15 to 25 percent per prescription.

Health savings accounts

- Taxpayers can establish health savings accounts allowing them to save and withdraw money tax-free for medical expenses.

Competition

- Private insurers can compete with the Medicare system in up to six metropolitan areas beginning in 2010.
- The government will *not* negotiate lower drug prices with drug companies.

Prescription Drug Costs Prescription drugs are more costly in United States than anywhere else in the developed world. The American pharmaceutical industry argues that the higher prices that Americans pay helped to fund research on new drugs, and that forcing down drug prices would curtail the development of new and potentially life-saving drugs. In effect, Americans are asked to subsidize drug research that benefits the entire world.

Many Americans have resorted to importing drugs from Canada or other nations that have much lower prices than those being charged in the United States. The Food and Drug Administration contends that this practice is illegal, and both the FDA and drug companies claim that imported drugs may not be safe (a highly dubious claim, inasmuch as they are the same drugs shipped by American drug companies to Canada and other nations).

Interest-Group Battles Interest-group battles over the details of health care policy have been intense. Virtually everyone has a financial stake in any proposal to reorganize the nation's health care system.

- Employers, especially small businesses, are fearful of added costs.

- Physicians strongly oppose price controls and treatment guidelines, as well as programs that take away patient choice of physician or force all physicians into health maintenance organizations (HMOs). Support is stronger among those physicians most likely to benefit from low-cost plans—general family practitioners—and weakest among those most likely to lose—medical specialists.

- Psychiatrists, psychologists, mental health and drug abuse counselors, physical therapists, chiropractors, optometrists, and dentists all want their own services covered. Providing such "comprehensive" services greatly increases costs.

- Drug companies want to see prescription drugs paid for, but they vigorously oppose price controls on drugs.

- Hospitals want all patients to be insured but oppose government payment schedules.

- Medical specialists fear that proposals for managed care will result in fewer consultations, and medical manufacturers fear it will limit use of high-priced equipment.

- The powerful senior citizens' lobby wants added benefits—including coverage for drugs, eyeglasses, dental care, and nursing homes—but fears folding Medicare into a larger health care system.

- Veterans' groups want to retain separate VA hospitals and medical services.

- Opponents of abortion rights are prepared to do battle to keep national coverage from including such procedures, whereas many supporters of abortion rights will not back any plan that excludes abortion services.

Although polls show that a majority of Americans are willing to pay higher taxes for comprehensive health care, many are willing to see increases only in "sin taxes"—taxes on alcohol, tobacco, and guns.

SUMMARY NOTES

- Social welfare policy largely determines who gets what from government; over half of the federal budget is devoted to "human resources." The government is a major redistributor of income from group to group.

- The poor are *not* the principal beneficiaries of social welfare spending. Only about one-third of all federal social welfare spending is means tested. Most social welfare spending, including the largest programs—Social Security and Medicare—goes to the middle class.

- About 11 to 15 percent of the U.S. population falls below the annual cash income level that the federal government sets as its official definition of poverty.

- Poverty is temporary for many families, but some poverty is persistent—lasting five years to a lifetime. Prolonged poverty and welfare dependency create an "underclass" beset by many social and economic problems. Poverty is most frequent among families headed by single mothers.

- Nearly one-third of the U.S. population receives some form of government payments or benefits. Entitlements are government benefits for which Congress has set eligibility criteria by law. Social Security and Medicare are the largest entitlement programs. The elderly are entitled to these benefits regardless of their income or wealth.

- Senior citizens are politically powerful; they vote more often than younger people and they have powerful lobbying organizations in Washington. Social Security is the largest single item in the federal budget. Yet proposals to modify Social Security or Medicare benefits are politically dangerous.

- Public assistance programs, including Family Assistance, Supplemental Security Income, and food stamps, require recipients to show that they are poor in order to claim benefits.

- Social welfare policies seek to alleviate hardship; at the same time they seek to avoid creating disincentives to work. Cash welfare payments may, for example, encourage teenage pregnancies, undermine family foundations, and contribute to long-term social dependency. Welfare reform centers on moving former welfare recipients into the work force. But doing so may require increased spending on education, job training, health care, and child care, and some recipients may never be able to work.

- Welfare reform in 1996 replaced federal entitlements to cash payments with block grants to the states. It also set time limits on welfare enrollment.

- Americans spend more on health care than citizens of any other nation, yet we fail to insure about 15 percent of the population. And the United States ranks below many other advanced nations in common health measures.

- Health care reform centers on two related problems—extending health insurance coverage to all Americans and containing the costs of health care. Proposals for extending coverage have included national health insurance and mandatory employer-sponsored health insurance. But only more modest proposals, for example, extending government programs to children and making insurance "portable," have been enacted.

- Managed care programs have succeeded in reducing the growth of health care costs in America. But these programs have generated complaints about coverage of medical conditions, bureaucratic interference in doctor-patient relationships, and the quality of medical care. The result is rising political support for a patients' bill of rights.

KEY TERMS

transfer payments 606
poverty line 606
means-tested spending 606
underclass 606
social insurance programs 610
public assistance programs 610

entitlements 610
Social Security 611
unemployment compensation 611
Supplemental Security Income (SSI) 611
Family Assistance 611
Food Stamp program 611

Earned Income Tax Credit (EITC) 611
Medicaid 612
dependency ratio 614
COLAs 614
Temporary Assistance to Needy Families 617
deductibles 620

managed care 623
preferred provider organizations (PPOs) 623
health maintenance organizations (HMOs) 623
Medicare 623
national health insurance 624

SUGGESTED READINGS

Bodenheimer, Thomas S. *Understanding Health Policy.* 3rd edition. New York: McGraw Hill, 2001. Leading text on health care policy, including cost containment, health insurance, managed care, and case histories.

DiNitto, Diana M. *Social Welfare Politics and Policy.* 8th ed. New York: Allyn & Bacon, 2003. A comprehensive overview of social welfare programs—Social Security, Medicare, SSI, cash assistance, Medicaid, food stamps, etc.—and the political controversies surrounding them.

Gilens, Martin. *Why Americans Hate Welfare.* Chicago: University of Chicago Press, 2000. An argument that racial stereotypes, aided by the media, encourage opposition to welfare.

Hays, Sharon. *Flat Broke With Children: Women in the Age of Welfare Reform.* New York: Oxford Press, 2003. Stories of single mothers and welfare workers trying to cope with the harsher rules of welfare reform.

MacManus, Susan A. *Young v. Old.* Boulder, Colo.: Westview Press, 1996. An argument based on polling data that "generational combat" is likely in the twenty-first century over taxing and spending for Social Security, Medicare, education, health care, etc.

Murray, Charles. *Losing Ground,* 10th American ed. New York: Basic Books, 1994. Controversial, classic thesis, first put forth in 1984, that government social welfare programs, by encouraging social dependence, had the unintended and perverse effect of slowing and even reversing earlier progress in reducing poverty, crime ignorance, and discrimination. Often cited as the inspiration for welfare reform.

Rector, Robert E., and Sarah E. Youssef. *The Impact of Welfare Reform.* Washington, D.C.: Heritage Foundation, 1999. Statistical analysis of the effects of welfare reform, including state-by-state data.

Weissert, Carol S. and William G. Weissert. *Governing Health: the Politics of Health Policy.* 2d edition. Baltimore: Johns Hopkins University Press, 2002. Health care policymaking, including the roles of Congress, the president, interest groups, and the bureaucracy.

Wilson, William Julius. *The Truly Disadvantaged.* Chicago: University of Chicago Press, 1987. Classic thesis that the growth of the underclass is primarily a result of the decline of manufacturing jobs and their shift to the suburbs, and the resulting concentration of poor, jobless, isolated people in the inner city.

18

POLITICS AND NATIONAL SECURITY

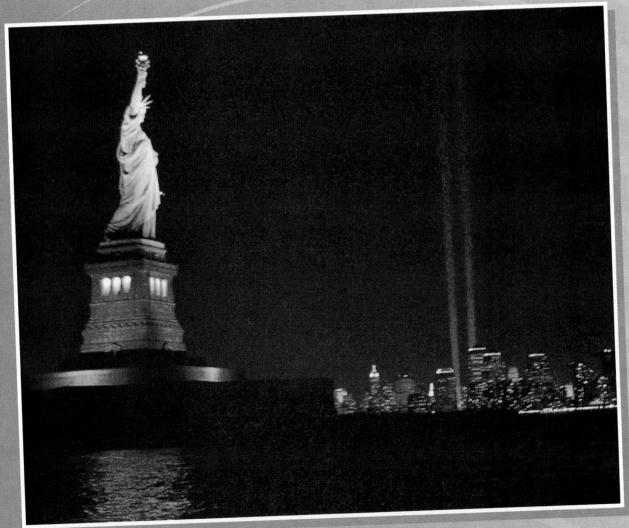

THINK
ABOUT POLITICS

1 Has the United Nations been effective in maintaining world peace?
Yes ● No ●

2 Should the United States and NATO intervene in regional conflicts in Eastern Europe?
Yes ● No ●

3 Should the United States build a ballistic missile defense system even if it is very costly?
Yes ● No ●

4 Is the president justified in placing U.S. troops in danger where U.S. vital interests are not at stake?
Yes ● No ●

5 Do you approve of the military attacks led by the United States against targets in Afghanistan?
Yes ● No ●

6 Do you favor the U.S. invading Iraq?
Yes ● No ●

7 Are U.S. military force levels today sufficient to deal with potential regional aggressors such as Iran, Iraq, and North Korea?
Yes ● No ●

8 Should the United States destroy all of its nuclear weapons now that the Cold War is over?
Yes ● No ●

America must decide how to use its national power in world affairs. Should we intervene with military forces in pursuit of humanitarian goals and to keep the peace in war-torn lands? Or should we only use military force when vital national interests are at stake?

Power among Nations

International politics, like all politics, is a struggle for power. The struggle for power is global; it involves all the nations and peoples of the world, whatever their goals or ideals. As the distinguished political scientist Hans Morgenthau once observed.

> Whatever the ultimate aims of international politics, power is always the immediate aim. Statesmen and peoples may ultimately seek freedom, security, prosperity or power itself. They may define their goals in terms of a religious, philosophic, economic, or social ideal. . . . But whenever they strive to realize their goal by means of international politics, they are striving for power.[1]

The struggle for power among nations has led to many attempts to bring order to the international system.

Collective Security Originally, **collective security** meant that *all* nations would join together to guarantee each other's "territorial integrity and existing political independence" against "external aggression" by any nation. This was the idea behind the League of Nations, established in 1919. However, opposition to international involvement was so great in the United States after World War I that, after a lengthy debate, the Senate refused to enroll the United States in the League of Nations. More important, the League of Nations failed to deal with acts of aggression by the Axis Powers—Germany, Japan, and Italy—in the 1930s. During that decade, Japan invaded Manchuria, Italy invaded Ethiopia, and Germany dismembered Czechoslovakia. The result was a devastating war: World War II cost more than 40 million lives, both civilian and military.

Formation of the United Nations Even after World War II, the notion of collective security remained an ideal of the victorious Allied Powers. The Charter of the United Nations, signed in 1945, provided for the following organization:

- The Security Council, with eleven member nations, five of them being permanent members—the United States, the **Soviet Union** (whose membership is now held by Russia), Britain, France, and China—and each having the power to veto any action by the Security Council.

- The General Assembly, composed of all the member nations, each with a single vote.

- The Secretariat, headed by a Secretary General with a staff at United Nations headquarters in New York.

collective security Attempt to bring order to international relations by all nations joining together to guarantee each other's "territorial integrity" and "independence" against "external aggression."

 State Department This U.S. Department of State Web site contains background notes on the countries and regions of the world. *www.state.gov/*

United Nations This United Nations site contains basic information about the world body's mission, member states, issues of concern, institutions, and accomplishments. *www.un.org/*

Soviet Union The Union of Soviet Socialist Republics (USSR) consisting of Russia and its bordering lands and ruled by the communist regime in Moscow, officially dissolved in 1991.

superpowers Refers to the United States and the Soviet Union after World War II, when these two nations dominated international politics.

regional security Attempt to bring order to international relations during the Cold War by creating regional alliances between a superpower and nations of a particular region.

North Atlantic Treaty Organization (NATO) Mutual-security agreement and joint military command uniting the nations of Western Europe, initially formed to resist Soviet expansionism.

- Organizations to handle specialized affairs—for example, the Economic and Social Council, the Trusteeship Council, and the International Court of Justice at The Hague in the Netherlands.

The Security Council has the "primary responsibility" for maintaining "international peace and security." The General Assembly has authority over "any matter affecting the peace of the world," although it is supposed to defer to the Security Council when the council has already taken up a particular security matter. No nation has a veto in the General Assembly; every nation has one vote regardless of its size or power. Most resolutions can be passed by a majority vote.

The United Nations in the Cold War The United Nations (UN) proved largely ineffective during the long Cold War confrontation between the communist nations, led by the Soviet Union, and the Western democracies, led by the United States. The UN grew from its original 51 member nations to more than 150, (191 in 2005), but most of those nations were headed by authoritarian regimes of one kind or another. The Western democracies were outnumbered in the General Assembly, and the Soviet Union frequently used its veto to prevent action by the Security Council. Anti-Western and antidemocratic speeches became common in the General Assembly.

During the Cold War, the UN was overshadowed by the confrontation of the world's two **superpowers**: the United States and the Soviet Union. Indeed, international conflicts throughout the world—in the Middle East, Africa, Latin America, Southeast Asia, and elsewhere—were usually influenced by some aspect of the superpower struggle.

Regional Security The general disappointment with the United Nations as a form of collective security gave rise as early as 1949 to a different approach; **regional security**. In response to aggressive Soviet moves in Europe, the United States and the democracies of Western Europe created the **North Atlantic Treaty Organization (NATO)**. In the NATO treaty, fifteen Western nations agreed to collective regional security: they agreed that "an armed attack against one or more [NATO nations] . . . shall be considered an attack against them all." The United States made a specific commitment to defend Western Europe in the event of a Soviet attack. A joint NATO military command was established (with Dwight D. Eisenhower as its first commander) to coordinate the defense of Western Europe.

After the formation of NATO, the Soviets made no further advances into Western Europe. The Soviets themselves, in response to NATO, drew up the Warsaw Pact, a comparable treaty with their own Eastern European satellite nations. But for many years the real deterrent to Warsaw Pact expansion was not the weak NATO armies but rather the pledge of the United States to use its strategic nuclear bomber force to inflict "massive retaliation" on the Soviet Union itself in the event of an attack on Western Europe.

The Warsaw Pact disintegrated following the dramatic collapse of the communist governments of Eastern Europe in 1989. Former Warsaw Pact nations—Poland, Hungary, Romania, Bulgaria, and East Germany—threw out their ruling communist regimes and demanded the withdrawal of Soviet troops from their territory. The Berlin Wall was dismantled in 1989, and Germany was formally reunified in 1990, bringing together the 61 million prosperous people of West Germany and the 17 million less affluent people of East Germany. (Unified Germany continues as a member of NATO.) The Communist Party was ousted from power in Moscow, and the Soviet Union collapsed in 1991.

NATO Today The United States and its Western European allies agree that NATO continues to play an important role in the security of Europe. Indeed, the continued deployment of some level of U.S. troops to NATO is widely considered to be reassurance that the United States remains committed to this security.

In recent years NATO has made the key decision to expand its security protections to the newly democratic nations of Eastern Europe. Three nations—Poland, Hungary, and the Czech Republic—were admitted to NATO in 1998. At that time Russia strongly objected to NATO expansion, viewing it as an incursion of Western powers in the East and a threat to Russia's security. A NATO-Russia Council was created in 2002 to calm Russian fears about NATO's intentions. In 2004 seven additional countries—Bulgaria, Estonia, Latvia, Lithuania, Romania, Slovakia, and Slovenia—were admitted to membership. All of these nations were formerly under the domination of the Soviet Union. NATO now has 26 members.

Yet another question confronting NATO is what role it should play in trying to resolve religious and ethnic conflicts in Eastern Europe. A combination of security and humanitarian concerns drew NATO, with heavy U.S. participation, into the former Yugoslavian province of Bosnia in 1995 to assist in resolving the war among the Serbs, Croats, and Moslems. This was the first deployment of NATO forces *outside* the national boundaries of NATO nations. NATO began acting militarily to halt ethnic conflicts in Kosovo in 1999. NATO forced Serbian President Slobodan Milosovic to withdraw his forces from the largely Muslim province. U.S. air power played the principal role in this engagement.

The UN Today The end of the Cold War has injected new vitality into the United Nations. Russia inherited the UN Security Council seat of the former Soviet Union, and its government has generally cooperated in UN efforts to bring stability to various regional conflicts. No longer are these conflicts "proxy" wars between the superpowers. Greater cooperation among the permanent members of the Security Council (the United States, Great Britain, France, China, and Russia) has brought "a new world order" to international politics. The UN has sent blue-helmeted "peacekeeping" forces to monitor cease-fires in many troubled areas of the world. But the United Nations and its Security Council must rely on "the last remaining superpower," the United States, to take the lead in enforcing its resolutions.

The Legacy of the Cold War

For more than forty years following the end of World War II, the United States and the Soviet Union confronted each other in the protracted political, military, and ideological struggle known as the **Cold War.**

Origins During World War II, the United States and the Soviet Union joined forces to eliminate the Nazi threat to the world. The United States dismantled its military forces at the end of the war in 1945, but the Soviet Union, under the brutal dictatorship of Josef Stalin, used the powerful Red Army to install communist governments in the nations of Eastern Europe in violation of wartime agreements to allow free elections. Stalin also ignored pledges to cooperate in a unified allied occupation of Germany; Germany was divided, and in 1948 Stalin unsuccessfully tried to oust the United States, Britain, and France from Berlin in a year-long "Berlin Blockade." Former British Prime Minister Winston Churchill warned the United States as early as 1946 that the Soviets were dividing Europe with an "Iron Curtain." When Soviet-backed communist forces threatened Greece and Turkey in 1947, President Harry S Truman responded with a pledge to "support free people

Kofi Annan, a native of Ghana, was appointed in 2002 to a second five-year term as Secretary General of the United Nations.

WWW NATO
The official "North Atlantic Treaty Organization" site contains basic facts about the alliance, current NATO news and issues, and important NATO policies.
www.nato.int/

Cold War Political, military, and ideological struggle between the United States and the Soviet Union following the end of World War II and ending with the collapse of the Soviet Union's communist government in 1991.

THINK AGAIN

Should the United States and NATO intervene in regional conflicts in Eastern Europe?

Truman Doctrine U.S. foreign policy, first articulated by President Harry S Truman, that pledged the United States to "support free peoples who are resisting attempted subjugation by armed minorities or by outside pressures."

containment Policy of preventing an enemy from expanding its boundaries and/or influence, specifically the U.S. foreign policy vis-à-vis the Soviet Union during the Cold War.

Marshall Plan U.S. program to rebuild the nations of Western Europe in the aftermath of World War II in order to render them less susceptible to communist influence and takeover.

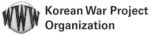 **Korean War Project Organization**

Dedicated to the memory of sacrifices of Americans in Korea, with links to battles, units, and memorials. **www.koreanwar.org**

Korean War Communist North Korea invaded non-Communist South Korea in June, 1950, causing President Harry S Truman to intervene militarily, with U.N. support. General Douglas MacArthur defeated the North Koreans, but with China's entry into the war, a stalemate resulted. An armistice was signed in 1953, with Korea divided along nearly original lines.

Cuban Missile Crisis The 1962 confrontation between the Soviet Union and the U.S. over Soviet placement of nuclear missiles in Cuba.

who are resisting attempted subjugation by armed minorities or by outside pressures," a policy that became known as the **Truman Doctrine**.

Containment The United States had fought two world wars to maintain democracy in Western Europe. The new threat of Soviet expansionism and communist world revolution caused America to assume world leadership on behalf of the preservation of democracy. In an influential article in the Council on Foreign Relations' journal, *Foreign Affairs*, the State Department's Russian expert George F. Kennan called for a policy of **containment**:

> It is clear that the main element of any United States policy toward the Soviet Union must be that of a long-term, vigilant containment of Russian expansive tendencies. . . . Soviet pressure against the free institutions of the western world is something that can be contained by the adroit and vigilant application of counterforce.[2]

To implement the containment policy, the United States first initiated the **Marshall Plan,** named for Secretary of State George C. Marshall, to rebuild the economies of the Western European nations. Marshall reasoned that *economically* weak nations were more susceptible to communist subversion and Soviet intimidation. The subsequent formation of NATO provided the necessary *military* support to contain the Soviet Union.

The Korean War The first military test of the containment policy came in June 1950, when communist North Korean armies invaded South Korea. President Truman assumed that the North Koreans were acting on behalf of their sponsor, the Soviet Union. The Soviets had already aided Chinese communists under the leadership of Mao Zedong in capturing control of mainland China in 1949. The United States quickly brought the Korean invasion issue to the Security Council. With the Soviets boycotting this meeting because the Council had refused to seat the new communist delegation from China, the Council passed a resolution calling on member nations to send troops to repel the invasion.

America's conventional (non-nuclear) military forces had been largely dismantled after World War II. Moreover, President Truman insisted on keeping most of the nation's forces in Europe, fearing that the Korean invasion was a diversion to be followed by a Soviet invasion of Western Europe. But General Douglas MacArthur, in a brilliant amphibious landing at Inchon behind North Korean lines, destroyed a much larger enemy army, captured the North Korean capital, and moved northward toward the Chinese border. Then in December 1950, disaster struck American forces as a million-strong Chinese army entered the conflict. Chinese troops surprised the Americans, inflicting heavy casualties, trapping entire units, and forcing U.S. troops to beat a hasty retreat. General MacArthur urged retaliation against China, but Truman sought to keep the war "limited." When MacArthur publicly protested political limits to military operations, Truman dismissed the popular general. The Korean War became a bloody stalemate.

Dwight Eisenhower was elected president in 1952 in large measure because he promised to "go to Korea" to end the increasingly unpopular war. He also threatened to use nuclear weapons in the conflict, but eventually agreed to a settlement along the original border between North and South Korea. Communist expansion in Korea was "contained," but at a high price: the United States lost more than 38,000 men in the war.

The Cuban Missile Crisis The most serious threat of nuclear holocaust during the entire Cold War was the Cuban missile crisis. In 1962 Soviet Premier Nikita Khrushchev sought to secretly install medium-range nuclear missiles in Cuba in an effort to give the Soviet Union nuclear capability against U.S. cities. In October 1962 intelligence photos showing Soviet missiles at Cuban bases touched off a thirteen-day crisis. President Kennedy rejected advice to launch an air strike to destroy the missiles before they could be activated. Instead, he publicly announced a naval blockade of Cuba, threatening to halt Soviet missile-carrying vessels at sea by force if necessary. The prospect of war appeared imminent; U.S. nuclear forces went on alert. Secretly, Kennedy proposed to withdraw U.S. nuclear missiles from Turkey in exchange for Soviet withdrawal of nuclear missiles from Cuba. Khrushchev's agreement to the deal appeared to the world as a backing down; Secretary of State Dean Rusk would boast, "We were eyeball to eyeball, and they blinked." Kennedy would be hailed for his statesmanship in the crisis; Khrushchev would soon lose his job.

The Vietnam War U.S. involvement in Vietnam grew out of the policy of containment. President Eisenhower had declined to intervene in the former French colony in 1956 when communist forces led by Ho Chi Minh defeated French forces at the battle of Dien Bien Phu. The resulting Geneva Accords divided that country into North Vietnam, with a communist government, and South Vietnam, with a U.S.-backed government. When South Vietnamese communist (Vietcong) guerrilla forces threatened the South Vietnamese government in the early 1960s, President Kennedy sent a force of more than 12,000 advisers and counterinsurgency forces to assist in every aspect of training and support for the Army of the Republic of Vietnam (ARVN). By 1964 units of the North Vietnamese Army (NVA) had begun to supplement the Vietcong guerrilla forces in the south. Unconfirmed reports of an attack on U.S. Navy vessels by North Vietnamese torpedo boats led the U.S. Congress to pass the Gulf of Tonkin Resolution, which authorized the president to take "all necessary measures" to repel any armed attack against any U.S. forces in Southeast Asia.

In February 1965 President Lyndon B. Johnson ordered U.S. combat troops into South Vietnam and authorized a gradual increase in air strikes against North Vietnam. Washington committed more than 500,000 troops to a war of attrition, a war in which U.S. firepower was expected to inflict sufficient casualties on the enemy to force a peace settlement. But over time, the failure to achieve any decisive military victories eroded popular support for the war.

On January 31, 1968, the Vietnam holiday of Tet, Vietcong forces blasted their way into the U.S. embassy compound in Saigon and held the courtyard for six

WWW Cuban Crises
The October 1962 nuclear missile crises described day to day, with photos. *www.cubacrisis.net*

Vietnam War War between non-Communist South Vietnam and Communist North Vietnam from 1956 to 1975, with increasing U.S. involvement, ending with U.S. withdrawal in 1973 and Communist victory in 1975. The war became unpopular in the U.S. after 1968 and caused President Johnson not to run for a second term. More than 58,000 Americans died in the war.

President Kennedy meeting with his cabinet during the Cuban missile crisis, which brought the United States and the Soviet Union to the brink of nuclear war in 1962.

hours. The attack was part of a massive, coordinated Tet offensive against all major cities of South Vietnam. U.S. forces responded and inflicted very heavy casualties on the Vietcong. By any military measure, the Tet offensive was a "defeat" for the enemy and a "victory" for U.S. forces. Yet the Tet offensive was Hanoi's greatest *political* victory. Television pictures of bloody fighting in Saigon and Hue seemed to mock President Johnson's promises of an early end to the war.

On March 31, 1968, President Johnson went on national television to make a dramatic announcement: he halted the bombing of North Vietnam and asked Hanoi for peace talks, concluding, "I shall not seek, and I will not accept, the nomination of my party for another term as your president." Formal peace talks opened in Paris on May 13.

The new president, Richard Nixon, and his national security adviser, Henry Kissinger, knew the war must be ended, but they sought to end it "honorably." Even in the absence of a settlement with the communists in Vietnam, Nixon began the withdrawal of U.S. troops under the guise of "Vietnamization" of the war effort. Unable to persuade Hanoi to make even the slightest concession at Paris, President Nixon sought to demonstrate American strength and resolve. In December 1972 the United States unleashed a devastating air attack directly on Hanoi for the first time. Critics at home labeled Nixon's action "the Christmas bombing," but when negotiations resumed in Paris in January, the North Vietnamese quickly agreed to peace on the terms that Kissinger and Le Duc Tho had worked out earlier.

The South Vietnamese government lasted two years after the agreement. In early 1975 Hanoi decided that the Americans would not "jump back in" and therefore "the opportune moment" was at hand for a new invasion. President Gerald Ford's requests to Congress for emergency military aid to the South Vietnamese fell on deaf ears. Saigon (now Ho Chi Minh City) fell to the North Vietnamese in April 1975, and the United States abandoned hundreds of thousands of loyal Vietnamese who had fought alongside the Americans for years.[3] The spectacle of U.S. Marines using their rifle butts to keep desperate Vietnamese from boarding helicopters on the roof of the U.S. embassy "provided a tragic epitaph for twenty-five years of American involvement in Vietnam."[4]

The Vietnam Syndrome America's humiliation in Vietnam had lasting national consequences. The United States suffered 47,378 battle deaths and missing-in-action among the 2.8 million U.S. personnel who served in Vietnam. A new isolationism permeated American foreign policy following defeat in Vietnam. The slogan "No more Vietnams" was used to oppose any U.S. military intervention, whether or not U.S. vital interests were at stake. Disillusionment replaced idealism. American leaders had exaggerated the importance of Vietnam; now Americans were unwilling to believe their leaders when they warned of other dangers.

In the late 1970s the Soviet Union rapidly expanded its political and military presence in Asia, Africa, the Middle East, Central America, and the Caribbean. The United States did little to respond to this new wave of Soviet expansionism until the Soviet invasion of Afghanistan in 1979, when President Jimmy Carter authorized the largest covert action in CIA history—the military support of the Afghan guerrilla forces fighting Soviet occupation. The Soviets suffered a heavy drain of human and economic resources in their nine-year war in Afghanistan, which some dubbed "Russia's Vietnam."

Rebuilding America's Defenses The decision to rebuild Western military forces and reassert international leadership on behalf of democratic values gained widespread support in the Western world in the early 1980's. President Ronald

Reagan, British Prime Minister Margaret Thatcher, French President François Mitterrand, and German Chancellor Helmut Kohl all pledged to increase their defense efforts and all held fast against a "nuclear freeze" movement that would have locked in Soviet superiority in European-based nuclear weapons.

The Reagan defense buildup extended through 1985—with increases in defense spending, improvements in strategic nuclear weapons, and, perhaps more important, the rebuilding and reequipping of U.S. conventional forces. The American and NATO defense buildup, together with the promise of a new, expensive, and technologically sophisticated race for ballistic missile defenses, forecast heavy additional strains on the weak economy of the Soviet Union. Thus, in 1985, when new Soviet President Mikhail Gorbachev came to power, the stage was set for an end to the Cold War.

Gorbachev announced reductions in the size of the Soviet military and reached agreements with the United States on the reduction of nuclear forces More important, in 1988 he announced that the Soviet Union would no longer use its military forces to keep communist governments in power in Eastern European nations. This stunning announcement, for which he received the Nobel Peace Prize in 1990, encouraged opposition democratic forces in Poland (the Solidarity movement), Czechoslovakia, Hungary, Bulgaria, Romania, and East Germany. Gorbachev refused to intervene to halt the destruction of the Berlin Wall, despite pleas by the East German hard-line communist leader Erich Honecker.

The Collapse of Communism Gorbachev's economic and political reforms threatened powerful interests in the Soviet Union—the Communist Party bureaucrats, who were losing control over economic enterprises; the military leaders, who opposed the withdrawal of Soviet troops from Germany and Eastern Europe, the KGB police, whose terror tactics were increasingly restricted, and central government officials, who were afraid of losing power to the republics. When hard liners in the Communist Party, the military, and the KGB attempted the forcible removal of Gorbachev in August 1991, democratic forces rallied to his support. Led by Boris Yeltsin, the first elected president of the Russian Republic, thousands of demonstrators took to the streets, Soviet military forces stood aside, and the coup crumbled. Yeltsin emerged as the most influential leader in the nation. The failed coup hastened the demise of the Communist Party. The party lost legitimacy with the peoples of Russia and the other republics.

The Vietnam War Memorial in Washington, D.C., is inscribed with the names of the nearly 50,000 Americans who died in Vietnam. America's defeat fostered a lasting skepticism about the wisdom of foreign military intervention, leading to a new isolationism in foreign policy.

The Disintegration of the Soviet Union Strong independence movements in the republics of the Soviet Union emerged as the authority of the centralized Communist Party in Moscow waned. Lithuania, Estonia, and Latvia—nations that had been forcibly incorporated into the Soviet Union in 1939—led the way to independence in 1991. Soon all of the fifteen republics of the Soviet Union declared their independence, and the Union of Soviet Socialist Republics officially ceased to exist after December 31, 1991. Its president, Mikhail Gorbachev, no longer had a government to preside over. The red flag with its hammer and sickle atop the Kremlin was replaced with the flag of the Russian Republic.

Russia after Communism The transition from a centralized state-run economy to free markets turned out to be more painful for Russians than expected. Living standards for most people declined, alcoholism and death rates increased, and even average life spans shortened. Ethnic conflict and political separatism, especially in the largely Muslim province of Chechnya, added to Russia's problems. Yeltsin was able to overcome these political challenges and win reelection as president in 1996. But corruption, embezzlement, graft, and organized crime continue to undermine democratic reforms. Poor health eventually forced Yeltsin to turn over power to Vladimir Putin, who himself won election as president of Russia in 2000.

The United States has a vital continuing interest in promoting democracy and economic reform in Russia. Russia remains the only nuclear power capable of destroying the United States.

Nuclear Threats

Nuclear weaponry has made the world infinitely more dangerous. During the Cold War, the nuclear arsenals of the United States and the Soviet Union threatened a human holocaust. Yet, paradoxically, the very destructiveness of nuclear weapons caused leaders on both sides to exercise extreme caution in their relations with each other. Scores of wars, large and small, were fought by different nations during the Cold War years, yet American and Soviet troops never engaged in direct combat against each other.

Deterrence To maintain nuclear peace during the Cold War, the United States relied primarily on the policy of **deterrence**. Deterrence is based on the notion

---

Russia EIN News
Business, cultural, political, and scientific news from Russia.
www.einnews.com/russia

THINK AGAIN

Should the United States destroy all of its nuclear weapons now that the Cold War is over?

---

deterrence U.S. approach to deterring any nuclear attack from the Soviet Union by maintaining a second-strike capability.

Russians face grim economic conditions as they try to transform their economic system from communism to free markets.

that a nation can dissuade a rational enemy from attacking by maintaining the capacity to destroy the enemy's homeland even *after* the nation has suffered a well-executed surprise attack by the enemy. Deterrence assumes that the worst may happen—a surprise first strike against a nation's nuclear forces. It emphasizes **second-strike capability**—the ability of a nation's forces to survive a surprise attack by the enemy and then to inflict an unacceptable level of destruction on the enemy's homeland. Deterrence is really a *psychological* defense against attack; no effective physical defense against a ballistic missile attack exists even today.

MAD Balance of Terror

By the early 1970s, a nuclear balance existed between the superpowers. Neither side could consider launching a nuclear attack because of the terrible consequences that the other side could inflict in retaliation. If neither side could be assured of destroying the other side's retaliatory missiles in a first strike, then a mutual "balance of terror" maintained the nuclear peace. In effect, the populations of each nation were being held hostage against a nuclear attack. Commentators labeled this balance of terror as **mutual assured destruction** deterrence, or MAD.

Limiting Nuclear Arms: SALT

The United States and the Soviet Union engaged in negotiations over nuclear arms control for many years. The development of reconnaissance satellites in the 1960s made it possible for each nation to monitor the strategic weapons possessed by the other. Space photography made cheating on agreements more difficult and thus opened the way for both nations to seek stability through arms control.

Following the election of Richard Nixon as president in 1968, the United States, largely guided by former Harvard professor Henry Kissinger (national security adviser to the president and later secretary of state), began negotiations with the Soviet Union over strategic nuclear arms. In 1972 the two nations concluded two and a half years of Strategic Arms Limitation Talks (SALT) about limiting the nuclear arms race. The agreement, **SALT I**, consisted of a treaty limiting antiballistic missiles (ABMs) and an agreement placing a numerical ceiling on offensive missiles. The **ABM Treaty** reflected the MAD theory that the populations of each nation should be *un*defended in order to hold them hostage against a first strike. Under the offensive-missiles

second-strike capability
Ability of a nation's forces to survive a surprise nuclear attack by the enemy and then to retaliate effectively.

mutual assured destruction (MAD) Nuclear peace maintained by the capability of each side's missile forces to survive a first strike and inflict heavy damages in retaliation against the aggressor's population.

SALT I First arms limitation treaty between the United States and the Soviet Union, signed in 1972, limiting the total number of offensive nuclear missiles; it included the ABM Treaty that reflected the theory that the population centers of both nations should be left *un*defended.

ABM Treaty A formal treaty in 1972 between the U.S. and the Soviet Union in which each side agreed *not* to build or deploy antiballistic missiles.

agreement, each side was frozen at the total number of offensive missiles, completed or under construction. Both sides could construct new and more destructive missiles as long as they dismantled an equal number of older missiles. Each nation agreed not to interfere in the satellite intelligence-gathering activities of the other nation.

SALT I was the first step forward on the control of nuclear arms; both sides agreed to continue negotiations. After seven years of difficult negotiations, the United States and the Soviet Union produced the lengthy and complicated **SALT II** treaty in 1979. It set an overall limit on "strategic nuclear launch vehicles"—ICBMs, SLBMs, bombers, and long-range Cruise missiles—at 2,250 for each side. It also limited the number of missiles that could have multiple warheads (MIRVs) and banned new types of ICBMs, with the exception of one new type of ICBM for each side. When the Soviet Union invaded Afghanistan in 1974, President Carter withdrew the SALT II treaty from Senate consideration. However, President Carter, and later President Reagan, announced that the United States would abide by the provisions of the unratified SALT II treaty as long as the Soviet Union did so.

Reducing Nuclear Arms: START In negotiations with the Soviets, the Reagan Administration established three central principles of arms control—reductions, equality, and verification. The new goal was to be *reductions* in missiles and warheads, not merely limitations on future numbers and types of weapons, as in previous SALT talks. To symbolize this new direction, President Reagan renamed the negotiations the Strategic Arms *Reduction* Talks, or START.

The **START I** Treaty signed in Moscow in 1991 by Presidents George Bush and Mikhail Gorbachev was the first agreement between the nuclear powers that actually resulted in the reduction of strategic nuclear weapons. (Earlier, the Intermediate-Range Nuclear Forces INF Treaty of 1987 eliminated missiles with an intermediate range, between 300 and 3,800 miles; although the portion of each side's nuclear weapons covered by the INF Treaty was small, it set the pattern for future arms control agreements in its provisions for reductions, equality, and verification.) The START I Treaty reduced the total number of deployed strategic nuclear delivery systems to no more than 1,600, a 30 percent reduction from the SALT II level.

A far-reaching **START II** agreement, signed in 1993 by U.S. President Bush and Russian President Yeltsin, promises to eliminate the threat of a first-strike nuclear attack by either side. Its most important provision is the agreement to eliminate all multiwarhead (MIRVed) land-based missiles. The Russians agreed to dismantle their powerful SS-18 missiles, the most dangerous threat to the nuclear balance of power. The United States agreed to dismantle the MX missile and convert the three-warheaded Minuteman IIIs into single-warhead missiles. START II also called for the reduction of overall strategic warheads to 3,500.

The Treaty of Moscow The capstone of strategic nuclear arms reductions is the Treaty of Moscow, signed by Russian President Vladimir Putin and U.S. President George W. Bush in 2002. This new treaty, which must be approved by the U.S. Senate and the Russian Federal Assembly, calls for an overall limit of nuclear warheads at 1,700–2,200 by 2012. Each side may determine for itself the composition and structure of its strategic forces consistent with this limit. The provisions of the START treaties remain unchanged. The effect of the Moscow Treaty, together with earlier reductions in nuclear weapons under the START treaties, will be to reduce the nuclear arsenals of the former adversaries by over 80 percent from Cold War levels (see Figure 18.1).

Nuclear Testing and Nonproliferation The United States and the former Soviet Union reached an agreement in 1963—the Limited Test Ban Treaty—that

SALT II Lengthy and complicated treaty between the United States and the Soviet Union, agreed to in 1979 but never ratified by the U.S. Senate, that set limits on all types of strategic nuclear launch vehicles.

START I First treaty between the United States and the Soviet Union that actually reduced the strategic nuclear arms of the superpowers, signed in 1991.

START II A treaty between the United States and Russia eliminating all multiwarhead land missiles and reducing nuclear weapons stockpiles; signed in 2003.

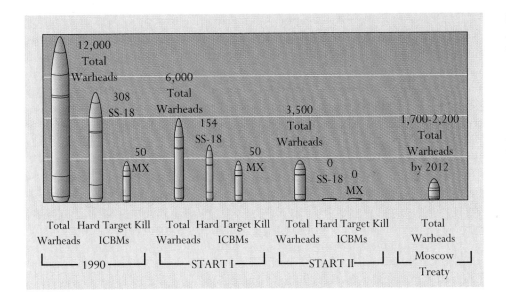

FIGURE 18.1 **Strategic Nuclear Arms under START Treaties**

Implementation of the Start II Treaty will reduce the total number of warheads in both the United States and Russia by over two-thirds and will completely eliminate bard target kill ICBMs.

prohibited nuclear testing in the atmosphere, under water, or in outer space. The effect was to allow only underground testing, which was believed to reduce radioactivity in the atmosphere. A Threshold Test Ban Treaty was signed in 1974 that prohibited tests of nuclear weapons with explosive power greater than 150 kilotons (equivalent to 150,000 tons of conventional explosives).

In 1992 the Russian government under President Yeltsin announced that it would discontinue *all* nuclear testing if the United States would do the same. President George Bush declined to make this pledge, but later President Bill Clinton placed an unofficial moratorium on U.S. nuclear testing. In 1996, President Clinton signed a **Comprehensive Test Ban Treaty**, a multilateral agreement that would prohibit all nuclear testing. Many non-nuclear-armed nations signed this treaty. But in 1999 the U.S. Senate voted against ratification. Opponents of the treaty noted that testing verified the safety and reliability of weapons, and that several other potentially threatening nuclear nations had refused to sign the treaty, including North Korea, Iran, Iraq, India, and Pakistan. Russia announced that it was awaiting U.S. ratification before signing the treaty, and China continued testing nuclear weapons.

Yet another **multilateral treaty**, the nuclear **Nonproliferation Treaty**, was signed by the United States and the former Soviet Union in 1968. It prohibits nuclear-armed nations from transferring weapons and technologies to nonnuclear nations. Nonnuclear signing nations pledged not to "receive, manufacture, or otherwise acquire nuclear weapons." But the Nonproliferation Treaty has been largely ignored, not only by nations that went on to acquire nuclear weapons (including India, Pakistan, China, and North Korea), but also by nations that have transferred nuclear technology to nonnuclear nations (including France and Russia). North Korea has demanded extensive U.S. foreign aid in exchange for dismantling its nuclear weapons facilities.

Nuclear Terrorism Even as the threat of a large-scale nuclear attack recedes, the threats arising from "nondeterrable" sources are increasing. Today, the principal nondeterrable threats are estimated to be (1) missiles launched by a terrorist nation; (2) unauthorized missile launches by elements within the former Soviet Union during periods of internal crisis and turmoil; and (3) accidental missile launches. Over time global nuclear and ballistic missile proliferation steadily increases the likelihood of these types of threats. Terrorist, unauthorized, and accidental launches are considered "nondeterrable" because the threat of nuclear retaliation is largely meaningless.

Comprehensive Test Ban Treaty A multilateral treaty prohibiting all nuclear testing.

multilateral treaty A treaty open to signature by more than two nations (as opposed to a bilateral treaty, signed by only two nations).

Nonproliferation Treaty A multilateral treaty in which nuclear nations pledged not to transfer nuclear weapons or technologies to nonnuclear nations, and nonnuclear nations pledged not to manufacture or acquire nuclear weapons.

The threat of mass terror weapons—nuclear, chemical, or biological weapons, especially those carried by medium- or long-range missiles—is likely to increase dramatically in the years ahead. North Korea is reported to possess nuclear weapons and to be developing long-range missiles to carry them. Defending against terrorist, unauthorized, or accidental missile attacks requires the development and deployment of **ballistic missile defense (BMD)** systems, weapons capable of detecting, intercepting, and destroying ballistic missiles while they are in flight. At present there is no defense against a ballistic missile attack on American cities (see *A Conflicting View:* "We Should Defend Ourselves against a Ballistic Missile Attack").

The Bush administration officially notified Russia in 2002 of its intent to withdraw from the provisions of the SALT I agreement that prohibited the development, testing, and deployment of antiballistic missiles. The Russian government objected (but provisions for a six-month notification of withdrawal were included in the original treaty). President Bush also announced that United States would begin the actual deployment of a limited number of ground-based and sea-based missile interceptors. This initial missile defense capability will be designed "to meet the near-term threat to our homeland, our deployed forces, and our friends and allies."

THINK AGAIN

Is the president justified in placing U.S. troops in danger where U.S. vital interests are not at stake?

When to Use Military Force?

All modern presidents have acknowledged that the most agonizing decisions they have made were to send U.S. military forces into combat. These decisions cost lives. The American people are willing to send their sons and daughters into danger—and even to see some of them wounded and killed—but *only* if a president convinces them that the outcome "is worth dying for." A president must be able to explain why they lost their lives and to justify their sacrifice.

To Protect Vital Interests The U.S. military learned many bitter lessons in its long bloody experience in Vietnam. Among those lessons are these:

- The United States should commit its military forces only in support of vital national interests.

- If military forces are committed, they must have clearly defined military objectives—the destruction of enemy forces and/or the capture of enemy-held territory.

- Any commitment of U.S. forces must be of sufficient strength to ensure overwhelming and decisive victory with the fewest possible casualties.

- Before committing U.S. military forces, there must be some reasonable assurances that the effort has the support of the American people and their representatives in Congress.

- The commitment of U.S. military forces should be a last resort, after political, economic, and diplomatic efforts have proven ineffective.

President George Bush argued that his decision to use military force in the Gulf War in 1990–91 met these guidelines: that preventing Iraq's Saddam Hussein from gaining control of the world's oil supply and developing nuclear and chemical weapons were vital national interests; that political and economic sanctions were not effective; and that he had defined clear military objectives—the removal of Iraqi troops from Kuwait and the destruction of Iraq's nuclear and chemical weapon capabilities (see *Up Close:* "The Use of Force: Operation Desert Storm"). And he authorized a large military commitment that led to a speedy and decisive victory.

ballistic missile defense (BMD) Weapons systems capable of detecting, intercepting, and destroying missiles in flight.

CIA World Factbook
Nations listed A–Z with geography, people, economy, government, military, etc., information.
www.cia.gov/publications/factbook

We Should Defend Ourselves against a Ballistic Missile Attack

For over a half-century, since the terrible nuclear blasts of Hiroshima and Nagasaki in Japan in 1945, the world has avoided nuclear war. Peace has been maintained by deterrence—by the threat of devastating nuclear attacks that would be launched in retaliation to an enemy's first strike. But in 1983 President Ronald Reagan urged that instead of deterring war through fear of retaliation, the United States should seek a technological defense against nuclear missiles.

> Our nuclear retaliating forces have deterred war for forty years. The fact is, however, that we have no defense against ballistic missile attack. . . . In the event that deterrence failed, a president's only recourse would be to surrender or to retaliate. Nuclear retaliation, whether massive or limited, would result in the loss of millions of lives. . . .
>
> If we apply our great scientific and engineering talent to the problem of defending against ballistic missiles, there is a very real possibility that future presidents will be able to deter war by means other than threatening devastation to any aggressor—and by a means which threatens no one.*

"Star Wars"

Reagan's Strategic Defense Initiative (SDI) was a research program designed to explore means of destroying enemy nuclear missiles in space before they could reach their targets. Following President Reagan's initial announcement of SDI in March 1983, the press quickly labeled the effort "Star Wars." In theory, a ballistic missile defense (BMD) system could be based in space, orbiting over enemy missile-launching sites. Should an enemy missile get through the space-based defense, a ground-based BMD system would attempt to intercept warheads as they reentered the atmosphere and approached their targets. SDI included research on laser beams, satellite surveillance, computerized battle-management systems, and "smart" and "brilliant" weapons systems. SDI under President Reagan was a very ambitious program with the goal of creating an "impenetrable shield" that would protect not only the population of the United States but the population of our allies as well.

Protection against Nuclear Terrorism

The end of the Cold War refocused SDI away from defense against a massive Russian missile attack to more limited yet more likely threats. Today the principal nuclear threats are missiles launched by terrorists or a "rogue state." President Bush redirected SDI toward defending against these more limited yet potentially devastating attacks.

The Gulf War experience demonstrated that deterrence may not protect the United States against a ballistic missile attack by a terrorist regime. The success of the Patriot antiballistic missile in destroying short-range Iraqi Scud missiles during the Gulf War demonstrated that enemy missiles could be intercepted in flight. (The Patriot is a ground-based "tactical" weapon designed to protect specific military targets.) However, developing an effective antiballistic missile that can intercept and destroy another missile in space has proven to be more difficult, although not impossible.

The Future of BMDs

As a Reagan-era initiative, partisanship has tended to cloud the debate over BMDs. In 1993 President Clinton announced the termination of the separate SDI organization, but he reassured the nation that research would continue on the ground-based ballistic missile defenses. President George W. Bush notified the Russians in 2002 that the United States was withdrawing from provisions of the SALT I Treaty of 1972 that prohibited the development, testing, or deployment of new ballistic missile defense systems.

Advanced testing has met with both successes and failures. Intercepting an incoming missile has been compared to "hitting a bullet with a bullet." Even this daunting challenge is further complicated by the likelihood of enemy decoys masking the real warhead; a reliable ballistic missile defense must be able to discriminate between decoys and actual warheads.

President George W. Bush announced a limited deployment of sea-based and ground-based missile interceptors and advanced Patriot missiles in 2004. The president spoke of an incremental growth of U.S. anti-ballistic missile capability directed at potential terrorist attacks.

*President Ronald Reagan, *The President's Strategic Defense Initiative*, The White House, January 3, 1985.

These guidelines for the use of military force are widely supported within the U.S. military itself.[5] Contrary to Hollywood stereotypes, military leaders are extremely reluctant to go to war when no vital interest of the United States is at stake, where there are no clear-cut military objectives, without the support of Congress or the American people, or without sufficient force to achieve speedy and decisive victory with minimal casualties. (See *People in Politics:* "Colin Powell, An American Journey.") They are wary of seeing their troops placed in danger merely to advance diplomatic goals, or to engage in "peacekeeping," or to "stabilize governments," or to "show the flag." They are reluctant to undertake humanitarian missions while being shot at. They do not like to risk their soldiers' lives under "rules of engagement" that limit their ability to defend themselves.

In Support of Important Political Objectives In contrast to military leaders, political leaders and diplomats often reflect the view that "war is a continuation of politics by other means"—a view commonly attributed to nineteenth-century German theorist of war Karl von Clausewitz. Military force may be used to protect interests that are important but not necessarily vital. Otherwise, the United States would be rendered largely impotent in world affairs. A diplomat's ability to achieve a satisfactory result often depends on the expressed or implied threat of military force. The distinguished international political theorist Hans Morgenthau wrote, "Since military strength is the obvious measure of a nation's power, its demonstration serves to impress others with that nation's power."[6]

Currently American military forces must be prepared to carry out a variety of missions in addition to the conduct of conventional war:

- Demonstrating U.S. resolve in crisis situations.

- Demonstrating U.S. support for democratic governments.

- Protecting U.S. citizens living abroad.

- Peacemaking among warring factions or nations.

- Peacekeeping where hostile factions or nations have accepted a peace agreement.

- Providing humanitarian aid often under warlike conditions.

- Assist in an international war against drug trafficking.

In pursuit of such objectives, recent U.S. presidents have sent troops to Lebanon in 1982 to stabilize the government (Reagan), to Grenada in 1983 to rescue American medical students and restore democratic government (Reagan), to Panama in 1989 to oust drug-trafficking General Manuel Antonio Noriega from power and to protect U.S. citizens (Bush), to Somalia in 1992–93 to provide emergency humanitarian aid (Bush and Clinton), to Haiti in 1994 (Clinton) to restore constitutional government and again to Haiti in 2004 (Bush), and to Bosnia and Kosovo for peacekeeping among warring ethnic factions (see Table 18.1).

Proponents of these more flexible uses of U.S. military forces usually deny any intent to be the "world's policeman." Rather, they argue that each situation must be judged independently on its own merits—weighing the importance of U.S. goals against expected costs. No military operation is without risk, but some risks may be worth taking to advance important political interests even though these interests may not be deemed "vital" to the United States.

In Support of the War on Terrorism The War on Terrorism creates new conditions for the use of military force.[5] Currently U.S. forces are prepared for:

terrorism Title 22 of the U.S. Code, Section 2656 (d): "The term 'terrorism' means premeditated, politically motivated violence perpetrated against noncombatant targets by subnational groups or clandestine agents, usually intended to influence an audience."

The Use of Force: Operation Desert Storm

Saddam Hussein's invasion of Kuwait on August 2, 1990, was apparently designed to restore his military prestige after an indecisive war against Iran, to secure additional oil revenues to finance the continued buildup of Iraqi military power, and to intimidate (and perhaps invade) Saudi Arabia and the Gulf states, thereby securing control over a major share of the world's oil reserves.

The Iraqi invasion met with a surprisingly swift response by the United Nations, with Security Council resolutions condemning the invasion, demanding an immediate withdrawal, and imposing a trade embargo and economic sanctions. President George Bush immediately set to work to stitch together a coalition military force that would eventually include thirty nations. Early on, the president described the U.S. military deployment as "defensive," but he soon became convinced that neither diplomacy nor an economic blockade would dislodge Saddam from Kuwait and so ordered the military to prepare an "offensive" option.

The top U.S. military commanders—including the chair of the Joint Chiefs of Staff, General Colin Powell, and the commander in the field, General Norman Schwartzkopf—had been field officers in Vietnam, and they were resolved not to repeat the mistakes of that war. They were reluctant to go into battle without the full support of the American people. If ordered to fight, they wanted to employ overwhelming and decisive military force; they wanted to avoid the gradual escalation, protracted conflict, target limitations, and political interference in the conduct of the war that had characterized the U.S. military's efforts in Vietnam. Accordingly, they presented the president with a plan that called for a very large military buildup involving nearly 500,000 troops. Coalition forces also included British and French heavy armored units, and Egyptian, Syrian, Saudi, and other Arab forces.

From Baghdad, CNN reporters Bernard Shaw and Peter Arnett were startled on the night of January 16 when Operation Desert Storm began with an air attack on key installations in the city. Iraqi forces were also surprised, despite the prompt timing of the attack; Saddam had assured them that the United States lacked the resolve to fight.

The success of the coalition air force was spectacular. American TV audiences saw videotapes of laser-guided bombs entering the doors and air shafts of enemy bunkers. Civilian damage was lower than in any previous air war. After five weeks of air war, intelligence estimated that nearly half the Iraqi tanks and artillery in the field had been destroyed, demoralized troops were hiding in deep shelters, and the battlefield had been isolated and "prepared" for ground operations.

General Schwartzkopf's plan for the ground war emphasized deception and maneuver. While Iraqi forces prepared for attacks from the south and the east coast, he sent heavily armed columns in a "Hail Mary" play—a wide sweep to the west, outflanking and cutting off Iraqi forces in the battle area. On the night of February 24, the ground attack began. Marines breached ditches and minefields and raced directly to the Kuwait airport; army helicopter air assaults lunged deep into Iraq; armored columns raced northward across the desert to outflank Iraqi forces and then attack them from the west, while a surge in air attacks kept Iraqi forces holed up in their bunkers. Iraqi troops surrendered in droves, highways from Kuwait city became a massive junkyard of Iraqi vehicles, and Iraqi forces that tried to fight were quickly destroyed. After 100 hours of ground fighting, President George Bush ordered a ceasefire.

The United States had achieved a decisive military victory quickly and with remarkably few casualties. The president resisted calls to expand the original objectives of the war and go on to capture Baghdad, to destroy the Iraqi economy, to encourage Iraq's disintegration as a nation, or to kill Saddam, although it was expected that his defeat would lead to his ouster. Although the war left many political issues unresolved, it was the most decisive military outcome the United States had achieved since the end of World War II.[*] President Bush chose to declare victory and celebrate the return of American troops.

---

[*] See Harry G. Summers. Jr., *On Strategy II: A Critical Analysis of the Gulf War* (New York: Dell, 1992).

Colin Powell, An American Journey

Secretary of State Colin Powell embodies the American dream: "a black kid of no early promise from an immigrant family of limited means who was raised in the South Bronx and somehow rose to become the National Security Adviser to the President of the United States and then Chairman of the Joint Chiefs of Staff." He also rose to be the American public's preferred choice for president of the United States in 1996, yet decided he did not have the "passion and commitment" for political life that he "felt every day of my thirty-five years as a soldier." But he answered his country's call again in 2001, this time to serve as secretary of state.

Born in Harlem to Jamaican immigrant parents, Powell recounts his youth as proof that "it is possible to rise above conditions." After graduation from Morris High School in the South Bronx, Powell enrolled at The City College of New York on a ROTC scholarship. In 1958 he graduated with a degree in geology at the top of his ROTC class and was commissioned a second lieutenant in the U.S. Army. Powell went to South Vietnam as a military adviser in 1962 and returned for a second tour of service in 1968. In Vietnam, he was awarded two Purple Hearts, a Bronze Star for Valor, and the Legion of Merit.

In 1972 Powell returned to the classroom to pursue a master's degree in business administration from George Washington University and accept an appointment to the prestigious White House Fellows Program. As a White House Fellow, Powell was assigned to the Office of Management and Budget, where he worked under Caspar Weinberger, later secretary of defense in the Reagan Administration. Powell's career was on a fast track after his White House duty. Powell was recalled to Washington in 1983 by Defense Secretary Weinberger to become senior military adviser to the secretary.

President George Bush chose General Powell in 1989 to head the Joint Chiefs of Staff, the nation's highest military position. It was Powell who helped convince the president that if military force were to be used to oust Saddam Hussein from Kuwait, it must be an overwhelming and decisive force, not gradual, limited escalation, as in Vietnam. Powell's televised press briefings during the war assured the American people of the competence and effectiveness of the U.S. military. The Gulf War victory restored the morale of U.S. military forces and the confidence of the American people in its military leadership.

To a great many Americans, Powell seemed to offer the nation what it most needed: a decisive leader with integrity and character, a political outsider untarnished by "politics as usual," and an African American whose "American journey"[*] could serve as a model for all and ease the nation's racial divisions. He was frequently compared to Dwight D. Eisenhower, whose military leadership in World War II ushered him into the White House. Like Ike, Powell waited until after army retirement to declare himself a Republican. He led all other candidates for president in public opinion polls in 1996, yet after "prayerful consideration," he announced that he would not be a candidate for president "or any elective office." For several years Powell devoted himself exclusively to volunteer activities, notably as chairman of a national campaign, "America's Promise—Alliance for Youth."

Powell's most challenging task as Secretary of State is to maintain the backing of other nations for the American-led war on terrorism. His advice to the president on the use of military force reflects his long-held belief, sometimes even referred to as the "Powell Doctrine," that military operations should be conducted only in the vital national interest, with clear goals and public support, and when overwhelming and decisive military force is to be employed.

[*]Source: Colin Powell, *My American Journey* (New York: Random House 1995).

- Direct attacks against terrorist forces to capture or kill them. These operations are usually carried out by highly trained Special Operations Forces.

- Attacks on nations that harbor terrorists, allow terrorists to maintain bases, or supply and equip terrorist organizations. In 1986, the United States struck at Libya in a limited air attack in response to various Libyan-supported acts of terrorism around the world. In 1993, the United States struck Iraq's intelligence center in Baghdad in response to a foiled plot to assassinate former President George Bush. In 2001, the United States relied principally on Special Forces working in con-

TABLE 18.1 Major Deployments of U.S. Military Forces Since World War II

Year	Area	President
1950–53	Korea	Truman
1958	Lebanon	Eisenhower
1961–64	Vietnam	Kennedy
1962	Cuban waters	Kennedy
1965–73	Vietnam	Johnson, Nixon
1965	Dominican Republic	Johnson
1970	Laos	Nixon
1970	Cambodia	Nixon
1975	Cambodia	Ford
1980	Iran	Carter
1982–83	Lebanon	Reagan
1983	Grenada	Reagan
1989	Panama	Bush
1990–91	Persian Gulf	Bush
1992–93	Somalia	Bush, Clinton
1994–95	Haiti	Clinton
1995–2000	Bosnia	Clinton
1999–2000	Kosovo	Clinton
2001–	Afghanistan	Bush
2002–	Philippines	Bush
2003–	Iraq	Bush
2004	Haiti	Bush

junction with tribal forces in Afghanistan to attack Al Qaeda terrorists and to topple the Taliban government that had harbored and supported Al Qaeda.

■ Preemptive attacks on regimes that threaten to use weapons of mass instruction—chemical, biological, or nuclear weapons—against the United States or its allies, or to supply terrorist organizations with these weapons. Preemptive military action represents a reversal of traditional U.S. policy. Historically the United States acted militarily only in response to a direct attack on its own forces or those of its allies. But it is argued that the Terrorist Attack of 9/11 initiated the current War on Terrorism and that American military actions in the Middle East, including those in Afghanistan and Iraq, are related to the 9/11 attack on America. The argument for preemptive military action was summarized by President Bush's National Security Adviser Condoleeza Rice: "We cannot wait until the smoking gun becomes a mushroom cloud."

The War on Terrorism

Terrorism is a political act. The deliberate targeting of civilians, the infliction of widespread destruction, and the resulting media portrayals of the pain and suffering of victims are designed to call attention to political grievances and to instill fear in people. (The Latin root of the term, *terrere*, means "to frighten.") The horror of terrorist acts and their unpredictability add to public fear—people can neither anticipate nor prepare for tragedies inflicted upon them. Terrorists hope to undermine the confidence of people in their government to protect them, and to conclude that

THINK AGAIN

Do you approve of the military attacks led by the United States against targets in Afghanistan?

THINK AGAIN

Do you favor the U.S. invading Iraq?

 Terrorism Research Center

The "Terrorism Research Center" Web site is dedicated to "informing the public of the phenomena of terrorism and information warfare." It contains news, analytical essays on terrorist issues, and many links to other terrorism materials and research sources. *www.terrorism.com*

submission to the terrorists' demands is preferable to living in a continuing climate of anxiety and uncertainty.

Global Terrorism Global terrorism has evolved over the years into highly sophisticated networks operating in many countries. The most notable terrorist attacks extend back over thirty years, but the death and destruction wrought by terrorists have dramatically increased (see Table 18.2). Prior to the attacks on New York's World Trade Center and the Pentagon on September 11, 2001, most Americans thought of terrorism as foreign. Terrorist acts on American soil had been rare; the most destructive attack—the Oklahoma City bombing of a federal building in 1995—had been carried out by domestic terrorists. But the 9/11 attacks were on an unprecedented scale and they revealed a sophisticated global plot against America.

A loose-knit network of terrorist cells (Al Qaeda) organized by a wealthy Saudi Arabian, Osama bin Laden, was engaged in global terrorism. Their political grievances included America's support of Israel in Middle East conflicts and an American presence in Islamic holy lands, notably Saudi Arabia. Several nations share these grievances and, more importantly, provided support and haven to Al Qaeda in similar terrorist organizations. The principal base of support and sanctuary for Al Qaeda was the repressive and violent Taliban regime of Afghanistan.

Declaring War on Terrorism On the evening of September 11, President George W. Bush spoke to the American people from the Oval Office in a nationally televised address:

> The pictures of airplanes flying into buildings, fires burning, huge structures collapsing, have filled us with disbelief, terrible sadness, and a quiet, unyielding anger. These mass murders were intended to frighten our nation into chaos and retreat. But they failed; our country is strong. . . . These deliberate and deadly attacks were more than acts of terror. They were acts of war.

The president outlined a broad "response to terrorism" to be fought both at home and abroad through diplomatic, military, financial, investigative, homeland security, and humanitarian means. He warned that the new war on terrorism would require a long-term sustained effort. It would require Americans to accept new restrictions on their lives (see "Terrorism's Threat to Democracy" in Chapter 1). It would require new legislation—an Airport Security Act federalizing security at U.S. airports and instituting new strict security measures, and a "Patriot" (anti-terrorism) Act expanding the authority of the attorney general and federal law-enforcement agencies to fight domestic terrorism (see *A Conflicting View*: "Terrorism Requires Restrictions on Civil Liberties" in Chapter 14). It would require the creation of a new Department of Homeland Security designed to coordinate many federal, state, and local law-enforcement agencies charged with responsibility for dealing with acts of terror (see "The Department of Homeland Security" in Chapter 12).

Operation "Enduring Freedom" The military phase of the war on terrorism began October 7, 2001, when U.S. Air Force and Navy aircraft began attacks on known Al Qaeda bases in Afghanistan and U.S. Special Forces organized and led anti-Taliban fighters, including several tribal groups calling themselves the Northern Alliance, in a campaign against the Taliban regime. A coalition of nations participated in Operation "Enduring Freedom"; some, including Britain and Canada, contributed troops, while others, including Pakistan, Saudi Arabia, and Uzbekistan, informally allowed U.S. forces to base operations on their territory. Kabul, the capital of Afghanistan, was occupied by anti-Taliban forces on November 13, 2001.

TABLE 18-2 Notable Global Terrorist Attacks

Date	Number of People Killed	Description	Prime suspect[s]
September 5, 1972	17	Israeli athletes are killed during the Olympics in Munich, Germany	Black September, a Palestinian guerrilla group
April 18, 1983	63	The American Embassy in Beirut, Lebanon, is bombed	Hezbollah [Party of God]
September 23, 1983	112	A plane crashes in United Arab Emirates after a bomb explodes in the baggage compartment	Unknown
October 23, 1983	299	Two truck bombs kill U.S. Marines and French paratroopers in Beirut, Lebanon	U.S. blames groups aligned with Iran and Syria
June 23, 1985	329	An Air India jet explodes over the Atlantic Ocean, off the coast of Ireland	The Royal Canadian Mounted Police charge Ajaib Singh Bagri and Ripudaman, two Sikh dissidents, in 2000
November 29, 1987	115	A Korean Air Lines jet explodes over the Burma coast	South Korea suspects North Korean involvement
December 21, 1988	270	Pan Am 103 explodes over Lockerbie, Scotland	One Libyan intelligence officer is convicted in a trial in The Hague in 2001, another is acquitted
September 19, 1989	171	A French U.T.A. jet explodes over Niger	The Lebanese Islamic Holy War claims responsibility, France holds Libya responsible
October 2, 1990	128	A hijacked Xiamen Airlines plane crashes into other parked planes in an airport in China	Unknown
March 17, 1992	29	A bomb demolishes the Israeli Embassy in Buenos Aires, Argentina	Unknown
February 26, 1993	6	A van filled with explosives explodes in the garage of the World Trade Center, leaving more than 1,000 people wounded	Ramzi Yousef receives a life sentence plus 240 years in 1998; the FBI suspects Osama bin Laden is behind the plot
April 19, 1995	168	Oklahoma City truck bomb destroys the Alfred P. Murrah federal building	Timothy McVeigh executed June 11, 2001
August 7, 1998	224	Car bombs destroy U.S. embassies in Nairobi, Kenya, and Dar Es Salaam, Tanzania	Al Qaeda (Osama bin Laden)
October 12, 2000	17	Rubber boat filled with explosives detonates next to USS Code in Yemen	Al Qaeda (Osama bin Laden)
September 11, 2001	3,000+	Four U.S. commercial airlines hijacked. Two destroy World Trade Center, one hits the Pentagon, one crashes in Pennsylvania	Al Qaeda (Osama bin Laden)
March 11, 2004	191	Bombing of train in Madrid, Spain	Al Qaeda
September 3, 2004	355 (155 children)	Chechen terrorists attack school in Breslan, Russia	Chechen

Source: U.S. Department of State, Office of Counterterrorism, October 2001.

President Bush made it clear that the United States was prepared to act militarily against governments that harbored or gave sanctuary to terrorists. The Taliban regime was ousted from power. By April 2002—six months into Operation Enduring Freedom—Al Qaeda and Taliban forces had been either destroyed or scattered into small groups in the mountainous areas of Afghanistan and neighboring Pakistan. Osama bin Laden himself, however, escaped capture.

A meeting in Bonn, Germany, of various Afghan political and military groups produced general agreement on the installation of a new government in Kabul, headed by Hamid Karzai. The Karzai government has less than full control over Afghanistan; various tribal military chiefs, or "warlords," exercise independent power throughout the country.

Operation Iraqi Freedom At the end of the Gulf War in 1991, the Iraqi regime of Saddam Hussein agreed to destroy all of its chemical and biological weapons and to end its efforts to acquire nuclear weapons. United Nations inspectors were to verify Iraqi compliance with these conditions. But Saddam's regime refused to cooperate; in 1998 he ordered the inspectors out of the country. Over a twelve-year period Iraq violated at least a dozen U.N. resolutions. Following a U.S. military buildup in the region in late 2002, Saddam allowed U.N. inspectors to return, but continued to obstruct their work. On March 19, 2003, after giving Saddam a forty-eight hour warning to leave Iraq, the United States and Great Britain launched air strikes designed to eliminate Saddam and his top command.

At different times President Bush stated the purposes of "Operation Iraqi Freedom" as (1) the elimination of Iraq's weapons of mass destruction, (2) a "regime change" for Iraq to end the threat that Saddam posed for his neighbors and to free the Iraqi people from his oppressive rule, and (3) to ensure that Saddam would not harbor or assist terrorist organizations. But President Bush and Secretary of State Colin Powell failed to secure U.N. Security Council approval for military action. Among the permanent members of the Security Counsel, only the British, with the strong support of Prime Minister Tony Blair, were prepared to offer significant military support for the war against Saddam. Public opinion in America supported military action, but public opinion in Europe opposed it (see *Compared to What:* "World Opinion about America's War against Terrorism"). France and Germany led the diplomatic opposition; Turkey refused to let U.S. troops use its territory to attack Iraq; and the U.S. was obliged to rely primarily on Kuwait, Qatar, and the other smaller Gulf states for regional support.

The U.S. military wanted to wage war in the fashion of the successful Gulf War—a period of heavy air bombardment to "prepare the battlefield," followed by a massive ground attack using overwhelming military force. But Secretary of Defense Donald Rumsfeld wanted a "leaner" fighting force in Iraq. He deployed fewer than half of the air, ground, and naval forces that had been used in the Gulf War. And he began the air and ground attacks simultaneously.

American and British soldiers and Marines took just twenty-one days to sweep the 350 miles from the Kuwait border to downtown Baghdad. The British 3rd Armored Division, with Australian support, captured the port city of Basra; the U.S. 3rd Infantry Division moved up the west side of the Euphrates River; and the U.S. 1st Marine Division moved up the east side. Special Operations Forces, together with elements of the 101st Airborne Division, joined Kurdish forces in northern Iraq. Special Operations Forces also acted quickly to secure Iraq's oil fields and prevent their destruction. At first progress was hindered by the requirement that soldiers wear heavy chemical protection gear and carry decontamination equip-

World Opinion about America's War against Terrorism

Europeans were generally sympathetic with the United States following the terrorist attack of 9/11, and generally supported the U.S. military campaign against terrorists in Afghanistan. But opinion in Europe, as well as in the Moslem world, opposed U.S. military action in Iraq. Indeed, over time ratings of the United States have grown markedly less favorable among Europeans, and United States is now strongly disliked in the Moslem world. An important factor in world opinion about America is the perception that the U.S. acts internationally without taking account of the interests of other nations.

Ratings Of The United States

	2002		2004	
	Favorable	Unfavorable	Favorable	Unfavorable
Great Britain	75	16	58	34
France	63	34	37	62
Germany	61	35	38	59
Russia	61	33	47	44
Turkey	30	42	30	45
Pakistan	10	58	21	50
Jordan	25	57	5	67
Morocco*	27	46	27	46

Source: Pew Research Center for the People and the Press. http://www.people-press.org. Reprinted by permission of Pew Research Center for the People and the Press.

ment. But neither chemical nor biological weapons were used against U.S. forces. The advance on Baghdad was speeded up and the city was captured with precious few casualties.

But the subsequent occupation of Iraq by American troops and attempts to reconstruct a more democratic government in that nation turned out badly. U.S. troops suffered more casualties in the aftermath of the war than during the war itself. Guerilla activity against American and British and other coalition nations' forces, and against Iraqis who appeared to cooperate in the reconstruction of their country, inflicted heavy damage and loss of life. The United States officially turned over sovereignty to an interim Iraqi government before June 30, 2004. But no plans were announced for the withdrawal of American troops from Iraq.

Military Force Levels

Overall military force levels in the United States are threat driven—that is, determined by the size and nature of the perceived threats to national security. It is true that particular weapons systems or base openings or closings may be driven by political forces such as the influence of defense contractors in Congress or the power of a member of Congress from a district heavily affected by defense spending. And not everyone in the White House and Congress, or even in the Defense Department, agrees on the precise nature of the threats confronting the United States now or in the future. Yet defense policy planning and the "sizing" of U.S. military forces are based on an assessment of the threats confronting the nation.

 American Security Council

Organization providing summary information on national security threats.
www.ascusa.org

THINK AGAIN

Are U.S. military force levels today sufficient to deal with potential regional aggressors such as Iran, Iraq, and North Korea?

For nearly a half-century the Soviet threat drove defense policy, force planning, training, strategy and tactics, weapons research and procurement, troop deployments, and defense budgeting. But over the last decade the fundamental change in the world balance of power inspired a complete reexamination of defense policy and force sizing.

Reductions in Forces Post–Cold War military force reductions began in 1990 in the Bush Administration. The initial plan called for a reduction of total U.S. military personnel from 2.1 million to 1.6 million. This plan envisioned a continuing "forward presence" in NATO but reduced U.S. forces in Europe by more than half. Consistent with the view that regional aggressors would be the most likely threats to U.S. interests in the future, forces designed principally to meet these threats, for example, the Marine Corps, suffered fewer cuts.

Iraqi-Equivalent Regional Threats Following the Gulf War (1991–92) military force levels were directed toward "Iraqi-equivalent" regional threats. U.S. military force levels were based on the experience of defeating Iraq speedily and decisively in the Gulf War. But planning also envisioned the possibility that a second aggressor might decide to challenge the United States somewhere else in the world while its forces were involved in an Iraqi-equivalent war. For example, if U.S. forces were involved in the Persian Gulf against Iraq or Iran, North Korea might decide to take advantage of the situation and launch an invasion of South Korea. Therefore the United States planned to maintain sufficient additional U.S. forces to "fight and win two nearly simultaneous major regional conflicts." The ambiguous wording—"nearly simultaneous"—recognized that the United States might not be able to airlift and sealift sufficient forces to fight and win two regional wars at the same time. American forces would be obliged to hold one aggressor (principally with air power) while defeating the other; once one aggressor was defeated, the United States could then redeploy sufficient forces to defeat a second aggressor.

Global Security
News and information about weapons, forces, and military conflicts around the world.
www.globalsecurity.org

Current Force Levels The Army fields ten active combat divisions. (A U.S. Army division includes 10,000 to 15,000 troops.) The Navy deploys eleven active carrier battle groups. (A carrier battle group typically includes one aircraft carrier with 75 to 85 aircraft, plus defending cruisers, destroyers, frigates, attack submarines, and support ships.) The Marine Corps is scheduled to retain all three of its Marine expeditionary forces (each includes one Marine division, one Marine air wing, and supporting services).

Criticism Although most defense experts agree on the assessment of the threat—the need to prepare to fight and win two major regional conflicts simultaneously—many believe the projected force levels are inadequate for these tasks. Opponents contend that the reduced numbers of Army and Air Force combat units and the limited transport and support services available to the military are inadequate for two major regional conflicts. Casualties can be kept low only when overwhelming military force is employed quickly and decisively, as it was in Operation Desert Storm. Lives are lost when minimal forces are sent into combat, when they have inadequate air combat support, or when they are extended over too broad a front. Potential regional foes—for example, Iran and North Korea—deploy modern heavy armor and artillery forces. The United States benefited from a six-month buildup of its heavy forces in the Gulf region before Operation

Desert Storm began; such a period of preparation is unlikely in a future conflict. The deployment of U.S. troops for humanitarian and "peacekeeping" missions detracts from their readiness to respond to a major regional threat. More important, perhaps, the minimal force levels projected would severely tax the nation's ability to respond to two conflicts simultaneously in opposing parts of the globe. Critics charge current-defense policy and military force levels were determined more by a desire to cut the defense budget than by a careful consideration of the forces required for national security.

Historical Trends in Defense Spending In the early Cold War years, defense spending claimed a major share of U.S. resources (see Figure 18.2). In 1955 defense spending in the United States was 58 percent of all federal expenditures and equaled 10.5 percent of the gross domestic product. By 1965 defense spending had shrunk to 40.1 percent of federal spending and to 7.5 percent of the GDP. The Vietnam War caused defense spending to temporarily surge upward but following President Nixon's decision to gradually withdraw U.S. forces from that conflict, defense spending began a long decline. By 1978 defense spending was down to 23 percent of federal spending and 4.5 percent of the GDP. Reagan's defense buildup brought defense spending up to 6.5 percent of the GDP and 29 percent of the total federal budget by 1986.

The achievement of the Cold War objectives of the U.S. national defense policy led to a welcome result—a lessening of the threat to national security and a reduction in national defense spending. U.S. defense spending steadily declined in real dollars after 1986, U.S. military strength was cut by nearly half. During the Clinton Administration defense spending declined to less than 15 percent of federal spending and less than 3 percent of the nation's GDP. These were levels roughly comparable to those than prevailed before Pearl Harbor was attacked in 1941. The War on Terrorism raised defense spending in 2005 to 19 percent of total federal spending and about 3.5 percent of the GDP.

FIGURE 18.2 The Price of Peace: National Defense Outlays as a Percentage of GDP

Current spending on defense is a much smaller percentage of the U.S. gross national product than it was during the Cold War. The 2003 defense budget increased spending for the first time in over a decade.

Source: Budget of the United States Government, 2005.

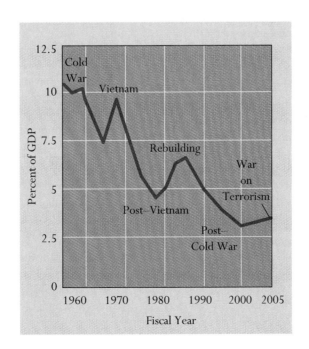

- The struggle for power is global. Leaders and peoples of the world protect and advance their goals and ideals through the exercise of power.

- There is no world government capable of legislating and enforcing rules of international politics. But various efforts to stabilize relations among nations have been attempted, including the balance-of-power system of alliances in the eighteenth and nineteenth centuries, the collective security arrangements of the League of Nations and the United Nations in the twentieth century, and the regional security approach of the North Atlantic Treaty Organization.

- The United Nations was largely ineffective during the Cold War, the confrontation between the Western democracies led by the United States and communist bloc nations led by the Soviet Union. During these years, the Western nations relied principally on the strength of the North Atlantic Treaty Organization (NATO) to deter war in Europe.

- For nearly fifty years, the Cold War largely directed U.S. foreign and defense policy. The United States sought to contain Soviet military expansionism and world communist revolutionary forces in all parts of the globe. U.S. involvement in the Korean and Vietnam wars grew out of this containment policy.

- During the Cold War years, U.S. and Soviet military forces never engaged in direct combat against each other, although many "proxy" conflicts took place throughout the world. The most serious threat of nuclear war occurred during the Cuban missile crisis in 1962.

- To maintain nuclear peace, the United States relied primarily on the policy of deterrence—dissuading the Soviets from launching a nuclear attack by maintaining survivable second-strike forces capable of inflicting unacceptable levels of destruction in a retaliating attack.

- In 1970 President Richard Nixon and National Security Adviser Henry Kissinger began negotiations with the Soviet Union with a view to limiting the nuclear arms race. These Strategic Arms Limitation Talks produced the SALT I agreement in 1972, and later, under President Jimmy Carter, the SALT II agreement in 1979. Both agreements set limits on future strategic weapons development but failed to reduce existing weapons stockpiles.

- President Ronald Reagan renamed the negotiations START, emphasizing the goal of reductions in weapons rather than limitations, and stressing equality and verification. The INF Treaty in 1987 was the first agreement that actually reduced nuclear arms, although it covered only intermediate-range weapons in Europe. Later the START I (1991) and START II (1993) treaties called for reducing nuclear arsenals by two-thirds from Cold War levels.

- The end of the Cold War followed the ouster of communist governments in Eastern Europe in 1989, the unification of Germany in 1990, the collapse of the Warsaw Pact communist military alliance in 1991, and the dissolution of the Soviet Union in 1991. Russia has inherited most of the nuclear weapons and military forces of the former Soviet Union as well as its seat in the UN Security Council.

- Current threats to peace and security are likely to be posed by regional aggressors. U.S. involvement in the Gulf War in 1990–91 is representative of the type of military action most likely to be undertaken in the future. Current defense policy calls for the United States to be prepared to fight two "Iraqi equivalent wars" "nearly simultaneously."

- The military phase of America's War on Terrorism began October 7, 2001, when U.S. aircraft began attacks on Al Qaeda bases in Afghanistan and U.S. special forces organized and led anti-Taliban Afghan fighters to oust the Taliban regime that had harbored the terrorists. These military actions largely destroyed the terrorist infrastructure in Afghanistan; yet scattered groups of terrorists remain in that country and neighboring Pakistan.

- President George W. Bush warned that the War on Terrorism would be a continuing one, but the variety of ways and means and places of potential terrorist attack make it impossible for the United States to guarantee an end to international terrorism.

- Following the Vietnam War, many military leaders argued that U.S. forces should be used only to protect vital American interests, only in support of clearly defined military objectives, only with sufficient strength to ensure decisive victory with the fewest possible casualties, only with the support of the American people and Congress, and only as a last resort.

- Recent presidents, however, have used military forces to carry out a variety of missions in addition to conventional war, including peacekeeping, antiterrorist, and humanitarian activities. They have argued that the risks were worth taking in light of the importance of the goals.

- U.S. military force levels and defense budgets are driven by perceived threats to national security. Thus, the end of the Cold War resulted in dramatic reductions in forces and budgets.

SUGGESTED READINGS

Clausewitz, Karl von. *On War*. Edited and translated by Michael Howard and Peter Paret. Princeton, N.J.: Princeton University Press, 1984. The classic theory of war and military operations, emphasizing their political character; first published in 1832.

Hastedt, Glenn P. *American Foreign Policy: Past, Present, Future*. 5th ed. Upper Saddle River, N.J.: Prentice Hall, 2003. A foreign policy text that deals with natural security issues within the broader context of foreign policy.

International Institute for Strategic Studies. *The Military Balance*. London: International Institute for Strategic Studies, published annually. Careful description of the military forces of more than 160 countries; this book is considered the most authoritative public information available.

Kegley, Charles W. *The New Global Terrorism*. Upper Saddle River, N.J.: Prentice Hall, 2003. Describing post-9/11 terrorism, its multiple roots, and leading ideas for winning the "war on global terrorism."

Magstadt, Thomas M. *An Empire If You Can Keep It: Power and Principle in American Foreign Policy*. Washington, D.C.: CQ Press, 2004. Comprehensive text on American foreign policy, describing its history, the Cold War, the Gulf War, September 11, and the War on Terrorism.

Snow, Donald M. *When America Fights: The Uses of U.S. Military Force*. Washington, D.C.: CQ Press, 2000. Questions U.S. military involvement in "peacekeeping" operations. Discusses the use of force in relation to U.S. national interests.

Summers, Harry G., Jr. *On Strategy II: A Critical Analysis of the Gulf War*. New York: Dell, 1992. Analysis of the Gulf War based on Clausewitz's classic principles of war. The strategic decisions leading to victory in the Gulf contrast markedly with the decisions in Vietnam that led to defeat, a topic covered in Summers's groundbreaking first book, *On Strategy: A Critical Analysis of the Vietnam War* (New York: Dell, 1984).

Wilson, George C. *This War Really Matters*. Washington, D.C.: CQ Press, 1999. A description of how defense budgets are constructed by the executive and approved by Congress and a questioning of whether the United States is adequately prepared for likely twenty-first-century wars.

MAKE IT REAL

THE IMPACT OF FOREIGN AID

The primary foreign policy goal of the United States remains, as it has been, to maintain our security and freedom. You are the Chief of Staff to the Secretary of the United States of America. In this simulation, you are presenting and arguing for the budget allocations for the next fiscal year for military aid, development aid, and human welfare.

Appendix

The Declaration of Independence

Drafted mainly by Thomas Jefferson, this document adopted by the Second Continental Congress, and signed by John Hancock and fifty-five others, outlined the rights of man and the rights to rebellion and self-government. It declared the independence of the colonies from Great Britain, justified rebellion, and listed the grievances against George the III and his government. What is memorable about this famous document is not only that it declared the birth of a new nation, but that it set forth, with eloquence, our basic philosophy of liberty and representative democracy.

IN CONGRESS, JULY 4, 1776 (The unanimous Declaration of the Thirteen United States of America)

Preamble

When, in the course of human events, it becomes necessary for one people to dissolve the political bands which have connected them with another, and to assume, among the powers of the earth, the separate and equal station to which the laws of nature and of nature's God entitle them, a decent respect to the opinions of mankind requires that they should declare the causes which impel them to the separation.

New Principles of Government

We hold these truths to be self-evident; that all men are created equal, that they are endowed by their Creator with certain unalienable rights, that among these are life, liberty, and the pursuit of happiness.

That, to secure these rights, governments are instituted among men, deriving their just powers from the consent of the governed.

That whenever any form of government becomes destructive of these ends, it is the right of the people to alter or to abolish it, and to institute new government, laying its foundation on such principles, and organizing its powers in such form, as to them shall seem most likely to effect their safety and happiness. Prudence, indeed will dictate that governments long established should not be changed for light and transient causes; and accordingly all experience hath shown that mankind are more disposed to suffer while evils are sufferable, than to right themselves by abolishing the forms to which they are accustomed. But when a long train of abuses and usurpations, pursuing invariably the same object, evinces a design to reduce them under absolute despotism, it is their right, it is their duty, to throw off such government, and to provide new guards for their future security.

Reasons for Separation

Such has been the patient sufferance of these colonies; and such is now the necessity which constrains them to alter their former systems of government. The history of the present king of Great Britain is a history of repeated injuries and usurpations, all having in direct object the establishment of an absolute tyranny over these states. To prove this, let facts be submitted to a candid world.

He has refused his assent to laws, the most wholesome and necessary for the public good.

He has forbidden his governors to pass laws of immediate and pressing importance unless suspended in their operation till his assent should be obtained; and when so suspended, he has utterly neglected to attend to them.

He has refused to pass other laws for the accommodation of large districts of people, unless those people would relinquish the right of representation in the legislature, a right inestimable to them, and formidable to tyrants only.

He has called together legislative bodies at places unusual, uncomfortable, and distant for the depository of their public records, for the sole purpose of fatiguing them into compliance with his measures.

He has dissolved representative houses repeatedly, for opposing, with manly firmness, his invasions on the rights of people.

He has refused, for a long time after such dissolutions, to cause others to be elected; whereby the legislative powers incapable of annihilation, have returned to the people at large for their exercise; the state remaining, in the mean-time, exposed to all the dangers of invasion from without and convulsions within.

He has endeavored to prevent the population of these states; for that purpose obstructing the laws of naturalization of foreigners, refusing to pass others to encourage their migration hither, and raising the conditions of new appropriations of lands.

He has obstructed the administration of justice, by refusing his assent to laws for establishing judiciary powers.

He has made judges dependent on his will alone for the tenure of their offices, and the amount and payment of their salaries.

He has erected a multitude of new offices, and sent hither swarms of officers to harass our people and eat out their substance.

He has kept among us, in times of peace, standing armies, without the consent of our legislature.

He has affected to render the military independent of, and superior to, the civil power.

He has combined with others to subject us to jurisdiction foreign to our constitution and unacknowledged by our laws, giving his assent to their acts of pretended legislation:

For quartering large bodies of armed troops among us;

For protecting them, by a mock trial, from punishment for any murders which they should commit on the inhabitants of these states;

For cutting off our trade with all parts of the world;

For imposing taxes on us without our consent;

For depriving us, in many cases, of the benefits of trial by jury;

For transporting us beyond seas, to be tried for pretended offenses;

For abolishing the free system of English laws in a neighboring province, establishing therein an arbitrary government, and enlarging its boundaries, so as to render it at once an example and fit instrument for introducing the same absolute rule into these colonies;

For taking away our charters, abolishing our most valuable laws, and altering, fundamentally, the forms of our governments;

For suspending our own legislatures, and declaring themselves invented with power to legislate for us in all cases whatsoever.

He has abdicated government here, by declaring us out of his protection and waging war against us.

He has plundered our seas, ravaged our coasts, burned our towns, and destroyed the lives of our people.

He is at this time transporting large armies of foreign mercenaries to complete the works of death, desolation, and tyranny already begun with circumstances of cruelty and perfidy scarcely paralleled in the most barbarous ages and totally unworthy of the head of a civilized nation.

He has constrained our fellow-citizens, taken captive on the high seas, to bear arms against their country, to become the executioners of their friends and brethren, or to fall themselves by their hands.

He has excited domestic insurrections among us, and has endeavored to bring on the inhabitants of our frontiers the merciless Indian savages, whose known rule of warfare is an undistinguished destruction of all ages, sexes, and conditions.

In every stage of these oppressions we have petitioned for redress in the most humble terms; our repeated petitions have been answered only by repeated injury. A prince whose character is thus marked by every act which may define a tyrant is unfit to be the ruler of a free people.

Nor have we been wanting in attention to our British brethren. We have warned them, from time to time, of attempts by their legislature to extend an unwarrantable jurisdiction over us. We have reminded them of the circumstances of our emigration and settlement here. We have appealed to their native justice and magnanimity; and we have conjured them, by the ties of our common kindred, to disavow these usurpations, which would inevitably interrupt our connections and correspondence. They, too, have been deaf to the voice of justice and of consanguinity. We must, therefore, acquiesce in the necessity which denounces our separation, and hold them, as we hold the rest of mankind, enemies in war, in peace, friends.

We, therefore, the representatives of the United States of America, in General Congress assembled, appealing to the Supreme Judge of the world for the rectitude of our intentions, do, in the name and by authority of the good people of these colonies, solemnly publish and declare, that these united colonies are, and of right ought to be, free and independent states; that they are absolved from all allegiance to the British crown, and that all political connection between them and the state of Great Britain is, and ought to be, totally dissolved; and that, as free and independent states, they have full power to levy war, conclude peace, contract alliances, establish commerce, and do all other acts and things which independent states may of a right do. And, for the support of this declaration, with a firm reliance on the protection of Divine Providence, we mutually pledge to each other our lives, our fortunes, and our sacred honor.

The Federalist, No. 10, James Madison

To the People of the State of New York: Among the numerous advantages promised by a well-constructed union, none deserves to be more accurately developed than its tendency to break and control the violence of faction. The friend of popular governments, never finds himself so much alarmed for their character and fate, as when he contemplates their propensity to this dangerous vice. He will not fail, therefore, to set a due value on any plan which, without violating the principles to which he is attached, provides a proper cure for it. The instability, injustice, and confusion introduced into the public councils, have, in truth, been the mortal diseases under which popular governments have everywhere perished; as they continue to be the favourite and fruitful topics from which the adversaries to liberty derive their most specious declamations. The valuable improvements made by the American constitutions on the popular models, both ancient and modern, cannot certainly be too much admired; but it would be an unwarrantable partiality, to contend that they have as effectually obviated the danger on this side, as was wished and expected. Complaints are everywhere heard from our most considerate and virtuous citizens, equally the friends of public and private faith, and of public and personal liberty, that our governments are too unstable; that the public good is disregarded in the conflicts of rival parties; and that measures are too often decided, not according to the rules of justice, and the rights of the minor party, but by the superior force of an interested and over-bearing majority. However anxiously we may wish that these complaints had no foundation, the evidence of known facts will not permit us to deny that they are in some degree true. It will be found, indeed, on a candid review of our situation, that some of the distresses under which we labour have been erroneously charged on the operation of our governments; but it will be found, at the same time, that other causes will not alone account for many of our heaviest misfortunes; and, particularly, for that prevailing and increasing distrust of public engagements, and alarm for private rights, which are echoed from one end of the continent to the other. These must be chiefly, if not wholly, effects of the unsteadiness and injustice, with which a factious spirit has tainted our public administrations.

By a faction, I understand a number of citizens, whether amounting to a majority or minority of the whole, who are united and actuated by some common impulse of passion, or of interest, adverse to the rights of other citizens, or to the permanent and aggregate interests of the community.

There are two methods of curing the mischiefs of faction: the one, by removing its causes; the other, by controlling its effects.

There are again two methods of removing the causes of faction: the one, by destroying the liberty which is essential to its existence; the other, by giving to every citizen the same opinions, the same passions, and the same interests.

It could never be more truly said, than of the first remedy, that it was worse than the disease. Liberty is to faction what air is to fire, an aliment without which it instantly expires. But it could not be a less folly to abolish liberty, which is essential to political life, because it nourishes faction, than it would be to wish the annihilation of air, which is essential to animal life, because it imparts to fire its destructive agency.

The second expedient is as impracticable, as the first would be unwise. As long as the reason of man continues fallible, and he is at liberty to exercise it, different opinions will be formed. As long as the connection subsists between his reason and his self-love, his opinions and his passions will have a reciprocal influence on each other; and the former will be objects to which the latter will attach themselves. The diversity in the faculties of men, from which the rights of property originate, is not less an insuperable obstacle to an uniformity of interests. The protection of these faculties is the first object of government. From the protection of different and unequal faculties of acquiring property, the possession of different degrees and kinds of property immediately results; and from the influence of these on the sentiments and views of the respective proprietors, ensues a division of the society into different interests and parties.

The latent causes of faction are thus sown in the nature of man; and we see them everywhere brought into different degrees of activity, according to the different circumstances of civil society. A zeal for different opinions concerning religion, concerning government, and many other points, as well of speculation as of practice; an attachment to different leaders ambitiously contending for preeminence and power; or to persons of other descriptions whose fortunes have been interesting to the human passions, have, in turn, divided mankind into parties, inflamed them with mutual animosity, and rendered them much more disposed to vex and oppress each other, than to cooperate for their common good. So strong is this propensity of mankind, to fall into mutual animosities, that where no substantial occasion presents itself, the most frivolous and fanciful distinctions have been sufficient to kindle their unfriendly passions and excite their most violent conflicts. But the most common and durable source of factions, has been the various and unequal distribution of property. Those who hold, and those who are without property, have ever formed distinct interests in society. Those who are creditors, and those who are debtors, fall under a like discrimination. A landed interest, a manufacturing interest, a mercantile interest, a moneyed interest, with many lesser interests, grow up of necessity in civilized nations, and divide them into different classes, actuated by different sentiments and views. The regulation of these various and interfering interests forms the principal task of modern legislation, and involves the spirit of the party and faction in the necessary and ordinary operations of the government.

No man is allowed to be a judge in his own cause; because his interest will certainly bias his judgment, and, not improbably, corrupt his integrity. With equal, nay, with greater reason, a body of men are unfit to be both judges and parties at the same time; yet what are many of the most important acts of legislation, but so many judicial determinations, not indeed concerning the right of single persons, but concerning the rights of large bodies of citizens? And what are the different classes of legislators, but advocates and parties to the causes which they determine? Is a law proposed concerning private debts? It is a question to which the creditors are parties on one side, and the debtors on the other. Justice ought to hold the balance between them. Yet the parties are, and must be, themselves the judges; and the most numerous party, or, in other words, the most powerful faction, must be expected to prevail. Shall domestic manufacturers be encouraged, and in what degree, by restrictions on foreign manufacturers are questions which would be differently decided by the landed and the manufacturing classes; and probably by neither with a sole regard to justice and the public good. The apportionment of taxes, on the various descriptions of property, is an act which seems to require the most exact impartiality; yet there is, perhaps, no legislative act, in which greater opportunity and temptation are given to a predominant party to trample on the rules of justice. Every shilling, with which they overburden the inferior number, is a shilling saved to their own pockets.

It is in vain to say, that enlightened statesmen will be able to adjust these clashing interests, and render them all subservient to the public good. Enlightened statesmen will not always be at the helm; nor, in many cases, can such an adjustment be made at all, without taking into view indirect and remote considerations, which will rarely prevail over the immediate interest which one party may find in disregarding the rights of another, or the good of the whole.

The inference to which we are brought is, that the *causes* of faction cannot be removed; and that relief is only to be sought in the means of controlling its *effects*.

If a faction consists of less than a majority, relief is supplied by the republican principle, which enables the majority to defeat its sinister views, by regular vote. It may clog the administration, it may convulse the society; but it will be unable to execute and mask its violence under the forms of the Constitution. When a majority is included in a faction, the form of popular government, on the other hand, enables it to sacrifice to its ruling passion or interest, both the public good and the rights of other citizens. To secure the public good, and private rights, against the danger of such a faction, and at the same time to preserve the spirit and the form of popular government, is then the great object to which our inquiries are directed. Let me add, that it is the great desideratum, by which alone this form of government can be rescued from the opprobrium under which it has so long laboured, and be recommended to the esteem and adoption of mankind.

By what means is this object attainable? Evidently by one of two only. Either the existence of the same passion or interest in a majority, at the same time, must be prevented; or the majority, having such coexistent passion or interest, must be rendered, by their number and local situation, unable to concert and carry into effect schemes of oppression. If the impulse and the opportunity be suffered to coincide, we well know that neither moral nor religious motives can be relied on as an adequate control. They are not found to be such on the injustice and violence of individuals, and lose their efficacy in proportion to the number combined together; that is, in proportion as their efficacy becomes needful.

From this view of the subject, it may be concluded, that a pure democracy, by which I mean a society consisting of a small number of citizens, who assemble and administer the government in person, can admit of no cure for the mischiefs of faction. A common passion or interest will, in almost every case, be felt by a majority of the whole; a communication and concert, results from the form of government itself; and there is nothing to check the inducements to sacrifice the weaker party, or an obnoxious individual. Hence, it is, that such democracies have ever been spectacles of turbulence and contention; have ever been found incompatible with personal security, or the rights of property; and have in general been as short in their lives, as they have been violent in their deaths. Theoretic politicians, who have patronized this species of government, have erroneously supposed, that by reducing mankind to a perfect equality in their political rights, they would, at the same time, be perfectly equalized and assimilated in their possessions, their opinions, and their passions.

A republic, by which I mean a government in which the scheme of representation takes place, opens a different prospect, and promises the cure for which we are seeking. Let us examine the points in which it varies from pure democracy, and we shall comprehend both the nature of the cure and the efficacy which it must derive from the union.

The two great points of difference, between a democracy and a republic, are, first, the delegation of the government, in the latter, to a small number of citizens, elected by the rest; secondly, the greater number of citizens, and greater sphere of country, over which the latter may be extended.

The effect of the first difference is, on the one hand, to refine and enlarge the public views, by passing them through the medium of a chosen body of citizens, whose wisdom may best discern the true interest of their country, and whose patriotism and love of justice, will be least likely to sacrifice it to temporary or partial considerations. Under such a regulation, it may well happen, that the public voice, pronounced by the representatives of the people, will be more consonant to the public good, than if pronounced by the people themselves, convened for the purpose. On the other hand the effect may be inverted. Men of factious tempers, of local prejudices, or of sinister designs, may by intrigue, by corruption, or by other means, first obtain the suffrages, and then betray the interest of the people. The question resulting is, whether small or extensive republics are most favourable to the election of proper guardians of the public weal; and it is clearly decided in favour of the latter by two obvious considerations.

In the first place, it is to be remarked that, however small the republic may be, the representatives must be raised to a certain number, in order to guard against the cabals of a few; and that however large it may be, they must be limited to a certain number, in order to guard against the confusion of a multitude. Hence, the number of representatives in the two cases not being in proportion to that of the constituents, and being proportionally greatest in the small republic, it follows, that if the proportion of fit characters be not less in the large than in the small republic, the former will present a greater option, and consequently a greater probability of a fit choice.

In the next place, as each representative will be chosen by a greater number of citizens in the large than in the small republic, it will be more difficult for unworthy candidates to practice with success the vicious arts, by which elections are too often carried; and the suffrages of the people being more free, will be more likely to centre in men who possess the most attractive merit, and the most diffusive and established characters.

It must be confessed, that in this, as in most other cases, there is a mean, on both sides of which inconveniences will be found to lie. By enlarging too much the number of electors, you render the representatives too little acquainted with all their local circumstances and lesser interests; as by reducing it too much, you render him unduly attached to these, and too little fit to comprehend and pursue great and national objects. The federal constitution forms a happy combination in this respect; the great and aggregate interests being referred to the national, the local and particular to the state legislatures.

The other point of difference is, the greater number of citizens, and extent of territory, which may be brought within the compass of republican, than of democratic government; and it is this circumstance principally which renders factious combinations less to be dreaded in the former, than in the latter. The smaller the society, the fewer probably will be the distinct parties and interests composing it; the fewer the distinct parties and interests, the more frequently will a majority be found of the same party; and the smaller the number of individuals composing a majority, and the smaller the compass within which they are placed, the more easily will they concert and execute their plans of oppression. Extend the sphere, and you take in a greater variety of parties and interests; you make it less probable that a majority of the whole will have a common motive to invade the rights of other citizens; or if such a common motive exists, it will be more difficult for all who feel it to discover their own strength, and to act in unison with each other. Besides other impediments, it may be remarked, that where there is a consciousness of unjust or dishonourable purposes, communication is always checked by distrust, in proportion to the number whose concurrence is necessary.

Hence, it clearly appears, that the same advantage, which a republic has over a democracy, in controlling the effects of faction, is enjoyed by a large over a small republic—is enjoyed by the union over the states composing it. Does this advantage consist in the substitution of representatives, whose enlightened views and virtuous sentiments render them superior to local prejudices, and to schemes of injustice? It will not be denied that the representation of the union will be most likely to possess these requisite endowments. Does it consist in the greater security afforded by a greater variety of parties, against the event of any one party being able to outnumber and oppress the rest? In an equal degree does the increased variety of parties, comprised within the union,

increase the security? Does it, in fine, consist in the greater obstacles opposed to the concert and accomplishment of the secret wishes of an unjust and interested majority? Here, again, the extent of the union gives it the most palpable advantage.

The influence of factious leaders may kindle a flame within their particular states, but will be unable to spread a general conflagration through the other states; a religious sect may degenerate into a political faction in a part of the confederacy; but the variety of sects dispersed over the entire face of it, must secure the national councils against any danger from that source; a rage for paper money, for an abolition of debts, for an equal division of property, or for any other improper or wicked project, will be less apt to pervade the whole body of the union than a particular member of it; in the same proportion as such a malady is more likely to taint a particular county or district, than an entire state.

In the extent and proper structure of the union, therefore, we behold a republican remedy for the diseases most incident to republican government. And according to the degree of pleasure and pride we feel in being republicans, ought to be our zeal in cherishing the spirit, and supporting the character of federalists.

The Federalist, No. 51, James Madison

To what expedient, then, shall we finally resort, for maintaining in practice the necessary partition of power among the several departments as laid down in the Constitution? The only answer that can be given is that as all these exterior provisions are found to be inadequate the defect must be supplied, by so contriving the interior structure of the government as that its several constituent parts may, by their mutual relations, be the means of keeping each other in their proper places. Without presuming to undertake a full development of this important idea I will hazard a few general observations which may perhaps place it

in a clearer light, and enable us to form a more correct judgment of the principles and structure of the government planned by the convention.

In order to lay a due foundation for that separate and distinct exercise of the different powers of government, which to a certain extent is admitted on all hands to be essential to the preservation of liberty, it is evident that each department should have a will of its own; and consequently should be so constituted that the members of each should have as little agency as possible in the appointment of the members of the others. Were this principle rigorously adhered to, it would require that all the appointments for the supreme executive, legislative, and judiciary magistracies should be drawn from the same fountain of authority, the people, through channels having no communication whatever with one another. Perhaps such a plan of constructing the several departments would be less difficult in practice than it may in contemplation appear. Some difficulties, however, and some additional expense would attend the execution of it. Some deviations, therefore, from the principle must be admitted. In the constitution of the judiciary department in particular, it might be inexpedient to insist rigorously on the principle: first, because peculiar qualifications being essential in the members, the primary consideration ought to be to select that mode of choice which best secures these qualifications; second, because the permanent tenure by which the appointments are held in that department must soon destroy all sense of dependence on the authority conferring them.

It is equally evident that the members of each department should be as little dependent as possible on those of the others for the emoluments annexed to their offices. Were the executive magistrate, or the judges, not independent of the legislature in this particular, their independence in every other would be merely nominal.

But the great security against a gradual concentration of the several powers in the same department consists in giving to those who administer each department the necessary constitutional means and personal motives to resist encroachments of the others. The provision for defense must in this, as in all other cases, be made commensurate to the danger of attack. Ambition must be made to counteract ambition. The interest of the man must be connected with the constitutional rights of the place. It may be a reflection on human nature that such devices should be necessary to control the abuses of government. But what is government itself but the greatest of all reflections on human nature? If men were angels, no government would be necessary. If angels were to governmen, neither external nor internal controls on government would be necessary. In framing a government which is to be administered by men over men, the great difficulty lies in this: you must first enable the government to control the governed; and in the next place oblige it to control itself. A dependence on the people is, no doubt, the primary control on the government; but experience has taught mankind the necessity of auxiliary precautions.

This policy of supplying, by opposite and rival interests, the defect of better motives, might be traced through the whole system of human affairs, private as well as public. We see it particularly displayed in all the subordinate distributions of power, where the constant aim is to divide and arrange the several offices in such a manner as that each may be a check on the other—that the private interest of every individual may be a sentinel over the public rights. These inventions of prudence cannot be less requisite in the distribution of the supreme powers of the State.

But it is not possible to give to each department an equal power of self-defense. In republican government, the legislative authority necessarily predominates. The remedy for this inconveniency is to divide the legislature into different branches; and to render them, by modes of election and different principles of action, as little connected with each other as the nature of their common functions and their common dependence on the society will admit. It may even be necessary to guard against dangerous encroachments by still fur-

ther precautions. As the weight of the legislative authority requires that it should be thus divided, the weakness of the executive may require, on the other hand, that it should be fortified. An absolute negative on the legislature appears, at first view, to be the natural defense with which the executive magistrate should be armed. But perhaps it would be neither altogether safe nor alone sufficient. On ordinary occasions it might not be exerted with the requisite firmness, and on extraordinary occasions it might be perfidiously abused. May not this defect of an absolute negative be supplied by some qualified connection between this weaker department and the weaker branch of the stronger department, by which the latter may be led to support the constitutional rights of the former, without being too much detached from the rights of its own department?

If the principles on which these observations are founded be just, as I persuade myself they are, and they be applied as a criterion to the several State constitutions, and to the federal Constitution, it will be found that if the latter does not perfectly correspond with them, the former are infinitely less able to bear such a test.

There are, moreover, two considerations particularly applicable to the federal system of America, which place that system in a very interesting point of view.

First. In a single republic, all the power surrendered by the people is submitted to the administration of a single government; and the usurpations are guarded against by a division of the government into distinct and separate departments. In the compound republic of America, the power surrendered by the people is first divided between two distinct governments, and then the portion allotted to each subdivided among distinct and separate departments. Hence a double security arises to the rights of the people. The different governments will control each other, at the same time that each will be controlled by itself.

Second. It is of great importance in a republic not only to guard the society

against the oppression of its rulers, but to guard one part of the society against the injustice of the other part. Different interests necessarily exist in different classes of citizens. If a majority be united by a common interest, the rights of the minority will be insecure. There are but two methods of providing against this evil: the one by creating a will in the community independent of the majority—that is, of the society itself; the other, by comprehending in the society so many separate descriptions of citizens as will render an unjust combination of a majority of the whole very improbable, if not impracticable. The first method prevails in all governments possessing an hereditary or $$$self-appointed authority. This, at best, is but a precarious security; because a power independent of the society may as well espouse the unjust views of the major as the rightful interests of the minor party, and may possibly be turned against both parties. The second method will be exemplified in the federal republic of the United States. Whilst all authority in it will be derived from and dependent on the society, the society itself will be broken into so many parts, interests and classes of citizens, that the rights of individuals, or of the minority, will be in little danger from interested combinations of the majority. In a free government the security for civil rights must be the same as that for religious rights. It consists in the one case in the multiplicity of interests, and in the other in the multiplicity of sects. The degree of security in both cases will depend on the number of interests and sects; and this may be presumed to depend on the extent of country and number of people comprehended under the same government. This view of the subject must particularly recommend a proper federal system to all the sincere and considerate friends of republican government, since it shows that in exact proportion as the territory of the Union may be formed into more circumscribed Confederacies, or States, oppressive combinations of a majority will be facilitated; the best security, under the republican forms, for the rights of every class of citizen, will be diminished; and consequently the stability and independence of some member of the government, the only other security, must be proportionally increased. Justice is the end of government. It is the end of civil society. It ever has been and ever will be pursued until it be obtained, or until liberty be lost in the pursuit. In a society under the forms of which the stronger faction can readily unite and oppress the weaker, anarchy may as truly be said to reign as in a state of nature, where the weaker individual is not secured against the violence of the stronger; and as, in the latter state, even the stronger individuals are prompted, by the uncertainty of their condition, to submit to a government which may protect the weak as well as themselves; so, in the former state, will the more powerful factions or parties be gradually induced, by a like motive, to wish for a government which will protect all parties, the weaker as well as the more powerful. It can be little doubted that if the State of Rhode Island was separated from the Confederacy and left to itself, the insecurity of rights under the popular form of government within such narrow limits would be displayed by such reiterated oppressions of factious majorities that some power altogether independent of the people would soon be called for by the voice of the very factions whose misrule had proved the necessity of it. In the extended republic of the United States, and among the great variety of interests, parties, and sects which it embraces, a coalition of a majority of the whole society could seldom take place on any other principles than those of justice and the general good; whilst there being thus less danger to a minor from the will of a major party, there must be less pretext, also, to provide for the security of the former, by introducing into the government a will not dependent on the latter, or, in other words, a will independent of the society itself. It is no less certain that it is important, notwithstanding the contrary opinions which have been entertained that the larger the society, provided it lie within a practicable sphere, the more duly capable it will be of self-government. And happily for the *republican cause*, the practicable sphere may be carried to a very great extent by a judicious modification and mixture of the *federal principle*.

Presidents and Vice Presidents

1. George Washington (1789)
   John Adams (1789)

2. John Adams (1797)
   Thomas Jefferson (1797)

3. Thomas Jefferson (1801)
   Aaron Burr (1801)
   George Clinton (1805)

4. James Madison (1809)
   George Clinton (1809)
   Elbridge Gerry (1813)

5. James Monroe (1817)
   Daniel D. Tompkins (1817)

6. John Quincy Adams (1825)
   John C. Calhoun (1825)

7. Andrew Jackson (1829)
   John C. Calhoun (1829)
   Martin Van Buren (1833)

8. Martin Van Buren (1837)
   Richard M. Johnson (1837)

9. William H. Harrison (1841)
   John Tyler (1841)

10. John Tyler (1841)

11. James K. Polk (1845)
    George M. Dallas (1845)

12. Zachary Taylor (1849)
    Millard Fillmore (1849)

13. Millard Fillmore (1850)

14. Franklin Pierce (1853)
    William R. King (1853)

15. James Buchanan (1857)
    John C. Breckinridge (1857)

16. Abraham Lincoln (1861)
    Hannibal Hamlin (1861)
    Andrew Johnson (1865)

17. Andrew Johnson (1865)

18. Ulysses S. Grant (1869)
    Schuyler Colfax (1869)
    Henry Wilson (1873)

19. Rutherford B. Hayes (1877)
    William A. Wheeler (1877)

20. James A. Garfield (1881)
    Chester A. Arthur (1881)

21. Chester A. Arthur (1881)

22. Grover Cleveland (1885)
    T.A. Hendricks (1885)

23. Benjamin Harrison (1889)
    Levi P. Morton (1889)

24. Grover Cleveland (1893)
    Adlai E. Stevenson (1893)

25. William McKinley (1897)
    Garret A. Hobart (1897)
    Theodore Roosevelt (1901)

26. Theodore Roosevelt (1901)
    Charles Fairbanks (1905)

27. William H. Taft (1909)
    James S. Sherman (1909)

28. Woodrow Wilson (1913)
    Thomas R. Marshall (1913)

29. Warren G. Harding (1921)
    Calvin Coolidge (1921)

30. Calvin Coolidge (1923)
    Charles G. Dawes (1925)

31. Herbert C. Hoover (1929)
    Charles Curtis (1929)

32. Franklin D. Roosevelt (1933)
    John Nance Garner (1933)
    Henry A. Wallace (1941)
    Harry S. Truman (1945)

33. Harry S. Truman (1945)
    Alben W. Barkley (1949)

34. Dwight D. Eisenhower (1953)
    Richard M. Nixon (1953)

35. John F. Kennedy (1961)
    Lyndon B. Johnson (1961)

36. Lyndon B. Johnson (1963)
    Hubert H. Humphrey (1965)

37. Richard M. Nixon (1969)
    Spiro T. Agnew (1969)
    Gerald R. Ford (1973)

38. Gerald R. Ford (1974)
    Nelson A. Rockefeller (1974)

39. James E. Carter, Jr. (1977)
    Walter F. Mondale (1977)

40. Ronald W. Reagan (1981)
    George H.W. Bush (1981)

41. George H.W. Bush (1989)
    James D. Quayle III (1989)

42. William J.B. Clinton (1993)
    Albert Gore (1993)

43. George W. Bush (2001)
    Richard Cheney (2001)

Supreme Court Justices

Current Supreme Court Justices

1. William H. Rehnquist (Chief Justice)
2. Antonin Scalia (Associate Justice)
3. John Paul Stevens (Associate Justice)
4. Sandra Day O'Connor (Associate Justice)
5. Anthony M. Kennedy (Associate Justice)
6. Ruth Bader Ginsburg (Associate Justice)
7. David H. Souter (Associate Justice)
8. Clarence Thomas (Associate Justice)
9. Stephen G. Breyer (Associate Justice)

Former Supreme Court Chief Justices

1. John Jay (1779–1795)
2. John Rutledge (1795)
3. Oliver Ellsworth (1996–1800)
4. John Marshall (1801–1835)
5. Roger Brooke Tancy (1836–1864)
6. Salmon Portland Chase (1864–1873)
7. Morrison R. Waite (1874–1888)
8. Melville Weston Fuller (1888–1910)
9. Edward Douglas White (1910–1921)
10. William Howard Taft (1921–1930)
11. Charles Evans Hughes (1930–1941)
12. Harlan Fiske Stone (1941–1946)
13. Fred M. Vison (1946–1953)
14. Earl Warren (1953–1969)
15. Warren E. Burger (1969–1986)

Former Supreme Court Associate Judges

1. James Wilson (1789–1798)
2. William Cushing (1790–1810)
3. John Blair, Jr. (1790–1796)
4. James Iredell (1790–1799)
5. Thomas Johnson (1792–1793)
6. William Paterson (1793–1806)
7. Samuel Chase (1796–1811)
8. Bushrod Washington (1799–1829)
9. Alfred Moore (1800–1804)
10. William Johnson (1804–1834)
11. H. Brockholst Livingston (1807–1328)
12. Thomas Todd (1807–1826)
13. Gabriel Duvall (1811–1835)
14. Joseph Story (1812–1845)
15. Smith Thompson (1823–1843)
16. Robert Trimble (1826–1828)
17. John McLean (1830–1861)
18. Henry Baldwin (1830–1844)
19. James M. Wayne (1835–1867)
20. Philip P. Barbour (1836–1841)
21. John Catron (1837–1865)
22. John McKinley (1838–1852)
23. Peter V. Daniel (1842–1860)
24. Samuel Nelson (1845–1872)
25. Levi Woodbury (1845–1851)
26. Robert C. Grier (1846–1870)
27. Benjamin R. Curtis (1851–1857)
28. John A. Campbell (1853–1861)
29. Nathan Clifford (1858–1881)
30. Noah H. Swayne (1862–1881)
31. Samuel F. Miller (1862–1890)
32. David Davis (1862–1877)
33. Stephen J. Field (1863–1897)
34. William Strong (1870–1880)
35. Joseph P. Bradley (1870–1892)
36. Ward Hunt (1873–1882)
37. John Marshall Harlan (1877–1911)
38. William B. Woods (1881–1887)
39. Stanley Matthews (1881–1889)
40. Horace Gray (1882–1902)
41. Samuel Blatchford (1882–1893)
42. Lucius Q. C. Lamar (1888–1893)
43. David J. Brewer (1890–1910)
44. Henry B. Brown (1891–1906)
45. George Shiras, Jr. (1892–1903)
46. Howell E. Jackson (1893–1895)
47. Rufus W. Peckham (1896–1909)
48. Joseph McKenna (1898–1925)
49. Oliver Wendell Holmes, Jr. (1902–1932)
50. William R. Day (1903–1922)
51. William H. Moody (1906–1910)
52. Horace H. Lurton (1910–1914)
53. Willis Van Devanter (1911–1937)
54. Joseph Rucker Lamar (1911–1916)
55. Mahlon Pitney (1912–1922)
56. James Clark McReynolds (1914–1941)
57. Louis D. Brandeis (1916–1939)
58. John H. Clark (1916–1922)
59. George Sutherland (1922–1938)
60. Pierce Butler (1923–1939)
61. Edward T. Sanford (1923–1930)
62. Owen J. Roberts (1930–1945)

63. Benjamin Nathan Cordozo (1932–1938)

64. Hugo Black (1937–1971)

65. Stanley F. Reed (1938–1957)

66. Felix Frankfurter (1939–1962)

67. William O. Douglas (1939–1975)

68. Frank W. Murphy (1940–1949)

69. James F. Byrnes (1941–1942)

70. Robert H. Jackson (1941–1954)

71. Wiley B. Rutledge (1943–1949)

72. Harold H. Burton (1945–1958)

73. Tom C. Clark (1949–1967)

74. Sherman Minton (1949–1956)

75. William J. Brennan, Jr. (1956–1990)

76. John Marshall Harlan II (1955–1971)

77. Charles E. Whittaker (1957–1962)

78. Potter Stewart (1958–1981)

79. Byron R. White (1962–1993)

80. Arthur J. Goldberg (1962–1965)

81. Abe Fortas (1965–1969)

82. Thurgood Marshall (1967–1991)

83. Harry A. Blackmun (1970–1994)

84. Lewis F. Powell, Jr. (1972–1987)

Presidential Elections and Voting

Year	Number of States	Candidates	Party	Popular Vote*	Electoral Vote[†]	Percentage of Popular Vote
1789	11	**George Washington**	No party designations		69	
		John Adams			34	
		Other Candidates			35	
1792	15	**George Washington**	No party designations		132	
		John Adams			77	
		George Clinton			50	
		Other Candidates			5	
1796	16	**John Adams**	Federalist		71	
		Thomas Jefferson	Democratic Republican		68	
		Thomas Pinckney	Federalist		59	
		Aaron Burr	Democratic Republican		30	
		Other Candidates			48	
1800	16	**Thomas Jefferson**	Democratic Republican		73	
		Aaron Burr	Democratic Republican		73	
		John Adams	Federalist		65	
		Charles C. Pinckney	Federalist		64	
		John Jay	Federalist		1	
1804	17	**Thomas Jefferson**	Democratic Republican		162	
		Charles C. Pinckney	Federalist		14	
1808	17	**James Madison**	Democratic Republican		122	
		Charles C. Pinckney	Federalist		47	
		George Clinton	Democratic Republican		6	
1812	18	**James Madison**	Democratic Republican		128	
		DeWitt Clinton	Federalist		89	
1816	19	**James Monroe**	Democratic Republican		183	
		Rufus King	Federalist		34	
1820	24	**James Monroe**	Democratic Republican		231	
		John Quincy Adams	Independent Republican		1	
1824	24	**John Quincy Adams**		108,740	84	30.5
		Andrew Jackson		153,544	99	43.1
		William H. Crawford		46,618	41	13.1
		Henry Clay		47,136	37	13.2
1828	24	**Andrew Jackson**	Democrat	647,286	178	56.0
		John Quincy Adams	National Republican	508,064	83	44.0
1832	24	**Andrew Jackson**	Democrat	687,502	219	55.0
		Henry Clay	National Republican	530,189	49	42.4
		William Wirt	Anti-Masonic		7	
		John Floyd	National Republican	33,108	11	2.6
1836	26	**Martin Van Buren**	Democrat	765,483	170	50.9
		William H. Harrison	Whig		73	
		Hugh L. White	Whig		26	
		Daniel Webster	Whig	739,795	14	49.1
		W. P. Mangum	Whig		11	
1840	26	**William H. Harrison**	Whig	1,274,624	234	53.1
		Martin Van Buren	Democrat	1,127,781	60	46.9

(continued on page A-12)

Presidential Elections and Voting

Year	Number of States	Candidates	Party	Popular Vote*	Electoral Vote†	Percentage of Popular Vote
1844	26	**James K. Polk**	Democrat	1,338,464	170	49.6
		Henry Clay	Whig	1,300,097	105	48.1
		James G. Birney	Liberty	62,300		2.3
1848	30	**Zachary Taylor**	Whig	1,360,967	163	47.4
		Lewis Cass	Democrat	1,222,342	127	42.5
		Martin Van Buren	Free Soil	291,263		10.1
1852	31	**Franklin Pierce**	Democrat	1,601,117	254	50.9
		Winfield Scott	Whig	1,385,453	42	44.1
		John P. Hale	Free Soil	155,825		5.0
1856	31	**James Buchanan**	Democrat	1,832,955	174	45.3
		John C. Frémont	Republican	1,339,932	114	33.1
		Millard Fillmore	American ("Know Nothing")	871,731	8	21.6
1860	33	**Abraham Lincoln**	Republican	1,865,593	180	39.8
		Stephen A. Douglas	Democrat	1,382,713	12	29.5
		John C. Breckinridge	Democrat	848,356	72	18.1
		John Bell	Constitutional Union	592,906	39	12.6
1864	36	**Abraham Lincoln**	Republican	2,206,938	212	55.0
		George B. McClellan	Democrat	1,803,787	21	45.0
1868	37	**Ulysses S. Grant**	Republican	3,013,421	214	52.7
		Horatio Seymour	Democrat	2,706,829	80	47.3
1872	37	**Ulysses S. Grant**	Republican	3,596,745	286	55.6
		Horace Greeley	Democrat	2,843,446	*	43.9
1876	38	**Rutherford B. Hayes**	Republican	4,036,572	185	48.0
		Samuel J. Tilden	Democrat	4,284,020	184	51.0
1880	38	**James A. Garfield**	Republican	4,453,295	214	48.5
		Winfield S. Hancock	Democrat	4,414,082	155	48.1
		James B. Weaver	Greenback-Labor	308,578		3.4
1884	38	**Grover Cleveland**	Democrat	4,879,507	219	48.5
		James G. Blaine	Republican	4,850,293	182	48.2
		Benjamin F. Butler	Greenback-Labor	175,370		1.8
		John P. St. John	Prohibition	150,369		1.5
1888	38	**Benjamin Harrison**	Republican	5,447,129	233	47.9
		Grover Cleveland	Democrat	5,537,857	168	48.6
		Clinton B. Fisk	Prohibition	249,506		2.2
		Alson J. Streeter	Union Labor	146,935		1.3
1892	44	**Grover Cleveland**	Democrat	5,555,426	277	46.1
		Benjamin Harrison	Republican	5,182,690	145	43.0
		James B. Weaver	People's	1,029,846	22	8.5
		John Bidwell	Prohibition	264,133		2.2
1896	45	**William McKinley**	Republican	7,102,246	271	51.1
		William J. Bryan	Democrat	6,492,559	176	47.7
1900	45	**William McKinley**	Republican	7,218,491	292	51.7
		William J. Bryan	Democrat; Populist	6,356,734	155	45.5
		John C. Woolley	Prohibition	208,914		1.5

Year	Number of States	Candidates	Party	Popular Vote*	Electoral Vote†	Percentage of Popular Vote
1904	45	**Theodore Roosevelt**	Republican	7,628,461	336	57.4
		Alton B. Parker	Democrat	5,084,223	140	37.6
		Eugene V. Debs	Socialist	402,283		3.0
		Silas C. Swallow	Prohibition	258,536		1.9
1908	46	**William H. Taft**	Republican	7,675,320	321	51.6
		William J. Bryan	Democrat	6,412,294	162	43.1
		Eugene V. Debs	Socialist	420,793		2.8
		Eugene W. Chafin	Prohibition	253,840		1.7
1912	48	**Woodrow Wilson**	Democrat	6,296,547	435	41.9
		Theodore Roosevelt	Progressive	4,118,571	88	27.4
		William H. Taft	Republican	3,486,720	8	23.2
		Eugene V. Debs	Socialist	900,672		6.0
		Eugene W. Chafin	Prohibition	206,275		1.4
1916	48	**Woodrow Wilson**	Democrat	9,127,695	277	49.4
		Charles E. Hughes	Republican	8,533,507	254	46.2
		A. L. Benson	Socialist	585,113		3.2
		J. Frank Hanly	Prohibition	220,506		1.2
1920	48	**Warren G. Harding**	Republican	16,143,407	404	60.4
		James M. Cox	Democrat	9,130,328	127	34.2
		Eugene V. Debs	Socialist	919,799		3.4
		P. P. Christensen	Farmer-Labor	265,411		1.0
1924	48	**Calvin Coolidge**	Republican	15,718,211	382	54.0
		John W. Davis	Democrat	8,385,283	136	28.8
		Robert M. La Follette	Progressive	4,831,289	13	16.6
1928	48	**Herbert C. Hoover**	Republican	21,391,993	444	58.2
		Alfred E. Smith	Democrat	15,016,169	87	40.9
1932	48	**Franklin D. Roosevelt**	Democrat	22,809,638	472	57.4
		Herbert C. Hoover	Republican	15,758,901	59	39.7
		Norman Thomas	Socialist	881,951		2.2
1936	48	**Franklin D. Roosevelt**	Democrat	27,752,869	523	60.8
		Alfred M. Landon	Republican	16,674,665	8	36.5
		William Lemke	Union	882,479		1.9
1940	48	**Franklin D. Roosevelt**	Democrat	27,307,819	449	54.8
		Wendell L. Willkie	Republican	22,321,018	82	44.8
1944	48	**Franklin D. Roosevelt**	Democrat	25,606,585	432	53.5
		Thomas E. Dewey	Republican	22,014,745	99	46.0
1948	48	**Harry S Truman**	Democrat	24,105,812	303	49.5
		Thomas E. Dewey	Republican	21,970,065	189	45.1
		J. Strom Thurmond	States' Rights	1,169,063	39	2.4
		Henry A. Wallace	Progressive	1,157,172		2.4
1952	48	**Dwight D. Eisenhower**	Republican	33,936,234	442	55.1
		Adlai E. Stevenson	Democrat	27,314,992	89	44.4
1956	48	**Dwight D. Eisenhower**	Republican	35,590,472	457*	57.6
		Adlai E. Stevenson	Democrat	26,022,752	73	42.1

(continued on page A-14)

Year	Number of States	Candidates	Party	Popular Vote*	Electoral Vote[†]	Percentage of Popular Vote
1960	50	**John F. Kennedy**	Democrat	34,227,096	303[†]	49.9
		Richard M. Nixon	Republican	34,108,546	219	49.6
1964	50	**Lyndon B. Johnson**	Democrat	42,676,220	486	61.3
		Barry M. Goldwater	Republican	26,860,314	52	38.5
1968	50	**Richard M. Nixon**	Republican	31,785,480	301	43.4
		Hubert H. Humphrey	Democrat	31,275,165	191	42.7
		George C. Wallace	American Independent	9,906,473	46	13.5
1972	50	**Richard M. Nixon‡**	Republican	47,165,234	520	60.6
		George S. McGovern	Democrat	29,168,110	17	37.5
1976	50	**Jimmy Carter**	Democrat	40,828,929	297	50.1
		Gerald R. Ford	Republican	39,148,940	240	47.9
		Eugene McCarthy	Independent	739,256		0.9
1980	50	**Ronald Reagan**	Republican	43,201,220	489	50.9
		Jimmy Carter	Democrat	34,913,332	49	41.2
		John B. Anderson	Independent	5,581,379		6.6
1984	50	**Ronald Reagan**	Republican	53,428,357	525	59.0
		Walter F. Mondale	Democrat	36,930,923	13	41.0
1988	50	**George H. W. Bush**	Republican	48,901,046	426	53.4
		Michael Dukakis	Democrat	41,809,030	111	45.6
1992	50	**Bill Clinton**	Democrat	43,728,275	370	43.2
		George Bush	Republican	38,167,416	168	37.7
		H. Ross Perot	United We Stand, America	19,237,247		19.0
1996	50	**Bill Clinton**	Democrat	45,590,703	379	49.0
		Bob Dole	Republican	37,816,307	159	41.0
		H. Ross Perot	Reform	7,866,284		8.0
2000	50	**George W. Bush**	Republican	50,456,169	271	48.0
		Al Gore	Democrat	50,996,116	266	48.0
		Ralph Nader	Green	2,767,176	0	3.0

*Percentage of popular vote given for any election year may not total 100 percent because candidates receiving less than 1 percent of the popular vote have been omitted.

[†]Prior to the passage of the Twelfth Amendment in 1904, the electoral college voted for two presidential candidates; the runner-up became Vice President. Data from Historical Statistics of the United States, Colonial Times to 1957 (1961), pp. 682–683, and The World Almanac.

*Because of the death of Greeley, Democratic electors scattered their votes.

*Walter B. Jones received 1 electoral vote.

[†]Harry F. Byrd received 15 electoral votes.

‡Resigned August 9, 1974: Vice President Gerald R. Ford became President.

Party Control of Congress

Congress	Years	Party and President	Senate DEM.	REP.	OTHER	House DEM.	REP.	OTHER
57th	1901–03	R T. Roosevelt	29	56	3	153	198	5
58th	1903–05	R T. Roosevelt	32	58	—	178	207	—
59th	1905–07	R T. Roosevelt	32	58	—	136	250	—
60th	1907–09	R T. Roosevelt	29	61	—	164	222	—
61st	1909–11	R Taft	32	59	—	172	219	—
62d	1911–13	R Taft	42	49	—	228	162	1
63d	1913–15	D Wilson	51	44	1	290	127	18
64th	1915–17	D Wilson	56	39	1	230	193	8
65th	1917–19	D Wilson	53	42	1	200	216	9
66th	1919–21	D Wilson	48	48	1	191	237	7
67th	1921–23	R Harding	37	59	—	132	300	1
68th	1923–25	R Coolidge	43	51	2	207	225	3
69th	1925–27	R Coolidge	40	54	1	183	247	5
70th	1927–29	R Coolidge	47	48	1	195	237	3
71st	1929–31	R Hoover	39	56	1	163	267	1
72d	1931–33	R Hoover	47	48	1	216	218	1
73d	1933–35	D F. Roosevelt	59	36	1	313	117	5
74th	1935–37	D F. Roosevelt	69	25	2	322	103	10
75th	1937–39	D F. Roosevelt	75	17	4	333	89	13
76th	1939–41	D F. Roosevelt	69	23	4	262	169	4
77th	1941–43	D F. Roosevelt	66	28	2	267	162	6
78th	1943–45	D F. Roosevelt	57	38	1	222	209	4
79th	1945–47	D Truman	57	38	1	243	190	2
80th	1947–49	D Truman	45	51	—	188	246	1
81st	1949–51	D Truman	54	42	—	263	171	1
82d	1951–53	D Truman	48	47	1	234	199	2
83d	1953–55	R Eisenhower	47	48	1	213	221	1
84th	1955–57	R Eisenhower	48	47	1	232	203	—
85th	1957–59	R Eisenhower	49	47	—	234	201	—
86th	1959–61	R Eisenhower	64	34	—	283	154	—
87th	1961–63	D Kennedy	64	36	—	263	174	—
88th	1963–65	D { Kennedy / Johnson	67	33	—	258	176	—
89th	1965–67	D Johnson	68	32	—	295	140	—
90th	1967–69	D Johnson	64	36	—	248	187	—
91st	1969–71	R Nixon	58	42	—	243	192	—
92d	1971–73	R Nixon	55	45	—	255	180	—
93d	1973–75	R { Nixon / Ford	57	43	—	243	192	—
94th	1975–77	R Ford	61	38	—	291	144	—
95th	1977–79	D Carter	62	38	—	292	143	—
96th	1979–81	D Carter	59	41	—	277	158	—
97th	1981–83	R Reagan	47	53	—	243	192	—
98th	1983–85	R Reagan	46	54	—	269	166	—
99th	1985–87	R Reagan	47	53	—	253	182	—
100th	1987–89	R Reagan	55	45	—	258	177	—
101st	1989–91	R Bush	55	45	—	260	175	—
102d	1991–93	R Bush	57	43	—	267	167	1
103d	1993–95	D Clinton	59	43	—	258	176	1
104th	1995–97	D Clinton	46	54	—	204	230	1
105th	1997–99	D Clinton	45	55	—	207	227	1
106th	1999–2001	D Clinton	45	55	—	211	223	1
107th	2001–2003	R Bush	50	50	—	212	221	2
108th	2003–2005	R Bush	49*	51	—	206	228	1

*Including Vermont independent Jim Jeffords.

Glossary

ABM Treaty A formal treaty in 1972 between the U.S. and the Soviet Union in which each side agreed not to build or deploy antiballistic missiles.

abolition movement Social movement before the Civil War whose goal was to abolish slavery throughout the United States.

access Meeting and talking with decision makers, a prerequisite to direct persuasion.

adjudication Decision making by the federal bureaucracy as to whether or not an individual or organization has complied with or violated government laws and/or regulation.

adversarial system Method of decision making in which an impartial judge or jury or decision maker hears arguments and reviews evidence presented by opposite sides.

advice and consent The constitutional power of the U.S. Senate to reject or ratify (by a two-thirds vote) treaties made by the president.

affirmative action Any program, whether enacted by a government or by a private organization, whose goal is to overcome the results of past unequal treatment of minorities and/or women by giving members of these groups preferential treatment in admissions, hiring, promotions, or other aspects of life.

affirmative racial gerrymandering Drawing district boundary lines to maximize minority representation.

agenda setting Deciding what will be decided, defining the problems and issues to be addressed by decision makers.

amendment Formal change in a bill, law, or constitution.

amicus curiae Literally, "friend of the court"; a person, private group or institution, or government agency that is not a party to a case but participates in the case (usually through submission of a brief) at the invitation of the court or on its own initiative.

Anti-Federalists Those who opposed the ratification of the U.S. Constitution and the creation of a strong national government.

appeal In general, requests that a higher court review cases decided at a lower level. In the Supreme Court, certain cases are designated as appeals under federal law; formally, these must be heard by the Court.

appellate jurisdiction Particular court's power to review a decision or action of a lower court.

apportionment The allocation of legislative seats to jurisdictions based on population. Seats in the U.S. House of Representatives are apportioned to the states on the basis of their population after every ten-year census.

appropriations act Congressional bill that provides money for programs authorized by Congress.

authorization Act of Congress that establishes a government program and defines the amount of money it may spend.

backdoor spending Spending by agencies of the federal government whose operations are not included in the federal budget.

bail Release of an accused person from custody in exchange for promise to appear at trial, guaranteed by money or property that is forfeited to court if defendant does not appear.

Bakke case U.S. Supreme Court case challenging affirmative action.

balanced budget Government budget in which expenditures and revenues are equal, so that no deficit or surplus exists.

ballistic missile defense (BMD) Weapons systems capable of detecting, intercepting, and destroying missiles in flight.

beliefs Shared ideas about what is true.

bicameral Any legislative body that consists of two separate chambers or houses; in the United States, the Senate represents 50 statewide voter constituencies, and the House of Representatives represents voters in 435 separate districts.

big-state strategy Presidential political campaign strategy in which a candidate focuses on winning primaries in large states because of their high delegate counts.

bill of attainder Legislative act inflicting punishment without judicial trial; forbidden under Article I of the Constitution.

Bill of Rights Written guarantees of basic individual liberties; the first ten amendments to the U.S. Constitution.

bipartisan Agreement by members of both the Democratic and the Republican parties.

bribery Giving or offering anything of value in an effort to influence government officials in the performance of their duties.

briefs Documents submitted by an attorney to a court, setting out the facts of the case and the legal arguments in support of the party represented by the attorney.

budget maximization Bureaucrats' tendencies to expand their agencies' budgets, staff, and authority.

budget resolution Congressional bill setting forth target budget figures for appropriations to various government departments and agencies.

bureaucracy Departments, agencies, bureaus, and offices that perform the functions of government.

cabinet The heads (secretaries) of the executive departments together with other top officials accorded cabinet rank by the president; only occasionally does it meet as a body to advise and support the president.

campaign strategy Plan for a political campaign, usually including a theme, an attempt to define the opponent or the issues, and an effort to coordinate images and messages in news broadcasts and paid advertising.

capital gains Profits from buying and selling property including stocks, bonds, and real estate.

capitalism Economic system asserting the individual's right to own private property and to buy, sell, rent, and trade that property in a free market.

capture theory of regulation Theory describing how some regulated industries come to benefit from government regulation and how some regulatory commissions come to represent the industries they are supposed to regulate rather than representing "the people."

careerism In politics, a reference to people who started young working in politics, running for and holding public office, and made politics their career.

casework Services performed by legislators or their staff on behalf of individual constituents.

caucus Nominating process in which party leaders select the party's nominee.

censure Public reprimand for wrongdoing, given to a member standing in the chamber before Congress.

centralized federalism Model of federalism in which the national government assumes primary responsibility for determining national goals in all major policy areas and directs state and local government activity through conditions attached to money grants.

chain of command Hierarchical structure of authority in which command flows downward; typical of a bureaucracy.

challengers In politics, a reference to people running against incumbent officeholders.

checks and balances Constitutional provisions giving each branch of the national government certain checks over the actions of other branches.

circuit courts The twelve appellate courts that make up the middle level of the federal court system.

civil cases Noncriminal court proceedings in which a plaintiff sues a defendant for damages in payment for harm inflicted.

civil disobedience Form of public protest involving the breaking of laws believed to be unjust.

class action suits Cases initiated by parties acting on behalf of themselves and all others similarly situated.

class conflict Conflict between upper and lower social classes over wealth and power.

class consciousness Awareness of one's class position and a feeling of political solidarity with others within the same class in opposition to other classes.

classical liberalism Political philosophy asserting the worth and dignity of the individual and emphasizing the rational ability of human beings to determine their own destinies.

clear and present danger doctrine Standard used by the courts to determine whether speech may be restricted; only speech that creates a serious and immediate danger to society may be restricted.

closed primaries Primary elections in which voters must declare (or have previously declared) their party affiliation and can cast a ballot only in their own party's primary election.

closed rule Rule that forbids adding any amendments to a bill under consideration by the House.

cloture Vote to end debate—that is, to end a filibuster—which requires a three-fifths vote of the entire membership of the Senate.

coalition A joining together of interest groups (or individuals) to achieve a common goal.

COLAs Annual cost-of-living adjustments mandated by law in Social Security and other welfare benefits.

Cold War Political, military, and ideological struggle between the United States and the Soviet Union following the end of World War II and ending with the collapse of the Soviet Union's communist government in 1991.

collective security Attempt to bring order to international relations by all nations joining together to guarantee each other's "territorial integrity" and "independence" against "external aggression."

commercial speech Advertising communications given only partial protection under the First Amendment to the Constitution.

common market Unified trade area in which all goods and services can be sold or exchanged free from customs or tariffs.

communism System of government in which a single totalitarian party controls all means of production and distribution of goods and services.

comparable worth Argument that pay levels for traditionally male and traditionally female jobs should be equalized by paying equally all jobs that are "worth about the same" to an employer.

Comprehensive Test Ban Treaty A multilateral treaty prohibiting all nuclear testing.

concurrent powers Powers exercised by both the national government and state governments in the American federal system.

concurring opinion Opinion by a member of a court that agrees with the result reached by the court in the case but disagrees with or departs from the court's rationale for the decision.

confederation Constitutional arrangement whereby the national government is created by and relies on subnational governments for its authority.

conference committee Meeting between representatives of the House and Senate to reconcile differences over provisions of a bill passed by both houses.

confirmation The constitutionally required consent of the Senate to appointments of high-level executive officials by the president and appointments of federal judges.

congressional hearings Congressional committee sessions in which members listen to witnesses who provide information and opinions on matters of interest to the committee, including pending legislation.

congressional investigation Congressional committee hearings on alleged misdeeds or scandals.

congressional session Each Congress elected in November of even-numbered years meets the following January 3 and remains in session for two years. Since the first Congress to meet under the Constitution in 1789, Congresses have been numbered by session (for example, 107th Congress 2001–2003, 108th Congress 2003–2005, 109th Congress 2005–2007).

conservatism Belief in the value of free markets, limited government, and individual self-reliance in economic affairs, combined with a belief in the value of tradition, law, and morality in social affairs.

constituency The votes in a legislator's home district.

constitution The legal structure of a political system, establishing governmental bodies, granting their powers, determining how their members are selected, and prescribing the rules by which they make their decisions. Considered basic or fundamental, a constitution cannot be changed by ordinary acts of governmental bodies.

constitutionalism A government of laws, not people, operating on the principle that governmental power must be limited and government officials should be restrained in their exercise of power over individuals.

containment Policy of preventing an enemy from expanding its boundaries and/or influence, specifically the U.S. foreign policy vis-à-vis the Soviet Union during the Cold War.

contingency fees Fees paid to attorneys to represent the plaintiff in a civil suit and receive in compensation an agreed-upon percentage of damages awarded (if any).

continuing resolution Congressional bill that authorizes government agencies to keep spending money for a specified period at the same level as in the previous fiscal year; passed when Congress is unable to enact final appropriations measures by October 1.

convention Nominating process in which delegates from local party organizations select the party's nominees.

cooperative federalism Model of federalism in which national, state, and local governments work together exercising common policy responsibilities.

covert action Secret intelligence activity outside U.S. borders undertaken with specific authorization by the president; acknowledgment of U.S. sponsorship would defeat or compromise its purpose.

Cuban missile crisis The 1962 confrontation between the Soviet Union and the U.S. over Soviet placement of nuclear missiles in Cuba.

de facto segregation Racial imbalances not directly caused by official actions but rather by residential patterns.

dealignment Declining attractiveness of the parties to the voters, a reluctance to identify strongly with a party, and a decrease in reliance on party affiliation in voter choice.

deductibles Initial charges in insurance plans, paid by beneficiaries.

defendants Parties against whom a criminal or civil suit is brought.

deferrals Items on which a president wishes to postpone spending.

deficit Imbalance in the annual federal budget in which spending exceeds revenues.

delegated, or enumerated, powers Powers specifically mentioned in the Constitution as belonging to the national government.

delegates Accredited voting members of a party's national presidential nominating convention.

democracy Governing system in which the people govern themselves, from the Greek term meaning "rule by the many."

democratic ideals Individual dignity, equality before the law, widespread participation in public decisions, and public decisions by majority rule, with one person having one vote.

Democratic Leadership Council Organization of party leaders who sought to create a "new" Democratic Party to appeal to middle-class, moderate voters.

Democratic Party One of the main parties in American politics; it traces its origins to Thomas Jefferson's Democratic-Republican Party, acquiring its current name under Andrew Jackson in 1828.

dependency ratio In the Social Security system, the number of recipients as a percentage of the number of contributing workers.

deregulation Lifting of government rules and bureaucratic supervision from business and professional activity.

deterrence U.S. approach to deterring any nuclear attack from the Soviet Union by maintaining a second-strike capability.

devolution Passing down of responsibilities from the national government to the states.

diplomatic recognition Power of the president to grant "legitimacy" to or withhold it from a government of another nation (to declare or refuse to declare it "rightful").

direct democracy Governing system in which every person participates actively in every public decision, rather than delegating decision making to representatives.

direct discrimination Now illegal practice of differential pay for men versus women even when those individuals have equal qualifications and perform the same job.

discharge petition Petition signed by at least 218 House members to force a vote on a bill within a committee that opposes it.

discretionary funds Budgeted funds not earmarked for specific purposes but available to be spent in accordance with the best judgment of a bureaucrat.

discretionary spending Spending for programs not previously mandated by law.

dissenting opinion Opinion by a member of a court that disagrees with the result reached by the court in the case.

district courts Original jurisdiction trial courts of the federal system.

divided party government One party controls the presidency while the other party controls one or both houses of Congress.

division of labor Division of work among many specialized workers in a bureaucracy.

drafting a bill Actual writing of a bill in legal language.

dual federalism Early concept of federalism in which national and state powers were clearly distinguished and functionally separate.

Earned Income Tax Credit Tax refunds in excess of tax payments for low-income workers.

Electoral College The 538 presidential electors apportioned among the states according to their congressional representation (plus 3 for the District of Columbia) whose votes officially elect the president and vice president of the United States.

elitism Theory that all societies, even democracies, are divided into the few who govern and the many who do not.

end of history The collapse of communism and the worldwide movement toward free markets and political democracy.

entitlement programs Social welfare programs that provide classes of people with legally enforceable rights to benefits.

entitlements Any social welfare program for which there are eligibility requirements, whether financial or contributory.

enumerated powers Powers specifically mentioned in the Constitution as belonging to the national government.

Equal Rights Amendment (ERA) Proposed amendment to the Constitution guaranteeing that equal rights under the law shall not be denied or abridged on account of sex. Passed by Congress in 1972, the amendment failed to win ratification by three of the necessary three-fourths of the states.

equality of opportunity Elimination of artificial barriers to success in life and the opportunity for everyone to strive for success.

equality of results Equal sharing of income and material goods regardless of one's efforts in life.

equal-time rule Federal Communications Commission (FCC) requirement that broadcasters who sell time to any political candidate must make equal time available to opposing candidates at the same price.

ex post facto law Retroactive criminal law that works against the accused; forbidden under Article I of the Constitution.

exclusionary rule Rule of law that evidence found in an illegal search or resulting from an illegally obtained confession may not be admitted at trial.

executive agreement Agreement with another nation signed by the president of the United States but less formal (and hence potentially less binding) than a treaty because it does not require Senate confirmation.

executive order Formal regulation governing executive branch operations issued by the president.

executive privilege Right of a president to withhold from other branches of government confidential communications within the executive branch; although posited by presidents, it has been upheld by the Supreme Court only in limited situations.

externalities Costs imposed on people who are not direct participants in an activity.

extremism Rejection of democratic politics and the assertion of the supremacy of the "people" over laws, institutions, and individual rights.

Fair Deal Policies of President Harry Truman extending Roosevelt's New Deal and maintaining the Democratic Party's voter coalition.

Family Assistance Public assistance program that provides monies to the states for their use in helping needy families with children.

fascism Political ideology in which the state and/or race is assumed to be supreme over individuals.

Federal Election Commission (FEC) Agency charged with enforcing federal election laws and disbursing public presidential campaign funds.

Federal Reserve Board (the Fed) Independent agency of the executive branch of the federal government charged with overseeing the nation's monetary policy.

federalism A constitutional arrangement whereby power is divided between national and subnational governments, each of which enforces its own laws directly on its citizens and neither of which can alter the arrangement without the consent of the other.

Federalists Those who supported the U.S. Constitution during the ratification process and who later formed a political party in support of John Adams's presidential candidacy.

"feeding frenzy" Intense media coverage of a scandal or event that blocks out most other news.

filibuster Delaying tactic by a senator or group of senators, using the Senate's unlimited debate rule to prevent a vote on a bill.

fiscal policy Economic policies involving taxing, spending, and deficit levels of the national government.

fiscal year Yearly government accounting period, not necessarily the same as the calendar year. The federal government's fiscal year begins October 1 and ends September 30.

focus group In a political context, a small number of people brought together in a comfortable setting to discuss and respond to themes and issues, allowing campaign managers to develop and analyze strategies.

Food Stamp program Public assistance program that provides low-income households with coupons redeemable for enough food to provide a minimal nutritious diet.

franking privilege Free use of the U.S. mails granted to members of Congress to promote communication with constituents.

Free Exercise Clause Clause in the First Amendment to the Constitution that prohibits government from restricting religious beliefs and practices.

free market Free competition for voluntary exchange among individuals, firms, and corporations.

free trade A policy of reducing or eliminating tariffs and quotas on imports to stimulate international trade.

freedom of expression Collectively, the First Amendment rights to free speech, press, and assembly.

free-riders People who do not belong to an organization or pay dues, yet nevertheless benefit from its activities.

front loading The scheduling of presidential primary elections early in the year.

front-end strategy Presidential political campaign strategy in which a candidate focuses on winning early primaries to build momentum.

gag order Order by a judge banning discussion or reporting of a case in order to ensure a fair and impartial trial.

gender gap Aggregate differences in political opinions of men and women.

general election Election to choose among candidates nominated by parties and/or independent candidates who gained access to the ballot by petition.

generation gap Differences in politics and public opinion among age groups.

generational effects Historical events that affect the views of those who lived through them.

gerrymandering Drawing district boundary lines for political advantage.

glass ceiling "Invisible" barriers to women rising to the highest positions in corporations and the professions.

GOP "Grand Old Party"—popular label for the Republican Party.

government bonds Certificates of indebtedness that pay interest and promise repayment on a future date.

government Organization extending to the whole society that can legitimately use force to carry out its decisions.

grand jury Jury charged only with determining whether sufficient evidence exists to support indictment of an individual on a felony charge; the grand jury's decision to indict does not represent a conviction.

grant of immunity from prosecution Grant by the government to an individual of freedom from prosecution on a particular charge in return for testimony by that individual that might otherwise be self-incriminating.

grants-in-aid Payments of funds from the national government to state or local governments or from a state government to local governments for specific purposes.

grass-roots lobbying Attempts to influence government decision making by inspiring constituents to contact their representatives.

Great Society Policies of President Lyndon Johnson that promised to solve the nation's social and economic problems through government intervention.

gridlock Political stalemate between the executive and legislative branches arising when one branch is controlled by one major political party and the other branch by the other party.

gross domestic product (GDP) Measure of economic performance in terms of the nation's total production of goods and services for a single year, valued in terms of market prices.

gross domestic product (GDP) The dollar sum of all the goods and services produced in a nation in a year.

halo effect Tendency of survey respondents to provide socially acceptable answers to questions.

health maintenance organizations (HMOs) Health care provider groups that provide a stipulated list of services to patients for a fixed fee that is usually substantially lower than such care would otherwise cost.

home rule Power of local government to pass laws affecting local affairs, so long as those laws do not conflict with state or federal laws.

home style Activities of Congress members specifically directed at their home constituencies.

honeymoon period Early months of a president's term in which his popularity with the public and influence with the Congress are generally high.

horse-race coverage Media coverage of electoral campaigns that concentrates on who is ahead and who is behind, and neglects the issues at stake.

ideological organizations Interest groups that pursue ideologically based (liberal or conservative) agendas.

ideological party Third party that exists to promote an ideology rather than to win elections.

ideology Consistent and integrated system of ideas, values, and beliefs.

impeachment Equivalent of a criminal charge against an elected official; removal of the impeached official from office depends on the outcome of a trial.

impersonality Treatment of all persons within a bureaucracy on the basis of "merit" and of all "clients" served by the bureaucracy equally according to rules.

implementation Development by the federal bureaucracy of procedures and activities to carry out policies legislated by Congress; it includes regulation as well as adjudication.

implied powers Powers not mentioned specifically in the Constitution as belonging to Congress but inferred as necessary and proper for carrying out the enumerated powers.

impoundment Refusal by a president to spend monies appropriated by Congress; outlawed except with congressional consent by the Budget and Impoundment Control Act of 1974.

incidence Actual bearer of a tax burden.

income transfers Government transfers of income from taxpayers to persons regarded as deserving.

incorporation In constitutional law, the application of almost all of the Bill of Rights to the states and all of their subdivision through the Fourteenth Amendment.

incremental budgeting Method of budgeting that focuses on requested increases in funding for existing programs, accepting as legitimate their previous year's expenditures.

incumbent gerrymandering Drawing legislative district boundaries to advantage incumbent legislators.

incumbent Candidate currently in office seeking reelection.

independent counsel ("special prosecutor") A prosecutor appointed by a federal court to pursue charges against a president or other high official. This position was allowed to lapse by Congress in 1999 after many controversial investigations by these prosecutors.

indexing Tying of benefit levels in social welfare programs to the general price level.

indictment Determination by a grand jury that sufficient evidence exists to warrant trial of an individual on a felony charge; necessary before an individual can be brought to trial.

individual income tax Taxes on individuals' wages and other earned income, the primary source of revenue for the U.S. federal government.

inflation Rise in the general level of prices; not just the prices of some products.

information overload Situation in which individuals are subjected to so many communications that they cannot make sense of them.

in-kind (noncash) benefits Benefits of a social welfare program that are not cash payments, including free medical care, subsidized housing, and food stamps.

interest groups Organizations that seek to influence government policy.

interest-group entrepreneurs Leaders who create organizations and market memberships.

intergovernmental relations Network of political, financial, and administrative relationships between units of the federal government and those of state and local governments.

iron triangles Mutually supportive relationships among interest groups, government agencies, and legislative committees with jurisdiction over a specific policy area.

issue ads Ads that advocate policy positions rather than explicitly supporting or opposing particular candidates.

Jim Crow Second-class-citizen status conferred on blacks by southern segregation laws; derived from a nineteenth-century song-and-dance act (usually performed by a white man in blackface) that stereotyped blacks

judicial activism Making of new law through judicial interpretations of the Constitution.

judicial review Power of the courts, especially the Supreme Court, to declare laws of Congress, laws of the states, and actions of the president unconstitutional and invalid.

judicial self-restraint Self-imposed limitation on judicial power by judges deferring to the policy judgments of elected branches of government.

jurisdiction Power of a court to hear a case in question.

Korean War Communist North Korea invaded non-Communist South Korea in June, 1950, causing President Harry S Truman to intervene militarily, with U.N. support. General Douglas MacArthur defeated the North Koreans, but with China's entry into the war, a stalemate resulted. An armistice was signed in 1953, with Korea divided along nearly original lines.

laboratories of democracy A reference to the ability of states to experiment and innovate in public policy.

left A reference to the liberal, progressive, and/or socialist side of the political spectrum.

legitimacy Widespread acceptance of something as necessary, rightful, and legally binding.

Lemon test To be constitutional, a law must have a secular purpose; its primary effect must neither advance nor inhibit religion; and it must not foster excessive government entanglement with religion.

Leninism The theories of Vladimir Lenin, among them that advanced capitalist countries turned toward war and colonialism to make their own workers relatively prosperous.

libel Writings that are false and malicious and are intended to damage an individual.

liberalism Belief in the value of strong government to provide economic security and protection for civil rights, combined with a belief in personal freedom from government intervention in social conduct.

life-cycle effects Changes in life circumstances associated with age that affect one's views.

limited government Principle that government power over the individual is limited, that there are some personal liberties that even a majority cannot regulate, and that government itself is restrained by law.

line-item veto Power of the chief executive to reject some portions of a bill without rejecting all of it.

literacy test Examination of a person's ability to read and write as a prerequisite to voter registration, outlawed by Voting Rights Act (1965) as discriminatory.

litigation Legal dispute brought before a court.

litmus test In political terms, a person's stand on a key issue that determines whether he or she will be appointed to public office or supported in electoral campaigns.

lobbying Activities directed at government officials with the hope of influencing their decisions.

lobbyist Person working to influence government policies and actions.

logrolling Bargaining for agreement among legislators to support each other's favorite bills, especially projects that primarily benefit individual members and their constituents.

machine Tightly disciplined party organization, headed by a boss, that relies on material rewards—including patronage jobs—to control politics.

majoritarianism Tendency of democratic governments to allow the faint preferences of the majority to prevail over the intense feelings of minorities.

majority leader In the House, the majority-party leader and second in command to the Speaker; in the Senate, the leader of the majority party.

majority opinion Opinion in a case that is subscribed to by a majority of the judges who participated in the decision.

majority Election by more than 50 percent of all votes cast in the contest.

malapportionment Unequal numbers of people in legislative districts resulting in inequality of voter representation.

managed care Programs designed to keep health care costs down by the establishment of strict guidelines regarding when and what diagnostic and therapeutic procedures should be administered to patients under various circumstances.

mandate Perception of popular support for a program or policy based on the margin of electoral victory won by a candidate who proposed it during a campaign; direct federal orders to state and local governments requiring them to perform a service or to obey federal laws in the performance of their functions.

mandatory spending Spending for program committments made by past congresses.

markup Line-by-line revision of a bill in committee by editing each phrase and word.

Marshall Plan U.S. program to rebuild the nations of Western Europe in the aftermath of World War II in order to render them less susceptible to communist influence and takeover.

Marxism The theories of Karl Marx, among them that capitalists oppress workers and that worldwide revolution and the emergence of a classless society are inevitable.

mass media All means of communication with the general public, including television, newspapers, magazines, radio, books, recordings, motion pictures, and the Internet.

means-tested spending Spending for benefits that is distributed on the basis of the recipient's income.

Medicaid Public assistance program that provides health care to the poor.

Medicare Social insurance program that provides health care insurance to elderly and disabled people.

merit system Selection of employees for government agencies on the basis of competence, with no consideration of an individual's political stance and/or power.

minority leader In both the House and Senate, the leader of the opposition party.

Miranda warning Requirement that persons arrested be informed of their rights immediately after arrest.

monetary policy Economic policies involving the money supply, interest rates, and banking activity.

"Motor Voter Act" Federal mandate that states offer voter registration at driver's licensing and welfare offices.

muckraking Journalistic exposés of corruption, wrongdoing, or mismanagement in government, business, and other institutions of society.

multilateral treaty A treaty open to signature by more than two nations (as opposed to a bilateral treaty, signed by only two nations).

mutual assured destruction (MAD) Nuclear peace maintained by the capability of each side's missile forces to survive a first strike and inflict heavy damages in retaliation against the aggressor's population.

name recognition Public awareness of a political candidate—whether they know his or her name.

national debt Total debt accumulated by the national government over the years.

national health insurance Government-provided insurance to all citizens paid from tax revenues.

National Security Council (NSC) "Inner cabinet" that advises the president and coordinates foreign, defense, and intelligence activities.

National Supremacy Clause Clause in Article VI of the U.S. Constitution declaring the constitution and laws of the national government "the supreme law of the land" superior to the constitutions and laws of the states.

nationalism Belief that shared cultural, historical, linguistic, and social characteristics of a people justify the creation of a government encompassing all of them, the resulting nation-state should be independent and legally equal to all other nation-states.

Necessary and Proper Clause Clause in Article I, Section 8, of the U.S. Constitution granting Congress the power to enact all laws that are "necessary and proper" for carrying out those responsibilities specifically delegated to it. Also referred to as the Implied Powers Clause.

negative campaigning Speeches, commercials, or advertising attacking a political opponent during a campaign.

New Deal Policies of President Franklin D. Roosevelt during the depression of the 1930s that helped form a Democratic Party coalition of urban working-class, ethnic, Catholic, Jewish, poor, and southern voters.

new federalism Attempts to return power and responsibility to the states and reduce the role of the national government in domestic affairs.

newsmaking Deciding what events, topics, presentations, and issues will be given coverage in the news.

No Establishment Clause Clause in the First Amendment to the Constitution that is interpreted to require the separation of church and state.

nomination Political party's selection of its candidate for a public office.

nominee Political party's entry in a general election race.

nonpartisan elections Elections in which candidates do not officially indicate their party affiliation; often used for city, country, school board, and judicial elections.

Nonproliferation Treaty A multilateral treaty in which nuclear nations pledged not to transfer nuclear weapons or technologies to nonnuclear nations, and nonnuclear nations pledged not to manufacture or acquire nuclear weapons.

nonviolent direct action Strategy used by civil rights leaders such as Martin Luther King, Jr., in which protesters break "unjust" laws openly but in a "loving" fashion in order to bring the injustices of such laws to public attention.

North Atlantic Treaty Organization (NATO) Mutual-security agreement and joint military command uniting the nations of Western Europe, initially formed to resist Soviet expansionism.

obligational authority Feature of some appropriations acts by which an agency is empowered to enter into contracts that will require the government to make payments beyond the fiscal year in question.

open primaries Primary elections in which a voter may cast a ballot in either party's primary election.

open rule Rule that permits unlimited amendments to a bill under consideration by the House.

open seat Seat in a legislature for which no incumbent is running for reelection.

organizational sclerosis Society encrusted with so many special benefits to interest groups that everyone's standard of living is lowered.

original intent Judicial philosophy under which judges attempt to apply the values of the Founders to current issues.

original jurisdiction Refers to a particular court's power to serve as the place where a given case is initially argued and decided.

outlays Actual dollar amounts to be spent by the federal government in a fiscal year.

override Voting in Congress to enact legislation vetoed by the president; requires a two-thirds vote in both the House and Senate.

oversight Congressional monitoring of the activities of executive branch agencies to determine if the laws are being faithfully executed.

packing Redistricting in which partisan voters are concentrated in a single district, "wasting" their majority vote and allowing the opposition to win by modest majorities in other districts.

paradox of democracy Potential for conflict between individual freedom and majority rule.

partial preemption Federal government's assumption of some regulatory powers in a particular field, with the stipulation that a state law on the same subject as a federal law is valid if it does not conflict with the federal law in the same area.

party identification Self-described identification with a political party, usually in response to the question, "Generally speaking, how would you identify yourself: as a Republican, Democrat, independent, or something else?"

party organization National and state party officials and workers, committee members, convention delegates, and others active in the party.

party polarization The tendency of the Democratic Party to take more liberal positions and the Republican Party to take more conservative positions on key issues.

party unity Percentage of Democrats and Republicans who stick with their party on party votes.

party vote Majority of Democrats voting in opposition to a majority of Republicans.

party-in-the-electorate Voters who identify themselves with a party.

party-in-the-government Public officials who were nominated by their party and who identify themselves in office with their party.

patronage Appointment to public office based on party loyalty.

petit (regular) juries Juries called to determine guilt or innocence.

photo ops Staged opportunities for the media to photograph the candidate in a favorable setting.

plaintiffs Parties initiating suits and claiming damages. In criminal cases, the state acts as plaintiff on behalf of an injured society and requests fines and/or imprisonment as damages. In civil suits, the plaintiff is the injured party and seeks monetary damages.

platform Statement of principles adopted by a political party at its national convention (specific portions of the platform are known as planks); a platform is not binding on the party's candidates.

plea bargaining Practice of allowing defendants to plead guilty to lesser crimes than those with which they were originally charged in return for reduced sentences.

pluralism Theory that democracy can be achieved through competition among multiple organized groups and that individuals can participate in politics through group memberships and elections.

plurality Election by at least one vote more than any other candidate in the race.

pocket veto Effective veto of a bill when Congress adjourns within ten days of passing it and the president fails to sign it.

policy networks Interaction in a common policy area among lobbyists, elected officials, staff personnel, bureaucrats, journalists, and private-sector experts.

political action committees (PACs) Organizations that solicit and receive campaign contributions from corporations, unions, trade associations, and ideological and issue-oriented groups, and their members, then distribute these funds to political candidates.

political alienation Belief that politics is irrelevant to one's life and that one cannot personally affect public affairs.

political culture Widely shared views about who should govern, for what ends, and by what means.

political equality Belief that the law should apply equally to all and that every person's vote counts equally.

political organizations Parties and interest groups that function as intermediaries between individuals and government.

political parties Organizations that seek to achieve power by winning public office.

political science The study of politics: who governs, for what ends, and by what means.

politically correct (PC) Repression of attitudes, speech, and writings that are deemed racist, sexist, homophohic (anti-homosexual), or otherwise "insensitive."

politics Deciding who gets what, when, and how.

poll taxes Taxes imposed as a prerequisite to voting; prohibited by the Twenty-fourth Amendment.

pork barreling Legislation designed to make government benefits, including jobs and projects used as political patronage, flow to a particular district or state.

poverty line Official standard regarding what level of annual cash income is sufficient to maintain a "decent standard of living"; those with incomes below this level are eligible for most public assistance programs.

power of the purse Congress's exclusive, constitutional power to authorize expenditures by all agencies of the federal government.

precedent Legal principle that previous decisions should determine the outcome of current cases; the basis for stability in law.

precinct Subdivision of a city, county, or ward for election purposes.

preemption Total or partial federal assumption of power in a particular field, restricting the authority of the states.

preferred position Refers to the tendency of the courts to give preference to the First Amendment rights to speech, press, and assembly when faced with conflicts.

preferred provider organizations (PPOs) Groups of hospitals and physicians who have joined together to offer their services to private insurers at a discount.

presidential primaries Primary elections in the states in which voters in each party can choose a presidential candidate for its party's nomination. Outcomes help determine the distribution of pledged delegates to each party's national nominating convention.

primary elections Elections to choose party nominees for public office; may be open or closed.

prior restraint Power of government to prevent publication or to require approval before publication, generally prohibited by the First Amendment.

prior restraint Government actions to restrict publication of a magazine, newspaper, or books on grounds of libel, obscenity, or other legal violations prior to actual publication of the work.

professionalism In politics, a reference to the increasing number of officeholders for whom politics is a full-time occupation.

program budgeting Identifying items in a budget according to the functions and programs they are to be spent on.

progressive taxation System of taxation in which higher income groups pay a larger percentage of their incomes in taxes than do lower income groups.

proportional (flat) taxation System of taxation in which all income groups pay the same percentage of their income in taxes.

proportional representation Electoral system that allocates seats in a legislature based on the proportion of votes each party receives in a national election.

protectionism A policy of high tariffs and quotas on imports to protect domestic industries.

protest party Third party that arises in response to issues of popular concern which have not been addressed by the major parties.

protests Public marches or demonstrations designed to call attention to an issue and motivate others to apply pressure on public officials.

public assistance programs Those social welfare programs for which no contributions are required and only those living in poverty (by official standards) are eligible; includes food stamps, Medicaid, and Family Assistance.

public goods Goods and services that cannot readily be provided by markets, either because they are too expensive for a single individual to buy or because if one person bought them, everyone else would use them without paying.

public opinion Aggregate of preferences and opinions of individuals on significant issues.

public relations Building and maintaining goodwill with the general public.

public-interest groups Interest groups that claim to represent broad classes of people or the public as a whole.

quota Provision of some affirmative action programs in which specific numbers or percentages of positions are open only to minorities and/or women.

radicalism Advocacy of immediate and drastic changes in society, including the complete restructuring of institutions, values, and beliefs. Radicals may exist on either the extreme left or extreme right.

raiding Organized efforts by one party to get its members to cross over in a primary and defeat an attractive candidate in the opposition party's primary.

ranking minority member The minority-party committee member with the most seniority.

ratification Power of a legislature to approve or reject decisions made by other bodies. State legislators or state conventions must ratify constitutional amendments submitted by Congress. The U.S. Senate must ratify treaties made by the president.

Reagan Coalition Combination of economic and social conservatives, religious fundamentalists, and defense-minded anticommunists who rallied behind Republican President Ronald Reagan.

realignment Long-term shift in social-group support for various political parties that creates new coalitions in each party.

recession Decline in the general level of economic activity.

redistricting Drawing of legislative district boundary lines following each ten-year census.

referenda Proposed laws or constitutional amendments submitted to the voters for their direct approval or rejection, found in state constitutions but not in the U.S. Constitution.

regional security Attempt to bring order to international relations during the Cold War by creating regional alliances between a superpower and nations of a particular region.

registration Requirement that prospective voters establish their identity and place of residence prior to an election in order to be eligible to vote.

regressive taxation System of taxation in which lower income groups pay a larger percentage of their incomes in taxes than do higher income groups.

regulation Development by the federal bureaucracy of formal rules for implementing legislation.

remedies and reliefs Orders of a court to correct a wrong, including a violation of the Constitution.

representational federalism Assertion that no constitutional division of powers exists between the nation and the states but the states retain their constitutional role merely by selecting the president and members of Congress.

representative democracy Governing system in which public decision making is delegated to representatives of the people chosen by popular vote in free, open, and periodic elections.

Republican Party One of the two main parties in American politics, it traces its origins to the antislavery and nationalist forces that united in the 1850s and nominated Abraham Lincoln for president in 1860.

republicanism Government by representatives of the people rather than directly by the people themselves.

rescissions Items on which a president wishes to cancel spending.

reserved powers Powers not granted to the national government or specifically denied to the states in the Constitution that are recognized by the Tenth Amendment as belonging to the state governments. This guarantee, known as the Reserved Powers Clause, embodies the principle of American federalism.

responsible party model System in which competitive parties adopt a platform of principles, recruiting candidates and directing campaigns based on the platform, and holding their elected officials responsible for enacting it.

restricted rule Rule that allows specified amendments to be added to a bill under consideration by the House.

retail politics Direct candidate contact with individual voters.

retrospective voting Voting for or against a candidate or party on the basis of past performance in office.

revolving doors The movement of individuals from government positions to jobs in the private sector, using the experience, knowledge, and contacts they acquired in government employment.

rider Amendment to a bill that is not germane to the bill's purposes.

right A reference to the conservative, traditional, anticommunist side of the political spectrum.

roll-call vote Vote of the full House or Senate on which all members' individual votes are recorded and made public.

rule of four At least four justices must agree to hear an appeal (writ of certiorari) from a lower court in order to get a case before the Supreme Court.

rule Stipulation attached to a bill in the House of Representatives that governs its consideration on the floor, including when and for how long it can be debated and how many (if any) amendments may be appended to it.

runoff primary Additional primary held between the top two vote-getters in a primary where no candidate has received a majority of the vote.

safe seat Legislative district in which the incumbent regularly wins by a large margin of the vote.

salient issues Issues about which most people have an opinion.

SALT I First arms limitation treaty between the United States and the Soviet Union, signed in 1972, limiting the total number of offensive nuclear missiles; it included the ABM Treaty that reflected the theory that the population centers of both nations should be left undefended.

SALT II Lengthy and complicated treaty between the United States and the Soviet Union, agreed to in 1979 but never ratified by the U.S. Senate, that set limits on all types of strategic nuclear launch vehicles.

search warrant Court order permitting law-enforcement officials to search a location in order to seize evidence of a crime; issued only for a specified location, in connection with a specific investigation, and on submission of proof that "probable cause" exists to warrant such a search.

second-strike capability Ability of a nation's forces to survive a surprise nuclear attack by the enemy and then to retaliate effectively.

selective perception Mentally screening out information or opinions with which one disagrees.

senatorial courtesy Custom of the U.S. Senate with regard to presidential nominations to the judiciary to defer to the judgment of senators from the president's party from the same state as the nominee.

seniority system Custom whereby the member of Congress who has served the longest on the majority side of a committee becomes its chair and the member who has served the longest on the minority side becomes its ranking member.

separate but equal Ruling of the Supreme Court in the case of Plessy v. Ferguson (1896) to the effect that segregated facilities were legal as long as the facilities were equal.

separation of powers Constitutional division of powers among the three branches of the national government—legislative, executive, and judicial.

set-aside program Program in which a specified number or percentage of contracts must go to designated minorities.

shield laws Laws in some states that give reporters the right to refuse to name their sources or to release their notes in court cases; may be overturned by the courts when such refusals jeopardize a fair trial for a defendant.

single-issue groups Organizations formed to support or oppose government action on a specific issue.

single-issue party Third party formed around one particular cause.

slander Oral statements that are false and malicious and are intended to damage an individual.

social contract Idea that government originates as an implied contract among individuals who agree to obey laws in exchange for protection of their rights.

social insurance programs Social welfare programs to which beneficiaries have made contributions so that they are entitled to benefits regardless of their personal wealth.

social mobility Extent to which people move upward or downward in income and status over a lifetime or generations.

Social Security Social insurance program composed of the Old Age and Survivors Insurance program, which pays benefits to retired workers who have paid into the program and their dependents and survivors, and the Disability Insurance program, which pays benefits to disabled workers and their families.

socialism System of government involving collective or government ownership of economic enterprise, with the goal being equality of results, not merely equality of opportunity.

socialization The learning of a culture and its values.

soft money Campaign contributions, not subject to regulated limits, given to a party for activities such as party building or voter registration, but not directly for campaigns. Soft-money contributions to national parties were banned in 2002.

solicitor general Attorney in the Department of Justice who represents the U.S. government before the Supreme Court and any other courts.

sound bites Concise and catchy phrases that attract media coverage.

sovereign immunity Legal doctrine that individuals can sue the government only with the government's consent.

Soviet Union The Union of Soviet Socialist Republics (USSR) consisting of Russia and its bordering lands and ruled by the communist regime in Moscow, officially dissolved in 1991.

Speaker of the House Presiding officer of the House of Representatives.

spin doctor Practitioner of the art of spin control, or manipulation of media reporting to favor one's own candidate.

splinter party Third party formed by a dissatisfied faction of a major party.

splintering Redistricting in which a strong minority is divided up and diluted to prevent it from electing a representative.

spoils system Selection of employees for government agencies on the basis of party loyalty, electoral support, and political influence.

standard partial preemption Form of partial preemption in which the states are permitted to regulate activities already regulated by the federal government if the state regulatory standards are at least as stringent as the federal government's.

standing committee Permanent committee of the House or Senate that deals with matters within a specified subject area.

standing Requirement that the party who files a lawsuit have a legal stake in the outcome.

stare decisis Judicial precept that the issue has already been decided in earlier cases and the earlier decision need only be applied in the specific case before the bench; the rule in most cases, it comes from the Latin for "the decision stands."

START I First treaty between the United States and the Soviet Union that actually reduced the strategic nuclear arms of the superpowers, signed in 1991.

START II A treaty between the United States and Russia eliminating all multi-warhead land missiles and reducing nuclear weapons stockpiles; signed in 2003.

statutory laws Laws made by act of Congress or the state legislatures, as opposed to constitutional law.

subcommittees Specialized committees within standing committees; subcommittee recommendations must be approved by the full standing committee before submission to the floor.

subcultures Variations on the prevailing values and beliefs in a society.

suffrage Legal right to vote.

Sullivan rule Court guideline that false and malicious statements regarding public officials are protected by the First Amendment unless it can be proven they were known to be false at the time they were made or were made with "reckless disregard" for their truth or falsehood.

superdelegates Delegates to the Democratic Party national convention selected because of their position in the government or the party and not pledged to any candidate.

superpowers Refers to the United States and the Soviet Union after World War II, when these two nations dominated international politics.

Supplemental Security Income (SSI) Public assistance program that provides monthly cash payments to the needy elderly (sixty-five or older), blind, and disabled.

survey research Gathering of information about public opinion by questioning a representative sample of the population.

swing states States that are not considered to be firmly in the Democratic or Republican column.

symbolic speech Actions other than speech itself but protected by the First Amendment because they constitute political expression.

tariff Tax imposed on imported products (also called a customs duty).

tax expenditures Revenues lost to the federal government because of exemptions, exclusions, deductions, and special-treatment provisions in tax laws.

taxes Compulsory payments to the government.

television malaise Generalized feelings of distrust, cynicism, and powerlessness stemming from television's emphasis on the negative aspects of American life.

Temporary Assistance to Needy Families Welfare reform program replacing federal cash entitlement with grants to the states for welfare recipients.

terrorism Title 22 of the U.S. Code, Section 2656 (d): "The term 'terrorism' means premeditated, politically motivated violence perpetrated against noncombatant targets by subnational groups or clandestine agents, usually intended to influence an audience."

third party Political party that challenges the two major parties in an election.

ticket splitter Person who votes for candidates of different parties for different offices in a general election.

total preemption Federal government's assumption of all regulatory powers in a particular field.

totalitarianism Rule by an elite that exercises unlimited power over individuals in all aspects of life.

trade associations Interest groups composed of businesses in specific industries.

transfer payments Direct payments (either in cash or in goods and/or services) by governments to individuals as part of a social welfare program, not as a result of any service or contribution rendered by the individual.

Truman Doctrine U.S. foreign policy, first articulated by President Harry S Truman, that pledged the United States to "support free peoples who are resisting attempted subjugation by armed minorities or by outside pressures."

trustees Legislators who feel obligated to use their own best judgment in decision making.

turnout Number of voters who actually cast ballots in an election, as a percentage of people eligible to register and vote.

turnover Replacement of members of Congress by retirement or resignation, by reapportionment, or (more rarely) by electoral defeat, usually expressed as a percentage of members newly elected.

unanimous consent agreement Negotiated by the majority and minority leaders of the Senate, it specifies when a bill will be taken up on the floor, what amendments will be considered, and when a vote will be taken.

underclass People who have remained poor and dependent on welfare over a prolonged period of time.

unemployment compensation Social insurance program that temporarily replaces part of the wages of workers who have lost their jobs.

unemployment rate Percentage of the civilian labor force who are not working but who are looking for work or waiting to return to or to begin a job.

unfunded mandates Mandates that impose costs on state and local governments (and private industry) without reimbursement from the federal government.

unitary system Constitutional arrangement whereby authority rests with the national government, subnational governments have only those powers given to them by the national government.

values Shared ideas about what is good and desirable.

veto Rejection of a legislative act by the executive branch; in the U.S. federal government, overriding of a veto requires a two-thirds majority in both houses of Congress.

Vietnam War War between non-Communist South Vietnam and Communist North Vietnam from 1956 to 1975, with increasing U.S. involvement, ending with U.S. withdrawal in 1973 and Communist victory in 1975. The war became unpopular in the U.S. after 1968 and caused President Johnson not to run for a second term. More than 58,000 Americans died in the war.

Wall-of-separation doctrine The Supreme Court's interpretation of the No Establishment Clause that laws may not have as their purpose aid to one religion or aid to all religions.

War Powers Act Bill passed in 1973 to limit presidential war-making powers; it restricts when, why, and for how long a president can commit U.S. forces and requires notification of and, in many cases, approval by Congress.

ward Division of a city for electoral or administrative purposes or as a unit for organizing political parties.

Watergate The scandal that led to the forced resignation of President Richard M. Nixon. Adding "gate" as a suffix to any alleged corruption in government suggests an analogy to the Watergate scandal.

whips In both the House and Senate, the principal assistants to the party leaders and next in command to those leaders.

whistle-blower Employee of the federal government or of a firm supplying the government who reports waste, mismanagement, and/or fraud by a government agency or contractor.

White House press corps Reporters from both print and broadcast media assigned to regularly cover the president.

white primary Democratic Party primary elections in many southern counties in the early part of the twentieth century that excluded black people from voting.

writ of certiorari Writ issued by the Supreme Court, at its discretion, to order a lower court to prepare the record of a case and send it to the Supreme Court for review. Most cases come to the Court as petitions for writs of certiorari.

writ of habeas corpus Court order directing public officials who are holding a person in custody to bring the prisoner into court and explain the reasons for confinement; the right to habeas corpus is protected by Article I of the Constitution.

zero-based budgeting Method of budgeting that demands justification for the entire budget request of an agency, not just its requested increase in funding.

Notes

Chapter One

1. For a discussion of various aspects of legitimacy and its measurement in public opinion polls, see M. Stephen Weatherford, "Measuring Political Legitimacy," *American Political Science Review* 86 (March 1992): 140–55.
2. Thomas Hobbes, *Leviathan* (1651).
3. For an explanation of the worldwide growth of democracy, see John Mueller, "Democracy and Ralph's Pretty Good Grocery Store," *American Journal of Political Science* 36 (November 1992): 983–1003.
4. John Locke, *Treatise on Government* (1688).
5. See Barbara S. Gamble, "Putting Civil Rights to a Popular Vote," *American Journal of Political Science* 41 (January 1997): 245–69.
6. James Madison, Alexander Hamilton, and John Jay, *The Federalist Papers* (New York: Mentor Books, 1961), No. 10, p. 81. Madison's *Federalist Papers*, No. 10 and No. 51, are reprinted in the Appendix.
7. E. E. Schattschneider, *Two Hundred Million Americans in Search of a Government* (New York: Holt, Rinehart & Winston, 1969), p. 63.
8. Harold Lasswell and Daniel Lerner, *The Comparative Study of Elites* (Stanford, Calif.: Stanford University Press, 1952), p. 7.
9. C. Wright Mills's classic study, *The Power Elite* (New York: Oxford University Press, 1956), is widely cited by Marxist critics of American democracy, but it can be read profitably by anyone concerned with the effects of large bureaucracies—corporate, governmental, or military—on democratic government.
10. In *Who Rules America?* (New York: Prentice Hall, 1967) and its sequel, *Who Rules America Now?* (New York: Prentice Hall, 1983), sociologist G. William Domhoff argues that America is ruled by an "upper class" who attend the same prestigious private schools, intermarry among themselves, and join the same exclusive clubs. In *Who's Running America?* (New York: Prentice Hall, 1976) and *Who's Running America? The Clinton Years* (New York: Prentice Hall, 1995), political scientist Thomas R. Dye documents the concentration of power and the control of assets in the hands of officers and directors of the nation's largest corporations, banks, law firms, networks, foundations, and so forth. Dye argues, however, that most of these "institutional elites" were not born into the upper class but instead climbed the ladder to success.
11. Yale political scientist Robert A. Dahl is an important contributor to the development of pluralist theory, beginning with his *Preface to Democratic Theory* (Chicago: University of Chicago Press, 1956). He often refers to a pluralist system as a *polyarchy*—literally, a system with many centers of power. See his *Polyarchy* (New Haven, Conn.: Yale University Press, 1971), and for a revised defense of pluralism, see his *Democracy and Its Critics* (New Haven, Conn.: Yale University Press, 1989).

Chapter Two

1. Gunnar Myrdal, *An American Dilemma* (New York: Harper, 1944).
2. See Martin Luther King, Jr., "Letter from Birmingham City Jail," April 16, 1963.
3. For a discussion of the sources and consequences of intolerance in the general public, see James L. Gibson, "The Political Consequences of Intolerance: Cultural Conformity and Political Freedom," *American Political Science Review* 86 (June 1992): 338–52.
4. Quoted in *The Ideas of Equality*, ed. George Abernathy (Richmond, Va.: John Knox Press, 1959), p. 185; also in Herbert McClosky and John Zaller, *The American Ethos: Public Attitudes toward Capitalism and Democracy* (Cambridge, Mass.: Harvard University Press, 1984), p. 72.
5. Quoted in Richard Hofstadter, *The American Political Tradition* (New York: Knopf, 1948), p. 45. Historian Hofstadter describes the thinking of American political leaders from Jefferson and the Founders to Franklin D. Roosevelt.
6. For a discussion of how people balance the values of individualism and opposition to big government with humanitarianism and the desire to help others, see Stanley Feldman and John Zaller, "The Political Culture of Ambivalence: Ideological Responses to the Welfare State," *American Journal of Political Science* 36 (February 1992): 268–307.
7. Robert E. Lane, "Market Justice, Political Justice," *American Political Science Review* 80 (June 1986): 383–402.
8. Greg J. Duncan, *Years of Poverty, Years of Plenty* (Ann Arbor: University of Michigan Press, 1984).
9. *New York Times*/CBS News polls, reported in *New York Times*, February 15, 1993. Copyright © 1993 by The New York Times Company.
10. American Security Council, *The Illegal Immigration Crisis* (Washington, D.C.: ASC, 1994).
11. *Sale v. Haitian Centers Council*, 125 L. Ed. 2d 128 (1993).
12. See Stephen Earl Bennett, "Americans' Knowledge of Ideology, 1980–92," *American Politics Quarterly* 23 (July 1995): 259–78.
13. For evidence that ideological consistency increases with educational level, see William G. Jacoby, "Ideological Identification and Issue Attitude," *American Journal of Political Science* 35 (February 1991): 178–205.
14. Richard Hofstadter, *The Paranoid Style in American Politics* (New York: Knopf, 1965).
15. Francis Fukuyama, *The End of History and the Last Man* (New York: Free Press, 1992).
16. See Robert Kimball, *Tenured Radicals* (New York: Harper & Row, 1990).
17. Herbert Marcuse, *One-Dimensional Man* (Boston: Beacon Press, 1964).
18. Allan Bloom, *The Closing of the American Mind* (New York: Simon & Schuster, 1987), p. 15.

Chapter Three

1. In *Federalist Papers*, No. 53, James Madison distinguishes a "constitution" from a law: a constitution is "established by the people and unalterable by the government, and a law established by the government and alterable by the government."

2. Another important decision on opening day of the Constitutional Convention was to keep the proceedings secret. James Madison made his own notes on the convention proceedings, and they were pub-lished many years later. See Max Ferrand, ed., *The Records of the Federal Convention of 1787* (New Haven, Conn.: Yale University Press, 1911).

3. See Edward Millican, *One United People: The Federalist Papers and the National Idea* (Lexington: University Press of Kentucky, 1990).

4. Charles A. Beard, *An Economic Interpretation of the Constitution* (New York: Macmillan, 1913).

5. Robert E. Brown, *Charles Beard and the Constitution* (Princeton, N.J.: Princeton University Press, 1956).

6. James Madison, *Federalist Papers*, No. 10, reprinted in the Appendix.

7. Alexander Hamilton, *Federalist Papers*, No. 78.

Chapter Four

1. The states are listed in the order in which their legislatures voted to secede. While occupied by Confederate troops, secessionist legislators in Missouri and Kentucky also voted to secede, but Unionist representatives from these states remained in Congress.

2. *Texas v. White*, 7 Wallace 700 (1869).

3. James Madison, *Federalist Papers*, No. 51, reprinted in the Appendix.

4. Ibid.

5. The arguments for "competitive federalism" are developed at length in Thomas R. Dye, *American Federalism: Competition among Governments* (Lexington, Mass.: Lexington Books, 1990).

6. David Osborne, *Laboratories of Democracy* (Cambridge, Mass.: Harvard Business School, 1988).

7. Morton Grodzins, *The American System* (Chicago: Rand McNally, 1966), pp. 8–9.

8. Ibid., p. 265.

9. Charles Press, *State and Community Governments in the Federal System* (New York: Wiley, 1979), p. 78.

10. *Garcia v. San Antonio Metropolitan Transit Authority*, 469 U.S. 528 (1985).

11. See Michael S. Greve, *Real Federalism: Why It Matters, How It Could Happen* (Washington, D.C.: AEI Press, 1999).

12. *U.S. v. Lopez*, 514 U.S. 549 (1995).

13. *Seminole Tribe of Florida v. Florida*, 517 U.S. 44 (1996).

14. *Alden v. Maine*, 67 U.S.L.W. 1401 (1999).

15. *Printz v. U.S.* 521 U.S. 890 (1997).

16. *Brzonkala v. Morrison* (2000).

17. *Federal-State-Local Relations: Federal Grants in Aid*, House Committee on Government Operations, 85th Cong., 2d sess., p. 7.

Chapter Five

1. See James A. Stimson, Michael B. Mackuen, and Robert S. Erikson, "Dynamic Representation," *American Political Science Review* 89 (September 1995): 543–61.

2. Robert S. Erikson and Kent L. Tedin, *American Public Opinion*, 6th ed. (New York: Addison Wesley Longman, 2001).

3. *Public Opinion* 9 (September/October 1986): 32.

4. Erikson and Tedin, *American Public Opinion*, pp. 58–61.

5. For a summary of literature on public opinion, see James Stimson, "Opinion and Representation," *American Political Science Review* 89 (March 1995): 179–83.

6. Sandra K. Schwartz, "Preschoolers and Politics," in *New Directions in Political Socialization*, eds. David C. Schwartz and Sandra K. Schwartz (New York: Free Press, 1975), p. 242.

7. M. Kent Jennings and Richard G. Niemi, *The Political Character of Adolescence* (Princeton, N.J.: Princeton University Press, 1974), p. 41.

8. David O. Sears and Carolyn Funk, "Evidence of the Long-Term Persistence of Adults' Political Predispositions" *Journal of Politics* 61 (February 1999): 1–28.

9. Robert D. Hess and Judith V. Torney, *The Development of Political Attitudes in Children* (Chicago: Aldine, 1977), p. 42.

10. See also Ted G. Jelen, "The Political Consequences of Religious Group Attitudes," *Journal of Politics* 55 (February 1993): 178–90.

11. Geoffrey C. Longman, "Religion and Political Behavior in the United States, "*Public Opinion Quarterly* 61 (Summer 1997): 288–316.

12. See John C. Green, "The Christian Right in the 1994 Elections," *P.S.: Political Science and Politics* 28 (March 1995): 5–23.

13. See M. Kent Jennings, "Residues of a Movement: The Aging of the American Protest Generation," *American Political Science Review* 81 (June 1987): 370–72; M. Kent, Jennings and Richard G. Niemi, *Generational Politics* (Princeton, N.J.: Princeton University Press, 1982).

14. See also James A. Stimson, *Public Opinion in America: Moods, Cycles, and Swings* (Boulder, Colo.: Westview Press, 1991).

15. V.O. Key Jr., *Public Opinion and American Democracy* (New York: Kuopf, 1967), p. 536.

16. *Smith V. Allwright*, 321 U.S. 649 (1944).

17. *Harper v. Virginia State Board of Elections*, 383 U.S. 663 (1966).

18. Congress had earlier passed the Voting Rights Act of 1970, which (1) extended the vote to eighteen-year-olds regardless of state law; (2) abolished residency requirements in excess of thirty days; and (3) prohibited literacy tests. However, there was some constitutional debate about the power of Congress to change state laws on voting age. Although Congress could end racial discrimination, extending the vote to eighteen-year-olds was a different matter. All previous extensions of the vote had come by constitutional amendment. Hence Congress quickly passed the Twenty-sixth Amendment.

19. Staci L. Rhine, "Registration Reform and Turnout," *American Politics Quarterly* 23 (October 1995): 409–26; Stephen Knack, "Does 'Motor Voter' Work?" *Journal of Politics* 57 (August 1995): 796–811; Michael D. Martinez and David B. Hill, "Did Motor Voter Work?" *American Politics Quarterly* 27 (February 1997): 296–315.

20. Richard G. Niemi and Paul S. Herrnson, "Beyond the Butterfly: The Complexity of U.S. Ballots," *Perspectives on Politics* 1 (June, 2003): 317–26.

21. *General Social Survey, 1998* (Chicago: National Opinion Research Center, 1999).

22. John E. Filer, Lawrence W. Kenny, and Rebecca B. Morton, "Redistribution, Income, and Voting," *American Journal of Political Science* 37 (February 1993): 63–87.

23. Sidney Verba, Kay Schlozman, Henry Brady, and Norman Nie, "Citizen Activity:

Who Participates? What Do They Say?" *American Political Science Review* 87 (June 1993): 303–18.

24. See Katherine Tate, "Black Political Participation in the 1984 and 1988 Presidential Elections," *American Political Science Review* 85 (December 1991): 1159–76.

25. John Stuart Mill, *Considerations on Representative Government* (Chicago: Regnery, Gateway, 1962; original publication 1859), p. 144.

26. Ibid., p. 130.

27. Attributed to Arthur Hadley by Austin Ranney in "Non-Voting Is Not a Social Disease," *Public Opinion* 6 (November/December 1983): 17.

28. Quoted in ibid., p. 18.

29. Francis Fox Piven and Richard Cloward, *Why Americans Don't Vote* (New York: Pantheon, 1987).

30. Jack Citrin, Eric Schickler, and John Sides, "What If Everyone Voted?," *American Journal of Political Science* 47 (January 2003) 75–90.

31. Martin Luther King, Jr., "Letter from Birmingham City Jail," April 16, 1963.

Chapter Six

1. For an overview of the mass media in American politics, see Doris A. Graber, *Mass Media and American Politics*, 6th ed. (Washington, D.C.: CQ Press, 2002).

2. Pew Research Center for People and the Press. http://people-press.org June, 2000.

3. See Lance Bennett, *News: The Politics of Illusion*, 4th ed. (White Plains, N.Y.: Longman, 2001).

4. E. E. Schattschneider, *The Semisovereign People* (New York: Holt, Rinehart & Winston, 1961), p. 68.

5. William A. Henry, "News as Entertainment," in *What's News*, ed. Elie Abel (San Francisco: Institute for Contemporary Studies, 1981), p. 133.

6. Shanto Iyengar, *Is Anyone Responsible? How Television Frames Political Issues* (Chicago: University of Chicago Press, 1991).

7. Graber, *Mass Media*, p. 35.

8. Matthew A. Baum, "Sex, Lies, and War: How Soft News Brings Foreign Policy to the Inattentive Public," *American Political Science Review* 96 (March, 2002): 91–109.

9. Larry Sabato, Mark Stencel, and S. Robert Lichter, *Peep Show? Media Politics in an Age of Scandal* (Lanham, Md.: Rowman & Littlefield, 2001).

10. Ben J. Wattenberg, *The Good News Is the Bad News Is Wrong* (New York: Simon & Schuster, 1984).

11. Ted Smith, "The Watchdog's Bite," *American Enterprise* 2 (January/February 1990): 66.

12. Larry Sabato, *Feeding Frenzy: How Attack Journalism Has Transformed American Politics* (New York: Free Press, 1991).

13. Graber, *Mass Media*, p. 946.

14. S. Robert Lichter, Stanley Rothman, and Linda S. Lichter, *The Media Elite* (Bethesda, Md.: Adler and Adler, 1986).

15. David Prindle, "Hollywood Liberalism" *Social Science Quarterly* 71 (March 1993): 121.

16. David C. Barker, "Rushed Decisions: Political Talk Radio and Vote Choice," *Journal of Politics* 61 (May 1999): 527–39.

17. Julianne F. Flowers, Audrey A. Haynes, and Michael H. Crespin, "The Media, the Campaign, and the Message," *American Journal of Political Science* 47 (April 2003): 259–73.

18. See David S. Castle, "Media Coverage of Presidential Primaries," *American Politics Quarterly* 19 (January 1991): 13–42; Christine F. Ridout, "The Role of Media Coverage of Iowa and New Hampshire," *American Politics Quarterly* 19 (January 1991): 43–58.

19. *Media Monitor* Vol. 14 (November/December, 2000).

20. Michael Robinson and Margaret Sheehan, *Over the Wire and on TV* (New York: Sage, 1983), p. 138. See also S. Robert Lichter, Daniel Amundson, and Richard Noyes, *The Video Campaign* (Washington, D.C.: American Enterprise Institute, 1988).

21. *New York Times v. U.S.*, 376 U.S. 713 (1971).

22. *New York Times v. Sullivan*, 376 U.S. 254 (1964).

23. *Reno v. American Civil Liberties Union* 117 S.Ct. 2329 (1997).

24. Bernard Cohen, *The Press and Foreign Policy* (Princeton, N.J.: Princeton University Press, 1963), p. 16.

25. Austin Ranney, *Channels of Power* (New York: Basic Books, 1983), p. 81.

26. Benjamin J. Page, Robert Y. Shapiro, and Glen R. Dempsey, "What Moves Public Opinion," *American Political Science Review* 81 (March 1987): 23–43.

27. National Institute of Mental Health, *Television and Behavior* (Washington, D.C.: Government Printing Office, 1982).

28. Brandon Centerwall, "Exposure to Television as a Risk Factor for Violence," *American Journal of Epidemiology* 129 (April 1989): 643–52.

Chapter Seven

1. Gaetano Mosca, *The Ruling Class* (New York: McGraw-Hill, 1939), p. 51.

2. James Madison, *Federalist Papers*, No. 10, reprinted in the Appendix.

3. George Washington, Farewell Address, September 17, 1796, in *Documents on American History*, 10th ed., eds. Henry Steele Commager and Milton Cantor (Upper Saddle River, N.J.: Prentice Hall, 1988), 1: 172.

4. E. E. Schattschneider, *Party Government* (New York: Holt, Rinehart & Winston, 1942), p. 1.

5. Geofrey C. Layman and Thomas M. Carsey, "Party Polarization and Conflict Extension in the American Electorate," *American Journal of Political Science* 46 (October, 2002): 786–802.

6. Since 1954, only Presidents Kennedy, Johnson, and Carter (all Democrats) worked with their party's majorities in both houses of Congress; President Clinton enjoyed Democratic Party control of the Congress in only his first two years in office. George W. Bush is the only Republican president in a half century to serve with a Republican majority in both the House and Senate. See Harold W. Stanley and Richard C. Niemi, *Vital Statistics on American Politics* (Washington, D.C.: CQ Press, 2003).

7. See Thomas R. Dye and Susan MacManus, *Politics in States and Communities*, 11th ed. (Upper Saddle River, N.J.: Prentice Hall, 2003).

8. *National Election Study*, 2000.

9. Conventions continue to play a modest role in nominations in some states:

   ■ Colorado: Parties may hold a preprimary convention to designate a candidate to be listed first on the primary ballot. All candidates receiving at least 30 percent of the delegate vote will be listed on the primary ballot.

- Connecticut: Party conventions are held to endorse candidates. If no one challenges the endorsed candidate, no primary election is held. If a challenger receives 20 percent of the delegate vote, a primary election will be held to determine the party's nominee in the general election.
- New York: Party conventions choose the party's "designated" candidate in primary elections. Anyone receiving 25 percent of the delegates also appears on the ballot.
- Utah: Party conventions select party's nominees.
- Illinois, Indiana, Michigan, and South Carolina: Party conventions nominate candidates for some minor state offices.

10. For an argument that primary elections force parties to be more responsive to voters, see John G. Geer and Mark E. Shere, "Party Competition and the Prisoner's Dilemma: An Argument for the Direct Primary," *Journal of Politics* 54 (August 1992): 365–74.

11. For an up-to-date listing of state primaries and relevant information about them, see *The Book of the States*, published biannually by the Council of State Governments, Lexington, Kentucky.

12. The U.S. Supreme Court declared that the blanket primary violated the First Amendment freedom of association right of political parties to choose their own candidates. California had adopted a primary system that gave all voters, regardless of party affiliation, ballots that included the names of *all* candidates in *both* parties. Candidates of each party who received the most votes were to become the nominees of those parties and move on to face each other in the general election. But the Court held that the blanket primary forced the parties to open their candidate-selection process "to persons wholly unaffiliated with the party, who may have different views from the party" and therefore violated the First Amendment associational rights of parties (*California Democratic Party v. Jones*, 530 U.S. 567 (2000).

13. Congressional Quarterly, *National Party Conventions 1831–1996* (Washington, D.C.: CQ Press, 1997).

14. For evidence that the national party conventions raise the poll standings of their presidential nominees, see James E. Campbell, Lynna L. Cherry, and Kenneth A. Wink, "The Convention Bump," *American Politics Quarterly* 20 (July 1992): 287–307.

15. See John A. Clark, John M. Bruce, John H. Kessel, and William G. Jacoby, "I'd Rather Switch Than Fight: Lifelong Democrats and Converts to Republicanism among Campaign Activists," *American Journal of Political Science* 35 (August 1991): 577–97.

16. For a scholarly debate over realignment, see Byron E. Schafer, ed., *The End of Realignment: Interpreting American Election Eras* (Madison: University of Wisconsin Press, 1991).

17. See Harold W. Stanley and Richard G. Niemi, "Partisanship and Group Support, 1952–1988," *American Politics Quarterly* 19 (April 1991): 189–210; Patricia Hurley, "Partisan Realignment in the 1980's," *Journal of Politics* 53 (February 1991): 55–63.

18. See Theodore J. Lowi and Joseph Romance, *A Republic of Parties: Debating the Two-Party System* (Lanham, MD: Rowman & Littlefield, 1998).

Chapter Eight

1. Gerald Pomper, *Elections in America* (New York: Dodd, Mead, 1968).

2. Morris P. Fiorina, *Retrospective Voting in American National Elections* (New Haven, Conn.: Yale University Press, 1988).

3. Quoted in *Congressional Quarterly Almanac, 1965* (Washington, D.C.: Congressional Quarterly, Inc., 1966), p. 267.

4. Alan Ehrenhalt, *The United States of Ambition: Politicians, Power and the Pursuit of Office* (New York: Random House, 1991), p. 22.

5. Alan I. Abramowitz, "Incumbency, Campaign Spending, and the Decline of Competition in U.S. House Elections," *Journal of Politics* 53 (February 1991): 55–70.

6. Herbert Alexander, as quoted in Richard R. Lau et al., "The Effects of Negative Political Advertisements," *American Political Science Review* 93 (December 1999): 851–75.

7. Quotation from Richard R. Lau, *op. cit*, p. 851.

8. Lee Sigelman and Emmett H. Buell, Jr., "You Take the High Road and I'll Take the Low Road? The Interplay of Attack Strategies and Tactics in Presidential Campaigns," *The Journal of Politics* 46 (May 2003): 518–31.

9. Richard R. Lau and Gerald M. Pomper, "Effectiveness of Negative Campaigning in U.S. Senate Elections," *American Journal of Political Science* 46 (January 2002): 47–66.

10. Center for Responsive Politics, *The Big Picture: The Money Behind the 2000 Elections* (Washington, D.C., 2001).

11. In the important U.S. Supreme Court decision in *Buckley v. Valeo* in 1976, James L. Buckley, former U.S. senator from New York, and his brother, William F. Buckley, the well-known conservative commentator, argued successfully that the laws limiting an individual's right to participate in political campaigns—financially or otherwise—violated First Amendment freedoms. Specifically, the U.S. Supreme Court held that no government could limit individuals' rights to spend money or publish or broadcast their own views on issues or elections. Candidates can spend as much of their own money as they wish on their own campaigns. Private individuals can spend as much as they wish to circulate their own views on an election, although their contributions to candidates and parties can still be limited. The Court, however, permitted governmental limitations on parties and campaign organizations and allowed the use of federal funds for financing campaigns. *Buckley v. Valeo*, 424 U.S. 1 (1976).

12. See Paul-Henri Guvian and Audrey A. Haynes, "Presidential Nominating Campaigns," *P.S. Political Science and Politics* 36 (April, 2003): 175–180.

13. Lynn Vavreck, Constantine J. Spiliotes and Linda L. Fowler, "The Effects of Retail Politics in the New Hampshire Primary," *American Journal of Political Science* 46 (July 2002): 595–610.

14. William G. Mayer, "Forecasting Presidential Nominations," *P.S. Political Science and Politics* 36 (April 2003): 153–58.

15. University-based political scientists rely heavily on a series of National Election Studies, originated at the Survey Research Center at the University of Michigan, which have surveyed the voting-age population in every presidential election and most congressional elections since 1952.

16. See Martin P. Wattenberg, *The Rise of Candidate-Centered Politics* (Cambridge, Mass.: Harvard University Press, 1991).

17. Responsibility for the economy, nonever, is also affected by the voters' partisanship, ideology, and views about whether the president or Congress is chiefly responsible. See Joseph J. Rudolph, "Who's Responsible for the Economy?," *American Journal of Political Science* 47 (October, 2003): 698–713.

18. For an argument that voters look ahead to the economic future and reward or punish the president based on rational expectations, see Michael B. MacKuen, Robert S. Erickson, and James A. Stimson, "Peasants or Bankers? The American Electorate and the U.S. Economy," *American Political Science Review* 86 (September 1992): 680–95.

Chapter Nine

1. Political scientist David Truman's classic definition of an interest group: "any group that is based on one or more shared attitudes and makes certain demands upon other groups or organizations in society." See *The Governmental Process* (New York: Knopf, 1971), p. 33.
2. James Madison, *Federalist Papers*, No. 10, reprinted in the Appendix.
3. Gale Research Company, *Encyclopedia of Associations* (Detroit: Gale Research, 2001).
4. Frank R. Baumgartner and Beth L. Leech, "Interest Niches and Policy Bandwagons: Patterns of Interest Group Involvement in National Politics," *The Journal of Politics* 63 (November, 2001): 1191–1213.
5. Jeffrey M. Berry, *The New Liberalism: The Rising Power of Citizen Groups* (Washington, D.C.: Brookings Institution Press, 1999).
6. For both theory and survey data on the sources of interest-group mobilization, see Jack L. Walker, *Mobilizing Interest Groups in America: Patrons, Professions, and Social Movements* (Ann Arbor: University of Michigan Press, 1991).
7. Kay Lehmann Scholzman, "What Accent the Heavenly Chorus? Political Equality and the American Pressure System," *Journal of Politics* 46 (November 1984): 1006–32; see also Jeffrey M. Berry, Kent E. Portney, and Ken Thomson, *The Case for Participatory Democracy* (Washington, D.C.: Brookings Institution Press, 1994).
8. Center for Responsive Politics, *Influence, Inc.* 2000 (Washington, D.C., 2001).
9. Quotation from Roger Kersh, "Corporate Lobbyists as Political Actors," in *Interest Group Politics*, 6th ed., eds. Allan J. Ciglar and Burdett A. Loomis (Washington, D.C.: CQ Press, 2002).
10. For evidence that vote buying on congressional roll calls is rare, see Janet M. Grenzke, "Shopping in the Congressional Supermarket: The Currency Is Complex," *American Journal of Political Science* 33 (February 1989): 1–24. But for evidence that committee participation by members of Congress is influenced by political action committee money, see Richard L. Hall and Frank W. Wayman, "Buying Time: Moneyed Interests and the Mobilization of Bias in Congressional Committees," *American Political Science Review* 84 (September 1990): 797–819.
11. See, for example, Mark E. Patterson, "The Presidency and Organized Interests: White House Patterns of Interest Group Liaison," *American Political Science Review* 86 (September 1992): 612–22.
12. Robert H. Salibury, "Who You Know versus what You Know: The use of Government Experience by Washington Lobbyists," *American Journal of Political Science*, vol. 33 (Feb. 1989): 175–95.
13. *Brown v. Board of Education of Topeka*, 349 U.S. 294 (1955).
14. Samuel Huntington, *Political Order in Changing Societies* (New Haven, Conn.: Yale University Press, 1965), p. 28.
15. Mancur Olson, *The Rise and Decline of Nations*. (New Haven, Conn.: Yale University Press, 1982).

Chapter Ten

1. James Madison, *Federalist Papers*, No. 10, reprinted in the Appendix.
2. Ibid.
3. Quoted in Jay M. Schafritz, *The HarperCollins Dictionary of American Government and Politics* (New York: HarperCollins, 1992), p. 56.
4. See David Auerswald and Forrest Maltzman, "Policymaking through Advice and Consent: Treaty Consideration by the United States Senate," *Journal of Politics* 65 (November 2003): 1097–1110.
5. *McGrain v. Doughtery*, 273 U.S. 13J (1927).
6. *Baker v. Carr*, 369 U.S. 186 (1962), *Wesberry v. Sanders*, 370 U.S. 1 (1964).
7. *Gray v. Sanders*, 322 U.S. 368 (1963).
8. *Department of Commerce v. U.S. House of Representatives* 525 U.S. 316 (1999).
9. *Gaffney v. Cummings*, 412 U.S. 763 (1973).
10. *Davis v. Bandemer*, 478 U.S. 109 (1986).
11. Scott W. Desposato and John R. Petrocik, "The Variable Incumbency Advantage: New Voters, Redistricting, and Personal Vote," *American Journal of Political Science* 47 (January 2003): 18–32
12. *Thornburg v. Gingles*, 478 U.S. 30 (1986).
13. *Shaw v. Reno*, 125 I. Ed. 2d 511 (1993).
14. *Miller v. Johnson*, 115 S. Ct. 2475 (1995).
15. See Roger H. Davidson and Walter J. Oleszek, *Congress and Its Members*, 9th ed. (Washington, D.C.: CQ Press, 2004).
16. David Lublin, *The Paradox of Representation: Racial Gerrymandering and Minority Interests in Congress* (Princeton, NJ.: Princeton University Press, 1997). See also David Lublin and D. Stephen Voss, "The Missing Middle," *Journal of Politics* 65 (February 2003). 227–37.
17. *Georgia v. Ashcroft*, June 26, 2003.
18. For an in-depth analysis of who decides to run for Congress and who does not, see Linda L. Fowler and Robert D. McClure, *Political Ambition: Who Decides to Run for Congress* (New Haven, Conn.: Yale University Press, 1990).
19. See Michael K. Moore and John R. Hibbing, "Situational Dissatisfaction in Congress: Explaining Voluntary Departures," *Journal of Politics* 60 (November 1998): 1088–1107.
20. *U.S. Term Limits v Thornton*, 115 S.C. 1842, (1995).
21. See Gary Jacobson, *The Politics of Congressional Elections*, 5th ed. (New York: HarperCollins, 2000).
22. See David Epstein and Peter Zemsky, "Money Talks: Deterring Quality Challengers in Congressional Elections," *American Political Science Review* 89 (June 1995): 295–322.
23. See Thomas E. Mann and Raymond Wolfinger, "Candidates and Parties in Congressional Elections," *American Political Science Review* 84 (September 1990): 545–64.
24. See Mary T. Hanna, "Political Science Caught Flat-Footed by Midterm Elections," *Chronicle of Higher Education*, November 30, 1994, pp. B1–2.
25. See Richard Fenno, *Going Home: Black Representatives and Their Constituents* (Chicago: University of Chicago Press, 2003).
26. Paul S. Herrnson, J. Celeste Lay, and Atiya Kai Stokes, "Women Running 'As Women'," *Journal of Politics* 65 (February 2003): 244–55.
27. U.S. House of Representatives, Commission on Administrative Review, *Administrative Reorganization and Legislative Management*, 95th Cong., 1st sess, H. Doc. 95–232, pp. 17–19.
28. Richard F. Fenno, *Home Style* (Boston: Little, Brown, 1978).
29. Roger H. Davidson and Walter J. Oleszak, *Congress and Its Members* 814 (Washington, D.C.: CQ Press, 2000), p. 19.
30. Glenn R. Parker, *Characteristics of Congress* (Upper Saddle River, N.J.: Prentice Hall, 1989), p. 30.
31. Richard F. Fenno, *The Making of a Senator: Dan Quayle* (Washington, D.C.: CQ Press, 1989), p. 119. Also cited in Davidson and Oleszak, *Congress and Its Members*, 9th ed., p. 120.
32. Davidson and Oleszak, *Congress and Its Members*, 9th ed., p. 129.
33. Ibid., p. 178.
34. Barbara Sinclair, "The Emergence of Strong Leadership in the House of Representatives," *Journal of Politics* 54 (August 1992): 657–84.
35. Gary W. Cox and Eric Magar, "How Much Is Majority Status in the U.S. Congress Worth?" *American Political Science Review* 93 (June 1999): 299–310.
36. Davidson and Oleszak, *Congress and Its Members*, 9th ed. p. 161.
37. John R. Hibbing, *Congressional Careers* (Chapel Hill: University of North Carolina Press, 1991).

38. See Charles Stewart and Tim Groseclose, "The Value of Committee Seats in the United States Senate," *American Journal of Political Science* 43 (July 1999): 963–73.

39. Larry Markinson, *The Cash Constituents of Congress* (Washington, D.C.: CQ Press, 1992).

40. Donald Matthews, *U.S. Senators and Their World* (New York: Vintage Books, 1960).

41. David Rohde, Norman J. Ornstein, and Robert L. Peabody, "Political Change and Legislative Norms," in *Studies of Congress*, ed. Glenn R. Parker (Washington, D.C.: CQ Press, 1985), p. 175.

42. See John R. Hibbing, "Contours of the Modern Congressional Career," *American Political Science Review* 85 (June 1991): 405–28.

43. Richard Fenno, *Power of the Purse* (Boston: Little, Brown, 1965), p. 620.

44. Ibid., p. 73.

45. See David R. Mayhew, *Divided We Govern* (New Haven, CT: Yale University Press, 1991); Sarah A. Binder, "The Dynamics of Legislative Gridlock," *American Political Science Review* 93 (September 1999): 519–33.

46. *Congressional Quarterly Weekly Report*, November 23, 1991, p. 3437.

Chapter Eleven

1. For an argument that presidents encourage people to think of them as "the single head of government and moral leader of the nation who speaks for all of the people," see Barbara Hinckley, *The Symbolic Presidency: How Presidents Portray Themselves* (New York: Routledge, 1991).

2. See Theodore Lowi, *The Personal President* (Ithaca, N.Y.: Cornell University Press, 1987).

3. Presidential address to Congress, September 20, 2001.

4. See Michael Less Benedict, *The Impeachment and Trial of Andrew Johnson* (New York: Norton, 1973).

5. William Howard Taft, *Our Chief Magistrate and His Powers* (New York: Columbia University Press, 1938), p. 138, reprinted in *The Presidency*, ed. John P. Roche (New York: Harcourt Brace Jovanovich, 1964), p. 23.

6. Quoted in Arthur B. Tourtellot, *Presidents on the Presidency* (New York: Doubleday, 1964), pp. 55–56.

7. Quoted in James MacGregor Burns, *John Kennedy: A Political Profile* (New York: Harcourt Brace, 1959), p. 275.

8. *Youngstown Sheet and Tube v. Sawyer*, 343 U.S. 579 (1952).

9. *United States v. Nixon*, 418 U.S. 683 (1974).

10. *Nixon v. Fitzgerald*, 457 U.S. 731 (1982).

11. *Clinton v. Jones*, 520 U.S. 681 (1997).

12. Quoted in Richard Neustadt, *Presidential Power* (New York: Wiley, 1960), p. 9.

13. See George C. Edwards, *The Public Presidency* (New York: St. Martin's Press, 1983).

See also Richard A. Brody, *Assessing Presidents: The Media, Elite Opinion, and Public Support* (Stanford, Calif.: Stanford University Press, 1991).

14. See Paul Brace and Barbara Hinckley, "The Structure of Presidential Approval," *Journal of Politics* 53 (November 1991): 993–1017.

15. See Suzanne L. Pancer, "Toward an understanding of 'Rally' Effect," *Public Opinion Quarterly* 59 (September, 1995): 526–46; Wave J. Aetherington and Michael Nelson: "Anatomy of a Rally Effect," *P.S. Political Science and Politics* 36 (January, 2003): 37–42.

16. John Mueller, *War, Presidents, and Public Opinion* (New York: Wiley, 1973).

17. See George C. Edwards and B. Dan Wood, "Who Influences Whom," *American Political Science Review* 93 (June 1999): 327–44.

18. George C. Edwards and Stephen J. Wayne, *Presidential Leadership*. 6th ed. (Belmont, Calif.: Wadsworth, 2003), p. 118.

19. *Youngstown Sheet and Tube v. Sawyer*, 343 U.S. 579 (1952).

20. Kenneth R. Mayer, "Executive Orders and Presidential Power," *Journal of Politics* 61 (May 1999): 445–66; Christopher J. Deering and Forrest Maltzman, "The Politics of Executive Orders," *Political Research Quarterly* 52 (December 1999): 767–83.

21. See also Jeffrey E. Cohen, *The Politics of the U.S. Cabinet* (Pittsburgh: University of Pittsburgh Press, 1988).

22. See Stanley Rothman and S. Robert Lichter, "How Liberal Are Bureaucrats?" *Regulation*, November–December 1983, pp.

16–22, for survey data on the voting behavior and political ideology of federal bureaucrats.

23. See Bradley H. Patterson, Jr., *The Ring of Power* (New York: Basic Books, 1988).

24. John Kingdon, *Agenda, Alternatives, and Public Policies* (Boston: Little, Brown, 1984), p. 25.

25. See Daniel E. Ingberman and Dennis A. Yao, "Presidential Commitment and the Veto," *American Journal of Political Science* 35 (May 1991): 357–89; and Samuel B. Hoff, "Saying No," *American Politics Quarterly* 19 (July 1991): 310–23.

26. For a discussion of the factors affecting the use of the presidential veto, see John T. Woolley, "Institutions, the Election Cycle, and the Presidential Veto," *American Journal of Political Science* 35 (May 1991): 279–304.

27. *Clinton v. City of New York*, 524 U.S. 417 (1998).

28. G.J.A. O'Toole, *Honorable Treachery: A History of U.S. Intelligence from the American Revolution to the CIA* (New York: Atlantic Monthly Press, 1991).

29. National Commission on Terrorist Attacks upon the United States, *The 9/11 Commission Report*, New York: W.W. Norton, 2004.

30. *Mora v. McNamara*, 389 U.S. 934 (1964); *Massachusetts v. Laird*, 400 U.S. 886 (1970). The Court specifically refused to intervene in the conduct of the Vietnam War by presidents Johnson and Nixon.

31. Jules Witcover, *Crap Shoot: Rolling the Dice on the Vice Presidency* (New York: Crow Publishing, 1992).

Chapter Twelve

1. "Red tape" derives its meaning from the use of reddish tape by seventeenth-century English courts to bind legal documents. Unwrapping court orders entangled one in "red tape." See Herbert Kaufman, *Red Tape: Its Uses and Abuses* (Washington, D.C.: Brookings Institution, 1977).

2. H. H. Gerth and C. Wright Mills, *From Max Weber* (New York: Oxford Press, 1958).

3. Max Neiman, *Defending Government: Why Big Government Works* (Upper Saddle River, N.J.: Prentice Hall, 2000).

4. James Q. Wilson, *Bureaucracy: What Government Agencies Do and Why They Do It* (New York: Basic Books, 1989).

5. William Niskanen, *Bureaucracy and Representative Government* (Chicago: Aldine, 1971).

6. The constitutional question of whether Congress can establish an executive branch commission and protect its members from dismissal by the president was settled in *Humphrey's Executor v. United States* (1935). Franklin Roosevelt fired Humphrey from the Federal Trade Commission despite a fixed term set by Congress. Humphrey died shortly afterward, and when the executors of his estate sued for his back pay, the Supreme Court ruled that his firing was illegal.

7. See Nicholas Henry, *Public Administration and Public Affairs*, 7th ed. (Upper Saddle River, N.J.: Prentice Hall, 1999), Chapter 11.

8. Quoted in U.S. Civil Service Commission, *Biography of an Ideal: A History of the Civil Service System* (Washington, D.C.: Government Printing Office, 1973), p. 16.

9. See U.S. House of Representatives Committee on Post Office and Civil Service,

The Senior Executive Service (Washington, D.C.: Government Printing Office, 1984).

10. Paul C. Light, *Thickening Government: Federal Hierarchy and the Diffusion of Accountability* (Washington, D.C.: Brookings Institution, 1995).

11. David Osborne and Ted Gaebler, *Reinventing Government* (New York: Addison-Wesley, 1992).

12. Al Gore, *Creating a Government That Works Better and Costs Less* (Washington, D.C.: Government Printing Office, 1993).

13. William G. Howell and David E. Lewis, "Agencies by Presidential Design," *Journal of Politics* 64 (November 2002): 1098–1114.

14. Aaron Wildavsky, *The New Politics of the Budgetary Process* (Glenview, Ill.: Scott, Foresman, 1988), p. 8.

15. Robert Crandell and Jerry Ellig, *Economic Deregulation and Consumer Choice* (Fairfax, Va.: Center for Market Processes, 1997).

16. General Accounting Office, *Regulatory Enforcement Fairness Act Report,* 1999.

17. Thomas D. Hopkins, *Regulatory Costs in Profile* (Washington, D.C.: Center for the Study of American Business, 1996).

18. Richard K. Vedder, "Federal Regulation's Impact on the Productivity Slowdown: A Trillion Dollar Drag," *Policy Study,* Center for the Study of American Business, July 1996.

19. For research suggesting that the appointive power is a more important instrument of political control of the bureaucracy than budgets or legislation, see B. Dan Wood and Richard W. Waterman, "The Dynamics of Political Control of the Bureaucracy," *American Political Science Review* 83 (September 1991): 801–28.

20. See Joel D. Aberbach, *Keeping a Watchful Eye: The Politics of Congressional Oversight* (Washington, D.C.: Brookings Institution, 1990).

21. Evidence of the effectiveness of interventions by members of Congress in local offices of federal agencies is provided by John T. Scholz, Jim Twombly, and Barbara Headrick, "Street-Level Political Controls over Federal Bureaucracy," *American Political Science Review* 85 (September 1991): 829–50.

22. Bradley Cannon and Michael Giles, "Recurring Litigants: Federal Agencies before the Supreme Court," *Western Political Quarterly* 15 (September 1972): 183–91; Reginald S. Sheehan, "Federal Agencies and the Supreme Court," *American Politics Quarterly* 20 (October 1992): 478–500.

Chapter Thirteen

1. Alexis de Tocqueville, *Democracy in America* (1835; New York: Mentor Books, 1956), p. 75.

2. Felix Frankfurter, "The Supreme Court and the Public," *Forum* 83 (June 1930): 332.

3. Alexander Hamilton, *Federalist Papers,* No. 78 (New York: Modern Library, 1937), p. 505.

4. *Marbury v. Madison,* 1 Cranch 137 (1803).

5. *Buckley v. Valeo,* 424 U.S. 1 (1976).

6. *U.S. v. Morrison* (May 15, 2000).

7. *Ex parte Milligan,* 4 Wallace 2 (1866).

8. *Youngstown Sheet and Tube Co. v. Sawyer,* 343 U.S. 579 (1952).

9. *United States v. Nixon,* 418 U.S. 683 (1974).

10. *Clinton v. Jones,* 520 U.S. 681 (1997).

11. *Brown v. Board of Education of Topeka,* 347 U.S. 483 (1954).

12. *Roe v. Wade,* 410 U.S. 113 (1973).

13. *Lawrence v. Texas* (June 26, 2003).

14. *West Virginia Board of Education v. Barnette,* 319 U.S. 624 (1943).

15. Quoted in Henry J. Abraham, *Justices and Presidents,* 3rd ed. (New York: Oxford University Press, 1992), p. 7.

16. Quoted in Charles P. Curtis, *Lions under the Throne* (Boston: Houghton Mifflin, 1947), p. 281.

17. Lee Epstein and Thomas G. Walker, *Constitutional Law for a Changing America,* 3rd ed. (Washington, D.C.: CQ Press, 1998), pp. 33–34.

18. William O. Douglas, "Stare Decisis," *Record,* April 1947, cited in Henry J. Abraham, *The Judicial Process* (New York: Oxford University Press, 1968), p. 58.

19. *Flast v. Cohen,* 392 U.S. 83 (1968).

20. *Gideon v. Wainright,* 372 U.S. 335 (1963).

21. *Missouri v. Jenkins,* 110 S.C. 1651 (1990).

22. *Morrison v. Olson,* 487 U.S. 654 (1988).

23. Robert Scigliano, *The Supreme Court and the Presidency* (New York: Free Press, 1971), pp. 147–48.

24. See Bryon J. Moraski and Charles R. Shipan, "The Politics of Supreme Court Nominations," *American Journal of Political Science* 43 (October 1999): 1069–95.

25. See Charles R. Shipan and Megan L. Shannon, "Delaying Justices, *American Journal of Political Science* 47 (October, 2003): 654–68; Sarah A. Binder and Forrest Maltzman, "Senotorial Delay in Confirming Federal Judges," *American Journal of Political Science* 46 (January 2002): 190–99.

26. At one time the U.S. Supreme Court was legally required to accept certain "writs of appeal," but today very few cases come to the Court in this fashion.

27. *University of California Regents v. Bakke,* 438 U.S. 265 (1978).

28. Thomas Marshall, *Public Opinion and the Supreme Court* (New York: Unwin Hyman, 1989), p. 97.

29. Lee Epstein and C. K. Rowland, "Debunking the Myth of Interest Group Invincibility," *American Political Science Review* 85 (1991): 205–17.

30. *Bush v. Gore,* December 12, 2000.

31. *Gore v. Harris,* Florida Supreme Court, December 8, 2000.

32. Gallup News Service, December 12, 2000.

33. James L. Gibson, et al., "Measuring Attitudes toward the United States Supreme Court," *American Journal of Political Science* 47 (April 2003): 354–67; Stephen P. Nicholson and Robert H. Howard, "Framing Support for the Supreme Court in the Aftermath of *Bush v. Gore," Journal of Politics* 65 (August, 2003): 676–95.

34. President Andrew Jackson's comments came in response to the Court's ruling in the case of *Cherokee Nation v. Georgia* (1831) and *Worcester v. Georgia* (1832), which forbade the federal or state governments from seizing Native American lands and forcing the people to move. Refusal by Jackson, an old "Indian fighter," to enforce the Court's decisions resulted in the infamous "Trail of Tears," the forced march of the Georgia Cherokees that left one-quarter of them dead along the path west.

35. *Grove City College v. Bell,* 465 U.S. 555 (1984).

36. *Pollock v. Farmer's Loan,* 158 U.S. 601 (1895).

Chapter Fourteen

1. James Madison, *Federalist Papers,* No. 10, reprinted in the Appendix.

2. *West Virginia Board of Education v. Barnette,* 319 U.S. 624 (1943).

3. *Slaughter-House Cases,* 16 Wallace 36 (1873).

4. *Hurtado v. California,* 110 U.S. 516 (1884).

5. *Gitlow v. New York,* 268 U.S. 652 (1925).

6. For an argument that Madison and some other framers not only were concerned with lessening religious conflict but also were hostile to religion generally, see Thomas Lindsay, "James Madison on Religion and Politics," *American Political Science Review* 85 (December 1991): 1051–65.

7. *Reynolds v. United States,* 98 U.S. 145 (1879).

8. *Pierce v. Society of Sisters,* 268 U.S. 510 (1925).

9. *Cantwell v. Connecticut,* 310 U.S. 296 (1940).

10. *Employment Division v. Smith,* 494 U.S. 872 (1990).

11. *Wisconsin v. Yoder,* 406 U.S. 295 (1972).

12. *Church of Lukumi Babalu Aye v. City of Hialeah* 508 U.S. 520 (1993).

13. *Bob Jones University v. United States,* 461 U.S. 574 (1983).

14. *Employment Division of Oregon v. Smith,* 494 U.S. 872 (1990).

15. *Goldman v. Weinberger,* 475 U.S. 503 (1986).

16. *Everson v. Board of Education,* 330 U.S. 1, 15, 16 (1947).

17. *Zorach v. Clausen,* 343 U.S. 306 (1952).

18. Opening public meetings with prayer was ruled constitutional as "a tolerable acknowledgment of beliefs widely held among the people of this country." *Marsh v. Chambers,* 463 U.S. 783 (1983).

19. *Lemon v. Kurtzman,* 403 U.S. 602 (1971).

20. *Muebler v. Adams,* 463 U.S. 388 (1983).

21. *Tilton v. Richardson,* 403 U.S. 672 (1971).

22. *Lambs Chapel v. Center Moriches Union Free School District,* 508 U.S. 384 (1993).

23. *Rosenberger v. University of Virginia,* 515 U.S. 819 (1995).

24. *Walz v. Tax Commission,* 397 U.S. 664 (1970).

25. *Board of Education v. Mergens,* 497 U.S. 111 (1990).

26. *McGowan v. Maryland,* 366 U.S. 429 (1961), and *Braunfeld v. Brown,* 366 U.S. 599 (1961).

27. *County of Allegbeny v. ACLU,* 492 U.S. 573 (1989).

28. *Edwards v. Aguillard,* 482 U.S. 578 (1987).

29. *Engle v. Vitale,* 370 U.S. 421 (1962).

30. *Abington School District v. Schempp,* 374 U.S. 203 (1963).

31. *Wallace v. Jaffree,* 472 U.S. 38 (1985).

32. *Lee v. Weisman,* 505 U.S. 577 (1992).

33. *Santa Fe Independent School District v. Doe,* 120 S.Ct. 2266 (2000).

34. *Zelman v. Simmons-Harris,* June 27, 2002.

35. *Schenck v. United States,* 249 U.S. 47 (1919).

36. *Gitlow v. New York,* 268 U.S. 652 (1925).

37. *Schenck v. United States,* 249 U.S. 47, 52 (1919).

38. *Whitney v. California,* 274 U.S. 357, 377 (1927), concurring opinion.

39. *Thomas v. Collins,* 323 U.S. 516 (1945).

40. *Dennis v. United States,* 341 U.S. 494 (1951).

41. *Yates v. United States,* 354 U.S. 298 (1957).

42. *Albertson v. Subversive Activities Control Board,* 382 U.S. 70 (1965).

43. *Whitebill v. Elkins,* 389 U.S. 54 (1967).

44. *United States v. Robel,* 389 U.S. 258 (1967).

45. *Aptheker v. Secretary of State,* 378 U.S. 500 (1964).

46. *Tinker v. Des Moines Independent Community School District,* 393 U.S. 503 (1969).

47. *Texas v. Johnson,* 491 U.S. 397 (1989).

48. *Chaplinsky v. New Hampshire,* 315 U.S. 568 (1942).

49. *Terminiello v. Chicago,* 337 U.S. 1 (1949).

50. *Coben v. California,* 403 U.S. 15 (1971).

51. Justice Louis D. Brandeis opinion in *Whitney v. California,* 274 U.S. 357 (1927).

52. *R. A. V. v. City of St. Paul, Minnesota,* 505 U.S. 377 (1992).

53. *Wisconsin v. Mitchell,* 508 U.S. 476 (1993).

54. *Virginia State Board of Pharmacy v. Virginia Consumer Council, Inc.,* 425 U.S. 748 (1976).

55. *Bates v. Arizona State Bar,* 433 U.S. 350 (1977).

56. *Linmark Associates, Inc. v. Township of Willingboro,* 431 U.S. 85 (1977).

57. *New York Times v. Sullivan,* 376 U.S. 254 (1964).

58. *Griswold v. Connecticut,* 381 U.S. 479 (1965).

59. *Roe v. Wade,* 410 U.S. 113 (1973).

60. *Harris v. McRae,* 448 U.S. 297 (1980).

61. *Planned Parenthood v. Casey,* 510 U.S. 110 (1992).

62. *Stenberg v. Carbart,* June 28, 2000.

63. *Bowers v. Hardwick,* 478 U.S. 186 (1986).

64. *Lawrence Texas* (June 26, 2003).

65. *Stanley v. Georgia* (1969).

66. *Washington v. Glucksberg,* 117 S.Ct. 2258 (1997).

67. *Gertz v. Robert Welch, Inc.,* 418 U.S. 323 (1974).

68. *Roth v. United States,* 354 U.S. 476 (1957).

69. *Jacobellis v. Ohio,* 378 U.S. 184 (1964).

70. *Jacobellis v. Ohio,* 378 U.S. 184 (1964).

71. *Roth v. United States,* 354 U.S. 476 (1957).

72. Bob Woodward and Scott Armstrong, *The Brethren* (New York: Avon, 1979), p. 233.

73. *Miller v. California,* 5413 U.S. 15 (1973).

74. *Barnes v. Glenn Theatre,* 501 U.S. 560 (1991).

75. *Reno v. American Civil Liberties Union,* 117 S.Ct. 2329 (1997).

76. *Near v. Minnesota,* 283 U.S. 697 (1931).

77. *New York Times v. United States,* 403 U.S. 713 (1971).

78. *Mutual Film Corp. v. Industrial Commission,* 236 U.S. 230 (1915).

79. *Times Film Corporation v. Chicago,* 365 U.S. 43 (1961).

80. *Freedman v. Maryland,* 380 U.S. 51 (1965).

81. *Young v. American Mini Theaters, Inc.,* 427 U.S. 50 (1976).

82. *Red Lion Broadcasting Co. v. Federal Communications Commission,* 395 U.S. 367 (1969).

83. *Miami Herald Publishing Co. v. Tornillo,* 418 U.S. 241 (1974).

84. *Branzburg v. Hayes,* 408 U.S. 665 (1972).

85. *NAACP v. Alabama ex rel. Patterson,* 357 U.S. 449 (1958).

86. *Healy v. James,* 408 U.S. 169 (1972).

87. *National Socialist Party of America v. Skokie,* 432 U.S. 43 (1977).

88. *Frisby v. Schultz,* 487 U.S. 474 (1988).

89. *Schenck v. Pro Choice Network of Western New York,* 519 U.S. 357 (1997).

90. James Madison, *Federalist Papers,* No. 46.

91. *Ex parte Milligan,* 4 Wallace 2 (1866).

92. *Duncan v. Kabanamosby,* 327 U.S. 304 (1946).

93. *Illinois v. Gates,* 462 U.S. 213 (1983).

94. *Arizona v. Hicks,* 480 U.S. 321 (1987).

95. *Knowles v. Iowa,* 525 U.S. 113 (1998).

96. *Olmstead v. U.S.,* 277 U.S. 438 (1928).

97. *Katz v. U.S.,* 309 U.S. 347 (1967).

98. *Veronia School District v. Acton,* 515 U.S. 646 (1995).

99. *Chandler v. Miller,* 520 U.S. 305 (1997).

100. *United States v. Watson,* 423 U.S. 411 (1976).

101. *Payton v. New York,* 445 U.S. 573 (1980).

102. *Spano v. New York,* 360 U.S. 315 (1959).

103. *Gideon v. Wainwright,* 372 U.S. 335 (1963).

104. *Escobedo v. Illinois,* 378 U.S. 478 (1964).

105. *Miranda v. Arizona,* 384 U.S. 436 (1966).

106. *Mapp v. Ohio,* 367 U.S. 643 (1961).

107. *United States v. Leon,* 468 U.S. 897 (1984).

108. *Illinois v. Perkins,* 497 U.S. 177 (1990).

109. *United States v. Salerno,* 481 U.S. 739 (1987).

110. *U.S. v. Marion,* 404 U.S. 307 (1971).

111. *Barker v. Wingo,* 407 U.S. 514 (1972).

112. *Illinois v. Allen,* 397 U.S. 337 (1970).

113. *Maryland v. Craig,* 497 U.S. 1 (1990).

114. *Brady v. Maryland,* 373 U.S. 83 (1963).

115. *Batson v. Kentucky,* 476 U.S. 79 (1986).

116. *Sheppard v. Maxwell,* 384 U.S. 333 (1966).

117. *Williams v. Florida,* 399 U.S. 78 (1970).

118. *Johnson v. Louisiana,* 406 U.S. 356 (1970); *Apodaca v. Oregon,* 406 U.S. 404 (1972).

119. U.S. Department of Justice, *The Prevalence of Guilty Pleas* (Washington, D.C.: Government Printing Office, 1984).

120. *U.S. v. Perez,* 9 Wheat. 579 (1824).

121. *Heath v. Alabama,* 474 U.S. 82 (1985).

122. *Furman v. Georgia,* 408 U.S. 238 (1972).

123. *Gregg v. Georgia,* 428 U.S. 153 (1976); *Proffitt v. Florida,* 428 U.S. 242 (1976); *Jurek v. Texas,* 428 U.S. 262 (1976).

124. *Ring v. Arizona,* June 24, 2002.

125. *Atkins v. Virginia,* June 20, 2002.

126. *McCleskey v. Kemp,* 481 U.S. 279 (1987).

127. *Felker v. Turpin,* 518 U.S. 1051 (1996).

Chapter Fifteen

1. *Dred Scott v. Sandford,* 60 U.S. 393 (1857).

2. See C. Vann Woodward, *Reunion and Reaction* (Boston: Little, Brown, 1951), and Woodward, *The Strange Career of Jim Crow* (New York: Oxford University Press, 1957).

3. *Civil Rights Cases,* 100 U.S. 3 (1883).

4. *Plessy v. Ferguson,* 163 U.S. 537 (1896).

5. *Sweatt v. Painter,* 339 U.S. 629 (1950).

6. *Brown v. Board of Education of Topeka,* 347 U.S. 483 (1954).

7. Kenneth Clark, *Dark Ghetto* (New York: Harper & Row, 1965), p. 75.

8. The Supreme Court ruled that Congress was bound to respect the Equal Protection Clause of the Fourteenth Amendment even though the amendment is directed at states, because equal protection is a liberty guaranteed by the Fifth

Amendment. *Bolling v. Sharpe*, 347 U.S. 497 (1954).

9. *Brown v. Board of Education of Topeka* (II), 349 U.S. 294 (1955).

10. *Alexander v. Holmes Board of Education*, 396 U.S. 19 (1969).

11. *Swann v. Charlotte-Mecklenburg County Board of Education*, 402 U.S. (1971).

12. *Milliken v. Bradley*, 418 U.S. 717 (1974).

13. *Board of Education v. Dowell*, 498 U.S. 550 (1991).

14. Martin Luther King, Jr., "Letter from Birmingham City Jail," April 16, 1963.

15. *University of California Regents v. Bakke*, 438 U.S. 265 (1978).

16. Bakke's overall grade point average was 3.46, and the average for special admissions students was 2.62. Bakke's MCAT scores were verbal, 96; quantitative, 94; science, 97; general information, 72. The average MCAT scores for special admissions students were verbal, 34; quantitative, 30; science, 37; general information, 18.

17. *United Steelworkers of America v. Weber*, 443 U.S. 193 (1979).

18. *United States v. Paradise*, 480 U.S. 149 (1987).

19. *Firefighters Local Union $$$1781 v. Stotts*, 467 U.S. 561 (1984).

20. *City of Richmond v. Crosen Co.*, 488 U.S. 469 (1989).

21. *Adarand Construction v. Pena*, 132 L. Ed., 2d 158 (1995).

22. *Wards Cove Packing Co., Inc., v. Antonio*, 490 U.S. 642 (1989).

23. *Hopwood v. Texas*, 116 S.Ct. 2581 (1996).

24. *Grutter v. Bollinger* (June 23, 2003).

25. *Gratz v. Bollinger* (June 23, 2003).

26. U.S. Department of Education, Office of Civil Rights, "Race-neutral Alternatives in Postsecondary Education," March, 2003.

27. State of California, Proposition 209 "Prohibition Against Discrimination or Preferential Treatment by State and Other Public Entities," http://vote96.ss.ca.gov.

28. *Coalition for Economic Equity v. Pete Wilson*, Ninth Circuit Court of Appeals, April 1997.

29. Rudolpho O. dela Garza et al., *Latino Voices: Mexican, Puerto Rican, and Cuban Perspectives on American Politics* (Boulder, Colo.: Westview Press, 1992).

30. See F. Luis Garcia, *Latinos in the Political System* (Notre Dame, Ind.: Notre Dame University Press, 1988).

31. Linda Chavez, "Tequila Sunrise: The Slow but Steady Progress of Hispanic Immigrants," *Policy Review* (Spring 1989): 64–67.

32. Peter Mathiessen, *Sal Si Puedes: Cesar Chavez and the New American Revolution* (New York: Random House, 1969).

33. *Plyer v. Doe*, 457 U.S. 202 (1982).

34. *Morton v. Mancari*, 417 U.S. 535 (1974).

35. See Joseph P. Shapiro, *No Pity: People with Disabilities Forging a New Civil Rights Movement* (New York: Times Books/Random House, 1993).

36. *U.S. News & World Report*, February 9, 1998.

37. *The Chronicle of Higher Education*, December 8, 2000.

38. *Bradwell v. Illinois*, 16 Wall 130 (1873).

39. *Reed v. Reed*, 404 U.S. 71 (1971).

40. *Stanton v. Stanton*, 421 U.S. 7 (1975).

41. *Craig v. Boren*, 429 U.S. 190 (1976).

42. *Dothard v. Rawlinson*, 433 U.S. 321 (1977).

43. *Arizona v. Norris*, 103 S.Ct. 3492 (1983).

44. *EEOC v. Madison Community School District*, 55 U.S.L.W. 2644 (1987).

45. *Michael M. v. Superior Court of Sonoma County*, 450 U.S. 464 (1981).

46. *Rostker v. Goldberg*, 453 U.S. 57 (1981).

47. *Statistical Abstract of the United States*, 2002, p. 440.

48. Susan Fraker, "Why Women Aren't Getting to the Top," *Fortune*, April 16, 1984, pp. 40–45.

49. *San Antonio Independent School District v. Rodriquez*, 411 U.S. 1 (1973).

50. *Williamson v. Lee Optical of Oklahoma*, 348 U.S. 483 (1955).

51. *Gideon v. Wainwright*, 372 U.S. 335 (1963).

52. *Harper v. Virginia State Board of Elections*, 383 U.S. 663 (1966).

53. *Harris v. McRae*, 448 U.S. 297 (1980).

54. *Rodriquez v. San Antonio Independent School District*, 411 U.S. 1 (1973).

55. *Serrano v. Priest*, 5 Cal. 3d 584 (1971).

Chapter Sixteen

1. Paul Samuelson, *Economics*, 12th ed. (New York: McGraw-Hill, 1985), p. 5.

2. For an argument that the money supply expands in election years in most democracies, see Edward R. Tufte, *Political Control of the Economy* (Princeton, N.J.: Princeton University Press, 1978).

3. GDP differs very little from gross national product, GNP, which is often used to compare the performance of national economies.

4. Richard B. Freeman, "Are Your Wages Set in Beijing?" *Journal of Economic Perspectives* 9 (Summer 1995): 15.

5. For a revealing case study of interest-group efforts to maintain tax breaks during the struggle over the Tax Reform Act of 1986, see Jeffrey H. Birnbaum and Alan S. Murray, *Showdown at Gucci Gulch* (New York: Random House, 1986).

6. "The Underground Economy," National Center for Policy Analysis, 1998.

7. Joseph A. Pechman, *Federal Tax Policy*, 5th ed. (Washington, D.C.: Brookings Institution, 1987).

Chapter Seventeen

1. Christopher Jenks and Paul E. Peterson, eds., *The Urban Underclass* (Washington, D.C.: Brookings Institution, 1991). See also William A. Kelso, *Poverty and the Underclass* (New York: New York University Press, 1994).

2. See William Julius Wilson, *The Truly Disadvantaged* (Chicago: University of Chicago Press, 1987).

3. See Michael B. Katz, *In the Shadow of the Poorhouse* (New York: Basic Books, 1996).

4. See Charles Murray, *Losing Ground* (New York: Basic Books, 1984).

5. National telephone poll, March 2001, reported in the *Los Angeles Times*.

Chapter Eighteen

1. Hans Morgenthau, *Politics among Nations*, 5th ed. (New York: Knopf, 1973), p. 27.

2. George F. Kennan, writing under the pseudonym "X," "Sources of Soviet Conduct," *Foreign Affairs* 25 (July 1947): 25.

3. Frank Snepp, *Decent Interval* (New York: Random House, 1977).

4. George C. Herring, *America's Longest War* (New York: Random House, 1979), p. 262.

5. See Caspar W. Weinberger, "The Uses of Military Force," *Defense* (Arlington, Va.: American Forces Information Services Survey, 1985), pp. 2–11.

6. Morgenthau, *Politics among Nations*, p. 80.

Photo Credits

Index

presidential campaign strategy and, 267
removing, 270–71
in representational federalism, 118
swing states and, 267, 269
12th Amendment and, 200, 202
2000 election and, 69, 266, 484–86
Electronic surveillance, 523–24
Eleventh Amendment, 79, 95
Elitism, 16–17, 20
intelligence and, 34
weak public opinion and, 147–48
Emancipation Proclamation, 539
EMILY's List, 257, 306
Encryption programs, 191
End of history, 48
Enemy combatants, 522
Engels, Friedrich, 46
Engle v. Vitale, 500
Enlightenment, 26
Entertainment Tonight, 178
Entitlement programs, 588, 589. *See also* Social Security
government spending on, 588
Entitlements, 124, 610–11
Enumerated powers, 77, 109
Environmental Defense Fund, 310
Environmentalism, 230
globalization and, 587
Environmental Protection Agency (EPA), 125, 309, 421, 430, 445–47
interest groups and, 452
Equal Employment Opportunity Commission (EEOC), 431, 445–47
affirmative action and, 550–51
disabled people and, 565
interest groups and, 452
women in, 568
Equality, 12, 537–75
affirmative action and, 550–56
Civil Rights Acts and, 545–48
definition of, 537
dilemmas in, 27–30
fairness and, 29, 30
gender, 566–70, 572
income/wealth and, 30–33
liberalism and, 42–43

of opportunity, 28, 537, 548–51
political, 28
politics of, 537
in politics vs. economics, 29–30
of results, 28–29, 537, 548–51
segregation and, 539–45
slavery and, 537–39
Equal Protection Clause, 323
affirmative action and, 552
death penalty and, 533
diversity and, 554–55
gay marriage and, 510–11
gerrymandering and, 326–27
reasonable classifications and, 571
women and, 566–67
Equal Rights Amendment (ERA), 79–80, 568
Equal time rule, 515
Equal-time rule, 187
Erlichman, John, 382
Ervin, Sam, 160
Escobedo v. Illinois, 526
Espionage Act (1917), 502
Estate taxes, 596
Ethics, congressional, 365–66
Ethics in Government Act, 310
Ethnic conflicts, 633, 638
Euro, the, 104
European Community, 104
European Parliament, 104
European Union, 104–5
Evers, Medgar, 546
Evidence, illegally obtained, 526–27
Exceptionalism, 138
Excise taxes, 596
Exclusionary rule, 526–27
Executive agreements, 402–3
Executive branch, U.S. *See* Bureaucracy; President
Executive orders, 391–93
Executive privilege, 382–83
Ex parte Milligan, 460–61
Ex post facto laws, 522–23
Exposure, media, 184
Externalities, 9
Extremism, 45

F

Factions
federalism and, 103, 106–7
interest groups as, 284–87
Madison on, 13–14, 75
political parties as, 199
Fair Deal, 205
Fair housing, 548

Fairness, 29, 30, 515
Falwell, Jerry, 292
Family, in socialization, 137
Family Assistance, 611
Family Channel, 292
Family Leave Act (1993), 351
Family Medical Leave Act, 44
Farm interest groups, 284, 290
Fascism, 46
Fat cats, 252
Faubus, Orval, 115, 410
Federal Advisory Council, 580
Federal Bureau of Investigation (FBI), 112, 191, 366
Federal Communications Commission (FCC), 248, 393
censorship by, 515
creation of, 186
disabled people and, 565
freedom of speech and, 508
media conglomerates and, 186–87
Federal courts, 465–70. *See also* Supreme Court, U.S.
of appeals, 465–66
appeals to state courts from, 467
caseload of, 467–70
circuit, 465–66
district, 465
jurisdiction of, 465, 467
Federal Election Campaign Act (1972), 250, 259
judicial review of, 460
Federal Elections Commission (FEC), 153, 233, 250, 253, 258–60
Federal Energy Regulatory Commission, 431
Federal Equal Credit Opportunity Act (1974), 568
Federal Highway Act (1916), 115
Federal Highway Act (1956), 362
Federal Home Loan Bank, 431
Federal Housing Administration (FHA), 588–89
Federalism, 67, 100–129
arguments for, 103–9
centralized, 116
coercion in, 125–27
confederation vs., 101, 103
cooperative, 113, 116
definition of, 101
devolution and, 123, 124–25
discrimination and, 108
dual, 113
evolution of American, 112–18

flow of money and power in, 120–25
new, 117
original design of, 109–12
representational, 117–18
revival of, 118–20
state-centered, 113
union and states in, 101–3
Federalist Papers, The (Madison, Hamilton, Jay), 74
on factions, 13–14, 75
on impeachment, 380
on the right to bear arms, 518
Federalists, 77, 199–202
Federal Maritime Commission, 431
Federal Register, 421, 448
Federal Reserve Banks, 580
Federal Reserve Board, 393, 580
Federal Reserve Notes, 580
Federal Reserve System, 430–31, 432, 577, 579–80
Federal Trade Commission, 431, 508
Feeding frenzies, 180
Feinstein, Dianne, 44, 338, 521
FICA. *See* Social Security
Field, Stephen J., 598
Fifteenth Amendment, 79, 96, 114, 150, 538
Fifth Amendment, 78, 94, 495
Double Jeopardy Clause, 112
illegal immigrants and, 39
shield laws and, 515–16
Fighting words doctrine, 505
Filibusters, 353, 475–76
Film rating system, 515
Filtering software, 191
Firefighters Local Union 1784 v. Stotts, 552
First Amendment, 78, 93
freedom of religion in, 494–502
freedom of speech in, 502–8
Internet and, 191
libel/slander and, 187–88
media and, 172–73
negative campaigns and, 246–47
obscenity and, 512–14
text of, 495
First Continental Congress (1774), 54, 59
Fiscal policy, 577, 578–79
Fiscal year, 439
Flag burning, 506
Flat taxation, 597, 598

single-issue, 230

splinter, 230–31

winner-take-all system and, 235

Thirteenth Amendment, 79, 96, 114, 497, 538

Thomas, Clarence, 475, 476, 477, 482–83

Thornburg v. Gingles, 327

Three-fifths Compromise, 62, 537–38

Thurmond, Strom, 364

Ticket splitters, 220

Tilden, Samuel, 270, 540

Tocqueville, Alexis de, 457

Torricelli, Robert, 366

Tort law, 289

Totalitarianism, 14

Total preemption, 125

Tower, John, 395, 429

Town meetings, 15

Trade. *See also* Globalization
free, 584, 586–87
international agreements on, 586
protectionism in, 583–84

Trade associations, 289

Trail of Tears, 562

Transfer payments, 605

Transportation Security Administration, 429

Treasury bonds, 590

Treasury Department, 112, 426, 579

Treaties, 321, 402

Treaty of Moscow (2002), 640

Trials, right to fair, 528–29. *See also* Judicial system, Texas; Judicial system, U.S.

Truman, Harry, 381, 384, 389
Cold War and, 633–34
desegregation and, 391
Fair Deal, 205
steel mill seizure by, 393, 461

Truman Doctrine, 362, 633–34

Trustees, 360

Tsongas, Paul, 391

Turner, Ted, 192

Turnover, congressional, 331

Tuskegee Institute, 542

Twelfth Amendment, 79, 95, 200, 202

Twentieth Amendment, 79, 97

Twenty-fifth Amendment, 79, 98–99, 153
presidential succession and, 374–75, 378

Twenty-first Amendment, 78, 79, 97

Twenty-fourth Amendment, 79, 98, 152

Twenty-second Amendment, 79, 98, 374

Twenty-seventh Amendment, 79, 99, 341

Twenty-sixth Amendment, 79, 99, 121

Twenty-third Amendment, 79, 98

Two-party system, 232–35

Tyler, John, 202

U

Unanimous consent agreement, 353

Underclass, 605, 606

Underground economy, 595–96

Unemployment compensation, 611

Unemployment rates, 581–92, 608

Unfunded mandates, 126–27

Unilateralism, 408–9

Unitary system, 101

United Farm Workers, 559

United Nations, 401–2, 402
formation of, 631–32
national security and, 631–32, 633
Operation Desert Storm and, 645

United States v. Morrison, 460

United States v. Paradise, 552

United States v. Richard m. Nixon, 382

United Steelworkers of America v. Weber, 552

United We Stand, 233

Universal coverage, 624–25

Universe, research, 132

University of California Regents v. Bakke, 479–80, 551–52

University of Michigan, 507, 554

U.S. Conference of Mayors, 294

U.S. Conference of Mayors, 285

U.S. marshals, 465

U.S. Postal Service, 432

U.S. vs. Lopez, 118–19

V

Values. *See also* Conservatism; Liberalism
conditions vs., 25
conflict over, 26

congressional voting and personal, 359–60

cultural consensus on, 233–34

definition of, 25

inconsistent application of, 26

media and, 175, 194

Van Buren, Martin, 202

Ventura, Jesse, 233

Versailles Treaty (1920), 402

Veterans of Foreign Wars, 285

Veterans' organizations, 284–85

Vetos, 399–401
line-item, 401
overriding, 70, 400
pocket, 400
as threat, 357–58

Vice president, 410–13
in presidential succession, 375
as presidents, 413
roles of, 411–13
selection of, 226, 410–11
in the Senate, 345–46

Victims' rights, 521

Vietnam Veterans Against the War, 390

Vietnam Veterans of America, 285

Vietnam War, 635–36
ACLU and, 503
aftermath of, 636
defense spending and, 653
Kerry and, 390
lessons from, 642
Nixon and, 403
Pentagon papers, 186
political parties and, 207
public confidence and, 6
symbolic speech and, 505
television in, 192
voting age and, 153
War Powers Act and, 82, 319, 407

Villa, Pancho, 378

Violence, protest and, 164

Violence Against Women Act (1994), 120, 460

Virginia Plan, 58, 60–61

Voices for Working Families, 261

Voltaire, 26

Voluntary exchange, 577

Voter registration
fraud and, 155
National Voter Registration Act on, 126
as obstacle to voting, 155
politics of, 156–57

racism in, 151–53

rates of, 155

Voters
candidate image and, 276, 278
Constitution on qualifications of, 62–63
decision factors for, 269–79
economy and, 278–79
gender and, 276, 277
by group, 276, 277
issues and, 279
party, 226–28
party identification and, 269, 273, 276
race and, 276, 277
ticket splitters, 220

Voter turnout, 149, 151, 154–56
for congressional elections, 332–33
definition of, 154
European, 158, 159
factors in, 158–60
in general elections, 333
importance of, 160–61
politics of, 156–58
in presidential primaries, 333
registration requirements and, 155, 156–57
running for office and, 163

Voting rights, 149–54
age and, 79, 99, 153
Constitution on, 28, 79–80
disenfranchisement and, 151–52
15th Amendment on, 114, 150
poll taxes and, 152
poverty and, 571
property qualifications in, 149–50
for women, 153
for 18-year-olds, 153

Voting Rights Act (1965), 152, 240, 362
gerrymandering and, 326–27
guarantees in, 538
language minorities and, 560

W

Wadsworth, John, 54

Wagner, Adolf, 423

Wallace, George, 108, 231, 232

Wallace, Mike, 188

Wall-of-separation doctrine, 498–99

Wall Street Journal, 170–71

Wards, 217–18

ELECTORAL COLLEGE VOTES IN THE 2004 ELECTION

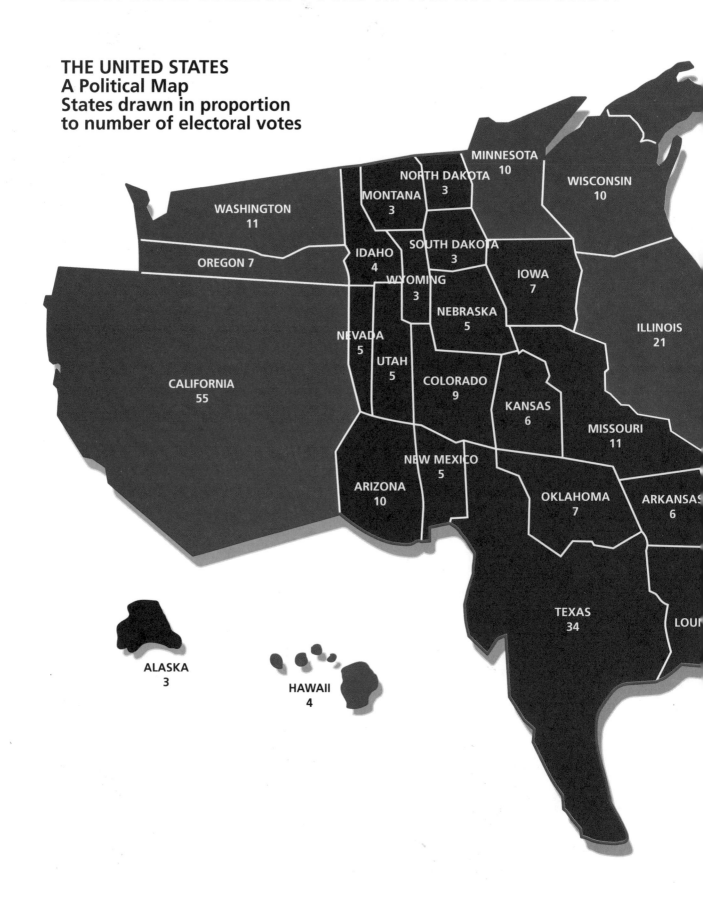

THE UNITED STATES
A Political Map
States drawn in proportion
to number of electoral votes

WASHINGTON 11

OREGON 7

IDAHO 4

MONTANA 3

NORTH DAKOTA 3

MINNESOTA 10

WISCONSIN 10

SOUTH DAKOTA 3

WYOMING 3

IOWA 7

NEVADA 5

NEBRASKA 5

ILLINOIS 21

UTAH 5

CALIFORNIA 55

COLORADO 9

KANSAS 6

MISSOURI 11

NEW MEXICO 5

ARIZONA 10

OKLAHOMA 7

ARKANSAS 6

TEXAS 34

LOUI

ALASKA 3

HAWAII 4